RXPREP COURSE BOOK
2016 EDITION

KAREN SHAPIRO, PHARMD, BCPS

SHERRY A. BROWN, PHARMD, MBA, BCPS

STEPHANIE D. GARRETT, PHARMD, BCPS

With JENNIFER S. SCHMITZ, PHARMD, BCPS

CONTRIBUTORS

PAUL BERINGER
PHARMD, BCPS, FASHP

HEATHER R. BREAM-ROUWENHORST
PHARMD, BCPS

KATIE E. CARDONE
PHARMD, BCACP, FNKF, FASN

GEORGE DEMAAGD
PHARMD, BCPS

PAULINA DEMING
PHARMD

CATRINA DERDERIAN
BS, PHARMD, BCACP

ROMIC ESKANDARIAN
PHARMD

CHRISTINE FITZGERALD
BS, PHARMD, BCPS

MUOI GI
PHARMD, BCPS, BCOP

JEFF GOAD
PHARMD, MPH, FAPHA, FCPHA, FCSHP

JEAN-VENABLE "KELLY" R. GOODE
PHARMD, BCPS, FAPHA, FCCP

SUSAN E. GORMAN
PHARMD, MS, DABAT, FAACT

PHILIP J. GREGORY
PHARMD, MS, FACN

MEGAN HEIM
PHARMD, BCACP

JAN D. HIRSCH
BSPHARM, PH.D

DARREL W. HUGHES
PHARMD, BCPS

ANN HYLTON
PHARMD, BCPS

KIM M. JONES
PHARMD, BCPS

JEFF LEE
PHARMD, FCCP

JOSEPH D. MA
PHARMD, FCP

JOEL C. MARRS
PHARMD, FCCP, FASHP, FNLA, BCPS-AQ CARDIOLOGY, BCACP, CLS

BETH A. MARTIN
PHD, MS, RPH

JESSE F. MARTINEZ
PHARMD, FASCP

EMI MINEJIMA
PHARMD

CHRISTINA L. MNATZAGANIAN
PHARMD, BCACP

CYNTHIA L. MORRIS-KUKOSKI
PHARMD, DABAT, FAACT

BETHANY L. MURPHY
PHARMD, BCACP

JAMES D. NASH
PHARMD, MPH, BCPS

TIEN M. H. NG
PHARMD, FCCP, BCPS (AQ-CARDIOLOGY)

NANCY N. NGUYEN
PHARMD, BCPS, AAHIVP, FCSHP

ELIZABETH POGGE
PHARMD, MPH, BCPS, FASCP

DOREEN PON
PHARMD, BCOP, BCPS

CHARLES D. PONTE
BS, PHARMD, FAADE, FAPHA, FASHP, FCCN, FNAP

ALLISON PROVINE
PHARMD, BCPS, BCPPS

SALLY RAFIE
PHARMD, BCPS

CHARLOTTE RICCHETTI
PHARMD, BCPS, CDE

KIMBERLY B. TALLIAN
PHARMD, BCPP, FASHP, FCCP, FCSHP

PAMELA TU
PHARMD

ROBIN WACKERNAH
PHARMD, BCPP

D. RAYMOND WEBER
PHARMD, BSPHARM, BCOP, BCPS, RPH

ANNIE WONG-BERINGER
PHARMD, FCCP, FIDSA

For information on additional pharmacy board and MPJE (law) review programs offered by RxPrep, visit our website at www.rxprep.com.

Cover design by creativeshoebox.com

Book production by midnightbookfactory.com

TABLE OF CONTENTS

EXAM OVERVIEW

INTRODUCTION
This section includes four topics:

- NAPLEX® Overview
- Format of the Exam
- How to Use this Book
- CPJE Pointers for CA Exam Takers

NAPLEX® OVERVIEW
The NAPLEX® Competency Statements are available on the National Association of Boards of Pharmacy (NABP) website at www.nabp.net. These provide a blueprint (or outline) of topics that are tested. The Competency Statements changed effective November 1, 2015. This is the summary of the 2015 blueprint, that will be in effect for 2016. Please visit the NABP website to stay up-to-date on the exam and any upcoming changes.

The exam now has two sections. Each section requires a passing score.

Area #1: Ensure Safe and Effective Pharmacotherapy and Health Outcomes (67% of the exam)

- This section includes drug mechanism of action, indications, side effects, contraindications and drug interactions. Trade/generics are tested, along with common dosage forms.

- Questions are largely asked in a patient-case format. It will be important to quickly identify pertinent information from the case (e.g., abnormal labs, past medical history, medication use history, etc.) and recognize appropriate or inappropriate treatments. Refer to the following chapters: Lab Values & Drug Monitoring and Patient Charts and Assessment & Healthcare Provider Education.

- The ability to monitor patient outcomes is assessed. This includes the patient's response to treatment and safety/efficacy of the chosen treatment. Improving medication adherence, recommending better treatment options and providing information to patients and healthcare providers are tested as well.

- Pharmacoeconomic factors may be important: if a patient cannot afford a drug and a less-expensive, but valid option is available, the pharmacist should recommend the preferable drug. It will be important to be able to read study summaries and interpret the data. Refer to the Biostatistics & Pharmacoeconomics Chapter.

- Be able to apply pharmacokinetic and pharmacogenomic parameters to individualize drug treatment. Refer to the following chapters: Pharmacokinetics and Pharmacogenomics.

- Be familiar with drug reference sources, how to administer and counsel on emergency care and vaccinations, and be able to make recommendations regarding common dietary supplements.

- Review self-care products and self-monitoring of health status by the patient.

- Medication safety concepts are tested in this section including quality improvement, evaluation of medication errors and the role of automated systems/technology. Refer to the Medication Safety & Quality Improvement chapter.

Area #2: Safe and Accurate Preparation, Compounding, Dispensing, and Administration of Medications and Provision of Health Care Products (33% of the exam)

- This includes <u>calculations</u>, including nutritional requirements and basic <u>PN calculations</u>. Flow rates for drugs administered by IV infusion <u>are essential</u>, along with drug concentrations, and the other general calculations in the section. Many of the math problems will require identifying necessary information from a patient case (dose, patient weight, IV flow rate, etc.) in order to perform the calculation. Poor math skills will result in an unacceptable grade on the exam. A math mistake in pharmacy is a dosing mistake. Accuracy in calculations is an important skill to demonstrate on the exam. Calculations are included throughout the RxPrep Course Book, but specifically in the following chapters: Calculations, Pharmacokinetics and Biostatistics & Pharmacoeconomics.

- Techniques, procedures and equipment for sterile and nonsterile compounding are assessed. Refer to the following chapters: Sterile Compounding and Nonsterile Compounding.

- Be familiar with storage, packaging, handling and medication disposal.

- Instructions and techniques for medication administration are tested in this section.

FORMAT OF THE EXAM

NAPLEX® is a computer-adaptive exam that currently consists of 185 questions. Of these, 150 questions are used to calculate the test score. The total test time is currently 4 hours and 15 minutes, which includes an optional 10-minute break after approximately 2 hours. Any other breaks that are needed will be subtracted from the total testing time.

NABP has announced that the number of questions on the exam will increase to 250 sometime in 2016. Watch the NABP website for information. We will post an announcement regarding any information that we receive.

- There are <u>5 question types</u> on NAPLEX®. Each of the 5 types are represented in the RxPrep Test Bank:

  ❑ Multiple-Choice: Select the one correct answer.

  ❑ Multiple-Response: Select all of the correct responses and no incorrect response(s) for credit.

  ❑ Constructed-Response: Enter the answer using the computer keyboard (usually for math problems).

  ❑ Ordered-Response: Put the items in a specified order.

  ❑ Hot Spot: Select the correct area on a diagram or picture by clicking on it.

- The majority of the questions (including calculations) are asked in a scenario-based format (such as patient profiles with accompanying questions). There are also stand alone questions.

- All questions must be answered in the order in which they are presented. It is not possible to skip questions, or to go back at a later time.

- A computer-adaptive exam assesses the answer to a given question in order to determine the level of difficulty for the following question. If you answer a question correctly, the computer will select a more difficult question from the test pool in an appropriate content area. If you answer a question incorrectly, an easier question will be selected by the computer. If you miss a calculation you are likely to get another similar item worth less and you may not accumulate enough points to pass.

- Personal calculators may not be used during the exam. The Pearson VUE testing center console uses an <u>on-screen calculator</u> which looks similar to the Texas Instruments TI-30XS Multiview and other similar hand-held calculators. The on-screen calculator can be opened in a pop-up window during the exam at any time (a similar on-screen calculator is available in the <u>RxPrep Test Bank</u> for practice). A candidate requesting a handheld calculator will be supplied a five function calculator by Pearson VUE. Some of the calculations require advanced functions only available on the on-screen calculator. Refer to the Calculations chapter for Math Tips.

- On the day of the exam, arrive 30 minutes prior to your appointment to get signed in (fingerprints will be taken, you will need 2 forms of ID, and do not bring prohibited items into the exam room). Acceptable forms of ID and the list of prohibited items is in the exam registration booklet.

- If you arrive 30 minutes or later than your scheduled appointment, and are refused admission to sit for the exam, you will be required to forfeit your appointment.

STUDY TIPS

- If you have not recently finished a year or more of clinical rotations in school or are coming from practice in a community setting review the Lab Values & Drug Monitoring and Patient Charts, Assessment and Healthcare Provider Communication chapters which discuss how to <u>interpret charts</u> (medical records); this is required in order to answer questions. The types of common case formats are in this course book at the end of most of the clinical chapters. Interpreting medical records requires an understanding of <u>lab values</u> (what the value is used for and the interpretation of common measurements).

- It is advisable to start with the beginning chapters in this text which represent the "foundation" material; the math should be done at the beginning of study and repeated (over and over) throughout the study period. Other foundation topics (such as drug interactions) will help make the clinical chapters easier to manage. For example, if you are familiar with the big inducers or big inhibitors you will have familiarity when reviewing them in the specific topic chapters in which they are used. It will make the process go smoother if the study is done in a logical fashion.

- Study the top selling drugs (group them together; you'll see all the statins are there, many ACE inhibitors, etc) and focus on the doses for the common agents. We have bolded most of them in this text. The RxPrep test bank can be used to check your retention of all the top sellers (and the essential others).

- When reading the case, you may wish to note allergies, abnormal labs and major enzyme inducers/inhibitors. They are there for a reason. You will have a dry erase board – you can quickly jot these things down – so they are in your mind when looking at the questions. Although time is limited it is easy to get cases confused after an hour or more of testing.

- Counseling is key; pharmacists must be able to make sure that patients use their drugs safely. In this text, counseling for key drugs is presented after the drug tables in each chapter. It is essential to be able to counsel on formulations that come in novel delivery vehicles, such as dry powder inhalers, self-injectables, patches and other formulations. These are each demonstrated in the videos, and are tested in the correlating test bank section. Most patients know how to swallow a compressed tablet (with a glass of water), but will not be able to figure out how to self-administer an enoxaparin injection or how to use a dry-powder inhaler. Increasingly, drugs are being given in alternative formulations.

- Conditions for which "lifestyle" is essential (heart failure, diabetes) will require that you know how to counsel on healthy-living and disease-monitoring.

- <u>Pharmacoeconomics</u> (with the necessary <u>biostatistics</u> equations) is a required competency; this area, similar to calculations, must be known well prior to sitting for licensure. <u>Pharmacokinetic calculations</u> must be known. The calculations in this area can be mastered through repetition; you must do the math repeatedly until you can do the math in all the sections <u>with decent speed</u>, and <u>with accuracy</u>. If you cannot manage to make this happen, please consider getting help with the RxPrep Online Course. The instructors explain each calculation in the simplest manner, step by step. The course also includes our assistance, as-needed.

- Dosing? What is important to know? Trade/generics? Use the <u>underlining</u> (for key information) and <u>bolding</u> (for key drugs) that is present throughout this text as our "best guess" on material that should be known prior to testing. Use your own judgement as well. When we decide, for example, that a dose is important, it is because our team here agrees that the drug is used commonly or is particularly toxic, and an unsafe dosing level would be <u>dangerous</u>. For example, if a patient begins a dopamine agonist at too high a dose the patient could get hurt, or could cause harm to others. Dopamine agonists cause excessive sedation, with onset that can be sudden. They must be started low and titrated carefully.

HOW TO USE THIS BOOK

This book is designed as a companion to our live or online courses and test bank. You can review these options on our website at www.rxprep.com. Select the online course without the text if you have the current version; this reduces the course cost by the price of the text and prevents another text from being sent.

If you are using the book as a stand-alone study tool, here are some pointers:

- If an item is bolded it is a <u>key drug</u> and if it is underlined it is <u>essential information</u>.

- Not all essential information is designated. Use the <u>top seller list</u> in the Appendix as a guide to must-know drugs. You will be tested on drugs that are not top sellers, but have safety considerations. Hospital drugs that are essential are noted in the text.

- This book is complete; you do not need to have a myriad of additional resources. If you are testing through most of 2016, this book is sufficient. However, if testing towards the latter part of the year, you should check for key updates. We often post these as they come along on our website. Only reputable resources should be used.

- At the end of many of the core chapters are patient cases with practice questions. These are designed to be somewhat similar to cases you might see on the exam – either in a written format, or the profile you might see on a pharmacy computer. The cases are designed to review key drug points and should not be missed. They do not overlap with the test bank questions.

- The questions in the RxPrep test banks match to the chapters in this text. The questions are designed to test the most basic drug competency knowledge. The knowledge in these questions, including calculations, should be at 100%. If you get something wrong do not skip it! Follow the instructions on "<u>How to Do Well on NAPLEX or CPJE</u>" that is under the "Announcements" section on your student Dashboard when logged into your account on the RxPrep website. You can access the announcements with the test bank or with the online course. Adult learners do not learn well passively by sitting in front of a text or computer screen; this announcement includes our best experience on how an adult learner can learn all this information, including how to remember oddball drug names (such as argatroban and *Ivacaftor*). It is possible. The exam is not complex; rather, there is much information to pack inside your brain, and the math must be done with good speed and accuracy.

CPJE POINTERS – FOR CA EXAM TAKERS

This text includes the topics that <u>overlap</u> with the CPJE (Medication Safety, ID, Immunizations, HIV, others). The clinical topics <u>not covered on that NAPLEX</u> that <u>are tested in the CPJE</u> are included in the separate CPJE course (therapeutic interchange, formulary, others). The California <u>law is covered completely</u>. The CPJE course is available at www.rxprep.com. We recommend, in addition, reading through Fred Weissman's book on California community law; this is a standard resource in California for community pharmacy law.

Best wishes for your exam preparation.

CALCULATIONS

TIPS FOR SUCCESS WITH MATH

If these tips are used consistently, accuracy will improve.

- Time permitting, double-check all math. It is very easy to make mistakes that will be caught when the calculation is repeated.

- When setting up <u>proportions</u>, make sure the units (including route and drug if applicable) in the <u>numerators match</u> and the units (route and drug) in the <u>denominators match</u>.

- If using proportions to solve the problem, place the answer directly back into the equation as an accuracy check. For example:

$$\frac{5\ g}{100\ g} = \frac{X\ g}{1{,}000\ g} \qquad X = 50\ g$$

Check: 5/100 = 0.05; 50/1,000 = 0.05

- When using <u>dimensional analysis</u>, make sure that units cancel out so the final answer is in the desired units. For example:

$$\frac{250\ mL}{400\ mg} \times \frac{1\ mg}{1000\ mcg} \times \frac{375\ mcg}{min} \times \frac{60\ min}{1\ hr} = 14\ mL/hr$$

- <u>Answer the question asked.</u> Many questions will require <u>multiple steps</u> to get to the correct answer and correct units.

- <u>Read the question again after solving the problem.</u> Be certain the answer has the correct units (g or mg, mEq, mL or L, etc.) and is rounded as specified in the question.

- If <u>rounding</u> is required, look at the number to the right of the one being rounded to; for example, if rounding to the nearest whole number look at the tenths column. If the number to the right is 0 to 4, round down. If the number to the right is 5 to 9, round up. For example, 31.27 rounded to the nearest whole number is 31, and 31.635 rounded to the nearest whole number is 32. <u>Round only at the end of the equation, not at each step.</u>

**In this chapter, some intermediate steps (that do not affect the final answer) may have been rounded for simplicity and space. The exam may also provide approximations without stating to do so; for example, if you calculated 13.567 and the answers are 2, 5, 14 and 32 you would select 14. In a similar problem, the question could ask you to round to the nearest whole number.

- The math in this section, and on the exam, is not complex. Most formulas are not provided. In the corresponding test bank sections each math problem presented here is repeated at least twice, but with different parameters and in a slightly different presentation. <u>Practice these problems repeatedly</u>; complete a math section, clear the score, and complete again. Each time this is done the speed and accuracy should increase. When all of the sections can be done with reasonable speed and accuracy, the math skills are acceptable. This method should be applied to each of the four calculation test bank sections, the biostatistics calculation test bank section and the PK calculation test bank section. There is also math included in other chapters, which is shown on the first page of this chapter in the Table of Contents, such as phenytoin adjustments in the Epilepsy/Seizures chapter. Every math problem that could be tested must seem simple by the exam date or the test date should be delayed. Math is worth a lot on a pharmacy exam; a math mistake in pharmacy means that the patient received an incorrect dose, and is not considered acceptable for passing.

- Most of the math problems on the exam will be in a <u>case-based</u> format. For this reason, the RxPrep Course Book includes math problems in the practice cases at the end of some of the other chapters. In this calculation chapter the math steps are explained; on the exam, it will be necessary to find the information located in the case and thus the math problem will not appear as simple. However, the math will be the same. Since finding the information takes time, each calculation should be able to be completed with reasonable speed, and with accuracy. For example, if the case states that 10 units of regular insulin was added to the fluid bag on 3/11 and the fluid bag ordered on 3/9 is chosen instead, the fluid will likely be a different volume and the answer will be incorrect. Or, if a patient weight is needed to calculate a dose, such as mg/kg, and several of the patient's weights are provided in the case, be careful to select the weight from the correct date.

- The RxPrep Calculations chapter incorporates <u>Calculation Practice</u> throughout the chapter. These problems provide practice utilizing several math techniques in multi-step problems.

- Math calculations and important formulas in the RxPrep Course Book are shown in two types of shaded boxes for easy identification:

Math Calculation

$$\frac{0.5 \text{ mg}}{2 \text{ mL}} = \frac{0.2 \text{ mg}}{X \text{ mL}} \qquad X = 0.8 \text{ mL}$$

Formula

$$\text{mmols} = \frac{\text{mg}}{\text{MW}}$$

EXAMPLE CASE

PATIENT PROFILE

| Patient Name | Roger Hadley |
| Address | 1345 Plum Street |

Age	67	**Sex**	M	**Race**	Caucasian	**Height**	5'10"	**Weight**	192 lbs
Allergies	NKDA
Vitals	BP: 184/94 mm/Hg	**HR:** 89 BPM	**Temp:** 98.6°F

DIAGNOSES

Chronic stable angina	Lower extremity cellulitis
Diabetes	New onset atrial fibrillation
Hypertension	

MEDICATIONS

Date	Prescriber	Drug & Strength	Sig
9/1/15	McMurphy	Glucophage XR	1 gram daily
9/1/15	McMurphy	Levemir FlexTouch pen	11 units SQ at HS daily
9/1/15	McMurphy	Diovan	160 mg daily
10/22/15	Ling	D51/2NS	50 ml/hr
10/22/15	Ling	Enoxaparin	40 mg SQ daily
10/22/15	Ling	Vancomycin	1250 mg IV Q12
10/22/15	Ling	Diltiazem	20 mg bolus IVP x 1
10/22/15	Ling	Diltiazem (100 mg/100 mL) drip	10 mg/hr

Example #1

At what rate (mL/hr) should Mr. Hadley's diltiazem drip be set at to provide the prescribed dose?

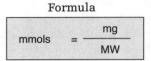

$$\frac{10 \text{ mg}}{\text{hr}} \times \frac{100 \text{ mL}}{100 \text{ mg}} = 10 \text{ mL/hr}$$

Example #2

Premixed bags of D5½NS (1 liter) are available on the floor. Mr. Hadley's infusion is started at 1300 on the day it was ordered. On what date and time will the premixed bag run out?

- a. 10/22/15 at 0100
- b. 10/22/15 at 1300
- c. 10/22/15 at 2000
- d. 10/23/15 at 1300
- e. 10/23/15 at 0900

The correct answer is (e).

$$1000 \text{ mL} \quad \times \quad \frac{hr}{50 \text{ mL}} \quad = \quad 20 \text{ hours}$$

The 1 liter bag will last 20 hours at the prescribed rate of 50 mL/hr. If the bag is started at 1300 (1pm) on 10/22/15, it will run out 20 hours later, at 0900 on 10/23/15. Refer to the Patient Charts, Assessment & Healthcare Provider Communication chapter for a discussion of military time.

EQUIVALENT MEASUREMENTS

The following equivalent measurements and metric conversions should be known in order to make necessary conversions in calculations problems. Approximate and actual conversions differ slightly. On the exam the conversion may be provided, the instructions may require rounding of the final answer so that either conversion will provide a correct answer or the problem may be multiple choice so the best answer can be selected.

MEASUREMENT	EQUIVALENT
tsp (t)	5 mL
tbsp (T)	15 mL
1 fl oz	30 mL (approx.); 29.57 mL (actual)
1 cup	8 oz 240 mL (approx.); 236.56 mL (actual)
1 pint	16 oz 480 mL (approx.); 473 mL (actual)
1 quart	2 pints 960 mL (approx.); 946 mL (actual)
1 gallon	4 quarts 3,840 mL (approx.); 3,785 mL (actual)

MEASUREMENT	EQUIVALENT
1 kg	2.2 pounds
1 oz	28.4 g
1 pound	454 g
1 in	2.54 cm
1 grain (gr)	65 mg (approx.); 64.8 mg (actual)

METRIC CONVERSIONS

PREFIX	DEFINITION
kilo	1,000 (one thousand), as in kg
deci	1/10 (one-tenth), as in dL
milli	1/1,000 (one-thousandth), as in mL
micro	1/1,000,000 (one-millionth), as in mcg
nano	1/1,000,000,000 (one-billionth), as in ng

CALCULATE THE CORRECT QUANTITY OF MEDICATION TO DISPENSE, ADMINISTER OR COMPOUND

Proportions

A proportion represents the equality of two ratios. Given any three values of a proportion, it is easy to calculate the fourth. Remember to keep the same units (route, drug, etc.) in the numerator and the same units (route, drug, etc.) in the denominator.

$$\frac{a}{b} = \frac{c}{d}$$

---

1. If 200 capsules contain 500 mg of an active ingredient, how many milligrams of the active ingredient will 76 capsules contain?

$$\frac{200 \text{ caps}}{500 \text{ mg}} = \frac{76 \text{ caps}}{X \text{ mg}} \qquad X = 190 \text{ mg}$$

---

2. A 10 gram packet of potassium chloride provides 20 mEq of potassium and 4 mEq of chloride. How many grams of powder would provide 8 mEq of potassium?

$$\frac{10 \text{ g}}{20 \text{ mEq K}} = \frac{X \text{ g}}{8 \text{ mEq K}} \qquad X = 4 \text{ g}$$

---

3. If one 10 mL vial contains 0.05 g of diltiazem, how many milliliters should be administered to provide a 25 mg dose of diltiazem?

First, convert grams to milligrams. It is usually best practice to convert to the units required for the answer when beginning the problem.

$$0.05 \text{ g of diltiazem} \times \frac{1,000 \text{ mg}}{1 \text{ g}} = 50 \text{ mg}$$

Use proportions to calculate the number of mL for a 25 mg dose.

$$\frac{50 \text{ mg}}{10 \text{ mL}} = \frac{25 \text{ mg}}{X \text{ mL}} \qquad X = 5 \text{ mL}$$

---

4. If phenobarbital elixir contains 18.2 mg of phenobarbital per 5 mL, how many grams of phenobarbital would be used in preparing a pint of the elixir? Round to the nearest tenth.

First, convert milligrams to grams.

$$18.2 \text{ mg} \times \frac{1 \text{ g}}{1,000 \text{ mg}} = 0.0182 \text{ g}$$

Use proportions to calculate the grams needed for 1 pint.

$$\frac{0.0182 \text{ g}}{5 \text{ mL}} = \frac{X \text{ g}}{473 \text{ mL}} \qquad X = 1.7 \text{ g}$$

Because of the rounding specifications in the question, the answer is the same regardless of the pint conversion used. Expect the same on the exam.

5. Digoxin injection is supplied in ampules of 500 mcg per 2 mL. How many milliliters must a nurse administer to provide a dose of 0.2 mg? Round to the nearest tenth.

First, convert 500 mcg to mg.

$$500 \text{ mcg} \times \frac{1 \text{ mg}}{1,000 \text{ mcg}} = 0.5 \text{ mg}$$

$$\frac{0.5 \text{ mg}}{2 \text{ mL}} = \frac{0.2 \text{ mg}}{X \text{ mL}} \qquad X = 0.8 \text{ mL}$$

---

6. A penicillin V 250 mg tablet equals 400,000 units of penicillin activity. A patient is taking penicillin V 500 mg tablets QID for 7 days. How much penicillin activity, in units, will this patient receive in the total prescription?

If 250 mg contains 400,000 units, then 500 mg contains 800,000 units. The patient is taking 4 tablets daily, for 7 days (or 28 total tablets), at 800,000 units each.

$$\frac{800,000 \text{ units}}{1 \text{ tab}} = \frac{X \text{ units}}{28 \text{ tabs}} \qquad X = 22,400,000 \text{ units}$$

---

7. A cough syrup contains 4 grams of brompheniramine maleate per liter. How many milligrams are contained in a teaspoonful dose of the elixir?

First, convert grams to milligrams.

$$4 \text{ g} \times \frac{1000 \text{ mg}}{1 \text{ g}} = 4,000 \text{ mg per 1 liter}$$

- 1 L = 1,000 mL

- 1 teaspoonful = 5 mL

Next, solve using proportions.

$$\frac{4,000 \text{ mg}}{1,000 \text{ mL}} = \frac{X \text{ mg}}{5 \text{ mL}} \qquad X = 20 \text{ mg}$$

---

8. A patient is to receive acyclovir 5 mg/kg every 8 hours for an acute outbreak of herpes zoster. What daily dose, in milligrams, should a 110 pound female receive?

Begin by converting the patient's weight in pounds (lbs) to kilograms (kg).

$$110 \text{ pounds} \times \frac{1 \text{ kg}}{2.2 \text{ pounds}} = 50 \text{ kg}$$

$$\frac{5 \text{ mg}}{1 \text{ kg}} = \frac{X \text{ mg}}{50 \text{ kg}} \qquad X = 250 \text{ mg/dose} \times 3 \text{ doses/day} = 750 \text{ mg/day}$$

9. MH is a 72 year old male patient hospitalized with decompensated heart failure and fever. Cultures are positive for aspergillosis. MH weighs 110 kg and will receive 0.25 mg/kg per day of amphotericin B (reconstituted and diluted to 0.1 mg/mL) by IV infusion. How many milliliters of amphotericin solution is required to deliver the daily dose?

Begin by calculating the total daily dose (mg) for this patient.

$$\frac{0.25 \text{ mg}}{1 \text{ kg}} = \frac{X \text{ mg}}{110 \text{ kg}} \qquad X = 27.5 \text{ mg daily}$$

Calculate the volume of reconstituted amphotericin B solution needed per day.

$$\frac{27.5 \text{ mg}}{X \text{ mL}} = \frac{0.1 \text{ mg}}{1 \text{ mL}} \qquad X = 275 \text{ mL}$$

10. An elixir of ferrous sulfate contains 220 milligrams of ferrous sulfate per 5 milliliters. If each milligram of ferrous sulfate contains the equivalent of 0.2 milligrams of elemental iron, how many milligrams of elemental iron would be in each 5 milliliters of elixir?

$$\frac{0.2 \text{ mg Fe}}{1 \text{ mg FeSO}_4} = \frac{X \text{ mg Fe}}{220 \text{ mg FeSO}_4} \qquad X = 44 \text{ mg elemental Fe}$$

Ferrous sulfate ($FeSO_4$) contains 20% elemental iron (Fe); this is given in the problem which states that 1 milligram has 0.2 milligrams of elemental iron, which is 20%. Oral iron products and percent elemental iron are reviewed in the Anemia chapter.

11. Oral potassium chloride 20% solution contains 40 mEq of potassium per 15 milliliters of solution. A patient needs 25 mEq of potassium daily. What is the amount, in milliliters, of 20% potassium chloride that the patient should take? Round to the nearest tenth.

$$\frac{40 \text{ mEq K}}{15 \text{ mL}} = \frac{25 \text{ mEq K}}{X \text{ mL}} \qquad X = 9.375, \text{ or } 9.4 \text{ mL}$$

Calculations Involving Prescriptions

12. A pharmacist receives this prescription for *Vicodin*. How many tablets should be dispensed?

   a. 6 tablets

   b. 8 tablets

   c. 12 tablets

   d. 16 tablets

   e. 24 tablets

The correct answer is (c). The dispense quantity is indicated and consistent with the "not to exceed" instructions. Generally, the acetaminophen component has the higher risk of toxicity (liver toxicity).

State of California
PRESCRIPTION BLANK

Joe Jackson, MD
927 Deep Valley Drive
Los Angeles, California
Phone (310) 555-3333

DEA#FJ 3829150
BATCH# HTS5058903765

CA LIC#568596

0200

Name: Edward Richards

D.O.B. May 15, 1949

Address: 177 Green Street

Date: November 29, 2013

Touch Rx symbol, color will disappear then reappear

Qty/Units

☑ 1-24 / 12
☐ 25-49 / ____
☐ 50-74 / ____
☐ 75-100 / ____
☐ 101-150 / ____
☐ 151 and over / ____

Rx Vicodin 5/325 mg #12

Sig: i-ii tabs PO q 4-6 hrs prn pain X 2 days. NTE 6/d.

SUBSTITUTION PERMISSABLE _____

DO NOT SUBSTITUTE _____

SIGNATURE OF PRESCRIBER

DO NOT REFILL ____ REFILL ____ TIMES

Prescription is void if more than one controlled substance is written per blank.

Security Features. Details on Back

13. A pharmacist receives a prescription for *"Vigamox* **0.5%. Dispense 3 mL. 1 gtt tid ou x 7d". How many drops will the patient use per day?**

    a. 1 drop

    b. 2 drops

    c. 3 drops

    d. 6 drops

    e. 21 drops

The correct answer is (d). Refer to the <u>Appendix</u> for common abbreviations used in prescriptions and medical charts. It is important to properly counsel patients on the correct technique for instilling eye drops. Refer to the Glaucoma, Ophthalmics & Otics chapter.

LABELING AND READING PRESCRIPTIONS
■ Prescriptions start with an instructive word (such as: Take, Place, Unwrap, Insert, Inhale).
■ Followed by the quantity and dosage form (such as: 1 capsule).
■ Followed by the location (such as: by mouth, rectally, vaginally, under tongue).
■ Followed by the frequency (such as: daily, twice daily, at meals and bedtime).
■ Finished with any noted instructions (such as: for pain, for cholesterol, on an empty stomach).

14. A 7 year old male child (3 feet, 4 inches and 48 pounds) presents to the urgent care clinic with a fever of 102°F, and nausea/vomiting that began the previous day. He will receive an acetaminophen 5 grain suppository for the fever. A pharmacist receives a prescription for the suppository with the instructions: Use 1 PR Q4-6H PRN temperature > 102 degrees. How many milligrams per kilogram (mg/kg) will the child receive per dose? Round to the nearest whole number.

    a. 3 mg/kg

    b. 15 mg/kg

    c. 89 mg/kg

    d. 60 mg/kg

    e. 325 mg/kg

The correct answer is (b). Five grains is 325 milligrams (65 mg/grain x 5 grains). The recommended weight-based acetaminophen dosing for children under 12 years of age is 10-15 mg/kg Q4-6H.

---

15. Which of the following are correct regarding the *Keflex* **prescription? (Select ALL that apply.)**

    a. If taken correctly, this prescription will last 14 days.

    b. The patient should be counseled to take the medication after meals and at bedtime.

    c. The patient should be counseled to finish all of the medication even if she starts to feel better.

    d. The patient should be counseled to take the medication every 6 hours around the clock.

    e. The pharmacist should verify whether the patient has any allergies.

> **JOE JACKSON, MD**
> 927 DEEP VALLEY DRIVE
> LOS ANGELES, CALIFORNIA
>
> PHONE (310) 555-3333   DEA NO. FJ3829150
>
> NAME *Melissa Atkins*   DATE *October 29, 2013*
>
> ADDRESS *18469 Lotus Circle*   AGE *57*
>
> **R̸**   *Keflex* 500 mg PO QID: ac and hs. #28
>
> ☐ LABEL
>
> REFILL ___0___ TIMES
>
> _____ , M.D.   _____ , M.D.
>
> DO NOT SUBSTITUTE   SUBSTITUTION PERMISSIBLE

The correct answers are (c) and (e). The patient should be counseled to finish all of the medication even if they start to feel better. Cephalexin *(Keflex)* is a first generation cephalosporin antibiotic that comes as tablets, capsules and powder for suspension. Allergies must be verified before dispensing any prescription.

16. How many milliliters (mL) of *Mylanta* suspension are contained in each dose of the prescription below? Round to the nearest whole number.

PRESCRIPTION	QUANTITY
Belladonna Tincture	10 mL
Phenobarbital	60 mL
Mylanta susp. qs. ad	120 mL
Sig. 5 mL BID	

The total prescription is 120 mL; 10 mL belladonna, 60 mL of phenobarbital, and that leaves 50 mL for the *Mylanta*.

$$\frac{50 \text{ mL } Mylanta}{120 \text{ mL total Rx}} = \frac{X \text{ mL } Mylanta}{5 \text{ mL total Rx dose}} \qquad X = 2.08, \text{ or 2 mL } Mylanta \text{ per dose}$$

After solving the problem, read the question again to be certain it was answered with the correct units (mL of *Mylanta* per dose).

---

17. A pharmacist received this sulfamethoxazole/trimethoprim prescription and dispensed 3 oz to Ms. Brooks. How many days of therapy will Ms. Brooks be short? Use 30 mL for 1 fluid ounce and round to the nearest whole number.

 a. 10 mL

 b. 90 mL

 c. 1 day

 d. 3 days

 e. 9 days

The correct answer is (c). Use caution with calculations like this where one step of the calculation is included as an answer choice. Always go back and read the question prior to selecting an answer.

5 mL (per dose) x 2 times/day x 10 days = 100 mL

Quantity dispensed: 3 oz x 30 mL/oz = 90 mL dispensed

Difference: 100 mL – 90 mL = 10 mL

Each tsp (t) is 5 mL. The patient must take 2 tsp (t) daily (10 mL), so she is 1 day short for her prescribed course of therapy.

Gene Tran, MD
5445 Grand Ave.
Fallbrook, California
Phone (760) 555-2112

005-1015

CA LIC. #A19666
D.E.A. #SK456789

Name   Angelina Brooks   Date   January 22, 2014

Address   33 Walden Rd. N Falls   D.O.B.   May 5, 1951

R̸x

TMP/SMX 40-200 mg/5 mL
Sig: 1 tsp PO BID x 10 days, until all taken.

❑ Do Not Substitute   Refill _____ Times

Quantity	Units
❑ 1-24	_____
❑ 25-49	_____
❑ 50-74	_____
❑ 75-100	_____
❑ 101-150	_____
❑ 151 and over	_____

Physician Signature

Prescription is void if more than one controlled substance is written per blank.

18. A pharmacist has tablets that contain 0.25 mg of levothyroxine per tablet. The tablets will be crushed and mixed with glycerol and water to prepare a prescription for a 36 pound child. How many levothyroxine tablets will be needed to compound the following prescription?

PRESCRIPTION	QUANTITY
Levothyroxine Liq.	0.1 mg/mL
Disp.	60 mL
Sig. 0.01 mg per kg PO BID	

$$60 \text{ mL total Rx} \times \frac{0.1 \text{ mg levo}}{\text{mL}} = 6 \text{ mg of levothyroxine needed}$$

$$6 \text{ mg levo} \times \frac{1 \text{ tab}}{0.25 \text{ mg levo}} = 24 \text{ tabs of levothyroxine needed}$$

The first step can also be performed as a proportion. <u>If the proportion is set up correctly, the answers will be the same.</u>

$$\frac{0.1 \text{ mg levo}}{1 \text{ mL}} = \frac{X \text{ mg levo}}{60 \text{ mL}} \qquad X = 6 \text{ mg of levothyroxine needed}$$

$$6 \text{ mg levo} \times \frac{1 \text{ tab}}{0.25 \text{ mg levo}} = 24 \text{ tabs of levothyroxine needed}$$

Or, it can be solved by <u>dimensional analysis</u>:

$$\frac{1 \text{ tab levo}}{0.25 \text{ mg levo}} \times \frac{0.1 \text{ mg levo}}{\text{mL}} \times 60 \text{ mL total Rx} = 24 \text{ tabs of levothyroxine needed}$$

After solving the problem, read the question again to be certain the question was answered with the correct units (tablets).

---

19. A pharmacist will prepare an *Amoxil* suspension to provide a 1600 mg daily dose for a child with an otitis media infection. The dose will be divided BID. To prepare an *Amoxil* suspension containing 200 mg/5 mL the pharmacist should add 76 mL of water to the powder for a final volume of 100 mL. The pharmacist should add approximately ¹⁄₃ of the water first, shake vigorously, add the remaining water, and shake again to form the suspension. The pharmacist mistakenly adds too much water and finds that the final volume is 110 mL. The pharmacy has no other bottles of *Amoxil,* so the pharmacist will dispense the bottle with the extra water added. How many mL should the patient take twice daily to receive the correct dose? Round to the nearest whole number.

Two methods to solve this calculation are shown:

$$\frac{200 \text{ mg}}{5 \text{ mL}} = \frac{X \text{ mg}}{100 \text{ mL}} \qquad X = 4{,}000 \text{ mg}$$

$$\frac{4{,}000 \text{ mg}}{110 \text{ mL}} = \frac{X \text{ mg}}{\text{mL}} \qquad X = 36.36 \text{ mg/mL}$$

$$\frac{4{,}000 \text{ mg}}{110 \text{ mL}} = \frac{800 \text{ mg}}{X \text{ mL}} \qquad X = 22 \text{ mL}$$

$$\frac{181.82 \text{ mg}}{5 \text{ mL}} = \frac{800 \text{ mg}}{X \text{ mL}} \qquad X = 22 \text{ mL}$$

20. How many milligrams of codeine will be contained in each capsule?

PRESCRIPTION	QUANTITY
Codeine Sulfate	0.6 g
Guaifenesin	1.2 g
Caffeine	0.15 g
M. ft. caps. no. 24	
Sig. One capsule TID PRN cough	

Begin by converting to the units requested in the answer (mg).

$$0.6 \text{ g codeine } \times \frac{1{,}000 \text{ mg}}{1 \text{ g}} = 600 \text{ mg of codeine for the total prescription}$$

The prescription order is for 24 capsules.

$$\frac{600 \text{ mg codeine total}}{24 \text{ caps}} = 25 \text{ mg of codeine/capsule}$$

After solving the problem, read the question again to be certain the question was answered with the correct units (mg of codeine per capsule).

---

21. A physician writes an order for aminophylline 500 mg IV, dosed at 0.5 mg per kg per hour for a patient weighing 165 pounds. There is only theophylline in stock. How many milligrams (mg) of theophylline will the patient receive per hour? Round to the nearest whole number.

$$\frac{0.5 \text{ mg Amino}}{\text{kg/hr}} \times \frac{1 \text{ kg}}{2.2 \text{ pounds}} \times 165 \text{ pounds } = 37.5 \text{ mg/hr aminophylline}$$

The aminophylline dose must now be converted to theophylline.

- <u>Aminophylline to theophylline</u>; multiply by 0.8
- <u>Theophylline to aminophylline</u>; divide by 0.8

$$37.5 \text{ mg/hr aminophylline} \times 0.8 = 30 \text{ mg/hr of theophylline}$$

After solving the problem, read the question again to be certain the question was answered with the correct units (mg per hour of theophylline).

---

22. How many grains of aspirin will be contained in each capsule? Round to the nearest tenth.

PRESCRIPTION	QUANTITY
Aspirin	6 g
Phenacetin	3.2 g
Caffeine	0.48 g
M. ft. no. 20 caps	
Sig. One capsule Q6H PRN pain	

$$6 \text{ g ASA} \times \frac{1,000 \text{ mg}}{1 \text{ g}} \times \frac{1 \text{ grain}}{65 \text{ mg}} = 92.3 \text{ grains}$$

We have 92.3 grains of aspirin that will be divided into 20 capsules.

$$\frac{92.3 \text{ grains}}{20 \text{ capsules}} = 4.6 \text{ grains/capsule}$$

After solving the problem, read the question again to be certain the question was answered with the correct units (grains per capsule).

---

23. A 45 milliliter nasal spray delivers 20 sprays per milliliter of solution. Each spray contains 1.5 mg of active drug. How many milligrams of drug are contained in the 45 mL package?

First calculate the amount of drug per mL.

$$\frac{1.5 \text{ mg drug}}{\text{spray}} \times \frac{20 \text{ sprays}}{\text{mL}} = 30 \text{ mg/mL}$$

Then solve for milligrams of drug in 45 mL.

$$\frac{30 \text{ mg}}{\text{mL}} = \frac{X \text{ mg}}{45 \text{ mL}} \qquad X = 1,350 \text{ mg}$$

---

24. A metered dose inhaler provides 90 micrograms of albuterol sulfate with each inhalation. The canister provides 200 inhalations. If the patient uses the entire canister, how many total milligrams will the patient have received?

$$200 \text{ inhalations} \times \frac{90 \text{ mcg}}{\text{inhalation}} = 18,000 \text{ mcg}$$

$$18,000 \text{ mcg} \times \frac{1 \text{ mg}}{1,000 \text{ mcg}} = 18 \text{ mg}$$

Percentage Strength

A percentage is a number or ratio as a fraction of 100. Expressions of concentration describe the amount of solute that will be contained in the total preparation. The percentage concentrations are defined as follows:

- Percent weight-in-volume (% w/v) is expressed as g/100 mL (a solid mixed into a liquid)
- Percent volume-in-volume (% v/v) is expressed as mL/100 mL (a liquid mixed into a liquid)
- Percent weight-in-weight (% w/w) is expressed as g/100 g (a solid mixed into a solid)

---

25. How many grams of NaCl are in 1 liter of normal saline (NS)?

Normal saline (NS) is 0.9% (w/v) NaCl solution

Remember (w/v) is always expressed as grams per 100 mL, therefore, NS contains 0.9 g NaCl per 100 mL of solution.

$$\frac{0.9 \text{ g}}{100 \text{ mL}} = \frac{X \text{ g}}{1,000 \text{ mL}} \qquad X = 9 \text{ g}$$

26. How many grams of NaCl are in 500 mL of ½NS? Round to the nearest hundredth.

NS is 0.9 g/100 mL; ½NS (called "half normal saline") is 0.45 g/100 mL.

$$\frac{0.45\ g}{100\ mL} = \frac{X\ g}{500\ mL} \qquad X = 2.25\ g$$

---

27. How many grams of dextrose are in 250 mL of D5W? Round to the nearest tenth.

D5W refers to 5% (w/v) dextrose in water solution.

$$\frac{5\ g}{100\ mL} = \frac{X\ g}{250\ mL} \qquad X = 12.5\ g$$

---

28. How many milligrams of triamcinolone should be used in preparing the following prescription? Round to the nearest whole number.

PRESCRIPTION	QUANTITY
Triamcinolone (w/v)	5%
Glycerin qs	60 mL
Sig. Two drops in right ear	

$$\frac{5\ g}{100\ mL} = \frac{X\ g}{60\ mL} \qquad X = 3\ g,\ or\ 3{,}000\ mg$$

---

29. A prescription reads as follows: "Prepare a 3% w/w coal tar preparation qs with petrolatum to 150 grams". How many grams of petrolatum are required to compound the prescription? Round to the nearest tenth.

$$\frac{3\ g\ coal\ tar}{100\ g\ preparation} = \frac{X\ g\ coal\ tar}{150\ g\ preparation} \qquad X = 4.5\ g\ coal\ tar$$

150 g (total weight of preparation) − 4.5 g (coal tar) = 145.5 g petrolatum

---

30. JL has mucositis secondary to methotrexate chemotherapy. His oncologist ordered lidocaine HCl 2% w/v solution; qs with pure water to 120 mL. How much lidocaine, in grams, is required to make the prescription? Round to the nearest tenth.

$$\frac{2\ g}{100\ mL} = \frac{X\ g}{120\ mL} \qquad X = 2.4\ g$$

31. SS is a 79 year old female with dry mouth and dry eyes from Sjögren's syndrome. She is picking up the prescription below. What is the maximum milligrams of pilocarpine she will receive per day?

PRESCRIPTION	QUANTITY
Pilocarpine	1% (w/v)
Sodium Chloride qs ad	15 mL
Sig: 2 gtts (0.1 mL) po TID prn up to 5 days for dry mouth	

First, calculate the amount of pilocarpine in the prescription.

$$\frac{1 \text{ g}}{100 \text{ mL}} = \frac{X \text{ g}}{15 \text{ mL}} \qquad X = 0.15 \text{ g}$$

Then, convert to mg since the problem asks for mg of pilocarpine.

$$0.15 \text{ g} \times \frac{1{,}000 \text{ mg}}{1 \text{ g}} = 150 \text{ mg of pilocarpine}$$

The patient will receive up to 3 doses per day (0.1 mL x 3 = 0.3 mL). Calculate the amount of pilocarpine in 0.3 mL.

$$\frac{150 \text{ mg pilocarpine}}{15 \text{ mL}} = \frac{X \text{ mg}}{0.3 \text{ mL}} \qquad X = 3 \text{ mg pilocarpine}$$

---

32. If 1,250 grams of a mixture contains 80 grams of drug, what is the percentage strength (w/w) of the mixture? Round to the nearest tenth.

$$\frac{80 \text{ g}}{1{,}250 \text{ g}} = \frac{X \text{ g}}{100 \text{ g}} \qquad X = 6.4 \text{ g, which is } 6.4\%$$

---

33. A mouth rinse contains $\frac{1}{12}$% (w/v) of chlorhexidine gluconate. How many grams of chlorhexidine gluconate should be used to prepare 18 liters of mouth rinse? Round to the nearest whole number.

- $\frac{1}{12}$% = 0.083 g per 100 mL (w/v)
- 18 L x 1,000 mL/L = 18,000 mL

$$\frac{0.083 \text{ g}}{100 \text{ mL}} = \frac{X \text{ g}}{18{,}000 \text{ mL}} \qquad X = 14.94 \text{ g, rounded to 15 g}$$

---

34. If 12 grams of lanolin are combined with 2 grams of white wax and 36 grams of petrolatum to make an ointment, what is the percentage strength (w/w) of lanolin in the ointment?

$$\frac{12 \text{ g lanolin}}{50 \text{ g ointment}} = \frac{X \text{ g}}{100 \text{ g}} \qquad X = 24\% \text{ w/w}$$

35. A pharmacist dissolves 6 tablets. Each tablet contains 250 mg of metronidazole. The pharmacist will put the drug into a liquid base to prepare 60 mL of a topical solution. What is the percentage strength (w/v) of metronidazole in the prescription? Round to the nearest tenth.

$$6 \text{ tablets} \times \frac{250 \text{ mg}}{1 \text{ tab}} = 1{,}500 \text{ mg, or } 1.5 \text{ g}$$

$$\frac{1.5 \text{ g}}{60 \text{ mL}} = \frac{X \text{ g}}{100 \text{ mL}} \qquad X = 2.5 \text{ g, which is } 2.5\% \text{ w/v}$$

---

36. A pharmacist adds 5.3 grams of hydrocortisone to 150 grams of a 2.5% hydrocortisone ointment. What is the percentage (w/w) of hydrocortisone in the finished product? Round to the nearest whole number.

First, determine the amount of hydrocortisone (HC) in the current product.

$$\frac{2.5 \text{ g HC}}{100 \text{ g ointment}} = \frac{X \text{ g HC}}{150 \text{ g ointment}} \qquad X = 3.75 \text{ g HC}$$

5.3 grams of hydrocortisone is being added to the existing product which contains 3.75 g of hydrocortisone: 5.3 g + 3.75 g = 9.05 g.

Next, find the percent concentration of the final product (5.3 g + 150 g = 155.3 g).

$$\frac{9.05 \text{ g HC}}{155.3 \text{ g ointment}} = \frac{X \text{ g HC}}{100 \text{ g ointment}} \qquad X = 5.8274 \text{ g, rounded to } 6\%$$

---

37. How many milliliters of hydrocortisone liquid (40 mg/mL) will be needed to prepare 30 grams of a 0.25% cream (w/w)? Round to the nearest hundredth.

First, calculate the amount of hydrocortisone needed in the final product.

$$\frac{0.25 \text{ g}}{100 \text{ g}} = \frac{X \text{ g}}{30 \text{ g}} \qquad X = 0.075 \text{ g or } 75 \text{ mg}$$

Then, solve for mL of hydrocortisone liquid needed.

$$\frac{40 \text{ mg}}{\text{mL}} = \frac{75 \text{ mg}}{X \text{ mL}} \qquad X = 1.875 \text{ mL, rounded to } 1.88 \text{ mL}$$

After solving the problem, read the question again to be certain the question was answered with the correct units (mL).

38. What is the percentage strength of imiquimod in the following prescription? Round to the nearest hundredth.

PRESCRIPTION	QUANTITY
Imiquimod 5% cream	15 g
Xylocaine	20 g
Hydrophilic ointment	25 g

First, calculate the amount of imiquimod (5%) in the prescription.

$$\frac{5 \text{ g}}{100 \text{ g}} \times 15 \text{ g} = 0.75 \text{ grams of imiquimod}$$

The total weight of the prescription is 60 g (15 g + 20 g + 25 g).

$$\frac{0.75 \text{ g}}{60 \text{ g}} = \frac{X \text{ g}}{100 \text{ g}} \quad X = 1.25 \text{ g, which is } 1.25\%$$

Ratio Strength

The concentration of weak solutions can be expressed in terms of ratio strength. Ratio strength describes the drug concentration in terms of a ratio (as the name suggests). It is denoted as one unit of solute contained in the total amount of the solution or mixture (e.g., 1:500). Ratio strength is another way of presenting a percentage strength. This makes sense because percentages are ratios of parts per hundred. When ratio strengths are involved in calculation problems, the ratio strength will often need to be converted to a percentage strength to solve calculation problems.

---

39. Express 0.04% as a ratio strength.

$$\frac{0.04}{100} = \frac{1 \text{ part}}{X \text{ parts}} \quad X = 2{,}500. \text{ Ratio strength is } 1{:}2{,}500$$

Convert back to 0.04% by taking 1/2,500 x 100 or simply 100/2,500. Try it.

---

40. Express 1:4,000 as a percentage strength.

$$\frac{1 \text{ part}}{4{,}000 \text{ part}} = \frac{X}{100} \quad X = 0.025, \text{ which is } 0.025\%$$

💡 SHORTCUT	
Convert a ratio strength to a percentage:	Convert a percentage to a ratio strength:
Percentage strength = 100 / ratio strength	Ratio strength = 100 / percentage strength

Problem #40 can be done using the shortcut above for converting between ratio and percentage strength:

Percentage strength = 100 / 4,000 = 0.025%

41. There are 50 mg of drug in 50 mL of solution. Express the concentration as a ratio strength (% w/v).

First, convert 50 mg to grams. 50 mg x 1 g/1,000 mg = 0.05 g

Then, calculate grams per 100 mL.

$$\frac{0.05 \text{ g}}{50 \text{ mL}} = \frac{X \text{ g}}{100 \text{ mL}} \qquad X = 0.1 \text{ g}$$

Now solve for ratio strength.

$$\frac{0.1 \text{ g}}{100 \text{ mL}} = \frac{1 \text{ part}}{X \text{ parts}} \qquad X = 1,000, \text{ or } 1:1,000$$

---

42. How many milligrams of iodine should be used in compounding the following prescription?

ITEM	QUANTITY
Iodine	1:400
Hydrophilic ointment ad	10 g
Sig. Apply as directed.	

First, convert the ratio strength to a percentage strength.

$$\frac{1 \text{ part}}{400 \text{ parts}} = \frac{X \text{ g}}{100 \text{ g}} \qquad X = 0.25\%$$

Then, determine how much iodine will be needed for the prescription.

$$\frac{0.25 \text{ g}}{100 \text{ g}} = \frac{X \text{ g}}{10 \text{ g}} \qquad X = 0.025 \text{ g, or } 25 \text{ mg}$$

Or, solve another way:

1:400 means 1 g in 400 g of ointment.

$$\frac{1 \text{ g}}{400 \text{ g}} = \frac{X \text{ g}}{10 \text{ g}} \qquad X = 0.025 \text{ g, or } 25 \text{ mg}$$

---

43. A 10 mL mixture contains 0.25 mL of active drug. Express the concentration as a percentage strength (% v/v) and a ratio strength.

First, find out how much drug is in 100 mL.

$$\frac{0.25 \text{ mL drug}}{10 \text{ mL}} = \frac{X \text{ mL drug}}{100 \text{ mL}} \qquad X = 2.5 \text{ mL, or } 2.5\% \text{ (v/v)}$$

Now solve for ratio strength.

$$\frac{2.5 \text{ mL drug}}{100 \text{ mL}} = \frac{1 \text{ part}}{X \text{ parts}} \qquad X = 40; \text{ or } 1:40$$

44. What is the concentration, in ratio strength, of a trituration made by combining 150 mg of albuterol sulfate and 4.05 grams of lactose?

First, add up the total weight of the prescription.

$$0.150 \text{ g} + 4.05 \text{ g} = 4.2 \text{ g}$$

Now solve for ratio strength.

$$\frac{0.150 \text{ g}}{4.2 \text{ g}} = \frac{1 \text{ part}}{X \text{ parts}} \qquad X = 28, \text{ or } 1{:}28$$

Parts Per Million

Parts indicate amount proportions. Parts per million (PPM) and parts per billion (PPB) are used to quantify strengths of very dilute solutions. It is defined as the number of parts of the drug per 1 million (or 1 billion) parts of the whole. The same default units are followed as for percentage systems (% w/w, % w/v and % v/v).

45. Express 0.00022% w/v as PPM. Round to the nearest tenth.

$$\frac{0.00022 \text{ g}}{100 \text{ mL}} = \frac{X \text{ parts}}{1{,}000{,}000} \qquad X = 2.2 \text{ PPM}$$

46. Express 30 PPM of copper in solution as a percentage.

$$\frac{30 \text{ parts}}{1{,}000{,}000} = \frac{X \text{ g}}{100 \text{ mL}} \qquad X = 0.003\%$$

47. Express 5 PPM of iron in water as a percentage.

$$\frac{5 \text{ parts}}{1{,}000{,}000} = \frac{X \text{ g}}{100 \text{ mL}} \qquad X = 0.0005\%$$

> **SHORTCUT**
>
> When converting from PPM to a percentage strength, move the decimal <u>left</u> 4 places.
>
> When converting from a percentage strength to PPM, move the decimal <u>right</u> 4 places.

48. A patient's blood contains 0.085 PPM of selenium. How many micrograms of selenium does the patient's blood contain if the blood volume is 6 liters?

$$\frac{0.085 \text{ parts}}{1{,}000{,}000} = \frac{X \text{ g}}{6{,}000 \text{ mL}} \qquad X = 0.00051 \text{ g, or } 510 \text{ mcg}$$

49. A sample of an intravenous solution is found to contain 0.4 PPM of DEHP. How much of the solution, in milliliters, will contain 50 micrograms of DEHP?

$$\frac{0.4 \text{ parts}}{1,000,000} = \frac{0.00005 \text{ g}}{X \text{ mL}} \qquad X = 125 \text{ mL}$$

If asked to express something in PPB (parts per billion), divide by 1,000,000,000 (9 zeros).

Specific Gravity

Specific gravity (SG) is the ratio of the density of a substance to the density of water. SG can be important for calculating doses of IV medications, in compounding, and in interpreting a urinalysis. Water has a specific gravity of 1 where 1 g water = 1 mL water. Substances with a SG < 1 are lighter than water and those with SG > 1 are heavier than water.

$$SG = \frac{\text{weight of substance (g)}}{\text{weight of equal volume of water (g)}} \qquad \text{or more simply:} \qquad SG = \frac{g}{mL}$$

---

50. What is the specific gravity of 150 mL of glycerin weighing 165 grams? Round to the nearest tenth.

$$SG = \frac{165 \text{ g}}{150 \text{ mL}} \qquad SG = 1.1$$

Check the answer: 150 mL x 1.1 = 165 g

---

51. What is the weight of 750 mL of concentrated acetic acid (SG = 1.2)?

$$1.2 = \frac{X \text{ g}}{750 \text{ mL}} \qquad X = 900 \text{ g}$$

Check the answer: 900 g/750 mL = 1.2

---

52. How many mL of polysorbate 80 (SG = 1.08) are needed to prepare a prescription that includes 48 grams of the surfactant/emulsifier (polysorbate)? Round to the nearest hundredth.

$$1.08 = \frac{48 \text{ g}}{X \text{ mL}} \qquad X = 44.44 \text{ mL}$$

Check the answer: 48 g/44.44 mL = 1.08

---

53. What is the specific gravity of 30 mL of a liquid weighing 23,400 milligrams? Round to the nearest hundredth.

$$SG = \frac{23.4 \text{ g}}{30 \text{ mL}} \qquad SG = 0.78$$

54. What is the weight of 0.5 L of polyethylene glycol 400 (SG = 1.13).

$$1.13 = \frac{X \text{ g}}{500 \text{ mL}} \qquad X = 565 \text{ grams}$$

---

55. Nitroglycerin has a specific gravity of 1.59. How much would 1 quart weigh in grams? Use 1 quart = 946 mL. Round to the nearest whole number.

$$1.59 = \frac{X \text{ g}}{946 \text{ mL}} \qquad X = 1{,}504 \text{ g}$$

Check the answer: 1,504 g/946 mL = 1.59

Note that the SG is <u>equivalent</u> to the <u>density in g/mL (with units)</u>. If asked for the density in the above problem, the answer would be 1.59 g/mL.

Calculation Practice

The following problem integrates multiple calculation concepts.

---

56. A pharmacist receives a prescription for a 1.5% (w/w) hydrocortisone cream using cold cream as the base. She will use hydrocortisone injection (100 mg/mL, SG 1.5) to prepare the prescription because she has no hydrocortisone powder in stock. How many grams of cold cream are required to compound 60 grams of the preparation?

First, calculate the grams of hydrocortisone required for the prescription.

$$\frac{1.5 \text{ g}}{100 \text{ g}} = \frac{X \text{ g}}{60 \text{ g}} \qquad X = 0.9 \text{ grams of hydrocortisone required}$$

Calculate the volume of hydrocortisone injection required.

$$\frac{100 \text{ mg}}{1 \text{ mL}} = \frac{900 \text{ mg}}{X \text{ mL}} \qquad X = 9 \text{ mL}$$

Calculate the weight of 9 mL of hydrocortisone injection using the SG provided.

$$1.5 = \frac{X \text{ g}}{9 \text{ mL}} \qquad X = 13.5 \text{ grams (weight of hydrocortisone injection)}$$

Calculate the grams of cold cream required.

60 g final product   −   13.5 g (weight of hydrocortisone)   =   46.5 g of cold cream

Dilution and Concentration

Often the strength of a product must be increased or decreased. Or, a new quantity is required. This formula can be used to change the strength or quantity. Be careful: <u>the units on each side must match</u> and one or more may need to be changed, such as mg to gram, or vice-versa.

$$Q_1 \times C_1 = Q_2 \times C_2$$

Q_1 = old quantity

C_1 = old concentration

Q_2 = new quantity

C_2 = new concentration

---

57. A pharmacist has an order for parenteral nutrition that includes 550 mL of D70%. The pharmacist checks the supplies and finds the closest strength he has available is D50%. How many mL of D50% will provide an equivalent energy requirement?

550 mL $\times$ 70% = Q_2 mL $\times$ 50%

Q_2 = 770 mL of D50%

---

58. How many grams of petrolatum (diluent) should be added to 250 grams of a 20% ichthammol ointment to make a 7% ichthammol ointment? Round to the nearest tenth.

Note the difference from the previous problem. In this example, the problem asks how much <u>diluent</u> should be added to make the final weight.

250 g $\times$ 20% = Q_2 $\times$ 7%

Q_2 = 714.3 g of 7% ichthammol ointment

Read the question again to be certain about what is being asked. Since the question did not ask how much of the 7% ointment can be prepared, but rather how much diluent is required, <u>an additional step is needed</u>:

714.3 g total weight – 250 g (already present) = 464.3 g petrolatum required

---

59. Using 20 grams of a 9% boric acid ointment base, the pharmacist will manufacture a 5% ointment. How much diluent is required?

20 g $\times$ 9% = Q_2 $\times$ 5%

Q_2 = 36 g of the 5% ointment can be prepared

36 g total weight – 20 g (already present) = 16 g diluent required

---

60. If 1 gallon of a 20% (w/v) solution is evaporated to a solution with a 50% (w/v) strength, what will be the new volume (in mL)? Round to the nearest 100 mL.

3,785 mL $\times$ 20% = Q_2 $\times$ 50%

Q_2 = 1,514 mL, rounded to the nearest 100 mL = 1500 mL

Note: This answer will be the same regardless of which conversion is used for gallon to mL.

61. A patient has been receiving 200 mL of an enteral mixture that contains 432 mOsm/L. The pharmacist will reduce the contents to 278 mOsm/L. How many mL of bacteriostatic water should be added to the bag? Round to the nearest mL.

$$200 \text{ mL} \times 432 \text{ mOsm/L} = Q_2 \times 278 \text{ mOsm/L} \quad X = 311 \text{ mL}$$

$$Q_2 = 311 \text{ mL of the 278 mOsm/L enteral mixture can be prepared}$$

There are 200 mL in the original bag. The final volume will be 311 mL.

$$311 \text{ mL} - 200 \text{ mL} = 111 \text{ mL of bacteriostatic water}$$

Calculation Practice

The following problems integrate multiple calculation concepts.

---

62. How many mL of a 1:2,500 (w/v) solution of aluminum acetate can be made from 100 mL of a 0.2% solution?

Both concentrations must be in the same units to use the $Q_1C_1 = Q_2C_2$ formula. So, 1:2,500 must be converted to a percentage strength first.

$$\frac{1 \text{ part}}{2,500 \text{ parts}} = \frac{X \text{ g}}{100 \text{ mL}} \qquad X = 0.04 \text{ g, or } 0.04\%$$

Now use the formula.

$$100 \text{ mL} \times 0.2\% = Q_2 \times 0.04\%$$

$$Q_2 = 500 \text{ mL}$$

---

63. What is the ratio strength (w/v) of 50 mL containing a 1:20 (w/v) ammonia solution diluted to 1 liter?

First, convert 1:20 to a percentage strength.

$$\frac{1 \text{ part}}{20 \text{ parts}} = \frac{X \text{ g}}{100 \text{ mL}} \qquad X = 5 \text{ g, or } 5\%$$

$$50 \text{ mL} \times 5\% = 1,000 \text{ mL} \times C_2$$

$$C_2 = 0.25\%$$

$$\text{Convert } 0.25\% \text{ to ratio strength} = 1:400$$

Alligation

Alligation is used to obtain a new strength (percentage) that is between two strengths the pharmacist has in stock. Occasionally, no math is required to solve this type of problem if the new strength needed is exactly in the middle of the 2 strengths that are given. If the prescription calls for an ingredient that is pure, the concentration is 100%. If given a diluent, such as petrolatum, lanolin, alcohol, "ointment base", etc., the concentration of the diluent is 0%.

64. A pharmacist must prepare 100 grams of a 50% hydrocortisone powder using the 25% and 75% powders that she has in stock. How much of each is required?

Since the desired strength is exactly in the middle of the strengths available, divide the desired quantity in half (100 g / 2 = 50 grams). Use 50 g of the 75% and 50 g of the 25% to prepare 100 g of a 50% powder.

---

65. A pharmacist is asked to prepare 80 grams of a 12.5% ichthammol ointment with 16% and 12% ichthammol ointments in stock.

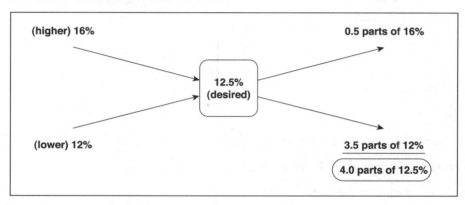

- To set up the X method:

    ☐ Put the more concentrated product at the top left (high goes high)

    ☐ Put the less concentrated product at the bottom left (low goes low)

    ☐ Place the desired concentration in the middle of the X

- Subtract along the "X" lines to obtain the number of parts on the right (16% – 12.5% = 3.5 parts; 12% – 12.5% = 0.5 parts).

- Add the number of parts on the right to find the total number of parts (4 parts).

- Divide the total weight (80 g) by the number of parts to obtain the weight per part.

$$\frac{80\ g}{4\ parts} = 20\ grams\ per\ part$$

- Take the amount per part (20 g) and multiply it by the parts from each of the concentrations (from the high, and from the low).

$$0.5\ parts\ of\ 16\% \times \frac{20\ g}{part} = 10\ g\ of\ the\ 16\%\ ichthammol\ ointment$$

$$3.5\ parts\ of\ 12\% \times \frac{20\ g}{part} = 70\ g\ of\ the\ 12\%\ ichthammol\ ointment$$

Mix together; the end product provides 80 g of a 12.5% ichthammol ointment.

66. A pharmacist is asked to prepare 1 gallon of tincture containing 5.5% iodine. The pharmacy has 3% iodine tincture and 8.5% iodine tincture in stock. How many mL of the 3% and 8.5% iodine tincture should be used? (Use 1 gallon = 3,785 mL)

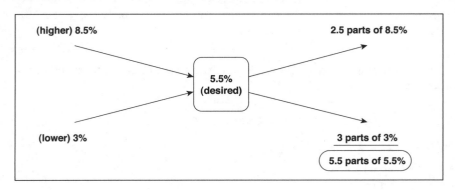

- To set up the X method:

  - Put the more concentrated product at the top left (high goes high)

  - Put the less concentrated product at the bottom left (low goes low)

  - Place the desired concentration in the middle of the X

- Subtract along the "X" lines to obtain the number of parts on the right (e.g., 8.5% – 5.5% = 3 parts; 3% – 5.5% = 2.5 parts for this problem).

- Add the number of parts on the right to find the total number of parts (5.5 parts in this problem).

Divide the total volume (3,785 mL) by the number of parts to obtain the volume per part.

$$\frac{3{,}785 \text{ mL}}{5.5 \text{ parts}} = 688.2 \text{ mL per part}$$

$$2.5 \text{ parts} \times \frac{688.2 \text{ mL}}{\text{part}} = 1{,}720 \text{ mL of the 8.5\% iodine tincture}$$

$$3 \text{ parts} \times \frac{688.2 \text{ mL}}{\text{part}} = 2{,}065 \text{ mL of the 3\% iodine tincture}$$

The end product provides 3,785 mL of a 5.5% iodine tincture. Alligation can also be used when the final volume is not known.

67. A hospice pharmacist received a prescription for 4% morphine sulfate oral solution. She has a 120 mL bottle of 12% morphine sulfate that was compounded this morning. How much diluent must be added to the 120 mL bottle to achieve the desired percentage strength for the patient?

Set up the X method in the same way:

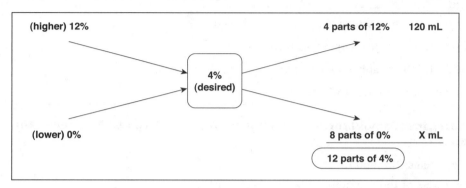

In this case, we do not know the final volume of the product, but we know the proper ratio of the parts.

$$\frac{4 \text{ parts of 12\%}}{8 \text{ parts of 0\%}} = \frac{120 \text{ mL of 12\%}}{X \text{ mL of 0\%}} \qquad X = 240 \text{ mL}$$

Therefore, 240 mL of diluent must be added to the 120 mL bottle of 12% morphine sulfate to get a 4% solution.

Osmolarity

The total number of particles in a given solution is directly proportional to its osmotic pressure. The particles are usually measured in milliosmoles. Osmolarity is the measure of total number of particles (or solutes) per liter (L) of solution, defined as osmoles/Liter (Osmol/L) or, more commonly as milliosmoles/Liter (mOsmol/L). Solutes can be either ionic (such as NaCl, which dissociates into 2 solutes in solution, Na^+ and Cl^-) or non-ionic, which do not dissociate (such as glucose and urea). The term for osmolarity when used to refer to the solute concentration of body fluids is tonicity, and solutions are thus isotonic (osmolarity is the same as blood, which is ~300 mOsmol/L), or is lower (hypotonic) or higher (hypertonic).

If the osmolarity is higher in one cellular compartment, it will cause water to move from the lower to the higher concentration of solutes. If a PN solution is injected with a higher osmolarity than blood, fluid will flow into the vein, resulting in edema, inflammation, phlebitis and possible thrombosis.

COMPOUND	# OF DISSOCIATION PARTICLES
Dextrose	1
Mannitol	1
Potassium chloride (KCl)	2
Sodium chloride (NaCl)	2
Sodium acetate ($NaC_2H_3O_2$)	2
Calcium chloride ($CaCl_2$)	3
Sodium citrate ($Na_3C_6H_5O_7$)	4

Milliosmole calculation problems differ from osmolarity calculation problems in that osmolarity will always need to be normalized to a volume of 1 liter. Some compounds for which it may be useful to know dissociations are listed in the table.

Osmolarity Calculations

Use this formula to find the mOsmol/L.

$$mOsmol/L = \frac{Wt\ of\ substance\ (g/L)}{MW\ (g/mole)} \times (\#\ of\ particles) \times 1{,}000$$

- Add up the number of particles into which the compound dissociates.
- Calculate the number of grams of the compound present in 1 L.
- Use the molecular weight (M.W.) to solve the problem.

Milliosmole calculations do not normalize to 1 liter.

---

68. What is the osmolarity, in mOsmol/L, of normal saline (0.9% NaCl)? M.W. = 58.5. Round to the nearest whole number.

NaCl dissociates into 2 particles; Na^+ and Cl^-.

Calculate the number of grams of the compound (NaCl) present in 1 L.

$$\frac{0.9\ g}{100\ mL} = \frac{X\ g}{1{,}000\ mL} \qquad X = 9\ g$$

Use the molecular weight to solve for mOsmol/L.

$$mOsmol/L = \frac{9\ g/L}{58.5\ g/mole} \times 2 \times 1{,}000 = 308\ mOsmol/L$$

---

69. What is the osmolarity, in mOsmol/L, of D5W? M.W. = 198. Round to the nearest tenth.

Dextrose does not dissociate and is counted as 1 particle.

$$\frac{5\ g}{100\ mL} = \frac{X\ g}{1{,}000\ mL} \qquad X = 50\ g$$

Use the molecular weight to solve for mOsmol/L.

$$mOsmol/L = \frac{50\ g/L}{198\ g/mole} \times 1 \times 1{,}000 = 252.5\ mOsmol/L$$

---

70. A solution contains 373 mg Na ions per liter. How many milliosmoles are represented in the solution? M.W. = 23. Round to the nearest tenth.

First, convert the units to match the formula.

$$\frac{373\ mg\ Na}{L} \times \frac{1\ g}{1{,}000\ mg} = 0.373\ g/L$$

$$mOsmol = \frac{0.373\ g/L}{23\ g/mole} \times 1 \times 1{,}000 = 16.2\ mOsmol$$

The problem asks for milliosmoles and not osmolarity. Since the problem provides the amount of Na ions in 1 liter, the numerical answer is the same (mOsmol or mOsmol/L).

71. Calculate the osmolar concentration, in milliosmoles, represented by 1 liter of a 10% (w/v) solution of anhydrous dextrose (M.W. = 180) in water. Round to the nearest tenth.

$$\frac{10 \text{ g}}{100 \text{ mL}} = \frac{X \text{ g}}{1,000 \text{ mL}} \qquad X = 100 \text{ g}$$

$$mOsmol = \frac{100 \text{ g/L}}{180 \text{ g/mole}} \times 1 \times 1,000 = 555.6 \text{ mOsmol}$$

The problem asks for milliosmoles and not osmolarity. Since the problem asks for mOsmol of dextrose in 1 liter, the numerical answer is the same (mOsmol or mOsmol/L).

---

72. How many milliosmoles of $CaCl_2$ (M.W.= 147) are represented in 150 mL of a 10% (w/v) calcium chloride solution? Round to the nearest whole number.

$$\frac{10 \text{ g}}{100 \text{ mL}} = \frac{X \text{ g}}{150 \text{ mL}} \qquad X = 15 \text{ g}$$

$$mOsmol = \frac{15 \text{ g}}{147 \text{ g/mol}} \times 3 \times 1,000 = 306 \text{ mOsmol}$$

Note that the problem is asking for milliosmoles and not osmolarity. Therefore, the answer is in milliosmoles and not mOsmol/L. It is not normalized to 1 liter.

---

73. A solution contains 200 mg Ca ions per liter. How many milliosmoles are represented in the solution? M.W = 40

$$mOsmol = \frac{0.2 \text{ g/L}}{40 \text{ g/mole}} \times 1 \times 1,000 = 5 \text{ mOsmol}$$

The problem is asking for milliosmoles and not osmolarity. Therefore, the answer is in milliosmoles and not mOsmol/L. It is not normalized to 1 liter.

---

74. How many grams of potassium chloride are needed to make 200 mL of a solution containing 250 mOsmol/L? Round to the nearest hundredth. (M.W. K = 39, M.W. Cl = 35.5)

First calculate the M.W. of KCl.

M.W. of KCl = M.W. of K + M.W. of Cl = 39 + 35.5 = 74.5

$$250 \text{ mOsmol/L} = \frac{X}{74.5} \times 2 \times 1,000 \qquad X = 9.31 \text{ g/L}$$

$$\frac{9.31 \text{ g}}{1,000 \text{ mL}} = \frac{X \text{ g}}{200 \text{ mL}} \qquad X = 1.86 \text{ g}$$

You may be provided with the molecular weight on the exam or asked to calculate it.

Isotonicity

Osmolarity is the measure of total number of particles (or solutes) per liter (L) of solution. Tonicity is the term used to describe osmolarity used in the context of body fluids. When solutions are prepared, they need to match the tonicity of the body fluid as closely as possible. Solutions that are not isotonic with the body fluid produce pain upon administration, and cause fluid transfer. In pharmacy, the terms hypotonic rather than hypo-osmotic, hypertonic rather than hyperosmotic, and isotonic rather than iso-osmotic, are used. Isotonicity is commonly used when preparing eye drops and nasal solutions.

Since isotonicity is related to the number of particles in solution, the dissociation factor (or ionization), symbolized by the letter i, is determined for the compound (drug). Non-ionic compounds do not dissociate and will have a dissociation factor, i, of 1. The table shows the dissociation factors (i) based on the percentage that dissociates into ions; for example, a dissociation factor of 1.8 means that 80% of the compound will dissociate in a weak solution.

NUMBER OF DISSOCIATED IONS	DISSOCIATION FACTOR (OR IONIZATION) i
1	1
2	1.8
3	2.6
4	3.4
5	4.2

As mentioned above, body fluids are isotonic, having an osmotic pressure equivalent to 0.9% sodium chloride. When making a medication to place into a body fluid, the drug provides solutes to the solvent and needs to be accounted for in the prescription in order to avoid making the prescription hypertonic. The relationship between the amount of drug that produces a particular osmolarity and the amount of sodium chloride that produces the same osmolarity is called the sodium chloride equivalent, or "E value" for short. This is the formula for calculating the E value of a compound:

$$E = \frac{(58.5)(i)}{(MW \text{ of drug})(1.8)}$$

The "E value" formula takes into account the molecular weight of NaCl (58.5) and the dissociation factor of 1.8 since normal saline is around 80% ionized; adding 0.8 for each additional ion beyond 1 into which the drug dissociates. The reason the compound is compared to NaCl is because NaCl is the major determinant of the isotonicity of body fluid.

Once the "E value" is determined, isotonicity problems can be calculated. The following steps outline the process of doing isotonicity problems:

1. Calculate the total amount of NaCl needed to make the final product/prescription isotonic. This is done by multiplying 0.9% NS by the desired volume of the prescription.

2. Multiply the total drug amount, in grams, by the "E value".

3. Subtract step 2 from step 1 to determine the total amount of NaCl needed to prepare an isotonic prescription.

---

75. Calculate the E value for mannitol (M.W. = 182). Round to the nearest hundredth.

$$\frac{(58.5)(i)}{(MW \text{ of drug})(1.8)} = \frac{58.5 \,(1)}{182 \,(1.8)} = 0.18$$

76. Calculate the E value for potassium iodide, which dissociates into 2 particles (M.W. = 166). Round to two decimal places.

$$\frac{(58.5)(i)}{(MW\ of\ drug)(1.8)} = \frac{58.5\ (1.8)}{166\ (1.8)} = 0.35$$

---

77. Physostigmine salicylate (M.W. = 413) is a 2- ion electrolyte, dissociating 80% in a given concentration (therefore, use a dissociation factor of 1.8). Calculate its sodium chloride equivalent. Round to two decimal places.

$$\frac{(58.5)(i)}{(MW\ of\ drug)(1.8)} = \frac{58.5\ (1.8)}{413\ (1.8)} = 0.14$$

---

78. The E-value for ephedrine sulfate is 0.23. How many grams of sodium chloride are needed to compound the following prescription? Round to 3 decimal places.

PRESCRIPTION	QUANTITY
Ephedrine sulfate	0.4 g
Sodium chloride	q.s.
Purified water qs	30 mL
Make isotonic soln.	
Sig. For the nose.	

Step 1. Determine how much NaCl would make the product isotonic.

$$\frac{0.9\ g}{100\ mL} = \frac{X}{30\ mL} \quad X = 0.27\ g$$

Step 2. Determine amount of sodium chloride represented from ephedrine sulfate.

0.4 g x 0.23 ("E value") = 0.092 g of sodium chloride

Step 3. Subtract step 2 from step 1.

0.27 g – 0.092 g = 0.178 g of NaCl are needed to make an isotonic solution

---

79. The pharmacist receives an order for 10 mL of tobramycin 1% ophthalmic solution. He has tobramycin 40 mg/mL solution. Tobramycin does not dissociate and has a M.W. of 468. Find the E value for tobramycin and determine the amount of NaCl needed to make the solution isotonic. Round to two decimal places.

$$\frac{(58.5)(i)}{(MW\ of\ drug)(1.8)} = \frac{58.5\ (1)}{468\ (1.8)} = 0.07, \text{ which is the "E value" for tobramycin}$$

The "E value" for tobramycin is 0.07. The prescription asks for 10 mL of 1% solution.

Step 1. Determine how much NaCl would make the product isotonic (if that is all you were using).

$$\frac{0.9 \text{ g}}{100 \text{ mL}} = \frac{X}{10 \text{ mL}} \qquad X = 0.09 \text{ g, or } 90 \text{ mg}$$

Step 2. Determine amount of sodium chloride represented from tobramycin.

$$\frac{1 \text{ g}}{100 \text{ mL}} = \frac{X}{10 \text{ mL}} \qquad X = 0.1 \text{ g, or } 100 \text{ mg}$$

$$100 \text{ mg} \times 0.07 \text{ ("E value")} = 7 \text{ mg of sodium chloride}$$

Step 3. Subtract step 2 from step 1.

You are using tobramycin, so you do not need all the NaCl. Subtract out the equivalent amount of tonicity provided by the tobramycin, which is 7 mg.

$$90 \text{ mg} - 7 \text{ mg} = 83 \text{ mg (83 mg additional sodium chloride is needed to make an isotonic solution)}$$

To calculate how much of the original stock solution is required, use the stock solution that is 40 mg/mL. The prescription is written for 10 mL of a 1% solution. In the previous steps it was found that 100 mg of tobramycin is needed to provide 10 mL of a 1% solution.

$$\frac{40 \text{ mg}}{1 \text{ mL}} = \frac{100 \text{ mg}}{X \text{ mL}} \qquad X = 2.5 \text{ mL of the original stock solution.}$$

Moles and Millimoles

A mole (mol) is the molecular weight of a substance in grams, or g/mole. A millimole (mmol) is 1/1,000 of the molecular weight in grams, or 1/1,000 of a mole. For monovalent species, the numeric value of the milliequivalent and millimole are identical.

$$\text{mols} = \frac{\text{g}}{\text{MW}} \qquad \text{or} \qquad \text{mmols} = \frac{\text{mg}}{\text{MW}}$$

80. How many moles of anhydrous magnesium sulfate (M.W. = 120.4) are present in 250 grams of the substance? Round to the nearest hundredth.

$$\text{mols} = \frac{\text{g}}{\text{MW}}$$

$$\text{mols} = \frac{250 \text{ g}}{120.4} = 2.076, \text{ or } 2.08 \text{ mols}$$

81. How many moles are equivalent to 875 milligrams of aluminum acetate (M.W. = 204)? Round to 3 decimal places.

First, convert 875 mg to grams.

$$875 \text{ mg} \times \frac{1 \text{ g}}{1,000 \text{ mg}} = 0.875 \text{ g}$$

Next, solve for mols.

$$mols = \frac{g}{MW} = \frac{0.875\ g}{204} = 0.004\ mols$$

---

82. How many millimoles of sodium phosphate (M.W. = 138) are present in 90 g of the substance? Round to the nearest whole number.

$$\frac{90,000\ mg}{138} = 652\ mmols$$

Or, solve another way:

$$\frac{90\ g}{138} = 0.652\ mols, \text{ which is } 652\ mmols$$

---

83. How many moles are equivalent to 45 grams of potassium carbonate (M.W. = 138)? Round to the nearest thousandth.

$$mols = \frac{g}{MW}$$

$$mols = \frac{45\ g}{138} = 0.326\ mols$$

---

84. How many millimoles of calcium chloride (M.W. = 147) are represented in 147 mL of a 10% (w/v) calcium chloride solution?

Step 1: Calculate the amount (g) of $CaCl_2$ in 147 mL of 10% $CaCl_2$ solution.

$$\frac{10\ g}{100\ mL} = \frac{X\ g}{147\ mL} \qquad X = 14.7\ g$$

Step 2: Calculate the mols of $CaCl_2$ in 147 mL of 10% $CaCl_2$ solution.

$$mols = \frac{14.7\ g}{147} \qquad X = 0.1\ mol$$

Step 3: Solve the problem by converting moles to millimoles; 0.1 mol x 1,000 = 100 mmols

---

85. How many milligrams of sodium chloride (MW = 58.5) represent 0.25 mmol? Do not round the answer.

$$0.25\ mmols = \frac{X\ mg}{58.5} \qquad X = 14.625\ mg$$

86. How many grams of sodium chloride (M.W. = 58.5) should be used to prepare this solution? Do not round the answer.

PRESCRIPTION	QUANTITY
Methylprednisolone	0.5 g
NaCl solution	60 mL
Each 5 mL should contain 0.6 mmols of NaCl	

$$\frac{0.6 \text{ mmols}}{5 \text{ mL}} = \frac{X \text{ mmols}}{60 \text{ mL}} \qquad X = 7.2 \text{ mmols}$$

$$7.2 \text{ mmols} = \frac{X \text{ mg}}{58.5} \qquad X = 421.2 \text{ mg or } 0.4212 \text{ g}$$

Milliequivalents

Drugs can be expressed in solution in different ways:

- Milliosmoles refers to the number of particles in solution.

- Millimoles refers to the molecular weight (MW).

- Milliequivalents (mEq) represent the amount, in milligrams (mg), of a solute equal to 1/1,000 of its gram equivalent weight, taking into account the valence of the ions. Like osmolarity, the quantity of particles is important – but so is the electrical charge. Milliequivalents refers to the chemical activity of an electrolyte and is related to the total number of ionic charges in solution and considers the valence (charge) of each ion.

COMPOUND	VALENCE
ammonium chloride (NH_4Cl)	1
potassium chloride (KCl^-)	1
potassium gluconate ($KC_6H_{11}O_7$)	1
sodium acetate ($NaC_2H_3O_2$)	1
sodium bicarbonate ($NaHCO_3$)	1
sodium chloride	1
calcium carbonate ($CaCO_3$)	2
calcium chloride ($CaCl_2$)	2
disodium phosphate	2
ferrous sulfate ($FeSO_4^{2-}$)	2
magnesium sulfate ($MgSO_4^{2-}$)	2

To count the valence, divide the compound into its positive and negative components, and then count the number of either the positive or the negative charges. For a given compound, the milliequivalents of cations equals that of anions. Some common compounds and their valence are listed in the table.

$$mEq = \frac{mg \times valence}{MW} \qquad or \qquad mEq = mmols \times valence$$

87. A 20 mL vial is labeled potassium chloride (2 mEq/mL). How many grams of potassium chloride (M.W. = 74.5) are present? Round to the nearest hundredth.

$$20 \text{ mL} \times \frac{2 \text{ mEq}}{mL} = 40 \text{ mEq KCl total}$$

$$mEq = \frac{mg \times valence}{MW}$$

$$40 \text{ mEq} = \frac{mg \times 1}{74.5} = 2{,}980 \text{ mg, which is } 2.98 \text{ g}$$

If asked to convert KCl liquid to tablets, use simple proportion since <u>KCl 10% = 20 mEq/15 mL</u>. For example, <u>if some-one is using Klor-Con 20 mEq BID, the total daily dose is 40 mEq. Convert to KCl 10%, by solving the following equation:</u>

$$\frac{40 \text{ mEq}}{X \text{ mL}} = \frac{20 \text{ mEq}}{15 \text{ mL}} \qquad X = 30 \text{ mL}$$

88. How many milliequivalents of potassium chloride are present in a 12 mL dose of a 10% (w/v) potassium chloride (M.W. = 74.5) elixir? Round to 1 decimal place.

$$\frac{10 \text{ g}}{100 \text{ mL}} = \frac{X \text{ g}}{12 \text{ mL}} \qquad X = 1.2 \text{ g, or } 1{,}200 \text{ mg}$$

$$\text{mEq} = \frac{1{,}200 \text{ mg} \times 1}{74.5} = 16.1 \text{ mEq}$$

89. Calculate the milliequivalents of a standard ammonium chloride (M.W. = 53.5) 21.4 mg/mL sterile solution in a 500 mL container.

$$\frac{21.4 \text{ mg}}{\text{mL}} \times 500 \text{ mL} = 10{,}700 \text{ mg}$$

$$\text{mEq} = \frac{10{,}700 \text{ mg} \times 1}{53.5} = 200 \text{ mEq}$$

90. How many milliequivalents of MgSO$_4$ (M.W. = 120.4) are represented in 1 gram of anhydrous magnesium sulfate? Round to the nearest tenth.

$$\text{mEq} = \frac{1{,}000 \text{ mg} \times 2}{120.4} = 16.6 \text{ mEq}$$

91. How many milliequivalents of sodium are in a 50 mL vial of sodium bicarbonate (M.W. = 84) 8.4%?

$$\frac{8.4 \text{ g}}{100 \text{ mL}} = \frac{X \text{ g}}{50 \text{ mL}} \qquad X = 4.2 \text{ g, or } 4{,}200 \text{ mg}$$

$$\text{mEq} = \frac{4{,}200 \text{ mg} \times 1}{84} = 50 \text{ mEq}$$

Calculation Practice

The following problem integrates multiple calculation concepts.

---

92. A pharmacist receives an order for sodium chloride 4 mEq/kg/day for a patient who weighs 165 pounds. Using ½NS, how many liters will the patient require per day? Round to the nearest tenth. (M.W. of Na = 23, M.W. of Cl = 35.5)

$$\frac{4 \text{ mEq}}{\text{kg}} \times 75 \text{ kg} = 300 \text{ mEq/day}$$

$$300 \text{ mEq} = \frac{X \text{ mg} \times 1}{58.5} = 17{,}550 \text{ mg, or } 17.55 \text{ g}$$

$$\frac{0.45 \text{ g}}{100 \text{ mL}} = \frac{17.55 \text{ g}}{X \text{ mL}} \quad X = 3{,}900 \text{ mL or } 3.9 \text{ L}$$

Body Mass Index

Overweight and obesity is a health problem associated with increased morbidity from hypertension, dyslipidemia, diabetes, coronary heart disease, stroke, gallbladder disease, osteoarthritis and some other conditions. Higher body weights are also associated with increases in all-cause mortality. Body mass index (BMI) is a measure of body fat based on height and weight that applies to adult men and women. BMI is a useful measure of body fat, but the BMI can over-estimate body fat in persons who are muscular, and can under-estimate body fat in frail elderly persons and others who have lost muscle mass. Waist circumference is used concurrently with BMI. If most of the fat is around the waist, there is higher disease risk. High risk is defined as a waist size > 35 inches for women or > 40 inches for men. Underweight can be a problem if a person is fighting a disease such as a frail, hospitalized patient with an infection.

BMI should be calculated as follows:

$$\text{BMI (kg/m}^2\text{)} = \frac{\text{weight (kg)}}{[\text{height (m)}]^2}$$

Alternatively, BMI can be calculated with weight in pounds and height in inches using a conversion factor to convert to units of kg/m²:

$$\text{BMI (kg/m}^2\text{)} = \frac{\text{weight (pounds)}}{[\text{height (in)}]^2} \times 703 \text{ (to convert to kg/m}^2\text{)}$$

BMI Classifications

BMI (kg/m²)	CLASSIFICATION
< 18.5	Underweight
18.5 - 24.9	Normal weight
25 - 29.9	Overweight
≥ 30	Obese

93. A male comes to the pharmacy and tells the pharmacist he is 6'7" tall and 250 pounds. His waist circumference is 43 inches. Calculate his BMI. Round to the nearest whole number. Is the patient underweight, normal weight, overweight, or obese?

- Convert weight to kg: 250 pounds x 1 kg/2.2 lbs = 113.6363 kg

- Convert height to cm: 6'7" = 79 inches x 2.54 cm/inch = 200.66 cm

$$200.66 \text{ cm} \quad \times \quad \frac{m}{100 \text{ cm}} \quad = \quad 2.0066 \text{ m}$$

$$\text{BMI (kg/m}^2) \quad = \quad \frac{113.6363 \text{ kg}}{(2.0066 \text{ m})^2} \quad = \quad 28.2 \text{ kg/m}^2, \text{ rounded to 28, which is overweight.}$$

Because of the rounding specifications in the question, the answer is the same regardless of the formula used. Expect the same on the exam.

---

94. Calculate the BMI for a male who is 6' tall and weighs 198 lbs. Round to the nearest tenth. Is the patient underweight, normal weight, overweight, or obese?

$$\text{BMI (kg/m}^2) \quad = \quad \frac{198 \text{ pounds}}{(72 \text{ in})^2} \quad \times \quad 703 \quad = \quad 26.9 \text{ kg/m}^2, \text{ which is overweight.}$$

Because of the rounding specifications in the question, the answer is the same regardless of the formula used. Expect the same on the exam.

Body Weight

Actual Body Weight or Total Body Weight

Actual body weight or total body weight (TBW) is the weight of the patient when weighed on a scale.

Ideal Body Weight

Ideal body weight (IBW) is the healthy (ideal) weight for a person. The IBW formula must be memorized:

IBW (males) = 50 kg + (2.3 kg)(number of inches over 5 feet)
IBW (females) = 45.5 kg + (2.3 kg)(number of inches over 5 feet)

There are alternate methods of calculating IBW in children and adults < 5 feet.

Adjusted Body Weight

Adjusted body weight is calculated when patients are obese or overweight. The adjusted body weight formula must be memorized:

$\text{AdjBW}_{0.4} = \text{IBW} + 0.4(\text{TBW} - \text{IBW})$

Adult doses are generally the same for all patients (e.g., lisinopril 10 mg daily, memantine 5 mg BID). Weight-based (mg/kg) dosing is common in pediatrics and is recommended for some medications in adult patients (see table). Total body weight is used for weight-based dosing of most drugs in adults, but there are some exceptions. Some drugs with a narrow therapeutic index (e.g., aminophylline, theophylline) are best dosed based on IBW to avoid toxicity. Dosing drugs in obese and overweight patients can be complicated; though these patients are known to have different pharmacokinetics and pharmacodynamics than normal weight patients, they are often excluded from clinical trials. Some drugs (e.g., enoxaparin, vancomycin, others) are dosed based on actual body weight (even if a patient is obese) because that has been determined in clinical trials to be the best weight to use. In clinical practice, it may be necessary to consult primary literature for the best dosing strategy in obese patients.

WHICH WEIGHT TO USE FOR DRUG DOSING (mg/kg)?*		
Underweight: TBW < IBW	**Normal Weight: TBW = IBW**	**Obese**: TBW >> IBW**
Use TBW to dose all medications (to avoid overdosing)	Use TBW to dose most medications	Use TBW for: LMWHs, UFH, vancomycin
	Use IBW for: Aminophylline, theophylline, acyclovir	Use IBW for: Aminophylline, theophylline, acyclovir
		Use AdjBW$_{0.4}$ for: Aminoglycosides#

*If a question specifies what weight to use, even if different from above, use it. Follow all instructions on the exam.

**Definition of obesity for drug dosing can differ, but is generally considered to be > 120 – 130% of IBW.

#Aminoglycosides are dosed based on total body weight or IBW, unless the patient is considered obese, then adjusted body weight is used.

Renal Function and Creatinine Clearance Estimation

The normal range for serum creatinine is approximately 0.6 to 1.2 mg/dL. A serum creatinine above this range usually indicates that the kidneys are not functioning properly. However, the values can appear normal even when renal function is compromised. Refer to the Lab Values & Drug Monitoring and Renal Disease Chapter.

Creatinine is a break-down product produced when muscle tissue makes energy. If kidney function declines and creatinine cannot be cleared (excreted), the creatinine level will increase in the blood and the creatinine clearance (CrCl) will decrease. This tells us that the concentration of drugs that are renally cleared will also increase and a dose reduction may be required.

Patients should be assessed for dehydration when the serum creatinine value is elevated. Dehydration can cause both the serum creatinine (SCr) and the blood urea nitrogen (BUN) values to increase. Generally, a BUN:SCr ratio > 20:1 indicates dehydration. Correcting the dehydration will reduce both BUN and SCr, and can prevent or treat acute renal failure. Signs of dehydration should also be assessed and these can include decreased urine output, tachycardia, tachypnea, dry skin/mouth/mucous membranes, skin tenting (skin does not bounce back when pinched into a fold) and possibly fever. Dehydration is usually caused by diarrhea, vomiting, and/or a lack of adequate fluid intake.

95. Looking at the laboratory values below, make an assessment of the patient's hydration status.

	PATIENT'S VALUE	REFERENCE RANGE
BUN	54 mg/dL	7–25 mg/dL
Creatinine	1.8 mg/dL	0.6–1.2 mg/dL

    a. The patient appears to be well hydrated.
    b. The patient appears to be too hydrated.
    c. The patient is not experiencing dehydration.
    d. The patient is experiencing dehydration and may need to be started on fluids.
    e. The patient has subjective information indicating dehydration but the patient needs to be assessed objectively as well.

The correct answer is (d). The patient's BUN:SCr ratio is 54/1.8 = 30:1. Since 30:1 > 20:1, the BUN is disproportionately elevated relative to the creatinine, indicating that the patient is dehydrated.

---

96. Nancy is receiving a furosemide infusion at 5 mg/hr. The nurse notices her urine output has decreased in the last hour. Laboratory values are drawn and the patient has a SCr of 1.5 mg/dL and a BUN of 26 mg/dL. The nurse wants to know if she should stop the furosemide infusion due to the patient becoming dehydrated. What is the correct assessment of the patient's hydration status?

    a. The patient appears to be too hydrated given the laboratory results.
    b. The patient is not experiencing dehydration given the laboratory results.
    c. The patient is experiencing dehydration and may need to be started on fluids.
    d. The patient has objective information indicating dehydration but the patient needs to be assessed subjectively as well.
    e. None of the above are correct.

The correct answer is (b). The BUN:SCr ratio is 26/1.5 = 17.3:1, which is < 20:1. Continue to monitor the patient.

The Cockcroft-Gault Equation

This formula is used by pharmacists to estimate renal function. However, it is not commonly used in very young children, ESRD patients or when renal function is fluctuating rapidly. There are different methods used to estimate renal function in these circumstances. The Cockcroft-Gault equation should be known, as it is commonly used in practice.

$$\text{CrCl} = \frac{140 - (\text{age of patient})}{72 \times \text{SCr}} \times \text{weight in kg (x 0.85 if female)}$$

WHICH WEIGHT TO USE FOR CALCULATING CrCl?		
Underweight: TBW < IBW	**Normal Weight: TBW = IBW**	**Overweight or Obese*: TBW > IBW**
Use <u>TBW</u> in CrCl calculation	Use <u>IBW</u> in CrCl calculation	Use <u>AdjBW</u>$_{0.4}$ in CrCl calculation

Overweight/obese determined by BMI

Once the CrCl has been calculated, it is used to renally adjust <u>all</u> necessary medications (unless serum creatinine changes). The proper weight to use in the Cockcroft-Gault equation <u>will not always be the same</u> weight used to calculate a weight-based (mg/kg) dose. The following examples illustrate this point.

Calculation Practice

The following problems integrate multiple calculation concepts. Refer to other chapters if you are unfamiliar with the dosing of the medications in the following questions.

---

97. A female patient is to receive 5 mg/kg/day of theophylline. The patient is 5'7" and weighs 243 pounds. Calculate the daily theophylline dose the patient should receive.

Theophylline and aminophylline should be <u>dosed on IBW</u> unless a different weight is specified in the problem. Check for instructions in the problem regarding rounding or which weight to use.

IBW (female) = 45.5 kg + (2.3 x 7 in) = 61.6 kg

Theophylline 5 mg/kg x 61.6 kg = 308 mg

---

98. A 64 year old female patient (height 5'5", weight 205 pounds) is hospitalized with a nosocomial pneumonia which is responding to treatment. Her current antibiotic medications include ciprofloxacin, *Primaxin* and vancomycin. Her morning laboratory values include: K 4 mEq/L, BUN 60 mg/dL, SCr 2.7 mg/dL and glucose 222 mg/dL. Based on the renal dosage recommendations from the package labeling below, what is the correct dose of *Primaxin* for this patient?

CrCl	≥ 71 mL/min	41–70 mL/min	21–40 mL/min	6–20 mL/min
Primaxin Dose	500 mg IV Q6H	500 mg IV Q8H	250 mg IV Q6H	250 mg IV Q12H

First determine which weight to use to calculate CrCl:

Actual Body Weight = 93.1818 kg

IBW = 45.5 kg + (2.3 x 5 in) = 57 kg

$$BMI = \frac{205 \text{ lbs}}{65^2} \times 703 = 34.1, \text{ or obese}$$

Now calculate her adjusted body weight:

AdjBW$_{0.4}$ = 57 + 0.4 (93.1818 − 57) = 71.47 kg

Then, solve using the Cockcroft-Gault equation:

$$CrCl = \frac{140 - 64}{72 \times 2.7} \times 71.47 (0.85) = 23.75 \text{ mL/min. The correct dose of } Primaxin \text{ is 250 mg IV Q6H.}$$

99. A 34 year old male (height 6'7", weight 287 pounds) is hospitalized after a motor vehicle accident. He develops a *Pseudomonas aeruginosa* infection. The physician orders tobramycin 2 mg/kg IV Q8H. Calculate the tobramycin dose. Round to the nearest 10 milligrams.

$$\text{Actual Body Weight} = 287 \text{ lb} \times \frac{1 \text{ kg}}{2.2 \text{ lbs}} = 130.4545 \text{ kg}$$

$$\text{IBW (male)} = 50 \text{ kg} + (2.3 \times 19 \text{ in}) = 93.7 \text{ kg}$$

$$\% \text{ above IBW} = \frac{130.4545 \text{ kg}}{93.7 \text{ kg}} = 1.39, \text{ he is } {\sim}39\% \text{ above his IBW}$$

Aminoglycosides are dosed on adjusted body weight in obese patients.

$$\text{AdjBW}_{0.4} = 93.7 + 0.4 (103.4545 - 93.7) = 108.4 \text{ kg}$$

$$\text{Tobramycin 2 mg/kg} \times 108.4 \text{ kg} = 216.8 \text{ mg, round to 220 mg IV Q8H}$$

---

100. Levofloxacin, dosing per pharmacy, is ordered for an 87 year old female patient (height 5'4", weight 103 pounds). Her labs include BUN 22 mg/dL and SCr 1 mg/dL. Choose the correct dosing regimen based on the renal dosage adjustments from the package labeling below.

CrCl	≥ 50 mL/min	20–49 mL/min	< 20 mL/min
Levofloxacin Dose	500 mg Q24 hours	250 mg Q24 hours	250 mg Q48 hours

First, determine which weight to use in calculating the CrCl.

$$\text{Actual Body Weight} = 46.8181 \text{ kg}$$

$$\text{IBW} = 45.5 \text{ kg} + (2.3 \times 4 \text{ in}) = 54.7 \text{ kg}$$

Use actual body weight for calculating CrCl since the patient's actual body weight is lower than her IBW.

$$\text{CrCl} = \frac{140 - 87}{72 \times 1} \times 46.8181 \text{ kg} (\times 0.85) = 29 \text{ mL/min. The correct dose of levofloxacin is 250 mg Q24H.}$$

---

101. A 50 year old male (height 6'1", weight 177 pounds) has HIV and is being started on tenofovir, emtricitabine and efavirenz therapy. His laboratory values include K 4.4 mEq/L, BUN 40 mg/dL, SCr 1.8 mg/dL, and CD4 count of 455 cells/mm^3. Using the renal dosage recommendations from the package labeling below, what is the correct dose of tenofovir for this patient.

CrCl	≥ 50 mL/min	30–49 mL/min	10–29 mL/min	< 10 mL/min
Tenofovir Dose	300 mg daily	300 mg Q48 hours	300 mg Q72-96 hours	300 mg weekly

First, determine which weight to use in calculating the CrCl.

Actual Body Weight = 80.4545 kg

IBW = 50 kg + (2.3 × 13 in) = 79.9, or 80 kg

The IBW is almost the same as the actual weight. Either weight will yield a similar CrCl.

Next, calculate the CrCl.

$$CrCl = \frac{140 - 50}{72 \times 1.8} \times 80 \text{ kg} = 55 \text{ mL/min}$$

The dose of tenofovir should be 300 mg daily.

PATIENT PROFILE

Patient Name	Carolyn Hoydt						
Address	13 Windgate Road						
Age:	37	Sex:	F	Race: Caucasian	Height: 5'6"	Weight:	175 pounds
Allergies	NKDA						

DIAGNOSES

DVT confirmed by ultrasound

MEDICATIONS

Date	Rx #	Prescriber	Drug/Strength/Sig
7/5/15	98732	Langston	*Ortho Tri-Cyclen* 1 PO Daily
7/5/15	98733	Langston	Centrum 1 PO Daily
11/15/15	102345	Mason	*Lovenox* 1 mg/kg SC Q12H
11/15/15	102347	Mason	D51/2NS @ 70 ml/hr

LAB/DIAGNOSTIC TESTS

Test	Normal Value	Date: 7/5/15	Results Date: 11/15/15	Date:
Na	135-146 mEq/L	136	142	
K	3.5-5.3 mEq/L	3.5	5.2	
Cl	98-110 mEq/L	109	105	
HCO3	22-28 mEq/L	25	26	
BUN	7-25 mg/dL	10	22	
Creatinine	0.6-1.2 mg/dL	0.7	1.4	
Glu	65-99 mg/dL	100	120	
Hgb	12-16 g/dL	12	13.6	
Hct	36-46%	37	41	

---

102. **The pharmacist reviews Ms. Hoydt's *Lovenox* order and labs above. At this hospital, pharmacists have the authority to make renal dosage adjustments per package labeling when necessary. What is the correct *Lovenox* dose for Ms. Hoydt?**

   a. 175 mg SC Q12H

   b. 175 mg SC once daily

   c. 80 mg SC once daily

   d. 80 mg SC Q12H

   e. 70 mg SC Q12H

The correct answer is (d). Actual body weight is used to determine the weight-based dose of LMWHs. Since the patient's BMI is 28.3 kg/m² (overweight), her adjusted body weight is used in the Cockcroft-Gault equation to calculate CrCl. Her CrCl is 58.5 ml/min (well above the threshold of 30 ml/min, for changing the interval of *Lovenox* to once daily).

PATIENT PROFILE

Patient Name	Jeremy Ross								
Address	22 Harris Lane								
Age:	41	**Sex:**	M	**Race:**	Hispanic	**Height:**	6'1"	**Weight:**	70 kg
Allergies	NKDA								

DIAGNOSES

Depression	Dyslipidemia
HIV	

MEDICATIONS

Date	Prescriber	Drug/Strength/Sig
5/5/15	Sangler	Nicotine patch 21 mg/day – apply 1 patch daily
5/5/15	Sangler	*Stribild* 1 tablet daily
6/15/15	Sangler	*Celexa* 20 mg 1 tablet daily
11/15/15	Mason	*Lipitor* 10 mg 1 tablet daily
12/1/15	Hern	*Bactrim* 20 mg TMP/kg/day IV divided Q6H

LAB/DIAGNOSTIC TESTS

Test	Normal Value	Results Date: 12/1/15	Date: 5/5/15	Date:
WBC	4,000-11,000 cells/mm³	10.7	9.5	
CD4	800-1,100 cells/mm³	187	226	
Na	135-146 mEq/L	139	142	
K	3.5-5.3 mEq/L	3.7	4.1	
Cl	98-110 mEq/L	109	105	
HCO3	22-28 mEq/L	24	26	
BUN	7-25 mg/dL	7	9	
Creatinine	0.6-1.2 mg/dL	0.6	0.8	
Glu	65-99 mg/dL	120	136	

103. The pharmacist reviews the order for IV *Bactrim* and the labs for Mr. Ross above. What dose should Mr. Ross receive given the renal dosage recommendations below?

CrCl	> 30 mL/min	15–30 mL/min	< 15 mL/min
Sulfamethoxazole/ trimethoprim (SMX/TMP)	No dosage adjustment required	Administer 50% of the recommended dose	Use is not recommended

a. 1400 mg TMP IV Q6H

b. 700 mg TMP IV Q6H

c. 400 mg TMP IV Q12H

d. 350 mg TMP IV Q6H

e. Mr. Ross should not receive *Bactrim*

The correct answer is (d). Mr. Ross is of normal weight (BMI = 20.4 kg/m²). His *Bactrim* dose will be calculated with his actual weight (20 mg TMP/kg/day x 70 kg = 1400 mg TMP/day or 350 mg TMP Q6H for normal renal function). His CrCl is calculated with his IBW and is > 130 ml/min. Renal dose adjustments will not be needed for any medications at this level of CrCl.

PATIENT PROFILE

Patient Name	Mike Kelly
Address	65 Laney Road
Age:	22 **Sex:** M **Race:** Caucasian
Allergies	NKDA

DIAGNOSES

Asthma
Allergies

MEDICATIONS

Date	Prescriber	Drug/Strength/Sig
8/23/15	Sanchez	*Singulair* 10 mg 1 tablet in the evening daily
8/23/15	Sanchez	*Qvar* 1 puff (40 mcg) BID
9/29/15	Williams	Methylprednisolone 40 mg IV Q12H
9/29/15	Williams	Aminophylline 0.5 mg/kg/hr
9/29/15	Williams	D5^1/$_2$NS at 80 ml/hr
9/29/15	Williams	Albuterol nebulization 2.5 mg Q6H

LAB/DIAGNOSTIC TESTS

Test	Normal Value	Results		
		Date: 9/1/14	Date: 1/7/15	Date: 9/29/15
Weight		125 pounds	141 pounds	152 pounds
Height		5'9"		5'9"
WBC	4,000-11,000 cells/mm^3	12,000		11,225
K	3.5-5 mEq/L	3.7	4.1	3.6
Glu	65-99 mg/dL	101		142

---

104. How many milligrams of aminophylline will Mike receive per day based on the order above? Round to the nearest whole number.

The aminophylline dose will be calculated based on Mike's IBW.

IBW (male) = 50 kg + (2.3 x 9 in) = 70.7 kg

Aminophylline 0.5 mg/kg/hr x 70.7 kg x 24 hrs = 848.4 mg/day, round to 848 mg/day

CALCULATE PATIENTS' NUTRITIONAL NEEDS

CALORIE SOURCES

A calorie is a measurement of the energy, or heat, it takes to raise the temperature of 1 gram of water by 1°C. Calories are associated with nutrition because humans obtain energy from the food they consume, or from enteral nutrition (EN) formulas delivered by "feeding" tubes into the stomach or intestine, or from parenteral nutrition (PN), which is delivered peripherally through a vein, or centrally through an artery. Calories from any of these nutrition sources are provided by these 3 components: carbohydrates, fat and protein.

A calorie is a very small unit, and these are therefore measured in kilocalories, or kcals, where 1,000 calories = 1 kcal. It is common to find the term "calories" used interchangeably for kcals. For example, the "Nutrition Facts" box on the side of a container of Honey Nut Cheerios® states that a serving of ¾ cup of the cereal provides 110 Calories. Precisely, this is 110 kcals. Looking at the box, the word "Calories" is written with a capital "C" which is sometimes used to indicate kcals, versus a lower case "c". For pharmacy calculations, "calories" or "Calories" are meant to refer to kilocalories, or kcals.

Carbohydrates

Glucose is the primary energy source. Unless a patient purchases glucose tablets or gel, carbohydrates are consumed as simple sugars, such as fruit juice, or complex "starchy" sugars, such as legumes and grains. These are hydrolyzed by the gut into the monosaccharides fructose, galactose and glucose, which are absorbed. The liver converts the first two into glucose, and excess glucose is stored as glycogen.

Carbohydrates from food or in EN formulas provide 4 kcal/gram, although the calories are measured together (carbs + fat + protein) in total kcal provided by each mL (kcal/mL) of the EN formula. In PN, dextrose monohydrate provides the carbohydrate source. This is the isomer of glucose (D-glucose) which can be metabolized for energy. The dextrose in PN provides 3.4 kcal/gram. Occasionally, glycerol is used as an alternative to dextrose in patients with impaired insulin secretion. Glycerol provides 4.3 kcal/gram and comes pre-mixed with amino acids.

Fat

Fats, or lipids, are used by the body for energy or for various critical functions, including being an essential component of cell membranes, a solvent for fat soluble vitamins, in hormone production and activity, in cell signaling, and other functions. In food or from EN formulas, fat is provided as four types: saturated, *trans*, monounsaturated and polyunsaturated. Each of these provides 9 kcal/gram. In PN, lipids are not measured in grams but in kcal/mL due to the caloric contribution provided by the egg phospholipid and glycerol components in the intravenous fat emulsion (IVFE). 10% IVFE provides 1.1 kcal/mL, 20% provides 2 kcal/mL and 30% provides 3 kcal/mL.

Protein

Protein is used either to repair or build muscle cells, or as a source of energy. Protein in enteral intake is present in various forms, and in PN as the constituent amino acids. If adequate energy is provided by carbohydrates and fat, the protein may be "spared" and can be used by muscle, (although the protein calories may not end up in the intended location). If "protein sparing" is used, the energy required by the patient will come from only the dextrose and lipids, which are the "non-protein calories" (NPC).

Protein calories from food, enteral nutrition formulas or as parenteral amino acid solutions each provide 4 kcal/gram. The kcal amounts in the chart below should be known:

USUAL DIET*			EN FORMULAS*		PN FORMULAS	
Carbs	Bread, Rice….	4 kcal/g	Corn syrup solids, cornstarch, sucrose….	The components contribute the same as from the diet, but are measured (together) as kcal/mL	Dextrose Monohydrate	3.4 kcal/gram
					Glycerol/ Glycerin**	4.3 kcal/gram
Fat	Butter, Oil….	9 kcal/g	Borage oil, canola oil, corn oil….		IV Fat Emulsion (IVFE) 10%	1.1 kcal/mL
					IVFE 20%	2 kcal/mL
					IVFE 30%	3 kcal/mL
Protein	Fish, Meat….	4 kcal/g	Casein, soy, whey….		Amino Acid Solutions (Aminosyn, Freamine….)	4 kcal/gram

*The diet and enteral formula components are common examples; there are others.

**Glycerol may be used to decrease hyperglycemia; more commonly, the dextrose load is decreased or the insulin dose is increased.

Parenteral Nutrition

It is preferable to use the <u>least invasive</u> and <u>most physiologic</u> method of feeding. Parenteral nutrition (PN) is neither and has a higher risk of complications, including infection and thrombosis. It may be indicated when the patient is not able to absorb adequate nutrition via the GI tract for > 5 days. Usual conditions that may require PN include bowel obstruction, ileus, severe diarrhea, radiation enteritis and untreatable malabsorption.

There are 2 types of PN admixtures. Mixtures that contain dextrose, amino acids, sterile water for injection, electrolytes, vitamins and minerals are referred to as 2-in-1 formulations, while the intravenous fat emulsion (IVFE) is infused separately. When the IVFE is contained in the same bag, it is referred to as a total nutrient admixture (TNA), or 3-in-1, or all-in-one formulation.

If the PN is expected to be short-term (< 1 week), peripheral administration may be possible, but has a high risk of phlebitis and vein damage. Central line placement allows for a higher osmolarity and a wider variation in pH. Common types of central lines include peripherally-inserted central catheters ("PICC" lines), Hickman, Broviac, Groshong and others.

The fluid, kcal, protein and lipid requirements, plus the initial electrolyte, vitamin and trace element requirements will be determined. Additional additives may be needed, such as insulin and histamine-2 receptor antagonists (H_2RAs). PN requires monitoring, including assessing the need, the degree of glucose intolerance and the risk of refeeding syndrome, which is an intracellular loss of electrolytes, particularly phosphate, which causes serious complications. The calculations for PN that follow are basic and should be known by pharmacists who work in the hospital setting. Nutrition pharmacy itself is more complex and is a specialty area.

Determining Fluid Needs

Fluid requirements are often calculated 1st when designing a PN regimen. Enough (but not too much) fluid needs to be given to maintain adequate hydration. Daily fluid needs can be calculated using this formula:

When weight > 20 kg: 1,500 mL + (20 mL)(Wt in kg − 20)

Alternatively, some institutions estimate adult fluid requirements using a general guideline of 30 – 40 mL/kg/day. The PN and fluid volume should be tailored to the patient. If the patient has problems with fluid accumulation (such as heart failure, renal dysfunction, etc.), the amount of fluid provided will be reduced. Fluid volume from medications (including IVPBs) should be included in the calculation of the overall volume the patient is receiving.

---

105. GG is a 57 year old female admitted to the hospital with bowel obstruction. She will be NPO for the next 5 – 7 days. The decision was made to start PN therapy. She weighs 65 kg and is 5′6″. The SCr is 1.3 mg/dL. Calculate GG's daily fluid requirements.

1,500 mL + (20 mL)(65 – 20) = 2,400 mL/day

---

106. A 76 year old, 154 lbs (IBW) patient is NPO and needs hydration. She is afebrile and does not have HF, renal disease, or ascites. What volume of fluid should the patient receive per day?

1,500 mL + (20 mL)(70 – 20) = 2,500 mL/day

Calculating Protein Calories

The typical protein requirement for a non-stressed, ambulatory patient is 0.8 – 1 g/kg/day. Protein requirements increase if the patient is placed under stress, which is defined as illness severity. The more severely ill, the greater the protein requirements will be. In patients with a high degree of metabolic stress the protein requirements can be as high as 1.8 – 2 g/kg/day.

CONDITION	PROTEIN REQUIREMENTS
Ambulatory, non-hospitalized (non-stressed)	0.8–1 g/kg/day
Hospitalized, or malnourished	1.2–2 g/kg/day

---

107. MK is a 62 year old female who has been admitted with enteritis and pneumonia. She has a history of Crohn's disease and COPD. She is 158 pounds, 5′4″. The staff gastroenterologist has ordered PN therapy with 1.5 g/kg IBW/day of protein. How many grams of protein will MK receive per day. Round to the nearest whole number.

First, calculate IBW: 45.5 + (2.3)(4) = 54.7 kg

Then, calculate the protein requirement: 54.7 kg x 1.5 g/kg IBW/day = 82 g protein/day

---

108. PP is a 46 year old male (207 pounds, 5′11″) who has been admitted for bowel resection surgery. Post surgery, he is to be started on PN therapy. The physician wants the patient to receive 1.3 g/kg/day of protein. Calculate his protein requirements using his actual weight. Round to the nearest whole number.

First, convert pounds to kg: 207 pounds x 1 kg/2.2 pounds = 94.1 kg

Then, calculate the protein requirement: 94.1 kg x 1.3 g/kg/day = 122 g protein/day

Calculating Non-Protein Calories

Basal Energy Expenditure and Total Energy Expenditure

The basal energy expenditure (BEE), otherwise referred to as the basal metabolic rate (BMR), is the energy expenditure in the <u>resting</u> state, exclusive of eating and activity. It is <u>estimated differently in male and female patients using the Harris-Benedict equations</u> below:

> BEE (males): 66.47 + 13.75 (weight in kg) + 5 (height in cm) − 6.76 (age in years)
>
> BEE (females): 655.1 + 9.6 (weight in kg) + 1.85 (height in cm) − 4.68 (age in years)

Total energy expenditure (TEE; or total daily expenditure, TDE) is a measure of basal energy expenditure plus excess metabolic demands as a result of stress, the thermal effects of feeding, and energy expenditure for activity. Once the BEE is calculated, calculate the TEE by taking the BEE calories and multiplying by the appropriate activity factor and stress factor. This will increase the calories required. Energy requirements are increased 12% with each degree of fever over 37° C.

> TEE = BEE x activity factor x stress factor

The activity factor is either 1.2 if confined to bed (non-ambulatory), or 1.3 if out of bed (ambulatory). Commonly used stress factors are listed in the table:

STATE OF STRESS	STRESS FACTOR
Minor surgery	1.2
Infection	1.4
Major trauma, sepsis, burns up to 30% BSA	1.5
Burns over 30% BSA	1.5–2

---

109. Using the Harris-Benedict equation, calculate the resting non-protein caloric requirement for a major trauma patient (stress factor 1.5) who is a 66 year old male, 174 pounds and 5'10" in height. Activity factor is 1.2. Round to the nearest whole number.

Height = 70 inches x 2.54 cm/inch = 177.8 cm. Weight 174 pounds x 1 kg/2.2 pounds = 79.0909 kg.

BEE (males): 66.47 + 13.75 (weight in kg) + 5 (height in cm) − 6.76 (age in years)

> BEE = 66.47 + (13.75 x 79.0909) + (5 x 177.8) − (6.76 x 66)

> BEE = 66.47 + 1,087.5 + 889 − 446.16 = 1,596.81, or 1,597 kcal/day

The BEE can be estimated using 15 – 25 kcal/kg (adults). It may be helpful to check the calculation with this estimate and see if the numbers are close. In this case, an estimation using 20 kcal/kg/day would provide 1,582 kcal/day (very close to 1,597 kcal/day as above).

---

110. Using the total energy expenditure equation, calculate the total non-protein caloric requirement for a major trauma patient (stress factor is 1.5, activity factor is 1.2) who is a 66 year old male, weighing 174 pounds and measuring 5'10" in height. (Use the BEE calculated from the patient in the previous problem.) Round to the nearest whole number.

TEE = BEE x activity factor x stress factor. BEE was calculated above.

> TEE = 1,597 kcal/day x 1.2 x 1.5 = 2,875 kcal/day

---

111. A 25 year old female major trauma patient survives surgery and is recovering in the surgical intensive care unit. The medical team wants to start PN therapy. She is 122 pounds, 5'7" with some mild renal impairment. Calculate her BEE using the Harris-Benedict equation and her TEE non-protein caloric requirements (stress factor = 1.7 and activity factor =1.2). Round each to the nearest whole number.

Height = 67 inches x 2.54 cm/inch = 170.18 cm. Weight 122 pounds x 1 kg/2.2 pounds = 55.4545 kg.

BEE (females): 655.1 + 9.6 (weight in kg) + 1.85 (height in cm) – 4.68 (age in years)

BEE = 655.1 + (9.6 x 55.4545) + (1.85 x 170.18) – (4.68 x 25)

BEE = 655.1 + 532.3636 + 314.833 – 117 = 1,385.2966, or 1,385 kcal/day

TEE = BEE x activity factor x stress factor

TEE = 1,385 kcal/day x 1.2 x 1.7 = 2,825 kcal/day

Calculating Amino Acids

Amino acids are the source of proteins in PN. Amino acids are used to build muscle mass and may not be counted as an energy source in critically ill patients because they are catabolic. Amino acids come in stock preparations of 5%, 8.5%, 10%, 15%, and others. Amino acids provide 4 kcal/gram.

---

112. If the pharmacy stocks *Aminosyn* 8.5%, how many mL will be needed to provide 108 grams of protein? Round to the nearest whole number.

$$\frac{8.5\ g}{100\ mL} = \frac{108\ g}{X\ mL} \qquad X = 1{,}270.58,\ or\ 1{,}271\ mL$$

---

113. How many calories are provided by 108 grams of protein?

$$\frac{4\ kcal}{g} \times 108\ g = 432\ kcal\ of\ protein$$

---

114. The pharmacy stocks *FreAmine* 10%. A patient requires 122 grams of protein per day. How many milliliters of *FreAmine* will the patient need?

$$\frac{10\ g}{100\ mL} = \frac{122\ g}{X\ mL} \qquad X = 1{,}220\ mL$$

---

115. JR requires 1.4 g/kg/day of protein and the pharmacy stocks *Aminosyn* 8.5%. JR is a 55 year old male (weight 189 pounds) who is confined to bed (activity factor 1.2) due to his current infection (stress factor 1.5). Calculate the amount of *Aminosyn*, in milliliters, JR should receive. Round to the nearest whole number.

First, convert weight to kg: 189 pounds x 1 kg/2.2 pounds = 85.90 kg

Next, calculate protein requirement: 1.4 g/kg/day x 85.9090 kg = 120.27 g/day

Then, calculate the amount of *Aminosyn* (mL) needed. Note the activity factor and stress factor are not required to calculate the protein requirement.

$$\frac{8.5\ g}{100\ mL} = \frac{120.27\ g}{X\ mL} \qquad X = 1{,}414.97,\ or\ 1{,}415\ mL$$

116. JR is receiving 97 grams of protein in an _Aminosyn_ 8.5% solution on day 8 of his hospitalization. How many calories are provided by this amount of protein?

$$\frac{4 \text{ kcal}}{g} \times 97 \text{ g} = 388 \text{ kcal of protein}$$

---

117. A PN order is written to add 800 mL of 10% amino acid solution. The pharmacy only has 15% amino acid solution in stock. Using the 15% amino acid solution instead, how many mL should be added to the PN bag? Round to the nearest whole number.

First, calculate the grams of protein that would be provided with the 10% solution.

$$\frac{10 \text{ g}}{100 \text{ mL}} = \frac{X \text{ g}}{800 \text{ mL}} \qquad X = 80 \text{ g}$$

Next, calculate how much of the 15% amino acid solution will supply 80 grams of protein.

$$\frac{15 \text{ g}}{100 \text{ mL}} = \frac{80 \text{ g}}{X \text{ mL}} \qquad X = 533 \text{ mL}$$

Nitrogen Balance

Determining The Grams Of Nitrogen From Protein

Nitrogen is released during protein catabolism and is mainly excreted as urea in the urine. Nitrogen balance is the difference between the body's nitrogen gains and losses. While grams of protein are calculated in a nutritional plan, grams of nitrogen are used as an expression of the amount of protein received by the patient. There is 1 g of nitrogen (N) for each 6.25 g of protein. To calculate the grams of nitrogen in a certain weight of protein, divide the protein grams by 6.25.

$$\text{Nitrogen intake} = \frac{\text{grams of protein intake}}{6.25}$$

---

118. A patient is receiving PN containing 540 mL of 12.5% amino acids per day. How many grams of nitrogen is the patient receiving? Round to the nearest tenth.

$$\frac{12.5 \text{ g}}{100 \text{ mL}} = \frac{X \text{ g}}{540 \text{ mL}} \qquad X = 67.5 \text{ g of protein}$$

$$\frac{67.5 \text{ g of protein}}{6.25} = 10.8 \text{ g of nitrogen}$$

Calculating the Non-Protein Calories to Nitrogen Ratio

The non-protein calorie to nitrogen ratio (NPC:N) is calculated as follows:

- First, calculate the grams of nitrogen supplied per day (1 g N = 6.25 g of protein).

- Then, divide the total non-protein calories (dextrose + lipids) by the grams of nitrogen.

Desirable NPC:N ratios are:

- 80:1 the most severely stressed patients

- 100:1 severely stressed patients

- 150:1 unstressed patient

119. A patient is receiving PN containing 480 mL of dextrose 50% and 50 grams of amino acids plus electrolytes. Calculate the non-protein calories to nitrogen ratio for this patient.

First, calculate the nitrogen intake.

$$\text{Nitrogen} = \frac{50 \text{ g of protein}}{6.25} = 8 \text{ g}$$

Next, calculate the non-protein calories.

$$\frac{50 \text{ g dextrose}}{100 \text{ mL}} = \frac{X \text{ g}}{480 \text{ mL}} \quad X = 240 \text{ g dextrose}$$

$$240 \text{ g dextrose} \times \frac{3.4 \text{ kcal dextrose}}{1 \text{ g}} = 816 \text{ kcal of dextrose}$$

Then, set up the NPC:N ratio.

NPC:N ratio is 816:8, or 102:1

Calculating Dextrose

Dextrose is the carbohydrate source in PN. The usual distribution of non-protein calories is 70 – 85% as carbohydrate (dextrose) and 15 – 30% as fat (lipids). Dextrose comes in concentrations of 5%, 10%, 20%, 30%, 50%, 70% and others. The higher concentrations are used for PN. When calculating the dextrose, do not exceed 4 mg/kg/min (some use 7 g/kg/day). These are conservative estimates of the maximum amount of dextrose that the liver can handle.

120. Using 50% dextrose in water, how many mL are required to fulfill a PN order for 405 grams of dextrose?

$$\frac{50 \text{ g}}{100 \text{ mL}} = \frac{405 \text{ g}}{X \text{ mL}} = 810 \text{ mL}$$

121. DF, a 44 year old male, is receiving 1,235 mL of D30W, 1,010 mL of *FreAmine* 8.5%, 200 mL of *Intralipid* 20% and 50 mL of electrolytes/minerals in his PN. How many calories from dextrose is DF receiving from the PN? Round to the nearest whole number.

$$\frac{30 \text{ g}}{100 \text{ mL}} \times \frac{1,235 \text{ mL}}{\text{day}} \times \frac{3.4 \text{ kcal}}{g} = 1,260 \text{ kcal/day}$$

122. A pharmacist has mixed 200 mL of D20% with 100 mL of D5%. What is the final concentration in the bag?

The 200 mL bag has 40 g of dextrose (20 g/100 mL x 2).

The 100 mL bag has 5 g of dextrose. There are a total of 45 g of dextrose in the bag.

$$\frac{45 \text{ g}}{300 \text{ mL}} = \frac{X \text{ g}}{100 \text{ mL}} \quad X = 15 \text{ g; the percentage is 15%}$$

123. **If a 50% dextrose injection provides 170 kcal in each 100 mL, how many milliliters of a 70% dextrose injection would provide the same caloric value? Round to the nearest tenth.**

$$\frac{70 \text{ g}}{100 \text{ mL}} = \frac{50 \text{ g}}{X \text{ mL}} = 71.4 \text{ mL}$$

$$\frac{100 \text{ mL}}{70 \text{ g}} \times \frac{1 \text{ g}}{3.4 \text{ kcal}} \times 170 \text{ kcal} = 71.4 \text{ mL}$$

Or, since the calories are from 50% dextrose, and the pharmacist is using 70% dextrose:

$$100 \text{ mL} \times 50\% = Q_2 \times 70\%$$

$$Q_2 = 71.4 \text{ mL}$$

---

124. **AH is receiving 640 mL of D50W in her PN. How many calories does this provide?**

$$\frac{50 \text{ g}}{100 \text{ mL}} \times \frac{640 \text{ mL}}{\text{day}} \times \frac{3.4 \text{ kcal}}{\text{g}} = 1{,}088 \text{ kcal}$$

---

125. **A PN order is written for 500 mL of 50% dextrose. The pharmacy only has D70W in stock. How many mL of D70W should be added to the PN bag? Round to the nearest whole number.**

First, calculate the grams of dextrose needed for the PN as written.

$$\frac{50 \text{ g}}{100 \text{ mL}} = \frac{X \text{ g}}{500 \text{ mL}} \qquad X = 250 \text{ g}$$

Next, calculate how much of the 70% dextrose solution provides 250 grams of dextrose.

$$\frac{70 \text{ g}}{100 \text{ mL}} = \frac{250 \text{ g}}{X \text{ mL}} \qquad X = 357 \text{ mL of D70W}$$

Calculating Lipids

Lipids are the source of fat in PN. The standard distribution of non-protein calories is 70 – 85% as carbohydrate (dextrose) and 15 – 30% as fat (lipids). Lipids are available as 10%, 20% or 30% emulsions. Do not exceed 2.5 g/kg/day of lipids. Lipids do not need to be given daily, especially if triglycerides are high. Due to the risk of infection, the recommended hang time limit for IV fat emulsions (IVFE) is 12 hours when infused alone. However, an admixture containing IVFE, such as a TNA, may be administered over 24 hours. Patients receiving lipids should have their triglycerides monitored. If lipids are given once weekly, then divide the total calories by 7 to determine the daily amount of fat the patient receives. Lipid emulsions cannot be filtered through 0.22 micron filters; 1.2 micron filters are commonly used for lipids. PN requires a filter itself due to the risk of a precipitate.

---

126. **A patient is receiving 500 mL of 10% lipids. How many calories is the patient receiving from the lipids? Round to the nearest whole number.**

$$\frac{1.1 \text{ kcal}}{\text{mL}} = \frac{X \text{ kcal}}{500 \text{ mL}} \qquad X = 550 \text{ kcal}$$

127. The total energy expenditure (TEE) for a patient is 2,435 kcal/day. The patient is receiving 1,446 kcal from dextrose and 810 kcal from protein. How many kcal should be provided by the lipids?

Remember that TEE refers to the non-protein calories.

2,435 kcal (total non-protein) − 1,446 kcal (dextrose) = 989 kcal remaining from lipids

---

128. Using a 20% lipid emulsion, how many mL are required to meet 989 calories? Round to the nearest whole number.

$$\frac{2 \text{ kcal}}{\text{mL}} = \frac{989 \text{ kcal}}{X \text{ mL}} \qquad X = 495 \text{ mL}$$

---

129. A patient is receiving 660 mL of 10% *Intralipid* on Saturdays along with his normal daily PN therapy of 1,420 mL of D20W, 450 mL *Aminosyn* 15%, and 30 mL of electrolytes. What is the daily amount of calories provided by the lipids? Round to the nearest whole number.

$$\frac{1.1 \text{ kcal}}{\text{mL}} = \frac{X \text{ kcal}}{660 \text{ mL}} \qquad X = 726 \text{ kcal/week. Divide by 7 to get kcal/day} = 104 \text{ kcal/day}$$

---

130. A patient is receiving 180 mL of 30% lipids. How many calories is the patient receiving from the lipids?

$$\frac{3 \text{ kcal}}{\text{mL}} = \frac{X \text{ kcal}}{180 \text{ mL}} \qquad X = 540 \text{ kcal}$$

---

131. A PN order calls for 475 calories to be provided by lipids. The pharmacy has 10% lipid emulsion in stock. How many mL should be administered to the patient? Round to the nearest whole number.

$$\frac{1.1 \text{ kcal}}{\text{mL}} = \frac{475 \text{ kcal}}{X \text{ mL}} \qquad X = 432 \text{ mL}$$

---

132. TE is a 35 year old female who is receiving 325 grams of dextrose, 85 grams of amino acids, and 300 mL of 10% lipids via her PN therapy. What percentage of calories is provided by the protein content? Round to the nearest whole number.

First, calculate the calories from all sources; dextrose, amino acids, and lipids.

DEXTROSE

$$\frac{3.4 \text{ kcal}}{\text{g}} \times 325 \text{ g} = 1{,}105 \text{ kcal of dextrose}$$

PROTEIN

$$\frac{4 \text{ kcal}}{\text{g}} \times 85 \text{ g} = 340 \text{ kcal of protein}$$

LIPIDS

$$\frac{1.1 \text{ kcal}}{\text{mL}} \times 300 \text{ mL} = 330 \text{ kcal of fat}$$

Then, add up the total calories from all the sources. 1,105 + 340 + 330 = 1,775 kcal
Finally, calculate the percent of calories from protein.

$$\frac{340 \text{ kcal}}{1{,}775 \text{ kcal}} \times 100 = 19\%$$

---

133. WC, a 57 year old male, is receiving 1,145 mL of D30W, 850 mL of *FreAmine* 8.5%, and 350 mL of *Intralipid* 10% in his PN therapy. What percentage of the non-protein calories are represented by dextrose? Round to the nearest whole number.

First, calculate the non-protein calories (dextrose and lipids).

DEXTROSE

$$\frac{3.4 \text{ kcal}}{\text{g}} \times \frac{30 \text{ g}}{100 \text{ mL}} \times 1{,}145 \text{ mL} = 1{,}168 \text{ kcal}$$

LIPIDS

$$\frac{1.1 \text{ kcal}}{\text{mL}} \times 350 \text{ mL} = 385 \text{ kcal}$$

Then, add up the calories from the non-protein sources. 1,168 + 385 = 1,553 kcal

Finally, calculate the percent of non-protein calories from dextrose.

$$\frac{1{,}168 \text{ kcal from dextrose}}{1{,}553 \text{ kcal non-protein}} \times 100 = 75\%$$

---

134. A 46 year old female with radiation enteritis is receiving 1,800 kcal from her parenteral nutrition. The solution contains amino acids, dextrose and electrolytes. There are 84.5 grams of protein in the PN and it is running at 85 mL/hour over 24 hours. What is the final concentration of dextrose in the PN solution? Round to the nearest whole number.

First, calculate the amount of dextrose the patient is receiving by subtracting out the protein component.

$$84.5 \text{ g} \times \frac{4 \text{ kcal}}{\text{g}} = 338 \text{ kcal}$$

$$1,800 \text{ kcal} - 338 \text{ kcal of protein} = 1,462 \text{ kcal from dextrose}$$

Next, calculate the grams of dextrose in this PN.

$$1,462 \text{ kcal} \times \frac{1 \text{ g}}{3.4 \text{ kcal}} = 430 \text{ grams of dextrose}$$

Then, calculate the final concentration. This requires calculating the total volume the patient is receiving.

$$\frac{85 \text{ mL}}{\text{hr}} \times 24 \text{ hours} = 2,040 \text{ mL or } 2.04 \text{ L}$$

$$\frac{430 \text{ g dextrose}}{2,040 \text{ mL}} = \frac{X \text{ g}}{100 \text{ mL}} \qquad X = 21\%$$

Determining the Amount of Electrolytes

Sodium Considerations

Sodium is the principal <u>extra</u>cellular cation. Sodium may need to be reduced in renal dysfunction or cardiovascular disease, including hypertension. Sodium chloride comes in many concentrations, such as 0.9% (NS), 0.45% (1/2 NS) and others. Sodium chloride 23.4% is used for PN preparation and contains 4 mEq/mL.

Sodium can be added to PN as either sodium chloride or sodium acetate. If a patient is acidotic, sodium acetate should be added. Sodium acetate is converted to sodium bicarbonate and may help correct the acidosis. A patient may require a certain quantity from each formulation or they may get sodium chloride alone. Hypertonic saline (greater than 0.9%) is dangerous if used incorrectly and is discussed in the Medication Safety & Quality Improvement chapter.

---

135. The pharmacist is going to add 80 mEq of sodium to the PN; half will be given as sodium acetate (2 mEq/mL) and half as sodium chloride (4 mEq/mL). How many mL of sodium chloride will be needed?

40 mEq will be provided by the NaCl.

$$\frac{4 \text{ mEq}}{\text{mL}} = \frac{40 \text{ mEq}}{X \text{ mL}} \qquad X = 10 \text{ mL}$$

---

136. The pharmacist is making PN that needs to contain 80 mEq of sodium and 45 mEq of acetate. The available pharmacy stock solutions contain 4 mEq/mL sodium as sodium chloride and 2 mEq/mL sodium as sodium acetate. The final volume of the PN will be 2.5 liters to be given at 100 mL/hr. What quantity, in milliliters, of each stock solution should be added to the PN to meet the requirements? Round to the nearest hundredth.

First, calculate the acetate component as this contributes sodium as well.

$$\frac{2 \text{ mEq}}{\text{mL}} = \frac{45 \text{ mEq}}{X \text{ mL}} \qquad X = 22.5 \text{ mL of sodium acetate}$$

Next, determine how many mEq of sodium are supplied by 22.5 mL sodium acetate.

$$\frac{2 \text{ mEq}}{\text{mL}} \text{ x } 22.5 \text{ mL sodium acetate} = 45 \text{ mEq of sodium}$$

So, 45 mEq of sodium acetate also supplies 45 mEq of sodium. How many mEq of sodium are left to be provided from sodium chloride?

80 mEq Na total – 45 mEq Na from Na Acetate = 35 mEq of sodium still needed from NaCl

Calculate how much sodium chloride will supply the remaining sodium (35 mEq).

$$\frac{4 \text{ mEq}}{\text{mL}} = \frac{35 \text{ mEq}}{\text{X mL}} \qquad \text{X} = 8.75 \text{ mL of sodium chloride}$$

---

137. A 2 liter PN solution is to contain 60 mEq of sodium and 30 mEq of acetate. The pharmacy has in stock sodium chloride (4 mEq/mL) and sodium acetate (2 mEq/mL). What quantity, in milliliters, of each solution should be added to the PN? Round to the nearest tenth.

First, calculate the amount of sodium acetate needed.

$$\frac{2 \text{ mEq}}{\text{mL}} = \frac{30 \text{ mEq}}{\text{X mL}} \qquad \text{X} = 15 \text{ mL of sodium acetate}$$

This amount (15 mL of sodium acetate) supplies 30 mEq of sodium (15 mL x 2 mEq/mL = 30 mEq). The additional amount of sodium required is 30 mEq from NaCl (60 mEq – 30 mEq).

Calculate the amount of sodium chloride needed.

$$\frac{4 \text{ mEq}}{\text{mL}} = \frac{30 \text{ mEq}}{\text{X mL}} \qquad \text{X} = 7.5 \text{ mL of NaCl}$$

Potassium, Calcium and Phosphate Considerations

Potassium

Potassium is the principal <u>intracellular</u> cation. Potassium may need to be reduced in renal or cardio-vascular disease. Potassium can be provided by potassium chloride (KCl), potassium phosphate (K Phos) or potassium acetate. <u>The normal range for serum potassium is 3.5 – 5 mEq/L.</u>

Calcium

Calcium is important for many functions including cardiac conduction, muscle contraction, and bone homeostasis. The normal serum calcium level is 8.5 – 10.5 mg/dL. Almost half of serum calcium is bound to albumin. <u>Low albumin</u> will lead to a <u>falsely low serum calcium concentration</u>. If albumin is low (< 3.5 g/dL), the calcium level must be corrected with this equation prior to the addition of calcium into the PN or providing calcium replacement in any manner:

$$Ca_{corrected} = calcium_{reported(serum)} + [(4.0 - albumin) \text{ x } (0.8)]$$

138. Calculate the corrected calcium value for a patient with the following lab values:

LAB	VALUE
Calcium	7.6 mg/dL (reference range 8.5–10.5 mg/dL)
Albumin	1.5 g/dL (reference range 3.5–5 g/dL)

$$Ca_{corrected} = 7.6 + [(4.0 - 1.5) \times (0.8)] = 9.6 \text{ mg/dL}$$

The corrected calcium provides an estimate of what the patient's serum calcium would be if the albumin was normal. In this example, the patient's corrected calcium is within the reference range for the lab.

Calcium and Phosphate Solubility

Phosphorus (or phosphate, PO_4) is present in DNA, cell membranes, ATP, acts as an acid-base buffer, and is vital in bone metabolism. Phosphate and calcium need to be added to the PN carefully, or they can bind together and precipitate which can cause a pulmonary embolus. This can be fatal. The following considerations can help reduce the risk of a calcium-phosphate precipitate:

- Choose calcium gluconate over calcium chloride ($CaCl_2$) because it is less reactive and has a lower risk of precipitation with phosphates. Calcium gluconate has a lower dissociation constant compared to calcium chloride, leaving less free calcium available in solution to bind phosphates.

- Add phosphate first (after the dextrose and amino acids), followed by other PN components, agitate the solution, then calcium should be added near the end to take advantage of the maximum volume of the PN formulation.

- The calcium and phosphate added together (units must be the same to do this) should not exceed 45 mEq/L.

- Maintain a proper pH (lower pH; less risk of precipitation) to eliminate binding and refrigerate the bag once prepared (PNs are kept in the refrigerator until they are needed). When temperature increases, more calcium and phosphate dissociate in solution and precipitation risk increases.

An additional safety consideration involves ordering the correct dose of phosphate. Phosphate can be ordered as potassium or sodium salts. The two forms do not provide equivalent amounts of phosphate. The order should be written in mmol (of phosphate), followed by the type of salt form (potassium or sodium).

---

139. The pharmacist has calculated that a patient requires 30 mmol of phosphate and 80 mEq of potassium. The pharmacy has stock solutions of potassium phosphate (3 mmol of phosphate with 4.4 mEq of potassium/mL) and potassium chloride (2 mEq K/mL). How much potassium phosphate and how much potassium chloride will be required to meet the patient's needs?

First, calculate the phosphate required (since phosphate can only be provided by KPO_4 and potassium will also be provided by this solution).

$$\frac{3 \text{ mmol phosphate}}{mL} = \frac{30 \text{ mmol phosphate}}{X \text{ mL}} \qquad X = 10 \text{ mL } KPO_4$$

Each mL of the potassium phosphate (KPO_4) supplies 4.4 mEq of potassium. Calculate the amount of potassium the patient will receive from the 10 mL of KPO_4.

> 10 mL x 4.4 mEq/mL = 44 mEq potassium from KPO_4

The remaining potassium will be provided by KCl.

> 80 mEq K required − 44 mEq potassium (from KPO_4) = 36 mEq to be obtained from KCl

> $$\frac{2 \text{ mEq K}}{\text{mL}} = \frac{36 \text{ mEq K}}{\text{X mL}} \qquad X = 18 \text{ mL KCl}$$

The patient requires 10 mL of potassium phosphate and 18 mL of potassium chloride.

---

140. A patient is to receive 8 mEq of calcium. The pharmacy has calcium gluconate 10% in stock which provides 0.465 mEq/mL. How many mL of calcium gluconate should be added to the PN? Round to the nearest whole number.

> $$8 \text{ mEq Ca} \quad \times \quad \frac{1 \text{ mL}}{0.465 \text{ mEq Ca}} = 17.2, \text{ or } 17 \text{ mL calcium gluconate}$$

---

141. A patient is receiving 30 mmol of phosphate and 8 mEq of calcium. The volume of the PN is 2,000 mL. There are 2 mEq PO_4/mmol. Confirm that the sum of the calcium and phosphorus does not exceed 45 mEq/L.

First, calculate mEq from the phosphate.

> $$\frac{2 \text{ mEq } PO_4}{\text{mmol}} \times 30 \text{ mmol } PO_4 = 60 \text{ mEq phosphate}$$

Then, add the phosphate and calcium. 60 mEq phosphate + 8 mEq calcium = 68 mEq.

Read the question again. Has it been answered?

The volume of the PN is 2,000 mL, or 2 L. Calculate the mEq per liter.

> 68 mEq/2 L = 34 mEq/L, which is less than 45 mEq/L.

Calculation Practice

The following problems integrate multiple calculation concepts.

---

142. A pharmacy receives the following PN order. Calculate the amount, in mL, of dextrose 70% that should be added to the PN. Round to the nearest whole number.

ITEM	QUANTITY	ITEM	QUANTITY
Dextrose 70%	250 g	Calcium	4.65 mEq
Amino acids	50 g	MVI-12	5 mL
Sodium chloride (M.W. 58.5)	44 mEq	Trace elements-5	1 mL
Sodium acetate (M.W. 82)	20 mEq	Vitamin K-1	0.5 mg
Potassium	40 mEq	Famotidine	10 mg
Magnesium sulfate	12 mEq	Regular insulin	20 units
Phosphate	18 mmol	Sterile water qs ad	960 mL

$$\frac{70 \text{ g}}{100 \text{ mL}} = \frac{250 \text{ g}}{X \text{ mL}} \qquad X = 357 \text{ mL of dextrose } 70\%$$

---

143. Using amino acids 10%, calculate the amount of amino acids that should be added to the PN.

$$\frac{10 \text{ g}}{100 \text{ mL}} = \frac{50 \text{ g}}{X \text{ mL}} \qquad X = 500 \text{ mL of } 10\% \text{ amino acids}$$

---

144. How many milliliters of 23.4% sodium chloride should be added to the PN.

$$44 \text{ mEq} = \frac{X \text{ mg} \times 1}{58.5} \qquad X = 2,574 \text{ mg, or } 2.574 \text{ g}$$

$$\frac{23.4 \text{ g}}{100 \text{ mL}} = \frac{2.574 \text{ g}}{X \text{ mL}} \qquad X = 11 \text{ mL of } 23.4\% \text{ NaCl}$$

This concentration of NaCl is hypertonic and is a high-alert drug due to heightened risk of patient harm when dosed incorrectly. Refer to the Medication Safety & Quality Improvement chapter.

---

145. Calculate the amount of 16.4% sodium acetate that should be added to the PN.

$$20 \text{ mEq} = \frac{X \text{ mg} \times 1}{82} \qquad X = 1,640 \text{ mg, or } 1.64 \text{ g}$$

$$\frac{16.4 \text{ g}}{100 \text{ mL}} = \frac{1.64 \text{ g}}{X \text{ mL}} \qquad X = 10 \text{ mL of } 16.4\% \text{ sodium acetate}$$

---

146. Using the potassium phosphate (3 mmol of phosphate and 4.4 mEq of potassium/mL) vials in stock, calculate the amount of potassium phosphate that should be added to the PN to meet the needs of the phosphate requirements.

$$\frac{3 \text{ mmol phosphate}}{\text{mL}} = \frac{18 \text{ mmol phosphate}}{X \text{ mL}} \qquad X = 6 \text{ mL potassium phosphate}$$

---

147. The PN contains 6 mL of potassium phosphate (3 mmol of phosphate and 4.4 mEq of potassium/mL). The daily potassium requirement from the PN order is 40 mEq. How much potassium chloride (2 mEq/mL), in milliliters, should be added to the PN? Round to the nearest tenth.

First, calculate the amount of K already required in the PN from potassium phosphate.

$$\frac{4.4 \text{ mEq K}}{\text{mL}} \times 6 \text{ mL} = 26.4 \text{ mEq K}$$

Total K needed is 40 mEq. 40 mEq – 26.4 mEq = 13.6 mEq still needed from KCl

$$\frac{2 \text{ mEq K}}{\text{mL}} = \frac{13.6 \text{ mEq K}}{X \text{ mL}} \qquad X = 6.8 \text{ mL KCl}$$

148. The PN order calls for 4.65 mEq of calcium. The pharmacy has calcium gluconate 10% (0.465 mEq/mL) in stock. How many mL of calcium gluconate 10% should be added to the PN?

$$\frac{0.465 \text{ mEq Ca}}{\text{mL}} = \frac{4.65 \text{ mEq Ca}}{X \text{ mL}} \qquad X = 10 \text{ mL calcium gluconate 10\%}$$

149. The PN calls for 18 mmol of phosphate and 4.65 mEq of calcium (provided by 10 mL of calcium gluconate 10%, as calculated in the previous problem) in a volume of 960 mL. There are 2 mEq PO$_4$/mmol. Confirm that the sum of the calcium and phosphorus do not exceed 45 mEq/L.

First, calculate mEq from the phosphate.

$$\frac{2 \text{ mEq PO}_4}{\text{mmol}} \times 18 \text{ mmol PO}_4 = 36 \text{ mEq phosphate}$$

Then, add the phosphate to the calcium. 36 mEq phosphate + 4.65 mEq calcium = 40.65 mEq.

The volume of the PN is 960 mL, or 0.96 L. Calculate the mEq per liter

$$40.65 \text{ mEq}/0.96 \text{ L} = 42.3 \text{ mEq/L, which is less than 45 mEq/L}$$

150. Calculate the amount of magnesium sulfate (4 mEq/mL) that should be added to the PN.

$$\frac{4 \text{ mEq}}{\text{mL}} = \frac{12 \text{ mEq}}{X \text{ mL}} \qquad X = 3 \text{ mL magnesium sulfate}$$

151. What percentage of the total calories from the above PN are represented by the protein component? Round to the nearest whole number.

First, calculate the total calories.

DEXTROSE

$$\frac{3.4 \text{ kcal dextrose}}{\text{g}} \times 250 \text{ g dextrose} = 850 \text{ kcal of dextrose}$$

PROTEIN

$$\frac{4 \text{ kcal protein}}{\text{g}} \times 50 \text{ g protein} = 200 \text{ kcal of protein}$$

Total calories = 850 + 200 = 1,050 kcal. Now, calculate the percent of calories from protein.

$$\frac{200 \text{ kcal}}{1,050 \text{ kcal}} \times 100 = 19\%$$

Multivitamins, Trace Elements, and Insulin

Multivitamins

There are 4 fat-soluble vitamins (A, D, E and K) and 9 water-soluble vitamins (thiamine, riboflavin, niacin, pantothenic acid, pyridoxine, ascorbic acid, folic acid, cyanocobalamin, biotin) in the standard MVI-13 mixture. The MVI-12 mixture does not contain vitamin K since certain patients may need less or more of this vitamin. If patients on PN therapy are using warfarin, the INR will need to be monitored.

Trace Elements

The standard mix includes zinc, copper, chromium and manganese (and may include selenium). Manganese and copper should be withheld in severe liver disease. Chromium, molybdenum and selenium should be withheld in severe renal disease. Iron is not routinely given in a PN.

Insulin

PNs may contain insulin, usually ≤ 50% of what the person is expected to require per day, supplemented by a sliding scale. A minimum dose to add is 10 units, and is usually increased in 10 unit increments. It is important to avoid adding too much insulin. Half the previous day's sliding scale or less can be used as a safe amount. PN formulas are often titrated on and off (e.g., started at less than the goal rate and not abruptly stopped) to facilitate physiologic glucose regulation.

Enteral Nutrition

Enteral nutrition (EN) is the provision of nutrients via the gastrointestinal (GI) tract through a feeding tube. Nasogastric (NG) tubes are often used, primarily for short-term administration. For longer-term, or if the stomach cannot be used, tubes are placed further down the GI tract. EN is the preferred route for patients who cannot meet their nutrition needs through voluntary oral intake. Tube feedings can range from providing adjunctive support to providing complete nutrition support. Several advantages of EN over PN include lower cost, using the gut which prevents atrophy and other problems, and a lower risk of complications (less infections, less hyperglycemia, reduced risk of cholelithiasis and cholestasis). The most common risk associated with enteral feeding is aspiration which can lead to pneumonia. Enteral feedings can cause drug interactions. The general rule for preventing drug/enteral feeding interactions is to hold the feedings one hour before or two hours after the drug is administered. Some drugs may require further separation.

Tube feeds do not, by themselves, provide enough water. Water is given in addition to the tube feeds. If fluid intake is inadequate, it will be uncomfortable for the patient and put them at risk for complications, including hypernatremia.

Drug-Nutrient interactions with enteral feedings (most common problems):

- Warfarin: many enteral products bind warfarin, resulting in low INRs and the need for dose adjustments. Hold tube feeds one hour before and one hour after warfarin administration. EN formulas contain varying amounts of vitamin K, which can complicate warfarin dosing in some patients.

- Tetracycline: will chelate with metals, including calcium, magnesium, and iron, which reduces drug availability; separate from tube feeds.

- Ciprofloxacin: the oral suspension is not used with tube feeds because the oil-based suspension adheres to the tube. The immediate-release tablets are used instead; crush and mix with water, flush line with water before and after administration.

- Phenytoin *(Dilantin suspen*sion): levels are reduced when the drug binds to the feeding solution, leading to less free drug availability and sub-therapeutic levels. Separate tube feeds by 2 hours.

Tube Names

- A tube in the nose to the stomach is called a nasogastric (NG), or nasoenteral, tube.

- A tube that goes through the skin into the stomach is called a gastrostomy, or percutaneous endoscopic gastrostomy (PEG, or G) tube.

- A tube into the small intestine is called a jejunostomy, or percutaneous endoscopic jejunostomy (PEJ, or J) tube.

Patient Case (For Questions 152 – 154)

Wilma is a patient starting enteral nutrition therapy. Wilma has a past medical history significant for type 2 diabetes. She will be started on *Glucerna* Ready-to-Drink Vanilla shakes. See the nutrient label provided.

152. According to the case above, what percent of calories will Wilma receive from the protein component? Round to the nearest whole number.

First, calculate the amount of calories provided by the protein component.

$$19.6 \text{ g protein} \times \frac{4 \text{ kcal}}{g} = 78.4 \text{ kcal}$$

Next, find the percentage of protein calories.

$$\frac{78.4 \text{ kcal}}{356 \text{ kcal}} \times 100 = 22\%$$

153. How many calories will Wilma receive from the fat component of 1 (8 fl oz.) shake? Round to the nearest whole number.

$$17.8 \text{ g} \times \frac{9 \text{ kcal}}{g} = 160.2, \text{ or } 160 \text{ kcal}$$

154. What percent of calories are derived from the fat component? Round to the nearest whole number.

$$\frac{160.2 \text{ kcal}}{356 \text{ kcal}} \times 100 = 45\%$$

Nutrition Facts	
Serving Size: 8 fl oz (237 mL)	
Amount Per Serving	
Calories	356 kcal
Total Fat 17.8 g	
Protein 19.6 g	
Total Carbohydrate 31.5 g	
Dietary Fiber 3.8 g	
L-Carnitine	51 mg
Taurine	40 mg
m-Inositol	205 mg
Vitamin A	
Vitamin C	
Iron	© RxPrep

Patient Case (For Questions 155 – 157)

Jonathan is a patient receiving *Osmolite* (a high-protein, low-residue formula) enteral nutrition through a PEG tube. See the nutrient label provided.

155. According to the case above, how many calories will Jonathan receive from the carbohydrate component in 4 fl oz? Round to the nearest whole number.

First, calculate the total calories from carbohydrates per 1 can (8 fl oz).

$$37.4 \text{ g carbohydrate} \times \frac{4 \text{ kcal}}{g} = 149.6 \text{ kcal from 8 fl oz}$$

The question asks about calories in 4 fl oz (1/2 can).

Nutrition Facts	
Serving Size: 8 fl oz (237 mL)	
Amount Per Serving	
Calories 285 kcal	
Total Fat 9.2 g	
Protein 13.2 g	
Total Carbohydrate 37.4 g	
L-Carnitine 36 mg	
Taurine 36 mg	
Vitamin A	
Vitamin C	
Iron	© RxPrep

$$\frac{149.6 \text{ kcal}}{2} = 74.8, \text{ or } 75 \text{ kcal from } 4 \text{ fl oz}$$

---

156. What percent of calories will Jonathan receive from the carbohydrate component? Round to the nearest whole number.

First, calculate the amount of calories from the carbohydrate component.

$$37.4 \text{ g carbohydrate} \times \frac{4 \text{ kcal}}{g} = 149.6 \text{ kcal}$$

Next, find the percentage of carbohydrate calories.

$$\frac{149.6 \text{ kcal}}{285 \text{ kcal}} \times 100 = 52.49, \text{ or } 52\%$$

---

157. The nurse was administering 1 can (8 fl oz.) of *Osmolite* to Jonathan when she accidentally spilled 2 fl oz. onto the floor. The remaining amount in the can was accurately delivered to Jonathan. How many calories did he actually receive? Do not round the answer.

$$\frac{8 \text{ fl oz}}{285 \text{ kcal}} = \frac{6 \text{ fl oz}}{X \text{ kcal}} \qquad X = 213.75 \text{ kcal}$$

CALCULATE RATES OF ADMINISTRATION

Flow Rates

Intravenous (IV) infusions or continuous infusions are commonly used to deliver medications in different settings, including hospitals. Flow rates are used to calculate the volume or amount of drug a patient will receive over a given period of time. An order can specify the rate of flow of continuous intravenous fluids in milliliters per minute, drops per minute, milligrams per hour, or as the total time to administer the entire volume of the infusion (e.g., give over 8 hours). IV tubing is set to deliver a certain number of drops per minute (gtts/min). There are various types of IV tubing and each has a hollow plastic chamber called a drip chamber. One can count the number of drops per minute by looking at the drip chamber. Also, it is important to know how big the drops are to calibrate the tubing in terms of drops/mL. This is called the <u>drop factor</u>. Calculating flow rates from a drop factor is not as common with the prevalence of programmable "smart" pumps. It is a good skill to know in the event a programmable pump is not available, fails, or simply as a double check.

---

158. The pharmacist has an order for heparin 25,000 units in 250 mL D5W to infuse at 1,000 units/hour. The pharmacy has the following premixed heparin bags in stock: 25,000 units in 500 mL ½ NS, 10,000 units in 250 mL D5W, and 25,000 units in 250 mL D5W. What should the infusion rate be set at in mL/hour?

The pharmacy has the heparin product that was ordered. First, calculate units per mL.

$$\frac{25,000 \text{ units}}{250 \text{ mL}} = 100 \text{ units/mL}$$

Next calculate the infusion rate.

$$\frac{1{,}000 \text{ units}}{1 \text{ hr}} \times \frac{1 \text{ mL}}{100 \text{ units}} = 10 \text{ mL/hr}$$

Since 1,000 units/hour must be delivered to the patient and there are 100 units in each mL, the pump should be programmed for an infusion rate of 10 mL/hr.

A second way to solve flow rate problems is using dimensional analysis, which combines individual steps into one calculation. If using dimensional analysis, make sure that all units cancel out to leave the correct units for the answer:

$$\frac{250 \text{ mL}}{25{,}000 \text{ units}} \times \frac{1{,}000 \text{ units}}{1 \text{ hr}} = 10 \text{ mL/hr}$$

Another way to solve these problems is to use a ratio:

$$\frac{25{,}000 \text{ units}}{250 \text{ mL}} = \frac{1{,}000 \text{ units}}{X \text{ mL}} \qquad X = 10 \text{ mL (10 mL/hr since we need to administered 1,000 units in 1 hour)}$$

Try solving the problems in this section both ways and decide which you prefer.

---

159. If 50 mg of drug are added to a 500 mL bag, what rate of flow, in milliliters per hour, will deliver 5 mg of drug per hour?

$$\frac{500 \text{ mL}}{50 \text{ mg}} \times \frac{5 \text{ mg}}{\text{hr}} = 50 \text{ mL/hour}$$

---

160. If 200 mg of drug are added to a 500 mL bag, what rate of flow, in milliliters per hour, will deliver 500 mcg of drug per hour? Round to the nearest hundredth.

$$200 \text{ mg} \times \frac{1{,}000 \text{ mcg}}{1 \text{ mg}} = 200{,}000 \text{ mcg}$$

$$\frac{200{,}000 \text{ mcg}}{500 \text{ mL}} = \frac{500 \text{ mcg}}{X} \qquad X = 1.25 \text{ mL/hour}$$

---

161. A 68 kg patient is receiving a drug in standard concentration of 400 mg/250 mL of 1/2 NS running at 15 mL/hr. Calculate the dose in mcg/kg/min. Round to the nearest hundredth.

$$\frac{15 \text{ mL}}{\text{hr}} \times \frac{400 \text{ mg drug}}{250 \text{ mL}} = 24 \text{ mg drug/hr}$$

$$\frac{24 \text{ mg drug}}{\text{hr}} \times \frac{1{,}000 \text{ mcg}}{1 \text{ mg}} = 24{,}000 \text{ mcg/hr}$$

$$\frac{24{,}000 \text{ mcg}}{\text{hr}} \times \frac{1 \text{ hr}}{60 \text{ min}} = 400 \text{ mcg/min}$$

$$\frac{400 \text{ mcg/min}}{68 \text{ kg}} = 5.88 \text{ mcg/kg/min}$$

162. The pharmacist has an order for heparin 25,000 units in 250 mL D5W to infuse at 1,000 units/hour. How many hours will it take to infuse the entire bag?

$$25{,}000 \text{ units} \times \frac{1 \text{ hr}}{1{,}000 \text{ units}} = 25 \text{ hrs}$$

The problem could ask how many drops will be administered per minute (or per hour). The problem would state the number of drops/mL, which depends on the infusion set used.

163. A physician orders an IV infusion of D5W 1 liter to be delivered over 8 hours. The IV infusion set delivers 15 drops/mL. How many drops/min will the patient receive? Round to the nearest whole number.

$$\frac{15 \text{ drops}}{1 \text{ mL}} \times \frac{1{,}000 \text{ mL}}{8 \text{ hr}} \times \frac{1 \text{ hr}}{60 \text{ min}} = 31.25 \text{ drops/min, rounded to 31 drops/min}$$

164. A nurse is hanging a 4% lidocaine drip for a patient. If the dose ordered is 6 mg/min, how many hours will a 250 mL bag last? Round to the nearest tenth.

$$\frac{4 \text{ g}}{100 \text{ mL}} = \frac{X \text{ g}}{250 \text{ mL}} \quad X = 10 \text{ g or } 10{,}000 \text{ mg}$$

$$\frac{6 \text{ mg}}{\text{min}} = \frac{10{,}000 \text{ mg}}{X \text{ min}} \quad X = 1{,}666.67 \text{ minutes} \qquad \text{Convert to hours} = 27.777 \text{ hrs, or } 27.8 \text{ hrs}$$

Or, solve another way:

$$\frac{1 \text{ hr}}{60 \text{ min}} \times \frac{1 \text{ min}}{6 \text{ mg}} \times \frac{1{,}000 \text{ mg}}{1 \text{ g}} \times \frac{4 \text{ g}}{100 \text{ mL}} \times 250 \text{ mL} = 27.8 \text{ hours}$$

165. A patient is to receive _Keppra_ at a rate of 5 mg/min. The pharmacy has a 5 mL _Keppra_ vial (100 mg/mL) which will be diluted in 100 mL of NS. What is the _Keppra_ infusion rate, in mL/min? Do not include the volume of the 5 mL additive.

First, calculate the amount of _Keppra_ in the vial.

$$\frac{100 \text{ mg}}{\text{mL}} = \frac{X \text{ mg}}{5 \text{ mL}} \quad X = 500 \text{ mg}$$

Then, solve for the answer in mL/min.

$$\frac{100 \text{ mL}}{500 \text{ mg}} \times \frac{5 \text{ mg}}{\text{min}} = 1 \text{ mL/min}$$

166. A physician orders 15 units of regular insulin to be added to a liter of D5W to be given over 10 hours. What is the infusion rate, in drops/minute, if the IV set delivers 15 drops/mL? Do not round the answer.

$$\frac{15 \text{ drops}}{\text{mL}} \times \frac{1{,}000 \text{ mL}}{10 \text{ hrs}} \times \frac{1 \text{ hr}}{60 \text{ min}} = 25 \text{ drops/min}$$

167. The pharmacy has insulin vials containing 100 units of insulin/mL. A physician orders 15 units of regular insulin to be added to a liter of D5W to be given over 10 hours. How many units of insulin will the patient receive each hour if the IV set delivers 15 drops/mL? Do not round the answer.

$$\frac{15 \text{ units}}{10 \text{ hrs}} = \frac{X \text{ units}}{1 \text{ hr}} \qquad X = 1.5 \text{ units/hr}$$

168. An order is written for 10 mL of a 10% calcium chloride injection and 10 mL of multivitamin injection (MVI) to be added to 500 mL of D5W. The infusion is to be administered over 6 hours. The IV set delivers 15 drops/mL. What should be the rate of flow in drops/minute to deliver this infusion? Round to the nearest whole number.

Total volume of the infusion = 500 mL (D5W) + 10 mL ($CaCl_2$) + 10 mL (MVI) = 520 mL

$$\frac{15 \text{ drops}}{mL} \times \frac{520 \text{ mL}}{6 \text{ hr}} \times \frac{1 \text{ hr}}{60 \text{ min}} = 22 \text{ drops/min}$$

169. RS is a 45 year old male, 5'5", 168 pounds, hospitalized with a diabetic foot infection. The pharmacist prepared a 500 mL bag of D5W containing 1 gram of vancomycin to be infused over 4 hours using a 20 gtts/mL IV tubing set. How many mg of vancomycin will the patient receive each minute? Round to the nearest tenth.

$$\frac{1,000 \text{ mg vanco}}{4 \text{ hrs}} \times \frac{1 \text{ hr}}{60 \text{ min}} = 4.16 \text{ mg/min, rounded to } 4.2 \text{ mg/min}$$

170. A patient is to receive 600,000 units of penicillin G potassium in 100 mL D5W. A vial of penicillin G potassium 1,000,000 units is available. The manufacture states that when 4.6 mL of diluent is added, a 200,000 units/mL solution will result. How many milliliters of reconstituted solution should be withdrawn and added to the bag of D5W?

$$\frac{200,000 \text{ units}}{mL} = \frac{600,000 \text{ units}}{X \text{ mL}} \qquad X = 3 \text{ mL}$$

171. A patient is to receive 1.5 liters of NS running at 45 gtts/min using a 15 gtts/mL IV tubing set. Calculate the total infusion time in hours. Round to the nearest tenth.

$$\frac{15 \text{ gtts}}{1 \text{ mL}} = \frac{45 \text{ gtts}}{X \text{ mL}} \qquad X = 3 \text{ mL}$$

$$\frac{3 \text{ mL}}{min} = \frac{1,500 \text{ mL}}{X \text{ min}} \qquad X = 500 \text{ min}$$

$$500 \text{ min} \times \frac{1 \text{ hr}}{60 \text{ min}} = 8.3 \text{ hrs}$$

172. An intravenous infusion contains 2 mL of a 1:1,000 (w/v) solution of epinephrine and 250 mL of D5W. At what flow rate, in mL/min, should the infusion be administered to provide 0.3 mcg/kg/min of epinephrine to an 80 kg patient? Round to the nearest whole number.

- 1:1,000 ratio strength = 0.1% (w/v)

$$\frac{0.1\ g}{100\ mL} = \frac{X\ g}{2\ mL} \qquad X = 0.002\ g,\ or\ 2\ mg$$

The patient is 80 kg x 0.3 mcg/kg/min = 24 mcg/min

$$\frac{252\ mL}{2\ mg} \times \frac{1\ mg}{1,000\ mcg} \times \frac{24\ mcg}{min} = 3\ mL/min$$

---

173. A patient is to receive *Flagyl* at a rate of 12.5 mg/min. The pharmacy has a 5 mL (100 mg/mL) *Flagyl* injection vial to be diluted in 100 mL of NS. How much drug in milligrams will the patient receive over 20 minutes?

$$\frac{12.5\ mg}{min} \times 20\ minutes = 250\ mg$$

---

174. A physician has ordered 2 grams of cefotetan to be added to 100 mL NS for a 56 year old female with an anaerobic infection. Using a reconstituted injection containing 154 mg/mL, how many milliliters should be added to prepare the order? Round to the nearest whole number.

$$2,000\ mg \times \frac{1\ mL}{154\ mg} = 13\ mL$$

---

175. JY is a 58 year old male hospitalized for a total knee replacement. He was given unfractionated heparin and developed heparin-induced thrombocytopenia (HIT). Argatroban was ordered at a dose of 2 mcg/kg/min. The pharmacy mixes a concentration of 100 mg argatroban in 250 mL of D5W. JY weighs 187 lbs. At what rate (mL/hour) should the nurse infuse argatroban to provide the desired dose? Round to the nearest whole number.

First, determine the amount of drug needed based on body weight.

$$2\ mcg/kg/min \times 85\ kg = 170\ mcg/min$$

Then, calculate mL/hr.

$$\frac{250\ mL}{100\ mg} \times \frac{1\ mg}{1,000\ mcg} \times \frac{170\ mcg}{min} \times \frac{60\ min}{hr} = 25.5\ mL/hr,\ rounded\ to\ 26\ mL/hr$$

---

176. The 8 a.m. medications scheduled for a patient include *Tygacil* dosed at 6 mg/kg. The patient weighs 142 pounds. The nurse has *Tygacil* labeled 500 mg/50 mL NS. The dose will be administered over thirty minutes. The IV tubing in the unit delivers 15 drops per milliliter. What is the correct rate of flow in drops per minute? Round to the nearest drop.

$$\frac{142\ pounds}{2.2\ pounds/kg} \times \frac{6\ mg}{kg} = 387.27\ mg\ required\ dose$$

$$387.27 \text{ mg} \times \frac{50 \text{ mL}}{500 \text{ mg}} = 38.727 \text{ mL}$$

$$\frac{38.727 \text{ mL}}{30 \text{ min}} \times \frac{15 \text{ drops}}{\text{mL}} = 19.36 \text{ drops/min, rounded to 19 drops/min}$$

177. A 165 pound patient is to receive 250 mL of a dopamine drip at a rate of 17 mcg/kg/min. The pharmacy has dopamine premixed in concentration of 3.2 mg/mL in D5W. Calculate the infusion rate in mL/minute. Round to the nearest tenth.

Step 1: Calculate amount of drug in the 250 mL bag.

$$\frac{3.2 \text{ mg}}{\text{mL}} \times 250 \text{ mL} = 800 \text{ mg}$$

Step 2: Calculate amount of drug the patient needs per minute.

$$\frac{17 \text{ mcg}}{\text{kg/min}} \times \frac{1 \text{ kg}}{2.2 \text{ lbs}} \times 165 \text{ lbs} = 1{,}275 \text{ mcg/min or } 1.275 \text{ mg/min}$$

Step 3: Solve for milliliters per minute.

$$\frac{250 \text{ mL}}{800 \text{ mg}} \times \frac{1.275 \text{ mg}}{\text{min}} = 0.4 \text{ mL/min}$$

178. An order is written for phenytoin IV. A loading dose of 15 mg/kg is to be infused at 0.5 mg/kg/min for a 33 pound child. The pharmacy has phenytoin injection solution 50 mg/mL in a 5 mL vial in stock. The pharmacist will put the dose into 50 mL NS. Over how many minutes should the dose be administered? Round to the nearest whole number.

First, calculate the child's body weight in kg.

$$33 \text{ lbs} \times \frac{1 \text{ kg}}{2.2 \text{ lbs}} = 15 \text{ kg}$$

Next, find the dose the child will receive.

$$\frac{15 \text{ mg}}{\text{kg}} \times 15 \text{ kg} = 225 \text{ mg}$$

Then, calculate the time it will take to infuse this amount of drug at the given rate.

$$0.5 \text{ mg/kg/min} \times 15 \text{ kg} = 7.5 \text{ mg/min}$$

$$\frac{1 \text{ min}}{7.5 \text{ mg}} \times 225 \text{ mg} = 30 \text{ minutes}$$

ADDITIONAL CALCULATION TYPES

pH, Arterial Blood Gas (ABG), Anion Gap, Buffer Systems and Ionization

pH

The pH refers to the acidity or basicity of the solution. As a solution becomes more acidic (the concentration of protons increases), the pH decreases. Conversely, when the pH increases, protons decrease, and the solution is more basic, or alkaline. Pure water is neutral at a pH of 7, and blood, with a pH of 7.4, is slightly alkaline. Stomach acid has a pH of ~2, is therefore acidic, with many protons in solution.

> **PH NOTES**
>
> A lower pH means more hydronium ions (H_3O^+, or H^+) in solution and is therefore more acidic. A higher pH is more basic and has less hydronium ions and more hydroxide (OH^-) ions in solution. The pH of 7 is said to be neutral. Blood is just slightly alkaline with a pH that should stay between 7.35–7.45.

Arterial Blood Gas

The acid-base status of a patient can be determined by an arterial blood gas (ABG). The primary buffering system of the body is the bicarbonate/carbonic acid system. The kidneys help to maintain a neutral pH by controlling bicarbonate (HCO_3) resorption and elimination. Bicarbonate acts as a buffer and a base. The lungs help maintain a neutral pH by controlling carbonic acid (which is directly proportional to the partial pressure of carbon dioxide or pCO_2) retained or released from the body. Carbon dioxide acts as a buffer and an acid. Alterations from the normal values lead to acid-base disorders. Diet and cellular metabolism lead to a large production of H^+ ions that need to be excreted to maintain acid-base balance. See Lab Values & Drug Monitoring chapter for ABG component reference ranges. ABGs are presented as follows in a written chart note:

ABG: $pH/pCO_2/pO_2/HCO_3/O_2$ Sat

An acid-base disorder that leads to a pH < 7.35 is called an acidosis. If the disorder leads to a pH > 7.45 it is called an alkalosis. These disorders are further classified as either metabolic or respiratory in origin. The primary cause of an acid-base disorder is determined from the abnormal component (HCO_3 or PCO_2) that tells the same story as the pH. The primary disturbance in a metabolic acid-base disorder is the plasma HCO_3 (bicarbonate) concentration. A metabolic acidosis is characterized primarily by a decrease in plasma HCO3 concentration. In a metabolic alkalosis, the plasma HCO_3 concentration is increased. Metabolic acidosis may be associated with an increase in the anion gap (see below). In respiratory acidosis, the pCO_2 is primarily elevated and in respiratory alkalosis, the pCO_2 is decreased. Each disturbance has a compensatory (secondary) response that attempts to correct the imbalance toward normal and keep the pH neutral.

---

179. A babysitter brings a 7 year old boy to the Emergency Department. He is unarousable. Labs are ordered and an ABG is drawn. The ABG results are as follows: 6.72/40/89/12/94%. What acid base disorder does the child have?

Based on the pH, this is an acidosis. The pCO_2 is normal and the HCO_3 is decreased (low bicarbonate indicates acidosis). This is a metabolic acidosis.

---

180. An elderly female is admitted to the hospital after a motor vehicle accident. She suffered a head injury and is in the ICU. An ABG is obtained and the results are as follows: 8.25/29/97/26/98%. What acid base disorder does the patient have?

Based on the pH, this is an alkalosis. The pCO_2 is decreased (low pCO_2 indicates alkalosis) and the HCO_3 is normal. This is a respiratory alkalosis.

Calculating Anion Gap

When a patient is experiencing metabolic acidosis, it is common to calculate an anion gap. The anion gap is the difference in the measured cations and the measured anions in the blood. An anion gap assists in determining the cause of the acidosis. A mnemonic to remember the causes of a gap acidosis is CUTE DIMPLES [cyanide, uremia, toluene, ethanol (alcoholic ketoacidosis), diabetic ketoacidosis, isoniazid, methanol, propylene glycol, lactic acidosis, ethylene glycol, salicylates]. The anion gap is considered high if it is > 12 mEq/L (meaning the patient has a gap acidosis). The anion gap can also be low, which is less common. A non-gap acidosis is caused by other factors, mainly hyperchloremic acidosis. Anion gap is calculated with this formula:

> Anion gap (AG) = $Na - Cl - HCO_3$

---

181. A patient in the ICU has recently developed an acidosis. Using the laboratory parameters below, calculate the patient's anion gap.

Na	139
Cl	101
K	4.6
HCO_3	19
SCr	1.6
BUN	38

Anion Gap = 139 − 101 − 19 = 19; therefore, the patient has a gap acidosis

---

182. SJ was recently admitted to the ICU with a pH of 7.27. Below is her laboratory data. Calculate SJ's anion gap.

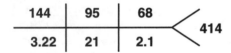

Anion Gap = 144 − 95 − 21 = 28; therefore, SJ has a gap acidosis

Buffer Systems and Ionization

Buffer systems help to reduce the impact of too few or too many hydrogen ions in body fluids. These hydrogen ions could cause harm including degrading some drugs, destabilizing proteins, inhibiting cellular functions, and with too much of a change outside of the narrow range, cells die and death can occur. Therefore, buffers minimize fluctuations in pH so that harm is avoided. Buffer systems are common in the body and are composed of either a weak acid and salt of the acid (e.g., acetic acid and sodium acetate), or weak base and salt of the base (e.g., ammonium hydroxide and ammonium chloride). An <u>acid</u> is a compound that dissociates, <u>releasing (donating) protons into solution</u>. Once the proton is released, the compound is now a conjugate base, or its salt form. For example, HCl in solution is an acid and dissociates (giving up the proton) into H^+ and Cl^-. <u>A base picks up, or binds, the proton</u>. For example, NH_3 is a base that can pick up a proton and become NH_4^+.

Acid-base reactions are equilibrium reactions; there is drug moving back and forth between the acid and base state. The pH and the pKa are used to determine if the drug is acting as an acid or a base. When the pH = pKa, the molar concentration of the salt form and the molar concentration of the acid form of the buffer acid-base pair will be equal: 50% of the buffer will be in salt form and 50% in acid form. Notice that the percentage of buffer in the acid form when added to the percentage of buffer in the salt form will equal 100%. When the pH = pKa, this is the point at which half the compound is protonated (ionized), and half is not protonated (un-ionized).

A 'strong' acid or base means 100% dissociation and a 'weak' acid or base means very limited dissociation. Any time a pKa is provided, it refers to the acid form losing protons to give to the base, or salt, form.

If the 'pKb' is provided, think base, 'base' simply because of the definitions of the two terms.

If the pH > pKa, more of the acid is ionized, and more of the conjugate base is un-ionized.

If the pH = pKa, the ionized and un-ionized forms are equal.

If the pH < pKa, more of the acid is un-ionized, and more of the conjugate base is ionized.

The percentage of drug in the ionized versus un-ionized state is important because an ionized drug is soluble but cannot easily cross lipid membranes. An un-ionized drug is not soluble but can cross the membranes and reach the proper receptor site. Most drugs are weak acids. They are soluble, and can pick up a proton to cross the lipid layer.

Most drug molecules are weak acids (or weak bases). These molecules can exist in either the un-ionized or the ionized state, and the degree of ionization depends on the dissociation constant (Ka) of the drug and the pH of the environment. This leads to the Henderson-Hasselbalch equation, also known as the buffer equation, which is used to solve for the pH.

WEAK ACID FORMULA

$$pH = pK_a + \log \left[\frac{salt}{acid} \right]$$

WEAK BASE FORMULAS

$$pH = (pK_w^* - pK_b) + \log \left[\frac{base}{salt} \right] \quad or \quad pH = pK_a + \log \left[\frac{base}{salt} \right]$$

where pKw = 14

---

183. What is the pH of a solution prepared to be 0.5 M sodium citrate and 0.05 M citric acid (pKa for citric acid = 3.13)? Round to the nearest hundredth.

$$pH = pK_a + \log \left[\frac{salt}{acid} \right]$$

$$pH = 3.13 + \log \left[\frac{0.5M}{0.05M} \right]$$

$$pH = 3.13 + \log[10]$$

$$pH = 3.13 + 1$$

$$pH = 4.13$$

184. What is the pH of a solution prepared to be 0.4 M ammonia and 0.04 M ammonium chloride (pKb for ammonia = 4.76)? Round to the nearest hundredth.

$$pH = (pK_w - pK_b) + \log\left[\frac{base}{salt}\right]$$

$$pH = (14 - 4.76) + \log\left[\frac{0.4}{0.04}\right]$$

$$pH = 9.24 + \log(10)$$

$$pH = 9.24 + 1$$

$$pH = 10.24$$

---

185. What is the pH of a buffer solution containing 0.5 M acetic acid and 1 M sodium acetate in 1 liter of solution (pKa for acetic acid = 4.76)? Round to the nearest hundredth.

$$pH = pK_a + \log\left[\frac{salt}{acid}\right]$$

$$pH = 4.76 + \log\left[\frac{1}{0.5}\right]$$

$$pH = 4.76 + \log(2)$$

$$pH = 4.76 + 0.301$$

$$pH = 5.06$$

---

186. What is the pH of a solution containing 0.2 mole of a weakly basic drug and 0.02 mole of its salt per liter of solution (pKa of the drug = 9.36)? Round to the nearest hundredth.

$$pH = pK_a + \log\left[\frac{base}{salt}\right]$$

$$pH = 9.36 + \log\left[\frac{0.2}{0.02}\right]$$

$$pH = 9.36 + 1$$

$$pH = 10.36$$

---

187. A buffer solution is prepared using 0.3 mole of a weakly basic drug and an unknown quantity of its salt (pKa of the drug = 10.1). The final solution has a pH of 8.99. How much of the salt was used? Round to the nearest hundredth.

$$pH = pK_a + \log\left[\frac{base}{salt}\right]$$

$$8.99 = 10.1 + \log \left[\frac{0.3}{X} \right]$$

$$8.99 - 10.1 = \log \left[\frac{0.3}{X} \right]$$

$$10^{-1.11} = \frac{0.3}{X}$$

$$X = 3.86 \text{ mole of the salt}$$

Percent of Ionization

The Henderson-Hasselbalch equation can be modified to calculate the percent of ionization of a drug.

To calculate the % ionization of a weak acid:

$$\% \text{ ionization} = \frac{100}{1+10^{(pKa-pH)}}$$

To calculate % ionization of a weak base:

$$\% \text{ ionization} = \frac{100}{1+10^{(pH-pKa)}}$$

---

188. What is the % ionization of amitriptyline, a weak base with a pKa = 9.4, at a physiologic pH of 7.4?

Use the weak base formula:

$$\% \text{ ionization} = \frac{100}{1+10^{(pH-pKa)}}$$

$$\% \text{ ionization} = \frac{100}{1+10^{(7.4-9.4)}}$$

$$\% \text{ ionization} = \frac{100}{1+10^{(-2)}}$$

$$\% \text{ ionization} = \frac{100}{1.01}$$

$$\% \text{ ionization} = 99\%$$

---

189. What is the % ionization of naproxen, a weak acid with a pKa of 4.2, in the stomach at a pH of 3? Round to the nearest whole number.

Use the weak acid formula:

$$\% \text{ ionization} = \frac{100}{1+10^{(pKa-pH)}}$$

$$\% \text{ ionization} = \frac{100}{16.85}$$

$$\% \text{ ionization} = 6\%$$

Calcium Formulations and Conversions

Calcium carbonate (*Oscal, Tums*, etc) has acid-dependent absorption and should be taken with meals. Calcium carbonate is a dense form of calcium and contains 40% elemental calcium. A tablet that advertises 500 mg of elemental calcium weighs 1,250 mg. If 1,250 mg is multiplied by 0.40 (which is 40%), it will yield 500 mg elemental calcium.

Calcium citrate (*Citracal*, etc) has acid-independent absorption and can be taken with or without food. Calcium citrate is less dense and contains 21% elemental calcium. A tablet that advertises 315 mg calcium weighs 1,500 mg. If 1,500 mg is multiplied by 0.21 (or 21%), it will yield 315 mg elemental calcium. This is why the larger calcium citrate tablets provide less elemental calcium per tablet. They may be preferred if the gut fluid is basic, rather than acidic.

Calcium acetate (*PhosLo*, etc) is used as a phosphate binder and not for calcium replacement. Though the capsules contain 25% elemental calcium, absorption from this formulation is poor. Calcium carbonate and citrate are most commonly used for calcium replacement.

---

190. A patient is taking 3 calcium citrate tablets daily (one tablet, TID). Each weighs 1,500 mg total (non-elemental) weight. She wishes to trade her calcium tablets for the carbonate form. If she is going to use 1,250 mg carbonate tablets (by weight), how many tablets will she need to take to provide the same total daily dose?

1,500 mg/tablet x 3 tablets/day x 0.21= 945 mg elemental calcium daily

Each of the carbonate tablets (1,250 mg x 0.4) has 500 mg elemental calcium per tablet.

$$\frac{945 \text{ mg elemental calcium}}{X \text{ tablets}} = \frac{500 \text{ mg elemental calcium}}{1 \text{ tablet}} \qquad X = 1.89 \text{ tablets}$$

She would need to take 2 tablets daily to provide a similar dose. Calcium absorption increases with lower doses, so this patient should be instructed to take one tablet with the morning meal and one with the evening meal.

Absolute Neutrophil Count

Neutrophils are our body's main defense against infection. The lower a patient's neutrophil count, the more susceptible that patient is to infection. The normal range for the absolute neutrophil count (ANC) is 2,200 – 8,000 cells/microliter. The microliter may be written as mm^3, or μL, but it is preferable to avoid the latter designation for safety reasons. Definitions vary, but an ANC < 1,000 cells/mm^3 would predispose a patient to infection; an ANC < 500 cells/mm^3 indicates very high risk for developing an infection. The Clozapine REMS Program is designed to reduce the risk of severe clozapine-induced neutropenia; clozapine cannot be refilled if the ANC is < 1,000 cells/mm^3. A neutropenic patient should be monitored for signs of infection, including fever, shaking, general weakness or flu-like symptoms. Precautions to reduce infection risk, such as proper hand-washing and avoiding others with infection, should be followed. Further information is in the Lab Values & Drug Monitoring chapter.

Calculating the ANC

Multiply the WBC (in total cells/mm³) by the percentage of neutrophils (the segs plus the bands) and divide by 100.

ANC (cells/mm³) = WBC x [(% segs + % bands)/100]

---

191. A patient is being seen at the oncology clinic today after her first round of chemotherapy one week ago. A CBC with differential is ordered and reported back as WBC = 14.8 x 10³ cells/mm³, segs 10% and bands 11%. Calculate this patient's ANC.

WBC = 14,800 cells/mm³, Segs = 10% Bands = 11%

ANC = 14,800 x [(10% + 11%)/100] = 14,800 x 0.21 = 3,108 cells/mm³

---

192. A patient is taking clozapine and is at the clinic for a routine visit. Today's labs include WBC = 4,300 cells/mm³ with 48% segs and 2% bands. Calculate this patient's ANC.

WBC = 4,300 cells/mm³, Segs = 48% Bands = 2%

ANC = 4,300 x [(48% + 2%)/100] = 4,300 x 0.5 = 2,150 cells/mm³

Calculation Practice

The following problems integrate multiple calculation concepts.

---

193. A patient is receiving D5½NS with potassium chloride at 20 drops/min. After 10 hours, the patient has received a total of 40 mEq of potassium chloride using tubing that delivers 15 drops/mL. What is the percentage concentration of potassium chloride in the patient's IV fluid? Round to 2 decimal places. (M.W. of K = 39, M.W. of Cl = 36)

$$40 \text{ mEq} = \frac{X \text{ mg} \times 1}{75} = 3,000 \text{ mg, or 3 g of KCl have been given in 10 hours}$$

$$\frac{20 \text{ drops}}{\text{min}} \times \frac{60 \text{ min}}{1 \text{ hr}} \times 10 \text{ hrs} = 12,000 \text{ drops infused in 10 hours}$$

$$\frac{15 \text{ drops}}{\text{mL}} = \frac{12,000 \text{ drops}}{X \text{ mL}} \quad X = 800 \text{ mL have infused in 10 hours}$$

$$\frac{3 \text{ g KCl}}{800 \text{ mL}} = \frac{X \text{ g}}{100 \text{ mL}} \quad X = 0.375 \text{ g, or } 0.38\%$$

---

194. An order is written for a dopamine drip in the ICU. The order reads: "Start dopamine drip at 3 mcg/kg/min, titrate by 5 mcg/kg/min Q5 minutes to achieve SBP > 100 mmHg. Page the critical care resident for additional orders if maximum dose of 20 mcg/kg/min is reached". The patient weighs 165 pounds and the ICU stocks premixed dopamine drips (400 mg/250 mL) in the automated dispensing cabinet (ADC). What rate (mL/hr) should the dopamine drip be started at? Round to the nearest whole number.

$$3 \text{ mcg/kg/min} \times 75 \text{ kg} = 225 \text{ mcg/min}$$

$$\frac{250 \text{ mL}}{400 \text{ mg}} \quad \times \quad \frac{1 \text{ mg}}{1000 \text{ mcg}} \quad \times \quad \frac{225 \text{ mcg}}{\text{min}} \quad \times \quad \frac{60 \text{ min}}{1 \text{ hr}} \quad = 8.4 \text{ mL/hr, or 8 mL/hr}$$

---

195. The patient in problem #194 is started on the dopamine drip as ordered. Later that day, the pharmacist checks on the patient and notes that the dopamine drip is running at 70 mL/hr and the patient's SBP is still < 100 mmHg. According to the original order, should the resident be paged?

$$20 \text{ mcg/kg/min} \quad \times \quad 75 \text{ kg} \quad = 1500 \text{ mcg/min}$$

$$\frac{250 \text{ mL}}{400 \text{ mg}} \quad \times \quad \frac{1 \text{ mg}}{1000 \text{ mcg}} \quad \times \quad \frac{1500 \text{ mcg}}{\text{min}} \quad \frac{60 \text{ min}}{1 \text{ hr}} \quad = 56.25 \text{ mL/hr – max rate per order}$$

The drip is running at 70 mL/hr and the maximum rate on the order was 56.25 mL/hr. According to the original order, the resident should be paged.

---

196. A pharmacist in an oncology clinic receives the following prescription for a patient with Hodgkin lymphoma: "Prednisone 40 mg/m²/day PO on days 1-14." The patient is 5'1" and weighs 116 pounds. The hospital uses the following formula for BSA (m²) = 0.007184 x height(cm)$^{0.725}$ x weight(kg)$^{0.425}$. How many 20 mg prednisone tablets should be dispensed to the patient?

$$\text{BSA (m}^2) = 0.007184 \quad \times \quad (154.94)^{0.725} \quad \times \quad (52.7272)^{0.425} = 1.5 \text{ m}^2$$

$$40 \text{ mg/m}^2\text{/day} \quad \times \quad 1.5 \text{ m}^2 = 60 \text{ mg/day}$$

Refer to Oncology II chapter for discussion of BSA.

The patient will take 60 mg of prednisone (three 20 mg tablets) per day for 14 days. The pharmacist should dispense 42 of the 20 mg prednisone tablets.

---

197. A nephrologist is treating a patient with hyponatremia. She estimates the patient's sodium deficit to be 210 mEq. How many mL of normal saline (M.W. Na = 23, M.W. Cl = 35.5) will be required to replace the deficit?

$$210 \text{ mEq} = \frac{\text{mg} \times 1}{58.5} \qquad 12,285 \text{ mg or 12.285 g}$$

$$\frac{0.9 \text{ g}}{100 \text{ mL}} = \frac{12.285 \text{ g}}{X \text{ mL}} \qquad X = 1,365 \text{ mL of NS are required}$$

---

198. A pharmacy technician is asked to compound three 500 mL doses of 5% albumin. How many 50 mL vials of 25% albumin will be required?

$$\frac{5 \text{ g}}{100 \text{ mL}} = \frac{X \text{ g}}{500 \text{ mL}} \qquad X = 25 \text{ g, or 75 g for the three required doses}$$

$$\frac{25 \text{ g}}{100 \text{ mL}} = \frac{X \text{ g}}{50 \text{ mL}} \qquad X = 12.5 \text{ g per 50 mL vial}$$

$$75 \text{ g required} \quad \times \quad \frac{1 \text{ vial}}{12.5 \text{ g}} \qquad X = 6 \text{ vials of 25\% albumin required}$$

199. A patient is to receive a potassium acetate infusion prepared by adding 9 mL of 39.2% potassium acetate ($KC_2H_3O_2$) to a 1 L infusion solution. The patient is to receive the potassium acetate at 5 mEq/hr. What rate in mL/hr will provide this dose? Round to the nearest whole number. (M.W. of K = 39, M.W of $C_2H_3O_2$ = 59)

$$\frac{39.2\ g}{100\ mL} = \frac{X\ g}{9\ mL} \qquad X = 3.528\ g\ or\ 3,528\ mg$$

$$X\ mEq = \frac{3,528\ mg \times 1}{98} = 36\ mEq$$

$$\frac{1,000\ mL}{36\ mEq} \times \frac{5\ mEq}{hr} = 138.88\ mL/hr,\ or\ 139\ mL/hr$$

PATIENT PROFILE

Patient Name	Helene Gudot							
Address	1365 Stephens Avenue							
Age:	64	Sex:	F	Race:	African American	Height:	5'5"	Weight: 135 pounds
Allergies	Bactrim							

DIAGNOSES

Type 2 Diabetes	Dyslipidemia
Hypertension	Heart Failure

MEDICATIONS

Date	Prescriber	Drug/Strength/Sig
12/10/15	Marks	Metformin 1 gram BID
12/10/15	Marks	Regular insulin sliding scale per protocol
12/11/15	Marks	*Lantus* 10 units at HS
12/12/15	Ventrakhan	D51/4NS + 20 mEq KCL at 75 mL/hr
12/12/15	King	*Coreg* 6.25 mg BID
12/13/15	Marks	D51/2NS + 10 mEq KCL at 60 mL/hr
12/13/15	Marks	Lasix 40 mg IV Q12H
12/13/15	Ventrakhan	*Altace* 5 mg BID

LAB/DIAGNOSTIC TESTS

Test	Normal Value	Results		
		Date: 12/13/15	Date: 12/12/15	Date: 12/11/15
WBC	4,000-11,000 cells/mm^3	10.7	10.1	12.2
Na	135-146 mEq/L	139	142	145
K	3.5-5.3 mEq/L	4.3	4.1	3.3
Cl	98-110 mEq/L	104	105	101
HCO3	22-28 mEq/L	26	26	25
BUN	7-25 mg/dL	23	26	28
Creatinine	0.6-1.2 mg/dL	1.1	1.3	1.4
Glu	65-99 mg/dL	180 @ 0700	140 @ 0700	260 @ 0700
Glu	65-99 mg/dL	280 @ 1100	280 @ 1100	320 @ 1100
Glu	65-99 mg/dL	220 @ 1700	300 @ 1700	280 @ 1700
Glu	65-99 mg/dL	100 @ 2100	220 @ 2100	220 @ 2100

200. Mrs. Gudot uses the following regular insulin sliding scale: "take 1 unit of insulin SQ for every 20 mg/dL of blood sugar > 160 mg/dL". How many units of sliding scale insulin should have been administered on December 12th?

140 mg/dL = no insulin

280 mg/dL – 160 mg/dL = 120 mg/dL; 120 mg/dL / 20 mg/dL = 6 units

300 mg/dL – 160 mg/dL = 140 mg/dL / 20 mg/dL = 7 units

220 mg/dL – 160 mg/dL = 60 mg/dL / 20 mg/dL = 3 units

Total sliding scale units for December 12th = 6 + 7 + 3 = 16 units

---

201. The pharmacist is asked to convert several of Mrs. Gudot's labs to different units so her case can be compared to a published case report. Convert her serum potassium level on December 13th to mg/dL. (M.W. of potassium = 39)

$$4.3 \text{ mEq} = \frac{X \text{ mg} \times 1}{39} \qquad X = 167.7 \text{ mg}$$

4.3 mEq = 167.7 mg. The patient's serum potassium is reported as 4.3 mEq/L, which equals 167.7 mg/L.

$$\frac{167.7 \text{ mg}}{1 \text{ L}} \times \frac{1 \text{ L}}{10 \text{ dL}} = 16.77 \text{ mg/dL}$$

---

202. Convert Mrs. Gudot's serum sodium level on December 11th to mmol/L. (M.W. of Na = 23)

$$145 \text{ mEq} = \frac{X \text{ mg} \times 1}{23} \qquad X = 3,335 \text{ mg}$$

$$X \text{ mmols} = \frac{3,335 \text{ mg}}{23} \qquad X = 145 \text{ mmols, therefore } 145 \text{ mEq/L} = 145 \text{ mmol/L for sodium}$$

Note that mmols = mEq in this problem. For Na and K, the mmol and mEq are the same; 1 mmol = 1 mEq.

NON-STERILE COMPOUNDING

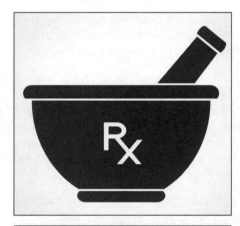

We gratefully acknowledge the assistance of Jesse Martinez, Clinical Associate Professor & Vice Dean, Western University College of Pharmacy, in preparing this chapter.

BACKGROUND

This chapter discusses non-sterile compounding requirements. Sterile compounding has other requirements, which are in the following chapter.

Compounding is when drugs are combined, mixed, or altered to create a medication tailored to the needs of an individual patient. If the health needs of a patient cannot be met by an FDA-approved medication, a compounded drug may be used. This can be done for medically necessary reasons, such as changing the form of the medication from a solid tablet to a liquid for a patient that has trouble swallowing, avoiding a non-essential ingredient that a patient cannot tolerate, or formulating a dose that is not commercially available. Compounding is useful for optional reasons, such as adding flavors to a medication or otherwise altering taste or texture.

Compounding is different from manufacturing since it is patient-specific (ordered by a prescriber for the patient) and regulated by the state boards of pharmacy. Compounded products do not have NDC numbers. Beyond use dates must be applied to each non-sterile compounded product, using USP 795 guidelines for Nonaqueous Liquids and Solid Formulations and for Water-Containing Formulations. For all other formulations, the beyond use date is no later than the intended duration of therapy or 30 days, whichever is earlier.

In contrast, FDA-approved and regulated drugs must be produced under Current Good Manufacturing Practices (CGMPs), have NDC numbers, and carry a manufacturer's expiration date.

Exceptions for compounding that are made to meet the needs of a shortage, or other exceptional circumstances that require bulk products made by a compounding pharmacist (and which are not labeled for specific patients), must be made in an FDA-registered facility using CGMPs, and must be labeled with a batch control number and expiration date. This type of compounding is distinguished from traditional compounding, and is referred to as "outsourcing". Another exception to traditional compounding requirements involves compounding dietary or nutritional supplements. These are foods, not drugs, and are regulated under the Dietary Supplement Health and Education Act (DSHEA). Dietary supplements, as food products, are not subject to the rigid requirements for drug manufacturing or compounding. Dietary supplements are not permitted to claim that they can treat or cure a condition. They must be made with safe components of food grade quality. Requirements for outsourcing facilities and for dietary supplements are described further in the RxPrep MPJE course manual.

Animal compounding requires a specialized knowledge of drug use in animals (metabolism, toxicity to different species, ADRs, others) and specifics, such as the length of time a food-producing animal must be off medications prior to that animal's products (e.g., milk, eggs, meat) entering the human food supply.

GENERAL NON-STERILE COMPOUNDING RULES

Personnel involved in compounding require training in USP 795, other applicable USP chapters, the safety data sheets (SDS–these include detailed information about the substances or mixtures), hazardous drug safety and handling, and the facility's policies and procedures. All training and compounding procedures must have oversight by a compounding supervisor who is skilled and has demonstrated knowledge of each step. The personnel must have demonstrated both verbal and functional knowledge (they need to demonstrate technique). A review of skills should be conducted for each staff member at least annually. Initial hires receive an orientation, then have specific training for their area of compounding, and then will require periodic inservices (training at the site), on a continual basis.

Hand hygiene is essential; refer to the Medication Safety chapter for proper hand hygiene for non-sterile compounding and routine patient care activities. Garb attire depends on the type of compounding and includes hair bonnets, gowns, gloves, shoe covers, face masks, beard covers and aprons. Hand hygiene and garbing is more detailed for sterile compounding, and is reviewed in the following chapter.

Compounding facilities must include adequate space designed for compounding, must be separate from other pharmacy activities, and the sterile area (which has very specific requirements) must be separate from the non-sterile areas. All areas require adequate heating, air conditioning and ventilation, hot and cold water, and hand soap/detergent. The hands should be dried with either an air dryer or single use (disposable) towels.

Compounding surfaces must not be reactive, additive or sorptive (a substance that can

---

CATEGORIES OF NON-STERILE COMPOUNDING

Simple compounding involves reconstituting or manipulating a commercial product by adding one or more ingredients (such as water or alcohol), as directed by the manufacturer. Example: Preparing *Benzamycin* for dispensing to a patient.

Moderate compounding requires calculations or procedures to determine the quantities of components for individualized dosage units or for which stability data is not available. Example: Mixing two prescription topical creams together that are not designed to be mixed by the manufacturer, and the stability of the final product is not available.

Complex compounding requires special training, environment, facilities, equipment, and procedures. Example: Preparing a transdermal drug delivery system.

COMPOUNDING RECORD

The compounding record is the log book of what products have been made, and includes:
-compound's official or assigned name
-strength & formulation
-reference for the master formula
-components with source, lot numbers & expiration dates
-the preparer
-the person who did quality control (QC).
-the pharmacist who approved the preparation with the date
-the control or prescription number
-a beyond-use date (BUD)
A copy of the prescription label is applied to the log, along with a description of the final preparation.

MASTER FORMULATION RECORD

A master formulation record is the "recipe" for the products compounded, and includes:
-compound's official or assigned name
-strength, dosage form, ingredients & quantities [the Active Pharmaceutical Ingredient (API) and all others]
-calculations/doses
-stability data
-references used
-equipment
-mixing instructions
-labeling information, with packaging and storage requirements
-description of final product,
QC procedures, with expected results.

penetrate another substance). Equipment should meet USP requirements for balances and volumetric measuring equipment and, if required, should be calibrated according to schedule. After each use, the equipment must be cleaned and stored. If possible, equipment used for certain purposes (such as chemotherapeutics) should be used only for that purpose. If equipment is used with other drugs, it must be cleaned meticulously prior to the next preparation.

The recommended source to find the correct ingredients that should be used in compounding preparations is the United States Pharmacopeia (USP)/National Formulary (NF), with the USP's Food Chemicals Codex (FCC–the materials compendium). Preferably, the approved substances should be manufactured in an FDA-registered facility. If any components come from a non-FDA registered facility, a Certificate of Analysis should be obtained for the product. If any component is not of "compendial quality" safety issues may be present.

The following documentation is required: the master formula, the compounding record (see boxes for each on previous page), equipment cleaning, calibration and maintenance records, temperature logs of the refrigerator, freezer and room (ambient) air, records of chemicals/bulk drug substances/drug products, and all other components. All components must be acquired from reputable sources.

Documentation must be detailed enough to enable another trained person to trace, evaluate, and replicate the steps involved in the preparation.

NON-STERILE COMPOUNDING EQUIPMENT

Balances

Required balances: a class III torsion balance (also known as a class A balance) utilizes both internal and external weights and requires the use of external weights for measurements exceeding 1 g. It contains two pans, as shown in the picture. The balance should have a sensitivity of 6 mg. The weights should not be touched because body oils can change the weight. For routine compounding, a simpler top-loading electronic balance is used most commonly. Calibration on the balances should be done frequently.

Torsion balance

Electronic balance

Measuring Devices

All equipment, including scales, measuring devices, slabs, spatulas and anything else used must be selected to avoid surfaces that can make contact with reactive, additive, or sorptive materials to avoid altering the safety, strength, quality, or purity of the preparation. When measuring ingredients, select a device equal to or slightly larger than the amount to be measured. If the volume to be measured is viscous, a syringe should be used (rather than a cylinder). Pipettes are thin glass tubes that are used for measuring some liquids, such as small amounts being placed into small containers, such as into test tubes.

The most accurate way to measure liquids is with a cylindrical graduate (also called a graduated cylinder, see figure), which has the same width (diameter) all the way down. When reading the volume in a graduated cylinder, use the measurement at the meniscus (the lowest point of the curve of the liquid) and read at eye level (bend knees, if needed).

A conical (cone-shaped) graduate has a wide mouth to enable the compounder to stir the components using a glass stirring rod. The wider the mouth, the lower the accuracy.

Pipette   Volumetric Flask   Graduated Cylinder
(measure from the bottom of the meniscus)

Mortar and Pestle

Compounding requires a minimum of two types of mortar and pestles: 1 glass and 1 Wedgewood (or porcelain or ceramic). Wedgewood or porcelain is used most commonly and is best for reducing particle size of dry powders and crystals. Porcelain has a smoother surface than Wedgewood and is preferred for blending powders or pulverizing soft materials. If Wedgewood is used for powders or crystals, the inside can be coated with lactose to fill in the crevice Glass is used for liquids and chemicals that are oily or that will stain the porcelain, including many chemotherapeutics. Glass is preferred for mixing liquids and semi-soft dosage forms.

Glass mortar and pestle   Ceramic mortar and pestle

Surfaces & Spatulas

Glassine weighing paper (as opposed to bond paper) should be used for weighing ointments and some dry chemicals. It is best to prepare creams and lotions using a slab and spatula because the water content will cause the paper to moisten, and possibly tear.

Generally, large metal (stainless steel) spatula blades are used, but small spatula blades (< 6 inches) can be used for removing product from the large spatula and putting the product into the container.

Plastic spatulas should be used for chemicals (e.g., potassium, iodine) that can react with stainless steel blades. The third type of spatula is the rubber spatula. Compounding slabs are also called ointment slabs. The slabs are often made of glass, which has a nonabsorbent surface.

COMPOUNDING INGREDIENTS

The active pharmaceutical ingredient (API) is the active ingredient/s in the preparation.

Added substances are the inactive ingredients (excipients), which are used for a variety of purposes, such as capsule fillers, lubricants, disintegrating substances, flavorings, preservatives and coloring.

A vehicle is the drug carrier, such as a capsule shell, or the diluent in which liquids or solids are placed. The USP monographs require that the product must contain +/- 10% of the labeled content. A water bath is used when heating to prevent over-heating.

If the type of alcohol is not specified, USP 95% ethyl alcohol is preferred.

Water from the most pure to less pure is: Sterile water for injection > purified water > potable water (sink water that is safe and unpolluted). Water can be potable for hand washing and equipment cleaning. Equipment should be rinsed with purified water. Water used in any other stage of the compounding process should be purified, with methods such as distillation, deionization, ion exchange, reverse osmosis, and filtration. Sterile Water for Injection can be used; it is of higher quality, and is used primarily for sterile compounding.

Ruminant animal components include any components from bovine (cattle), caprine (goat), and ovine (sheep) that can contain prions, which cause severe muscle-wasting disease. The supplier is responsible for providing written assurance that the component complies with all federal and state laws, and importation requirements for ruminant animal components.

FLAVORING

Products or preparations that have an unpleasant taste will result in decreased adherence. Flavor is one of the key attributes in determining the palatability of drugs given in oral liquid and oral semi-solid dosage forms. Salty or sweet tastes can be used to mask a bitter flavor. Mint and spices can be used to mask poor flavor. Acids (such as citric acid) are used to enhance fruit flavors. A few concerns with sweeteners used in chewables is described under tablets.

PRESERVATIVES

Liquid preparations, unless they are single-use, will commonly contain a preservative to inhibit microbial growth. The preservative must be compatible with the mixture, be relatively stable and have an acceptable color, taste and odor. Antioxidants are used commonly to prevent oxidation, the reaction of a substance with oxygen. Light and temperature catalyze oxidation and many sensitive liquid compounds will require avoidance of light or the use of refrigeration to maintain stability. Unsaturated fatty acids are prone to oxidation and will turn rancid, which produces an odor and discoloration. Common preservatives and antioxidants include benzalkonium chloride (BAK, commonly used in eye drops), benzyl alcohol, chlorhexidine, thimerosal (contains mercury), sodium benzoate, benzethonium chloride, propylparaben and others.

Compounding Preparation and Techniques

See the Drug Formulations chapter for definitions and purpose for various drug formulations. This section reviews basic preparation for commonly made compounded formulations. For all compounded products, the following steps should be followed:

1. Work out the calculations to determine the quantities of each component required. Get all the equipment needed.

2. Garb and wash hands.

3. Clean the equipment, if needed.

4. Assemble all materials.

5. Compound the product.

6. Keep the compounding record.

7. Validate the weight, check the prescription for mixing adequacy, color, clarity, odor, consistency and pH. Enter all in the compounding record.

FORMULATION	PREPARATION
Powders - Powders are finely divided drugs, or other chemicals. Powders range in size from very coarse (No. 8) to very fine (No. 80).	Levigation is the process of reducing the size of a particle of a solid by triturating it (grinding it down to smaller particles) in a mortar or spatulating it on an ointment slab with a small amount of liquid (the wetting agent) in which the solid is not soluble. The goal is to transfer a product from a solid to a uniform paste. A levigating agent will help incorporate the solid into a cream or ointment base. It also makes the solid more uniform throughout the base and reduces a gritty consistency.
	The levigating agent must be miscible (compatible) with the ointment base. For example, sulfur ointment 10% USP uses 10% mineral oil to prepare a white petrolatum-based ointment. The mineral oil is the levigating agent. The petrolatum is used as the base to deliver the medication (the sulfur, used to treat dermatitis or scabies). Oil-in-water is written as o/w. Water-in-oil is w/o.
	Levigating Agents used in preparing ointments are:
	For aqueous systems (o/w dispersions) – Glycerin, propylene glycol, polyethylene glycol 80.
	For oleaginous systems (w/o dispersions) – Mineral oil (light and heavy), castor oil, cottonseed oil, *Tween 80*.
	Mineral oil is good to use for levigating a hydrophobic ointment such as white petrolatum.
	If heat is used (to mix things easier), the use should be limited and the ingredient with the higher melting point should be heated. Otherwise, there is a possibility of undesired chemical reactions. Use a water bath to help prevent overheating.
	Trituration is the process of reducing fracturable powder substances into fine particles by rubbing (or grinding) them with a mortar and pestle, or on an ointment slab.
	A eutectic mixture is two or more components that melt at a temperature lower than the melting temperature for the individual components. Eutectic mixtures can be formed between two compounds or between a compound and an excipient, such as salt and water. Traditional ice cream makes take advantage of the mixture of salt and water to make ice cream, which freezes because the melting temperature of the eutectic mixture is lower than either the salt or the water.

Compounding Preparation and Techniques Continued

FORMULATION	PREPARATION
Capsules - Capsules are unit doses made in soluble shells of <u>gelatin</u>, or hypromellose (a non-animal product to accommodate cultural and dietary requirements). Unpleasant tastes and odors can be masked by the capsule shell.	Capsules are made by triturating the powders to a small particle size, mixing by <u>geometric dilution</u>, and calculating the weight needed to fill a capsule. <u>Glycerol</u> and <u>sorbitol</u> are used as "plasticizers" to <u>soften</u> the capsule. Capsules can be prepared either with a machine or by hand using the <u>punch</u> method. First, the ingredients are triturated to produce a fine particle size, then mixed with geometric dilution. Holding the capsule base, the components are put into the capsule to half the length of the capsule. The components are punched down, and repeated, until the base is filled. Lastly, the cap is placed and air pockets are tapped out. The smaller the size, the higher the number of the capsule. The smallest capsule size is 5 and the largest capsule size is 000.
Tablets - Compressed tablets are commonly made with large-scale manufacturing, are the least expensive to make, and the most common dosage form dispensed. They are also made in compounding. <u>Sorbitol</u> is used often in chewable tablets because it is sweet. Sorbitol is also used as a plasticizer, and as a thickening agent in liquids. Sorbitol can cause considerable <u>GI distress in some patients with IBS</u> due to laxative properties. <u>Lactose</u> is a commonly used filler, and is a sweetener. Lactose can cause <u>GI distress</u> in patients with <u>lactose-intolerance</u>.	Tablets include compressed tablets, troches (lozenges; these are described separately next), sublingual formulations, and vaginal inserts. With these methods, a vehicle (an excipient, which is a binder to <u>keep the tablet compressed</u> (together) after it has been formed) is combined with the drug. <u>Binders</u> include starch (cellulose), gelatin, and various sugars, including lactose. Preparing tablets with the <u>dry granulation</u> method: The components are mixed by <u>geometric dilution</u> and <u>compressed</u> in a heavy-duty tablet machine. The product initially formed is called a slug, which is formed and compressed into tablets. This method is commonly used and avoids the drying steps required with the wet granulation method. Preparing tablets with the <u>wet granulation</u> method: This method requires geometric dilution followed by wetting and kneading to produce a wet mass, which is forced through a granulator or screen, and then dried.
Troches (oral lozenges) are designed to deliver drug to the oral mucosa. The troche dissolves in the mouth.	Troches are made in molds and can include flavorings or colorings. To prepare a troche, add a <u>flavoring oil</u> with a few drops of <u>glycerin</u> or other solvent before adding the <u>drug</u> to a <u>base</u>. Common bases include PEG for soft lozenges, glycerin gelatin bases for chewable lozenges and sucrose syrup bases for hard lozenges.
Solutions	<u>Solutions</u> are liquid preparations of <u>soluble</u> chemicals <u>dissolved in solvents such as water, alcohol, or propylene glycol</u>. When alcohol is used as a solvent in a systemic formulation, the pharmacist should consider effects on the patient, and if the alcohol could interact with medications.

Compounding Preparation and Techniques Continued

FORMULATION	PREPARATION
Suspensions	Suspensions are a <u>two-phased system</u> of a finely divided <u>solid in a liquid</u> medium. The drug must be uniformly dispersed in the medium. The suspension should be <u>deflocculated</u>: this means that the repulsive forces between particles predominate so that the particles in the suspension repel each other and remain as discrete, single particles. Suspensions should <u>settle slowly</u>, be easy to <u>redisperse by gently shaking</u> and have <u>uniform particles that are of small size.</u>
	Suspending agents: Natural <u>hydrocolloids</u> are <u>emulsifiers</u> from plant or animal products. These also increase the viscosity and add structure to the suspension since the droplets are less likely to merge. <u>Vegetable</u> hydrocolloids include acacia, tragacanth, agar, pectin and carrageenan. <u>Animal</u> hydrocolloids include gelatin, lanolin, cholesterol and lecithin. Semi-synthetic hydrocolloids include methylcellulose and carboxymethylcellulose. Synthetic hydrocolloids (the <u>strongest</u>) include carbomers and polyvinyl alcohol clays, including bentonite and veegum.
Syrups	Syrups are concentrated, aqueous preparations of sugar or a sugar-substitute, flavoring and the drug/s, such as cough syrups.
Elixirs	Elixirs are clear, sweetened, hydroalcoholic solutions suitable for water-insoluble drugs, such as mouthwashes.
Emulsions & Emulsifiers Emulsions are a two-phase system of two immiscible liquids, one of which is dispersed through the other as small droplets. <u>Emulsions are immiscible</u> (they do not form a suspension – which means the <u>two liquids stay separate</u> when combined).They can be oil-in-water, or water-in-oil. An emulsifier ("emulgent") is used to stabilize the emulsion. Emulsifiers are usually surfactants ("wetting agents") that reduce the surface tension between the two liquids so that the two different substances can move closer to each other. <u>Emulsifiers</u> include agar, pectin, lipophilic esters of sorbitan *(Arlacel and Span)* and the hydrophilic esters *(Myrj and Tween)*. Other emulsifier names that may be good to recognize are <u>polyethylene glycol (PEG</u>, which is also commonly used as a laxative), <u>acacia, glyceryl monostearate and sodium laurel sulfate</u>. Emulsion (in the internal phase) can mask a bad taste since the drug is less likely to interact with the patient's taste buds.	The <u>Continental or dry gum method</u> of preparing an emulsion uses oil, purified water and gum (such as acacia) in the ratio of 4:2:1. The <u>English, or wet gum method</u> uses the same ingredients (oil, water, gum) but the order of mixing is different. In the dry gum method, the gum is mixed rapidly with oil, and then the water is added all at once. The wet gum method is a slower process in which the gum is dissolved in water first, and then the oil is slowly added. The <u>hydrophilic-lipophilic balance (HLB) number</u> is used to choose which surfactant to select when preparing an emulsion to provide good "emulsification". The HLB number is provided for the oil or can be taken from a reference list. <u>Agents with a low HLB number are more oil-soluble. Agents with a high HLB number are more water-soluble. The HLB scale range is 0-20</u> and a value of 10, the midpoint, is the breakpoint between water and oil solubility. A value less than 10, therefore, is lipid-soluble, and a value greater than 10 is water-soluble. The most common type of emulsion is an oil-in-water (o/w) emulsion, where the oil is dispersed in an aqueous phase. The surfactant will have a high HLB number, which means the surfactant is water-soluble. A value less than 10 is used for water-in-oil (w/o) emulsions, which means the surfactant is oil-soluble. Using a list of HLB values, such as the short group provided here, a pharmacist can choose a surfactant to prepare an o/w (HLB > 10) or w/o emulsion (HLB < 10). {{TABLE}}

Commercial Name	Chemical Name	HLB Value
Glyceryl monostearate	Glyceryl monostearate	3.8
PEG 400 Monooleate	Polyoxyethylene monooleate	11.4
Span 65	Sorbitan tristearate	2.1
Tween 81	Polyoxyethylene sorbitan monooleate	10
Tween 85	Polyoxyethylene sorbitan trioleate	11

Compounding Preparation and Techniques Continued

FORMULATION	PREPARATION
Lotions have the most water, and are most often oil-in-water (with a small amount of oil). They absorb quickly and are easy to spread on the skin. Since lotions contain a lot of water, they often come in pumps.	An emollient is a single agent that is used to soften and smooth the skin, and come in different formulations. Lotions, creams, ointments and pastes are all water and oil emulsions (either oil-in-water, or water-in-oil), but in different amounts and for different uses.
Creams are emulsions of about half oil and half water. They spread easily and are reasonably hydrating. Creams are packaged in tubes, and sometimes in tubs.	Creams are water-based, ointments are oil-based.
Ointments - Ointments are ~80% oil and 20% water. There are five classes or types of ointment bases which are differentiated on the basis of their physical composition. These are oleaginous bases, absorption bases, water-in-oil emulsion bases, oil-in-water emulsion bases, and water soluble or water miscible bases (PEG ointment). **Pastes** are the thickest ointments and are also used as protective barriers.	The key to a homogenous, even preparation (versus an uneven preparation that feels gritty) is to incorporate the drug on an ointment slab with spatulation into the vehicle using geometric dilution. In order to put a component into the delivery vehicle, a wetting or levigating agent such as mineral oil or glycerin is often used first in order to make the particle size smaller, and easier to incorporate. The smallest quantity of active ingredient is mixed well with an equal volume of the diluent or base on the ointment slab. More diluent (base) is added in amounts equal to the volume of the mixture on the ointment slab. Repeat this process until all of the diluent is mixed in. If heat is used: when melting a number of ingredients, melt the ingredient with the highest melting point first. Use the lowest temperature that will work, for the shortest period of time. Slowly reduce the heat to melt the ingredient with the next lowest melting point. Cooling is important; do not try to speed it up with ice or cold water as this will alter the consistency.
Gels	Gels are oil-in-water emulsions, usually with an alcohol base. They are easy to spread and dry into a thin film. Gels are also used as thickeners. They include a solid and a liquid that are dispersed evenly throughout a material (the suspension is interpenetrated by the liquid). Common gels used as thickeners are the alginates (including Na+, K+, Ca+ alginate, agar, carrageenan, gelatin, carbomer, tragacanth, bentonite).

Compounding Preparation and Techniques Continued

FORMULATION	PREPARATION
Suppositories are solid dosage forms used to deliver medicine into the rectum, vagina or urethra. They are formed in a mold. They melt, soften or dissolve in the body cavity. Suppositories bypass the oral route and avoid first pass metabolism. The base must be compatible with the medication, must not melt too quickly (such as in the hands while inserting), must be stable and must not have a disagreeable look or scent. Examples include the following rectal suppositories: acetaminophen suppository, hemorrhoid suppository, mesalamine suppository, and various types of vaginal suppositories. Suppository removal is easier if a lubricant is used. Use glycerin if vegetable oil or cocoa butter is the base or mineral oil or *PAM* vegetable spray if PEG is the base.	A base is the bulk of the suppository and is either an oleaginous (lipid) or a water soluble/miscible base. Oleaginous bases include either cocoa butter (theobroma oil), which is commonly used, or synthetic triglyceride bases, which are made of hydrogenated vegetable oil. Water soluble bases include glycerinated glycerin and polyethylene glycol (PEG) polymers. *Carbowax* is a commonly used PEG base that comes in many products which are designated by the molecular weight (e.g., PEG 200, PEG 300, etc.) If a small number of suppositories are needed, cocoa butter can be handrolled and a tip for insertion ease can be shaped with a knife. The cocoa butter should not be melted, and the compounding must be quick or the heat from the hands will melt the base. Commonly, molds are used, and two methods of making suppositories with molds are called compression molding and fusion molding. Suppositories include the addition of a drug. The drug will displace part of the base, and the amount displaced is calculated using the density factor. If the drug has the same density as the base, it will displace an equal amount of volume. If the density is greater, it will displace less, and if lower, it will displace more. The density factor of drugs that are used in suppositories is found in compounding references, or the density factor can be calculated. The melted base should be poured into the mold when the mold has reached room temperature. When using plastic disposable molds, be sure the temperature of the melt is lower than that which will melt the mold.

Labels on Pharmacy-Compounded Products

In the absence of stability information that is applicable to a specific drug and preparation, the following table presents maximum beyond use dates (BUDs) recommended for non-sterile compounded drug preparations that are packaged in tight, light-resistant containers and stored at controlled room temperature or under cold refrigeration (as specified in the following table), unless otherwise indicated. Drugs or chemicals known to be labile to decomposition will require shorter BUDs. The BUD shall not be later than the expiration date on the container of any component.

FORMULATION	BEYOND USE DATE
Nonaqueous Formulations	Not later than the time remaining until the earliest expiration date of any API or 6 months, whichever is earlier.
Water-Containing Oral Formulations	Not later than 14 days when stored at controlled cold temperatures.
Water-Containing Topical/Dermal and Mucosal Liquid and Semisolid Formulations	Not later than 30 days.

Auxiliary Labels for Compounded Creams and Lotions

- Refrigerate, Shake Well (emulsions, suspensions), External Use Only

The product label must include generic or chemical name of active ingredients, strength or quantity, pharmacy lot number, beyond-use date, and any special storage requirements.

A statement that the product has been compounded by the pharmacy must be placed on the label of the container.

For capsules, the label must include mcg or mg/capsule.

For liquids, the strength should be in concentration (e.g., 125 mg/5 mL), or provided as a percentage.

The coining of short names for marketing or convenience (e.g., Johnson's Solution) is strongly discouraged.

Expiration Dates on Bulk Product Containers

If any ingredients are moved from the original container to a different container, the new container should be labeled with the component name, original supplier, lot or control number, transfer date and expiration date. If there is a component without an expiration date, use a conservative (cautious) date which is no more than 3 years from the date of receipt, and label the container with the date of receipt.

Storage and Handling

Compounding bulk products/ingredients should be stored and handled according to the manufacturer's storage requirements, or per USP, NF, or FCC monograph requirements, with all stated temperature and humidity requirements, labeled appropriately. Store off the floor (on shelves) and rotate the stock so the oldest (nearest expiration date) is in front and will be used first.

IF TEMPERATURE CONTROL IS REQUIRED, USE:	F°	C°
Room	68° to 77°	20° to 25°
Refrigerator	36° to 46°	2° to 8°
Freezer	-13° to 14°	-25° to -10°

Hazardous drug storage and handling is managed according to National Institute of Occupational Safety and Health (NIOSH) guidelines (not EPA). This includes chemotherapeutics (antineoplastics) and others which must be compounded in a separate area with negative air pressure. Only personnel trained in hazardous drugs can compound or handle these agents, including janitorial (custodial) staff, who must know how to safely dispose of the waste. Federal and state requirements apply. Waste of any type cannot "gather" in the facility and must be disposed of routinely and promptly.

Quality Assurance

A quality assurance (QA) or quality control (QC) plan must include records of the personnel (staff) orientation and training, variances/trends, Standard Operating Procedures (SOPs), documentation, verification, testing, cleaning and disinfection, packaging, repackaging, labeling, storage and personnel involved in the process.

Red Flags for Possible Inappropriate Compounding/Safety Concerns

If the same product is already available commercially, or was withdrawn for safety reasons, then the compounding form should not be made. Dosage forms that are difficult to make can be a red flag. Another red flag is the use of components without USP, NF, or FCC standards or use of products from suppliers that are not FDA-registered.

Patient Counseling

The pharmacist must counsel the patient or patient's agent about proper use and be instructed to report any ADR; if any are reported, they should be recorded in the Compounding Record.

4

STERILE COMPOUNDING

Biological safety cabinet in an ISO Class 5 cleanroom.

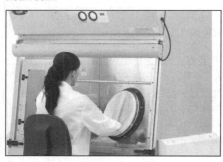

Isolator device, substitutes for ISO Class 5, hands go through the holes in front.

We gratefully acknowledge the assistance of Romic Eskandarian, PharmD, Director of Pharmacy, Glendale Adventist Medical Center, in preparing this chapter.

Note: Master formulation records and compounding log requirements are discussed in the Non-Sterile Compounding chapter.

BACKGROUND

It is advisable to first review the terminology on the following page (in the gray shaded box); these terms are used throughout this chapter. Preparing compounded sterile preparations (CSPs) is a fundamental part of hospital pharmacy practice. Medications that must be prepared in a sterile manner include opthalmics, inhalations, tissue soaks (for organ transplants), other implants, irrigations and IV medications. About half of medications given in the hospital setting are given IV; these bypass the protective mechanisms of the skin barrier and gastrointestinal tract. If the medication is contaminated, the patient will suffer severe adverse effects and possible death.

GUIDELINES/REFERENCES

USP Chapter 797, Pharmaceutical Compounding, Sterile Preparations

ASHP Guidelines on Compounding Sterile Preparations – *Am J Health Syst Pharm.* 2014:71(2):145-166.

Kienle, PC. Q&A: Understanding Beyond-Use Dating for Compounded Sterile Preparations. http://www.pppmag.com/documents/V4N3/p2_4_5.pdf> (accessed 2015 Nov 10).

Vial/Bag System, No risk level.

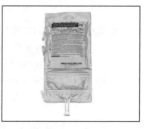

Ready-to-Use IV Bag, No risk level.

DEFINITIONS

Ante room, or Ante: Refers to the space outside the sterile compounding area where the sink and garbing items are located. Garbing and hand washing must be done in the ante room.

Buffer area: Referred to as the cleanroom. This is where the sterile compounding takes place. If performing high-risk compounding this must be in a separate room, or done with an isolator barrier device (both types shown above).

Biological safety cabinet: This is called the "hood" and is where low, medium and high-risk compounding is done. It is located in the cleanroom.

CSP: Compounded sterile preparation (the IV drugs made in the cleanroom).

Garb: The clothes and protective gear required in a cleanroom. "Garbing" is putting them on prior to entering the cleanroom.

Hazardous drugs: Refers to drugs that cause cell death; primarily chemotherapy drugs (antineoplastics).

Positive pressure: Keeps contaminated air from entering the hood to protect the CSP from contamination. Positive pressure is required for most sterile drug preparation.

Negative pressure: For hazardous drugs; keeps contaminated air away from the compounding staff and from exiting the hood. The air is vented to the outside.

ISO classification: Refers to the number of particles that are permitted per volume of air. The smaller the number, the cleaner the air. All primary engineering controls (PECs) must be ISO 5, the buffer area must be ISO 7, the ante area can be ISO 8 if it opens only into a positive pressure ISO 7 cleanroom, or must be ISO 7 if it opens into a negative pressure cleanroom.

Primary Engineering Control (PEC), refers to the isolator device or the room that provides the ISO Class 5 area for compounding CSPs. PECs all rely on a high-efficiency particulate air (HEPA) filter.

HEPA filters: High-efficiency particulate air (HEPA) filters which are >99.97% efficient in removing particles as small as 0.3 microns (μm). The air flow goes in one direction (unidirectional, either horizontal or vertical) to move particles away from CSPs.

CSP Risk Levels

USP sets risk levels at low, low with a 12-hour or less beyond use date (BUD), medium, high, and a special category called immediate use. The risk categories correlate with the risk of contamination and is determined by the compounding location, the complexity of the preparation, the stability of the components, and the storage temperature. The contamination can be either bacterial, fungal, physical, chemical or endotoxins, which are toxins released (primarily) from certain Gram-negative bacteria which cause numerous adverse effects, including septic shock.

Two forms of IVs that do not have a CSP Risk Level:

- Ready-to-use IVs are premixed and do not require any preparation at the pharmacy other than labeling the bag for a patient.

- Vial/bag systems (such as *Add-Vantage*) where the drug vial is attached to the IV bag and is squeezed into the bag when it is ready for use.

CSP Risk Level Classification

- Immediate use is only intended for emergency administration, such as providing stat IV administration in a medical setting or ambulance. It must be for administration within 1 hour.

- Low-risk CSPs require an ISO Class 5 within an ISO 7 environment, using only sterile ingredients and equipment. Limited to transfer, measuring, and mixing manipulations.

- Low-risk with 12-hour or Less BUD is a special type of low-risk compounding that permits the preparation outside of a hood, but in a segregated compounding area. The staff preparing the product are required to use similar requirements to those required within an ISO environment: proper hand hygiene, garbing, cleaning and disinfecting, and environmental sampling.

- Medium-risk involves individual or small doses of sterile products with complex aseptic manipulations.

- High-risk involves nonsterile ingredients or equipment.

Level, ISO Requirements and Beyond Use Dates*

RISK	COMPOUNDING LOCATION	BUD ROOM TEMP	BUD REFRIG	BUD FROZEN (≤ 10 °C)	EXAMPLES
Low-risk	ISO Class 5, ISO Class 7 buffer area. ISO Class 8 ante area	48 hours	14 days	45 days	Small volume injections, IV fluids with max of 3 components, single dose vial reconstitution, etc.
Low-risk with < 12-hr BUD	ISO Class 5 segregated from other operations	12 hours	12 hours	N/A	Same as Low-Risk—what is different is the space
Medium-risk	ISO Class 5 ISO Class 7 buffer area, ISO Class 8 ante area	30 hours	9 days	45 days	Batched syringes, parenteral nutrition, Opthalmics made from sterile products, etc.
High-risk	ISO Class 5 PEC, ISO Class 7 buffer area, ISO Class 7 ante area	24 hours	3 days	45 days	CSPs from bulk drug containers, preparations that require sterilization, products made with non-sterile components, etc.
Immediate-use	"Clean, uncluttered, functionally separate area" per USP	1 hour	N/A	N/A	Used in patient care & procedural units, medical offices, ambulances

*ASHP Guidelines on Comp Sterile Preparations. – Am J Health Syst Pharm. 2014: 71(2): 145-166.

Beyond Use Dates and Label Requirements

The beyond use date (BUD) is the date or time after which the CSP should not be used or started. The BUDs for sterile products are usually shorter than those for nonsterile products. With either type of product, stability testing and expirations of the individual components can override the recommended BUD. Minimum label requirements are provided in USP 797 and, in some states, there are additional requirements from the state's board of pharmacy. CSP minimal label requirements include: the generic name and concentration of active ingredients, the route and recommended administration rate (e.g., flow rate) storage and handling instructions, preparation date, beyond use date, name or initials of responsible compounding personnel, and auxiliary labels. All chemotherapy preparations must have a label that reads "Chemotherapy--dispose of properly" or similar. If the product has been prepared in a batch (25 or more units) the label must include the control or lot number, device-specific instructions (if appropriate) and auxiliary labels. Auxiliary labels should be placed on CSPs that are not refrigerated, if a filter is required and if light protection is required. High-alert medications are drugs that have a heightened risk of causing significant patient harm when used incorrectly. High-alert medications should have auxiliary labels such as "Contains Potassium" or "Warning: Paralyzing drug."

CSP Preparation, Visual Inspection and Sterility Testing

IV solutions should be <u>isotonic</u> (osmotic pressure matches to human blood by having the same number of particles in solution), measured via milliosmoles (mOsm) or mOsm/Liter. Human blood has an osmolarity of <u>285 mOsm/L</u>. This prevents fluid transfer across the (biological) semipermeable membranes. The pH should be close to <u>neutral</u> (pH of 7); blood is slightly alkaline at a pH of 7.35 - 7.45. When preparing CSPs, no eating, drinking, coughing or talking is permitted. No distractions or interruptions should be present. <u>Non-PVC bags</u> should be used for medications that have <u>leaching or sorption</u> issues (refer to the IV Administration & Storage chapter). The IV set must be sterile and nonpyrogenic.

Products that are prepared for injection into a patient go directly into the bloodstream and <u>bypass the protection from the skin and gut</u>. If organisms are present, the risk for severe infection is high. Most sterile product contamination comes from the compounding <u>personnel violating procedures</u>, such as wearing a contaminated object into the cleanroom, touching their face, fixing their hair, or improper garbing (gowning) procedures.

CSPs intended for storage outside the limits described in the previous table must have <u>sterility testing</u>. Generally, high-risk CSPs require sterility testing prior to use, and must include the types in the bullet point. The sterility testing should use either <u>tryptic soy broth</u> (TSB) or <u>fluid thioglycollate medium</u> (FTM), and include <u>bacterial endotoxin</u> (pyrogen) testing prior to use.

- Batches of high-risk CSPs prepared as multiple-dose vials for multiple patients, batches of high-risk CSPs that have been left for > 12 hours at 2 to 8 °C (36 to 46 °F) or for > 6 hours at > 8 °C (46 °F) before sterilization, or batches of > 25 identical, single-dose, high-risk CSPs.

- Finished CSPs are individually <u>inspected</u> immediately after preparation against a dark background for particulates, foreign matter, precipitates and cloudiness. The container should be lightly squeezed to check for leakage.

Sterilization Methods: Steam (Wet Heat, Autoclaving), Dry Heat, Filtration

- For high-risk CSPs (primarily), terminal sterilization is applied with pressurized steam sterilization using an <u>autoclave</u> (described below) to the sealed container. CSPs that are heat-labile (e.g., hormones, other proteins) will not be able to tolerate this method can be sterilized with <u>filtration</u> using a <u>0.22 micron</u> filter. This will achieve a lower sterility level than steam filtration, but is used when required. If filtering is used, the <u>filter integrity</u> must be tested with the <u>bubble-point test</u>. This test uses pressure to force liquid to "bubble" out of the filter.

Courtesy of NuAire, Inc. 2015

Laminar Flow Hood with Positive Pressure.

- Steam sterilization is conducted inside a machine called an autoclave. It is preferred and is used commonly but can only be used for heat-stable solutions. The <u>steam will damage heat-labile</u> (sensitive) drug solutions and moisture will damage moisture-sensitive materials.

- Dry heat sterilization can be used for products that would be damaged by moisture. The air is circulated through an oven by radiation or with a blower. Gas sterilization using ethylene oxide is sometimes used when heat would damage the contents. The gas has safety concerns, including toxic residues that may remain on the product, and the gas (if not mixed with other gases) is flammable. Another type of sterilization is ionizing radiation.

CLEAN ROOMS AND LAMINAR FLOW HOODS

Hoods are ventilation devices used to keep CSPs free of contaminants, and are used to keep the pharmacy area free of noxious fumes. Vertical flow hoods (also called biological safety cabinets or chemotherapy hoods) blow air from the top down to maintain sterility and to protect the pharmacist or technician. The hoods use a High Efficiency Particulate Air (HEPA) filter that catches particulates with a laminar air flow that keeps air moving in one direction with either positive or negative pressure.

Positive pressure air flow is used for most CSPs and is designed to keep contaminants out of the hood area (to protect the drugs). Negative pressure is when contaminated air emitted from a chemotherapeutic, radionuclide other toxic drug is pulled out of the hood (to protect the compounding staff from the contaminants). The cabinet is stainless steel with a smooth design to keep out contaminants and is designed to reduce the risk of joints/connections and other spaces where spores might accumulate.

Laminar Flow Hood Procedures

- Laminar flow hoods are kept running and continuously cleaned. Prior to use (at least at beginning of each work shift and as-scheduled) all surfaces are thoroughly cleaned with 70% isopropyl alcohol (IPA) in a side-to-side motion, starting from the back of the hood. If a spill occurs or whenever the hood looks like it requires cleaning, it is cleaned again.

- Prior to preparation, all components are gathered and checked for discoloration, particulates (discard) and leaks, and the expiration dates are checked to make sure that the drug products remain suitable for use.

- Only required items can be placed in the hood, side by side (not behind each other except possibly for items such as consecutive bags that additives are being placed into, for example – if this is done, place the larger items behind the smaller ones and do not put more than a few in this manner) and do not block three inches from the back of the hood.

- Leave six inches from the front edge of the hood clear (this is where the air starts to mingle), with no blockage to the HEPA filter. Only essential objects and materials necessary for product preparation should be placed in the airflow hood (no pens or calculators.) Do not tear open components. Open along seal within the hood. Do not touch the syringe tip or plunger, even with gloved hands.

- Work in the center and place critical items reasonably close to the air source.

- Nothing should pass behind a sterile object and the HEPA filter in a horizontal airflow hood or above a sterile object in a vertical airflow hood. Chemotherapy must be done in a vertical hood.

- For greatest accuracy, use the smallest syringe that can hold the desired amount of solution. The syringe should not be larger than twice the volume to be measured.

- The volume of solution drawn into a syringe is measured at the point of contact between the rubber piston and the side of the syringe barrel.

- Powders are reconstituted by introducing a diluent such as sterile water for injection.

- Prior to withdrawing any liquid from a vial, first inject a volume of air equal to the volume of fluid removed. Exception: do not inject air prior to removing cytotoxic drugs from vials.

- Swab the rubber top (or ampule neck) with sterile isopropyl alcohol, and wait for it to air-dry; do not blow on or wave over it to dry faster.

- Puncture the rubber top of the vial with the needle bevel up. Then bring the syringe and needle straight up, penetrate the stopper, and depress the plunger of the syringe, emptying the air into the vial. Invert the vial with the attached syringe. Draw up from the vial the amount of liquid required. Withdraw the needle from the vial. In the case of a multi-dose vial, the rubber cap will close, sealing the contents of the vial.

- If the medication is in a glass ampule, open the ampule by forcefully snapping the neck away from you, then tilt the ampule, place the needle bevel of a filter needle or tip of a filter straw in the corner near the opening, and withdraw the medication. Use a needle equipped with a filter for filtering out any tiny glass particles, fibers, or paint chips that may have fallen into the ampule. Before injecting the contents of a syringe into an IV, the needle must be changed to avoid introducing glass or particles into the admixture. A standard needle could be used to withdraw the drug from the ampule; it is then replaced with a filter device before the drug is pushed out of the syringe.

- Instruct the technicians to keep all the additives with the bag and the syringes used (pulled up to the precise volume that was injected into the bag) for the pharmacist to check.

Cleaning and Disinfecting

- Personnel who perform cleaning in this area must demonstrate cleaning and disinfection competency for an ISO Class 5 environment, with proper gloving and garbing. The compounding supervisor should watch the cleaning process.

- The disinfectant used should be a germicidal detergent. If the cleaner is being used inside the buffer area and it requires dilution, sterile water is used.

- All water used for cleaning surfaces must be sterile water, followed by sterile 70% IPA.

- Clean from the cleanest to dirtiest areas (opposite of garbing procedure). First clean the buffer area, then the ante area, then the general supply area, with low-shedding dedicated mops and cleaners for each area. Hazardous drugs require decontamination, which involves additional steps.

- The work areas must be cleaned according to the following schedule.

SPACE	CLEANING SCHEDULE
Buffer area	At the beginning of each shift
	Before and after each batch
	After spills
	Every 30 minutes of continuous use
	Anytime contamination is suspected
Counters, work surfaces and floors	Daily
Walls, ceiling, storage shelves	Monthly

GARBING

Remove garbing before crossing the line of demarcation: Outer garments (coats), jewelry, any piercings above the neck and make-up should be removed prior to working in the clean room. Artificial or long nails are not permitted. Use sterile, powder-free gloves only for sterile compounding. If double gloving is used the 2nd pair donned will need to be the next largest size, and the outer glove goes over the cuff of the gown. Whenever the gloves touch non-sterile surfaces and routinely during compounding, disinfect the glove surfaces with 70% isopropyl alcohol (IPA) and inspect for tears routinely.

All garb must be used with an isolator unless the isolator manufacturer provides written documentation, based on validated environmental testing, that any garb component is not required.

Garbing Order

1. Hair cover, facemask and beard/eye cover (in any order)

2. Shoe covers (donned 1 at a time, stepping over the line of demarcation) or change every two hours

3. Hand hygiene (30 seconds, use nail pick to clean under nails)

4. Don low-linting gown (does not have to be sterile)

5. Perform hand cleaning with alcohol based surgical hand scrub with persistent activity

6. Don sterile, powder-free gloves

Regarb Required:

- When garb is exposed to less than ISO Class 8 conditions (garb is not supposed to be worn outside of the ante room).

- If compounders leave the ante room, they must completely re-garb, including handwashing.

When and Which Garb can be Reused:

- If not visibly soiled and if the person has not left the ante room, the gown may be reused for current work shift only. Disposable gowns are preferred but not required. If gowns are reusable, they must be laundered prior to reuse.

- Task-specific eye shields and dedicated shoes may be reused, but they must be stored in the ante area and routinely cleaned with germicidal disinfectant.

RECALLS, QUALITY ASSURANCE AND STERILITY DOCUMENTATION

Recalls are discussed further with the MPJE law course; a summary of the recall classes is included here since the drugs involved are often those used for sterile compounding, and include issues such as a lack of sterility data or the presence of particulates in the solution. Recalls are carried out by the manufacturer, as the FDA generally lacks the immediate legal authority to simply require a manufacturer to recall the drug. Recalls may be initiated by FDA request, by an FDA order under statutory authority or at the company's own initiative. There are times when the FDA is slow to act and the company will pull the drug first to avoid patient harm and probable lawsuits.

CLASS	DESCRIPTION
Class I Recall	A situation in which there is a reasonable probability that the use or exposure will cause serious adverse health consequences or death. For example, a morphine tablet manufactured with ten times the amount of active ingredient.
Class II Recall	A situation in which use or exposure can cause temporary or reversible adverse health consequences or where the probability of harm is remote. For example, ketorolac injections have been recalled in 2010 and 2015 due to the possibility of particles in the vials.
Class III Recall	A situation in which use of or exposure is not likely to cause adverse health consequences. For example, the coloring on tablets may have been applied inconsistently.

Every facility that does sterile compounding must have a quality assurance (QA) plan that evaluates, corrects and improves the quality processes. The plan should minimally include:

- Personnel training and assessment

- Environmental monitoring

- Equipment calibration and maintenance

Every process must be documented and follow-up actions identified that have assigned personnel responsible for each item, with expected dates of completion. If a problem has been identified or a medication error or safety issue has occurred the analysis should be started as soon as possible with a root cause analysis, discussed in the Medication Safety chapter. A failure mode and effects analysis of new techniques can help to identify problems with new procedures in advance.

Personnel Training

All personnel require orientation, hands-on, written tests, a "live" skills assessment where technique must be demonstrated, and continuous inservices (on-site training). Most contamination comes from the personnel (themselves, or their technique). Improper garbing is a common contributor to contamination.

Environmental Monitoring

Each of the following tests will provide a number of colony forming units (CFUs) and the number will determine the course of action to take. Certification by an outside expert is required every 6 months (semi-annually).

- Temperature (discussed previously under Room Requirements) must be documented at least daily.

- Air (viable agar sampling) to check for microbial growth is required every 6 months.

- Surfaces (media-fill testing, with agar plates tests) for viable contamination on surfaces. USP 797 requires the test to be done periodically in all ISO spaces, using plates containing tryptic soy agar with polysorbate 80 and lecithin. Use sample surfaces at the end of the day to simulate the dirtiest condition. After the plates have been incubated, the results should indicate zero CFUs (preferred); action must be taken if > 3 CFUs in the ISO Class 5 area.

- Personnel are tested with gloved fingertip sampling, which is used to verify proper donning technique. This method uses two agar-filled plates (one for each hand) that is incubated and then investigated for microbial growth. This test is required during the initial hand hygiene and garbing competency training, and on an ongoing basis (annually for low and medium risk operations and semi-annually for high risk operations). Sample immediately after donning sterile gloves and before disinfecting with sterile 70% IPA. Passing requires 3 consecutive gloved fingertip samples with zero CFUs for both hands. The tests are done in the buffer area or ante area.

Pyrogen (Bacterial Endotoxin) Testing

Endotoxins are produced by both Gram-positive and Gram-negative bacteria and fungi. Endotoxins from Gram-negative bacteria are more potent and represent a serious threat to patient safety. Intrathecal CSPs contaminated with endotoxins have been implicated in cases of both septic and aseptic meningitis and shock because the intrathecal space does not have the same immunological and biological defense mechanisms as the intravenous system. Pyrogens can come from using equipment (such as glassware and utensils) that has been washed with tap water. Filtration using typical 0.22 micron filters or steam sterilization will not eliminate endotoxins after introduction into a solution. To avoid this issue, glassware and utensils should be rinsed with sterile water and de-pyrogenated using dry-heat oven sterilization.

The reagent for the bacterial endotoxins test (BET) is called the Limulus Amebocyte Lysate (LAL), which is based on clotting properties of the horseshoe crab's blood.

Environmental Monitoring Summary

Temperature	Daily (at a minimum)
Qualified certifier must certify the area	Every 6 months (semi-annually)
Air sampling by compounding personnel or certifier	At least every 6 months
Gloved fingertip sampling	Verify at initial training
Passing requires 3 samples (2 plates each) with zero CFUs	Low and medium risk (annually)
	High risk (semi-annually)
Surface sampling	Periodically
HEPA filter pressure	Each shift (preferably) or daily (minimally)

5

MEDICATION SAFETY & QUALITY IMPROVEMENT

CDC/Amanda Mills

GUIDELINES/REFERENCES

Institute for Safe Medication Practices.
www.ismp.org (accessed 2015 Dec 1).

The Joint Commission.
www.jcintcommission.org (accessed 2015 Dec 1).

MMWR Guideline for Hand Hygiene in Health-Care Settings October 25, 2002, 51(RR16);1-44.

Additional guidelines included with the video files (RxPrep Online).

BACKGROUND

Awareness of the prevalence of medical errors increased after the release of a study from the Institute of Medicine (IOM), *To Err is Human* (1999), which found that up to 98,000 Americans die each year in U.S. hospitals due to preventable medical errors, 7,000 from medication errors alone. These numbers understated the problem because they did not include preventable deaths due to medical treatments outside of hospitals. Since the release of the IOM study, there has been a greater focus on the quality of healthcare provided in the U.S. and the need to reduce medical errors, which are preventable. Pharmacists are most concerned with errors involving medications.

This chapter begins with an overview of medication errors, followed by specific measures to limit these errors in the community and institutional settings. Included are select "high risk" drugs that require implementation of specific safety measures to avoid patient harm. Technology and automation are important tools in medication safety. This chapter includes discussion of barcoding, clinical decision support (CDS), automated dispensing cabinets (ADCs) and patient controlled analgesia (PCA) devices.

A component of patient safety includes reducing infection risk. Essential methods to reduce infections, such as proper hand-washing technique, enforcing universal precautions and using safe injection technique are included. The chapter concludes with a discussion of The Joint Commission (TJC), which provides accreditation for healthcare facilities. A primary focus of TJC is patient safety.

MEDICATION ERRORS

The formal definition of a medication error developed by the National Coordinating Council on Medication Error Reporting and Prevention (NCC MERP) is "any preventable event that may cause or lead to inappropriate medication use or patient harm while the medication is in the control of the healthcare professional, patient, or consumer. This can include errors made in prescribing, order communication, product labeling and packaging, compounding, dispensing, administration, education and monitoring.

**EXAMPLE OF AN ADR
(NOT A MEDICATION ERROR)**

A 55-year old female has a history of herpes zoster. She has no other known medical conditions. The patient reports considerable "shingles pain" that "runs from my back through my left breast". She received a prescription for pregabalin. The patient returned to the clinic with complaints of ankle swelling, which required drug discontinuation.

This problem would not be attributable to a medication error made by the prescriber of pregabalin or by the pharmacist who dispensed it. Rather, this is a side effect that can occur with the use of this drug.

ERRORS OF OMISSION AND COMMISSION

Error of Omission	Error of Commission
Something was left out that is needed for safety	Something was done incorrectly
Example: Failing to warn a patient about an important side effect with a new medication	Example: Prescribing bupropion to a patient with a history of seizures

Do not confuse medication errors with adverse drug reactions (ADRs). ADRs are generally not avoidable although they may be more likely to occur if the drug is given to a patient at high risk for certain complications. Refer to the Drug Sensitivities, Allergies, Desensitization & Reporting chapter for a discussion of ADRs.

A sentinel event is an unexpected occurrence involving death or serious physical or psychological injury, or risk thereof. When a sentinel event occurs, it is important to find out what went wrong and implement measures to prevent it from happening again.

System-Based Causes of Medication Errors

Experts in medication safety concur that the most common cause of medication errors is not individual error but problems with the design of the medical system itself. Currently, instead of blaming the "inexperienced pharmacist" or the "lazy technician" (or the prescriber), healthcare professionals should find ways to improve the system in order to reduce the chance that the error will occur again. Errors will always occur, but the goal is to design systems to prevent medication errors from reaching the patient. Some "at risk" behaviors that can compromise patient safety are included on the following page.

Response to Medication Errors

Institutions should have a plan in place for responding to medication errors. The plan should address the following:

- Internal notification: Who should be notified within the institution and within what time frame?

- External reporting: Who should be notified outside of the institution? See below.

- Disclosure: What information should be shared with the patient/family? Who will be present when this occurs?

- Investigation: What is the process for immediate and long-term internal investigation of an error?

- Improvement: What process will ensure that immediate and long-term preventative actions are taken?

Reporting

Medication errors, preventable adverse drug reactions, hazardous conditions and "close calls" or "near misses" should be reported. We report medication errors so that changes can be made to the system to prevent similar errors in the future. Without reporting, these events may go unrecognized and will likely happen again because others will not learn from the incident.

In a community pharmacy, the staff member who discovers the error should immediately report it (using the established reporting structure) to the corporate office or in the case of an independently owned pharmacy, the owner, who is involved with the quality assurance program. These are mandated by many state boards of pharmacy and have the purpose (in the words of the California Board) "to develop pharmacy systems and workflow processes designed to prevent medication errors." Error investigations need to take place quickly (often as soon as within 48 hours of the incident) so that the sequence of events remains clear to those involved. Many states mandate the ethical requirement that errors be reported to the patient and the prescriber as soon as possible.

In a hospital setting, the staff member should report a medication error through the hospital's specific medication event reporting system. Many medication error reporting systems within hospitals are electronic; however, some hospitals still maintain a paper reporting system. The hospital's Pharmacy and Therapeutics (P&T) committee and Medication Safety Committee (or similar entity) should be informed of the error.

Reporting to Organizations that Specialize in Error Prevention

The Patient Safety and Quality Improvement Act of 2005 (Patient Safety Act) authorized the creation of Patient Safety Organizations (PSOs) to improve the quality and safety of health care delivery in the United States. The Patient Safety Act encourages clinicians and healthcare organizations to voluntarily report and share quality and patient safety information without fear of the information being used in legal proceedings. The Agency for Healthcare Research and Quality (AHRQ) administers the provisions of the Patient Safety Act and the Patient Safety Rule dealing with PSO operations.

Organizations that specialize in error prevention can analyze the system-based causes of the errors and make recommendations to others who can learn from the mistakes. Every pharmacist should make it a practice to read medication error reports in order to use this history to improve their own practice settings. Information sources include the Institute for Safe Medication Practices (ISMP) newsletters which have information about medication-related errors, adverse drug reactions, as well as recommendations that will help reduce the risk of medication errors and other adverse drug events at the practice site.

The ISMP National Medication Errors Reporting Program (MERP) is a confidential national voluntary reporting program that provides expert analysis of the system causes of medication errors and disseminates recommendations for prevention.

On the ISMP website (www.ismp.org), medication errors and close calls can be reported. Click on "Report Errors." Professionals and consumers should be encouraged to report medication errors using this site even if the error was reported internally. When there are many reports of a particular error, the manufacturer may take measures to increase safety (e.g., REMS program, name change, packaging change, etc.).

> **Those who cannot remember the past are condemned to repeat it.**
>
> *Poet and Philosopher George Santayana 1863-1952*

Evaluating Medication Errors and Quality Improvement

A root cause analysis (RCA) is a retrospective investigation of an event that has already occurred which includes reviewing the sequence of events that led to the error. The information obtained in the analysis is <u>used to design changes that will hopefully prevent future errors</u>. Findings from the RCA can be applied proactively to analyze and improve processes and systems before they fail again.

The RCA can be of enormous value in capturing both the big-picture perspective and the details of the error. This type of analysis facilitates system evaluation and the need for corrective action. <u>Targeting corrective measures at the identified root causes</u> is the best way to prevent similar problems from occurring in the future. However, it is recognized that complete prevention of recurrence by a single intervention is not always possible. Thus, <u>RCA</u> is often considered to be a <u>repetitive process</u>, and is frequently viewed as an important <u>continuous quality improvement (CQI)</u> tool.

An analysis can also be done <u>prospectively</u> to identify pathways that could lead to errors and to identify ways to reduce the error risk. <u>Failure Mode and Effects Analysis (FMEA) is a proactive method</u> used to reduce the frequency and consequences of errors. FMEA is used to analyze the design of the system in order <u>to evaluate the potential for failures</u>, and to determine what potential effects could occur when the medication delivery system changes in any substantial way or if a potentially dangerous new drug will be added to the formulary.

COMMON METHODS USED TO REDUCE MEDICATION ERRORS

Avoid "Do Not Use" Abbreviations, Symbols, and Dosage Designations

<u>Abbreviations are unsafe and contribute to many medical errors.</u> TJC standards include recommendations against the use of unsafe abbreviations. The <u>minimum list</u> of "Do Not Use" abbreviations <u>per TJC</u> is shown in the table. ISMP also publishes a list of error-prone abbreviations, symbols, and dosage designations which includes those on TJC's list (designated by **) and many others. Try writing the number 5.0 on lined paper and it is clear how easily the number could be mistaken for 50; this is why trailing zeros (zeros after a whole number) are not permitted. Leading zeros are required because it would be easy to miss a decimal point placed before a number (such as .5) if the leading zero was not present (the correct way to write this is 0.5). The other items on the list are important enough that it is almost misleading to give one example – such as the long history of mix-ups between morphine and magnesium and resultant fatalities. All institutions accredited by TJC are required to have a list of abbreviations that may not be used in the facility. This list must include <u>all</u> of the abbreviations from the TJC "Do Not Use" list, and any additonal abbreviations <u>selected by the institution</u> (e.g., those that have resulted in significant errors at the site in the past). The unapproved abbreviation list should be readily accessible in the institution (e.g., wall charts, pocket cards, etc.). It is best to try to avoid abbreviations entirely.

The ISMP's list of error-prone abbreviations is available at: http://www.ismp.org/tools/errorproneabbreviations.pdf

DO NOT USE	POTENTIAL PROBLEM	USE INSTEAD
U, u (unit)	Mistaken for "0" (zero), the number "4"(four) or "cc"	Write "unit"
IU (International Unit)	Mistaken for IV (intravenous) or the number 10 (ten)	Write "International Unit"
Q.D., QD, q.d., qd (daily)	Mistaken for each other	Write "daily"
Q.O.D., QOD, q.o.d., qod (every other day)	Period after the Q mistaken for "I" and the "O" mistaken for "I"	Write "every other day"
Trailing zero (X.0 mg)	Decimal point is missed	Write X mg
Lack of leading zero (.X mg)		Write 0.X mg
MS	Can mean morphine sulfate or magnesium sulfate	<u>Write "morphine sulfate"</u>
		<u>Write "magnesium sulfate"</u>
MSO_4 and $MgSO_4$	Confused with one another	

Tall Man Lettering

Look-alike, sound-alike (LASA) medications are a common cause of medication errors. Poor handwriting and similar product labeling aggravate the problem of pulling a look-alike or sound-alike agent instead of the intended medication. Drug dictionaries within computer systems are being built with alerts that can double-check that the correct medication is being ordered or withdrawn. For example a warning may appear on the screen of the ADC which will state: "This is DILAUDID. Did you want hydro-MORPHONE? (To avoid confusion with morphine.)

Drugs that are easily mixed up should be labeled with tall man letters (e.g., CeleXA, CeleBREX). Using tall man letters, which mix upper and lower case letters, draws attention to the dissimilarities in the drug names. The letters that are upper cases are the ones that are different between the two look-alike, sound-alike drugs. Tall man lettering makes the drugs with names that look or sound like others less prone to mix-ups. ISMP, FDA, TJC, and other safety-conscious organizations have promoted the use of tall man letters as one means of reducing confusion between similar drug names. If receiving a verbal order for a drug that is easily confused with another be sure to repeat the drug name back, with spelling if helpful, to the prescriber. It may be possible to remove a drug that is easily confused with another from the institution's formulary.

Use the ISMP "high-alert" list to determine which medications require special safeguards to reduce the risk of errors. It is available at: http://www.ismp.org/Tools/highAlertMedicationLists.asp. Keep in mind that the ISMP's list represents the most common agents that are high risk, and need special precautions. An institution's list may include additonal drugs based on experience in that setting.

The FDA's and ISMP's approved tall man lettering information is available at: http://www.ismp.org/tools/tallmanletters.pdf

Special Bins and Labeling for High-Alert Drugs

Drugs that bear a heightened risk of causing significant patient harm when used in error should be designated as "High-Alert". Any drug that is high risk for significant harm if dispensed incorrectly can be placed in a medication bin that provides a visual alert to the person pulling the medication. The bin can be labeled with warnings and include materials (placed inside the bin) that should be dispensed with the drug (such as oral syringes or MedGuides). In the hospital setting certain drugs are classified as "high-alert" and these can be placed in bins labeled with dispensing requirements.

There are many drugs considered high-alert. Some examples include: insulin and oral hypoglycemics, opioids, anticoagulants, antiarrhythmics, anesthetics, chemotherapeutics, concentrated electrolytes (injectable KCl, phosphate, magnesium and hypertonic saline), inotropic medications and epidural/intrathecal medications.

Select High-Alert Drugs and Safe-Use Precautions

DRUG	PRECAUTIONS
Hypertonic Saline	Use premixed products; store in pharmacy
	Limit options; do not stock the 3% sodium chloride injection
	Develop a protocol for administering sodium chloride for hyponatremia; address the rate and volume of administration and the frequency of serum sodium monitoring
	Limit addition of sodium to enteral feedings to the pharmacy
	In dialysis units, stock a single hypertonic concentration and store in a locked area with limited access and affix special hazard labeling
Insulin	Eliminate insulin pens from the inpatient setting
	If U-500 is stocked, specify conditions under which it is to be used
	Standardize all insulin infusions to one concentration
	Develop protocols for insulin infusions, transition from infusion to SC and sliding scale orders; use standard orders for management of hypoglycemia
	Do not use "U" for units; always label with "units" or "units = mL", but never just "mL"
	Do not place insulin in ADCs; all insulin orders should be reviewed by a pharmacist prior to dispensing
Heparin	Standardize heparin solutions; use premixed and reduce the number of concentrations available
	Standardize administration procedures; place dose stickers on heparin bags and double check all rate changes.
	Differentiate all look-alike products
	Separate the storage of all drugs ordered in units
	Develop and follow standard treatment protocols; standardize the weight-based dosing
	Have infusion pump rate settings and line placement on dual-channel pumps checked by two persons; use only 'free flow' protected pumps
	Do not use "U" for units
Potassium Chloride	Remove all KCl vials from floor stock; centralize KCl infusion preparation in the pharmacy
	Use premixed containers
	Use protocols for KCl delivery which include indications for IV administration, maximum rate of infusion, maximum allowable concentration, guidelines for when cardiac monitoring is required, stipulation that all KCl infusions must be given via a pump, prohibition of multiple simultaneous KCl solutions (e.g., no IV KCl while KCl is being infused in another IV)
	Allow for automatic substitution of oral KCl for IV KCl, when appropriate
	Label all fluids containing potassium with a "Potassium Added" sticker
Opioids	Use of tools to screen patients for risk factors for oversedation and respiratory depression
	Monitor vitals, use of telemetry when indicated, and sedation scales per protocol
	Build red flag alerts into e-prescribing systems for dosing limits
	Use of tall man lettering
	Separate look-alike, sound-alike agents
	Use conversion support systems to calculate correct doses
	Use infusion pump technology when administering IV

Patient Profiles

Pharmacies should maintain current patient profiles that include all prescription drugs, over the counter (OTC) medications, and anything else the patient is taking such as natural products and other supplements. Allergies and the type of allergic reaction (e.g., rash, lip swelling) should be recorded. Intolerances should be noted and the drug avoided, if possible, or the intolerance can be proactively managed (such as using an antiemetic agent if the intolerance is nausea from an opioid). See the Drug Sensitivities, Allergies, Desensitization & Reporting chapter for pointers on proper documentation. The most common use of the profile is to check for allergies and drug interactions, but it can also be used for monitoring appropriateness of therapy, checking for polypharmacy (meaning "many drugs" and refers to problems that can occur when a patient is taking more medications than are necessary) and assessing patient adherence with their medication regimen.

Medication Therapy Management

Errors may be discovered during a more comprehensive medication review (CMR), through the process of medication therapy management (MTM). A personal medication record (PMR) is prepared, and a medication-related action plan (MAP) is developed, preferably by a pharmacist-led team. The next steps involve interventions, referrals, documentation and plans for follow-up. This is a program mandated under the Medicare drug benefit (Medicare Part D) to promote safe and effective medication use. Medicare's drug benefit provides outpatient prescription drug coverage. It is available only through private companies. At a minimum, beneficiaries targeted for MTM include members with multiple chronic conditions who are taking multiple drugs and are likely to incur annual costs for covered drugs that exceed a predetermined level. Computer databases are used to identify patients with certain high-risk conditions (such as heart failure or uncontrolled diabetes) who are generally using many medications (some systems tag patients taking many chronic medications daily) and assign a pharmacist (preferably) to review profiles for proper use. Since this is a Medicare requirement the majority of MTM programs exist within Medicare-funded healthcare plans. MTM may also apply to populations outside of Medicare.

The pharmacist can form a partnership with the patient and prescriber to remedy any issues or lapses. Often, these reviews identify missed therapy such as lack of an ACE inhibitor or ARB in patients with diabetes, missing beta blocker therapy post-MI, missing bisphosphonate therapy with high-dose chronic steroids, and others, since these are easily searchable in databases. A popular MTM initiative is to improve nonadherence in heart failure patients due to the high-rate of ED visits due to decompensated heart failure. MTM is also used to identify cost-savings, by promoting switches to generics or more affordable brands, or by suggesting patient assistance programs or low income subsidies for eligible members.

Drug Utilization Reviews and Retrospective Analysis

Drug utilization reviews (DURs) are reviews of prescribing used by medical groups, insurance or localities that try to identify some combination of inappropriate medication use, including therapeutic duplications, drug-drug and drug-disease contraindications, incorrect dosage or treatment durations, abuse and clinical misuse, such as prescribing out of formulary for unnecessary indications.

Medication Reconciliation

According to TJC, "medication reconciliation is the process of comparing a patient's medication orders to all of the medications that the patient has been taking." This reconciliation is done to avoid medication errors such as omissions, duplications, dosing errors, or drug interactions. Medication reconciliation ("med rec") was previously done on paper forms, but it is now usually performed within the electronic health record (EHR). Prescribers can view side-by-side lists of home medications and ordered medications and address any discrepancies. This process if most effective when complete and accurate information is entered into the patient's medical record (PMR). For this reason, pharmacy departments are often actively involved in documenting home medication use and performing medication reconciliation. In many hospitals, admission orders for a patient cannot be entered into the electronic system <u>until medication reconciliation is completed</u> by a physician, pharmacist or nurse.

Medication reconciliation should be done at <u>every transition of care</u> in which new medications are ordered or existing orders are rewritten. Transitions of care include changes in setting, service, practitioner or level of care. This process comprises five steps:

1. Develop a list of current medications;

2. Develop a list of medications to be prescribed;

3. Compare the medications on the two lists;

4. Note discrepancies and make clinical decisions based on the comparison; and

5. Communicate the new list to appropriate caregivers and to the patient

At discharge, medication reconciliation will occur again. This is an opportunity for the prescriber to address any of the patient's home medications that were "on hold" during the hospitalization and which medications used during the hospitalization should be be continued when the patient goes home. Discrepancies are addressed and the patient is educated. Though most often discussed in the hospital context, medication reconciliation can be equally important in ambulatory care, as many patients receive prescriptions from more than one outpatient provider and may go to several pharmacies. Medication reconciliation is a part of the National Patient Safety Goals (NPSGs) issued by The Joint Commission (TJC).

Include Indications for Use and Proper Instructions on Prescriptions

An <u>indication for use</u> that is written on the prescription (such as lisinopril 10 mg once daily for hypertension) <u>helps pharmacists ensure appropriate prescribing and drug selection</u>. If the pharmacist does not know the indication for the prescribed medication, the prescriber should be contacted.

Using <u>the term "as directed" is not acceptable</u> on prescriptions because the patient often has no idea what this means and the pharmacist cannot verify a proper dosing regimen. Occasionally, this term is used on the bottle along with a separate dosing calendar, such as with warfarin. It would be preferable to write "use per instructions on the dosing calendar" since the patient may not understand how to take the medication and may not be aware that a separate dosing calendar exists.

Use of the Metric System

<u>Measurements should be recorded in the metric system only</u>. Prescribers should use the metric system to express all weights, volumes and units. Computer systems generally have a drop-down menu for selecting the correct units (lb vs kg, for example) and easily converting between units. It is critical to record the correct units, since many calculations (CrCl or eGFR) and dosing checks are performed automatically by the EHR system based on the height and/or weight recorded for the patient. With the increasing prevalence of overweight and obesity in the U.S., it is not uncommon to care for patients weighing 100 kg (or more); but serious errors can occur if this weight was intended to be 100 pounds. Unfortunately, these types of errors do occur in healthcare facilities.

EXAMPLE OF THE BENEFIT OF MEDICATION RECONCILIATION

Ann is an 82 year-old female. Her only medication for the previous ten years has been atenolol 25 mg daily. Ann recently developed influenza. She began to have trouble breathing and was taken to the hospital. It was discovered that Ann had pneumonia and heart failure. She was prescribed lisinopril, carvedilol and furosemide. Ann was discharged to transitional care and received the new medications plus her home medication (atenolol). The consultant pharmacist conducted a medication review to reconcile the medications and, after discussion with the physician, the pharmacist wrote an order to discontinue the atenolol.

Do Not Rely on Medication Packaging for Identification Purposes

Look-alike packaging can contribute to errors. If unavoidable, separate look-alike drugs in the pharmacy and patient care units, or repackage. Never rely on the package to identify the right drug product. Pharmacies frequently have to purchase products from different manufacturers (and these may look vastly different).

Avoid Multiple-Dose Vials, If Possible

These pose risk for cross-contamination (infection) and over-dosing. If used, they should be (ideally) designated for a single patient and labeled appropriately. Discard the remainder when the patient is done with the medication, or is discharged.

Use Safe Practices for Emergency Medications/Crash Carts

Staff must be properly trained to handle emergencies and use crash cart medications. The medications should be unit dose and age-specific, including pediatric-specific doses. A weight-based dosing chart can be placed in the trays used in the pediatric units. If a unit dose medication is not available it is best to have prefilled syringes and drips in the cart (to the extent possible) because it is easy to make a mistake under the stress of a code. The emergency medications should be stored in sealed or locked containers in a locked room and re-placed as soon as possible after use (through a cart exchange so that the area is not left without required medications). Monitor the drug expiration dates. Trained pharmacists should be present at codes when possible.

EXAMPLE OF AN ERROR DUE TO MISIDENTIFICATION OF A CONCENTRATION BASED ON THE PACKAGING

The intravenous catheters of three neonates in a NICU unit in Los Angeles were flushed with the adult therapeutic dose of heparin (10,000 units/mL) rather than the heparin flush dose of 10 units/mL. This accident did not result in fatalities although two of the babies required the reversal agent protamine. Three babies died from a similar incident the previous year at a different hospital. The overdose was administered because the nurse thought she was using a lower concentration of heparin.

Due to the high risk associated with heparin overdose, high concentration heparin vials should not be present in patient care areas. Instead, therapeutic doses should be sent by the pharmacy department.

CODE BLUE

A code blue refers to a patient requiring emergency medical care, typically for cardiac or respiratory arrest. The overhead announcement will provide the patient's location. The code team (often including a pharmacist) will rush to the room and begin immediate resuscitative efforts.

Dedicate Pharmacists to the ICU, Pediatric Units and Emergency Departments

These are units with a high incidence of preventable medication errors, and pharmacists working in these units can assist in identifying and preventing medication errors by developing process improvements designed to reduce errors.

Develop and Use Protocols

Protocols for high-risk drugs increase the rate of appropriate prescribing and reduce the chance of errors due to inappropriate prescribing. TJC requires that standard order sets be used for all antithrombotics. The standard order set (which can be on paper or electronic depending on the institution) should include instructions for initial doses of heparin and other high-risk antithrombotics, monitoring for bleeding, using appropriate antidotes, monitoring for HIT and discontinuing heparin if HIT is suspected. The prescriber should be required to justify any order outside the protocol and a pharmacist should approve or reject the request.

Monitor for Drug-Food Interactions

Check for drug-food interactions routinely and have nutrition (also called "dietary") involved with this effort when drugs with a high rate of food interactions (such as warfarin) are ordered.

Education

Staff education programs such as "in-services" should be provided whenever new high-alert drugs are being used in the facility, to introduce new procedural changes aimed at preventing medication errors and to introduce any new guidelines. The information provided in these "in-services" should be unbiased and should not be provided in a skewed manner by drug company representatives. Many hospitals now limit access of pharmaceutical companies and representatives due to the inherent bias.

Patients can play a vital role in preventing medication errors when they have been encouraged to ask questions and seek satisfactory answers about their medications before drugs are dispensed at a pharmacy. If a patient questions any part of the medication dispensing process, whether it is about the drug's appearance, or dose, or something else, the pharmacist must be receptive and responsive (not defensive). All patient inquiries should be thoroughly investigated before the medication is dispensed. The written information about the medications should be at a reading level that is comprehensible for the patient.

It may be necessary to provide pictograms or other means of instruction to patients who do not speak English or are unable to read English. Attempts must be made to communicate to the patient in their language, using on-site staff or dial-in services. Refer to the Patient Charts, Assessment & Healthcare Provider Communication chapter.

Follow Requirements for Risk Evaluation and Mitigation Strategies (REMS) Drugs

REMS is an FDA program that requires specified training and various restrictions (patient requirements, user registries, etc.) on certain drugs. Examples include the clozapine patient registry, the APPRISE program for erythropoietin use in oncology, the iPLEDGE program for isotretinoin, and others. In 2011 the FDA began new REMS to reduce the misuse of long-acting opioids due to the inherent danger with these drugs. The list of REMS drugs continues grow. When studying from this book note the many drugs that have REMS requirements.

Medication Guides

Medication Guides (or MedGuides) present important adverse events that can occur with over 300 medications. MedGuides are FDA-approved patient handouts and are considered part of the drug's labeling. If a medication has a MedGuide, it should be dispensed with the original prescription and with each refill. Some medications dispensed while inpatient require MedGuides and these should be available to the patient or family upon request. It is not necessary to dispense them to inpatients routinely because the patient is being monitored. MedGuides are required for many individual agents and some entire classes of medications (including anticonvulsants, antidepressants, long-acting opioids, NSAIDs and the ADHD stimulants and atomoxetine).

USE OF TECHNOLOGY AND AUTOMATED SYSTEMS

Computerized Prescriber Order Entry and Clinical Decision Support

Computerized physician/provider order entry (CPOE) is a computerized process that allows direct entry of medical orders by prescribers. Directly entering orders into a computer has the benefit of reducing errors by minimizing the ambiguity resulting from hand-written orders. A much greater benefit is seen with the combination of CPOE and clin-

CITALOPRAM DOSE RANGE

FDA notified healthcare professionals and patients that the antidepressant Celexa (citalopram) should no longer be used at doses greater than 40 mg per day because it can cause abnormal changes in the electrical activity of the heart. In addition, studies did not show a benefit in the treatment of depression at doses higher than 40 mg per day. Read the MedWatch safety alert by clicking "References" linked to the FDA Drug Safety Communication.
Thank you

Alert Action

○ Cancel citalopram
○ Override

[References]   [OK]

ical decision support (CDS) tools. Clinical guidelines and patient labs can be built into the CPOE system and alerts can notify a prescriber if the drug is inappropriate, or if labs indicate that the drug could be unsafe (such as a high potassium level and a new order for a potassium-sparing agent). CPOE can include standard order sets and protocols. In addition to medication orders, CPOE is used for laboratory orders and procedures. An example of an on-screen alert from a CDS system is shown. The alert in this example pops-up when a prescriber attempts to order citalopram with a dose greater than 40 mg/day. In most hospitals, pharmacists are actively involved in creating, updating and monitoring the CDS tools. One aspect of QI is monitoring, reporting trends and addressing alert overrides.

Barcoding

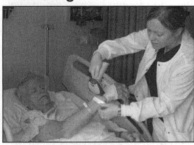

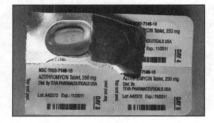

Barcoding may be the most important medication error reduction tool available right now. The barcode follows the drug through the medication use process to make sure it is being properly stocked (such as in the right space in the pharmacy or in the right pocket in the dispensing cabinet), through compounding (if required), and to the patient. The barcode is used at the bedside to identify that the correct drug (by scanning the code on the drug's packaging) is going to the right patient (by scanning the patient's wristband) and confirms that the dose is being given at the right time. The nurse may have a badge barcode to track who administered the dose. Barcodes are now on many pumps and can prevent errors involving medications being given IV that are not meant to be administered in this manner. When a medication is scanned and administered using barcode technology the administration can automatically populate on the medication administration record (MAR), thus avoiding the time associated with manual charting of medication administration.

Automated Dispensing Cabinet Overview and Safety Concerns

Most pharmacy interns will have seen automated dispensing cabinets (ADCs) while on clinical rotations. Common names are *Pyxis, Omnicell, ScriptPro* and *AccuDose*. Over half of the hospitals in the U.S. now use ADCs. In many hospitals the ADCs have replaced patient cassettes that had to be filled at least once daily and exchanged.

Practical Benefits of ADCs

The drug inventory and medication can be automated when drugs are placed into the cabinet and removed. Controlled drug security can be improved (versus the previous method of keeping the controlled drugs locked in a metal cabinet or in a drawer in the nurses' station). The drugs are easily available at the unit and do not require individual delivery from the pharmacy. ADCs provide alerts, usage reports and work well with bar-coding.

Important Safety Considerations with ADCs

- Stocking errors, such as a drug being placed in an incorrect drawer or bin, can lead to the wrong drug being dispensed (barcode scanning can be used to make sure that the correct drug is being placed into the ADC or dispensed).

- The wrong drug can be selected from the screen or ADC.

- The wrong dose can be selected from the screen.

- Errors can occur due to overrides that are not subject to a pharmacist's prospective order review.

Methods to Improve ADC Safety

- TJC requires that the pharmacist review the order before the medication can be removed from the ADC for a patient, except in special circumstances. The override function should be limited to true emergencies and all overrides should be investigated.

- The most common error associated with ADC use is giving the wrong drug or dose to a patient. The patient's MAR should be accessible to practitioners while they are removing medications from the ADC. Barcode scanning improves ADC safety. The drug can be scanned to make sure it is going into the right place in the cabinet and can ensure that the right drug is being pulled. Prior to administration the patient's wrist band can be scanned to make sure the drug is going to the right patient.

- Look-alike and sound-alike medications should be stored in different locations within the ADC. Using computerized alerts, ideally pop-ups that require a confirmation, when medications with high potential for mix-up in a given setting are selected, can help reduce error risk.

- Certain medications should <u>not</u> be put into the ADCs, including insulin, warfarin and high-dose narcotics (such as hydromorphone 10 mg/mL and morphine 20 mg/mL).

- Nurses should not be permitted to put medications back into the medication compartment because it might be placed in the wrong area; it is best to have a separate drawer for all "returned" medications.

- If the machine is in a busy, noisy environment, or in one with poor lighting, errors increase.

The California board specifically states that all drugs that are stocked in the ADC in a nursing facility are restocked by a pharmacist or by an intern or technician working under the supervision of a pharmacist. Removable pockets or drawers transported between the pharmacy and a stocking facility must be transported in a secure tamper-evident container.

Patient Controlled Analgesia Device Overview and Safety Concerns

Opioids are effective agents used for moderate to severe post-surgical pain and are the mainstay of treatment. These may be administered with patient controlled analgesia (PCA) devices. PCAs allow the patient to treat pain quickly (there is no need to call the nurse and wait for the dose to arrive) and allow the administration of small doses, which helps reduce side effects (particularly over-sedation). However, as some patients will be opioid-naïve or receiving higher-than-normal doses post-surgically, antiemetics or antihistamines may be required. PCA drug delivery can mimic the pain pattern more closely and provide good pain control. Increasingly, the PCA is administered with anesthetics for a synergistic benefit in pain relief.

PCA Safety Considerations

- The devices can be complex and require set-up and programming. This is a significant cause of preventable medication errors. PCAs should be used only by well-coordinated healthcare teams.

- Patients may not be appropriate candidates for PCA treatment. They should be cooperative and should have a cognitive assessment prior to using the PCA to ensure that they can follow instructions.

- Friends and family members should not administer PCA doses. This is a TJC requirement.

- PCAs do not frequently cause respiratory depression, but the risk is present. Advanced age, obesity and concurrent use of CNS depressants (in addition to higher opioid doses) increases risk.

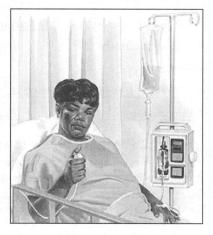

PCA Safety Steps
- <u>Limit the opioids</u> available in floor stock. <u>Use standard order sets</u> (set drug dosages, especially for opioid-naïve patients) so that drugs are not over-dosed.
- <u>Educate staff</u> about HYDROmorphone and morphine mix-ups.
- Implement PCA <u>protocols</u> that include independent double-checking of the drug, pump setting, and dosage. The concentration on the <u>Medication Administration Record (MAR)</u> should match the PCA label.
- Use <u>bar-coding</u> technology. Some infusion pumps incorporate bar-coding technology. Scanning the bar-code on the PCA bag would help ensure the correct concentration is entered during PCA programming. It will also ensure that the right patient is getting the medication.
- Assess the patient's <u>pain, sedation and respiratory rate</u> on a scheduled basis.

INFECTION CONTROL IN HOSPITALS

Nearly two million infections occur in hospitals annually – about one infection for every twenty patients. It is somewhat incredulous that so many patients enter hospitals for treatment of a condition and contract a different condition at the same facility.

The organisms in healthcare settings are highly pathogenic, meaning that resistant bacteria are present in hospitals because that is where the sickest patients are. Certain organisms grow in hospital settings, such as *Pseudomonas* in the moist environment of the ventilator.

Hospital infections cause avoidable illness and death and add enormous financial costs. The worst part of this sad state of affairs is that many of these infections are preventable if proper techniques (which are often simple measures) are followed. Many states now require hospitals to report infection rates and Medicare has begun to refuse reimbursement for hospital-acquired infections that are largely avoidable.

It is important to properly clean surfaces, including bed rails, eating trays, and other room surfaces. Health care professionals should be careful not to be sources of infection from contaminated clothing (including white coats and ties). Organisms that spread via surface contact include VRE, *C. difficile*, noroviruses and other intestinal tract pathogens.

Common Types of Hospital (Nosocomial) Acquired Infections
- Urinary tract infections, from indwelling catheters (very common), <u>remove the catheter as soon as possible)</u> – preventing catheter associated infections is one of TJC's National Patient Safety Goals (NPSG).
- Blood stream infections <u>from IV lines (central lines have the highest risk) and catheters</u>
- Surgical site infections (<u>see Surgical Prophylaxis in the Infectious Diseases II chapter</u>)
- Decubitus ulcers
- Hepatitis
- *<u>Clostridium difficile</u>,* other GI infections
- <u>Pneumonia (mostly due to ventilator use)</u>, bronchitis

Universal Precautions for the Spread of Infectious Agents in the Healthcare Setting
Universal precautions is an approach to infection control that treats human blood and body fluids as if they are known to be infectious for HIV, HBV and other bloodborne pathogens. Contact with bodily fluids should be avoided through the use of good hand hygiene and, in select cases, the use of gowns, masks, or patient isolation.

There are 3 categories of transmission-based precautions defined by the CDC:

Contact Precautions

- Intended to prevent transmission of infectious agents which are spread by direct and indirect contact with the patient and the patient's environment.

- Single patient rooms are preferred. If not available, keep ≥ 3 feet spatial separation between beds to prevent inadvertent sharing of items between patients.

- Healthcare personnel caring for these patients wear a gown and gloves for all interactions that may involve contact with the patient or contaminated areas in the patient's room.

- Contact precautions are recommended for patients colonized with MRSA and VRE.

Droplet precautions

- Intended to prevent transmission of pathogens spread through close respiratory contact with respiratory secretions.

- Single patient rooms are preferred. If not available, keeping ≥ 3 feet spatial separation and drawing a curtain between beds is especially important for diseases transmitted via droplets.

- Healthcare personnel wear a mask (a respirator is not necessary) for close contact with the patient. The mask is donned upon entry to the patient's room.

- Droplet precautions are recommended for patients with active *B. pertussis*, influenza virus, adenovirus, rhinovirus, *N. meningitides*, and group A streptococcus (for the first 24 hours of antimicrobial therapy).

Airborne Precautions

- Intended to prevent transmission of infectious agents that remain infectious over long distances when suspended in the air.

- Patient should be placed in an airborne infection isolation room (AIIR). An AIIR is a single-patient room that is equipped with special air and ventilation handling pressure rooms. The air is exhausted directly to the outside or re-circulated through HEPA filtration before return.

- Healthcare personnel wear a mask or respirator (N95 level or higher), depending on the disease, which is donned prior to room entry.

- Airborne precautions are recommended for patients with rubella virus (measles), varicella virus (chickenpox), or *M. tuberculosis*.

Prevention Of Catheter Associated Bloodstream Infections (CRBSI)

- The most important and most cost-effective strategy to minimize catheter-associated bloodstream infections is through aseptic technique during catheter insertion, including proper handwashing and utilization of standard protocols/catheter insertion checklist.

- It is also important to minimize use of intravascular catheters, if possible, through intravenous to oral route protocols and setting appropriate time limits for catheter use. For example, peripheral catheters should be removed/replaced every 2 – 3 days to minimize risk for infection.

- Other strategies shown to reduce the risk of CRBSI, include the use of skin antiseptics (2% chlorhexidine), antibiotic impregnated central venous catheters, and antibiotic/ethanol lock therapy, but must be weighed against the potential risk for increased rates of resistance.

Hand Hygiene

Many hospital infections are spread by hospital worker's hands and numerous studies show that proper hand hygiene reduces the spread of nosocomial infection. Alcohol-based hand rubs (gel, rinse or foam) are considered more effective in the healthcare setting than plain soap or antimicrobial soap and water, but soap and water are preferable in some situation. Do not wear jewelry under gloves, as it can harbor bacteria and tear the gloves. Keep fingernails clipped short and clean.

CDC/Amanda Mills

Antimicrobial hand soaps that contain chlorhexidine (*Hibiclens,* others) may be preferable to soap and water to reduce infections in healthcare facilities. Triclosan may also be better but this compound gets into the water supply and has environmental concerns.

When to Wash Hands

- Before entering and after leaving patient rooms.
- Between patient contacts if there is more than one patient per room.
- Before and after removing gloves (new gloves with each patient).
- Before handling invasive devices, including injections.
- After coughing or sneezing.
- Before handling food and oral medications.

Use Soap and Water (not alcohol-based rubs) in These Situations

- Before eating.
- After using the restroom.
- Anytime there is visible soil (anything noticeable on the hands).
- After caring for a patient with diarrhea or known *C. difficile* or spore forming organisms; alcohol-based hand rubs have poor activity against spores.
- Before caring for patients with food allergies.

Soap and Water Technique

- Wet both sides of hands, apply soap, rub together for at least 15 (slow) seconds.
- Rinse thoroughly.
- Dry with paper towel and use the towel to turn off the water.

Alcohol-Based Hand Rubs Technique

- Use enough gel (2 – 5 mL or about the size of a quarter).
- Rub hands together until the rub dries (15 – 25 seconds).
- Hands should be completely dry before putting on gloves.

Hand-Hygiene for Sterile Compounding

- Refer to the Sterile Compounding chapter.

Safe Injection Practices

Outbreaks involving the transmission of blood borne pathogens or other microbial pathogens to patients (and occasionally to healthcare workers) continue to occur due to unsafe injection technique. The majority of safety breaches involve the reuse of syringes in multiple patients, contamination of IV bags with used syringes, failure to follow basic injection safety when administering IV medications and inappropriate care or maintenance of glucometer equipment that is used on multiple patients.

The following practices ensure safe injection of medications. These recommendations are meant for healthcare facilities; see the Drug Disposal chapter for more information on syringe disposal for patients.

- Never administer an oral solution/suspension intravenously. Many medication errors (sometimes fatal) have occurred this way. Always use oral syringes (which are difficult or impossible to attach a needle to for IV injection) and label oral syringes "for oral use only".

- Never reinsert used needles into a multiple-dose vial or solution container (whenever possible, use of single-dose vials is preferred over multiple-dose vials, especially when medications will be administered to multiple patients).

- Needles used for withdrawing blood or any other body fluid, or used for administering medications or other fluids should preferably have "engineered sharps protection" which reduces the risk of an exposure incident by a mechanism such as drawing the needle into the syringe barrel after use.

- To avoid contamination to the patient, never touch the tip or plunger of a syringe.

- Disposable needles contaminated with drugs, chemicals or blood products should never be removed from their original syringes unless no other option is available. Throw the entire needle/syringe assembly (needle attached to the syringe) into the red plastic sharps container (a non-reusable plastic container that is puncture resistant, leak proof on the sides and bottom, properly labeled and closable).

- Never remove a needle by unscrewing it.

- Used disposable needles/sharps should be discarded immediately after use without recapping into a sharps container.

- Sharps containers should be easily accessible, replaced routinely, and not allowed to overfill. Never compress or "push down" on the contents of any sharps container.

- If someone is stuck with a needle the proper department at the facility should be contacted immediately.

THE JOINT COMMISSION ON ACCREDITATION OF HEALTHCARE ORGANIZATIONS (JOINT COMMISSION, OR TJC)

The Joint Commission is an independent, not-for-profit organization that accredits and certifies more than 17,000 health care organizations and programs in the U.S., including hospitals, healthcare networks, longterm care facilities, homecare organizations, office-based surgery centers and independent laboratories. TJC focuses on the highest quality and safety of care and sets standards that institutions must meet to be accredited. An accredited organization must undergo an on-site survey at least every three years and surveys can be unannounced.

National patient safety goals (NPSGs) are set annually by TJC for different types of healthcare settings in order to improve patient safety. Each goal includes defined measures called "Elements of Performance" that must be met. These will be included in the institution's protocol. There are other NPSGs not discussed here, such as a goal for conducting a preprocedure verification process and another for identifying patients at risk of suicide. Pharmacists focus on medication-related NPSGs. Hospital NPSGs related to medication safety for 2016 include the following:

NPSG 03.04.01: Label all medications, medication containers and other solutions on and off the sterile field in perioperative and other procedural settings.

Numerous errors, sometimes fatal, have occurred due to medications and other solutions that were removed from their original containers and placed into unlabeled containers. This is of particular concern in perioperative and other procedural areas. Pharmacists should ensure that all medications and medication containers are labeled. The exception is when an agent is to be immediately administered without a break in the medication use process. Medication and solution labels should contain medication name, strength, quantity, diluent and volume and expiration date/time.

NPSG 03.05.01: Reduce the likelihood of harm associated with anticoagulant therapy.

There are many elements to this goal, including the requirement to use standardized dosing protocols, monitoring INRs, using programmable pumps for heparin, and providing education to patients and families. In the protocol, starting dose ranges are included; if the prescriber requests a dose out of the range the pharmacist will need to confirm agreement. The protocol will note alternative dosing ranges for a drug that increases or decreases the therapeutic effect of the anticoagulant. For example, if a drug that inhibits warfarin metabolism is being used concurrently, a lower starting dose will be required. INR monitoring frequency (plus baseline INR) will be in the protocol, along with the requirement to notify dietary.

NPSG 03.06.01: Maintain and communicate accurate patient medication information.

This includes medication reconciliation, providing written information to the patient and conducting discharge counseling. In conducting the reconciliation the medication name, dose, frequency, route, and purpose (at the minimum) should be confirmed. Refer to Medication Reconciliation earlier in this chapter.

NPSG 02.03.01: Report critical results of tests and diagnostic procedures on a timely basis.

This includes identifying and acting upon critical lab values, blood culture results, and other critical results as defined in the protocol. It should state the acceptable length of time between the availability and the reporting. The process should be evaluated to make sure the time is being met. Pharmacists should play an active role in this communication process.

NPSG 07.01.01: Comply with the Centers for Disease Control (CDC) hand hygiene guidelines.

Proper hand hygiene technique as described previously in this chapter. The goals for improving compliance should be stated, and the frequency of monitoring to ensure the goals are being met must be included.

NPSG 07.03.01; 07.04.01; 07.05.01; 07.06.01: Implement evidence-based practices to reduce health-care associated infections.

These include recommendations to reduce the likely sources of infection, such as from urinary catheters: only use if warranted, proper hand hygiene prior to insertion by qualified personnel only, properly secure the indwelling catheter, use the smallest bore catheter possible, with good drainage (to minimize tissue damage – all insertion and removal should be done according to the institution's protocol), continue to assess the need for continued catheter use in order to remove the catheter as soon as it is no longer needed. Reducing risk of healthcare-associated infection with multidrug-resistant organisms is addressed. To reduce infections with ventilator use: elevate head-of-bed 30-45 degrees, assess readiness to wean off ventilator at least daily, use breaks or reductions in sedation use if possible, consider DVT prophylaxis, use stress-ulcer prophylaxis judiciously and only in patients who meet requirements for use; see the Critical Care & Fluids/Electrolytes chapter.

NPSG 01.01.01: Use at least two patient identifiers when providing care, treatment and services.

There have been countless medication errors (and surgical misadventures) due to patient misidentification. Two identifiers (such as name and medical record number) must be verified prior to administering medications, blood or blood components, taking lab samples or providing any treatment or procedure. The identifiers must be patient-specific – things like doctor's name, zip code or patient location should not be used in a hospital setting. In the community setting (which does not require adherence to NPSG requirements but in which the use of <u>two identifiers</u> is very important to prevent someone receiving someone else's medication) the two identifiers used most commonly are the patient's name and the home address (sometimes DOB is used, but the name and DOB can be the same as another person).

6

DRUG SENSITIVITIES, ALLERGIES, DESENSITIZATION & REPORTING

ANAPHYLACTIC REACTION

Antigen

Plasma cell

IgE

B-cell

Histamine

Mast cell

GUIDELINES/REFERENCES

Food and Drug Administration Med-Watch program http://www.fda.gov/Safety/MedWatch/ (accessed 2015 November 3)

Drug Allergy: An Updated Practice Parameter. *Ann Allergy Asthma Immunol.* 2010 Oct;105:259-273.

BACKGROUND

Adverse drug reaction (ADR) is a term that encompasses all unintended pharmacologic effects of a drug when it is administered correctly and used at recommended doses. Note: ADRs should not be confused with medication errors, which can include overdose and administration mistakes, and are discussed in the Medication Safety chapter. ADRs result in substantial morbidity and mortality and reports are increasing; 711,232 reports with serious outcomes were logged with the FDA in 2013 (including 117,752 deaths).

Boxed warnings are the FDA's strictest warning about a drug's safety risks and are used in some prescription drugs that can cause serious injury or death. The boxed warning is designed to inform healthcare prescribers about the risk/s, and is displayed prominently in a black box at the beginning of the package labeling. Drugs that increase mortality risk may still be used in select patients or under certain conditions [e.g., long-acting beta agonists have a boxed warning for asthma-related death, but only if they are used alone (without a steroid)]; thus, the boxed warning is to avoid using them alone. In other cases, the drug should not be used if there are other options available (e.g., tigecycline). Other boxed warnings are designed to avoid mishaps due to prescribing or dispensing errors (e.g., cyclosporine has a boxed warning to avoid using the incorrect formulation, which can lead to rejection of the transplant). If a boxed warning concerns an adverse effect that the patient could experience (e.g., suicide risk in adolescents using antidepressants), the patient or caregiver must be informed of the risk and methods to use the drug in the safest manner possible (such as monitoring for changes in mood).

ADRs are categorized into predictable (Type A) and unpredictable (Type B) reactions. Type A reactions are dose-dependent, related to the known pharmacologic actions of the drug, can occur in any patient, and range from mild to severe. Type A reactions are the most common and account for an estimated 80% of ADRs. An example of a Type A reaction is orthostatic hypotension with doxazosin. If a patient starts doxazosin at 1 mg QHS they will have much less orthostatic hypotension and dizziness than if the medication is started at a 4 mg dose; thus, this drug is slowly titrated upward to reduce the severity of the side effect.

Type B reactions are generally not dose-dependent, are unrelated to the pharmacologic actions of the drug, and are influenced by patient-specific susceptibility factors (e.g., rash with lamotrigine). Type B reactions involve a drug intolerance (e.g., nausea with codeine), idiosyncratic reactions (Stevens-Johnson syndrome), drug allergy, and pseudoallergic reaction (itching after opioid administration or redman syndrome with rapid vancomycin infusion).

Although side effects or adverse effects can occur in anyone, likelihood may increase if a drug is used in a patient who is at high risk for a certain condition. For example, some degree of renal damage is not unexpected with use of an aminoglycoside for longer than 7 days. However, if given to a patient with underlying renal impairment, nephrotoxicity may be more likely to occur and may happen sooner.

Drug allergy

Drug allergy, one category of adverse drug reactions, refers to an immune-mediated response to a medication or excipient (inactive ingredient). True drug allergies, or hypersensitivity reactions, are classified into four types. Type I reactions are immediate (within 15 – 30 minutes of exposure) and involve an IgE-mediated immune response. Reactions can include urticaria (hives), angioedema, bronchospasm and anaphylaxis. The severity can range from minor inconvenience to death. Type II reactions occur minutes to hours after exposure. Examples include hemolytic anemia and thrombocytopenia. Type III describes immune-complex reactions, which have an onset of 3 – 10 hours after exposure. Examples include drug-induced lupus and serum sickness. Type IV reactions are delayed hypersensitivity reactions. They can occur anywhere from 48 hours to several weeks after exposure. The classic example of a type IV reaction is the PPD skin test for tuberculosis; the intradermal response peaks at 48 – 72 hours.

Assessing Causality of an Adverse Drug Reaction

When an adverse reaction occurs, it can sometimes be difficult to determine whether a particular drug is the cause. The Naranjo Scale is a validated causality assessment scale that can help determine the likelihood that a drug caused an ADR. Based on the questionnaire, a probability score is calculated. A score > 9 = definite ADR; 5 – 8 = probable ADR; 1 – 4 = possible ADR; 0 = doubtful ADR.

QUESTION	YES	NO	DO NOT KNOW
Are there previous conclusive reports on this reaction?	+1	0	
Did the adverse event appear after the suspected drug was given?	+2	-1	
Did the adverse reaction improve when the drug was discontinued or a specific antagonist was given?	+1	0	
Did the adverse reaction appear when the drug was readministered?	+2	-1	
Are there alternative causes that could on their own have caused the reaction?	-1	+2	
Did the reaction reappear when a placebo was given?	-1	+1	
Was the drug detected in any body fluid in toxic concentrations?	+1	0	
Was the reaction more severe when the dose was increased or less severe when the dose was decreased?	+1	0	
Did the patient have a similar reaction to the same or similar drugs in any previous exposure?	+1	0	
Was the adverse event confirmed by any objective evidence?	+1	0	

Characterizing an Adverse Drug Reaction

In order to properly characterize an adverse reaction, sensitivity to a drug or a true drug allergy, pharmacists must ask the right questions. When patients report an "allergy" to a drug, these questions can help place the reaction into the proper context:

- What reaction occurred (a mild rash, a severe rash with blisters, trouble breathing)?

- When did it occur? About how old were you?

- Can you use similar drugs in the same class? For example, if a penicillin allergy is reported, ask if they have ever used *Keflex*.

- Ask about and include any food allergies and latex allergies in the patient record. Latex allergies should be recorded because some drugs require tubing, have latex vial stoppers, or require gloves for administration.

ADR REPORTING

Side effects, adverse events and allergies should be reported to the FDA's MedWatch program, which is called the FDA Adverse Event Reporting System (FAERS), that provides a central collection point for problems caused by drugs. Note that vaccines are an exception that are not reported under FAERS; vaccine adverse drug reactions are reported under a different program called VAERS. See the Immunizations chapter for information.

- The FDA conducts Phase IV (post-marketing safety surveillance programs) for approved drugs and biologics and collects and analyzes the reports to better understand the drug safety profile in a real world setting. When drugs are studied in trials, high-risk patients are typically excluded. Yet in real life settings, some high risk patients will receive the medication. If a drug causes a reaction in 1 out of every 3,000 people, the problem may not be apparent in a smaller clinical trial. For this reason, community-based adverse event reporting is critical.

EXAMPLE OF "REAL LIFE" ADVERSE EVENT INCIDENCE VERSUS THAT IN A CLINICAL TRIAL SETTING

When spironolactone was studied in heart failure patients during the RALES trial, patients with renal insufficiency or elevated potassium levels were excluded due to the known risk of additional hyperkalemia from the use of spironolactone. The drug was found to have benefit in advanced heart failure patients and doctors in the community began to use it in their heart failure patients. In this real life setting, patients with renal insufficiency or elevated potassium were occasionally prescribed spironolactone, and arrhythmias and sudden death due to hyperkalemia were reported.

- Reporting is voluntary but has important implications for safe medication use. Healthcare professionals and patients may also report adverse events to the drug manufacturer, who is required by law to send the report to the FDA. The MedWatch form used for reporting can be found online via the link provided in the references at the beginning of this chapter. Reports can also be made by calling the FDA directly. MedWatch is not only used to report problems with drugs; it is also used for reporting problems with biologics, medical devices and some dietary supplements and cosmetics.

EXAMPLE: AN ADR WAS ADDED TO THE PACKAGE INSERT MANY YEARS AFTER THE DRUG HAD BEEN RELEASED DUE TO ADR REPORTS RECEIVED BY THE FDA

Oseltamivir *(Tamiflu)* was initially released without any warning of unusual behavior in children. The FDA received enough reports that they issued a warning to prescribers in 2006. After many more reports, in 2008, the FDA required the manufacturer to update the prescribing information to include a precaution about hallucinations, confusion and other strange behavior in children.

- If the FDA receives enough reports that a drug is linked to a particular problem they may require that the product's drug information, such as the package insert, be changed. In especially risky cases, a safety alert is issued to prescribers, usually before the labeling is changed.

Example of a Posting on the FDA Website of a Drug that is Being Monitored Under Phase IV

DRUG	USAGE	ADVERSE EVENT REPORTS	NOTES
Canagliflozin (*Invokana*)	An adjunct to diet and exercise to improve glycemic control in adults with type 2 diabetes mellitus.	Angioedema, serious UTI, renal failure, diabetic ketoacidosis and nephrolithiasis	FDA continues to evaluate the identified adverse events. A drug safety communication (DSC) was issued for ketoacidosis and diabetic ketoacidosis.

INTOLERANCES, SENSITIVITIES AND IDIOSYNCRATIC REACTIONS

Stomach Upset/Nausea

Stomach upset or nausea is often incorrectly reported as an allergy. It should be listed on the patient profile because the drug bothered the patient and, if possible, should be avoided in the future; but this is not an allergy and should not prevent drugs in the same class from being used. This is more accurately categorized as an intolerance. Modern electronic medical records often allow for documentation of intolerances separately from allergies. An example of an intolerance is the patient who has stomach upset with codeine (but not hydrocodone or other drugs in the morphine class) or from erythromycin (but not azithromycin or other macrolides).

Mild Rash

Opioids cause a non-allergic release of histamine from mast cells in the skin in all patients, causing itching and rash in some. This is particularly problematic in the inpatient setting after surgery, when opioid-naïve patients receive the medication or when non-naïve patients receive higher-than-normal doses. Pruritus due to this or other causes, if not severe, can be reduced or avoided if the patient is pre-medicated with an antihistamine, such as diphenhydramine.

Photosensitivity

Photosensitivity can occur when sunlight reacts with a drug in the skin and causes tissue damage that looks like a severe sunburn on sun-exposed areas; this occurs within hours of sun exposure. A type IV (delayed hypersensitivity) reaction can also occur with sun exposure and some medications. It appears as a red, itchy rash that can spread to areas that were not exposed to sun and occurs within days of sun exposure.

When dispensing medications that can cause photosensitivity, it is important to advise the patient and/or their caregivers to limit sun exposure and to use sunscreens that block both UVA and UVB radiation (these are labeled broad spectrum).

EXAMPLE: STOMACH UPSET DUE TO CODEINE REPORTED INCORRECTLY AS A DRUG ALLERGY

Carmen received acetaminophen 300 mg-codeine 30 mg *(Tylenol #3)* for pain relief after a dental extraction. Carmen got very nauseated from the medicine. When she was admitted to the hospital several years later for a left hip replacement, she reported to the intake coordinator that she was "allergic" to codeine. The intake coordinator did not attempt to clarify the reaction. The hospital's pain management protocol calls for hydromorphone in a patient-controlled analgesic device for postoperative pain control. The physician used a less desirable option for pain control due to the reported allergy.

DRUGS MOST COMMONLY ASSOCIATED WITH PHOTOSENSITIVITY

Amiodarone	**Oral and topical retinoids**
Carbamazepine	
Chloroquine	Quinidine
Coal Tar	**Quinolones**
Cyclosporine	St. John's wort
Diuretics, thiazides and loops	**Sulfa antibiotics**
Fluorouracil, topical	**Tacrolimus**
Griseofulvin	**Tetracyclines**
NSAIDs	Tigecycline
	Voriconazole

Severe Skin Rashes

There are several severe skin rashes that can be caused by drugs, including <u>Stevens-Johnson syndrome (SJS)</u>, <u>toxic epidermal necrolysis (TEN)</u>, drug reaction with eosinophilia and systemic symptoms (DRESS) and thrombotic thrombocytopenic purpura (TTP). <u>All of these can be life-threatening and require prompt treatment.</u> SJS and TEN generally occur 1 - 3 weeks after drug administration, and almost always more than 72 hours after

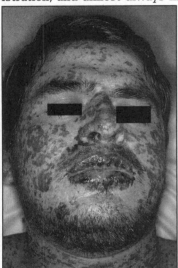

administration. These rashes can result in severe mucosal erosions, a high body temperature and organ damage (eyes, liver, kidney, lungs). SJS and TEN are not easily distinguishable from one another; SJS can lead to TEN, and the key to treating both is <u>stopping the offending agent as soon as possible</u>. In addition, patients will receive fluid and electrolyte replacement, wound care and pain medi-

Patient with Stevens-Johnson Syndrome

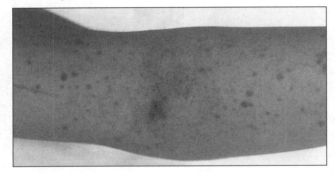

Patient with Thrombotic Thrombocytopenic Purpura

cations. <u>Systemic steroids</u> may be used in SJS, though benefit is controversial, but are <u>contraindicated in TEN</u>. Due to the severity of the mucosal involvement, antibiotics are often necessary to prevent infection. DRESS can include a variety of skin eruptions as well as systemic symptoms such as fever, hepatic dysfunction, renal dysfunction and lymphadenopathy. Treatment consists of <u>stopping the offending agent</u>, although <u>symptoms may</u> continue to <u>worsen</u> for a period of time after the agent has been discontinued. TTP can cause purpura (bruises) and petechiae (dots) on the skin. These are caused by bleeding under the skin. TTP should be treated immediately with plasma exchange. A table listing the drugs most commonly associated with severe skin reactions is included on this page. Cases of severe reaction have also been associated with the use of the OTC analgesics acetaminophen and ibuprofen, which are generally considered to be safe medications.

DRUGS COMMONLY ASSOCIATED WITH SEVERE SKIN REACTIONS

SJS/TEN	DRESS
Abacavir	Carbamazepine
Allopurinol	Celecoxib
Carbamazepine	Doxycycline
Clindamycin	Ethosuximide
Clopidogrel	Fosphenytoin
Deferasirox	Gabapentin
Ethosuximide	Ibuprofen
Fosphenytoin	Lacosamide
Hydroxychloroquine	Lamotrigine
Isavuconazonium	Minocycline
Letrozole	Oxcarbazepine
Lamotrigine	Phenytoin
Minocycline	Sulfasalazine
Nevirapine	Sulfamethoxazole
Oseltamivir	Terbinafine
Oxcarbazepine	Valproate
Penicillins	Vancomycin
Peramivir	
Phenobarbital	**TTP**
	Acyclovir
Phenytoin	**Clopidogrel**
Piroxicam	Famciclovir
Quinine	**Ticlopidine**
Sulfamethoxazole	Sulfamethoxazole
Terbinafine	Quinine
Ticlopidine	Valacyclovir
Tiagabine	
Varenicline	
Voriconazole	
Zonisamide	

DRUG ALLERGIES AND ANAPHYLAXIS

Some drugs are more commonly associated with drug allergies than others. Penicillins and sulfon-amides are two classes that cause the most drug allergies. For a true drug allergy to occur the person must have taken the drug previously. Initial exposure will cause a Type I hypersensitivity reaction, resulting in IgE production, which primes the body to release excessive histamine at the next drug exposure. This section describes drug allergy reactions and treatment, but keep in mind that similar treatment may be used for non-drug allergies, and the pharmacist who is dispensing an epinephrine self-injector for other types of allergies will provide the same instructions.

Some medications (e.g., phytonadione, contrast media) are associated with a pseudoallergic reaction sometimes called an anaphylactoid reaction. It is not IgE-mediated, but the clinical appearance and treatment are similar to that of anaphylaxis.

A reaction without breathing difficulty can sometimes be treated by simply stopping the offending drug. Antihistamines can be used to counteract the histamine release that causes itching, swelling and rash. Systemic steroids, and sometimes NSAIDs, can be used to decrease swelling. Severe swelling may necessitate a steroid injection. Epinephrine is used to reverse bronchoconstriction if the patient is wheezing or has other signs of trouble breathing.

Anaphylaxis

Anaphylaxis is a severe, life-threatening allergic reaction that occurs seconds to minutes after taking the drug. Anaphylaxis can occur after an initial exposure and subsequent immune response, but some drugs can cause anaphylaxis with the first exposure. A patient experiencing anaphylaxis may have generalized urticaria (hives), swelling of the mouth and throat, difficulty breathing or wheezing sounds, abdominal cramping and hypotension (which can cause dizziness or light-headedness). They can become unconscious or go into shock. Symptoms can develop quickly, within seconds or minutes; treatment must be administered immediately.

Anyone with serious allergies to food, drugs or serious medical conditions (including hypoglycemia that may require glucagon) should wear a *Medic Alert* bracelet. These are available in many pharmacies, and link the patient and reactions to a 24-hour information line.

Anaphylaxis Treatment

An anaphylactic reaction requires immediate emergency medical care. The patient or family should be instructed to call 911 if anaphylaxis occurs. Treatment includes epinephrine injection ± diphenhydramine ± steroids ± IV fluids. To avoid blocking the airway, nothing should be placed under the head or in the mouth. Swollen airways can be quickly fatal; patients who have had such a reaction should carry injectable single-use epinephrine (*EpiPen, EpiPen Jr, Adrenaclick, Auvi-Q*) if they may be at future risk. These are available in dosages of 0.3 mg or 0.15 mg of epinephrine. The patient's emergency kit should also include diphenhydramine tablets (25 mg x 2) and emergency contact information.

Patient Counseling for Epinephrine Auto-Injectors

- Tell your family, caregivers and others where you keep your epinephrine auto-injector and how to use it, as you may not be able to speak in an allergic emergency.

- For *Auvi-Q*, pull off the outer case, then follow the voice instructions to administer.

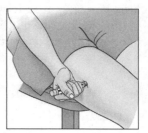

- For others *(EpiPen, Adrenaclick)*:

  - Grasp the epinephrine shot injector in one fist with the black tip pointing down. Do not touch the black tip. (Color may be different).

  - With the other hand, pull off the cap.

- ❑ Hold the tip close to your outer thigh. Swing and jab the tip into your outer thigh (through clothing if necessary). The injector should be at a 90-degree angle to your thigh.
- ❑ Keep the injector in your outer thigh while slowly counting to 10.
- ❑ Remove the injector and <u>rub the area</u> where the medicine entered your skin.
- ❑ Look at the tip: If the needle is showing, you received the dose. If not, you need to inject again. It is normal for some of the liquid to remain in the injector. Do not try to inject the remaining liquid.
- ❑ If you have two pens, you may need to use the second (in the opposite thigh) to maintain breathing prior to the arrival of medical help.

- ■ Take the antihistamine tablets (2 x 25 mg) in your allergy kit (only if there is no tongue/lip swelling).

- ■ Seek emergency medical care (call 911), additional care may be needed.

COMMON DRUG CLASSES THAT CAN CAUSE ALLERGIC REACTIONS

While any drug can lead to an allergic reaction, some are known to do so more than others. These are discussed below. Often the drug that caused a reaction can be replaced with another drug. Patch testing by an allergist is the most reliable way to determine if a person is truly allergic to a drug, but it does not provide any information regarding certain types of rashes (e.g., Stevens-Johnson syndrome or toxic epidermal necrolysis).

Beta-Lactam Allergy

Penicillin is a beta-lactam antibiotic and there are many related compounds in this family, including nafcillin, oxacillin, ampicillin, amoxicillin, ticarcillin, piperacillin and others. Anyone who is <u>allergic to one</u> of the penicillins should be presumed to be <u>allergic to all penicillins</u> and should <u>avoid the entire group</u>, unless they have been specifically evaluated for this problem.

Cephalosporins are related to penicillin. People with a history of <u>penicillin allergy</u> have a <u>small risk</u> of having an allergic reaction to a <u>cephalosporin or carbapenem</u>. Risk of cross-reactivity is low, however, it is prudent on the exam to <u>avoid</u> any beta-lactam with a stated allergy to another, <u>unless there is no alternative agent</u>. A notable exception is in acute otitis media (AOM); the American Academy of Pediatrics recommends use of 2nd or 3rd generation cephalosporins in patients with a non-severe penicillin allergy, due to toxicities and decreased efficacy of alternative AOM therapies in children.

Sulfa Allergies

Reactions are most <u>commonly reported</u> with <u>sulfamethoxazole</u> (in *Bactrim, Septra)*, and the patient should <u>avoid using sulfapyridine, sulfadiazine and sulfisoxazole</u>. "Non-arylamine" sulfonamides (thiazide diuretics, loop diuretics, sulfonylureas, acetazolamide, zonisamide and celecoxib) usually do not cross react with a sulfamethoxazole allergy, but on the exam you will likely have to recognize the possible interaction. Since the cross-reactivity between sulfamethoxazole and thiazides and loops is very small, the reaction is usually not considered when the need for these drugs is present; even so, the patient should be aware to watch for a possible reaction. There are other sulfa-type groups that also have low cross-reactivity. <u>Sulfite or sulfate allergies do not cross react with a sulfonamide</u>. The rotigotine patch, orphenadrine injection, the *Rowasa* mesalamine enema, some dobutamine formulations and some eye drops contain sulfites.

Opioid Allergy

The following agents cross-react: morphine, oxymorphone, codeine, hydrocodone, hydromorphone, oxycodone, nalbuphine, buprenorphine, butorphanol, levorphanol, naloxone and heroin (diacetyl-morphine). Although tapentadol does not have an opioid-allergy contraindication in the U.S. package labeling, tramadol does, and the two agents are structurally similar. Use caution if recommending either in an opioid allergy. If allergic to tramadol, an allergy to tapentadol is likely, and vice-versa. If a patient has a known or suspected morphine-group allergy, choose (if appropriate): fentanyl, meperidine, methadone, tramadol, tapentadol. Meperidine and fentanyl are cross-reactive. The bottom line is safety; if used, monitor the patient.

Heparin-Induced Thrombocytopenia

See Anticoagulation chapter for information on heparin-induced thrombocytopenia (HIT).

Biologics

Biologics (e.g., rituximab and others) can cause hypersensitivity reactions, among other ADRs. Desensitization is possible for some agents in patients who need a biologic but have had a prior poor reaction. See the following page for more information regarding desensitization.

Breathing Difficulties and NSAIDs

Reactions to NSAIDS, including aspirin, can either be a drug sensitivity or a true allergic reaction. A drug sensitivity can cause rhinitis, mild asthmatic-type reactions, or skin reactions. If a true allergy is present, the patient will experience urticaria, angioedema, and occasionally anaphylaxis. COX-2 selective NSAIDs are used clinically, but on licensing exams it may be prudent to avoid all NSAIDs.

Contrast Media

Contrast media (used in CT scans, etc.) can cause anaphylactoid reactions and delayed skin reactions. Systemic steroids and antihistamines are sometimes used to prevent reactions if contrast media is needed in a patient who has had a prior reaction.

Peanut and Soy Allergy

It is important for the pharmacist to be aware if a patient has a peanut allergy. Peanuts and soy are in the same family and can have cross-reactivity. Soy is used in some medications. Parents of children with peanut allergies should be trained in CPR and an *EpiPen* may need to be kept within close reach. Most likely, a reaction will be due to consuming peanuts or soy unknowingly in food products.

Drugs to avoid with peanut or soy allergy: Clevidipine *(Cleviprex)*, propofol *(Diprivan)*, progesterone in *Prometrium* capsules

Egg Allergy

If a patient has a true allergy to eggs (which means they cannot enjoy birthday cake), they cannot use:

- Clevidipine *(Cleviprex)*
- Propofol *(Diprivan)*
- Yellow Fever vaccine (chicken eggs are used in vaccine production)
- Influenza vaccine (chicken eggs are used in vaccine production) – Per ACIP, people who have experienced only hives from consuming eggs can receive inactivated vaccine (the shot, given IM), as long as they are treated by a healthcare provider who is familiar with the potential manifestations of egg allergies and can be observed in a healthcare setting for at least 30 minutes after receiving each dose. A person who has more severe symptoms (such as wheezing, requiring epinephrine, hypotension, cardiovascular changes) may need to receive a different formulation of the vaccine, but should be evaluated further by an allergist physician. *Flublok* is the first seasonal influenza vaccine made using recombinant techniques and does not use eggs at all in its production.

Penicillin Skin Testing

A penicillin allergy is the most common drug allergy in the U.S., reported in about 10% of the general population. A true penicillin allergy has been found to be present in only about 10% of those that are reported. Some patients report a penicillin "allergy" when their reaction was more properly categorized as an intolerance (e.g., nausea or diarrhea). In other cases, patients may have had a true allergic reaction to penicillin in the past, but over time, the antibodies can wane and the patient may be able to safely receive penicillins. Due to concerns of cross-reactivity with cephalosporins and carbapenems, a penicillin allergy can severely limit the selection of antibiotics available to treat infectious diseases. Patients who report a penicillin allergy have been shown to more often receive broad-spectrum antibiotics that cause more collateral damage, such as quinolones, and antibiotics with greater toxicity potential, such as vancomycin. The goal of penicillin skin testing is to identify patients who are at the greatest risk of a Type I hypersensitivity reaction if they received systemic penicillin.

The penicillin skin test uses the components of penicillin that most often cause an immune (allergic) response, which includes products of penicillin metabolism (these are called major determinants of reaction). A specific product containing the major determinants *(Pre-Pen)* is used in addition to diluted penicillin G and a step-wise skin test is done. First, a drop of test solution is placed on the skin (usually on the inside of the forearm) and the skin is barely punctured through the solution. The site is then observed for 15 minutes. If there is no localized reaction (redness, swelling) at the test site, a small amount of test solutions are injected intradermally and the test sites are observed. If the patient develops a localized reaction around the *Pre-Pen* or penicillin G test site, they are at high risk of a reaction to systemic penicillin and should not receive it. If the skin test is negative with no reaction to the test solutions, they can be considered to be at the same risk as a patient in the general population who does not report a penicillin allergy. It is important that drugs that could interfere with a skin reaction be held before beginning the test (e.g., H_1RA and vasopressors), as this could cause a false-negative test. Note that skin testing only predicts an IgE-mediated reaction. Regardless of skin test results, a patient should never be re-challenged with an agent that caused SJS or TEN.

Induction of Drug Tolerance (Desensitization)

In many cases when a drug allergy is present an alternative medication can be chosen. When no acceptable alternative is available, induction of drug tolerance (often referred to as desensitization) may be recommended. This is a step-wise process that begins by administering a very small dose of the medication and then incrementally increasing the dose at regular time intervals up to the target dose. This modifies the patient's response to the medication and temporarily allows safe treatment. Treatment of syphilis in a penicillin-allergic pregnant patient is a place for desensitization. The CDC guideline recommends that the patient undergo desensitization and subsequent penicillin treatment, rather than using second-line agents. The desensitization procedure must take place in a medical setting where emergency care can be provided if a serious reaction occurs. Treatment with the agent must start immediately following the desensitization procedure and must not be interrupted until therapy is complete. A drug-free period allows the immune system to re-sensitize to the drug and serious hypersensitivity reactions (including anaphylaxis) could occur with subsequent doses. Induction of drug tolerance is a more accurate term than desensitization, because the process does not "cure" the patient of an allergy, and the reaction should not be removed from the patient's medical record. If the drug is required again, the process must be repeated. Desensitization protocols exist for a number of antimicrobial agents, some biologics and a few others medications (such as aspirin). Desensitization should never be attempted if an agent has previously caused SJS or TEN.

PHARMACOKINETICS

We gratefully acknowledge the assistance of Paul Beringer, PharmD, BCPS, FASHP, Associate Professor of Clinical Pharmacy and Clinical Medicine, University of Southern California, in preparing this chapter.

BACKGROUND

Pharmacokinetics is what the human body does to a drug and pharmacodynamics is what the drug does to the human body. Pharmacokinetics involves the study of the time course of drug absorption, distribution, metabolism and excretion. Mathematical relationships are used to describe these processes. Clinicians use pharmacokinetics to assess drug levels and optimize drug therapy. Pharmacodynamics refers to the relationship between the drug concentration at the site of action and both therapeutic and adverse effects. Pharmacodynamics is also used to explain the effect of the drug on an organism (such as a bacteriostatic or bactericidal effect).

ABSORPTION

There are two main sites for drug administration: intravascular, where the drug is placed directly into the blood either intravenously or intra-arterially, and extravascular. Some examples of extravascular administration include oral, sublingual, buccal, intramuscular, subcutaneous, transdermal, inhaled, topical, ocular, intraocular, intrathecal and rectal. If a drug is administered extravascularly, drug absorption occurs as the drug moves from the site of administration to the systemic circulation (bloodstream). When a drug is administered intravascularly, the drug directly enters the systemic circulation and absorption is not necessary.

Absorption of oral drugs into the systemic circulation occurs via two primary processes: passive diffusion across the gut wall or active transport. Passive diffusion occurs when a high concentration of drug in the gut lumen moves across the gut wall to equalize drug concentration (or reach an equilibrium). Drug particles move through the gut wall into the portal vein, unassisted by cellular machinery. Active transport occurs when drugs are moved across the gut wall via transporter proteins that are normally used to absorb nutrients from food.

Extravascular Drug Administration

Drugs administered extravascularly can be divided into two categories: drugs intended for local effects and drugs intended for systemic effects. Drugs intended for local effects are often applied topically where the drug effect is needed. Examples of this include eye drops for glaucoma (e.g., latanoprost), dermal preparations for psoriasis (e.g., coal tar preparations), and nasal sprays for allergies (e.g., fluticasone nasal spray). Topical administration of a drug can produce therapeutic effects while minimizing systemic toxicity due to lower systemic exposure, but some topical formulations are designed to deliver a systemic dose (e.g., *Duragesic* patch). The extent of topical absorption is affected by many factors, including presence of open wounds on the skin (increased absorption) and the amount of drug applied. Drugs intended for systemic effects are generally administered to facilitate absorption to the circulatory system. Examples of drugs intended for systemic effects are oral tablets for seasonal allergies (e.g., loratadine), suppositories for fever (e.g., acetaminophen) and sublingual tablets for angina (nitroglycerin SL). Some percentage of a drug intended for systemic effect will move from the site of administration into the systemic circulation.

Dosage Form Dissolution and Drug Solubility

When an oral dosage form is ingested, it begins to dissolve in the gastrointestinal (GI) tract and the active ingredient is released from the dosage form which is typically a compressed tablet or a capsule. This is called <u>dissolution</u>. Dissolution is a function of the inactive matrix that is used to formulate the drug dosage form. Many pharmaceutical companies utilize biocompatible polymers to develop controlled release drug products with a predefined dissolution process. This can provide less variability in drug concentrations and reduce the dosing frequency. Most immediate release formulations dissolve and get absorbed rapidly, but some can be destroyed in the gut (<u>primarily by hydrolysis</u>, or lysis with water) making them less available for absorption. Drug formulations have been developed with protective coatings to <u>limit drug degradation</u> in the acidic medium of the stomach but permit dissolution in the basic medium of the intestine. Examples of drugs with these protective coatings include enteric coated formulations such as *Dulcolax* and *Entocort EC*.

If a drug has poor absorption, one of the methods used to increase the dissolution rate is to <u>reduce particle diameter</u>, which <u>increases surface area</u>. Drugs with very small particle diameters are referred to as <u>micronized</u>, which means the diameter was measured in micrometers, but may now refer to even smaller particle sizes measured in nanometers. Drugs with poor absorption that are micronized include progesterone and fenofibrate formulations. Without micronization, these drugs would be poorly absorbed. The <u>rate of dissolution</u> is described by the <u>Noyes-Whitney</u> equation.

Following dissolution, the drug that is released from the dosage form can be <u>dissolved</u> in GI fluids. The rate and extent to which the drug dissolves depends on the drug's <u>solubility</u>. Poorly soluble drugs are generally lipophilic, or lipid-loving. Freely soluble drugs are generally hydrophilic, or water-loving. As a drug moves through the GI tract, <u>only dissolved drug is absorbed into the bloodstream</u>. Thus poorly soluble drugs generally have poor systemic absorption, and highly soluble drugs often have good systemic absorption.

Bioavailability

The extent to which a drug is absorbed into the systemic circulation is called bioavailability. <u>Bioavailability is the percentage of drug absorbed from extravascular</u> administration (e.g., oral) <u>relative to intravascular administration</u> (e.g., IV). It is affected by absorption, dissolution, route of administration and other factors. Bioavailability is reported as a percentage from 0 to 100%. If the oral dose of a drug is the same as the IV dose (such as with levofloxacin or linezolid), then the bioavailability is 1, or 100%. With these two drugs, nearly 100% is absorbed and it is simple to convert from IV to PO dosing. In many hospitals, these drugs are automatically converted from IV to oral in the same dose under the hospital's <u>therapeutic interchange</u> or IV to PO protocol. With most drugs given orally, not all of the dose is absorbed, and the bioavailability is < 100%. In this case, the oral dose must be higher than the IV dose to produce the same effect. A drug with good absorption characteristics will generally have a high bioavailability (> 70%), while a drug with poor absorption will have low bioavailability (< 10%). Levofloxacin has high bioavailability; the oral and IV drug doses are the same. Bisphosphonates, like ibandronate, have low oral bioavailability, and the recommended IV dose (3 mg IV every 3 months) is substantially lower than the oral dose (150 mg PO monthly).

Bioavailability can be calculated using the area under the plasma concentration time curve, or AUC. The AUC represents the total exposure of drug following administration.

Absolute bioavailability, represented by F, is calculated using the following equation:

$$F\ (\%) = 100 \times \frac{AUC_{extravascular}}{AUC_{intravenous}} \times \frac{Dose_{intravenous}}{Dose_{extravascular}}$$

1. **A pharmacokinetic study of an investigational drug was conducted in healthy volunteers. Following an IV bolus dose of 15 mg, the AUC was determined to be 4.2 $^{mg \times hr}/_L$. Subjects were later given an oral dose of 50 mg and the AUC was determined to be 8 $^{mg \times hr}/_L$. Calculate the absolute bioavailability of the investigational drug. Round to the nearest whole number.**

$$F\ (\%) = 100 \times \frac{\dfrac{8\ mg \times hr}{L}}{\dfrac{4.2\ mg \times hr}{L}} \times \frac{15\ mg}{50\ mg} = 57\%$$

Different dosage forms of the same drug (e.g., tablet vs solution) may have different bioavailabilities. The formula below can be used to calculate an equivalent dose of a drug when the dosage form is changed:

$$\text{Dose of New Dosage Form} = \frac{\text{Amount Absorbed from Current Dosage Form}}{\text{F of New Dosage Form}}$$

DISTRIBUTION

Distribution is the process by which drug molecules move from the systemic circulation to the various tissues and organs of the body. Distribution occurs for intravascular and extravascular routes of administration and depends on the physical and chemical properties of the drug molecule and interactions with membranes and tissues throughout the body. In general, drugs distribute throughout the body based on the drug's lipophilicity, molecular weight, solubility, ionization status and the extent of protein binding. Factors that favor passage across membranes and greater drug distribution to the tissues include high lipophilicity, low molecular weight, unionized status and low protein binding. Human plasma contains many proteins, and albumin is the primary protein responsible for drug binding. If a drug is highly protein-bound (> 90%) and serum albumin is low (< 3.5 g/dL), then a higher percentage of the drug will be in the unbound form. Only the unbound (free) form is able to interact with receptors and exert therapeutic or toxic effects.

Though the unbound form of the drug is responsible for the therapeutic effect, many drug assays cannot differentiate between bound and unbound (active) drug. When assessing levels of highly protein bound compounds (e.g., phenytoin, calcium), a patient with low serum albumin will have more of the unbound (active) compound in the serum, and may experience therapeutic or even adverse effects at what appears to be a normal or below normal drug level. This issue can be overcome by obtaining a "free" phenytoin level or ionized calcium level. If the free phenytoin or ionized calcium is reported, there is no adjustment required for hypoalbuminemia. Otherwise, adjustment of the total level is required. The adjustment formulas allow us to determine what the concentration would be if albumin was normal. With hypoalbuminemia, the corrected level will be higher than the total level reported by the lab. The formulas to adjust these levels for low albumin are in the Calculations chapter (calcium) and Epilepsy/Seizures chapter (phenytoin).

2. A pharmacist receives a call from a provider asking for assistance with two patients in the clinic. Both patients have a seizure disorder and are taking phenytoin. Patient A is seizure free, but is experiencing symptoms of toxicity. Patient B has a higher phenytoin level and is doing fine. Which of the following statements are true of this scenario? (Select ALL that apply.)

LAB	REFERENCE RANGE	PATIENT A	PATIENT B
Phenytoin level (total)	10-20 mcg/mL	14.3	17.8
Albumin	3.5-5 g/dL	2.1	4.2

    a. Patient B's corrected phenytoin level will be lower than the total level reported.

    b. Patient A's corrected phenytoin level will be lower than the total level reported.

    c. Patient A's corrected phenytoin level will be higher than the total level reported.

    d. Patient A has a greater percentage of bound phenytoin.

    e. Patient A has a greater percentage of unbound phenytoin.

The correct answers are (c and e). The corrected phenytoin level for Patient A (using the formulas found in the Epilepsy/Seizure chapter) is 27.5 mcg/mL. Increased unbound phenytoin is contributing to the patient's side effects.

Volume of Distribution

The volume of distribution (V or Vd) is how large an area in the patient's body the drug has distributed into, and is based on the properties of that drug. The volume of distribution relates the amount of drug in the body to the concentration of drug measured in plasma (or serum). When a dose of drug is administered (e.g., 1,000 mg), a concentration (e.g., 12 mcg/mL) from a sample of biological fluid can be measured and reported. To convert between amounts and concentrations, a volume is needed. The equation for volume of distribution is:

> **SUBSCRIPTS IN FORMULAS**
>
> Vd can be written as V_d and ke can be written as k_e. In this chapter the subscripts are not used for Vd and ke for simplicity.

$$\text{Vd} = \frac{\text{Amount of drug in body}}{\text{Concentration of drug in plasma}}$$

The Vd is determined from the amount of drug in the body after the dose has been given.

---

3. A 500 mg dose of gentamicin is administered to a patient, and a blood sample is drawn immediately after administration. The concentration of gentamicin is measured as 25 mcg/mL (which is the same as 25 mg/L). What is the volume of distribution of gentamicin in this patient?

$$\text{Vd} = \frac{500 \text{ mg}}{25 \text{ mg/L}} = 20 \text{ L}$$

Vd is a theoretical value, which is why it is sometimes called the "apparent" volume of distribution. Vd is not an exact physical volume that has been measured, but is a helpful parameter because it is used to make inferences regarding the distribution of the drug throughout the body. The Vd of a drug can be very small, such as with aminoglycosides (Vd = ~14 L), or very large, such as with chloroquine (Vd = 15,000 L). Drugs that have a low Vd can be highly protein bound; the protein-binding limits diffusion through the lipid bilayer. More of the drug remains in the intravascular space (within the blood compartment). Chloroquine has an enormous Vd; chloroquine is lipophilic and becomes sequestered or stuck in the fatty tissue outside of the blood compartment.

METABOLISM

Metabolism is the process by which a drug is converted from its original chemical structure into other forms to facilitate elimination from the body. The original chemical form is called the parent drug and the additional forms are called metabolites. Metabolism can occur throughout the body; however, the gut and liver are primary sites for drug metabolism due to high levels of metabolic enzymes in these tissues.

Enzyme metabolism involves <u>Phase I reactions</u> (oxidation, reduction and hydrolysis), followed by <u>Phase II</u> (conjugation) reactions. Phase I reactions, which can terminate the activity of the drug or convert a prodrug into its active form, provide a reactive functional group on the compound that permits the drug to be attacked by Phase II enzymes. For example, breaking carbon bonds or <u>adding a hydroxyl group</u> to a drug will make the drug <u>more hydrophilic</u> – this means more of the drug will stay in the blood, the blood then passes through the kidneys, and the drug can be renally excreted. Glucuronidation and other Phase II reactions create compounds that are more readily excreted in the urine and bile. Cytochrome P450 (CYP450) enzymes, located mainly in the liver and intestines, metabolize the majority of drugs. Metabolism is described in detail in the Drug Interactions chapter.

Some drugs are partially or extensively metabolized by the liver before they reach the systemic circulation. This is called <u>first-pass metabolism</u>. First-pass metabolism <u>reduces the bioavailability</u> of an oral formulation. For a drug with extensive first-pass metabolism (e.g., propranolol), the IV dose will be much lower than the equivalent oral dose even if the oral formulation is well absorbed.

EXCRETION

Excretion is the process of irreversible removal of drugs from the body. Excretion can occur through the kidney (urine), liver (bile), gut (feces), lungs (exhaled air) and skin (sweat). The primary route of excretion for most drugs is the kidney (renal excretion). P-glycoprotein (P-gp) efflux pumps play a role in absorption and excretion of many drugs. Drugs affected by P-gp are discussed in the Drug Interactions chapter. Renal excretion is described in detail in the Renal Disease and Dosing Considerations chapter, and in the Calculations chapter.

Clearance and Area Under the Curve

Clearance (Cl) describes the rate of drug removal in a certain volume of plasma over a certain amount of time. Since the liver and kidneys clear most of the drug (and these organs do not usually speed up or slow down), most drug elimination occurs at a <u>steady rate</u> (called the <u>rate of elimination</u>). This is true of drugs that follow first-order kinetics (discussed later in the chapter). The term <u>clearance</u> is used to describe the efficiency of drug removal from the body. Clearance is generally described by the following equation:

$$Cl = \frac{\text{Rate of Elimination (Re)}}{\text{Concentration}}$$

4. A dose of gentamicin is given to a patient and urine is collected from the patient for 4 hours after drug administration. It is determined that 300 mg of gentamicin was eliminated during that time period, and the measured plasma concentration at the midpoint of the collection was 12.5 mg/L. Calculate the patient's gentamicin clearance.

$$Cl = \frac{300 \text{ mg of gentamicin} / 4 \text{ hours}}{12.5 \text{ mg/L}} = 6 \text{ L/hr}$$

or

$$Cl = \frac{300 \text{ mg of gentamicin}}{4 \text{ hours}} \times \frac{L}{12.5 \text{ mg}} = 6 \text{ L/hr}$$

The rate of elimination (Re) has units of mass per time (e.g., mg/hr), and drug concentration has units of amount per volume (e.g., mg/L); units of mass (mg) cancel out and clearance has units of volume per time (e.g., L/hr). Because the rate of elimination is difficult to assess clinically, another method is used to calculate the clearance of a drug from the body:

$$F \times Dose = Cl \times AUC$$

The area under the curve (AUC) is the most reliable measurement of a drug's bioavailability because it directly represents the amount of the drug that has reached the systemic circulation. The clearance for extravascular administration is calculated with this formula:

$$Cl = \frac{F \times Dose}{AUC}$$

Following IV administration, $F = 1$, which can be inserted into the previous equation to determine clearance for a drug given intravenously:

$$Cl = \frac{Dose}{AUC}$$

---

5. A patient is currently receiving 400 mg of gentamicin IV once daily and, based on measured serum concentrations, the AUC is determined to be 80 $^{mg \times hr}/_{L}$. Calculate the patient's gentamicin clearance.

$$Cl = \frac{400 \text{ mg}}{80 \frac{\text{mg} \times \text{hr}}{L}} = 5 \text{ L/hr}$$

ZERO-ORDER AND FIRST-ORDER PHARMACOKINETICS

Most drugs follow first-order elimination or "first-order kinetics", where a constant percent of drug is removed per unit of time. For example, a 325 mg dose of acetaminophen is eliminated at the same rate as a 650 mg dose. With zero-order elimination, a constant amount of drug (mg) is removed per unit of time no matter how much drug is in the body. The following table provides an example of zero-order and first-order elimination of a 2 gram dose of a drug.

Zero-Order vs First-Order Pharmacokinetics

HOUR	ZERO-ORDER			FIRST-ORDER		
	Amount of Drug (mg)	Percent Removed in Previous Hour	Amount (mg) Removed in Previous Hour	Amount of Drug (mg)	Percent Removed in Previous Hour	Amount (mg) Removed in Previous Hour
0	2,000			2,000		
1	1,700	0.1500	300	1,600	0.2	400
2	1,400	0.1765	300	1,280	0.2	320
3	1,100	0.2143	300	1,024	0.2	256

Michaelis-Menten Kinetics

Michaelis-Menten kinetics, or saturable kinetics, begin as first-order, but at higher concentrations the rate of metabolism approaches maximum capacity. At this point, any increase in dose leads to a disproportionate increase in drug concentration at steady state. The maximum rate of metabolism is defined as the Vmax (see figure). The concentration at which the rate of metabolism is half maximal is defined as the Michaelis-Menten constant (Km). At concentrations less than the Km, the rate of metabolism is first-order. At concentrations above the Km, the rate of metabolism becomes mixed (first-order and zero order) and at high concentrations relative to the Km, the rate of metabolism becomes zero order (e.g., Vmax). Phenytoin, theophylline and voriconazole have this type of saturable kinetics. Phenytoin experiences saturable kinetics even at drug concentrations within the accepted therapeutic range. Because of this, phenytoin dose adjustments should be made in small increments (30 - 50 mg) when the serum concentration is > 7 mg/L.

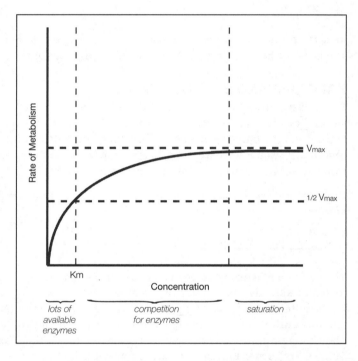

---

6. A patient has been using phenytoin 100 mg three times daily. The phenytoin level was drawn and found to be 8.8 mcg/mL (reference range 10 - 20 mcg/mL). The prescriber doubled the dose to 200 mg three times daily. The patient started to slur her words, felt fatigued and returned to the clinic. The level was repeated and found to be 23.7 mcg/mL. Which of the following statements is accurate regarding the most likely reason for the change in phenytoin level?

  a. Phenytoin half-life is reduced at higher doses.

  b. Phenytoin volume of distribution increases at higher doses.

  c. The patient's serum albumin level likely increased.

  d. Phenytoin bioavailability can decrease at higher doses.

  e. Phenytoin metabolism can become saturated at higher doses.

The correct answer is (e). The most likely explanation for the increase in phenytoin level is that when the dose was doubled, the metabolism became partially or completely saturated, and the steady-state level increased dramatically.

ELIMINATION RATE CONSTANT

The elimination rate constant (ke) is the fraction of the drug that is eliminated (cleared) per unit of time. It is calculated from the Vd and the clearance:

$$ke = \frac{Cl}{Vd}$$

---

7. A drug has the following pharmacokinetic parameters: Vd = 50 liters and Cl = 5,000 mL/hour. Calculate the elimination rate constant of the drug.

$$ke = \frac{5 \text{ L/hr}}{50 \text{ L}} = 0.1 \text{ hr}^{-1}$$

Be certain that the values have been converted to units that will properly cancel out in the equation. The ke is 0.1 hr^{-1} (meaning that 10% of the drug remaining is cleared per hour).

HALF-LIFE AND STEADY STATE

The time required for the drug concentration (and drug amount) to decrease by 50% is called the elimination half-life (t$_{1/2}$). For example, it takes 5 hours for theophylline concentrations to fall from 16 to 8 mg/L. Thus the half-life of theophylline is 5 hours. It would take 5 more hours for the drug concentration to fall from 8 mg/L to 4 mg/L. It is important to note that the half-life is independent of the drug concentration (for drugs exhibiting first-order kinetics).

Half-life is more clinically meaningful than ke. The half-life of a drug can be calculated from the ke:

$$t_{1/2} = \frac{0.693}{ke}$$

The half-life of a drug can be used to calculate the time required for drug washout or the time required to achieve steady-state (refer to table). The most clinically useful information is obtained from drug levels collected at steady state. When a fixed dose is administered at regular intervals, the drug accumulates until it reaches steady state where the rate of drug intake equals the rate of drug elimination. The time required to reach steady state depends on the elimination half-life of the drug. If the drug follows first-order kinetics (described previously) in a one-compartment distribution model (the drug is rapidly and evenly distributed throughout the body) and if a loading dose has not been given, it takes ~5 half-lives to reach steady state.

# OF HALF-LIVES	ELIMINATION % OF DRUG REMAINING IN THE BODY	ACCUMULATION % OF STEADY-STATE ACHIEVED
1	50	50
2	25	75
3	12.5	87.5
4	6.25	93.8
5	3.13	96.9

8. Tetracycline has a clearance of 7.014 L/hr and a volume of distribution of 105 L. Calculate the half-life of tetracycline (round to the nearest tenth) and the time required for elimination of greater than 95% of the drug from the body.

$$ke = \frac{Cl}{Vd} = \frac{7.014 \text{ L/hr}}{105 \text{ L}} = 0.0668 \text{ hr}^{-1}$$

$$t_{1/2} = \frac{0.693}{ke} = \frac{0.693}{0.0668 \text{ hr}^{-1}} = 10.4 \text{ hours}$$

Notice that <u>5 half-lives are required to eliminate more than 95% of the drug</u>. Thus, the time required is 5 x 10.4 hours = 52 hours.

---

9. A patient receives 200 mg of a drug with a half-life of 5 hours. How much of the drug still remains in the patient after 10 hours?

- 10 hours = 2 half-lives

- 50 mg of drug remains after 10 hours

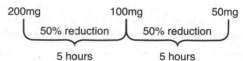

---

10. The serum concentration of Drug A over time is plotted in the figure. What is the half-life of Drug A?

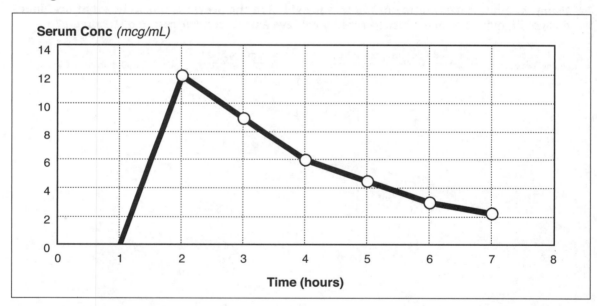

Choose two times (in hours) where the drug concentration has decreased by half to find the half-life.

- At 2 hours the concentration is 12 mcg/mL and at 4 hours the concentration is 6 mcg/mL.

- It takes 2 hours for the concentration to decrease by 50%, so the half-life is 2 hours.

LOADING DOSE

Administration of a loading dose may be necessary to rapidly achieve therapeutic concentrations of a drug. When the half-life of a drug is long relative to the frequency of administration, it will take several doses before steady state is achieved.

---

11. A patient will be started on daily oral digoxin for management of atrial fibrillation. The following pharmacokinetic parameters for oral digoxin are known: F = 0.6, Vd = 500 L and Cl = 120 L/day. When would steady state be reached? Round to the nearest day.

$$ke = \frac{Cl}{Vd} = \frac{120 \text{ L/day}}{500 \text{ L}} = 0.24 \text{ days}^{-1}$$

$$t_{1/2} = \frac{0.693}{ke} = \frac{0.693}{0.24 \text{ days}^{-1}} = {\sim}2.89 \text{ days}$$

Steady state would be achieved after 5 half-lives = 5 x 2.89 days = ~14 days. Therefore, it is beneficial to administer a loading dose to achieve the targeted levels more quickly in some cases.

$$\text{Loading Dose} = \frac{\text{Desired Concentration} \times Vd}{F}$$

---

12. Using the pharmacokinetic parameters provided in the previous question, what oral loading dose of digoxin is appropriate to rapidly achieve a peak concentration of 1.5 mcg/L?

$$\text{Loading Dose} = \frac{\text{Desired Concentration} \times Vd}{F} = \frac{1.5 \text{ mcg/L} \times 500 \text{ L}}{0.6} = 1{,}250 \text{ mcg or } 1.25 \text{ mg}$$

Questions

1. A patient is currently receiving ciprofloxacin 400 mg IV Q12H. The pharmacist recommends a conversion to oral therapy in preparation for hospital discharge. Ciprofloxacin tablets are available in 250, 500 and 750 mg strengths. If the bioavailability of ciprofloxacin is 70%, which of the following is the closest equivalent oral dose?

    a. 250 mg PO once daily
    b. 250 mg PO BID
    c. 500 mg PO BID
    d. 750 mg PO BID
    e. 250 mg PO Q8H

2. A patient will be started on gentamicin for an infection. The patient weighs 176 pounds and the volume of distribution of gentamicin is 0.25 L/kg. What is an appropriate IV loading dose to achieve a peak concentration of 10 mcg/mL?

    a. 2.5 mg IV
    b. 200 mg IV
    c. 440 mg IV
    d. 2,000 mg IV
    e. 2,500 mg IV

3. The AUC of an IV drug is 600 $^{mg\,x\,hr}/_L$. When the same dose is given orally, the AUC is 240 $^{mg\,x\,hr}/_L$. What is the drug's bioavailability?

    a. 2.5 mg IV
    b. 200 mg IV
    c. 440 mg IV
    d. 2,000 mg IV
    e. 2,500 mg IV

4. A patient is to be initiated on intravenous vancomycin for treatment of a bloodstream infection. Based on the patient's renal function the estimated clearance is 5 L/hr. What is an appropriate dose to achieve a 24 hour AUC of 400 $^{mg\,x\,hr}/_L$?

    a. 1 gram IV Q24H
    b. 2 grams IV Q12H
    c. 1 gram IV Q8H
    d. 500 mg IV Q12H
    e. 1 gram IV Q12H

5. A patient has been receiving phenytoin 300 mg PO QHS for one month for treatment of a seizure disorder. A plasma sample is obtained and measures 10 mg/L. If the goal is to achieve a steady-state concentration of 15 mg/L, which recommendation is most appropriate?

    a. Increase dose to 450 mg PO QHS.
    b. Increase dose to 330 mg PO QHS.
    c. Increase dose to 500 mg PO QHS.
    d. Reduce dose to 250 mg PO QHS.
    e. Maintain current dose.

6. A patient is currently receiving an intravenous infusion of theophylline at a rate of 40 mg/hr. The patient begins to experience nausea/vomiting and agitation and the decision is made to stop the infusion. If the estimated elimination rate constant is 0.17 hr^{-1}, approximately how long will it take for the medication to be completely removed (> 95%) from the body?

    a. 4 hours
    b. 7 hours
    c. 20 hours
    d. 48 hours
    e. 235 hours

Answers

1-c, 2-b, 3-c, 4-e, 5-b, 6-c

DRUG INTERACTIONS

BACKGROUND

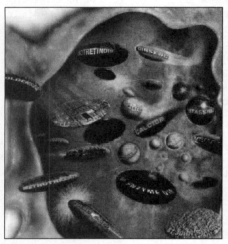

The cytochrome P450 enzymes (abbreviated as CYP) contain many forms, but about a dozen of them are involved in the metabolism of most drugs. This discussion begins with the most common isoenzymes that are well known to pharmacists. Enzyme metabolism involves Phase I reactions (oxidation, reduction and hydrolysis), followed by Phase II, which normally terminates the activity of the drug. (Phase I provides a reactive functional group on the compound that permits the drug to be attacked by the Phase II enzymes.) Drugs are considered by the body to be foreign, similar to a toxin, which must be eliminated either through a pump that pushes the drug back into the gut (for elimination in the feces via the P-gp efflux pumps – efflux means "to flow out"), or in the bile (which eliminates through the gallbladder) or through the kidney via renal elimination. For most drugs to be excreted renally, they must be first converted (metabolized) into a more hydrophilic form, which occurs by the process of enzyme metabolism, described here.

CYP enzymes are found in many cells, but are primarily located in the liver and intestines. The majority of medications (75%) are metabolized by CYP 450 enzymes, and of these, greater than 80% are metabolized by CYP 450 3A4 alone, or 3A4 and other enzymes.

All enzymes in the body work using an enzyme-substrate system. The enzyme is a protein that performs some action. The substrate is a chemical that is acted upon. Drug molecules, foods, and toxins are substrates for CYP enzymes. In the following figure, warfarin (the substrate) is joined with the CYP 2C9 enzyme in a manner similar to puzzle pieces. The enzyme converts the warfarin into an inactive metabolite (this is generally the case; however sometimes the conversion produces a toxic metabolite or an active or beneficial metabolite). The metabolite is generally more water-soluble than the

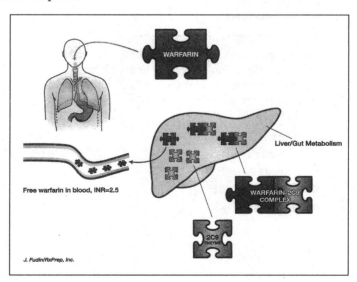

Free warfarin in blood, INR=2.5

WARFARIN

Liver/Gut Metabolism

WARFARIN-2C9 COMPLEX

2C9 ENZYME

J. Fudin/RxPrep, Inc.

parent compound, which facilitates excretion (exit from the body) via filtration through the kidneys. Warfarin causes an increase in the INR (a pharmacologic action), but warfarin metabolites do not. Thus <u>each time warfarin molecules pass through the liver, some are captured by the CYP 2C9 enzyme and converted into inactive metabolites</u>, leaving less warfarin to elicit its beneficial effects of increasing the INR. Most of this reaction occurs during the "<u>first pass</u>" when the drug (substrate) passes through the gut wall and liver prior to reaching the systemic circulation.

<u>Inducers</u> are compounds (many of which are drugs) that either increase the production of the enzyme (by increasing the expression of the gene sequence that codes for the enzyme), or, increase the activity of the enzyme. The net effect of an <u>inducer is to increase</u> the degree of drug <u>metabolism</u>, which results in <u>lower blood levels</u> of the substrate. In the figure to the right, rifampin has caused induction of the enzyme 2C9, which causes more of the enzyme to be present, resulting in more drug metabolism. The warfarin metabolism increases, less warfarin is available systemically, and the INR will decrease. <u>Rifampin</u> is used as an example here because it <u>is one of</u>

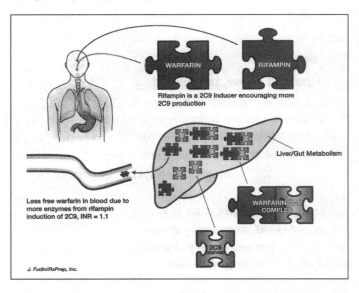

the strongest inducers and induces many enzymes [1A2, 2C8, 2C9, 2C19, 3A4 and the P-glycoprotein (P-gp) pump]. If rifampin is given to a patient on warfarin the warfarin dose will need to be increased between 100-300% to keep the INR therapeutic.

In the case of prodrugs, the inducer can increase an enzyme that is responsible for converting the substrate into a <u>more</u> active form (instead of a <u>less</u> active or inactive form). Prodrug conversion is technically referred to as bioactivation.

<u>Inhibitors</u> are compounds (many of which are drugs) that inhibit the activity of the enzyme. The <u>enzyme inhibition</u> results in <u>less drug metabolism</u>. The drug serum level (and therapeutic effect) will <u>increase</u>. This can result in drug toxicity. In the next figure, amiodarone, a 2C9 inhibitor is given to a patient using warfarin. Amiodarone inhibits the metabolism of warfarin. The warfarin level in the serum will increase

and there will be a corresponding increase in the INR. This interaction would cause a supratherapeutic INR with risk of bleeding. This reaction is well known to pharmacists; when amiodarone is given to a patient who has been using warfarin (which is done commonly) the reaction is anticipated and the INR dose is decreased 30-50%. If they are started concurrently, a lower dose of warfarin will be given.

In the case of a prodrug, an inhibitor of the enzyme involved in bioactivation would block the production of the active form of the drug. Inhibitors <u>decrease</u> the levels of the <u>prodrug's</u> active form.

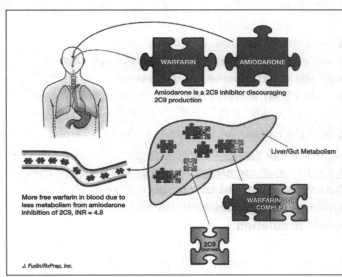

Prodrugs

As discussed above, <u>inducers decrease the concentration of the substrate – except with prodrugs</u>. <u>Inhibitors increase the concentration of the substrate – except with prodrugs</u>. Here, the opposite occurs because prodrugs are taken by the patient in an inactive form and are converted by bioactivation (enzyme conversion) into the active form. With prodrugs, inhibitors decrease the active form (the enzyme conversion is blocked) and inducers increase the active form (more enzymes available to convert more of the drug).

In the figure, codeine is an inactive substrate that requires metabolism by the 2D6 enzymes to various metabolites, which include morphine. Much of the analgesic efficacy of codeine is due to the morphine metabolite. When codeine is dispensed to a patient who has not had a pharmacogenomic analysis the pharmacist will have no way of predicting the dose required of the drug: the 2D6 enzyme is not inducible but is subject to a wide variability in 2D6 expression due primarily to ethnic variations in gene expression. Patients could be 2D6 ultrarapid metabolizers

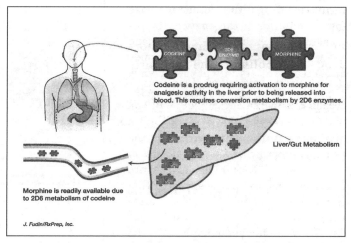

Codeine is a prodrug requiring activation to morphine for analgesic activity in the liver prior to being released into blood. This requires conversion metabolism by 2D6 enzymes.

Liver/Gut Metabolism

Morphine is readily available due to 2D6 metabolism of codeine

J. Fudin/RxPrep, Inc.

(UMs, producing a lot of the enzyme), extensive metabolizers (EMs, producing a lot of the enzyme but less than the UMs), intermediate metabolizers (IMs) or poor metabolizers (PMs). Even within ethnic groups there is wide variability in the gene expression. About 25% of drugs go through the 2D6 system, including many <u>pain and psychiatric</u> drugs. These two conditions, more than most others, typically involve multiple medications given concurrently for the same condition – which makes drug interaction analysis essential. Although diminished analgesic efficacy is a clinical concern, tragedies have occurred repeatedly because of the use of codeine in an UM, and resultant death from morphine overdose. In one case, a breastfeeding mother had taken codeine and (unknown to anyone) she was an UM of 2D6. Morphine passes readily into breast milk and the infant suffered fatal respiratory depression. Recently several children received a morphine overdose after receiving codeine for post-tonsillectomy pain.

In this figure the 2D6 inhibitor paroxetine blocks the conversion of codeine to morphine, resulting in lower analgesia.

<u>Practical Considerations</u>: Discontinuation of an inhibitor or inducer can have dangerous consequences. If a patient is using methadone and the dose has been increased to compensate for induction and the inducer is stopped, the methadone level could become lethal. In the warfarin and rifampin example, if the rifampin is stopped the warfarin levels would become supratherapeutic – and potentially very dangerous.

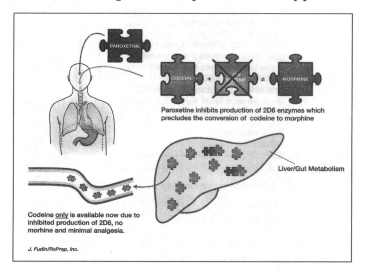

Paroxetine inhibits production of 2D6 enzymes which precludes the conversion of codeine to morphine

Liver/Gut Metabolism

Codeine <u>only</u> is available now due to inhibited production of 2D6, no morphine and minimal analgesia.

J. Fudin/RxPrep, Inc.

"Lag" Time for Inhibition and Induction

Inhibition of an enzyme is fast and at most takes a few days to take effect and will end quickly when the inhibitor is discontinued. Induction most often requires additional enzyme production, which takes time. The full effect may not be present for up to two weeks. When the inducer is stopped it could take 2-4 weeks for the induction to disappear completely; the enzymes have been produced and will die off based on their half-lives.

FDA DEFINITIONS		
TERM	**INDUCERS**	**INHIBITORS**
Strong	≥ 80% ↓ in AUC	≥ 5-fold ↑ in AUC
Moderate	50-80% ↓ in AUC	≥ 2 but < 5-fold ↑ in AUC
Weak	20-50% ↓ in AUC	≥ 1.25 but < 2-fold ↑ in AUC

P-glycoproteins (P-gp)

P-gp's are efflux transporters found in the gut and other organs. They pump drugs back into the gut (to exit out of the body). If a drug is subject to efflux, and the transporter is inhibited by a different drug, the substrate drug concentration will increase in the plasma. If an inducer is given that causes the production of more pumps, the blood levels of the substrate will decrease. The following figure is a schematic representation of this activity. Many of the P-gp drug interactions are not yet included in various pharmacy software packages, which warrants caution.

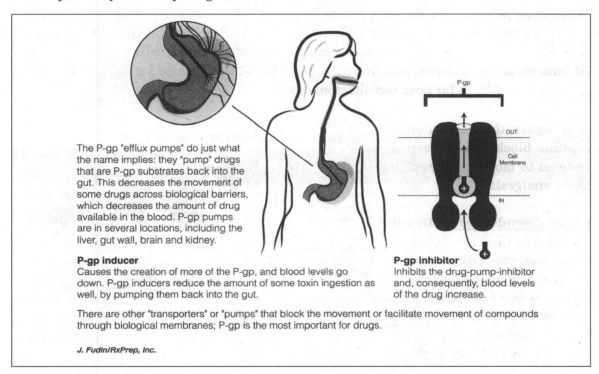

The P-gp "efflux pumps" do just what the name implies: they "pump" drugs that are P-gp substrates back into the gut. This decreases the movement of some drugs across biological barriers, which decreases the amount of drug available in the blood. P-gp pumps are in several locations, including the liver, gut wall, brain and kidney.

P-gp inducer
Causes the creation of more of the P-gp, and blood levels go down. P-gp inducers reduce the amount of some toxin ingestion as well, by pumping them back into the gut.

P-gp inhibitor
Inhibits the drug-pump-inhibitor and, consequently, blood levels of the drug increase.

There are other "transporters" or "pumps" that block the movement or facilitate movement of compounds through biological membranes; P-gp is the most important for drugs.

J. Fudin/RxPrep, Inc.

The following table provides a list of P-glycoprotein efflux pump substrates, inhibitors and inducers. This is not a complete list but includes many clinically important drugs.

P-gp Efflux Pump (Partial List)

STRONG INHIBITORS	STRONG INDUCERS	SUBSTRATES
Itraconazole	Rifampin	Aliskiren
Ketoconazole	Avasimibe	Colchicine
Verapamil	Carbamazepine	Dabigatran
Ritonavir	Phenytoin	Cyclosporine
Lopinavir/Ritonavir	St John's wort	Digoxin
Indinavir/Ritonavir	Tipranavir /Ritonavir	Fexofenadine
Conivaptan		Posaconazole
Clarithromycin		Ranolazine
Erythromycin		Rivaroxaban
Amiodarone		Saxagliptin
Quinidine		Tacrolimus

Cytochrome P 450 Substrates, Inducers, and Inhibitors (Partial List)

CLASS	SUBSTRATES	INDUCERS	INHIBITORS
3A4	alfentanil, alfuzosin, alprazolam, amiodarone, amlodipine, amprenavir, apixaban, aprepitant, atazanavir, apomorphine, aripiprazole, atazanavir, atorvastatin, buprenorphine, buspirone, carbamazepine, citalopram, clarithromycin, dapsone, delavirdine, diazepam, diltiazem, dronedarone, dutasteride, efavirenz, eplerenone, erythromycin, escitalopram, esomeprazole, estrogens, felbamate, fentanyl, fosamprenavir, haloperidol, hydrocodone, indinavir, ketoconazole, lansoprazole, levonorgestrel, lidocaine, lopinavir, losartan, lovastatin, mirtazapine, modafinil, nateglinide, nelfinavir, nevirapine, nifedipine, omeprazole, ondansetron, oxycodone, progesterone, propoxyphene, quinidine, rabeprazole, ranolazine, repaglinide, ritonavir, rivaroxaban, saquinavir, sildenafil, simvastatin, sirolimus, tadalafil, tipranavir, tramadol, trazodone, vardenafil, venlafaxine, verapamil, (R)-warfarin, zolpidem	carbamazepine, oxcarbazepine, phenytoin, phenobarbital, primidone, rifabutin, rifampin, rifapentine, smoking, St. John's wort	amiodarone, amprenavir, aprepitant, atazanavir, cimetidine, clarithromycin, cyclosporine, delavirdine, diltiazem, dronedarone, efavirenz, erythromycin, fluconazole, fluvoxamine, fosamprenavir, grapefruit juice, haloperidol, indinavir, isoniazid, itraconazole, ketoconazole, lidocaine, metronidazole, nefazodone, nelfinavir, nevirapine, posaconazole, propofol, quinidine, ranolazine, ritonavir, saquinavir, sertraline, telithromycin, verapamil, voriconazole
1A2	alosetron, amitriptyline, clozapine, cyclobenzaprine, duloxetine, estradiol, methadone, mirtazapine, olanzapine, pimozide, propranolol, rasagiline, ropinirole, theophylline, (R)-warfarin	carbamazepine, estrogen, phenobarbital, phenytoin, primidone, rifampin, ritonavir, smoking, St. John's wort	cimetidine, ciprofloxacin, clarithromycin, erythromycin, fluvoxamine, gemfibrozil, isoniazid, ketoconazole, zileuton

CLASS	SUBSTRATES	INDUCERS	INHIBITORS
2C8	amiodarone, pioglitazone, repaglinide, rosiglitazone	carbamazepine, phenobarbital, phenytoin, rifampin	atazanavir, gemfibrozil, irbesartan, ritonavir
2C9	carvedilol, celecoxib, diazepam, fluvastatin, phenytoin, ramelteon, (S)-warfarin	aprepitant, carbamazepine, phenobarbital, phenytoin, primidone, rifampin, rifapentine, St. John's wort	amiodarone, cimetidine, trimethoprim/ sulfamethoxazole, fluconazole, fluvoxamine, isoniazid, ketoconazole, metronidazole, voriconazole, warfarin, zafirlukast
2C19	clopidogrel, phenytoin, thioridazine, voriconazole	carbamazepine, phenobarbital, phenytoin, rifampin	cimetidine, esomeprazole, etravirine, efavirenz, fluoxetine, fluvoxamine, ketoconazole, modafinil, omeprazole, topiramate, voriconazole
2D6	amitriptyline, aripiprazole, atomoxetine, carvedilol, clozapine, codeine, desipramine, dextromethorphan, donepezil, doxepin, fentanyl, flecainide, haloperidol, hydrocodone, imipramine, lidocaine, meperidine, methadone, methamphetamine, mirtazapine, nortriptyline, oxycodone, propafenone, propoxyphene, propranolol, thioridazine, tramadol, trazodone, venlafaxine		amiodarone, cimetidine, darifenacin, duloxetine, fluoxetine, paroxetine, propafenone, quinidine, ritonavir, sertraline

SELECT DRUGS WITH SIGNIFICANT INTERACTIONS – WATCH FOR THESE

This is only some, but not all of the common drug interactions – refer to the individual chapters.

Amiodarone

The following medications must have the doses δεχρεασεδ 30 - 50% when starting amiodarone: digoxin, warfarin, quinidine and procainamide. Use lower doses of simvastatin, lovastatin and atorvastatin. Digoxin and warfarin are likely drugs to be given with amiodarone (for heart failure, and for arrhythmia). If the drugs are started concurrently the lower dose of the digoxin or warfarin is used. If warfarin or digoxin is on board first, the pharmacist must recognize the interaction and decrease the dose when amiodarone is started.

Digoxin

The digoxin level increases mostly due to a decline in renal function or hypokalemia. The drug interaction with amiodarone is described previously; although a minority of digoxin is hepatically cleared, enzyme interactions are important because digoxin is kept in a narrow therapeutic range. Another consideration with digoxin is additive drugs that lower heart rate (< 60 BPM). These are primarily beta blockers and the non-DHP calcium channel blockers (diltiazem and verapamil). Other drugs that lower heart rate are amiodarone, dexmedetomidine (Precedex), clonidine and opioids. Bradycardia is one of the symptoms of organophosphate poisoning, which occurs most commonly with farm workers due to pesticide exposure.

Grapefruit Juice/Fruit Interactions

Concurrent use with grapefruit and some drugs (including simvastatin, lovastatin and atorvastatin and CCBs) will cause an increase in the drug concentration which may or may not be clinically relevant. With some drugs, it could be quite clinically relevant. For example, with rivaroxaban or ticagrelor there would be increased bleeding risk and with QT prolongers there would be risk of torsades (lurasidone, quinidine, many others). If there is any risk, safety is paramount. Counsel the patient to avoid grapefruit. This is not a "gut interaction" problem; the drug metabolizing enzymes are inactivated.

QUICK STUDY TOOL FOR CYP INTERACTIONS
SEE MORE COMPLETE LIST OF INDUCERS AND INHIBITORS BELOW

PS PORCS (BIG INDUCERS)

Phenytoin

Smoking

Phenobarbital

Oxcarbazepine (and eslicarbazepine)

Rifampin (and rifabutin, rifapentine)

Carbamazepine (and is an auto-inducer)

St. John's wort

G ♥ PACMAN (BIG INHIBITORS)

Grapefruit

♥

PIs Protease Inhibitors (don't miss ritonavir) but check all PIs since many are potent inhibitors

Azole antifungals, the agents that are used oral and IV: fluconazole, itraconazole, ketoconazole, posaconazole, voriconazole and isavuconazonium

C – cyclosporine and cimetidine, the H_2RA that is the most difficult to use due to DIs and androgen-blocking effects (that can cause gynecomastia – swollen, painful breast tissue or impotence)

Macrolides (clarithromycin and erythromycin), not azithromycin, but DO include the related compound telithromycin

Amiodarone (and dronedarone)

Non-DHP CCBs diltiazem and verapamil

Lamotrigine & Valproate

This combination has high risk for severe rash and requires a careful titration with patient or parent monitoring. The interaction should not be missed by pharmacists because the rash may occur in children (seizures may require this combination) and the parents need to know that this is an emergency. Any inhibitor of lamotrigine will require a lower dose titration that is included in the packaging. Inducers require a higher dose; this would not cause as much risk with severe rash, but it would impair seizure control.

Monoamine Oxidase Inhibitors (MAO Inhibitors)

The non-selective MAO inhibitors have drug interactions that can cause serotonin syndrome, hypertensive crisis, and potentially be fatal. Monoamines that would have reduced metabolism with monoamine oxidase inhibitors include dopamine, epinephrine, norepinephrine, serotonin (and tyramine, which is also a monoamine and thus the problem with foods rich in tyramine). This is mostly a risk with the antidepressants (which raise levels of the monoamines) and other agents that have a similar effect. There is some degree of risk with the Parkinson agents; refer to the chapter for specifics.

- Do not use MAO inhibitors with ephedrine and analogs (pseudoephedrine, etc.), bupropion, buspirone, linezolid, lithium, meperidine, SSRIs, SNRIs, TCAs, tramadol, levodopa, mirtazapine, dextromethorphan, cyclobenzaprine (and other skeletal muscle relaxants), some of the triptans, St. John's wort, procarbazine, lorcaserin, and some others.

- The non-selective MAO inhibitors, the selegiline patch (at the two higher doses) and rasagiline should not be used with tyramine-rich foods, which include aged cheeses, air-dried meats, certain wines and beers and other foods which have been aged, fermented, pickled or smoked.

Hydrocodone and Tramadol

Both of these opioids are metabolized by 2D6; patients without this enzyme (~10% of Caucasians, others) or those on 2D6 inhibitors (fluoxetine, paroxetine, others) would be at increased risk of respiratory depression and, at the least, have increased side effects with hydrocodone. Tramadol requires conversion by 2D6 to the main active (analgesic) metabolite.

Codeine

Codeine is a partial prodrug for morphine and undergoes conversion by the 2D6 enzyme. Patients who have a lot of 2D6 will produce morphine rapidly, which could be fatal to the patient, or to the infant if the mother is using codeine and is breastfeeding. Patients who lack 2D6 or those on 2D6 inhibitors would have a lack of analgesic efficacy from the drug.

Fentanyl, Hydrocodone, Oxycodone, Methadone

These opioids are primarily metabolized by 3A4; patients on 3A4 inhibitors could suffer fatality. This is a black box warning for oxycodone (to avoid use with 3A4 inhibitors) and a product labeling warning for methadone. Using 3A4 inducers could cause a subtherapeutic response.

PDE5-Inhibitors

These are used for erectile dysfunction, pulmonary arterial hypertension, benign prostatic hypertrophy, and a few off label uses. They are contraindicated with nitrates due to severe hypotension. The nitrate most commonly used in the outpatient setting is the sublingual formulations, which are not dosed on a regular basis; it may be necessary to review further back in the dispensing history to find if the patient has the drug. Increasingly, patients use more than one pharmacy and the pharmacy computer will not contain the complete history unless it is collected at intake and entered manually.

These drugs cause orthostasis with headache and dizziness – and are used commonly in older men, who may also be taking alpha blockers for prostate enlargement – and which have similar side effects. The additive effect could be dangerous. When adding one class to another, it is done cautiously with lower dosing. Another complication would occur if too high a dose is given; the product labeling warns against using higher doses with 3A4 inhibitors as these are 3A4 substrates and this interaction would have the effect of providing a higher dose, with more dizziness, orthostasis, flushing and headache. These side effects are related to the action of the drug; blood is moving outward, towards the periphery.

Chelation Risk – Quinolones, Tetracyclines

Antacids, didanosine, sucralfate, bile acid resins, magnesium, aluminum, calcium, iron, zinc, multivitamins or any product containing these multivalent cations can chelate and inhibit absorption; the quinolone separation times vary. The tetracycline class (including doxycycline and minocycline) have the chelation interaction and require separation.

Statins

When the statin dose is increased, the risk is higher for muscle toxicity: muscle aches, soreness, or worse, including a rapid breakdown of muscle tissue (rhabdomyolysis), which can cause renal failure as the muscle "breakdown" products enter the blood and travel to the kidneys, causing damage. The statins that have the most risk for drug interactions are the ones that go through the highest degree of 3A4 metabolism: atorvastatin, simvastatin and lovastatin. Drugs that increase statin levels (including the inhibitor gemfibrozil, macrolides, others) will increase the risk.

Calcineurin Inhibitors (Tacrolimus & Cyclosporine)

The calcineurin inhibitors (CNIs) are important because they are the central immunosuppressants used chronically (with some combination of adjuvants) and they are subject to many drug interactions. Transplant patients are immune-suppressed and this results in illness: fungal infections may be treated with systemic azoles (which are inhibitors), bacterial infections may be treated with macrolides (most are inhibitors) or with rifampin (a strong inducer) or with aminoglycosides or other nephrotoxic drugs – and the calcineurin inhibitors themselves are nephrotoxic. Depression is common post-transplant; many of the SSRIs are inhibitors. Grapefruit juice is an absolute "do not take" with the CNIs. With transplant drugs the serum level needs to remain constant, around-the-clock, to reduce the risk of graft rejection.

ADDITIVE DRUG INTERACTIONS

These involve classes of drugs which may (or may not) pose a problem individually, but can become dangerous when used with other drugs that cause similar side effects. The MAO inhibitors discussed previously could be placed in this section since the toxic effect is generally additive. For example, a patient using fluoxetine 60 mg Q daily, bupropion 150 mg BID and (due to a recent infection) is given linezolid 600 mg IV Q 12. Consider the additive effect with substantial doses.

Bleeding Risk

Anticoagulants (warfarin, dabigatran, rivaroxaban, heparin and others) and antiplatelets (aspirin, dipyridamole, clopidogrel, prasugrel, ticagrelor) and other agents that increase bleeding risk have an additive effect: the more agents being used concurrently that increase bleeding risk, the higher the bleeding risk.

In some high-risk cases (such as a patient on warfarin who had a stroke) there may even be use of an anticoagulant with an antiplatelet (such as warfarin plus aspirin). However, the use of this combination may be inadvertent; the cardiologist may have prescribed the warfarin (or other anticoagulant) and the patient is using the aspirin OTC on their own – or is using it based on an old recommendation.

Other agents that increase bleeding risk which should be avoided in patients on the above agents, or at higher bleeding risk for other reasons (such as having had a previous bleed): OTC or prescription NSAIDs, SSRIs (and some SSRIs are inhibitors that will increase warfarin levels) and SNRIs, natural products, including ginkgo biloba (commonly used agent that inhibits platelet activating factor and must be stopped in advance of surgery); ginkgo biloba increases bleeding risk with no effect on the INR. Ginkgo is one of the "5 Gs" that can raise bleeding risk: ginkgo biloba, garlic, ginger, glucosamine and ginseng. Other natural products with known risk for bleeding include fish oils (at higher doses), vitamin E and willow bark. Others included in the warfarin package insert are listed in the Anticoagulation chapter.

Hyperkalemia Risk

Potassium is renally cleared; severe renal disease causes hyperkalemia by itself. The largest increases among the drugs listed here would be expected from the aldosterone blockers (spironolactone and eplerenone) since aldosterone regulates potassium excretion; if aldosterone is blocked, hyperkalemia is a significant risk. The American Heart Association has issued recommendations to minimize the risk of hyperkalemia in patients treated with these agents, which includes avoiding use if the potassium is high at baseline (> 5 mEq/L), monitoring renal function and avoiding the use of concurrent NSAIDs. This is discussed further in the Heart Failure chapter.

- Additive potassium accumulation: ACE inhibitors, ARBs, aliskiren, amiloride, triamterene, eplerenone, spironolactone, salt substitutes (KCl), and the drospirenone-containing oral contraceptives.

- Additional drugs that can cause or worsen hyperkalemia include the calcineurin inhibitors (tacrolimus and cyclosporine), canaglifozin, pentamidine and sulfamethoxazole/trimethoprim, due to the trimethoprim component.

CNS Depression

CNS side effects are caused by drugs that enter the CNS (lipophilic) and primarily involve drugs that cause sedation (somnolence), dizziness, confusion (↓ cognitive function) and altered consciousness. CNS side effects can be activating (such as with the use of stimulants), but are primarily sedating. CNS depressants that are legal and dispensed in the pharmacy are one of the top causes of automobile accidents. It is not only alcohol and illicit drug use that causes car crashes. In some cases, the two are mixed, such as the use of opioids and illicit drugs, or opioids taken with alcohol. Any agent will be worse if dosed higher and taken with other CNS depressants. Pain drugs, primarily opioids, cause more accidental death (by overdose) than deaths due to car accidents, whatever the cause. There is regional variance in the risk of death from opioids: this occurs everywhere, but the Southwest and Appalachia region are the hardest-hit. The rate of drug-related deaths more than quadrupled between 1999 and 2010 in several states, including Kentucky, Indiana and Iowa.

- Additive CNS effects: alcohol, most pain medications (all of the opioids, some of the NSAIDs, other pain drugs), skeletal muscle relaxants, anticonvulsants, benzodiazepines, barbiturates, hypnotics, mirtazapine, trazodone, dronabinol, nabilone, propranolol, clonidine, and others, and many illicit substances.

QT Prolongation & Torsade De Pointes (TdP)

QT risk drugs and QT risk conditions are listed in the Arrhythmia chapter. The risk of drug-induced TdP is low relative to other drug-induced effects, but the lethality is high. TdP is always preceded by QT prolongation; yet it is only within the last ten years that the FDA set a requirement that new drugs had to be tested for the effect on the QT interval. In some cases, the drug (alone) has high QT risk (such as with dofetilide and sotalol) but with many others with lower risk the danger develops when the risk is additive, especially in an at-risk patient, such as those with underlying cardiac disease or long QT syndrome. Most commonly, the effect is additive.

Ototoxicity

Many other additive interactions are described in the individual chapters, but ototoxicity is not described elsewhere and is included here. Ototoxicity is disturbing to patients: hearing loss can cause social isolation and impair relationships. Tinnitus can become chronic and cause a large decrease in the quality of life. A loss of equilibrium and dizziness, including increased falls, can decrease confidence and cause injury. The risk increases with concurrent ototoxic drugs, higher drug levels and the duration of exposure. Drugs with known ototoxic risk include:

- Salicylates, vancomycin, aminoglycosides, cisplatin and loop diuretics. If mefloquine (anti-malarial agent) causes tinnitus, it will be present with other symptoms of neurotoxicity.

Additive ototoxic drugs are given inpatient and audiology should be consulted to conduct a baseline hearing exam and throughout treatment on a scheduled basis. With some drugs an audiology consult is ordered after a certain period of time when damage would be expected.

Practice Questions

1. Drug A is a substrate of enzyme X. Drug B is an inducer of enzyme X. A patient has been using Drug A with good results. The patient has now started therapy with Drug B. What will happen to the concentration of Drug A?

   a. Increase
   b. Decrease
   c. Stay the Same
   d. There is not enough information given
   e. None of the above

2. Drug A is a substrate of enzyme X. Drug B is an inhibitor of enzyme X. A patient has been using Drug A with good results. The patient has now started therapy with Drug B. What will happen to the concentration of Drug A?

   a. Increase
   b. Decrease
   c. Stay the Same
   d. This is not enough information given
   e. None of the above

3. Drug A is a substrate of enzyme X. Drug A is also an inducer of enzyme Y. Drug B is a substrate of enzyme Y. Drug B is also an inhibitor of enzyme X. When these drugs are both administered, what will happen to the concentrations of Drug A and Drug B?

   a. Levels of both Drug A and Drug B will increase
   b. Levels of Drug A will increase and levels of Drug B will decrease
   c. Levels of Drug A will decrease and levels of Drug B will increase
   d. Levels of Drug A will increase and levels of Drug B will stay the same
   e. There is not enough information given.

4. A patient with heart failure is using many medications, including digoxin, warfarin and pravastatin. She is started on amiodarone therapy. Which statement is correct?

   a. The INR will increase; the warfarin dose will need to be reduced
   b. The digoxin will increase; the digoxin dose will need to be reduced
   c. The pravastatin level will increase; the pravastatin dose will need to be reduced
   d. A and B
   e. All of the above

5. A patient has been using warfarin for DVT treatment. She was hospitalized for afibrillation and started on amiodarone therapy. While hospitalized, she developed an infection and was prescribed trimethoprim/sulfamethoxazole and ketoconazole. Which of the following agents will increase the INR and could result in bleeding?

   a. Amiodarone
   b. Trimethoprim/sulfamethoxazole
   c. Ketoconazole
   d. A and B
   e. All of the above

6. The pharmacist is dispensing a prescription for ciprofloxacin. The only medication the patient is using is a daily multivitamin, which she takes with breakfast and an iron supplement, which she takes with dinner. She has yogurt or cheese every day with lunch. Which counseling statement is correct?

   a. She will need to separate the ciprofloxacin from the multivitamin
   b. She will need to separate the ciprofloxacin from the iron supplement
   c. She will need to separate the ciprofloxacin from the yogurt and cheese
   d. A and B
   e. All of the above

7. A major drug interaction can occur with the use of grapefruit juice and which of the following medications?

   a. Atorvastatin and Amiodarone
   b. Celecoxib and Felodipine
   c. Lovastatin and Lithium
   d. Levetiracetam and Topiramate
   e. Duloxetine and Mirtazapine

Answers

1-b, 2-a, 3-b, 4-d, 5-e, 6-e, 7-a

PHARMACOGENOMICS

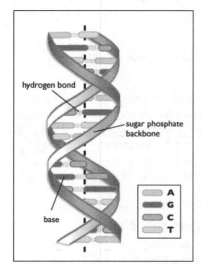

We gratefully acknowledge the assistance of Joseph D. Ma, PharmD, FCP, Associate Professor of Clinical Pharmacy at the University of California San Diego, Skaggs School of Pharmacy and Pharmaceutical Sciences, in preparing this chapter.

BACKGROUND

Pharmacogenomics is the science which examines <u>inherited variations in genes</u> that dictate drug response and explores ways that the variations can be used <u>to predict</u> whether a patient will have a <u>good, bad, or no response to a drug</u>. It is estimated that genetic factors contribute between 20 – 40% of the differences in drug metabolism and response between patients. The goal of pharmacogenomics is to identify these factors and develop optimized treatment strategies to improve efficacy while reducing adverse reactions. Pharmacogenomics is called "<u>personalized medicine</u>" where drugs are tailored for a person's unique <u>genotype</u>. Since pharmacogenomic information and testing recommendations are rapidly changing, two suggested references to acquire up-to-date information are the FDA Table of Pharmacogenomic Biomarkers in Drug Labeling and Clinical Pharmacogenetics Implementation Consortium (CPIC).

DEFINITIONS

<u>Deoxyribonucleic acid (DNA)</u>: Deoxyribonucleic acid (DNA) is the genetic information, or characteristics of each individual, that has been inherited from both parents. The DNA is composed of long macromolecules that are the main components of the chromosomes. It consists of two long chains of nucleotides twisted into a double helix and joined together by hydrogen bonds.

<u>Chromosome</u>: The DNA is wrapped around proteins and packaged into chromosomes, which appear as threadlike structures. In a human cell there are usually 46 chromosomes, organized into two pairs of 23 – one pair has been inherited from the father and the other pair has been inherited from the mother.

<u>Nucleotides</u>: These consist of a nitrogenous base [adenine (A), thymine (T), guanine (G) and cytosine (C)], a five-carbon sugar, and a phosphate group. Nucleotides are the building blocks of DNA. In DNA, A binds to T and G binds to C, holding the double-helix form together. Similarly, RNA, which is single-stranded, has four bases but uracil (U) replaces the thymine (T).

Gene: The DNA can be divided into specific sequences of nucleotides that code for a single protein. The sequences of the nucleotides are called genes, which are the code, or instructions, for the synthesis of RNA, which is then translated into proteins. The proteins make up the life form; this is why the gene is called the basic unit of heredity.

Allele: The specific form of a gene. The genes have different forms because each person has two alleles (one from the mother and one from the father) for each gene. Alleles are also described as wild-type or variants. A wild-type allele is the usual (or normal) sequence that is most prevalent in humans. A mutation and/or polymorphism is referred to as a variant allele.

Genotype: The genetic constitution of an organism or cell. The specific 2 alleles inherited for a specific gene. A wild-type genotype is when both alleles are the usual (or normal) sequence. If one of the alleles is a variant, then the individual has a heterozygous genotype. If both of the alleles are variants, then the individual has a homozygous genotype.

Phenotype: A phenotype is the set of observable traits of an individual that results from his/her particular genotype. As an example, variations in the cytochrome P450 2D6 gene may result in phenotypes of ultra-rapid metabolizers (UMs), intermediate metabolizers (IMs), and poor metabolizers (PMs) of particular drugs.

Haplotype: A group of genes or DNA variations that exist on the same chromosome and are likely to be inherited together.

Polymorphism: An inherited variation in the DNA sequence. Polymorphisms occur with fairly high frequency, but most do not result in a change in phenotype. Polymorphisms most commonly involve variation at a single base pair within the DNA. This is called a single nucleotide polymorphism (SNP, pronounced "snip"). Polymorphisms can also involve larger stretches of DNA called structural variations (SV). Human leukocyte antigens (HLAs) have structural variations which are clinically significant. HLAs alert the immune system to target a pathogen for destruction, and certain HLA variants put patients at higher risk for hypersensitivity reactions.

SINGLE NUCLEOTIDE POLYMORPHISMS (SNPS) AND NOMENCLATURE

SNPs are the most common genetic polymorphisms in DNA. They occur every 100 – 300 base pairs and account for about 90% of all differences in human DNA. Whether the SNP has an effect on function (and subsequent action of a drug) depends on the location and presence within a patient's DNA. Pharmacogenomic testing can identify a specific SNP, with the results of such testing being used to predict what type of response a patient may have to a drug. Numerous nomenclatures are used to describe SNPs. One example of a SNP can be described by the following ABCB1 3435 C>T. The ABCB1, or adenosine-triphosphate binding cassette protein B1, are letters and numbers that refers to a specific gene. ABCB1 is the gene that codes for drug transporter, P-glycoprotein. The numbers 3435 refer to the location of the SNP on the DNA or gene. The letter C (cytosine) is the original nucleotide, while the next letter T (thymine) is the variant nucleotide.

EXAMPLES OF CHANGES IN DRUG RESPONSE OR TOXICITY

Genetic polymorphisms can significantly alter the response or toxicity of a drug. These examples of genetic polymorphisms are well known:

- Codeine and CYP2D6: Based on the presence or absence of CYP2D6 polymorphisms, patients can be CYP2D6 ultra-rapid metabolizers (UMs), extensive metabolizers (EMs), intermediate metabolizers (IMs) or poor metabolizers (PMs). Codeine is metabolized to morphine by CYP2D6; morphine provides the analgesic (e.g., pain relief) and toxic (e.g., oversedation, nausea/vomiting) effects. UMs will have higher morphine levels while PMs will have low, or absent morphine levels. UMs will likely experience more morphine-related toxicity. PMs will likely experience a lack of efficacy resulting in a lack of pain relief.

- Carbamazepine and HLA-B*1502: If this polymorphism is present, the risk of a severe skin reaction to carbamazepine increases from <1% (wild type) to 5-10%.

- Trastuzumab and HER2/neu: If the breast cancer tumor overexpresses HER2, trastuzumab *(Herceptin)* and ado-trastuzumab *(Kadcyla)* will be efficacious.

Drugs With Required/Strongly Recommended Genetic Testing

The Drugs With Pharmacogenomic Testing table includes drugs where genetic testing is routinely done and/or required according to the product labeling. Following this list are the drugs known to have genetic factors, but where standardized testing is not yet routine.

DRUG	INDICATIONS	TESTING AND/OR RECOMMENDATIONS	CLINICAL SIGNIFICANCE
Abacavir *(Ziagen)* Abacavir + lamivudine *(Epzicom)* Abacavir + zidovudine + lamivudine *(Trizivir)* Abacavir + dolutegravir + lamivudine *(Triumeq)*	HIV	HLA-B*5701 If test positive, do not use abacavir.	Serious and fatal hypersensitivity reactions have occurred. Test for HLA-B*5701 prior to starting abacavir. Patients who are HLA-B*5701 positive are at ↑ risk for a hypersensitivity reaction. Contraindicated in HLA-B*5701 positive patients. Discontinue as soon as a hypersensitivity reaction is suspected.
Clopidogrel *(Plavix)*	Acute coronary syndromes, PAD, stroke	CYP2C19 genotype Consider alternative treatment in patients identified as CYP2C19 poor metabolizers (have 2C19*2 or *3 alleles).	The CYP2C19*1 allele is fully functional (able to convert clopidogrel to the active metabolite) whereas *2 and *3 alleles are reduced/loss of function alleles, A CYP2C19 poor metabolizer will have a loss of function allele. Poor metabolizers exhibit higher cardiovascular event rates than patients with normal CYP2C19 function.
Carbamazepine *(Tegretol,* others)	Seizures, neuralgia	HLA-B*1502 in Asian patients. If test positive, do not use carbamazepine unless benefit clearly outweighs risk.	Serious skin reactions, including Stevens-Johnson syndrome (SJS) and toxic epidermal necrolysis (TEN), have occurred. Patients with the HLA-B*1502 allele are at an ↑ risk of these skin reactions and this allele is more common in Asian populations. Testing for HLA-B*1502 should be done in Asian patients prior to starting carbamazepine.
Trastuzumab *(Herceptin)*, Ado-trastuzumab emtansine *(Kadcyla)*, Lapatinib *(Tykerb)*, Pertuzumab *(Perjeta)*	Breast and gastric cancer	HER2 protein overexpression Must be positive (2+ or 3+) to use drug	HER2 overexpression required for use. The test must be 2+ or 3+ positive on immunohistochemical (IHC) testing. HER2 negative status and those with weakly positive (1+) tumors do not respond well to therapy.
Cetuximab *(Erbitux)*, Panitumumab *(Vectibix)*	Colorectal cancer	KRAS If positive for a KRAS mutation on codon 12 or 13, do not use drugs	These agents are not effective in patients with colorectal cancer who have a KRAS mutation (~40% of patients). Therefore, only patients who are KRAS mutation-negative (wild type) should receive these medications.
Afatinib *(Gilotrif)*, Cetuximab *(Erbitux)*, Erlotinib *(Tarceva)*, Panitumumab *(Vectibix)*	Non-small cell lung cancer	EGFR If EGFR protein positive, can use these drugs	These medications have enhanced effectiveness in tumors expressing EGFR or who have EGFR exon 19 deletion or exon 21 substitution mutations.
Imatinib *(Gleevec)*	Gastrointestinal stromal tumors (GIST)	Kit (CD117) If positive, can use drug	Patients with Kit (CD117) positive gastrointestinal stromal tumors (GIST) will respond to therapy.

Drugs With Required/Strongly Recommended Genetic Testing Continued

DRUG	INDICATIONS	TESTING AND/OR RECOMMENDATIONS	CLINICAL SIGNIFICANCE
Imatinib *(Gleevec)*, Dasatinib *(Sprycel)*, Nilotinib *(Tasigna)*, PONATinib *(Iclusig)*, Bosutinib *(Bosulif)*	Chronic myelogenous leukemia (CML)	BCR-ABL Must be BCR-ABL positive to use drug	In CML, the Philadelphia chromosome is a specific abnormality which leads to a fusion protein of abl (Abelson) with bcr (breakpoint cluster region), termed BCR-ABL.
Imatinib *(Gleevec)*	Myelodysplastic/ myeloproliferative disease (MDS/ MPD)	Platelet-derived growth factor receptor (PDGFR) If PDGFR gene rearrangement positive, can use drug	Adults patients with myelodysplastic/ myeloproliferative diseases (MDS/MPD) associated with PDGFR gene rearrangements will respond to imatinib.
Maraviroc *(Selzentry)*	HIV	HIV tropism with Trofile test If CCR5-positive, can use drug	Adult patients infected with only CCR5-tropic HIV-1 should use maraviroc. Do not use in patients with dual/mixed or CXCR-4-tropic HIV-1 disease.
Rituximab *(Rituxan)*, Obinutuzumab *(Gazyva)*, Ofatumumab *(Arzerra)*, Tositumomab *(Bexxar)*	Non-Hodgkin lymphomas, Hodgkin lymphoma, chronic lymphocytic leukemia, etc.	B-Cell CD20 Expression If positive, can use drug	Directed against CD-20 receptor site on malignant cells but also normal lymphocytes resulting in efficacy and toxicity with antibody dependent cell mediated cytotoxicity (ADCC), complement fixation, natural killer cell activation and apoptosis.
Simeprevir *(Olysio)*	Hepatitis C	NS3 Q80K polymorphism If positive, do not use drug	Screen patients with HCV genotype 1a infection for the NS3 Q80K polymorphism at baseline. Patients with this polymorphism will not respond and alternative therapy should be given.
Crizotinib *(Xalkori)*, Ceritinib *(Zykadia)*	Locally advanced or metastatic non-small cell lung cancer (NSCLC)	Anaplastic lymphoma kinase (ALK) Must be ALK positive to use the drug	Tyrosine kinase inhibitors indicated for the treatment of patients with locally advanced or metastatic NSCLC that is ALK positive as detected by an FDA-approved test.
Vemurafenib *(Zelboraf)*, Dabrafenib *(Tafinlar)*, Trametinib *(Mekinist)*	Unresectable or metastatic melanoma	BRAF V600E or BRAF V600K mutation Must be positive to use drug	These agents are contraindicated in patients with wild-type BRAF melanoma.
Azathioprine, Mercaptopurine	Solid organ cancers, leukemia, Crohn's disease, ulcerative colitis	Thiopurine methyltransferase (TPMT) If positive for loss of function TPMT allele, find alternative treatment or start at a very low dose	Patients with a genetic deficiency of TPMT may have ↑ risk of myelosuppressive effects; those patients with low or absent TPMT activity are at risk for severe myelotoxicity; occurs in ~10% of patients.
Lenalidomide *(Revlimid)*	Myelodysplastic syndrome (MDS)	5q deletion If positive, can use drug	Patients with 5q deletion MDS have ↑ risk of hematologic toxicity (neutropenia and thrombocytopenia) from their MDS but also a better response to lenalidomide therapy.

Drugs With Required/Strongly Recommended Genetic Testing Continued

DRUG	INDICATIONS	TESTING AND/OR RECOMMENDATIONS	CLINICAL SIGNIFICANCE
Ivacaftor *(Kalydeco)*	Cystic fibrosis transmembrane conductance regulator (CFTR)	CFTR G551D, G1244E, G1349D, G178R, G551S, S1251N, S1255P, S549N, S549R, R117H mutation carriers If positive, can use drug	Cystic fibrosis patients age two years and older who have the specific mutations in the CFTR gene.
Denileukin diftitox *(Ontak)*	Cutaneous T-cell lymphoma	IL2RA (CD-25 antigen) If positive, can use drug	Directed against CD-25 receptor site on positive malignant cells.

Select Drugs Where Pharmacogenomic Testing Should Be Considered

DRUG	INDICATIONS	TESTING AND/OR RECOMMENDATIONS	CLINICAL SIGNIFICANCE
Allopurinol *(Aloprim, Zyloprim)*	Gout	HLA-B*5801 Consider testing prior to starting therapy in high-risk individuals (Korean patients with significant renal impairment or those of Han Chinese or Thai ancestry).	Increased risk of severe skin reactions (SJS) in patients testing positive for HLA-B*5801. Discontinue at 1st appearance of skin rash or other signs which may indicate an allergic reaction.
Codeine	Pain, cough	CYP2D6 Consider testing. Per CPIC recommendations: In CYP2D6 ultra-rapid metabolizers, avoid codeine due to potential for toxicity. In CYP2D6 poor metabolizers, avoid codeine due to lack of efficacy.	Codeine (a prodrug) is metabolized to morphine via CYP2D6. Ultra-rapid metabolizers may have exaggerated response due to extensive conversion to morphine metabolite. Over-production of morphine can result in $\uparrow$ CNS effects, including an $\uparrow$ risk of respiratory depression. Case reports exist of infant deaths due to nursing mothers who are ultra-rapid metabolizers taking codeine for pain. Excessive amounts of morphine were present in breastmilk and passed on to the infant resulting in respiratory depression and death. See more information in Pain chapter.
Warfarin *(Coumadin, Jantoven)*	Clot prevention	CYP 2C9 and VKORC1 If not testing, use caution by selecting a low starting dose, increasing slowly, and monitoring INR frequently. If the test indicates variations, a safer, lower starting dose can be selected.	Increased bleeding risk due to decreased function alleles and haplotypes (CYP 2C9*2 and CYP 2C9*3) and VKORC1 G > A variant.
Capecitabine *(Xeloda)*, Fluorouracil *(Adrucil)*	Breast, colon, pancreatic cancers	Dihydropyrimidine dehydrogenase (DPD) deficiency If positive, do not use drug	A deficiency in DPD can $\uparrow$ toxicity (diarrhea, neutropenia, neurotoxicity) associated with these agents. The incidence is low but potentially fatal.

Drugs With Required/Strongly Recommended Genetic Testing Continued

DRUG	INDICATIONS	TESTING AND/OR RECOMMENDATIONS	CLINICAL SIGNIFICANCE
Phenytoin (*Dilantin*), Fosphenytoin (*Cerebyx*)	Seizures	HLA-B*1502 for Asian patients If positive, do not use unless benefit clearly outweighs risk.	Strong association between developing Stevens-Johnson Syndrome (SJS) and Toxic Epidermal Necrolysis (TEN) and the presence of the HLA-B*1502 allele.
Atomoxetine (*Strattera*)	ADHD	CYP2D6 genotype No recommendation, but use caution.	Atomoxetine concentrations have been measured at 5-fold higher concentrations in poor metabolizers versus extensive metabolizers. This can lead to an increase in adverse effects. See ADHD chapter.
Fluorouracil, Methotrexate	Lymphomas, leukemias, psoriasis, RA, others	Methylenetetrahydrofolate reductase (MTHFR) If positive, consider reducing dose	MTHFR polymorphisms influence the metabolism of folates and could modify the pharmacodynamics of antifolates and many other drugs whose metabolism, biochemical effects, or target structures require methylation reactions.
Irinotecan (*Camptosar*)	Colon cancer and other cancers	UGT1A1*28 If positive, consider reducing dose	Patients homozygous for the UGT1A1*28 allele are at ↑ risk of neutropenia; initial one-level dose reduction should be considered. Heterozygous carriers of the UGT1A1*28 allele may also be at risk, however, most patients tolerate normal starting doses.
Many pain and psych drugs – see Drug Interactions chapter	Various psychiatric disorders	CYP2D6 genotype If poor metabolizer, consider reducing dose	CYP2D6 poor metabolizers are at ↑ risk of variable response to therapies; reduce dosage by 25% for some antipsychotics and reduce doses when co-administered with CYP2D6 inhibitors.
Cisplatin (*Platinol*)	Several cancers	TPMT If positive, can use drug with caution and monitor closely for ototoxicity	TPMT intermediate or poor metabolizers are at ↑ risk for ototoxicity, particularly in children. All patients undergoing cisplatin treatment have a risk of ototoxicity; recommend audiometric testing.
Tamoxifen (*Nolvadex, Soltamox*)	Breast cancer	Estrogen receptor 1 If positive, can use drug	Available evidence indicates that patients whose tumors are estrogen receptor positive are more likely to benefit from tamoxifen therapy.
Chloroquine (*Aralen*), Dapsone (*Aczone*), Methylene blue, Nitrofurantoin, Primaquine, Probenecid, Quinidine, Quinine and Sulfonamides	Infectious diseases	Glucose-6-phosphate dehydrogenase (G6PD) deficiency If positive, can use drug with caution and monitor blood counts	Hemolytic anemia is more common in G6PD deficient patients.
Isoniazid	Tuberculosis	NAT1, NAT2 If positive, can use drug with caution and monitor liver function monthly	Neuropathy and liver toxicity more common in NAT1/NAT2 slow acetylators.

PRACTICE QUESTIONS

1. A 15 year-old female of Asian ancestry presents with a seizure disorder. The physician plans to initiate carbamazepine therapy, but first orders genetic testing in order to determine if she is at an increased risk for the following adverse drug reaction:

    a. Gastrointestinal bleeding
    b. Hemorrhage
    c. Serious skin reactions
    d. Neuropathy
    e. Tendon rupture

2. When initiating carbamazepine in a patient of Asian descent, which is the appropriate allele and/or polymorphism to test for?

    a. HLA-B *5701
    b. HLA-B *1502
    c. CYP450 2C9
    d. HER2
    e. TPMT activity

3. Trastuzumab is indicated in cancers with an overexpression of this gene:

    a. ALK
    b. BCR ABL+
    c. BRAF
    d. HER2
    e. BRCA2

4. A patient was started on warfarin 5 mg once daily. She presents to the clinic 2 weeks later and is found to have an INR of 4.7 with excessive oral bleeding when she brushes her teeth. Which of the following most likely describes the patient's genotype?

    a. CYP 2C9 *1/*1
    b. CYP 2C9 *3/*3
    c. CYP 3A4 *1/*1
    d. CYP 2D6 *1/*1
    e. CYP 2D6 *1/*2

5. Which of the following statements regarding abacavir is correct? (Select **ALL** that apply.)

    a. Testing for HLA-B*5701 is recommended on initiation or re-initiation of therapy.
    b. If the testing is positive for HLA-B*5701, abacavir cannot be used.
    c. Abacavir is a protease inhibitor that should be boosted with ritonavir.
    d. Abacavir can be taken with or without food.
    e. Abacavir is recommended as a preferred first line agent as part of a combination regimen for newly diagnosed HIV+ patients.

Questions 6-7 apply to the following case.

A 33 year old mother gave birth to full term, healthy male infant, delivered vaginally. The mother was prescribed acetaminophen with codeine for episiotomy pain and took the medication for 2 weeks. Her infant had intermittent periods of breastfeeding. On Day 7, her infant was noted for lethargy; on Day 10, her infant had grey colored skin, decreased milk intake; on Day 11, her infant was found dead. A postmortem analysis revealed no anatomical abnormalities. Morphine blood concentrations postmortem in the infant were 70 ng/mL (average concentrations in breast fed neonates are 0 to 2.2 ng/mL).

6. Which CYP enzyme predominately metabolizes codeine?

    a. CYP2D6
    b. CYP2C9
    c. CYP2C19
    d. CYP3A4
    e. CYP1A2

7. Which metabolizer phenotype of the mother best correlates with the symptoms experienced by her infant?

    a. Poor metabolizer
    b. Intermediate metabolizer
    c. Extensive metabolizer
    d. Ultra-rapid metabolizer
    e. The mother lacked CYP2D6 enzymes

Answers

1-c, 2-b, 3-d, 4-b, 5-a,b,d,e, 6-a, 7-d

10

BIOSTATISTICS & PHARMACOECONOMICS

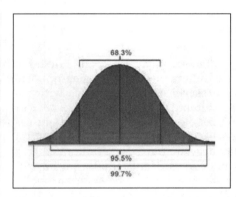

We gratefully acknowledge the assistance of Jeff Lee, PharmD, FCCP, Associate Professor, Lipscomb University College of Pharmacy, and Jan D. Hirsch, BSPharm, PhD, Associate Professor at the University of California San Diego, Skaggs School of Pharmacy and Pharmaceutical Sciences, in preparing this chapter.

BIOSTATISTICS

Background

Health care is evolving at an exponential rate. The development of new technologies and care delivery strategies has contributed to an explosion in the sheer quantity of evidence being created and published in the health care field. As pharmacists, the "drug experts," it is our responsibility to review and evaluate biomedical literature assessing safety, efficacy and value of new drugs and innovative uses of current drugs. Biomedical literature presents clinical data, and uses statistical methods and tools to answer research questions and aid in the development of clinical guidelines and consensus statements on the optimal treatment of various medical conditions. While there are a few types of studies that do not require statistical analysis (e.g., case studies, case series), most robust studies include statistical analyses and pharmacists should acquire the basic knowledge of statistical methods to best interpret available data.

Descriptive Statistics

Descriptive statistics are designed to describe the basic features of the data and provide simple summaries in a meaningful way. Measures of central tendency estimate the "center" of a distribution of values. There are three ways of estimating central tendency: the mean, the median and the mode. Although they all estimate the "center" of a group of data, the values obtained can be quite different.

Mean

The mean is the <u>average</u> value of a data set. It is calculated by adding up the values in a list, and dividing by the number of values present. The mean will reflect (or be sensitive to) the outlying (extreme) values which may not be representative of the norm. <u>Means can be used when the data are not skewed</u>. The mean is used for <u>continuous data</u>.

$$\text{Mean} = \frac{\text{Sum of all values}}{\text{Number of values}}$$

Median

The median is the value in the middle of a ranked list. To calculate the median, arrange all the numbers/values in numerical order (lowest to highest) and pick the middle number/value. Half of the values will be above the median, and half will be below. If the list contains an even number of values, then select the 2 values in the middle of the ranked list, add them together and divide by 2 to get the median. Unlike the mean, the median is less influenced by outliers. Another term for the median is the 50th percentile, where 50% of the values are below the median and the other 50% are above the median. The median should be used when data are skewed. When the mean and the median values are very different, the data set is skewed. Median values can be used with both continuous and ordinal, or ranked, data.

Mode

The mode is the value that occurs most frequently in a set of data. A data set can have zero, one or multiple modes.

Range

The range is the difference between the highest and the lowest values.

Example: Mean, Median, Mode, and Range

From the given data set, calculate the mean, median, mode and range.

Data = 4, 3, 7, 8, 1, 11, 6, 12, 15, 8

$$\text{Mean} = \frac{4+3+7+8+1+11+6+12+15+8}{10} = 7.5$$

$$\text{Median} = 1, 3, 4, 6, 7, 8, 8, 11, 12, 15 = \frac{(7+8)}{2} = 7.5$$

Mode = 8 (value that occurs most frequently)

Range = 15 − 1 = 14

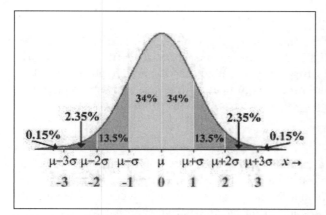

Normal Distribution

A "normal" distribution is also known as a bell-shaped curve or Gaussian curve. Generally, clinical studies rely on "sample" populations that appear to be representative of the population since the entire population cannot be studied and, therefore, an approximation has to be made. When the sample group with continuous data is large, the distribution approximates a normal, bell shaped curve (see picture) where μ is the mean, and σ is the standard deviation (SD). In a Gaussian or normal distribution, the mean, mode and median would all have the same (or similar) value and would look like the figure above. Notice the curve is symmetric around the mean and the skew is zero.

Standard Deviation

The standard deviation (SD) shows how much variation, or dispersion, there is from the mean. The closer the numbers cluster around the mean, the smaller the standard deviation. If the SD is small, one would conclude that the drug being studied had a similar effect on most subjects. SD is a positive number expressed in the same units as the data and it is used for continuous data that is normally distributed. In a normal distribution, roughly 68% of the values are within 1 standard deviation from the mean and 95% of the values are within 2 standard deviations. Standard deviation is calculated by taking the square root of the variance.

Skewness

Data that do not have a normal distribution are skewed and have an asymmetric curve (see curves A and C below). This means the data has extremes, or outliers. Data that are skewed to the right have a positive skew (curve C below) and data that are skewed to the left have a negative skew (curve A below). The direction of the skew refers to the direction of the longer tail, not to the bulk of the data or curve hump. Notice that in curve B, the right and left are perfect mirrors of one another indicating symmetrical data.

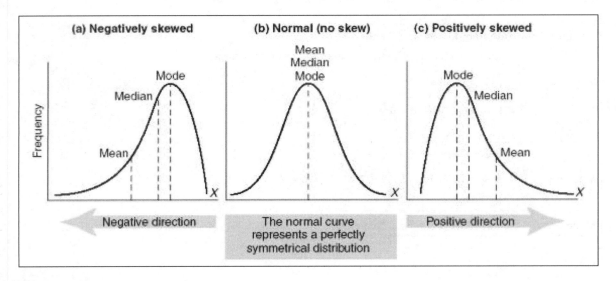

Statistical Inference and Error

Null Hypothesis (H₀)

The null hypothesis of a clinical trial states that there is no difference (or relationship) between groups (i.e., Drug A = Drug B). A study is designed to disprove this assertion by testing for a statistically significant difference between Drug A and Drug B (this is called the alternate hypothesis or H_A). If the study data concluded that there was a statistically significant difference between Drug A and Drug B, then the null hypothesis would fail to be accepted (therefore, it would be rejected).

Alternative Hypothesis (H_A)

The alternative hypothesis states that there is a treatment difference (or a relationship between the intervention and the outcome or endpoint) between groups in the trial (i.e., Drug A ≠ Drug B). When statistical significance of the primary endpoint is met, we fail to accept the null hypothesis. If you fail to accept (or reject) the null hypothesis (H_0), you are accepting the alternative hypothesis.

P-value

The p-value is the likelihood (or probability) that chance would produce a difference as large or larger than the one found in the study, if the null hypothesis is true. In simple terms, it is the probability that the result obtained was due to chance. Generally, a p-value of < 0.05 (and sometimes < 0.01 or other values, depending on the trial design) indicates statistical significance. If the p-value is < 0.05, there is < 5% probability that the result occurred by chance. In other words, the p-value is the probability of a random difference, given that the null hypothesis is true.

If there is a low probability the result was obtained by chance (e.g., p-value < 0.05) we can state that the conclusion is "statistically significant" (i.e., unlikely to have occurred by chance). When the p-value is smaller than the predetermined significance level (or alpha level), the difference found between groups is statistically significant and the study failed to accept (or reject) the null hypothesis. Again, the study would fail to accept (or reject) the null hypothesis when the p-value is less than the predetermined significance level, indicating that the observed result is highly unlikely under the null hypothesis. The p-value provides no information about the size of the effect or its clinical significance, only statistical significance.

Confidence Interval (CI)

The confidence interval (CI) is a range of values derived from the sample data that has a given probability of encompassing the "true" value. It reflects the margin of error that inherently exists when a sample statistic is used to estimate the true value of the population. Therefore, CIs help determine the validity of the sample statistic by attempting to capture the true population parameter. The confidence interval states that there is a given probability that the population's true value is contained within this interval. The most common confidence level used in medicine is 95%; however, other levels may be used. As the confidence level increases, the confidence interval becomes wider. A 95% CI can also be stated as a 5% degree of uncertainty. The confidence level is equal to 1 – alpha (type I error), or CI = 1 – type I error.

CIs can be used descriptively or inferentially. An example of descriptive use: a study reports that the mean weight of newborns at one hospital in the past 12 months was 7.7 lbs, with a 95% confidence interval (6.6 – 8.8 lbs) – meaning the researcher is 95% confident that the confidence interval contains the sample statistic. Inferential use looks at the values as a way of comparing groups and determining level of significance. A few rules apply when looking at CIs for inferential use:

- When the 95% CI for the estimated difference between groups (or within the same group over time) does not include zero, the results are significant at the 0.05 level.

- When the 95% CI for an odds ratio, risk ratio or hazard ratio that compares 2 groups does not include one, the results are significant at the 0.05 level.

See examples of inferential use of CIs and p-values using the difference and RR in the tables below.

LUNG FUNCTION	ROFLUMILAST (N = 745)	PLACEBO (N = 745)	DIFFERENCE (95% CI)	P-VALUE
Change in pre-bronchodilator FEV$_1$ (mL)	46	8	38 (18 – 58)	p = 0.0003
Change in pre-bronchodilator FEV$_1$/FVC (%)	0.314	0.001	0.313 (-0.26 – 0.89)	p = 0.2858

EXACERBATIONS	ROFLUMILAST	PLACEBO	RELATIVE RISK (95% CI)	P-VALUE
Severe (mean rate, per patient per year)	0.11 (n = 69)	0.12 (n = 81)	RR 0.92 (0.61 – 1.29)	p = 0.5275
Moderate (mean rate, per patient per year)	0.94 (n = 299)	1.11 (n = 343)	RR 0.85 (0.72 – 0.99)	p = 0.0325

The use of p-values and confidence intervals is complementary. P-values allow a quick decision about whether a result is statistically significant or not. Confidence intervals provide information on statistical significance plus estimates the effect size as well as the variability of the estimate.

Clinical Significance

A measure of statistical significance is not the same as "clinical significance". Statistical significance reflects the influence of chance on the outcome; clinical significance reflects the clinical value of the outcome. For example, if a blood pressure drug lowers SBP by 3 mmHg, it may be statistically significant (with a p-value < 0.05) versus placebo, but clinically the drug will not be used since other drugs lower BP to a greater degree. It would not be "clinically significant" because it does not measure up to other available drugs and would not have an advantageous clinical benefit.

Correlation

Correlation describes the relationship between two or more variables which is then plotted on a linear scale. The direction and magnitude of the linear correlation can be quantified with a correlation coefficient. The most widely-used type of correlation coefficient is the Pearson Correlation Coefficient, abbreviated r. Values of the correlation coefficient vary from -1 to 1. If the coefficient is 0, then the two variables have no relationship or correlation. If the coefficient is positive, the 2 variables tend to increase or decrease together. If the coefficient is negative, the 2 variables are inversely related, that is, as one variable decreases, the other variable increases. If the coefficient is 1 or -1, the two variables have perfect correlation and the data points form a straight line.

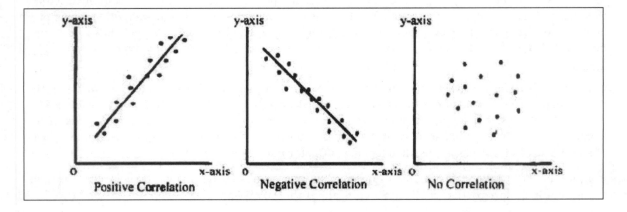

Type I error

The Greek letter, alpha (α) is the probability of a type I error. The alpha value is chosen by the researcher before the study starts, to be the acceptable threshold of statistical significance. Commonly, α is set to equal 0.05, which means < 5% of the time the null hypothesis will be rejected in error. A type I error occurs when the null hypothesis is true, yet it is rejected in error. Said another way, it was concluded that there was a difference between two groups when, in fact, there was not. When a researcher chooses the p-value of < 0.05 for statistical significance, the researcher accepts the fact that this error will occur < 5% of the time. A type I error is also known as a false positive (e.g., a drug is concluded to be better than placebo when it is not). Confidence interval is related to type I error: CI = 1 – type I error (alpha).

Type II error

The Greek letter, beta (β) is the probability of a type II error. Beta is generally set at 0.1 or 0.2, indicating a willingness to accept a type II error 10 or 20 times in 100 comparisons. A type II error occurs when the null hypothesis is false, yet it is accepted in error. Said another way, it was concluded that there was no difference between two groups when, in fact, there was. A type II error is also known as a false negative (e.g., a drug is concluded not to have benefit over placebo when it actually has benefit). Beta is usually expressed in terms of statistical power, which is calculated as 1 – beta.

The Importance of Type I and Type II Errors is Dependent on the Situation

Consider a screening test for a biological marker known to give a good estimate of whether or not a particular disease will develop within the next 5 years. There is a prophylactic medication that can be given if the patient is at risk, but the medication is very expensive and can have serious side effects. The null hypothesis (H_0) is that the patient does not have the biological marker.

A false positive test (type I error – testing positive for the marker of the disease when indeed the patient does not have the biological marker) may make the patient anxious and seek unnecessary treatments and/or surgery. A false negative (type II error – testing negative for the marker of the disease when indeed the patient has the biological marker) may be more serious since the patient may not seek further treatment that could have prevented or halted the disease.

DECISION BASED ON SCREENING TEST	UNDERLYING "TRUTH" IS BIOLOGICAL MARKER PRESENT?	
	H_0 TRUE – DO NOT HAVE THE MARKER	H_0 FALSE – DO HAVE THE MARKER
Accept (fail to reject) H_0 No biological marker, therefore, no disease	No error (necessary treatment given)	Type II error "false negative" (necessary treatment not given)
Reject H_0 Have biological marker and will develop disease	Type I error "false positive" (unnecessary treatment given)	No error (no unnecessary treatment given)

Statistical Power

Power of a statistical test is the probability that the test will reject the null hypothesis when the null hypothesis is false (avoiding a type II error). As the power increases, the chance of a type II error occurring decreases. Therefore, power is equal to 1 – beta. A higher statistical power means that we can be more certain that the null hypothesis was correctly rejected. The power of a study is determined by several factors including the sample size, the number of events (MIs, strokes, deaths, etc.), the effect size and the statistical significance criterion used.

Variables and Data Types

Dependent & Independent Variables

A <u>dependent variable</u> is the <u>outcome of interest</u>, which should change in response to some intervention. An <u>independent variable is the intervention</u>, or what is being manipulated. For example, aspirin is compared to placebo to see if it leads to a reduction in coronary events. The dependent variable (or outcome of interest) is the number of coronary events while the independent variable (the intervention) is aspirin.

Discrete & Continuous Data

NAME	DESCRIPTION

Discrete Data – can have only a limited, or finite, set of values (i.e., not continuous) and can assume only whole numbers. There are 2 types of discrete data:

Nominal	Consists of <u>categories</u>, where the order of the categories is arbitrary (e.g., marital status, gender, ethnicity). The numbers do not have a true numerical, or quantitative, value (e.g., 0 = male, 1 = female).
Ordinal	Consists of <u>ranked categories</u>, where the order of the ranking is important. However, the difference between categories cannot be considered to be equal. These are usually scoring systems that are ranked by severity (e.g., Apgar score, Likert scales, NYHA functional class) but cannot be measured/quantified. There is no consistent correlation between the rank and the degree of severity. For example, a trauma score of 4 does not necessarily mean you are twice as ill as a trauma score of 2.

Continuous Data – can take an infinite number of possible values (such as height, weight, A1C, blood pressure) within a defined range. Continuous data can include fractional data (e.g., A1C of 7.3%). Types of continuous data include:

Interval	Interval data is used to measure continuous data that have legitimate mathematical values. The difference between 2 consecutive values is consistent along any point of the scale, but the zero point is arbitrary and does not mean "none" of the variable (e.g., Celsius temperature scale).
Ratio	Ratio data has equal intervals between values and a meaningful zero point; meaning there is none of the variable (e.g., height, weight, time, length).

Determining the appropriate statistical test depends on many factors, including the type of data, the number of groups being compared, whether the samples are independent or paired and the assumptions within a specific test. Below is a chart outlining some of the statistical tests commonly used in clinical trials.

Comparison of Statistical Tests*

NUMBER OF GROUPS COMPARED	INDEPENDENT SAMPLES	PAIRED SAMPLES	CORRELATION

Nominal Data

NUMBER OF GROUPS COMPARED	INDEPENDENT SAMPLES	PAIRED SAMPLES	CORRELATION
2	Chi-squared test or Fisher's Exact test	McNemar test	Phi
3 or more	Chi-squared test	Cochran Q	

Comparison of Statistical Tests Continued*

Ordinal Data

NUMBER OF GROUPS COMPARED	INDEPENDENT SAMPLES	PAIRED SAMPLES	CORRELATION
2	Wilcoxon rank sum test or Mann-Whitney U test‡	Wilcoxon signed-rank test‡	Spearman's
3 or more	Kruskal-Wallis test‡	Friedman test‡	

Continuous Data

2	Student's t-test**	Paired Student's t-test** or Wilcoxon signed-rank test‡	Pearson's
3 or more	Analysis of variance (ANOVA)** or Kruskal-Wallis test‡	ANOVA**	

* Other tests may also apply. Specific test utilized also depends on distribution of data.
** Parametric test
‡ Nonparametric test

Risk

Relative Risk/Risk Ratio (RR)

The relative risk (or risk ratio) is the probability of an unfavorable event occurring in the treatment group versus the control group. First, the risk of developing the event must be calculated for both groups. Risk is defined as the probability of an unfavorable event occurring by the end of a clinical trial. Once the risk for each arm is determined, the relative risk can be calculated by comparing the risk calculated for the treatment group (numerator) to the risk calculated for the control group (denominator). The RR is generally expressed as a decimal but can also appear as a percentage. RR is simply the ratio of risks in the 2 groups.

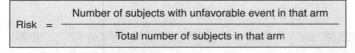

$$\text{Risk} = \frac{\text{Number of subjects with unfavorable event in that arm}}{\text{Total number of subjects in that arm}}$$

$$\text{RR} = \frac{\text{Risk in treatment group}}{\text{Risk in control group}}$$

INTERPRETING RR

- RR = 1: no difference in risk between the 2 groups

- RR < 1: fewer events are occurring in the treatment group compared to the control group

- RR > 1: more events are occurring in the treatment group compared to the control group

Example #1: A randomized, double-blind placebo-controlled study was performed to evaluate whether metoprolol reduced disease progression in heart failure (HF) patients. A total of 10,111 patients were enrolled and followed for over 12 months. Using the results below, calculate the relative risk of HF progression.

RESULTS	METOPROLOL (N = 5,123)	PLACEBO (N = 4,988)
Incidence of HF progression	16%	28%
Death rate	1.9%	3.3%

If heart failure progression occurred in 28% of placebo-treated patients and in 16% of metoprolol-treated patients, then the relative risk is $0.16/0.28 = 0.57$, or 57%. Therefore, subjects treated with metoprolol were only 57% as likely as placebo-treated patients to have heart failure progression.

Example #2: A pilot study was conducted to evaluate a new drug, Drug A, for the prevention of chemotherapy-induced nausea and vomiting (CINV) in patients receiving a doxorubicin-containing regimen. The study included a total of 245 patients. Using the results below, calculate the risk ratio of CINV.

RESULTS	DRUG A (N = 120)	PLACEBO (N = 125)
Diarrhea (# of patients)	8	11
CINV (# of patients)	6	20

The risk of CINV in the Drug A arm is 6 patients divided by 120 patients in this arm, or 5% ($6/120 = 0.05$ x 100 = 5%). The risk of CINV in the placebo arm is 20 patients divided by 125 patients in this arm, or 16% ($20/125 = 0.16$ x 100 = 16%). The risk ratio can be calculated as $0.05/0.16 = 0.3125$, or 31%. Therefore, subjects treated with Drug A were only 31% as likely as placebo-treated patients to have CINV.

By reporting only the relative risk (as opposed to absolute risk), the value of the treatment may be overstated (as is often done in the lay press).

Here is another formula that can be used for calculating RR:

$$RR = \frac{a/(a + b)}{c/(c + d)}$$

EXPOSURE OR TREATMENT	DISEASE	
	PRESENT	ABSENT
Present (Drug group)	a	b
Absent (Placebo group)	c	d

Example #3: A prospective, cohort study was initiated to evaluate the risk of developing lung cancer (CA) in heavy smokers (> 2 packs of cigarettes/day). The study enrolled 200 patients and the duration of follow up was 15 years. Using the results below, calculate the relative risk of developing lung CA from smoking.

RESULTS	LUNG CA PRESENT	LUNG CA ABSENT
Smokers (n = 100)	40	60
Non-smokers (n = 100)	10	90

$$RR = \frac{40/(40 + 60)}{10/(10 + 90)} = 4$$

The RR of 4 means that smokers are 4 times as likely to develop lung CA than non-smokers.

Relative Risk Reduction (RRR)

Relative risk reduction measures how much the risk is reduced in the treatment group compared to the control group. It can be calculated by either dividing the absolute risk reduction by the control group risk rate or by subtracting the relative risk (expressed as a decimal) from 1.

$$RRR = \frac{(\% \text{ risk in control group} - \% \text{ risk in treatment group})}{\% \text{ risk in the control group}} \quad \text{or} \quad 1 - RR$$

Using Example #1 from above: A randomized, double-blind placebo-controlled study was performed to evaluate whether metoprolol reduced disease progression in heart failure (HF) patients. A total of 10,111 patients were enrolled and followed for over 12 months. Using the results below, calculate the relative risk reduction of HF progression.

RESULTS	METOPROLOL (N = 5,123)	PLACEBO (N = 4,988)
Incidence of HF progression	16%	28%
Death rate	1.9%	3.3%

The RRR is calculated by: (28% – 16%)/28% = 0.43 or 1 – 0.57 = 0.43, or 43%. Therefore, there is a 43% relative risk reduction of heart failure progression in patients being treated with metoprolol. Patients taking metoprolol are 43% less likely to experience heart failure progression.

Using Example #2 from above: A pilot study was conducted to evaluate a new drug, Drug A, to evaluate the prevention of chemotherapy-induced nausea and vomiting (CINV) in patients receiving doxorubicin-containing regimen. The study included a total of 245 patients. Using the results below, calculate the relative risk reduction of CINV.

RESULTS	DRUG A (N = 120)	PLACEBO (N = 125)
Diarrhea (# of patients)	8	11
CINV (# of patients)	6	20

The RRR is calculated by: (16% – 5%)/16% = 0.69 or 1 – 0.31 = 0.69, or 69%. Therefore, there is a 69% relative risk reduction of CINV in patients being treated with Drug A. Patients taking Drug A are 69% less likely to experience CINV.

Expressing the result as a relative risk reduction is more intuitively understandable. RR and RRR are limited in that these data do not reflect how important, or large, the treatment effect is in the population at-large. They only provide a measure of what the risk of an event is in one group (treatment or exposed) compared to the risk of that event in a comparison (or control) group.

Absolute Risk Reduction (ARR)

Absolute risk reduction, or attributable risk, is the difference between the control group's event rate and the treatment group's event rate.

> ARR =   (% risk in control group) – (% risk in treatment group)

Using Example #1 from above: A randomized, double-blind placebo-controlled study was performed to evaluate whether metoprolol reduced disease progression in heart failure (HF) patients. A total of 10,111 patients were enrolled and followed for over 12 months. Using the results below, calculate the attributable risk of HF progression.

RESULTS	METOPROLOL (N = 5,123)	PLACEBO (N = 4,988)
Incidence of HF progression	16%	28%
Death rate	1.9%	3.3%

The ARR is 28% – 16% = 12%. The ARR is 12%. This is the difference in risk that can be attributed to the intervention (drug). For every 100 patients treated with metoprolol, 12 fewer patients experience heart failure progression.

Using Example #2 from above: A pilot study was conducted to evaluate a new drug, Drug A, to evaluate the prevention of chemotherapy-induced nausea and vomiting (CINV) in patients receiving doxorubicin-containing regimen. The study included a total of 245 patients. Using the results below, calculate the absolute risk reduction of CINV.

RESULTS	DRUG A (N = 120)	PLACEBO (N = 125)
Diarrhea (# of patients)	8	11
CINV (# of patients)	6	20

The ARR is 16% – 5% = 11%. The ARR is 11%. For every 100 patients treated with Drug A, 11 fewer patients experience CINV.

Number Needed to Treat (NNT)

The number needed to treat represents the number of people who would need to be treated with the intervention (drug) for a certain period of time (e.g., one year) in order to achieve the desired outcome (e.g., prevent adverse event) in one patient.

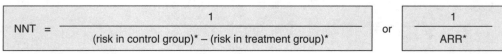

$$NNT = \frac{1}{(\text{risk in control group})^* - (\text{risk in treatment group})^*} \quad or \quad \frac{1}{ARR^*}$$

*expressed as a decimal

Example #1 from above: 1/0.12 = 8.3, or 9 (<u>must always round up</u> since you cannot divide a person into fractions). Therefore, for every 9 patients who received metoprolol for 1 year, heart failure progression is prevented in one patient.

Example #2 from above: 1/0.11 = 9.09 or 10 (<u>must always round up</u>). Treating 10 patients with Drug A will prevent CINV in 1 patient. The NNT puts the results of a trial in a clinically relevant context. When the treatment or exposure causes harm (e.g., cigarette smoking, *Vioxx*, etc), the term NNT does not work and it is more accurate to report the results as the <u>number needed to harm (NNH)</u> which is calculated the same way as NNT. However, with NNH, we always <u>round down</u>.

Odds

Odds are not the same as risk. Risk is the probability that a person who has not developed the event will develop the event whereas odds represent the probability of the event occurring compared with the probability that it will not occur. Using the example of 100 smokers, if 40 smokers developed lung cancer and 60 smokers did not develop lung cancer, the risk would be 40/100, or 40%, and the odds would be 40:60, 40/60 or 67%.

Odds Ratio (OR)

The odds ratio is the ratio of two odds, or the ratio of the odds of an event occurring in the treatment group to the odds of an event occurring in the control group. It is a measure of association between an exposure and an outcome. Odds ratios are used mostly in case-control studies, but they are the unit of outcome provided by logistic regression analysis which is a valuable statistical tool.

$$\text{Odds Ratio (OR)} = \frac{ad}{bc}$$

EXPOSURE OR TREATMENT	DISEASE	
	PRESENT	ABSENT
Present (Drug group)	a	b
Absent (Placebo group)	c	d

Using Example #3 from above: A prospective, cohort study was initiated to evaluate the risk of developing lung cancer (CA) in heavy smokers (> 2 packs of cigarettes/day). The study enrolled 200 patients and the duration of follow up was 15 years. Using the results below, calculate the odds ratio of developing lung CA from smoking.

RESULTS	LUNG CA PRESENT	LUNG CA ABSENT
Smokers (n = 100)	40	60
Non-smokers (n = 100)	10	90

The odds of a smoker developing lung CA would be 40/60 = 0.67, whereas the odds of a non-smoker developing lung CA would be 10/90 = 0.11. The odds ratio is then 0.67/0.11, or 6, meaning that smokers are 6 times as likely to develop lung cancer than non-smokers. An odds ratio of 1 indicates no difference between groups. The smaller the event rate, the closer the odds ratio is to the relative risk.

Hazard Ratio (HR)

Hazard ratios are often used when clinical trials present data related to the time survived to an event (e.g., mortality, cure, specified level of symptom reduction).

A hazard rate is the chance of an unfavorable event occurring by a given point in time. A hazard ratio is the hazard or chance of an event occurring at any given time during the study in the treatment group as compared to a comparator group. <u>Hazard ratios</u> are used in clinical trials with <u>time-to-event (or sur-</u>

vival) analysis. Hazard ratios assume that the ratio is constant over time. Hazard ratios are a specific type of RR with the distinction that HR ratios are the relative likelihood of an event in the treated vs comparator group at any given point in time during the trial and the RR is the likelihood of an event in the treated vs comparator group at the end of the trial.

$$HR = \frac{\text{Hazard rate in the treatment group}}{\text{Hazard rate in the control group}}$$

Interpreting HR

- HR = 1: Event rates are the same in both arms over time

- HR < 1: At any given time, relatively fewer patients in the treatment group have had an event compared to the control group

- HR > 1: At any given time, relatively more patients in the treatment group have had an event compared to the control group

For example, in a clinical trial assessing the cure rate provided by Drug A vs. placebo the hazard ratio (HR) is reported to be 4.0. This means that a treated patient who has not been cured by a certain time point has four times the chance of being cured by the next time point compared to someone in the placebo group.

Sensitivity and Specificity

Sensitivity and specificity are concepts often applied to diagnostic testing for diseases. Sensitivity is the proportion of time a test is positive in patients who have the disease; also stated as the ability of the test to correctly identify patients who are known to have the disease in question. If a test has high sensitivity, it will pick up nearly everyone with the disease. A test with 100% sensitivity will recognize all patients with the disease by testing positive. Therefore, a negative test would definitely rule out the presence of the disease. Sensitivity is the percentage of "true-positive" results and is equal to 1 – type II error. Specificity is the proportion of time a test is negative in patients who do not have the disease; also stated as the ability of the test to correctly identify patients who are known to not have the disease. If a test has high specificity, it will not mistakenly give a positive result to many people without the disease. A test with 100% specificity will read negative and accurately exclude disease from all healthy patients. Specificity is the percentage of "true-negative" results and is equal to 1 – type I error. Sensitivity and specificity can be described using a simple 2x2 table:

	PATIENTS WITH DISEASE	PATIENTS WITHOUT DISEASE
Test is positive	a (True +)	b (False +)
Test is negative	c (False -)	d (True -)
	a + c	b + d

Using this table, sensitivity may be calculated using the following formula:

$$\text{Sensitivity} = \frac{a}{(a + c)}$$

Specificity, then, can be calculated using the following formula:

$$\text{Sensitivity} = \frac{d}{(b + d)}$$

Overview of Study Designs

There are many types of study designs used in evidence-based medicine. Each trial design has certain strengths and weaknesses. Clinical study designs include observational designs (such as case reports, case series, cross-sectional, case-control, cohort) and experimental designs (such as a randomized, controlled trial). A placebo, or an inert compound indistinguishable from the active drug, may be used in experimental trials to minimize bias. This practice is called "blinding" or "masking" the treatment allocation in a clinical trial. In a single-blind trial, generally the subject (the patient) is unaware of the treatment allocation, whereas the investigator is aware of the treatment the patient is receiving. In a double-blind trial, neither the subjects nor the researchers know who is receiving active drug or placebo. The hierarchy presented in the picture is indicative of the confidence in results that is generally attributed to each type of study.

Observational Studies

An observational study is a type of trial in which individuals are enrolled and observed and/or certain outcomes are measured under precisely defined conditions in a systematic and objective manner. No attempt is made to affect the outcome (no intervention). Observational studies follow subjects with a certain condition or those who receive a particular treatment over time. They may be compared to another group who are not affected by the condition or are not taking the particular treatment. Large observational studies can clarify the tolerability profile of marketed medicines. An example of an observational study is the Women's Health Initiative trial. Types of observational studies are listed below.

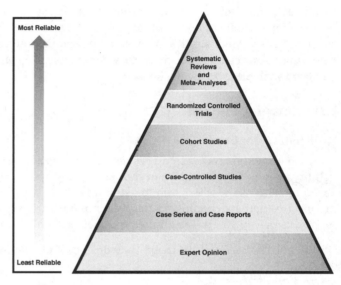

Case Report or Case Series

A simple descriptive account of observations of a single patient (case report) or series of patients (case series) can be useful from a clinical perspective for unusual or rarely observed events. Based on observed clinical aspects of a patient(s) and intervention, the possibility of an association between treatment and effect may be proposed. However, no conclusion can be drawn from these small studies. They may generate hypotheses that can then be studied in larger trials with more robust study designs (e.g., prospective cohort or randomized controlled trial).

Case-Control Study

Case-control studies compare patients who have a disease or outcome of interest (the cases) to patients who do not have the disease or outcome (the controls), and look back retrospectively to compare exposure to a risk factor. Risk factor exposure is compared in each group to determine if a relationship between the risk factor and the disease exists. Case-control studies are observational because no intervention is implemented and no attempt is made to alter the course of the disease. For example, did subjects exposed to statins have a higher incidence of liver damage? Case-control studies are good for studying rare diseases or outcomes, can be conducted in less time since the condition has already occurred, and are useful to establish an association. They are often used to generate hypotheses that can then be studied via a prospective cohort or other studies.

Cohort Study

A cohort is a group of people who share a common characteristic(s) or experience within a defined period of time (e.g., year born, exposure to pollutant/drug/vaccine, or having undergone a certain procedure). <u>This study type follows the cohort over time (longitudinal) and the outcomes are compared to a subset of the group who were not exposed to the intervention such as a drug (e.g., the Framingham studies)</u>. Cohort members must be at risk of experiencing the event and they must not have had the outcome of interest at the start of the study. A cohort study is a good trial design when conducting a randomized trial would be considered unethical. Cohort studies may be <u>prospective</u> in design (carried out into the future) but can be done <u>retrospectively</u> as well (e.g., by reviewing patient medical charts).

Cross-Sectional Study

Cross-sectional studies are descriptive, observational trials and are used to estimate the relationship between an outcome of interest and population variables as they exist at a cross-section (one point in time). Cross-sectional studies are used to determine prevalence of disease. By identifying associations between exposures and outcomes, they can be used to generate hypotheses about causation that can be tested with other study designs.

Experimental Studies

Randomized Controlled Trial (RCT)

This experimental trial design involves randomization, which minimizes bias and increases internal validity, thereby increasing the overall strength of the study conclusions. These are generally designed as superiority trials, which aim to determine if one treatment is better than another. RCTs are always prospective and are considered the gold standard trial design in evaluating safety and efficacy of an intervention (e.g., drug). The clinical trial setting can be controlled in many ways.

Within a RCT, there are different study designs and a few are listed below:

PARALLEL STUDY DESIGN
Subjects are randomized to either the treatment group or the placebo group only and stay in that group for the duration of the study. This is the most common design used in Phase III comparative trials for FDA drug approval. A larger sample size is needed compared to the crossover design; however, this trial design can be done in a shorter period of time.

CROSSOVER STUDY DESIGN
Subjects are randomized to a treatment sequence and each subject receives all of the interventions. With this type of design, every patient serves as his or her own control. For example, comparing drugs A and B, half of the subjects are randomly allocated to receive them in the order A then B, and half of the subjects are to receive them in the order B then A. A washout period between treatments is required. A washout period is the time between discontinuing the first treatment and before the initiation of the second treatment and is needed to reduce the effects of the 1st drug taken in the 2nd phase of the trial.

FACTORIAL DESIGN
Subjects are randomized to multiple assignments within the study and it is designed to evaluate multiple interventions in a single experiment. For example, in a simple 2x2 factorial design, patients can be assigned to 1 of 2 drug doses (e.g., 100 mg or 200 mg) and 1 of 2 drugs (Drug A or Drug B).

Intention-To-Treat (ITT) vs. Per Protocol (PP) Analyses

Data from clinical trials can be analyzed in two different ways; intention-to-treat or per protocol. Intention-to-treat analysis includes data for all patients originally allocated to each treatment group (active and control) regardless if the patient did not complete the trial according to the study protocol (e.g., due to non-compliance, protocol deviations or study withdrawal). This method provides a conservative estimate of the treatment effect. A per protocol analysis is conducted for the subset of the trial population who completed the study according to the protocol (or at least without any major protocol violations). This method may provide an optimistic estimate of treatment effect since it is limited to the subset of patients who were adherent to the protocol. In practice, both methods are often used to analyze the results of a clinical trial.

Composite Endpoints

A composite endpoint is a single measure of effect, comprised of multiple individual endpoints or outcomes being collected in a trial. Composite endpoints are common in reporting clinical trial results. They can be helpful in instances where there is no single primary outcome variable that adequately portrays efficacy. A more common rationale for using composite endpoints is to reduce the sample size needed to show an effect by increasing the event rate in the control group.

Despite these potential advantages, the use of composite endpoints may complicate the interpretation of the results, as it blends individual endpoint results into a single endpoint. When assessing the appropriateness of a composite endpoint in a clinical trial, the reader should ensure that the individual endpoints comprising the composite endpoint are similar in importance to patients, they occur with similar frequency, and are affected to a similar degree by the intervention.

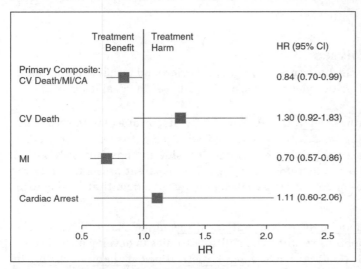

In this example, the primary composite endpoint encompasses the endpoints of cardiovascular death (CV death), myocardial infarction (MI), and cardiac arrest (CA) and is statistically significant, although only one of the individual components (MI) shows a statistically significant treatment benefit. By reporting both the composite and individual endpoints, the reader can evaluate the relative contribution of each component to the composite result.

Pogue, et al. PLoS One, 2012, 7(4): e34785.

Noninferiority and Equivalence Trial Designs

The terms "noninferiority" and "equivalence" are often used interchangeably (incorrectly) in describing trial designs where the objective is to demonstrate that a new treatment is similar to the standard treatment. In reality, these two terms define different trial designs. An equivalence trial represents a study designed to demonstrate that two interventions do not differ in either direction (more or less effective) by more than a prespecified equivalence margin (two-way margin). A noninferiority trial, in contrast, seeks to determine whether a new treatment is not worse than a reference treatment by more than a prespecified noninferiority margin (one-way margin). Noninferiority trials are much more common than equivalence trials.

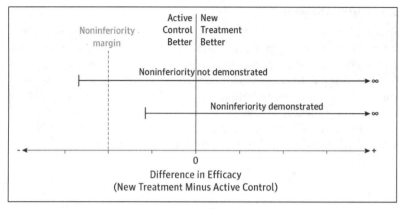

Kaji and Lewis, JAMA, 2015. 313(23): 2371-2372.

In this example, the prespecified noninferiority margin is between 0 and the dashed line. In the top example, the lower limit of the confidence interval falls to the left of the noninferiority margin, so noninferiority is not demonstrated. In the lower example, the lower limit of the confidence interval does not cross the noninferiority margin, thus noninferiority is demonstrated.

Clinical trials may not provide "real life" comparisons

Patients in clinical trials may not be reflective of those treated in everyday clinical practice. Patients in clinical trials tend to be younger, more compliant with therapy, more likely to reach target doses of the drug, and do so more quickly than in everyday practice. They are not as likely to have as complex a presentation as real-life patients. For example, practitioners use a drug that is cleared renally in patients with moderate to severe renal impairment, when this subgroup of patients was excluded from clinical trials related to the drug in question. Therefore, it will not be known how to use the drug safely in this patient population.

Systematic Reviews and Meta-Analyses

When there are many studies available in the literature, a systematic review and possible meta-analysis is useful to summarize the main findings in order to guide evidence-based medical decisions.

A systematic review is a structured literature review that uses a step-by-step protocol with preset criteria for selecting and rigorously evaluating studies. Systematic reviews attempt to identify all studies that meet the pre-defined criteria, evaluate the validity of findings (considering possible bias within the study design), and then synthesize the results into a meaningful, transparent presentation of results. A systematic review study may also conduct a meta-analysis to present a quantitative synthesis of results across studies.

META-ANALYSIS CAN BE USED:

- To establish statistical significance with studies that have conflicting results

- To develop a more correct estimate of effect magnitude

- To provide a more complex analysis of harms, safety data, and/or benefits

- To examine subgroups from multiple studies with individual numbers that are not statistically significant

Meta-analysis is a statistical technique that can be used to combine results from multiple studies to develop a single conclusion that has greater statistical power than is possible in the individual smaller studies. The validity and usefulness of a meta-analysis is largely dependent on the quality of the systematic review that identified which studies to include. A meta-analysis considers the differing sizes and quality of trials for a treatment, giving more weight to the findings from larger, more rigorous studies. The technique also considers how the studies differ and the possible contribution of differing factors to driving treatment outcomes.

Although there are many potential flaws in this type of pooled data analysis, if the studies included in the meta-analysis are rigorous, randomized, controlled trials, the results could provide the highest level of evidence for medical decisions.

Results of a meta-analysis are presented in a diagram called a <u>forest plot</u>. The forest plot provides information about each study included in the meta-analysis as well as a combined summary effect of the results overall. Several columns are used to summarize the meta-analysis results in the forest plot.

Looking at the figure below, a forest plot from Larsson et al that compared the risk of atrial fibrillation between groups of subjects with the highest vs. lowest category of coffee consumption.

The first three columns are:

1. List of studies, by author name, included in the meta-analysis.

2. Year of each study was published

3. Population studied (i.e. men, women or both)

Results of each study are plotted to the right.

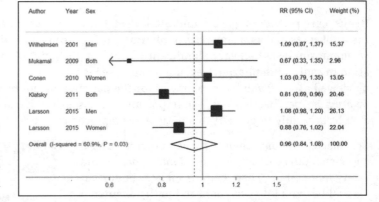

- The values on the x-axis are the study outcomes (relative risk in this study) and the solid vertical line at 1.0 is the "line of no effect". This line would be at 1.0 if study outcomes were expressed as odds ratios but at zero if expressed as weighted mean differences.

- The point estimate of the result in each study is plotted as a square. The size of the square represents the weight given to the study in the summary result. Larger studies with smaller confidence intervals will be given more weight and have a larger square. The confidence interval for each study is expressed as a horizontal line running through the box; longer lines indicate wider confidence interval, thus less precision and if the line crosses the "line of no effect" it is possible the intervention had no effect.

The meta-analysis combined summary effect is presented as a diamond with a dotted vertical line running through the center representing the point estimate of the combined summary effect.

- The width of the diamond indicates the confidence interval for the combined effect.

- If the diamond does not cross the "line of no effect" then the differences between groups can be interpreted as statistically significant. Note, in this study the diamond does cross the "line of no effect" thus the authors conclude no overall association between coffee consumption and atrial fibrillation risk.

The two columns to the right of the plotted data contain the numeric results of each study (same as graphed) and then the weight given to the study in the overall analysis.

PHARMACOECONOMICS

Background

Health care costs in the United States rank among the highest of all industrialized countries. In 2013 (the most recent data available), total health care expenditures reached 2.9 trillion dollars, which translates to an average of $9,255 per person, or about 17.4% of the nation's gross domestic product. The increasing costs have highlighted the need to understand how our limited resources can be used most effectively and efficiently in the care of our patients and society as a whole. Therefore, it is necessary to scientifically evaluate the value (e.g., costs vs. outcomes) of interventions such as drug therapy.

Definitions

Pharmacoeconomics is a collection of descriptive and analytic techniques for evaluating pharmaceutical interventions (drugs, devices, procedures, etc.) in the health care system. <u>Pharmacoeconomic research identifies, measures, and compares the costs (direct, indirect and intangible) and consequences (clinical,</u>

economic and humanistic) of pharmaceutical products and services. Various research methods can be used to determine the impact of the pharmaceutical product or service. These methods include: cost-effectiveness analysis, cost-minimization analysis, cost-utility analysis, and cost-benefit analysis. Although the term "pharmacoeconomics" is frequently referred to as "outcomes research", they are not the same thing. Pharmacoeconomic methods are specific to assessing the costs and consequences of pharmaceutical products and services, whereas outcomes research represents a broader research discipline that attempts to identify, measure, and evaluate the end result of health care services generally.

Health care providers, payers and other decision makers use these methods to evaluate and compare the total costs and consequences of pharmaceutical products and services. As the results of pharmacoeconomic analyses can vary significantly based on the point of view of the analyst, a critical consideration in evaluating pharmacoeconomic analyses is to clearly identify the study perspective. What may be viewed as good value for society or for the patient may not be deemed as such from an institutional or provider perspective (e.g., the importance of assessing the costs of lost productivity due to illness may be critically important to a patient or employer, but perhaps less so to a health plan).

Pharmacoeconomic analyses can provide useful supplemental evidence to traditional efficacy and safety endpoints. They help translate important clinical benefits into economic and patient-centered terms, and can assist providers and payers in determining where, if at all, a drug fits into the treatment paradigm for a specific condition. Pharmacoeconomic studies serve to guide optimal healthcare resource allocation, in a standardized and evidence-based manner.

The ECHO model (Economic, Clinical and Humanistic Outcomes) provides a broad evaluative framework to assess the outcomes associated with disease and its treatment.

- Economic outcomes: Include direct, indirect and intangible costs of the drug compared to a medical intervention.

- Clinical outcomes: Include medical events that occur as a result of the treatment or intervention.

- Humanistic Outcomes: Include consequences of the disease or treatment as reported by the patient or caregiver (e.g., patient satisfaction, quality of life).

Average and Incremental Cost Effectiveness Ratios

Commonly, the results of a pharmacoeconomic analysis will be expressed in terms of a cost ratio, representing the costs incurred to achieve a particular outcome [e.g., cost per case cured, cost per treatment success, cost per quality-adjusted life year (QALY) gained]. Two fundamental cost ratios are commonly used to communicate results of a pharmacoeconomic analysis.

COSTS

Direct Medical Costs
Costs associated with the detection, prevention, or treatment of a disease or illness. Direct cost examples include medications, medication administration, hospitalizations, clinic visits, emergency room visits, and nursing services.

Direct Non-Medical Costs
Costs for non-medical services associated with disease and treatment. Direct non-medical costs include travel costs (gas, bus, hotel stays for family), child care services (for children of patients), or costs for other household services required due to illness.

Indirect Costs
Costs that result from the effects of morbidity or mortality on production capacity, including costs of time lost from work, or working at a lower productivity level due to disease or treatment. Indirect costs can occur at both the patient and caregiver level.

Intangible costs
Costs incurred that represent the nonfinancial outcomes of disease and treatment, including pain and suffering, anxiety, and fatigue.

Average Cost Effectiveness Ratios

Average cost ratios reflect the cost per outcome of one treatment alternative independent of other alternatives. For example, if a treatment costs $50 to generate two successful outcomes, the average cost ratio is $25/treatment success ($50/2 successfully treated).

Incremental Cost Effectiveness Ratios

Incremental cost ratios represent the change in costs and outcomes when two treatment alternatives are compared. An incremental cost ratio is calculated when evaluating costs and outcomes between competing alternatives, and represents the additional costs required to produce an additional unit of effect. Mathematically, it is calculated as follows where C is for costs and E is for effects:

$$\text{Incremental Cost Ratio} = \frac{(C_2 - C_1)}{(E_2 - E_1)}$$

For example, if spending $200 on Drug A results in 5 treatment successes while spending $300 on Drug B results in 7 treatment successes, the incremental cost ratio of Drug B relative to Drug A is $50 for each additional treatment success:

$$\frac{(\$300 - \$200)}{(7 - 5)} = \frac{\$100}{2} = \$50 \text{ per additional success with Drug B}$$

Pharmacoeconomic Methodologies

Cost-Minimization Analysis

Cost-minimization analysis (CMA) is used when two or more interventions have already demonstrated equivalency in outcomes and the costs of each intervention are being compared. CMA measures and compares the input costs of treatment alternatives that have been deemed as equivalent from an outcomes perspective. This determination of equivalence is a key consideration in adopting this methodology. Ideally, evidence will exist to support the clinical equivalence of the alternatives. In some instances, assumptions will be made in the absence of relevant evidence. For example, two ACE-inhibitors, captopril and lisinopril, are considered therapeutically equivalent in the literature, but the acquisition cost (the price paid for the drug) and administrative costs may be different (captopril is administered TID and lisinopril is administered once daily). A CMA would look at "minimizing costs" when multiple drugs have equal efficacy and tolerability. Another example of CMA is looking at the same drug regimen given in two different settings (e.g., hospital versus home health care). CMA is considered the easiest analysis to perform. However, the use of this method is limited given its ability to compare only alternatives with demonstrated equivalent outcomes.

Cost-Benefit Analysis

Cost-benefit analysis (CBA) is a systematic process for calculating and comparing benefits and costs of an intervention in terms of monetary units. CBA consists of identifying all the benefits from an intervention and converting them into dollars in the year that they will occur. Also, the costs associated with the intervention are identified and are allocated to the year when they occur. All costs are then discounted back to their present day value. Given that all other factors remain constant, the program with the largest present day value of benefits minus costs is the best economic value. In CBA, both benefits and costs are expressed in terms of dollars and are adjusted to their present value. This can be difficult when required to measure the benefits and then assign a dollar amount to that benefit (e.g., when measuring the benefit of patient quality of life, an outcome difficult to measure and assign a dollar value to it). One advantage to using CBA is the ability to determine if the benefits of the intervention exceed the costs of implementation. CBA can also be used to compare multiple programs for similar or unrelated outcomes, as long as the outcome measures can be converted to dollars.

Cost-Effectiveness Analysis

Cost-effectiveness analysis (CEA) is defined as a series of analytical and mathematical procedures that aid in the selection of a course of action from various alternative approaches. Inputs are usually measured in dollars and outputs are usually measured in natural units (e.g., LDL values in mg/dL, % clinical cures, length of stay). The main advantage of this method is that the outcomes are easier to quantify when compared to other analyses, and clinicians and <u>decision makers are familiar</u> with these types of <u>outcomes</u> since they are <u>similar to outcomes seen in clinical trials</u> and practice. Therefore, CEA is the <u>most common</u> methodology seen in the literature today. A disadvantage of CEA is the <u>inability</u> to directly <u>compare different types of outcomes</u>. For example, one cannot compare the cost effectiveness of implementing a diabetes program with implementing an asthma program where the outcome units are different (e.g., blood glucose values versus asthma exacerbations). It is also difficult to combine two or more outcomes into one value of measurement (e.g., comparing one chemotherapeutic agent that prolongs survival but has significant side effects to another chemotherapeutic agent that has less effect on prolonging survival and has fewer side effects).

Cost-Utility Analysis

<u>Cost-utility analysis (CUA)</u> is a specialized form of CEA that includes a <u>quality-of-life</u> component associated with morbidity using common health indices such as <u>quality-adjusted life years (QALYs) and disability-adjusted life years (DALYs)</u>. With CEA, you can measure the quantity of life (years gained) but not the "quality" or "utility" of those years. In a CUA, the intervention outcome is measured in terms QALY gained. QALY takes into account both the quality (morbidity) and the quantity (mortality) of life gained. CUA measures outcomes based on years of life that are adjusted by utility weights, which range from 1 for "perfect health" to 0 for "dead". These weights can take into account patient and society preferences for specific health states; however, there is no consensus on the measurement, since both patient and society preferences may vary based on culture. An advantage of CUA is that different types of outcomes and diseases with multiple outcomes of interest can be compared (unlike CEA) using one common unit, like QALY. In addition, CUA combines morbidity and mortality into one unit without having to assign a dollar value to it (unlike CBA).

Four Basic Pharmacoeconomic Methodologies

METHODOLOGY	COST MEASUREMENT UNIT	OUTCOME UNIT
Cost-minimization analysis	Dollars	Demonstrated or assumed to be equivalent in comparative groups
Cost-benefit analysis	Dollars	Dollars
Cost-effectiveness analysis	Dollars	Natural units (e.g., life-years gained, mmHg blood pressure, % at treatment goal)
Cost-utility analysis	Dollars	Quality-adjusted-life-year (QALY) or other utilities

Health-Related Quality of Life

Health-related quality of life (HRQOL) refers to the effects of a disease and its treatment on an individual's functioning and well being as perceived by that individual. It is commonly included under a broad umbrella of assessments known as patient-reported outcomes (PROs). HRQOL is comprised of several important domains, including physical and mental functioning, role functioning, vitality, social functioning, and general health perceptions, among others.

HRQOL assessments can provide important patient-centered information related to the effects of a disease or treatment on patient functioning and well-being. These assessments are typically developed as either general (or generic) health status instruments that can be used across a number of disease areas (e.g., SF-36 Health Survey can be used for asthma and diabetes, among others) or disease-specific measures applicable to a limited disease population (e.g., Asthma Quality of Life Questionnaire). Prior to their use in practice, it is critical that the reliability and validity of HRQOL assessments in specific patient populations has been documented.

PRACTICE CASE

The NEW ENGLAND JOURNAL of MEDICINE

ESTABLISHED IN 1812   NOVEMBER 15, 2007   VOL. 357   NO. 20

Prasugrel versus Clopidogrel in Patients with Acute Coronary Syndromes

Stephen D. Wiviott, M.D., Eugene Braunwald, M.D., Carolyn H. McCabe, B.S., Gilles Montalescot, M.D., Ph.D.,
Witold Ruzyllo, M.D., Shmuel Gottlieb, M.D., Franz-Joseph Neumann, M.D., Diego Ardissino, M.D.,
Stefano De Servi, M.D., Sabina A. Murphy, M.P.H., Jeffrey Riesmeyer, M.D., Govinda Weerakkody, Ph.D.,
C. Michael Gibson, M.D., and Elliott M. Antman, M.D., for the TRITON–TIMI 38 Investigators*

ABSTRACT

BACKGROUND

Dual-antiplatelet therapy with aspirin and a thienopyridine is a cornerstone of treatment to prevent thrombotic complications of acute coronary syndromes and percutaneous coronary intervention.

METHODS

To compare prasugrel, a new thienopyridine, with clopidogrel, we randomly assigned 13,608 patients with moderate-to-high-risk acute coronary syndromes with scheduled percutaneous coronary intervention to receive prasugrel (a 60-mg loading dose and a 10-mg daily maintenance dose) or clopidogrel (a 300-mg loading dose and a 75-mg daily maintenance dose), for 6 to 15 months. The primary efficacy end point was death from cardiovascular causes, nonfatal myocardial infarction, or nonfatal stroke. The key safety end point was major bleeding.

RESULTS

The primary efficacy end point occurred in 12.1% of patients receiving clopidogrel and 9.9% of patients receiving prasugrel (hazard ratio for prasugrel vs. clopidogrel, 0.81; 95% confidence interval [CI], 0.73 to 0.90; P<0.001). We also found significant reductions in the prasugrel group in the rates of myocardial infarction (9.7% for clopidogrel vs. 7.4% for prasugrel; P<0.001), urgent target-vessel revascularization (3.7% vs. 2.5%; P<0.001), and stent thrombosis (2.4% vs. 1.1%; P<0.001). Major bleeding was observed in 2.4% of patients receiving prasugrel and in 1.8% of patients receiving clopidogrel (hazard ratio, 1.32; 95% CI, 1.03 to 1.68; P=0.03). Also greater in the prasugrel group was the rate of life-threatening bleeding (1.4% vs. 0.9%; P=0.01), including nonfatal bleeding (1.1% vs. 0.9%; hazard ratio, 1.25; P=0.23) and fatal bleeding (0.4% vs. 0.1%; P=0.002).

CONCLUSIONS

In patients with acute coronary syndromes with scheduled percutaneous coronary intervention, prasugrel therapy was associated with significantly reduced rates of ischemic events, including stent thrombosis, but with an increased risk of major bleeding, including fatal bleeding. Overall mortality did not differ significantly between treatment groups. (ClinicalTrials.gov number, NCT00097591.)

QUESTIONS

1. Looking at the results of the trial above, which of the following statements is correct?

   a. Clopidogrel has demonstrated a statistically significant benefit over prasugrel in reducing the primary efficacy endpoint

   b. Prasugrel has demonstrated a statistically significant benefit over clopidogrel in reducing the primary efficacy endpoint

   c. Prasugrel has demonstrated a statistically significant benefit over clopidogrel in preventing major bleeding

   d. Clopidogrel has demonstrated a statistically significant benefit over prasugrel in reducing the primary efficacy endpoint and preventing major bleeding

   e. There is no statistical difference between clopidogrel and prasugrel in the primary efficacy endpoint.

2. In the trial above, what is the absolute risk reduction in the primary efficacy endpoint?

   a. 22%
   b. 2.2%
   c. 9.9%
   d. 200%
   e. 28%

3. In the trial above, what is the relative risk reduction of experiencing the primary efficacy endpoint?

   a. 81.8%
   b. 50%
   c. 18.2%
   d. 122%
   e. 69%

4. In the trial above, what is the number of people needed to treat with prasugrel to achieve the primary efficacy measure in one patient?

   a. 40
   b. 45
   c. 4.5
   d. 46
   e. 14

5. In the trial above, the hazard ratio for non-fatal bleeding of 1.25 can be interpreted as:

   a. At any time a patient in the prasugrel group was 1.25 times as likely to experience nonfatal bleeding as a patient in the clopidogrel group.

   b. At any time a patient in the prasugrel group was 75% more likely to experience nonfatal bleeding as a patient in the clopidogrel group.

   c. At any time a patient in the clopidogrel group was 1.25 times as likely to experience nonfatal bleeding as a patient in the prasugrel group.

   d. At any time a patient in the clopidogrel group was 75% more likely to experience nonfatal bleeding as a patient in the prasugrel group.

   e. At only this point in time a patient in the prasugrel group was 1.25 times more likely to experience nonfatal bleeding as a patient in the clopidogrel group.

Questions 6-14 do not relate to the case.

6. A trial is conducted between 2 different beta blockers, referred to as Drug A and Drug B. The null hypothesis is that both drugs will be equal in their effects on lowering BP. The study concluded that the effects of Drug A were better than Drug B in lowering BP (p-value < 0.01). Which of the following statements is correct?

   a. We can accept the null hypothesis.
   b. We can fail to accept the null hypothesis.
   c. There is a 10% chance that Drug A is superior.
   d. There is a 0.1% chance that Drug B is superior.
   e. This trial did not reach statistical significance.

7. Correlation in a clinical trial describes:

   a. The ability of 1 or more variables to predict another
   b. The relationship between 2 variables
   c. Nominal data
   d. Confounding variables
   e. A cause and effect relationship

8. Which of the following statements concerning a Type I error is correct?

   a. A type I error means that the null hypothesis is accepted in error.
   b. A type I error means that the null hypothesis is rejected in error.
   c. A type I error means failing to reject the null hypothesis in error.
   d. A type I error means that the null hypothesis is accepted.
   e. A type I error is a beta error.

9. Which of the following statements concerning case-control studies is correct? (Select **ALL** that apply)

   a. They are retrospective.
   b. The patient serves as their own control.
   c. The researcher analyzes individual patient cases.
   d. They include cases without the intervention.
   e. They provide conclusive evidence of cause and effect.

10. Which of the following statements regarding the median is correct? (Select **ALL** that apply)

    a. It is the value in the middle of a ranked list.
    b. It is not appropriate to use with skewed data.
    c. It is not sensitive to outliers.
    d. It is a measure of dispersion.
    e. In a normal distribution, it is the same as the mean.

11. Choose the example that represents a direct medical cost: (Select **ALL** that apply)

    a. Lost productivity
    b. Quality of life
    c. Clinic visit
    d. Nursing services
    e. Cost of taking the bus to the hospital

12. Choose the best description of the purpose of a pharmacoeconomic analysis:

    a. To measure and compare the costs and outcomes of drug therapy and other medical interventions.
    b. To reduce health care expenditures by limiting medication use to only those who need it most.
    c. To get the best treatments available to as many people as possible.
    d. To examine the indirect costs of medical care in each medical specialty within hospitals, clinics, and outpatient surgery centers.
    e. To reduce the pharmacy drug budget within a hospital setting as a way to control health care costs.

13. Which of the following statements regarding average and incremental cost ratios is correct? (Select **ALL** that apply)

    a. Average cost ratios represent the average cost per outcome between competing alternatives.
    b. Incremental cost ratios represent the cost per additional unit of outcome between competing alternatives.
    c. Average cost ratios represent the average cost per outcome within a single alternative.
    d. Incremental cost ratios represent the cost per additional unit of outcome within a single alternative
    e. In most instances, incremental and average cost ratios are equal.

14. A pharmacist is conducting an analysis to determine the best way to manage patients with diabetes based on A1C values. Three treatment regimens will be evaluated based on cost and effects on A1C reduction. Choose the type of analysis the pharmacist should perform:

    a. A cost-utility analysis
    b. A cost-minimization analysis
    c. A cost-optimization analysis
    d. A cost-benefit analysis
    e. A cost-effectiveness analysis

Answers

1-b, 2-b, 3-c, 4-d, 5-a, 6-b, 7-b, 8-b, 9-a,c,d, 10-a,c,e, 11-c,d, 12-a, 13-b,c, 14-e

11

DRUG MECHANISMS, CLASSES & STRUCTURES

Functional Group	Structure
Hydroxyl	R—O—H
Methyl	R—CH₃
Carbonyl	R—C(=O)—R′
Carboxyl	R—C(=O)—OH
Amino	R—N(H)(H)
Phosphate	R—O—P(=O)(OH)—OH
Sulfhydryl	R—S—H

Please go to www.rxprep.com and click on the Student Resources tab and <u>print</u> out the document called <u>Chemical Structures and Functional Groups</u>. Keep with this chapter. These correlate to the structure questions in the RxPrep test bank.

Drugs are referred to by mechanism of action or purpose (such as ACE inhibitors, or antihypertensives) and by route of administration (such as topicals or oral suspensions). Primary mechanisms of action include local direct action (e.g., an emollient), chemical reactants (e.g., antacids), chelators (e.g., deferoxamine), and drugs that interact with receptors on the cell surface in the targeted tissue.

Drugs that Interact with Receptors

An agonist refers to a drug that behaves in a similar manner to a naturally occurring <u>endogenous</u> (produced by the body) <u>ligand</u>; the ligand (or substrate) is the compound that would normally bind to the receptor. An agonist will generally activate a receptor that starts a chain reaction that produces an effect, such as altering a second <u>messenger system</u>. For example, theophylline blocks phosphodiesterase (PDE), which increases the second messenger cyclic adenine monophosphate (cAMP), which in turn induces the release of epinephrine (which causes the bronchioles to open).

A drug that blocks the endogenous substrate is an <u>antagonist</u> (or blocker), such as beta blockers which block beta adrenergic transmitters such as epinephrine, which normally increases heart rate and blood pressure. Drugs can activate or inhibit enzymes, such as heparin which binds to antithrombin, an enzyme that inactivates thrombin. The interaction of the enzyme with the drug can be competitive or non-competitive. Competitive interaction occurs when a drug binds to the receptor which blocks the active site where the substrate would normally bind, preventing the activity (such as aspirin binding to cyclooxygenase in platelets which blocks thromboxane synthesis). In non-competitive interaction the drug binds to the enzyme at a site other than the active site, and reduces the activity of the substrate.

Except for the drugs that affect GABA, most seizure drugs bind to a receptor to alter <u>ion entry or departure</u> from a cell, which (in this case) reduces the excessive electrical activity (seizures). Antiarrhythmics work by a similar mechanism.

Many drugs interfere with normal cell duplication by binding to the DNA or some type of protein (such as ribosomes) or intercalating (inserting) itself into the DNA to prevent replication. Antibodies and hormones can amplify or provide a normal cellular process, such as erythropoietin injection to stimulate RBC production or testosterone gel to provide a substitute for low endogenous testosterone. Monoclonal antibodies are identical clones to a parent cell, and are used to interact with a cell receptor and block the receptor [such as infliximab, which inhibits tumor necrosis factor (TNF)-alpha] or as an agonist (such as immune globulin).

This chapter includes a drug chart of common mechanisms. Under the entry, there is an explanation designed to provide further information to aid memorization, followed by graphic representations of common hormone pathways, and common neurotransmitters (NT) and complications resulting from excess catecholamines [EPI, norepinephrine (NE), dopamine (DA) and serotonin (5HT)].

DRUG/CLASS	EXAMPLE	MECHANISM OF ACTION

ID I, Bacterial Infections

DRUG/CLASS	EXAMPLE	MECHANISM OF ACTION
Beta-lactams/monobactams *Gram-positives have more layers in the cell wall than Gram-negatives; beta lactams bind to penicillin-binding proteins (PBPs) in the wall, which prevents x-linking & makes the wall weak. This causes it to burst. Gram-negatives' wall is between 2 membrane layers made of x-linked peptidoglycans. Beta-lactams bind to PBPs & cause a similar method of cell death.*	Penicillin	Inhibits cell wall synthesis by binding to penicillin-binding proteins - bactericidal.
Quinolones *The enzyme DNA gyrase (also called topoisomerase II) stabilizes the DNA when it is unwinding in order to replicate. Without this stability, the DNA breaks apart and the bacteria is not able to replicate.*	Ciprofloxacin	Binds to topoisomerase IV and inhibits DNA gyrase causing DNA strands to break apart - bactericidal.
Tetracyclines *Each ribosome has subunits: 30S (small) and 50S (large). Binding to the 30S prevents the ribosomes from making proteins, which halts replication. Tetracyclines and aminoglycosides block the 30S subunit, and aminoglycosides also block the larger 50S subunit.*	Doxycycline	Reversibly binds to the 30S ribosomal subunit preventing reproduction - bacteriostatic.
Sulfonamides *Bacteria synthesize folate they need (humans get folate through the diet). Sulfonamides block an enzyme involved in the synthesis of folate, and without folate there is no replication.*	Sulfamethoxazole	Inhibits enzymes of the folate pathway to interfere with bacterial folate synthesis - bactericidal with trimethoprim.
Macrolides *Macrolides, chloramphenicol and clindamycin prevent the bacteria's ribosomes from making proteins by binding to the larger part of the ribosome, the 50S subunit. This halts replication.*	Azithromycin	Binds to the 50S ribosomal subunit preventing reproduction - bacteriostatic.
Glycopeptides *Peptidoglycans form a layer of the bacteria's cell wall. Glycopeptides block the peptidoglycans from forming, which blocks the cell wall formation.*	Vancomycin	Inhibits cell wall synthesis by blocking peptidoglycan polymerization - bactericidal.
Lipopeptides *Binding (inserting itself into the cell membrane) creates holes in the bacterial membrane, causing the ions to leak out. This destroys the bacteria.*	Daptomycin	Binds to the cell membrane causing rapid depolarization and inhibits DNA/RNA, and protein synthesis - bactericidal.
Oxazolidinones *Binding to a section of the 50S subunit of the ribosome, the 23S portion, blocks initiation, the first step in protein synthesis. This is a unique MOA, and thus cross-resistance with other drugs is rare.*	Linezolid	Binds to 23S ribosomal RNA of the 50S subunit inhibiting bacterial translation and synthesis - bacteriostatic.
Lincosamides *Macrolides, chloramphenicol and clindamycin prevent the bacteria's ribosomes from making proteins by binding to the 50S subunit, which halts replication.*	Clindamycin	Reversibly binds to the 50S ribosomal subunit inhibiting bacterial protein synthesis - bacteriostatic.
Anti-protozoal/Anti-bacterial *Treats many different kinds of infections primarily in the intestine, and STIs, including protozoa, giardia, trichomonas, bacteroides, clostridium, and anaerobic bacterial infections.*	Metronidazole	Affects the structure of DNA and causes strand breakage, which inhibits protein synthesis.
Aminoglycosides *Prevents the bacteria's ribosomes from making proteins by binding to the 30S and 50S subunits. This halts replication. Tetracyclines and aminoglycosides block the 30S, and aminoglycosides also block the larger 50S.*	Gentamicin	Binds to the 30S and 50S ribosomal subunits blocking bacterial protein synthesis; concentration-dependent.

Drug Mechanisms and Tips Continued

DRUG/CLASS	EXAMPLE	MECHANISM OF ACTION

ID III, Fungal and Viral Infections Chapter (Fungal)

DRUG/CLASS	EXAMPLE	MECHANISM OF ACTION
Polyene antifungals *Ergosterol is the equivalent to cholesterol in the fungal cell membrane. Amphotericin B binds to ergosterol, which causes ion channels to form and the cell contents to leak, leading to cell death..*	Amphotericin	Binds to ergosterol, which causes ion channels to form (leaky cell, components leak out), which leads to cell death.
Uracil blockers *Flucytosine turns into fluorouracil, which competes with uracil in the fungal RNA; this interferes with replication and protein synthesis.*	Flucytosine	Penetrates fungal cell wall to compete with uracil inhibiting fungal RNA and protein synthesis- fungicidal.
Azole antifungals *Blocks the enzyme that forms ergosterol, which is a fungi alternative of cholesterol and is required as part of the fungi's cell membrane.*	Fluconazole	↓ ergosterol synthesis and inhibits cell membrane formation- fungistatic.

ID III, Fungal and Viral Infections Chapter (Viral)

DRUG/CLASS	EXAMPLE	MECHANISM OF ACTION
Neuraminidase inhibitors *The influenza virus has two proteins on the surface of the membrane: hemagglutinin and neuraminidase. Once the virus has replicated, it needs to get out of the cell it has used for replication. To separate from the host's cell membrane so it can go infect other cells, the virus uses the neuraminidase enzyme like a scissors to cut itself loose.*	Oseltamivir	Inhibits the neuraminidase enzyme, preventing viral reproduction.
Viral replication blockers *The mechanism for antivirals is similar to the HIV drugs: blocking some part of the process inside the cell that the virus is using to replicate itself (such as blocking fusion into the cell, blocking the proteases, etc.)*	Acyclovir	Inhibits viral replication by competively binding to the enzymes that assemble the viral DNA.

Diabetes Chapter

DRUG/CLASS	EXAMPLE	MECHANISM OF ACTION
Insulin *See diagram.*	Aspart	
Biguanides *The glucose in the plasma cannot get into the cells that need it, so the cells send signals to the liver to release more glucose, which is not needed. The biguanides ↓the liver's output of glucose (primarily), ↓ glucose absorption in the gut and ↑ glucose entry into muscle cells (↑ insulin sensitivity).*	Metformin	↓ hepatic glucose production and intestinal absorption of glucose; ↑ insulin sensitivity.
Sulfonylureas *↑ pancreas' insulin production; daytime agent (covers > 1 meal).*	Glipizide	Stimulates insulin secretion from the pancreatic beta cells.
Meglitinides *↑ pancreas' insulin production; short-acting (postprandial for 1 meal).*	Repaglinide	Stimulates insulin secretion from the pancreatic beta cells.
Thiazolidinediones "Glitazones" *PPAR (pronounced pee-par) receptors are required for the uptake of some hormones, including insulin. A specific type, the PPAR-gamma subtype, activates fat & muscle cells, which causes more glucose to enter, and blocks glucose in the liver (from glycogen) from releasing into the blood. The glitazones are PPAR-g agonists. The mechanism requires transcription, which takes time; it can take over a month to see the full effect. These also affect PPAR receptors in the kidneys, which causes Na and H2O retention (edema).*	Pioglitazone	↑ peripheral insulin sensitivity through PPARy agonism.
Alpha-glucosidase inhibitors *Binds to enzymes in the small intestine which ↓ carbohydrate digestion (into monomers, including glucose), which ↓ absorption. This occurs with a meal; these drugs ↓ postprandial (after meal) hyperglycemia.*	Miglitol	Reversibly inhibits intestinal alpha-glucosidase.
SGLT-2 inhibitors "Glifozlins" *Normally, the kidneys reabsorb most of the glucose back into the blood. The SGLT-2 pump exchanges glucose (into the blood) for sodium (into the urine). Inhibiting the SGLT-2 pump results in glucose being excreted instead of reabsorbed. This ↑ diuresis, which can cause dizziness. The urine will have a higher glucose content, which provides a food source for fungi. These sometimes cause fungal (Candida) infections.*	Canagliflozin	Inhibit SGLT-2 in the proximal renal tubules ↓ reabsorption of glucose and ↑ urinary glucose excretion.

Drug Mechanisms and Tips Continued

DRUG/CLASS	EXAMPLE	MECHANISM OF ACTION
GLP-1 agonists *GLP (which is incretin) and GIP are 2 hormones released into the gut when a person eats, which go into the pancreas and cause the beta cells to release more insulin. The higher the glucose level, the more these hormones trigger insulin release. Both enzymes are quickly degraded in the gut by the enzyme DPP-4. GLP-1 agonists acts like more GLP, and the DPP-4 inhibitors block the enzyme from destroying these 2 enzymes (GLP and GIP). GLP also ↓ the release of glucagon. Just like insulin causes plasma BG to ↓, glucagon will ↑ the BG. GLP also slows the passage of food through the gut; this causes nausea, but also causes food satiety (less hunger, since the food is staying around longer).*	Exenatide	Incretin mimetics; GLP-1 analog ↑ insulin secretion and ↓ glucagon secretions and slows gastric emptying.
DPP-4 inhibitors *See above; these drugs prevent the breakdown of GLP.*	Sitaglipt n	Prevents DPP-4 enzyme from breaking down the incretin hormones, GLP and GIP.

Autoimmune Chapter

DRUG/CLASS	EXAMPLE	MECHANISM OF ACTION
Methotrexate *High doses have an anti-proliferative effect, which means it ↓ cell replication (to treat cancer). When used for autoimmune conditions (much lower doses), the mechanism is not well defined, but has an anti-inflammatory effect.*	Methotrexate	Inhibits folate synthesis by inhibiting DNA synthesis, repair, and cellular replication
TNF inhibitors *TNF plays an important role in inflammatory processes; blocking TNF ↓ inflammation.*	Etanercept	Binds tumor necrosis factor (TNF) and blocks its interaction with cell surface receptors.

Hepatitis & Liver Disease Chapter

DRUG/CLASS	EXAMPLE	MECHANISM OF ACTION
Interferons *Interferons are natural hormones released in response to pathogens. Interferon alpha (used for hepatitis) and beta (used for multiple sclerosis) cause the cells to release substances that ↓ viral protein synthesis.*	Interferon-alpha-2b	Interacts with cells through high affinity cell surface receptors causing multiple effects like cellular growth inhibition, induction of gene transcription, alters the state of cellular differentiation, etc.

Thyroid Disorders Chapter

DRUG/CLASS	EXAMPLE	MECHANISM OF ACTION
Levothyroxine *See diagram.*	Levothyroxine	T4, used to replace thyroid hormone, which is no longer being produced due to an auto-immune destruction of the thyroid gland (Hashimoto's)
Thionamides *See diagram.*	Propylthiouracil	Inhibits the synthesis of thyroid hormones by blocking the oxidation of iodine in the thyroid gland; for hyperthyroidism (such as Grave's).

Transplant Chapter

DRUG/CLASS	EXAMPLE	MECHANISM OF ACTION
Steroids *Steroids used short-term can ↓ acute inflammation & be life-saving; used long term, they are one of the hardest drugs to take (ruins bone health, ↑ BG, ↑ BP, Cushingoid Sx, etc) & are used when other alternatives are insufficient.*	Prednisone	↓ inflammation, suppresses the immune system, suppresses the adrenal gland function with chronic administration.
Calcineurin inhibitors *Basic drugs used to block rejection of a transplanted organ; given with another agent to ↓ many toxicities (including nephrotoxicity--which is important since a kidney may have been the transplant).*	Tacrolimus	Suppresses cellular immunity by inhibiting T-lymphocyte activation.

Drug Mechanisms and Tips Continued

DRUG/CLASS	EXAMPLE	MECHANISM OF ACTION

Osteoporosis and Hormone Therapy Chapter

DRUG/CLASS	EXAMPLE	MECHANISM OF ACTION
Estrogen *See diagram. Estrogen taken by pills or a patch works by negative feedback on LH and FSH, which ↓ vasomotor symptoms (hot flashes, in the perimenopause, prevents ovulation (for contraception), ↓ bone resorption (for osteoporosis prevention) & replenishes the vaginal mucosa.*	Estradiol	The 2 female sex hormones are estrogen [*estriol (weakest), estrone & estradiol (most potent)]* and progesterone (P).
Progestin *Progestins are used for other indications, including contraception, either alone (DepoProvera, IUD implant, and in progestin-only pills) or in combination with estrogen. The progestins used the most in birth control pills are levonorgestrel and norethindrone. The progestins used to prevent endometrial hyperplasia (see right) is commonly given as a separate drug (Provera) or in combination with the estrogen (Prempro, Premphase).*	Medroxyprogesterone	Unopposed E (given alone) causes the endometrial lining to grow; this can lead to endometrial cancer. Most women using E for menopausal symptoms have a uterus & will need to use a P with the E to prevent endometrial hyperplasia.
Bisphosphonates *Osteoclasts break down (dissolve and absorb) bone, osteoblasts build (synthesize) bone. The bisphosphonates prevent bone break down.*	Alendronate	Inhibits osteoclasts, ↓ bone resorption.
PTH Analog *Teriparatide prevents bone breakdown, and helps build new bone. This is a recombinant form of parathyroid hormone (PTH); and is given by injection.*	Teriparatide	Stimulates osteoblasts, ↓ osteoclast activity, ↑ GI Ca-absorption & renal Ca-reabsorption.
Testosterone *In some men it is used to improve hypogonadism (low T), which is the recommended use; in other men, it is used to ↑ vitality/virility (without low T level).*	Testosterone Gel	Primary androgen (male sex hormone), indicated for replacement in androgen-deficiency.

Pain Chapter

DRUG/CLASS	EXAMPLE	MECHANISM OF ACTION
Acetaminophen *Unlike NSAIDs, does not ↓ inflammation to a significant effect. Both acetaminophen and NSAIDs provide analgesia (↓ pain) and are antipyretic (↓ fever). Acetaminophen is safer, except in overdose (due to hepatotoxicity).*	Acetaminophen	↓ pain and fever. Mechanism not clear, but ↓ PG formation.
Aspirin *Used primarily for cardio-protection; same mechanism as other NSAIDs.*	Aspirin	Blocks the synthesis of COX-1 and COX-2 enzymes. Aspirin forms an irreversible (covalent) bond with the COX-1 enzyme, which provides an antiplatelet effect.
NSAIDS, nonselective *Prostaglandins (PGs) are made from arachidonic acid by the action of COX enzymes. Blocking PG formation ↓ fever (antipyretic), pain (analgesic) and inflammation. In the gastric mucosa, PGE-1 is gut protective; PGs with chronic NSAID use can cause gastric ulceration. While COX-1 is the predominant form affecting PG formation in the gut, the expression of COX-2 is inducible (it can be up-regulated) and COX-2 selective NSAIDs do not eliminate GI risk.*	Ibuprofen	Blocks the synthesis of COX-1 and COX-2 enzymes, which ↓ PG formation.
NSAIDS, selective *See above. Has less of an effect on the GI mucosa, but may be worse for the heart and kidneys.* .	Celecoxib	Blocks COX-2 only, which ↓ PG formation.
Opioids *Morphine is the prototypical mu opioid receptor agonist.*		Agonist at the mu, kappa, and delta opioid receptors. The primary receptor for analgesia is the mu receptor.
Opioid antagonist *Used for overdose (respiratory depression), and will also reverse analgesia.*	Naloxone	
Opioid partial agonist *Occupies the opioid receptor; often given with naloxone (Subutex, others) to block the high from opioids.*	Buprenorphine	Partial agonist at the mu receptor.

Drug Mechanisms and Tips Continued

DRUG/CLASS	EXAMPLE	MECHANISM OF ACTION
Tramadol *Tramadol affects dual mechanisms: opiate agonist, and monoamine reuptake inhibitor (5HT and NE); it must be used cautiously with other serotonergic drugs. Due to effect on NE is less sedating (in some it is activating) than other opioids.*	Tramadol	Binds to mu opiate receptors and inhibits the reuptake of serotonin and norepinephrine.
Tapentadol *Tapentadol is similar to tramadol (affects opiate and NE receptors), but is for more severe pain than tramadol (between tramadol and full scale agonists like morphine). Similar to tramadol, it can contribute to serotonergic toxicity, and can cause physical dependence.*	Tapentadol	Binds to mu opiate receptors and inhibits the reuptake of norepinephrine. Full mechanism not well defined; may affect other NTs.
Skeletal muscle relaxants *The different drugs in this group have different mechanisms of action; they all are highly sedating (strong CNS depressant effects). Carisoprodol's mechanism makes it highly addictive, and dangerous when mixed with other agents; it is scheduled federally as C-IV.*	Carisoprodol	Primarily works as a strong CNS depressant; metabolized to meprobamate, a strong anxiolytic with depressant properties.

Gout Chapter

DRUG/CLASS	EXAMPLE	MECHANISM OF ACTION
Xanthine oxidase inhibitors *By blocking a key enzyme required to produce uric acid, the end product (from an earlier step in the process) is harmless.*	Allopurinol	Blocks uric acid production by inhibiting xanthine oxidase (blocks conversion of xanthine --> hypoxanthine --> uric acid).

Hypertension Chapter

DRUG/CLASS	EXAMPLE	MECHANISM OF ACTION
Thiazides *Most combo drugs (with another BP drug) end in IDE, ZIDE, ETIC or HCT. They are used for hypertension. They do not cause the water loss loops cause, and are not useful for diuresis in heart failure.*	Chlorthalidone	Inhibits Na and Cl reabsorption in the distal convoluted tubules of the nephron increasing excretion of Na, water, and K.
DHP-calcium channel blockers (DHP CCBs) *Ends in DIPINE. Amlodipine and nifedipine ER used commonly; nifedipine IR is avoided due to side effects (peripheral edema, reflex tachycardia, etc.) They do not ↓ HR like the non-DHP CCBs.*	Amlodipine	Inhibits Ca movement through calcium channels, causing vasodilation and ↓ BP.
Non-DHP calcium channel blockers *Two in class: Verapamil is used mainly for hypertension; diltiazem is used mainly to control heart rate in tachycardia d/t arrhythmias (rate control). Both ↓ BP. Do not use with a non-DHP CCB (same mechanism).*	Diltiazem	Inhibits Ca from entering the "slow" channels of smooth muscle and myocardium causing coronary vasodilation.
ACE inhibitors *Ends in PRIL. Angiotensin II is the active form of angiotensin that can stimulate aldosterone release. Aldosterone --> sodium and water retention, which ↑ blood pressure. Angiotensin II is a potent vasoconstrictor (↑ BP) & interacts with the sympathetic nervous system to ↑ vascular tone.*	Benazepril	Inhibits angiotensin-converting enzyme preventing the conversion of angiotensin I to angiotensin II
ARBs *Ends in ARTAN. Usually used as alternative to ACE I (no cough), otherwise similar.*	Irbesartan	Blocks angiotensin II from binding to the angiotensin II type-1 (AT1) receptor.
Beta blockers, selective *Ends in OLOL. The alpha and beta blocker (labetalol) has a ends in ALOL. "A" for alpha blocking.*	Metoprolol	Competitively blocks beta-1 adrenergic receptors (heart) with minimal effect on beta-2 receptors (lung).
Beta blocker, nonselective *Ends in OLOL, like propranolol. Propranolol is also lipophilic, and it has a role for conditions where CNS penetration (due to lipophilicity) is required, such as essential tremor or stage fright.*	Propranolol	Competitive blocker of beta-1 and beta-2 receptors (to block NE) in (primarily) the heart and lung.
Alpha-2 agonists *Used for hypertension (see NT diagram). Only antihypertensive that comes in a patch. Used for ADHD for symptom management, and helps with nighttime sleep; the MOA for ADHD is not well defined.*	Clonidine	Stimulates alpha-2 receptors in the brain resulting in ↓ sympathetic outflow from the CNS.

Dyslipidemia Chapter

DRUG/CLASS	EXAMPLE	MECHANISM OF ACTION
HMG-CoA reductase inhibitor *Some cholesterol comes from the diet, but most is synthesized, which requires the enzyme that statins block.*	Simvastatin	Block the enzyme, which catalyzes the rate-limiting step in cholesterol synthesis, which ↓ cholesterol.

Drug Mechanisms and Tips Continued

DRUG/CLASS	EXAMPLE	MECHANISM OF ACTION
Fibrates *FIBR in middle of name. Primarily used to ↓ triglycerides (TG).*	Fenofibrate	Induces lipoprotein lipolysis and hepatic fatty acid uptake, ↑ removal of LDL, stimulates reverse cholesterol transport, and ↓ neutral lipid exchange between VLDL and HDL.
Omega-3 fatty acids *In addition to TGs, have antithrombotic, anti-arrhythmic & anti-inflammatory effects, and ↓ BP. Many people use OTC fish oils primarily for CV benefits.*	*Lovaza*	↓ the hepatic synthesis of TGs.

Heart Failure Chapter

DRUG/CLASS	EXAMPLE	MECHANISM OF ACTION
Aldosterone Receptor Antagonists (ARAs) *Blocking aldosterone ↓ K excretion, which ↑ potassium, possibly to dangerous levels. Since K is cleared renally, if renal impairment is present hyper-K is more likely.*	Spironolactone	Aldosterone ↑ sodium and water retention, and ↑ potassium excretion (blocking aldosterone is used to lower BP and for benefit in HF.
Nitrates *Used in MI ↓ preload and afterload, which ↓ myocardial (heart) oxygen demand. Oral forms used for angina, and in blacks (with hydralazine) for HF.*	*Nitrostat.*	↑ nitric oxide causing venous vasodilation.
Digoxin *Inhibiting pump causes ↑Na inside muscle cells, which ↑ Ca in cells, which ↑ contraction force (positive inotrope). Also ↓ heart rate (negative chronotrope).*	Digoxin	Inhibits Na/K ATPase pump; ↑ CO, ↓ HR.

Antiarrhythmics Chapter

DRUG/CLASS	EXAMPLE	MECHANISM OF ACTION
Amiodarone *Prolonging repolarization (when the heart recharges) slows the electrical impulses, which ↓ arrhythmias. Contains iodine, and has a structure similar to levothyroxine; can cause hypo or hyperthyroidism.*	Amiodarone	Prolongs repolarization with effects on Na, K & Ca channels & alpha and beta receptors inhibitor.

Anticoagulation Chapter

DRUG/CLASS	EXAMPLE	MECHANISM OF ACTION
Indirect Xa inhibitors *Factor Xa is at the start of the coagulation cascade where the intrinsic & extrinsic pathways meet, and is central to the coagulation process.*	Fondaparinux	Converts prothrombin to thrombin (active form).
Direct thrombin inhibitors (DTIs) *Argatroban is given IV, and is the key anticoagulant used for inpatients with heparin induced thrombocytopenia (HIT). Dabigatran is an oral DTI.*	Argatroban	Directly inhibits thrombin (factor IIa).
Heparin, Unfractionated (UFH) *Antithrombin is a natural anticoagulant that inhibits coagulation by lysing thrombin and factor Xa. Heparin and the LMWHs markedly increase the power of antithrombin.*	Heparin	Binds to antithrombin; antithrombin inactivates thrombin and activated factor X (factor Xa).
Low molecular weight heparin (LMWH) *Like heparin, LMWHs bind to & accelerate the activity of antithrombin. Compared to UFH, LMWH's have ↓ binding to plasma proteins & endothelial cells, ↓ interpatient variability, a more predictable response and longer duration of action. Can be given SC (& can be self-administered).*	Enoxaparin	Binds to antithrombin and inactivates thrombin Factor Xa > Factor IIa
Protamine *Reversal agent (antidote) for heparin and LMWH. Binds to heparin and LMWHs to form a compound with no anticoagulant activity; it is used if bleeding occurs, or when surgery must take place quickly in a patient using either heparin or a LMWH.*	Protamine	Binds with strongly acidic heparin to form a stable complex (salt), which neutralizes the anticoagulant activity.
Warfarin *The liver requires vitamin K to make blood clotting proteins (factors). Warfarin blocks vitamin K from working, and the liver produces clotting proteins that work less effectively. Too much clotting, such as with a DVT or a PE, blocks blood vessels and can be fatal. The catch is that when the blood is artificially anticoagulated, clotting is poor, and slight injury to a blood vessel can cause severe blood loss.*	*Coumadin*	Inhibits VKORC1 reducing the regeneration of vitamin K and depleting Factors II, VII, IX, and X & proteins C and S.
Vitamin K *Reversal agent (antidote) for warfarin. In bleeding or with a very high risk of bleeding in a patient who has taken warfarin, vitamin K can be given directly to override the effect of the warfarin.*	*Mephyton (phytonadione)*	Promotes liver synthesis of clotting Factors II, VII, IX, X.

Drug Mechanisms and Tips Continued

DRUG/CLASS	EXAMPLE	MECHANISM OF ACTION

Acute Coronary Syndrome (ACS) Chapter

P2Y-12 inhibitors *P2Y-12 plays a central role in amplification and stabilization of ADP-induced platelet aggregation.*	Clodipogrel	Inhibits P2Y-12 receptor on platelets.
GIIb/IIIa inhibitors *The platelet receptor GPIIb/IIIa is critical in thrombosis & hemostasis by mediating interactions between platelets & ligands, primarily fibrinogen. The receptor has 2 subunits, GPIIb & GPIIIa. When fibrinogen binds to the activated GPIIb/IIIa receptor, it x-links (aggregates) adjacent platelets.*	Eptifibatide	Blocks glycoprotein IIb/IIIa receptors, preventing platelet aggregation and thrombosis.
Fibrinolytics *Fibrinolytics are also called thrombolytics, since they lyse (dissolve) a thrombus (clot). They do this by activating plasminogen, which forms plasmin- an enzyme that acts like a scissors and cuts the x-links formed by fibrin that provides the structure to a clot.*	Alteplase	Causes fibrinolysis by binding to fibrin & converts plasminogen to plasmin.

Sexual Dysfunction Chapter

| **PDE-5 inhibitors**
cGMP causes the smooth muscle in the penis to relax so that the corpus cavernosum (inside compartment) can fill with blood, which forms the erection. PDE-5 makes cGMP inactive; inhibiting PDE-5 keeps the penis relaxed so it can fill. | Sildenafil | Inhibits phospohodiesterase-5 (PDE-5) preventing the degradation of cGMP in the corpus cavernosum. |

Asthma/COPD Chapters

Beta-2 agonists *Just as beta blockers that block beta-2 receptors cause bronchoconstriction, beta-2 agonists cause broncho-relaxation, and are used for acute (fast) relief for trouble breathing.*	Albuterol	Binds beta-2 receptors causing relaxation of bronchial smooth muscles.
Inhaled steroids *Asthma has a pattern of inflammation (with various inflammatory mediators) that causes the classic symptoms of shortness of breath, wheezing, chest tightness and cough. Suppressing the inflammation with inhaled steroids is the most effective chronic treatment.*	Budesonide	Depresses migration of leukocytes and fibroblasts causing inhibition of the inflammatory response.
Theophylline *Theophylline relaxes bronchial smooth muscle (to let air flow in) and ↓ the inflammation pathways. It works well, but is difficult to use due to many drug and disease interactions, and toxicity.*	Theophylline	Blocks PDE-III and IV, causing ↑ cAMP, and likely has other mechanism/s not well defined.
Anticholinergics *Acetylcholine causes bronchoconstriction; blocking acetylcholine in salivary glands causes the primary side effect of dry mouth. Tiotropium causes more dry mouth, but is given less frequently (Q daily) than ipratropium (QID).*	Ipratropium	Blocks acetylcholine and ↓ cGMP at parasympathetic sites in the bronchial smooth muscle.

Allergic Rhinitis/Cough & Cold Chapter

Antihistamines, sedating *H1 agonism causes pruritus (itching), vasodilation and bronchoconstriction. Diphenhydramine (H1 antagonist) is helpful for itching/allergic reactions, nausea, motion sickness, and for bronchial relaxation (for allergic reaction).*	Diphenhydramine	Blocks histamine at histamine-1 receptor site. Non-selective.
Antihistamines, nonsedating *Non-sedating antihistamines (2nd-generation) block histamine release; they do not bind to histamine-releasing cells in the CNS which cause sedation.*	Cetirizine	Blocks histamine at histamine-1 receptor. Selective.
Decongestants *Vasoconstriction helps to ↓ swollen nasal mucous membranes, edema and nasal congestion in the respiratory tract mucosa.*	Pseudoephedrine	Alpha-adrenergic agonists (sympathomimetics) which cause vasoconstriction.
Dextromethorphan *At high doses is an NMDA receptor antagonist, which --> hallucinations (used as a drug of abuse). Memantine is an NMDA (NaMenDA) receptor antagonist.*	Delsym	*Binds to the medullary cough center in the brain, ↓ cough.*
Guaifenisen *↑ amount and ↓ the viscosity (thins) the respiratory tract secretions (phlegm), which may ↑ the effectiveness of the cough reflex.*	Mucinex	Hydrates throat and ↓ phlegm viscosity.

Drug Mechanisms and Tips Continued

DRUG/CLASS	EXAMPLE	MECHANISM OF ACTION
Anemia Chapter		
Erythropoietin stimulating agents (ESAs) *The kidney produces erythropoietin, but not with very poor renal function. No erythropoietin --> ↓ RBCs --> anemia. Also used for cancer, but less commonly than in past; can contribute to tumor growth.*	*Epoetin alfa*	Stimulates erythropoiesis (to produce RBC's) in the bone marrow.
Depression Chapter		
SSRIs *See diagram for antidepressant NTs. Escitalopram is the left entantiomer (S-stereoisomer) of the racemic (both left and right) compound citalopram. Steroisomers are generally half the dose of the racemic compound (e.g., escitalopram 10 mg is ~20 mg citalopram.)*	Escitalopram	Inhibits serotonin reuptake in CNS neurons.
SNRIs *Similar to effects of SSRIs on serotonin; effects on NE can contribute to side effects, including ↑ BP and sweating.*	Venlafaxine	Inhibits serotonin and norepinephrine reuptake in CNS neurons..
MAO inhibitors *Highest risk for hypertensive crisis with the non-selective MAO inhibitors used for depression; other MAO inhibitors have risk, especially in combination with other drugs that raise these activating NTs.*	Tranylcypromine	Inhibits the monoamine oxidase enzyme responsible for breaking down NE, DA & 5HT.
Schizophrenia/ Psychosis Chapter		
Antipsychotics, phenothiazines *Phenothiazines, depending on the activity at different receptors, have antipsychotic, antiemetic, sedative antipruritic and anticholinergic effects. The ones that block DA D2 receptors (like chlorpromazine) are used as antipsychotics. The ones that do not (like promethazine) are not useful as antipsychotics; promethazine is used primarily for nausea.*	Chlorpromazine	Blocks D2 receptors in the CNS; strong alpha blocking; may depress the reticular activating system (regulates wakefulness).
Antipsychotics, butyrophenones *First generation (typical) antipsychotics include different drug classes, including phenothiazines and butyrophenones. All block dopamine D2 receptors. A butyrophenone that has fallen out of favor due to QT risk is droperidol, which was previously a common antiemetic in the hospital setting. Haloperidol also has QT risk and both have many other complications, including sedation and a high risk of EPS.*	Haloperidol	Blocks D2 receptors in the brain; has minimal 5HT-2A effect.
Antipsychotics, second generation *The primary difference between the typicals and atypicals is that while both block DA, atypicals also block 5HT. Aripiprazole was the 1st atypical that is markedly different; it is a D2 & 5-HT1A partial agonist & 5-HT2A antagonist.*	Aripiprazole	Blocks D2 and 5HT-2A receptors.
Bipolar Chapter		
Lithium *Lithium is an old, useful bipolar drug (primarily for mania), and is increasingly used as augmentive (add-on) treatment for depression; this is likely d/t ↑ 5HT transmission. Lithium is serotonergic; use cautiously with other 5HT drugs.*	Lithobid	Alters cation transport, improves reuptake of 5HT & NE, ↑ glutamate clearance, inhibits second messenger systems.
Parkinson's Chapter		
Carbidopa/levodopa *Levodopa is converted to dopamine in the CNS, but before it gets to the CNS, it will get destroyed by the enzyme dopa-decarboxylase. It is given with carbidopa, which blocks this enzyme.*	*Sinemet*	Carbidopa inhibits dopa decarboxylase preventing metabolism of levodopa.
Dopamine agonists *Sinemet works well, but long-term is plagued by response fluctuations (movement freezes up), and produces free radicals that seem to destroy DA-producing cells. DA-agonists do not produce cytotoxic free radicals. They are not without adverse effects, including excessive sedation/sudden sleep.*	Pramipexole	Acts like dopamine at the dopamine receptor.
Anticholinergics *Used early in disease, and is avoided in elderly due to poor tolerability. The mechanism for benefit is not well known but may be due to restoring a balance in the CNS between DA and Ach.*	Benztropine	Blocks acetylcholine at cerebral synapses; similar to the effects of atropine.

Drug Mechanisms and Tips Continued

DRUG/CLASS	EXAMPLE	MECHANISM OF ACTION

Alzheimers Chapter

DRUG/CLASS	EXAMPLE	MECHANISM OF ACTION
Acetylcholinesterase inhibitors *Acetylcholine is reduced in AD, and the dementia is thought to be partially due to dysfunction in cholinergic signal transmission. Blocking the enzyme ↑ ACh.*	Donepezil	Inhibits acetylcholinesterase, the enzyme responsible for breakdown of acetylcholine.
Memantine *Activation (by glutamate, other compounds) of CNS NMDA receptors may contribute to Alzheimer's disease symptoms. Memantine (NaMeNDa) is thought to provide NMDA receptor antagonism.*	Namenda	Blocks NMDA which inhibits glutamate from binding to NMDA receptors; ↓ abnormal activation.

ADHD Chapter

DRUG/CLASS	EXAMPLE	MECHANISM OF ACTION
Stimulants *Low levels of DA and NE in the prefrontal cortex are thought to contribute to ADHD symptoms; stimulants ↑ levels of both NTs.*	Methylphenidate	Blocks reuptake of norepinephrine and dopamine in the CNS.
Atomoxetine *See above. Antidepressants modestly improve ADHD symptoms; others in this or the SSRI class may be approved for ADHD in the future.*	Strattera	Selective norepinephrine reuptake inhibitor.

Sleep Disorders Chapter

DRUG/CLASS	EXAMPLE	MECHANISM OF ACTION
Non-Benzodiazepines *Thought for many years to be safer than the benzodiazepines (and do cause ↓ dependence) but now should be used less due to known health risks. Both groups affect GABA, which causes inhibition of the CNS, including sedation. Lacks anxiolytic (anti-anxiety) effect.*	Zolpidem	Potentiates GABA, causing inhibition by binding to a benzodiazepine receptor subtype specific for sedation.
Benzodiazepines *Difficult to use chronically due to dependence, tolerance and risk of abuse. ↑ efficiency of GABA. Sedating and anxiolytic effect.*	Temazepam	↑ the efficiency of GABA, which ↑ the inhibitory effect (↓ motor activity, ↑ sedation, ↑ anticonvulsant activity, etc.)

CLASS/EXAMPLE	NTS/CHANNELS AFFECTED	MECHANISM OF ACTION

Epilepsy/Seizures Chapter

CLASS/EXAMPLE	NTS/CHANNELS AFFECTED	MECHANISM OF ACTION
Barbiturates/Phenobarbital	GABA (agonist)	Antiepileptic Drugs (AEDs) ↓ the abnormal electrical activity that causes seizures by 5 primary mechanisms: 1. ↑ GABA, which inhibits the neuron from firing (via blocking Cl-channels), 2. ↓ Glutamate, an excitatory NT, by blocking glutamate reuptake into the neuron or by another mechanism, 3. Inhibiting Na ion channels; Na channels along the neurons affect how electrical signals travel. Changing the amount of ions inside and outside of the neuron affects the action potential, which causes the neurons to fire. Binding to the Na channel (lamotrigine, phenytoin, carbamazepine, oxcarbazepine), causes the neuron to slow down or stop firing repeatedly. 4. Modulating calcium channels; Ca ions control the electrical signal going from one neuron to another, and binding to the channel slows down or stops the transmission. 5. Decreasing entry of K into the cells; K entry ↑ excitation.
Benzodiazepines/Clobazam	GABA (↑ efficiency)	
Carbamazepine	Na channels	
Oxcarbazepine	Na, Ca channels	
Valproate	GABA channels	
Ethosuximide	Ca channels	
Lamotrigine	Glutamate, Na channels	
Topiramate	Na channels	
Phenytoin/Fosphenytoin	Na channels	
Levetiracetam	GABA, Ca channels	
Pregabalin/Gabapentin	Glutamate, Ca channels	

Drug Mechanisms and Tips Continued

DRUG/CLASS	EXAMPLE	MECHANISM OF ACTION

Gastroesophageal Reflux Disease & Peptic Ulcer Disease Chapter

DRUG/CLASS	EXAMPLE	MECHANISM OF ACTION
Antacids *Antacids, histamine type-2 receptor antagonists and PPIs are the usual choices to ↓ reflux symptoms. Antacids are fastest (they do not require absorption as they work in the gut) but are short-acting; they have to be in the stomach to have an effect.*	Ca-carbonate	Neutralizes gastric acid via a reaction that produces salt and water; this ↑ gastric pH (↓ acidity).
Histamine-2 receptor antagonists (H2RAs) *H2 receptors are located on the gastric mucosa parietal (acid-secreting) cells. Lasts longer than antacids (works systemically, versus in the gut alone), but less effective than PPIs for decreasing acid secretion. They slow down, rather than inactivate, the proton pump.*	Famotidine	Reversibly inhibits H2 receptors on the gastric parietal cells which ↓ gastric acid secretion.
Proton pump inhibitors (PPIs) *Binds to and inactivates the proton pump (versus H2-blockers which ↓ acid secretion). Used commonly; strong acid suppression has health risks (↑ infection risk, ↓ bone density).*	Omeprazole	Irreversibly binds to gastric H/K ATPase pump in parietal cells, blocking gastric acid secretion.

Constipation Chapter

DRUG/CLASS	EXAMPLE	MECHANISM OF ACTION
Bulk forming laxatives *Bulk agents soften hard stool to permit defecation (taken with adequate fluids), and soaks up fluid to harden liquid stool (to help with diarrhea).*	Psyllium	Soaks up fluid in loose stools to form gel matrix & adds bulk to hard stools.
Stool softeners *Docusate is a common OTC agent used chronically by many to soften hard stool. It is similar to an emollient & makes the stool easier to pass out.*	Docusate	Lubricates and softens fecal mass.
Stimulant laxatives *Irritation to the lining causes contractions, which helps push the stool out, in addition to a water "rush" that acts like a wave, carrying the stool out.*	Sennosides	↓ water and electrolyte absorption by stimulating colonic neurons and irritating the mucosal lining of the colon.
Polyethylene glycol (PEG) *PEG is used for a variety of purposes: to make compounds larger (to escape the immune system, and ↑ the duration of action (such as Pegfilgrastim) & as solvents/excipients in compounding. Taken orally, it works as a laxative.*	Miralax	Causes fluids to be retained in the bowel lumen with a net ↑ of fluid secretions in the small intestines.
Glycerin *Glycerin suppositories are non-systemic, work quickly, and come in pede and adult sizes.*	Pedia-Lax	Osmotic pressure ↑ to draw fluids into the colon and stimulate fecal evacuation.
PAMORAs *Blocks opioids in the GI tract to relieve constipation; little of the drug enters the CNS, and these do not block analgesia or cause opioid withdrawal symptoms.*	Naloxegol	Peripherally-Acting Mu Opioid Receptor Antagonists (PAMORA) block the opioid in the gut to ↓ opioid-induced constipation. They do not affect opioid receptors in the CNS, and do not ↓ analgesia.

Irritable Bowel Syndrome Chapter

DRUG/CLASS	EXAMPLE	MECHANISM OF ACTION
Mesalamine *Mesalamine is a salicylate that inhibits COX synthesis (↓ PGs), and has both anti-inflammatory and immunosuppressive properties. Is given topically (and sometimes systemically) depending on the location of the condition.*	Canasa	Controls inflammatory mechanisms, acts as a free radical scavenger and inhibits TNF.
Dicyclomine *By blocking acetylcholine in the GI tract, the parasympathetic "rest and digest" response is reduced (↓ intestinal movement, muscle spasms/cramping).*	Bentyl	Blocks acetylcholine at parasympathetic sites (anticholinergic).

Drug Mechanisms and Tips Continued

DRUG/CLASS	EXAMPLE	MECHANISM OF ACTION

Benign Prostatic Hyperplasia Chapter

DRUG/CLASS	EXAMPLE	MECHANISM OF ACTION
Alpha blockers, non-selective *Non-selective alpha blockers affect volume receptors and cause orthostasis; the selective blockers (such as tamsulosin) are designed to ↓ orthostasis by attaching specifically to alpha-1a receptors on the prostate.*	Doxazosin	Inhibits alpha-1 adrenergic receptors and relaxes the smooth muscles of the bladder neck, reducing obstruction (↑ urine outflow).
5-alpha reductase inhibitors *DHT is the hormone that primarily effects normal (and abnormal) prostate growth. The inhibition of this process means the prostate stops growing, it shrinks with time, and ↓ BPH symptoms.*	Finasteride	Inhibits 5 alpha-reductase, which blocks the conversion of testosterone to active dihydrotestosterone (DHT).

Overactive Bladder Chapter

DRUG/CLASS	EXAMPLE	MECHANISM OF ACTION
Anticholinergics *A bothersome side effect of anticholinergics used for other purposes is urinary retention; in this case, drugs are used for the same effect (to ↓ urination). Using agents with a high affinity for a subtype of the muscarinic receptor (M3) ↓ side effects; however, the M3 subtype is in the salivary glands & dry mouth is common.*	Oxybutynin	Competitive antagonist of the muscarinic receptors, which inhibits binding of acetylcholine.

Glaucoma Chapter

DRUG/CLASS	EXAMPLE	MECHANISM OF ACTION
Beta blockers *Glaucoma medications either ↓ aqueous humor production (which ↓ IOP, the fluid pressure in eyes) and/or ↑ the flow of the fluid out of the eyes (outflow).*	Timolol	Blocks beta-1 and beta-2 adrenergic receptors to ↓ aqueous humor production.
Prostaglandin analogs *See previous; affects both mechanisms, are strong ↓ of IOP. Also darkens pupils/lengthens eyelashes, which may or may not be welcome to the patient.*	Latanoprost	↑ outflow to ↓ IOP.
Carbonic anhydrase inhibitors (CAIs) *See above.*	Dorzolamide	Inhibits carbonic anhydrase, ↓ production to ↓ IOP.

Critical Care Chapter

DRUG/CLASS	EXAMPLE	MECHANISM OF ACTION
Vasopressors *See diagram. Vasopressors inotropes ↑CO (pushes more blood from the heart to the body) during a critical condition when the CO has fallen. All are catecholamines (in this case DA) and are agonists at alpha & beta receptors.*	Dopamine	Stimulates vasoconstriction to ↑ systemic vascular resistance to ↑ blood pressure & ↑ CO.
Inotropes *Dobutamine is a synthetic catecholamine (see above, and diagram) and is a strong agonist at beta receptors.*	Dobutamine	↑ contractility of the heart to ↑ heart rate and cardiac output.
Neuromuscular blockers (non-depolarizing) *These paralyze muscles (e.g., for surgery so patient can't move) by blocking acetylcholine. Have no effect on pain; analgesics must be given b/c the patient cannot report pain. They keep diaphragm from moving; a ventilator is required to force breathing.*	Cisatracurium	Binds to the acetylcholine receptor to block the action of acetylcholine.
Neuromuscular blockers (depolarizing) *Depolarizing, like the non-depolarizing, have to stop Ach, which causes opening of a cation channel to generate an action potential --> muscle contraction. Succinylcholine makes the ACh receptor insensitive to Ach.*	Succinylcholine	Activates acetylcholine receptors (continuously) which desensitizes them.
Vasopressin antagonists *Vasopressin (antidiuretic hormone, ADH), causes vasoconstriction and ↓ water reabsorption.*	Vasopressin	↑ excretion of water while maintaining Na by antagonizing vasopressin receptors.
Alpha-2 agonist, selective *Used for sedation in the ICU. This agent is preferred by some b/c patients are more easily arousable (& can communicate pain) & ↓ ventilation time compared to other 2 other primary sedation agents, midazolam & propofol.*	Dexmedetomidine	↓ NE release, which ↑ firing of inhibitory neurons, which causes sedative & anxiolytic (relaxing) effects.

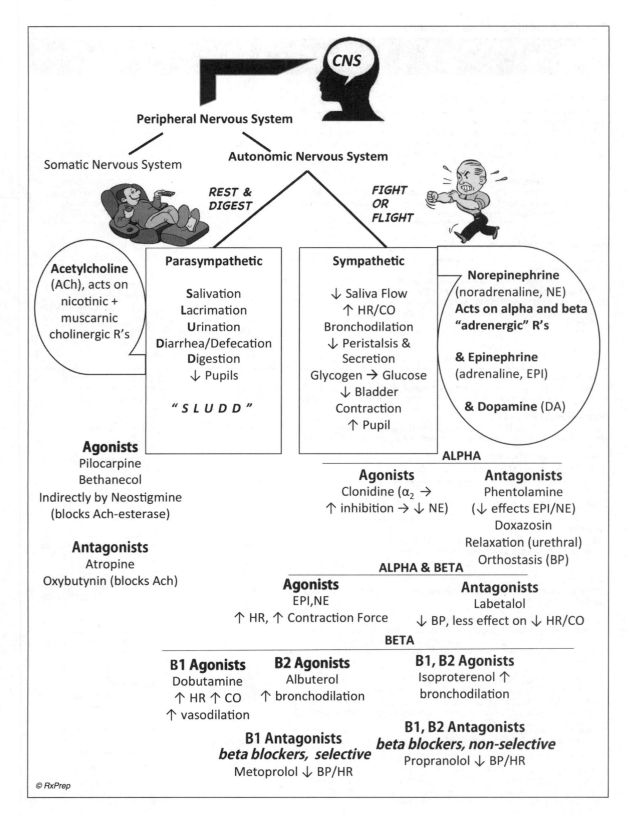

EPI, NE, DA (CATECHOLAMINES)
& HYPERTENSIVE CRISIS

These NTs are monoamines and are metabolized by monoamine oxidase (MAO) or catechol-o-methyl transferase (COMT).

The older MAO inhibitor antidepressants are non-selective (MAO A and B), and they bind irreversibly to the MAO enzyme—and destroy it.. The newer drugs are specific for MAO A or MAO B...but the specificity is dose-related. MAO inhibitors & drugs metabolized by MAO → catecholamine excess → hypertension, hyperthermia, tachycardia, agitation...coma, death.

Remedy: Wait 14 days or longer between a MAO-metabolized drug and an MAO inhibitor.

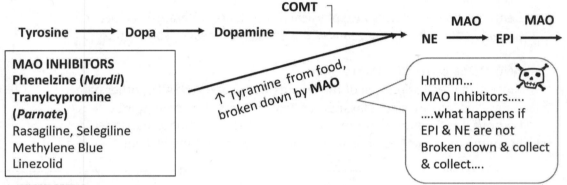

Tyrosine → Dopa → Dopamine → NE → EPI →

COMT

MAO   MAO

MAO INHIBITORS
Phenelzine (*Nardil*)
Tranylcypromine (*Parnate*)
Rasagiline, Selegiline
Methylene Blue
Linezolid

↑ Tyramine from food, broken down by **MAO**

Hmmm...
MAO Inhibitors.....
....what happens if
EPI & NE are not
Broken down & collect
& collect....

RISK WITH

Ephedrine and analogs (pseudoephedrine, etc.), bupropion, buspirone, lithium, meperidine, SSRIs, SNRIs, TCAs, tramadol, levodopa, mirtazapine, dextromethorphan, cyclobenzaprine (and other skeletal muscle relaxants), some of the triptans, St. John's wort, procarbazine, lorcaserin, others.

SEROTONIN: 5HT
& SEROTONIN SYNDROME

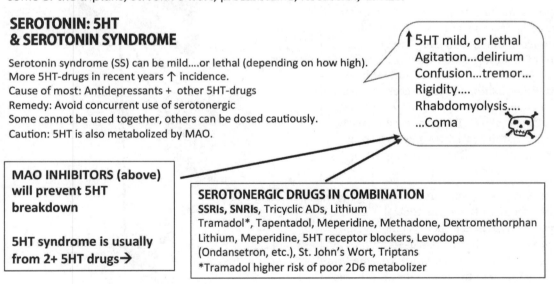

Serotonin syndrome (SS) can be mild....or lethal (depending on how high).
More 5HT-drugs in recent years ↑ incidence.
Cause of most: Antidepressants + other 5HT-drugs
Remedy: Avoid concurrent use of serotonergic
Some cannot be used together, others can be dosed cautiously.
Caution: 5HT is also metabolized by MAO.

↑ 5HT mild, or lethal
Agitation...delirium
Confusion...tremor...
Rigidity....
Rhabdomyolysis....
...Coma

MAO INHIBITORS (above) will prevent 5HT breakdown

5HT syndrome is usually from 2+ 5HT drugs→

SEROTONERGIC DRUGS IN COMBINATION
SSRIs, SNRIs, Tricyclic ADs, Lithium
Tramadol*, Tapentadol, Meperidine, Methadone, Dextromethorphan
Lithium, Meperidine, 5HT receptor blockers, Levodopa
(Ondansetron, etc.), St. John's Wort, Triptans
*Tramadol higher risk of poor 2D6 metabolizer

© RxPrep

GABA is the primary INHIBITORY NT.
GABA ↓Brain Stimulation, Fear & Anxiety.

CNS DEPRESSANT EFFECTS
Common & cause of many auto accidents & injuries
Often additive...some drugs on their own can knock a person out, including GABA drugs:

GABA Agonists or ↑ GABA Effect
Barbiturates
Benzodiazepines...both cause physical dependence, tolerance can occur and addiction/abuse (especially with benzodiazepines) is common.

AND THESE cause CNS Depression:
Most pain medications (all of the opioids, some of the NSAIDs, other pain drugs), skeletal muscle relaxants, anticonvulsants, benzodiazepines, barbiturates, hypnotics, mirtazapine, trazodone, dronabinol, nabilone, propranolol, clonidine, others, many illicit substances and alcohol.

© RxPrep

INSULIN

Insulin works primarily on 3 areas: the liver (makes the liver convert glucose into glycogen, to store for later use--and also prevents the glycogen from breaking back down into glucose after a person eats and the glucose in the blood increases), the muscle cells (which need a lot of insulin; insulin brings glucose into the cells for energy) and adipose (fat) cells (insulin causes excess glucose to be converted into fat, which is stored in adipose cells). To supply cells with energy, insulin activates glucose transporters on the cells so glucose can get in; this reduces hyperglycemia.

Normally, the pancreas releases the right amount of insulin that the body requires. When the beta cells in the pancreas have been destroyed (type 1) the patient must take insulin. In type 2, there is less insulin over time, and there can be resistance to insulin in the cells, which means more insulin is required in order to open up the glucose transporters and let glucose get into the cells.

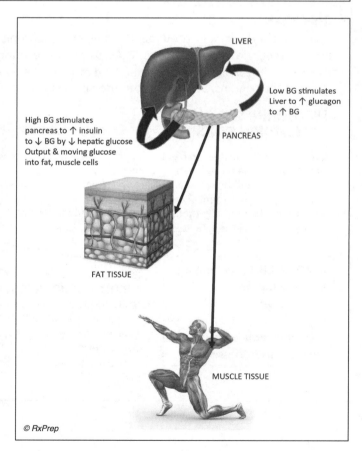

LIVER

Low BG stimulates Liver to ↑ glucagon to ↑ BG

High BG stimulates pancreas to ↑ insulin to ↓ BG by ↓ hepatic glucose Output & moving glucose into fat, muscle cells

PANCREAS

FAT TISSUE

MUSCLE TISSUE

© RxPrep

THYROID

The thyroid gland produces triiodothyronine (T3) and thyroxine (T4). Both require iodine; if iodine is low, the thyroid will increase in size in an attempt to overcome the deficiency, producing a goiter. Propylthioruracil and methimazole block iodine oxidation to block production of thyroid hormones (to treat hyperthyroidism).

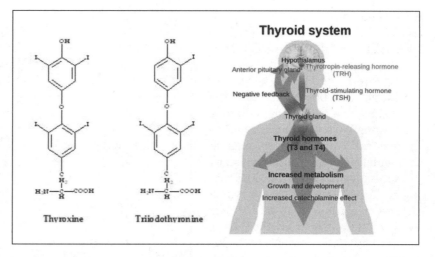

The thyroid gland is controlled by the hypothalamus and the pituitary gland. The hypothalamus produces thyrotropin-releasing hormone (TRH), which stimulates the production of TSH, which increases production of T3 and T4. Over-production of thyroid hormones has the reverse effect by decreasing production through "feedback inhibition," in which the end product (thyroid hormone) is high, and the thyroid hormone reduces it's own synthesis.

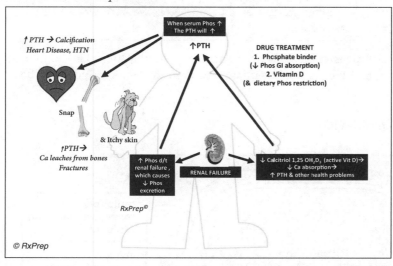

PARATHYROID HORMONE & HYPER-PARATHYROIDISM

Hyperparathyroidism can be caused by several conditions, and is commonly a secondary complication of severe renal disease.

Both high phosphate and low vitamin D contribute to hyperparathyroidism—both are treated:

Initially, dietary restriction of phosphate is tried (which does not provide a large reduction), followed by the addition of phosphate binders which bind the phosphate in the gut and prevent absorption. These are taken with each meal.

When the kidney is unable to activate Vitamin D, either the active form (calcitriol) or a calcium mimetic (such as *Sensipar*) is used as a substitute.

CORTISOL

Hypothalamus--> anterior pituitary--> ACTH--> adrenal gland--> cortisol. Physical and emotional stress increases cortisol production, with effects shown in the diagram. Notice that endogenous steroids cause the same effects, but dysregulated.

Giving steroids chronically has the reverse effect, and shuts down cortisol production through negative feedback, causing Cushing's.

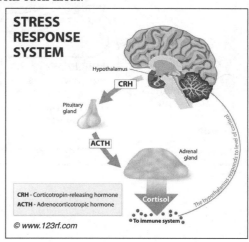

ESTROGEN, PROGESTERONE AND THE FEMALE MENSTRUAL CYCLE

The menstrual cycle has 3 phases: 1st: The follicular phase begins on the 1st day bleeding (the start of the period). Follicle stimulating hormone (FSH) stimulates egg (follicle) development, and increases estrogen. 2nd: The ovulatory phase, which is a short phase. It begins when the luteinizing hormone (LH) level surges, which triggers ovulation 24-36 hours later (release of the egg from the ovary), and the end of the phase. 3rd: The luteal phase, which begins with ovulation and lasts about 14 days.

Notice in phase 1 that estrogen (E) and progesterone (P) are low, and this triggers bleeding. E and P causes the endometrium to thicken, and when low, the lining drips off. Estrogen increases, which causes LH to surge

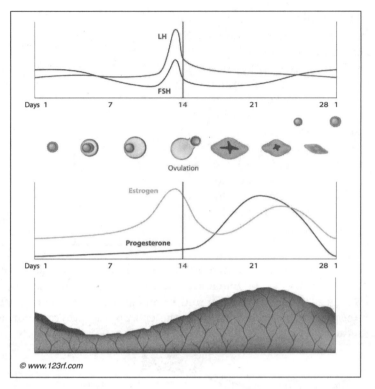

© www.123rf.com

and trigger ovulation. Estrogen and Progesterone cause the endometrium (the lining of the uterus) to thicken to prepare for an embryo, and P causes the cervical mucus to thicken and increases body temperature.

ANTIBIOTICS MECHANISM OF ACTION

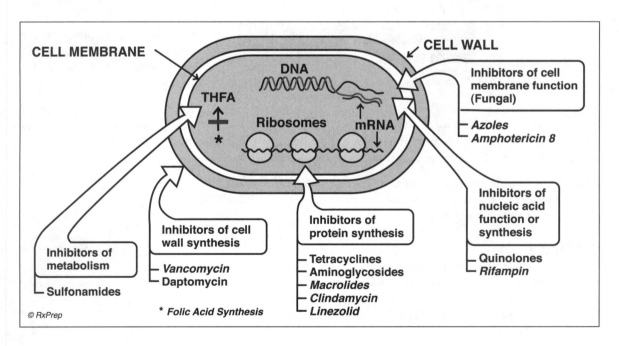

DRUG FORMULATIONS

DRUG FORMULATION CONSIDERATIONS

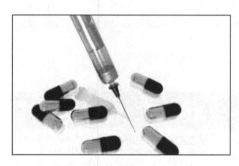

Compressed tablets are the least expensive drug formulation to manufacture and the most common formulation type. Capsules are also relatively inexpensive to make. If a pharmaceutical company develops a drug in any other formulation the cost will be higher – and a patient group that would benefit from the new formulation would be required. Prednisolone 10 mg tablets cost < 25¢ per tablet. A similar steroid in an oral disintegrating formulation (ODT), *Orapred ODT*, is branded and is ~$16 per tablet. The higher-priced formulation might be beneficial in a child with facial swelling who might choke on a hard tablet or who cannot yet swallow tablets.

It is helpful to recall a drug's formulation types by asking two questions:

1) Who typically uses this drug?

2) Would there be a reason to have this type of formulation for this patient population?

This can be useful on the exam if unsure if the formulation exists.

Examples

Olanzapine

Olanzapine is an antipsychotic with various formulations available: immediate-release (IR) tablet, oral disintegrating tablet, short-acting injection, and long-acting injection.

Who uses this drug? People with schizophrenia, bipolar disorder or some type of psychosis.

What types of formulations would be beneficial? The majority of patients with schizophrenia discontinue antipsychotics. It is useful to deliver the drug in a long-acting injection to improve adherence. A few of the antipsychotics come as orally disintegrating tablets (ODTs) – these are useful to block the patient from hiding the medication in the mouth ("cheeking") and then spitting it out when no one is watching. The ODT formulations dissolve in the mouth quickly which prevents cheeking. The fast-acting injection works quickly and is useful for acute agitation.

Ondansetron

Ondansetron, a 5-HT$_3$-receptor antagonist used to prevent or treat nausea is available in with various formulations available: IR tablet, short-acting injection, oral solution, ODT and oral film.

<u>Who uses this drug</u>? Patients receiving emetogenic chemotherapy or any other emetogenic drug, post-surgical patients, opioid-naïve patients using opioids acutely or with any condition that causes nausea/vomiting.

<u>What types of formulations would be beneficial</u>? If vomiting is an issue, oral medications would be useless and the <u>injection</u> would be used instead. If there is nausea alone, the <u>ODT or the film or the injection</u> can be given. ODTs are preferred if there is dysphagia, which could be present due to age and/or a medical condition, including cancer. It would be difficult to swallow tablets with painful esophageal ulcers, strictures or tumors. Films can be placed on or under the tongue or along the inside of the cheek and provide similar benefit to ODTs. With some film formulations the <u>loss to first-pass metabolism is reduced</u>. The <u>oral solution</u> would be preferable if the patient has an NG-tube or any dysphagia or pain from solid oral formulations. The solution can be swallowed directly and is sweetened with sorbitol to mask the bitter taste of the medicine. One of the 5-HT_3-receptor antagonists comes in a long-acting <u>patch</u> (*Sancuso*) that reduces nausea for up to seven days; this would be useful for a patient with nausea from chemotherapy that lasts awhile. The patch is put on prior to chemo (not useful for nausea happening when the patch is first applied) since, like most patches, it takes time for drug absorption through the skin. This summary chart contains select medications and the reasoning behind the unique formulation(s).

Select Medications in Unique Formulations

FORMULATION	EXAMPLES	REASONS FOR USE
ODTs – placed on the tongue and disintegrate rapidly in saliva	*Niravam* – alprazolam *Abilify Discmelt* – aripiprazole *Parcopa* – carbidopa/levodopa *Zyrtec Allergy Children* – cetirizine *FazaClo* – clozapine *Aricept ODT* – Donepezil *Prevacid SoluTab* – lansoprazole *Lamictal ODT* – lamotrigine *Metozolv ODT* – metoclopramide *Remeron SolTab* – mirtazapine *Zyprexa Zydis* – olanzapine *Zofran ODT* – ondansetron *Orapred ODT* – prednisone *Risperdal M-TAB* – risperidone *Maxalt-MLT* – rizatriptan *Zelapar* – selegiline *Staxyn* – vardenafil *Zomig-ZMT* – zolmitriptan	<u>Dysphagia</u> – trouble swallowing due to a variety of reasons: Stroke is the #1 cause of dysphagia due to paralysis of the throat muscles. Dysphagia can be due to esophagitis, esophageal tumors, ↓ LES pressure/reflux, facial swelling from an allergic reaction, or with other conditions that worsen motor function, including multiple sclerosis and Parkinson disease. <u>Children</u> are often too young to swallow tablets or capsules. <u>Nausea</u> can make it difficult to tolerate anything orally, however, ODTs cause less nausea than oral formulations swallowed whole. If vomiting is present or is likely a non-oral route should be used. <u>Non-adherence</u> – ODTs prevent holding the drug in the corner of the mouth to spit out shortly afterward – the tablet would dissolve quickly and the caregiver could follow with a drink of water.
Films that use gut absorption	*Zuplenz* – ondansetron Many OTC products used for children come as films, and films are used for some adult OTC drugs and for breath fresheners.	Films have similar benefits to ODTs; they dissolve in the mouth easily and do not have issues associated with swallowing.
Lozenges for oral mucosa drug administration	*Mycelex* – clotrimazole troche	Used to treat a condition in the oral mucosa – the drug is held in the mouth while the troche slowly dissolves.

Common (Select) Medications Given in Unique Formulations Continued

FORMULATION	EXAMPLES	REASONS FOR USE
Sublingual (SL) or buccal delivery with tablets, film, or sprays	*Saphris* – asenapine SL tablet *Edluar* – zolpidem SL tablet *Intermezzo* – zolpidem SL tablet *Nitrostat* – nitroglycerin SL tablet *Nitrolingual, NitroMist* – nitroglycerin SL spray *Bunavail* – buprenorphine/naloxone buccal film *Onsolis* – fentanyl buccal film *Subsys* – fentanyl SL spray *Actiq* – fentanyl buccal lozenge *Fentora* – fentanyl buccal tablet *Abstral* – fentanyl SL tablet	SL and buccal absorption has a faster onset than a tablet or capsule that is swallowed; the drug is readily absorbed into the venous circulation right under the absorption site (e.g., under the tongue). Less of the drug is lost to gut degradation and first-pass metabolism.
Nasal sprays (NS)	*Lazanda* – fentanyl NS *Fortical, Miacalcin* – calcitonin NS *Flumist* – influenza live vaccine NS *Nascobal* – cyanocobalamin (vitamin B 12) NS *Sprix* – ketorolac NS *Imitrex* – sumatriptan NS *Zomig* – zolmitriptan NS *Afrin* – oxymetazoline NS *Flonase* – fluticasone NS	Nasal sprays such as *Afrin* and *Flonase* are used primarily to treat localized nasal symptoms. The nasal route has a faster onset than the GI route, and is useful for acute conditions that should be treated quickly, including pain. Nasal sprays bypass gut absorption; proteins that would get destroyed in the gut (calcitonin) can be given nasally. A compound that requires a gut factor for absorption can also be given nasally (vitamin B12).
Creams, ointments, gels, solutions for topical conditions	*Abreva* – docosanol cream *Latisse* – bimatoprost gel *Bactroban* – mupirocin ointment Many others, including topical retinoids and benzoyl peroxide or salicylic acid products for acne, psoriasis treatments, first aid products, steroid creams and ointments & topical antifungals.	Topical treatments used for topical conditions have a decreased incidence of systemic side effects and generally provide faster relief. Common conditions treated topically include cold sores, acne, eczema, inflammation, mild infections, hair loss, rash, fungal infections, viral sores, hypotrichosis.
Topicals for systemic conditions	*Nitro-Bid* – nitroglycerin ointment *AndroGel* and other hormones	
Injections that patients can self-administer (mostly SC)	*Imitrex* – sumatriptan *Arixtra* – fondaparinux *Lovenox* – enoxaparin *Humira* – adalimumab *EpiPen* – epinephrine *Enbrel* – etanercept *Evzio* – naloxone *Simponi* – golimumab *Copaxone* – glatiramer *Peg-Intron, Rebif* – and other interferons *Physicians EZ Use B-12* – cyanocobalamin (vitamin B12) *Aranesp* – darbepoetin alfa *Epogen/Procrit* – epoetin alfa	SC administration is used for acute relief (such as pain, with triptans) or for stat treatment of a severe condition (such as opioid overdose with *Evzio* or bronchoconstriction with the *EpiPen*) or, for drugs that would get destroyed or not absorbed if given by oral administration (enoxaparin). The erythropoiesis stimulating agents (ESAs) are given SC by patients with impaired renal function, and if in ESRD, are given IV at the dialysis center.

Common (Select) Medications Given in Unique Formulations Continued

FORMULATION	EXAMPLES	REASONS FOR USE
Chewable Tablets	Many OTCs *(Pepto-Bismol, Immodium, Claritin)* *Augmentin* – amoxicillin/clavulanate *Suprax* – cefixime *Amoxil* – amoxicillin *Dilantin Infatabs* – phenytoin *Fosrenol* – lanthanum (must chew for drug to bind gut phosphate) *Singulair* – montelukast *Lamictal CD* – lamotrigine *Methylin* – methyphenidate	These are primarily used for children who are unable to swallow tablets. A few are for adults; calcium citrate tablets are large, and chewable calcium products are easier to tolerate. Note that *Pepto-Bismol* and *Immodium* are used for diarrhea; with a gut infection, nausea could be present.
Long-Acting Oral Tablets/Capsules Some capsules can be opened and the beads put in a small amount of soft food- instruct the patient to swallow without chewing. Note the danger if long-acting formulations are crushed: a fatal dose could be released. This includes ER opioids. Be sure to look for the suffix and counsel. There are a few long-acting formulations that can be cut at the score line – but still NOT crushed, such as *Toprol XL* and *Sinemet CR*.	*Concerta* *Detrol LA* Do not crush or chew any drug that has the following suffix that indicates it is a long-acting formulation: XR, ER, LA, SR, CR, CRT, SA, TR, TD, or have 24 in the name, or the ending –cont (for controlled release), or timecaps or sprinkles.	Certain drugs are designed as slow release or are enteric-coated to avoid irritation to the GI lining or are designed to dissolve in the small intestine. Or, the drug may be designed to release drug slowly to avoid nausea or to provide a long-duration of action to avoid repeated day-time dosing. Providing a smooth level of drug release over time reduces high "peaks" which reduces side effects due to too much drug hitting the "wrong" receptor and provides a safe level of drug over the dosing interval. This is required for conditions that require steady drug levels such as with epilepsy, hypertension, and with many others.

Common (Select) Medications Given in Unique Formulations Continued

FORMULATION	EXAMPLES	REASONS FOR USE
Granules, powders or capsules that can be opened and sprinkled into soft food or water Typically these are long-acting beads - if they sit in soft food the liquid will ruin the slow release. The food must not be warm or the beads will dissolve. Instruct patients to consume right after they sprinkle or stir; do not chew if long-acting or an irritant. To swallow <u>without chewing</u> requires that the drug be placed in a <u>small amount of soft food</u>.	*Avinza* – morphine, on applesauce or soft food *Kadian* – morphine, on applesauce or soft food *Monurol* – fosfomycin, in 3-4 ounces cool water *Micro-K* – potassium, on applesauce or pudding *Coreg CR* – carvedilol, on applesauce *Creon, Lip-Prot-Amyl, Pancreaze, Pertzye, Ultresa, Viokace, Zenpep* – pancrelipase, on soft food with low pH (applesauce, pureed pears or banana) *Depakote Sprinkle* – valproic acid, on soft food *Namenda XR* – memantine, on applesauce *Ritalin LA, Metadate CD, Adderall XR* – methylphenidate, on applesauce *Focalin XR* – dexmethylphenidate, on applesauce *Adderall XR* – dextroamphetamine/amphetamine ER, on applesauce *Vyvanse* – lisdexamfetamine, in water, yogurt or orange juice *Singulair* – montelukast granules, in 5 mL baby formula or breast milk or in a spoonful of applesauce, carrots, rice or ice cream *Topamax Sprinkle* – topiramate, on soft food *Dexilant* – dexlansoprazole, in applesauce or acidic juice *Prevacid* – lansoprazole, in applesauce or acidic juice *Nexium* – esomeprazole, in applesauce or acidic juice *Prilosec* – omeprazole, in applesauce or water *Welchol* – colesevelam, in 4-8 oz water, fruit juice or diet soda *Colestid* – colestipol, in at least 3 oz of liquid *Questran, Questran Light, Prevalite* – cholestyramine, in 2-6 oz water or non-carbonated liquid	These are used primarily for geriatric and pediatric patients who have some type of swallowing issue. Sometimes the capsule or tablet is too large to swallow. Instruct patient <u>not to chew</u> any long-acting pellets or beads that are emptied out from a capsule, <u>not to let the mixture sit too long</u> (take within the time directed) and <u>not to add to anything warm or hot</u> (the contents will dissolve too quickly).
Patches	See chart of common patches later in this chapter; a few examples are listed here: *Exelon* – rivastigmine *Duragesic* – fentanyl *Sancuso* – granisetron	Provides drug for a longer period of time (up to 1 week), Less side effects ($\downarrow$ nausea, $\downarrow$ GI irritation) and $\downarrow$ side effects from high peak levels with frequent oral dosing. Useful option if vomiting. Helps with adherence if family member can apply patch.
Intravenous (IV) Infusion	Many, acute care drugs	Fast response, achieves high concentrations and/or avoid poor absorption with critical illness, bypasses the oral route, avoids loss of drug due to N/V.

Common (Select) Medications Given in Unique Formulations Continued

FORMULATION	EXAMPLES	REASONS FOR USE
Long-Acting Intramuscular (IM) Injections	*Haldol* – haloperidol decanoate *Zyprexa Relprevv* – olanzapine *Risperdal Consta* – risperidone *Abilify Maintena* – aripiprazole *Invega Sustenna* – paliperidone *Lupron Depot* – leuprolide	Various drugs come as long-acting injections to improve adherence (such as antipsychotics) or to ↓ the need for more frequent (painful) injections.
Suppositories/ Enemas	*Rowasa* – mesalamine enema *Canasa* – mesalamine suppository *Babylax* – glycerin suppository *Dulcolax* – bisacodyl suppository *Fleet Enema* – sodium phosphates enema *Preparation H* – phenylephrine/cocoa butter suppository *FeverAll* – acetaminophen suppository	Used either for localized treatment (treating constipation, hemorrhoids) or for systemic treatment (such as mesalamine rectal forms for distal ulcerative colitis. Suppositories can be used when the patient is NPO and systemic treatment is needed (such as acetaminophen for treating pain or fever in an infant).

PATCHES

Medications are increasingly being delivered via transdermal delivery systems. Common concerns with their use includes non-adhesion (patches falling off the skin), patients inappropriately cutting patches, improper disposal, MRI burns, heat exposure leading to toxicity, and lag-time to effect. This list contains the more commonly used patches and how to address common issues concerning patches.

Common Patches, Application Sites

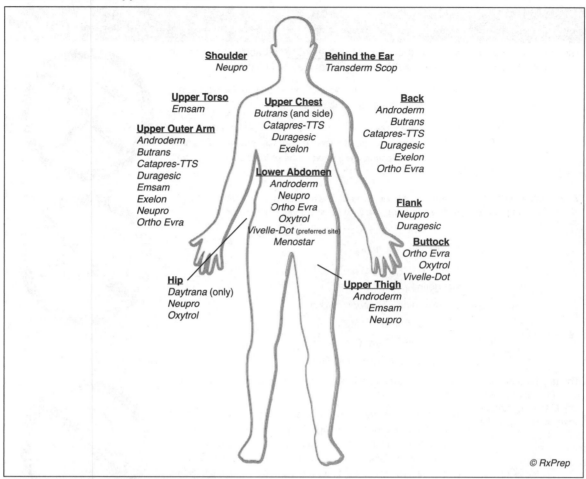

Shoulder
Neupro

Behind the Ear
Transderm Scop

Upper Torso
Emsam

Upper Chest
Butrans (and side)
Catapres-TTS
Duragesic
Exelon

Back
Androderm
Butrans
Catapres-TTS
Duragesic
Exelon
Ortho Evra

Upper Outer Arm
Androderm
Butrans
Catapres-TTS
Duragesic
Emsam
Exelon
Neupro
Ortho Evra

Lower Abdomen
Androderm
Neupro
Ortho Evra
Oxytrol
Vivelle-Dot (preferred site)
Menostar

Flank
Neupro
Duragesic

Buttock
Ortho Evra
Oxytrol
Vivelle-Dot

Hip
Daytrana (only)
Neupro
Oxytrol

Upper Thigh
Androderm
Emsam
Neupro

© RxPrep

Common Concerns with Patches

QUESTION	RESPONSE	
Can I cut the patch into pieces?	■ Usually no, except *Lidoderm*, which is designed to be cut and applied over the painful regions. ■ Some patients are instructed by their healthcare providers to cut matrix patches, such as fentanyl. This is not advisable since prescribed doses can change and medication errors can happen. Fentanyl patches are available in five different doses and as less expensive generics, which should make cutting unnecessary.	
Can the patch be exposed to heat from an electric blanket, heating pad, or body temperature > 38 °C (> 100.4 °F)?	In almost all cases no heat exposure; this causes the drug to pour out of the patch, resulting in toxicity. With fentanyl and buprenorphine this can be quickly toxic (fatal).	

Common Concerns with Patches Continued

QUESTION	RESPONSE	
The patch is bothering my skin. What can I do?	■ Check if the patient is <u>alternating</u> the application site. An alternative site (if permitted) may be beneficial. ■ The skin should not be shaved shortly before applying; shaving is irritating to the skin. ■ In some cases a topical steroid, such as hydrocortisone (OTC) can be applied <u>after</u> the patch is removed; if applied before application it will prevent the patch from sticking well.	
Which patches need to be removed prior to an MRI?	Patches containing metal, such as aluminum, need to be removed prior to an MRI or else it will burn the skin. Testosterone *(Androderm)* Clonidine *(Catapres-TTS)* Fentanyl *(Duragesic*, generics) Rotigotine *(Neupro)* Scopolamine *(Transderm-Scop)* *Salonpas Power Plus* (OTC) Nicotine (*NicoDerm CQ*) Check package insert; this can change.	
The patch does not stick (it falls or peels off). Can the patch be covered with tape if it will not stick?	With most patches, if it comes off, a new patch is reapplied to the same or a different site. ■ Most patches cannot be covered with tape. A few patches permit tape around the edges. If patches are placed on lubricated skin they will not stick. Place on dry, non-lubricated skin. No moisturizer or bath oils beforehand. Press down for the right amount of time, with palm over the patch. Some require a rather long time, such as the fentanyl patch which takes 30 seconds of pressure to adhere to the skin. ■ Hairy skin will block some of the drug from touching the skin, and can prevent the patch from sticking well. Although patches are not placed on hairy skin, do not shave right before the patch application. This can cause little bumps on delicate skin, and patches cannot be placed on irritated or broken skin. Cut hair close to the skin or shave in advance. Or, use a permitted site that is not hairy. ■ Try not to touch the sticky-side of the patch. ■ Warning: Do not cover patches with the exception of fentanyl *(Duragesic)* or buprenorphine *(Butrans),* which can be covered only with the <u>permitted</u> adhesive film dressings *Bioclusive* or *Tegaderm.* ■ *Catapres-TTS* comes with its own adhesive cover, which goes over the patch to hold it in place.	

Common Concerns with Patches Continued

QUESTION	RESPONSE
How often do I need to apply my patch?	Clonidine (*Catapres-TTS*): Weekly Estradiol (*Climara, Menostar*): Weekly Estradiol (*Alora, Vivelle-Dot*): Twice weekly Estradiol/levonorgestrel (*ClimaraPro*): Weekly Fentanyl (*Duragesic*): Q72H, if it wears off after 48 hours, change to Q48H Diclofenac (*Flector*): Twice daily Lidocaine (*Lidoderm*): 1-3 patches on for 12 hours, then off 12 hours Methylphenidate (*Daytrana*): Q AM, 2 hours prior to school, alternate hips daily Nicotine (*NicoDerm CQ*): Daily Nitroglycerin (*Minitran, Nitro-Dur*): On 12-14 hours/day, off 10-12 hours/day Ethinyl estradiol/norelgestromin (*Ortho Evra*): Weekly for 3 weeks, off for the 4th week Oxybutynin (*Oxytrol*): Twice weekly Rivastigmine (*Exelon*): Daily Rotigotine (*Neupro*): Daily Scopolamine (*Transderm-Scop*): Q72H, if needed Selegiline (*Emsam*): Daily Testosterone (*Androderm*): Nightly, not on scrotum
Where is the patch applied?	Check individual agent. Common application sites include upper chest or upper/sides of back (below the neck), upper thigh, upper outer arm. Most require alternating sites to reduce skin irritation. ■ *Daytrana* is on hip, alternating right and left hips daily. ■ *Transderm Scop* is behind the ear, alternating ears Q 72H. ■ Estrogen patches are mostly lower abdomen; some can be applied to upper buttock. Never to breasts. ■ Testosterone patch is never to scrotum (testicles and surrounding sac). ■ Topical pain patches, such as *Flector*, *Lidoderm* and *Salonpas* are over the painful area(s). ■ Systemic pain patches, such as *Duragesic,* are applied to the chest, back, flank, or upper arm.
How do I dispose of used patches?	■ In most cases, remove and fold patch to press adhesive surfaces together, then discard but not in the toilet for most patches. The DEA permits flushing of highly potent narcotic patches (*Duragesic, Daytrana, Butrans*), since these are dangerous and a child or animal could ingest a fatal amount. ■ Alternatively, the fentanyl patch can be cut up and mixed with noxious substance, then disposed in the trash. See Drug Disposal chapter for more information. ■ The *Butrans* patch can be placed and sealed into the Patch-Disposal Unit that comes with the drug, then disposed in the trash.

13

DIETARY SUPPLEMENTS, NATURAL & COMPLEMENTARY MEDICINE

We gratefully acknowledge the assistance of Philip J. Gregory, PharmD, MS, FACN and Aleah M. Rodriguez, PharmD, Center for Drug Information & Evidence-Based Practice, Creighton University School of Pharmacy, in preparing this chapter.

BACKGROUND

<u>Complementary</u> medicine refers to a non-mainstream practice that is used together <u>with conventional medicine</u> (such as physician visits, lab work, diagnostic and surgical procedures, and prescription medications). For example, most Americans with cancer will use conventional chemotherapy, and many of these will use complementary medicine approaches to manage side effects and promote healing. These could include the use of melatonin or valerian to help with sleep, or marijuana to help reduce nausea and improve appetite. Some of the cancer treatment centers offer complementary approaches that include popular "mind-body" practices to help the patient develop strength and handle the stressors of treatment, such as yoga, meditation and massage.

The term *alternative* medicine is used when <u>conventional medicine is not used</u>. Most Americans practice complementary medicine, which commonly includes natural medicines.

NATURAL MEDICINE

'Natural medicine' is a general umbrella term that includes herbals (plant products), vitamins, minerals, and many substances that are not plant-derived but exist in nature, such as glucosamine from shellfish. The FDA uses the term "dietary supplements."

GUIDELINES/REFERENCES

Natural Medicines, available at www.naturalmedicines.com

Questions and answers on dietary supplements. U.S. Food and Drug Administration. http://www.fda.gov/Food/DietarySupplements/QADietarySupplements/ucm191930.htm#FDA_role. (accessed 2015 Sept 27).

Baker RD, Greer FR. Diagnosis and prevention of iron deficiency and iron-deficiency anemia in infants and young children (0-3 years of age). *Pediatrics.* 2010;126(5):1040-50.

Addtl guidelines included with the video files (RxPrep Online).

Dietary supplements are regulated by the Dietary Supplement Health and Education Act (DSHEA) of 1994. By this law, the dietary supplement manufacturer is responsible for ensuring that their products are safe before they are marketed. In contrast, drugs must be proven safe and effective for the intended use before they can be sold. Under DSHEA, once the product is marketed, the FDA has the responsibility for showing that a dietary supplement is "unsafe," before it can take action to restrict the product's use or removal from the marketplace. The company selling or distributing the product is required to record, investigate and forward to the FDA reports they receive of any serious adverse events. Patients and healthcare providers can also submit reports about adverse events from dietary supplements via the FDA's MedWatch program (see the Drug Allergies chapter for information on MedWatch).

Since dietary supplements do not need to be proven effective before they are marketed, the manufacturers cannot make claims that the product treats or cures a condition. Manufacturers are only allowed to make claims about the nutrient content, the relationship to health, and can describe the role of an ingredient that affects normal body structure or function, such as "calcium builds strong bones", "fiber maintains bowel regularity" or "antioxidants maintain cell integrity." Products that make structure/function claims are required to include the warning: "This statement has not been evaluated by the FDA. This product is not intended to diagnose, treat, cure, or prevent any disease."

Although dietary supplement manufacturers are required by law to follow current good manufacturing practices (CGMPs), many do not adequately comply with this requirement. There have been many reports of dietary supplements that are adulterated with incorrect ingredients, including prescription drugs. Pharmacists can help consumers choose a reputable product. The United States Pharmacopeia (USP) establishes standards for dietary supplements. Products that are awarded the USP Verified mark have met requirements for CGMPs. In recent years, other third party organizations have put in place programs that will issue a grade or put a seal of approval on products made by a company following CGMPs.

Some natural medicines pose safety risks in some people. Three areas of particular safety concern are natural medicines that increase bleeding risk, those that interact with prescription drugs, and those that cause cardiotoxicity or hepatotoxicity.

Increased Bleeding Risk

Several natural medicines have the potential to increase bleeding risk, especially in those with other risk factors. Some of the most prominent are known as the "5 Gs:" ginkgo biloba, garlic, ginger, glucosamine and ginseng. Other natural products with known risk for bleeding include fish oils (at higher doses), vitamin E and willow bark. Other natural medicines that may pose a risk with warfarin are discussed in the Anticoagulation chapter.

Interactions with Drugs

Natural medicines interact with prescription medications through pharmacokinetic and pharmacodynamic interactions. Pharmacokinetic interactions are most often due to induction or inhibition of metabolic enzymes and drug transporters. St. John's wort is a good example of a dietary supplement that interacts with many prescription drugs. This herbal product is a "broad-spectrum" inducer and should be avoided or used cautiously with oral contraceptives, transplant drugs, or warfarin, among many others. St. John's wort induces CYP 3A4, p-glycoprotein (P-gp). It is also an inducer of other CYP enzymes: CYP 2C19 >> 2C9 > 1A2. St. John's wort has pharmacodynamic interactions due to serotonergic effects, and can cause serotonin syndrome when taken with MAO inhibitors (including linezolid), SSRIs, SNRIs, triptans, and some others. St. John's wort causes photosensitivity, and requires counseling on sun protection and avoidance. It can lower the seizure threshold and should be avoided in anyone with a seizure history.

Liver toxicity

Natural products can be hepatotoxic, including chaparral, comfrey and kava. If liver enzymes are elevated, check with the patient – sometimes the use of "tea blends" or mixtures can be contributory. The liver toxicity may be due to an additive in the mixture.

Cardiac toxicity

Some natural medicines can cause cardiotoxicity. Ephedra was removed from the market due to reports of cardiac toxicity related to its stimulant effects. Bitter orange (also known as *Citrus aurantium* or synephrine) replaced ephedra in many products promoted for weight loss. Bitter orange has stimulant effects and there are case reports of cardiac toxicity, including myocardial infarction, stroke and arrhythmias. Other products promoted for weight loss or those used as "pre-workout" supplements often contain stimulants (e.g., dimethylamylamine) that can raise the risk of cardiac toxicity.

COMMONLY USED NATURAL MEDICINES

CONDITION	TREATMENT
Anxiety	Valerian, lemon balm, passionflower, chamomile, theanine, skullcap, St. John's wort (many drug interactions), SAMe, kava [avoid due to hepatotoxicity), hops, roseroot, 5-HTP (avoid due to eosinophilia myalgia syndrome (EMS)], and L-tryptophan (avoid due to EMS).
Insomnia/Sleep	Melatonin, valerian, lemon balm, passionflower, chamomile, skullcap, St. John's wort (if due to depression; many drug interactions), coenzyme Q-10 (if due to heart failure), kava (avoid due to hepatotoxicity), hops, lavender, sour cherry, 5-HTP (avoid due to EMS), and L-tryptophan (avoid due to EMS). Melatonin used for jet-lag.
ADHD	Fish oil (or DHA), evening primrose oil, flaxseed oil, zinc, iron, magnesium, L-carnitine, caffeine, dimethylamylamine (avoid due to cardiotoxicity), and SAMe.
Cancer prevention	Beta-carotene, fish oil, black or green tea, coffee, garlic (increases bleeding risk), soy, vitamins A, D, and E (don't exceed 400 IU daily), lycopene, calcium, and fibers (barley, blond psyllium, oat bran, oats, wheat bran).
Canker sores/apthous ulcers	L-lysine, propolis, rhubarb, sage, lavendar oil.
Cholesterol	Red yeast rice (contains low dose HMG-CoA reductase inhibitors), artichoke extract, garlic, niacin, fish oil (or EPA; good for hypertriglyceridemia but may raise LDL), plant sterols/stanols, and fibers (barley, blond psyllium, and oat bran), or beta glucans, which come from oats or barley.
Depression	St. John's wort (inducer; many drug interactions), SAMe, fish oil (or EPA/DHA), 5-HTP (avoid due to EMS), L-tryptophan (avoid due to EMS), saffron, folate or L-methylfolate, and DHEA (may increase prostate and/or breast cancer risk; has steroid-like effects).
Colds and Flu	Prevention: Echinacea, andrographis, garlic (increases bleeding risk), ginseng (American has more research than Panax; both increase bleeding risk), zinc (nasal products can cause loss of smell), vitamin C, and some probiotics (*Bifidobacterium animals, Lactobacillus acidophilus*, and *Lactobacillus rhamnosus GG*). Treatment: Echinacea, andrographis, elderberry, bee propolis, zinc, and vitamin C.
Dementia/Memory	Ginkgo (increases bleeding risk), huperzine A, folate, vitamin E (don't exceed 400 IU QD), coconut oil (or medium chain triglycerides), evening primrose oil, vinpocetine, phosphatidylserine, alpha-GPC, and acetyl-L-carnitine.
Diabetes	Bitter melon, berberine, gymnema, chromium, magnesium (avoid in renal impairment), ginseng (American has more research than Panax; both increase bleeding risk), agaricus mushroom, alpha lipoic acid, cinnamon, blond psyllium, oat bran, fenugreek, and acetyl-l-carnitine (for neuropathy).
Energy/Weight Loss	Bitter orange (avoid due to cardiotoxicity), raspberry ketone (similar to bitter orange), dimethylamylamine (avoid due to cardiotoxicity), caffeine, guarana (contains caffeine), green coffee bean extract (contains caffeine), blond psyllium (can help with GI side effects of orlistat), barley, calcium, 7-keto-DHEA, and conjugated linoleic acid.
UTI	Cranberry, blueberry, bearberry (may be carcinogenic with long-term use), garlic (avoid topical use), echinacea, stinging nettle, asparagus, yogurt, and some probiotics (Bifidobacteria and Lactobacillus strains).
Dyspepsia	Calcium, magnesium, phosphate salts, peppermint, caraway, chamomile, lemon balm, mastic, and artichoke.

Commonly Used Natural Medicines Continued

CONDITION	TREATMENT
IBD	Cascara (avoid, may worsen IBD), senna (avoid, may worsen IBD), fibers [for diarrhea; examples: blond psyllium, barley, and oat bran (or beta glucans)], peppermint, chamomile, some probiotics (Lactobacillus strains, *Saccharomyces boulardii*, or *Bifidobacterium infantis*), fish oil (or EPA/DHA), glutamine, belladonna (avoid due to toxicities) and indian frankincense.
Heart Health/Heart Failure	Coenzyme Q10, L-arginine, pomegranate, casein peptides, fish oil, hawthorne, dandelion (diuretic), taurine, L-carnitine (or propionyl-L-carnitine), magnesium (if deficient), and thiamine (if deficient).
Hypertension	Fish oil (or EPA/DHA), alpha-linolenic acid (better if from diet), fiber (blond psyllium, oats, and wheat bran), hibiscus, pomegranate, black, green, or oolong tea, L-arginine, coenzyme Q10, garlic, potassium, and vitamin D.
Liver Disease	Milk thistle
Menopause	Black cohosh, chasteberry, Panax ginseng, sage, DHEA (may increase breast cancer risk; has steroid-like effects), St. John's wort (many drug interactions), dong quai (may increase INR), red clover, soy, flaxseed, and evening primrose oil.
Migraine/Headache	Prevention: Feverfew, butterbur, fish oil, magnesium, coenzyme Q10, 5-HTP (avoid due to EMS), melatonin, caffeine, and riboflavin. Treatment: Caffeine, guarana (contains caffeine), willow bark (increases bleeding risk), peppermint oil (topical), chasteberry (if related to premenstrual syndrome), magnesium, and 5-HTP (avoid due to EMS).
Motion Sickness/Nausea	Ginger (increases bleeding risk), peppermint, pyridoxine, and GABA.
Osteoporosis	Calcium, vitamin D, soy, black cohosh, ipriflavone, DHEA (may increase prostate and/or breast cancer risk; has steroid-like effects), flaxseed, magnesium, zinc, and green, black, or oolong tea.
Osteoarthritis	Glucosamine (sulfate salts have the best evidence), chondroitin, SAMe, ginger (increases bleeding risk), devil's claw, cat's claw, capsicum (topical), turmeric, willow bark (increases bleeding risk), indian frankincense, methylsulfonylmethane, and avocado/soybean unsaponifiables (ASU).
Prostate Enlargement	Saw palmetto (most used but may be ineffective), pygeum, beta-sitosterol, african wild potato extract (contains beta-sitosterol; can cause hypoglycemia), pumpkin seed (contains beta-sitosterol), rye grass pollen (contains beta-sitosterol), stinging nettle, selenium, vitamin E, lycopene, and garlic.
Skin Conditions	Aloe vera (used for lichen planus, psoriasis, HSV, burns), tea tree oil (used for acne, dandruff, fungal infections), topical vitamin D (used for psoriasis, seborrheic keratosis), and biotin (used for hairloss or increasing nail and hair thickness.

VITAMIN SUPPLEMENTATION

People who consume an adequate diet typically do not require vitamin supplementation. Many people have poor diets that are low in nutritional value, and may require a vitamin supplement to prevent nutrient deficiencies. It is concerning to healthcare professionals that calcium and vitamin D intake remains insufficient for the majority of adults and children. Folate intake among women of child-bearing age can be insufficient. If thiamine (vitamin B1) is insufficient, this can cause Wernicke's encephalopathy. Symptoms of Wernicke's include mental confusion, ataxia, tremor and vision changes. A lack of thiamine is common in alcoholism, and can be due to malabsorption, including from Crohn's, and can occur after obesity surgery, with advanced HIV, and from a few other conditions. As the symptoms of Wernicke's fade, Korsakoff syndrome tends to develop (also called Korsakoff psychosis), which is permanent neurologic (mental) damage. Pharmacists are part of the solution to problems associated with vi-

VITAMINS	NAMES
Vitamin A	Retinol
Vitamin B1	Thiamine
Vitamin B12	Cobalamin
Vitamin B2	Riboflavin
Vitamin B3	Niacin
Vitamin B6	Pyridoxine
Vitamin B9	Folic Acid
Vitamin C	Ascorbic Acid

tamin deficiencies. Anticonvulsants can contribute to _calcium deficiency_ and may require calcium and vitamin D supplementation. There are other individual drugs that deplete nutrients, require a supplement to work properly or require a supplement to reduce toxicity (see table at end of chapter).

Calcium & Vitamin D Supplementation

All prescription medicines for low bone density recommend adequate calcium and vitamin D supplementation taken concurrently (if dietary intake is inadequate). Vitamin D supplementation alone does not reduce fracture risk, but low levels of vitamin D can impair calcium absorption. Patients who do not receive enough vitamin D from the sun or their diet can benefit from supplementation with both calcium and vitamin D. Calcium and vitamin D supplementation is an essential topic for pharmacists since they are often recommending OTC products, which are required with many prescription drugs; product type and selection is discussed in the Osteoporosis and Hormone Therapy chapter.

Folic Acid (Folate)

Any woman planning to <u>conceive</u> (and all <u>women of child-bearing age</u>) should be taking a folate supplement (<u>400 – 800 mcg/daily</u>, which is 0.4-0.8 mg/daily) to help <u>prevent birth defects</u> of the brain and spinal cord (neural tube defects). Folate needs to be taken <u>at least one month before pregnancy</u> and continued for the first 2-3 months of pregnancy. Once pregnant, the woman is likely taking a prescription prenatal vitamin and this is continued throughout since it also contains calcium (not enough, about 200 mg) and some iron. Folate is in many healthy foods, including fortified cereals (some of which are not healthy), dried beans, leafy green vegetables and orange juice. Multivitamins usually contain an amount in the recommended range. Prescription prenatal vitamins usually contain 1000 mcg, or 1 mg, of folate. The newer birth control pill _Beyaz_ contains folate, however it is less expensive to use a different birth control pill with a supplement. _Beyaz_ contains the potassium-sparing progestin drospirenone, with ethinyl estradiol and levomefolate.

Vitamin E

It is unusual to have a vitamin E deficiency, since it is present in many foods. Vitamin E in foods is considered healthy, but excess intake in supplements is considered a health risk (particularly CVD risk); patients should not be exceeding 400 IU daily.

Vitamin Requirements For Infants & Children

Most children do not need vitamins, except as listed per the American Academy of Pediatrics (AAP):

- <u>Exclusively breastfed</u> infants or babies drinking less than 1 liter of baby formula need 400 IU of vitamin D daily (can use _Poly-Vi-Sol_ or generic).

- Older children who do not drink at least 4 cups of Vitamin D fortified milk also need Vitamin D supplements.

Iron Requirements For Infants & Children

CONDITION	TREATMENT
0 – 4 months	Supplemental iron not required.
4 – 6 months	Formulas contain adequate iron; supplementation not required. <u>Breast-fed babies need 1 mg/kg/day from 4-6 months old and until consuming iron-rich foods.</u> At about 6 months most breast-fed babies get about half their calories from other foods, which may be adequate.
6 – 12 months	Need 11 mg/day of iron. Food sources are preferred; supplement as-needed.
1 – 3 years	Need 7 mg/day of iron. Food sources are preferred; supplement as-needed.

Pre-term infants

- Preterm (< 37 weeks) breast-fed infants should receive 2 mg/kg/day of elemental iron supplementation from age 1 to 12 months. Most preterm formula-fed infants receive enough iron from formula, but some may still require supplementation.

Adolescent girls

- At risk of anemia once they begin menstruating.

Iron-only supplements (generics available) – check bottle on iron drops because the iron mg/dropper ranges from 10-15 mg

- *Fer-In-Sol* Iron Supplement Drops
- *Feosol* Tablets and Caplets

Vitamin Supplements with Iron

- *Poly-Vi-Sol* Vitamin Drops With Iron: use if they need the vitamin D and iron
- Or others, such as: *Flintstones* Children's Chewable Multivitamin plus Iron, *Pokemon* Children's Multiple Vitamin with Iron, and store brands

Drugs that Cause Clinically Significant Nutrient Depletion

A supplement is needed for most patients. *Calcium should be given with vitamin D, if needed.

DRUG	DEPLETED NUTRIENT	CHAPTER
Acetazolamide	Calcium, potassium	Travelers' Medicine, Glaucoma
Amphotericin B	Magnesium, potassium	Infectious Disease
Carbamazepine	Calcium*	Epilepsy, Bipolar
Isoniazid	Vitamin B6	Infectious Disease
Lamotrigine	Calcium*	Epilepsy, Bipolar
Loop diuretics	Potassium	Hypertension, CHF
Methotrexate	Folate	Autoimmune Conditions, Oncology
Orlistat	Beta-carotene, fat-soluble vitamins	Weight Loss
Oxcarbazepine	Calcium*	Epilepsy
Phenobarbital/Primidone	Calcium*	Epilepsy
Phenytoin	Calcium*	Epilepsy
PPIs	Magnesium, vitamin B12 (> 2 yrs tx)	GERD
Sulfamethoxazole	Folate	Infectious Disease
Topiramate	Calcium*	Epilepsy, Weight Loss
Valproic Acid/Divalproex	Calcium*	Epilepsy, Bipolar
Zonisamide	Calcium*	Epilepsy

Conditions with Recommended Supplements

CONDITION	RECOMMENDED SUPPLEMENT	CHAPTER
Alcoholism	Vitamin B1, folate	Hepatitis
Microcytic Anemia	Ferrous sulfate	Anemia
Macrocytic Anemia	Vitamin B12 and/or folate	Anemia
Pregnancy	Folate, calcium, vitamin D, pyridoxine (for nausea)	Pregnancy
Osteopenia/Osteoporosis	Calcium, vitamin D	Osteoporosis, Pregnancy
Osteomalacia (Rickets)	Calcium, vitamin D	Vitamin deficiency
Chronic Kidney Disease	Vitamin D	Renal Disease, Bipolar Disorder (for Lithium side effect)
Scurvy	Vitamin C	Vitamin deficiency
Crohn's Disease (and possibly ulcerative colitis)	Patient specific-depends on levels; can require iron, zinc, folate, calcium, vitamin D, B vitamins	IBD
Bariatric Surgery	Various; patient-specific, refer to chapter	Weight Loss

Safety Comments on Homeopathic Products and Medical Foods

Homeopathic Products: Homeopathy is based on "the law of similars" or the concept that "like is cured by like". This is the belief that giving very small amounts of a substance, which in its undiluted form causes similar symptoms of the illness, will protect the patient or cure them of the illness. The quantity of homeopathic substances in a product are reported in X or C dilution scales. X represents a 1:10 dilution and C represents a 1:100 dilution of solute:solvent. The number in front of the X or C is the number of subsequent dilutions. The more dilute a substance is, the more "potent" it is considered.

Most evidence does not support validity to homeopathy, however many adherents (including the Queen of England) are advocates. The remedies may be providing a placebo benefit, or, may actually be labeled as homeopathic but contain measurable concentrations of drugs, nutrients or dietary supplement ingredients. In 2010, *Hyland's Teething Tablets* were recalled due to cases of belladonna toxicity. The amount of belladonna could be measured and was unsafe. It is tempting to use the term "homeopathic" on a label. It sounds nice, and if a manufacturer labels a product "homeopathic", they are permitted to make health claims, while dietary supplements are not allowed by law to claim benefit for particular conditions. There have been other recent examples of products labeled as homeopathic which actually were not. Always check the quantity of ingredients.

Medical Foods: These are products that are supposed to meet a nutritional need for certain patient groups for a specific condition. A recent medical food that many pharmacists will have seen is a formulation of folate called *Deplin* that is being marketed for help in treating depression. The advertisement for this product states that "*Deplin* is a medical food containing L-methylfolate, the active form of the vitamin, folate. It is the only folate that can be taken up by the brain where it helps balance the chemical messengers that affect mood (serotonin, norepinephrine and dopamine)." It is less expensive to use over-the-counter folate supplements and there is no evidence that this supplement would provide more benefit, however the manufacturer can make this claim since it is a medical food. In a medical food, all ingredients must be Generally Recognized as Safe (G.R.A.S.) or be approved food additives. Most of the medical foods have Rx-only on the label and have NDC numbers.

DRUG REFERENCES

BACKGROUND

Providing drug information to patients as well as other healthcare professionals is one of the critical functions of pharmacists, regardless of the practice setting. In order to perform this function effectively and efficiently, it is important to be able to choose the most appropriate and specific resources based on the type of information needed. The following section is intended to highlight some of the key resources based on the type of information needed. It is not intended to be a comprehensive review of drug information resources available, but should provide a basic understanding for licensure.

It is important to continually evaluate new drug information resources and technology, and incorporate them into your practice to insure the resources being reviewed are current, and are reflecting the most current information available.

It is also important to recognize that patients also have access to many of the same drug information resources. As healthcare providers, pharmacists need to be aware of what patients are reading and be able to provide context as-needed to clarify the information as it applies to their case. Pharmacists must also be able to recognize when the medical information requested is outside the scope of normal pharmacy practice/expertise. These questions should be referred to the appropriate healthcare provider for follow up.

SOURCES, BY CATEGORY

General Drug Information

American Hospital Formulary Service (AHFS) Drug Information

Lexicomp's Drug Information Handbook, and online resource

Drug Topics: Red Book

- The Red Book is a useful resource to determine product presentations (i.e., dosage form, strength, and package size) and availability.

Food and Drug Administration (FDA): Orange Book:

- The Orange Book indicates if a generic is therapeutically equivalent to the brand at www.accessdata.fda. gov/scripts/cder/ob/See FDA Drug Approval & Therapeutic Equivalence chapter for more information.

FDA: Purple Book

- The Purple Book lists biological products, including any biosimilar and interchangeable biological products at www.fda.gov

FDA: National Drug Code (NDC) Directory

- The National Drug Code (NDC) is the universal product identifier for human drugs at http://www.accessdata.fda.gov/scripts/cder/ndc/default.cfm

FDA: Drugs Home page at www.fda.gov/Drugs

FDA: Drugs@FDA at www.accessdata.fda.gov/scripts/cder/drugsatfda

Facts and Comparisons

Micromedex

National Library of Medicine (NLM): Dailymed

- Database of Product Package Inserts at dailymed.nlm.nih.gov/dailymed

NLM: Drug Information Portal at druginfo.nlm.nih.gov/drugportal

Physician's Desk Reference (PDR)

- Collection of product package inserts

Pharmacist's Letter

Drugs of Choice from the Medical Letter

Sanford Guide to Antimicrobial Therapy

Toxicology

Micromedex: POISINDEX

Lexicomp's: Poisoning and Toxicology: Lexi-Tox

NLM: TOXNET at toxnet.nlm.nih.gov/

Adverse Drug Reactions

Individual product package inserts, PDR, DailyMed, Lexicomp, or in any of the general drug resources

ASHP: Drug-Induced Diseases: Prevention, Detection, and Management

Drug Shortages

ASHP: Drug Shortages at www.ashp.org/drugshortages

FDA: Drug Shortages at www.fda.gov/drugs/drugsafety/drugshortages/

Centers for Disease Control and Prevention (CDC): Vaccines and Immunizations – Current Vaccine Shortages & Delays at www.cdc.gov/vaccines/vac-gen/shortages/

FDA Drug and Biologic Recalls

Drug Recalls at www.fda.gov/Drugs/DrugSafety/DrugRecalls/default.htm

Biologic Recalls at www.fda.gov/BiologicsBloodVaccines/SafetyAvailability/Recalls/

General Medical Information (Professional)

CDC: Diseases & Conditions at www.cdc.gov/diseasesconditions

Harrison's Principles of Internal Medicine

National Cancer Institute (NCI) at www.cancer.gov

The Merck Manual at www.merckmanuals.com/professional/

Washington Manual of Medical Therapeutics

General Medical/Drug Information (Consumer)

CDC: Diseases & Conditions at www.cdc.gov/diseasesconditions

FDA: Consumer pages at www.fda.gov/ForConsumers

NIH: MedlinePlus at www.nlm.nih.gov/medlineplus

Medication Safety (see Medication Safety chapter)

FDA: Drug Safety Communications at www.fda.gov/Drugs/DrugSafety

FDA: Medication Guides at www.fda.gov/Drugs/DrugSafety/ucm085729.htm

FDA: MedWatch at www.fda.gov/Safety/MedWatch

Institute for Safe Medication Practices (ISMP) at www.ismp.org

Reporting Adverse Drug Reactions

Drugs/Devices: FDA: MedWatch Adverse Event Reporting System (FAERS) at www.fda.gov/medwatch or 1-800-FDA-1088 (1-800-332-1088)

Vaccines: CDC/FDA: Vaccine Adverse Event Reporting System (VAERS) at vaers.hhs.gov/index

Reporting Medical Errors

In Hospital

- To the P&T Committee, at staff meetings (as defined by facility), to the Medication Safety Committee

In any setting

- ISMP's Medication Errors Reporting Program (MERP)
- FDA's MedWatch
- MedMARx program

Drug Interactions

Drug Interaction Facts

Hansten and Horn's Drug Interactions Analysis and Management

Micromedex

Lexicomp Online Database

IV Stability, Compatibility & Sterile Compounding

Trissel's Handbook on Injectable Drugs

AHFS Drug Information, King Guide, Micromedex, Product Package Inserts

Beyond use dates for compounded sterile products: US Pharmacopoeia National Formulary (USP-NF) Chapter 797 (Sterile Compounding) and ASHP Guidelines on Compounding Sterile Preparations

- USP sets standards for quality, purity, identity, and strength of medicines, food ingredients and dietary supplements

Compounding, Manufacturing & Non-Sterile Compounding Stability

Beyond use dates for compounded non-sterile products: US Pharmacopoeia National Formulary (USP-NF) Chapter 795 (Non-Sterile Compounding)

Allen's Compounded Formulations

Extemporaneous Formulations for Pediatric, Geriatric, and Special Needs Patients, International Journal of Pharmaceutical Compounding, bimonthly publication, and Pediatric Drug Formulations

Remington: The Science and Practice of Pharmacy

- Includes a chapter on extemporaneous prescription compounding

Trissel's Stability of Compounded Formulations

Drug Identification

Facts and Comparisons

Therapeutic Research Center's Ident-A-Drug at identadrug.therapeuticresearch.com

Micromedex: IDENTIDEX

PDR

NLM: PillBox at pillbox.nlm.nih.gov

Foreign Drug Identification

Diccionario de Especialidades Farmacéuticas, printed in Spanish

International Drug Directory (Index Nominum)

Martindale

Micromedex

USP Dictionary of USAN and International Drug Names

Natural Products/Alternative Medicine

Micromedex

Natural Medicines Comprehensive Database

PDR for Herbal Medicines

US Pharmacopoeia

SOURCES, BY CATEGORY *Continued*

Immunizations

- The CDC's Pink Book, Epidemiology and Prevention of Vaccine Preventable Disease, is published every 2 years and is available at www.cdc.gov i

- CDC Advisory Committee on Immunization Practices (ACIP). Updates are published in the Morbidity and Mortality Weekly Report (MMWR).

- APhA Immunization Resources at www.pharmacist. com/imz

- Immunization Action Coalition at www.immunize.org

Travel Medicine

CDC: Travelers' Health at www.cdc.gov/travel

CDC: Yellow Book

- The Yellow Book is the CDC's reference book for healthcare professionals who advise international travelers about health risks.

International Society of Travel Medicine (ISTM) at www.istm.org

Association For Medical Assistance To Travelers (IA-MAT) at www.iamat.org

Pregnancy and Lactation

Breastfeeding: A Guide for the Medical Profession

Briggs' Drugs in Pregnancy and Lactation

CDC: Medications and Pregnancy at www.cdc.gov/pregnancy/meds/

Hale's Medications and Mothers' Milk at www.medsmilk.com/

Micromedex

NLM: LactMed at toxnet.nlm.nih.gov/newtoxnet/lactmed.htm

Women's Health

CDC: Women's Health at www.cdc.gov/women

Department of Health and Human Services (DHHS) Women's Health at http://www.hrsa.gov/womenshealth/index.html

FDA: For Women at www.fda.gov/ForConsumers/ByAudience/ForWomen

NLM: Women's Health at www.nlm.nih.gov/medlineplus/womenshealth.html

World Health Organization (WHO): Women's Health at www.who.int/topics/womens_health/en

Geriatrics

FDA: Medicines and You: A Guide for Older Adults at www.fda.gov/Drugs/ResourcesForYou/ucm163959.htm

Lexicomp: Geriatric Dosage Handbook

NIH: Senior Health at nihseniorhealth.gov

The American Geriatrics Society (AGS) Guidelines & Recommendations at www.americangeriatrics.org/health_care_professionals/ clinical_practice/clinical_guidelines_recommendations/

Pediatrics

AHFS Drug Information

CDC: Vaccines & Immunizations at www.cdc.gov/vaccines

Harriet Lane Handbook

Micromedex

Nelson: Textbook of Pediatrics

Neofax

Lexicomp's Pediatric & Neonatal Dosage Handbook

ASHP: Pediatric Injectable Drugs

Psychiatry

Clinical Handbook of Psychotropic Drugs

Diagnostic and Statistical Manual of Mental Disorders: Fifth edition (DSM-5)

SOURCES, BY CATEGORY *Continued*

Pharmacology/Pharmacy Text Books

Koda-Kimble's Applied Therapeutics: The Clinical Use of Drugs

Goodman and Gilman's: The Pharmacological Basis of Therapeutics

Handbook of Nonprescription Drugs (OTC)

DiPiro's Pharmacotherapy: A Pathophysiologic Approach

Pharmaceutics

Handbook of Pharmaceutical Excipients

Merck Index

Remington: The Science and Practice of Pharmacy

Guidelines

National Guideline Clearinghouse at www.guideline.gov

Select Key Guidelines

- ACC/AHA Guideline on the Treatment of Blood Cholesterol to Reduce Atherosclerotic Cardiovascular Risk in Adults (2013)

- 2014 Evidence-based guideline for the management of high blood pressure in adults. Report from the panel members appointed to the Eighth Joint National Committee (JNC 8)

- American Diabetes Assoc (ADA) Clinical Practice Recommendations and American Association of Clinical Endocrinologists/American College of Endocrinology Consensus Statement (AACE), both for diabetes

- CHEST guidelines for antithrombotic therapy

Refer to the professional organization websites (e.g., AACE, ACG, ACOG, others)

Clinical Trials

NIH: ClinicalTrials.gov at www.clinicaltrials.gov

Professional Organizations

American Academy of Pediatrics (AAP) at www.aap.org

American Cancer Society (ACS) at www.cancer.org

American Diabetes Association (ADA) at www.diabetes.org

American Heart Association (AHA) at www.heart.org

American Society of Clinical Oncology (ASCO) at www.asco.org

Infectious Diseases Society of America (IDSA) at www.idsociety.org/

For Additional Professional Organizations

NLM: Professional Organizations at: www.nlm.nih.gov/medlineplus/organizations/all_organizations.html

Pharmacy Organizations

Academy of Managed Care Pharmacy (AMCP) at www.amcp.org

American College of Clinical Pharmacy (ACCP) at www.accp.com

American Pharmacists Association (APhA) at www.pharmacist.com

American Society of Health-System Pharmacists (ASHP) at www.ashp.org

Literature Search

Excerpta Medica (EMBASE)

International Pharmaceutical Abstracts (IPA)

NLM: PubMed at www.ncbi.nlm.nih.gov/pubmed

Miscellaneous Resources

NLM: Gallery of Mobile Apps and Sites www.nlm.nih.gov/mobile

Legislative and Business Developments

The Pink Sheet: biopharma regulatory, legislative, legal & business developments

Pharmacist's Letter

FDA: Center for Drug Evaluation and Research (CDER) at www.fda.gov/Drugs/default.htm

15

LAB VALUES & DRUG MONITORING

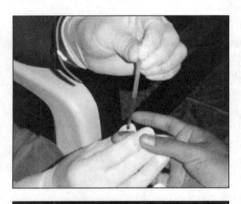

GUIDELINES/REFERENCES

Lab Tests Online. www.labtestsonline.org (accessed 2015 Dec 7).

Lee M. Basic Skills in Interpreting Laboratory Data. 5th ed. Betheseda, MD: ASHP; 2013.

Schmidt J, Wieczorkiewicz J. Interpreting Laboratory Data: A Point-of-Care Guide. Betheseda, MD: ASHP; 2012.

BACKGROUND

Laboratory values assist healthcare providers in diagnosing and monitoring diseases and drug therapies. In addition to typical blood or other samples sent to a hospital or outside laboratory, there are newer ways to conduct tests and obtain results. Point-of-care (POC) testing provides quick results right at the site of patient care. There are many POC tests including tests for cardiac enzymes, A1C, INR, various infections and others. Home testing kits provide convenience and privacy and are available to test for pregnancy, ovulation, HIV infection, herpes, and presence of illicit substances or opioids. Many are available OTC.

Therapeutic drug monitoring (TDM) involves obtaining a drug level and related labs to monitor for efficacy and minimize toxicity. For example, if a patient is receiving traditional dosing of gentamicin, the healthcare team will monitor both the gentamicin trough level and the patient's renal function since aminoglycosides can cause nephrotoxicity. Pharmacists in California (as of January, 2014), as part of the provider legislation, can order and interpret lab tests for a variety of purposes, including tests to screen for and diagnose disease, to check for medication adherence or to screen for drugs of abuse. Prescribing privilege is advancing in many states.

TEST RESULTS

Test results are usually a numerical value, such as sodium = 139 mEq/L. Other lab results are "positive" or "negative" or indicate a specific item, such as "Gram-positive cocci". Reference ranges can vary slightly from one lab to another due to slight variances in products and techniques. Reference ranges also differ between pediatric and adult populations in many cases. A patient's lab results may be within the normal ranges or may indicate a serious condition that needs to be addressed rapidly. A value that is termed critical can be life-threatening unless a corrective action is taken quickly. The Joint Commission requires that all accredited facilities create and follow a protocol to identify and report critical values to the responsible caregiver, who has an established time frame to manage the result. This applies to critical lab values and diagnostic procedure results.

TEST DEFINITIONS

Complete Blood Cell Count

The <u>complete blood count (CBC)</u> is a commonly ordered lab panel that analyzes the white blood cells (WBCs), or neutrophils, the red blood cells (RBCs), and the platelets (PLTs). The CBC includes the hemoglobin (oxygen-carrying protein in RBCs) and the hematocrit (the level of RBCs in the fluid component of the blood, or plasma). A low WBC count is called leuko<u>penia</u>. A high WBC count is leuko<u>cytosis</u>. When a <u>CBC with differential</u> is ordered, the types of neutrophils are analyzed. RBCs have an average life span of <u>120 days</u>. A high RBC count is called erythrocytosis. Anemia occurs if there is decreased production, loss (bleeding), or destruction (hemolysis) of RBCs. Platelets have an average life span of <u>7 – 10 days</u>. A high PLT count is called thrombocytosis and a low PLT count is called <u>thrombocytopenia</u>.

The stick diagram below is used in practice when writing a paper chart note to denote the four primary components of the CBC:

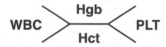

Basic Metabolic Panel / Comprehensive Metabolic Panel

The <u>basic metabolic panel (BMP)</u> includes seven or eight tests that analyze electrolytes and glucose, acid/base (with the HCO_3, or bicarbonate) and renal function. Some labs calculate and report the anion gap along with the BMP (see Calculations chapter). The stick diagram below is used to denote seven of the BMP components:

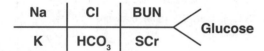

A comprehensive metabolic panel (CMP) includes the tests in the BMP plus albumin, alanine aminotransferase (ALT), aspartate aminotransferase (AST), total bilirubin and total protein. The additional tests are used primarily to assess liver function. The BMP and CMP are groups of labs that are ordered together for convenience. Clinicians should be aware of cost and not order a panel if single lab tests would be sufficient.

COMMON ADULT LABORATORY REFERENCE RANGES

Drugs specifically indicated to treat a lab abnormality (e.g., urate lowering therapies) are not included in Notes.

ITEM	COMMON REFERENCE RANGE	NOTES

BMP and Electrolytes

ITEM	COMMON REFERENCE RANGE	NOTES
Calcium, total Calcium, ionized	8.5–10.5 mg/dL 4.5–5.1 mg/dL	Calculate corrected calcium if albumin is low (see Calculations chapter for formula). Correction is not needed for ionized calcium. ↑ due to calcium supplementation, vitamin D, thiazide diuretics. ↓ due to systemic steroids, long-term heparin, loop diuretics, bisphosphonates, calcitonin, foscarnet, topiramate. Supplement in pregnancy, other conditions and with certain drugs (see Osteoporosis & Hormone Therapy and Dietary Supplements & Natural and Complementary Medicine chapters).
Chloride (Cl)	95–106 mEq/L	Used with other labs to assess acid-base status and fluid balance.

Common Adult Laboratory Reference Ranges Continued

ITEM	COMMON REFERENCE RANGE	NOTES
Magnesium (Mg)	1.3–2.1 mEq/L	↑ due to magnesium-containing antacids and laxatives plus renal impairment. ↓ due to PPIs, diuretics, amphotericin, foscarnet, echinocandins, diarrhea, chronic alcohol intake.
Phosphate (PO_4)	2.3–4.7 mg/dL	↑ in renal failure. ↓ due to phosphate binders, foscarnet, oral calcium intake.
Potassium (K)	3.5–5 mEq/L	↑ due to ACE inhibitors, ARBs, aldosterone receptor antagonists (ARAs), aliskiren, NSAIDs, cyclosporine, tacrolimus, mycophenolate, potassium supplements, drospirenone-containing oral contraceptives, sulfamethoxazole/trimethoprim, chronic heparin use, canagliflozin, pentamidine. ↓ due to steroids, beta-2 agonists, conivaptan, diuretics, insulin, mycophenolate (both ↑ and ↓ reported).
Sodium (Na)	135–145 mEq/L	↑ due to lithium, hypertonic saline. ↓ due to carbamazepine, oxcarbazepine, SSRIs, diuretics, desmopressin.
Bicarbonate (HCO_3 or "bicarb")	Venous: 24–30 mEq/L Arterial: 22–26 mEq/L (varies by method)	Used to assess acid-base status (see Acid-Base in this chapter). ↑ due to loop diuretics, systemic steroids. ↓ due to topiramate, zonisamide, salicylate overdose.
BUN (Blood Urea Nitrogen)	7–20 mg/dL	Used with SCr (e.g., BUN/SCr ratio) to assess fluid status and renal function.
SCr (Serum Creatinine)	0.6–1.3 mg/dL	↑ due to many drugs that impair renal function (e.g., amphotericin B, cisplatin, colistimethate, cyclosporine, loop diuretics, NSAIDs, radiocontrast dye, tacrolimus, and vancomycin). False ↑ due to sulfamethoxazole/trimethoprim, H_2RAs. ↓ with low muscle mass, amputation, hemodilution.
Anion Gap (AG)	5–12 mEq/L	A calculated value, but often reported on the BMP (see Calculations chapter). Presence of ↑ anion gap suggests metabolic acidosis.

WBC and Differential

WBC	4,000–11,000 cells/mm³	Used to diagnose and monitor infection/inflammation. Can ↑ as an acute phase reactant, indicating a systemic reaction to inflammation or stress. ↑ due to systemic steroids, colony stimulating factors, epinephrine. ↓ due to clozapine, chemotherapy that targets the bone marrow, carbamazepine, cephalosporins, procainamide, vancomycin.
Neutrophils	45–73%	Neutrophils and bands are used with clinical s/sx to assess likelihood of infection and with WBC in absolute neutrophil count (ANC) calculation (see Calculations chapter).
Bands	3–5%	Neutrophils are also called polymorphonuclear cells (PMNs or polys) and segmented neutrophils (segs). Bands are immature neutrophils released from bone marrow to fight infection (called a "left shift").

Common Adult Laboratory Reference Ranges Continued

ITEM	COMMON REFERENCE RANGE	NOTES
Eosinophils	0–5%	↑ in drug allergy, asthma, inflammation, parasitic infection.
Basophils	0–1%	↑ in inflammation, hypersensitivity reaction, leukemia.
Lymphocytes	20–40%	↑ in viral infections, lymphoma. ↓ in bone marrow suppression, HIV, or due to systemic steroids.
Monocytes	2–8%	↑ in chronic infections, inflammation, stress.

Anemia

ITEM	COMMON REFERENCE RANGE	NOTES
RBC (Red Blood Cells)	Males: 4.5–5.5 x 10^6 cells/μL Females: 4.1–4.9 x 10^6 cells/μL	↑ due to erythropoiesis-stimulating agents (ESAs), smoking, and in polycythemia (a condition that causes high RBCs). ↓ due to chemotherapy that targets the bone marrow, low production, blood loss, deficiency anemias (e.g., B12, folate), hemolytic anemia, sickle cell anemia.
Hgb, Hb (Hemoglobin)	Males: 13.5–18 g/dL Females: 12–16 g/dL	Hgb is the iron-containing protein that carries oxygen in the RBCs. The Hct mirrors the Hgb result (providing the same clinical information). ↑ due to ESAs (see Anemia chapter). ↓ due to bleeding, risk with anticoagulants, antiplatelets, P2Y$_{12}$ inhibitors, fibrinolytics or due to drug-induced aplastic anemia (e.g., carbamazepine, chloramphenicol, felbamate, others).
Hct (Hematocrit)	Males: 38–50% Females: 36–46%	
MCV (Mean Corpuscular Volume)	80–100 mm^3	↑ due to B12 or folate deficiency. ↓ due to iron deficiency.
MCH (Mean Corpuscular Hemoglobin)	26–34 pg/cell	Additional tests used in an anemia work-up. Together MCV, MCHC and RDW are called "RBC indices".
MCHC (Mean Corpuscular Hgb Conc.)	31 - 37 g/dL	
RDW (RBC Distribution Width)	11.5–14.5%	RDW measures the variability in the RBC size.
Iron	65–150 mcg/dL	↑ due to iron supplementation. ↓ due to blood loss or poor nutritional intake.
TIBC (Total Iron Binding Capacity)	250–400 mcg/dL	Monitored as part of the workup and treatment for iron deficiency anemia, anemia of chronic disease or anemia of chronic kidney disease (CKD). Often parenteral iron is required in conjunction with an ESA for patients on dialysis (see Anemia chapter).
Transferrin	> 200 mg/dL	
TSAT (Transferrin Saturation)	Males: 15–50% Females: 12–45%	
Ferritin	11–300 ng/mL	
Erythropoietin	2–25 mIU/mL	

Common Adult Laboratory Reference Ranges Continued

ITEM	COMMON REFERENCE RANGE	NOTES
Folic acid (folate)	5–25 mcg/L	B12 and folate are ordered for further workup of macrocytic anemia. ↓ due to phenytoin/fosphenytoin, phenobarbital, primidone, methotrexate, sulfasalazine, sulfamethoxazole/trimethoprim. Supplement folate in pregnancy, alcoholism (see Dietary Supplements & Natural and Complementary Medicine chapter).
Vitamin B12	> 200 pg/mL	↓ due to PPIs, metformin, colchicine, chloramphenicol.
MMA Methylmalonate	Varies	Used for further workup of macrocytic anemia when B12 deficiency is suspected. Schilling test has also been used.
Reticulocyte count	0.5–2.5%	Immature red blood cells; the test can determine if the bone marrow production of RBCs is acceptable.
Coombs Test, Direct Also known as: Direct Antiglobulin Test (DAT)	Negative Positive Coombs test (risk for hemolytic anemia) If positive, discontinue the offending drug	Used to determine cause of hemolytic anemia (autoimmune vs. drug-induced) and in assessment of transfusion compatibility. <u>Positive</u> in drug-induced hemolysis caused by <u>penicillins and cephalosporins</u> (prolonged use/high concentrations), <u>isoniazid, levodopa, methyldopa, nitrofurantoin, quinidine, quinine, rifampin and sulfonamides</u>.
G6PD (Glucose-6-phosphate dehydrogenase)	5–14 units/gram Patients with G6PD deficiency should avoid drugs known to cause hemolysis. If hemolysis occurs with these drugs, test for G6PD deficiency.	If hemolytic anemia occurs, the test can be done to see if it is due to a G6PD deficiency (the result will be low). The RBC destruction (with G6PD deficiency) is triggered by stress, foods (<u>fava beans</u>) or these drugs: <u>chloroquine, dapsone, methylene blue, nitrofurantoin, primaquine, probenecid, quinidine, quinine, rasburicase and sulfonamides</u>.

Anticoagulation

Item	Reference	Notes
Anti-Xa (Antifactor Xa Activity)	Obtain a peak anti-Xa <u>4 hours</u> after LMWH dose for proper interpretation. Refer to Therapeutic Drug Monitoring table at end of chapter.	To monitor low molecular weight heparins (LMWHs). Monitoring is recommended in pregnancy and mechanical heart valves and possibly in obesity, low body weight, pediatrics, elderly, or renal insufficiency (see Anticoagulation chapter). ↑ due to heparin, LMWHs and fondaparinux.
PT/INR (Prothrombin Time/International Normalized Ratio)	PT: 10–13 seconds (varies) INR: < 1.2 (for those not on warfarin)	To monitor warfarin. INR ↑ (without warfarin) due to liver disease. False ↑ from daptomycin, oritavancin, telavancin (no ↑ risk of bleeding). Many drugs ↑ or ↓ INR (see Anticoagulation chapter).
aPTT or PTT (Activated Partial Thromboplastin Time)	22–38 seconds (varies – this is called the "control") Treatment goal (on UFH): 1.5–2.5x control	To monitor unfractionated heparin (UFH) and direct thrombin inhibitors (e.g., argatroban). False ↑ from oritavancin, telavancin.
ACT (Activated Clotting Time)	70–180 seconds (varies)	To monitor anticoagulation in the cardiac catheterization lab during percutaneous coronary intervention (PCI) and in surgery.

Common Adult Laboratory Reference Ranges Continued

ITEM	COMMON REFERENCE RANGE	NOTES
Platelets	150,000–450,000/mm³	Platelets are required for clot formation. Spontaneous bleeding can occur when platelets are < 20,000/mm³. ↓ due to heparin, LMWHs, fondaparinux, glycoprotein IIb/IIIa receptor antagonists, linezolid, valproic acid, chemotherapy that targets the bone marrow, rarely other drugs.
Heparin-induced platelet antibodies: 1st ELISA test, then 2nd Serotonin release assay (SRA)	Negative	To confirm diagnosis of heparin-induced thrombocytopenia (HIT). If the ELISA test is positive, a positive SRA is confirmatory.

Liver and Gastroenterology

Albumin	3.5–5 g/dL	↓ due to cirrhosis and malnutrition. Highly protein bound drugs (e.g., warfarin) are impacted by changes in albumin; phenytoin, valproic acid and calcium serum concentrations requires correction for low albumin (see Epilepsy/Seizures and Calculations chapters).
Alk Phos or ALP (Alkaline Phosphatase)	33–131 IU/L	Used with other labs to assess liver, biliary tract (cholestatic) and bone disease.
AST (Aspartate Aminotransferase)	10–40 units/L	AST and ALT are enzymes released from injured hepatocytes (liver cells). Numerous medications and herbals can ↑ AST and ALT (see Hepatitis & Liver Disease chapter).
ALT (Alanine Aminotransferase)	10–40 units/L	
GGT (Gamma-Glutamyl Transpeptidase)	9–58 units/L	Used with other labs to assess liver, biliary tract (cholestatic) and pancreas.
T Bili (Bilirubin, total)	0.1–1.2 mg/dL	Used along with other liver tests to monitor drug toxicity, determine other cause of liver damage and detect bile duct blockage.
Ammonia	19–60 mcg/dL	Though not diagnostic, often measured in suspected hepatic encephalopathy (HE). ↑ due to valproic acid, topiramate. ↓ due to lactulose.

Pancreatitis

Amylase	60–180 units/L	↑ due to pancreatitis.
Lipase	5–160 units/L	

Common Adult Laboratory Reference Ranges Continued

ITEM	COMMON REFERENCE RANGE	NOTES

Cardiovascular

ITEM	COMMON REFERENCE RANGE	NOTES
CK or CPK (Creatine Kinase or Creatine Phosphokinase)	Males: 55–170 IU/L Females: 30–135 IU/L	To assess muscle inflammation (myositis) or more serious muscle damage and to diagnose cardiac conditions. ↑ due to <u>daptomycin</u>, quinupristin/dalfopristin, <u>statins</u>, fibrates (especially if given with a statin), emtricitabine, <u>tenofovir</u>, tipranavir, <u>raltegravir</u>, <u>dolutegravir</u>, telbivudine.
CK-MB isoenzymes, total	≤ 6.0 ng/mL	As a group, these are called "cardiac enzymes" and are used in the <u>diagnosis of MI</u>. The troponins can be elevated with a few other conditions (sepsis, PE, CKD).
TnT (Troponin T)	0–0.1 ng/mL (assay dependent)	BNP and NT-proBNP are both <u>markers of cardiac stress</u>. They are not HF nor heart disease-specific but the <u>higher the values, the higher the likelihood of HF</u>. Renal failure is the second most common cause of ↑ in BNP and NT-proBNP.
TnI (Troponin I)	0–0.5 ng/mL (assay dependent)	
BNP (B-Type Natriuretic Peptide)	< 100 pg/mL or ng/L	Myoglobin and CK-MB are not interchangeable; they are 2 separate markers. Myoglobin is a sensitive marker for muscle injury but has relatively low specificity for acute MI and therefore is not routinely used for diagnosis (see Acute Coronary Syndrome chapter).
NT-proBNP (N-Terminal-ProBNP)	Males: < 61 pg/mL Females: 12–151 pg/mL	

Lipids and Cardiovascular Risk

ITEM	COMMON REFERENCE RANGE	NOTES
TC (Total Cholesterol)	< 200 mg/dL	For complete discussion, see Dyslipidemia chapter. Fasting begins 9-12 hours prior to lipid blood draw.
HDL (High Density Lipoprotein)	< 40 mg/dL, low ≥ 60 mg/dL, high	Guidelines do not support specific TC, HDL or TG goals; they support a statin intensity level for LDL-C reductions based on those most likely to benefit.
LDL (Low Density Lipoprotein)	LDL: 70–189, depending on risk factors	↑ Lp(a) and ↑ ApoB are being used more commonly; these are associated with ↑ coagulation and ↑ risk of CVD.
TG (Triglycerides)	< 150 mg/dL	↑ CRP indicates inflammation, which could be due to many conditions (infection, trauma, malignancy). High-sensitivity CRP (hs-CRP) is more sensitive for CVD.
Lipoprotein-a, Lp(a)	< 10 mg/dL	The coronary artery calcium score measures calcium build-up in the coronary arteries.
Apoliprotein-B, Apo B	< 130 mg/dL	The ankle brachial index measures the ratio of the BP in the lower legs to the BP in the arms. It is used to assess severity of peripheral artery disease (PAD). An ABI < 1 indicates some degree of PAD.
CRP (C-reactive Protein)	0–0.5 mg/dL; higher levels indicate ↑ risk	
Coronary Artery Calcium score	< 300 Agatston units or < 75 percentile for age, sex and ethnicity; higher is at risk	
ABI (Ankle Brachial Index)	1–1.4	

Common Adult Laboratory Reference Ranges Continued

ITEM	COMMON REFERENCE RANGE	NOTES

Diabetes

ITEM	COMMON REFERENCE RANGE	NOTES
FPG (Fasting Plasma Glucose)	≥ 126 mg/dL is positive for diabetes 100–125 mg/dL is positive for pre-diabetes	Fasting is 8+ hours (see Diabetes chapter for complete information).
eAG (Estimated Average Glucose)	< 154 mg/dL (ADA)	An eAG of 154 mg/dL corresponds to an A1C of 7%; used to assist patients by making the average glucose over-time correspond to a finger stick value that corresponds to the current glucose level.
A1C (Hemoglobin A1C)	< 7% (ADA), ≤ 6.5% (AACE)	Average blood glucose over the past 3 months; based on attachment of glucose to hemoglobin; ↑ glucose = ↑ BG attached to Hgb = ↑ A1C.
Preprandial blood glucose	70–130 mg/dL (ADA), < 110 mg/dL (AACE)	Blood glucose measurement taken before a meal.
Postprandial blood glucose	< 180 mg/dL (ADA), < 140 mg/dL (AACE)	Blood glucose measurement taken after a meal (1-2 hours after the start of eating).
C-peptide (fasting)	0.78–1.89 ng/mL	Insulin breakdown product used to evaluate beta-cell function (distinguish type 1 from type 2 diabetes).
UACR or ACR (Urine Albumin to Creatinine Ratio or Albumin to Creatinine Ratio) or UAE (Urinary Albumin Excretion)	Males: < 17 mg/gram Females: < 25 mg/gram < 30 mg/24 hours	See Diabetes and Renal Disease chapters.

Thyroid Function

ITEM	COMMON REFERENCE RANGE	NOTES
TSH (Thyroid Stimulating Hormone)	0.3–3 mIU/L	TSH is used with FT4 to diagnose hypothyroidism and is used alone (sometimes with FT4) to monitor patients being treated. Low iodine intake is a cause of hypothyroidism; this is rare in the U.S. because iodine is added to table salt (NaCl). ↑ or ↓ due to amiodarone, lithium
Total thyroxine (T4)	4.5–10.9 mcg/dL	T4 and FT4 are two of several tests used for a detailed assessment of thyroid function.
Free thyroxine (FT4)	0.9–2.3 ng/dL	↓ due many drugs (e.g., phenytoin, rifampin, SSRIs, estrogen, others) (see Thyroid chapter for additional interacting drugs).

Uric Acid/Gout

ITEM	COMMON REFERENCE RANGE	NOTES
Uric acid	Males: 3.5–7.2 mg/dL Females: 2–6.5 mg/dL	Used in diagnosis/treatment of gout. ↑ due to diuretics, niacin, high doses of aspirin, pyrazinamide, cyclosporine, tacrolimus, ribavirin, some pancreatic enzyme products.

Common Adult Laboratory Reference Ranges Continued

ITEM	COMMON REFERENCE RANGE	NOTES

Inflammation/Autoimmune Disease

ITEM	COMMON REFERENCE RANGE	NOTES
CRP (C-Reactive Protein)	Normal: 0–0.5 mg/dL High risk: > 3 mg/dL	Nonspecific tests used in autoimmune disorders, inflammation and infections. Drug-induced lupus erythematosus (DILE) can be caused by many drugs. More likely with anti-TNF agents, hydralazine, isoniazid, methimazole, methyldopa, minocycline, procainamide, propylthiouracil, quinidine and terbinafine. If ANA is positive, histone antibody and anti-dsDNA tests will be help establish diagnosis. Causative drug will require discontinuation.
RF (Rheumatoid Factor, serum)	< 40 IU/mL	
ESR (Erythrocyte Sedimentation Rate)	Males: ≤ 20 mm/hr Females: ≤ 30 mm/hr	
ANA (Antinuclear Antibodies)	Negative (titers may be provided)	
Antihistone Antibodies (Detected by ELISA)	Negative	

HIV

ITEM	COMMON REFERENCE RANGE	NOTES
HIV Antibody	Negative (non-reactive)	Detects infection with the virus; may not become positive until several weeks after exposure.
HIV DNA PCR	Negative	Useful for early detection.
CD4+ T Lymphocyte Count	800–1,100 cells/mm^3	Used to monitor HIV treatment (see HIV chapter).
HIV RNA Concentration (Viral Load)	Undetectable	
HIV p24 Antigen	Undetectable	Useful for early detection.

Acid-Base (arterial sample)

ITEM	COMMON REFERENCE RANGE	NOTES
pH	7.35–7.45	Values for arterial blood gas (ABG) sample (see Calculations chapter for interpretation). Bicarbonate on the ABG is a calculated value and reference range may differ from venous samples.
pCO_2	35–45 mmHg	
pO_2	80–100 mmHg	
HCO_3	22–26 mEq/L	
O_2 Sat	> 95%	

Hormonal

ITEM	COMMON REFERENCE RANGE	NOTES
Testosterone total, free	Males: 300–950 ng/dL	
PSA (Prostate-Specific Antigen)	< 4 ng/mL	Can ↑ with testosterone supplementation.

Common Adult Laboratory Reference Ranges Continued

ITEM	COMMON REFERENCE RANGE	NOTES
hCG (Human Chorionic Gonadotropin)	Varies by test	Tested in blood or urine to determine pregnancy.
LH (Luteinizing Hormone)	Varies during cycle	Rises mid-cycle causing egg release from the ovaries. Tested in urine with ovulation predictor kits for women attempting pregnancy.
PTH (Parathyroid Hormone)	Varies	Used in evaluation of parathyroid disorders, hypercalcemia and chronic kidney disease (CKD) (see Renal Disease chapter).

Other

Cosyntropin Stimulation Test	Baseline and timed increase are measured	Used to test for adrenal suppression; medications that affect baseline cortisol or suppress adrenal response will impact test and may need to be held prior (e.g., steroids).
Lactic acid (lactate)	0.5–2.2 mEq/L	Indicates anaerobic metabolism/lactic acidosis. ↑ due to NRTIs (see HIV chapter), metformin (low risk/mostly with renal disease and heart failure), alcohol, cyanide.
Procalcitonin	≤ 0.15 ng/mL	↑ due to systemic bacterial infections like sepsis or severe localized infections
Prolactin	1–25 ng/mL	Secretion is regulated by dopamine; can ↑ with haloperidol, risperidone, paliperidone, methyldopa. Can ↓ with bromocriptine.
PPD (Purified Protein Derivative or Mantoux test)	No induration; induration is measured for diagnosis of TB exposure.	TB test administered by intradermal injection. Response is measured by diameter (mm) of induration at 48-72 hours.
Serum osmolality	275–290 mOsm/kg H_2O	Used with Na, BUN/SCr, and clinical volume status to evaluate hypo/hypernatremia. ↑ due to mannitol, toxicities (e.g., ethylene glycol, methanol, propylene glycol, others).
TPMT (Thiopurine Methyltransferase)	≥ 15 units/mL	Those with genetic deficiency of TPMT are at ↑ risk for myelosuppression (bone marrow suppression) and may require lower doses with azathioprine and mercaptopurine.
Vitamin D, serum 25(OH)	> 30 ng/mL	↓ levels increase risk of osteoporosis, osteomalacia (rickets), CVD, diabetes, hypertension, infectious diseases & other conditions. Supplement vitamin D with various conditions and drugs (see Osteoporosis & Hormone Therapy, Renal Disease and Dietary Supplements & Natural and Complementary Medicine chapters).

USING LAB PATTERNS TO DETERMINE THE LIKELY DIAGNOSIS

LIKELY DIAGNOSIS	ABNORMAL LAB OR PATTERN
Heart Failure	↑ BNP / NT-proBNP with s/sx of heart failure
Anemia	↓ Hgb / Hct / RBC. Abnormal RBC indices will indicate type of anemia.
Blood Loss	↓ Hgb / Hct / RBC (sometimes ↓ is dramatic). RBC indices should be normal. ↑ Reticulocyte count if bone marrow is normal.

Using Lab Patterns to Determine the Likely Diagnosis Continued

LIKELY DIAGNOSIS	ABNORMAL LAB OR PATTERN
Liver Injury (acute)	↑ AST / ALT (released from injured hepatocytes)
Liver Disease (chronic)	↑ INR, ↓ albumin, ↓ platelets (all reflect ↓ functional capacity of the liver)
Alcoholic Hepatitis	↑ AST > ↑ ALT / ↑ GGT
Cholestasis (biliary)	↑ Alk Phos / T Bili / GGT with normal or slightly ↑ AST / ALT
Pancreatitis	↑ Amylase and lipase
Acute Kidney Injury	↑ BUN / SCr, possibly ↑ K (BUN:SCr ratio and urinalysis are helpful)
Chronic Kidney Disease, untreated	↑ BUN / SCr / K / PO_4 / PTH with ↓ Hgb / Hct / Ca
Infection, bacterial	↑ WBC with ↑ neutrophils and/or bands (often ↑ lactate / ESR / CRP depending on severity)
Infection, viral	↑ or normal WBC without ↑ neutrophils and/or bands
Infection, parasitic	↑ Eosinophils
Autoimmune	↑ ESR / CRP / ANA
Muscle Damage / Rhabdomyolysis	↑ CPK (and ↑ SCr in rhabdomyolysis)
Lactic Acidosis	↑ Lactic acid, ↑ AG and metabolic acidosis by ABGs

THERAPEUTIC DRUG MONITORING

Drug levels or other values (such as anti-Xa levels for LMWHs) are used to reach dosing goals and to avoid toxicity. Therapeutic drug monitoring (TDM) is increasingly common due to the need to target highly resistant organisms and dose medications in overweight and obese patients. The peak level is the highest concentration in the blood the drug will reach and requires time for the drug to distribute in the body's tissues. The trough level is the lowest concentration the drug will reach in the blood and is drawn right before the next dose or some short period of time before the next dose (30 minutes is common). This allows time for assessment of the level before another dose is given and time to hold the next dose if the level is high. Timing of drug levels is critical to correct interpretation. For example, a tobramycin level of 6 mcg/mL would be interpreted differently if the level was a trough vs a peak.

Obtaining drug levels at steady state is often (but not always) the preferred time. Steady state occurs when the amount of drug going in (for example, when the patient swallows their daily dose) equals the amount of drug going out (from metabolism and clearance). It takes ~5 half-lives for a drug to reach steady state.

Narrow therapeutic index (NTI) drugs have a narrow separation between the level at which the drug provides a benefit and a high (supratherapeutic, and likely toxic) level or a low (subtherapeutic) level. Whether a drug has a NTI can affect generic substitution because a few states do not permit generic substitution of NTI drugs; the FDA, however, does not separate NTI drugs from other drugs in the reference for acceptable generic substitution, the *Orange Book*. The following table lists drugs that are commonly monitored. The table does not include the transplant drugs tacrolimus, cyclosporine, sirolimus and everolimus. These are NTI drugs and are monitored, but the target level will depend on the transplant type, sampling method, concurrent drugs and time since transplant.

TDM is Common for These Drugs that Require Levels

DRUG	USUAL THERAPEUTIC RANGE
Amikacin (traditional dosing)	Peak: 20–30 mcg/mL Trough: < 5 mcg/mL
Carbamazepine	4–12 mcg/mL
Digoxin	0.8–2 ng/mL (AFib) 0.5–0.9 ng/mL (HF)
Gentamicin (traditional dosing)	Peak: 5–10 mcg/mL Trough: < 2 mcg/mL
Lithium	0.6–1.2 mEq/L (up to 1.5 mEq/L for acute symptoms)
Enoxaparin	VTE treatment with daily therapy. Anti-Xa: 1–2 anti-Xa units/mL VTE treatment with Q12H therapy. Anti-Xa: 0.6–1 anti-Xa units/mL Recurrent VTE prophylaxis in pregnancy. Anti-Xa: 0.2–0.6 anti-Xa units/mL
Phenobarbital/Primidone	20–40 mcg/mL (adults)
Phenytoin/Fosphenytoin	10–20 mcg/mL; if low albumin correct serum level; see Epilepsy/Seizures chapter.
Free Phenytoin	1–2.5 mcg/mL
Procainamide	4–10 mcg/mL
NAPA	15–25 mcg/mL
Combined	10–30 mcg/mL
Theophylline	5–15 mcg/mL 5–10 mcg/mL (neonates)
Tobramycin (traditional dosing)	Peak: 5–10 mcg/mL Trough: < 2 mcg/mL
Valproic acid	50–100 mcg/mL (up to 150 mcg/mL in some patients); if low albumin correct serum level; see Epilepsy/Seizures chapter.
Vancomycin	Trough: 15–20 mcg/mL for most serious infections (pneumonia, endocarditis, osteomyelitis, meningitis, and bacteremia) Trough: 10–15 mcg/mL for others
Voriconazole	Trough: 1–5 mcg/mL (target trough may vary depending on MIC for pathogen)
Warfarin	Goal INR is 2–3 for most indications, use higher range (2.5–3.5) with mechanical mitral valves

16

PATIENT CHARTS, ASSESSMENT & HEALTHCARE PROVIDER COMMUNICATION

GUIDELINES/REFERENCES

American Society of Health-System Pharmacists. ASHP Guidelines on Pharmacist-Conducted Patient Education and Counseling. *Am J Health-Syst Pharm.* 1997;54:431-4.

Office of Disease Prevention and Health Promotion. Health Literacy and Communication at http://health.gov/communication/ (accessed 2015 Oct 25).

Agency for Healthcare Research and Quality (AHRQ). Pharmacy Health Literacy Center at http://www.ahrq.gov/ (accessed 2015 Oct 25).

Additional guidelines included with the video files (RxPrep Online).

BACKGROUND

The increased use of electronic health records (EHRs) has provided pharmacists with greater access to patient-specific information, including labs, test results and notes from other healthcare providers.

This is welcome news to the profession, and assists with the pharmacists' involvement in improving patient outcomes, and in assisting patients with health literacy and empowerment in improving their health.

THE PATIENT MEDICAL RECORD

Electronic Health Records

The patient medical record (PMR) provides complete documentation of a patient's medical history at a particular institution. The PMR can be referred to using older terminology such as the medical record or the patient chart. These terms are from the heyday of paper records, when all records of the patient's medical care were gathered into ring binders. Paper charts remain in some healthcare settings, but are being phased out and replaced by EHRs. Once implemented, EHRs improve accuracy and efficiency. EHRs are not without drawbacks; they can be subject to hacking and confidentiality breaches, discussed further.

The EHR is expedient and simpler to review: if, for example, a patient is admitted to the hospital with an elevated SCr, the EHR provides current and previous lab results (by selecting a date range that can go back years in time) which are used to determine if this is a new or an old finding, and what recent work-up has been completed. With a paper chart, time is required to look back through the chart to find this history. With paper charts, papers can be missing – even the entire chart can be lost, and time is required to transport the chart to wherever the patient is going next or to gather history with calls and faxes. Labs and tests are often duplicated because it may be easier to reorder them rather than locating them in the paper records. Procedures with results recorded on paper can be quickly scanned into the EHR. EHRs allow providers to have immediate access to information when they are off-site.

The Health Insurance Portability and Accountability Act of 1996 (HIPAA) security protections for paper records remain the same with electronic records. Access is limited with PINs and passwords, information is encrypted so unauthorized users cannot read it, and an "audit trail" is used to track access. Security can still be violated. Individuals can access medical records for patients they are not involved with, an employee can have the screen visible or forget to log out, and the system can be hacked from the outside. All personnel using the EHR are responsible for security, education on security must be continual, and the software must be evaluated for breaches. As part of the HIPAA requirements, patients have a right to fill out a signed request for their medical records that are kept in either paper or electronic formats.

When the EHR is linked to Computerized Prescriber Order Entry (CPOE) and electronic prescribing (e-prescribing), the problem of illegible handwriting is eliminated. The CPOE system can be designed to present only formulary drugs with proper dosing as options. As a result, pharmacists spend less time clarifying orders or changing to a formulary drug. Clinical decision support (CDS) tools can be built into the order entry process. Examples include order sets, pathways, limited drop-down menus that reflect the preferred drug(s), drug interaction and dose checking alerts, and others. The alerts can appear to the prescriber and/or the pharmacist. Alerts can be constructed that require the user to take action to respond to the alert. An example is checking a box stating that the user is aware of a potential drug interaction and wishes to proceed with the order anyway. Critical results (e.g., aPTT ≥ 150 secs., platelets < 50,000/mm³) can be linked to alert systems, including automatic texts to providers. Electronic information is easier to pool together to measure clinical outcomes and perform quality improvement (QI) activities. EHR implementation at a facility does not occur without complaints; a few primary issues have involved safeguards for patient privacy, the increased time required for training and charting, and the implementation costs for the facility. A common complaint in all practice settings is "alert fatigue" or reduced sensitivity to the alerts. This can cause users to bypass important alerts and compromise patient safety. Refer to the Medication Safety & Quality Improvement chapter for additional information.

HIPAA & PHI

The HIPAA Privacy Rule covers all individually identifiable health information, which is called "protected health information" (PHI).

PHI includes the patient's address (anything more specific than the state they live in), the patient's physical and psychological conditions, the care received or planned, and information that could be used to identify that patient, including name, address, date of birth, medical record number, social security number, phone, fax and email.

It is acceptable to use PHI for treatment decisions, payment (insurance purposes) and for the specific facility operations (such as QI, infection control, etc.) and, if legally warranted (such as with an abuse case) or if required for public health.

Patient's can request their own PHI. If the PHI is used for other purposes (e.g., research), an authorization by the patient is required and identifiers are removed.

Sections of the Patient Medical Record

The first additions to the PMR (paper or EHR) are the patient's demographic data (including insurance information), admission sheet, a service agreement form ("this is what I am having done at this facility"), a page describing the patient's rights (a Joint Commission requirement), and an advanced directive to document the patient's wishes concerning medical treatment if he or she is unable to make decisions on their own behalf.

Certain religious groups will request a refusal form for blood transfusions and blood products. Blood products primarily involve albumin and immune globulins, but some patients will refuse drugs buffered in blood *(Epogen/Procrit, Kogenate* – used for hemophilia), natural clotting factors/tissue adhesives/interferons and a few other uncommon agents. A few vaccines contain porcine-derived gelatin as a stabilizer. The major religious groups consider this use acceptable, but a specific patient may not.

Other forms in the PMR include progress notes, the vital signs record, clinical pathway sheets used for some conditions, medication records used for some medications (such as warfarin to track the INR history), medication administration records and procedure records, including the diagnostic and operating room (OR) records. The list of "Do Not Use" abbreviations should be easily available. It is important to avoid abbreviations that could be interpreted to mean something else – all hospitals will include their own group of unsafe abbreviations and the Joint Commission's list of unsafe abbreviations, acronyms and symbols; see the Medication Safety & Quality Improvement chapter for further discussion. Some institutions give prescribers laminated cards of the unapproved abbreviation list to keep in their pocket, hang the list on the wall near the computer, or make the list visible on the computer screen when making entries. At the end of the hospital stay the planning and discharge forms are added to the EHR.

Requirements for Reimbursement: Documentation and Quality of Care

Pharmacists are involved with many patient care activities and frequently make verbal recommendations concerning patient care. While verbal recommendations may be effective, they are not part of the PMR and do not allow the information to be shared with other healthcare providers involved in the patient's care who are not present at that time. Interventions require documentation for reimbursement since the quality of the care is (increasingly) tied to the payment. Departments of pharmacy should have policies in place that describe the authority of pharmacists to document in the PMR, what activities will be documented, and the proper format for documentation. Some activities that pharmacists document in the PMR include patient counseling, medication histories, consultations (e.g., pharmacokinetics, anticoagulation) and dosage adjustments. Documenting in the PMR is critical to establishing pharmacists as central members of the healthcare team.

The federal health insurance program is called the Affordable Care Act (ACA) or is referred to as "Obamacare". The ACA includes a "National Quality Strategy" which assesses the improvement in quality of care by determining if the members are healthier and if the costs are lower. Since the Centers for Medicare and Medicaid Services (CMS) provides health insurance to many Americans, CMS is directly involved with quality measurements and cost control. CMS has penalties for poor care and incentives for quality care. Two areas in which the penalties are steep are the rate of hospital-acquired infections and the hospital's readmission rate. These measures are chosen because they are expensive and are often, but not always, avoidable.

The Joint Commission, The Pharmacy Quality Alliance (PQA) and The Agency for Healthcare Research and Quality (AHRQ) are also involved in setting the criteria to measure the quality of care. The PQA quality measurements focus on medications. Specific goals that involve medications include increasing adherence, avoiding unnecessary or unsafe medications (such as high-risk medications in the elderly) and increasing the use of medications indicated for certain conditions.

> **MEDICARE & MEDICAID**
>
> Medicare is the federal health insurance program for people ≥ 65 yrs, < 65 yrs with disability and all ages with end stage renal disease (ESRD).
>
> The prescription drug benefit under Medicare is called Part D.
>
> Part A covers the hospital visit and Part B covers medical costs, such as doctor visits, and some vaccines.
>
> Medicaid provides health insurance for all ages with very low income (< 133% of the federal poverty level). Medicaid is a federal and state program. A senior who qualifies for both Medicare and Medicaid has "dual coverage."

THE SOAP FORMAT FOR PROGRESS NOTES

A progress note records a patient encounter. The SOAP note format is organized into four parts: Subjective, Objective, Assessment and Plan (SOAP). Paper charts and EHRs often use this format. Prior to the use of SOAP notes it was difficult to understand patient chart entries because the format was not standardized. The SOAP note was developed to provide a standard structure for recording the patient encounter. Pharmacists may write SOAP notes to document their activities and read the SOAP notes of others while providing patient care. An example SOAP note from an EHR is included at the end of this chapter.

Subjective

The 1st section in a SOAP note is the subjective information recorded from the patient. It is the patient's own narrative of their symptoms. Only the relevant information is recorded. The person conducting the interview should use only direct questions and avoid leading questions. For example, the leading question: "You always take your blood pressure pills, right?" is not likely to get a useful response. Phrasing the question in a direct manner that is worded to avoid a yes or no response will elicit a more useful response: "In a typical week, about how many mornings do you forget to take the blood pressure pills?"

The subjective section begins with a one-line Chief Complaint (CC), the specific reason the patient is being seen today, such as "I've had a stabbing pain in my right hip for three days" or "I feel like I need to go all the time but nothing much comes out." The subjective section includes the history of the present illness (HPI): the onset and duration of the specific complaint, the quality and severity (for example, with a pain complaint, descriptive words should be used to identify the type of pain, with a numerical pain rating), any modifying factors (what reduces or aggravates the condition), and treatment that has been tried to resolve the condition and the effect of the treatment, if any.

This section includes the past medical history (PMH), social history (alcohol, tobacco and illicit drug use), family history (first-degree relatives only – parents and siblings), allergies and medication use. Medication use includes prescriptions, samples, and OTCs, including vitamins and natural products. Information on start date and last refill is important when recording medication information.

Objective

The 2nd section in a SOAP note is the objective information obtained by the clinician, either through observation or analysis. This includes the vital signs (respiration rate, heart rate, blood pressure, temperature). Note that on the top of the sample EHR at the end of this chapter the vitals are recorded at the top of the page – but they are part of the objective section. Any other measurements (for example, height and weight, spirometry), physical findings, tests performed (e.g., ECG, chest x-ray, urinalysis) and laboratory results go into this section. If medications are obtained from a source other than the patient (recording information from prescription bottles, calling another pharmacy, etc.) they are occasionally recorded in the objective section of the SOAP because they were objectively verified.

SIGNS AND SYMPTONS (S/Sx)

A symptom is subjective information, described by the patient, such as "My lower back hurts."

A sign is generally objective (described by the clinician), such as recording the patient's vital signs.

Occasionally objective evidence (such as a skin rash), can be seen by either the patient or family members or the clinician.

CRITICAL RESULTS

Critical results are levels significantly outside the normal range and can indicate a life-threatening situation.

They need to be reported to a health-care provider right away and must be responded to quickly.

This is a Joint Commission National Patient Safety Goal.

Units of Measure

It is important to document measurements according to the policies of the institution. Documentation is generally done in metric system units (kg, cm, etc.). Recording weights and heights with incorrect units (150 pounds vs 150 kg) can have fatal consequences in terms of dosing medications. Refer to the Calculations chapter for common height and weight conversions. In the U.S., temperatures are still frequently recorded in degrees Fahrenheit and may need to be converted to degrees Celsius.

Temperature Conversions

$$°C = (°F - 32)/1.8$$

$$°F = (°C \times 1.8) + 32$$

Assessment

The 3rd section is the assessment. This is the provider's thought process of possible causes of the current situation. Many conditions present with similar signs and symptoms; the assessment will often include multiple possible diagnoses. The differential diagnosis is a list of possible diagnoses that could explain the patient's current signs and symptoms. Each diagnosis on the list will be investigated.

Plan

The 4th section is the plan. This is how the problem(s) will be addressed. The plan should be as specific as possible. Labs might be ordered, the patient might require diagnostic exams, referrals may be requested, or the patient may require education. Education could be required for a variety of reasons, such as suspected non-adherence, to remedy poor device technique or to provide nutritional education or smoking cessation support. If there is a differential diagnosis there will be multiple steps in the plan to eliminate ("rule out") some of the possible conditions. Patients often have many medical problems that must be addressed, and they may be vastly different from the complaint that prompted the patient to seek medical attention.

MILITARY TIME

12-Hr clock	24-Hr clock
12:00 midnight	24:00
1:00 am	01:00
...(continuing).	(pronounced "Oh-100")
7:00 pm	19:00
8:00 pm	20:00
9:00 pm	21:00
10:00 pm	22:00
11:00 pm	23:00
12:00 midnight	24:00

Military Time

In all medical records, including the SOAP note, time is recorded with a 24-hour clock, rather than splitting the day into two 12-hour segments (AM/PM). The 24-hour clock is called "military time." The day begins at midnight, which is called 24:00 (pronounced twenty-four hundred). This is actually the start of the day and is sometimes referred to as 00:00. One minute past midnight is 00:01, thirty minutes is 00:30, one hour is 01:00, and so on. After 12:00 noon the time continues on the same number scale for the rest of the day: 1:00 PM is 1300, 2:00 PM is 1400, and so on. The last minute of the day is 23:59, then 24:00 (midnight), and then the next day begins.

This text contains three EHR SOAP notes; one at the end of this chapter and the patient cases at the end of the Chronic Heart Failure and Inflammatory Bowel Disease chapters.

ASSESSMENT OF TREATMENT PLANS

Pharmacists caring for patients are often faced with complex medication regimens. In order to provide the best care possible, a systematic approach to assessment of the treatment plan and medication regimen is warranted. Pharmacists should assess for medication therapy problems (see table), intervene when appropriate, and document the intervention(s) in the PMR as policy permits.

Medication Therapy Problems

Untreated medical condition	Adverse drug reaction
Medication used without an indication	Drug interactions
Improper drug selection	Improper use of medication
Subtherapeutic dose	Failure to receive medication
Overdosage	Lack of understanding of the medication therapy by the patient
Therapeutic duplication	Nonadherence with the medication therapy
Drug allergy	

HEALTHCARE PROVIDER COMMUNICATION

Health Literacy

Good communication skills are essential for pharmacists and are linked to patient satisfaction and trust. Despite providing valuable information to patients, much of the information that pharmacists provide may not be understood. Only about 12% of adults have proficient health literacy, an example of this is being able to correctly interpret a prescription label. Health literacy is the degree to which individuals are able to obtain, process and understand basic health and medication information to make appropriate health decisions. Health literacy is different than simply being able to read or being well educated; many educated people have difficulty understanding medical information. Low health literacy is common in the elderly, minority populations, those with lower income, poor health, and limited English proficiency but can be an issue for any patient. A person's health literacy is dependent on age, communication skills, knowledge, experience and culture. Low health literacy is linked to poor health outcomes.

Effective Communication and Education Strategies

- Approach all patients as if they are at risk of not understanding the health information presented. Do not assume that it is easy to tell who has low health literacy.

- Use everyday, non-medical language that patients can understand.
  Example: Say "high blood pressure" instead of "hypertension" or "tired" instead of "fatigued".

- Ask open-ended questions that require more than a "yes" or "no" answer.
  Example: Ask "what questions can I answer about your new medication today?" instead of "do you have any questions?"

- Avoid leading questions.
  Example: Ask "what about your high blood pressure concerns you?" instead of "are you most concerned about the side effects from the high blood pressure medication?"

- Confirm understanding. Ask the patient to repeat the information or ask what they would tell their spouse or friend about the new medication.

- Use different communication strategies (verbal, written, visual aids) to enhance understanding. Ask the patient how he/she prefers to receive the information.

- Use active listening. Clarifying or summarizing what the patient has said is helpful and gives the patient an opportunity to offer correction.

- Speak clearly, make eye contact, introduce yourself and refer to patients by their name. Avoid "sweetie", "dear" and other similar terms.

Communication Challenges

Communicating medical information to patients with language/cultural differences and disabilities presents additional challenges. Be creative to ensure that all patients receive the education they need. Use interpreters or interpreter services (computer or phone services) when needed. Family members and friends (especially children) should not be used to interpret, if this can be avoided. They might edit or incorrectly relay the information. Strategies to enhance communication with certain patient types are included in the table.

PATIENT TYPE OR DISABILITY	STRATEGIES TO ENHANCE COMMUNICATION
Blindness or visual impairment	Provide information electronically when possible (some technology can "read" this aloud or convert to Braille).
	Use large text in written information.
	Speak normally.
Hearing impairment	Conduct counseling in a quiet, well-lit area.
	Speak directly to the patient; avoid explaining and demonstrating at the same time (many patients read lips and have difficulty focusing on two things at the same time).
Older adults	Issues above with visual and hearing impairment may apply.
	Older adults may not trust young healthcare providers. Earn their trust by being professional, competent and caring.
	Older adults may have difficulty with child-resistant caps and complicated devices. Recommend alternatives as needed.
Different cultures	Some cultures rely heavily on complementary and alternative medicine. Be sure to ask patients about this.

Juanita Burrows (PRN: JB747114): SOAP Note for 09/25/2014
Age on DOS: 40 yrs, DOB: 03/13/1974

San Diego Medical Group
35 La Jolla Drive Suite 100 San Diego, CA 92130
(444) 444-4444

seen by: Alison James
seen on: Thursday 25 September 2014

VS

Height:	Weight:	BMI:	Blood Pressure:	Temp:	Pulse:	Resp Rate:
67.0 in	195.0 lb	30.5	154 / 92 mmHg	97.9 F	80 bpm	12 rpm

CC "I feel limp"

S JB is a 40 y/o female who presents with a 3 month history of increasing fatigue. She first noticed that she felt tired when she was working long hours to get a job done at work, but has been working her usual 8 hours a day for the past 2 months and has not regained her energy. She describes her fatigue as "feeling limp". It is present throughout the day, but worse with significant exertion (e.g., walking > 3-4 blocks or going up stairs). She has tried to go to bed earlier, but even sleeping up to 10 hours/night (increased from 8 hours/night) has not helped. She is concerned that there is something seriously wrong, as she is usually full of energy and her family and friends are starting to ask if she is sick. She has also not been able to exercise, which she usually enjoys. She denies chest pain, SOB, abdominal pain, N/V/D, or changes in her stool. She has no alopecia or skin changes. She has had no fever, chills or night sweats. She has gained about 6-7 lbs in the last few months, which she attributes to inactivity due to fatigue. She denies depressed mood, sadness, or anhedonia. She states that she goes to bed at 10pm and wakes feeling tired at 6am on weekdays and 8am on weekends. Her husband states that she has "always" snored quite loudly. Her menses are regular in timing, heavy flow for 1-2 days, then lighter for another 2-3 days. This pattern is unchanged from prior to the onset of her fatigue. Her last menstrual period was one week ago. When asked about compliance with her medications, she states that she takes everything regularly "except the one for her blood pressure because she doesn't feel like her pressure is high".

She reports a history of GERD, HTN, and depression.
Her medications include: Zantac 150 mg PO QHS, Chlorthalidone 25 mg PO Daily,
Zoloft 100 mg Daily, and Caltrate + D 600 mg BID.

O Well-appearing black female in no acute distress.
SKIN: not pale, no rashes
NECK: no thyromegaly or thyroid nodules
NODES: no cervical, axillary or inguinal lymphadenopathy
CHEST: clear to auscultation and percussion bilaterally
CV: RRR, 2/6 systolic ejection murmur heard best at the LLSB that radiates to the apex, no S3 or S4
ABD: normal active bowel sounds, no hepatosplenomegaly by palpation or percussion, no abdominal tenderness
EXT: no edema, pulses normal

A Recent onset of fatigue with no obvious inciting event. Hypothyroidism is possible especially given her weight gain, though this also may have occurred from her inactivity. It is possible that she is anemic though her menstrual periods have not lengthened or increased and there is no other obvious source of blood loss. A recent menses makes pregnancy unlikely. Given her history of snoring, sleep apnea is possible, but her history of snoring over many years is not entirely consistent with her more recent onset of fatigue. She does not seem to have a recurrence of her depression since she has no new symptoms. She does not have symptoms of infection, nor has her murmur changed, so subacute bacterial endocarditis is possible but unlikely. BP is elevated and she has been noncompliant with prescribed therapy for HTN.

P #1. Check TSH to rule out hypothyroidism
#2. Check CBC to rule out anemia
#3. If the above are unremarkable, consider a sleep study to rule out sleep apnea
#4. Consider blood cultures to rule out subacute bacterial endocarditis
#5. Pharmacy consult for medication adherence
#6. Follow-up visit in 1 week to discuss test results and further work-up

26 September 2014 5:23 PM
page 1 of 1

PRACTICE CASE

PATIENT PROFILE

Patient Name	Celene Molina
Address	456 Washington Drive

Age:	58	Sex:	F	Race:	Hispanic	Height:	5'2"	Weight:	146 pounds

Allergies NKDA

Date	Prescriber	Drug/Strength/Sig/Quantity
12/11/15	Williams	Captopril 25 mg 1 tab PO TID #90
12/11/15	Williams	Furosemide 40 mg 1 tab with breakfast and lunch #60
12/11/15	Williams	*Klor-Con* 20 mEq 1 tab PO QAM #30
12/11/15	Williams	Metoprolol tartrate 50 mg 1 tab BID #60
12/11/15	Williams	Sertraline 50 mg 1 tab PO BID #60
12/11/15	Williams	Metformin 500 mg 1 tab PO TID #90
12/11/15	Williams	Simvastatin 20 mg 1 tab PO QHS #30
12/11/15	Williams	Albuterol inhaler 1 puff QID PRN #1 inhaler
12/11/15	Williams	*Advair Diskus* 1 puff BID #1 inhaler

ADDITIONAL INFORMATION

Date: 12/11/15 **Notes:** Patient out of medications. Provided refills for all medications. Follow-up in one month. Instructed patient to bring medication bottles to next clinic appointment.

Date: 1/15/16 **Notes:** Follow-up visit. Patient accompanied by daughter. Each bottle has 10-20 tabs remaining. Daughter states that her mother does not know how to use the inhalers. Vital signs today: BP 158/98, HR 82, Glucose (not fasting) 258 mg/dL

QUESTIONS

1. Celene speaks very little English and has limited health literacy. According to her daughter, she does not understand how to use her prescribed inhalers. All of the following methods are helpful to assist patients with limited English language proficiency EXCEPT:

    a. Use a translator or translator service.

    b. Reinforce the counseling with Celene's daughter.

    c. Talk loudly with exaggerated speech when explaining key points.

    d. Provide written information in the patient's language.

    e. Use pictures and diagrams, or pictograms, as aids during counseling.

2. The patient's daughter explained that the person who helped them in the clinic in December was not very friendly and "scared" her Mom. The pharmacist and nursing team leader will work together to prepare an educational program to help the staff improve relationships with the patients. Each of the following strategies can improve relationships between healthcare professionals and patients EXCEPT:

    a. Use short words and sentences.

    b. Adopt a friendly rather than a business-like attitude.

    c. Use medical terminology when educating patients (e.g., use "hypertension" instead of "high blood pressure").

    d. Repeat instructions to patients if they look confused.

    e. Have patients repeat back the instructions.

3. Which of the following techniques would be most helpful to assist with Celene's medication adherence at this time?

   a. Switch the *Advair Diskus* to *Flovent HFA*.

   b. Simplify the medication regimen.

   c. Instruct the patient to move the simvastatin dose to the morning.

   d. Have the patient repeat back how to take each medication.

   e. Change the albuterol to oral tablets to reduce inhaler use.

4. Celene has reviewed her medications with the pharmacist and will leave for home shortly. The pharmacist would like to verify that Celene has received proper instruction on how to use her inhalers. Which of the following is the best method?

   a. Have the patient use pictures or pictograms to explain the technique to the pharmacist.

   b. The pharmacist should follow-up the visit with a telephone call.

   c. Celene's daughter should explain back the technique that her mother will use.

   d. Celene should demonstrate to the pharmacist how the inhaler is used.

   e. Have Celene watch video instructions before she goes home.

Answers

1-c, 2-c, 3-b, 4-d

17

DRUG DISPOSAL

Courtesy of Appalachian Voices

GUIDELINES/REFERENCES

Drug Enforcement Administration. Drug Disposal Information. http://www.deadiversion.usdoj.gov/drug_disposal/ (accessed 2015 October 12)

Food and Drug Administration. How to Dispose of Unused Medicines. http://www.fda.gov/forconsumers/consumerupdates/ucm101653.htm (accessed 2015 October 12)

U.S. Environmental Protection Agency. How to Dispose of Medicines Properly. http://water.epa.gov/scitech/swguidance/ppcp/upload/ppcpflyer.pdf (accessed 2015 October 12)

BACKGROUND

It is important to dispose of drugs properly to avoid accidental ingestion, environmental pollution and limit drug abuse. More Americans currently abuse prescription drugs than the number of those using cocaine, hallucinogens, heroin, and inhalants combined. Children and pets can accidently ingest drugs. Drugs that are flushed down the toilet can be found in the waterways, from the east to west coast.

There are safe and responsible ways to dispose of drugs through law enforcement-sponsored take-back events, collection receptacles and mail-back packages.

If the above disposal options are not available, patients can be instructed to follow local guidelines for Home Hazardous Waste (HHW) collection. HHW is any waste, produced in the home, which contains hazardous substances that can harm the environment, wildlife, and human health, and includes unwanted drugs. Cities and/or states have regulations on how to dispose of home hazardous waste, including prescription drugs.

If programs are not available, it is sometimes possible to dispose of unwanted drugs in the household trash if certain precautions are taken. Some drugs cannot be discarded in household trash due to higher risk, and these drugs can be flushed down the toilet instead. The complete list of drugs that should be flushed is at the end of this chapter. Drug disposal instructions are included in the package labeling.

NATIONAL AND LOCAL DRUG TAKE-BACK EVENTS

Courtesy of Penn State

In 2010, the DEA implemented the <u>National Prescription Drug Take-Back Day program</u> at over 3,000 collection sites nationwide, which provided consumers a safe way to dispose of unused controlled substances. Take-Back events are a significant part of the government's effort to reduce prescription drug diversion and abuse by removing unwanted or expired medications from America's home medicine cabinets. Pharmacists volunteer at these events to help collect unwanted medications. The first four years of the program collected over 2,400 tons of unused drugs. The National Prescription Drug Take-Back Days were temporarily discontinued but are now reinstated.

Local law enforcement can host community take-back events. If these are available, the information should be known to local law enforcement and waste management services.

COLLECTION RECEPTACLES

Courtesy of Sharps Compliance, Inc.©

Until recently, federal law did not provide a legal method for controlled drug disposal, except to return them to law enforcement. This caused unwanted drugs to be flushed or otherwise discarded or kept at home and subject to diversion. Currently, the Secure and Responsible Drug Disposal Act allows manufacturers, distributors, reverse distributors, narcotic treatment programs, hospitals/clinics with an on-site pharmacy, and retail pharmacies to voluntarily register with the DEA to collect controlled drugs (and non-controlled drugs) from patients for destruction. This is a welcome change since patients will have more disposal options and do not need to wait for a specific Take-Back Day to dispose of their unused medications. These DEA-authorized collection receptacles are to collect unused/unwanted drugs from patients only. Pharmacies and hospitals cannot dispose of unused/unwanted controlled substances from their inventory into the collection receptacle.

The drugs collected should not be individually counted or inventoried. The patient or patient's agent should place the drugs directly into the collection receptacle themselves.

MAIL-BACK PROGRAMS

Courtesy of Sharps Compliance, Inc.©

Pharmacies and other DEA-authorized collectors can provide envelopes for patients to return drugs to a mail-back program. The medications are placed into the envelope and dropped off in the mail. The package is plain and does not have markings or other information that indicates what is inside the envelope.

The package should be pre-addressed with the collector's registered address or the participating law enforcement's address. The cost of shipping the package is postage paid.

DISPOSING DRUGS IN THE HOUSEHOLD TRASH

If no disposal instructions are given on the prescription drug labeling, and if there are no local disposal options or take-back programs in the local area, the U.S. Environmental Protection Agency and the FDA recommend throwing away drugs in the household trash by following these steps:

Courtesy of the Substance Abuse and Mental Health Services Administration

1. Remove the drugs from their original containers and mix them with an undesirable substance, such as used coffee grounds, dirt or kitty litter. This makes the drug less appealing to children and pets, and not easily recognizable to people who may intentionally go through the trash to look for drugs.

2. Scratch out all identifying information on the prescription label to make it unreadable if the container is being discarded. This will help protect the patient's identity.

3. Place the mixture in a sealable bag, empty can or other container to prevent the drug from leaking or breaking out of a garbage bag.

4. Place in trash can.

FLUSHING DRUGS DOWN THE TOILET OR SINK

In most cases, drugs should not be disposed of by flushing them down the sink or toilet because this will contaminate the water supply or soil. However, some medications can be particularly fatal if accidently ingested by others (especially children and pets), causing respiratory depression, and possibly death. The FDA recommends flushing specific drugs down the sink or toilet so the risk can be immediately and permanently removed from the home only when it is not possible for the drugs to be disposed of through a take-back program, collection receptacle, or mail-back program. With these drugs only the health risks from accidental ingestion will outweigh the environmental risks.

The FDA list of unwanted medicines that should be flushed down the sink or toilet (as of September 2015):

ACTIVE INGREDIENT	DRUG
Buprenorphine	*Belbuca,* soluble film (buccal) *Butrans*, transdermal patch (extended-release) Buprenorphine, tablet (sublingual)*
Buprenorphine/Naloxone	*Bunavail*, buccal film *Suboxone*, film (sublingual) *Zubsolv*, tablet (sublingual) Buprenorphine/Naloxone, tablet (sublingual)*
Diazepam	*Diastat/Diastat AcuDial*, rectal gel
Fentanyl	*Abstral*, tablet (sublingual) *Actiq*, oral transmucosal lozenge* *Duragesic*, patch (extended-release)* *Fentora*, tablet (buccal) *Onsolis*, soluble film (buccal)
Hydromorphone	*Dilaudid*, tablet* *Dilaudid*, oral liquid* *Exalgo*, tablets (extended-release)
Hydrocodone	*Hysingla ER*, tablet (extended-release) *Zohydro ER*, capsule (extended-release)
Meperidine	*Demerol*, tablet* *Demerol*, oral solution*
Methadone	*Dolophine*, tablet* *Methadose*, tablet* *Methadose,* oral solution*
Methylphenidate	*Daytrana*, transdermal patch system
Morphine	*Avinza*, capsule (extended-release) *Kadian*, capsule (extended-release) *Morphabond*, tablet (extended-release) *MS Contin*, tablet (extended-release)* Morphine, tablet (immediate-release)* Morphine, oral solution*
Morphine/Naltrexone	*Embeda*, capsule (extended-release)
Oxycodone	*Oxaydo*, tablet (immediate-release) *Oxycontin*, tablet (extended-release) Oxycodone, capsule Oxycodone, oral solution
Oxycodone/Acetaminophen	*Percocet*, tablet* *Xartemis XR*, tablet
Oxycodone/Aspirin	*Percodan*, tablet*
Oxycodone/Naloxone	*Targiniq ER*, tablets (extended-release)
Oxymorphone	*Opana*, tablet (immediate-release) *Opana ER*, tablet (extended-release)
Sodium Oxybate	*Xyrem*, oral solution
Tapentadol	*Nucynta ER*, tablet (extended-release)

* These medicines have generic versions available or are only available in generic formulations.

SHARPS DISPOSAL

Used needles and other sharps cause injuries and spread infections, including hepatitis B and C, and HIV. Sharps should be disposed of in an FDA-cleared sharps container, which are puncture resistant, labeled or color-coded appropriately, closeable, and leak-proof. They come marked with a line that indicates when the container should be considered full (about ¾ full); never overfill or press down to fit in more waste. Patients who use sharps should have a disposal container and be instructed to put needles and other sharps in the container immediately after use.

The entire assembly is discarded (needle plus syringe). Do not instruct patients to remove the needle or attempt to cut it. The only time that recapping a needle is permitted is when the sharps container is not immediately available; in that case, use the one-hand method to recap until the sharps container can be reached: Place the cap on a table or counter next to something firm to push the cap against: 2. Hold the syringe with the needle attached and slip the needle into the cap without using the other hand. Push the capped needle on the firm surface to "seat" the cap onto the needle using only the one hand.

Anyone using syringes should be instructed not to contaminate the injection by touching the tip or plunger, and not to share needles with others. Needles are not meant to be reused. Sharps disposal guidelines and programs vary. The local trash removal services or health department should have the available service/s, and the pharmacy can relate this information to patients. These include drop boxes or supervised collection sites (such as in a hospital, pharmacy, police or fire station), household hazardous waste collection sites, mail-back programs and residential special waste services pick-up. If someone is stuck with a used needle, the proper department at a healthcare facility, and may require post exposure prophylaxis (PEP) for HIV and hepatitis B. In the outpatient setting, instruct the patient to wash the area right away with soap and water, and contact their healthcare provider.

IV DRUG COMPATIBILITY, ADMINISTRATION & DEGRADATION

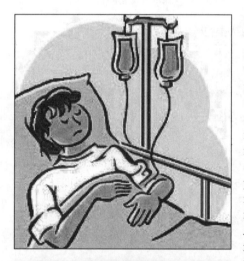

GUIDELINES/REFERENCES

Handbook on Injectable Drugs.
18th Ed. American Society of Health-System Pharmacists. 2014

King Guide to Parenteral Admixtures.
https://www.kingguide.com/online.html
(accessed 2015 November 18)

Package inserts, various (accessed 2015 November 18)

BACKGROUND

The pharmacist is the primary consult for questions concerning the compatibility and stability of parenteral medications. There are many drugs and the information changes; reputable resources are required. The *Handbook on Injectable Drugs* (formerly called *Trissel's*) or the *King Guide to Parenteral Admixtures* (commonly called *King's*) are the primary compatibility and stability resources, along with the drug's package insert. Some drug information databases, including *Micromedex*, *Clinical Pharmacology* and *Lexi-Comp* have an IV compatibility database that can be used in the clinical setting. A reputable group of pharmacists prepares lists of compatibility issues on a periodic basis that are published in *Pharmacy Practice News* and in *Hospital Pharmacy*. These lists are used for handy reference purposes; however, the pharmacist must verify the information as it may have changed.

INCOMPATIBILITIES

Chemical incompatibility causes drug degradation or toxicity due to a hydrolysis, oxidation or decomposition reaction. Physical incompatibility is commonly due to compounds binding together and forming a precipitate which may or may not be visible, and can be quickly fatal if the precipitate travels to the lungs.

Physical incompatibilities can occur with the following:

■ The container (drugs that cannot be placed into PVC containers)

■ The solution (diluents – primarily dextrose or saline) and

■ Other drugs, such as phenytoin binding to dextrose or calcium binding to phosphate; drug-drug incompatibility can occur when drugs are mixed in the same syringe or container, or during Y site administration.

Drugs and Intravenous Polyvinyl Chloride Containers

The majority of polyvinyl chloride (PVC) containers use diethylhexyl phthalate (<u>DEHP</u>) as a "plasticizer" to make the plastic flexible. The DEHP compound is of concern, as it may affect male fertility. The two primary concerns with the use of PVC containers are <u>leaching</u> (DEHP leaches from the PVC container into the solution) and <u>sorption</u> (the drug moves into the PVC container). Drugs that have incompatibility with PVC containers can be placed in <u>polyolefin</u> containers, or with some drugs, in <u>glass</u> containers (although glass is heavy and can break). Review the list of drugs with sorption issues on the page 249.

DRUGS THAT LEACH INTO PVC
Mnemonic: "Two Tiny Tots Came Dressed In Elephant Pajamas"

Tacrolimus	**I**xabepilone
Temsirolimus	**E**toposide
Teniposide	**P**aclitaxel
Cabazitaxel	
Docetaxel	

Drugs and Incompatible IV Solutions (Saline or Dextrose)

When drugs are put into solution for IV administration in the pharmacy they are commonly placed into 50 mL or larger IV "piggybacks" that contain 5% dextrose or 0.9% saline. With many drugs either solution is acceptable but with others only dextrose or only saline is compatible (see table).

Incompatibility During Y-Site Administration

COMMON DRUGS THAT REQUIRE EITHER DEXTROSE OR SALINE	
Saline Only (No Dextrose)	**Dextrose Only (No Saline)**
<u>Ampicillin</u>	<u>Amphotericin B</u> (all formulations)
Abatacept (*Orencia*)	Carfilzomib (*Kyprolis*)
<u>Ampicillin/Sulbactam</u> (*Unasyn*)	Mycophenolate (*CellCept IV*)
Azacitidine (*Vidaza*) NS or LR	Pentamidine
Belimumab (*Benlysta*)	<u>Quinupristin/Dalfopristin</u> (*Synercid*)
Bevacizumab (*Avastin*)	<u>Sulfamethoxazole/ Trimethoprim</u> (*Bactrim*)
<u>Caspofungin</u> (*Cancidas*) NS or LR	
<u>Daptomycin</u> (*Cubicin*) NS or LR	
Idarucizumab (*Praxbind*)	
<u>Phenytoin</u>	
Ertapenem (*Invanz*)	
Infliximab (*Remicade*)	
Iron Sucrose (*Venofer*)	
Sodium Ferric Gluconate Complex (*Ferrlecit*)	
Natalizumab (*Tysabri*)	
Trastuzumab (*Herceptin*)	

When a patient is receiving medication through an IV line, sometimes another medication needs to be given at the same time. If another IV line is not available, more than one medication can often be given through a single IV line using "<u>Y-site</u>" administration (see figure). The <u>drugs mix together briefly in the common portion of the IV tubing</u>, and a drug may come in contact with an incompatible drug or solution. Nursing staff (who hang the infusion bags) commonly consult with the pharmacist to check for compatibility issues.

When a pharmacist references a resource to check whether drugs can be co-administered, several types of compatibility listings are available. "Additive compatibility" (drugs are mixed in the same container) and "syringe compatibility" (drugs are mixed in a syringe) are listed separately from Y-site compatibility. Y-site incompatibilities are important in pharmacy because this type of administration is common and many drugs that cannot be mixed in the same container are compatible to mix in the line.

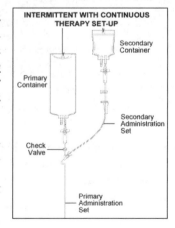

In the following examples, the reference drug is listed above the table (cefepime) with the manu-facturer and concentration listed directly below. The drug tested with it is listed in the left column (gentamicin).

Additive Compatibility

In this example, the pharmacist looks to see if cefepime can be mixed with gentamicin in the same container. Based on the information below, cefepime and gentamicin are incompatible when mixed to-gether in either D5W or NS at the concentrations listed. This is indicated by the "I" in the final column and the remarks, which indicate that a precipitate formed in the reference that is cited.

Cefepime

DRUG	MFR*	CONC/L	MFR	CONC/L	TEST SOLN	REMARKS	REF	C/I
Gentamicin	ES	1.2 g	BR	40 g	D5W, NS	Cloudiness forms in 18 hr at room temp	588	I

Y-Site Injection Compatibility (1:1 Mixture)

In this example, a nurse called to ask the pharmacist whether cefepime can be given in the same line while gentamicin is infusing. The pharmacist finds that cefepime and gentamicin are compatible for Y-site administration at the concentrations listed, indicated by the "C" in the far right column and by the remarks.

Cefepime

DRUG	MFR*	CONC	MFR	CONC	REMARKS	REF	C/I
Gentamicin	ES	6 mg/mL	BMS	120 mg/mL	Physically compatible with less than 10% cefepime loss. Gentamicin was not tested.	2212	C

C = compatible; I = incompatible

Information is extensive for incompatibilities; this is a discussion of a select few. Amphotericin B is incompatible with the majority of IV drugs with any type of IV administration. The common hospital IV drug piperacillin/tazobactam (discussed further below) forms a precipitate when it mixes with acyclovir, amphotericin B and many other IV drugs.

Heparin is incompatible when administered with many drugs, including those which are often given concurrently in a patient requiring heparin (nitroglycerin, alteplase and hydromorphone). Caspofungin, another common hospital drug for treating *Candida* infections, has many Y-site in-compatibilities. All of the IV quinolones are incompatible with Y-site infusion with <u>many</u> drugs. When incompatibili-ties exist, particularly with long or continuous infusions, additional IV sites may be required.

Maintenance Fluid Bag

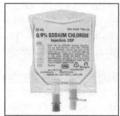

IV Piggyback

FILTERS

In-line filters (inside the IV tubing) are used with drugs that have a risk of particulates, precipitates, crystals, contaminants or entrapped air in the final solution. The size of the filter required is deter-mined by the size of the particles to be removed. The majority of drugs in which filters are necessary use a <u>0.22 micron filter</u> (1 micron = 1/1,000 mm); another common filter size is <u>1.2 microns</u> which is used for most <u>lipids</u>. Some drugs come packaged with the filter that should be used. If compounding IV medications in a sterile hood and glass ampules are used, filter <u>needles</u> are used to prevent particu-lates from entering the IV bag and a filter may be required in the line.

COMMON DRUGS WITH FILTER REQUIREMENTS

Filter during administration (0.22 micron, unless noted):

Abatacept (Orencia)

Abciximab (ReoPro)

Amiodarone (continuous infusions)

Digoxin Immune Fab (DigiFab)

Golimumab (Simponi)

Infliximab (Remicade)

Isavuconazonium (Cresemba)

Lipids (not all, 1.2 micron)

Lorazepam (Ativan)

Mannitol (Osmitrol)

Phenytoin (Dilantin)

Parenteral Nutrition

Thiotepa

Filter during preparation only:

Amphotericin B, liposomal and lipid complex (Abelcet, AmBisome)

SELECT IV DRUGS THAT DO NOT REQUIRE REFRIGERATION

Acetaminophen (Ofirmev)

Acyclovir – refrigeration causes crystallization

Deferoxamine (Desferal)

Dexmedetomidine (Precedex)

Enoxaparin (Lovenox)

Furosemide – refrigeration causes crystallization

Hydralazine

Levetiracetam (Keppra)

Metronidazole

Pentamidine

Propofol (Diprivan)

Moxifloxacin (Avelox)

Phenytoin

Sulfamethoxazole/Trimethoprim (Bactrim)

Valproate

Stability – Effects of Time, Temperature, Light, Agitation

A drug that is "stable" at room temperature will be stable only for a certain time, at a certain temperature, with a certain degree of light exposure, and sometimes varies based on the concentration. Compounded sterile products (CSPs) have variable storage requirements due to sterility concerns. See Sterile Products chapter.

As a drug remains in solution longer the likelihood of a chemical reaction occurring increases. Compatibility concerns due to longer infusion times have become an important issue in recent years with piperacillin/tazobactam (Zosyn) extended infusions. Zosyn is also commonly used with shorter, intermittent infusions (which cause fewer compatibility issues). The longer infusion period is used to obtain a higher time above the minimum inhibitory concentration (T > MIC) in order to counter drug resistance with some of the common nosocomial pathogens, including *Pseudomonas*, *Enterobacter* and *Acinetobacter*. The higher T > MIC is beneficial, but the longer infusion times result in more significant compatibility issues with some of the other drugs that the hospitalized patient receives. Interactions with piperacillin/tazobactam, azithromycin, ciprofloxacin, tobramycin, vancomycin, other antibiotics, insulin and some vasopressors occur more commonly when given as a longer infusion.

Higher temperatures promote chemical reactions, which is why the majority of compounded IV drugs are kept cold (refrigerated) in order to extend the time that the drug is stable. There are exceptions; for example, furosemide crystallizes if kept cold and is stored at room temperature. See the table of IV drugs that do not require refrigeration.

Light exposure causes photo-degradation that can destroy the drug and in some cases will increase the toxicity. Many medications should be protected from light during storage to avoid degradation. Some medications are supplied in amber vials, while others should be kept in their original packaging (foil overwrap or box) until administration. A small number of drugs are so light-sensitive that they require protection from light during administration. Pharmacy staff dispense these medications in a light-protective cover. Additionally, in some cases, light-protective tubing (generally amber colored) is required. See the table for a list of "photosensitive" drugs that require light-protection during administration.

Agitation destroys some drugs, particularly hormones and other proteins. Drugs that are easily destroyed include alteplase, immune globulins, insulins, rasburicase and some vaccines, including zoster. Quinupristin/dalfopristin *(Synercid)*, etanercept *(Enbrel)* are some of the drugs that form a foam and should only be swirled when reconstituting. Do not shake; wait for the foam to dissolve.

IV Drug Discoloration. What Does it Mean?

In some cases discoloration can be of little or no consequence. However, in <u>most</u> cases, discoloration indicates <u>oxidation</u> or another type of <u>decomposition</u>. Some examples include:

- Nitroprusside – Light causes decomposition, which is visible as an orange, dark brown or blue liquid. A blue color indicates nearly complete decomposition. If discolored, do not use.

- Chlorpromazine – A slightly yellowed color is acceptable. Do not use if <u>darker</u> than light yellow.

- Dacarbazine – Turns pink if drug has decomposed; do not use.

- Dobutamine – <u>Oxidation</u> turns the liquid slightly pink, but <u>potency is not lost</u>.

- Dopamine – A slightly yellowed color is acceptable. Do not use if <u>darker</u> than light yellow.

- Norepinephrine – <u>Oxidation</u> turns the liquid <u>brown</u>. If discolored, do not use.

- Epinephrine – <u>Oxidation</u> turns the liquid pink, then <u>brown</u>. If discolored, do not use.

- Isoproterenol – Exposure to air, light or ↑ temperature turns the liquid pink or darker. If discolored, do not use.

- Morphine – If the solution is dark, do not use.

- Tigecycline – Reconstituted solution is yellow/orange, do not use if green/black.

<u>And the opposite</u>: Do not use the antidote *Cyanokit* if the solution is not dark red.

What About "Particulate" Matter in the Solution?

Drugs in solution decompose faster than other formulations. The clinician (or the patient if using a self-injectable) should be instructed to check for particulate matter. If <u>particulates</u> are present, the product <u>should not be used</u>.

PROTECT FROM LIGHT DURING ADMINISTRATION
Anthracyclines
Dacarbazine (if extravasates, protect exposed tissues from light)
<u>Doxycycline</u>
<u>Epoprostenol *(Flolan)*</u>
<u>Micafungin *(Mycamine)*</u>
<u>Nitroprusside *(Nitropress)*</u>
Pentamidine
Phytonadione

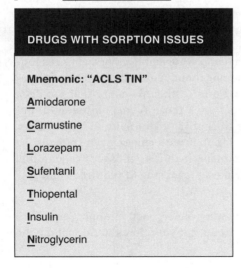

DRUGS WITH SORPTION ISSUES
Mnemonic: "ACLS TIN"
Amiodarone
Carmustine
Lorazepam
Sufentanil
Thiopental
Insulin
Nitroglycerin

EMERGENCY PREPAREDNESS, TOXICOLOGY & ANTIDOTES

KEEP CALM AND ASK A PHARMACIST AT THE POISON CONTROL CENTER

GUIDELINES/REFERENCES

National Library of Medicine TOXNET. http://toxnet.nlm.nih.gov/(accessed 2015 Oct 4).

Lexi-Comp Toxicology Online. http://online.lexi.com/lco/action/home/tox (accessed 2015 Oct 4).

CDC, Emergency Preparedness, at http://emergency.cdc.gov/ (accessed 2015 Oct 12).

ASHP Best Practices, ASHP Statement on the Role of Health-System Pharmacists in Emergency Preparedness. 2015-2016 Ed., Bethesda, MD: ASHP; 2015.

We gratefully acknowledge the assistance of Susan E. Gorman, PharmD, MS, DABAT, FAACT, Past-President, American Board of Applied Toxicology, and Cynthia L. Morris-Kukoski, PharmD, DABAT, FAACT, Former Past-President, American Board of Applied Toxicology, in preparing this chapter.

EMERGENCY PREPAREDNESS

This section reviews the involvement that could be expected of the pharmacy staff in response to a disaster, which can include natural disasters (e.g., floods), industrial accidents, terrorist attacks that involve the release of biological and chemical agents, and disasters from radioactive, nuclear, or explosive devices.

Pharmacists should be primarily involved in the areas in which they have expertise: drug management required for the specific disaster (e.g., antidotes) and in the usual drug management of patients during and after a disaster. Legal issues regarding dispensing a drug during an emergency (such as with the Emergency Prescription Assistance Program), are discussed under the legal requirements in RxPrep's MPJE course.

It is most important for the pharmacy staff involved in preparing for an emergency to be well informed about likely threats in their locality and to coordinate the drug components that will be included in the emergency response plans with the federal, regional and state and local agencies responsible for the plan development and maintenance. The pharmacists involved with these efforts should ensure that the drug stockpile is in agreement with these plans, and should discourage inappropriate stockpiling by individual institutions. Pharmacists should be familiar with emergency protocols for their institution or workplace, including those for evacuation, disaster preparedness, mass dispensing (if required), and poisoning emergencies.

Communications concerning emergency planning and response requires an electronic network that should include the hospital pharmacy department directors and local pharmacies that can serve the needs of the community. The network should be used to transmit urgent information related to emergency preparedness and counterterrorism, and to circulate important new information related to the pharmacist involvement on disaster response teams, such as a new biological threat, or a heightened state of emergency. Pharmacists involved from a hospital setting should be familiar with the recommendations of the American Society of Health System Pharmacists (ASHP), which is referenced on the first page of this chapter. The CDC pages on Emergency Preparedness (also referenced) include recommendations for the treatment of likely toxins, and includes sections on current disease outbreaks, and treatment for chemical and radiation exposure. One of the antidotes for exposure to radioactive iodine (KI, potassium iodide) is discussed in the thyroid chapter.

TOXICOLOGY AND ANTIDOTES

Toxic means poisonous, and toxicology is the study of poisonous chemicals, which includes drugs at unsafe doses. Antidotes are substances that stop the harmful effects of the poison (or overdosed drug).

Children are the most common victims of accidental poisoning in the United States. The top categories of substances in accidental pediatric exposures are cosmetics/personal care products, analgesics and cleaning substances. Accidental poisoning is common among the elderly and is primarily due to mental or physical impairment, the use of multiple drugs, and reduced elimination. Poisoning can be intentional, such as with attempted suicide or as an act of revenge, or in situations such as rape (drug-facilitated sexual assault).

Prevention of Accidental Poisoning

To reduce accidental poisoning in children, child-resistant (C-R) containers are helpful, but are not foolproof. These are required for prescription drugs unless waived by the patient or with specific substances that are excluded from this requirement, such as nitroglycerin sublingual tablets. Non-prescription drugs that require C-R containers include anything containing iron, diphenhydramine, acetaminophen, salicylates, NSAIDs, "imidazoline" vasoconstrictors such as naphazoline and oxymetazoline and drugs that have been switched from Rx to OTC. Non-drug compounds that are dangerous if swallowed require C-R packaging, such as turpentine. A complete list of drugs that must have C-R packaging (and those that do not need to have this type of packaging) is provided in the RxPrep MPJE course, since this is a federal legal requirement. Common C-R packaging includes screw caps that require more than a simple turn to open (such as having the user press down with the palm when turning to open), unit-

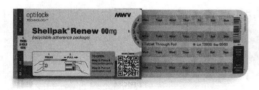

dose packaging and the card adherence and safety packaging that require the user to press on one side while pulling the medication card out of the other side. The picture demonstrates the *Optilock* packaging, which, additionally, can help with adherence when the day of the week that the dose should be taken is specified next to the dose.

Early Suspicion, Actions and Decontamination

For any questionable exposure the national poison control line (phone # 800-222-1222) can be contacted. With topical exposure, remove any contaminated clothing and run water over the skin for 10 minutes, then soap and rinse. For ocular exposure, remove contact lenses and rinse eye (or eyes) with water from a tap or hose with a gentle stream for at least 15 minutes. With oral ingestion, remove anything in the mouth and collect any suspect containers to bring to the emergency department. If unconscious, place the patient on the left side to more easily clear vomit if emesis (vomiting) occurs. Ipecac syrup was used previously to induce emesis for certain exposures, but is no longer commercially available, and is no longer recommended. Instruct others not to give ipecac syrup (it remains in many home medicine cabinets) or use any other mechanism to induce vomiting.

If the patient is unconscious, having difficulty breathing, appears agitated or is having a seizure, emergency help should be contacted (call 911). If the patient is not breathing and/or has no pulse CPR should be initiated. Upon arrival to the acute care facility, cardiovascular support and breathing support, including assisted ventilation, may be required. Cardiac monitoring with an ECG will be needed with drugs that affect heart rate or rhythm or with any cardiac abnormality present. With some substances, specific antidotes or dialysis may be used.

Decontamination with Activated Charcoal

For some orally ingested compounds taken in potentially toxic amounts, activated charcoal can be administered and is most effective within one hour of the ingestion. Activated charcoal can be aqueous, or combined with sorbitol as a cathartic and sweetener. Sorbitol should be avoided because it can induce vomiting and cause electrolyte disturbances. Prior to the use of activated charcoal, it may be necessary to protect the airway in patients who are unconscious or likely to become unconscious with intubation. This will prevent vomiting and aspiration. Activated charcoal is contraindicated when the airway is unprotected, or if the ingested compound may increase the risk of aspiration (such as with hydrocarbons). Drugs will bind to the activated charcoal and should be separated by at least two hours. Alcohols, heavy metals (iron, lead, lithium, mercury) and corrosives (alkalis, acids) do not bind to charcoal. The dose of activated charcoal is 1 g/kg.

Caution: Symptoms of Overdose May Not Be Present

Several of the most dangerous compounds do not cause immediate symptoms when toxic. To identify whether a patient is at risk, the clinician should determine the time(s) of ingestion, the quantity, and the formulation ingested. For example, in an acetaminophen overdose the patient can remain asymptomatic for up to two days – until end organ toxicity (liver failure) is apparent. When the serum acetaminophen level is available, and the exposure has occurred within the past 24 hours, the level is used as the basis for treatment. In some instances, the antidote may be given immediately. In certain overdoses, drug levels can be useful to guide treatment and monitoring of the patient; however, in most drug overdose situations, clinical evaluation of the patient's signs and symptoms will guide treatment. In many cases of overdose, more than one drug is involved; for example, acetaminophen is often combined with an opioid and treatment for both may be required (i.e., naloxone and n-acetylcysteine).

Antidotes for Common Drug and Non-Drug Poisonings

DRUG/TOXIN	ANTIDOTE	COMMENTS
Acetaminophen	**N-acetylcysteine** (oral or *Acetadote*, IV)	N-acetylcysteine restores hepatic glutathione (acts as a glutathione substrate). It should be initiated immediately if overdose is suspected regardless of symptoms.
		Oral: 140 mg/kg x 1, followed by 70 mg/kg every 4 hours x 17 additional doses. Repeat the dose if emesis occurs within 1 hour of administration.
		Intravenous: 150 mg/kg IV over 60 minutes, followed by 50 mg/kg IV over 4 hours, followed by 100 mg/kg IV over 16 hours.
Animal bites	Rabies vaccine (*Imovax, Rabavert*) and human rabies immune globulin (*Imogam Rabies HT, HyperRAB S/D*)	High risk animal bites or exposures; vaccine given 1 mL IM deltoid (adults) or thigh (children, infants) on days 0, 3, 7, 14 and immune globulin is given 20 units/kg on day 0, infiltrated around wound site or separate site from vaccine. HRIG not useful after day 7 of vaccine or in previously immunized individuals. Clean wound with soap and water. Tetanus shot required if not within past 10 years.

Antidotes for Common Drug and Non-Drug Poisonings Continued

DRUG/TOXIN	ANTIDOTE	COMMENTS
Organophosphates (OPs), include industrial insecticides (malathion, others) and nerve (warfare) gases (sarin, others)	**Atropine** and **pralidoxime**, or in combination *(DuoDote)*	OPs block acetylcholinesterase, which increases acetylcholine (Ach) levels. Atropine is an anticholinergic and blocks the effects of Ach to reduce the cholinergic SLUDGE symptoms: salivation, lacrimation, urination, diarrhea, gastrointestinal distress and emesis. Pralidoxime treats the muscle weakness and relieves paralysis of respiratory muscles secondary to the toxicity.
Botulism	Botulism antitoxin (heptavalent), supportive care (ventilator for respiratory support)	Toxin causes neuroparalysis; respiratory support is central. Heptavalent botulism antitoxin is only available through the CDC. BabyBIG (botulism immune globulin) is used for infant botulism (different than foodborne botulism) and is available through the California Department of Public Health.
Black Widow spider bites	Antivenin *for Latrodectus mactans*, supportive care	Predominantly found in southern and western states. Children and frail elderly at highest risk for severe injury. The spiders are non-aggressive if left alone. Supportive care is the mainstay of therapy (opioids for pain management and benzodiazepines for muscle spasms).
Carbon monoxide (CO)	Oxygen, possibly hyperbaric	Accidental exposure from gas heaters, wood or charcoal stoves, CO-emitting kerosene heaters (colorless, odorless) or automobile exhaust.
Ethanol (alcoholic drinks)	Supportive care, correct hypoglycemia	If any question if chronic alcohol user, administer thiamine (vitamin B1) to prevent Wernicke syndrome (neurological damage).
Ethylene glycol, diethylene glycol, methanol	**Fomepizole *(Antizol)*,** preferred or Ethanol (2nd line)	Fomepizole and ethanol inhibit alcohol dehydrogenase (ADH). Caution: children are very prone to hypoglycemia. Methanol or ethylene glycol toxicity should be suspected with anion-gap metabolic acidosis along with an osmolar gap.
Anticholinergic overdose (atropine, diphenhydramine, dimenhydrinate, *Atropa belladonna* (deadly nightshade), jimson weed, scopolamine	Supportive care, rarely physostigmine	Physostigmine inhibits acetylcholinesterase, which increases the affects of acetylcholine, reducing the anticholinergic toxicity but is not routinely recommended. It may be used in severe cases of delirium if no contraindications are present (cardiac conduction defects, seizures). Benzodiazepines/anticonvulsants if seizures present. Anticholinergic overdose symptoms can be remembered with the mnemonic, "red as a beet, dry as a bone, blind as a bat, mad as a hatter, and hot as a hare" for the symptoms of flushing, dry skin and mucous membranes, mydriasis with double or blurry vision, altered mental status and fever. Severe symptoms include tachycardia, hypertension, psychosis, seizures, respiratory and cardiovascular collapse.
Benzodiazepines	**Flumazenil**	Flumazenil is used off-label for non-benzodiazepine hypnotic overdose (e.g., zolpidem) but is not routinely recommended. Flumazenil can precipitate seizures when used in benzodiazepine-dependent patients.

Antidotes for Common Drug and Non-Drug Poisonings Continued

DRUG/TOXIN	ANTIDOTE	COMMENTS
Beta blockers	Supportive care, possibly glucagon and/or high dose insulin with glucose	Treat bradycardia, hypotension and seizures. Glucagon may be used if unresponsive to standard supportive care. High dose insulin with glucose may be used in patients refractory to glucagon therapy.
Calcium channel blockers	Supportive care (see beta blockers above), Calcium (chloride or gluconate), possibly glucagon and/or high dose insulin with glucose	Administer calcium IV only, avoid fast infusion, monitor ECG, do not infuse calcium in same line as phosphate-containing solutions. Glucagon may be used if unresponsive to standard care. High dose insulin with glucose may be used in patients refractory to glucagon therapy.
Cyanide	2 IV antidotes Hydroxocobalamin *(Cyanokit)* Sodium thiosulfate + Sodium nitrite *(Nithiodote)*	Cyanide overdose is due to high dose, or long treatment duration or renal impairment treatment with nitroprusside, or from ingestion of amygdalin, a synthetic form of laetrile (used as a cancer remedy – is ineffective), or most commonly, due to smoke inhalation. Do not use *Cyanokit* if solution is not dark red.
Dabigatran	Idarucizumab *(Praxbind)*	Idarucizumab is a reversal agent for dabigatran *(Pradaxa)*. Use if urgent surgery is required or with life-threatening/uncontrolled bleeding. Dose is 5 mg IV (2.5 mg vial x 2).
Digoxin, oleander, foxglove	**Digoxin Immune Fab (DigiFab)**	*DigiFab* 40 mg vial binds ~0.5 mg digoxin. Interferes with digoxin levels drawn after its use. When neither amount ingested nor digoxin level is known, adult dose is 20 vials.
Heavy metals, including arsenic, copper, gold, lead, mercury	**Dimercaprol** or Penicillamine or Calcium disodium edetate (EDTA) **Succimer** (Dimercaptosuccinic acid, DMSA)	Succimer is a water-soluble, oral chelating agent that is used in asymptomatic children with serum lead levels > 45 mcg/dL. EDTA is a parenteral chelating agent. It does not cross the blood-brain barrier and can exacerbate encephalopathy; dimercaprol, which does cross the blood-brain barrier, is given first. Do not use disodium EDTA; use $CaNa_2$ EDTA. Lead poisoning is initially asymptomatic; toxicity results in cognitive deficits, highest risk in children with exposure to lead-containing paint chips.
Heparin, Low Molecular Weight Heparin (LMWH)	**Protamine**	1 mg will reverse ~100 units of heparin; is used as a reversal agent for LMWHs. See Anticoagulation chapter.
Insulin or other hypoglycemics, severe low blood glucose	**Dextrose** Glucagon if unconscious and outpatient	Dextrose injection or infusion (drip): do not exceed 12.5 or 25% peripherally due to risk of thrombosis, may require co-administration of potassium (IV dextrose will result in hypokalemia). Sulfonylureas: octreotide (*SandoSTATIN*) may be given with dextrose.
Isoniazid	**Pyridoxine (Vitamin B6)**	Oral pyridoxine 10 – 50 mg is used daily with isoniazid to prevent neuropathies, and in higher intravenous doses to treat toxicity.

Antidotes for Common Drug and Non-Drug Poisonings Continued

DRUG/TOXIN	ANTIDOTE	COMMENTS
<u>Iron</u> Aluminum (unlabeled)	**Deferoxamine *(Desferal)*** Deferiprone *(Ferriprox)* and Deferasirox *(Exjade)* – for iron overload from blood transfusions	Overdose can be due to accidental ingestion or secondary to multiple transfusions. Childhood iron overdose: iron tablets look like candy and toddlers put almost anything into their mouths; most lethal ingestion is due to exposure to prenatal multivitamins and OTC iron tablets. Deferoxamine is used for iron and aluminum toxicity (off label use).
Local anesthetics (bupivacaine, mepivacaine, ropivacaine) and other lipophilic drugs (buproprion, TCAs, CCBs, beta blockers)	Lipid emulsion 20%	Enhanced elimination of some lipophilic drugs using 20% lipid emulsion bolus, followed by continuous infusion (not FDA-approved).
Methotrexate	Leucovorin (Folinic acid), Levoleucovorin *(Fusilev)* Glucarpidase *(Voraxaze)*	Leucovorin/levoleucovorin: For rescue after high-dose methotrexate treatment (in cancer treatment) and to diminish the toxicity and counteract the effects of impaired methotrexate elimination or with a change to accidental overdose. Note: Glucarpidase availability may be limited.
Methemoglobinemia	Methylene blue	Drugs that cause methemoglobinemia (an altered form of hemoglobin) include anesthetics, dapsone, phenytoin, chloroquine and silver sulfadiazine; this condition is rare, and is more likely to occur if multiple drugs listed are used together or can be due to a congenital condition. Chemicals that can cause methemoglobinemia include amyl nitrite and other nitrites, including illicit "poppers". Antidote is contraindicated in patients with G6PD deficiency.
Amatoxin-containing mushrooms	Supportive care, Silibinin (*Legalon SIL*) ± Atropine	There are various types of mushrooms; some are poisonous, many are not. Treatment is guided by symptoms, such as hallucinations. Atropine if severe muscarinic symptoms (bradycardia). Silibinin is the flavonoid in milk thistle, sometimes used for hepato-protection.
Napthalene, from mothballs	Supportive care, Methylene blue	Methylene blue is indicated for drug-induced methemoglobinemia and as an indicator dye; this is off-label use.
Neostigmine, pyridostigmine	Pralidoxime	Pralidoxime counteracts the muscle weakness and/or respiratory depression secondary to overdose of anticholinesterase medications used to treat myasthenia gravis.
Nicotine, including e-cigarettes	<u>Supportive care</u>, **Atropine**	Atropine is a nicotinic receptor antagonist and should be given to treat symptomatic bradycardia. Benzodiazepines should be given to treat seizures.
<u>Opioids, legal and illicit</u> (e.g., heroin)	**Naloxone (*Narcan, Narcan NS, Evzio*)**	*Evzio* is an auto injector for emergency treatment outside of the hospital. See Pain chapter.
Petroleum distillates (gasoline, kerosene, mineral oil, paint thinners)	Oxygen, supportive care	Do <u>not</u> use gastric emptying. Keep patient NPO due to aspiration risk.

Antidotes for Common Drug and Non-Drug Poisonings Continued

DRUG/TOXIN	ANTIDOTE	COMMENTS
Plants: Castor beans, jequirity beans, oleander and foxglove, hemlock	Supportive care, *DigiFab* if oleander or foxglove	Castor beans contain ricin. Jequirity beans contain abrin; structurally has the same two-subunit configuration as ricin. Oleander and foxglove contain digitalis glycosides.
Salicylates	**Sodium bicarbonate**	Salicylates may cause metabolic acidosis; sodium bicarbonate is an alkalinizing agent and is given to alkalinize the urine. This will decrease the drug reabsorption and increase the excretion of the salicylates and other weak acids.
Scorpion stings	Antivenin immune FAB *Centruroides (Anascorp)*, supportive care.	Scorpions producing clinical symptoms are found mainly in the southwest.
Snake bites: Eastern coral snake, Texas coral snake, Copperhead snake, Rattlesnake	Antivenin *Micrurus fulvius* for coral snake bites; *CroFab* for Copperhead and Rattlesnake bites	Do not use ice; Do not cut/suck out venom; transport patient to healthcare facility.
Stimulant overdose from amphetamines, including ADHD and weight loss drugs, cocaine, ephedrine, caffeine, theophylline, MDMA (ecstasy), alcohol withdrawal	Supportive care, possibly Benzodiazepines	Symptoms of overdose include tachycardia, hypertension, mydriasis, agitation, possible seizures, hyperthermia and psychosis. Benzodiazepines (e.g., lorazepam) may be administered for agitation and/or seizures.
Tricyclic Antidepressants	Supportive care	Overdose can cause several conditions that must be managed, including arrhythmias, seizures and respiratory depression. IV hypertonic sodium bicarbonate can be administered to decrease a widened QRS complex. Benzodiazepines may be used for symptom relief, seizures. Vasopressors may be used for hypotension.
Valproate-induced hyperammonemia	L-Carnitine (Levocarnitine)	Treat if symptomatic (changes in mental status, elevated ammonia level).
Warfarin, rat poison (rodenticides)	**Phytonadione (vitamin K) (Mephyton)**	See Anticoagulation chapter (note this is given as vitamin K1, the precursor of other vitamin K forms).

CRITICAL CARE & FLUIDS/ ELECTROLYTES

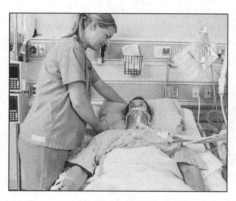

We gratefully acknowledge the assistance of Darrel W. Hughes, PharmD, BCPS, Clinical Specialist, Emergency Medicine at University Health System and University of Texas Health Science Center San Antonio, in preparing this chapter.

BACKGROUND

Patients with life-threatening injuries or illnesses require specialized care that is often initiated pre-hospital or in an emergency department and continued in the intensive care unit (ICU). Large hospitals have specialized ICUs for different types of patients: medical, surgical, cardiovascular, trauma, pediatric, neonatal, etc. Patients in the ICU receive most of their medications by the intravenous (IV) route. This route provides rapid onset of effect and easy titration, avoids gut/absorption issues, and permits administration when the patient is sedated. Although patients in the ICU are very sick, many recover and eventually go home. The ICU mortality rate in the U.S. is ~15%. Conditions that are common in the ICU are addressed in this chapter.

SHOCK

Shock is a medical emergency characterized by <u>hypoperfusion</u> usually in the setting of <u>hypotension</u>, defined as systolic blood pressure (SBP) < 90 mmHg or mean arterial pressure (MAP) < 70 mmHg. There are four main types of shock: (1) hypovolemic (e.g., hemorrhagic), (2) distributive (e.g., septic), (3) cardiogenic (e.g., post-myocardial infarction), and (4) obstructive (e.g., massive pulmonary embolism). Diagnosis of shock is based on hemodynamic parameters. Patients may experience more than one type of shock at a time. Drugs used for shock may also be used for advanced cardiac life support (ACLS)/cardiac arrest, hypotension during surgery/anesthesia, acute decompensated heart failure (ADHF), and other critical conditions. Most of the medications discussed must be administered by an infusion pump, ideally through a central line.

GENERAL PRINCIPLES FOR TREATING SHOCK

1. Fill the Tank - optimize preload with 30 mL/kg of crystalloid bolus or central venous pressure (CVP) > 8 mmHg
2. Squeeze the Pipes - peripheral vasoconstrictor to ↑ systemic vascular resistance (SVR)
3. Kick the Pump - beta-1 agonist to ↑ myocardial contractility and cardiac output (CO)

Hypovolemic Shock

Treatment of hypovolemic shock requires restoring intravascular volume (with crystalloids) and improving oxygen-carrying capacity with blood transfusion when indicated. Fluid resuscitation with crystalloids is generally recommended as first-line therapy in patients with hypovolemic shock that is not caused by hemorrhage. Blood products (packed red blood cells and fresh frozen plasma) should be administered in hypovolemic shock for patients with hemoglobin < 7 g/dL (< 10 g/dL in patients with cardiovascular disease) or patients who have a significant active bleed. If the patient does not respond to the initial crystalloid therapy ("fluid challenge"), then vasopressors may be indicated. Vasopressors will not be effective unless intravascular volume is adequate (at least 30 mL/kg of crystalloid or CVP > 8 mmHg).

Crystalloids vs Colloids

Hospitalized patients frequently receive IV fluids to replace patient losses and treat various conditions. IV fluids are categorized as crystalloids or colloids. Crystalloids contain various concentrations of sodium and/or dextrose that pass freely between semipermeable membranes. Most of the administered volume does not remain in the intravascular space (inside the blood vessels). It goes into the extravascular space or interstitial space. Crystalloids are less costly and generally have fewer adverse reactions than colloids. Some data suggest that balanced solutions (chloride-restrictive) may be preferred in certain disease states like sepsis. The chloride load provided to ICU patients can be high enough to contribute to cell injury, including renal damage. Colloids are large molecules (typically protein or starch) dispersed in solutions that primarily remain in the intravascular space and ↑ oncotic pressure. Colloids provide greater intravascular volume expansion than equal volumes of crystalloids, but are more expensive and provide questionable clinical benefit over crystalloids.

FLUID	COMMENTS

Crystalloids

FLUID	COMMENTS
Dextrose 5% (D5W)*	Slightly hypotonic, equivalent to "free water" (crosses membranes easily), useful in dehydration, avoid in head injury (can ↑ intracranial pressure)
NaCl 0.9% (normal saline, NS)*	Isotonic, useful for fluid resuscitation, risk of hypernatremia and hyperchloremic metabolic acidosis
Lactated Ringer's (LR) Chloride-restrictive	Isotonic, contains NaCl, KCl, CaCl, Na-lactate (lactate is converted to bicarbonate to help correct acidosis), risk for hyperkalemia, equally effective to NS
Multiple electrolyte injection (*Plasma-Lyte A*, others) Chloride-restrictive	Isotonic, *Plasma-Lyte A* contains electrolytes and acetate (acetate is converted to bicarbonate to help correct acidosis), risk for hyperkalemia

Colloids

FLUID	COMMENTS
Albumin 5%, 25% (Albuked, Albuminar, Albutein, AlbuRx, Flexbumin, others)	Natural colloid, more expensive than crystalloids with no evidence of superiority
	Remains in the intravascular space; useful with significant edema (cirrhosis). Albumin 5% and 25% are isotonic; 25% albumin pulls water into the intravascular space; not effective for nutritional supplementation
	Prepare 5% albumin by diluting 25% albumin with normal saline, not sterile water (sterile water may cause hemolysis/renal damage due to hypotonicity), do not use if sediment present, do not begin administration > 4 hours after puncturing the container
Dextran (*Dextran 40, Dextran 70*)	Used infrequently. High risk for ADRs (urticaria, acute renal failure, increased bleeding time), can cause anaphylaxis, impairs hemostasis (sometimes used as an anticoagulant)
Hydroxyethyl starch (*Hespan, Hextend*)	Used infrequently. Semi-synthetic colloid, can cause anaphylaxis, impairs hemostasis. Boxed Warning: avoid use in critically ill patients (including sepsis) due to mortality and renal injury

*   There are various crystalloid concentrations and combinations including: D50, D5NS, D5½NS, ½NS

Distributive Shock

Distributive shock is characterized by low SVR, and initially high CO followed by low or normal CO. Septic, anaphylactic, and neurogenic shock are examples of distributive shock.

Sepsis and Septic Shock

Sepsis is the presence of or suspected infection in the setting of systemic manifestations of infection which include temperature > 38.3°C or < 36°C, heart rate > 90 BPM, WBC > 12,000 cells/mm³ or < 4,000 cells/mm³, altered mental status, hyperglycemia (blood glucose > 140 mg/dL without diabetes), significant edema/positive fluid balance and others. Severe sepsis is the presence of sepsis-induced tissue hypoperfusion or organ dysfunction and septic shock is IV fluid-resistant hypotension which requires vasopressor treatment to maintain blood pressure. The Surviving Sepsis Campaign is an initiative that prompts the use of selected evidence-based interventions (called "bundles") to reduce mortality from sepsis and septic shock. The use of early goal-directed therapy, administration of broad-spectrum antibiotics, 30 mL/kg of crystalloid, CVP > 8 mmHg and MAP > 65 mmHg were associated with lower overall mortality than standard of care.

Vasopressors work by vasoconstriction (think "pressing down on the vasculature") and therefore they ↑ systemic vascular resistance (SVR), which ↑ blood pressure. Phenylephrine is a pure alpha agonist that ↑ SVR without increasing heart rate. Epinephrine and norepinephrine are mixed alpha and beta agonists. Norepinephrine is considered the vasopressor of choice in septic shock, while epinephrine is a mainstay in advanced cardiac life support and anaphylactic shock states. Dopamine is a natural precursor of norepinephrine that stimulates different receptors depending on the dose (see table on next page). High doses of dopamine are required to stimulate alpha receptors and exert vasopressor effects. At medium doses, dopamine stimulates beta-1 receptors and acts as a positive inotrope along with other actions. At low doses, dopamine stimulates dopaminergic (D-1) receptors in the kidney causing vasodilation.

GUIDELINES/REFERENCES

Dellinger RP, Levy MM, Rhodes A, et al. Surviving Sepsis Campaign: International Guidelines for Management of Severe Sepsis and Septic Shock: 2012. *Crit Care Med.* 2013; 41(2):580-637.

Vasopressors

DRUG	DOSING/MOA	SAFETY/SIDE EFFECTS/MONITORING
DOPamine	**Low dose: D-1 agonist** 1-4 mcg/kg/min **Med dose: Beta-1 agonist** 5-10 mcg/kg/min **High dose: Alpha-1 agonist** 10-20 mcg/kg/min	**BOXED WARNING** Dopamine and norepinephrine have a boxed warning regarding extravasation; all vasopressors are <u>vesicants</u> when administered IV, treat extravasation with phentolamine **WARNINGS** Use extreme caution in patients taking an MAO inhibitor; prolonged hypertension may result (dopamine, epinephrine and norepinephrine)
EPINEPHrine (*Adrenalin*) *Auvi-Q, EpiPen, Adrenaclick* for anaphylaxis	**Alpha-1, beta-1, beta-2 agonist** 0.1-2 mcg/kg/min IV **ACLS: 1 mg IV Q3-5 min**	**SIDE EFFECTS** <u>Arrhythmias, tachycardia</u> (especially with dopamine, epinephrine, vasopressin), <u>bradycardia</u> (with phenylephrine), tachyphylaxis, <u>peripheral/gut ischemia, necrosis (gangrene), hyperglycemia (with epinephrine)</u>, hyponatremia (with vasopressin)
Norepinephrine (*Levophed*)	**Alpha-1 agonist > beta-1 agonist** 0.1-3 mcg/kg/min	**MONITORING** <u>Continuous BP</u> monitoring (with continuous infusions), HR, MAP, ECG, urine output, infusion site for extravasation, serum and urine sodium (vasopressin)
Phenylephrine (*Vazculep* for hypotension during anesthesia)	**Alpha-1 agonist** 0.5-9 mcg/kg/min	**NOTES** No clear evidence that low dose dopamine (renal dosing) provides benefit. Epinephrine used for <u>IV route is 1:10,000</u> ratio strength or <u>0.1 mg/mL</u>. Epinephrine used for <u>IM route is 1:1,000</u> ratio strength or <u>1 mg/mL</u>. Lidocaine with epinephrine is discussed with Anesthetics in this chapter.
Vasopressin (*Vasostrict*)	**Vasoconstrictor, no inotropic or chronotropic effects** Shock: 0.01-0.03 units/min ACLS: 40 units IV x 1	Norepinephrine: <u>Protect from light</u> to improve stability. Vasopressin: known as <u>arginine vasopressin</u> (AVP) and <u>antidiuretic hormone</u> (ADH). Taper dose to avoid rebound hypotension/maintain target blood pressure. Solutions should not be used if they are discolored or contain precipitate(s).

Treatment of Extravasation

Vasopressors are <u>vesicants</u> that cause severe tissue damage/necrosis with extravasation. This is a <u>medical emergency</u>. To reduce the risk, every attempt should be made to infuse vasopressors through a central line. Treat vasopressor extravasations with <u>phentolamine</u>, an <u>alpha-adrenergic blocker</u> that antagonizes the effects of the vasopressor. If extravasation occurs with norepinephrine, epinephrine or phenylephrine, stop the infusion but do not disconnect the needle/canula and do not flush the line. Gently aspirate out the drug. Nitroglycerin ointment is sometimes used topically (off-label) as an alternative if phentolamine is unavailable.

Acute Decompensated Heart Failure and Cardiogenic Shock

Heart failure patients may experience episodes of worsening symptoms such as sudden weight gain, inability to lie flat without becoming short of breath, decreasing functionality (unable to perform their daily routine), increasing shortness of breath and fatigue. This is called ADHF, and when hypotension and hypoperfusion are also present, it is called cardiogenic shock.

Clinical Presentation and Assessment

ADHF is caused by worsening HF, a cardiac event (MI, arrhythmia, valvular disease, uncontrolled hypertension) or a non-cardiac cause (e.g., non-adherence with medications or dietary restrictions, worsening renal function, infection, illicit drug use). Use of drugs that can worsen cardiac function can also cause/exacerbate ADHF. Examples include negative inotropes, NSAIDs/COX-2 inhibitors, drugs which cause fluid retention and direct cardiotoxic drugs.

Patients with ADHF present with worsening congestion, hypoperfusion, or both. Evidence of congestion includes elevated jugular venous distention, lower extremity or pulmonary edema, rales and ascites. Evidence of hypoperfusion includes cool extremities, hypotension, decreased renal function and impaired mental function. Some patients with ADHF require invasive monitoring with a catheter that is guided through the right side of the heart into the pulmonary artery, called a Swan-Ganz or pulmonary artery (PA) catheter. The catheter provides hemodynamic measurements of congestion (pulmonary capillary wedge pressure or PCWP), hypoperfuson (cardiac output) and other measurements (SVR, CVP) useful for guiding treatment. Treatment of ADHF generally consists of diuretics, inotropes and vasodilators in various combinations depending on the patient's signs/symptoms.

In ADHF, counsel on the importance of medication adherence and optimize drug therapy/doses (see Chronic Heart Failure chapter). Beta blockers should only be stopped in an ADHF episode if hypotension or hypoperfusion is present.

Treating Congestion

The majority of patients with ADHF present with congestion. Congestion is treated with diuretics and possibly IV vasodilators. Loop diuretics are initially given IV since congestion can decrease their absorption. If diuretic resistance develops, the dose can be increased or a thiazide-type diuretic (e.g., metolazone, chlorothiazide) can be added to the loop.

IV vasodilators include nitroglycerin, nitroprusside and nesiritide. Frequent or continuous blood pressure monitoring is required when using vasodilators and dose must be decreased if hypotension or worsening of renal function is noted. Nitroglycerin (NTG) is a venous vasodilator (at low doses), but an effective arterial vasodilator at high doses. NTG is often used when there is active myocardial ischemia or uncontrolled hypertension, but effectiveness may be limited after 24 – 48 hours due to tachyphylaxis.

Nitroprusside is a mixed (equal) arterial and venous vasodilator at all doses. It has greater effect on BP than NTG, but it should not be used in active myocardial ischemia because it can cause blood to be diverted away from the diseased coronary arteries ("coronary steal"). Metabolism of nitroprusside results in formation of thiocyanate and cyanide, both of which can cause toxicity (especially in renal and hepatic insufficiency, respectively). Renal and hepatic function must be monitored during treatment. Though tachyphylaxis does not occur with nitroprusside, prolonged administration and use of high doses are discouraged due to increased risk of toxicity. Hydroxocobalamin can be administered to reduce risk of thiocyanate toxicity and sodium thiosulfate is used for cyanide toxicity (see Toxicology, Antidotes & Emergency Preparedness chapter).

Nesiritide (*Natrecor*) is a recombinant B-type natriuretic peptide that binds to vascular smooth muscle, increases cGMP resulting in smooth muscle relaxation which causes vasodilation. Nesiritide produces both arterial and venous vasodilation. It has not been found to reduce mortality or hospitalizations compared to other treatments and is not commonly used.

Vasodilators

DRUG	DOSING	SAFETY/SIDE EFFECTS/MONITORING
Nitroglycerin (*Nitronal*) See Chronic Stable Angina chapter for other formulations	Initial: 5 mcg/min Max: 400 mcg/min Continuous IV infusion due to short t½ Titrate to effect	**CONTRAINDICATIONS** SBP < 90 mmHg, concurrent use with PDE-5 inhibitors or riociguat **WARNINGS** Severe hypotension and ↑ intracranial pressure **SIDE EFFECTS** Hypotension, headache, lightheadedness, tachycardia, tachyphylaxis (within 24-48 hours of continuous administration) **MONITORING** BP, HR **NOTES** Prepare in glass bottles, PAB™, EXCEL™ (polyolefin) containers. PVC can cause adsorption of drug. Use administration sets (tubing) intended for NTG.
Nitroprusside (*Nitropress, Nipride*)	Initial dose varies by indication ADHF: 5-10 mcg/min Titrate to effect Requires light protection during administration. A blue-color indicates degradation to cyanide – do not use	**BOXED WARNINGS** Metabolism produces cyanide (use the lowest dose for the shortest duration necessary), excessive hypotension (continuous BP monitoring required), not for direct injection (must be further diluted; D5W preferred). **WARNINGS** ↑ intracranial pressure **SIDE EFFECTS** Hypotension, headache, tachycardia, thiocyanate/cyanide toxicity (especially in renal and hepatic impairment) **MONITORING** BP (continuous), HR, renal function, urine output, thiocyanate/cyanide toxicity, acid-base status, venous oxygen concentration
Nesiritide (*Natrecor*)	Bolus: 2 mcg/kg; draw bolus only from prepared (reconstituted) IV bag Infusion: 0.01 mcg/kg/min; max 0.03 mcg/kg/min	**CONTRAINDICATIONS** Persistent SBP < 100 mmHg prior to treatment, cardiogenic shock (if used as the primary treatment) **SIDE EFFECTS** Hypotension, ↑ SCr **MONITORING** BP, renal function, urine output **NOTES** Limited experience with infusions lasting longer than 96 hours

Treating Hypoperfusion

The most common cause of cardiogenic shock (or ADHF with hypoperfusion) is myocardial infarction (MI) with resulting failure of the left ventricle. Cardiogenic shock requires treatment with vasopressors and/or inotropes. The IV vasodilators previously discussed are generally contraindicated (since low blood pressure has already compromised perfusion). Dopamine (discussed previously) in medium doses is the inotrope of choice in heart failure when SBP < 90 mmHg.

Inotropes work by increasing contractility of the heart. Dobutamine is a beta-1 agonist and ↑ heart rate and force of contraction, which ↑ cardiac output. It has weak beta-2 (vasodilation) and alpha-1 agonist activity. Milrinone is a selective phosphodiesterase-3 inhibitor in cardiac and vascular tissue. It produces inotropic effects with significant vasodilation and less chronotropic effect (less of an effect on heart rate) compared to dobutamine. Because both dobutamine and milrinone produce vasodilation, they should only be used when BP is adequate. Milrinone requires dose adjustment in renal insufficiency. The vasodilatory + inotropic properties of dobutamine and milrinone make them uniquely suited to treat ADHF in patients with both congestion and hypoperfusion. Inotropes are associated with worse outcomes in heart failure and should be stopped as soon as the patient is stabilized.

Inotropes with Vasodilatory Effects

DRUG	DOSING	SAFETY/SIDE EFFECTS/MONITORING
DOBUTamine	**Beta-1 agonist with some beta-2 and alpha-1 agonism (both weak)** Initial: 0.5-1 mcg/kg/min Maintenance: 2-20 mcg/kg/min	**SIDE EFFECTS** Dobutamine: hyper and hypotension, ventricular arrhythmias, tachycardia, angina Milrinone: ventricular arrhythmias, hypotension **MONITORING** Continuous BP and ECG monitoring, HR, CVP, MAP, urine output, LFTs and renal function (with milrinone)
Milrinone	**Phosphodiesterase-3 (PDE-3) inhibitor** Maintenance: 0.125-0.75 mcg/kg/min; may consider a 50 mcg/kg loading dose (often omitted due to propensity to cause hypotension)	**NOTES** Milrinone: dose must be reduced for renal impairment. Dobutamine may turn slightly pink due to oxidation, but potency is not lost. Dobutamine and milrinone often referred to as "inodilators". Because of risk of hypotension, dobutamine may be used for inotropic effect only after adequate perfusion is achieved.

Pain, Agitation and Delirium

Pain

Opioids given IV (such as morphine and fentanyl) are first-line for analgesia (to reduce pain) in the ICU, but the principles of pain management are the same for all patients (see Pain chapter for a full discussion of the opioids). The pharmacokinetic properties of the drug and the renal/hepatic function of the patient will dictate the choice of agent, because all IV opioids exhibit similar analgesic efficacy when used correctly. Adjuvants (acetaminophen, NSAIDs, others) may be appropriate depending on the type of pain. Assessment of pain (with a validated pain scale) should be performed as frequently as every 2 - 4 hours in the ICU, and

GUIDELINES/REFERENCES

Barr J, Fraser GL, Puntillo K, et al. Clinical Practice Guidelines for the Management of Pain, Agitation, and Delirium in Adult Patients in the Intensive Care Unit. *Crit Care Med.* 2013; 41(1):263-306.

all ICU patients should be evaluated for pain at rest. Analgesia-based sedation or "analgosedation" is a sedation strategy that uses analgesia first to relieve pain and discomfort, which are primary causes of agitation. Analgosedation is associated with less time on the ventilator and shorter ICU length of stay.

Agitation

Sedation (to reduce distress, fear and anxiety) is necessary in most ICU patients to maintain synchronized breathing if on a ventilator (prevent "bucking" the ventilator), and to limit suffering in the harsh ICU environment. Agitation is managed with benzodiazepines (lorazepam, midazolam) and/or hypnotics (propofol, dexmedetomidine). Nonbenzodiazepines (propofol and dexmedetomidine) are associated with improved ICU outcomes, shorter duration of mechanical ventilation, and ↓ length of stay (LOS), though they are more expensive than benzodiazepines. Dexmedetomidine *(Precedex)* is the only sedative approved for use in non-intubated patients. Benzodiazepines will always have an important role in sedation of the ICU patient with seizures or alcohol/benzodiazepine withdrawal. Benzodiazepines are discussed in the Anxiety chapter.

Sedatives are used with validated sedation scales that allow for titration to light or deep sedation. Light sedation (unless contraindicated) is associated with improved outcomes. Some commonly used sedation

RICHMOND AGITATION AND SEDATION SCALE (RASS)		
Score	**Term**	**Description**
+4	Combative	Overtly combative, violent, immediate danger to staff
+3	Very agitated	Pulls or removes tube(s) or catheter(s); aggressive
+2	Agitated	Frequent non-purposeful movement, fights ventilator
+1	Restless	Anxious but movements not aggressive, vigorous
0	Alert and calm	
-1	Drowsy	Not fully alert, but has sustained awakening (eye opening/eye contact) to voice (≥ 10 seconds)
-2	Light sedation	Briefly awakens with eye contact to voice (< 10 seconds)
-3	Moderate sedation	Movement or eye opening to voice (but no eye contact)
-4	Deep sedation	No response to voice, but movement or eye opening to physical stimulation
-5	Unarousable	No response to voice or physical stimulation

scales include the Richmond Agitation Sedation Scale (RASS – see table), the Ramsay Agitation Scale (RAS), and the Riker Sedation-Agitation Scale (SAS). Patients should be monitored every 2 – 3 hours while receiving a sedation protocol to make sure they are receiving the minimal amount of drug(s) to keep them calm and pain-free. Daily interruptions of continuous infusions of sedative drugs ("sedation vacations") are used to assess the readiness to wean off/stop the sedative as soon as medically feasible.

Delirium

Delirium affects up to 80% of ventilated ICU patients and is associated with ↑ mortality and ↑ LOS. Delirium assessment is required. Early mobilization and control of the patient's environment (light, noise, stimuli) is recommended to ↓ incidence of delirium, but no medications are recommended for prevention. There is little evidence to support the use of haloperidol for treatment of ICU delirium, although this practice is commonplace. Atypical antipsychotics (primarily quetiapine, which is mildly sedating and has little risk for movement disorders) can be useful. Providing sedation with non-benzodiazepines may ↓ the incidence of delirium and/or shorten the duration in patients who already have it. Antipsychotics are discussed in the Schizophrenia/Psychosis chapter.

Agents for Pain, Agitation, and Delirium in the ICU

DRUG	DOSING	SAFETY/SIDE EFFECTS/MONITORING

Sedation/Agitation

DRUG	DOSING	SAFETY/SIDE EFFECTS/MONITORING
LORazepam (***Ativan***, *LORazepam Intensol*) Benzodiazepine	LD: 0.02-0.04 mg/kg IV push (max 2 mg) MD: 0.02-0.06 mg/kg IV Q2-6H PRN or an infusion 0.01-0.1 mg/kg/hr (max 10 mg/hr) Dose varies by indication; often used off-label	Total daily dose as low as 1 mg/kg/day can cause propylene glycol toxicity (acute renal failure and metabolic acidosis). In critical care patients monitor BP, HR, RR, sedation scale, s/sx of propylene glycol toxicity if receiving continuous infusion (BUN, SCr, lactate, anion gap). Limit use for delirium. See Anxiety chapter for additional information.
Midazolam (*Versed*) Benzodiazepine used specifically in acute care settings; injection only	LD: 0.01-0.05 mg/kg IV push MD: 0.02-0.1 mg/kg/hr IV Dose varies per indication Shorter acting than lorazepam if patient has normal organ function (no hepatic or renal impairment or HF) Highly lipophilic, can accumulate in obese patients Active metabolite that accumulates in renal impairment (caution with continuous infusion) Major 3A4 substrate; caution/use lower dose if used with 3A4 inhibitors	**BOXED WARNINGS** Respiratory depression, respiratory arrest, or apnea; start at lower end of dosing range in debilitated patients and geriatric population, do not administer by rapid IV injection in neonates **CONTRAINDICATIONS** Intrathecal or epidural administration due to benzoyl alcohol in the formulation, acute narrow angle glaucoma, use of potent CYP 3A4 inhibitors **SIDE EFFECTS** Respiratory depression, apnea, oversedation, hypotension **MONITORING** BP, HR, RR, sedation scale
Propofol (*Diprivan*) Short-acting general anesthetic FDA permits importation of *Fresenius Propoven* (propofol formulation) due to drug shortage	Initial Infusion: 5 mcg/kg/min IV, ↑ by 5-10 mcg/kg/min until desired level of sedation achieved MD: 5-50 mcg/kg/min IV Oil-in-water emulsion (provides 1.1 kcal/mL)	**CONTRAINDICATIONS** Hypersensitivity to egg, egg product, soy and soy product **SIDE EFFECTS** Hypotension, apnea, hypertriglyceridemia, green urine/hair/nail beds, propofol-related infusion syndrome (PRIS – rare but can be fatal), myoclonus, pancreatitis, pain on injection (particularly peripheral vein), QT prolongation **MONITORING** BP, HR, RR, sedation scale, triglycerides (if administered longer than 2 days), signs and symptoms of pancreatitis **NOTES** Shake well before use. Do not use if there is separation of phases in the emulsion. Use strict aseptic technique due to potential for bacterial growth. Discard vial and tubing within 12 hours of use. If transferred to a syringe prior to administration, must discard syringe within 6 hours. Do not use a filter < 5 micron for administration. Does not require refrigeration.

Agents for Pain, Agitation, and Delirium in the ICU Continued

DRUG	DOSING	SAFETY/SIDE EFFECTS/MONITORING
Dexmedetomidine (*Precedex*) Alpha-2 adrenergic agonist Used for sedation in intubated and non-intubated patients; patients are arousable and alert when stimulated (less respiratory depression than other sedatives)	LD: 0.5-1 mcg/kg IV over 10 minutes (may be omitted) MD: 0.2-1.5 mcg/kg/hr IV for 24 hours (rate can be adjusted until desired level of sedation achieved) Duration of infusion should not exceed 24 hours	**WARNINGS** Use with caution in patients with hepatic impairment, diabetes, heart block, bradycardia, severe ventricular dysfunction, hypovolemia or chronic hypertension **SIDE EFFECTS** Hypo and hypertension, bradycardia, dry mouth, nausea, constipation **MONITORING** BP, HR, sedation scale **NOTES** Does not require refrigeration
Etomidate (*Amidate*) Nonbarbiturate hypnotic Ultra short-acting; used as an induction agent for anesthesia Minimal cardiovascular effects	Sedation: 0.1-0.2 mg/kg IV followed by 0.05 mg/kg every 3-5 minutes	**WARNING** Inhibits 11-B-hydroxylase which can lead to ↓ cortisol production for up to 24 hours **MONITORING** Monitor for adrenal insufficiency (hypotension, hyperkalemia), respiratory status, BP, HR, infusion site, sedation scale
Ketamine (*Ketalar*) NMDA receptor antagonist Used as an induction agent for anesthesia	Sedation: 0.2-0.8 mg/kg IV (may follow with continuous infusion) Pretreatment with benzodiazepine can ↓ incidence of emergence reactions (see warnings) by 50%	**WARNINGS** Emergence reactions (vivid dreams, hallucinations, delirium), cerebrospinal fluid (CSF) pressure elevation, respiratory depression/apnea, may cause dependence/tolerance **MONITORING** BP, HR, respiratory status, emergence reactions, sedation scale

Pain/Analgesia

Morphine	LD: 2-4 mg IV push MD: 2-30 mg/hr	See Pain chapter for additional information. In critical care patients monitor BP, HR, respiration, pain and sedation for all.
FentaNYL	LD: 0.35-0.5 mcg/kg slow IV push Q30-60 min (25-35 mcg for ~70 kg patient) MD: 0.7-10 mcg/kg/hr	Fentanyl: less hypotension (no histamine release) than morphine (perferred for hemodynamically unstable patients), 100x more potent that morphine; rapid onset and short duration of action (half-life increases with duration of infusion), can accumulate in hepatic impairment; 3A4 substrate and potential for numerous drug interactions.
HYDROmorphone (*Dilaudid*)	LD: 0.2-0.6 mg IV push MD: 0.5-3 mg/hr	Hydromorphone: very potent, dose carefully.
Remifentanil (*Ultiva*)	LD: 1.5 mcg/kg over 1 min MD: 0.5-15 mcg/kg/hr	

Agents for Pain, Agitation, and Delirium in the ICU Continued

DRUG	DOSING	SAFETY/SIDE EFFECTS/MONITORING

Delirium

| Haloperidol *(Haldol)* | 0.5-10 mg IV push at 5 mg/minute; may repeat Q15-30 minutes until calm, then administer 25% of last dose Q6H | See Schizophrenia/Psychosis chapter. Not recommended for treatment of delirium in recent guidelines. |
| QUEtiapine *(SEROquel)* | 50 mg PO Q12H; may increase by 50-100 mg/day every 24 hours up to 200 mg Q12H | See Schizophrenia/Psychosis chapter. May decrease duration of delirium. |

RISK FACTORS FOR THE DEVELOPMENT OF STRESS ULCERS
Mechanical ventilation
Coagulopathy
Sepsis
Traumatic brain injury
Burn patients
Acute renal failure
High dose systemic steroids

Stress Ulcer Prophylaxis

Stress ulcers can result from the metabolic stress experienced by a patient in an ICU. Patients with critical illness have reduced blood flow to the gut as blood flow is diverted to the major organs of the body. This results in a breakdown of gastric mucosal defense mechanisms including prostaglandin synthesis, bicarbonate production and cell turnover.

Histamine-2 receptor antagonists (H$_2$RAs) and proton pump inhibitors (PPIs) are the recommended agents for prevention of stress-related mucosal damage. H$_2$RAs can cause thrombocytopenia and mental status changes in the elderly or those with renal/hepatic impairment. Tachyphylaxis (tolerance) has also been reported. PPIs have been associated with an increased risk of GI infections *(C. difficile)*, fractures and nosocomial pneumonia. These agents are discussed in the GERD and PUD chapters. Patients without risk factors for stress ulcers should not receive stress ulcer prophylaxis (see risk factors in table).

ADDITIONAL DRUGS USED IN THE ICU AND OPERATING ROOM

Anesthetics

COMMONLY USED ANESTHETICS

Local – lidocaine *(Xylocaine)*, benzocaine, liposomal bupivacaine *(Exparel)*

Inhaled – desflurane *(Suprane)*, sevoflurane *(Ultane)*, isoflurane *(Forane)*, nitrous oxide, others

Injectable – bupivacaine *(Marcaine, Sensorcaine)*, lidocaine *(Xylocaine)*, ropivacaine *(Naropin)*, others

Anesthetics are used for a variety of effects including numbing of an area (local anesthesia), to block pain (regional anesthesia), or to cause a reversible loss of consciousness and sleepiness during surgery (general anesthesia). Anesthetics can be given via several routes of administration: topical, inhaled, intravenous, epidural or spinal. Increasingly, anesthetics are being used with opioids to reduce the opioid requirement for pain control. They work by blocking the initiation and conduction of nerve impulses by decreasing the neuronal permeability to sodium ions. Most patients receiving anesthetics must be continuously monitored (vital signs and respiration). The main side effects of anesthetics include hypotension, bradycardia, nausea and vomiting and a mild drop in body temperature that can cause shivering. Overdose can cause respiratory depression. Allergic reactions are possible. Inhaled anesthetics can rarely cause malignant hyperthermia (MH). See side bar for some commonly used anesthetics.

Epidurals containing bupivacaine can quickly be fatal if given intravenous. Do not give bupivacaine epidurals by IV infusion. Lidocaine should not be given by dual routes of administration (IV and topical). Lidocaine/epinephrine combination products are used for some local procedures that require an anesthetic, such as inserting an IV line. The epinephrine is added for vasoconstriction, which keeps the lidocaine localized to the area where the numbing is needed. Deaths have occurred due to mix-ups with epinephrine products and lidocaine/epinephrine products. Be careful to use the proper product, concentration and route of administration.

Neuromuscular Blocking Agents

These agents cause skeletal muscle paralysis. Patients can require the use of a paralytic agent in surgery conducted under general anesthesia, to facilitate mechanical intubation, manage increased intracranial pressure, treat muscle spasms (tetany) and prevent shivering in patients undergoing therapeutic hypothermia after cardiac arrest. The use of neuromuscular blocking agents (NMBAs) is typically recommended when other methods have proven ineffective; they are not routinely used in all critically ill patients. These agents do not provide sedation or analgesia. Therefore, patients should receive adequate sedation and analgesia prior to starting a NMBA. Patients must be mechanically ventilated as these agents paralyze the diaphragm. These are considered high risk medications by ISMP. All NMBAs should be labeled with a bright red auxiliary label stating "WARNING, PARALYZING AGENT".

Patients receiving paralytics are unable to breath, move, blink, or cough. Special care must be taken to protect the skin, lubricate the eyes, and suction frequently to clear secretions while NMBAs are being used. Glycopyrrolate *(Robinul)* is an anticholinergic agent that can be used to reduce secretions. Numerous medications can enhance the neuromuscular blocking activity of the NMBAs leading to toxicity (aminoglycosides, calcium channel blockers, colistimethate, cyclosporine, inhaled anesthetics, lithium, quinidine, vancomycin, others). Monitoring for the appropriate depth of paralysis is recommended.

There are 2 types of NMBAs – depolarizing and non-depolarizing. Succinylcholine is the <u>only available depolarizing agent</u> and is typically reserved for intubation. It is not used for continuous neuromuscular blockade. Succinylcholine has been rarely associated with causing malignant hyperthermia (particularly when used with inhaled anesthetics). Resembling acetylcholine, succinylcholine <u>binds to and activates the acetylcholine receptors and desensitizes them</u>. The <u>non-depolarizing</u> NMBAs work by binding to the acetylcholine receptor and blocking the actions of endogenous acetylcholine.

DRUG	SAFETY/SIDE EFFECTS/MONITORING

Depolarizing NMBA

Succinylcholine *(Anectine,* ***Quelicin****, Quelicin-1000)*	Short-acting, fast onset (30-60 seconds)

Non-depolarizing NMBAs

For all non-depolarizing NMBAs	**SIDE EFFECTS** Flushing, bradycardia, hypotension, tachyphylaxis, acute quadriplegic myopathy syndrome (AQMS) with long-term use **MONITORING** Peripheral nerve stimulator to assess depth of paralysis during continuous infusions [also called train-of-four (TOF)], vital signs (BP, HR, RR)
Atracurium	Short t½; intermediate-acting; metabolized by Hofmann elimination (independent of renal and hepatic function)
Cisatracurium *(Nimbex)*	Short t½; intermediate-acting; metabolized by Hofmann elimination (independent of renal and hepatic function)
Pancuronium	Long-acting agent, can accumulate in renal or hepatic dysfunction, ↑ HR
Rocuronium *(Zemuron)*	Intermediate-acting agent
Vecuronium	Intermediate-acting agent; can accumulate in renal or hepatic dysfunction

Hemostatic Agents

The term hemostasis means causing bleeding to stop. A variety of hemostatic methods can be used, ranging from simple manual pressure with one finger to electrical tissue cauterization, or the systemic administration of blood products (transfusions) or hemostatic agents. The systemic hemostatic drugs work by inhibiting fibrinolysis or enhancing coagulation. Several factor products are available to treat hemorrhage in patients with hemophilia or rare factor deficiencies (*FEIBA, Coagadex*). Newer hemostatic drugs (*Kcentra* and *Praxbind*) have been approved as reversal agents for specific anticoagulants. See Anticoagulation chapter.

Systemic Hemostatic Agents

DRUG	SAFETY/SIDE EFFECTS/MONITORING
Aminocaproic acid *(Amicar)* Tablet, solution, injection	**CONTRAINDICATIONS** Disseminated intravascular coagulation (without heparin); active intravascular clotting process **SIDE EFFECTS** Injection-site reactions, thrombosis **NOTES** FDA-approved for excessive bleeding associated with cardiac surgery, liver cirrhosis, and urinary fibrinolysis. Do not use in patients with active clots, do not give with factor IX complex concentrates due to ↑ risk for thrombosis.
Tranexamic acid *(Cyklokapron,* injection) *(Lysteda,* oral)	**CONTRAINDICATIONS** IV: acquired defective color vision, active intravascular clotting, subarachnoid hemorrhage Oral: previous or current thromboembolic disease, current use of combination hormonal contraception **SIDE EFFECTS** Injection: vascular occlusion, thrombosis Oral: retinal clotting *Lysteda* (oral) is approved for heavy menstrual bleeding (menorrhagia). The injection is approved for bleeding with hemophilia and is often used off-label to control surgical bleeding.
Recombinant Factor VIIa *(NovoSeven RT)* Injection	**BOXED WARNING** Risk of thrombotic events, particularly when used off-label **NOTES** FDA-approved for hemophilia and factor VII deficiency; has been used successfully off-label for patients with hemorrhage from trauma and warfarin-related bleeding events.

Topical Agents: There are many and most are used surgically. These include thrombin in bandages, liquids and spray forms, fibrin sealants, acrylates and a few others (names often include "throm": <u>Recothrom, Evithrom)</u>. A few topical hemostatics are OTC.

Intravenous Immunoglobulin

Intravenous immune globulin (IVIG or IGIV) contains pooled <u>immunoglobulin (IgG),</u> administered intravenously. The IgG is extracted from the plasma of a thousand or more blood donors (this is the FDA's minimum; typically the IVIG is derived from between 3,000-10,000 donors). IVIG is given as plasma protein replacement therapy (IgG) for immune deficient patients who have decreased or abolished antibody production capabilities. Initially, IVIG was used only for immunodeficiency conditions. Currently, IVIG has several FDA-approved indications and is used for a variety of off-label indications (multiple sclerosis, myasthenia gravis, Guillaine-Barré, others) with varying results.

DRUG	DOSING	SAFETY/SIDE EFFECTS/MONITORING
Intravenous immunoglobulin (*Bivigam*, **Carimune NF,** *Flebogamma*, **Flebogamma DIF**, **Gammagard**, *Gammagard S/D*, *Gammaked*, *Gammaplex*, **Gamunex-C,** *Hizentra*, *Hyqvia*, **Octagam**, **Privigen**)	Indication and product specific <u>Use IBW to calculate dose</u> <u>Use slower infusion rate in renal and cardiovascular disease</u> Do not freeze, shake or heat	**BOXED WARNINGS** <u>Acute renal dysfunction</u> can rarely occur and has been associated with fatalities; usually within 7 days of use (<u>more likely with products stabilized with sucrose</u>). <u>Use with caution in the elderly, patients with renal disease, diabetes mellitus, volume depletion, sepsis, paraproteinemia, and nephrotoxic medications</u> due to risk of renal dysfunction. <u>Thrombosis</u> may occur with IVIG products even in the absence of risk factors. For patients at risk, administer at the minimum dose. Monitor all patients. **CONTRAINDICATIONS** <u>IgA deficiency (can use product with lowest amount of IgA)</u> **WARNINGS** Use with caution in patients with cardiovascular disease (use isotonic products and low infusion rate) **SIDE EFFECTS** <u>Headache, nausea, diarrhea, injection site reaction, infusion reaction (facial flushing, chest tightness, fever, chills, hypotension – slow/stop infusion), renal failure or blood dyscrasias (both rare)</u> **MONITORING** <u>Renal function, urine output, volume status, Hgb</u> **NOTES** Patients should be asked about past IVIG infusions, including product used and any reactions that occurred. The pharmacy must keep track of IVIG lot numbers used for each patient.

ELECTROLYTE DISORDERS

Any patient (including outpatients) can experience electrolyte abnormalities, but these are common in critically ill patients. Some drugs deplete electrolytes and cause acute deficiency. Some electrolyte abnormalities can be fatal when severe (seizures, cardiac arrhythmias, coma). Protocols to replace electrolytes should be followed in order to avoid toxicity. Electrolytes and their reference ranges are discussed in the Lab Values & Drug Monitoring chapter.

Sodium

Hyponatremia

Hyponatremia (Na < 135 mEq/L) may develop from many causes and is usually not symptomatic until < 120 mEq/L, unless the serum level falls rapidly. Hyponatremia is classified first according to serum osmolality and then by clinical volume status:

- Hypotonic <u>hypovolemic</u> hyponatremia is caused by diuretic use, salt-wasting syndromes, adrenal insufficiency, blood loss, vomiting/diarrhea. The treatment is typically to <u>correct the underlying cause</u> and to administer <u>saline</u> solutions.

- Hypotonic <u>hypervolemic</u> hyponatremia is caused by fluid overload, usually with cirrhosis, heart failure, or renal failure. <u>Diuresis with fluid restriction</u> is the preferred treatment.

■ Hypotonic isovolemic (euvolemic) hyponatremia is usually caused by the syndrome of inappropriate antidiuretic hormone (SIADH). It is treated with fluid restriction or diuresis. Demeclocycline is frequently used off-label for hyponatremia associated with SIADH.

The <u>arginine vasopressin (AVP) receptor antagonists (conivaptan or tolvaptan)</u> may be used to treat <u>SIADH and hypervolemic hyponatremia</u>. They increase excretion of free water while maintaining sodium. The role for these agents is still being determined, as they are <u>more expensive than 3% saline</u> and use beyond 30 days with the oral product, tolvaptan *(Samsca)*, is not recommended. Caution should be taken in treating patients with hyponatremia to prevent correcting too quickly. <u>Correcting sodium more rapidly than 12 mEq/L over 24 hours can cause osmotic demyelination syndrome or central pontine myelinolysis, which can cause paralysis, seizures and death</u>. Conservative correction goals are advised as accidental overcorrection is common. Administration of desmopressin reduces water diuresis and may help avoid overcorrection.

DRUG	DOSE	SAFETY/SIDE EFFECTS/MONITORING
Conivaptan *(Vaprisol)* Injection Dual AVP antagonist [vasopressin 1A (V1A) and vasopressin 2 (V2)]	LD: 20 mg IV over 30 minutes MD: 20 mg continuous IV infusion over 24 hours. May increase to 40 mg IV daily if Na does not ↑ at desired rate. Do not use longer than 4 days CrCl < 30 mL/min: avoid ↓ dose in moderate hepatic impairment	**CONTRAINDICATIONS** Allergy to <u>corn</u> or corn products, <u>hypovolemic hyponatremia</u>, concurrent use with strong 3A4 inhibitors, <u>anuria</u> **WARNING** <u>Overly rapid correction of hyponatremia (> 12 mEq/L/24 hours) associated with osmotic demyelination syndrome (life-threatening)</u> **SIDE EFFECTS** Orthostatic hypotension, fever, hypokalemia, <u>infusion site reactions (> 60%)</u> **MONITORING** Rate of Na increase, BP, volume status, urine output
Tolvaptan *(Samsca)* Tablet Selective AVP antagonist [vasopressin 2 (V2) only]	15 mg PO daily; max 60 mg PO daily; <u>for up to 30 days due to hepatotoxicity</u> Not recommended if CrCl < 10 mL/min Avoid fluid restriction in first 24 hours of therapy	**BOXED WARNINGS** Should be initiated and re-initiated in a hospital under close monitoring of serum Na <u>Overly rapid correction of hyponatremia (> 12 mEq/L/24 hours) associated with osmotic demyelination syndrome (life-threatening)</u> **CONTRAINDICATIONS** <u>Patients who are unable to sense or respond appropriately to thirst, urgent need to raise Na</u>, hypovolemic hyponatremia, concurrent use with strong 3A4 inhibitors, <u>anuria</u> **WARNINGS** <u>Hepatotoxicity (avoid use > 30 days and in liver disease/cirrhosis)</u> **SIDE EFFECTS** <u>Thirst, nausea, dry mouth, polyuria, weakness</u>, hyperglycemia, hypernatremia **MONITORING** Rate of Na increase, BP, volume status, urine output; signs of drug-induced hepatotoxicity

Hypernatremia

Hypernatremia (Na > 145 mEq/L) is associated with a water deficit and hypertonicity.

- Hypovolemic hypernatremia is caused by dehydration, vomiting, diarrhea and is treated with fluids.

- Hypervolemic hypernatremia is caused by intake of hypertonic fluids and is treated with diuresis.

- Isovolemic (euvolemic) hypernatremia is frequently caused by diabetes insipidus (DI), which can ↓ antidiuretic hormone (ADH). It is treated with desmopressin.

Potassium

Treatment of hyperkalemia is discussed in the Renal Disease and Dosing Considerations chapter. Hypokalemia (K < 3.5 mEq/L) is a common occurrence in hospitalized patients. Management includes treating the underlying cause [e.g., metabolic alkalosis, overdiuresis, some medications (amphotericin, insulin)] and administering oral or IV potassium. The oral route is preferred for replacement when feasible. Oral potassium salt formulations are reviewed in the Chronic Heart Failure chapter. In general, a drop of 1 mEq/L in serum K below 3.5 mEq/L represents a total body deficit of 100 – 400 mEq. Hospitals use K sliding scales that allow a healthcare provider (usually a nurse) to administer a certain dose of potassium based on various ranges of low serum K (e.g., for K 3.5 – 3.7 mEq/L, give 20 mEq KCl PO x 2 doses; for K 3.3 – 3.4 mEq/L, give 20 mEq KCl PO x 3 doses, etc.). Potassium chloride premixed IVs are generally used for IV replacement. Safe recommendations for IV potassium replacement through a peripheral line include an infusion rate ≤ 10 mEq/hr and maximum concentration of 10 mEq/100 mL. More rapid infusions and higher concentrations may be warranted in severe or symptomatic hypokalemia; these require a central line and cardiac monitoring. IV potassium can be fatal if administered undiluted or IV push. When hypokalemia is resistant to treatment, serum magnesium should be checked and replaced as needed. Magnesium is necessary for potassium uptake.

Magnesium

Hypomagnesemia (Mg < 1.3 mEq/L) is more common than hypermagnesemia. Common causes of hypomagnesemia include chronic alcohol use, diuretics, vomiting, and diarrhea. Hypermagnesemia is most commonly due to renal insufficiency. When serum Mg is < 1 mEq/L with life-threatening symptoms (seizures or arrhythmias), IV replacement is recommended. Magnesium sulfate is used for IV replacement. When serum Mg is < 1 mEq/L without life-threatening symptoms, therapy can be administered IV or IM. When serum Mg is > 1 mEq/L and < 1.5 mEq/L, there are many options including oral replacement. Magnesium replacement regimens should continue for 5 days to fully replace body stores.

Phosphorous

Treatment of hyperphosphatemia is discussed in the Renal Disease and Dosing Considerations chapter. Hypophosphatemia is considered severe and usually symptomatic when serum PO_4 is < 1 mg/dL. Hypophosphatemia can be associated with phosphate-binding drugs (calcium, sevelamer, anatacids), chronic alcohol intake, and hyperparathyroidism. When serum PO_4 is < 1 mg/dL, IV phosphorus is used for replacement. Many regimens can be used, but 0.08 – 0.16 mmol/kg in 500 mL of NS over 6 hours is common. Patients must be carefully monitored and additional doses may be necessary. Patients with hypophosphatemia often have hypokalemia and hypomagnesemia that will require correction. Less severe hypophosphatemia can be treated orally and full replacement often takes one week or longer.

PRACTICE CASE

JL is a 65 y/o female in the ER with pneumonia. Over the past hour, she has had increasing difficulty breathing and oxygen saturation is not markedly improving with nasal administration of O_2. ER staff believes she will require admission to the ICU for intubation and mechanical ventilation. Past medical history includes COPD, chronic kidney disease, and diabetes.

Home Medications:
Lantus 30 units SC at HS
Novolog 5 units TID with meals
Lisinopril 10 mg daily
Symbicort 2 inhalations BID
Albuterol nebulizer PRN
Oxygen at 1 liter (delivered via home health company)

Labs:
Na (mEq/L) = 138 (135-145)
K (mEq/L) = 5.1 (3.5-5)
Cl (mEq/L) = 100 (95-103)
HCO_3 (mEq/L) = 33 (24-30)
BUN (mg/dL) = 24 (7-20)
SCr (mg/dL) = 1.7 (0.6-1.3)
Glucose (mg/dL) = 202 (100-125)
WBC (mm^3) = 14.6 (4,000-11,000)
Hgb (g/dL) = 11.2 (13.5-18 male, 12-16 female)
Hct (%) = 33.5 (38-50 male, 36-46 female)
Plt (mm^3) = 227,000 (150,000-450,000)
PMN (%) = 85 (45-73)
Bands (%) = 1 (3-5)
MCV (mm^3) = 78 (80-96)
RDW (%) = 15 (11.5-14.5)

Vitals and Tests:
BP: 138/87 HR: 98 RR: 25 Temp: 101.2°F O_2 Saturation on 1 liter = 92%
CXR: RML infiltrate

QUESTIONS

1. Based on this patient's past medical history and labs, which of the following medications may accumulate and cause side effects? (Select **ALL** that apply.)

   a. Dexmedetomidine
   b. Lorazepam
   c. Midazolam
   d. Propofol
   e. Remifentanil

2. Propofol and fentanyl continuous IV infusions were started for this patient. What general principle is correct regarding management of these medications for this patient?

   a. Heavier sedation is preferred to minimize risk to staff.
   b. Pain and sedation should be monitored with validated scales at least weekly.
   c. Daily sedation vacations are recommended to reduce the duration of mechanical ventilation.
   d. Propofol may be sufficient as a single agent since it also has analgesic properties.
   e. Benzodiazepines are preferred over propofol or dexmedetomidine because they cause less delirium.

3. The patient's respiratory status worsened and she is now requiring cisatracurium to maintain adequate oxygenation. Which of the following is correct regarding the propofol and fentanyl?

   a. Propofol may be discontinued since the patient should not be agitated while receiving a neuromuscular blocking drug.
   b. Fentanyl may be discontinued since pain should be well controlled while receiving a neuromuscular blocking drug.
   c. Haloperidol should be added to propofol and fentanyl since cisatracurium will cause delirium.
   d. Propofol and fentanyl should be continued and sedation and analgesia assessed prior and during cisatracurium therapy.
   e. Propofol and fentanyl should be continued, but succinylcholine is a better choice of neuromuscular blocking drug for this patient.

Questions 4-15 do not apply to the case.

4. Which of the following statements about colloids is/are true? (Select **ALL** that apply.)

   a. Sodium chloride 0.9% is a colloid
   b. Approximately 25% of the volume of a colloid remains intravascularly after administration
   c. Colloids are significantly more expensive than crystalloids
   d. Patients receiving colloids have a higher risk of developing pulmonary edema compared to patients receiving crystalloids.
   e. Albumin 25% is a colloid

5. Which of the following vasopressors is considered first-line in treating patients with sepsis?

   a. Norepinephrine
   b. Vasopressin
   c. Epinephrine
   d. Phenylephrine
   e. Ephedrine

6. Which of the following is an antidote for morphine overdose?

   a. Naloxone
   b. Sodium thiosulfate
   c. Flumazenil
   d. Protamine
   e. Deferoxamine

7. Which of the following statements is true regarding neuromuscular blocking agents (NMBAs)?

   a. Cisatracurium is a non-depolarizing agent.
   b. Patients receiving these drugs do not require sedation/analgesia.
   c. These drugs should be used routinely in critically ill patients.
   d. NMBAs are not associated with significant adverse effects.
   e. NMBAs are monitored using the Ramsay agitation scale.

8. Which of the following is true of *Precedex*?

   a. It is a benzodiazepine.

   b. It can only be used in intubated patients.

   c. It is an oil-in-water emulsion.

   d. It is an alpha-2 antagonist.

   e. It can be used in both intubated and non-intubated patients.

9. What effect can be expected from dopamine at medium doses (5 – 10 mcg/kg/min)?

   a. Alpha-1 antagonist, vasoconstriction

   b. Alpha-1 agonist, vasoconstriction

   c. Beta-1 agonist, positive inotropic effect

   d. Beta-2 agonist, positive inotropic effect

   e. D-1 agonist, vasodilation

10. Which of the following electrolyte disorders is conivaptan approved to treat?

    a. Hypovolemic hypotonic hyponatremia

    b. Euvolemic hyponatremia

    c. Hypervolemic hypernatremia

    d. Diabetes insipidus

    e. Euvolemic hypernatremia

11. How much of a change in sodium should be <u>avoided</u> in patients with sodium imbalances?

    a. > 6 mEq/L/day

    b. > 10 mEq/L/day

    c. > 12 mEq/L/day

    d. > 12 mEq/L/hr

    e. > 20 mEq/L/hr

12. The medical team will start a dobutamine drip at 10 mcg/kg/min for a patient weighing 60 kg. The standard concentration of dobutamine in the pharmacy is 250 mg/250 mL bag. Calculate how many hours the bag will last at the prescribed rate?

    a. 3 hours

    b. 5 hours

    c. 7 hours

    d. 10 hours

    e. 15 hours

13. Which of the following medications used for ICU sedation has a high concentration of propylene glycol, which may lead to metabolic acidosis?

    a. *Diprivan*

    b. *Precedex*

    c. *Ativan*

    d. *Haldol*

    e. Midazolam

14. Which of the following is important to monitor before and during haloperidol administration for ICU delirium?

    a. Blood glucose

    b. Potassium

    c. Cortisol

    d. QT interval

    e. Lactate

15. A 75 year-old is admitted with ADHF. He presents with congestion, altered mental status and poor urine output. His vital signs are BP 80/57, HR 112, RR 24 and oxygen saturation 93%. He is started on bumetanide 1 mg IV Q12H. Which of the following medications is most appropriate to start at this time?

    a. Dopamine

    b. Nitroprusside

    c. Nitroglycerin

    d. Milrinone

    e. Clevidipine

Answers

1-b,c, 2-c, 3-d, 4-c,e, 5-a, 6-a, 7-a, 8-e, 9-c, 10-b, 11-c, 12-c, 13-c, 14-d, 15-a

DRUG USE IN PREGNANCY AND LACTATION

© Artisticco, LLC

We gratefully acknowledge the assistance of Ann Hylton, PharmD, BCPS, Assistant Professor & Residency Program Director, Appalachian College of Pharmacy, in preparing this chapter.

BACKGROUND

Pregnancy typically lasts 9 months and is divided into 3 trimesters. The first trimester is when the embryo is most susceptible to birth defects caused by teratogens. For drugs to be teratogenic, the drug has to cross the placenta into fetal circulation. A positive human chorionic gonadotropin (hCG+) lab result confirms pregnancy. Teratogenic drugs should be discontinued prior to pregnancy, if possible.

LIFESTYLE MANAGEMENT

Lifestyle modifications should always be considered first when treating pregnant patients. Encourage alcohol cessation: alcohol in pregnancy can cause growth retardation and cognitive impairment. Encourage smoking cessation: tobacco use in pregnancy can cause spontaneous abortion, low birth weight and sudden infant death syndrome. Behavioral intervention is a safe and sometimes effective strategy for prenatal smoking cessation.

GUIDELINES/REFERENCES

CDC STI/STD recommendations, available at www.cdc.gov

VA/DoD clinical practice guideline for management of pregnancy. Washington (DC); 2009.

American College of Obstetricians and Gynecologists (ACOG) Practice Guidelines, available at www.acog.org

Folic Acid Supplements in Women of Childbearing Age

Women of childbearing age should consume adequate folic acid (400 - 800 mcg daily), calcium (1,000 mg daily) and vitamin D (600 IU daily). Folic acid (folate) can prevent birth defects of the brain and spinal cord (neural tube defects). Folate should be taken at least one month prior to pregnancy and continued for the first 2 - 3 months in order to cover organogenesis. An OTC prenatal vitamin that contains 600 - 800 mcg would supply the recommended amount. Prescription prenatal vitamins (e.g., *PrimaCare ONE, Zenate*) usually contain 800 mcg. Folic acid at 1 mg and higher is usually by prescription, although there are a few OTC products with this dose available. Folic acid is in many healthy foods, including fortified cereals, dried beans, leafy green vegetables and orange juice.

VACCINATION DURING PREGNANCY

- Inactivated influenza vaccine is recommended in pregnancy, regardless of the trimester.

- Tdap is recommended between 27 - 36 weeks of each pregnancy. If the woman has not been vaccinated or if the history is unclear, a 3-dose series is needed (one with Tdap, the other two with Td only). If the woman delivers and has not received vaccination, she should receive it post-delivery. Vaccination protects the baby and mother from pertussis (whooping cough), which is severe in infants.

- No live vaccines (e.g., MMR, varicella, live influenza nasal) one month before and during pregnancy.

- Other vaccines may be needed in unusual circumstances (e.g., foreign travel); refer to the CDC guidelines.

DRUG TREATMENT

Drug selection during pregnancy should consider the following:

- The use of lifestyle measures first

- Selecting drugs carefully, and only when necessary after failure of lifestyle measures

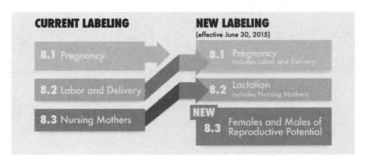

FDA Pregnancy Categories

As of June 30, 2015, the FDA has implemented new pregnancy and lactation labeling requirements. All newly approved prescription drugs and biologics are required to comply with the updated labeling immediately, and drugs approved on or after June 30, 2001 will gradually adopt the new labeling requirements over the next 5 years. Labeling for over-the-counter medications will not change. The new labeling is intended to provide patients and clinicians with more detailed benefit/risk data in order to make informed decisions.

SECTION	DESCRIPTION
8.1 Pregnancy	Risk summary is required for all medications. This section highlights the risk of adverse developmental outcomes based on all relevant human and animal data as well as the drug's pharmacology. If applicable, clinical considerations such as dose adjustments, maternal/fetal adverse reactions and disease-associated risks are discussed.
	Pregnancy exposure registry statement and contact information is provided in this subsection. Healthcare providers should encourage patients to participate in registries, which exist for select disease states and drugs. The registries collect health information from women who take prescription medications and vaccines when they are pregnant and breastfeeding. Information is also collected on the newborn baby.
8.2 Lactation	A lactation risk summary is required. This section summarizes information on the presence of the drug and/or active metabolites in human milk, the effects on the breastfed infant, and the effects on milk production. If applicable, clinical considerations such as minimizing exposure and monitoring for adverse reactions are included.
8.3 Females & Males of Reproductive Potential	If applicable, includes information when there are requirements for pregnancy testing and/or contraception before, during, or after drug use. Human and/or animal data suggesting drug-associated effects on fertility are included.

The old pregnancy categories were viewed as confusing and overly simplistic, and lacking in detailed information to assist clinicians and patients. With some drugs, ratings were applied incorrectly due to a lack of available information. Although these categories are being transitioned to the new labeling, they are currently included on many drugs, and will be referred to by clinicians and patients.

CATEGORY	INTERPRETATION OF THE PREVIOUS PREGNANCY CATEGORIES
A	Controlled studies in animals and women have shown no risk in the first trimester, and possible fetal harm is remote.
B	Either animal studies have not demonstrated a fetal risk but there are no controlled studies in pregnant women, or animal studies have shown an adverse effect that was not confirmed in controlled studies in women in the 1st trimester.
C	No controlled studies in humans have been performed and animal studies have shown adverse events, or studies in humans and animals are not available; give only if potential benefit outweighs the risk.
D	Positive evidence of fetal risk is available, but the benefits may outweigh the risk of life-threatening or serious disease.
X	Studies in animals or humans show fetal abnormalities; use in pregnancy is contraindicated.

Common Teratogens

Teratogenic drugs should be discontinued in pregnancy (and preferably prior to pregnancy), whenever possible. Well-known teratogens include: alcohol, ACE inhibitors, angiotensin receptor blockers, benzodiazepines, carbamazepine, dutasteride, ergot-derivatives such as DHE, finasteride, isotretinoin, lenalidomide, leflunomide, lithium, methimazole, methotrexate, misoprostol, nafarelin, NSAIDs, paroxetine, phenobarbital, phenytoin, propylthiouracil, quinolones, ribavirin, statins, tazarotene, tetracyclines, thalidomide and related compounds, topiramate, valproate, and warfarin.

With any medication, the drug's potential harm must be weighed against the risk of the condition not being adequately treated. In 2011, the FDA issued a warning regarding SSRI use during pregnancy and the potential risk of persistent pulmonary hypertension of the newborn (PPHN). Paroxetine is considered to have the highest risk of cardiac abnormalities of the SSRIs. Although each medication carries unknown risk, untreated depression during pregnancy can have harmful consequences for the mother and child. Newer data has shown most SSRI/SNRIs to be relatively safe in pregnancy (with the exception of paroxetine). It is important to assess the risk of disease with the risk of treatment.

Some medications should not be handled by pregnant healthcare professionals (e.g., 5-alpha reductase inhibitors, testosterone, mycophenolate, ganciclovir, and chemotherapeutics).

Select Conditions and Preferred Management during Pregnancy and Lactation

CONDITION	PREFERRED MANAGEMENT	NOTES
Morning Sickness, Nausea, Vomiting	Eat smaller, more frequent meals, avoid spicy or odorous foods, take more frequent naps, and reduce stress, including working long hours. If lifestyle measures fail, ACOG recommends pyridoxine (vitamin B6) +/- doxylamine first line.	Ginger is rated "possibly effective" for treating morning sickness in the Natural Medicines Database. Hyperemesis gravidarum is severe N/V, causing weight loss, dehydration and electrolyte imbalance. It will be treated under the care of an obstetrician and may require hospitalization.
GERD/Heartburn	Eat smaller, more frequent meals, avoid foods that worsen GERD. If symptoms occur while sleeping, recommend elevating the head of the bed and not eating 3 hours prior to sleep. If lifestyle measures fail, recommend antacids. Calcium antacids, such as calcium carbonate in *Tums*, are a good choice since calcium intake is often deficient in pregnancy. H$_2$RAs are Pregnancy Category B. PPIs are Pregnancy Categories B or C.	Use caution with excessive use of antacids containing aluminum or magnesium if renal disease is present. Do not recommend sodium bicarbonate or magnesium trisilicate (which comes in combination with aluminum hydroxide in *Gaviscon*).
Flatulence	Simethicone (*Gas-X, Mylicon*).	
Constipation	↑ fluid intake, ↑ dietary fiber intake, ↑ physical activity If lifestyle measures fail, fiber (psyllium, calcium polycarbophil, methylcellulose) with adequate amounts of fluids is first line.	
Cough, Cold, Allergies	First line: first-generation antihistamines. Chlorpheniramine (drug of choice) and diphenhydramine are Pregnancy Category B. The non-sedating 2nd generation agents loratadine and cetirizine are often recommended by obstetricians during the second and third trimesters. If nasal steroids are needed for chronic allergy symptoms, budesonide (*Rhinocort*) and beclomethasone (*Beconase AQ*) are considered safest.	The oral decongestants should not be recommended during the first trimester. Decongestants (pseudoephedrine, phenylephrine, oxymetazoline), the cough-suppressant dextromethorphan and the mucolytic guaifenesin have limited safety data in pregnancy/lactation, but may be recommended by the physician.
Pain	Acetaminophen (Pregnancy Category C) is the analgesic and antipyretic drug of choice during pregnancy and is considered safe to use if breastfeeding. The FDA is currently investigating the link between acetaminophen and the risk of attention deficit hyperactivity disorder (ADHD) in children born to women who took acetaminophen at any time during pregnancy.	Avoid aspirin for management of pain. Ibuprofen is Pregnancy Category C/D > 30 weeks gestation, and naproxen is Pregnancy Category C. The FDA is currently investigating the link between NSAIDs and the risk of miscarriage in the first half of pregnancy. Use of NSAIDs in pregnancy should be avoided. Consider the safety risk with opioid metabolism in pregnant or lactating women (see Drug Interactions and Pain chapters). If codeine is given to a breastfeeding mother who is a CYP 2D6 rapid metabolizer, the infant could suffer fatality. Use a short-acting opioid formulation, at the lowest effective dose, taken after feedings to reduce the risk to the infant.

Select Conditions and Preferred Management during Pregnancy and Lactation Continued

CONDITION	PREFERRED MANAGEMENT	NOTES
Infection	Generally considered safe to use: penicillins (including amoxicillin and ampicillin), cephalosporins, erythromycin and azithromycin. **VAGINAL FUNGAL INFECTIONS** Topical antifungals (creams, suppositories) x 7 days. **URINARY TRACT INFECTIONS** Cephalexin 500 mg PO Q6H x 7 days Ampicillin 500 mg PO Q6H x 7 days Nitrofurantoin and SMX/TMP should be considered last line during the 1st trimester, and should not be used in the last 2 weeks of pregnancy. Must treat bacteriuria, even if asymptomatic with negative urinalysis. Untreated bacteriuria can lead to premature birth, pyelonephritis, and neonatal meningitis.	Do not use: quinolones (due to cartilage damage) and tetracyclines (due to teeth discoloration). **VAGINAL FUNGAL INFECTIONS** Avoid fluconazole. **URINARY TRACT INFECTION** SMX/TMP is Pregnancy Category D, but data on birth defects is mixed and ACOG recommendations state that the use in pregnancy (if necessary) may be acceptable. See Infectious Disease chapters for STI/STD management in pregnancy.
Asthma	Maintenance therapy (steroid): inhaled budesonide Rescue therapy (short-acting beta agonist): inhaled albuterol	Budesonide is also the preferred steroid for infants in the *Respules*, which are put in a nebulizer.
Venous Thromboembolism/ Mechanical Valves	Low molecular weight heparin (LMWH) is Pregnancy Category B and is preferred. Unfractionated heparin (UFH) is Pregnancy Category C and is used during last month of pregnancy or if delivery appears imminent. UFH has a shorter half life than LMWH. Use pneumatic compression devices prior to delivery in women with thrombosis if they are getting a C-section.	The newer anticoagulants are category B or C and are not recommended. Warfarin is Pregnancy Category D (women with mechanical heart valves) and Pregnancy Category X (other indications).
Hypothyroidism	Levothyroxine (Pregnancy Category A). Will require a 30-50% dose increase during pregnancy.	Serious consequences of untreated hypothyroidism include: spontaneous abortion/miscarriage, preeclampsia, stillbirth, growth/cognitive impairment, low birth weight.
Hyperthyroidism	Mild hyperthyroid cases will not require treatment. Preferable to normalize the mother's thyroid function prior to pregnancy. Contraception should be used until the condition is controlled. If drugs are necessary (i.e., Graves' disease): propylthiouracil is preferred if trying to conceive and in the 1st trimester, methimazole is preferred during the 2nd and 3rd trimester. Both drugs are Pregnancy Category D.	Both drugs are high risk for hepatic injury, readily cross the placenta, and can cause congenital defects. Uncontrolled maternal hyperthyroidism can cause premature delivery and low birth weight.
Iron Deficiency Anemia	Supplemental iron, prenatal vitamins with iron.	
Hypertension	Labetalol, methyldopa, nifedipine.	ACE inhibitors, ARBs and direct renin inhibitors are contraindicated in pregnancy.
Diabetes	Insulin is preferred. Metformin and glyburide (Pregnancy Category B) are also commonly used.	

Managing hypertension, diabetes, HIV and bipolar disorder during pregnancy are discussed further in the respective chapters.

PEDIATRIC CONDITIONS

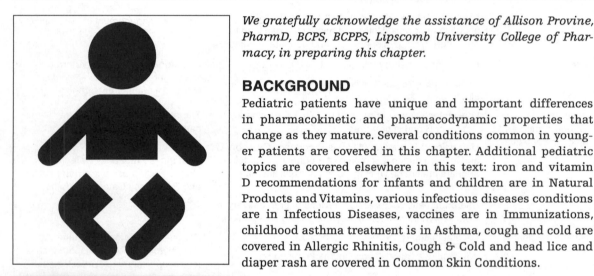

We gratefully acknowledge the assistance of Allison Provine, PharmD, BCPS, BCPPS, Lipscomb University College of Pharmacy, in preparing this chapter.

BACKGROUND

Pediatric patients have unique and important differences in pharmacokinetic and pharmacodynamic properties that change as they mature. Several conditions common in younger patients are covered in this chapter. Additional pediatric topics are covered elsewhere in this text: iron and vitamin D recommendations for infants and children are in Natural Products and Vitamins, various infectious diseases conditions are in Infectious Diseases, vaccines are in Immunizations, childhood asthma treatment is in Asthma, cough and cold are covered in Allergic Rhinitis, Cough & Cold and head lice and diaper rash are covered in Common Skin Conditions.

An infant can become seriously ill very quickly. The box indicates conditions in which a child should be referred for urgent care.

Various studies have demonstrated that when parents measure liquid doses, the dose is often incorrect. Household spoons should not be used for measuring medication. All liquid medications should be dispensed with an oral dosing syringe or dosing cup. The parent (or caregiver) should be able to read the markings on the device when it contains medication. Instruct the parents how to draw up the correct dose.

When dispensing liquid medications that carry high risk, follow safe practice recommendations:

GUIDELINES/REFERENCES

Cherry JD. Clinical practice: Croup. *N Engl J Med*. 2008; 358(4):384-391.

Vande Walle J, Rittig S, Bauer S, et al. Practical consensus guidelines for the management of enuresis. *Eur J Pediatr*. 2012; 171(6):971-983.

Addtl guidelines included with the video files (RxPrep Online).

- Stock one strength if a dangerous drug comes in a variety of strengths. Place the container into a high-risk bin with instructions attached to the container.
- The prescription should be written in terms of total mg and in mg/kg per dose.
- The pharmacist should check that the dose is accurate with the child's weight. Ask the parent for the child's weight if it is not available.

AGE CLASSIFICATIONS	
Neonate	0 – 28 days
Infant	1 month – 12 months
Child	1 – 12 years
Adolescent	13 – 18 years

REFER FOR URGENT CARE WITH ANY OF THE FOLLOWING SIGNS OR SYMPTOMS

Age < 3 months old with a temperature of 100.4°F (rectal)

Age 3 – 6 months with a temperature of 101°F (rectal)

Age > 6 months with a temperature of 103°F (rectal)

Any cough/cold that worsens or does not improve in several days

Unusual, severe, or persistent pain that does not go away after several hours

Blood in the urine or stool

Inability to sleep or drink

Rash that looks severe or any rash with fever

Abrasions that are dirty or deep (requiring sutures)

Limping or unable to move an extremity

Seizure

- The container label should include the dose (mg) and the volume (mL). Dispense with a measuring device.

With some high-risk drugs, it is preferable to administer at a medical facility, where help is available if needed.

BACTERIAL MENINGITIS

This infectious disease topic is included in the Infectious Diseases II chapter and is additionally covered here for three primary conditions that are specific to neonates: the fatality rate if untreated is close to 100%; organisms that cause the condition differ, which changes the drug treatment; and because of safety issues with ceftriaxone use in neonates.

The classic signs of meningitis are uncommon in neonates (age 0 – 28 days). Bulging fontanelles and nuchal rigidity will be present in < 25% of cases; otherwise, the symptoms are non-specific and a definite diagnosis in a suspected case can be made with a lumbar puncture.

The likely pathogens causing bacterial meningitis in a neonate differ from other ages due to the vertical transmission of organisms from the mother to the baby in the birth canal. The predominant pathogens are Group B streptococcus (GBS – predominantly type III), *Escherichia coli* and *Listeria monocytogenes*. A few other common organisms that should be treated empirically and listed in the table below with their recommended treatment. Ceftriaxone, which is used in adults, is generally <u>avoided</u> in neonates: ceftriaxone displaces bilirubin from albumin, which can cause bilirubin-induced brain damage (kernicterus). Ceftriaxone and calcium-containing solutions can precipitate, causing an embolus and death. Therefore, concurrent use in neonates is contraindicated. See Infectious Diseases II chapter for empiric treatment of bacterial meningitis.

AGE	COMMON BACTERIAL PATHOGENS	EMPIRIC TREATMENT
< 1 month	*Streptococcus agalactiae (Group B strep), Escherichia coli, Listeria monocytogenes, Klebsiella*	Ampicillin + Cefotaxime or Ampicillin + Aminoglycoside (Gentamicin)
1 – 23 months	*Streptococcus pneumoniae, Neisseria meningitidis, S. agalactiae, Haemophilus influenza, E. coli*	Vancomycin + 3rd generation cephalosporin (Ceftriaxone or Cefotaxime)
2+ years	*N. meningitidis, S. pneumoniae*	Vancomycin + 3rd generation cephalosporin (Ceftriaxone or Cefotaxime)

RESPIRATORY SYNCYTIAL VIRUS

Respiratory Syncytial Virus (RSV) infection occurs commonly and nearly all children have been infected by the age of two years. In older, healthier children, the symptoms mimic the common cold, but in premature babies and neonates, RSV can be deadly. RSV is a common cause of bronchiolitis (swelling and mucus build up in the bronchioles). Symptoms include low-grade fever, cough, dyspnea and cyanosis (bluish skin due to lack of oxygen). Similar to other viral infections the treatment is primarily supportive (supplemental oxygen, IV fluids, suctioning of secretions).

RSV Prophylaxis

No vaccine is available for RSV and no lasting immunity develops after infection, therefore risk remains high. Palivizumab (*Synagis*) is a humanized monoclonal antibody indicated for the prevention of serious lower respiratory tract disease caused by RSV in children at high risk of the disease. The American Academy of Pediatrics (AAP) recommends considering palivizumab prophylaxis during RSV season (late fall, early winter, early spring) for infants born before 29 weeks gestation who are younger than 12 months at the start of the RSV season, and for infants with chronic illness [primarily congenital heart disease or chronic lung disease (CLD)]. Palivizumab is dosed monthly at 15 mg/kg per dose. Infants should not receive more than 5 monthly doses during the RSV season. In addition to premature infants, palivizumab is used for certain infants and children < 24 months with select medical conditions that affect respiration. If the baby becomes infected with RSV, no further doses of palivizumab should be given.

Palivizumab is given by intramuscular (IM) injection. In neonates and infants, the IM injection site is the anterolateral thigh muscle. The deltoid can be used in children > 1 year if the muscle mass is adequate, but this is unlikely until the child is older (usually around 3 years of age).

CROUP

Croup, or laryngotracheobronchitis, is a viral or bacterial infection which causes inflammation of the upper airway, larynx, trachea and bronchi. The inflammation results in the hallmark signs of inspiratory stridor (high pitched breathing sound), barking cough, and hoarseness. Croup is most common in children < 6 years old and is often worse at night. The illness is classified and treated by the severity of the symptoms.

Supportive Care

In mild cases, a child may present with only a croupy cough, which can be managed at home and should resolve within a few days. Cool mist or steam (avoid spilling hot water on infants) and adequate hydration may help alleviate symptoms.

Drug Treatment for Mild (if Warranted), Moderate or Severe Illness

Systemic steroids and nebulized epinephrine are used in mild, moderate, and severe cases of croup. Some severe symptoms can require breathing support such as intubation.

In a typical croup case presenting to an acute care setting with moderate-to-severe symptoms, a patient having difficulty breathing will be given a steroid (oral if tolerated, or by injection) and then nebulized racemic epinephrine, if needed. Nebulized racemic epinephrine is a 1:1 mixture of dextro (D) isomers and levo (L) isomers (the L-isomer is the active component). If racemic epinephrine is not available L-epinephrine is used; this is ½ of the drug (one of the isomers) and the dose is, consequently, ½ of the racemic formulation.

Epinephrine is an <u>adrenergic agonist</u> that will relax the bronchial smooth muscle and cause <u>broncho-dilation</u>. When given with a nebulizer (or as an injection – these are used occasionally in an outpatient self-administered device for other conditions) the onset of action is fast but lasts at most up to 2 hours; a child receiving epinephrine will need to be monitored for a return of bronchospasm and for tachycardia. The child should not be discharged until breathing is easy with no stridor at rest and after receiving steroids to reduce the inflammation (usually dexamethasone). Antibiotics are used only if there is a lack of improvement due to a secondary bacterial infection.

DRUG	DOSING	SAFETY/SIDE EFFECTS/MONITORING
Dexamethasone Oral solution, injection (other forms not used in infants)	0.6 mg/kg x 1 PO/IM/IV, max 16 mg/dose	See Asthma chapter for steroid safety issues. This refers to acute use only.
Either given via nebulizer: Racemic epinephrine 2.25% solution L-epinephrine solution 10 mg racemic epinephrine = 5 mg L-epinephrine	<u>Racemic epinephrine</u> 0.05 – 0.1 mL/kg (max 0.5 mL) diluted in 2 mL NS, can repeat Q 20 min PRN <u>L-epinephrine</u> 0.5 mL/kg of 1:1000 solution (maximum dose: 5 mL) diluted in NS, can repeat Q 20 min PRN	**WARNINGS** Caution with cardiovascular disease, cerebrovascular disease, thyroid disease, diabetes (can ↑ blood glucose), extravasation (IV) **SIDE EFFECTS** ↑ BP, HR, anxiety, arrhythmia **NOTES** Monitor for recurrent bronchospasm.

NOCTURNAL ENURESIS

Nocturnal enuresis, or bed-wetting, is a normal part of a child's development and is not generally treated before age 5. Boys (more often than girls) can still be developing nighttime bladder control until 7 years old. The two "treatments" are alarm therapy and desmopressin. Prior to either of these, behavioral approaches are used first. Embarrassment should be minimized. Bladder training exercises (such as attempting to hold the urine during the day for a set time period) are not recommended.

Behavioral approaches that can be effective include <u>positive reinforcement</u>, establishing a <u>normal day-time voiding pattern</u> and a normal bowel pattern, and establishing a <u>normal hydration pattern</u>. Fluid intake should be limited prior to bedtime. Behavioral approaches are effective in many children and should be tried for up to 3 months. If <u>behavioral methods do not result in dryness</u>, either <u>alarm therapy</u> or <u>alarm therapy with drug treatment</u> (desmopressin) can be tried.

Alarm therapy can be useful and should be considered for a minimum of 3 consecutive months. If unsuccessful initially, alarm therapy might work when the child is older and more motivated. Alarm therapy is effective in about 2/3 of children initially; many will relapse and require the intervention repeated. There are numerous alarms available that attach to the underwear or pajamas and sound an alarm when wet. The child may sleep through the alarm but will generally stop voiding. When the alarm sounds a parent should wake the child and escort him or her to the bathroom.

Drug Treatment

Desmopressin (oral tablet) is the only preferred medication for enuresis. <u>Desmopressin is a synthetic analogue of antidiuretic hormone</u> (ADH); simulating ADH will ↓ nocturnal urine production. Desmopressin can be used in combination with alarm therapy.

DRUG	DOSING	SAFETY/SIDE EFFECTS/MONITORING
Desmopressin *(DDAVP)* – used in tablets for enuresis, and in tablets, nasal spray or injection for diabetes insipidus and hemophilia A (to control bleeding)	Start 0.2 mg PO QHS, can titrate to 0.6 mg max	**CONTRAINDICATIONS** Hyponatremia or history of hyponatremia CrCl < 50 mL/min **SIDE EFFECTS** Headache, fatigue, possible ↓ sodium due to water retention **NOTES** Limit fluid intake 1 hour before dose and until the next morning.

OVER THE COUNTER PRODUCTS FOR CHILDREN < 12 MONTHS OLD

If the condition does not require urgent care, there are several over the counter (OTC) products approved that are deemed generally safe for use in infants.

Intestinal Gas

Intestinal gas is a common condition with infants and causes distress post-feedings. <u>Simethicone drops</u> can offer mild, if any, benefit. The drug is not absorbed and is safe to use. Typically, as the child's digestive tract grows, the crying and fussiness will resolve. Parents can be comforted that symptoms will generally dissipate when the child is around 6 – 8 months old.

Nasal Congestion

Nasal congestion is very common in babies and is generally not serious. Children < 2 years old breathe mostly through their nose; they have not yet learned to breathe through their mouths. Smoke, including that from e-cigarettes, will cause irritation; do not permit anyone to smoke near children. Using a car seat indoors to sit the child upright may help. A cool mist humidifier near the bedside may reduce congestion – especially in the winter months when the home is heated. Some parents will help reduce congestion by steaming the bathroom up with the shower while a parent sits with the baby <u>outside of the shower</u> (in the steamy bathroom). Be careful <u>not to let hot steam</u> get near the child's skin.

OTC cough and cold medicines <u>should not be used</u> in children <u>< 2 years old</u> (per the FDA) and <u>< 6 years old</u> (per the AAP). Compared to placebo (sweet syrup with no medicine in it) these are no more effective in babies but do have more toxicities. Gentle <u>suctioning with saline drops or spray</u> to loosen the mucus can provide relief. Suction bulbs are sold in pharmacies.

Mild Pain and Fever

Never recommend aspirin or any salicylate-containing product (bismuth subsalicylate, others) for ages < 16 years who are recovering from chickenpox or flu symptoms due to the association with Reye's syndrome. It is best not to recommend these at all because it may not be clear if the child is recovering from a virus. The infant drops and children's suspensions <u>both contain the same dosage for acetaminophen</u> to help reduce toxicity in older children; previously, the infant drops were more concentrated. Acetaminophen is the most common cause of liver failure when used in doses above the safe amount. Accidental acetaminophen overdose can be due to the parent's inadvertent use of acetaminophen in multiple products. Take the time to counsel parents about this danger and the various names under which acetaminophen is packaged. This is discussed further in the Allergic Rhinitis, Cough & Cold chapter. Ibuprofen comes in <u>different dosage strengths</u> for infants and children and should be avoided in infants <6 months old for pain/fever due to the risk of nephrotoxicity. With either acetaminophen or ibuprofen infant drops, the medicine can be squirted into the child's mouth. It is acceptable to mix with a small amount of formula, but if the child might not drink the entire dose, it will be difficult to know how much of the dose was taken. The branded acetaminophen and ibuprofen are more expensive than the store's own formulations, which contain the same active ingredients, and are less costly.

Constipation

Community pharmacists commonly recommend pediatric-size glycerin suppositories for "stat" removal of feces in a quite uncomfortable baby. Previously, there had not been a recommendation available for treating constipation in the youngest patients. In 2011, a guideline on the use of laxatives in children by the Canadian Paediatric Society was developed. This guideline recommends oral polyethylene glycol (*Miralax*) as an option for intermittent constipation prevention. This is an unlabeled use and assumes the child will be able to swallow the medication. *Miralax* (or the less-expensive store brand) is started at 0.5 to 1 g/kg/day and titrated up, if needed. Dietary measures (prunes or pears, as the fruit or juice) are helpful. Any child with continuing issues with constipation should be seen by the pediatrician.

Select OTC Products for Infants

DRUG	DOSING	SAFETY/SIDE EFFECTS/MONITORING
Intestinal Gas		
Simethicone *(Mylicon Infants' Gas Relief Drops, Baby Gas-X Infant Drops)*	20 mg, 1-4 times/day PRN	Take after meals for mild gas pains. Shake drops before using. Can mix with water, formula, or other liquids.
Nasal dryness/congestion		
NaCl 0.9% intranasal saline solution *(Little Remedies Saline Nasal Drops, Ocean for Kids)*	2-6 drops per nostril PRN	See Allergic Rhinitis chapter; saline can be used with a suction bulb.
Fever		
Acetaminophen *(Children's Tylenol, PediaCare Infants' Fever Reducer/Pain Reliever, others)*	10-15 mg/kg/dose every 4-6 hours (max 75 mg/kg/day) All acetaminophen liquid (infants and children) is the same concentration: 160 mg/5 mL	For simplicity, age and weight-based dosing for infants is on the side of the dropper container. Caution for overdose from a variety of products, or incorrect dosing.
Ibuprofen *(Motrin Infant Drops, Infants' Advil Drops, Motrin* or *Advil* children's suspension, others)*	5-10 mg/kg/dose every 6-8 hours (max 40 mg/kg/day) Infant drop strength: 50 mg/1.25 mL	Indicated for infants > 6 months old. Caution for nausea.
Constipation		
Glycerin suppositories *(Babylax, Pedia-Lax)*	1 pediatric suppository. Insert high into the rectum. Retain for ~15 minutes.	Instruct parent to check with the pediatrician if using more than occasionally.
Polyethylene glycol *(MiraLax)*	Age ≥ 6 months: 0.2-1 gram/kg (max 17 grams). Dissolve in at least 4 oz water or other beverage. The capful, which is ~1 heaping tablespoon, contains ~17 grams.	Instruct parent to check with the pediatrician if using more than occasionally.

Systemic Drugs Not Generally Used in Pediatrics

- Quinolones are not routinely used in pediatric patients due to the possibility of adverse musculo-skeletal adverse effects. In special cases, such as anthrax treatment, cystic fibrosis or in the treatment of multidrug-resistant organisms, they are used on a case-by-case basis.

- Tetracyclines are not generally used in children < 8 years of age due to permanent discoloration of teeth and retardation of skeletal development and bone growth. One notable exception is in tick-borne Rickettsial diseases (Rocky Mountain spotted fever, erlichiosis and anaplasmosis). Doxycycline is the most effective treatment and is recommended by AAP and the CDC for this indication in pediatric patients, as the risk of severe illness or death outweighs the risk of tooth discoloration. See the Infectious Diseases II chapter.

- Promethazine is contraindicated in children < 2 years of age due to the potential for severe and potentially fatal respiratory depression.

- Codeine is metabolized to morphine by the CYP450 2D6 enzyme; certain children over-express this enzyme – and consequently, would produce a higher than expected amount of morphine. This can result in toxicity and a possible lethal overdose. Codeine has a boxed warning to avoid use with two childhood surgeries that are done routinely (tonsillectomy, adenoidectomy); codeine is dangerous if used for any condition if the child over-expresses this enzyme. It is preferable to avoid this analgesic in children.

- Several OTC products are not safe in young children; even OTC diphenhydramine can quickly become toxic if used in ages < 6 years. Consult drug information sources prior to recommending OTC or Rx drugs for use in children.

Primary Toxicities From Accidental Overdose in Children

Iron and acetaminophen are two common culprits of accidental overdose in children. Toddlers put anything in their mouths, especially if it looks like it could be candy. One dose of several drug classes, including sulfonylureas, can be fatal to an infant. It is important to counsel older patients about the safe storage of medications to prevent accidental overdoses. If the child has ingested anything that could be toxic (even if the ingestion is suspected only) the poison control center should be contacted immediately for advice. Review the Antidote chapter for further information on pediatric poisoning.

Vaccine-Preventable Childhood Diseases

Vaccine-preventable illness is, unfortunately, being seen more commonly than in previous years due to a lack of immunizations in certain communities. Additionally, recent immigrants who have not received vaccination in their home countries can bring in disease. The vaccine information on these conditions is in the Immunization chapter. The symptoms of the more common vaccine-preventable illnesses are listed below so that the pharmacist can recognize the illness if it presents in a child. Each of the conditions below can lead to severe, permanent damage except for chickenpox, which generally dissipates without long-term consequences for most of the person's life. Eventually, when the child who has had chickenpox when younger becomes an older person (> 50 years old) they will be at risk for shingles, which can be quite painful. Shingles only occurs in patients who have had chickenpox.

ILLNESS	EMBLEMATIC SYMPTOMS	SYMPTOM DESCRIPTION
Measles	Koplik spots are small <u>white spots</u> on the <u>inside of the cheeks</u> (inside the mouth) and appear 2-5 days prior to the rash seen below.	<u>Koplik spots in mouth, maculopapular rash</u>, fever, malaise, cough, rhinitis, conjunctivitis. Transmission is airborne and measles are highly contagious. If not immune, 90% of people who are in contact with an infected person will also become infected.
Mumps	Swollen and tender salivary glands under the ears (parotitis)	Swollen salivary glands, fever, headache, myalgia, fatigue, loss of appetite; up to 50% of patients have mild or no symptoms.
Rubella		Fever, rash, swollen glands, cold-like symptoms, aching joints; up to 50% of patients have mild or no symptoms. Can cause birth defects if contracted by a pregnant woman.
Polio	Child with poliomyelitis	Fever, sore throat, fatigue, nausea, headache, abdominal pain; the majority have no symptoms and never know they were infected – others get severe nerve damage (paralytic polio) and later in life, post-polio syndrome, which causes progressive weakness and cognitive issues.

Vaccine-Preventable Childhood Diseases Continued

ILLNESS	EMBLEMATIC SYMPTOMS	SYMPTOM DESCRIPTION
Pertussis	"WHOOP" Listen to a child making whooping sounds on YouTube; several parents have posted videos.	Sudden cough outbursts, fever, rhinitis, bluish skin (cyanosis), vomiting, fatigue. Can cause respiratory failure and death, especially in infants.
Chicken Pox (Varicella)	Chicken pox rash (spots) CDC/ Susan Lindsley	Itchy rash, fever, malaise. The rash appears as crops of sores (head, then trunk, then arms & legs), that turn into blisters, burst, then form crusts. Long-term implications include shingles (Herpes zoster) with risk of ophthalmic involvement and post-herpetic neuralgia (severe pain after the infection).

Questions

1. An 8 year old male weighs 55 pounds. Select an appropriate acetaminophen dose to recommend for this child:

   a. 1000 mg PO Q6 hours PRN pain

   b. 650 mg PO Q6 hours PRN pain

   c. 325 mg PO Q6 hours PRN pain

   d. 120 mg PO Q6 hours PRN pain

   e. 80 mg PO Q6 hours PRN pain

2. HY is a 2 year old female who presents to the emergency department with a frequent barking cough, prominent inspiratory stridor, marked sternal retractions, and agitation. She is afebrile with some rhinorrhea. Which of the following drug treatments is most likely warranted for her severe condition, based on the presentation?

   a. Dexamethasone and nebulized racemic epinephrine

   b. Dexamethasone only

   c. Nebulized budesonide and dextromethorphan

   d. Dexamethasone, pseudoephedrine, and nebulized racemic epinephrine

   e. Nebulized racemic epinephrine

3. MS is a 6 year old female (37.4 pounds) who presents to your pharmacy with a prescription for cefpodoxime written by her pediatrician for presumed bacterial pneumonia. She has a history of rash with penicillin. The pediatrician chose to use a cephalosporin. The dose of cefpodoxime recommended in the drug information reference is 10 mg/kg/day divided every 12 hours. The pharmacist should counsel the parent/caregiver to give the following milligrams for each dose:

   a. 15 mg

   b. 25 mg

   c. 55 mg

   d. 85 mg

   e. 115 mg

4. A 4 day-old male presents to the hospital with increased lethargy, poor feeding, and hypothermia. Blood and urine cultures are obtained along with a lumbar puncture to evaluate his cerebrospinal fluid. The most appropriate empiric regimen for suspected meningitis would be:

   a. Vancomycin and ampicillin
   b. Ampicillin and ceftriaxone
   c. Vancomycin and ceftriaxone
   d. Ampicillin and gentamicin
   e. Ceftriaxone and gentamicin

5. Which of the following statements concerning respiratory syncytial virus (RSV) are correct? (Select **ALL** that apply.)

   a. A patient presenting with RSV should be given nebulized corticosteroids early in the course to improve respiratory function.
   b. All patients requiring hospital admission due to RSV should be given nebulized ribavirin.
   c. An 11 month old infant with chronic lung disease on home oxygen should receive prophylaxis against RSV with palivizumab (*Synagis*).
   d. Palivizumab (*Synagis*) should be given once a week for the duration of RSV season for patients who meet criteria for prophylaxis.
   e. The treatment for RSV infection is primarily supportive and does not routinely require drug treatment.

6. Which of the following statements concerning croup are correct? (Select **ALL** that apply.)

   a. Clinical manifestations are caused by inflammation of the upper airway leading to narrowing of the trachea.
   b. Croup is most common in children 6-10 years of age.
   c. Croup is most commonly caused by a fungal infection.
   d. Mild cases are treated with supportive care, including possible use of nebulized albuterol or an albuterol MDI.
   e. Antibiotics should generally be given in children presenting with croup in order to prevent severe consequences.

7. A 14 year old male who weighs 132 lbs is diagnosed with a deep vein thrombosis and started on a heparin continuous infusion at 20 units/kg/hour. The heparin concentration in the IV bag is 25,000 units in 250 mL. How many milliliters of heparin should this patient receive each hour?

   a. 12 mL
   b. 22 mL
   c. 32.5 mL
   d. 55 mL
   e. 111.5 mL

8. A father brings his 2 month old daughter to the pharmacy. The girl weighs 14 pounds. The father states she has a rectal temperature of 100.6°F (38.1°C) and wants advice on an over-the-counter medication to treat her fever. The most appropriate recommendation is:

   a. Recommend ibuprofen 5-10 mg/kg/dose every 6-8 hours as needed until her fever subsides.
   b. Recommend putting his daughter in a cold bath to lower her temperature.
   c. Recommend acetaminophen 10-15 mg/kg/dose every 4-6 hours as needed until her fever subsides.
   d. Recommend he seek immediate medical care for his daughter.
   e. Recommend he continue monitoring her and seek medical care only if her temperature rises to 103°F (39.4°C).

9. Which of the following would be an appropriate over-the-counter recommendation for an infant?

   a. Simethicone drops for gas
   b. Dextromethorphan for a dry cough
   c. Bisacodyl suppository for constipation
   d. Fexofenadine (*Allegra Allergy Children's*) for runny nose/sneezing
   e. Loperamide for diarrhea

Answers

1-c, 2-a, 3-d, 4-d, 5-c, e, 6-a, d, 7-a, 8-d, 9-a

23

IMMUNIZATIONS

© Tamara Radavanavich

We gratefully acknowledge the assistance of Jeff Goad, PharmD, MPH, FAPhA, FCPhA, FCSHP, Chapman University School of Pharmacy, in preparing this chapter.

BACKGROUND

Immunizations in the United States over the past century are one of public health's greatest achievements. Since vaccines are medications, pharmacists should review immunization histories with patients. Vaccines prevent patients from acquiring serious or potentially fatal diseases. Many formerly prevalent childhood diseases (diphtheria, measles, meningitis, polio, tetanus) are rare because many children are vaccinated to prevent the illness, and others are protected by herd immunity (people around them are protected – thus they are less likely to catch the illness). If immunization rates drop below 85% to 95%, vaccine-preventable diseases may once again become common threats, as recent scattered pertussis outbreaks in the United States demonstrate.

GUIDELINES/REFERENCES

Immunization recommendations are written by the CDC Advisory Committee on Immunization Practices (ACIP) and the Committee on Infectious Diseases of the American Academy of Pediatrics (AAP). The pediatric and adult schedules are updated annually and published in January. Updates are published in the Morbidity and Mortality Weekly Report (MMWR).

The CDC's Pink Book, Epidemiology and Prevention of Vaccine Preventable Disease is published every 2 years and is available at www.cdc.gov.

Helpful resources for immunizing pharmacists are available on the following websites:

- American Pharmacists Association www.pharmacist.com/immunization-center (Accessed 2015 Dec 8)

- Centers for Disease Control and Prevention/Vaccines and Immunizations www.cdc.gov/vaccines and www.cdc.gov/travel (Accessed 2015 Dec 8)

- Immunization Action Coalition www.immunize.org (Accessed 2015 Dec 8)

Read through the background information before reviewing the individual vaccines. Immunization is currently taught in most pharmacy schools and has become standard pharmacy practice in many settings, especially in the community pharmacy. Principles of immunization should be well understood.

Travel vaccines are discussed in more detail in the Travelers chapter.

The CDC Advisory Committee on Immunization Practices (ACIP) develops written recommendations for the routine administration of vaccines to children and adults in the civilian population. The Immunization Action Coalition's (IAC) website has useful information for clinicians, such as vaccine records and clinic tools.

Safety Concerns

Some parents withhold vaccines due to misconceptions about the risk of autism, a developmental disorder. There is no evidence that vaccines cause autism. Thimerosal, a mercury-containing preservative used in vaccines, was alleged to be a possible cause since mercury has been linked to some brain disorders. Evidence does not suggest that thimerosal poses a risk for or is linked to autism. Thimerosal has been removed from most childhood vaccines. Andrew Wakefield, a one time British researcher, falsified research concluding that MMR caused autism. This lead to a decrease in MMR vaccination in the UK and a resurgence in measles in that country and around the world. It is important for pharmacists to provide patients with credible sources of information to counter erroneous information found on the internet and in the media. Promoting vaccination requires open communication and education.

Usually, vaccine adverse effects are minor and include mild fever, soreness or swelling at the injection site. Some vaccines may cause headache, loss of appetite and dizziness – but these quickly dissipate. Very rarely, anaphylaxis can occur. Anyone giving vaccines must screen for previous reactions and be prepared to treat a severe reaction. Some vaccines have specific contraindications to use, such as a true egg allergy with some of the influenza vaccines (this has been modified in recent years; see allergy discussion in this chapter), and with yellow fever and in one brand of the rabies vaccine.

Federal law requires that patients receive the most up-to-date version of the Vaccine Information Statement (VIS) before each vaccine is administered. The VIS standardized forms describe the risk and benefit of the vaccines, purpose of the vaccine, who should receive it and who should not, and what the patient can expect for both mild and serious adverse effects. VISs are created by the CDC and updated versions are available on the CDC and IAC websites.

Gelatin in Vaccines

Gelatin is used in some vaccines as a stabilizer, which is porcine-derived. For observant Muslims, Jews and Seventh Day Adventists who follow dietary rules that prohibit pork products, most religious leaders permit the use of gelatin-containing vaccines because the gelatin is injected, not ingested, and the end-product has been rendered pure.

Pharmacist's Role in Immunization

Pharmacists in the community setting have increased immunization rates, particularly by providing influenza, meningococcal, pneumococcal, pertussis (in Tdap) and herpes zoster (shingles) vaccinations. The pharmacist's role is expanding to include more vaccines and management of immunization clinics in healthcare settings. Pharmacists have become increasingly involved in pre-travel health services, providing travel advice, medications and immunizations per protocol for international travel. During comprehensive medication therapy management (MTM) sessions and in many inpatient and community pharmacy settings, pharmacists routinely screen and order vaccines (e.g., pneumococcal, Tdap, and influenza), per protocols.

PRINCIPLES OF IMMUNITY

Immunity is the ability of the human body to tolerate the presence of material indigenous to the body ("self"), and to recognize and eliminate foreign ("nonself") material. This discriminatory ability provides protection from infectious disease, since most microbes are identified as foreign by the immune system. Immunity to a microbe is usually indicated by the presence of antibody to that organism. There are two basic mechanisms for acquiring immunity, active and passive.

Active and Passive Immunity

Active immunity is protection that is produced by the person's own immune system. This type of immunity is usually permanent. One way to acquire active immunity is to survive an infection. Another way to produce active immunity is by vaccination. Passive immunity is protection by antibody containing products produced by an animal or human and transferred to a human, usually by injection. Passive immunity is useful when quick protection is required, such as providing rabies immune globulin to a patient who has been bit by a rabid animal. This will be administered concurrently with the rabies vaccine, which takes time to offer protection. Protection from passive immunity wanes with time, usually within a few weeks or months. Common forms of passive immunity are immune globulin injections and the antibodies an infant receives from the mother shortly before birth. The mother's antibodies provide passive protection from illness while the child is building its own immunity.

Live Attenuated and Inactivated Vaccines

SEPARATION TIME BETWEEN LIVE VACCINES AND ANTIBODY-CONTAINING PRODUCTS

PRODUCT GIVEN FIRST	ACTION
Vaccine	Wait 2 weeks before giving antibody
Antibody	Wait 3 months or longer before giving vaccine

*Except zoster vaccine

GENERAL RULE

The more similar a vaccine is to the natural disease, the better the immune response to the vaccine.

Live attenuated (weakened) vaccines are produced by modifying a disease-producing ("wild") virus or bacterium in a laboratory; they retain the ability to replicate (grow) and produce immunity, but usually do not cause illness. Administering live vaccines to immunocompromised patients may be contraindicated since uncontrolled replication of the pathogen could take place (see other chapters for immunization recommendations in specific populations, such as with HIV/AIDS). Live attenuated vaccines produce a strong immune response since the body's response to the vaccine is similar to actual disease.

Inactivated vaccines can be composed of either whole viruses or bacteria, or fractions of either. Immunity can diminish with time. As a result, some inactivated vaccines may require periodic supplemental doses to increase, or "boost" immunity.

Polysaccharide and Conjugate Vaccines

Inactivated vaccines are available in polysaccharide or conjugate formulations or, for some of the vaccines, in both forms (such as pneumococcal and meningococcal vaccines). Because the immune system in infants and young children is not completely developed, polysaccharide vaccines do not consistently produce an effective immune response (via the antibody production) in children under 2 years of age, and the antibodies that are made are less effective. For this reason, polysaccharide vaccines are not given to infants and young children. When the polysaccharide is chemically combined (conjugated) with a protein molecule, the antibody response improves and the vaccine is viable for this patient population. This is why infants and young children receive the pneumococcal conjugate vaccine (*Prevnar 13*) as infants, and may receive the pneumococcal polysaccharide vaccine (*Pneumovax*) when older than 2 years old, if indicated.

TIMING AND SPACING OF VACCINES

Vaccines and antibody products may require a separation period. The presence of circulating antibody to a vaccine antigen may reduce or completely eliminate the immune response to the vaccine. The amount of interference produced by circulating antibody generally depends on the type of vaccine administered and the amount of antibody.

Inactivated antigens are generally not affected by circulating antibody, so they can be administered before, after, or at the same time as the antibody. Live vaccines, however, must replicate in order to cause an immune response and antibody against injected live vaccine antigen may interfere with replication. If the live vaccine is given first, it is necessary to wait at least 2 weeks before giving the antibody.

The necessary interval between an antibody-containing blood product and MMR or varicella-containing vaccine (except zoster vaccine – this is not affected by circulating antibody) is a minimum of 3 months and may be up to 11 months. The specific blood product and dose administered determines the time interval. Consult "The Pink Book" to determine the specific recommended interval. During pregnancy maternal antibodies are passed from the mother to the baby and may reduce the subsequent live vaccine response in the baby. This is why live vaccines are withheld until the child is 12 months. Inactivated vaccines may be started at the age of 2 months, with the exception of hepatitis B vaccine which can be started at birth.

Simultaneous administration of antibody (in the form of immune globulin) and vaccine is recommended for postexposure prophylaxis of certain diseases, such as hepatitis A and B, rabies and tetanus.

Simultaneous Administration

Administering the most common live or inactivated vaccines simultaneously (on the same day or at the same visit) does not decrease antibody response and does not increase the rate of adverse reactions. Simultaneous administration of all vaccines for which a child is eligible is very important in childhood vaccination programs. It increases the probability that a child will be fully immunized at the appropriate age.

According to the ACIP, with one exception, simultaneous administration of the vaccines currently available in the United States is acceptable, and every effort should be made to provide all necessary vaccinations at one visit to improve compliance. The one exception is in children with functional or anatomic asplenia, the pneumococcal conjugate vaccine (PCV13) and *Menactra* brand meningococcal conjugate vaccine should not be administered at the same visit, but should be separated by at least 4 weeks.

Non-Simultaneous Administration of Different Vaccines

In some situations, vaccines that could be given at the same visit are not. If live injected vaccines (MMR, MMRV, varicella, zoster, and yellow fever) and live intranasal influenza vaccine (LAIV) are not administered at the same visit, they should be separated by at least 4 weeks.

Intervals of Doses between Vaccines Given in Series

Increasing the interval between doses of a multidose vaccine does not diminish the effectiveness of the vaccine after completion of all doses. It may, however, delay more complete protection. Decreasing the interval between doses of a multidose vaccine may interfere with antibody response and protection.

Interval for Administration of Live Vaccines and TB Skin Test

The tuberculin skin test (TST) is used to determine if a person is infected with *Mycobacterium tuberculosis*. The test is performed by injecting 0.1 ml of tuberculin purified protein derivative (PPD) into the inner surface of the forearm. Live vaccines can be administered on the same day and is the preferred method to avoid a false negative response to the skin test. Although a theoretical risk, interferon-gamma release assay (IGRA) tests (which may be used to detect TB infection) and live vaccines should be done on the same day or the IGRA drawn before administration of a live vaccine. If a live vaccine has been given recently (but not on the same day) as the PPD, wait 4 weeks before placing the PPD in order to avoid a false negative TB test result. False negative TB test results delay treatment of tuberculosis infection and are a significant risk to the patient and to public health. Alternatively, administer the PPD test first, then wait 48-72 hours and determine the PPD results before administering the live vaccine.

VACCINE ADVERSE REACTIONS

Vaccine adverse reactions fall into three general categories: local, systemic, and allergic. Local reactions are generally the least severe and most frequent. Allergic reactions can be the most severe, but are the least frequent.

The most common type of adverse reactions are local reactions, such as pain, swelling and redness at the site of injection. Local reactions may occur with up to 80% of vaccine doses, depending on the vaccine type. Local reactions are most common with inactivated vaccines, particularly those, such as DTaP, that contain an adjuvant. These reactions generally occur within a few hours of the injection and are usually mild and self-limited. Rarely, local reactions may be very exaggerated or severe.

Systemic adverse reactions are more generalized events and include fever, malaise, myalgias (muscle pain), headache, loss of appetite, and mild manifestations similar to the actual disease being prevented (such as a few chicken pox vesicles after receiving the varicella vaccine). These symptoms are common and may be nonspecific. Systemic adverse reactions following live vaccines are usually mild, and often occur 7–21 days after the vaccine was given (i.e., after an incubation period of the vaccine virus). Intranasal LAIV is cold adapted, meaning it can replicate in the cooler temperatures of upper airways (nose and throat) but not in the higher temperatures of the lower airways and the lungs. Mild cold-like symptoms such as a runny nose may occur.

A third type of vaccine adverse reaction is an allergic reaction. The allergic reaction may be caused by the vaccine antigen itself or some other component of the vaccine, such as cell culture material, stabilizer, preservative, or antibiotic used to inhibit bacterial growth. Minor allergic reactions are self-limited and can be treated with diphenhydramine. Minor allergic reactions are not a contraindication to subsequent vaccination. Severe allergic reactions, like anaphylaxis, may be life-threatening if not managed correctly. Fortunately, they are rare, occurring at a rate of less than one in half a million doses. The risk of an allergic reaction can be minimized by good screening prior to vaccination. A severe, anaphylactic allergic reaction following a dose of vaccine is a contraindication to a subsequent dose of that vaccine. Anaphylactic allergies are those that are mediated by IgE, occur within minutes or hours of receiving the vaccine, and require immediate medical attention. Examples of symptoms and signs typical of an anaphylactic reaction can include generalized urticaria (hives), swelling of the mouth and throat, difficulty breathing, wheezing, abdominal cramping, hypotension, or shock. In the event of an anaphylactic reaction, the appropriate emergency protocols should be followed and epinephrine should be immediately accessible. Immunizations should never be administered if epinephrine is not available.

All patients should be monitored for at least 15 minutes after vaccination. Providers should report clinically significant adverse events to the FDA's Vaccine Adverse Event Reporting System (VAERS) even if they are unsure whether a vaccine caused the event.

All providers who administer vaccines must have emergency protocols and supplies to treat anaphylaxis. If symptoms are generalized, a second person should activate the emergency medical system (EMS), by calling 911 and notifying the on-call physician. The primary healthcare provider should remain with the patient, assessing the airway, breathing, circulation, and level of consciousness.

- Administer aqueous epinephrine 1:1,000 (1 mg/mL) dilution intramuscularly, 0.01 mL per kg of body weight per dose, up to a 0.5 mL maximum per dose.

- Most pharmacies use prefilled epinephrine auto-injection devices. At least three adult (0.3 mg) auto-injectors should be available. While patients taking beta blockers may need higher or more frequent doses of epinephrine, emergency guidelines for use of epinephrine do not vary. Most adults will require 1 to 3 doses spaced every 5-10 minutes until paramedics arrive.

- In addition, for systemic anaphylaxis such as generalized urticaria, diphenhydramine may be administered either orally or by injection after the epinephrine has been administered. Due to the risk of choking, no drug should be administered orally if the patient is exhibiting signs of mouth, throat or lip swelling or difficulty breathing.

- Monitor the patient closely until EMS arrives. Perform cardiopulmonary resuscitation (CPR), if necessary, and maintain the airway. Keep patient in a supine position (flat on back) unless he or she is having breathing difficulty. If breathing is difficult, the patient's head may be elevated, provided blood pressure is adequate to prevent loss of consciousness. If blood pressure is low, elevate legs. Monitor blood pressure and pulse every 5 minutes.

- If EMS has not arrived and symptoms are still present, repeat dose of epinephrine.

- Record all vital signs, medications administered to the patient, including the time, dosage, response, the name of the medical personnel who administered the medication and other relevant clinical information.

- Notify the patient's primary care physician.

- Report reaction to VAERS.

- Immunizing pharmacists should always maintain a current basic life support (BLS or CPR) certification.

SYSTEMIC STEROID-INDUCED IMMUNOSUPPRESSION
CORTICOSTEROIDS
■ 20 mg or more per day of prednisone*
■ 2 mg/kg or more per day of prednisone*
■ NOT intra-articular injections, metered-dose inhalers, topical, alternate day or short course < 14 days
For 14 days or longer

CONTRAINDICATIONS AND PRECAUTIONS

Contraindications and precautions to vaccination generally specify circumstances when vaccines should not be given. Most precautions are temporary, and the vaccine can be given at a later time.

A contraindication is a condition that greatly increases a potential vaccine recipient's chance of a serious adverse reaction. It is a condition related to the recipient, not with the vaccine per se. For instance, administering influenza vaccine (except *Flublok)* to a person with a true anaphylactic allergy to egg could cause serious illness or death. In general, vaccines should not be administered when a contraindicated condition is present.

Two important contraindications to vaccination with live vaccines are pregnancy and immunosuppression. Two conditions are temporary precautions to vaccination: moderate or severe acute illness (all vaccines), and having recently received an antibody-containing blood product (live vaccines only).

ALTERED IMMUNOCOMPETENCE

Altered immunocompetence includes immunocompromised, immunosuppressed, and other conditions that affect immunocompetence (such as asplenia). Live vaccines can cause severe or fatal reactions in immunocompromised (due to disease/s) or immunosuppressed (by drug/biologic) people due to uncontrolled replication of the vaccine virus or reduced vaccine efficacy. Live vaccines should not be administered to this population of people. Certain drugs may cause immunosuppression. For instance, persons receiving

INVALID CONTRAINDICATIONS TO VACCINATION
VACCINATIONS MAY BE GIVEN, IF REQUIRED & INDICATED

- Mild acute illness (slight fever, mild diarrhea)
- Antimicrobial treatment (exceptions are certain antiviral medications and oral typhoid vaccine)
- Local skin reactions (mild/moderate)
- Allergies: bird feathers, penicillin, allergies to products not in the vaccine, allergies that are not anaphylactic

- Pregnancy, breastfeeding, preterm birth
- Tuberculin skin test (see text for timing and spacing with live vaccines only)
- Multiple vaccines being administered simultaneously
- Immunosuppressed person in the household, recent exposure to the disease, or convalescence
- Family history of adverse events to the vaccine

most cancer treatments should not be given live vaccines. Live vaccines can be given after chemotherapy has been discontinued for at least 3 months. Anyone receiving large doses of systemic steroids should not receive live vaccines (see the box on previous page). MMR and Varicella, both of which are live vaccines, are only contraindicated for HIV patients with CD4+ T lymphocyte counts < 200 cells/mm³. Both the pneumococcal conjugate vaccine (PCV13) and the 23-valent pneumococcal polysaccharide vaccine (PPSV23) should be given to adult patients with functional or anatomical asplenia). Live vaccines, when indicated, may be administered to asplenic patients.

VACCINATION OF PREGNANT WOMEN

- Live vaccines should not be administered to women 1 month before or during pregnancy

- In general, inactivated vaccines may be administered to pregnant women for whom they are indicated

- HPV vaccine should be deferred during pregnancy

- Pregnant women should receive the influenza vaccine (in season) and Tdap

---

VACCINATIONS DURING PREGNANCY

The most frequent vaccines administered to pregnant women are the influenza (inactivated) vaccine and Tdap. The influenza shot is indicated in all trimesters of pregnancy. Pregnant women should receive Tdap with each pregnancy. The optimum time for Tdap vaccination is between weeks 27 and 36 of the pregnancy. If the woman has not been vaccinated or her vaccination history is unclear, a 3-dose series is needed; one Tdap then two Td doses at 1 – 2 months and 6 months. If the woman delivers and has not received vaccination, she should receive it post-delivery. Tdap vaccination is given to protect the baby from pertussis (whooping cough) before the child is old enough to be fully vaccinated. In addition to the mother, other family members and close caregivers should receive pertussis vaccination.

VACCINATIONS FOR HEALTHCARE PROFESSIONALS

Hepatitis B

If there is no documented evidence of a complete hepatitis B vaccine series or no serologic evidence of immunity then the healthcare professional should:

- Receive the 3-dose series (dose #1 now, #2 in 1 month, #3 approximately 5 months after #2).

- If required by the institution, have anti-HBs antibody tested 1 – 2 months after dose #3.

Flu (Influenza)

- Influenza vaccine annually.

MMR (Measles, Mumps, & Rubella)

- If born in 1957 or later and have not had the MMR vaccine or if lacking an up-to-date blood test showing immunity to measles, mumps, and rubella, receive 2 doses of MMR, 4 weeks apart.

Varicella (Chickenpox)

- If no varicella vaccine received, or without positive serology to varicella, receive 2 doses of varicella vaccine, 4 weeks apart.

Tdap (Tetanus, Diphtheria, Pertussis)

- Get a one-time dose of Tdap as soon as possible if no Tdap previously (regardless of when previous dose of Td was received). Get Td boosters every 10 years thereafter. Pregnant healthcare workers need to get a dose of Tdap during each pregnancy.

SCREENING PRIOR TO VACCINE ADMINISTRATION

Use a screening form to rule out specific contraindications and precautions to the vaccine in adults. Note that a "yes" response to some of these questions will indicate a type of vaccine to use, rather than a contraindication to all (e.g., if a person has diabetes and selects "yes" to question #4, they should receive the inactivated influenza vaccine rather than the live influenza vaccine).

1. Are you sick today?

2. Do you have allergies to medications, food, a vaccine component, or latex?

3. Have you ever had a serious reaction after receiving a vaccination?

4. Do you have a long-term health problem with heart disease, lung disease, asthma, kidney disease, metabolic disease (e.g., diabetes), anemia, or other blood disorder?

5. Do you have cancer, leukemia, AIDS, or any other immune system problem?

6. Do you take cortisone, prednisone, other steroids, or anticancer drugs, or have you had radiation treatments?

7. Have you had a seizure or nervous system problem?

8. During the past year, have you received a transfusion of blood or blood products, or been given immune (gamma) globulin or an antiviral drug?

9. For women: Are you pregnant or is there a chance you could become pregnant during the next month?

10. Have you received any vaccinations in the past 4 weeks?

IMMUNIZATION REGISTRIES

Immunization registries are computerized information systems that collect vaccination histories and help ensure correct and timely immunizations, especially for children. They are useful for healthcare providers who use the registries to obtain the patient's history, produce vaccine records, manage vaccine inventories, among other benefits. It helps the community at-large to identify groups who are not receiving vaccines in order to target outreach efforts. Some systems are able to notify parents if vaccines are needed. Where allowed, pharmacists should strive to report all vaccines administered to their state or local registry.

VACCINES

VACCINE	ADMINISTER TO	STORAGE/ADMINISTRATION

Diphtheria Toxoid-, Tetanus Toxoid- and acellular Pertussis-Containing Vaccines
The pediatric formulations (with the upper-case D, as in DTaP) have 3-5 times as much of the diphtheria component than the adult formulation. The adult formulations have a lower case d (Tdap, or Td).

DTaP: *Daptacel, Infanrix* DTaP-IPV: *Kinrix* DTaP-HepB-IPV: *Pediarix* DTaP-IPV/Hib: *Pentacel*	Children get 5 doses of DTaP at age 2, 4, 6, 12-18 months and 4-6 years, then the Tdap x 1 at age 11-12 years. (see Tdap section). DTaP series given to children younger than 7 years of age.	Store in refrigerator. Do not freeze. Shake the prefilled syringe or vial before use. Give IM.

Vaccines Continued

VACCINE	ADMINISTER TO	STORAGE/ADMINISTRATION

Haemophilus influenzae type b-Containing Vaccines

Hib: *ActHIB, Hiberix, PedvaxHIB* DTaP-IPV/Hib: *Pentacel* MenCY-Hib: *Menhibrix* (Meningococcal serogroups C and Y-Hib)	Hib: Given to children. Sometimes in adults after splenectomy. *Menhibrix* is only for high risk infants ages 6 weeks-18 months.	Store in refrigerator. Do not freeze. Shake the prefilled syringe or vial before use. Give IM.

Hepatitis-Containing Vaccines

HepA: *Havrix, Vaqta* **HepB: *Engerix-B, Recombivax HB*** 10, 20, 40 mcg/mL (40 is for dialysis patients) **HepA-HepB: *Twinrix*** DTaP-HepB-IPV: *Pediarix*	**Hep A** Hep A is given to children at 1 year of age as a routine vaccination (2 doses). Hep A is given to adults: men who have sex with men, IV drug abusers, chronic disease, travelers to countries with high Hep A incidence. **Hep B** Hep B is a 3-dose series given at 0, 1 and 6 months for all children and adolescents, and certain adults: health care workers (required by OSHA), men who have sex with men, anyone who has sex with multiple partners, IV drug users, ESRD, chronic liver disease, diabetes (19-59 yrs).	Store in refrigerator. Do not freeze. Shake the vial or prefilled syringe before use. Give IM.

Human Papillomavirus Vaccines: Prevents ~90% of cervical cancers, as well as vulvar, vaginal, oropharyngeal and anal cancers.

HPV2: *Cervarix* Bivalent vaccine. Only provides immunity against the HPV strains that cause cancer. Female only. **HPV4: *Gardasil* (4-valent)** Quadrivalent vaccine. Provides immunity against HPV strains responsible for causing certain cancers and genital warts. **HPV9: *Gardasil* (9-valent)** Either vaccine recommended for females. Only *Gardasil* 4 or 9 is indicated for males.	HPV vaccine is indicated for females age 9-26 years. <u>ACIP recommends the 3 dose series between the age of 11-12 years, with catch-up vaccination at age 13-26 years. Vaccination can begin at age 9 years and ideally prior to sexual activity.</u> <u>Males 9-26 years to reduce the likelihood of genital warts or anal cancers. (HPV4 or HPV9).</u> <u>Requires 3 doses.</u> The 2nd dose is 1-2 months after the 1st and the 3rd 6 months after the 1st. Primary prevention of cervical CA is via vaccination. PAP smears are still necessary in sexually active women. Cervical CA has high mortality. *Gardasil* 4-valent is being replaced by *Gardasil 9*; both will be available initially.	Store in refrigerator. Do not freeze. Protect from light. Shake the prefilled syringe or vial before use. Give IM. Caution for fainting (similar risk to other vaccines); administer to seated patient and monitor after vaccination.

Vaccines Continued

VACCINE	ADMINISTER TO	STORAGE/ADMINISTRATION

Influenza Vaccines: Most illness occurs in young children, most severe illness occurs in people > 65 years or those with comorbid conditions. See the influenza section at the end of this chapter for additional information.

LAIV (Live Attenuated Influenza Virus) Quadrivalent nasal spray: For healthy people ages 2-49 years *FluMist* **IIV (Inactivated Influenza Vaccine given IM)** Quadrivalent, grown in eggs: *Fluarix, Flulaval, Fluzone* Trivalent, grown in eggs (IIV3): Various ages (youngest 6 months), grown in eggs *Afluria, Fluarix, Flulaval, Fluvirin, Fluzone* Trivalent, grown in cell culture (ccIIV3): Approved for ≥ 18 years *Flucelvax* Trivalent, high-dose, grown in eggs (IIV3): Approved for age ≥ 65 years *Fluzone High-Dose* **RIV3 (Trivalent, Recombinant Egg-Free)** Approved for ≥ 18 years *Flublok* **IIV (Inactivated Influenza Vaccine given intradermal)** Quadrivalent, grown in eggs: Approved for ages 18-64 years (IIV4) *Fluzone Intradermal* **Adjuvanted Inactivated Influenza vaccine** Trivalent, grown in eggs: Approved for ages ≥ 65 years (ACIP review pending as of 12/2015)	The CDC recommends that everyone 6 months of age and older get a seasonal flu vaccine. The CDC does not have a preference for any particular flu vaccine, when used within FDA indications. Children aged 6 months through 8 years who have not previously received a total of ≥ 2 doses of influenza vaccine before July 1, 2015 require 2 doses for 2015–16 given 4 weeks apart. Seasonal vaccine recommendations are updated annually and can be found at www.cdc.gov. Chronic, non-immunocompromising illnesses are a precaution, not a contraindication to the use of LAIV4, and LAIV4 has specific indications when it can be used: healthy (no underlying medical conditions that predisposes them to influenza complications), in ages 2-49 years. Trivalent flu vaccines protect against three influenza viruses: two influenza A's (an H1N1 and an H3N2) and one influenza B. The quadrivalent flu vaccines protect against two influenza A's and two influenza B's. *Fluzone Intradermal* uses smaller needle (30 gauge, 1.5 mm vs 22 to 25 gauge, 15.8-38.1 mm), but more redness, swelling, itching. Pregnancy Category B (other influenza shots are Pregnancy Category C).	Store in the refrigerator. Do not freeze. Give vaccine as soon as it is available, even if it arrives in late summer and preferably before October. Offer throughout the influenza season; outbreaks usually peak by February, but can be later. Revaccinate each year. The adjuvanted formulation contains an oil-in-water emulsion of MF59, to improve antibody response. **PRECAUTIONS:** 1. Defer if patient has a moderate-severe acute illness. 2. Refer to physician if patient had Guillain-Barré within 6 weeks of a prior dose of flu vaccine. Those who can eat lightly cooked eggs without reactions or if they experience only hives after eating eggs can receive inactivated vaccine and be observed for 30 minutes. See "Allergy to Vaccine Components" for details. *Flublok* is completely egg-free (recombinant vaccine). *Afluria*: Note the product is labeled for children > 5 years old, but ACIP recommends giving it after age 9 years or older due to reports of febrile seizure in young children. If vaccine shortage occurs, discuss risks/benefits of using *Afluria* in younger children with parents. Can be given with needle-free jet injector. *FluMist Quadrivalent* is given as 0.2 mL, divided between the two nostrils; see diagram later in chapter.

Vaccines Continued

VACCINE	ADMINISTER TO	STORAGE/ADMINISTRATION

Measles, Mumps and Rubella-Containing Vaccines

MMR: *M-M-R II* MMRV: *ProQuad*	Given to children and non-immune adults. *ProQuad*: 12 months-12 years. Adults born before 1957 generally are considered immune to measles and mumps. Healthcare providers born before 1957 must prove immunity or receive 2 doses MMR vaccine at least 4 weeks apart. Live vaccine, not used in pregnancy.	MMR: Store in refrigerator or freezer. MMRV: Store in freezer only due to varicella component. Always store diluents in refrigerator. Protect from light. Give SC.

Meningococcal Vaccines

MCV4: **Menactra, Menveo** MPSV4: **Menomune** Adults usually 1 dose; revaccination if high-risk: HIV+, asplenia, complement component deficiencies. In high-risk the conjugate vaccine (MCV4) is preferred. MenB-4c: *Bexsero* 10-25 years MenB-FHbp: *Trumenba* 10-25 years	Vaccinate: ■ 1 dose for 11-12 year old adolescents with one booster dose at age 16-18 years. ■ 2-55 years old if at high risk, such as: College freshman in dormitories, asplenia/sickle cell disease, military service, immunodeficiencies (specifically complement deficiency), travelers to high-risk countries like the meningitis belt in Sub-Saharan Africa, lab workers with *N. meningitidis* exposure. People with continued risk of meningococcal disease should be revaccinated every 5 years. *Menomune*: ≥ 2 years *Menactra*: 9 months-55 years *Menveo*: 2 months-55 years *Bexsero*: 2 dose series 1 month apart, *Trumenba*: 3 dose series (0, 2, 6 months), either for ≥ 10 years in specific groups requiring protection against invasive meningococcal disease.	Store in refrigerator. Protect from light. MCV give IM, MPSV give SC. *Menactra, Menveo & Menomune*: Both vials (the powder and the diluent) contain vaccine; use only the supplied diluent for reconstitution. *Bexsero* or *Trumenba* cover the group b strain and are used in addition to one of the other meningococcal vaccines. Required by Saudi Arabia for travel to the Hajj and Umrah pilgrimages; must have proof of vaccination.

Pneumococcal Vaccines

13-valent conjugate vaccine (PCV13): *Prevnar 13* **23-valent polysaccharide vaccine (PPSV23):** *Pneumovax 23*	PCV13: All children < 6 years, all adults > 64 years, Minimum age at immunization: 6 weeks PPSV23: All adults > 64 years and some children and adults age 2-64 years Minimum age at immunization: 2 years; PPSV23 does not invoke immunity in patients < 2 years old. See below for recommendations.	Store in refrigerator. Do not freeze. Shake the vial or prefilled syringe prior to use. Do not mix with other vaccines in the same syringe. **PCV13** Give IM. **PPSV23** Give IM or SC.

Universal Concepts

■ Patients who received the PCV13 pediatric series: it is not recommended to receive any more PCV13 doses for life.

■ Patients > 6 years old who never received the PCV13 pediatric series and are indicated now: it is recommended to receive only 1 lifetime dose of PCV13.

■ The maximum number of PPSV23 doses is 2 before 65 age years (spaced at least 5 years apart), and 1 after age 65 years (maximum 3 lifetime doses).

Vaccines Continued

VACCINE	ADMINISTER TO	STORAGE/ADMINISTRATION

Summary of *Prevnar 13* **(PCV13)/***Pneumovax 23* **(PPSV23) Recommendations**

AGE	PATIENT POPULATIONS	REGIMEN	CLINICAL EXAMPLE
2 – 15 months	All children	PCV13 – 4 doses Schedule: 2, 4, 6, 12-15 months	Any newborn with or without comorbidities should receive the PCV13 series (see schedule at left).
2 – 5 years	High risk children with altered immunocompetence*	PPSV23 – 2 doses Sequence: PPSV23 → 5 years → PPSV23	A 3 year old female with sickle cell disease should get PPSV23 x 2 (see sequence at left).
2 – 64 years	High risk, with no altered immunocompetence*	PPSV23 – 1 dose before age 65	A 50 year old patient newly diagnosed with diabetes should get PPSV23 x1.
6 – 64 years	High risk children and adults with altered immunocompetence	PCV13 – 1 dose if no previous PCV13 PPSV23 – 2 doses Sequence: PCV13 → 8 weeks → PPSV23 → 5 years → PPSV23**	A 43 year old patient newly diagnosed with HIV should get PCV13 x1, then PPSV23 x2 (see sequence at left).
≥ 65 years	All adults	PCV13 – 1 dose, if no previous PCV13 PPSV23 – 1 dose Sequence: <u>PCV13 → 1 year → PPSV23</u>***	A 65 year old patient should get PCV13 now, then PPSV23 (see sequence at left).

* See table in MMWR Weekly (June 28, 2013 / 62(25);521-524) www.cdc.gov/mmwr/preview/mmwrhtml/mm6225a3.htm

** If PPSV23 has been received but PCV13 has not, administer 1 dose of PCV13 at least 8 weeks after the most recent dose of PPSV23 (PPSV23 → 8 weeks → PCV13)

*** If have not received PCV13 but have received a dose of PPSV23 at age 65 years or older: Administer PCV13 at least 1 year after the dose of PPSV23 received at age 65 years or older (PPSV23 → 1 year → PCV13)

Poliovirus-Containing Vaccines

IPV: *IPOL* DTaP-HepB-IPV: *Pediarix* DTaP-IPV: *Kinrix, Quadracel* DTaP-IPV/Hib: *Pentacel*	Vaccine series to ALL children.	**Inactivated Poliomyelitis Vaccines (IPV)** Store in refrigerator. Do not freeze. Shake the prefilled syringe or vial before use. Give IM or SC.

Rotavirus Vaccines

RV1: *Rotarix* RV5: *RotaTeq*	Oral vaccine series given to all infants. Do not initiate the series after age 15 weeks.	Store in refrigerator. Do not freeze. Protect from light. Oral suspensions.

Vaccines Continued

VACCINE	ADMINISTER TO	STORAGE/ADMINISTRATION

Tetanus Toxoid- and Diphtheria Toxoid-Containing Vaccines

The pediatric formulations (with the upper-case D, as in DTaP) have 3-5 times as much of the diphtheria component than the adult formulation. The adult formulations have a lower case d (Tdap, or Td).

VACCINE	ADMINISTER TO	STORAGE/ADMINISTRATION
Td: *Tenivac* DT: *Diphtheria and Tetanus Toxoid*	May be used in wound prophylaxis and for <u>routine boosting Q 10 years</u>. If the wound is <u>deep or dirty</u>, revaccination if <u>more than 5 years</u> since the last dose. They may also require tetanus immunoglobulin (TIG) if no previous tetanus vaccines.	Store in refrigerator. Do not freeze. DT is for primary series in infants and children < 7 years old who have a contraindication to the acellular pertussis antigen. Give IM.
Tdap: *Adacel, Boostrix* See previous table for DTaP series, indicated for children 6 weeks to 6 years of age. Single Tdap dose for ages 7-10 years who were not fully vaccinated with DTaP series (missed dose in series). Tdap is the one time booster for ages 11 years and up with no previous record of Tdap, then one dose of Td every 10 years.	<u>Administer a one-time dose of Tdap to adults who have not received Tdap previously</u>, and as soon as feasible to all 1) pregnant or postpartum women, 2) close contacts of infants younger than age 12 months (e.g., grandparents and child-care providers), and 3) health-care personnel with direct patient contact. <u>Pregnant women (weeks 27-36) should receive Tdap with each pregnancy.</u> If the woman has not been vaccinated or the history is unclear, a 3-dose series is needed (one with Tdap, the other 2 with Td only at 0, 1 month, and 6-12 months). If the woman delivers and has not received vaccination, she should receive it post-delivery. Vaccination protects the baby and mother from pertussis (whooping cough).	All tetanus, diphtheria, and pertussis containing vaccines: Store in refrigerator. Do not freeze. Shake the prefilled syringe or vial before use. Give IM.

Varicella-Containing Vaccines

VACCINE	ADMINISTER TO	STORAGE/ADMINISTRATION
VAR: *Varivax* (chickenpox) **ZOS:** *Zostavax* (herpes zoster/shingles) MMRV: *ProQuad*	Children get varicella vaccine at 12 months & again at 4-6 yrs. All adults without evidence of immunity to varicella should receive <u>2 doses</u> of varicella vaccine at least <u>4 weeks</u> apart. Varicella vaccines are live vaccines; do not use in pregnancy or if immunocompromised. Herpes zoster vaccination (potency 14 times greater than varicella in order to elicit needed immune response). The FDA indication for zoster vaccine is for adults 50+ years. ACIP recommends use in 60+ years. *Zostavax* is indicated for prevention of shingles and not for treatment of active case. Also reduces complications such as severity of postherpetic neuralgia following infections. Vaccinate even if history of zoster infection since you can get it again.	Varicella-containing vaccines have 2 components: vaccine & diluent. Store vaccine <u>in freezer</u> & protect <u>from light</u> (keep in original container). Store diluent <u>in refrigerator</u> or room temp. Do not give if hypersensitivity to <u>gelatin or neomycin</u>. <u>Give SC.</u> Reconstituted; reconstitute immediately upon removal from freezer and inject; short stability. SC injection in adults for vaccines is in the fatty tissue at triceps; see diagram at end of chapter.

NON-ROUTINE VACCINES

DRUG	ADMINISTER TO	STORAGE/ADMINISTRATION
Rabies *Imovax, RabAvert*	May be given preventively if high risk exposure (animal handlers, traveling to high risk area, etc.) or given with rabies exposure.	Reconstitute with provided diluent. Give IM. Refrigerate. Prevention: 3 vaccine doses Exposure, without previous vaccination: Rabies Ig with vaccine x 1, then 3 more vaccine doses Exposure, with previous vaccination: 2 vaccine doses
Typhoid *Vivotif Berna* (oral capsules) Live attenuated vaccine. *Typhim Vi* (Injection) Polysaccharide (inactivated)	Typhoid fever caused by *Salmonella Typhi* exposure from food or drink beverages handled by infected person who is shedding or from contaminated sewage. Travelers from U.S. to Asia, Africa, and Latin America at risk. To reduce risk: "Boil it, cook it, peel it, or forget it."	Live vaccine, capsules <u>refrigerated</u>. 4 capsules: Take 1 capsule PO on alternate days (day 1, 3, 5 & 7); take on an empty stomach with cold or lukewarm water, complete at least 1 week prior to exposure. Injection: Give IM x1 (every 5 years if at risk).
Japanese Encephalitis *Ixiaro*	Not recommended for all travelers to Asia. May be given if spending 1 month+ in endemic areas during transmission season, especially if travel will include rural areas.	2 doses 28 days apart, complete at least 1 week prior to potential exposure. Give IM.
Tuberculosis bacille Calmette-Guerin (BCG)	Not used often in U.S. Often given to infants and small children in countries with higher TB incidence. Weak protection provided by the vaccine for pulmonary TB. Can cause false positive reaction to TB skin test.	Live vaccine.
Yellow Fever *(YF-VAX)* After vaccination provide International Certificate of Vaccination (yellow card) valid 10 days after vaccination, may be required to enter endemic areas.	In tropical and subtropical areas South America and Africa. Transmitted by mosquito. Use insect repellent, wear protective clothing, and consider vaccination.	<u>Give SC</u>. <u>Reconstituted</u>. Live virus vaccine. Contraindicated in patients with a severe (life-threatening) allergy to eggs or gelatin, immunosuppression, or breastfeeding. Avoid donating blood for 2 weeks after receiving vaccine.

Vaccines: Miscellaneous Tips

- The CDC does not recommend using acetaminophen routinely before or at vaccination as it may decrease the immune response. It can be used to treat pain and fever <u>after</u> vaccination.

- Never mix different vaccines in the same syringe yourself.

- Most vaccines can be given simultaneously. If a vaccine is missed, then any 2 live vaccines not given at the same time must be given at least 4 weeks apart.

STORAGE

Store refrigerated vaccines immediately upon arrival. Vaccines are stored in refrigerator and freezer units designed for storing biologics, including vaccines, or the frozen and refrigerated vaccines are stored in separate, free-standing freezer and refrigerator units. At a minimum, a household-style unit can be used if there is a separate exterior door for the freezer and separate thermostats for the freezer and refrigerator. Dormitory-style refrigerators should not be used. Keep a calibrated thermometer or a digital data logger connected to a glycol encased probe in the refrigerator and freezer. Post "Do Not Unplug" signs next to electrical outlets and "Do Not Stop Power" signs near circuit breakers to maintain a consistent power source. Store vaccines on the shelves away from the walls. Vaccines should never be stored in the door of the freezer or refrigerator as the temperature there is unstable. Read and document refrigerator and freezer temperatures at least twice each workday: in the morning and before the end of the workday. The CDC recommends using glycol encased probes and digital data loggers for more accurate temperature assessment and monitoring. Keep temperature logs for at least 3 years. Rotate stock so vaccine and diluent with the earliest expiration date is used first. Place vaccine with the longest expiration date behind the vaccine that will expire the soonest.

Staff can easily confuse the vaccines within the storage unit. Use labels & separate containers.

Store refrigerated vaccines between 35°F and 46°F (2°C and 8°C). Store frozen vaccines between -58°F and +5°F (-50°C and -15°C).

ADMINISTRATION

See the chart at the end of this chapter for injection technique. In adults intramuscular (IM) injections are given in the deltoid muscle at the central and thickest portion above the level of the armpit and below the acromion (emerging evidence suggests providers may be giving IM vaccines too high on the deltoid, make sure to give in the thickest, most central part of the deltoid). Adults require a 1" needle (or a 1½" needle for women greater than 200 lbs or men greater than 260 pounds). Use a 22-25 gauge needle inserted at a 90 degree angle. The higher the gauge, the thinner the needle.

Subcutaneous (SC) vaccinations are given in the fatty tissue over the triceps with a 5/8", 23-25 gauge needle at a 45 degree angle.

Administering Vaccines to Adults:
Dose, Route, Site, and Needle Size

VACCINE	DOSE	ROUTE
Hepatitis A (HepA)	≤18 yrs: 0.5 mL ≥19 yrs: 1.0 mL	IM
Hepatitis B (HepB)	≤19 yrs: 0.5 mL ≥20 yrs: 1.0 mL	IM
HepA-HepB (Twinrix)	≥18 yrs: 1.0 mL	IM
Human papillomavirus (HPV)	0.5 mL	IM
Influenza, live attenuated (LAIV)	0.2 mL (0.1 mL into each nostril)	NAS (Intranasal spray)
Influenza, inactivated (IIV) and recombinant (RIV)	0.5 mL	IM
Influenza (IIV) Fluzone Intradermal, for ages 18 through 64 years	0.1 mL	ID (Intradermal)
Measles, Mumps, Rubella (MMR)	0.5 mL	SubCut
Meningococcal conjugate (MenACWY)	0.5 mL	IM
Meningococcal protein (MenB)	0.5 mL	IM
Meningococcal serogroup B (MenB)	0.5 mL	IM
Meningococcal polysaccharide (MPSV)	0.5 mL	SubCut
Pneumococcal conjugate (PCV13)	0.5 mL	IM
Pneumococcal polysaccharide (PPSV)	0.5 mL	IM or SubCut
Tetanus, Diphtheria (Td) with Pertussis (Tdap)	0.5 mL	IM
Varicella (VAR)	0.5 mL	SubCut
Zoster (HZV)	0.65 mL	SubCut

Intramuscular (IM) injection

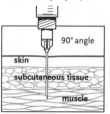

90° angle

skin

subcutaneous tissue

muscle

Subcutaneous (SubCut) injection

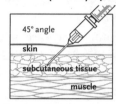

45° angle

skin

subcutaneous tissue

muscle

Intradermal (ID) administration of Fluzone ID vaccine

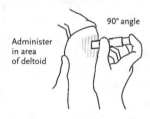

90° angle

Administer in area of deltoid

Intranasal (NAS) administration of Flumist (LAIV) vaccine

NOTE: Always refer to the package insert included with each biologic for complete vaccine administration information. CDC's Advisory Committee on Immunization Practices (ACIP) recommendations for the particular vaccine should be reviewed as well. Access the ACIP recommendations at www.immunize.org/acip.

Injection Site and Needle Size

Subcutaneous (SubCut) injection – Use a 23–25 gauge, ⁵/8" needle. Inject in fatty tissue over triceps.

Intramuscular (IM) injection – Use a 22–25 gauge needle. Inject in deltoid muscle of arm. Choose the needle length as indicated below:

Gender/Weight	Needle Length	
Female or male less than 130 lbs	⁵/8"*–1"	* A ⁵/8" needle may be used for patients weighing less than 130 lbs (<60 kg) for IM injection in the deltoid muscle **only** if the subcutaneous tissue is not bunched and the injection is made at a 90-degree angle.
Female or male 130–152 lbs	1"	
Female 153–200 lbs	1–1¹/2"	
Male 153–260 lbs	1–1¹/2"	
Female 200+ lbs	1¹/2"	
Male 260+ lbs	1¹/2"	

INFLUENZA

Influenza (the flu) is the most common vaccine preventable illness in the U.S. Make sure patients know:

- The influenza vaccine cannot cause the flu. They may get a sore arm, or mild systemic reactions that go away.

- Chronic diseases are a precaution to receiving the intranasal live-attenuated influenza vaccine (LAIV).

- Everyone 6 months and older should be vaccinated annually – patients at highest risk will get vaccinated first if there is a vaccine shortage; check the CDC vaccination website if a shortage is present.

- Pregnant women are at risk for severe disease and should be vaccinated.

- Individuals can and should be vaccinated for influenza even if it is late in the season.

Influenza A and B are the two types of influenza viruses that cause epidemic human disease. Influenza A viruses are further categorized into subtypes on the basis of two surface antigens: hemagglutinin and neuraminidase. Immunity to the surface antigens, particularly the hemagglutinin, reduces the likelihood of infection and severity of disease if infection occurs. Frequent development of antigenic variants through antigenic drift is the virologic basis for seasonal epidemics and is the reason the influenza vaccine generally changes from year to year. It is given annually. More dramatic antigenic changes, or shifts, occur approximately every 30 years and can result in the emergence of a novel influenza virus with the potential to cause a pandemic.

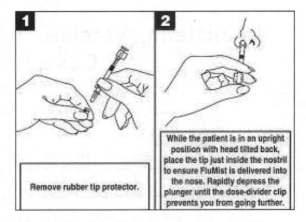

Influenza (inactivated) injection – annually, each fall

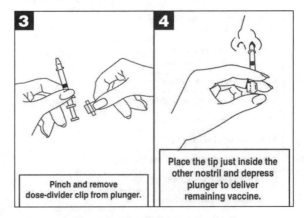

Influenza – live nasal vaccine, annually, each fall, if healthy, ages 2-49 years

The virus spreads from person to person, primarily through respiratory droplet transmission. This can happen when an infected person coughs or sneezes in close proximity to an uninfected person. If someone sneezes in their hands and touches something it is possible to spread illness. Influenza illness is characterized by the abrupt onset of these symptoms: fever, myalgia, headache, malaise, nonproductive cough, sore throat, and rhinitis. Among children, otitis media, nausea, and vomiting also are commonly reported with influenza illness.

Uncomplicated influenza illness typically resolves after 3 – 7 days for the majority of persons, although cough and malaise can persist for more than 2 weeks. However, for certain people, influenza can exacerbate underlying medical conditions (e.g., pulmonary or cardiac disease), lead to secondary bacterial pneumonia or primary influenza viral pneumonia (older and immunocompromised), and ultimately hospitalization and death. See the Infectious Diseases 3 chapter for antiviral medications in influenza.

TRAVELERS

We gratefully acknowledge the assistance of Catrina Derderian, BS, PharmD, BCACP, Clinical Pharmacist, Cambridge Health Alliance, in preparing this chapter.

BACKGROUND

International travel involves millions of travelers to all places in the world. Reasons for international travel are diverse, including tourism, business and research, study abroad, and visiting with family. Each of these distinct travel purposes predisposes the traveler to higher risks of certain diseases. Travelers often do not recognize the associated health risks and may not seek consultation with an appropriate healthcare professional prior to travel. Pharmacists are accessible, and many now provide formal advice to the traveling public, administer and supply travel vaccines, and provide malaria prophylaxis and other medications. Consultative services provided by pharmacists can include educational awareness of country-specific risks, and ways to prevent and address them.

Patients should be advised to <u>pack medications and medical supplies in carry-on luggage</u> and stored in the original prescription containers. They should bring copies of all prescriptions and a <u>list of all medications and medical conditions</u>. It is prudent for travelers to check with their health insurance company to find out if their policy will cover medical care internationally or while on board a ship. Travel health information, including insurance recommendations, is available on the CDC's travel information website where the "<u>Yellow Book</u>" (the CDC's <u>standard resource on travel information)</u> is located. Travel advisories and visa requirements can be checked on the U.S. State Department website. Additional information on vaccinations is in the Immunizations chapter.

GUIDELINES/REFERENCES

Centers for Disease Control (CDC) Center on Travelers Health. Available at http://wwwnc.cdc.gov/travel (accessed 2015 Sept 9).

International Society of Travel Medicine (ISTM), Pharmacist Professional Group of the ISTM, Available at www.istm.org (accessed 2015 Sept 9).

MAJOR CONCERNS FOR TRAVELING INDIVIDUALS

When preparing a patient for travel, a few matters are routinely considered. Common concerns include 1) diseases spread through <u>food and water</u>, 2) diseases spread through <u>blood and bodily fluids</u>, and 3) diseases transmitted by <u>insects</u>. Traveler's risk for contracting disease should be assessed based upon travel duration, country and region specific risks, patient itinerary, and patient specific health concerns.

Diseases Transmitted through Contaminated Food and Water

Travelers' Diarrhea Prevention

Contracting travelers' diarrhea (TD) is the most common concern of patients who travel abroad. TD is caused by unclean food and/or water, and usually presents as 3 or more unformed stools per day plus 1 or more associated symptoms, such as abdominal cramping. Symptoms usually occur within 6 - 72 hours if caused by a bacterial or viral pathogen. Most cases of TD (> 80%) are <u>bacterial</u> and <u>E. coli</u> is the primary bacterial pathogen. Travelers to developing countries are at highest risk due to limited access to sanitary water and inadequate practices for handling foods. Areas of highest risk include most of Asia, the Middle East, Africa, Mexico, and Central and South America.

Safe food and water habits can reduce risk. The adage <u>"cook it, peel it, or forget it"</u> when discussing food consumption is helpful. The following food and water precautions can be recommended:

- Eat only food that is cooked and served hot. Avoid food that has been sitting on a buffet.

- Avoid raw or undercooked meats and fish.

- Eat raw fruits and vegetables only if washed in clean water or peeled (e.g., oranges).

- When drinking water, buy it bottled or bring it to a boil for approximately 1 minute before drinking. Avoid ice.

- Keep hands clean; wash hands often with soap and water, especially after using the bathroom and before eating. If soap and water are not available, use an alcohol-based hand sanitizer. Keep hands out of the mouth.

Eating at well known restaurants may help reduce risk. Poor hygiene practice in small, local restaurants can increase the risk of contracting TD. <u>Hydration is essential</u> for all TD cases. In serious cases with prolonged diarrhea or vomiting, oral rehydration solution can be used for fluid replacement. The packets are available in pharmacies throughout the world and can be prepared by mixing 1 packet with 1 liter of boiled purified water. <u>Over-the-counter loperamide *(Imodium)* can be used to decrease the frequency and urgency of bowel movements</u>, and can make it easier for a person with diarrhea to ride on a bus or airplane while waiting for an antibiotic to take effect. It should <u>not be used in children < 2 years old without a physician's authorization</u> due to the risk of toxic megacolon. Another option to help symptoms of TD is bismuth subsalicylate, which is the active ingredient in *Pepto Bismol*. Bismuth subsalicylate can reduce the incidence of TD by ~50%.

Bismuth subsalicylate (which is a salicylate) should not be used with <u>anticoagulants or with a salicylate allergy</u>, with renal insufficiency, or in children who are < 12 years old or who may have a viral infection (due to the risk of Reye's syndrome). Patients should be aware that the tongue (and possibly stool) can <u>blacken</u>, which resolves with drug discontinuation. If used excessively or with other salicylates, toxicity could occur, and can present as tinnitus.

TD caused by a bacterial infection can be treated with a quinolone or other antibiotic; refer to the Infectious Diseases chapters. Untreated bacterial diarrhea can last 3 - 7 days.

Typhoid Fever

Typhoid fever is caused by the bacterium *Salmonella* Typhi. The disease is potentially severe and can be life-threatening. The highest areas of risk for contracting typhoid fever include east and southeast Asia, Africa, the Caribbean, and Central and South America.

Humans are the only source of the bacteria, which is shed through feces and spread primarily through <u>consumption of water or food that has been contaminated by the feces</u> of someone with either <u>an acute infection</u> or from a <u>chronic, asymptomatic carrier</u>.

The incubation period of typhoid (and paratyphoid infection, a similar disease) is 6 – 30 days. Symptoms of illness include gradually increasing fatigue, malaise, fever, earache and anorexia, with possible hepatosplenomegaly. A transient, macular rash may be present on the trunk. Intestinal hemorrhage or perforation can occur 2 – 3 weeks later and can be fatal.

Typhoid vaccines are recommended but are only 50 – 80% effective; therefore, even vaccinated travelers should follow safe food and water precautions and wash hands frequently. These precautions are the only prevention method for paratyphoid fever, for which there is no vaccine. There are two typhoid vaccines: *Vivotif Berna*, taken as oral capsules, or *Typhim Vi*, an intramuscular injection.

Vivotif Berna is an oral, live, attenuated vaccine and consists of 4 capsules, 1 taken every other day. The capsules are refrigerated (not frozen). Each capsule is taken with cool liquid (not warm), 1 hour before a meal. The oral vaccine should not be considered if a patient is on antibiotics or has an extremely sensitive stomach. The regimen should be completed 1 week prior to travel and is not used in children < 6 years. Revaccination is recommended every 5 years.

Typhim VI, the injectable vaccine, is one 0.5-mL dose given intramuscularly ≥ 2 weeks before the expected exposure. The injectable vaccination is not recommended for children < 2 years. Revaccination with *Typhim VI* is recommended every 2 years.

Hepatitis A

Hepatitis A is one of the most common vaccine-preventable infections acquired during international travel. Persons from developed countries who travel to developing countries are at highest risk. The virus is transmitted when a person ingests fecal matter, even in microscopic amounts, from objects, food, or drinks contaminated by the feces of an infected person. Once infected, the presentation is either asymptomatic or can have symptoms of fever, malaise, jaundice, nausea and abdominal discomfort that can persist for up to 7 weeks. Symptomatic presentation is less common in children.

Vaccination is recommended for susceptible travelers to countries with high or intermediate risk of hepatitis A. There are two monovalent (hepatitis A only) vaccines *(Havrix, Vaqta)* and a combination hepatitis A/B vaccine *(Twinrix)*. *Havrix* and *Vaqta* are both 2 dose series and approved for those > 12 months. *Twinrix* is a 3 dose series approved for adults > 18 years of age. No booster is required for either Hepatitis A vaccine. Immunoglobulin is given with the Hepatitis A vaccine in some high-risk groups.

Diseases Transmitted Through Blood and Bodily Fluids

Hepatitis B

Hepatitis B is transmitted through contact with contaminated blood or other body fluids. The risk for travelers who do not participate in high risk behaviors is low. Hepatitis B has an incubation period of about 90 days. Infection may present as malaise, jaundice, nausea and abdominal discomfort. Chronic infection with Hepatitis B can result in chronic liver disease and liver cancer.

Vaccination for Hepatitis B is extremely important to consider for travelers who plan to have sexual encounters with new partners, patients who may be traveling to receive medical care, or patients who may be volunteering to provide medical work. Piercings and tattoos can transmit the virus and should be avoided.

The vaccine is a 3-dose series on a 0-, 1-, and 6-month schedule. Due to the extended amount of time needed to receive the full vaccination series, many travelers are unable to receive all three doses before departure. Therefore, as many doses as possible should be administered before departure and the series should be completed when the traveler returns to the U.S. In instances of high risk, an accelerated series may be administered. There are three vaccines available for traveling adults; the single antigen vaccines *(Engerix-B, Recombivax HB)* and the Hepatitis A/B *Twinrix* combination. Boosters are not recommended for vaccinated individuals with normal immune status.

Diseases Transmitted By Insect Bites

Insects that transmit disease are vectors; a vector carries the disease to an individual, causing infection. A reservoir is any place (such as an animal, insect, soil or plant) in which the disease lives and can multiply. The primary insect that causes infection to travelers are various types of mosquitos, which carry parasites for Japanese encephalitis, yellow fever, dengue and malaria. The tsetse fly spreads African sleeping sickness. Insect bites should be avoided as much as possible.

Mosquito-Borne Illness Prevention: Recommendations to Reduce Insect Bites

- Stay and sleep in screened or air-conditioned rooms.

- Cover exposed skin by wearing long-sleeved shirts, long pants and hats.

- Use a bed net, which can be pre-treated with mosquito repellant.

- Use proper application of mosquito repellents containing 20% to 50% DEET as the active ingredient on exposed skin and clothing. DEET also protects against ticks. Other insect repellants that can be used topically for mosquitos (but not for ticks) are picaridin, oil of lemon, eucalyptus or IR3535. Permethrin can be used to treat clothing, gear and bed nets but should not be applied directly to the skin.

Dengue: No Vaccine, Transmitted By Mosquito

Dengue is transmitted between people by the mosquitoes *Aedes aegypti* and *Aedes albopictus*. In many parts of the tropics and subtropics, dengue is endemic; it occurs every year, usually during a season when mosquito populations are high and rainfall is optimal for breeding. Sequential infections put people at greater risk for dengue hemorrhagic fever and dengue shock syndrome, both of which can be fatal. Protection from mosquito bites with non-drug measures (mentioned above) are essential since there are no vaccines available against dengue, and there are no specific medications to treat a dengue infection.

Malaria: Prophylactic Medication Available, Transmitted By Mosquito

Cases of malaria in travelers has been increasing over the past 4 years. Malaria is transmitted by the *Anopheles* mosquito. It is endemic in Asia, Latin America, North Africa, Eastern Europe, and the South Pacific. *Plasmodium vivax* is the most common of four human malaria species (*P. falciparum*, *P. malariae*, *P. ovale*, and *P. vivax*). *P. vivax* causes up to 65% of malaria cases in India and is becoming increasingly resistant to malaria drugs. By contrast, *P. falciparum* is the most deadly species and the subject of most malaria-related research. The CDC website includes maps of malaria presence by country and the species of malaria, and specific medication recommendations for that area. Recommendations may change year-to-year.

DRUG	DOSING	SAFETY/SIDE EFFECTS/MONITORING
Atovaquone/Proquanil *(Malarone)* For *P. falciparum*, all areas, including chloroquine-resistant Advantages: Well tolerated Start right before travel Short treatment Disadvantages: Daily dosing Not used in pregnancy Cost	Adult prophylactic dose: 250/100 mg PO daily with food or milk Start: 1-2 days pre-travel Stop: 7 days post-travel	**CONTRAINDICATIONS** Do not use for prophylaxis with CrCl < 30 mL/min **SIDE EFFECTS** Abdominal pain, nausea, headache, ↑LFTs **NOTES** Consider monitoring LFTs and renal function Per CDC, not recommended in pregnancy

Malaria Drugs Continued

DRUG	DOSING	SAFETY/SIDE EFFECTS/MONITORING
Mefloquine *(Lariam)* For *P. falciparum*, all areas, including chloroquine-resistant Advantages: Once weekly dosing Used in pregnancy Disadvantages: Start 1-2 weeks prior to travel Long treatment (for short trip) Side effects	Adult prophylactic dose: 250 mg PO weekly with food and water Start: 2-3 weeks pre-travel Stop: 4 weeks post-travel	**BOXED WARNING** Neuropsychiatric effects; discontinue if symptoms occur during treatment **WARNINGS** Arrhythmias, QT prolongation, agranulocytosis/aplastic anemia, caution with liver impairment **CONTRAINDICATIONS** Seizure history **SIDE EFFECTS** Chills, dizziness, fatigue, nausea **MONITORING** Psychiatric symptoms: anxiety, depression, hallucinations Neurologic symptoms: dizziness, tinnitus, loss of balance, seizures)
Chloroquine *(Aralen)* Advantages: Once weekly dosing Long trip itineraries May already take for rheumatoid arthritis Used in pregnancy Disadvantages: Long treatment (for short trip) Start 1-2 weeks prior to travel	Adult prophylactic dose: 500 mg PO weekly with food CrCl < 10 mL/min: 50% dose, or do not use Start: 1-2 weeks pre-travel Stop: 4 weeks post-travel	**WARNINGS** Retinopathy, macular degeneration: discontinue with retinal changes/blurry vision Arrhythmias, QT prolongation Skeletal muscle myopathy/weakness, extrapyramidal reactions, hematologic effects (agranulocytosis, others) **SIDE EFFECTS** Nausea, exacerbation of psoriasis, anxiety, visual changes/damage, hearing loss/tinnitus, alopecia. blue-gray skin pigmentation Uncommon: risk rash/DRESS syndrome **MONITORING** CBC with long-term use, seizures, hepatic damage, auditory damage, blood disorders **NOTES** Avoid use with hypersensitivity to quinine compounds, G6PD+ (risk hemolytic anemia, bleeding)
Primaquine For *P. vivax, P. ovale, P. falciparum* Advantages: Short treatment Start right before travel—if G6PD ruled out Disadvantages: Daily dosing Not used in pregnancy	30 mg Q daily for prophylaxis Take with food to ↓ nausea CDC requires screening for G6PD prior to use Start: 1 day pre-travel Stop: 7 days post-travely	**CONTRAINDICATIONS** Concurrent drugs that can cause hemolytic anemia or bone marrow suppression/agranulocytosis, current or recent use of quinacrine, acute illness **WARNINGS** Hemolytic anemia, other hematologic effects, arrhythmias/QT prolongation **SIDE EFFECTS** Nausea **NOTES** Per CDC, not recommended in pregnancy

Malaria Drugs Continued

DRUG	DOSING	SAFETY/SIDE EFFECTS/MONITORING
Doxycycline *(Vibramycin)* For *P. falciparum*, all areas, including chloroquine-resistant Advantages: Long trip itineraries Last minute travelers (start 1-2 days prior) Inexpensive May already take for acne Disadvantages: Long treatment (for short trip) Side effects Not used in pregnancy	100 mg Q daily for prophylaxis Take with food to ↓ nausea Start: 1-2 days pre-travel Stop: 4 weeks post-travel	**CONTRAINDICATIONS** Pregnancy, children < 8 years **SIDE EFFECTS** Nausea, photosensitivity See Infectious Disease chapter for further information.

Japanese Encephalitis: Vaccine Available, Transmitted By Mosquito

The Japanese Encephalitis (JE) vaccination is sometimes recommended with travel to Asia and parts of the western Pacific. JE can cause asymptomatic infection, or can develop into encephalitis, with rigors and risk of seizures, coma and death. Travelers are most likely to become infected when visiting rural agricultural areas. The best prevention is to reduce exposure to mosquitos. The vaccine is recommended for travelers older than 2 months of age who plan to spend at least 1 month in endemic areas during the JE virus transmission season or for those with extended exposure to the outdoors (e.g., campers). The vaccine (*IXIARO*) is a two-dose series. The last dose should be given at least 1 week before travel. For adults planning additional travel, a booster is recommended 1 year after the primary series.

Yellow Fever: Vaccine Available, Transmitted By Mosquito

Yellow fever is caused by a virus found in tropical and subtropical areas in South America and Africa. Reducing mosquito exposure is essential. Most infections are asymptomatic. If symptoms develop, the initial illness presents as an influenza-like syndrome. Most patients will improve, but ~15% progress to a more toxic form of the disease with risk of shock and organ failure. There is no specific treatment for acute infection except symptomatic relief with fluids, analgesics and antipyretics. Aspirin and other NSAIDs cannot be used due to an increased risk for bleeding. Infected patients should be protected from further mosquito exposure (staying indoors or under a mosquito net) during the first few days of illness, or they will contribute to the transmission cycle.

Vaccination is rcommended only in travelers who are at a high risk of exposure or who require proof of vaccination to enter a country. This is due to the high risk of serious adverse effects after the vaccination, including low grade fever, headache, and in rare cases, yellow fever vaccine-associated neurologic disease. After vaccination, the patient is provided an "International Certificate of Vaccination or Prophylaxis", which is called the "yellow fever card." The card is valid only if the vaccination is completed 10 days before arrival.

The vaccine is contraindicated in infants < 6 months who are at higher risk for significant complications, and in patients with hypersensitivity to eggs, egg products, chicken proteins or gelatin. Additional contraindications include a thymus disorder or myasthenia gravis. This is a live vaccine and cannot be used with immunosuppression, including HIV patients with a CD4+ count < 200/mm^3, anyone using strong immune-suppressants (TNF-inhibitors, high-dose systemic steroids, certain chemotherapy agents, and IL-1 and IL-6 antagonists). The contraindications and precautions to the yellow fever vaccine should be reviewed prior to administration.

ACIP recommends that a woman wait 4 weeks after receiving the vaccine before conceiving. Yellow fever vaccine safety has not been tested during pregnancy. The CDC recommends advising pregnant women who would require vaccination to avoid travel to at-risk regions.

African Sleeping Sickness: No Vaccine, Transmitted By Tsetse Fly

The tsetse fly lives in sub-Saharan Africa and spreads African sleeping sickness (African trypanosomiasis). Tsetse fly protection is different from mosquito protection. The insect can bite through thin fabric. Clothing should be medium-weight and be neutral in color as the fly is attracted to bright colors, dark colors, metallic fabric and the color blue. Insect repellants described above should be used, but there is limited evidence they work against this insect.

ADDITIONAL CONCERNS FOR TRAVELING INDIVIDUALS

Meningitis

Meningitis is spread by respiratory secretions and is widespread in many parts of the world. Vaccination is recommended by the CDC for people who travel to or reside in countries where *N. meningitidis* is hyperendemic or epidemic, particularly if contact with the local population will be prolonged. Hyperendemic regions include the meningitis belt of Africa during the dry season (December – June). Additionally, the meningococcal vaccine is required by the government of Saudi Arabia for annual travel during the period of the Hajj and Umrah pilgrimages.

Bacterial meningitis has high fatality and is a medical emergency. Patients with symptoms of fever, severe, unrelenting headache, nausea, stiff neck and mental status changes require urgent treatment to avoid the risk of permanent neurological damage and death. There are four vaccines approved for use in the United States. The meningococcal vaccines are a routine part of children's vaccination, and are reviewed in detail in the Immunizations chapter.

Polio

Most people in the U.S. have received polio vaccination as children; regrettably, the virus has not been eradicated and there have been recent outbreaks. Five countries remain endemic (Afghanistan, Nigeria, Cameroon, Somalia and Pakistan). The CDC recommends that adult travelers to regions with wild poliovirus (WPV) receive a single lifetime booster dose. As of May 2015, travelers to polio-infected countries may be required to show proof of polio vaccination when leaving the polio-infected country. The booster should be administered at least 4 weeks prior to travel. Polio vaccination should be documented on an International Certificate of Vaccination (ICVP), which provides proof of vaccination during travel. This documentation is similar to the documentation required for the yellow fever vaccine.

Venous Thromboembolism Prevention

Travelers are at increased risk for deep vein thrombosis (DVT) and pulmonary embolism (PE) due to limited movement with intercontinental air travel. Wearing compression stockings during long trips reduces risk; these are sold in pharmacies. Travelers should be instructed to get up and walk (choosing an aisle seat is helpful) and to perform lower leg exercises when sitting.

Patients should know symptoms of DVT and PE and be instructed to seek immediate medical care if suspected. DVT risk factors, symptoms and treatment are discussed in the Anticoagulation chapter.

Motion Sickness, Altitude Sickness, Jet Lag

Motion Sickness is common among travelers and is discussed in the Motion Sickness chapter. Acute mountain sickness (AMS) occurs when people climb rapidly to a high altitude. It occurs commonly above 8,000 feet and is more likely in individuals who live close to sea level and those who had the condition previously. Primary symptoms are dizziness, headache, tachycardia and shortness of breath.

The primary prophylactic medication is <u>acetazolamide</u> *(Diamox)* 125 mg twice daily, started the day before (preferred) or on the day of ascent. Higher doses are used for treatment. This can improve breathing, but is not without side effects (polyuria, taste alteration, risk of dehydration, photosensitivity, urticaria and a possibility of severe skin rashes). <u>Acetazolamide is contraindicated with a sulfa allergy</u>. Sun protection and hydration is recommended. In acute cases, oxygen, inhaled beta-agonists and dexamethasone is given to reduce cerebral edema.

For treatment of jet lag, refer to the Dietary Supplements chapter.

THE RETURNED TRAVELER

If a patient is ill upon returning from travel, it is imperative that he or she is aware that it is necessary to see a healthcare provider.

Incubation periods of different diseases vary and some symptoms can present weeks or months after the initial infection. Due to extended incubation periods, travelers often return home before their symptoms present, which can lead to epidemics and the spread of disease from country to country.

An example of this is illustrated by the 2014 outbreak of Ebola in West Africa, which was the largest Ebola outbreak in history. Ebola is transmitted by direct contact with blood or bodily fluids of a symptomatic person. The Ebola symptoms (fever, headache, diarrhea, and hemorrhaging) can appear from 2 - 21 days after exposure. It is very likely that a person can be infected, but asymptomatic, when returning to the U.S. Immediate isolation is required to reduce transmission.

Important information for a patient to relay to the healthcare provider includes the travel itinerary (where they went), the trip duration, where they stayed, what they did and what precautions they took to reduce infection risk, including vaccination history prior to leaving the U.S.

RENAL DISEASE

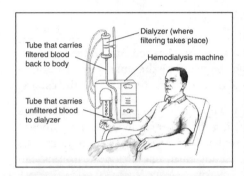

Tube that carries filtered blood back to body

Dialyzer (where filtering takes place)

Hemodialysis machine

Tube that carries unfiltered blood to dialyzer

GUIDELINES/REFERENCES

Kidney Disease: Improving Global Outcomes (KDIGO) CKD Work Group. KDIGO 2012 Clinical Practice Guideline for the Evaluation and Management of Chronic Kidney Disease. *Kidney Inter.*, Suppl. 2013;3:1-150.

Additional guidelines included with the video files (RxPrep Online).

We gratefully acknowledge the assistance of Katie E. Cardone, PharmD, BCACP, FNKF, FASN, Albany Nephrology Pharmacy Group (ANephRx), Albany College of Pharmacy and Health Sciences, in preparing this chapter.

BACKGROUND

The prevalence of chronic kidney disease (CKD) has increased from 12.3% to 14% in the U.S. over the past twenty years. The most common causes of CKD are diabetes and hypertension. Patients with CKD have a higher risk of cardiovascular morbidity and mortality. The pharmacist's role in treating patients with CKD includes modifying medication regimens based on the degree of kidney function, initiating treatment to minimize disease progression and treating the complications of CKD (anemia, bone and mineral metabolism disorders, hypertension and acid-base and electrolyte disturbances).

RENAL PHYSIOLOGY

The nephron is the functional unit of the kidney and there are roughly one million nephrons in each kidney. A primary function of the nephron is to control the concentration of water and Na. The nephrons reabsorb what is needed (to go back into the circulation) and the remainder is excreted as urine. This regulates the blood volume, and in turn, the blood pressure. The parts of the nephron include the glomerulus, the proximal tubule, the loop of Henle, the distal tubule and the collecting duct (see figure on the following page).

Glomerulus

Blood is delivered into the glomerulus, a large filtering unit that is located within Bowman's capsule. Substances with a molecular weight < 40,000 daltons, including most drugs, can pass through the glomerular capillaries into the filtrate. If the glomerulus is healthy, larger substances (e.g., proteins and protein bound drugs) are not filtered and stay in the blood. If the glomerulus is damaged, some albumin passes into the urine. The amount of albumin in the urine can be used to gauge the severity of kidney damage in patients with kidney disease or nephropathy. Glomerular filtration rate (GFR) and degree of proteinuria are used to stage the severity of kidney disease.

Proximal Tubule

Proximal means "close to", and the proximal tubule is the part of the nephron closest to Bowman's capsule. Large amounts of water are reabsorbed here, along with Na, Cl and Ca. The pH is regulated by exchange of hydrogen ions and bicarbonate ions. Water, Na and Cl reabsorption continues further along the nephron.

Loop of Henle

As filtrate moves down the loop of Henle (the descending limb), water is reabsorbed, but Na and Cl ions are not; this increases the concentration of Na and Cl in the lumen (the inside of the nephron "tube"). As the filtrate

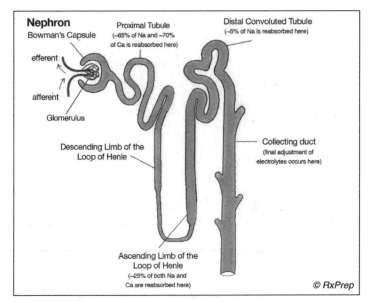

moves up the loop of Henle (the ascending limb), Na and Cl ions are reabsorbed but water is not. If antidiuretic hormone (ADH) is present, water will pass through the walls of the duct and will not be eliminated. The more ADH present, the more water is reabsorbed back into the blood (anti-diuresis).

Loop diuretics inhibit the Na-K pump in the ascending limb of the loop of Henle (the part that goes back up). About 25% of the sodium is reabsorbed here and inhibiting these pumps leads to a significant increase in the tubular concentration of Na and less water is reabsorbed. By blocking the pump, the electrical gradient is altered and reabsorption of Ca decreases. Long-term use of loop diuretics can deplete Ca and have a harmful effect on bone.

Distal Convoluted Tubule

Distal means "farthest away" and the distal convoluted tubule is the farthest away from the entry point to the nephron. The distal tubule is also involved in regulating K, Na, Ca and pH. Thiazide diuretics inhibit the Na-Cl pump in the distal tubule. Only about 5% of the sodium is reabsorbed at this point, which makes thiazides weaker diuretics than loops. Thiazides increase Ca reabsorption by affecting the Ca pump in the distal convoluted tubule. Consequently, the long-term use of thiazide diuretics has a protective effect on bone.

Collecting Duct

The collecting duct is a network of tubules and ducts that connect the nephrons to the ureter. Urine passes from the ureter into the bladder, and from there out of the body via the urethra. The collecting duct is involved with water and electrolyte balance and is affected by levels of ADH and aldosterone. Aldosterone works in the distal tubule to increase Na and water retention and decrease K. By blocking aldosterone (with antagonists like spironolactone or eplerenone), serum K increases.

DRUG-INDUCED KIDNEY DISEASE

Drug-induced kidney disease (DIKD) is linked to numerous medications; it can be acute and reversible if the medication is stopped, but the injury can be irreversible and progress to CKD. DIKD is especially prevalent in the hospital setting and contributes to morbidity and mortality. Risk factors for DIKD include use of multiple nephrotoxic medications, baseline reduction in renal blood flow (e.g., preexisting kidney disease, heart failure, dehydration, hypotension, others), large doses or frequent use of nephrotoxic medications, increased age and others. Common medications associated with DIKD include aminoglycosides, amphotericin B, cisplatin, colistimethate, cyclosporine, loop diuretics, NSAIDs, radiographic contrast dye, tacrolimus and vancomycin.

ESTIMATING KIDNEY FUNCTION

Two common labs used to estimate kidney function are the blood urea nitrogen (BUN) and serum creatinine (SCr). BUN measures the amount of nitrogen that comes from urea, a waste product. As kidney function declines, BUN increases. BUN is not used independently to measure reduced kidney function because other factors besides renal impairment increase BUN (primarily dehydration).

Creatinine, a waste product of muscle metabolism, is easily measured and mostly filtered by the kidneys. The concentration correlates inversely with kidney function; as kidney function decreases, creatinine increases (similar to BUN). The normal range of serum creatinine (SCr) is approximately 0.6 to 1.3 mg/dL. An important issue clinically is that SCr can be decreased in elderly patients with low muscle mass. This is especially true of frail, elderly patients who are bedridden.

Creatinine Clearance Estimation

The Cockcroft-Gault equation for calculating creatinine clearance (CrCl) is the most commonly used equation for estimating kidney function. This equation is reviewed in the Calculations chapter. The accuracy of creatinine-based estimation equations is limited when a patient has very low or high muscle mass, is obese, has liver disease, is pregnant or with other conditions that cause abnormal muscle turnover. In addition, although creatinine is mostly filtered, it is partially secreted. The contribution of tubular secretion to creatinine elimination is more significant when kidney function is impaired. The Cockcroft-Gault formula may not be preferable in very young children, in end-stage renal disease (ESRD) or when renal function is fluctuating rapidly. Drug dosing recommendations provided by manufacturers are generally based on CrCl (calculated with Cockcroft-Gault), while the utility of GFR is mostly in staging kidney disease (see below).

Other Measures of Kidney Function

The gold-standard methods to estimate the GFR utilize inulin or radioactive substances. These markers are largely limited to the research setting due to the cost, inconvenience and the availability of alternative estimation methods. Other equations, such as the MDRD and CKD-EPI equations, provide an estimate of GFR and are recommended to stage CKD. The MDRD-derived GFR is being reported more frequently by many labs. KDIGO recommends staging CKD based on the cause of CKD, the GFR and albuminuria as shown in the tables.

GFR and Albuminuria Categories

GFR (mL/min/1.73m²)	TERMS	GFR CATEGORY (KDIGO 2012)	CKD STAGE (KDOQI 2002)
≥ 90 + kidney damage*	Normal or high	G1	Stage 1
60-89 + kidney damage*	Mild decrease	G2	Stage 2
45-59	Mild - moderate decrease	G3a	Stage 3
30-44	Moderate - severe decrease	G3b	
15-29	Severe decrease	G4	Stage 4
< 15 or dialysis dependent	Kidney failure	G5	Stage 5

*Markers of kidney damage include history of kidney transplant, structural abnormalities on imaging, albuminuria and others

ACR (mg/g) OR AER (mg/24hr)	TERMS	ALBUMINURIA CATEGORY (KDIGO 2012)
< 30	Normal to mild increase (previously called microalbuminuria)	A1
30-300	Moderate increase (previously called microalbuminuria)	A2
> 300	Severe increase (previously called macroalbuminuria)	A3

ACR: albumin to creatinine ratio; AER: albumin excretion rate

Proteinuria, Blood Pressure Control, and the Use of ACE Inhibitors and ARBs

Uncontrolled blood pressure, diabetes and proteinuria are all risk factors for the progression of CKD. Strict glycemic control is critical to preserve kidney function in patients with diabetes. ACE inhibitors or ARBs are used to prevent kidney disease progression in diabetic and non-diabetic patients with proteinuria. According to KDIGO, the goal blood pressure in kidney disease is ≤ 140/90 mmHg if no proteinuria is present (albuminuria category A1) and ≤ 130/80 mmHg if proteinuria is present (categories A2 or A3).

ACE inhibitors and ARBs reduce pressure in the glomerulus, help preserve kidney function, reduce proteinuria and provide cardiovascular protection. These drugs inhibit the renin-angiotensin-aldosterone system (RAAS), causing efferent arteriolar dilation. Note that the use of ACE inhibitors and ARBs can cause a 30% increase in SCr during the initiation of treatment. This rise is generally acceptable and is not a reason to stop treatment. If the SCr increase is > 30%, the treatment should be discontinued and the patient should be evaluated for hemodynamic factors that may need to be addressed. ACE inhibitors or ARBs may cause hyperkalemia. It is important to counsel patients on adherence to potassium-restricted diets in order to maximize the dose of ACE inhibitor/ARB. It is recommended that the serum creatinine and potassium be monitored 1 – 2 weeks after initiating ACE inhibitors or ARBs in patients with CKD. ACE inhibitors and ARBs are discussed in more detail in the Hypertension and Chronic Heart Failure chapters.

MODIFYING DRUG THERAPY

Drug regimens will often require modification (e.g., by a dose reduction and/or extending the interval) in patients with impaired kidney function since some medications can accumulate and cause side effects/toxicity. Medications can directly cause or worsen kidney disease and, in some cases, they can be less effective. Dose reductions reduce peak concentrations but maintain trough concentrations. This strategy is effective for drugs whose pharmacodynamic effect is governed by a minimum concentration over the dosing interval. Beta-lactams are a classic example of drugs that are dosed based on time above the minimum inhibitory concentration (MIC), exhibiting time-dependent killing properties. Extending the interval of a regimen maintains peak concentrations and reduces the trough concentration. This strategy is most useful for drugs that rely on achieving a specific peak concentration, such as quinolones and aminoglycosides, which exhibit concentration-dependent bacterial killing.

SELECT DRUGS THAT REQUIRE ↓ DOSE OR ↑ INTERVAL WITH IMPAIRED KIDNEY FUNCTION

Antimicrobials/Antivirals/Antifungals

Acyclovir, valacyclovir

Amantadine

Amphotericin

Aminoglycosides (↑ dosing interval)

Azole antifungals

Anti-tuberculosis medications ethambutol, pyrazinamide

Aztreonam

Beta-lactam antibiotics (most)

Ganciclovir, valganciclovir

Maraviroc

NRTIs, including tenofovir

Polymyxins

Quinolones (except moxifloxacin)

Sulfamethoxazole/trimethoprim

Vancomycin

Cardiovascular

Antiarrhythmics (digoxin, disopyramide, procainamide, sotalol*)

Dabigatran* (for AFib)

LMWHs (enoxaparin)

Rivaroxaban* (for AFib)

Statins (most)

Pain/Gout

Allopurinol

Colchicine

Gabapentin, pregabalin

Morphine and codeine

Tramadol IR

Gastrointestinal

Famotidine, ranitidine

Metoclopramide

Other

Bisphosphonates*

Cyclosporine

Lithium

*Medication has indication-specific recommendations

COMPLICATIONS IN CHRONIC KIDNEY DISEASE

Anemia of CKD

Erythropoietin is produced by the kidneys and stimulates production of reticulocytes (immature red blood cells) in the bone marrow. As kidney function declines, the production of erythropoietin declines and anemia results. Further exacerbating the problem is a pro-inflammatory state caused by CKD that can result in anemia of chronic disease. Nutritional deficiencies may be present requiring iron, folate or vitamin B12 supplementation. Anemia identification and treatment is discussed in the Anemia chapter. Key points related to anemia treatment in CKD:

SELECT DRUGS THAT ARE CONTRAINDICATED IN KIDNEY IMPAIRMENT		
CrCl < 50 mL/min	Duloxetine	**Other#**
Chlorpropamide	Fondaparinux	Dofetilide
Cidofovir	NSAIDs	Foscarnet
Ribavirin*	Potassium-sparing diuretics	Glyburide
Voriconazole IV		Meperidine
	Ribavirin (product specific)	Metformin
CrCl < 30 mL/min	Rivaroxaban*	Nitrofurantoin
Avanafil	Tadalafil*	Sotalol* *(Betapace AF)*
Bisphosphonates*	Tramadol ER	
Dabigatran*	SGLT2 inhibitors	

*Medication has indication or formulation-specific recommendations
#Not specified, another CrCl cut-off is used, or based on SCr alone

- The treatment of anemia of CKD generally involves a combination of erythropoiesis-stimulating agents (ESAs) and iron supplementation.

- Intravenous iron is preferred over oral iron for patients on hemodialysis, but may also be required for other patients with CKD due to poor iron absorption in the GI tract in advanced CKD.

- ESAs, including epoetin alfa (*Epogen, Procrit*) and darbepoetin alfa (*Aranesp*) are generally necessary to treat anemia of CKD to prevent the need for blood transfusions.

- For patients using ESAs, the serum hemoglobin level should not be corrected to the "normal" level of patients without CKD due to an increased risk of cardiovascular events, stroke and death. See Anemia chapter.

CKD Mineral and Bone Disorder

CKD mineral and bone disorder (CKD-MBD) is common in patients with CKD and affects almost all patients receiving dialysis. Studies have shown an association between CKD-MBD and fractures, cardiovascular disease and mortality. Patients with advanced kidney disease require screening for abnormalities associated with parathyroid hormone (PTH), phosphorus, calcium and vitamin D at regular intervals, according to disease severity. Therapeutic targets for phosphorus, calcium and PTH are dependent on the severity of CKD. The KDIGO CKD-MBD practice guideline suggests maintaining PTH between 2 and 9 times the normal range for patients on dialysis, but fails to provide specific targets for predialysis CKD patients. Calcium should be maintained in the normal range for all CKD patients. Phosphorus should be maintained in the normal range for non-dialysis CKD patients, and "toward" the normal range in dialysis patients.

Hyperphosphatemia

Bone metabolism abnormalities are initially caused by elevations in serum phosphorus, which is renally excreted. To compensate for hyperphosphatemia, the parathyroid gland increases the release of PTH. Elevated PTH concentrations over time lead to secondary hyperparathyroidism and high turnover bone disease (see Drug Mechanisms, Classes & Structures chapter). Treatment of secondary hyperparathyroidism is initially focused on controlling serum phosphorus by restricting dietary phosphate (avoiding dairy products, cola, chocolate and nuts). Eventually, phosphate binders may be required. <u>Phosphate binders bind meal-time phosphate in the gut</u> that is coming from the diet. <u>If a dose is missed</u> (and the food is absorbed), <u>the dose of phosphate binder should be skipped</u>, and the patient should resume normal dosing at the next meal or snack. There are three types of phosphate binders:

- <u>Aluminum-based agents</u> (*ALternaGEL,* others): potent phosphate binders, but aluminum can accumulate in CKD and is <u>toxic</u> to the nervous system and bone, and may lead to "dialysis dementia"; these should only be <u>used short-term, if at all</u>, and are not used commonly.

- <u>Calcium-based agents</u> (primarily calcium acetate and carbonate): effective first line agents for hyperphosphatemia in CKD. <u>The dose-limiting effect is hypercalcemia, which is especially problematic in patients taking vitamin D (which increases calcium absorption)</u>.

- <u>Aluminum-free, calcium-free agents</u>: newer agents approved for hyperphosphatemia utilize <u>iron (Auryxia)</u> or other compounds to bind phosphorus in the gut. Because <u>they do not contain aluminum or calcium</u>, they do not cause problems with excess aluminum load and cause less of a problem with excess calcium load. They are the most <u>expensive</u>.

Phosphate Binders

DRUG	DOSE	SAFETY/SIDE EFFECTS/MONITORING

Aluminum-based: one of the most potent phosphate binders but due to risk of accumulation the treatment duration is limited to 4 weeks.

| Aluminum hydroxide (*ALternaGEL, Amphojel,* others)

Suspension | 300-600 mg TID with meals | **SIDE EFFECTS**
Constipation, poor taste, nausea, aluminum intoxication, "dialysis dementia" and osteomalacia

MONITORING
Ca, PO_4, serum aluminum concentrations, PTH |

Calcium-based: <u>first line</u> for hyperphosphatemia of CKD.

| Calcium acetate (*PhosLo, Phoslyra,* others)

Tablet, capsule, solution | 667-1,334 mg TID with meals | **SIDE EFFECTS**
Constipation, nausea, hypercalcemia

MONITORING
Ca, PO_4, PTH |
| Calcium carbonate (*Tums,* store brands, others)

Tablet, chewable tablet | 500 mg TID with meals, chewable or not | **NOTES**
Calcium acetate binds more dietary phosphorus on an elemental calcium basis compared to calcium carbonate. |

Aluminum-free, calcium-free

| Sucroferric oxyhydroxide (*Velphoro*)

Chewable tablet | 500 mg TID with meals | **SIDE EFFECTS**
Diarrhea, discolored (black) feces

MONITORING
PO_4; iron, ferritin, TSAT (only with ferric citrate) |
| Ferric Citrate (*Auryxia*)

Tablet | 2,000 mg TID with meals, up to 12 grams per day | **NOTES**
Iron <u>absorption</u> occurs with <u>ferric citrate</u> (not with sucroferric oxyhydroxide); dosage reduction of IV iron may be necessary. |

Phosphate Binders Continued

DRUG	DOSE	SAFETY/SIDE EFFECTS/MONITORING
Lanthanum carbonate *(Fosrenol)* Chewable tablet, packet	500-1,000 mg TID with meals, chewable – <u>must chew thoroughly</u>	**CONTRAINDICATIONS** Bowel obstruction, fecal impaction, ileus **SIDE EFFECTS** N/V, diarrhea and constipation, abdominal pain **MONITORING** Ca, PO_4, PTH **NOTES** Long-term safety has not been established.

Sevelamer: a non-calcium, non-aluminum based phosphate binder that is not systemically absorbed. Also, has the benefit of <u>lowering total cholesterol and LDL by 15-30%</u>. Sevelamer carbonate may have an advantage over sevelamer hydrochloride of maintaining bicarbonate concentrations.

Sevelamer carbonate **(Renvela)** Tablet, packet Sevelamer hydrochloride *(Renagel)* Tablet	800-1,600 mg three times daily with meals	**CONTRAINDICATIONS** Bowel obstruction **SIDE EFFECTS** N/V/D (all > 20%), constipation, abdominal pain **MONITORING** Ca, PO_4, HCO_3, Cl, PTH

Vitamin D Deficiency & Secondary Hyperparathyroidism

After controlling hyperphosphatemia, <u>elevations in PTH</u> are <u>treated primarily with vitamin D</u>. Vitamin D deficiency occurs when the kidney is unable to hydroxylate 25-OH vitamin D to its final active form, 1,25-dihydroxy vitamin D. Vitamin D deficiency exacerbates bone disease, impairs immunity and increases cardiovascular disease.

Vitamin D occurs in two primary forms: <u>vitamin D3 or cholecalciferol</u>, which is synthesized in the <u>skin</u> after exposure to ultraviolet light, and <u>vitamin D2 or ergocalciferol</u>, which is produced from plant sterols and is the <u>primary dietary source</u> of vitamin D. <u>Calcitriol *(Rocaltrol)* is the active form of vitamin D3</u> and is <u>used in patients with CKD</u> to <u>increase calcium absorption from the gut</u>, raise serum calcium concentrations and <u>inhibit PTH secretion</u>. Newer <u>active vitamin D analogs</u> such as paricalcitol and doxercalciferol cause <u>less hypercalcemia than calcitriol</u>. These agents are summarized in the table.

Agents for the Treatment of Secondary Hyperparathyroidism

DRUG	DOSING	SAFETY/SIDE EFFECTS/MONITORING

Vitamin D analogs: ↑ **intestinal absorption of Ca and provide a negative feedback to the parathyroid gland.**

Calcitriol *(Rocaltrol, Calcijex)*	CKD: 0.25 mcg PO three times weekly to daily	**CONTRAINDICATIONS** Hypercalcemia, vitamin D toxicity
Capsule, solution, injection	Dialysis: 0.5-1 mcg PO daily or 0.5-4 mcg IV three times weekly	**SIDE EFFECTS** N/V/D (> 10%), hypercalcemia, hyperphosphatemia
Doxercalciferol *(Hectorol)* Capsule, injection	CKD: 1 mcg PO three times weekly to daily Dialysis: 2.5-10 mcg PO three times weekly; 1-4 mcg IV three times weekly	**MONITORING** Ca, PO_4, PTH
Paricalcitol *(Zemplar)* Capsule, injection	CKD: 1 mcg PO three times weekly to daily Dialysis: 2.8-7 mcg IV three times weekly; 2-4 mcg PO three times weekly	**NOTES** Take with food or shortly after a meal to ↓ GI upset (calcitriol).

Calcimimetic – ↑ **sensitivity of calcium-sensing receptor on the parathyroid gland, thereby** ↓ **PTH,** ↓ **Ca,** ↓ **PO_4 and preventing progressive bone disease**

Cinacalcet *(Sensipar)* Tablet	30-180 mg PO daily with food	**CONTRAINDICATIONS** Hypocalcemia **WARNING** Caution in patients with history of seizure **SIDE EFFECTS** Hypocalcemia, N/V/D, paresthesia, fatigue, depression, anorexia, constipation, bone fracture, weakness, arthralgia, myalgia, limb pain, URTIs **MONITORING** Ca, PO_4, PTH **NOTES** Take tablet whole, do not crush or chew.

Supplementation with oral vitamin D2 (ergocalciferol) or D3 (cholecalciferol) may also be necessary (especially in patients with Stage 3 and 4 CKD) if vitamin D levels are reduced. The dosing depends on the severity of the deficiency. Treatment of vitamin D deficiency can result in hypercalcemia or hyper-phosphatemia. These values must be monitored during treatment. Further information on vitamin D is contained in the Dietary Supplements & Natural and Complementary Medicine and Osteoporosis chapters.

Hyperkalemia

A normal potassium level is 3.5 – 5 mEq/L. Hyperkalemia, depending on the source, can be defined as a potassium level above 5.3 or above 5.5 mEq/L, although clinicians will be concerned with any level above 5 mEq/L.

Potassium is the most abundant intracellular cation and is essential for life. Humans obtain potassium through the diet from many foods, including meats, beans and fruits. Daily intake through the GI tract is about 1 mEq/kg/day. Excess intake is excreted partially via the gut and primarily via the kidneys. Potassium excretion is increased by aldosterone, diuretics (strongly by loops, weakly by thiazides), by a high urine flow (via osmotic diuresis), and by negatively charged ions in the distal tubule (via bicarbonate).

Even if a person intakes a very rich potassium load, the acute rise in potassium would be offset by the release of insulin, which would cause potassium to shift into the cells. This is why excessive intake is not normally a cause of hyperkalemia unless there is significant renal damage. The most common cause of hyperkalemia is decreased renal excretion due to kidney failure. This can be in combination with a high potassium intake or can be partially due to the use of drugs that interfere with potassium excretion. Drugs that raise potassium levels include ACE inhibitors, ARBs, aldosterone receptor antagonists (ARAs), aliskiren, NSAIDs, cyclosporine, tacrolimus, everolimus, mycophenolate, potassium supplements, glyco-pyrrolate, drospirenone-containing oral contraceptives, sulfamethoxazole/trimethoprim, chronic hepa-rin use, canagliflozin, pentamidine and potassium present in IV fluids, including parenteral nutrition.

Patients with diabetes often have a diet high in sodium and low in potassium and are taking ACE in-hibitors or ARBs. The insulin deficiency reduces the ability to shift potassium into the cells. These fac-tors put patients with diabetes at higher risk for hyperkalemia. Hospitalized patients, primarily due to the use of drugs, are at higher risk of hyperkalemia than outpatients. Rarely, acute hyperkalemia can be due to tumor lysis, rhabdomyolysis or succinylcholine administration.

A patient with elevated potassium, depending on the level, may be asymptomatic or symptomatic. Muscle weakness and bradycardia may be present. Fatal arrhythmias can develop. If the potassium is high or the heart rate/rhythm is abnormal, the patient will generally be monitored with an ECG. The risk for severe, negative outcomes increases as the potassium level increases.

Treatment of Hyperkalemia

If hyperkalemia is severe the urgent clinical need is to stabilize the myocardial cells and to rapidly shift potassium intracellularly. Inter-ventions to enhance potassium elimination may be initiated, though these generally take longer to work. All sources of potassium must be discontinued.

> **STEPS FOR TREATING SEVERE HYPERKALEMIA**
>
> 1. Stabilize the Heart
> 2. Move it
> 3. Remove it

1. Stabilize the Myocardial Cells

Calcium gluconate is administered IV to stabilize the heart. It does not lower total body potassium.

2. Move It: Shift Excess Potassium Intracellularly

Several medications move potassium from the extracellular compartment to intracellular compart-ment. These agents work quickly. One or more of these methods should be used in severe hyperkale-mia. They do not lower total body potassium.

- Insulin co-administered with dextrose or glucose. Dextrose or glucose prevents hypoglycemia from insulin and stimulates endogenous insulin secretion. Dextrose and glucose do not lower potassium on their own.

- If metabolic acidosis is present, administer sodium bicarbonate.

- Consider beta-agonists, such as nebulized albuterol. Monitor for tachycardia and chest pain.

3. Remove It: Enhance Potassium Removal from the Body

These methods generally take longer to reduce potassium. They are commonly used in conjunction with the methods above in severe hyperkalemia or alone in less severe situations.

- Loop diuretic, such as furosemide. Monitor volume status.

- Sodium polystyrene sulfate or *Veltassa*. These bind potassium in the GI tract and increase fecal excretion. Effective lowering of potassium with these agents when given orally may take hours to days. Rectal administration (sodium polystyrene only) may be used in acute (emergency) treatment.

- Fludrocortisone (*Florinef*), especially in a patient with hypoaldosteronism.

■ Dialysis can be used if the hyperkalemia could be fatal or for patients with kidney failure. Because setting up and completing dialysis takes time (usually several hours), other methods of lowering potassium are generally used in conjunction with dialysis.

INTERVENTION	ROUTE OF ADMINISTRATION	ONSET	MECHANISM OF BENEFIT
Calcium gluconate	IV	1-2 minutes	Stabilize the myocardial cells (reverse ECG changes)
Regular insulin	IV	30 minutes	Shifts K intracellularly
Dextrose	IV	30 minutes	Shifts K intracellularly by stimulating insulin release
Sodium bicarbonate	IV	30 minutes	Shifts K intracellularly
Albuterol	Nebulized	30 minutes	Shifts K intracellularly
Furosemide	IV	5 minutes	Elimination (urine)
Sodium polystyrene sulfonate	Oral or rectal	1 hour; oral not for acute emergency	Elimination (GI)
Patiromer	Oral	~7 hours; not for acute emergency	Elimination (GI)
Hemodialysis		Immediate, but may take several hours to set-up procedure	Elimination (blood)

Treatment of Hyperkalemia

DRUG	DOSE	SAFETY/SIDE EFFECTS/MONITORING
Sodium polystyrene sulfate (*SPS, Kayexalate, Kalexate, Kionex*) Powder for oral suspension, suspension (oral and rectal) Non-absorbed cation exchange resin	Oral: 15 grams 1-4 times/day Rectal: 30-50 grams Q6H	**WARNINGS** Electrolyte disturbances including hypokalemia, fecal impaction; do not mix oral products with sorbitol (↑ risk of GI necrosis) **SIDE EFFECTS** Hypernatremia, hypocalcemia, hypokalemia, hypomagnesemia, N/V, constipation or diarrhea **MONITORING** K, Mg, Na, Ca **NOTES** Do not mix oral products with fruit juices containing K
Patiromer (Veltassa) Powder for oral suspension Non-absorbed cation exchange polymer	8.4 grams PO once daily with food. Max 25.2 grams once daily. Adjust by 8.4 grams per day PRN at one week intervals to obtain desired K Instructions: pour 30 mL of water into an empty cup, empty *Veltassa* packet contents into water and stir well, add an additional 60 mL of water to the mixture and stir well (mixture will be cloudy), drink right away. If powder remains in cup, add additional water and drink. Repeat as needed.	**WARNINGS** Binds to many oral drugs; give other drugs at least 6 hours before or 6 hours after. If ≥ 6 hr separation is not possible, choose only one drug to administer. Can worsen GI motility and cause hypomagnesemia. **SIDE EFFECTS** Constipation, hypomagnesemia, hypokalemia, N/D **MONITORING** K, Mg **NOTES** Delayed onset of action (~7 hrs); not for emergency use Store in refrigerator. If stored at room temperature, use within 3 months.

Metabolic Acidosis

The ability of the kidney to generate bicarbonate decreases as CKD progresses and may result in the development of metabolic acidosis. In the ambulatory care setting, treatment of metabolic acidosis is initiated when the serum bicarbonate concentration is < 22 mEq/L. Agents to replace bicarbonate are summarized below.

DRUG	DOSING	SAFETY/SIDE EFFECTS/MONITORING
Sodium bicarbonate Tablets, granules, powder	1-2 tabs PO 1-3 times a day	**CONTRAINDICATIONS** Alkalosis, hypernatremia, hypocalcemia, pulmonary edema, unknown abdominal pain **WARNINGS** Use caution in patients with HTN, cardiovascular disease, fluid retention due to Na load **SIDE EFFECTS** N/V/D, hypernatremia **MONITORING** Na, HCO_3
Sodium citrate/citric acid (*Bicitra, Cytra-2, Oracit, Shohl's* solution) Solution	10-30 mL PO with water, taken after meals and at bedtime Take after meals and at bedtime to avoid laxative effect Chilled solution improves taste	**CONTRAINDICATIONS** Alkalosis, Na restricted diet, hypernatremia **SIDE EFFECTS** N/V/D, metabolic alkalosis, tetany **MONITORING** Na, HCO_3, urinary pH **NOTES** Metabolized to bicarbonate by the liver, may not be effective in concomitant liver failure Avoid concurrent use with aluminum containing products (e.g., antacids)

DIALYSIS

If kidney disease progresses to end-stage kidney disease, then renal replacement using dialysis will be required to remove waste products, electrolytes and excess fluid unless the patient receives a kidney transplant. The two primary types of dialysis are hemodialysis (HD) and peritoneal dialysis (PD).

In HD, the patient is connected to a dialysis machine via vascular access such as a catheter, arterio-venous fistula (more permanent) or graft. Blood leaves the patient's body and is pumped through the dialysis circuit in the machine. The blood enters the dialyzer and toxic waste products, electrolytes and water are removed through two processes; diffusion and convection. Solutes diffuse across the semipermeable membrane and the cleansed blood is returned back to the patient. Convection is a process in which the pressure generated in the dialyzer generates filtration of water and solutes. HD is typically a 3 – 4 hour process, done several times (usually three times) per week. Increasingly, patients are choosing home HD, which can be done more frequently (typically 5 – 6 times per week).

In PD, a dialysis solution (usually containing glucose) is pumped into the peritoneal cavity (the abdominal cavity surrounding the internal organs), and the peritoneal membrane acts as the semipermeable membrane (i.e., as the dialyzer). The solution is left in the abdomen to "dwell" for a period of time, then drained. This cycle is repeated throughout the day, every day. PD is performed by the patient at home. There are two main types of PD: 1) continuous ambulatory peritoneal dialysis (CAPD), which is done without a machine, and requires the dialysate to be exchanged (by the patient) at scheduled intervals throughout the day, and 2) automated peritoneal dialysis (APD), where the patient uses a machine in the home to exchange the dialysate several times throughout the night.

Factors Affecting Drug Removal During Dialysis

When a patient is on dialysis, the pharmacist needs to consider how much of the patient's medications are removed by dialysis in order to recommend a reasonable dosing regimen and/or schedule the dosing of the medications after dialysis. Drug removal during dialysis depends primarily on the factors in the table below. In general, <u>small, hydrophilic, non-protein bound molecules are readily removed</u> by dialysis. If a drug has a very large volume of distribution, only a small fraction of the total drug will reside in the bloodstream and be removed by dialysis.

FACTOR	EFFECT

Drug Characteristics

Molecular weight/size	Smaller molecules tend to be more readily removed by dialysis
Volume of distribution	Drugs with large Vd are less likely to be significantly removed by dialysis
Protein-binding	Highly protein-bound drugs are less likely to be removed by dialysis

Dialysis Factors

Membrane	High-flux (large pore size) and high-efficiency (large surface area) HD filters remove substances more than conventional/low-flux filters
Blood flow rate	Higher dialysis blood flow rates increase drug removal during dialysis over a given time interval

HEPATITIS & LIVER DISEASE

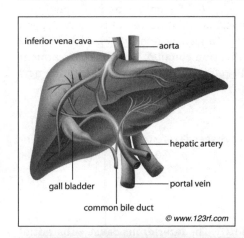

inferior vena cava — aorta

— hepatic artery

gall bladder — portal vein

common bile duct

© www.123rf.com

We gratefully acknowledge the assistance of Paulina Deming, PharmD, Associate Professor at the University of New Mexico College of Pharmacy, in preparing this chapter.

HEPATITIS

Background

The term hepatitis means inflammation of the liver. Hepatitis viruses are the most common cause, but alcohol, certain drugs, autoimmune diseases and other viruses/infections can also cause hepatitis. Viruses that damage the liver include hepatitis A through E (most cases of viral hepatitis are caused by hepatitis A, B and C), along with herpes, CMV, Epstein-Barr virus, and adenoviruses. Symptoms and treatment differ depending on the cause of hepatitis and extent of liver damage (see discussion of cirrhosis in this chapter). Many patients with hepatitis B and C do not know they are infected.

Hepatitis A

Hepatitis A virus (HAV) is a <u>vaccine preventable disease</u> that causes an <u>acute, self-limiting illness</u> in most patients. Transmission is primarily via the <u>fecal-oral</u> route through improper hand washing after exposure with an infected person or <u>via contaminated food/water</u>. Symptoms are generally mild and non-specific. The hepatitis A vaccine *(Havrix, Vaqta)* is given to children beginning at one year of age (2 shots are required), and to older persons if risk factors are present: household members and close personal contacts of adopted children from high or intermediate HAV endemicity, men who have sex with men, users of illegal injection and noninjection drugs, if someone lives in or travels to areas with high prevalence, if liver disease is present, if receiving blood products, or if working with HAV infected animals. <u>Treatment of hepatitis A is supportive and no antiviral agents are needed</u>. Immunoglobulin (IgG) can be given for post-exposure prophylaxis in select cases.

GUIDELINES/REFERENCES

AASLD/IDSA/IAS – USA. Recommendations for testing, managing, and treating hepatitis C. http://www.hcvguidelines.org. Accessed 2015 Dec 1.

Hepatitis B

Hepatitis B virus (HBV) is a <u>vaccine preventable disease</u> that <u>causes acute illness and may lead to chronic infection, cirrhosis of the liver, liver cancer, liver failure, and death</u>. Transmission requires contact with infectious blood, semen, or other body fluids by having sex with an infected person, sharing contaminated needles to inject drugs, or from an infected mother to her newborn (perinatal transmission). For recommendations on HBV vaccination and the vaccination schedules see the Immunizations chapter. <u>Interferons and select nucleoside/tide reverse transcriptase inhibitors (NRTIs) are used</u> for treatment of chronic HBV. Treatment <u>duration</u> is <u>not well defined</u>. <u>Hepatitis B reactivation</u> is a concern in patients with prior HBV exposure undergoing certain <u>immunosuppressive therapies</u> and requires <u>screening</u>, monitoring, and managing patients to minimize the risk of HBV reactivation.

Hepatitis C

Hepatitis C virus (HCV) is a <u>non-vaccine preventable</u> disease that can cause <u>acute disease</u>, <u>but more commonly</u> is associated with <u>chronic disease</u>, with consequences similar to hepatitis B. HCV is the most common indication for liver transplant. Transmission is through <u>blood</u> and it is most commonly transmitted in the United States via intravenous drug use. <u>There are 6 different</u> hepatitis C <u>genotypes</u> (1 – 6) and various subtypes (for example 1a or 1b). Treatment options and duration of therapy depend on the genotype and include <u>peginterferons, ribavirin and direct acting antivirals (DAAs)</u>. DAAs include protease inhibitors, NS5B polymerase inhibitors and NS5A replication complex inhibitors. Treatment of HCV is rapidly evolving; new drugs are being approved and preferred regimens change as the new drugs are studied.

NON-DRUG TREATMENT

Counseling of patients with HBV and HCV is essential to prevent disease transmission to others. Alcohol cessation is recommended.

DRUG TREATMENT

Interferon Alfa

Interferon alfa (INF-alfa) is indicated for <u>treatment of HBV and HCV</u>. The interferons cause substantial toxicities and laboratory abnormalities limiting their use. The pegylated forms (PEG-INF-alfa) have polyethylene glycol added to the interferon via pegylation, which prolongs the half-life, reducing the dosing frequency to once weekly. Interferons are naturally-produced cytokines that have antiviral, antiproliferative, and immunomodulatory effects. Interferon-βs are used for Multiple Sclerosis; see Systemic Steroids & Autoimmune chapter.

DRUG	DOSING	SAFETY/SIDE EFFECTS/MONITORING
Interferon-α-2b (*Intron A*) – for HBV, HCV, many cancers Pegylated interferon-α-2a (*Pegasys*) – for HBV and HCV Pegylated interferon-α-2b (*Peg-Intron*) – for HCV Interferon-βs are used for Multiple Sclerosis; see Systemic Steroids & Autoimmune Conditions chapter	Dosing varies based on indication. HCV dosing example: *Intron A:* 3 million units SC 3 times weekly *Peg-Intron:* 1.5 mcg/kg SC weekly *Pegasys:* 180 mcg SC weekly + ribavirin (different doses depending on interferon type used) Treatment duration depends on the genotype Dose reduction required in the setting of thrombocytopenia and neutropenia (withhold treatment when ANC < 500/mm³ or platelets < 25,000/mm³) and for renal dysfunction (CrCl < 50 for *Peg-Intron* and CrCl < 30 for *Pegasys*)	**BOXED WARNINGS** May cause or exacerbate <u>neuropsychiatric, autoimmune, ischemic or infectious</u> disorders; combination treatment with <u>ribavirin may cause birth defects and/or fetal mortality and/or hemolytic anemia</u> **CONTRAINDICATIONS** Autoimmune hepatitis, decompensated liver disease in cirrhotic patients, infants and neonates *(Pegasys)* **WARNINGS** Neuropsychiatric events, cardiovascular events, endocrine disorders (aggravates hypo/hyperthyroidism, hypo/hyperglycemia), ophthalmologic disorders (retinopathy, decrease in vision), pancreatitis, myelosuppression and serious skin reactions **SIDE EFFECTS** Interferons can cause <u>many</u> adverse effects. <u>CNS effects</u> (fatigue, anxiety, depression, weakness), <u>GI upset</u> (N/V, anorexia, weight loss), ↑ LFTs (5-10x ULN during treatment), myelosuppression, mild alopecia <u>Flu-like syndrome</u> (starting 1-2 hrs after administration with <u>fever, chills, HA, malaise, arthralgia, myalgia, diaphoresis</u> which can last 24 hrs). <u>Pre-treat with acetaminophen and antihistamine.</u> **MONITORING** CBC with differential and platelets, LFTs, uric acid, SCr, electrolytes, TGs, thyroid function tests, serum HBV DNA or HCV-RNA levels **NOTES** MedGuide required

Nucleoside/Tide Reverse Transcriptase Inhibitors (NRTIs)

These agents inhibit HBV replication by inhibiting HBV polymerase resulting in DNA chain termination. Prior to starting HBV therapy, all patients should be tested for HIV. Antivirals used for HBV can have activity against HIV and if a patient is co-infected with both HIV and HBV, it is important that the chosen therapy is appropriate for both viruses to minimize risk of HIV antiviral resistance.

DRUG	DOSING	SAFETY/SIDE EFFECTS/MONITORING
Entire Class	CrCl < 50 mL/min: ↓ dose or frequency	**BOXED WARNINGS (FOR ENTIRE CLASS)** Lactic acidosis and severe hepatomegaly with steatosis, which may be fatal. Exacerbations of HBV may occur upon discontinuation, monitor closely. See HIV chapter for further information.
LamiVUDine (*Epivir HBV*) Tablet, solution	100 mg daily 150 mg BID or 300 mg daily if co-infected with HIV CrCl < 50 mL/min: ↓ dose	**BOXED WARNING** Do not use *Epivir HBV* for treatment of HIV (contains lower dose of lamivudine); can result in HIV resistance. **SIDE EFFECTS** HA, N/V/D, fatigue, insomnia, myalgias, ↑ LFTs
Adefovir (*Hepsera*) Tablet	10 mg daily CrCl < 50 mL/min: ↓ frequency	**BOXED WARNING** May cause HIV resistance in patients with unrecognized or untreated HIV infection. Use caution in patients with renal impairment or those at risk of renal toxicity (including concurrent nephrotoxic agents or NSAIDs). **SIDE EFFECTS** HA, weakness, abdominal pain, hematuria, rash, nephrotoxicity
Tenofovir **(*Viread*)** Tablet, powder (oral) 1st line agent	300 mg daily CrCl < 50 mL/min: ↓ frequency	**WARNINGS** Renal toxicity including acute renal failure and/or Fanconi's syndrome, osteomalacia and ↓ bone mineral density **SIDE EFFECTS** N/V/D, HA, depression, renal impairment, ↓ bone mineral density, ↑ LFTs, ↑ CPK
Entecavir (*Baraclude*) Tablet, oral solution 1st line agent	Nucleoside-treatment naïve: 0.5 mg daily Lamivudine-resistant: 1 mg daily Take on empty stomach CrCl < 50 mL/min: ↓ dose or frequency	**BOXED WARNING** May cause HIV resistance in patients with unrecognized or untreated HIV infection. **SIDE EFFECTS** Peripheral edema, pyrexia, ascites, ↑ LFTs, hematuria, nephrotoxicity, ↑ SCr **NOTES** Food reduces AUC by 18-20%; take on an empty stomach (2 hours before or after a meal).
Telbivudine (*Tyzeka*) Tablet	600 mg daily CrCl < 50 mL/min: ↓ frequency	**SIDE EFFECTS** ↑ CPK, fatigue, headache, ↑ LFTs

NRTI Drug Interactions

- Ribavirin can ↑ hepatotoxic effects of all NRTIs; lactic acidosis can occur.
- Lamivudine: SMX/TMP can ↑ lamivudine levels due to ↓ excretion.
- Tenofovir: Avoid concomitant treatment with didanosine or adefovir due to ↑ risk of virologic failure and potential for ↑ side effects.

- Telbivudine: Avoid concomitant interferon alpha treatment due to ↑ risk of peripheral neuropathy from telbivudine.

NRTI Counseling

- *Epivir HBV* tablets and oral solution are not interchangeable with *Epivir* tablets and solution (which have higher doses).

- Entecavir: Food ↓ the absorption of this drug; take on an empty stomach (take 2 hours before or after a meal).

- Some people (rarely) have developed a serious condition called lactic acidosis (a buildup of an acid in the blood). Lactic acidosis is a medical emergency and must be treated in the hospital. Be seen right away if you feel very weak or tired, have unusual muscle pain, have trouble breathing, have stomach pain with nausea and vomiting, and/or feel dizzy or light-headed.

- Lamivudine: Some people (rarely) have developed pancreatitis, which is a medical emergency and must be treated in the hospital. Be seen right away if you have upper abdominal pain that radiates to your back, or abdominal pain that feels worse after eating with or without nausea or vomiting.

Ribavirin

Ribavirin (RBV) is an oral antiviral agent that inhibits replication of RNA and DNA viruses. It is indicated for HCV in combination with other agents and never as monotherapy. Aerosolized ribavirin has been used for respiratory syncytial virus (RSV).

DRUG	DOSING	SAFETY/SIDE EFFECTS/MONITORING
Ribavirin *(Copegus, Moderiba, Rebetol, Ribasphere, Ribasphere RibaPak)* Capsule, tablet, solution (oral) *Virazole* for RSV	400-600 mg BID, varies based on indication, patient weight and genotype ↑ tolerability if given with food When Hgb < 10 g/dL, ↓ dose (avoid if Hgb < 8.5 g/dL) Capsule should be not be crushed, chewed, open, or broken.	**BOXED WARNINGS** Significant teratogenic effects (avoid in pregnancy or women wishing to become pregnant) Monotherapy is not effective for HCV Hemolytic anemia (primary toxicity of oral therapy mostly occurring within 4 weeks of therapy) Caution with inhalation formulation in patients on a ventilator (precipitation of drug may interfere with ventilation) **CONTRAINDICATIONS** Pregnancy, women of childbearing age who will not use contraception reliably, male partners of pregnant women, hemoglobinopathies, CrCl < 50 mL/min *(Ribasphere, Rebetrol)*, autoimmune hepatitis, concomitant use with didanosine **SIDE EFFECTS** Hemolytic anemia (can worsen cardiac disease and lead to MIs; do not use in unstable cardiac disease), fatigue, HA, insomnia, N/V/D, anorexia, myalgias, hyperuricemia **MONITORING** CBC with differential and PLTs, electrolytes, uric acid, bilirubin, LFTs, HCV-RNA levels, TSH, monthly pregnancy tests **NOTES** Pregnancy Category X; highly teratogenic Can stay in body for as long as 6 months. Avoid pregnancy in female patients and female partners of male patients during therapy and for 6 months after completing therapy. At least two reliable forms of effective contraception must be utilized during treatment and during the 6-month post-treatment follow-up period. MedGuide required

Ribavirin Drug Interactions

- Do not use with didanosine due to cases of fatal hepatic failure, peripheral neuropathy and pancreatitis.

- Ribavirin can ↑ hepatotoxic effects of all NRTIs; lactic acidosis can occur.

- Zidovudine can ↑ risk and severity of anemia from ribavirin.

Ribavirin Counseling

- Dispense MedGuide and instruct patient to read it. Ribavirin can cause birth defects or death of an unborn child. If you are pregnant or your sexual partner is pregnant, do not use. If you could become pregnant, you must not become pregnant during therapy and for 6 months after you have stopped therapy. During this time, you must use 2 forms of birth control, and you must have pregnancy tests that show that you are not pregnant.

- Female sexual partners of male patients being treated must not become pregnant during treatment and for 6 months after treatment has stopped. Therefore, you must use 2 forms of birth control during this time.

- If you or a female sexual partner becomes pregnant, tell your healthcare provider immediately. There is a Ribavirin Pregnancy Registry that collects information about pregnancy outcomes in female patients and female partners of male patients exposed to ribavirin. You or your healthcare provider should contact the Registry at 1-800-593-2214. All information is confidential.

- If using the oral solution, wash the measuring cup or spoon to avoid swallowing of the medicine by someone other than the person to whom it was prescribed.

- This medicine can cause a dangerous drop in your red blood cell count, called anemia. Your healthcare provider should check your red blood cell count before you start therapy and often during the first 4 weeks of therapy. Your red blood cell count may be checked more often if you have any heart or breathing problems.

- Do not take ribavirin alone to treat hepatitis C infection. Ribavirin is used in combination for treating hepatitis C infection.

Direct Acting Antiviral Agents

Direct acting antiviral agents (DAAs) are indicated for the treatment of chronic HCV infection in adult patients and act by directly inhibiting various steps in hepatitis C viral replication. Currently available classes of DAAs include NS3/4A protease inhibitors (simeprevir, paritaprevir), NS5B polymerase inhibitors (sofosbuvir, dasabuvir) and NS5A replication complex inhibitors (daclatasvir, ledipasvir, ombitasvir). Ombitasvir is co-formulated with ritonavir-boosted paritaprevir (PrO) as the brand name *Technivie* and co-packaged with dasabuvir (PrOD) as *Viekira Pak*. The combination of sofosbuvir and ledipasvir is also available as *Harvoni*.

Protease Inhibitors

These drugs inhibit the HCV NS3/4A protease which is essential for HCV viral replication. They must be used in combination with other DAAs to prevent the development of resistance. Simeprevir *(Olysio)* was previously used in combination with PEG-INF-alfa and ribavirin, but the toxicities associated with interferons limit the ongoing use of interferon-based therapies. It is currently used in combination with sofosbuvir. Paritaprevir is currently available only in combination products. Historically other PIs (telaprevir and boceprevir) were used with interferons, but these have been removed from the market in the United States.

DRUG	DOSING	SAFETY/SIDE EFFECTS/MONITORING
Simeprevir **(Olysio)** Capsule	150 mg daily with food Screening for <u>NS3 Q80K polymorphism</u> is <u>recommended</u> at baseline for patients with HCV genotype 1a who will be treated with simeprevir + RBV and PEG-INF-alfa; if positive, consider alternate therapy Polymorphism screening may also be considered if starting simeprevir + sofosbuvir	**CONTRAINDICATIONS** When used in combination with ribavirin or interferon the contraindications to those agents are applicable to combination treatment regimens with simeprevir **WARNINGS** Serious symptomatic <u>bradycardia</u> in patients receiving <u>sofosbuvir + amiodarone and another DAA</u> (particularly in patients taking beta blockers, with underlying cardiac conditions and/or advanced liver disease); hepatic decompensation and hepatic failure (in advanced and/or decompensated cirrhosis), photosensitivity, rash **SIDE EFFECTS** Rash (photosensitivity), pruritus, myalgia, dyspnea, ↑ serum bilirubin, nausea, fatigue **MONITORING** CBC with differential (to monitor anemia and neutropenia), electrolytes, LFTs, HCV-RNA levels **NOTES** <u>Monotherapy</u> with simeprevir is <u>not recommended</u>. Discontinue treatment with combination simeprevir, PEG-INF-alfa and RBV if HCV-RNA is ≥ 25 units/mL at treatment weeks 4 or 12 (treatment is inadequate). <u>No treatment stopping rules apply to the simeprevir + sofosbuvir</u> combination.

Simeprevir Drug Interactions

- Simeprevir is a 3A4 substrate (major); <u>do not administer</u> with moderate or strong inducers or inhibitors of 3A4.

- Simeprevir mildly inhibits 1A2 and intestinal 3A4 activity, but does not affect hepatic 3A4 activity.

- Simeprevir inhibits P-gp; can ↓ concentrations of P-gp substrates.

- Can ↑ bradycardic effect of amiodarone.

Other DAAs and Combination Products for HCV

Sofosbuvir is a nucleotide inhibitor of HCV NS5B polymerase <u>indicated for hepatitis C only</u>. It is combined with an NS5A inhibitor (ledipasvir, daclatasvir) in many recommended HCV regimens. Combination products target HCV by different mechanisms; some include ritonavir, which is <u>not active for HCV</u> but <u>increases levels</u> of HCV protease inhibitors used with it. In the following table, all safety/side effects/monitoring of individual components apply to combination products. See table of recommended treatment regimens for treatment-naive patients with HCV at the end of this section.

DRUG	DOSING	SAFETY/SIDE EFFECTS/MONITORING
Sofosbuvir (Sovaldi) Tablet **+ ledipasvir (Harvoni)**	400 mg daily with or without food	**CONTRAINDICATIONS** When used in combination with ribavirin or interferon the contraindications to those agents are applicable to combination treatment regimens with sofosbuvir **WARNINGS** Serious symptomatic bradycardia in patients receiving sofosbuvir + amiodarone and another DAA (particularly in patients taking beta blockers, with underlying cardiac conditions and/or advanced liver disease) **SIDE EFFECTS** Fatigue, HA, nausea, insomnia, anemia, chills, irritability, pruritus, skin rash, weakness, myalgia **MONITORING** LFTs, bilirubin, CBC, HCV-RNA levels **NOTES** Monotherapy with sofosbuvir is not recommended
Sofosbuvir + ledipasvir (Harvoni) Tablet	1 tablet daily (90 mg ledipasvir + 400 mg sofosbuvir) with or without food	See above **NOTES** Ledipasvir requires acidic environment for absorption. Acid suppressive therapy should be avoided or minimized during therapy. Ledipasvir is only available in combination with sofosbuvir. *Harvoni* is a complete HCV regimen.
Daclatasvir (Daklinza) Tablet	60 mg daily with or without food combination with sofosbuvir 30 mg daily with strong 3A4 inhibitors 90 mg daily with moderate 3A4 inducers	**CONTRAINDICATIONS** Use with strong 3A4 inducers **WARNINGS** Serious symptomatic bradycardia in patients receiving sofosbuvir + amiodarone and another DAA (particularly in patients taking beta blockers, with underlying cardiac conditions and/or advanced liver disease) **SIDE EFFECTS** Fatigue, HA, N/D **MONITORING** LFTs, SCr, cardiac monitoring (if used with amiodarone), HCV RNA **NOTES** Monotherapy with daclatasvir is not recommended

Other DAAs and Combination Products for HCV Continued

DRUG	DOSING	SAFETY/SIDE EFFECTS/MONITORING
Paritaprevir/ ritonavir/ombitasvir *(Technivie)* Tablet	2 tablets once daily in the morning with a meal	**CONTRAINDICATIONS** Moderate-severe hepatic impairment, concomitant use with drugs highly dependent on <u>3A4</u> for elimination (if ↑ levels can cause serious events) and moderate-strong inducers of <u>3A4</u>, all contraindications to ribavirin apply when used in combination regimens **WARNINGS** <u>Hepatic decompensation and hepatic failure in patients with cirrhosis</u> (not indicated in cirrhosis); <u>risk of ↑ LFTs</u> (> 5 x ULN) within 4 wks of treatment, female patients taking <u>ethinyl estradiol</u> products are at ↑ risk; <u>significant drug interaction potential</u>, risk of HIV protease inhibitor resistance **SIDE EFFECTS** Asthenia, fatigue, nausea, insomnia, pruritus, skin reactions **MONITORING** CBC, LFTs, bilirubin, HCV-RNA levels **NOTES** <u>MedGuide required</u>
Paritaprevir/ ritonavir/ombitasvir + dasabuvir *(Viekira Pak)* Tablet Paritaprevir + ritonavir + ombitasvir fixed dose combination tablet copackaged with dasabuvir (250 mg) tablets	2 tablets of paritaprevir/ritonavir/ombitasvir <u>once daily</u> in the morning and 1 dasabuvir tablet <u>twice daily</u> with meals	**CONTRAINDICATIONS** Moderate-severe hepatic impairment; concomitant use with drugs highly dependent on <u>3A4</u> for elimination (if ↑ levels can cause serious events), moderate-strong inducers of <u>3A4</u>, and strong inducers or inhibitors of <u>2C8</u>; all contraindications to ribavirin apply when used in combination regimens **WARNINGS** <u>Hepatic decompensation and hepatic failure in patients with cirrhosis</u>; <u>risk of ↑ LFTs</u> (> 5 x ULN) within 4 wks of treatment, female patients taking <u>ethinyl estradiol</u> products are at ↑ risk; <u>significant drug interaction potential</u>, risk of HIV protease inhibitor resistance **SIDE EFFECTS** Fatigue, HA, pruritus, skin reactions, insomnia, nausea **MONITORING** CBC, LFTs, bilirubin, HCV RNA, SCr **NOTES** <u>MedGuide required</u>

Drug Interactions

Sofosbuvir

- Sofosbuvir is a substrate of P-gp; avoid with potent P-gp inducers (e.g., St. John's wort, rifampin).

- Avoid co-administration with carbamazepine, oxcarbazepine, phenobarbital, phenytoin, rifapentine, rifabutin and tipranavir/ritonavir.

- Can ↑ bradycardic effect of amiodarone.

Harvoni

Interactions for sofosbuvir apply to *Harvoni* and:

- Antacids, H$_2$RAs and PPIs can ↓ concentrations of ledipasvir. Separate *Harvoni* from antacids by 4 hrs; take H$_2$RAs at the same time as *Harvoni* or 12 hrs apart and use ≤ famotidine 40 mg BID or equivalent; take PPIs at the same time as *Harvoni*. Avoid PPIs at doses ≥ omeprazole 20 mg/day or equivalent and avoid use of PPI with food.

- Avoid co-administration with rosuvastatin.

Daclatasvir

- Daclatasvir is a substrate of 3A4 (major) and P-gp; avoid strong 3A4 inducers (see recommended dose adjustments in table).

- Can ↑ bradycardic effect of amiodarone.

Technivie and Viekira Pak

- *Technivie* and *Viekira Pak* are substrates (major) and inhibitors (strong) of 3A4 and P-gp; avoid concomitant use with drugs highly dependent on 3A4 for elimination (if ↑ levels can cause serious events) and avoid moderate-strong 3A4 inducers due to ↓ efficacy of HCV therapy.

- Monitoring is required because of potential for numerous drug-drug interactions. See HIV chapter for additional ritonavir drug interactions.

- *Viekira Pak* is a substrate (major) of 2C8; avoid strong inducers or inhibitors of 2C8.

Technivie and *Viekira Pak* Counseling

- Dispense MedGuide and instruct patient to read it. This medication can cause increases in liver function blood tests. Get immediate medical help if you develop any of the following: yellowing of the white part of your eyes or yellowing of your skin, dark-colored urine, light colored stool, or bad stomach pain with severe nausea.

- *Viekira Pak* contains 2 different types of tablets. You must take both types of tablets exactly as prescribed to treat your chronic hepatitis C virus (HCV) infection.

  - The pink tablet contains the medicines ombitasvir, paritaprevir, and ritonavir
  - The beige tablet contains the medicine dasabuvir

- *Technivie* and *Viekira Pak:* Certain medications cannot be used with this medication. Ethinyl estradiol-containing medicines must be stopped before starting it. Use another method of birth control during treatment and for ~2 weeks after. Examples of ethinyl estradiol products include:

  - Combination oral contraceptive pills or patches like *Lo Loestrin FE, Norinyl, Ortho Tri-Cyclen Lo, Ortho Evra*
  - Hormonal vaginal rings like *Nuvaring*
  - Hormone replacement therapy like *Fem HRT*

Recommended HCV Treatment Regimens (for Treatment-Naïve Patients)*

Duration of treatment with recommended regimens is <u>12 weeks</u> for patients <u>without cirrhosis</u> and extended to <u>16 or 24 weeks</u> in patients <u>with cirrhosis</u>.

	GENOTYPE					
REGIMEN	la	lb	2	3**	4	5-6
Sofosbuvir + Daclatasvir	12 wks					
	24 wks (+/- RBV)			24 wks (+/-RBV)		
Sofosbuvir + Ledipasvir	12 wks				12 wks	
Sofosbuvir + Simeprevir	12 wks					
	24 wks (+/- RBV)					
PrOD		12 wks				
PrOD + RBV	12 wks					
	24 wks					
PrO + RBV					12 wks	
Sofosbuvir + RBV			12 wks		24 wks	
			16 wks			

*Check for guideline updates at: http://www.hcvguidelines.org

**Another recommended regimen for genotype 3 is sofosbuvir + RBV + PEG-INF-alfa x 12 weeks for patients eligible for interferon

RBV = ribavirin; PrOD = paritaprevir + ritonavir + ombitasvir + dasabuvir *(Viekira Pak);* PrO = paritaprevir + ritonavir + ombitasvir *(Technivie)*

LIVER DISEASE AND CIRRHOSIS

Background

Cirrhosis is advanced and irreversible <u>fibrosis (scarring)</u> of the liver. There are many causes, but the most common in the U.S. are hepatitis C and alcohol consumption. As scar tissue replaces the healthy liver tissue, blood flow through the liver is impaired leading to numerous complications including portal hypertension, varices, ascites, hepatic encephalopathy and others.

Clinical Presentation

Symptoms can include nausea, loss of appetite, vomiting, diarrhea, malaise, pain in the upper right quadrant of the abdomen, yellowed skin and yellowed whites of the eyes (jaundice), darkened urine and/or lightened color (white or clay-colored) stool caused by low bile in the stool due to decreased production or a blocked bile duct.

Objective Criteria

Cirrhosis is definitively diagnosed with a liver biopsy, but certain labs can suggest cirrhosis or liver damage. Aspartate aminotransferase (AST) and alanine aminotransferase (ALT) are liver enzymes. The normal range for both AST and ALT is 10 – 40 units/L. There is some slight variance in these ranges on different lab reports. In general, the higher the values, the more active (acute) the liver disease. Clinical signs of liver disease, in addition to ↑ ALT and ↑ AST, include ↓ albumin (protein produced by the liver; normal range 3.5 – 5.5 g/dL), ↑ alkaline phosphatase (Alk Phos or ALP), ↑ total bilirubin (Tbili), ↑ lactate dehydrogenase (LDH), and ↑ in prothrombin time (PT). Albumin and PT/INR are markers of synthetic (production ability) liver function. Liver disease can be classified as hepatocellular (↑ ALT and ↑ AST), cholestatic (↑ Alk Phos and ↑ Tbili), or mixed (↑ AST, ALT, Alk Phos and Tbili).

Assessing Severity of Liver Disease

It is important to assess the severity of the liver disease as it serves as a predictor of patient survival, surgical outcomes, and the risk of complications such as variceal bleeding. The Child-Pugh classification system is widely used which has a scoring system that ranges from 0 – 15. Class A (mild disease) is defined as a score < 7; Class B (moderate disease) is a score of 7 – 9, and Class C (severe disease) is a score of 10 – 15. The model for end-stage liver disease (MELD) is another scoring system with a scoring system that ranges from 0 – 40, with higher numbers indicating a greater risk of death within three months. Noninvasive tests are increasingly used to predict fibrosis and cirrhosis. Unlike drug dosing in renal failure, little data are available to guide drug dosing of hepatically cleared agents with liver failure. In general, caution is advised when using hepatically cleared agents in severe liver disease (Class C) and, in select cases, dose adjustment may be necessary. In general, for drugs that are extensively hepatically metabolized, it is best to start at lower doses and titrate to clinical effect.

Natural Products

Milk thistle, an extract derived from a member of the daisy family, is sometimes used by patients with liver disease. Although there are limited data to demonstrate efficacy of milk thistle for alcoholic liver disease, hepatitis B or C, milk thistle does not appear to be harmful. A possible side effect is mild diarrhea and there are concerns for possible drug interactions with milk thistle and antiviral hepatitis C medications. Kava, comfrey, flavocoxid (Limbrel, a medical food) are known hepatotoxins

Drug-Induced Liver Injury

Many drugs can cause liver damage. If this occurs, the primary treatment (in most cases) is to stop the drug. Hepatotoxic drugs are typically discontinued when the LFTs are > 3 times the upper limit of normal (> 150 units/L of ALT or AST), however clinical judgment is warranted. Rechallenging with the potential agent can be considered if clinically necessary. An excellent reference for drug-induced liver injury (DILI) is http://livertox.nih.gov.

Acetaminophen is a known hepatotoxic agent and can cause severe injury. Acetaminophen may be used by patients with cirrhosis, however for limited periods of time and at lower dosages. Patients with alcoholic cirrhosis who are actively drinking and/or malnourished may be more susceptible to further liver damage. NSAIDs should be avoided with cirrhosis because these agents can lead to decompensation, including bleeding.

ALCOHOLIC LIVER DISEASE

Alcoholic liver disease is caused by excessive drinking, and can include fatty liver, alcoholic hepatitis, and chronic hepatitis with hepatic fibrosis or cirrhosis. Chronic alcohol ingestion over a long period of time causes "steatosis" or fatty liver, due to fat deposition in the hepatocytes. This can be reversible

SELECT DRUGS WITH BOXED WARNING FOR LIVER DAMAGE

Acetaminophen (acute, high doses)	Methotrexate
	Mipomersen
Amiodarone	Nefazodone
Bosentan	NNRTIs (highest risk with nevirapine)
Felbamate	
Flutamide	NRTIs (highest risk with didanosine, stavudine, zidovudine)
Isoniazid	
Ketoconazole (highest risk), other azoles	PIs (highest risk with tipranavir)
Leflunomide and Teriflunomide	Propylthiouracil
Lomitapide	Tolcapone
Maraviroc	Valproic acid

and self-limited (if drinking is stopped) or can lead to fibrosis and cirrhosis. Some patients develop alcoholic hepatitis, an acute process with poor short-term survival. Of all chronic heavy drinkers, only 15 – 20% develop hepatitis or cirrhosis, which can occur simultaneously or in succession.

Alcohol-induced liver disease is the most common type of drug-induced liver disease. Risk increases with amount consumed, and duration. Women have higher risk than men. Treatment programs use mainly <u>benzodiazepines</u> for alcohol withdrawal in <u>inpatients</u> whereas anticonvulsants are used for outpatients. Naltrexone *(ReVia)*, acamprosate *(Campral)* and disulfiram *(Antabuse)* are <u>used to prevent relapses</u>. There are a few off-label treatments.

Chronic consumption of alcohol results in the secretion of pro-inflammatory cytokines (TNF-alpha, IL-6 and IL-8), oxidative stress, lipid peroxidation, and acetaldehyde toxicity. These factors cause inflammation, apoptosis (cell death) and eventually fibrosis of liver cells. This can cause portal hypertension, ascites, variceal bleeding and hepatic encephalopathy. Drinking habits of patients need to be assessed routinely. If alcohol consumption is ceased the liver can possibly regenerate to some extent.

Treatment
The most important part of treatment is alcohol <u>cessation</u>. Maintenance of abstinence is essential to improving outcomes and should include the use of drug treatment to control cravings. An alcohol rehabilitation program and a <u>support group</u> whose members share common experiences and problems are extremely helpful in breaking the addiction to alcohol. Proper nutrition is essential to help the liver recover. Vitamins and trace minerals, including vitamin A, vitamin D, thiamine (vitamin B1), folate, pyridoxine (vitamin B6) and zinc can help reverse malnutrition. <u>Thiamine</u> is used to prevent and treat <u>Wernicke-Korsakoff syndrome.</u> Wernicke's encephalopathy and Korsakoff syndrome are different conditions that are both due to brain damage caused by a <u>lack of vitamin B1</u>. Last, avoidance of hepatotoxic agents and/or adjusting/limiting the dose of hepatotoxic agents should be utilized.

COMPLICATIONS OF LIVER DISEASE AND CIRRHOSIS

Portal Hypertension and Variceal Bleeding
Portal hypertension, or increased blood pressure in the portal vein, can cause further complications including the development and bleeding of esophageal varices. These are enlarged veins in the lower part of the esophagus. They are most commonly caused by cirrhosis. The scarring blocks the blood flow through the liver, which causes blood to flow up through the veins in the esophagus. The veins balloon out and will bleed if they break open.

Acute variceal bleeding can be <u>fatal</u>. Patients should be stabilized by providing supportive therapy such as blood volume resuscitation/blood products, mechanical ventilation, correction of coagulopathy, and attempts to stop the bleeding and preventing rebleeding. Band ligation or sclerotherapy are recommended first-line treatments for bleeding varices. In addition, <u>vasoactive</u> therapy is used to stop or minimize the bleeding by decreasing portal blood flow and pressure by splanchnic vasoconstriction. <u>Octreotide is selective</u> for the splanchnic vessels whereas <u>vasopressin is non-selective</u>. Surgical interventions may be considered if the patient is not responding to treatment or to prevent future rebleeding episodes. Common surgical procedures include balloon tamponade (may help control current bleeding) or transjugular intrahepatic portosystemic shunt (TIPS). Short-term antibiotic prophylaxis (ceftriaxone or quinolone for up to 7 days) should be provided to cirrhotic patients with variceal bleed to reduce bacterial infections and mortality. <u>Non-selective beta-blockers should be added after resolution</u> of variceal bleeding for <u>secondary prevention</u> of variceal bleeding recurrence.

DRUG	DOSING	SAFETY/SIDE EFFECTS/MONITORING
Octreotide *(SandoSTATIN)* Analogue of somatostatin – has greater potency and longer duration of action	Bolus: 25-100 mcg IV (usual 50 mcg), may repeat in 1 hr if hemorrhage not controlled Infusion: followed by 25-50 mcg/hr continuous IV infusion x 2-5 days	**SIDE EFFECTS** Bradycardia, chest pain, fatigue, HA, pruritus, hyperglycemia, hypoglycemia (highest risk in type 1 diabetes), N/V/D, hypothyroidism, abdominal pain, malaise, fever, dizziness, flatulence, cholelithiasis, biliary sludge, constipation, injection site pain, arthropathy, myalgias, URTIs **MONITORING** Blood glucose, HR, ECG
Vasopressin *(Pitressin, Vasostrict)* <u>Antidiuretic hormone analog</u> Not 1ˢᵗ line (usually used with nitroglycerin IV to prevent myocardial ischemia)	Infusion: 0.2-0.4 units/min IV (max 0.8 units/min), max duration 24 hours	**SIDE EFFECTS** Arrhythmias, chest pain, MI, ↓ cardiac output, ↑ BP, nausea, vomiting **MONITORING** BP, HR, ECG, fluid balance

<u>Non-selective</u> beta blockers (<u>such as nadolol and propranolol</u>) or endoscopic variceal ligation (EVL) are used for primary prevention of variceal bleeding. <u>Beta blockers reduce portal pressure</u> by reducing portal venous inflow by two mechanisms: 1) decreased cardiac output (via beta-1 blockade), and 2) decreased splanchnic blood flow by vasoconstriction (via beta-2 blockade and unopposed alpha activity). The beta blocker should be titrated to the maximal tolerated dose (<u>target HR 55 – 60 BPM</u>) and continued indefinitely.

DRUG	DOSING	SAFETY/SIDE EFFECTS/MONITORING
Nadolol *(Corgard)*	20-40 mg PO daily	Refer to Hypertension chapter for a complete review of beta blockers. **BOXED WARNING** Do not withdraw beta blockers abruptly (particularly in patients with CAD), gradually taper over 1-2 weeks to avoid acute tachycardia, HTN, and/or ischemia. **CONTRAINDICATIONS** Sinus bradycardia, 2ⁿᵈ or 3ʳᵈ degree heart block, sick sinus syndrome (unless patient has a functioning artificial pacemaker) or cardiogenic shock. Do not initiate in patients with active asthma exacerbation.
Propranolol (Inderal LA, Inderal XL, InnoPran XL)	20 mg PO BID	<u>Non-selective</u> agents are used for portal hypertension; use extreme caution with asthma or severe COPD or peripheral vascular disease and Raynaud's disease. May mask signs of hyperthyroidism; may aggravate psychiatric conditions, and use caution in patients with diabetes particularly with recurrent hypoglycemia. Monitor <u>HR</u> and <u>BP</u>.

Hepatic Encephalopathy

Hepatic encephalopathy (HE) is a syndrome of neuropsychiatric abnormalities caused by acute or chronic hepatic insufficiency. Symptoms include <u>musty odor of the breath</u> and/or urine, <u>changes in thinking, confusion, forgetfulness</u>, mood changes, poor concentration, drowsiness, disorientation, worsening handwriting and hand tremor (asterixis), sluggish movements, and many others, including risk of coma. The <u>symptoms of HE result from an accumulation of gut-derived nitrogenous substances</u>

in the blood (such as <u>ammonia</u>, glutamate, others) due to decreased hepatic functioning and shunting through the porto-systemic collaterals, which bypass the liver. Treatment includes identifying and treating precipitating factors and <u>reducing blood ammonia levels through diet (limiting the amount of animal protein) and drug therapy.</u>

Patients should have a daily protein intake of 1 – 1.5 g/kg. Vegetable and dairy sources of protein are preferred to animal sources due to the lower calorie to nitrogen ratio. Branched-chain amino acids (BCAAs) (e.g., leucine, isoleucine, valine) are favored over aromatic amino acids (AAAs); they interfere with AAAs ability to cross the blood-brain barrier and increase hepatocyte growth factor synthesis.

Drug therapy consists of nonabsorbable disaccharides (such as lactulose) and antibiotics (rifaximin, neomycin, others) for acute and chronic therapy. <u>Lactulose is first line therapy for both acute and chronic (prevention) therapy, followed by rifaximin.</u> Lactulose works by converting ammonia produced by intestinal bacteria to ammonium, which is polar and therefore cannot readily diffuse into the blood. Lactulose also enhances diffusion of ammonia into the colon for excretion. Antibiotics work by inhibiting the activity of urease-producing bacteria, which decreases the ammonia production. Zinc (220 mg PO BID) may be used; it can serve as a cofactor for enzymes of the urea cycle and further decrease ammonia concentrations and correct a zinc deficiency.

DRUG	DOSING	SAFETY/SIDE EFFECTS/MONITORING
Lactulose (*Constulose, Enulose, Generlac, Kristalose*) Oral solution and packet	Treatment: 30-45 mL (or 20-30 grams) PO every hour until evacuation; then 30-45 mL (20-30 grams) PO 3-4 times/day titrated to produce 2-3 soft bowel movements daily Enema: Q4-6H PRN Prevention: 30-45 mL (or 20-30 grams) PO 3-4 times/day titrated to produce 2-3 soft bowel movements daily	**SIDE EFFECTS** <u>Flatulence, diarrhea, dyspepsia, abdominal discomfort,</u> dehydration, hypernatremia, hypokalemia **MONITORING** Mental status, bowel movements, ammonia, fluid status, electrolytes
Rifaximin (*Xifaxan*) Tablet	Treatment (off-label): 400 mg PO Q8H x 5-10 days Prevention: 550 mg PO BID	**SIDE EFFECTS** Peripheral edema, dizziness, fatigue, nausea, ascites, flatulence, headache **MONITORING** Mental status, ammonia
Neomycin (*Neo-Fradin*)	500-2,000 mg PO Q6-8H x 5-6 days	**BOXED WARNINGS** <u>Neurotoxicity,</u> (hearing loss, vertigo, ataxia); nephrotoxicity (particularly in renal impairment or with concurrent use of other nephrotoxic drugs); may cause neuromuscular blockade and respiratory paralysis especially when given soon after anesthesia or with muscle relaxants **SIDE EFFECTS** <u>GI upset,</u> ototoxicity, nephrotoxicity, irritation/soreness of mouth/rectal area **MONITORING** Mental status, renal function, hearing, ammonia
MetroNIDAZOLE (*Flagyl, Flagyl ER, Metro*)	250 mg PO Q6-12H	**NOTES** Do not use long term due to <u>peripheral neuropathies</u> See Infectious Diseases I for additional information

Ascites

Ascites is fluid accumulation within the peritoneal space that can lead to the development of spontaneous bacterial peritonitis (SBP) and hepatorenal syndrome (HRS). Ascites is a common occurrence when the portal hypertension leads to an increase in systemic and splanchnic vasodilation, which results in increased arterial pressure, sodium and water retention, and renal vasoconstriction.

There are many treatment approaches to managing ascites, which are chosen based on the severity. Patients with ascites due to portal hypertension should restrict dietary sodium intake to < 2 grams/day, avoid sodium-retaining medications (including NSAIDs), and use diuretics to increase fluid loss. Restriction of fluid is recommended only in patients with symptomatic severe hyponatremia (serum Na < 120 mEq/L).

Diuretic therapy for ascites can be initiated with either spironolactone monotherapy or with a combination of furosemide and spironolactone. Spironolactone is initiated at a single daily dose of 50 – 100 mg and increased to a maximum of 400 mg per day. When used in combination, the drugs should be titrated to a maximal weight loss of 0.5 kg/day with a ratio of 40 mg furosemide to 100 mg spironolactone to maintain potassium balance, if possible. Furosemide by itself is ineffective. All patients with cirrhosis and ascites should be considered for liver transplantation. In severe cases abdominal paracentesis may be needed to directly remove ascitic fluid. Large volume paracentesis (removal of > 5 L) has been associated with significant fluid shifts and the addition of albumin (6 – 8 grams per liter of fluid removed) is recommended to prevent paracentesis-induced circulatory dysfunction and progression to hepatorenal syndrome.

Spontaneous Bacterial Peritonitis

Spontaneous bacterial peritonitis (SBP) is an acute infection of the ascitic fluid. Diagnosis is guided by cell and microbiologic analysis. In general, targeting *Streptococci* and enteric Gram-negative pathogens with ceftriaxone (or equivalent) for 5 – 7 days is recommended. The addition of albumin (1.5 grams/kg of body weight on day 1 and 1 gram/kg on day 3) can improve survival in some patients. Primary prophylaxis with norfloxacin or sulfamethoxazole/trimethoprim to prevent SBP is indicated in select cases. The same agents are used to prevent SBP recurrence. Norfloxacin is not readily available and ciprofloxacin is used as an alternative.

Hepatorenal Syndrome

Hepatorenal syndrome (HRS) is the development of renal failure in patients with advanced cirrhosis. HRS is the result of renal vasoconstriction mediated by activation of the renin-angiotensin-aldosterone system (RAAS) and the sympathetic nervous system (SNS) through a feedback mechanism known as hepatorenal reflex. Appropriately treating the various stages and complications of cirrhosis, and avoiding nephrotoxins and renal hypoperfusion help prevent progression to HRS. HRS can be directly treated with albumin, octreotide, and midodrine, but prevention is critical given the difficulty in managing HRS in this patient population.

PRACTICE CASE

PM is a 44 y/o male patient being seen in the gastroenterology clinic for follow-up. He was recently diagnosed with HCV and expected to started treatment this week with Harvoni. His past medical history is significant for depression and GERD. PM stopped using alcohol and IV drugs 5 years ago. He has repeatedly tested negative for HIV over many years.

Allergies: NKDA

Medications:
Celexa 40 mg daily
Pepcid 20 mg daily
Tums 1-2 tabs PRN heartburn

Vitals:
Height: 5'9" Weight: 196 pounds
BP: 131/82 mmHg HR: 75 BPM RR: 13 BPM Temp: 98.°F Pain: 3/10

Labs:	
Na (mEq/L) = 140 (135 - 145)	WBC (cells/mm³) = 6.1 (4 - 11 x 10^3)
K (mEq/L) = 4.1 (3.5 - 5)	Hgb (g/dL) = 14.1 (13.5 - 18 male, 12 - 16 female)
Cl (mEq/L) = 101 (95 - 103)	
HCO_3 (mEq/L) = 29 (24 - 30)	Hct (%) = 42.3 (38 - 50 male, 36 - 46 female)
BUN (mg/dL) = 17 (7 - 20)	
SCr (mg/dL) = 1.1 (0.6 - 1.3)	Plt (cells/mm³) = 187 (150 - 450 x 10^3)
Glucose (mg/dL) = 132 (100 - 125)	AST (IU/L) = 87 (1 - 40)
Ca (mg/dL) = 10.1 (8.5 - 10.5)	ALT (IU/L) = 75 (1 - 40)
Mg (mEq/L) = 1.5 (1.3 - 2.1)	Albumin (g/dL) = 3.7 (3.5 - 5)
PO_4 (mg/dL) = 4.2 (2.3 - 4.7)	T Bili (mg/dL) = 1.1 (0.1 - 1.2)
	TSH (mIU/L) = 1.9 (0.3 - 3)

Refer to the clinical pharmacist for review of medication side effects and additional counseling.

Questions

1. PM is starting *Harvoni*. What are the components of *Harvoni*?

    a. Ledipasvir + sofosbuvir
    b. Paritaprevir + ritonavir + ombitasvir
    c. Paritaprevir + ritonavir + ombitasvir + dasabuvir
    d. Simeprevir + sofosbuvir
    e. Sofosbuvir + daclatasvir

2. Upon review of PM's medication list, which medication/s pose a potential drug-drug interaction risk with *Harvoni*?

    a. *Celexa*
    b. *Tums*
    c. *Pepcid*
    d. *Celexa* and *Pepcid*
    e. *Tums* and *Pepcid*

Questions 3 – 7 do not apply to the above case.

3. Which of the following is the most serious and primary toxicity of ribavirin?

   a. Hemolytic anemia
   b. Hemorrhagic cystitis
   c. Pancreatitis
   d. Agranulocytosis
   e. Gastrointestinal hemorrhage

4. A patient is scheduled to start immunosuppressive therapy for chronic inflammatory bowel disease. Testing for which of the following is indicated? (Select **ALL** that apply.)

   a. Latent Hepatitis A virus infection
   b. Latent Hepatitis B virus infection
   c. Latent Hepatitis C virus infection
   d. HIV
   e. Herpes Simplex Virus

5. A patient with liver failure presents with acute hepatic encephalopathy. Which of the following is considered first-line treatment for acute hepatic encephalopathy?

   a. Decreasing protein intake to < 1 gram/kg/day
   b. Lactulose
   c. Furosemide
   d. Neomycin
   e. Metronidazole

6. Which of the following is correct regarding daclatasvir treatment? (Select **ALL** that apply.)

   a. Test for Q80k polymorphism prior to starting treatment.
   b. Avoid acid suppressive therapy while on treatment.
   c. It is used in combination with sofosbuvir.
   d. The brand name is *Sovaldi.*
   e. It is indicated for treatment of acute variceal bleeding.

7. Which of the following medications can lead to renal insufficiency and osteomalacia?

   a. Adefovir
   b. Tenofovir
   c. Daclatasvir
   d. Lamivudine
   e. Entecavir

Answers
1-a, 2-e, 3-a, 4-b, 5-b, 6-c, 7-b

INFECTIOUS DISEASES I: BACKGROUND & ANTIBACTERIALS BY DRUG CLASS

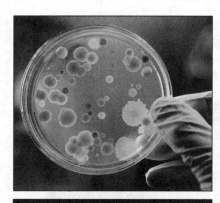

We gratefully acknowledge the assistance of Emi Minejima, PharmD, Assistant Professor and Annie Wong-Beringer, PharmD, FCCP, FIDSA, Associate Dean and Professor, University of Southern California School of Pharmacy, in preparing this chapter.

BACKGROUND

An infectious disease is caused by one or more pathogenic (disease-causing) viruses, bacteria, fungi, protozoa, parasites, and/or infectious proteins (prions). Infectious diseases are transmitted through various mechanisms, including physical contact with an infected individual or their body fluids, consuming contaminated food or water, or by touching contaminated objects. Some conditions are transmitted by airborne inhalation and others are spread by a vector (carrier). Transmissible diseases that are spread from <u>person to person</u> are referred to as <u>communicable</u> or <u>contagious</u>, and can be highly infective; these involve special care from the patient and the facility to stop the infection from spreading. To successfully treat an infectious disease, multiple factors must be considered. The three primary factors are the pathogen characteristics (the <u>bug</u>), the medication properties (the <u>drug</u>), and any patient-specific information (the <u>host</u>). Patient-specific information includes medication allergies, immune function, and chronic diseases that put a patient at risk for certain types of infections or which can change the treatment approach (e.g., the presence of renal failure may require a change in the drug or the dose).

GUIDELINES/REFERENCES

Barlett JG, Auwaerter PG, Pham PA. Johns Hopkins Antibiotic Guide: Diagnosis & Treatment of Infectious Diseases 3rd Ed. Massachusetts: Jones and Bartlett Learning; 2012.

Addtl. guidelines by disease state; with online course videos.

Bacterial Organism Identification

One of the first steps in bacterial identification is the Gram stain. Bacteria stain differently based on the composition of their cell wall. <u>Gram-positive</u> organisms have a thick cell wall and stain dark <u>purple, or bluish</u> in color from the crystal violet stain. <u>Gram-negative</u> organisms have a thin cell wall and take up the safranin counterstain, resulting in a <u>pink or reddish</u> color. In addition to revealing the cell wall composition, the Gram stain outlines the organism, so it can be categorized by <u>shape</u> (or <u>morphology</u>). Gram stain results can help determine the appropriate <u>empiric</u> antibiotic regimen, which is based on a best-guess of the <u>likely organism/s</u> causing the infection. Empiric treatment is usually <u>broad-spectrum</u>, which means it covers several different types of bacteria. Antibiotic <u>streamlining</u> is the process of converting patients from a broad-spectrum regimen to treatment that is targeted to the organism (<u>narrow spectrum</u>). Streamlining is important to <u>limit drug resistance</u> and improve <u>patient care</u>.

Selected Bacterial Organisms

GRAM-POSITIVE ORGANISMS	
COCCI	
Clusters	**Pairs/Chains**
Staphylococcus aureus (MSSA, MRSA, CA-MRSA) Staphylococcus epidermidis (Coagulase-negative Staph)	Streptococcus pneumoniae Streptococcus pyogenes (Group A) Streptococcus agalactiae (Group B) Viridans group Streptococcus Enterococcus faecalis (including VRE) Enterococcus faecium (including VRE)
RODS	**ANAEROBES**
Bacillus anthracis Corynebacterium species Listeria monocytogenes Nocardia asteroides (branched appearance)	Peptostreptococcus Actinomyces israelii (branched appearance) Clostridium difficile Clostridium perfringens Lactobacillus species Propionibacterium acnes

GRAM-NEGATIVE ORGANISMS	
COCCI	**COCCOBACILLI**
Neisseria gonorrhoeae Neisseria meningitidis	Acinetobacter baumannii Bordetella pertussis Pasteurella multocida Moraxella catarrhalis
RODS	
Enterobacteriaceae (colonize the gut)	**Non-Enterobacteriaceae (do not colonize the gut)**
Escherichia coli Klebsiella species Enterobacter cloacae Proteus mirabilis Serratia species Citrobacter species Morganella morganii Salmonella species Shigella species	Pseudomonas aeruginosa Burkholderia cepacia Stenotrophomonas maltophilia Legionella pneumophila Haemophilus influenzae Eikenella corrodens Providencia species Campylobacter jejuni (curved rod) Helicobacter pylori (curved rod) Vibrio cholerae Yersinia pestis
ANAEROBES	**ATYPICAL ORGANISMS**
Bacteroides fragilis Prevotella species Fusobacterium species	Chlamydia/Chlamydophila pneumoniae Mycoplasma pneumoniae Mycobacterium tuberculosis (acid-fast bacillus)

MSSA = methicillin-susceptible Staphylococcus aureus; MRSA = methicillin-resistant Staphylococcus aureus; CA-MRSA = Community-associated methicillin-resistant Staphylcoccus aureus; VRE = Vancomycin-resistant Enterococcus

COMMON BACTERIAL PATHOGENS FOR SELECTED SITES OF INFECTION

CNS/Meningitis
Streptococcus pneumoniae
Neisseria meningitidis
Haemophilus influenzae
Streptococci/E. coli (young)
Listeria (young/old)

Upper Respiratory
Moraxella catarrhalis
Haemophilus influenzae
Streptococci

Bone & Joint
Staphylococcus aureus
Staphylococcus epidermidis
Streptococci
Neisseria gonorrhoeae
± GNR

Mouth/ENT
Mouth flora *(Peptostreptococcus, Actinomyces)*
Anaerobic GNR
± *Haemophilus influenzae* and aerobic GNR

Skin/Soft Tissue
Staphylococcus aureus
Streptococcus pyogenes
Staphylococcus epidermidis
Pasteurella multocida
± aerobic/anaerobic GNR (diabetics)

Intra-abdominal
E. coli, Proteus, Klebsiella
Enterococci/Streptococci
Bacteroides species

Lower Respiratory (Community)
Streptococcus pneumoniae
Haemophilus influenzae
Atypicals: *Legionella, Mycoplasma*
Enteric GNR (alcoholics, IC, HCA)

Lower Respiratory (Hospital)
Enteric GNR *(E. coli, Klebsiella, Proteus)*
Streptococcus pneumoniae
Pseudomonas aeruginosa
Enterobacter species
S. aureus, including MRSA

Urinary Tract
E. coli, Proteus, Klebsiella
Staphylococcus saprophyticus
Enterococci/Streptococci

CNS = central nervous system, ENT = ear, nose and throat, GNR = Gram-negative rods, HCA = healthcare associated, IC = immunocompromised

ANTIBIOTIC RESISTANCE

Antibiotic resistance is the ability of an organism to multiply in the presence of a drug that would normally limit its growth or kill it. The CDC estimates that there are ~2,000,000 infections a year where the causative organism is resistant to the usual treatment. These infections are difficult to treat and often require drugs that are costly and/or toxic.

There are a variety of mechanisms that cause resistance. It can be <u>inherent</u> to the organism. For example, atypical organisms lack a cell wall, so they are inherently resistant to drugs that target the cell wall, such as beta-lactams. It can be due to <u>selection pressure</u>; antibiotics kill off the susceptible bacteria, leaving behind the more resistant strains to multiply. For example, normal GI flora includes *Enterococcus*, a subset of which is vancomycin-resistant *Enterococcus* (VRE), which can become predominant after the use of antibiotics that have eliminated susceptible organisms. Beta-lactamases are the primary method of resistance to beta-lactam antibiotics. Beta-lactamases are enzymes (produced by the bacteria) which break down the antibiotic before it can bind to the site of activity. Some beta-lactamases can break down all penicillins and most cephalosporins. These are called <u>extended-spectrum beta-lactamases (ESBLs)</u>. Organisms that produce ESBLs are a therapeutic challenge, and serious infections involving these organisms are <u>treated with carbapenems</u>, or newer <u>cephalosporin/beta-lactamase inhibitors</u>.

Carbapenem-resistant *Enterobacteriaceae* (CRE) are a group of very multidrug-resistant (MDR) Gram-negative organisms that are becoming more common. CRE produce enzymes that break down penicillins, most cephalosporins, and carbapenems and are most commonly found in *Klebsiella* spp. (a part of the normal GI flora). Infections with *Klebsiella* are normally treatable with older, safer drugs. Carbapenem-resistant *Klebsiella pneumoniae* infections typically require treatment with a combination of antibiotics that can include a polymyxin, an older drug class which was not used for many years because less toxic drugs became available. The emergence of CRE and some other resistant Gram-negative infections (including *Acinetobacter baumannii* and *Pseudomonas aeruginosa*), pulled polymyxins back into use, with the need to manage the toxicity that came with them. Another treatment option is a newer, costly drug [the combination agent ceftazidime/avibactam *(Avycaz)*], which is active against some types of carbapenemase-producing organisms.

COMMON RESISTANT PATHOGENS	
S. aureus (MRSA)	*K. pneumoniae (ESBL, CRE)*
E. faecalis, E. faecium (VRE)	*Acinetobacter baumannii*
E. coli, extended-spectrum beta-lactamase producing (ESBL, CRE)	*Pseudomonas aeruginosa*

ANTIBIOTICS AND COLLATERAL DAMAGE

Collateral damage refers to the unintended consequences of antibiotic use, including altered GI flora, which can lead to antibiotic resistance and can cause superinfections such as *C. difficile* infections (CDI). Antibiotics kill the pathogens and normal, healthy GI flora, resulting in overgrowth of organisms that are resistant to the drug. *C. difficile* spores are normally present as part of the flora in the inactive form. When an antibiotic kills off the normal flora, the *C. difficile* spores can become activated and infectious. The activated spores produce toxins that inflame the GI mucosa. The symptoms depend on the degree of inflammation, which can be mild (loose stools and some cramping) to pseudomembranous colitis (which can be fatal). Older, sicker patients are at a higher risk of developing a *C. difficile* infection. They are also more likely to do poorly once the infection is contracted. In recent years, *C. difficile* infections have become more common, more severe, and more difficult to treat. All antibiotics are associated with risk for CDI, and include a warning of risk of superinfection. Certain antibiotic classes are associated with high risk for CDI, such as clindamycin, which has a boxed warning for CDI. When appropriate, antibiotic treatment should be streamlined, or discontinued.

INFECTIOUS DISEASES CONCEPTS

- Minimum inhibitory concentration (MIC): Lowest drug concentration that prevents visible microbial growth after a 24 hour incubation. The MIC is usually reported on the culture and susceptibility report, with the susceptibility interpretation (S, I, or R, described below).

- Breakpoint: The MIC at which an organism is deemed either susceptible or resistant to an antibiotic. Breakpoints vary for different antibiotic classes. Breakpoints are established by the FDA and Clinical and Laboratory Standards Institute (CLSI), not by individual hospitals.

- Synergy: When two or more agents combine to produce a greater effect than the sum of their individual effects (in contrast to an additive effect, which is the sum of the effect of the individual agents). Synergy is important for treating certain types of infections.

Culture and Susceptibility

Culture and Susceptibility (C & S) reports are provided by the microbiology laboratory. Patient specimens (lung secretions, urine, blood, tissue from a wound or fluid from an abscess) are sent to the lab, where bacteria are Gram-stained (to reveal the cell wall type and shape). Once an organism has grown in culture, it is identified, and tested against different concentrations of antibiotics to determine the MIC. In the report, each antibiotic has a susceptibility interpretation: S (susceptible or sensitive), I (intermediate) or R (resistant), and the MIC in mg/L (or µg/mL). Refer to the following chart.

Susceptible means that the drug inhibits the organism and is likely a good treatment option. Drugs listed as Intermediate may be effective with a high dose (which may be toxic), or if the drug reaches high concentrations at the site of infection. A drug rated as intermediate would not be expected to achieve as good a result as a drug rated as susceptible. Resistant means the drug is unlikely to reach effective levels at the site of the infection and is not a treatment option. It is best to use a drug that is sensitive. MICs are specific to each antibiotic and organism and should not be compared among different classes of antibiotics. In addition to the susceptibility interpretation and the MIC, the choice of antibiotic will depend upon the site of infection, plus patient-specific characteristics and cost.

Sample Culture and Susceptibility Report

> 100,000 CFU/ML *E. COLI*

DRUG	MIC INTERPRETATION	MIC (MG/L)
Ampicillin	R	> 32
Ampicillin/sulbactam	S	< 2
Cefazolin-UTI	S	< 16
Cefepime	S	< 1
Ceftriaxone	S	< 1
Ciprofloxacin	S	1
Gentamicin	S	< 1
Piperacillin/tazobactam	S	< 4
Meropenem	S	< 0.25
Nitrofurantoin	S	< 32
Tobramycin	S	< 1
Sulfamethoxazole/trimethoprim	R	> 76/4

CFU = colony-forming units; S = susceptible; I = intermediate; R = resistant

Antibiogram

An antibiogram combines the C & S data from individual patients at an institution into one chart (such as all Gram-positive organisms cultured at that hospital). This provides the susceptibility patterns at the hospital over a specific time period (generally 1 year). The bacteria types are shown on the y-axis. The x-axis lists the drugs and the percentage of each organism that are susceptible to each drug. Antibiograms aid in selecting empiric treatment (for example, if a patient has a Gram-positive cocci lung infection, a drug that covers a high percentage of the likely organism/s can be chosen from the antibiogram. They are also used to monitor resistance trends over time).

Antibiogram Example (abridged)

HOSPITAL ANTIBIOGRAM JANUARY 2014-DECEMBER 2014 REPORTED AS % SUSCEPTIBLE	# OF ISOLATES	PENICILLIN	OXACILLIN	AMPICILLIN	CEFOTAXIME	CEFTRIAXONE	CLINDAMYCIN	ERYTHROMYCIN	GENTAMICIN	LEVOFLOXACIN	LINEZOLID	TETRACYCLINE	SMX/TMP	VANCOMYCIN
GRAM-POSITIVE ORGANISMS ALL ISOLATES														
Staphylococcus aureus	1360													
MSSA	830	–	100	–	–	–	88	78	98§	87	100	93	98	100
MRSA	530	–	–	–	–	–	78	10	92§	15	100	93	92	100
Streptococcus pneumoniae	42	91* 83**	–	–	100* 92**	100* 92**	–	79	–	97	–	85	80	100
Enterococcus spp.	663	–	–	93	–	–	–	–	69§	–	99	–	–	100
Enterococcus faecalis	99	–	–	98	92	–	–	–	62§	–	99	–	–	87
Enterococcus faecium	164	–	–	10	100	–	–	–	90§	100	99	–	–	15
URINE ISOLATES														
Enterococcus spp.	153	–	–	79	–	–	–	–	–	61	100	–	–	81

*Non-meningitis; **Meningitis; §Synergy only

ANTIMICROBIAL STEWARDSHIP PROGRAMS

- Antimicrobial stewardship programs (ASP) involve efforts to 1) improve patient safety and outcomes, 2) curb resistance, and 3) promote cost-effectiveness.

- ASPs are a <u>team effort</u> among ID physicians, ID pharmacists, microbiology lab personnel, infection prevention and control, information technology, and prescribers. Teams work toward the <u>optimal antibiotic selection, dosage, route of administration, and duration</u>.

- ASPs use guidelines with local antibiograms to establish antibiotic guidance for their hospital.

- Most ASPs conduct audits of prescribing habits and provide education to change suboptimal prescribing habits and improve care.

- Other aspects of an ASP can include 1) discontinuation or <u>de-escalation</u> of broad-spectrum antibiotics (based on C & S results), 2) automatic <u>intravenous-to-oral interchange</u>, and 3) restriction- or criteria-based authorization policies for certain drugs (to limit use to specific situations).

Antibiotic Mechanism of Action

Knowledge of the mechanism of action (MOA) can help distinguish what types of organisms can be treated by a given antibiotic. In addition, it generally predicts the <u>bacteriostatic</u> (inhibits bacterial growth) or <u>bactericidal</u> (kills bacteria) activity (see figure below). While bactericidal activity can be predicted by the MOA, it also depends on other factors, including the organism and MIC, achievable concentrations of the antibiotic at the site of infection, duration of exposure and amount of bacteria present. It is important to know which agents are bactericidal and bacteriostatic; however, for most infections, bactericidal activity does not imply improved patient outcomes in a patient who is not immunocompromised. Guidelines typically prioritize bactericidal antibiotics when it is of particular importance, such as in immunocompromised patients, or for deep-seated infections (e.g., bloodstream infections, endocarditis).

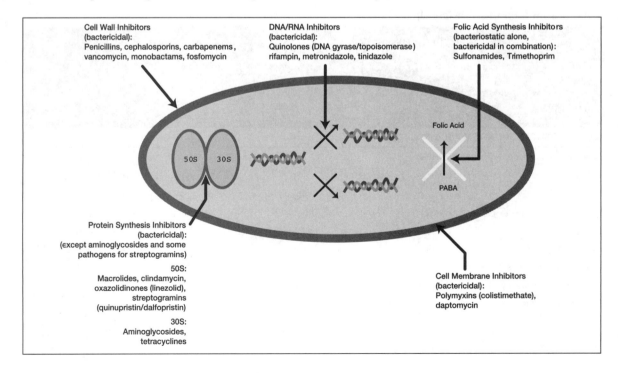

Cell Wall Inhibitors (bactericidal): Penicillins, cephalosporins, carbapenems, vancomycin, monobactams, fosfomycin

DNA/RNA Inhibitors (bactericidal): Quinolones (DNA gyrase/topoisomerase) rifampin, metronidazole, tinidazole

Folic Acid Synthesis Inhibitors (bacteriostatic alone, bactericidal in combination): Sulfonamides, Trimethoprim

Folic Acid

PABA

Protein Synthesis Inhibitors (bactericidal): (except aminoglycosides and some pathogens for streptogramins)

50S: Macrolides, clindamycin, oxazolidinones (linezolid), streptogramins (quinupristin/dalfopristin)

30S: Aminoglycosides, tetracyclines

Cell Membrane Inhibitors (bactericidal): Polymyxins (colistimethate), daptomycin

ANTIBIOTIC PHARMACOKINETICS AND PHARMACODYNAMICS

The appropriate selection of an antibiotic regimen requires an understanding of pharmacokinetic (PK) principles (absorption, distribution, metabolism and excretion) and pharmacodynamic principles (concentration-dependent or time-dependent killing). Refer to the Pharmacokinetics chapter.

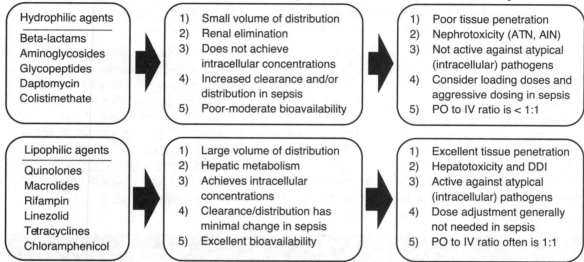

Hydrophilic agents		
Beta-lactams		
Aminoglycosides		
Glycopeptides		
Daptomycin		
Colistimethate		

1) Small volume of distribution
2) Renal elimination
3) Does not achieve intracellular concentrations
4) Increased clearance and/or distribution in sepsis
5) Poor-moderate bioavailability

1) Poor tissue penetration
2) Nephrotoxicity (ATN, AIN)
3) Not active against atypical (intracellular) pathogens
4) Consider loading doses and aggressive dosing in sepsis
5) PO to IV ratio is < 1:1

Lipophilic agents
Quinolones
Macrolides
Rifampin
Linezolid
Tetracyclines
Chloramphenicol

1) Large volume of distribution
2) Hepatic metabolism
3) Achieves intracellular concentrations
4) Clearance/distribution has minimal change in sepsis
5) Excellent bioavailability

1) Excellent tissue penetration
2) Hepatotoxicity and DDI
3) Active against atypical (intracellular) pathogens
4) Dose adjustment generally not needed in sepsis
5) PO to IV ratio often is 1:1

ATN = acute tubular necrosis, AIN = acute interstitial nephritis, PO = oral, IV = intravenous, DDI = drug-drug interaction

Hydrophilic or Lipophilic Agents

Hydrophilicity or lipophilicity of the antibiotic can be used to predict a number of PK parameters (see following figure). Lipophilic drugs generally have enhanced penetration of bone, lung, and brain tissues.

Dose Optimization

Pharmacodynamics of selected agents are displayed in the following figure. Agents that exhibit time-dependent killing (such as beta-lactams) are generally dosed more frequently to maximize the time above the MIC, while concentration-dependent agents (such as aminoglycosides) are generally dosed less frequently and in higher doses to maximize the concentration above the MIC. The <u>pharmacodynamics of beta-lactam antibiotics can be maximized</u> by more frequent dosing, extending the infusion time (such as over 4 hours) or administering as a <u>continuous infusion</u> which can lead to <u>greater time spent above the MIC</u>. Studies have documented that extended/continuous infusion of beta-lactams can reduce length of stay, mortality, and costs particularly when treating pneumonia caused by multidrug-resistant Gram-negative pathogens like *Pseudomonas*.

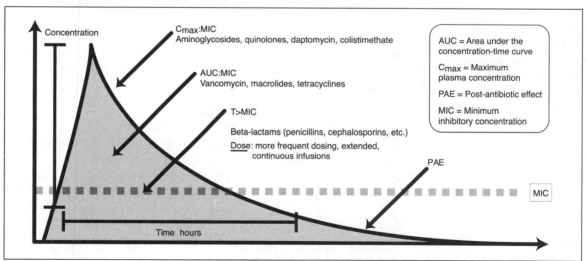

PENICILLINS

Penicillins (PCNs) are <u>beta-lactam antibiotics</u>, whose chemical structure is characterized by a beta-lactam ring. They <u>inhibit bacterial cell wall synthesis</u> by binding to penicillin-binding proteins (PBPs), which prevents the final transpeptidation step of peptidoglycan synthesis in bacterial cell walls. PCNs exhibit <u>time-dependent killing</u> and are <u>bactericidal, except against *Enterococci* species</u> where amino-glycosides (gentamicin and streptomycin) are needed for bactericidal activity.

- Coverage: Natural penicillins are mainly active against Gram-positive cocci, including *Enterococcus* and anaerobes (mouth flora), with little Gram-negative activity. Addition of the amino group to form the aminopenicillins expands coverage to include the Gram-negative bacilli *Haemophilus, Neisseria, Proteus, E. coli, Klebsiella* (HNPEK). The <u>addition of a beta-lactamase inhibitor</u> adds activity against MSSA, <u>increased Gram-negative coverage</u> (more resistant strains of HNPEK) and Gram-negative <u>anaerobes</u> (*B. fragilis*). Extended-spectrum penicillins, <u>piperacillin/tazobactam</u> and ticarcillin/cla-vulanate have very broad coverage with <u>expanded Gram-negative coverage</u> including *Citrobacter, Acinetobacter, Providencia, Enterobacter, Serratia* (CAPES) and *Pseudomonas aeruginosa*. Nafcillin, oxacillin, and dicloxacillin have enhanced activity against methicillin-susceptible *Staphylococcus aureus* (MSSA), but lack *Enterococcus* activity. Class trends: <u>No atypical coverage</u>.

Select Penicillins

DRUG	DOSING	SAFETY/SIDE EFFECTS/MONITORING
Natural Penicillins – *Streptococci* (↑ resistance with *S. pneumoniae*), *Enterococci*, Gram-positive anaerobes (<u>mouth flora</u>)		**BOXED WARNING** Penicillin G benzathine: Not for intravenous (IV) use, can cause cardiorespiratory arrest and death.
Penicillin *(Pen VK)* Tablet, suspension	125-500 mg PO Q6-12H on empty stomach	
Penicillin G Benzathine (*Bicillin L-A*) Pen G Benzathine and Pen G Procaine *(Bicillin C-R)*	1.2-2.4 million units IM x 1 (frequency varies)	**CONTRAINDICATIONS** *Augmentin/Unasyn*: History of cholestatic jaundice or hepatic dysfunction associated with previous use; severe renal impairment (CrCl < 30 mL/min)
Penicillin G Aqueous *(Pfizerpen-G)*	2-4 million units IV Q4-6H	**WARNINGS** Anaphylaxis/hypersensitivity reactions, do not use in PCN-allergic patients.
Aminopenicillins – *Streptococci, Enterococci,* HNPEK and Gram-positive anaerobes (mouth flora). <u>Beta-lactamase inhibitor combos</u> are active against <u>MSSA</u>, <u>more resistant</u> strains of HNPEK plus Gram-negative anaerobes (*B. fragilis*)		**SIDE EFFECTS** <u>GI upset, diarrhea, rash</u>/allergic reactions/anaphylaxis, acute interstitial nephritis, myelosuppression with prolonged use, ↑ LFTs, <u>seizures with accumulation</u>
Amoxicillin *(Amoxil, Moxatag)* Tablet, capsule, <u>chewable</u>, suspension **+ clavulanate (*Augmentin, Augmentin ES-600, Augmentin XR, Amoclan*)** Tablet, <u>chewable</u>, suspension	Amoxicillin: 250-500 mg PO Q8H or 500-875 mg PO Q12H or 775 mg XR *(Moxatag)* PO daily Amox/clav: 500 mg PO TID, 875 mg PO BID, or 2,000 XR PO BID with food For Amox/Clav, use a 14:1 ratio to ↓ diarrhea due to the clavulanate component.	**MONITORING** Renal function, symptoms of anaphylaxis with 1st dose, CBC and LFTs with prolonged courses **NOTES** Pregnancy Category B
Ampicillin Injection, capsule, suspension **+ sulbactam (*Unasyn*)** Injection *Unasyn* 3 g = 2 g ampicillin/1 g sulbactam *Unasyn* 1.5 g = 1 g ampicillin/0.5 g sulbactam	Ampicillin: 250-500 mg PO Q6H <u>on empty stomach 1 hr before or 2 hrs after meals</u> or 1-2 grams IV/IM Q4-6H Ampicillin/sulbactam: 1.5-3 grams IV Q6H	When CrCl < 30 mL/min, avoid amoxicillin 875 mg and 775 mg XR formulations. Amoxicillin – DOC in acute otitis media, *H. pylori* regimens, prophylaxis for endocarditis Some chewable tablets contain phenylalanine – do not dispense to patients with phenylketonuria.

DRUG	DOSING	SAFETY/SIDE EFFECTS/MONITORING
Extended-Spectrum Penicillins – *Streptococci*, MSSA, *Enterococci*, more resistant strains of HNPEK, CAPES, Gram-positive anaerobes (mouth flora) and Gram-negative anaerobes (*B. fragilis*), <u>Pseudomonas</u>		See previous.
Piperacillin **+ tazobactam *(Zosyn)*** *Zosyn* 3.375 g = 3 g piperacillin/0.375 g tazobactam *Zosyn* 4.5 g = 4 g piperacillin/0.5 g tazobactam	3.375 grams IV Q6H or 4.5 grams IV Q6-8H <u>Prolonged or extended infusion</u> regimen: 3.375-4.5 grams IV Q8H (each dose infused <u>over 4 hours</u>)	
Ticarcillin **+ clavulanate *(Timentin)*** *Timentin* 3.1 g = 3 g ticarcillin/ 0.1 g clavulanic acid	Ticarcillin/Clav: 3.1 grams IV Q4-6H	
Antistaphylococcal Penicillins – *Streptococci, Staphylococci* (<u>MSSA</u> only); no coverage of *Enterococcus* or Gram-negatives		**NOTES** Used for skin, soft tissue, bone, and joint infections <u>Nafcillin/oxacillin/dicloxacillin do not require renal dosage adjustment.</u> Nafcillin is a vesicant – if extravasation occurs, use cold packs and hyaluronidase injections. Administration through a central line is preferred.
Nafcillin	1-2 grams IV/IM Q4-6H	
Oxacillin	250-2,000 mg IV Q4-6H	
Dicloxacillin	125-500 mg PO Q6H	

See lab interactions, storage requirements, renal dosage information near the end of this chapter.

Penicillin Drug Interactions

- Probenecid can ↑ levels of PCNs by interfering with renal excretion. This combination can be used to ↑ penicillin levels for severe infections.

- Tetracyclines and other bacteriostatic agents can ↓ effectiveness of penicillins by slowing bacterial growth (penicillins work best against actively growing bacteria).

- Penicillins can ↑ the serum concentration of methotrexate.

- Penicillins can ↓ serum concentrations of the active metabolites of mycophenolate due to impaired enterohepatic recirculation.

- Nafcillin is a moderate CYP3A4 inducer.

- Dicloxacillin and nafcillin can ↓ INR through ↑ metabolism of warfarin; other PCNs may ↑ anticoagulant effect of warfarin.

CEPHALOSPORINS

Cephalosporins are beta-lactams that inhibit bacterial cell wall synthesis by binding to penicillin-binding proteins (PBPs), which prevents the final transpeptidation step of peptidoglycan synthesis in bacterial cell walls. Cephalosporins exhibit time-dependent killing with bactericidal activity.

- Coverage: The spectrum of activity is variable by cephalosporin generation. The spectrum summary is contained in the drug table. First generation cephalosporins excel against Gram-positive cocci (in most cases 1st generation is preferred if a cephalosporin is used for MSSA infection), with activity against some Gram-negative rods: *Proteus, E. coli, Klebsiella* (PEK). Second generation cephalosporins are split into two groups. Agents such as cefuroxime cover more resistant *S. pneumoniae* and *Haemophilus, Neisseria, Proteus, E. coli, Klebsiella* (HNPEK), where the cephamycin second generation drugs (cefotetan and cefoxitin) have added anaerobic coverage (*B. fragilis*). Third generation cephalosporins are also best thought of in two groups: ceftriaxone, cefotaxime and oral agents provide coverage of more resistant *Streptococci* along with enhanced Gram-negative coverage, plus *Citrobacter, Acinetobacter, Providencia, Enterobacter, Serratia* (CAPES). The second group of 3rd generation agents includes ceftazidime, which lacks Gram-positive activity but covers *Pseudomonas*, and the newer beta-lactamase inhibitor combinations ceftazidime/avibactam and ceftolozane/tazobactam, which have added activity against MDR *Pseudomonas* and other Gram-negative rods. The fourth generation drug, cefepime, has broad Gram-negative activity including *Pseudomonas*, and Gram-positive activity similar to ceftriaxone. The fifth generation agent, ceftaroline, is similar to ceftriaxone, but is the only beta-lactam with MRSA activity. Class trends: Cephalosporins are not active against *Enterococcus* spp. or atypicals.

DRUG	DOSING	SAFETY/SIDE EFFECTS/ MONITORING
1st Generation – *Streptococci, Staphylococci* (MSSA), PEK, Gram-positive anaerobes (mouth flora). Overall, ↑ Staphylococci, ↓ Gram-negative activity compared to 2nd/3rd/4th generations. Generally, 1st generation is preferred for MSSA.		**CONTRAINDICATIONS** Ceftriaxone: Hyperbilirubinemic neonates (causes biliary sludging), concurrent use with calcium-containing IV products in neonates ≤ 28 days old
Cefadroxil	500-1,000 mg PO Q12H	
CeFAZolin (Ancef, Kefzol)	1-1.5 grams IV/IM Q8H	**WARNINGS** Anaphylaxis/hypersensitivity reactions
Cephalexin (Keflex)	250-1,000 mg PO Q6H	Some agents may ↑ INR in patients taking warfarin.
2nd Generation – Same as 1st generation plus: *Haemophilus, Neisseria* (HNPEK). Cephamycin group (cefotetan and cefoxitin) have additional activity against Gram-negative anaerobic bacteria (*Bacteroides fragilis*).		Cross sensitivity (< 10%) with PCN allergy – do not use in patients who have a type-1 PCN allergy (swelling, angioedema, anaphylaxis).
Cefaclor (Ceclor)	250-500 mg PO Q8H	Cefotetan contains a N-methylthiotetrazole (NMTT or 1-MTT) side chain, which can ↑ risk
Cefprozil (Cefzil)	250-500 mg PO Q12-24H	of hypoprothrombinemia (bleeding) and a disulfiram-like reaction with
Cefuroxime (Ceftin, Zinacef)	250-1,500 mg PO/IV/IM Q8-12H, take suspension with food	alcohol ingestion.
CefoTEtan (Cefotan)	1-2 grams IV/IM Q12H	**SIDE EFFECTS** GI upset, diarrhea, rash/allergic
CefOXitin (Mefoxin)	1-2 grams IV/IM Q6-8H	reactions/anaphylaxis, acute interstitial nephritis, myelosuppression with prolonged use, ↑ LFTs, seizures
3rd Generation Group 1 – *Streptococci* (covers more resistant *S. pneumoniae* and Viridans group *Strep.*), *Staphylococci* (MSSA), more resistant strains of HNPEK, Gram-positive anaerobes (mouth flora).		with accumulation, drug fever
Cefdinir (Omnicef)	300 mg PO Q12H or 600 mg PO daily	**MONITORING** Renal function, signs of anaphylaxis with 1st dose, CBC, LFTs
Cefditoren (Spectracef)	200-400 mg PO Q12H with food	
Cefixime (Suprax)	400 mg PO divided Q12-24H	**NOTES** Pregnancy Category B
Cefpodoxime (Vantin)	100-400 mg PO Q12H	Ceftriaxone does not require renal adjustment.
Ceftibuten (Cedax)	400 mg PO daily on empty stomach	Cefixime available in chewable tablet
CefTRIAXone (Rocephin)	1-2 grams IV/IM Q12-24H	Some chewable tablets contain phenylalanine – do not dispense to patients with phenylketonuria
Cefotaxime (Claforan)	1-2 grams IV/IM Q4-12H	Ceftazidime/avibactam covers some carbapenem-resistant *Enterobacteriaceae* (CRE).
3rd Generation Group 2 – Ceftazidime has very little Gram-positive activity, ↑ Gram-negative activity, including *Pseudomonas*. Beta-lactamase inhibitor combos ceftazidime/avibactam and ceftolozane/tazobactam have extended coverage of MDR Gram-negative rods, including *Pseudomonas*.		
CefTAZidime (Fortaz, Tazicef)	1-2 grams IV/IM Q8-12H	
+ avibactam (Avycaz) *Avycaz* 2.5 grams = 2 g ceftazidime/0.5 g avibactam	Ceftazidime/avibactam: 2.5 grams IV Q8H	
Ceftolozane/tazobactam (Zerbaxa) *Zerbaxa* 1.5 g = 1 g ceftolozane/0.5 g tazobactam	1.5 gram IV Q8H	

DRUG	DOSING	SAFETY/SIDE EFFECTS/MONITORING
4ᵗʰ Generation – Gram-negative activity includes HNPEK, *Citrobacter*, <u>*Acinetobacter*</u>, *Providencia*, <u>*Enterobacter*</u> and *Serratia* species (CAPES) and <u>*Pseudomonas*</u>. Gram-positive activity similar to 3ʳᵈ generation.		See previous page
Cefepime *(Maxipime)*	1-2 grams IV/IM Q8-12H	
5ᵗʰ Generation – Broadest Gram-positive activity; *Staphylococci* (<u>covers MRSA</u>), Gram-negative activity similar to ceftriaxone (no *Pseudomonas* coverage).		
Ceftaroline fosamil *(Teflaro)*	600 mg IV Q12H	

See lab interactions, storage requirements, renal dosage information near the end of this chapter.

Cephalosporin Drug Interactions

■ Probenecid can ↑ levels of cephalosporins by interfering with renal excretion. This combination may be used to ↑ cephalosporin levels.

■ Cephalosporins may enhance the anticoagulant effect of warfarin by inhibiting the production of vitamin K-dependent clotting factors.

■ Drugs that ↓ stomach acid can ↓ the bioavailability of some cephalosporins. Cefuroxime, cefpodoxime, cefdinir and cefditoren should be separated by 2 hours from short-acting antacids. H₂RAs and PPIs should be avoided.

CARBAPENEMS

Carbapenems are <u>beta-lactams</u> that <u>inhibit bacterial cell wall synthesis</u> by binding to one or more penicillin-binding proteins (PBPs), which in turn prevents the final transpeptidation step of peptidoglycan synthesis in bacterial cell walls. Carbapenems exhibit <u>time-dependent killing with bactericidal activity</u>.

■ Coverage: Very broad spectrum ("big gun") generally reserved for MDR Gram-negative infections. Activity against most Gram-positive, Gram-negative (including <u>ESBL producing bacteria</u>), and anaerobic pathogens. <u>No coverage</u> of <u>atypical pathogens, MRSA, VRE</u>, *C. difficile* and *Stenotrophomonas*. <u>Ertapenem is different</u> from other carbapenems; it has <u>no activity against *Pseudomonas*, *Acinetobacter* or *Enterococcus*</u>.

DRUG	DOSING	SAFETY/SIDE EFFECTS/MONITORING
Doripenem *(Doribax)* Injection	500 mg IV Q8H	**CONTRAINDICATIONS** Anaphylactic reactions to beta-lactam antibiotics **WARNINGS** Carbapenems have been associated with CNS adverse effects, including confusional states and seizures.
Imipenem/ Cilastatin *(Primaxin)* Injection	250-1,000 mg IV Q6-8H	Doripenem: Do not use for the treatment of pneumonia including healthcare-associated pneumonia (HAP) and ventilator-associated pneumonia (VAP). Do not use in patients with PCN allergy; cross-reactivity has been reported to be as high as 50%, but newer studies show rates < 10%.
Meropenem *(Merrem)* Injection	500-1,000 mg IV Q8H Dilute with SWFI – stable for 3 hours at room temperature	**SIDE EFFECTS** Diarrhea, rash, and seizures with higher doses and in patients with impaired renal function (mainly imipenem), bone marrow suppression with prolonged use, ↑ LFTs **MONITORING** Renal function, symptoms of anaphylaxis with 1ˢᵗ dose, CBC, LFTs **NOTES** Pregnancy Category B (meropenem/doripenem)/C (imipenem) Imipenem is combined with cilastatin to prevent drug degradation by renal tubular dehydropeptidase. Common uses: ESBL-producing bacteria, *Pseudomonas* infections, broad-spectrum empiric coverage
Ertapenem *(INVanz)* Injection	1 gram IV/IM daily Stable in NS	See above **NOTES** Pregnancy Category B No coverage of *Pseudomonas, Acinetobacter* or *Enterococcus* Common uses: ESBL-producing bacteria, diabetic foot infections

See lab interactions, storage requirements, renal dosage information near the end of this chapter.

Carbapenem Drug Interactions

- Probenecid can ↑ levels of carbapenems by interfering with renal excretion.

- Carbapenems can ↓ serum concentrations of valproic acid leading to a loss of seizure control.

- Use with caution in patients at risk for seizures or with other agents known to lower seizure threshold (e.g., ganciclovir, quinolones, bupropion, tramadol). See Epilepsy/Seizures chapter for a complete list.

MONOBACTAM

Aztreonam

Inhibits bacterial cell wall synthesis by binding to one or more of the penicillin-binding proteins (PBPs), which inhibits the final transpeptidation step of peptidoglycan synthesis in bacterial cell walls, thus inhibiting cell wall synthesis; bactericidal. The monobactam structure makes cross-reactivity with beta-lactam allergy unlikely. Primarily used when beta-lactam allergy present.

- Coverage: Similar to ceftazidime, encompassing many Gram-negative organisms including *Pseudomonas*. It has no Gram-positive activity.

DRUG	DOSING	SAFETY/SIDE EFFECTS/MONITORING
Aztreonam *(Azactam IV)* *Cayston* – inhaled for CF	500-2,000 mg IV Q6-12H CrCl 10-30 mL/min: ↓ dose by 50% after the 1st dose CrCl < 10 mL/min: ↓ dose by 75% after the 1st dose	**SIDE EFFECTS** Similar to penicillins, including rash, N/V/D, ↑ LFTs **NOTES** Pregnancy Category B

See lab interactions, storage requirements, renal dosage information near the end of this chapter.

Beta-Lactam Spectrum of Activity

MRSA	S. AUREUS (MSSA)	S. PNEUMONIAE	VIRIDANS GROUP STREPTOCOCCUS	ENTEROCOCCUS	PEK	HNPEK	CAPES	PSEUDOMONAS	GRAM-POSITIVE ANAEROBES (MOUTH FLORA)	BACTEROIDES FRAGILIS	ATYPICAL ORGANISMS
		Penicillin	Penicillin	Penicillin					Penicillin		
		Amoxicillin	Amoxicillin	Amoxicillin	Amoxicillin				Amoxicillin		
	Oxacillin Nafcillin	Oxacillin Nafcillin	Oxacillin Nafcillin								
	Amoxicillin/clavulanate Ampicillin/sulbactam	Amoxicillin/clavulanate Ampicillin/sulbactam	Amoxicillin/clavulanate Ampicillin/sulbactam	Amoxicillin/clavulanate Ampicillin/sulbactam	Amoxicillin/clavulanate Ampicillin/sulbactam	Amoxicillin/clavulanate Ampicillin/sulbactam			Amoxicillin/clavulanate Ampicillin/sulbactam	Amoxicillin/clavulanate Ampicillin/sulbactam	
	Piperacillin/tazobactam Ticarcillin/clavulanate	Piperacillin/tazobactam Ticarcillin/clavulanate	Piperacillin/tazobactam Ticarcillin/clavulanate	Piperacillin/tazobactam Ticarcillin/clavulanate	Piperacillin/tazobactam Ticarcillin/clavulanate	Piperacillin/tazobactam Ticarcillin/clavulanate	Piperacillin/tazobactam Ticarcillin/clavulanate	Piperacillin/tazobactam Ticarcillin/clavulanate	Piperacillin/tazobactam Ticarcillin/clavulanate	Piperacillin/tazobactam Ticarcillin/clavulanate	
	Cefazolin Cephalexin	Cefazolin Cephalexin	Cefazolin Cephalexin		Cefazolin Cephalexin				Cefazolin Cephalexin		
	Cefuroxime Cefotetan Cefoxitin	Cefuroxime Cefotetan Cefoxitin	Cefuroxime Cefotetan Cefoxitin		Cefuroxime Cefotetan Cefoxitin	Cefuroxime Cefotetan Cefoxitin			Cefotetan Cefoxitin	Cefotetan Cefoxitin	
	Cefotaxime Ceftriaxone	Cefotaxime Ceftriaxone	Cefotaxime Ceftriaxone		Cefotaxime Ceftriaxone	Cefotaxime Ceftriaxone	Cefotaxime Ceftriaxone		Cefotaxime Ceftriaxone		
					Ceftazidime Aztreonam	Ceftazidime Aztreonam	Ceftazidime Aztreonam	Ceftazidime Aztreonam			
	Cefepime	Cefepime	Cefepime		Cefepime	Cefepime	Cefepime	Cefepime			
Ceftaroline	Ceftaroline	Ceftaroline	Ceftaroline		Ceftaroline	Ceftaroline	Ceftaroline		Ceftaroline		
	Ceftazidime/avibactam Ceftaroline/tazobactam	Ceftazidime/avibactam Ceftaroline/tazobactam	Ceftazidime/avibactam Ceftaroline/tazobactam		Ceftazidime/avibactam Ceftaroline/tazobactam	Ceftazidime/avibactam Ceftaroline/tazobactam	Ceftazidime/avibactam Ceftaroline/tazobactam	Ceftazidime/avibactam Ceftaroline/tazobactam			
	Imipenem/cilastatin* Meropenem* Doripenem*	Imipenem/cilastatin* Meropenem* Doripenem*	Imipenem/cilastatin* Meropenem* Doripenem*	Imipenem/cilastatin* Meropenem* Doripenem*	Imipenem/cilastatin* Meropenem* Doripenem*	Imipenem/cilastatin* Meropenem* Doripenem*	Imipenem/cilastatin* Meropenem* Doripenem*	Imipenem/cilastatin* Meropenem* Doripenem*	Imipenem/cilastatin* Meropenem* Doripenem*	Imipenem/cilastatin* Meropenem* Doripenem*	
	Ertapenem	Ertapenem	Ertapenem		Ertapenem	Ertapenem	Ertapenem		Ertapenem	Ertapenem	

*E. faecalis, only
PEK = Proteus, E. coli, Klebsiella; HNPEK = Haemophilus, Neisseria, Proteus, E. coli, Klebsiella
CAPES = Citrobacter, Acinetobacter, Providencia, Enterobacter, Serratia

AMINOGLYCOSIDES

Aminoglycosides (AMGs) interfere with bacterial protein synthesis by binding to the 30S and 50S ribosomal subunits resulting in a defective bacterial cell membrane. AMGs exhibit <u>concentration-dependent killing</u> and demonstrate <u>a post-antibiotic effect</u> (PAE). The PAE is defined as the continued suppression of bacterial growth when antibiotic levels fall below the MIC of the organism. Extended interval dosing of AMGs allows use of higher doses that reliably achieve the desired peak (≥ 10x the MIC) for <u>Gram-negative organisms</u>, while preventing accumulation which can lead to toxicity. In extended interval dosing nomograms, a random level is drawn after the first dose and the result is used to determine the appropriate dosing interval. The dosing interval is always rounded up if it falls on the line, to avoid potential toxicity. Extended interval dosing has also been shown to ↓ <u>nephrotoxicity</u>, ↓ <u>cost, and ↑ bactericidal activity</u>, but has not been shown to be clinically superior in efficacy relative to traditional dosing.

- Coverage: Mainly Gram-negative bacteria (<u>including *Pseudomonas*</u>); gentamicin and streptomycin are used for synergy when treating Gram-positive cocci (e.g., *Staphylococcus* and *Enterococcus*, in the setting of endocarditis) in combination with a beta-lactam or vancomycin. Streptomycin and amikacin are used as second line therapy for *Mycobacterial* infections.

DRUG	DOSING	SAFETY/SIDE EFFECTS/MONITORING
Gentamicin IV, IM, ophthalmic, topical **Tobramycin** IV, IM, ophthalmic, inhaled Tobramycin inhalation for CF – *TOBI, TOBI Podhaler, Bethkis, Kitabis Pak* **Amikacin** IV, IM Streptomycin IM	If <u>underweight</u>, use <u>actual body weight</u> for dosing If not obese, ideal body weight or actual body weight can be used for dosing (follow hospital's protocol) If <u>obese</u>, use <u>adjusted body weight</u> for dosing (see notes) **Traditional Dosing** Gent/tobra: 1-2.5 mg/kg/dose (lower doses for Gram-positive infections; higher doses for Gram-negative infections) Amikacin: 5-7.5 mg/kg/dose **Renal Adjustments:** CrCl ≥ 60 mL/min: Q8H CrCl 40-60 mL/min: Q12H CrCl 20-40 mL/min: Q24H CrCl < 20 mL/min: Loading dose, then dose per levels **Extended Interval Dosing** Gent/tobra: 4-7 mg/kg/dose Amikacin: 15-20 mg/kg/dose Frequency determined by nomogram (example on next page) Do not use extended interval dosing nomograms with these conditions: Pregnancy, ascites, burns, cystic fibrosis, CrCl < 30 mL/min (including end-stage renal disease on dialysis), or when using for synergy in Gram-positive infections	**BOXED WARNINGS** <u>Nephrotoxicity, ototoxicity,</u> (hearing loss, vertigo, ataxia), <u>neuromuscular blockade</u> and <u>respiratory paralysis</u>, fetal harm if given in pregnancy (tobramycin). <u>Avoid concurrent therapy with other neurotoxic/nephrotoxic drugs</u>. **WARNINGS** Use with caution in patients with impaired renal function, in the elderly, and those on other nephrotoxic drugs (amphotericin B, cisplatin, colistimethate, cyclosporine, loop diuretics, NSAIDs, radiocontrast dye, tacrolimus and vancomycin). **SIDE EFFECTS** Nephrotoxicity (acute tubular necrosis), hearing loss (early toxicity associated with high-pitched sounds), vestibular toxicity (resulting in balance deficits) **MONITORING** Renal function, urine output, hearing tests, drug levels Traditional dosing: Draw trough level right before the 4th dose, draw peak level ½ hour after the end of drug infusion of the 4th dose (follow hospital's protocol). Extended interval dosing: Draw random level per timing on the nomogram (example of nomogram follows). **NOTES** Pregnancy Category D. Amikacin has the broadest spectrum of activity. The clinical definition of obesity varies. For exam purposes, obesity will be obvious, and may be stated in the question, indicating that adjusted body weight should be used for weight-based dosing.

See lab interactions, storage requirements, renal dosage information near the end of this chapter.

Traditional Dosing Target Drug Concentrations

DRUG	PEAK	TROUGH
Gentamicin		
Gram-negative infection:	5-10 mcg/mL	< 2 mcg/mL
Gram-positive infection:	3-4 mcg/mL	< 1 mcg/mL
Tobramycin	5-10 mcg/mL	< 2 mcg/mL
Amikacin	20-30 mcg/mL	< 5 mcg/mL

Organism-specific peak goals are typically ≥10 times the MIC of the bacteria causing the infection.

Example of Extended Interval Dosing Nomogram

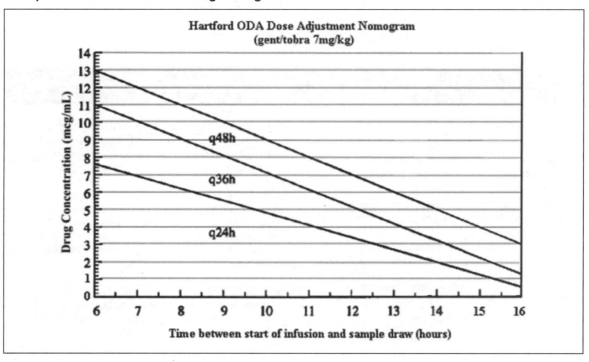

QUINOLONES

Quinolones <u>inhibit bacterial DNA topoisomerase IV and inhibit DNA gyrase</u> (topoisomerase II). This prevents supercoiling of DNA and promotes breakage of double-stranded DNA. Quinolones exhibit <u>concentration-dependent killing</u> with <u>bactericidal</u> activity.

- Coverage: Broad spectrum agents with activity against a variety of Gram-negative, Gram-positive, and atypical pathogens. <u>Gemifloxacin, levofloxacin and moxifloxacin</u> are often referred to as <u>respiratory quinolones</u> due to <u>enhanced coverage of *S. pneumoniae*</u> and atypical coverage. <u>Ciprofloxacin and levofloxacin</u> have enhanced Gram-negative activity, including *Pseudomonas*, but are typically used in combination with another agent (e.g., a beta-lactam) when treating *Pseudomonas* infections. Moxifloxacin has enhanced Gram-positive and <u>anaerobic</u> activity and can be used alone for mixed infections (intra-abdominal infections). Quinolones are noted in some resources to have activity against *Staphylococcus* species, including MRSA; however, because of high rates of resistance, quinolones should generally be avoided for treatment of MRSA.

DRUG	DOSING	SAFETY/SIDE EFFECTS/MONITORING
Ofloxacin Tablet, ophthalmic, otic	200-400 mg PO Q12H CrCl < 30 mL/min: 400 mg Q24H	**BOXED WARNINGS** <u>Tendon inflammation and/or rupture</u> (most often in Achilles tendon); ↑ risk with concurrent systemic steroid use, organ transplant patients, > 60 years of age May exacerbate muscle weakness related to myasthenia gravis.
Norfloxacin *(Noroxin)* Tablet	400 mg PO BID or 800 mg PO daily CrCl ≤ 30 mL/min: 400 mg daily	**CONTRAINDICATIONS** Concurrent administration of tizanidine (with ciprofloxacin) **WARNINGS** <u>QT prolongation</u>; avoid use in patients at risk for QT prolongation. Use caution with agents that prolong QT interval including Class Ia and Class III antiarrhythmics (<u>highest risk with moxifloxacin</u>).
Ciprofloxacin *(**Cipro, Cipro XR**, Ciloxin* eye drops, *Cetraxal* ear drops)* Tablet, suspension, injection, ointment, ophthalmic, otic + dexamethasone *(Ciprodex* ear drops)	250-750 mg PO or 200-400 mg IV Q8-12H CrCl 30-50 mL/min: Q12H CrCl < 30 mL/min: Q18-24H	<u>Peripheral neuropathy</u> (with systemic formulations) – can last months to years after the drug has been discontinued. In some cases, it may become permanent. If symptoms, discontinue the drug. CNS effects [tremor, restlessness, confusion, and very rarely hallucinations, ↑ intracranial pressure (including pseudotumor cerebri) or <u>seizures</u>]; use with caution in patients with known or suspected CNS disorder.
Levofloxacin *(**Levaquin**, Quixin* eye drops)* Tablet, solution, injection, ophthalmic	250-750 mg IV/PO daily CrCl < 50 mL/min: Extend dosing interval and/or ↓ dose. Adjustment varies based on indication and renal function.	<u>Hypoglycemia/hyperglycemia</u> ↑LFTs <u>Photosensitivity/phototoxicity</u> Risk of arthropathy, <u>use in children should be avoided</u> due to concerns of musculoskeletal toxicity, may use if benefit outweighs the risk (such as anthrax) per the American Academy of Pediatrics
Gatifloxacin *(Zymaxid* eye drops)	No oral formulation	**SIDE EFFECTS** <u>GI upset/diarrhea</u>, headache, dizziness, insomnia, crystalluria and interstitial nephritis (rare)
Moxifloxacin *(Avelox, Avelox ABC Pack, Moxeza* eye drops, ***Vigamox*** eye drops)* Tablet, injection, ophthalmic	400 mg IV/PO Q24H	**NOTES** Pregnancy Category C. MedGuide required. *Cipro* oral susp should not be given through a <u>NG or other feeding tube</u> (the oil-based suspension adheres to the tubing). Shake vigorously for 15 seconds each time before use. Do not chew the microcapsules. <u>Do not refrigerate the oral suspension.</u>
Gemifloxacin *(Factive)* Tablet	320 mg PO daily CrCl ≤ 40 mL/min: 160 mg daily	*Cipro* – can crush immediate-release tablets, mix with water and give <u>via feeding tube</u>. Hold tube feedings at least 1 hour before and 2 hours after dose.
Finafloxacin *(Xtoro)* Otic suspension	Acute otitis externa (swimmer's ear): 4 drops in affected ear/s BID x 7 days If using an otowick, initial dose is 8 drops	Moxifloxacin does not reach adequate concentrations in the urine and should not be used for UTIs. Most quinolones require dose adjustment for renal impairment (<u>except moxifloxacin</u>).

See lab interactions, storage requirements, renal dosage information near the end of this chapter.

Quinolone Drug Interactions

- Antacids, didanosine, sucralfate, bile acid resins, magnesium, aluminum, calcium, iron, zinc, multivitamins or any product containing these multivalent cations can chelate and inhibit absorption. Separate as follows:

  ❑ Give ciprofloxacin 2 hours before or 6 hours after these agents

  ❑ Give levofloxacin 2 hours before or 2 hours after these agents

  ❑ Give moxifloxacin 4 hours before or 8 hours after these agents

- Although the actual influence of dairy products on quinolone absorption varies, it is generally recommended that concomitant intake of calcium-rich foods (dairy products) be avoided due to the potential of chelation.

- Lanthanum *(Fosrenol)* can ↓ the serum concentration of quinolones; take oral quinolones at least 2 hours before or after lanthanum.

- Sevelamer *(Renagel)* can ↓ the serum concentration of quinolones; take oral quinolones at least 2 hours before or 6 hours after sevelamer.

- Can ↑ the effects of warfarin, sulfonylureas/insulin and QT-prolonging drugs (moxifloxacin prolongs the QT interval the most).

- Probenecid and NSAIDs can ↑ quinolone levels.

- Ciprofloxacin is a P-glycoprotein substrate, strong 1A2 inhibitor and weak 3A4 inhibitor; ciprofloxacin can ↑ the levels of caffeine and theophylline by reducing metabolism.

MACROLIDES

Macrolides bind to the <u>50S ribosomal subunit</u>, resulting in inhibition of RNA-dependent protein synthesis with <u>bacteriostatic</u> activity related to total exposure of the drug (AUC/MIC).

- Coverage: Good <u>atypical</u> coverage (*Legionella, Chlamydia, Mycoplasma* and some *Mycobacterium* species) and *Haemophilus*. Macrolides are treatment options for community-acquired upper and lower respiratory tract infections and certain sexually transmitted infections, but utility against *S. pneumoniae, Haemophilus, Neisseria,* and *Moraxella* is limited due to increasing resistance.

DRUG	DOSING	SAFETY/SIDE EFFECTS/MONITORING
Azithromycin *(Zithromax, Z-Pak,* Zmax, Zithromax Tri-Pak, AzaSite *ophthalmic)* Tablet, suspension, injection, ophthalmic Better Gram-negative coverage compared to erythromycin	PO: 500 mg on day 1, then 250 mg on days 2-5 *(Z-Pak)* or 500 mg daily x 3 days or 1-2 grams x 1 *(Zmax)* or 600 mg daily Prophylaxis: 600 mg daily or 1,200 mg PO weekly IV: 250-500 mg daily No adjustment in renal impairment	**CONTRAINDICATIONS** History of cholestatic jaundice/hepatic dysfunction with prior use Clarithromycin and erythromycin: Concomitant use with pimozide, ergotamine or dihydroergotamine, lovastatin or simvastatin Clarithromycin: Concurrent use with colchicine in patients with renal or hepatic impairment, history of QT prolongation or ventricular arrhythmia **WARNINGS** <u>QT prolongation</u>; use with caution in patients at risk of prolonged cardiac repolarization; avoid use in patients with uncorrected hypokalemia or hypomagnesemia, clinically significant bradycardia, and patients receiving Class Ia or Class III antiarrhythmic agents (<u>highest risk with erythromycin</u>). <u>Hepatotoxicity</u>; use caution in patients with liver disease.
Clarithromycin *(Biaxin, Biaxin XL, Biaxin XL Pac)* Tablet, suspension Better Gram-positive coverage	250-500 mg PO Q12H or 1 gram *(Biaxin XL)* PO daily CrCl < 30 mL/minute: ↓ dose by 50%	
Erythromycin *(E.E.S., Ery-Tab, EryPed, Erythrocin, PCE)* Capsule, tablet, suspension, injection, ophthalmic, topical	E.E.S.: 400-800 mg PO Q6-12H Erythromycin base/stearate: 250-500 mg PO Q6-12H Erythromycin lactobionate: 15-20 mg/kg/day IV Q6H (max 4 grams/day) 400 mg E.E.S. = 250 mg base or stearate No adjustment in renal impairment IV is stable in NS	**SIDE EFFECTS** <u>GI upset</u> (diarrhea, abdominal pain and cramping especially with erythromycin), taste perversion, ↑ LFTs, ototoxicity (reversible and rare) **NOTES** Pregnancy Category B/C (clarithromycin) *AzaSite* – viscous solution for ophthalmic use. Store at room temp once dispensed (cold makes solution more viscous). Azithromycin ER suspension *(Zmax)* is not bioequivalent with *Zithromax* and should not be interchanged.

See lab interactions, storage requirements, renal dosage information near the end of this chapter.

Macrolide Drug Interactions

- Erythromycin and clarithromycin are substrates of 3A4 (major) and 3A4 inhibitors (moderate/strong); use caution or avoid with many medications metabolized by 3A4 including apixaban, colchicine, conivaptan, cyclosporine, dabigatran, digoxin, quetiapine, quinidine, rifabutin, rivaroxaban, theophylline, warfarin and others. See Drug Interactions chapter for more information.

- <u>Azithromycin</u> is a substrate of 3A4 (minor) and inhibitor of 1A2 (weak) and P-gp; it has <u>fewer clinically significant drug interactions</u>.

- <u>All macrolides</u>: Do not use concurrently with agents that can <u>prolong the QT interval</u>.

TETRACYCLINES

Tetracyclines inhibit bacterial protein synthesis by reversibly binding to the 30S ribosomal subunit with bacteriostatic activity related to the total exposure of the drug (AUC/MIC). Doxycycline is used more often in practice due to improved tolerability and broader indications, including for respiratory tract infections, tick-borne/rickettsial diseases, spirochetes and *Chlamydia* infections. Doxycycline is also an option for the treatment of MRSA in mild skin infections and VRE in urinary tract infections. Minocycline has enhanced Gram-positive coverage and is often preferred for skin infections, including acne. Tetracycline is rarely used in practice, but is used as part of *H. pylori* regimens.

- Coverage: Many Gram-positive bacteria, including *Staphylococci, Streptococci, Enterococci, Nocardia, Bacillus* and *Propionibacterium* spp., Gram-negative bacteria, including respiratory flora *(Haemophilus, Moraxella,* atypicals) and other unique pathogens (spirochetes, *Rickettsiae, Bacillus anthracis, Treponema pallidum,* etc.).

DRUG	DOSING	SAFETY/SIDE EFFECTS/MONITORING
Doxycycline *(Adoxa, Atridox, Doryx, Monodox, Oracea, Vibramycin,* others) Capsule, tablet, suspension, syrup, injection	100-200 mg PO/IV in 1-2 divided doses Take *Oracea* on an empty stomach (1 hr before or 2 hrs after meals). Take other forms with food to ↓ GI irritation No adjustment in renal impairment	**WARNINGS** Children < 8 years of age, pregnancy and breastfeeding (Pregnancy Category D – suppresses bone growth and skeletal development, permanently discolors teeth) Drug Rash with Eosinophilia and Systemic Symptoms syndrome (DRESS), exfoliative dermatitis ↑ BUN Photosensitivity Drug-induced lupus erythematosus (DILE) with minocycline
Minocycline *(Minocin, Solodyn)* Capsule, tablet, injection	200 mg PO/IV x 1, then 100 mg PO/IV Q12H No adjustment in renal impairment	**SIDE EFFECTS** N/V/D, rash
Tetracycline Capsule	250-500 mg PO Q6H on an empty stomach CrCl ≤ 80 mL/min: Extend dosing interval	**MONITORING** LFTs, renal function, CBC **NOTES** Pregnancy Category D

See lab interactions, storage requirements, renal dosage information near the end of this chapter.

Tetracycline Drug Interactions

- Tetracycline absorption is impaired by antacids containing magnesium, aluminum, or calcium or medications that contain divalent cations such as iron-containing preparations, sucralfate, bile acid resins, or bismuth subsalicylate – separate doses (take 1 – 2 hours before or 4 hours after). Doxycycline and minocycline are less likely to be of clinical concern. These can be taken with food to reduce GI upset, but do not administer with dairy products (calcium). Do not eat or drink dairy products within 1 hour before or 2 hours after tetracycline products.

- Lanthanum *(Fosrenol)* can ↓ the concentration of tetracycline derivatives; take at least 2 hours before or after lanthanum.

- Tetracycline is a substrate of 3A4 (major) and 3A4 (moderate) inhibitor. Caution with the use of 3A4 inhibitors which ↑ levels, and 3A4 inducers which ↓ levels.

- Doxycycline is a weak 3A4 inhibitor.

- Tetracyclines can enhance the anticoagulant effects in patients taking warfarin.

- Tetracycline derivatives can enhance the effects of neuromuscular blocking agents.

- Avoid concomitant use with retinoic acid derivatives due to the risk of pseudotumor cerebri.

- Tetracyclines can ↓ the effectiveness of penicillins by slowing bacterial growth (penicillins work best against actively growing bacteria).

SULFONAMIDES

Sulfamethoxazole (SMX) interferes with bacterial folic acid synthesis via inhibition of dihydrofolic acid formation from para-aminobenzoic acid and trimethoprim (TMP) inhibits dihydrofolic acid reduction to tetrahydrofolate resulting in inhibition of the folic acid pathway. Individually they are bacteriostatic, however collectively they are bactericidal.

- Coverage: Gram-positive bacteria, including *Staphylococci*/MRSA, however *S. pneumoniae* and Group A Strep coverage is unreliable. Active against many Gram-negative bacteria, including *Haemophilus, Proteus, E. coli, Klebsiella, Enterobacter, Shigella, Salmonella,* and *Stenotrophomonas*. Coverage also includes some opportunistic pathogens (*Nocardia, Pneumocystis, Toxoplasmosis*), but lacks *Pseudomonas, Enterococci*, atypical or anaerobic coverage.

DRUG	DOSING	SAFETY/SIDE EFFECTS/MONITORING
Sulfamethoxazole/ Trimethoprim (Bactrim, Bactrim DS, Septra DS, Sulfatrim, others) **Single Strength (SS)** 400 mg SMX/80 mg TMP **Double Strength (DS)** 800 mg SMX/160 mg TMP Sulfamethoxazole: Trimethoprim dose is always a 5:1 ratio	Dose is based on the TMP component **Severe Infections** 10-20 mg/kg/day TMP divided Q6-8H (2 DS tabs BID-TID) **Adult Female Uncomplicated UTI** 1 DS tab BID x 3 days **PCP Prophylaxis** 1 DS or SS tab daily **PCP Treatment** 15-20 mg/kg/day TMP IV/PO divided Q6H CrCl 15-30 mL/min: ↓ dose by 50% CrCl < 15 mL/min: Not recommended	**CONTRAINDICATIONS** Sulfa allergy, pregnancy (at term), breastfeeding, anemia due to folate deficiency, marked renal or hepatic disease, infants < 2 months of age **WARNINGS** Blood dyscrasias including agranulocytosis and aplastic anemia SJS/TEN, thrombotic thrombocytopenic purpura (TTP), and other dermatologic reactions G6PD deficiency; use caution and discontinue drug if hemolysis occurs. **SIDE EFFECTS** N/V/D, anorexia, skin reactions (rash, urticaria, SJS/TEN), crystalluria (take with 8 oz of water), photosensitivity, ↑ K, hypoglycemia, ↓ folate, positive Coombs test, myelosuppression with prolonged use, false elevations in SCr due to inhibition of tubular secretion of creatinine (pseudoazotemia), interstitial nephritis, CNS (confusion, drug fever, seizures), ↑ LFTs **MONITORING** Renal function, LFTs, electrolytes, CBC **NOTES** Weight based doses should always be expressed as mg/kg of the trimethoprim component. Pregnancy Category C or D, varies by source. Should be used last line in the first trimester and should be avoided in the last 2 weeks of pregnancy. Risk for kernicterus and spinal cord defects.

See lab interactions, storage requirements, renal dosage information near the end of this chapter.

Sulfonamide Drug Interactions

- Sulfonamides are inhibitors of 2C8/9 (moderate/strong). Can cause significantly ↑ INR, caution with concurrent use of warfarin. See Drug Interactions chapter for more 2C8/9 substrates.

- Can ↑ levels/effects of sulfonylureas, metformin, fosphenytoin/phenytoin, dofetilide, azathioprine, methotrexate and mercaptopurine.

- Levels of SMX/TMP can be ↓ by 2C8/9 inducers and the therapeutic effects may be diminished by the use of leucovorin/levoleucovorin.

- ACE inhibitors, ARBs, aliskiren, potassium-sparing diuretics, drospirenone-containing oral contraceptives, cyclosporine, tacrolimus and canagliflozin will ↑ risk for hyperkalemia when used concurrently; monitor. See Drug Interactions chapter for expanded list.

ANTIBIOTICS FOR GRAM-POSITIVE INFECTIONS

Vancomycin

Glycopeptide: Inhibits bacterial cell wall synthesis by blocking peptidoglycan polymerization by binding to the D-alanyl-D-alanine portion of cell wall precursor.

- Coverage: Gram-positive bacteria, including *Staphylococcus* (MRSA), *Streptococci*, *Enterococci* (not VRE), and *C. difficile*.

DRUG	DOSING	SAFETY/SIDE EFFECTS/MONITORING
Vancomycin *(Vancocin)* Injection, capsule, solution kit	**MRSA infections:** 15-20 mg/kg IV Q8-12H Dosed on actual body weight CrCl 20-49 mL/min: Q24H CrCl < 20 mL/min: Give loading dose, then dose per levels Infuse peripheral IV at a concentration not to exceed 5 mg/mL ***C. difficile*-associated diarrhea** 125-500 mg PO QID x 10-14 days (upper end used for recurrent or severe, complicated disease) PO: No adjustment in renal impairment	**WARNINGS** Caution with the use of other nephrotoxic or ototoxic drugs **SIDE EFFECTS** GI upset (oral route), infusion reaction/red man syndrome (maculopapular rash from too rapid of an infusion rate, hypotension, flushing, chills – every 500 mg of drug should be infused over a minimum of 30 minutes), nephrotoxicity, myelosuppression (neutropenia/thrombocytopenia), drug fever, ototoxicity **MONITORING** Renal function, WBC, trough concentration at steady state (generally before the 4th dose) Target troughs of 15-20 mcg/mL – pneumonia, endocarditis, osteomyelitis, meningitis, bacteremia Target troughs of 10-15 mcg/mL for other infections **NOTES** Pregnancy Category B (oral)/C (IV) First-line treatment for MRSA infections Consider alternative agent when MRSA MIC ≥ 2 mcg/mL.

See lab interactions, storage requirements, renal dosage information near the end of this chapter.

Vancomycin Drug Interactions

- Vancomycin can ↑ toxicity of other nephrotoxic drugs (e.g., aminoglycosides, amphotericin B, cisplatin, colistimethate, cyclosporine, loop diuretics, NSAIDs, radiographic contrast dye, tacrolimus and vancomycin). Vancomycin can ↑ toxicity of other ototoxic drugs (e.g., aminoglycosides, cisplatin, loop diuretics, others).

Lipoglycopeptides

Inhibit bacterial cell wall synthesis by 1) blocking polymerization and cross-linking of peptidoglycan by binding to the D-Ala-D-Ala portion of the cell wall, and 2) disrupting bacterial membrane potential and changing cell permeability due to the presence of a lipophilic side chain moiety. Exhibit concentration-dependent killing and are bactericidal.

- Coverage: Similar to vancomycin.

DRUG	DOSING	SAFETY/SIDE EFFECTS/MONITORING
Telavancin (*Vibativ*) Injection Approved for complicated skin and soft-tissue infections (SSTI) and hospital-acquired pneumonia	10 mg/kg IV daily CrCl ≤ 50 mL/min: ↓ dose or extend interval Infuse over 60 minutes to prevent infusion reaction REMS – warning of ↑ mortality in patients with pre-existing renal dysfunction and risk of fetal developmental toxicity	**BOXED WARNINGS** Fetal risk – obtain pregnancy test prior to starting therapy. Nephrotoxicity ↑ mortality versus vancomycin in some patients with pre-existing moderate-to-severe renal impairment (CrCl ≤ 50 mL/minute) **WARNINGS** Can cause falsely ↑ PT/INR readings but the drug does not ↑ bleeding risk. Does not interfere with factor Xa monitoring. Rapid IV administration may result in red man syndrome. **SIDE EFFECTS** Metallic taste, N/V, ↑ SCr, QT prolongation, red man syndrome **MONITORING** Renal function, pregnancy status **NOTES** Pregnancy Category C (there is a pregnancy registry) MedGuide required
Oritavancin (*Orbactiv*) Injection Coverage: Gram-positives including *Staphylococci* (MRSA), *Streptococci*, and *Enterococcus faecalis* (not VRE) Approved for SSTI	Single-dose regimen 1,200 mg IV x 1 Infuse over 3 hours CrCl < 30 mL/min: Has not been studied, use with caution Extremely long half-life, therefore a single-dose regimen	**CONTRAINDICATIONS** Oritavancin: Use of intravenous unfractionated heparin for 48 hours after oritavancin administration due to interference with aPTT laboratory results **WARNINGS** Oritavancin: May ↑ risk of bleeding in patients receiving warfarin. Enhanced monitoring is recommended. Can cause falsely ↑ PT/INR reading for up to 24 hours and aPTT for up to 48 hours after a dose. Osteomyelitis developed more often in the oritavancin group.
Dalbavancin (*Dalvance*) Injection Coverage: Gram-positives including *Staphylococci* (MRSA) and *Streptococci* Approved for SSTI	Two-dose regimen 1,000 mg IV x 1, then 500 mg IV one week later Infuse over 30 minutes CrCl < 30 mL/min: 750 mg IV x 1, followed by 375 mg IV one week later Extremely long half-life, therefore a two-dose regimen	Dalbavancin: Infusion reactions: rapid IV administration may result in red man syndrome – infuse over 30 minutes, ↑ ALT levels > 3 times the upper limit of normal **SIDE EFFECTS** N/V/D, headache, rash, infusion reaction (red man syndrome) **MONITORING** Signs of osteomyelitis (oritavancin), LFTs, renal function **NOTES** Pregnancy Category C

See lab interactions, storage requirements, renal dosage information near the end of this chapter.

Telavancin Drug Interactions

■ Avoid in patients with congenital long QT syndrome, known QT prolongation, or uncompensated heart failure. Caution with the use of other medications known to prolong the QT interval (see Arrhythmias chapter).

Oritavancin Drug Interactions

■ Weak inhibitor of 2C9 and 2C19 and weak inducer of 3A4 and 2D6. Use caution when coadministered with drugs metabolized by these enzymes.

Daptomycin *(Cubicin)*

Daptomycin is a cyclic lipopeptide agent that binds to cell membrane components causing rapid depolarization, inhibiting all intracellular replication processes including protein synthesis. Daptomycin exhibits concentration-dependent killing and bactericidal activity.

■ Coverage: Most Gram-positive bacteria, including *Staphylococci* (MRSA) and *Enterococci,* including VRE (*E. faecium* and *E. faecalis).*

DRUG	DOSING	SAFETY/SIDE EFFECTS/MONITORING
DAPTOmycin *(Cubicin)* Injection Approved for complicated skin and soft-tissue infections (SSTI) and *S. aureus* (MRSA) bloodstream infections, including right-sided endocarditis	SSTI: 4 mg/kg IV daily Bacteremia/right-sided endocarditis: 6 mg/kg IV daily CrCl < 30 mL/min: Extend dosing interval to Q48H	**WARNINGS** Eosinophilic pneumonia – generally develops 2-4 weeks after therapy initiation. Myopathy – discontinue in patients with signs and symptoms along with an increase in CPK > 1,000 units/L (5x ULN) or in asymptomatic patients with a CPK ≥ 2,000 units/L (10x ULN). **SIDE EFFECTS** N/V/D, constipation, anemia, headache, dizziness, ↑ CPK and myopathy, dyspnea, hypo/hyperkalemia, hyperphosphatemia, ↑ LFTs **MONITORING** CPK level weekly (more frequently if on a statin); muscle pain/ weakness **NOTES** Pregnancy Category B Can cause falsely ↑ PT/INR readings but the drug does not ↑ bleeding risk. Compatible with NS and LR only Do not use to treat pneumonia as drug is inactivated in the lungs by surfactant.

See lab interactions, storage requirements, renal dosage information near the end of this chapter.

Daptomycin Drug Interactions

■ Daptomycin can have additive risk of muscle toxicity when used in conjunction with statins.

Oxazolidinones

Bind to the 50S subunit of the bacterial ribosome inhibiting bacterial translation and protein synthesis and exhibit generally <u>bacteriostatic activity</u>.

- Coverage: Similar to vancomycin, but also cover <u>VRE</u> (*E. faecium* and *E. faecalis*).

DRUG	DOSING	SAFETY/SIDE EFFECTS/MONITORING
Linezolid *(Zyvox)* Tablet, suspension, injection	600 mg PO/IV Q12H	**CONTRAINDICATIONS** <u>Linezolid: Concurrent or use within 2 weeks of MAO inhibitors</u> **WARNINGS** <u>Linezolid: Duration-related myelosuppression</u>, peripheral and optic neuropathy when treated > 28 days, serotonin syndrome, hypoglycemia – caution in patients on insulin or hypoglycemia agents Tedizolid: Consider alternative therapy in patients with neutropenia.
Tedizolid *(Sivextro)* Tablet, injection Approved for SSTI	200 mg IV/PO daily for 6 days Infuse over 1 hour, stable in NS	**SIDE EFFECTS** Myelosuppression, anemia ($\downarrow$ Hgb), <u>thrombocytopenia</u>, <u>headache, nausea, diarrhea</u>, dizziness, insomnia, $\uparrow$ pancreatic enzymes, $\uparrow$ LFTs, neuropathy **MONITORING** Weekly CBC, visual function **NOTES** Pregnancy Category C Less GI and myelotoxicity expected with tedizolid compared to linezolid No adjustment in renal impairment <u>Do not shake</u> linezolid suspension.

See lab interactions, storage requirements, renal dosage information near the end of this chapter.

Linezolid Drug Interactions

- Linezolid is a weak monoamine oxidase inhibitor. Caution in patients taking concurrent serotonergic or adrenergic drugs.

- Avoid tyramine-containing foods and serotonergic drugs. See Drug Interactions chapter.

- Linezolid can exacerbate hypoglycemic episodes, caution in patients receiving insulin or oral hypoglycemic agents.

Tedizolid Drug Interactions

- Potential interaction with serotonergic drugs, less than with linezolid.

Quinupristin/Dalfopristin *(Synercid)*

Streptogramin class – binds to the 50S ribosomal subunit inhibiting protein synthesis; bactericidal.

- Coverage: Most Gram-positive bacteria, including *Staphylococci* (MRSA), *Enterococcus faecium* (VRE, but <u>not active against *E. faecalis*</u>). Approved for complicated skin and soft-tissue infections, but is <u>not well-tolerated</u> and <u>use is typically limited</u> to vancomycin-resistant *E. faecium* infections.

DRUG	DOSING	SAFETY/SIDE EFFECTS/MONITORING
Quinupristin/ Dalfopristin *(Synercid)* Injection	7.5 mg/kg IV Q8-12H No adjustment in renal impairment	**SIDE EFFECTS** Arthralgias/myalgias (up to 47%), infusion reactions, including edema and pain at infusion site (up to 44%), phlebitis (40%), hyperbilirubinemia (up to 35%), CPK elevations, GI upset, ↑ LFTs **NOTES** Pregnancy Category B

See lab interactions, storage requirements, renal dosage information near the end of this chapter.

Quinupristin/Dalfopristin Drug Interactions

- Quinupristin/Dalfopristin is a weak 3A4 inhibitor; can ↑ levels of CCBs, cyclosporine, dofetilide and others.

Tigecycline *(Tygacil)*

Glycylcycline class – binds to the 30S ribosomal subunit inhibiting protein synthesis; <u>structurally related to the tetracyclines</u>; <u>bacteriostatic</u>.

- Coverage: Very broad spectrum activity against Gram-positive bacteria including *Staphylococci* (<u>MRSA</u>), *Enterococci* (including <u>VRE</u>), <u>Gram-negative, anaerobic,</u> and <u>atypical</u> organisms. Among the Gram-negatives, <u>no activity against the "3 P's"</u>: *Pseudomonas, Proteus, Providencia* species. Approved for complicated skin and soft-tissue infections/intra-abdominal infections and community-acquired pneumonia; however, an FDA warning suggests to <u>use only when other alternatives are not possible</u>.

DRUG	DOSING	SAFETY/SIDE EFFECTS/MONITORING
Tigecycline *(Tygacil)* Injection Derivative of minocycline	100 mg IV x 1 dose, then 50 mg IV Q12H Severe hepatic impairment: 100 mg IV x 1, then 25 mg IV Q12H <u>No adjustment in renal impairment</u>	**BOXED WARNING** ↑ risk of death, use only when alternative treatments are not suitable. **WARNINGS** Hepatotoxicity, pancreatitis, photosensitivity, teeth discoloration in children < 8 years old (avoid use) **SIDE EFFECTS** N/V/D, headache, dizziness, ↑ LFTs, rash **NOTES** Pregnancy Category D Lower cure rates in ventilator-associated pneumonia <u>Avoid use in bloodstream infections</u>. It does not achieve adequate concentrations in the blood since it is lipophilic (drug distributes quickly out of blood into tissues). <u>Reconstituted solution should be yellow-orange; discard if not this color.</u>

See lab interactions, storage requirements, renal dosage information near the end of this chapter.

Tigecycline Drug Interactions

- Tigecycline can ↑ INR in patients taking warfarin.

ADDITIONAL BROAD SPECTRUM AGENTS

Polymyxins

The polymyxin class consists of two main agents, colistimethate (also called colistin) and polymyxin B. Colistimethate is an inactive prodrug that is hydrolyzed to colistin, which acts as a cationic detergent and damages the bacterial cytoplasmic membrane causing leaking of intracellular substances and cell death (this is thought to be the mechanism of nephrotoxicity as well). These antibiotics exhibit concentration-dependent killing and are bactericidal.

- Coverage: Gram-negative bacteria such as *Enterobacter* spp., *E. coli*, *Klebsiella pneumoniae*, and *Pseudomonas aeruginosa*; used primarily in setting of MDR Gram-negative pathogens. These do not cover *Proteus* spp.

- Should be used in combination with another antibiotic due to emergence of resistance.

DRUG	DOSING	SAFETY/SIDE EFFECTS/MONITORING
Colistimethate sodium or colistin *(Coly-Mycin M)* Injection (also used for inhalation)	2.5-5 mg/kg/day IV/IM in 2-4 divided doses Dose is expressed in terms of colistin base activity CrCl < 80 mL/min: ↓ dose and extend interval Solutions for inhalation must be mixed immediately prior to administration.	**WARNING** Dose-dependent nephrotoxicity (monitor renal function and electrolytes), neurotoxicity **SIDE EFFECTS** Nephrotoxicity (proteinuria, ↑ SCr), neurologic disturbances (dizziness, headache, tingling, oral paresthesia, vertigo) **NOTES** Pregnancy Category C Assess dose carefully, as dosage can be represented in units of colistimethate sodium, mg colistimethate sodium, or mg of colistin base activity. Avoid use with other nephrotoxic medications. The neurotoxicity of colistimethate can result in respiratory paralysis from neuromuscular blockade.
Polymyxin B Sulfate Injection (IM/IV, intrathecal)	15,000-25,000 units/kg/day IV divided every 12 hours CrCl < 80 mL/min: ↓ frequency and extend interval	**BOXED WARNINGS** Nephrotoxicity (dose-dependent) Neurotoxicity Safety in pregnancy is not established. Intramuscular/intrathecal administration only to hospitalized patients Avoid concurrent or sequential use of other neurotoxic or nephrotoxic drugs The neurotoxicity of polymyxin B sulfate can result in respiratory paralysis from neuromuscular blockade. **SIDE EFFECTS** Nephrotoxicity, neurologic disturbances (dizziness, tingling, numbness, paresthesia, vertigo), fever, urticaria **MONITORING** Renal function **NOTES** 1 mg = 10,000 units polymyxin B

See lab interactions, storage requirements, renal dosage information near the end of this chapter.

Polymyxin Drug Interactions

- Other nephrotoxic agents can enhance the nephrotoxic effect.

Chloramphenicol

Reversibly binds to the 50S subunit of the bacterial ribosome inhibiting protein synthesis; bactericidal.

- Coverage: Activity against Gram-positives, Gram-negatives, anaerobes, and atypicals.

DRUG	DOSING	SAFETY/SIDE EFFECTS/MONITORING
Chloramphenicol Injection Rarely used due to side effects	50-100 mg/kg/day IV in divided doses Q6H (max 4 g/day) No adjustment in renal impairment but use with caution	**BOXED WARNING** Serious and fatal blood dyscrasias (aplastic anemia, thrombocytopenia, granulocytopenia) **WARNINGS** Gray syndrome – characterized by circulatory collapse, cyanosis, acidosis, abdominal distention, myocardial depression, coma, and death; associated with high serum levels **SIDE EFFECTS** Myelosuppression (pancytopenia), aplastic anemia, dermatologic (angioedema, rash, urticaria) **MONITORING** CBC at baseline and every 2 days during therapy, LFTs and renal function, serum drug concentrations

See lab interactions, storage requirements, renal dosage information near the end of this chapter.

Telithromycin *(Ketek)*

A ketolide antibiotic, telithromycin binds to the 50S subunit of the bacterial ribosome inhibiting protein synthesis (structurally related to macrolides). Telithromycin exhibits concentration-dependent killing and is bactericidal.

- Coverage: Gram-positive bacteria, primarily *Streptococci* species, including macrolide-resistant strains, Gram-negative, some anaerobic, and atypical organisms. FDA approved for community acquired pneumonia only.

DRUG	DOSING	SAFETY/SIDE EFFECTS/MONITORING
Telithromycin *(Ketek)* Tablet	800 mg PO daily CrCl < 30 mL/min: 600 mg PO daily CrCl < 30 mL/min + hepatic impairment: 400 mg PO daily	**BOXED WARNING** Contraindicated in patients with myasthenia gravis due to respiratory failure **CONTRAINDICATIONS** Allergy to macrolides, history of hepatitis or jaundice from macrolides, myasthenia gravis, concurrent use with colchicine (if patient has renal or liver impairment), lovastatin, simvastatin or pimozide **WARNINGS** Acute hepatic failure (can be fatal), QT prolongation, visual disturbances (blurry vision, diplopia), syncope **SIDE EFFECTS** N/V/D, dizziness, headache, ↑ LFTs, rash **MONITORING** LFTs and visual acuity **NOTES** Pregnancy Category C

See lab interactions, storage requirements, renal dosage information near the end of this chapter.

- Telithromycin is a substrate of 1A2 (minor), 3A4 (major) and an inhibitor of 2D6 (weak) and 3A4 (strong). Avoid with moderate/strong 3A4 inhibitors and 3A4 substrates with a narrow therapeutic window or significant toxicity (e.g., simvastatin, lovastatin). Avoid with class Ia and class III antiarrhythmics and other major QT prolonging drugs. See Drug Interactions chapter for more information.

MISCELLANEOUS ANTIBIOTICS

Clindamycin *(Cleocin)*

Lincosamide class – reversibly binds to the 50S subunit of the bacterial ribosome inhibiting protein synthesis; bacteriostatic.

- Coverage: Most aerobic and anaerobic Gram-positive bacteria (including some community-associated MRSA). Does not cover *Enterococcus*.

DRUG	DOSING	SAFETY/SIDE EFFECTS/MONITORING
Clindamycin *(Cleocin)* Injection, capsule, suspension Topical: Foam, gel, lotion, kit, solution, swab (*Cleocin-T, Clindagel, ClindaMax, Clindacin ETZ, Clindacin Pac, Clindacin-P, Evoclin*) Vaginal: Cream, suppository (*Clindesse, Cleocin* ovule)	150-450 mg PO Q6H 600-900 mg IV Q8H No adjustment in renal impairment	**BOXED WARNING** Colitis (*C. difficile*) **WARNING** Severe or fatal skin reactions (SJS/TEN) **SIDE EFFECTS** N/V/D, rash, urticaria, ↑ LFTs (rare) **NOTES** Pregnancy Category B. An induction test (D-test) should be performed on bacteria that are susceptible to clindamycin but resistant to erythromycin. A flattened zone between the disks (positive D-test) indicates inducible clindamycin resistance is present and clindamycin should not be used.

See lab interactions, storage requirements, renal dosage information near the end of this chapter.

Metronidazole *(Flagyl)* and Tinidazole *(Tindamax)*

These antibiotics cause a loss of helical DNA structure and strand breakage resulting in inhibition of protein synthesis; bactericidal.

- Coverage: Metronidazole has activity against anaerobes and protozoal infections; effective for bacterial vaginosis, trichomoniasis, giardiasis, amebiasis, *Clostridium difficile*, and is used in combination regimens for intra-abdominal infections. Tinidazole is structurally related to metronidazole, but activity is limited to protozoa (giardiasis, amebiasis), trichomoniasis and bacterial vaginosis organisms.

DRUG	DOSING	SAFETY/SIDE EFFECTS/MONITORING
Metronidazole *(Flagyl, Flagyl ER, Metro)* Tablet, capsule, injection Topical: *MetroCream, MetroGel, MetroGel Vaginal, MetroLotion, Noritate, Vandazole*	500-750 mg IV/PO Q8-12H or 250-500 mg IV/PO Q6-8H **Mild-to-Moderate CDI:** <u>500 mg IV/PO TID for 10-14 days</u> No adjustment in renal impairment Take immediate-release tablets with food to ↓ GI upset. Take extended-release tablets on empty stomach	**BOXED WARNING** Possibly carcinogenic based on animal data **CONTRAINDICATIONS** Pregnancy (1st trimester), breastfeeding (tinidazole), use of disulfiram within the past 2 weeks (metronidazole), <u>use of alcohol or propylene glycol-containing products during therapy or within 3 days of therapy discontinuation</u> **WARNINGS** CNS effects – seizures, peripheral/optic neuropathies, aseptic meningitis (metronidazole), encephalopathy (metronidazole)
Tinidazole *(Tindamax)* Tablet	2 grams PO daily Take with food to minimize GI effects No adjustment in renal impairment	**SIDE EFFECTS** N/V/D, <u>metallic taste</u>, furry tongue, darkened urine, rash, headache, dizziness **NOTES** Pregnancy Category B metronidazole/C (tinidazole)

See lab interactions, storage requirements, renal dosage information near the end of this chapter.

Metronidazole/Tinidazole Drug Interactions

■ Metronidazole is an inhibitor of 3A4 (weak) and 2C9 (weak). Tinidazole is a substrate of 3A4 (minor).

■ <u>Metronidazole and tinidazole should not be used with alcohol (during and for 3 days after discontinuation of therapy) due to a potential disulfiram-like reaction.</u>

■ Metronidazole, and potentially tinidazole, can ↑ INR in patients taking warfarin.

Fidaxomicin *(Dificid)*

Inhibits RNA polymerase resulting in inhibition of protein synthesis and cell death; bactericidal.

■ Coverage: Used for *Clostridium difficile* infection. Although it has shown benefit in preventing recurrence of disease, it is currently used most often in select cases due to high cost (e.g., recurrent disease, treatment failure with vancomycin or metronidazole).

DRUG	DOSING	SAFETY/SIDE EFFECTS/MONITORING
Fidaxomicin *(Dificid)* Tablet	200 mg PO BID x 10 days No adjustment in renal impairment	**SIDE EFFECTS** N/V, abdominal pain, GI bleeding, anemia **NOTES** Pregnancy Category B <u>Not effective for systemic infections</u> – absorption is minimal.

See lab interactions, storage requirements, renal dosage information near the end of this chapter.

Rifaximin *(Xifaxan)*

Rifaximin inhibits bacterial RNA synthesis by binding to bacterial DNA-dependent RNA polymerase. It is structurally related to rifampin and is bactericidal.

- Coverage: *E. coli*

DRUG	DOSING	SAFETY/SIDE EFFECTS/MONITORING
Rifaximin *(Xifaxan)* Tablet	**Travelers' diarrhea:** 200 mg PO TID x 3 days **Reduction of hepatic encephalopathy recurrence:** 550 mg PO BID **Irritable bowel syndrome w/diarrhea (IBS-D):** 550 mg PO TID x 14 days No adjustment in renal impairment	**SIDE EFFECTS** Peripheral edema, dizziness, headache, flatulence, nausea, abdominal pain, rash/pruritus **NOTES** Pregnancy Category C Not effective for systemic infections – < 1% absorption May be used as salvage treatment in patients with *C. difficile* infection

See lab interactions, storage requirements, renal dosage information near the end of this chapter.

URINARY AGENTS

Fosfomycin *(Monurol)*

Inhibits bacterial cell wall synthesis by inactivating the enzyme pyruval transferase, which is critical in the synthesis of cell walls; bactericidal. Single-dose regimen used for uncomplicated UTI (cystitis only).

- Coverage: *E. coli* (including ESBLs) and *E. faecalis* (including VRE).

DRUG	DOSING	SAFETY/SIDE EFFECTS/MONITORING
Fosfomycin *(Monurol)* 1 packet granules = 3 grams	**Female, Uncomplicated UTI** 3 grams PO x 1, mixed in 3-4 oz of cold water	**SIDE EFFECTS** Headache, diarrhea, nausea **NOTES** Pregnancy Category B

See lab interactions, storage requirements, renal dosage information near the end of this chapter.

Nitrofurantoin *(Macrodantin, Macrobid, Furadantin)*

Bacterial cell wall inhibitor; bactericidal. Used for uncomplicated UTI (cystitis only).

- Coverage: *E. coli, Klebsiella, Enterobacter, S. aureus,* and *Enterococcus* (VRE).

DRUG	DOSING	SAFETY/SIDE EFFECTS/MONITORING
Nitrofurantoin *(Macrodantin, Macrobid, Furadantin)* Capsule, suspension	*Macrodantin:* 50-100 mg PO QID with food x 3-7 days; 50-100 mg PO QHS with food for prophylaxis *Macrobid:* 100 mg PO BID x 7 days The macrocrystal formulation *(Macrobid)* dissolves more slowly and is given BID CrCl < 60 mL/min: Contraindicated Per revised 2015 Beers Criteria: Use can be considered when CrCl > 30 mL/min	**CONTRAINDICATIONS** Renal impairment (CrCl < 60 mL/min) due to inadequate urinary concentrations and risk for accumulation of neurotoxins, a previous history of cholestatic jaundice/ hepatic dysfunction, pregnancy (at term) **WARNINGS** Optic neuritis, hepatotoxicity, peripheral neuropathy, pulmonary toxicity, hemolytic anemia (use caution in patients with G6PD deficiency) and positive Coombs test **SIDE EFFECTS** GI upset, headache, rash, brown urine discoloration (harmless) **NOTES** Pregnancy Category B (used last line in 1st trimester, contraindicated in last 2 weeks of pregnancy)

See lab interactions, storage requirements, renal dosage information near the end of this chapter.

TOPICAL DECOLONIZATION

Mupirocin Nasal Ointment *(Bactroban)*

Topical antimicrobial ointment used to eliminate *Staphylococci* (MRSA) colonization of the nares. See Common Skin Conditions chapter for discussion regarding mupirocin topical use for infected skin lesions.

DRUG	DOSING	SAFETY/SIDE EFFECTS/MONITORING
Mupirocin Nasal *(Bactroban Nasal)* 1 g tubes	Decolonization: ½ tube in each nostril BID x 5 days	**SIDE EFFECTS** Headache, burning, localized irritation, rhinitis, pharyngitis

See lab interactions, storage requirements, renal dosage information near the end of this chapter.

DRUGS ACTIVE AGAINST SPECIFIC PATHOGENS

Community-associated methicillin-resistant *Staphylococcus aureus* (CA-MRSA) skin & soft tissue infections (SSTI)

SMX/TMP *(Bactrim DS)*

Doxycycline, Minocycline

Clindamycin*

For more severe SSTI requiring IV treatment or hospitalization

Vancomycin

Linezolid, tedizolid

Daptomycin

Ceftaroline

Telavancin

Oritavancin

Dalbavancin

Quinupristin/dalfopristin

Tigecycline

Nosocomial MRSA

Vancomycin (consider using alternative if MIC ≥ 2)

Linezolid

Telavancin

Daptomycin (not in pneumonia)

Rifampin (used in combination therapy only)

VRE *(E. faecalis)*

Pen G or ampicillin

Linezolid

Daptomycin

Tigecycline

Cystitis only: nitrofurantoin, fosfomycin, doxycycline

VRE *(E. faecium)*

Daptomycin

Linezolid

Quinupristin/Dalfopristin

Tigecycline

Cystitis only: nitrofurantoin, fosfomycin, doxycycline

Pseudomonas aeruginosa

Ceftazidime

Ceftazidime/avibactam

Ceftolozane/tazobactam

Cefepime

Piperacillin/tazobactam, ticarcillin/clavulanate

Carbapenems (except ertapenem)

Ciprofloxacin, levofloxacin

Aztreonam

Aminoglycosides

Colistimethate

Acinetobacter baumannii

Carbapenems (except ertapenem)

Ampicillin/sulbactam

Minocycline

Tigecycline

Quinolones

SMX/TMP

Colistimethate

Extended spectrum beta-lactamase producing Gram-negative rods (ESBL GNR) – *E. coli, Klebsiella pneumoniae, P. mirabilis*

Carbapenems

Ceftolozane/tazobactam

Ceftazidime/avibactam

Cefepime (high-dose)

Quinolones

Aminoglycosides

Carbapenem-resistant Gram-negative rods (CRE, KPC)

Ceftazidime/avibactam

Colistimethate

Bacteroides fragilis

Metronidazole

Beta-lactam/beta-lactamase inhibitor combos

Cefotetan, cefoxitin

Carbapenems

Tigecycline

Others (reduced activity): clindamycin, moxifloxacin

Clostridium difficile Infection

Metronidazole

Vancomycin (oral)

Fidaxomicin

Atypical Organisms

Azithromycin, clarithromycin

Doxycycline, minocycline

Quinolones

HNPEK

Amoxicillin (if beta-lactamase negative)

Beta-lactam/beta-lactamase inhibitor combos

Cephalosporins (except 1st generation)

Carbapenems

SMX/TMP

Aminoglycosides

Quinolones

A D-test must be performed before using clindamycin. Never use quinolones for MRSA, regardless of susceptibility report.

STORAGE REQUIREMENTS

REFRIGERATION REQUIRED AFTER RECONSTITUTION		
Penicillin VK	Cefadroxil *(Duricef)*	Cefaclor *(Ceclor)*
Ampicillin	Cefpodoxime *(Vantin)*	Ceftibuten *(Cedax)*
Amoxicillin/Clavulanate *(Augmentin)*	Cefprozil *(Cefzil)*	Vancomycin (oral)
Cephalexin *(Keflex)*	Cefuroxime *(Ceftin)*	Valacyclovir*

REFRIGERATION RECOMMENDED
Amoxicillin (*Amoxil*) – improves taste

DO NOT REFRIGERATE		
Cefdinir *(Omnicef)*	Ciprofloxacin *(Cipro)*	Sulfamethoxazole/Trimethoprim *(Septra, Sulfatrim)*
Azithromycin *(Zmax)*	Levofloxacin *(Levaquin)*	Fluconazole *(Diflucan)**
Clarithromycin *(Biaxin)* – bitter taste, thickens/gels	Clindamycin *(Cleocin)* – thickens, may crystallize	Posaconazole *(Noxafil)**
Doxycycline *(Vibramycin)*	Linezolid *(Zyvox)*	Voriconazole *(Vfend)**
		Nystatin*

These agents are discussed in Infectious Diseases Chapter III

RENAL DOSE ADJUSTMENT

Many antibiotics are cleared through the kidneys and require adjustment based on renal function. Most beta-lactams and quinolones require adjustment for renal impairment. See the following table of antibiotics that do not require renal adjustment.

NO RENAL DOSE ADJUSTMENT REQUIRED	
Dicloxacillin, nafcillin, oxacillin	Clindamycin
Ceftriaxone	Metronidazole, tinidazole
Moxifloxacin	Fidaxomicin
Azithromycin, erythromycin	Vancomycin (PO only)
Doxycycline, minocycline, tigecycline	Rifaximin
Linezolid, tedizolid	Rifampin*
Quinupristin/dalfopristin	Chloramphenicol

This agent is discussed in Infectious Diseases Chapter II

DRUG-LABORATORY INTERACTIONS

Some antibiotics can cause abnormalities in laboratory values. This can arise in several situations. An antibiotic can cause a true change in the lab value, which indicates a problem and often necessitates a change in therapy (e.g., a positive Coombs test in combination with bleeding indicates that a patient could be experiencing drug-related hemolysis and the antibiotic should be discontinued). In other cases, a drug should not be started in patients with certain conditions (sulfonamides in patients with G6PD deficiency). And in some situations, medications can interfere with the result of the test, even if there are no clinical effects (daptomycin can cause a falsely elevated INR reading, but does not cause bleeding).

LAB TEST	IMPLICATIONS	ANTIBIOTICS
G6PD deficiency	Discontinue drug if present or bleeding (hemolysis) of unknown cause	Chloroquine*, primaquine* Dapsone** Nitrofurantoin Quinine* Sulfamethoxazole
Coombs test, positive	Discontinue drug; can cause hemolysis Increased risk with higher doses/prolonged infusions	Penicillins Cephalosporins Imipenem, meropenem Nitrofurantoin Rifampin Sulfamethoxazole Quinine* Isoniazid**
Drug-Induced Lupus Erythematosus (DILE), evidenced by either butterfly rash, achy joints, lab tests (RF+, ↑ ANA, ESR, CRP)	Discontinue drug; lupus damages joints/organs	Isoniazid** Minocycline Terbinafine**
False-positive urine glucose tests (with copper reduction tests)	Positive urinary glucose may be due to drug (rather than ↑ BG)	Penicillins Cephalosporins Imipenem Isoniazid**
Changes in coagulation tests (PT & INR, aPTT)	Use alternate assay (Factor Xa) or alternative anticoagulant not requiring aPTT or PT/INR monitoring	Oritavancin Telavancin
False elevation in INR	Use alternate assay (Factor Xa) or alternative anticoagulant not requiring PT/INR monitoring	Daptomycin
Elevated CPK	Monitor at least weekly, or more if current or prior statin use. Discontinue daptomycin if CPK > 5x the upper limit of normal (ULN) or 1,000 units/L along with symptoms of myopathy or when CPK > 10x ULN if asymptomatic.	Daptomycin

* These agents are discussed in Travelers
**These agents are discussed in Infectious Diseases II – IV

SPECIAL REQUIREMENTS	DRUG	
Most antibiotics can be taken with food to ↓ GI upset; except these, which are different	Within one hour of finishing a meal: *Moxatag* (amoxicillin formulation) Empty stomach: Ampicillin oral capsules and suspension, azithromycin (*Zmax,* extended-release oral suspension), ceftibuten suspension, levofloxacin oral solution, metronidazole extended-release, penicillin, itraconazole solution*, voriconazole*	
Oral to IV Dosing Ratios 1:1 (Oral and IV dose is the same)	Levofloxacin, moxifloxacin Doxycycline, minocycline Sulfamethoxazole/trimethoprim Linezolid, tedizolid Metronidazole Fluconazole*, isavuconazonium*, posaconazole* (oral capsules and IV), voriconazole*	
Light Protection Required During Administration	Doxycycline Micafungin* Pentamidine*	
Compatible with Dextrose only	Dalbavancin, oritavancin Pentamidine* Quinupristin/dalfopristin Sulfamethoxazole/trimethoprim Amphotericin B* (conventional, *Abelcet*, *Amphotec, Ambisome*)	5% Dextrose Injection, USP

Special Requirements Continued

SPECIAL REQUIREMENTS	DRUG	
Compatible with Saline only	Ampicillin Ampicillin/sulbactam Ertapenem	0.9% Sodium Chloride Injection, USP
Compatible with NS/LR only	Caspofungin* Daptomycin	Lactated Ringer's Injection, USP
IV antibiotics that should NOT be refrigerated	Acyclovir* – refrigeration causes crystallization Clindamycin – refrigeration causes crystallization Metronidazole Moxifloxacin Sulfamethoxazole/trimethoprim	

* These agents are discussed in Infectious Diseases Chapter II-IV

Patient Counseling

Counseling That Applies to All Antibiotics

- <u>Antibiotics only treat bacterial infections</u>. They do not treat viral infections such as the common cold and are not recommended in most cases of acute bronchitis and sinusitis.

- Skipping doses or not completing the full course of therapy may ↓ effectiveness of treatment, cause the infection to return, and increase the likelihood that this medicine will not work for you in the future.

- If your symptoms worsen, contact your healthcare provider.

- Many antibiotics can cause <u>rash</u>. If you experience a rash, contact your healthcare provider.

- Many antibiotics cause <u>GI upset</u>. Taking medication <u>with food</u> will usually help, however some antibiotics need to be taken on an empty stomach.

- Measure liquid doses carefully using a <u>measuring device/syringe</u> which came with the medicine. Ask your pharmacist if you do not have one. <u>Household spoons should not be used</u>, as they often fail to deliver the correct dose.

- Contact your healthcare provider if you have <u>watery diarrhea</u> several times a day, with or without abdominal cramping. This can occur during treatment, or weeks after the antibiotic treatment has finished. You should not self-treat with anti-diarrheal medicine.

- Some oral liquid and chewable dosage forms contain phenylalanine. Let the pharmacist know if you have phenylketonuria (inability to metabolize phenylalanine).

Amoxicillin products

- Amoxicillin may be taken with food, usually every 8 or 12 hours. *Moxatag* is taken within 1 hour of finishing a meal. *Augmentin* is taken with food to ↑ absorption and ↓ stomach upset. Amoxicillin/clavulanate extended release tablets should be administered with food.

- The suspensions should be refrigerated (especially important for *Augmentin).*

Azithromycin *(Zithromax)*

- Common dosing is two 250 mg tablets on day 1, followed by one 250 mg tablet daily on days 2 – 5, or 500 mg daily for 3 days.

- The tablets and immediate release oral suspension can be taken with or without food, extended release suspension should be taken on an empty stomach (1 hour before or 2 hours after a meal).

- The suspension should be stored at room temperature and should not be refrigerated.

Cephalexin *(Keflex)* / Cefuroxime *(Ceftin)* / Cefdinir *(Omnicef)*

- Cephalexin: Take this medication by mouth with or without a meal or snack every 6 hours. The suspension should be refrigerated.

- Cefuroxime: Take this medication by mouth with a meal or snack every 12 hours. The suspension should be refrigerated.

- Cefdinir: Can be taken with or without food. The suspension should not be refrigerated.

Clarithromycin *(Biaxin)*

- Common side effects include abnormal (metallic) taste, diarrhea and GI upset.

- The tablets and oral suspension are taken twice daily with or without food or with milk.

- *Biaxin XL* tablets should be taken with food.

- The liquid suspension should not be refrigerated.

Ciprofloxacin *(Cipro)*

- Rarely, seizures can occur, especially in those with seizure disorders (quinolones should be avoided with a seizure history).

- This medicine can make your skin more sensitive to the sun, and you can burn more easily. Use sunscreen, wear protective clothing, and avoid the sun.

- This medicine can rarely cause a serious problem called tendon rupture or swelling of the tendon (tendonitis). If you notice, pain, swelling and inflammation of the tendons on the back of the ankle (Achilles), shoulder, hand or other sites, stop the medicine and contact your healthcare provider immediately. This occurs more frequently in people over age 60, and in patients who have had transplants and use systemic steroid medicine, such as prednisone.

- This medicine can rarely cause weakness or tingling/painful sensations in the arms and legs. If this occurs, contact your healthcare provider immediately.

- Take this medication 2 hours before or 6 hours after taking antacids, vitamins, magnesium, calcium, iron or zinc supplements, dairy products, bismuth subsalicylate or the medicines sucralfate or didanosine *(Videx).*

- This is not a first choice medicine in patients under 18 years of age due to a risk of bone and joint problems. However, it is used occasionally on a short-term basis for certain conditions.

- Do not use this medicine if you take a different medicine called tizanidine *(Zanaflex).* Please tell your pharmacist about all medicines you are using, since this medicine can interact with many others. The liquid suspension should not be refrigerated. Maintain adequate hydration to prevent crystalluria.

Clindamycin *(Cleocin)*

- Take by mouth with or without food, 3 – 4 times a day.
- Take with a full glass of water to avoid GI irritation.
- The liquid suspension <u>should not be refrigerated</u>.

Doxycycline *(Doryx*, others)

- This medicine can make your skin more sensitive to the sun, and you can burn more easily. Use sunscreen, wear protective clothing, and avoid the sun.
- Take with a full glass of water to avoid GI irritation.
- This medicine should be taken twice daily 1 – 2 hours before, or 4 – 6 hours after taking antacids, vitamins, magnesium, calcium, iron or zinc supplements, dairy products, bismuth subsalicylate.
- *Oracea* should be taken on an empty stomach (1 hour before or 2 hours after meals)
- Do not use this medicine if you are pregnant, if you could become pregnant, or if you are breastfeeding.
- The liquid suspension <u>should not be refrigerated</u>.

Erythromycin

- The liquid suspension combination with sulfisoxazole should be refrigerated.

Levofloxacin *(Levaquin)*

- Take this medication once daily, with or without food. The suspension is taken 1 hour before or 2 hours after eating. Maintain adequate hydration to prevent crystal formation in the urine.
- If you use blood sugar-lowering medicines, your blood sugar may get unusually low. Be sure to check your blood sugar level frequently and treat a low blood sugar if it occurs.
- This medicine should be taken 2 hours before, or 2 hours after taking antacids, vitamins, magnesium, calcium, iron or zinc supplements, dairy products, bismuth subsalicylate or the medicines sucralfate *(Carafate)* or didanosine *(Videx)*.
- The liquid formulation <u>should not be refrigerated</u>.

Metronidazole *(Flagyl)*

- Common side effects include nausea and unusual (metallic) taste.
- Do not use any alcohol products while using this medicine, and for at least 3 days afterward.
- Immediate-release tablets and capsules may be taken with food to minimize stomach upset. Take extended release tablets on an empty stomach (1 hour before or 2 hours after meals); do not split, crush, or chew.

Minocycline *(Minocin, Solodyn)*

- Take this medication with or without food, 1– 2 times daily.
- Swallow tablet or capsule whole.
- Take with a full glass of water to decrease GI irritation.
- Do not use this medication if you are pregnant, if you could become pregnant, or if you are breastfeeding.

Mupirocin Ointment *(Bactroban Nasal)* **1 gram tube**

- Place ½ the ointment from the tube into one nostril and the other ½ into the other nostril. Press the nostrils at the same time and let go many times (for about a minute) to spread the ointment into the nose.

- Wash your hands after use.

- The most common side effects are burning and itching.

Nitrofurantoin *(Macrodantin, Macrobid)*

- Take this medication with food to improve absorption and ↓ side effects. Swallow the medication whole.

- Do not use magnesium trisilicate-containing antacids while taking this medication. These antacids can bind with nitrofurantoin, preventing its full absorption into your system.

- Side effects including nausea and headache may occur.

- This medication may cause your urine to turn dark yellow or brown in color. This is usually a harmless, temporary effect and will disappear when the medication is stopped. However, dark brown urine can also be a sign of liver damage. Seek immediate medical attention if you notice dark urine along with any of the following symptoms: persistent nausea or vomiting, pale stools, unusual fatigue or if your skin and whites of your eyes become yellow.

- This medication may rarely cause very serious (possibly fatal) lung problems. Lung problems may occur within the first month of treatment or after long-term use of nitrofurantoin (generally for 6 months or longer). Seek immediate medical attention if you develop symptoms of lung problems including: persistent cough, chest pain, shortness of breath/trouble breathing, joint/muscle pain or bluish/purplish skin.

Penicillin VK

- Take this medication by mouth one hour before or two hours after a meal, usually every 6 hours.

- The suspension should be refrigerated.

Sulfamethoxazole and Trimethoprim *(Bactrim, Septra)*

- Do not use this medication if you have an allergy to sulfa medicines.

- Take with a full glass of water to prevent crystal formation in the urine. Take with or without food. If stomach upset occurs, take with food or milk.

- Do not use this medication if you are pregnant, if you could become pregnant, or if you are breast-feeding.

- This medicine can make your skin more sensitive to the sun, and you can burn more easily. Use sunscreen, wear protective clothing, and avoid the sun.

- Shake the suspension prior to use. The suspension <u>should not be refrigerated</u>.

Questions

1. Which of the following statements regarding linezolid is correct?

    a. It is in a new class called cyclic lipo-peptides.

    b. It is a MAO inhibitor and should be avoided with serotonergic agents.

    c. It is a combination product consisting of quinupristin and dalfopristin.

    d. It needs to be dose adjusted in patients with renal impairment.

    e. It is not effective for treating infections in the lung.

2. Which of the following statements regarding the intravenous formulation of *Bactrim* is/are correct? (Select **ALL** that apply.)

    a. *Bactrim* IV should be protected from light during administration

    b. *Bactrim* IV should be refrigerated

    c. *Bactrim* IV is compatible with Dextrose 5% (D5W)

    d. *Bactrim* IV needs to be dose adjusted in patients with significant renal impairment

    e. *Bactrim* IV can be converted to *Bactrim* PO in a 1:1 fashion

3. Which one of the following antibiotics does not require dose adjustment in renal impairment?

    a. Gentamicin

    b. Clarithromycin

    c. Cefixime

    d. Tigecycline

    e. Daptomycin

4. Which one of the following antibiotics should be refrigerated?

    a. *Cipro*

    b. *Keflex*

    c. *Levaquin*

    d. *Septra*

    e. *Zithromax*

5. The pharmacist should counsel a patient to use sunscreen when taking which of the following medication(s)? (Select **ALL** that apply.)

    a. *Cleocin*

    b. *Biaxin*

    c. *Avelox*

    d. *Minocin*

    e. *Tamiflu*

6. Which one of the following antimicrobials in the IV formulation is stable in and preferred to be reconstituted in normal saline (NS)?

    a. Quinupristin/dalfopristin

    b. Ertapenem

    c. Ampicillin

    d. SMX/TMP

    e. Azithromycin

7. An infection caused by *E. coli* that produces extended-spectrum beta-lactamases could be treated with which of the following antibiotics: (Select **ALL** that apply.)

    a. *Invanz*

    b. *Rocephin*

    c. *Unasyn*

    d. *Zerbaxa*

    e. *Avycaz*

8. All of the following have activity against *Pseudomonas aeruginosa* except: (Select **ALL** that apply.)

    a. Cefepime

    b. Meropenem

    c. Ertapenem

    d. Piperacillin/tazobactam

    e. Aztreonam

9. Which of the following antibiotics can interfere with coagulation or coagulation assays: (Select **ALL** that apply)

    a. *Vibativ*
    b. *Tygacil*
    c. *Primaxin*
    d. *Sivextro*
    e. *Orbactiv*

10. Which of the following antibiotics is not matched with a possible side effect/warning/interaction:

    a. Daptomycin –increased CPK/myopathy
    b. Telavancin – fetal risk
    c. Vancomycin – seizures
    d. Metronidazole – disulfiram-like reaction with alcohol consumption
    e. Doripenem – decreased valproic acid concentrations

Answers

1-b, 2-c,d,e, 3-d, 4-b, 5-c,d, 6-b,c, 7-a,d,e, 8-c, 9-a,e, 10-c

INFECTIOUS DISEASES II: BACTERIAL INFECTIONS

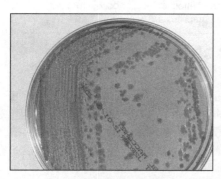

We gratefully acknowledge the assistance of Emi Minejima, PharmD, Assistant Professor and Annie Wong-Beringer, PharmD, FCCP, FIDSA, Associate Dean and Professor, University of Southern California School of Pharmacy, in preparing this chapter.

BACKGROUND

Infectious Diseases I should be reviewed prior to this chapter, to gain a working knowledge of bacterial pathogens, microbiology reports, resistance, and antibiotic agents, including spectrum of activity (coverage), and pharmacokinetics/pharmacodynamics, which play an important role in selecting optimal treatment of infections.

Antibiotic Selection Principles

- <u>Presence of infection</u> is based on <u>signs and symptoms</u>. For example, a positive urine culture does not determine the presence of infection. The diagnosis of an infection must be made initially based on symptoms of dysuria, urgency, leukocytosis, fever, etc. and a urinalysis. Once the diagnosis of infection is made, the culture can help guide an appropriate antibiotic choice.

- A broad spectrum regimen is often used empirically to ensure adequate therapy for likely pathogens. Local resistance patterns and antibiotic use guidelines should always be considered.

- Infection characteristics include <u>infection site</u>, infection <u>severity</u>, and whether it is <u>community-</u> or <u>hospital-acquired</u>.

- Antibiotic characteristics include spectrum of activity and <u>adequate penetration to the site of infection</u>. Lipophilic antimicrobials have enhanced tissue penetration. Antibiotics that are cleared hepatically may not achieve adequate drug concentrations in the urine.

- Patient characteristics can affect treatment choice. These include <u>age, body weight, renal/hepatic function, allergies</u>, recent antibiotic use, colonization with resistant bacteria, recent environmental exposure, vaccination status, pregnancy status, immune function, and <u>comorbid</u> conditions.

GUIDELINES/REFERENCES

Bratzler DW, Dellinger EP, Olsen KM et al. Clinical practice guidelines for antimicrobial prophylaxis for surgery. *Am J Health-Syst Pharm.* 2013; 70:195-283.

Lieberthal AS, Carroll AE, Chonmaitree T et al. The Diagnosis and Management Acute Otitis Media; *Pediatrics.* 2013; 131:e964-e999.

Workowski KA, Golan GA. Sexually Transmitted Diseases Treatment Guidelines, 2015. *MMWR Recomm Rep* 2015;64(No. RR-3):1-137

Guidelines available at the Infectious Diseases Society of America website (www.idsociety.org)

Additional references included with the video files (RxPrep Online).

■ When susceptibilities are available, empiric antibiotics should be streamlined to narrower spectrum treatment in order to limit collateral damage associated with broad spectrum agents.

Assessment of Treatment

MONITORING TREATMENT RESPONSE	REASONS FOR LACK OF RESPONSE
Clinical status of the patient: 1. Fever trend (and other vital signs) 2. WBC trend 3. Reduction in signs and symptoms of infection Radiographic findings (such as CXR) Negative cultures Pain/inflammation – markers of inflammation include procalcitonin levels (more specific to bacterial infection), C-reactive protein (CRP), and the erythrocyte sedimentation rate (ESR)	Antibiotic factors: Inadequate spectrum and/or dose, poor tissue penetration, drug-drug interaction/s, non-adherence, inadequate duration of therapy Microbiologic factors: Resistance, superinfection *(C. difficile)*, alternative etiology (viral, fungal, non-infectious cause) Host factors: Uncontrolled source of infection (e.g., abscess or fluid collection), immunocompromised

ANTIMICROBIAL AGENTS FOR SELECT INFECTIOUS CONDITIONS

Perioperative Antimicrobial Prophylaxis

■ A dose of antibiotics given immediately prior to procedures can obtain therapeutic levels in both serum and tissue to reduce the incidence of surgical site infections. This should be initiated within 60 minutes before the incision, or 120 minutes before the incision if using quinolones or vancomycin, which require longer infusion times to avoid serious adverse effects.

■ In order to maintain therapeutic levels throughout the surgery, additional doses may be required for longer surgeries (> 3 – 4 hours) or in cases of major blood loss during the procedure.

■ Controversy exists regarding the duration of prophylaxis necessary after the surgery is complete. In most circumstances, no additional doses are required. If continued postoperatively, prophylactic agents should be discontinued within 24 hours. In general, first or second generation cephalosporins (e.g., cefazolin) are the drugs of choice for most procedures. Vancomycin is used as an alternative in beta-lactam allergic patients or is added when MRSA is a concern.

■ Surgeries involving the bowel or with a risk of an anaerobic infection commonly require antibiotics with anaerobic coverage such as cefotetan, cefoxitin, ertapenem or (ceftriaxone + metronidazole).

SURGICAL PROCEDURE	RECOMMENDED ANTIBIOTICS*	IF BETA-LACTAM ALLERGY
Cardiac or vascular surgeries	Cefazolin or cefuroxime	Vancomycin or clindamycin
Hip fracture repair/ total joint replacement	Cefazolin	Vancomycin or clindamycin
Colon (colorectal)	Cefotetan, cefoxitin, ampicillin/ sulbactam, ertapenem or Metronidazole + (cefazolin or ceftriaxone)	Clindamycin + (aminoglycoside or quinolone or aztreonam) or Metronidazole + (aminoglycoside or quinolone)
Hysterectomy	Cefotetan, cefazolin, cefoxitin or ampicillin/sulbactam	Clindamycin or vancomycin + (aminoglycoside or quinolone or aztreonam) or Metronidazole + (aminoglycoside or quinolone)

For procedures and/or patients where MRSA is a likely pathogen consider adding vancomycin to routine prophylaxis.

Meningitis

Meningitis is inflammation of the meninges (membranes) that cover the brain and spinal cord. The meninges swell, causing three classic symptoms: Severe <u>headache</u>, nuchal rigidity (<u>stiff neck</u>) and <u>altered mental status</u>. Not every patient will demonstrate all three symptoms. Other symptoms could include chills, vomiting and photophobia. Meningitis is mostly caused by viral infections, but can be due to bacteria or fungi. Meningitis symptoms must be quickly recognized and treated to avoid severe complications, including death.

- Diagnosis is made by a lumbar puncture (LP), which is a sampling of the cerebral spinal fluid (CSF) to help guide antibiotic choices before the culture and susceptibility results are available. In some patients a computed tomography (CT) scan is performed prior to the LP to avoid potentially fatal complications. It is preferable to get the LP prior to starting antibiotics, however antibiotics should be given promptly, even if the LP is delayed.

- Antibiotic dosages are higher to penetrate the CNS.

- The most likely organisms causing bacterial meningitis are *Streptococcus pneumoniae*, *Neisseria meningitidis*, *Haemophilus influenzae* and *Listeria monocytogenes*. Likely pathogens and empiric antibiotics largely depend on the patient's age and immune status (see table).

Acute Bacterial Meningitis Treatment (Community-Acquired)

- Dexamethasone is given 15 – 20 min prior to or with the 1st dose of antibiotics to prevent neurological complications of meningitis. The adult dexamethasone dose is 0.15 mg/kg (commonly rounded to 10 mg) IV Q6H x 4 days.

- Antibiotic durations are pathogen-dependent: 7 days for *N. meningitidis* and *H. influenzae*, 10 – 14 days for *S. pneumoniae* and 21 days for *Listeria monocytogenes*.

AGE/RISK GROUP	EMPIRIC THERAPY
Age < 1 month Common pathogens: *S. agalactiae, E. coli, Listeria monocytogenes, Klebsiella* spp.	Ampicillin* 150-200 mg/kg/day in divided doses **plus** Cefotaxime 100-200 mg/kg/day in divided doses or Gentamicin 5-7.5 mg/kg/day, in divided doses
Age 1-23 months Common pathogens: *S. pneumoniae, N. meningitidis, S. agalactiae, H. influenzae, E. coli*	Cefotaxime 225-300 mg/kg/day in divided doses or Ceftriaxone 80-100 mg/kg/day in divided doses **plus** Vancomycin 60 mg/kg/day, divided Q6H
Age 2-50 Years Common pathogens: *S. pneumoniae, N. meningitidis*	Cefotaxime 2 grams IV Q4-6H or Ceftriaxone 2 grams IV Q12H **plus** Vancomycin 30-45 mg/kg/day in divided doses
Age > 50 years or Immunocompromised Common pathogens: *S. pneumoniae, N. meningitidis, L. monocytogenes*, aerobic gram-negative bacilli	Vancomycin + ampicillin* + (ceftriaxone or cefotaxime)
If Severe PCN Allergy	Quinolone (moxifloxacin or levofloxacin) + vancomycin (± SMX/TMP 10-20 mg/kg/day IV divided Q6-12H for *Listeria* coverage)

*Ampicillin is added for *Listeria* coverage

UPPER RESPIRATORY TRACT INFECTIONS

Acute Otitis Media

Acute otitis media (AOM) is the most common childhood infection in the United States requiring antibiotic treatment. Signs and symptoms often have a rapid onset and can include bulging tympanic membranes, otorrhea (middle ear effusion/fluid), otalgia (ear pain), fever, crying and tugging or rubbing the ears.

- Systemic agents are preferred for pain (acetaminophen or ibuprofen). In children age > 5 years, procaine, lidocaine or topical benzocaine *(Americaine Otic)* can be used.

- Many of the infections are viral, therefore antibiotics will be ineffective.

- Observation without antibiotics may be an option for non-severe AOM depending on age, diagnostic certainty, and illness severity. An observation period of 48 – 72 hours is used to assess clinical improvement without antibiotics. The decision for observation should involve both the pediatrician and parent/s.

AOM Treatment

AGE	OTORRHEA WITH AOM	UNILATERAL OR BILATERAL AOM WITH SEVERE SYMPTOMS*	BILATERAL AOM WITHOUT OTORRHEA	UNILATERAL AOM WITHOUT OTORRHEA
6 months-2 years	Antibiotics	Antibiotics	Antibiotics	Antibiotics or additional observation
≥ 2 years	Antibiotics	Antibiotics	Antibiotics or additional observation	Antibiotics or additional observation

Severe symptoms include otalgia > 48 hrs, temperature ≥ 39°C (102.2°F) in past 48 hrs

INITIAL ANTIBIOTIC TREATMENT		ANTIBIOTIC TREATMENT AFTER 48-72 HOURS OF FAILURE OF INITIAL THERAPY
Recommended First-line Treatment	Alternative Treatment (if Penicillin Allergy)	Recommended First-line Treatment
Amoxicillin 80-90 mg/kg/day in 2 divided doses or	Cefdinir 14 mg/kg/day in 1 or 2 doses	Amox/clav* (90 mg/kg/day of amoxicillin with 6.4 mg/kg/day of clavulanate) in 2 divided doses or
Amox/clav 90 mg/kg/day of amoxicillin with 6.4 mg/kg/day of clavulanate (amoxicillin to clavulanate ratio is 14:1) in 2 divided doses	Cefuroxime 30 mg/kg/day in 2 divided doses	Ceftriaxone 50 mg/kg IM/IV daily for 3 days
	Cefpodoxime 10 mg/kg/day in 2 divided doses	
	Ceftriaxone 50 mg/kg IM/IV daily for 1 or 3 days	

May be considered in patients who have received amoxicillin in the past 30 days

- First line treatment is high-dose amoxicillin (80 – 90 mg/kg/day divided Q12H) or amoxicillin/clavulanate (90 mg/kg/day of amoxicillin divided Q12H). The higher dose will cover most *S. pneumoniae*.

- Recommended agents in the setting of amoxicillin failure include amoxicillin/clavulanate 90 mg/kg/day of amoxicillin component x 5 – 10 days (see recommendations for duration below) or ceftriaxone 50 mg/kg IM/IV daily x 3 days.

- When using high dose amoxicillin/clavulanate, the formulation with less clavulanate should be used, as it is less likely to cause diarrhea. *Augmentin ES-600* (amoxicillin 600 mg and clavulanate 42.9 mg per 5 mL) has a lower ratio of amoxicillin/clavulanate than the other suspension formulations.

- Recommended duration of treatment for amoxicillin, amoxicillin/clavulanate and oral cephalosporins: < 2 years of age = 10 days; 2 – 5 years of age = 7 days; and ≥ 6 years of age = 5 – 7 days.

- Ceftriaxone (50 mg/kg) can be given IM/IV daily for 1 or 3 days (1 or 3 days for initial treatment or 3 days for treatment failure) for those who cannot tolerate oral medication due to GI side effects.

- In patients with a non-severe penicillin allergy, the American Academy of Pediatrics (AAP) recommends use of a cephalosporin, as stated above. Although there is some risk of cross-reactivity, it is thought to be much lower than old estimates and is negligible with second and third generation cephalosporins (cefuroxime, cefdinir, cefpodoxime and ceftriaxone). In addition, non-beta-lactam antibiotics that are suitable for use in children have limited efficacy against typical pathogens, due to resistance.

AOM Prevention

The pneumococcal conjugate vaccine (PCV13, *Prevnar 13*) is recommended for all children, with the series starting at 2 months of age, and pneumococcal polysaccharide vaccine (PPSV23, *Pneumovax 23*) is recommended in select patients. See the Immunizations chapter for detailed information. Annual influenza vaccine should be given to all patients age ≥ 6 months. Prophylactic antibiotics should not be prescribed to reduce frequency of AOM.

Overview of Non-AOM Upper Respiratory Tract Infection Management

The majority of upper respiratory tract infections are viral, therefore, antibiotics will not impact the disease course. If severe/chronic symptoms and/or microbiologic/diagnostic evidence of a bacterial infection are present, antibacterials may be used for pharyngitis and sinusitis (see table below).

	COMMON COLD	INFLUENZA	PHARYNGITIS	SINUSITIS
Typical Etiology	Respiratory viruses (Rhinovirus, coronavirus)	Influenza virus	Respiratory viruses *S. pyogenes*	Respiratory viruses, *S. pneumoniae, H. influenzae, Moraxella catarrhalis. Staphylococci* species, anaerobes and Gram-negative rods may also be implicated in chronic sinusitis.
Indications for Anti-infective Treatment	None	< 48 hours since symptom onset Risk factors for severe disease Outbreak scenario	Positive rapid antigen diagnostic test or positive *S. pyogenes* culture	> 7-10 days of symptoms Tooth/face pain Nasal drainage/discharge Congestion or severe/worsening symptoms
Anti-infective options	None	Oseltamivir Zanamivir	Penicillin Amoxicillin 1st/2nd generation cephalosporin If beta-lactam allergy: Clarithromycin or azithromycin or clindamycin	**First Line** Amoxicillin/clavulanate **Second Line if Failure to Above** Oral 2nd or 3rd generation cephalosporins + clindamycin, doxycycline Respiratory quinolone (gemifloxacin, moxifloxacin, levofloxacin)
Treatment Duration	Per symptoms	5 days	10 days unless using azithromycin (5 days)	Variable depending on severity and chronicity Acute sinusitis: Adults: 5-7 days Children: 10-14 days Chronic sinusitis: ≥ 21 days ± surgical intervention

LOWER RESPIRATORY TRACT INFECTIONS

Bronchitis

Bronchitis is an inflammation of the mucous membranes of the bronchi. It is classified as acute and chronic. Chronic bronchitis is treated with antibiotics only when exacerbations occur.

Acute Bronchitis

- Symptoms of acute bronchitis are usually self-limited and can include cough lasting more than 5 days (up to 3 weeks) with or without sputum production, fatigue, headache and watery eyes. Systemic symptoms such as fever are rare.

- Acute bronchitis is <u>primarily</u> (90% of cases) <u>caused by respiratory viruses</u> including:

  - Respiratory syncytial virus (RSV), adenovirus, rhinovirus, coronavirus, influenza virus, parainfluenza virus

- For severe cases bacterial etiology can be considered with the following pathogens:

  - *Mycoplasma pneumoniae, Haemophilus influenzae, Bordetella pertussis, Chlamydophila pneumoniae*

- Diagnosis is usually made by ruling out other causes of acute cough (common cold, acute asthma, pneumonia). Cultures are not routinely performed.

Acute Bacterial Exacerbation of Chronic Bronchitis

- Acute bacterial exacerbation of chronic bronchitis (ABECB), or chronic obstructive pulmonary disease (COPD) exacerbations, are diagnosed based on clinical presentation. Exacerbations can be triggered by infections (70 – 80% are due to bacterial or viral causes), environmental pollution, pulmonary embolism, or unknown causes.

- The Global Initiative for Chronic Obstructive Lung Disease (GOLD) defines an acute exacerbation as an acute increase in symptoms beyond normal day-to-day variation and necessitates a change in medications. If there is increased sputum purulence and increased sputum volume, increased dyspnea, or if mechanical ventilation is required, antibiotics should be utilized for 5 – 10 days.

BRONCHITIS NOTES & TREATMENT

Acute Bronchitis
Mild-to-moderate disease:

- <u>Supportive treatment</u> – fluids to prevent dehydration, antipyretics for fever, antitussive agents, vaporizers, etc.

For patients with confirmed or probable *Bordetella pertussis* (whooping cough):

- Azithromycin 500 mg x 1, then 250 mg daily x 2-5 days or

- Clarithromycin 500 mg BID or 1 g ER daily x 7 days or

- SMX/TMP DS 1 tab BID x 14 days

Acute Bacterial Exacerbation of Chronic Bronchitis (ABECB)

- Supportive treatment – supplemental oxygen, increase dose and/or frequency of short-acting beta-2 adrenergic agonists, anticholinergic agents, IV or PO steroids (prednisone 40 mg PO daily x 5 days)

- Antibiotics indicated if three cardinal symptoms present: increase in dyspnea, sputum volume, and sputum purulence; or if mechanical ventilation is required

  - <u>Amoxicillin/clavulanate</u> or

  - Azithromycin or

  - Doxycycline

  - Duration 5-10 days

Community-Acquired Pneumonia

Community-acquired pneumonia (CAP) is contracted outside of healthcare facilities and is one of the most common types of pneumonia. Causes could be bacterial, viral or fungal (rare). Most bacterial cases are caused by *Streptococcus pneumoniae*, *Haemophilus influenzae* and *Moraxella catarrhalis*. Patients often present with fever, productive cough with purulent sputum and pleuritic chest pain. Rales (crackling noises) can be heard over the infected lobe on auscultation. A chest x-ray is the gold standard for the diagnosis of CAP; findings of "infiltrates" or "consolidations" are indicative of pneumonia. The antibiotic recommendations for pneumonia are designed to provide reliable empiric coverage of *S. pneumoniae*, atypical bacteria and if indicated, risk factors for additional pathogens (*Pseudomonas*, MRSA). There are subtle differences in coverage that are important when treating pneumonia. Coverage must be considered by specific antibiotic, rather than using class trends. A good example is ciprofloxacin; because ciprofloxacin does not reliably cover *S. pneumoniae*, it is not a respiratory quinolone, and is not used for CAP unless *Pseudomonas* risk exists. The following chart is intended to clarify the role of the different antibiotics in a regimen.

ORAL ANTIBIOTICS FOR CAP

Amoxicillin *(Amoxil)* 875 mg Q12H or 500 mg-1,000 mg Q8H

Amoxicillin/clavulanate *(Augmentin)* 875/125 mg Q12H or 500 mg/125 mg Q8H

Amoxicillin/clavulanate *(Augmentin XR)* 2 grams/125 mg Q12H

Cefuroxime *(Ceftin)* 500 mg Q12H

Cefpodoxime (Vantin) 200 mg Q12H

Cefdinir (Omnicef) 300 mg Q12H

Azithromycin *(Zithromax)* 500 mg x1, then 250 mg daily (days 2-5)

Clarithromycin *(Biaxin)* 250 mg Q12H

Clarithromycin *(Biaxin XL)* 1,000 mg daily

Erythromycin base 250 mg Q6H or 500 mg Q12H

Doxycycline *(Vibramycin)* 100 mg Q12H

Gemifloxacin *(Factive)* 320 mg daily

Levofloxacin *(Levaquin)* 500-750 mg daily

Moxifloxacin (Avelox) 400 mg daily

CAP Antibiotic Coverage

S. PNEUMONIAE	ATYPICAL ORGANISMS	PSEUDOMONAS COVERAGE FOR PNEUMONIA**
Amoxicillin, ampicillin, ampicillin/sulbactam		
Ceftriaxone, cefotaxime		
Azithromycin, clarithromycin, erythromycin*	Azithromycin, clarithromycin, erythromycin*	
Doxycycline*	Doxycycline*	
Levofloxacin, moxifloxacin, gemifloxacin	Levofloxacin, moxifloxacin, gemifloxacin	Ciprofloxacin, levofloxacin
Piperacillin/tazobactam		Piperacillin/tazobactam
Cefepime		Cefepime
Imipenem/cilastatin, meropenem		Imipenem/cilastatin, meropenem
		Aztreonam
		Tobramycin, gentamicin

* Monotherapy is used only for outpatients.
** Empiric therapy with a combination of two agents is recommended. May be narrowed to one drug when culture and susceptibility results are available.

CAP Treatment Recommendations

SETTING	COMMON PATHOGENS	EMPIRIC TREATMENT
Outpatient	*S. pneumoniae, Mycoplasma pneumoniae, H. influenzae, Chlamydophila pneumoniae,* respiratory viruses	If previously healthy and no antibiotic use in past 3 months: ■ Macrolide (azithromycin, clarithromycin, erythromycin) or ■ Doxycycline If comorbidities or risk for drug-resistant *S. pneumoniae* (chronic heart, lung, liver, or renal disease; diabetes mellitus; alcoholism; malignancies; asplenia; immunosuppression or use of immunosuppressants; use of antimicrobials within the previous 3 months): ■ Beta-lactam + macrolide ❑ Preferred beta-lactam: Amoxicillin (high-dose) or amoxicillin/clavulanate ❑ Alternatives: Cefpodoxime, cefdinir, cefuroxime, ceftriaxone ❑ Doxycycline is an alternative to a macrolide ■ Respiratory quinolone monotherapy ❑ Moxifloxacin, gemifloxacin, or levofloxacin (750 mg)
Inpatient (non-ICU) IV or PO antibiotics	*S. pneumoniae, Mycoplasma pneumoniae, H. influenzae, Chlamydophila pneumoniae, Legionella spp.,* respiratory viruses, aspiration (mouth flora)	■ Beta-lactam + macrolide ❑ Preferred beta-lactam: Ceftriaxone, cefotaxime, ampicillin ❑ Doxycycline is an alternative to a macrolide ■ Respiratory quinolone monotherapy (consider reserving quinolone for beta-lactam allergies) ❑ Moxifloxacin, gemifloxacin, or levofloxacin – IV/PO
Inpatient (ICU) IV antibiotics preferred	*S. pneumoniae, S. aureus, H. influenzae,* Gram-negative bacilli, *Legionella* spp.	Beta-lactam + (azithromycin or a respiratory quinolone) ❑ Beta-lactams: Ceftriaxone, cefotaxime, ampicillin/sulbactam ■ For PCN allergic: Aztreonam + respiratory quinolone
If *Pseudomonas* is a consideration		■ Antipneumococcal, antipseudomonal beta-lactam + (ciprofloxacin or levofloxacin) ❑ Beta-lactams: Piperacillin/tazobactam, cefepime, imipenem/cilastatin, meropenem or ■ The above beta-lactam + an aminoglycoside + azithromycin
If MRSA is a consideration		■ Add vancomycin or linezolid

Duration

The duration of treatment can be as short as 5 days, depending on the patient's condition. Most are treated successfully in 5 – 7 days.

Hospital-Acquired/Ventilator-Associated/Healthcare-Associated Pneumonias

Hospitalized patients and those with chronic exposure to the healthcare system are at risk of more resistant pathogens. Ventilated patients are at especially high-risk. Hospital-acquired pneumonia (HAP) is the leading infectious cause of death in ICUs. HAP can be reduced by proper hand-washing, elevating the head of bed by ≥ 30 degrees, weaning off the ventilator, removing nasogastric (NG) tubes, and discontinuing unnecessary stress ulcer prophylaxis.

PNEUMONIA DEFINITIONS
Community-acquired pneumonia (CAP): Contracted outside of a healthcare facility
Hospital-acquired pneumonia (HAP): Onset > 48 hours after hospital admission
Ventilator-associated pneumonia (VAP): Occurs > 48 hours after intubation (mechanical ventilation)
Healthcare-associated pneumonia (HCAP): Onset is proximal to healthcare exposure, putting patient at higher risk of drug-resistant bacteria. Specific criteria: ■ Nursing home residence ■ Hospitalized within past 90 days (length of stay ≥ 48 hours) ■ Receiving IV antibiotics, chemotherapy, or wound care (within 30 days) ■ Receiving chronic hemodialysis

Overview of HAP/VAP/HCAP Etiology and Management

ONSET	COMMON PATHOGENS	RECOMMENDED EMPIRIC REGIMEN		
Early onset HAP or VAP (< 5 days) and no risk factors for multidrug-resistant pathogens	*S. pneumoniae*, MSSA, *H. influenzae*, *E. coli*, *Proteus*, *Klebsiella*, *Enterobacter*, *Proteus*, *Serratia*	Ceftriaxone or Ampicillin/sulbactam or Ertapenem or Levofloxacin, moxifloxacin (preferred) or ciprofloxacin		
Late onset HAP, VAP, or HCAP (≥ 5 days) or risk factors for MDR pathogens	Above pathogens plus: MRSA, *Pseudomonas aeruginosa*, *Acinetobacter spp.*, *Enterobacter spp.*, + other nosocomial pathogens	Antipseudomonal Beta-lactam (choose 1) +	2nd Antipseudomonal Agent (choose 1) +	Anti-MRSA if patient has risk factors for MRSA (choose 1)
		Cefepime Ceftazidime Piperacillin/ tazobactam Imipenem/cilastatin Meropenem	Gentamicin Tobramycin Amikacin Levofloxacin Ciprofloxacin	Vancomycin Linezolid

Severe Beta-lactam Allergy

■ Early onset: Use levofloxacin or moxifloxacin

■ Late onset: Substitute aztreonam 2 grams IV Q8H for the beta-lactam

Duration of Treatment

Treat for 7 – 8 days, or 14 days if caused by *Pseudomonas* or *Acinetobacter*, or when blood cultures are positive.

Tuberculosis

Tuberculosis (TB) is caused by *Mycobacterium tuberculosis* (aerobic, non-spore forming bacillus). Active TB is transmitted by aerosolized droplets (sneezing, coughing, talking, etc.) and is highly contagious. TB primarily attacks the lungs, but can also disseminate to other organs. Tuberculosis can be fatal if not treated properly. Incidence of strains that are resistant to multiple drugs continues to increase. The disease has two phases: latent and active. Latent disease occurs when the immune system is able to contain the disease, and is characterized by a complete lack of symptoms. Active pulmonary disease is highly contagious and most often manifested as cough/hemoptysis (with blood), purulent sputum and fever/night sweats. Hospitalized patients with active pulmonary TB should be isolated in a single negative pressure room and healthcare workers must wear N95 respirator masks.

Latent Tuberculosis Diagnosis and Treatment

Latent disease is diagnosed using the tuberculin skin test (TST), also called a purified protein derivative (PPD) test. The solution is injected intradermally and the area is inspected for induration (raised area) 48 – 72 hours later. False positive TST can occur in those who have received the bacille Calmette-Guerin (BCG) vaccine (used in areas of the world with high TB rates). A diagnostic blood test for latent tuberculosis is also available. The interferon-gamma release assay (IGRA) does not require a follow-up visit and can be used in patients who have received the BCG vaccine. Treatment of latent TB with one of the following regimens greatly reduces the risk of developing of active disease:

- Isoniazid (INH) 300 mg PO daily (or 15 mg/kg PO twice weekly, max 900 mg/dose) for 9 months. These regimens are preferred for HIV+ and children), or

- Rifampin 600 mg daily for 4 months if INH-resistant/INH not tolerated, or

- INH and rifapentine *(Priftin)* once weekly for 12 weeks (not used in HIV+, children < 2 years old, or pregnant women). The older combination of rifampin + pyrazinamide is no longer recommended due to risk of hepatotoxicity.

POSITIVE TB SKIN TEST (TST) CRITERIA

≥ 5 mm induration:
Close contacts of recent TB cases

Significant immunosuppression (e.g., HIV)

≥ 10 mm induration:
Recent immigrants

IV drug users

Residents/employees of "high-risk" congregate settings (e.g., inmates, healthcare workers)

Moderate immunosuppression

≥ 15 mm induration:
Patients with no risk factors

Induration = raised area

RIPE THERAPY TIPS

Monitoring:

Sputum culture

Chest X-ray

CBC

LFTs (including total bilirubin)

Renal function

Uric acid

Vision tests (monthly)

Mental status

Other:

Pyridoxine 25 mg PO daily is given to reduce risk of INH-associated peripheral neuropathy

Rifabutin – used instead of rifampin if unacceptable drug-drug interactions

---

Active Tuberculosis Diagnosis and Treatment

Active TB is a public health issue because it is highly contagious and can be difficult to treat. It is diagnosed through a sputum culture (not TST). *M. tuberculosis* (MTB) are acid fast bacilli (AFB) and can be detected by AFB stain in the laboratory. However, the acid fast test is not specific to MTB; definitive diagnosis must be made using polymerase chain reaction (PCR) testing or culture results. MTB is a slow-growing organism; final culture and susceptibility results can take up to 6 weeks.

Active disease treatment is divided into two treatment phases (initial and continuation). To avoid treatment failure due to resistance, preferred initial treatment consists of a 4-drug regimen of rifampin, isoniazid, pyrazinamide and ethambutol (RIPE).

Use of Directly Observed Treatment (DOT) is preferred to increase medication adherence, and alternate dosing regimens (weekly or twice weekly) can be used in this setting. Daily dosing regimens are strongly encouraged if DOT is not possible.

In multidrug-resistant TB (MDR-TB), moxifloxacin is often added and the RIPE regimen becomes PRIME. Streptomycin given IM is an alternative agent to ethambutol, but it has associated toxicities (see Infectious Diseases I Chapter) and resistance is increasing. In extremely drug-resistant TB (XDR-TB), bedaquiline *(Sirturo)* may be used, but it has boxed warnings for QT prolongation and increased risk of death compared to placebo.

TB Disease Treatment Regimens

PREFERRED REGIMEN

Initial Phase – Take all 4 drugs for about 8 weeks (when cultures and susceptibilities are available)

	Rifampin (RIF) + Isoniazid (INH) + Pyrazinamide + Ethambutol* (RIPE)
	Duration: 56 daily doses (8 weeks)

Continuation Phase – Once susceptibilities are known

Susceptible to INH and RIF	Continue INH and RIF daily or twice weekly (18 weeks)
	Total duration: 26 weeks (6 months)
Resistant to INH	RIF + Pyrazinamide + Ethambutol ± Moxifloxacin (18 weeks)
	Total duration: 26 weeks (6 months)
If resistant to RIF	Isoniazid + Ethambutol + Quinolone + (Pyrazinamide x 2 months)
	Total duration: 12-18 months
MDR-TB (resistant to RIF and INH)	Quinolone** + Pyrazinamide + Ethambutol + AMG (streptomycin/amikacin/kanamycin) ± alternative agent***
	Total duration: 18-24 months

*   Ethambutol can be discontinued if drug susceptibility studies demonstrate susceptibility to first-line drugs

** Quinolone = levofloxacin or moxifloxacin

*** Alternative agents include cycloserine, capreomycin, ethionamide and others

RIPE Therapy for Active TB

DRUG	DOSING	SAFETY/SIDE EFFECTS/MONITORING
Rifampin *(Rifadin)* + isoniazid *(Rifamate)* + isoniazid + pyrazinamide *(Rifater)*	10 mg/kg (max 600 mg) PO daily or 2-3x/week	**CONTRAINDICATIONS** Concurrent use with protease inhibitors (PIs) **SIDE EFFECTS** ↑ LFTs, GI upset, rash/pruritus, orange-red discoloration of body secretions, flu-like syndrome, positive Coombs test **NOTES** Orange-red discoloration of body secretions (sputum, urine, sweat, tears) – can stain contact lenses and clothing. Rifabutin dosed 5 mg/kg/day (300 mg) can replace rifampin to avoid significant drug-drug interactions (e.g., HIV patient on PIs).

RIPE Therapy for Active TB Continued

DRUG	DOSING	SAFETY/SIDE EFFECTS/MONITORING
Isoniazid (INH) + rifampin *(Rifamate)* + pyrazinamide/ rifampin *(Rifater)*	5 mg/kg (max 300 mg) PO daily or 15 mg/kg (max 900 mg) 2-3x/week Take on an empty stomach <u>Use pyridoxine 25 mg PO daily to ↓ risk of INH-associated peripheral neuropathy</u>	**BOXED WARNING** Severe (and fatal) hepatitis **CONTRAINDICATIONS** Active liver disease, previous severe adverse reaction to INH **SIDE EFFECTS** <u>Headache, GI upset, ↑ LFTs (usually asymptomatic), peripheral neuropathy, drug-induced lupus erythematosus (DILE), positive Coombs test</u>, hyperglycemia, agranulocytosis, hemolytic and aplastic anemia, thrombocytopenia **NOTES** Store oral solution at room temperature. Peripheral neuropathy is rare, but occurs more commonly in patients predisposed to neuropathy (diabetes, HIV, renal failure, alcoholism). These patients and patients who are pregnant or breastfeeding should always receive pyridoxine supplementation.
Pyrazinamide + rifampin + isoniazid *(Rifater)*	20-25 mg/kg/day PO 40-55 kg: 1 g/day 56-75 kg: 1.5 g/day 76-90 kg: 2 g/day (max dose); 3-4 grams given 2-3x/week Extend interval for CrCl < 30 mL/min	**CONTRAINDICATIONS** Acute gout, severe hepatic damage **SIDE EFFECTS** <u>GI upset, malaise, increased LFTs, hyperuricemia</u>, gout, arthralgias, myalgias, rash
Ethambutol *(Myambutol)*	15-20 mg/kg (max 1.6 grams) PO daily or 25-30 mg/kg (max 2.4 grams) 3x/week or 50 mg/kg (max 4 grams) 2x/week Take without regards to meals Extend interval for CrCl < 50 mL/min	**CONTRAINDICATIONS** Optic neuritis (risk vs benefit decision); use in young children, unconscious patients, or any patient who cannot discern and report visual changes. **SIDE EFFECTS** <u>Optic neuritis (dose-related)</u>, ↑ LFTs, visual acuity, scotoma and/or color blindness (usually reversible); rash, headache, confusion, hallucinations, N/V, abdominal pain

Tuberculosis Agents Drug Interactions

■ Rifampin is a <u>potent inducer</u> of CYP450 1A2, 2C8, 2C9, 2C19, <u>3A4</u> and P-glycoprotein. Significantly <u>↓ concentrations and effect of many other drugs</u> (100+ are documented). Three notable interactions involve ↓ serum concentrations of <u>protease inhibitors</u> (rifabutin is substituted) and warfarin (a <u>very large ↓ in INR</u> is common) and <u>↓ efficacy of oral contraceptives</u>. It is <u>important to screen all concurrent medications for drug interactions</u> with rifampin due to its extremely high potential for interactions. See the Drug Interactions chapter.

■ INH is an <u>inhibitor</u> of 1A2 (weak), 2C19 (moderate), 2C9 (weak), 2D6 (moderate), and 3A4 (weak). Use of INH can ↑ levels and toxicity of many other drugs. Also notable, enzyme inhibition can decrease activation of other drugs that require conversion to active metabolites. Manufacturer recommends avoiding tyramine and histamine containing foods (low clinical significance). ↑ dietary intake of folic acid, niacin, and magnesium while taking INH.

Infective Endocarditis

Infective endocarditis (IE) is an infection of the inner tissue of the heart, most commonly the heart valves, and is generally fatal if untreated. The majority of patients present with fever with or without heart murmur. IE is diagnosed by the Modified Duke Criteria which includes an <u>echocardiogram</u>, allowing for visualization of the vegetation. The three most common organisms that cause IE are *Staphylococcus*, *Streptococcus*, and *Enterococcus* species.

Empiric treatment often includes vancomycin and ceftriaxone. Definitive treatment and antibiotic duration for IE are dependent on the pathogen, the type of infected valve (native or prosthetic) and the susceptibility results. In general, 4 – 6 weeks of IV antibiotic treatment is required; when prosthetic valves and/or more resistant organisms are involved, durations will be at the upper end of this range.

Gentamicin is added to primary antimicrobial therapy for synergy when feasible. It is most important in infections that are more difficult to eradicate, such as prosthetic valve infections, and with more resistant organisms. In some cases the risk of additive nephrotoxicity with vancomycin outweighs the benefit and it is left off of the regimen (e.g., when vancomycin is used for Streptococcal endocarditis in beta-lactam allergy). The duration of gentamicin varies based on the presence of a prosthetic valve (2 weeks), or on the pathogen (4 – 6 weeks for *Enterococcus*). When <u>gentamicin</u> is used for <u>synergy</u>, target <u>peak levels of 3 – 4 mcg/mL</u> and <u>trough levels < 1 mcg/mL</u>. <u>Extended interval dosing</u> is <u>not used for</u> AMG when treating <u>endocarditis</u>.

Some bacteria will form a biofilm (slime layer), especially on prosthetic valves, which can be difficult to penetrate with antibiotics. Rifampin can be used in cases of *Staphylococcal* prosthetic valve endocarditis due to its ability to treat organisms in a biofilm.

ORGANISM	PREFERRED ANTIBIOTIC REGIMEN
Viridans group *Streptococci*	Penicillin, ampicillin, or ceftriaxone ± gentamicin for synergy
	If beta-lactam allergy, use vancomycin monotherapy
Staphylococci (MSSA)	Nafcillin or cefazolin (if beta-lactam allergy, use vancomycin) + gentamicin for synergy
	(Gentamicin is used only for prosthetic valve)
Staphylococci (MRSA)	Vancomycin + gentamicin for synergy
	(Gentamicin is used only for prosthetic valve)
Enterococci	Penicillin or ampicillin (if beta-lactam allergy or resistance, use vancomycin) + gentamicin for synergy

Dental Procedures and IE Prophylaxis

The mouth contains bacteria that are released during dental work and travel into the bloodstream where they can settle on the heart lining, a heart valve or a blood vessel. IE after dental procedures is rare, but risk is increased with certain cardiac conditions. Antibiotics should be used before all dental procedures that involve manipulation of gingival tissue (gums) or the periapical region (near the root of the tooth) or perforation of the oral mucosa in patients with the highest risk of contracting IE. See the following table for the risk criteria and prophylaxis regimens.

IE Dental Prophylaxis

PATIENTS AT HIGH RISK OF IE	ADULT PROPHYLAXIS REGIMENS*
Artificial (prosthetic) heart valve or heart valve repaired with artificial material	Given as a single dose 30-60 min before dental procedure
	Oral:
History of endocarditis	Amoxicillin 2 grams
Heart transplant with abnormal heart valve function	
Certain congenital heart defects including:	If unable to take oral medication:
■ Cyanotic congenital heart disease (birth defects with oxygen levels lower than normal), that has not been fully repaired, including children who have had surgical shunts and conduits.	Ampicillin 2 grams IM/IV or
	Cefazolin 1 gram IM/IV
■ Congenital heart defect that has been completely repaired with artificial material or a device for the first six months after the repair procedure.	If allergic to penicillins and can take oral medication:
	Cephalexin or cefadroxil** 2 grams or
	Clindamycin 600 mg or
■ Repaired congenital heart disease with residual defects, such as persisting leaks or abnormal flow at or adjacent to a prosthetic patch or prosthetic device.	Azithromycin or clarithromycin 500 mg
	If allergic to penicillins and unable to take oral medication:
	Cefazolin or ceftriaxone 1 gram IM/IV
	Clindamycin 600 mg IM/IV

*In pediatric patients use weight-based doses of the same antibiotics.
**Cephalosporins should not be used in an individual with a history of anaphylaxis, angioedema, or urticaria with penicillins or ampicillin.

Intra-Abdominal Infections

Intra-abdominal infections are a common cause of hospital admissions and the second most common cause of infectious mortality in ICUs. Intra-abdominal infections are usually polymicrobial and can occur in any intra-abdominal organ or space. The range of infections includes: primary (spontaneous bacterial), secondary and tertiary peritonitis, and biliary tract infections (cholecystitis and cholangitis).

■ Primary peritonitis (AKA spontaneous bacterial peritonitis, SBP) is an infection of the peritoneal space and often occurs in patients with liver disease. The most likely pathogens are *Streptococci* and enteric Gram-negative organisms (PEK) and, rarely, anaerobes. The drug of choice is ceftriaxone for 5 – 7 days. Alternatives include ampicillin, gentamicin or a quinolone, among other options. SMX/TMP, ofloxacin and/or ciprofloxacin can be used for primary or secondary prophylaxis of SBP.

■ Secondary peritonitis is caused by a traumatic event (e.g., ulceration, ischemia, obstruction, or surgery). Abscesses are common and should be drained and damaged tissue may require surgery. The most likely pathogens are *Streptococci*, enteric Gram-negatives and anaerobes *(Bacteroides fragilis)*. In more severe cases (critically ill patients in the ICU), coverage of *Pseudomonas* and CAPES organisms may be necessary.

■ Cholecystitis is an acute inflammation of the gallbladder due to an obstructive stone and is generally surgically managed through cholecystectomy. Infection may not be the precipitating factor, but complicates half of cases. If infection is present, likely pathogens and antimicrobial selection are similar to primary peritonitis. Cholangitis is an infection of the common bile duct and is generally managed with bile decompression and antimicrobial therapy. Likely pathogens and antimicrobial selection are similar to secondary peritonitis.

Treatment consists of selecting an agent or combination that will cover the likely pathogens, which includes anaerobes. This can be accomplished with a single drug in some cases; however, if the antibiotic selected does not have anaerobic coverage, an additional antibiotic (generally metronidazole) must be added. See Infectious Diseases I chapter for detailed discussion of antibiotic coverage. Duration of treatment is generally 4 – 7 days for mild to moderate cases with adequate source control. Longer courses (7 – 14 days) may be needed in more severe cases. If an intra-abdominal abscess is present, ≥ 14 days may be required.

Management of Secondary Peritonitis and Cholangitis

MILD-TO-MODERATE INFECTIONS	HIGH-SEVERITY INFECTIONS/ICU
Cover PEK + anaerobes + *Streptococci* ± *Enterococci*	Cover PEK + CAPES + anaerobes + *Streptococci* ± *Enterococci*
Possible regimens include:	Possible regimens include:
Cefoxitin, ertapenem, moxifloxacin	Carbapenem (except ertapenem)
(Cefazolin or cefuroxime or ceftriaxone) + metronidazole	Piperacillin/tazobactam
(Ciprofloxacin or levofloxacin) + metronidazole	(Cefepime or ceftazidime) + metronidazole
	(Ciprofloxacin or levofloxacin) + metronidazole
	(Aztreonam or AMG) + metronidazole

AMG = aminoglycosides; CAPES (nosocomial GNRs) = Citrobacter, Acinetobacter, Pseudomonas, Enterobacter, Serratia; ICU = intensive care unit; PEK (enteric GNRs) = Proteus, E. coli, Klebsiella

Skin and Soft-Tissue Infections

Skin and soft-tissue infections (SSTIs) may involve any or all layers of the skin (epidermis, dermis, and subcutaneous fat), fascia, and muscle. SSTIs usually result from introduction of bacteria through breaks in the skin barrier, and less frequently from an infection that spreads from the bloodstream to the skin. Minor local trauma (small cuts, insect bites) can be the provoking event, which can progress to deeper infection. SSTIs can be broadly divided into nonpurulent (cellulitis, erysipelas, necrotizing infections) and purulent (furuncle, carbuncle, abscess) infections and are further categorized as mild, moderate or severe.

Cellulitis is an acute nonpurulent infection that extends down to the subcutaneous tissues. Lesions are usually painful, erythematous, and feel hot and tender. The infected area has poorly defined margins and may extend. *S. pyogenes* and *S. aureus* are the most frequent pathogens, including community-associated MRSA (CA-MRSA). Non-pharmacologic treatment involves measures to decrease swelling (elevation and immobilization of the area) and cool sterile saline dressings to decrease the pain. Blood culture or wound cultures are not routinely recommended for mild to moderate nonpurulent infections, unless the patient has significant risk factors such as immunosuppression, immersion injuries, or animal bites. Mild nonpurulent infections may be treated with oral antibiotics that primarily target *Streptococci*. If cellulitis is secondary to penetrating trauma, coverage of *S. aureus* and *Streptococci* is recommended.

SSTI CLASSIFICATIONS
Mild infection
Systemic symptoms* absent
Moderate infection
Systemic symptoms* present
Severe infection
Any of the following:
Failed I&D (if purulent) + oral antibiotics
Signs of deeper infection (fluid-filled blisters, skin sloughing, hypotension or evidence of organ dysfunction)
Patient is immunocompromised

Systemic symptoms: temperature > 100.4° F, heart rate >90 BPM, WBC < 12,000 or < 400 cells/mm³

In _purulent_ SSTI, abscesses should have an incision and drainage (I&D) and cultures should be sent for Gram stain and culture in moderate, severe or recurrent infections. If antibiotics are indicated, then _target S. aureus_ (including MRSA if patient has previously failed initial antibiotic treatment or is immunosuppressed or septic). For recurrent SSTIs in patients colonized with _S. aureus_, consider decolonization with intranasal mupirocin _(Bactroban Nasal)_ BID for 5 days, daily chlorhexidine washes, and daily decontamination of personal items.

SSTI Treatment

INFECTION/ SEVERITY	ADULT TREATMENT OPTIONS	COMMENTS

Empiric antibiotics for nonpurulent infection

INFECTION/ SEVERITY	ADULT TREATMENT OPTIONS	COMMENTS
Mild Target _Streptococci_	Penicillin VK 250-500 mg PO Q6H Cephalexin 500 mg PO Q6H or Dicloxacillin 500 mg PO QID or Clindamycin 300-450 mg QID	Duration of therapy = 5 days (extend if infection has not improved within 5 days).
Moderate Target _Streptococci_ ± MSSA	Penicillin 2-4 million units IV Q4-6H or Ceftriaxone 1 g IV Q24H or Cefazolin 1 g IV Q8H or Clindamycin 600-900 mg IV Q8H	IV antibiotics preferred initially. Once the patient is clinically stabile, can transition to PO antibiotics. Duration of therapy = 5 days (extend if infection has not improved within 5 days).
Severe or necrotizing Broad coverage	Vancomycin + beta-lactam: Vancomycin 15 mg/kg IV Q12H + Piperacillin/tazobactam 3.375 g IV Q6H or Imipenem/cilastatin 1 g IV Q6-8H or Meropenem 1 g IV Q8H	Treatment of choice for Group A Strep _(S. pyogenes)_ necrotizing fasciitis is penicillin G with clindamycin added for toxin suppression. Management of diabetic foot ulcers/infections is addressed later in this chapter.

Empiric oral therapy for purulent infection. All purulent infections (abscesses) should have I & D.

INFECTION/ SEVERITY	ADULT TREATMENT OPTIONS	COMMENTS
Moderate purulent SSTI Target CA-MRSA	SMX/TMP 1-2 DS tabs BID or Doxycycline 100 mg BID or Minocycline 200 mg x 1, then 100 mg BID or Clindamycin 300-450 mg QID or Linezolid 600 mg BID	Mild purulent infections – primary treatment is I & D; antibiotics are not indicated in many cases. If systemic signs and symptoms present (moderate infection), consider oral antibiotics. Defined treatment based on C & S: If MSSA, narrow to cephalexin or dicloxacillin If MRSA, narrow to SMX/TMP
Severe purulent SSTI Target MRSA	Vancomycin 15 mg/kg IV Q12H (goal trough 10-15 mg/L) or Daptomycin 4 mg/kg IV daily or Linezolid 600 mg IV/PO BID or Telavancin 10 mg/kg/dose IV daily or Ceftaroline 600 mg IV Q12H or Tedizolid 200 mg IV/PO daily or Dalbavancin 1,000 mg IV x 1, then 500 mg IV one week later or Oritavancin 1,200 mg IV x 1	If systemic signs and symptoms present, failed oral antibiotics, or immunocompromised, consider IV antibiotics. Once the patient is clinically stable, can transition to PO antibiotics. Bite infections require broader antibiotic coverage (e.g. ampicillin/sulbactam, amoxicillin/clavulanate) for aerobic Gram-negatives (including _Pasteurella_ spp.), Gram-positives and anaerobes. Duration of therapy = 7 to 14 days.

Diabetic Foot Infections

Diabetic patients are at high risk for foot infections because of compromised blood flow to the lower extremities and neuropathic damage. Foot infections are the most common cause of amputation in diabetic patients. Grading systems are used to evaluate ulcers for presence of inflammation, purulence and infection, and to classify severity, which guides management (surgery and/or antibiotics). *Staphylococcus* spp. and *Streptococcus* spp. are the predominant pathogens in diabetic foot infections (DFIs), however, they can be polymicrobial infections, thus empiric therapy is usually broad. It is imperative that patients follow proper foot care and evaluation, as discussed in the Diabetes chapter. If deeper infection, such as <u>osteomyelitis</u>, is present, <u>longer courses of antibiotics</u> (often IV) will be required.

ETIOLOGY	GRAM-POSITIVE	GRAM-NEGATIVE
Aerobic	*S. aureus* (including MRSA) Group A *Streptococcus* *Viridans* group *Streptococci* *S. epidermidis*	*E. coli* *Klebsiella pneumoniae* *Proteus mirabilis* *Enterobacter cloacae* *Pseudomonas aeruginosa*
Anaerobic	*Peptostreptococcus* *Clostridium perfringens*	*Bacteroides fragilis* and others

Treatment of Moderate-Severe (Life or Limb-threatening) Diabetic Foot Infections

TYPE OF REGIMEN	TREATMENT REGIMEN	COMMENTS
Combination	Vancomycin plus one of the following: Ceftazidime*, cefepime*, piperacillin-tazobactam*, aztreonam* or a carbapenem* Vancomycin alternatives: Daptomycin or Linezolid Note: Consider adding anaerobe coverage (metronidazole) if ceftazidime, cefepime, or aztreonam selected	<u>Duration</u>: 7-14 days More severe, deep tissue infection: treat for 2-4 weeks. Severe, limb-threatening or bone/joint infection: treat for 4-6 weeks. Osteomyelitis requires longer courses of therapy, and may include chronic suppressive therapy.
Monotherapy	Ampicillin/sulbactam or Piperacillin/tazobactam* or Ticarcillin/clavulanate* or Imipenem/cilastatin* or Meropenem* or Ertapenem or Tigecycline** or Moxifloxacin	

* Has Pseudomonas coverage
** Tigecycline should only be used when all other alternatives have been exhausted

Urinary Tract Infections

Most urinary tract infections (UTIs) occur in the bladder (cystitis) and urethra, which is called the lower urinary tract. More severe infections can occur in the kidneys (pyelonephritis), or the upper urinary tract. UTIs are more common in females than males, as the female urethra provides a shorter route for organisms to travel up into the bladder. Sexual intercourse can facilitate this movement; women who develop UTIs commonly after intercourse may be prescribed prophylactic antibiotics after sexual intercourse. UTIs are classified as uncomplicated and complicated. Uncomplicated UTIs are those that occur in non-pregnant, premenopausal women who have no urologic abnormalities or comorbidities. An infection in males is considered to be complicated because it is likely due to some type of abnormality or obstruction, such as an enlarged prostate. Complicated infections can also result from a neurogenic bladder (e.g., spinal cord injury, stroke, multiple sclerosis), an obstruction (e.g., a stone) or the presence of an indwelling catheter. All patients are at risk for catheter-associated infections, see the Medication Safety & Quality Control chapter for a discussion of ways to reduce this common (and often preventable) infection.

UTI SYMPTOMS
Lower UTI (cystitis)   Dysuria, urgency, frequency, burning, nocturia, suprapubic heaviness, and/or hematuria (fever is uncommon)
Upper UTI (pyelonephritis)   Flank pain/costovertebral angle pain, abdominal pain, fever, nausea, vomiting, and malaise

A urinalysis is considered positive when there is evidence of pyuria (positive leukocyte esterase or > 10 WBC/mm^3) and bacteriuria ($\geq 10^5$ bacteria/mL in asymptomatic patients, $\geq 10^3$ bacteria/mL in symptomatic males, and $\geq 10^2$ bacteria/mL in symptomatic females and catheterized patients).

Aside from antibiotics, other products used for this condition include cranberry, blueberry, bearberry, garlic, echinacea, stinging nettle, asparagus, yogurt and some probiotics (*Bifidobacteria* and *Lactobacillus* strains). See the Natural Products chapter.

UTI Treatment

DIAGNOSIS	DRUGS OF CHOICE/GUIDELINES	COMMENTS
Acute uncomplicated cystitis in females of child bearing age (~15-45 years of age) Common pathogens: *E. coli* (vast majority), *Proteus*, *Klebsiella* (PEK) *S. saprophyticus*, *Enterococcus*	Nitrofurantoin 100 mg BID with food x 5 days (less collateral damage) or SMX/TMP 1 DS tab BID x 3 days (avoid if *E. coli* resistance rate in community/institution is ≥ 20% or if sulfa allergy) or Fosfomycin 3 grams x 1 in 4 oz water (lower efficacy) or Alternatives: Ciprofloxacin 250 mg BID x 3 days or Ciprofloxacin ER 500 mg daily x 3 days or Levofloxacin 250 mg daily x 3 days Beta-lactam agents (amoxicillin/clavulanate and oral cephalosporins) x 3-7 days are appropriate choices when other recommended agents cannot be used. Treat pregnant women for 3-7 days.	Usually empirically treated as an outpatient If no response with a 3 day course, perform urinary culture and treat accordingly. Do not use moxifloxacin for UTIs (does not reach high levels in the urine) or gemifloxacin (limited activity against normal UTI pathogens). Prophylaxis: If ≥ 3 episodes in 1 yr, can use 1 SMX/TMP SS daily, nitrofurantoin 50 mg PO daily, or 1 SMX/TMP DS post coitus. May add phenazopyridine 200 mg PO TID x 2 days to relieve dysuria.

UTI Treatment Continued

DIAGNOSIS	DRUGS OF CHOICE/GUIDELINES	COMMENTS
Acute uncomplicated pyelonephritis Common pathogens: *E. coli, Enterococci, P. mirabilis, K. pneumoniae, P. aeruginosa*	Moderately ill outpatient (PO): If local quinolone resistance < 10% - Ciprofloxacin 500 mg PO BID or ciprofloxacin ER 1,000 mg daily x 7 days or levofloxacin 750 mg daily x 5 days If local quinolone resistance > 10% - Ceftriaxone 1 gram IV x 1 or AMG IV x 1, followed by SMX/TMP (if susceptible) or beta-lactam (amox/clav, cefdinir, cefaclor, or cefpodoxime) – treat for 14 days Severe – hospitalized patient (IV): Initial: Ceftriaxone; ampicillin + gentamicin; ciprofloxacin or levofloxacin; or pip/tazo. Step down to oral options based on susceptibility results. Treatment duration: 14 days total (including IV & PO)	If risk for or documented *Pseudomonas* infection, consider piperacillin/tazobactam or meropenem ± aminoglycoside.
Complicated UTI Common pathogens: *E.coli, Klebsiella, Enterobacter, Serratia, Pseudomonas, Enterococcus, Staphylococcus*	Similar to options noted above for pyelonephritis If ESBL producers are present, use a carbapenem Treat for 7 days if there is prompt symptom relief Treat for 10-14 days with delayed response	Urinalysis, urine and blood cultures should be done. May be due to obstruction, catheterization – remove or change catheter if possible.

Bacteriuria and Pregnancy

Bacteriuria in pregnant women must be treated (for 3 – 7 days) even if asymptomatic with negative urinalysis. If not treated, bacteriuria can lead to pyelonephritis, premature birth and neonatal meningitis.

■ Generally, beta-lactams are used (amoxicillin/clavulanate or oral cephalosporins).

■ Nitrofurantoin and SMX/TMP can be used with a beta-lactam allergy, although they are typically last line agents in the 1st trimester and are contraindicated late in pregnancy (last 2 weeks before delivery). There is concern that SMX/TMP could cause hyperbilirubinemia and kernicterus in the newborn (Pregnancy Category D near term); otherwise, category C. Nitrofurantoin is contraindicated in the late pregnancy, due to the possibility of hemolytic anemia in the infant. Fosfomycin is Pregnancy Category B and can also be considered for use.

■ In pregnant women, avoid quinolones (cartilage toxicity and arthropathies) and tetracyclines (teratogenic). See Drug Use in Pregnancy chapter for more information.

Urinary Analgesic

Phenazopyridine may be given for symptomatic relief of dysuria (pain or burning with urination). Appropriate antibiotic treatment will resolve symptoms promptly. It is occasionally given to reduce pain from vaginal procedures.

DRUG	DOSING	SAFETY/SIDE EFFECTS/MONITORING
Phenazopyridine (*Azo, Uristat, Pyridium,* others) OTC/RX	100-200 mg TID x 2 days (max)	**CONTRAINDICATIONS** Do not use in patients with renal impairment or liver disease. **SIDE EFFECTS** Headache, dizziness, stomach cramps, body secretion discoloration **NOTES** Pregnancy Category B. Take with or following food and 8 oz of water to minimize stomach upset. May cause red-orange coloring of the urine and other body fluids. Contact lenses and clothes can be stained. Can cause hemolytic anemia in patients with G6PD deficiency (discontinue if hemolysis occurs).

Clostridium difficile Infection

The GI tract contains > 1,000 species of organisms. The use of antibiotics eliminates much of the "healthy" bacteria, allowing an overgrowth of *Clostridium difficile* bacteria, a Gram-positive rod, obligate anaerobic, spore-forming bacteria. Some types releases toxins that attack the intestinal lining, causing colitis. Symptoms of *C. difficile* infection (CDI) include abdominal cramps, profuse diarrhea (can be bloody), and fever. *C. difficile* overgrowth can lead to inflammation of the colon and pseudomembranous colitis, which can progress to toxic megacolon and colectomy or death. Rates of CDI have increased in recent years due to overuse of antibiotics. In addition to antibiotics, other risk factors include recent healthcare exposure, use of proton pump inhibitors, advanced age, immunocompromised state, obesity and previous CDI.

CDI Treatment and Isolation Principles

- Discontinue antibiotics, if possible.

- Review the medication profile for other medications that could cause diarrhea.

- Antimotility agents should not be used for CDI diarrhea due to the risk of toxic megacolon.

- Patient should be isolated to prevent transmission (single-patient rooms, contact precautions: gloves, gowns).

- Wash hands with soap and water to remove spores from the hands and prevent transmission. Hand sanitizers containing alcohol do not kill or remove *C. difficile* spores.

- Metronidazole should not be used beyond the 1st recurrence or for long-term therapy due to the potential for cumulative neurotoxicity.

- Probiotics *(Lactobacillus, Saccharomyces)* are not beneficial for treatment, but may have some benefit for prophylaxis.

- Although not currently part of the IDSA guidelines, fidaxomicin or fecal stool transplant are alternative therapies for recurrent or relapsing CDI.

CDI Treatment*

SEVERITY OF INFECTION	1ST INFECTION	2ND INFECTION (1ST RECURRENCE)	3RD INFECTION (2ND RECURRENCE)
Mild-moderate disease	Metronidazole 500 mg PO TID x 10-14 days	Same as 1st infection if same severity	Vancomycin taper/pulse therapy 125 mg PO QID x 10-14 days, BID x 1 week, daily x 1 week, then 125 mg every 2-3 days/week for 2-8 weeks
Severe disease WBC ≥ 15,000 or SCr ≥ 1.5x baseline level	Vancomycin 125 mg PO QID x 10-14 days	Same as 1st infection if same severity	Vancomycin taper/pulse therapy
Severe, complicated disease Hypotension, shock, ileus, or toxic megacolon	Vancomycin 500 mg PO QID + metronidazole 500 mg IV Q8H If complete ileus, add vancomycin per rectum (500 mg in 100 mL NS PR Q6H)	Same as 1st infection if same severity	Vancomycin taper/pulse therapy

* In clinical trials, fidaxomicin was non-inferior to vancomycin oral therapy, but with lower recurrence rates. Consider fidaxomicin instead of vancomycin for patients at high risk of recurrence (patients receiving chemotherapy or immuno-suppressed patients) – place in therapy not fully established.

Traveler's Diarrhea

Traveler's diarrhea (TD) is the most common travel-related illness. Bacteria causes 80% of TD cases, including enterotoxigenic *Escherichia coli*, followed by *Campylobacter jejuni*, *Shigella spp.*, and *Salmonella spp.* Viral diarrhea can involve a number of pathogens, most commonly norovirus and rotavirus. Less commonly, protozoa including *Giardia*, *Entamoeba histolytica*, *Cryptosporidium* and *Cyclospora*, cause TD. Bacterial and viral diarrhea presents with sudden onset of symptoms, including cramps and urgent loose stools to severe abdominal pain, fever, vomiting, and bloody diarrhea. Protozoal diarrhea, such as that caused by *Giardia* or *E. histolytica*, generally has a more gradual onset of low-grade symptoms, with 2 – 5 loose stools per day.

The primary source of infection is ingestion of fecally contaminated food and water. Antibiotic treatment can reduce duration of diarrhea, but most cases are benign and resolve in 3 – 5 days without treatment. Preventive measures should be taken:

- Avoid eating foods or drinking beverages from street vendors or other places of unhygienic conditions
- Avoid eating raw or under cooked meat/seafood and raw fruits (e.g., oranges, bananas, avocados) and vegetables unless the traveler peels them
- Avoid tap water, ice, unpasteurized milk and dairy products

A simple rule is "boil it, cook it, peel it, or forget it." Well-cooked and packaged foods are generally safe. Safe beverages include bottled, carbonated drinks, hot tea or coffee, beer, wine, boiled water or treated water (with iodine or chlorine).

TRAVELER'S DIARRHEA TREATMENT

Ciprofloxacin 750 mg PO x 1 or 500 mg PO BID x 1-3 days or

Levofloxacin 500 mg PO daily x 1-3 days or

Norfloxacin 400 mg PO BID x 1-3 days or

Ofloxacin 200 mg PO BID x 1-3 days or

Rifaximin 200 mg PO TID x 3 days or

Azithromycin 1,000 mg PO x 1 or 500 mg PO daily x 1-3 days – drug of choice in pregnancy and children

Bismuth subsalicylate 524 mg (2 tablets) every 30 min to 1 hour up to 8 doses/day x 2 days

Plus

Loperamide 4 mg x 1, then 2 mg after each loose stool – max 8 mg/day for traveler's (max 16 mg/day for acute diarrhea). Loperamide is not recommended if patient has dysentery, high fever or blood in stool.

Prophylactic antibiotics are not recommended due to concerns of toxicity, resistance, lack of activity against viral pathogens and because most cases of TD are self-limiting without antibiotic treatment. Bismuth subsalicylate (BSS) taken as either 2 tablets QID (or liquid) reduces the incidence of TD (not to be used longer than 3 weeks). BSS commonly causes blackening of the tongue and stool and may cause nausea, constipation, and rarely tinnitus. BSS should be avoided in those with an aspirin allergy, renal insufficiency, and by those taking anticoagulants, probenecid, or methotrexate. The role of probiotics for the prevention of TD is unclear at this time. The most important treatment is oral rehydration therapy, especially in young children, elderly or those with chronic medical conditions. A 1 – 3 day course of quinolones or macrolides are generally effective in treating TD (see box). Adjunctive therapy, including antimotility agents (loperamide) provide symptomatic relief, but generally should be avoided for bloody diarrhea or for patients with a fever. Diphenoxylate is no longer recommended due to concerns of toxicity (risks > benefit).

Sexually Transmitted Infections

Sexually transmitted infections (STIs) encompass a variety of clinical syndromes and infections caused by pathogens acquired through sexual activity and are a major public health concern. Screening and prevention counseling should be done for timely diagnosis of STIs and prevention of complications, including cervical cancer, infertility, or transmission to partners. Sexual partners should be treated concurrently to prevent re-infection, except in bacterial vaginosis. The most common STIs and their treatment recommendations are listed below.

INFECTION	DOC	DOSING/DURATION	ALTERNATIVES/NOTES
Syphilis – caused by *Treponema pallidum*, a spirochete Primary, secondary, or early latent (< 1 year duration)	Penicillin G benzathine *(Bicillin L-A, do not substitute with Bicillin C-R)*	2.4 million units IM x 1	Doxycycline 100 mg PO BID or Tetracycline 500 mg PO QID x 14 days Pregnant patients allergic to PCN should be desensitized and treated with PCN.
Syphilis – Late latent (> 1 year duration), tertiary, or latent syphilis of unknown duration	Penicillin G benzathine *(Bicillin L-A – do not substitute with Bicillin C-R)*	2.4 million units IM weekly x 3 weeks (7.2 million units total)	Doxycycline 100 mg PO BID or Tetracycline 500 mg PO QID x 28 days Pregnant patients allergic to PCN should be desensitized and treated with PCN.
Neurosyphilis (including ocular syphilis)	Penicillin G aqueous crystalline	3-4 million units IV Q4H or continuous infusion (18-24 million units/day) x 10-14 days	Penicillin G procaine 2.4 million units IM daily + probenecid 500 mg PO QID x 10-14 days
Congenital syphilis	Penicillin G aqueous crystalline	Newborns: 50,000 units/kg IV Q12H x 7 days, then Q8H for 10 days total Infants ≥ 1 month old: 50,000 units/kg IV Q4-6H x 10 days	Penicillin G procaine 50,000 units/kg IM daily x 10 days

Sexually Transmitted Infections Drugs Continued

INFECTION	DOC	DOSING/DURATION	ALTERNATIVES/NOTES
Gonorrhea – caused by *Neisseria gonorrhoeae*, a Gram-negative diplococcus Urethral, cervical, rectal, pharyngeal	<u>Ceftriaxone</u> plus either Azithromycin (preferred) or Doxycycline	<u>250 mg IM x 1</u> 1 gram PO x 1 100 mg PO BID x 7 days	<u>Monotherapy</u> is <u>not recommended</u> due to resistance. Recommended therapy also covers co-infection with *Chlamydia*. Ceftriaxone is most effective for pharyngeal infections. If ceftriaxone is not available, can use cefixime *(Suprax)* 400 mg PO x 1 + azithromycin (or doxycycline) with a test for cure in 1 week. If severe cephalosporin allergy, azithromycin 2 g PO x 1 plus either gemifloxacin 320 mg PO x 1 or gentamicin 240 mg IM x 1 with a test for cure in 1 week.
Chlamydial Infections – caused by *Chlamydia trachomatis*, intracellular obligate Gram-negative organism	<u>Azithromycin</u> or Doxycycline	<u>1 gram PO x 1</u> 100 mg PO BID x 7 days	Erythromycin base 500 mg PO QID x 7 days or Levofloxacin 500 mg PO daily x 7 days or Ofloxacin 300 mg PO BID x 7 days Pregnancy: Azithromycin (preferred) or amoxicillin 500 mg PO TID x 7 days
Bacterial Vaginosis – caused by many different organisms	<u>Metronidazole</u> or <u>Metronidazole 0.75% gel</u> or Clindamycin 2% cream	500 mg PO BID x 7 days 5 g intravaginally daily x 5 days 5 g intravaginally at bedtime x 7 days	Clindamycin 300 mg PO BID x 7 days or Clindamycin ovules* 100 mg intravaginally at bedtime x 3 days or Tinidazole 2 g PO daily x 2 days or Tinidazole 1 g PO daily x 5 days
Trichomoniasis – caused by *Trichomonas vaginalis*, a flagellated protozoan	Metronidazole or Tinidazole	2 grams PO x 1 2 grams PO x 1	Metronidazole 500 mg PO BID x 7 days
Herpes Simplex Virus (HSV 1 and HSV 2)			See Infectious Diseases III chapter.

*Clindamycin ovules use a base that can weaken latex or rubber products (i.e., condoms).
Condom use within 72 hours of clindamycin ovules should not be considered adequate protection.

Rickettsial Diseases and Related Infections

Rickettsial infections are caused by a variety of bacteria that are carried by many ticks, fleas, and lice and cause diseases in humans such as those found below. Rocky Mountain spotted fever is the most common and most fatal rickettsial illness in the U.S. Initial signs and symptoms include fever, headache, muscle pain followed by the development of a rash.

DISEASE	ORGANISM	TREATMENT
Rocky Mountain Spotted Fever	*Rickettsia rickettsii* Gram-negative obligate intracellular bacteria	Doxycycline 100 mg PO/IV BID x 5-7 days
Typhus	*Rickettsia typhi* Gram-negative obligate intracellular bacteria	Doxycycline 100 mg PO/IV BID x 7 days
Lyme Disease	*Borrelia burgdorferi* Spirochete	Doxycycline 100 mg PO BID x 10-21 days or Amoxicillin 500 mg PO TID x 14-21 days or Cefuroxime 500 mg PO BID x 14-21 days
Ehrlichiosis	*Ehrlichia chaffeensis* Obligate intracellular bacteria	Doxycycline 100 mg PO/IV BID x 7-14 days
Tularemia	*Francisella tularensis* Aerobic Gram-negative coccobacilli	Gentamicin or tobramycin 5 mg/kg/d IV divided Q8H x 7-14 days

PRACTICE CASE

MJ is a previously healthy 43 y/o black female who presents to the urgent care clinic with complaints of fever, runny nose, congestion, productive cough and body aches. She reports that she has been feeling this way for the past 36 hours and she needs to get better quickly to return to work. She noticed a lot of people coughing on the bus this week and figures that is where she picked this up. Her past medical history is significant for GERD and depression.

Allergies: Sulfa (extreme rash and hives)

Medications:
Prozac 20 mg PO daily
Zantac 150 mg PO BID
Tums 1-2 tabs PRN heartburn

Vitals:
Height: 5'6" Weight: 192 pounds BMI: 31
BP: 164/81 mmHg HR: 114 BPM RR: 24 BPM Temp: 102.3°F Pain: 2/10

Labs:

Na (mEq/L) = 142 (135 - 145)
K (mEq/L) = 3.5 (3.5 - 5)
Cl (mEq/L) = 97 (95 - 103)
HCO_3 (mEq/L) = 27 (24 - 30)
BUN (mg/dL) = 13 (7 - 20)
SCr (mg/dL) = 1.1 (0.6 - 1.3)
Glucose (mg/dL) = 129 (100 - 125)
Ca (mg/dL) = 10.1 (8.5 - 10.5)
Mg (mEq/L) = 2.0 (1.3 - 2.1)
PO_4 (mg/dL) = 4.2 (2.3 - 4.7)

WBC (cells/mm^3) = 15.3 (4 - 11 x 10^3)
Hgb (g/dL) = 13.3 (13.5 - 18 male, 12 - 16 female)
Hct (%) = 42 (38 - 50 male, 36 - 46 female)
Plt (cells/mm^3) = 315 (150 - 450 x 10^3)
PMNs (%) = 90 (45 - 73)
Bands (%) = 7 (3 - 5)
Eosinophils (%) = 2 (0 - 5)
Basophils (%) = 0 (0 - 1)
Lymphocytes (%) = 37 (20 - 40)
Monocytes (%) = 3 (2 - 8)

Tests:
Chest x-ray: left middle lobe infiltrate

Assessment and Plan:
CAP confirmed by chest x-ray. Start antibiotic and have patient stay home from work for 2 days.

Questions

1. Based on the information provided in the case, what is the most appropriate antibiotic for MJ?

   a. *Zithromax* 500 mg PO x 1, then 250 mg PO daily x days 2-5

   b. *Avelox* 400 mg IV daily x 5-7 days

   c. *Levaquin* 500 mg PO x 1, then 250 mg PO daily x 5-7 days

   d. *Ceftin* 500 mg PO Q12H x 5-7 days

   e. *Bactrim* 1 DS tab PO Q12H x 5-7 days

2. MJ has accidentally lost the prescription and she cannot afford another office visit. She decides to tough it out and goes back to work. Two days later, MJ is admitted to the hospital due to worsening symptoms. What is the best regimen to treat her community-acquired pneumonia in the inpatient setting?

   a. Ciprofloxacin 500 mg PO daily

   b. Ceftriaxone 1 gram IV daily

   c. Ceftriaxone 1 gram IV daily + azithromycin 500 mg IV daily

   d. Vancomycin 1 gram IV Q12H + imipenem/cilastatin 500 mg Q6H

   e. Gemifloxacin 320 mg PO daily + clarithromycin 500 mg PO Q12H

3. While in the hospital, MJ's course is complicated by a bacteremia due to an infected central line with *Pseudomonas aeruginosa*. Which of the following antibiotics would be an appropriate treatment for her bacteremia

   a. Ampicillin

   b. *Cubicin*

   c. *Invanz*

   d. *Merrem*

   e. *Tygacil*

4. MJ has turned the corner and was discharged home a few weeks later. After about 3-4 months, she returns to the clinic complaining of intense burning on urination, dysuria, and frequent bathroom visits. The diagnosis is confirmed as a urinary tract infection caused by *E. coli,* which is susceptible to all antibiotics tested. Which of the following is the best choice to treat MJ's UTI?

   a. *Bactrim* SS 1 tab PO BID x 3 days

   b. *Bactrim* DS 1 tab PO BID x 3 days

   c. Nitrofurantoin 100 mg PO BID x 3 days

   d. Nitrofurantoin 100 mg PO BID x 5 days

   e. Phenazopyridine 200 mg TID x 2 days

Questions 5 – 10 do not apply to the case

5. The pharmacist is working in the ER when an intern asks how to treat the patient in room 4 who has a gonorrheal STD infection. What is the best recommendation to treat this patient?

   a. Levofloxacin 750 mg PO x 1

   b. Doxycycline 100 mg PO BID x 7 days

   c. Benzathine penicillin G 2.4 million units IM x 1

   d. Metronidazole 2 grams PO x 1

   e. Ceftriaxone 250 mg IM x 1 + azithromycin 1 gram PO x 1

6. Tommy is taking isoniazid (INH) for latent tuberculosis treatment. Which of the following is/are correct regarding INH? (Select **ALL** that apply.)

   a. INH should be taken 1 hour before or 2 hours after a meal on an empty stomach.

   b. INH is a potent enzyme inducer.

   c. INH is contraindicated in acute gout.

   d. INH can be used alone to treat latent TB.

   e. INH requires dose adjustments in renal impairment.

7. Which of the following medications can help prevent peripheral neuropathies in patients taking isoniazid?

    a. Pyrazinamide
    b. Pyridoxine
    c. *Pyridium*
    d. Pyridostigmine
    e. Pyrimethamine

8. A patient comes into your clinic. She is 5 months pregnant and has a UTI. She is allergic to cephalexin. Which of the following regimens would be a treatment option for her? (Select **ALL** that apply.)

    a. *Bactrim* 1 DS tab BID x 3 days
    b. *Cipro ER* 500 mg PO daily x 7 days
    c. Nitrofurantoin 100 mg PO BID x 7 days
    d. Cefpodoxime 100 mg PO Q12H x 7 days
    e. Do not treat since she is pregnant.

9. A 26 year old male presents to the clinic complaining of pain in his right foot. On exam, there is no focal abscess, just diffuse redness and warmth on the bottom of big toe spreading to the arch of his foot. He recalls stepping on a staple the week prior. He denies having a fever and his vital signs are normal. Which one of the following antibiotics would be a good choice for his skin infection? (Select **ALL** that apply.)

    a. *Bactrim* SS 1 tab PO BID x 7 days
    b. Ceftriaxone 1 g IV x 1
    c. Dicloxacillin 500 mg PO Q6H x 5 days
    d. Sivextro 200 mg PO Q24H x 7 days
    e. Cephalexin 500 mg PO Q6H x 5 days

10. A 45 year old male with history of Hepatitis C cirrhosis presents to the hospital with a 6 day history of fever and chills. He has significant ascites and he has diffuse tenderness to palpation in his abdomen. The physician orders 2 sets of blood cultures, which grow Gram-negative rods, pending identification and susceptibilities. Which of the following would be the best choice for empiric therapy?

    a. *Bactrim DS* PO BID
    b. Ceftriaxone 1 gram IV daily
    c. Ofloxacin 200 mg IV Q12H
    d. Cefixime 200 mg PO BID
    e. Erythromycin 250 mg IV Q6H

Answers

1-a, 2-c, 3-d, 4-d, 5-e, 6-a,d, 7-b , 8-a,c, 9-c,e, 10-b

INFECTIOUS DISEASES III: ANTIFUNGALS, ANTIVIRALS & ANTIPARASITICALS

CDC/Dr. Lucille K. Georg

We gratefully acknowledge the assistance of Emi Mineji-ma, PharmD, Assistant Professor and Annie Wong-Beringer, PharmD, FCCP, FIDSA, Associate Dean and Professor, University of Southern California School of Pharmacy, in preparing this chapter.

GUIDELINES/REFERENCES

Walsh TJ, Anaissie EJ, Denning DW, eg al. Treatment of Aspergillosis *Clinical Infectious Diseases.* 2008;46:327-360

Pappas PG, Kauffman CA, Andes, D, et al. Guidelines for the Management of Candidiasis: 2009 Update by the Infectious Diseases Society of America. *linical Infectious Diseases.* 2009;48:503-535

Additional guidelines available at: http://www.idsociety.org

SYSTEMIC FUNGAL INFECTIONS

Fungal infections cause a wide spectrum of disease, from severe infections such as meningitis or pneumonia, to mild infections such as nail bed infections. Invasive fungal infections are associated with high morbidity and mortality. Candidemia, the 4th most common cause of nosocomial bloodstream infections in the U.S., has a mortality rate up to 30%. Diagnosis of fungal infections can be made by culture, serologic studies, or histologic features of a tissue specimen.

Fungi are classified as either yeasts, molds, or dimorphic (see box). Dimorphic fungi exist as mold forms at lower temperatures and yeast forms at higher temperatures ("Mold in the cold, yeast in the heat"). *Zygomycetes* refers to a class of fungi which includes *Mucor* spp. and *Rhizopus* spp.; invasive disease with this group is commonly referred to as "mucormycosis".

Certain types of fungi (including yeasts such as *Candida)* may colonize body surfaces and are considered to be normal flora in the intestine. They do not normally cause serious infections unless the immune system is weakened, or compromised, by drugs or diseases (HIV, malignancy). See Infectious Diseases IV for more information on opportunistic infections. Some fungi reproduce by spreading microscopic spores. These spores are often present in the air, where they can be inhaled or come into contact with the skin, causing lung and skin infections and in some cases central nervous system infections. Systemic and long-term therapy is necessary for certain fungal infections (*Cryptococcal* meningitis, *Coccidioides)* in the chronically immunosuppressed host.

FUNGAL CLASSIFICATIONS

Yeasts
Candida spp. (includes *C. albicans, C. tropicalis, C. glabrata, C. krusei)*

Cryptococcus neoformans

Molds
Aspergillus spp.

Zygomycetes (Mucor spp., *Rhizopus* spp.)

Dimorphic fungi
Histoplasma capsulatum

Blastomyces dermatitidis

Coccidioides immitis

In general, _C. albicans_ is the most susceptible of the _Candida_ species. _C. glabrata_ and _C. krusei_ tend to be more difficult to treat due to resistance patterns. Of the molds, _Aspergillus_ and _Zygomycetes_ require the use of specific agents that have adequate activity.

Amphotericin B Deoxycholate and Lipid Formulations

Amphotericin B is broad spectrum and fungicidal, binding to ergosterol, altering cell membrane permeability and causing cell death. Amphotericin B deoxycholate (the conventional form) has many toxicities. Lipid formulations are a complex of the active medication and a lipid component, which are used clinically because they are associated with fewer toxicities. Amphotericin B products are active against yeasts, molds and dimorphic fungi. They are used as initial treatment for many invasive infections, including _Cryptococcal_ meningitis, histoplasmosis and mucormycosis.

AMPHOTERICIN B FORMULATIONS	DOSING	SAFETY/SIDE EFFECTS/MONITORING
Conventional Formulation		**BOXED WARNINGS** Medication errors from confusion between lipid-based forms of amphotericin _(Abelcet, Amphotec, AmBisome)_ and conventional amphotericin B for injection have resulted in death. Conventional amphotericin B for injection doses should not exceed 1.5 mg/kg/day; verify product name and dosage if dose exceeds 1.5 mg/kg/day. Overdose may result in cardiopulmonary arrest.
Amphotericin B deoxycholate Injection	0.1-1.5 mg/kg/day	
		SIDE EFFECTS Infusion-related: fever, chills, HA, malaise, rigors, ↓ K, ↓ Mg, nephrotoxicity, anemia, hypotension/hypertension, thrombophlebitis, N/V
Lipid Formulations		_AmBisome_ has had rare reports of severe back/chest pain with 1st dose.
Amphotericin B Lipid Complex _(Abelcet)_ Injection	5 mg/kg/day	**MONITORING** Renal function, LFTs, electrolytes (especially K and Mg), CBC **NOTES** Pregnancy Category B.
Liposomal Amphotericin B _(AmBisome)_ Injection	3-6 mg/kg/day	Amphotericin B deoxycholate (conventional formulation) requires pre-medication to reduce infusion-related reactions. Give the following 30-60 minutes prior to infusion: ■ Acetaminophen or NSAID ■ Diphenhydramine and/or hydrocortisone ■ Meperidine to ↓ duration of severe rigors
Amphotericin B cholesteryl sulfate complex _(Amphotec)_ Injection	3-4 mg/kg/day	■ NS boluses to ↓ risk of nephrotoxicity Lipid formulations have ↓ infusion reactions and ↓ nephrotoxicity compared to conventional formulation. While lipid formulations are more expensive than conventional amphotericin B, most institutions use lipid formulations due to ↓ toxicity and ↓ need for premedication.

Amphotericin B Drug Interactions

■ Additive ↑ risk of nephrotoxicity when used with other nephrotoxic agents such as aminoglycosides, cisplatin, colistimethate, cyclosporine, flucytosine, loop diuretics, NSAIDs, radiocontrast dye, tacrolimus, vancomycin and others.

■ May ↑ risk of digoxin toxicity due to hypokalemia. Use caution with any agent that ↓ potassium or magnesium since amphotericin decreases both. Scheduled replacement of potassium or magnesium should be considered.

Flucytosine

Flucytosine is fungicidal. After penetrating fungal cells it is converted to fluorouracil, which competes with uracil, interfering with fungal RNA and protein synthesis. Due to development of resistance when used alone, flucytosine is recommended for use <u>in combination with amphotericin B</u> for treatment of invasive *Cryptococcal* (meningitis) or *Candida* infections.

DRUG	DOSING	SAFETY/SIDE EFFECTS/MONITORING
Flucytosine, 5-FC *(Ancobon)* Spectrum: covers yeasts, including *Candida* and *Cryptococcus*	50-150 mg/kg/day, divided Q6H CrCl < 40 mL/min: reduce dose and extend interval	**BOXED WARNING** Use with extreme caution in patients with renal dysfunction. Closely monitor hematologic, renal, and hepatic status. **SIDE EFFECTS** Dose-related <u>myelosuppression</u>, (anemia, neutropenia, thrombocytopenia), ↑ SCr, ↑ BUN, <u>hepatitis</u> , ↑ bilirubin, many CNS effects, hypoglycemia, ↓ K, aplastic anemia, and others **NOTES** Avoid use as monotherapy due to rapid resistance.

Azole Antifungals

Azole antifungals decrease ergosterol synthesis and inhibit cell membrane formation and are typically fungistatic, but may be fungicidal for select fungal pathogens. Azoles are inhibitors of the fungal CYP450 system and also interact with the human CYP450 enzymes (mainly 3A4) resulting in <u>significant drug interactions as a class</u>. The coverage and indications of azoles vary widely. Ketoconazole was the first azole, but due to toxicities and many significant drug interactions it is most often used topically. <u>Fluconazole</u> has reliable activity against *Candida albicans* and *Candida tropicalis*. It is useful for oropharyngeal candidiasis (thrush) in HIV patients or in moderate-severe disease in non-HIV infected patients. Itraconazole can be used as an alternative to fluconazole in some cases, as it is active against *C. albicans*, *C. tropicalis* and *Cryptococcus neoformans*, but use is often limited by drug interactions, less data and expense. The primary uses for itraconazole are for the dimorphic fungi *Blastomycosis* and *Histoplasmosis* and for nail bed infections (onychomycosis). <u>Voriconazole</u> has additional mold activity and is the drug of choice for *Aspergillus* infections. The newer azoles (<u>posaconazole and isavuconazonium</u>) also cover *Aspergillus* and are the only azoles with activity against *Zygomycetes*. See the Common Skin Conditions chapter for treatment of non-invasive fungal infections, including onychomycosis.

DRUG	DOSING	SAFETY/SIDE EFFECTS/MONITORING
Ketoconazole *(Nizoral, Nizoral AD, Ketodan, Extina, Xolegel* – all brands are topicals) Tablet, cream, foam, gel, shampoo Used off-label to treat advanced prostate cancer due to anti-androgenic activity (dosing differs for this indication)	200-400 mg PO daily No adjustment in renal impairment See Common Skin Conditions chapter.	**BOXED WARNINGS** **Ketoconazole** Hepatotoxicity which has led to liver transplantation and/or death. Concomitant use with cisapride, dofetilide, pimozide, and quinidine is contraindicated due risk of life-threatening ventricular arrhythmias such as torsades de pointes. Use oral tablets only when other effective antifungal therapy is unavailable or not tolerated and the benefits outweigh risks (hepatotoxicity, adrenal insufficiency, drug interactions). **Itraconazole** Contraindicated for treatment of onychomycosis in patients with ventricular dysfunction or a history of HF.
Fluconazole *(Diflucan)* Tablet, suspension, injection Spectrum: yeasts (including *Candida albicans Candida tropicalis, Cryptococcus*) and *Coccidioides* Limited efficacy for *C. glabrata* due to resistance *C. krusei* is considered fluconazole-resistant	100-800 mg PO/IV daily Vaginal candidiasis: 150 mg PO x 1 CrCl ≤ 50 mL/min: ↓ dose by 50%	Coadministration with itraconazole can cause ↑ plasma concentrations of certain drugs and can lead to QT prolongation and ventricular tachyarrhythmias, including torsades de pointes. Coadministration with methadone, disopyramide, dofetilide, dronedarone, quinidine, ergot alkaloids, irinotecan, lurasidone, oral midazolam, pimozide, triazolam, felodipine, nisoldipine, ranolazine, eplerenone, cisapride, lovastatin, simvastatin and, in subjects with renal or hepatic impairment, colchicine, is contraindicated. **SIDE EFFECTS** Headache, N/V, abdominal pain, rash/pruritus, ↑ LFTs, ↑ triglycerides, QT prolongation, ↓ K, hypertension, edema, dizziness, hair loss (or possible hair growth) and altered hair texture with ketoconazole shampoo
Itraconazole *(Sporanox, Sporanox PulsePak, Onmel)* Tablet, capsule, solution Spectrum: yeasts *(C. albicans, C. tropicalis)*, dimorphic fungi, *Aspergillus*	200-400 mg PO daily-BID Capsules and oral solution are not interchangeable. Solution is taken without food. Capsule and tablet are taken with food. Limited data on use in renal impairment (use with caution). See Common Skin Conditions chapter for use in treatment of onychomycosis.	**NOTES** All azoles are cleared hepatically except fluconazole, which requires renal dose adjustment. Fluconazole and voriconazole penetrate the CNS adequately to treat fungal meningitis. Voriconazole is often associated with CNS toxicities (headache, dizziness, hallucinations or ocular toxicity). Pregnancy Category C (itraconazole, ketoconazole, single dose fluconazole 150 mg for vulvovaginal candidiasis) Pregnancy Category D – Fluconazole (all other doses and indications)

Azole Antifungals Continued

DRUG	DOSING	SAFETY/SIDE EFFECTS/MONITORING
Voriconazole *(Vfend)* Tablet, suspension, injection Spectrum similar to itraconazole but better coverage of *Aspergillus* species, *C. glabrata,* and *C. krusei,* compared to itraconazole/fluconazole. No activity against *Zygomycetes* (*Mucor, Rhizopus*). Drug of choice for Aspergillosis	Loading dose: 6 mg/kg IV Q12H x 2 doses Maintenance dose: 4 mg/kg IV Q12H or 200 mg PO Q12H – use actual body weight for dosing **Therapeutic Range** Trough levels: 1-5 mcg/mL CrCl < 50 mL/min: Oral dosing is preferred after the initial IV loading doses. The IV vehicle, SBECD (sulfobutyl ether beta-cyclodextrin), may accumulate and worsen renal function. Suspension – shake for 10 seconds before each use. Do not refrigerate.	**CONTRAINDICATIONS** Coadministration with barbiturates (long-acting), carbamazepine, efavirenz (≥ 400 mg/day), ergot alkaloids, pimozide, quinidine, rifabutin, rifampin, ritonavir (≥ 800 mg/day), sirolimus and St. John's wort **WARNINGS** Liver damage, visual disturbances (optic neuritis and papilledema), fetal harm, QT prolongation (correct K, Ca, and Mg prior to initiating treatment), serious skin reactions (SJS/TEN), phototoxicity (malignancy has been reported in patients with prior photosensitivity reactions on long-term voriconazole), skeletal adverse effects (fluorosis, periostitis) **SIDE EFFECTS** Visual changes (~20% – blurred vision, photophobia, altered color perception, altered visual acuity), ↑ LFTs, ↑ SCr, CNS toxicity (hallucinations, headache, dizziness), rash (SJS/TEN), photosensitivity, ↓ K, ↓ Mg, skeletal pain **MONITORING** LFTs, renal function, electrolytes, visual function (for therapy > 28 days), CBC, trough concentrations **NOTES** Pregnancy category D Caution driving at night due to vision changes. Avoid direct sunlight. Hold tube feedings for 1 hour before and 1 hour after doses.
Posaconazole *(Noxafil)* Tablet, suspension, injection Spectrum similar to voriconazole plus *Zygomycetes* (*Mucor* and *Rhizopus*)	Suspension: 200 mg TID or 400 mg BID Give with a full meal (during or within 20 minutes following a meal) Tablets: 300 mg PO BID on day 1, then 300 mg PO daily with food. Based on indication, can range from 100-400 mg/day, divided in 1-3 doses IV: 300 mg BID x 1 day, then 300 mg daily CrCl < 50 mL/min: Oral dosing is preferred. The IV vehicle, SBECD (sulfobutyl ether beta-cyclodextrin), may accumulate and worsen renal function.	**CONTRAINDICATIONS** Coadministration with sirolimus, ergot alkaloids, pimozide, quinidine, atorvastatin, lovastatin or simvastatin **WARNINGS** QT prolongation – correct K, Ca, and Mg prior to initiating therapy **SIDE EFFECTS** N/V/D, fever, headache, ↑ LFTs, rash, ↓ K, ↓ Mg, hyperglycemia **MONITORING** LFTs, renal function, electrolytes, CBC **NOTES** Pregnancy Category C Suspension and tablet are not interchangeable, as dosing regimens differ. Tablet is better absorbed.

Azole Antifungals Continued

DRUG	DOSING	SAFETY/SIDE EFFECTS/MONITORING
Isavuconazonium (Cresemba) Capsules, injection Prodrug of isavuconazole Similar spectrum to posaconazole	IV/PO: 372 mg Q8H for 6 doses, then 372 mg daily No adjustment for renal dysfunction, use with caution in severe hepatic impairment Can be taken without regard to food	**CONTRAINDICATIONS** Concurrent use of strong CYP3A4 inhibitors or inducers, familial short QT syndrome **WARNINGS** Hepatic adverse drug reactions, infusion reaction (DC infusion if occurs), hypersensitivity reactions (anaphylaxis, SJS/TEN), embryo-fetal toxicity, drug interactions, <u>particulates (undissolved drug)</u> **SIDE EFFECTS** N/V/D, HA, infusion reactions (hypotension, dyspnea, chills, dizziness, tingling and numbness), peripheral edema, ↓ K, ↑ LFTs **MONITORING** LFTs, electrolytes **NOTES** Pregnancy Category C <u>Requires a filter</u> (0.2-1.2 micron) <u>during administration</u> due to possible particulates

Azole Antifungals Drug Interactions

- <u>All azoles are 3A4 inhibitors</u> (moderate-strong). Itraconazole is an inhibitor of 3A4 (strong) and P-glycoprotein (P-gp). Ketoconazole inhibits 1A2 (weak), 2C9 (moderate), 2C19 (moderate), 2D6 (moderate), 3A4 (strong) and P-gp. Fluconazole is an inhibitor of 2C9 (moderate), 2C19 (strong), and 3A4 (moderate). Voriconazole is an inhibitor of 2C9 (moderate), 2C19 (moderate) and 3A4 (strong). Posaconazole is an inhibitor of 3A4 (strong). Isavuconazonium is an inhibitor of 3A4 (moderate), inducer of 2C8/9 (weak/moderate), 3A4 (weak).

- <u>Itraconazole and ketoconazole have pH-dependent absorption;</u> ↑ pH causes ↓ absorption. Antacids should be spaced 2 hours from doses. If PPIs and H2RAs must be used during antifungal therapy, administer itraconazole or ketoconazole with 8 oz. non-diet cola to provide an acidic environment for absorption.

- <u>PPIs and cimetidine</u> can <u>decrease absorption of posaconazole suspension</u> and <u>should be stopped</u> during therapy to avoid treatment failure.

- Voriconazole is metabolized by several CYP 450 enzymes (2C19, 2C9 and 3A4); the <u>voriconazole concentration can ↑ dangerously</u> when given with drugs that inhibit voriconazole's metabolism or with small dose increases – it exhibits <u>first-order, followed by zero-order (non-linear) kinetics.</u>

- <u>Avoid concurrent use</u> of voriconazole with the following drugs: barbiturates (long-acting), carbamazepine, efavirenz (≥ 400 mg/day), ergot alkaloids, pimozide, quinidine, rifabutin, rifampin, ritonavir (≥ 800 mg/day), sirolimus and St. John's wort.

- Avoid use of isavuconazonium with strong 3A4 inhibitors or inducers.

- All azoles can ↑ INR in patients on warfarin – greatest risk with fluconazole, ketoconazole and voriconazole. Monitor INR.

Echinocandins

Echinocandins inhibit synthesis of $\beta(1,3)$-D-glucan, an essential component of the fungal cell wall, and are considered to be <u>fungicidal</u>. They are effective against <u>most Candida spp.</u>, including non-albicans strains that are resistant to azoles (e.g., *C. glabrata* and *C. krusei*). Activity includes *Aspergillus* spp., but other agents are generally preferred. Should be used as part of a combination regimen if used for *Aspergillus* spp. Echinocandins are generally <u>well-tolerated</u> and are not associated with significant renal or hepatic toxicity. Echinocandins are available only as injections.

DRUG	DOSING	SAFETY/SIDE EFFECTS/MONITORING
Caspofungin *(Cancidas)* Injection	70 mg IV on day 1, then 50 mg IV daily Moderate hepatic impairment: 70 mg IV on day 1, then 35 mg IV daily ↑ dose to 70 mg IV daily when used in combination with rifampin or other strong enzyme inducers	**WARNINGS** Histamine-mediated symptoms (rash, pruritus, facial swelling, flushing, hypotension) have occurred; anaphylaxis **SIDE EFFECTS** ↑ LFTs, hypotension, fever, N/V/D, ↓ K, ↓ Mg, hypoglycemia, anemia, ↑ SCr, rash **MONITORING** LFTs
Micafungin *(Mycamine)* Injection	**Candidemia** 100 mg IV daily **Esophageal Candidiasis** 150 mg IV daily	**NOTES** All are given once daily and <u>do not require dose adjustment in renal impairment</u>. Very few drug interactions.
Anidulafungin *(Eraxis)* Injection	**Candidemia** 200 mg IV on day 1, then 100 mg IV daily **Esophageal Candidiasis** 100 mg IV on day 1, then 50 mg daily	Caution use of caspofungin with cyclosporine due to ↑ hepatotoxicity. Pregnancy Category C/B (anidulafungin)

Other Antifungal Agents

Systemic agents for treatment of superficial fungal infections are typically considered second line to topical products. Griseofulvin is a less favorable agent, as it has a narrow antifungal spectrum, is less effective than other systemic agents (e.g., itraconazole or terbinafine), and requires prolonged courses. <u>Nystatin</u> suspension and <u>clotrimazole</u> troches/lozenges are useful for treating mild, <u>localized *Candida* infections</u> (thrush) in <u>immunocompetent patients</u>. Local agents can be used in <u>immunosuppressed patients</u> for prophylaxis, but <u>systemic treatment (e.g., fluconazole) is required</u> if an infection occurs.

DRUG	DOSING	SAFETY/SIDE EFFECTS/MONITORING
Griseofulvin *(Grifulvin V, Gris-PEG)* Tablet, suspension Griseofulvin binds to the keratin precursor cells which prevents fungal invasion; indicated for dermatomycosis and tinea infections of skin, hair and nails.	*Grifulvin V:* 500-1,000 mg/day in 1-2 divided doses *Gris-PEG:* 375-750 mg/day in 1-2 divided doses Take with a fatty meal to ↑ absorption or with food/milk to avoid GI upset	**CONTRAINDICATIONS** Severe liver disease, porphyria, pregnancy **SIDE EFFECTS** HA, rash, urticaria, dizziness, <u>photosensitivity</u>, ↑ LFTs, leukopenia, severe skin reactions **MONITORING** LFTs, renal function, CBC **NOTES** <u>Pregnancy Category X</u> Cross reaction possible with PCN allergy Duration of therapy depends on site of infection. Tinea corporis: 2-4 weeks. Tinea pedis: 4-8 weeks

Other Antifungal Agents Continued

DRUG	DOSING	SAFETY/SIDE EFFECTS/MONITORING
Terbinafine *(LamISIL, Terbinex)* Tablet, oral granule, topical Topical forms (Rx, OTC) Inhibits squalene epoxidase, a key enzyme in sterol biosynthesis in fungi, resulting in a deficiency of ergosterol within the cell wall leading to cell death	250 mg/day in 1-2 divided doses without regards to meals Confirm fungal infection prior to use for onychomycosis or dermatomycosis See Common Skin Conditions chapter	**WARNINGS** Liver failure, taste/smell disturbance (including loss of taste or smell that can be permanent), depression, neutropenia, serious skin reactions (SJS/TEN/DRESS/erythema multiforme) Can cause or exacerbate systemic lupus erythematosus **SIDE EFFECTS** HA, ↑ LFTs, skin rashes, abdominal pain, pruritus, diarrhea, dyspepsia, taste disturbance **MONITORING** CBC, LFTs
Clotrimazole *(Mycelex)* 10 mg troche/lozenge	**Oral Candidiasis** Prophylaxis: 10 mg 3x/day Treatment: 10 mg 5x/day x 14 days Allow troche to dissolve slowly over 15-30 minutes	**SIDE EFFECTS** ↑ LFTs, nausea, dysgeusia **MONITORING** LFTs **NOTES** Pregnancy Category C
Nystatin *(Bio-Statin)* Suspension, tablet	**Oral Candidiasis** Suspension: 400,000-600,000 units 4 times/day; swish in the mouth and retain for as long as possible (several minutes) before swallowing **Intestinal infections** Oral tablets: 500,000-1,000,000 units Q8H	**SIDE EFFECTS** N/V/D, stomach pain **NOTES** Pregnancy Category C

Drug Interactions

- Griseofulvin: Induces 1A2, 2C9, 3A4 (all weak/moderate). Griseofulvin may ↓ the metabolism of hormonal (estrogen and progestin) contraceptives which may lead to <u>contraceptive failure</u>. Use an alternative, nonhormonal form of contraception.

- Terbinafine is a strong 2D6 inhibitor and a weak/moderate 3A4 inducer.

Treatment Recommendations for Selected Fungal Pathogens

PATHOGEN	FIRST-LINE TREATMENT
Candida albicans	If HIV-negative and oropharyngeal involvement only: fluconazole or topicals (clotrimazole, nystatin) If HIV-positive or esophageal or invasive infection: fluconazole or echinocandin or amphotericin B
Candida glabrata or Candida krusei	Echinocandins or amphotericin B
Aspergillus	Voriconazole, liposomal amphotericin B, isavuconazonium

Treatment Recommendations for Selected Fungal Pathogens Continued

PATHOGEN	FIRST-LINE TREATMENT
Cryptococcus neoformans	Induction in serious infections (primarily causes meningitis): amphotericin B + flucytosine (5-FC)
	Consolidation: fluconazole (prolonged)
Coccidioides immitis	Fluconazole or amphotericin B
Histoplasma capsulatum	Liposomal amphotericin B or itraconazole
Zygomycetes class *(Rhizopus, Mucor*, etc.)*	Amphotericin B ± posaconazole, isavuconazonium
Dermatophytes	Nail bed infections: itraconazole, terbinafine, or fluconazole (confirm fungal infection prior to treatment)

Antifungal Patient Counseling

All azoles

- Common side effects include headache, nausea and abdominal pain.
- This drug can (rarely) damage the liver. Get immediate medical help if you develop any of the following: yellowing of the white part of your eyes or yellowing of your skin, dark-colored urine, light colored stool, or severe stomach pain with nausea.
- The liquid suspension should <u>not</u> be refrigerated.

Ketoconazole *(Nizoral)* and itraconazole *(Sporanox)*

- With ketoconazole and itraconazole: <u>do not use with antacids</u> (need two hour separation). These medicines will reduce the amount of the antifungal medicine that gets absorbed.
- Itraconazole tablets and capsules should be taken with food.
- Itraconazole solution should be taken on an empty stomach.

Voriconazole *(Vfend)*

- Avoid driving at night because this medicine may cause <u>vision problems</u> like blurry vision. If you have any change in your eyesight, avoid all driving or using dangerous machinery. Vision changes are temporary and reversible.
- Avoid sunlight. Your skin may burn more easily. Your eyes may hurt in bright sunlight.
- Take this medication by mouth <u>on an empty stomach</u>, at least 1 hour before or 1 hour after meals, usually every 12 hours or as directed.
- The liquid suspension should <u>not</u> be refrigerated.
- There are many interactions with this drug and other medicines. Please discuss with your pharmacist to make sure this will not pose a problem.
- Do not use this medication if you are pregnant, if you could become pregnant, or if you are breastfeeding.

Posaconazole *(Noxafil)*

- Posaconazole tablets should be taken with food; posaconazole suspension should be administered during or within 20 min following a full meal or oral liquid nutritional supplement to maximize absorption.

Nystatin

- If you are using the suspension form of this medication, shake well before using. Be sure to swish the medication around in your mouth for several minutes before swallowing.

Terbinafine *(Lamisil)*

- The most common side effect is headache. Temporary change or loss of taste and appetite and loss of smell can also occur.

- Terbinafine is used to treat certain types of fungal infections (e.g., fingernail or toenail). It works by stopping the growth of fungus.

- Take this medication by mouth with or without food, usually once a day. Dosage and length of treatment depend on the location of the fungus and the response to treatment.

- It may take several months after you finish treatment to see the full benefit of this drug. It takes time for your new healthy nails to grow out and replace the infected ones.

- Skipping doses or not completing the full course of therapy may ↓ effectiveness of treatment, cause the infection to return, and increase the likelihood that this medicine will not work for you in the future.

- This drug can (rarely) damage the liver. Get immediate medical help if you develop any of the following: yellowing of the white part of your eyes or yellowing of your skin, dark-colored urine, light colored stool, or bad stomach pain with severe nausea.

VIRAL INFECTIONS

Viruses are obligate intracellular parasites, depending on the host cell's metabolic processes for survival. Therapies available to treat viral infections work by either directly inhibiting viruses (antiviral agents) or augmenting or modifying host defenses to the viral infection (immunomodulating agents). Antivirals target critical steps in the viral life cycle, such as entry into the cell or replication. As viruses depend on hosts for metabolism/replication, antivirals may injure or destroy the host cells.

Many viral infections have no effective drug treatment. Medications are available to treat influenza virus, herpes simplex virus [genital herpes, herpes labialis (cold sores), and systemic herpes virus infections], varicella-zoster virus (VZV) and cytomegalovirus (CMV).

Influenza

Influenza is a respiratory virus that affects 5 – 20% of the U.S. population annually, with peak activity between late November and March. Influenza A and B are the strains that commonly infect humans and can cause severe illness, leading to hospitalization and death, particularly in at-risk patients (pregnant women, children age < 5 years, adults age > 65 years, immunocompromised patients and those with co-morbid conditions such as diabetes, asthma or cardiovascular disease). Influenza spreads via respiratory droplets generated by coughing and sneezing. A person with influenza can be contagious one day prior to developing symptoms and for up to 5 – 7 days after becoming ill. Influenza commonly presents with symptoms that include fever, chills, fatigue, body aches, cough, sore throat and headaches. The seasonal influenza vaccine is the most effective prevention for influenza infection and is recommended for all age ≥ 6 months. See Immunizations chapter.

Antivirals for Influenza

The Centers for Disease Control and Prevention (CDC) updates antiviral treatment recommendations based on the type of circulating virus during influenza season. Neuraminidase inhibitors (oseltamivir, zanamivir and peramivir) reduce the amount of virus in the body by inhibiting the enzyme which enables the release of new viral particles from infected cells. They are active against both influenza A and B and decrease the duration of symptoms by about 1 day. To be effective neuraminidase inhibitors should be started within 48 hours of illness onset. There is less benefit if started later, after the virus has already caused damage to respiratory epithelial cells. Adamantanes (rimantadine and amantadine) are only effective for influenza A, and in recent years have not been recommended as monotherapy due to resistance.

Neuraminidase Inhibitors

DRUG	DOSING	SAFETY/SIDE EFFECTS/MONITORING
Oseltamivir (*Tamiflu*) 30, 45, 75 mg capsules 6 mg/mL (60 mL) suspension 	**Treatment, age > 12 years:** 75 mg BID x 5 days **Prophylaxis, age > 12 years:** 75 mg daily x 10 days Pediatric patients (age 2 weeks-12 years): Dose is based on body weight. CrCl ≤ 60 mL/min: ↓ dose and/or extend interval	**WARNINGS** Neuropsychiatric events (sudden confusion, delirium, hallucinations, unusual behavior, or self-injury), serious skin reactions (SJS/TEN), anaphylaxis **SIDE EFFECTS** N/<u>V</u>/D, abdominal pain **NOTES** Pregnancy Category C
Zanamivir *(Relenza Diskhaler)* 	**Treatment, age ≥ 7 years:** 10 mg (two 5 mg inhalations) BID x 5 days **Prophylaxis, age ≥ 5 years:** 10 mg (two 5 mg inhalations) once daily x 10 days (household setting) or 28 days (community outbreak)	**WARNINGS** Neuropsychiatric events, <u>bronchospasm (do not use in asthma/COPD or</u> with any <u>breathing problems)</u>. Stop the drug if wheezing or breathing problems develop. **SIDE EFFECTS** Headache, throat pain, cough **NOTES** Pregnancy Category C
Peramivir *(Rapivab)* Injection	**Treatment (adult):** 600 mg IV as a single dose CrCl 30-49 mL/min: 200 mg IV x 1 CrCl 10-29 mL/min or intermittent hemodialysis: 100 mg IV x 1	**WARNINGS** Neuropsychiatric events (sudden confusion, delirium, hallucinations, unusual behavior, or self-injury), serious skin reactions (SJS/TEN), anaphylaxis **SIDE EFFECTS** Hypertension, insomnia, increased blood glucose, diarrhea, constipation, neutropenia,↑ AST/ALT **NOTES** Pregnancy Category C

Adamantanes

Rimantadine *(Flumadine)* Tablet Amantadine can be used for influenza prophylaxis and treatment, but has higher incidence adverse effects, and greater dose reductions are needed in renal impairment.	**Treatment/Prophylaxis:** 100 mg BID CrCl < 30 mL/min: 100 mg daily	**WARNINGS** Seizures – use with caution in patients with a history of seizure disorder. Psychosis – avoid use. **SIDE EFFECTS** N/V, loss of appetite, dry mouth, insomnia, impaired concentration. Amantadine has greater incidence of these side effects. **NOTES** See Parkinson Disease chapter for further information on amantadine.

Herpes Simplex Virus and Varicella Zoster Virus

Herpes simplex type 1 (HSV-1) is most commonly associated with oropharyngeal disease, and HSV-2 is associated more closely with genital disease. However, each virus is capable of causing infections clinically indistinguishable at both anatomic sites.

Infection with varicella zoster virus is commonly called chickenpox. After an occurrence of varicella zoster infection, the virus lies dormant in the nerve root and can later cause herpes zoster infection, often referred to as shingles.

The table below contains drug information on the antivirals used for herpes simplex and varicella zoster infections. Regimens used to treat different types of herpes virus infections and shingles, complete with dosing information, are detailed later.

DRUG	SAFETY/SIDE EFFECTS/MONITORING

Antivirals Used for Treatment of Herpes Simplex Virus (HSV), Varicella Zoster Virus (VZV)

Acyclovir (Zovirax, Sitavig) Capsule, tablet, buccal tablet, suspension, injection, topical Zovirax cream, Denavir, Sitavig – for cold sores (herpes simplex labialis)	**WARNINGS** Thrombocytopenic purpura/hemolytic uremic syndrome (TTP/HUS) has been reported in immunocompromised patients. Caution in patients with renal impairment, the elderly, and/or those receiving nephrotoxic agents. Infuse acyclovir over at least 1 hour and maintain adequate hydration to reduce risk of renal tubular damage. **SIDE EFFECTS** Malaise, headache, N/V/D, rash, pruritus, ↑ LFTs, neutropenia, ↑ SCr/BUN (crystal nephropathy), ↑ seizures (especially with IV formulation), transient burning or stinging with topical formulation
ValACYclovir (Valtrex) Tablet Prodrug of acyclovir	**MONITORING** Renal function, LFTs, CBC **NOTES** Pregnancy Category B
Famciclovir (Famvir) Tablet Prodrug of penciclovir	Acyclovir dose is based on IBW in obese patients. Infuse acyclovir over 1 hour to prevent renal damage. ↓ dose and/or extend interval in renal impairment. Store valacyclovir oral suspension in a refrigerator.

Cytomegalovirus

Cytomegalovirus (CMV) is a double-stranded DNA virus within the herpes virus family (HHV-5). It occurs in advanced immunocompromised states (e.g., HIV-AIDS, transplant recipients) and most commonly causes retinitis, colitis or esophagitis. Ganciclovir and valganciclovir are the treatments of choice for CMV disease. Foscarnet and cidofovir should be reserved for refractory cases of CMV infection, treatment limiting toxicities due to ganciclovir, and/or when the CMV strain is found to be resistant to (val)ganciclovir. Secondary prophylaxis (also called maintenance) is necessary in some patients (e.g., HIV patients with CMV retinitis and CD4+ counts < 50 cells/mm^3); valganciclovir is preferred.

DRUG	DOSING	SAFETY/SIDE EFFECTS/MONITORING

Antivirals Used for Treatment of Cytomegalovirus (CMV)

DRUG	DOSING	SAFETY/SIDE EFFECTS/MONITORING
Ganciclovir (*Cytovene* injection, *Zirgan* ophthalmic gel)	Treatment: 5 mg/kg IV BID Maintenance/secondary prophylaxis: 5 mg/kg IV daily ↓ dose and extend interval when CrCl < 70 mL/min Prepare in sterile water, <u>not</u> bacteriostatic (ganciclovir) Hazardous agents: Special handling required	**BOXED WARNINGS** <u>Myelosuppression</u>; carcinogenic and teratogenic effects and inhibition of spermatogenesis in animals **SIDE EFFECTS** Fever, N/V/D, anorexia, thrombocytopenia, neutropenia, <u>leukopenia, anemia</u>, ↑ SCr, seizures (rare), retinal detachment (valganciclovir) **MONITORING** CBC with differential, PLT, SCr, retinal exam (valganciclovir) **NOTES** Patients of reproductive potential: Females should use contraception during treatment and for 30 days after, males for 90 days. Pregnancy Category C (Ganciclovir) Potentially teratogenic; consider risk/benefit. (Valganciclovir) IV ganciclovir 5 mg/kg = PO valganciclovir 900 mg <u>Ganciclovir and valganciclovir are the drugs of choice for CMV disease.</u>
ValGANciclovir (*Valcyte*) Tablet, suspension <u>Prodrug of ganciclovir</u> with better bioavailability than oral ganciclovir.	Treatment: 900 mg PO BID x21 days Maintenance/secondary prophylaxis: 900 mg PO daily ↓ dose and extend interval when CrCl < 60 mL/min Hazardous agents: Special handling required	
Cidofovir (*Vistide*) Injection CMV retinitis in HIV patients <u>only</u>	5 mg/kg/wk IV x 2 weeks, then 5 mg/kg once every 2 weeks Hazardous agent: Special handling required Renal impairment: ↓ dose or discontinue based on level of SCr increase (also see Contraindications)	**BOXED WARNINGS** Dose-dependent <u>nephropathy</u>, neutropenia, carcinogenic/teratogenic **CONTRAINDICATIONS** SCr > 1.5 mg/dL, CrCl ≤ 55 mL/min, urine protein ≥ 100 mg/dL (> 2+ proteinuria), sulfa allergy, use with or within 7 days of other nephrotoxic drugs, direct intraocular injection **SIDE EFFECTS** Similar to ganciclovir with risk of <u>nephrotoxicity</u>; lower risk for myelosuppression, metabolic acidosis **NOTES** Pregnancy Category C Patient should receive hydration before each dose. Can decrease tenofovir clearance.
Foscarnet (*Foscavir*) Injection CMV, resistant HSV	Induction: 90 mg/kg IV Q12H or 60 mg/kg Q8H x 2-3 weeks Maintenance: 90-120 mg/kg IV daily Resistant HSV infection: 40 mg/kg Q8-12H x 2-3 weeks Renal impairment: ↓ dose and extend interval	**BOXED WARNINGS** <u>Renal impairment</u> occurs to some degree in <u>majority of patients</u>; seizures due to <u>electrolyte imbalances</u> **SIDE EFFECTS** Electrolyte abnormalities (↓ K, ↓ Ca, ↓ Mg, ↓ Phos), <u>↑ SCr</u>, ↑ BUN **NOTES** Vesicant (central line preferred)

Genital Herpes

Genital herpes is a chronic, life-long viral infection. One in six people in the U.S. have HSV-2. The first episode of genital herpes usually begins within 2-14 days post exposure, but up to 50% of patients are asymptomatic. Symptoms of the first episode can include flu-like symptoms, fever, headache, malaise, myalgia, and development of pustular or ulcerative lesions on external genitalia. Lesions usually begin as papules or vesicles that rapidly spread and clusters of lesions form, crust, and re-epithelialize. Lesions are described as painful. Itching, dysuria, and vaginal or urethral discharge are common symptoms. Recurrent infections are not associated with systemic manifestations. Symptoms are localized to the genital area, milder, and of shorter duration. Patients typically experience a prodrome prior to symptoms.

Treatment must be initiated during prodrome or within 1 day of lesion onset for the patient to experience the full benefit. Suppressive therapy reduces the frequency of genital herpes recurrences by 70-80% among patients who have frequent recurrences (e.g., > 6 recurrences/year) and many report no symptomatic outbreaks. Viral transmission is also reduced. Acyclovir *(Zovirax)* is the least expensive regimen, however, it must be dosed up to 5 times per day. Valacyclovir *(Valtrex)* is a prodrug of acyclovir that results in higher concentrations than with oral acyclovir and less frequent dosing that may enhance adherence. In general, 5 mg/kg IV acyclovir = 1,000 mg PO valacyclovir. If the virus is found to be resistant to acyclovir, it will be resistant to valacyclovir. Famciclovir *(Famvir)* is a pro-drug of penciclovir. Strains resistant to acyclovir are generally resistant to famciclovir. Infections caused by acyclovir-resistant HSV are treated with foscarnet until the lesions heal.

In addition to causing genital herpes, HSV is the most commonly identified cause of acute, sporadic viral encephalitis in the United States. Clinical symptoms include acute onset of fever and focal neurologic symptoms. Diagnosis can be difficult; the most sensitive noninvasive method is by the detection of HSV DNA by PCR of CSF fluid. Intravenous therapy is used for up to 3 weeks for this indication.

Herpes Simplex Virus Treatment In Non-HIV Patients

HSV INFECTION	ACYCLOVIR	VALACYCLOVIR	FAMCICLOVIR
Primary – initial episode			
Genital HSV	400 mg PO TID x 7-10 days or 200 mg PO 5x daily x 10 days Treatment can be extended if healing is incomplete after 10 days of therapy	1 gram PO BID x 10 days	250 mg PO TID x 10 days
Oral HSV	200 mg PO 5x daily or 400 mg TID x 7-10 days		
HSV encephalitis	10 mg/kg IV q8h x 14-21 days		
Recurrent episodes			
Genital HSV	400 mg PO TID x 5 days or 800 mg PO BID x 5 days or 800 mg PO TID x 2 days	500 mg PO BID x 3 days or 1 gram PO daily x 5 days	125 mg PO BID x 5 days or 1 gram PO BID x 1 day or 500 mg PO x 1, then 250 mg PO BID x 2 days
Oral HSV	200 mg PO 5x daily x 5 days or 400 mg PO TID x 5 days or 800 mg PO BID x 5 days	1-2 grams PO BID x 1 day	1.5 grams PO x 1 dose
Chronic suppression (daily therapy)			
Genital HSV	400 mg PO BID	500 mg PO daily or 1 gram PO daily	250 mg PO BID
Oral HSV	400 mg PO BID		

Varicella Zoster Virus and Herpes Zoster

Most people in the U.S. have had varicella zoster virus (chickenpox) infection during childhood. The virus can lie dormant in the nerve for decades without causing any symptoms. The recurrence of viral symptoms is called herpes zoster or shingles. The risk of herpes zoster increases with age, and older patients are more likely to experience postherpetic neuralgia, non-pain complications, hospitalizations, and interference with activities of daily living. An outbreak may occur as the patient ages, and is often due to acute stress. Although herpes zoster can occur at any age, adults > 60 years old are most often affected. The shingles rash is distinctive – it can be itchy or tingly, is very painful and often manifests unilaterally. Pharmacists should be able to recognize a shingles rash and inform patients to see a physician; refer to the following image.

Shingles vaccine *(Zostavax)* can prevent shingles and shingles-related complications. It is FDA approved for use in patients 50+ years of age and is recommended by ACIP for patients age 60+ years of age. It can be used in patients who have experienced a previous shingles outbreak to decrease likelihood of recurrence and postherpetic neuralgia. See Immunizations chapter.

Antiviral therapy should be initiated at the earliest sign or symptom of shingles and is most effective when started within 72 hours of the onset of zoster rash. Pain can be treated with topical agents (*Lido-*

derm patch, lidocaine viscous gel) or with neuropathic pain agents (anticonvulsants, antidepressants), and sometimes with NSAIDs or opioids. Most recover without long-term aftereffects; 5 – 10% have chronic pain, which can be debilitating.

Herpes Zoster (Shingles) Treatment

DRUG	DOSING	DESCRIPTION
Acyclovir *(Zovirax)*	800 mg PO 5x daily for 7-10 days	
Famciclovir *(Famvir)*	500 mg PO TID for 7 days	
Valacyclovir *(Valtrex)*	1 gram PO TID for 7 days	A cluster of fluid-filled blisters, often in a band around one side of the waist or on one side of the forehead, or around an eye or on the neck (less commonly anywhere else on the body).

Herpes Simplex Labialis (Cold Sores)

Cold sores are ubiquitous and are highly contagious. Children often pick up the infection from family members. Infection is usually due to HSV-1 in children, but can be caused by HSV-2 when older due to oral/genital sex. Virus can be shed when asymptomatic but is most commonly spread with active lesions; kissing, sharing drinks should be avoided when lesions are oozing. Sore eruption is preceded by prodromal symptoms (tingling, itching, soreness). In most patients the sore appears in the same location repeatedly. The most common site is the junction between the upper and lower lip. Triggers that cause sore outbreaks include fatigue/stress, stress to the skin (sun exposure, acid peels) and dental work. Patients should identify their own trigger/s and attempt to avoid them. The prodromal period is the optimal time to apply topical or take oral medication to reduce blister duration. If recurrences are frequent (> 4 times/year), chronic suppression, taken daily, can be used. OTC and Rx topicals shorten the duration by up to one day; oral (systemic) antivirals shorten the duration by up to two days. The *Natural Medicines Database* lists lysine as possibly effective for cold sore prevention.

DRUGS	DOSING	NOTES
Docosanol *(Abreva)* OTC	Apply 5x daily at first sign of outbreak, continue until healed.	Systemic antivirals are more effective.
Acyclovir topical cream *(Zovirax)* Rx	Apply 5x daily for 4 days (can be used on genital sores).	
Acyclovir buccal tablet *(Sitavig)* Rx	Apply 50 mg tablet as a single dose to the upper gum region.	
Penciclovir topical cream *(Denavir)* Rx	Apply every 2 hours during waking hours for 4 days.	

Epstein-Barr Virus

This virus, also called EBV, is a member of the herpes virus family. Infectious EBV is called <u>mononucleosis</u> or "mono" and most people get infected with EBV at some point in their lives. It is transmitted through bodily fluids, primarily saliva, and can <u>spread by kissing</u>, sharing drinks or food, or contact with an object that has been in the mouth of an infected person (e.g., children's toys). Common symptoms are fatigue, fever, sore throat and swollen lymph nodes, and usually resolve in 2 – 4 weeks. No drug treatment or vaccine exists for mononucleosis.

West Nile Virus

West Nile Virus (WNV) is part of the Japanese encephalitis virus antigenic complex and is transmitted via mosquitos. Most patients remain asymptomatic; only ~20% show symptoms of fever, headache, or other flu-like symptoms but < 1% can develop encephalitis or meningitis. Treatment of WNV is primarily supportive as there are no antivirals with good activity against WNV. Prevention while outdoors is key:

- Use mosquito repellent with DEET, picaridin, oil of lemon eucalyptus (CDC recommended products only) or IR3535.

- Wear protective clothing (long sleeves and pants).

- Avoid/eliminate standing or stagnant water which are breeding grounds for mosquitos.

Antiviral Patient Counseling

Oseltamivir (Tamiflu)

- Treatment should begin within 2 days of onset of influenza symptoms.

- The most common side effects are nausea and vomiting. Take with or without food. There is less chance of stomach upset if you take it with a light snack, milk, or a meal.

- Patients with the flu, particularly children and adolescents, may be at an ↑ risk of self-injury and confusion shortly after taking this medicine and should be closely monitored for signs of unusual behavior. Contact your healthcare provider immediately if you or your loved ones show any signs of unusual behavior.

- Tell your healthcare provider if you have received the nasally administered influenza virus vaccine during the past two weeks (there is a risk that *Tamiflu* may inhibit replication of the live virus vaccine).

Acyclovir (Zovirax)

- This medicine works best when taken at the first sign of an outbreak within the first day.

- The most common side effects are malaise (a generally ill feeling), headache, nausea and diarrhea.

- Take this medication by mouth with or without food, usually 2 to 5 times daily, as directed. The intervals should be evenly spaced.

- Drink plenty of fluids while taking this medication.

- The topical cream may cause temporary burning or stinging.

Valacyclovir (Valtrex)

- *Valtrex* is used daily to manage herpes simplex, and when used along with the following safer sex practices can lower the chances of passing genital herpes to your partner.
  - ❏ Do not have sexual contact when you have any symptom or outbreak of genital herpes.
  - ❏ Use a condom made of latex or polyurethane whenever you have sexual contact.

- This medication does not cure herpes infections (cold sores, chickenpox, shingles, or genital herpes).

- This medication can be taken with or without food. If stomach upset occurs, take with meals.

- Start treatment during prodrome or within 24 hours of the onset of symptoms. This medication is less helpful if you start treatment too late.

- The most common side effects are tiredness and headache. These side effects are usually mild and do not cause patients to stop taking the medication.

- Store suspension in a refrigerator. Discard after 21 days.

Malaria

Drugs used for malaria prophylaxis are in the Travelers Chapter. Check the CDC website for updated resistance patterns.

ANTIPARASITICALS

Pinworm *(Vermicularis)* Infection

Approximately 40 million persons in the U.S. are infected with *Enterobius vermicularis* (pinworms). Pinworm infection most commonly occurs in children age 5 – 10 years and presents as perianal itching, predominantly at night. Person-to-person transmission can occur by eating contaminated food or handling contaminated clothes; hands should be washed frequently. The "tape" test is used to identify eggs: stick a piece of tape around the anus in the morning prior to voiding/defecating. It can take up to 3 morning tape tests to identify the eggs. Reinfection after treatment is common.

Pinworm Treatment

DRUGS	DOSING	SAFETY/NOTES
Pyrantel pamoate (*Pamix, Pin-X, Reeses*) – OTC Tablet, chewable, suspension	11 mg/kg x1. Max: 1 gram	**SIDE EFFECTS** HA (both agents), dizziness (pyrantel), nausea and ↑ LFTs (albendazole)
Albendazole (*Albenza*) – Rx Tablet, chewable	400 mg PO x1, then repeat in 2 weeks Take with a high-fat meal. Can also be used at different dose/duration for neurocysticercosis (parasite infection in the brain). Neurocysticercosis: give concurrently with anticonvulsants and high-dose glucocorticoids to decrease CNS inflammation.	

Questions

1. A patient is on amphotericin B for treatment of cryptococcal meningitis. Which of the following electrolyte abnormalities need to be monitored during therapy?

   a. Hypocalcemia and hypomagnesemia
   b. Hyponatremia and hypokalemia
   c. Hypernatremia and hyperkalemia
   d. Hypokalemia and hypernatremia
   e. Hypokalemia and hypomagnesemia

2. Which of the following statements is/are correct regarding *Vfend*? (Select **ALL** that apply.)

   a. *Vfend* can cause visual changes and patients should be instructed not to operate heavy machinery while taking the medication.
   b. *Vfend* must be taken on an empty stomach.
   c. *Vfend* oral tablets should not be used in patients with poor renal function.
   d. *Vfend* oral suspension should be refrigerated.
   e. *Vfend* is a preferred agent for *Aspergillosis* infections.

3. An intern in the ED asks about treating genital herpes simplex virus and *Valtrex*. Which of the following statements is correct regarding *Valtrex*?

   a. *Valtrex* is a prodrug of acyclovir and can be used as suppressive therapy in patients with herpes simplex virus.
   b. *Valtrex* is a prodrug of penciclovir and should not be used as suppressive therapy in patients with herpes simplex virus.
   c. *Valtrex* should only be used for herpes zoster virus.
   d. *Valtrex* needs to be taken with a fatty meal for best absorption.
   e. *Valtrex* is contraindicated in patients with a CrCl < 30 mL/min.

4. A patient has been receiving *Noxafil* suspension for antifungal prophylaxis during cancer chemotherapy treatment. She has a new prescription for *Noxafil* tablets because she experienced nausea with the suspension and her mucositis has improved to the point that she can now swallow a tablet. Which of the following statements is incorrect?

   a. An appropriate maintenance dose for posaconazole tablets is 300 mg PO daily.
   b. An appropriate dose for posaconazole suspension is 200 mg PO TID.
   c. The suspension is better absorbed than the tablets.
   d. Atorvastatin is contraindicated with posaconazole.
   e. Posaconazole suspension should not be refrigerated.

5. The medical resident in the clinic asks the pharmacist for a recommendation for shingles treatment in a 71 year old female. She is 5'3" tall, weighs 118 pounds and has a serum creatinine of 1.0 mg/dL. Which of the following would be an appropriate regimen? (Select ALL that apply).

   a. Famciclovir 500 mg PO TID for 7 days
   b. Acyclovir 800 mg PO 5x daily for 7-10 days
   c. Valganciclovir 1,000 mg PO TID for 7 days
   d. Acyclovir cream applied 5x daily for 7-10 days
   e. Valacyclovir 500 mg PO TID for 10 days

Answers

1-e, 2-a,b,e, 3-a, 4-c, 5-a,b

INFECTIOUS DISEASES IV: OPPORTUNISTIC INFECTIONS

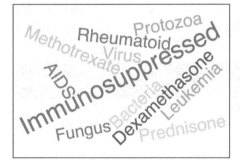

We gratefully acknowledge the assistance of Emi Minejima, PharmD, Assistant Professor, and Annie Wong-Beringer, PharmD, FCCP, FIDSA, Associate Dean and Professor, University of Southern California School of Pharmacy, in preparing this chapter.

BACKGROUND

Immunocompromised patients are predisposed to infections with a variety of pathogens, including <u>bacteria, fungi, viruses</u> and <u>protozoa</u>. These are called <u>opportunistic infections (OIs)</u> because they occur primarily when the <u>immune system is unable to respond</u> in a normal manner. The risk can be related to a disease or to drug treatment that suppresses the immune system. Immunocompromised states include:

- <u>Diseases</u> that destroy key components of the immune response (primarily HIV patients with a CD4+ T lymphocyte count < 200 cells/microliter).

- Systemic <u>steroids</u> taken for 14 days or longer at a dose ≥ 2 mg/kg/day or ≥ 20 mg prednisone or prednisone equivalent.

- <u>Asplenia</u> (lack of a functioning spleen), as with sickle cell disease or following a splenectomy.

- Use of strong <u>immunosuppressants</u> for autoimmune conditions or transplant (e.g., TNF-alpha inhibitors).

- Use of <u>cancer chemotherapy</u> agents that destroy white blood cells.

PRIMARY PROPHYLAXIS IN PATIENTS WITH MALIGNANCIES

Patients with malignancies undergoing chemotherapy are at high risk for opportunistic infections, which contributes to morbidity and mortality. Severe neutropenia (<u>ANC <500</u>) is a <u>major risk factor for the development of infections</u> and effective strategies to anticipate, prevent, and manage infectious complications can greatly improve outcomes. Without neutrophils, patients are highly susceptible to Gram-negative pathogens, fungal infections, and viral infections. Antimicrobials are used for prevention of these infectious diseases. Patients are stratified by their malignancy, anticipated duration of neutropenia, and the risk for the particular infection. Antibiotic prophylaxis often consists of a quinolone (primarily levofloxacin). Antifungal prophylaxis commonly involves fluconazole or an echinocandin. In higher risk patients where mold/*Mucor* coverage is necessary, amphotericin B, voriconazole or posaconazole may be used. Antivirals are used for patients at intermediate-to-high risk of infection and typical agents include acyclovir, valacyclovir and famciclovir. Patients who develop a fever while neutropenic receive presumptive treatment with specific antimicrobial regimens based on current guidelines.

PRIMARY PROPHYLAXIS IN PATIENTS WITH HIV

HIV-infected patients not taking antiretroviral therapy (ART) are at risk for developing OIs as a result of uncontrolled HIV infection and progressive immunosuppression. Patients are at higher risk for specific OIs as CD4+ counts decline. The table below outlines select OIs, CD4+ count at which the patient becomes at risk for the infection, and the primary prophylaxis regimen that should be initiated to prevent the first episode of the infection. Oropharyngeal and esophageal *Candida* infections (also called thrush) also occur when the CD4+ count is < 200 cells/mm³. These infections are generally less severe (low morbidity and mortality) and resolve quickly with fluconazole treatment. No prophylaxis (primary or secondary) is recommended for candidiasis. Note that although the species name of *Pneumocystis* was changed from *carinii* to *jirovecii*, pneumonia caused by this organism is still commonly referred to as PCP, or sometimes PJP.

PATHOGEN	INDICATION	PRIMARY PROPHYLAXIS REGIMEN	CRITERIA FOR DISCONTINUING PRIMARY PROPHYLAXIS
Pneumocystis pneumonia (PCP)	CD4+ count < 200 cells/mm³ or oropharyngeal candidiasis	Preferred: SMX/TMP 1 DS tab PO daily or 1 SS PO daily Alternative: SMX/TMP 1 DS PO TIW or dapsone 100 mg PO daily or 50 mg PO BID, or (dapsone 50 mg PO daily + pyrimethamine 50 mg PO weekly + leucovorin 25 mg PO weekly), or aerosolized pentamidine, or atovaquone	CD4+ count ≥ 200 cells/mm³ for > 3 months on ART
Toxoplasma gondii	Toxoplasma IgG positive patients with CD4+ count < 100 cells/mm³	Preferred: SMX/TMP 1 DS tab PO daily Alternative: SMX/TMP 1 DS PO TIW or 1 SS PO daily or (dapsone 50 mg PO daily + pyrimethamine 50 mg PO weekly + leucovorin 25 mg PO weekly) or (atovaquone alone, or with pyrimethamine + leucovorin)	CD4+ count > 200 cells/mm³ for > 3 months on ART
Mycobacterium avium complex (MAC)	CD4+ count < 50 cells/mm³ after active disseminated MAC disease is ruled out	Preferred: azithromycin 1,200 mg PO weekly or clarithromycin 500 mg PO BID or azithromycin 600 mg PO twice weekly	CD4+ count > 100 cells/mm³ for ≥ 3 months on ART

TREATMENT OF OPPORTUNISTIC INFECTIONS

Treatment for each infection remains the same, regardless of the cause of immunosuppression. Newly diagnosed patients with HIV and an OI should be monitored closely for immune reconstitution inflammatory syndrome (IRIS) when antiretroviral therapy (ART) is started (see Human Immunodeficiency Virus chapter). The table below lists select OIs and the recommended agents for treatment. Secondary prophylaxis is given to prevent future episodes/recurrence of the infection, and should be started after completing initial treatment for the infection in patients who continue to be at risk.

PATHOGEN	FIRST LINE TREATMENT	ALTERNATIVE TREATMENT	SECONDARY PROPHYLAXIS
Candidiasis (oropharyngeal/ esophageal)	Fluconazole	Itraconazole Posaconazole	None

PATHOGEN	FIRST LINE TREATMENT	ALTERNATIVE TREATMENT	SECONDARY PROPHYLAXIS
Cytomegalovirus (CMV)	Valganciclovir Ganciclovir	For resistant strains: Foscarnet, cidofovir	Valganciclovir
Cryptococcal meningitis	Induction: Amphotericin B deoxycholate + flucytosine	Induction: Liposomal amphotericin B + flucytosine or Fluconazole ± flucytosine	Fluconazole (low dose)
Mycobacterium avium complex infection	(Clarithromycin or azithromycin) + ethambutol	Add a 3rd or 4th agent using rifabutin, amikacin or streptomycin, moxifloxacin or levofloxacin	Same as treatment regimens
Pneumocystis pneumonia (PCP)	SMX/TMP ± prednisone or methylprednisolone Duration: 21 days	Atovaquone or (clindamycin + primaquine) or pentamidine IV or (dapsone + trimethoprim)*	SMX/TMP or dapsone or (dapsone + pyrimethamine**) or atovaquone or inhaled pentamidine
Toxoplasmosis meningoencephalitis	Pyrimethamine** + sulfadiazine	SMX/TMP, (pyrimethamine** + either clindamycin or azithromycin), (atovaquone alone, or with sulfadiazine or with pyrimethamine**)	Same agents at reduced dosed

* Selection of alternative therapy for PCP depends on severity of illness and patient specific factors (allergies and G6PD deficiency). For example, atovaquone, clindamycin + primaquine or pentamidine are all potential options in the setting of sulfa allergy, however only atovaquone (mild-to-moderate disease) and pentamidine (moderate-severe disease) are available options in the setting of G6PD deficiency.

** Leucovorin added as rescue therapy to reduce risk for myelosuppression associated with pyrimethamine.

Questions

Questions 1 and 2 refer to the following case:

RY is a 24 year old male with AIDS who presents to the HIV clinic for a routine follow-up visit. He states that he was unable to pick up his prescriptions and hasn't taken his antiretroviral therapy for the past 4 months. His CD4 count is found to be 94 cells/mm³.

1. Prophylaxis for which opportunistic infection/s should be initiated in RY? (Select **ALL** that apply.)

   a. *Toxoplasmosis* only

   b. *Pneumocystis* pneumonia, *Toxoplasmosis* and *Mycobacterium avium* complex

   c. *Pneumocystis* pneumonia and *Toxoplasmosis*

   d. *Mycobacterium avium* complex only

   e. *Toxoplasmosis* and *Mycobacterium avium* complex

2. Choose the statements that are true regarding the prophylaxis regimen that should be started for RY: (Select **ALL** that apply.)

   a. SMX/TMP DS PO daily will cover both *Pneumocystis* pneumonia and *Toxoplasmosis*

   b. SMX/TMP DS PO daily is the preferred regimen

   c. Dapsone could be used in place of SMX/TMP if the patient had G6PD deficiency

   d. Azithromycin should be dosed at 600 mg PO daily

   e. Prophylaxis should continue until the CD4 count is > 200 cells/mm³

3. A patient is receiving azithromycin for prophylaxis of *Mycobacterium avium* complex. Which of the following would be concerning if added to the patient's medications?

   a. Nystatin swish and swallow

   b. Amiodarone

   c. Omeprazole

   d. Lisinopril

   e. Spironolactone

Answers

1-c, 2-a,b,e, 3-b

HUMAN IMMUNODEFICIENCY VIRUS

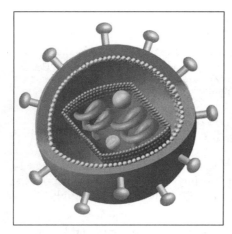

We gratefully acknowledge the assistance of Nancy N. Nguyen, PharmD, BCPS, AAHIVP, FCSHP, Clinical Professor at the University of the Pacific Thomas J. Long School of Pharmacy and Health Sciences, in preparing this chapter.

BACKGROUND

The first cases of Human Immunodeficiency Virus (HIV)/Acquired Immunodeficiency Syndrome (AIDS) were reported in 1981. The Centers for Disease Control and Prevention now estimates that there are more than 1.2 million people in the United States living with HIV infection, and about 1 out of every 8 persons is unaware that they are infected. HIV is an RNA retrovirus that attacks the immune system, mainly the CD4+ T-helper cells, causing a progressive decrease in CD4+ T cell count. Once CD4+ counts fall below a critical level, the person becomes more susceptible to opportunistic infections (OIs) and certain malignancies due to the loss of cell-mediated immunity. CD4+ count is the major laboratory indicator of immune function in HIV-1 infected patients and serves as a key factor in determining the need for prophylaxis against OIs. See Infectious Diseases IV chapter for more information on OIs. Plasma HIV-1 RNA (viral load) should be measured in all HIV-1 infected patients at baseline and on a regular basis thereafter, especially in patients who are on treatment, since viral

GUIDELINES/REFERENCES

Panel on Antiretroviral Guidelines for Adults and Adolescents. Guidelines for the use of antiretroviral agents in HIV-1-infected adults and adolescents. Department of Health and Human Services. Available at: http://aidsinfo.nih.gov/contentfiles/lvguidelines/adultandadolescentgl.pdf. Accessed 2015 November 18.

Panel on Treatment of HIV-Infected Pregnant Women and Prevention of Perinatal Transmission. Recommendations for Use of Antiretroviral Drugs in Pregnant HIV-1-Infected Women for Maternal Health and Interventions to Reduce Perinatal HIV Transmission in the United States. Available at: http://aidsinfo.nih.gov/contentfiles/lvguidelines/perinatalgl.pdf. Accessed 2015 November 7.

Panel on Opportunistic Infections in HIV-Infected Adults and Adolescents. Guidelines for the prevention and treatment of opportunistic infections in HIV-infected adults and adolescents: recommendations from the Centers for Disease Control and Prevention, the National Institutes of Health, and the HIV Medicine Association of the Infectious Diseases Society of America. Available at: http://aidsinfo.nih.gov/contentfiles/lvguidelines/adult_oi.pdf. Accessed 2015 November 7.

Addtional guidelines included with the video files (RxPrep Online).

load is the most important <u>indicator of response to antiretroviral therapy</u>. The <u>viral load</u> quantifies the degree of viremia by measuring the copies of HIV RNA in the blood. It is used to <u>assess response to drug therapy, disease progression</u> (along with CD4+ count) and <u>possible medication adherence problems or drug resistance</u>.

TRANSMISSION

HIV can be spread through infected <u>blood</u>, <u>semen</u>, and <u>vaginal secretions</u>. Unprotected intercourse and sharing needles with HIV-infected individuals are the two most common means of HIV transmission. The entry of the virus via sexual exposure may be facilitated through the presence of sores or cuts in the vagina, penis, rectum, or mouth. Vertical transmission (from mother to child) may also occur, either during <u>pregnancy</u>, <u>at birth</u>, or through <u>breastfeeding</u>.

DIAGNOSIS

In an acute HIV infection, there is an initial burst of viremia immediately following the initial contraction/infection. Persons with acute HIV infection may experience non-specific flu-like symptoms, such as fever, fatigue/malaise, myalgias/arthralgias, lymphadenopathy, and rash, although many persons may not recognize that they have developed an acute HIV infection since symptoms, if present, are self-limiting. <u>Anti-HIV antibodies (HIV Ab)</u> are undetectable at this time, however, HIV RNA and HIV p24 antigen will be present. Following this acute phase of the infection, HIV Ab test will usually become positive about 4 – 8 weeks after contracting the disease; for some individuals, it may take up to 3 – 6 months for HIV Ab to be detected. Recent infection is generally considered the phase up to 6 months after the onset of the infection during which HIV Ab are detectable.

The <u>gold standard</u> diagnostic test is the HIV immunoassay screening test [also referred to as <u>HIV ELISA</u> (enzyme-linked immunosorbent assay)] which tests for the presence of HIV Ab in a person's blood sample. A positive HIV screening test may not always represent true infection (due to rare chance of false-positive tests) and therefore all positive screening tests must be followed by a second supplemental test. <u>Diagnosis of HIV is confirmed when both the HIV immunoassay screening and supplemental tests are positive.</u> As of June 2014, the CDC recommends the following HIV testing algorithm:

- Initial HIV screening should be conducted using a FDA-approved combination HIV Ab and HIV p24 antigen immunoassay test.

- If the initial screening test is reactive (positive), then a supplemental testing with a secondary HIV Ab immunoassay test should be performed.

- If the initial test is reactive but the secondary test is non-reactive or indeterminate, then a third test should be conducted using the HIV-1 nucleic acid test.

HIV rapid tests are essentially simplified HIV ELISA tests which screen for the presence of HIV Ab using either a fingerstick blood or an oral swab sample. These tests are available for point of care testing and as in-home test kits (see Over-the-Counter HIV Testing below). Of note, the CDC testing recommendations do not include HIV rapid test in the testing algorithm. Therefore, all patients with positive HIV rapid tests should undergo further HIV testing using the recommended testing algorithm.

The CDC recommends routine HIV screening for patients aged 13 – 64 years old in all healthcare settings (unless the patient declines testing). Additionally, pregnant women and patients initiating treatment for tuberculosis or sexually transmitted infections should also be tested for HIV. Persons at high risk for HIV (e.g., injection drug users, persons with high-risk sexual behaviors) should be tested for HIV at least annually. Persons with positive HIV tests should be referred for HIV medical care and receive initial evaluation, including testing for CD4+ counts and HIV viral load.

Over-the-Counter HIV Testing

There are 2 over-the-counter HIV tests patients can do at home. The *Home Access Express HIV-1 Test System* is a blood test where the patient collects the sample of blood from a fingerstick, ships the sample in a pre-paid overnight envelope, and obtains results the next day (excluding weekends and holidays). The *OraQuick In-Home HIV Test* is an oral swab test where results are obtained in 20-40 minutes. Individuals with a positive OTC HIV home test result must follow-up with their healthcare provider for a confirmatory HIV Ab laboratory-based test. These are HIV Ab screening tests, meaning they can detect the presence of HIV Ab which may take up to 3 months after onset of infection to develop. The tests are most accurate after 3 months from the risk event; therefore, testing sooner than 3 months can lead to a false negative result.

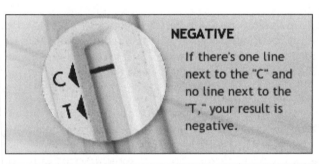

NEGATIVE

If there's one line next to the "C" and no line next to the "T," your result is negative.

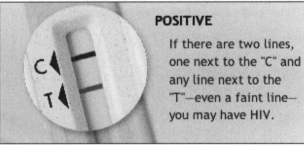

POSITIVE

If there are two lines, one next to the "C" and any line next to the "T"—even a faint line—you may have HIV.

HOW TO TAKE THE *ORAQUICK* TEST

- Do not eat, drink, or use oral care products at least 30 minutes before taking the test. Remove dental products such as dentures that cover your gums.

- Tear open the packet labeled "Test Tube". There is liquid in this tube so be careful upon opening not to spill the liquid. Pop off the cap, do not twist.

- Open the packet labeled "Test Stick". Do not touch the pad with your fingers. Gently swipe the pad along your upper gums once and your lower gums once. You may use either side on the flat pad. Make sure you swipe each gum only once or your results could be wrong (do not swab the roof of the mouth, inside of the cheek, or the tongue).

- Insert the test stick into the test tube which contains liquid at the bottom. Write down your start time. Then add 20 minutes and write down this number, which is your read time.

- Read the results after 20 minutes but not later than 40 minutes. Do not remove the test stick from the liquid while the test is running.

- If there is one line next to "C" and no line next to "T", your test result is negative. If there are 2 lines, one next to "C" and any line next to "T" (even a faint one), your test result is positive for HIV Ab; consult with your healthcare provider for a confirmatory test. The test is considered invalid if no line appears next to "C" or no lines appear at all.

Initial Evaluation and Monitoring

Initial evaluation of newly infected patients should include a discussion on the benefits of ART for the patient's health and to prevent transmission. It is recommended that the following laboratory parameters be measured for all HIV-infected individuals:

- CD4+ count and HIV viral load (an increase in viral load generally indicates inadequate treatment response and/or drug resistance while a decrease in the CD4+ count is a predictor of disease progression) – prior to ART initiation or modification, 2 – 8 weeks post initiation, then every 3 – 6 months thereafter

- Drug resistance testing – at entry into care regardless of ART initiation, at ART initiation and at ART modification

- Comprehensive metabolic panel (includes LFTs, SCr, glucose), CBC with differential, and lipid panel – prior to ART initiation or modification and every 6 – 12 months thereafter

HIV Replication Cycle Stages and the Antiretrovirals Site of Action

It is <u>very important to understand the steps (or stages)</u> involved in <u>HIV viral replication</u> and know where <u>each drug class works</u>. See following diagram.

STAGE	DESCRIPTION OF STAGE	DRUG CLASS TARGETING THIS STAGE
Stage 1: Binding/Attachment	HIV attaches to a CD4 receptor and either a CCR5 or CXCR4 co-receptor on the surface of the CD4+ host cell. The virus must bind/attach to both a CD4 receptor and a co-receptor in order for the next step of viral replication to occur.	CCR5 Antagonist (blocks only the CCR5 co-receptor but not the CXCR4 co-receptor)
Stage 2: Fusion	Fusion of the HIV viral envelope with the CD4+ host cell membrane allows HIV to enter the host cell, where uncoating of the virus releases HIV RNA and viral proteins and enzymes needed for HIV replication into the host cell's cytoplasm.	Fusion Inhibitors
Stage 3: Reverse Transcription	HIV RNA is converted to HIV DNA by reverse transcriptase.	Nucleoside/Nucleotide Reverse Transcriptase Inhibitors (NRTIs) and Non-Nucleoside Reverse Transcriptase Inhibitors (NNRTIs)
Stage 4: Integration	HIV DNA is transported across the host cell nuclear membrane and is integrated into the host cell's DNA.	Integrase Strand Transfer Inhibitors (INSTIs)
Stage 5: Transcription and Translation	HIV DNA is transcribed and translated into new HIV RNA as well as new viral proteins such as envelope proteins and non-functional long-chain proteins.	
Stage 6: Assembly	New HIV RNA, viral envelope proteins, and non-functional long-chain viral proteins migrate to the host cell surface to begin forming new, immature HIV virus. Protease enzyme is also incorporated into this newly forming HIV virus.	
Stage 7: Budding and Maturation	Newly formed, immature HIV virus buds off from the host cell. During the maturation process, protease cleaves the long-chain viral proteins into smaller, functional viral proteins and enzymes. The mature HIV virus is now able to move on to infect other CD4+ host cells.	Protease Inhibitors (PIs)

ANTIRETROVIRAL THERAPY

Treatment for HIV requires combination antiretroviral therapy (ART). <u>ART has dramatically reduced HIV-associated morbidity and mortality</u> and, although <u>not curative</u>, has transformed HIV disease into a chronic, manageable condition. Without treatment, the vast majority of HIV-infected individuals will eventually develop progressive immunosuppression (as evident by low CD4+ count), leading to OIs and premature death. <u>The primary goals of ART are to: restore and preserve the immune system, suppress HIV viral load to undetectable levels, reduce HIV-associated morbidity, prolong survival and prevent HIV transmission</u>.

<u>ART is recommended in all HIV-infected individuals</u> to reduce risk of disease progression and, in combination with safer sex/behavior risk reduction practices, to prevent transmission of HIV to non-HIV-infected individuals. On a case-by-case basis, ART may be deferred due to clinical and/or psychosocial factors, but therapy should be initiated

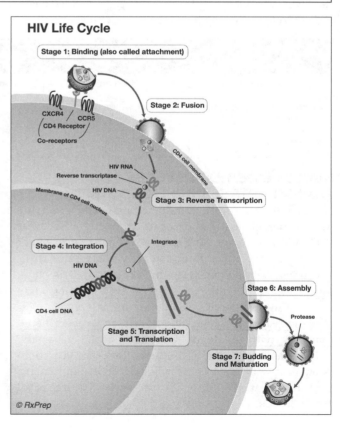

HIV Life Cycle

Stage 1: Binding (also called attachment)

Stage 2: Fusion

CXCR4 / CCR5
CD4 Receptor
Co-receptors

CD4 cell membrane

HIV RNA
Reverse transcriptase
HIV DNA
Membrane of CD4 cell nucleus

Stage 3: Reverse Transcription

Stage 4: Integration
Integrase
HIV DNA
CD4 cell DNA

Stage 5: Transcription and Translation

Stage 6: Assembly
Protease

Stage 7: Budding and Maturation

© RxPrep

as soon as is feasible. Patients starting ART should be willing and able to commit to treatment and understand the benefits and risks of therapy and the importance of adherence. Patients need to be advised that they need to have an adherence rate of 95% or higher in order for their ART regimen to be effective long-term. An example of 95% or higher adherence is no more than 1 missed dose per month for a patient who is taking a once daily regimen.

Recommended Regimens For Antiretroviral-Naïve HIV-1 Infected Patients

Selection of an ART regimen should be individualized based on efficacy, toxicity, pill burden, dosing frequency, drug interaction potential, resistance test results, and comorbid conditions. Below lists currently recommended initial ART regimen options for treatment-naive patients. Recommended regimens have optimal and durable efficacy, favorable tolerability and toxicity profile and ease of use. These regimens are listed in alphabetical order, not by order of preference. [Note: HIV treatment guidelines are updated frequently. Check for guideline updates at: http://aidsinfo.nih.gov]

REGIMENS	COMMENTS
INSTI-BASED REGIMEN Dolutegravir/abacavir/lamivudine	Abacavir should not be used in patients who test positive for HLA-B*5701
Dolutegravir + emtricitabine/tenofovir	Tenofovir should be used with caution in patients with renal insufficiency
Elvitegravir/cobicistat/emtricitabine/tenofovir	Elvitegravir/cobicistat/emtricitabine/tenofovir *(Stribild)* should only be initiated in patients with baseline CrCl ≥ 70 mL/min
Elvitegravir/cobicistat/emtricitabine/tenofovir alafenamide	Elvitegravir/cobicistat/emtricitabine/tenofovir alafenamide *(Genvoya)* should only be initiated in patients with baseline CrCl ≥ 30 mL/min
Raltegravir + emtricitabine/tenofovir	
PI-BASED REGIMEN Darunavir + ritonavir + emtricitabine/tenofovir	Lamivudine may be substituted for emtricitabine, and vice versa

Recommended Regimens for HIV-1 Infected Pregnant Women

Regimen must include 2 NRTIs (see recommended combos in chart) plus either a boosted-PI, NNRTI or INSTI. Preferred drugs per class are listed below:

2 NRTIs	+ PI	or NNRTI	or INSTI
Abacavir/lamivudine or	Atazanavir + ritonavir or	Efavirenz	Raltegravir
Tenofovir with emtricitabine (or lamivudine) or	Darunavir + ritonavir		
Zidovudine/lamivudine			

NUCLEOSIDE/TIDE REVERSE TRANSCRIPTASE INHIBITORS (NRTIs)

NRTIs are structurally similar to naturally occurring nucleosides/nucleotides needed to synthesize viral DNA. NRTIs compete for binding at the catalytic site of reverse transcriptase, interfering with HIV viral RNA-dependent DNA polymerase which results in DNA chain termination and halts further viral DNA synthesis (see Stage #3 in the HIV life cycle diagram). All NRTIs have a boxed warning for lactic acidosis and severe hepatomegaly with steatosis, sometimes fatal (especially didanosine, stavudine and zidovudine). If the patient is suspected to have lactic acidosis or hepatotoxicity, stop treatment with NRTI. Please see key features of all NRTIs in box.

KEY FEATURES OF NRTIs

Boxed Warning: lactic acidosis and hepatomegaly with steatosis (zidovudine, stavudine, didanosine > other NRTIs)

Renal dose adjustment (except abacavir)

No CYP450 drug interactions

Take without regards to meals (except didanosine and certain combination tablets)

DRUG	DOSING	SAFETY/SIDE EFFECTS/MONITORING
Abacavir, ABC **(Ziagen)** Tablet, oral solution (20 mg/mL) **+ lamivudine (Epzicom)** + lamivudine and zidovudine *(Trizivir)* **+ lamivudine and dolutegravir (Triumeq)**	300 mg BID or 600 mg daily No renal dose adjustments required *Epzicom:* 1 tab daily *Trizivir:* 1 tab BID *Triumeq:* 1 tab daily and keep in the original container All formulations: Take without regards to food	**BOXED WARNINGS** Serious, sometimes fatal, hypersensitivity reactions – look for fever, rash, fatigue, malaise, GI symptoms (N/V/D, abdominal pain), and/or respiratory symptoms (dyspnea, cough); discontinue drug and do not re-challenge regardless of HLA-B*5701 status Screen for the HLA-B*5701 allele before starting abacavir therapy – if positive, use is contraindicated due to ↑ risk for hypersensitivity reactions. Record as abacavir allergy in patient record and do not use. **CONTRAINDICATIONS** Previous hypersensitivity to abacavir, moderate to severe hepatic impairment **WARNINGS** Caution in CVD due to increased risk of MIs **SIDE EFFECTS** N/V, HA, rash, ↑ LFTs, hypersensitivity reaction, hyperlipidemia **MONITORING** LFTs, s/sx of hypersensitivity **NOTES** Pregnancy Category C Caution with alcohol (↑ abacavir AUC) MedGuide and warning card (summarizing symptoms of hypersensitivity) should be dispensed with each prescription and refill (for abacavir alone and abacavir combination pills) Abacavir/lamivudine with either efavirenz or atazanavir + ritonavir should not be used in patients with pre-treatment HIV viral load > 100,000 copies/mL
Didanosine, ddI *(Videx, Videx EC)* Capsule, solution (10 mg/mL)	≥ 60 kg: 400 mg daily < 60 kg: 250 mg daily Take on an empty stomach (at least 30 minutes before or 2 hours after a meal) CrCl < 60 mL/min: ↓ dose Oral soln: Stable for 30 days if refrigerated	**BOXED WARNINGS** Pancreatitis (sometimes fatal) **CONTRAINDICATIONS** Concurrent use with allopurinol or ribavirin **WARNINGS** Noncirrhotic portal hypertension, retinal changes and optic neuritis **SIDE EFFECTS** N/V/D, peripheral neuropathy (potentially irreversible), ↑ amylase, ↑ LFTs, insulin resistance/diabetes **MONITORING** LFTs, eye exam, CBC, blood chemistry, renal function, amylase and lipase (with pancreatitis) **NOTES** Pregnancy Category B Avoid didanosine and stavudine combination due to ↑ risk of pancreatitis, peripheral neuropathy, and lactic acidosis Avoid use with tenofovir due to resistance and virologic failure as well as ↑ didanosine concentrations MedGuide required

Nucleoside Reverse Transcriptase Inhibitors (NRTIs) Continued

DRUG	DOSING	SAFETY/SIDE EFFECTS/MONITORING
Emtricitabine, FTC **(Emtriva)** Capsule, oral solution (10 mg/mL) **+ tenofovir (Truvada)** **+ efavirenz and tenofovir (Atripla)** **+ tenofovir and rilpivirine (Complera)** **+ tenofovir and elvitegravir and cobicistat (Stribild)** **+ tenofovir alafenamide and elvitegravir and cobicistat (Genvoya)**	Cap: <u>200 mg daily</u> Soln: 240 mg daily (refrigerate; stable for 3 months at room temp) Take without regards to food CrCl < 50 mL/min: ↓ dose or frequency <u>1 tab daily for Truvada, Atripla, Complera, Stribild, and Genvoya</u> Take *Truvada* without regards to food Take *Atripla* on an <u>empty stomach</u>, preferably at <u>bedtime</u> Take *Complera*, *Stribild* and *Genvoya* with food	**BOXED WARNINGS** <u>Severe acute exacerbation of hepatitis B (HBV) can occur when drug is discontinued in patients with HBV infection</u> **SIDE EFFECTS** N/V/D, rash, dizziness, HA, insomnia, <u>hyperpigmentation</u> primarily of palms and/or soles (mainly in children), ↑ CPK, ↑ LFTs **MONITORING** LFTs, renal function, HBV status prior to initiation **NOTES** Pregnancy Category B Avoid combining with lamivudine; antagonistic interaction as both are cytosine analogs: FT<u>C</u> and 3T<u>C</u> Capsule and oral solution are not bioequivalent *Truvada, Atripla, Complera, Stribild, Genvoya:* keep in original container (contains desiccant to protect from moisture) MedGuide required (for *Truvada*)
LamiVUDine, 3TC **(Epivir)** Tablet, oral solution (10 mg/mL) **+ zidovudine (Combivir)** **+ abacavir (Epzicom)** **+ abacavir and zidovudine (Trizivir)** **+ abacavir and dolutegravir (Triumeq)**	150 mg BID or 300 mg daily CrCl < 50 mL/min: ↓ dose 1 tab daily for *Epzicom* and *Triumeq* 1 tab BID for *Combivir* and *Trizivir* Take without regards to food *Triumeq:* Keep in original container	**BOXED WARNINGS** <u>Do not use *Epivir-HBV* for treatment of HIV (contains lower dose of lamivudine); can result in HIV resistance</u> Severe acute exacerbation of hepatitis B (HBV) can occur when drug is discontinued in patients with HBV infection **SIDE EFFECTS** Headache, N/V/D, fatigue, insomnia, myalgias, ↑ LFTs **MONITORING** LFTs, renal function, HBV status prior to initiation **NOTES** Pregnancy Category C Avoid combining with emtricitabine; antagonistic interaction as both are cytosine analogs: FT<u>C</u> and 3T<u>C</u>) Has activity against HBV. In HIV/HBV co-infection, must dose lamivudine at the higher, HIV treatment dose; use correct dosage strength/product (*Epivir* is not equivalent to *Epivir-HBV*)

Nucleoside Reverse Transcriptase Inhibitors (NRTIs) Continued

DRUG	DOSING	SAFETY/SIDE EFFECTS/MONITORING
Stavudine, d4T *(Zerit)* Capsule, oral solution (1 mg/mL)	≥ 60 kg: 40 mg Q12H < 60 kg: 30 mg Q12H CrCl ≤ 50 mL/min: ↓ dose and/or frequency Oral soln: Stable for <u>30 days in refrigerator</u>. <u>Shake</u> vigorously before use Take without regards to food	**BOXED WARNINSG** Pancreatitis (sometimes fatal) has occurred during combination therapy with didanosine **WARNINGS** Neurologic symptoms including motor weakness (mimics Guillian-Barre syndrome) and hepatotoxicity **SIDE EFFECTS** <u>HA, N/V/D, peripheral neuropathy (can be irreversible), ↑ LFTs, hyperbilirubinemia, lipoatrophy</u>, pancreatitis, insulin resistance/diabetes, hyperlipidemia **MONITORING** LFTs, renal function, s/sx of peripheral neuropathy, lipids **NOTES** Pregnancy Category C Avoid stavudine and didanosine combination due to ↑ risk of peripheral neuropathy, pancreatitis, and lactic acidosis Do not combine with zidovudine; antagonist interaction as both are thymidine analogs: d4<u>T</u> and AZ<u>T</u> Lipoatrophy: stavudine > zidovudine > other NRTIs MedGuide required
Tenofovir **disoproxil fumarate**, TDF *(Viread)* Tablet, oral powder (40 mg/g) **+ emtricitabine** *(Truvada)* **+ emtricitabine and efavirenz** *(Atripla)* **+ emtricitabine and rilpivirine** *(Complera)* **+ emtricitabine and elvitegravir and cobicistat** *(Stribild)* **Tenofovir alafenamide + emtricitabine and elvitegravir and cobicistat** *(Genvoya)*	<u>300 mg daily</u> CrCl < 50 mL/min: ↓ frequency <u>1 tab daily</u> for *Truvada, Atripla, Complera, Stribild* and *Genvoya* Take *Viread* tablets and *Truvada* without regards to food Take *Atripla* on an <u>empty stomach</u>, preferably at <u>bedtime</u> Take *Complera, Stribild* and *Genvoya* <u>with food</u> <u>Dispense in original container</u>	**BOXED WARNINGS** <u>Severe acute exacerbation of hepatitis B (HBV) can occur when drug is discontinued in patients with HBV infection</u> **WARNINGS** <u>Renal toxicity including acute renal failure and/or Fanconi's syndrome, osteomalacia and ↓ bone mineral density</u> **SIDE EFFECTS** N/V/D, HA, depression, <u>renal impairment, ↓ bone mineral density</u>, ↑ LFTs, ↑ CPK **MONITORING** LFTs, CBC, renal function, CPK, bone density (long-term), HBV status prior to initiation **NOTES** Pregnancy Category B Avoid use with didanosine due to resistance and virologic failure as well as ↑ didanosine concentration Has activity against HBV (same treatment dose as HIV infection) Powder should be mixed with 2-4 oz of soft food (applesauce, yogurt) to avoid bitter taste. Do not mix powder with liquid. Consider vitamin D and calcium supplementation MedGuide required (for *Truvada*) Tenofovir alafenamide, a new form of tenofovir, was approved November 2015 in combination with emtricitabine + elvitegravir + cobicistat *(Genvoya)*. This new form achieves lower blood levels but higher intracellular levels of tenofovir and appears to have lower rates of renal and bone toxicity compared to the older form of tenofovir *(Viread)*.

Nucleoside Reverse Transcriptase Inhibitors (NRTIs) Continued

DRUG	DOSING	SAFETY/SIDE EFFECTS/MONITORING
Zidovudine, ZDV or AZT *(Retrovir)* Capsule, tablet, oral solution (10 mg/mL), injection + lamivudine *(Combivir)* + abacavir and lamivudine *(Trizivir)*	PO: 300 mg BID IV: 1 mg/kg Q4H CrCl < 15 mL/min: ↓ dose and/or change frequency 1 tab BID for *Combivir* and *Trizivir* Take without regards to food (although generally better tolerated when taken with food)	**BOXED WARNINGS** Hematologic toxicities (neutropenia and anemia) especially in advanced HIV Prolonged use has been associated with symptomatic myopathy and myositis **SIDE EFFECTS** N/V, anorexia, HA, malaise, insomnia, skin/nail hyperpigmentation (blue), myopathy, macrocytic anemia, lipoatrophy, ↑LFTs, insulin resistance/diabetes, hyperlipidemia **MONITORING** CBC, LFTs, lipids, blood glucose **NOTES** Pregnancy Category C Avoid combining with stavudine; antagonist interaction as both are thymidine analogs: d4T and AZT Erythropoietin is indicated to manage zidovudine-induced anemia Lipoatrophy: stavudine > zidovudine > other NRTIs IV zidovudine should be administered in the setting of labor for HIV-infected pregnant women, with HIV viral load > 1,000 copies/mL (or unknown HIV viral load)

NRTI Drug Interactions

NRTIs do not undergo hepatic transformations via the CYP metabolic pathway, therefore, they have fewer significant drug interactions compared to PIs and NNRTIs. Some NRTIs have other mechanisms of drug interactions (e.g., P-glycoprotein, overlapping toxicities). Here are a few notable drug interactions:

- Avoid concurrent use of ribavirin with didanosine (↑ risk of liver failure, pancreatitis), and ribavirin with zidovudine (significantly ↑ risk and severity of anemia).

- Avoid didanosine (ddI) and stavudine (d4T) combination due to ↑ risk of peripheral neuropathy, pancreatitis, and lactic acidosis.

- Avoid didanosine and tenofovir combination due to resistance and virologic failure as well as increased didanosine concentration.

- Allopurinol can ↑ didanosine levels; avoid combination.

- Avoid emtricitabine and lamivudine combination (antagonistic interaction as both cytosine analogs: FTC and 3TC).

- Avoid zidovudine and stavudine (antagonistic interaction as both are thymidine analogs: d4T and AZT).

- Methadone can ↑ zidovudine levels; monitor for zidovudine toxicity.

- Caution when using ledipasvir with tenofovir due to ↑ tenofovir levels; monitor renal function closely.

NON-NUCLEOSIDE REVERSE TRANSCRIP-TASE INHIBITORS (NNRTIs)

NNRTIs work by non-competitive binding to reverse transcriptase and blocking the RNA-dependent and DNA-dependent DNA polymerase activities including HIV-1 replication (see Stage #3 in the HIV life cycle diagram). All NNRTIs can cause hepatotoxicity and rash including SJS/TEN (monitor for erythema, facial edema, skin necrosis, blisters, tongue swelling)

KEY FEATURES OF NNRTIs

Hepatotoxicity and rash (including SJS/TEN) (nevirapine > other NNRTIs)

No renal dose adjustment needed (avoid *Atripla* and *Complera* if CrCl < 50 mL/min)

Primarily CYP450 inducers (exceptions: delavirdine - inhibitor, efavirenz - inducer > inhibitor, rilpivirine - substrate)

Food requirements:
- With food – etravirine, rilpivirine
- Without food – efavirenz
- Without regards to food – delavirdine, nevirapine

DRUG	DOSING	SAFETY/SIDE EFFECTS/MONITORING
Delavirdine, DLV *(Rescriptor)* Tablet	400 mg TID Patients with achlorhydria should take with acidic beverage; separate dose from antacids by 1 hour Take without regards to food	**CONTRAINDICATIONS** Concurrent use of alprazolam, ergot alkaloids, midazolam, rifampin, triazolam, others **SIDE EFFECTS** Nausea, headache, depression, fever, rash, ↑ LFTs **NOTES** Pregnancy Category C Rarely used due to TID dosing, drug interactions, and suboptimal response (compared to other antiretrovirals)
Efavirenz, EFV *(Sustiva)* Capsule, tablet **+ emtricitabine and tenofovir *(Atripla)***	600 mg daily 1 tab daily for *Atripla* Take on an empty stomach (to ↓ risk of CNS effects), preferably at bedtime Capsule contents may be sprinkled onto 1-2 teaspoons of food *Atripla:* Keep in original container (contains desiccant to protect from moisture)	**WARNINGS** Fetal toxicity, serious psychiatric symptoms (suicidal ideation, depression), CNS symptoms (generally resolve in 2-4 weeks), convulsions **SIDE EFFECTS** CNS effects (impaired concentration, abnormal dreams, confusion, dizziness), rash, HA, N/V, fatigue, insomnia **MONITORING** Lipids, CNS and psychiatric effects, LFTs **NOTES** Pregnancy Category D – potential teratogenicity (e.g., neural tube defects) in animal studies. Efavirenz is not recommended for initiation in ART-naive women who may become pregnant or are in their first 8 weeks of pregnancy. Efavirenz may be continued in pregnant women who present for prenatal care in the first trimester, as long as the HIV viral load is undetectable on the efavirenz-based regimen since changing regimens may lead to loss of viral control and increase risk of perinatal transmission May cause false positive cannabinoid and benzodiazepine on drug screening tests Efavirenz should not be used with abacavir/lamivudine (or emtricitabine) in patients with pre-treatment HIV viral load > 100,000 copies/mL

Non-Nucleoside Reverse Transcriptase Inhibitors (NNRTIs) Continued

DRUG	DOSING	SAFETY/SIDE EFFECTS/MONITORING
Etravirine, ETR *(Intelence)* Tablet	200 mg BID <u>after meals</u> Protect from moisture Tablets may be dispersed in water to ease administration	**SIDE EFFECTS** Nausea, rash (including SJS/TEN), ↑ cholesterol, ↑ LDL, ↑ TGs, hyperglycemia, ↑ LFTs, peripheral neuropathy **MONITORING** LFTs, lipids, blood glucose **NOTES** Pregnancy Category B Typically used in patients who are treatment-experienced and have resistance to first line ART regimens
Nevirapine, NVP *(Viramune, Viramune XR)* Tablet, oral suspension (10 mg/mL)	200 mg daily x 14 days, then 200 mg BID *(Viramune)* or 400 mg daily *(Viramune XR)* <u>Need 14 day lead-in period (may ↓ risk of rash, hepatotoxicity)</u> Take without regards to food	**BOXED WARNINGS** <u>Hepatotoxicity (liver failure, death)</u> – risk highest during the first 6 weeks of therapy but may be seen out to 18 weeks (or more); more common in women and with higher CD4+ counts as noted below <u>Serious skin reactions (SJS/TEN)</u> – risk highest during the first 18 weeks of therapy and intensive monitoring is required **CONTRAINDICATIONS** Moderate-to-severe hepatic impairment, use in post-exposure prophylaxis regimens **SIDE EFFECTS** <u>Rash (SJS/TEN)</u>, nausea, diarrhea, <u>↑ LFTs</u> **MONITORING** CBC, LFTs, rash **NOTES** Pregnancy Category B Do not initiate therapy in women with CD4+ counts > 250 cells/mm^3 or in men with CD4+ counts > 400 cells/mm^3 due to ↑ risk of hepatotoxicity; never use for post-exposure prophylaxis in non-HIV-infected persons MedGuide required

Non-Nucleoside Reverse Transcriptase Inhibitors (NNRTIs) Continued

DRUG	DOSING	SAFETY/SIDE EFFECTS/MONITORING
Rilpivirine, RPV *(Edurant)* Tablet **+ emtricitabine and tenofovir *(Complera)***	25 mg daily <u>with a meal</u> <u>Keep in original container</u>; protect from light 1 tab daily <u>with food</u> *(Complera)*	**CONTRAINDICATIONS** Concurrent use with PPIs, rifampin, rifapentine, carbamazepine, oxcarbazepine, phenobarbital, phenytoin, St. John's wort, and dexamethasone (more than a single dose) **WARNINGS** QT prolongation, serious skin reactions, multiorgan hypersensitivity reactions (DRESS), depressive disorders, hepatotoxicity **SIDE EFFECTS** <u>Depressive disorders, mood changes, insomnia</u>, headache, rash **MONITORING** LFTs, rash, lipids, CNS effects **NOTES** Pregnancy Category B Higher rates of failure if viral load > 100,000 copies/mL and/or CD4+ counts < 200 cells/mm³ at treatment initiation H_2RAs should be administered at least 12 hours before or 4 hours after rilpivirine Antacids should be given at least 2 hours before or 4 hours after rilpivirine Protein supplement drinks should not be substituted for normal to high calorie meal (does not increase rilpivirine absorption)

NNRTI Drug Interactions

All NNRTIs are cleared non-renally and metabolized in the liver via the CYP 450 system and have <u>many</u> drug interactions. <u>They are all 3A4 substrates and may also be an inducer (nevirapine and etravirine)</u>, inhibitor (delavirdine) <u>or both inducer and inhibitor (efavirenz)</u>. Many of the NNRTIs inhibit other isoenzymes. You should always run a drug interaction check on all patients receiving NNRTIs. Below are some notable drug interactions:

- Delavirdine: Strong inhibitor of 2C9, 2C19 and 2D6, moderate inhibitor of 3A4 and major 3A4 substrate.

- Efavirenz: Moderate inhibitor of 2C8/9 and 2C19; moderate inducer of 3A4 and a major substrate of 3A4. Avoid concurrent use with carbamazepine, itraconazole, ketoconazole, posaconazole, simeprevir, St. John's wort, others.

- Etravirine: Moderate inhibitor of 2C9 and 2C19; moderate inducer of 3A4; and major substrate of 3A4, 2C9, and 2C19. Avoid concurrent use with clopidogrel, carbamazepine, phenobarbital, phenytoin, rifampin, St. John's wort, others.

- Nevirapine: Weak 3A4 inducer and major 3A4 substrate. Avoid concurrent use with atazanavir, carbamazepine, dolutegravir, itraconazole, ketoconazole, rifampin, St. John's wort, others.

- Rilpivirine: Major substrate of 3A4. <u>Contraindicated with strong 3A4 inducers</u> (carbamazepine, oxcarbazepine, phenobarbital, phenytoin, rifampin, St. John's wort, systemic dexamethasone (more than a single dose) <u>and PPIs</u>. Caution with other acid suppressants: H_2RAs should be administered at least 12 hours before or 4 hours after rilpivirine; antacids should be given at least 2 hours before or 4 hours after rilpivirine.

- <u>Methadone levels can be ↓ by efavirenz and nevirapine. Monitor for signs and symptoms of possible methadone withdrawal.</u>

- <u>Hormonal contraceptive levels may be decreased by efavirenz and nevirapine</u> and result in unintended pregnancy. Patients should be counseled to use alternative or additional contraception.

PROTEASE INHIBITORS (PIs)

PIs work by inhibiting HIV-1 protease and rendering the enzyme incapable of cleaving the Gag-Pol polyprotein, resulting in non-functional viral proteins which lead to the production of immature, non-infectious virions (see Stage #7 in the HIV life cycle diagram). The generic names of PIs end in "-navir".

KEY FEATURES OF PIs
Hepatotoxicity (highest risk with tipranavir)
Metabolic abnormalities such as hyperlipidemia, insulin resistance/hyperglycemia, lipohypertrophy (atazanavir, darunavir < other PIs)
Increased CVD risk (lowest with atazanavir and darunavir)
Bleeding events (in patients with hemophilia)
ECG changes (especially saquinavir, lopinavir/ritonavir and atazanavir)
GI upset (N/V/D)
Hypersensitivity reactions have been reported (rare)
No renal dose adjustment needed (avoid atazanavir + cobicistat and darunavir + cobicistat if CrCl < 70 mL/min)
Primarily CYP450 inhibitors (always check for drug interactions; also see PI Drug Interactions section)
Generally take with food (also helps decrease GI side effects; exceptions: fosamprenavir and lopinavir/ritonavir)
Take with ritonavir or cobicistat to increase levels of the other PI

DRUG	DOSING	SAFETY/SIDE EFFECTS/MONITORING
Darunavir, DRV *(Prezista)* Tablet, oral suspension (100 mg/mL) + cobicistat *(Prezcobix)* Tablet	Treatment naïve: <u>800 mg + 100 mg ritonavir daily</u> Treatment-experienced: 600 mg + 100 mg ritonavir BID 1 tablet daily *(Prezcobix)* <u>Take with food</u> <u>Swallow whole</u> If CrCl < 70 mL/min, do not give *Prezcobix* as part of a regimen that includes tenofovir disoproxil fumarate	**WARNINGS** <u>Drug-induced hepatitis, serious skin reactions (SJS/TEN), use caution in patients with a sulfa allergy</u> **SIDE EFFECTS** <u>N/V/D, rash, ↑ LFTs, HA</u>, ↑ SCr (with *Prezcobix*) **MONITORING** LFTs, rash, blood glucose, lipids, SCr (with *Prezcobix*) **NOTES** Pregnancy Category C <u>Must be given with ritonavir or cobicistat</u> (cobicistat only FDA approved with darunavir daily dose) Compared to other PIs, less likely to cause lipodystrophy or affect blood glucose and lipids

Protease Inhibitors (PIs) Continued

DRUG	DOSING	SAFETY/SIDE EFFECTS/MONITORING
Atazanavir, ATV **(Reyataz)** Capsule, oral powder + cobicistat *(Evotaz)* Tablet	300 mg + 100 mg ritonavir daily (or 150 mg cobicistat) 400 mg daily if therapy-naïve, not on tenofovir, and unable to tolerate ritonavir 1 tablet daily *(Evotaz)* Take with food (better absorption) If CrCl < 70 mL/min, do not give *Evotaz* as part of a regimen that includes tenofovir disoproxil fumarate	**WARNINGS** PR interval prolongation, severe skin reactions, hyperbilirubinemia, hepatoxicity, nephrolithiasis and cholelithiasis **SIDE EFFECTS** Indirect hyperbilirubinemia (jaundice or scleral icterus – think "bananavir" – reversible), HA, N/V/D, rash, depression, myalgia, ↑ SCr (with *Evotaz*) **MONITORING** ECG in at-risk patients, LFTs (including bilirubin), blood glucose, lipids, SCr (with *Evotaz*) **NOTES** Pregnancy Category B Compared to other PIs, less likely to cause lipodystrophy or affect blood glucose and lipids Caution with acid-suppressive agents as they can reduce the absorption (and blood levels) of atazanavir **With H$_2$RAs** Atazanavir alone (unboosted): Take at least 2 hours before or 10 hours after H$_2$RA Atazanavir with ritonavir: Take together or at least 10 hours after H$_2$RA **With Antacids** Take atazanavir at least 2 hours before or 1 hour after antacids **With PPIs** Atazanavir with ritonavir: Take at least 12 hours after PPIs. The dose should not be > 20 mg of omeprazole (or equivalent) per day (PPIs are not recommended if atazanavir unboosted or in treatment-experienced patients)
Fosamprenavir, FPV *(Lexiva)* Tablet, oral suspension (50 mg/mL)	Treatment naïve: 1,400 mg ± 100-200 mg ritonavir daily or 700 mg + 100 mg ritonavir BID Treatment-experienced: 700 mg + 100 mg ritonavir BID Oral suspension: Take without food (adults) Tablets: Take without regards to meals (unboosted); Take with food (boosted with ritonavir)	**WARNINGS** Use caution in patients with a sulfa allergy, nephrolithiasis, hemolytic anemia, hypersensitivity reactions (SJS/TEN) **SIDE EFFECTS** N/V/D, HA, rash, hyperlipidemia (especially TG) **MONITORING** LFTs, GI symptoms, glucose, lipids **NOTES** Pregnancy Category C Prodrug of amprenavir Caution when dispensing: Potential for medication error among *Lexiva*, *Lexapro*, and *Levitra* Unboosted fosamprenavir not recommended due to inferior potency compared to boosted PIs

Protease Inhibitors (PIs) Continued

DRUG	DOSING	SAFETY/SIDE EFFECTS/MONITORING
Indinavir, IDV *(Crixivan)* Capsule	Without ritonavir: 800 mg every 8 hours. Take on empty stomach (1 hour before or 2 hours after a meal) With ritonavir: 800 mg + 100-200 mg ritonavir BID. <u>Take with food due to ritonavir component and with 48 oz. of water</u> Swallow whole; do not break, crush, or chew	**WARNINGS** Hyperbilirubinemia, hemolytic anemia, <u>nephrolithiasis/urolithiasis</u> **SIDE EFFECTS** <u>N/V/D, HA, nephrolithiasis</u>, ↑ LFTs, rash, metallic taste, abdominal pain **MONITORING** LFTs (including bilirubin), urinalysis, CBC, blood glucose, lipids **NOTES** Pregnancy Category C Compared to other PIs, indinavir (and lopinavir/ritonavir) have highest risk of causing hyperglycemia, including insulin resistance/diabetes <u>Must dispense in the original container with the desiccant to protect from moisture</u> Avoid high fat/high calorie meal as indinavir absorption is decreased
Lopinavir + Ritonavir, LPV/r *(Kaletra)* Tablet, oral solution (80 mg lopinavir + 20 mg ritonavir/mL)	Treatment naïve: <u>800 mg lopinavir/200 mg ritonavir daily or 400/100 mg BID</u> Treatment-experienced: 400/100 mg BID Solution: Take <u>with food</u>. <u>Refrigerate</u>; Stable for 2 months at room temp. <u>Contains 42% alcohol</u>. Tablets: Take without regards to meals. Store at room temperature; swallow whole; do not break, crush, or chew.	**WARNINGS** Pancreatitis, hepatotoxicity, QT and/or PR interval prolongation, caution in patients with CVD due to increased risk of MIs **SIDE EFFECTS** N/V/D, abdominal pain, hyperlipidemia (especially TG), hyperglycemia **MONITORING** LFTs, blood glucose, lipids, ECG in at-risk patients **NOTES** Pregnancy Category C Compared to other PIs, lopinavir/ritonavir (and indinavir) have highest risk of causing hyperglycemia, including insulin resistance/diabetes Avoid once daily dosing with carbamazepine, phenytoin, phenobarbital and in pregnant women MedGuide required
Nelfinavir, NFV *(Viracept)* Tablet	750 mg TID or 1,250 mg BID <u>Take with food</u>	**SIDE EFFECTS** <u>Diarrhea</u> (up to 20% in adults), flatulence, nausea, rash, ↑ LFTs **MONITORING** LFTs, GI symptoms (and electrolytes, hydration status if diarrhea), blood glucose, lipids **NOTES** Pregnancy Category B Boosting with ritonavir not recommended (high enough absorption on its own) If difficulty with swallowing, tablets may be dissolved in small amount of water and consumed immediately Do not use with PPIs

Protease Inhibitors (PIs) Continued

DRUG	DOSING	SAFETY/SIDE EFFECTS/MONITORING
Ritonavir, RTV (Norvir) Capsule, tablet, oral solution (80 mg/mL) Primarily used as a booster agent and not as a sole PI	100-400 mg/day (booster dose), given in 1 to 2 divided doses Take with food Capsules: Refrigerate; stable at room temperature up to 30 days Tablets: Store at room temp; swallow whole; do not break, crush, or chew Solution: Store at room temp.; contains 43% alcohol; shake well before use Keep in original container	**BOXED WARNING** Ritonavir interacts with many medications, including antiarrhythmics, ergot alkaloids, and sedatives/hypnotics, resulting in potentially serious and/or life-threatening adverse events **WARNINGS** Pancreatitis, hepatotoxicity, PR interval prolongation **SIDE EFFECTS** N/V/D, paresthesias, asthenia, arthralgias, ↑ CPK **MONITORING** LFTs, CPK, glucose, lipids **NOTES** Pregnancy Category B Capsules and tablets are not bioequivalent; when switching from capsules to tablets (dose 1:1), patients may experience more GI side effects initially due to higher ritonavir levels with tablet form Can mix oral soln with chocolate milk or liquid nutritional supplement to mask unpleasant taste
Saquinavir, SQV (Invirase) Capsule, tablet	1,000 mg + ritonavir 100 mg BID Take with food (or within 2 hours of a full meal) Must be given with ritonavir	**CONTRAINDICATIONS** Severe hepatic impairment, congenital or acquired QT prolongation, complete AV block or at high-risk for AV block, and refractory hypokalemia or hypomagnesemia **WARNINGS** PR and QT interval prolongation (avoid use if QT > 450 msec), photosensitivity reaction **SIDE EFFECTS** N/V/D, HA, abdominal pain, fatigue, hyperglycemia **MONITORING** ECG (baseline and ongoing), electrolytes (esp K, Mg), blood glucose, lipids **NOTES** Pregnancy Category B Capsules may be opened and mixed with syrup or jam immediately before taking MedGuide required

Protease Inhibitors (PIs) Continued

DRUG	DOSING	SAFETY/SIDE EFFECTS/MONITORING
Tipranavir, TPV *(Aptivus)* Capsule, oral solution (100 mg/mL)	500 mg + ritonavir 200 mg BID Take with food Swallow whole; do not break, crush, or chew Must be given with ritonavir Capsules: Refrigerate; can store at room temp. up to 60 days; need to discard 60 days after opening bottle Solution: Store at room temperature; need to discard 60 days after opening bottle	**BOXED WARNINGS** Clinical hepatitis and hepatic decompensation (sometimes fatal) and intracranial hemorrhage **CONTRAINDICATIONS** Moderate or severe hepatic impairment **WARNINGS** Use caution in patients with a sulfa allergy, intracranial hemorrhage (caution in those with bleeding risk) **SIDE EFFECTS** N/V/D, HA, ↑ CPK, hyperlipidemia (especially TG) **MONITORING** LFTs, blood glucose, lipids **NOTES** Pregnancy Category C Capsules contain 7% alcohol. Oral solution contains vitamin E; additional vitamin supplements should be avoided.

PI Drug Interactions

All PIs are metabolized in the liver via the CYP 450 system and have many drug interactions. All PIs are 3A4 substrates and most are strong inhibitors of 3A4. Ritonavir is a potent 3A4 inhibitor used at low doses to increase, or boost, the level of other PIs. Cobicistat *(Tybost)* is a strong 3A4 inhibitor and FDA-approved to pharmacokinetically enhance, or boost, levels of atazanavir and darunavir. However, cobicistat itself is not a protease inhibitor and also not interchangeable with ritonavir. The drug interaction list below highlights the most important interactions and contraindications and is not all-inclusive.

- The following drugs are contraindicated with all PIs: alfuzosin, cisapride, ergot derivatives, flecainide, lovastatin, midazolam (oral), pimozide, propafenone, quinidine, rifampin, sildenafil (when used for the treatment of pulmonary arterial hypertension), simvastatin, St. John's wort, and triazolam. Voriconazole is contraindicated with ritonavir ≥ 800 mg/day. Many of the PIs should not be used with simeprevir or amiodarone.

- Caution with concurrent use of 3A4 inducers as they can lower the concentration of PIs. Avoid concurrent use with rifampin.

- PIs can alter the INR (mainly ↓) in patients taking warfarin due to 2C9 induction; the INR should be closely monitored.

- PIs ↑ the levels of trazodone and many tricyclic antidepressants. Start with low doses and then titrate anti-depressant doses based upon clinical response.

- Atazanavir: caution with the use of acid-suppressive agents. See PI table above.

- Nelfinavir cannot be used with PPIs.

- Phosphodiesterase-5 inhibitors (PDE-5 inhibitors): <u>PIs can ↑ levels of PDE-5 inhibitors and ↑ risk of toxicity</u>. PDE-5 inhibitors should be initiated at lowest dose and the dosing interval should be extended.

- Hormonal contraceptives (especially those containing ethinyl estradiol and norethindrone): Ritonavir may ↓ levels via CYP induction. Patients should be counseled to use additional/alternative contraceptive methods.

- <u>Methadone: Levels may be ↓ by ritonavir (via CYP induction). Monitor for possible methadone withdrawal.</u>

- Statins: PIs can ↑ statin levels. Concurrent use of <u>lovastatin or simvastatin with PIs is contraindicated</u>. Start statin therapy with a low dose and titrate to response. Monitor closely for statin toxicity. Darunavir can significantly ↑ pravastatin levels, therefore consider alternative statin.

INTEGRASE STRAND TRANSFER INHIBITORS (INSTIs)

INSTIs block the integrase enzyme needed for viral DNA to integrate with the host cell DNA/human genome (see Stage #4 in the HIV life cycle diagram). <u>The generic names of INSTIs end in "-tegravir".</u>

KEY FEATURES OF INSTIs
<u>Headache</u>
<u>Insomnia</u>
<u>↑ CPK (raltegravir > other INSTIs)</u>
No renal dose adjustment needed (avoid *Stribild* if CrCl < 70 mL/min, avoid *Genvoya* if CrCl < 30 mL/min)
No major CYP interactions (exception: elvitegravir + cobicistat or ritonavir)
<u>Interact with polyvalent cations – must separate dose</u>
<u>Take without regards to meals (exception: elvitegravir with food)</u>

DRUG	DOSING	SAFETY/SIDE EFFECTS/MONITORING
Dolutegravir, DTG *(Tivicay)* Tablet	50 mg PO daily (not indicated for weight < 40 kg) 50 mg PO BID (for treatment-experienced patients or those with INSTI resistance or those taking certain UGT1A or 3A inducers) Take without regard to meals	**CONTRAINDICATION** Coadministration with dofetilide **SIDE EFFECTS** Insomnia, HA, diarrhea, rash, ↑ CPK, ↑ LFTs among hepatitis B/C patients, <u>↑ SCr without affecting GFR</u> **MONITORING** CPK, LFTs (especially in hepatitis B/C patients) **NOTES** Pregnancy Category B

Integrase Strand Transfer Inhibitors (INSTIs) Continued

DRUG	DOSING	SAFETY/SIDE EFFECTS/MONITORING
Elvitegravir, EVG *(Vitekta)* Tablet **+ cobicistat and emtricitabine and tenofovir disoproxil fumarate** *(Stribild)* Tablet **+ cobicistat and emtricitabine and tenofovir alafenamide** *(Genvoya)* Tablet	85 mg daily with ritonavir + either atazanavir or lopinavir 150 mg daily with ritonavir + either darunavir, fosamprenavir, or tipranavir *Stribild*: 1 tablet daily; Do not initiate if CrCl < 70 mL/min; discontinue when CrCl < 50 mL/min *Genvoya*: 1 tablet daily; do not initiate if CrCl < 30 mL/min Keep in original container Take with food	**BOXED WARNINGS (FOR *STRIBILD* AND *GENVOYA* ONLY)** Lactic acidosis with severe hepatomegaly with steatosis Acute exacerbation of HBV can occur when drug is discontinued in patients with HBV (specific for emtricitabine and tenofovir) **CONTRAINDICATIONS** For *Stribild* and *Genvoya* only: Concurrent use of alfuzosin, cisapride, ergot derivatives, lovastatin, midazolam (oral), pimozide, rifampin, sildenafil (when used for pulmonary arterial hypertension), simvastatin, St. John's wort and triazolam **WARNINGS** For *Stribild* and *Genvoya* only: New onset or worsening renal impairment, decrease in bone density (likely due to tenofovir) **SIDE EFFECTS** Proteinuria, nausea and diarrhea, hyperlipidemia, HA, insomnia, ↑ SCr (with *Stribild* and *Genvoya*: without effect on GFR due to cobicistat; with effect on GFR due to tenofovir) **MONITORING** CPK, LFTs, renal function with *Stribild/Genvoya* **NOTES** Pregnancy Category B Cobicistat is a booster similar to ritonavir Elvitegravir/cobicistat/emtricitabine/tenofovir alafenamide *(Genvoya)* was approved in Nov. 2015
Raltegravir, RAL *(Isentress)* Tablet (including chewable), powder packet for oral suspension	400 mg BID Take without regard to meals Chewable tablets: Keep in original container Oral suspension: Keep in original container, do not open foil packet until ready for reconstitution and use	**SIDE EFFECTS** Nausea, HA, insomnia, fatigue, ↑ CPK, myopathy and rhabdomyolysis **MONITORING** CPK (if symptomatic), LFTs **NOTES** Pregnancy Category C

INSTI Drug Interactions

- INSTIs should be taken 2 hours before or 6 hours after taking cation-containing antacids or laxatives, sucralfate, iron supplements, calcium supplements or buffered medications. Exception for raltegravir and calcium carbonate: no dose separation needed. H₂RAs and PPIs do not pose an interaction with INSTIs.

- Raltegravir: Metabolized by the UGT1A1-mediated glucuronidation pathway. Rifampin, a strong inducer of UGT1A1, will ↓ levels of raltegravir. When given concurrently with rifampin, use raltegravir 800 mg BID. PPIs can ↑ levels of raltegravir although dosage adjustment is not needed.

- *Stribild* and *Genvoya:* Cobicistat, a component in these co-formulated tablets, is an inhibitor of 3A4 (strong), 2D6 (weak) and P-gp. Cobicistat interactions are very similar to ritonavir interactions. Elvitegravir is a major 3A4 substrate and an inducer of 2C9 (weak/moderate) and may ↓ the plasma concentrations of 2C9 substrates. *Stribild* and *Genvoya* should not be co-administered with any other ART.

CCR5 ANTAGONIST

CCR5 inhibitors bind to the CCR5 co-receptor on the CD4+ cells and prevent HIV cell entry (see Stage #1 in the HIV life cycle diagram). Unlike the other antiretroviral drug classes, CCR5 inhibitors do not directly target the HIV cell but rather blocks the human host cell receptor.

DRUG	DOSING	SAFETY/SIDE EFFECTS/MONITORING
Maraviroc, MVC *(Selzentry)* Tablet	300 mg BID Take without regard to meals CrCl < 30 mL/min: ↓ dose Dose adjust if concurrent CYP 3A4 inhibitor or inducer Prior to starting therapy, patients must undergo a tropism test, to determine the tropism (or preference) of the HIV for the CCR5 co-receptor. Maraviroc will only work in patients with CCR5-tropic disease (not CXCR4- or dual/mixed-tropic disease)	**BOXED WARNING** Hepatotoxicity, may occur with severe rash or other allergic type features **CONTRAINDICATIONS** Patients with severe renal impairment (CrCl < 30 mL/min) taking potent 3A4 inhibitors/inducers **WARNINGS** Hypersensitivity reactions (including SJS), CV events (including MI), orthostatic hypotension in patients with renal impairment **SIDE EFFECTS** URTIs, fever, cough, rash, abdominal pain, dizziness **MONITORING** Tropism testing prior to initiation, LFTs, s/sx of infection, skin reactions **NOTES** Pregnancy Category B Swallow tablets whole; do not chew, break, or crush MedGuide required

CCR5 Antagonist Drug Interactions

Maraviroc is a P-gp and major 3A4 substrate. Maraviroc concentrations can be significantly ↑ in the presence of strong 3A4 inhibitors and ↓ with 3A4 inducers, and maraviroc dosage may need to be adjusted. Avoid use with St. John's wort.

FUSION INHIBITORS

Fusion inhibitors block the fusion of the HIV-1 virus with the CD4+ cells by blocking the conformational change in gp41 required for membrane fusion and entry into CD4+ cells (see Stage #2 in the HIV life cycle diagram). The currently available fusion inhibitor, enfuvirtide, is not metabolized through CYP and, therefore, has no significant drug interactions.

DRUG	DOSING	SAFETY/SIDE EFFECTS/MONITORING
Enfuvirtide, T20 (Fuzeon) Powder for injection	90 mg SC BID Reconstituted solution should be refrigerated and used within 24 hours	**WARNINGS** ↑ risk of bacterial pneumonia, hypersensitivity reaction **SIDE EFFECTS** Local injection site reactions in 98% of patients (pain, erythema, nodules and cysts, ecchymosis), diarrhea, nausea, fatigue **NOTES** Pregnancy Category B Patient should be counseled regarding proper reconstitution and injection technique and to rotate injection sites Typically used in patients who are treatment-experienced with resistance to multiple other ART

COMBINATION PRODUCTS

GENERIC NAME	BRAND NAME	DOSE
Abacavir 600 mg + lamivudine 300 mg	Epzicom	1 tab daily
Emtricitabine 200 mg + tenofovir 300 mg	Truvada	1 tab daily
Abacavir 600 mg + dolutegravir 50 mg + lamivudine 300 mg	Triumeq	1 tab daily
Lamivudine 150 mg + zidovudine 300 mg	Combivir	1 tab BID
Abacavir 300 mg + lamivudine 150 mg + zidovudine 300 mg	Trizivir	1 tab BID
Efavirenz 600 mg + emtricitabine 200 mg + tenofovir 300 mg	Atripla	1 tab at bedtime on empty stomach
Emtricitabine 200 mg + rilpivirine 25 mg + tenofovir 300 mg	Complera	1 tab daily with food
Elvitegravir 150 mg + cobicistat 150 mg + emtricitabine 200 mg + tenofovir 300 mg	Stribild	1 tab daily with food
Elvitegravir 150 mg + cobicistat 150 mg + emtricitabine 200 mg + tenofovir alafenamide 10 mg	Genvoya	1 tab daily with food

ADMINISTRATION				
With food				**Without food**
Atazanavir	*Kaletra* oral soln	Tipranavir		*Atripla*
Complera	Nelfinavir	Tenofovir powder (to avoid bitter taste)		Didanosine
Darunavir	Rilpivirine			Efavirenz (small amount of non-fatty food is okay)
Etravirine (after meals)	Ritonavir			
Genvoya	Saquinavir			Fosamprenavir (oral suspension)
Indinavir (boosted)	*Stribild*			Indinavir (unboosted)

Select Complications of ART

Lactic acidosis and severe hepatomegaly with steatosis: Stop treatment in any patient who develops clinical or laboratory findings suggestive of lactic acidosis or hepatotoxicity ($\uparrow$ LFTs may/may not accompany hepatomegaly and steatosis). Most commonly associated with NRTIs.

Immune reconstitution inflammatory syndrome (IRIS): Paradoxical worsening of a preexisting OI or malignancy when ART is initiated. Since ART leads to an improvement in immune function, an inflammatory reaction may occur at the site of the preexisting infection. Patients at highest risk for IRIS are those with low CD4+ counts and high viral loads. IRIS generally develops within 1 – 3 months of ART initiation. Commonly found pathogens associated with IRIS include *M. tuberculosis*, *M. avium*, *Pneumocystis jiroveci* pneumonia (PCP), herpes simplex virus (HSV), herpes zoster, cytomegalovirus (CMV), *Cryptococcus*, and HBV.

Lipodystrophy: Changes in fat distribution in the body and is further subcategorized as lipoatrophy (fat loss or wasting) or lipohypertrophy (fat accumulation).

Lipoatrophy: Loss of subcutaneous fat in the face, arms, legs, and buttocks and is most commonly associated with NRTIs, specifically with stavudine (and zidovudine to a lesser extent).

Lipohypertrophy: Fat accumulation in the upper back and neck ("buffalo hump"), abdominal area, and breast area in both men and women and is most commonly associated with PIs. Breast enlargement with efavirenz has been reported.

Diarrhea: Diarrhea is a common side effect of ART. All ARTs have been associated with GI toxicity, however, PIs are generally the most problematic especially nelfinavir and lopinavir/ritonavir.

MANAGEMENT OF IRIS
Start or continue therapy for the underlying opportunistic pathogen or malignancy.
Continue ART if the patient is currently receiving ART. Among patients newly diagnosed with HIV with OI, ART may be intentionally delayed while treating the OI to minimize risk for IRIS. However, ART should be started within 2 weeks of OI treatment initiation for PCP and *M. tuberculosis* secondary to mortality benefits.
In select circumstances, the addition of corticosteroids may be appropriate.

Therapies for HIV Complications

DRUG AND INDICATION	DOSING	SAFETY/SIDE EFFECTS/MONITORING
Poly-L-Lactic Acid (*Sculptra*) Injection Lipoatrophy (facial)	About 20 injections (given intradermal or SC) per cheek Typical treatment course can require 3-6 treatments. Treatments should be separated by ≥ 2 weeks.	**SIDE EFFECTS** Injection site reactions (e.g., bleeding, bruising, erythema, edema, inflammation), photosensitivity, hematoma, discomfort
Calcium hydroxylapatite (*Radiesse*) Injection Lipoatrophy (facial)	Intradermal injection Typical treatment course may require 1-3 treatments. In clinical trials, multiple treatments were separated by at least 1 month.	**SIDE EFFECTS** Injection site reactions (e.g., bruising, erythema, edema), pain, pruritus, nodules
Tesamorelin (*Egrifta*) Injection HIV-associated lipodystrophy (specifically reduction of excess abdominal fat)	2 mg SC daily	**SIDE EFFECTS** Injection site reactions (e.g., pruritus, erythema, bruising, pain), rash, peripheral edema, hyperglycemia, arthralgias, development of IgG antibodies **NOTES** This medication is a growth hormone releasing factor
Crofelemer (*Fulyzaq*) Tablet Non-infectious diarrhea due to ART	125 mg PO BID	**SIDE EFFECTS** URTIs, bronchitis, cough, flatulence, ↑ bilirubin/LFTs **NOTES** Due to cost, first consider trial of loperamide (*Imodium*) or diphenoxylate/atropine (*Lomotil*)
Megestrol (*Megace, Megace ES*) Tablet, suspension *Megace* 40 mg/mL, *Megace ES* 625 mg/5 mL Anorexia or cachexia associated with AIDS	400 – 800 mg suspension PO daily	**SIDE EFFECTS** Hyperglycemia, adrenal suppression, hypertension, HA, rash, N/V/D **NOTES** Available as oral suspension (used in HIV-associated anorexia/cachexia) and tablets (used in cancer treatment) – dispense correct strength and formulation. *Megace* and *Megace ES* are not equivalent on a mg-per-mg basis. Pregnancy Category X (suspension)/D (tablets)
Dronabinol (*Marinol*) C-III Capsule AIDS-related anorexia	2.5 mg PO BID (before lunch and dinner), max 20 mg/day Refrigerate capsules Swallow capsule whole. Do not chew, break, or crush.	**SIDE EFFECTS** CNS effects (e.g., euphoria, somnolence, abnormal thinking, confusion), dizziness, abdominal pain, paranoia, N/V **NOTES** Causes positive cannabinoid drug test. Caution in patients with underlying cardiac or liver disease or seizure disorders.

PRE-EXPOSURE PROPHYLAXIS (PrEP)

PrEP is a new HIV prevention method in which people who do not have HIV take emtricitabine/tenofovir *(Truvada)* 1 tab PO daily, in combination with safer sex/behavior risk reduction practices, to reduce their risk of becoming infected. PrEP is recommended for both homosexual and heterosexual individuals who are at very high risk for sexual exposure to HIV as well as for active intravenous drug users.

Before Initiating PrEP

- Confirm HIV negative status through HIV antibody test

- Confirm CrCl ≥ 60 mL/min

- Confirm patient very high risk for acquiring HIV

- Screen for hepatitis B and STIs

Once PrEP is initiated, follow-up visits are needed at least every 3 months with the following recommendations during each visit:

- HIV test and document negative result

- Provide no more than 90-day supply at a time (renew Rx only once HIV negative status is confirmed)

- Pregnancy test (for non-HIV-infected women taking PrEP)

- Counseling on PrEP adherence and safe sex/behavior risk reduction practices

- Every 6 months, check SCr and calculate CrCl, and test for bacterial STIs (regardless of symptoms)

NONOCCUPATIONAL POSTEXPOSURE PROPHYLAXIS (nPEP)

Nonoccupational exposure is the use of ART prophylaxis after sexual, injection drug use, or some other nonoccupational exposure to HIV. Regardless of whether or not nPEP is prescribed, the exposed patient should be tested for HIV Ab at baseline, 4 – 6 weeks, 3 months, and 6 months after the exposure event.

Nonoccupational Postexposure Prophylaxis (nPEP) Recommendations

PREFERRED REGIMENS	CRITERIA TO QUALIFY	DURATION
NNRTI-BASED Efavirenz + (Lamivudine or emtricitabine) + (Zidovudine or tenofovir) **PI-BASED** Lopinavir/ritonavir + (Lamivudine or emtricitabine) + Zidovudine	≤ 72 hours since exposure Known HIV (+) status of source (If HIV status unknown, then case-by-case determination) Exposed patient is HIV (–) or being tested for HIV Type of exposure is also factored into decision to initiate nPEP	28 days

OCCUPATIONAL POST-EXPOSURE PROPHYLAXIS RECOMMENDATIONS (PEP)

Occupational exposure typically refers to exposure of health care personnel to blood or body fluids that may potentially be contaminated with HIV. ART prophylaxis for occupational exposure is generally only recommended if the source of contaminated blood or body fluid is known to be HIV infected. If the source patient's HIV status is unknown, the HIV status should be determined, if possible, to guide need for HIV PEP. Therapy should be started right away, ideally within 72 hours, when treatment is indicated. Per the 2013 updated guideline, a three drug regimen including raltegravir (Isentress) + tenofovir/emtricitibine (Truvada) for a 4-week course is the preferred regimen. The exposed health care personnel should be tested for HIV Ab at baseline, 4 – 6 weeks, 3 months, and 6 months after the exposure event. If PEP is initiated, then CBC, renal and liver function should be tested at baseline and repeated at 2 weeks post-exposure.

STRATEGIES TO IMPROVE ADHERENCE TO ANTIRETROVIRAL THERAPY

Multidisciplinary team approach (e.g., nurses, social workers, pharmacists, psychologists, physicians)

Accessible, non-judgmental health care team, establish trusting relationship with patient

Evaluate patient's knowledge of HIV disease, prevention and treatment, and provide information as needed; establish patient readiness to start ART and involve in ART regimen selection

Identify potential barriers to adherence (e.g., psychosocial or cognitive issues, substance abuse, low literacy, busy daily schedule, lack of prescription coverage and/or social support)

Assess adherence at every clinic visit, and simplify ART regimen when possible; provide positive reinforcement to foster adherence success

Identify non-adherence and reasons for non-adherence (e.g., adverse effects from medications, complex regimen, difficulty swallowing large pills, forgetfulness, pill fatigue, food requirements, stigma)

Provide resources (e.g., referrals for mental health and/or substance abuse treatment, prescription drug assistance programs, pillboxes, reminder tools, medication lists or calendars)

PATIENT COUNSELING

All HIV Medications

- This medication is not a cure for HIV and, when used alone, does not prevent the spread of HIV to others through sexual contact or blood contamination (such as sharing used needles).

- It is very important to continue taking this medication (and other HIV medications in your regimen) exactly as prescribed by your healthcare provider. Do not skip doses or stop taking your HIV medication regimen even for a short time unless directed to do so by your healthcare provider. Skipping or stopping your medication, or taking only some but not all of the HIV medications in your full regimen, may cause the amount of HIV virus to increase and make the infection more difficult to treat (resistant). Refill all HIV medications before you run out.

- If you are taking HIV medications for the first time, you may experience symptoms of an old infection. This may happen as your immune system begins to work better. Contact your healthcare provider immediately if you notice any of the following symptoms: new cough, trouble breathing, fever, new vision problems, new headaches or new skin problems.

- Rarely, this medication can cause severe liver problems. Tell your healthcare provider immediately if you develop symptoms such as persistent nausea/vomiting, loss of appetite, stomach/abdominal pain, pale stools, dark urine, yellowing eyes/skin, or unusual tiredness.

- If you have hepatitis B and are taking a regimen containing lamivudine, emtricitabine, and/or tenofovir, your hepatitis symptoms may become worse or become very serious if you stop taking any of these medications. Talk with your healthcare provider before stopping the medication(s). Tell your healthcare provider immediately if you develop symptoms of worsening liver problems.

NRTIs Patient Counseling

- This medication can cause changes in body fat, such as loss of fat from legs, arms and face. These symptoms occur after you have been on the medication for a long time.

- Rarely, this medication can cause a build-up of acid in your blood; report any symptoms such as stomach pain, nausea, vomiting, troubled breathing, weakness or muscle pain.

- If you have hepatitis B and are taking a regimen containing lamivudine, emtricitabine, and/or tenofovir, your hepatitis symptoms may become worse or become very serious if you stop taking any of these medications. Talk with your healthcare provider before stopping the medication(s). Tell your healthcare provider immediately if you develop symptoms of worsening liver problems.

Emtricitabine

- Rarely, this medication can cause darkening skin color on palms of hands and on soles of feet.

- This medication may cause rash in some people who take it. If you develop a rash, notify your healthcare provider as soon as possible.

- Take this medication with or without food.

Tenofovir

- Tell your healthcare provider immediately if any of these rare but serious side effects occur: signs of kidney problems such as a change in the amount of urine, unusual thirst, muscle cramps/weakness, bone pain, or easily broken bones.

- Tenofovir tablets (or *Truvada*): Take this medication with or without food.

- Tenofovir powder: This medication comes with a dosing scoop; use only the dosing scoop to measure the oral powder. Mix the oral powder with soft foods that can be swallowed without chewing (e.g., applesauce, baby food or yogurt). Do not mix with liquid as the powder may float to the top even after stirring. Give the entire dose right away after mixing to avoid a bad taste.

NNRTIs Patient Counseling

- This medication may cause a rash in some people who take it. If you develop a rash, notify your healthcare provider right away. If the rash is very severe, accompanied with a fever, or you develop skin blistering, seek care immediately.

- This medication may interact with many other medications. Tell your healthcare provider about all the medications you are taking, including any over-the-counter medications and herbal supplements. Do not start, stop, or change the dosage of any medication before checking with your healthcare provider or pharmacist first.

Efavirenz

- Take this medication by mouth on an empty stomach, usually once daily at bedtime. Taking efavirenz with food especially fatty foods, can increase the blood level of this medication, which may increase your risk of certain side effects.

- Headache, nausea, vomiting, and diarrhea may occur.

- Dizziness, drowsiness, unusual or vivid dreams/nightmares, trouble sleeping, tiredness/fatigue, and trouble concentrating may occur. These side effects may begin 1 – 2 days after starting this medication and usually go away in 2 – 4 weeks. They are also reduced by taking efavirenz on an empty stomach at bedtime. If any of these effects persist or worsen, tell your healthcare provider promptly.

- Because efavirenz may impair thinking or reactions, use caution when driving or performing tasks that requires you to be awake and alert. Avoid drinking alcohol.

- Infrequently, serious <u>psychiatric symptoms</u> may occur during efavirenz treatment, especially in people who have mental health conditions. Tell your healthcare provider immediately if any of these unlikely but serious side effects occur: mental/mood changes such as depression, thoughts of suicide, nervousness, angry behavior, or hallucinations.

- This medication may decrease the effectiveness of hormonal birth control pills, patch, or ring and may result in pregnancy. To reduce the risk of unintended pregnancy, and also the risk of spreading HIV to others, use barrier protection during all sexual activity.

- This medication can cause harm to an unborn baby. Do not use efavirenz without your healthcare provider's consent if you are pregnant or planning to get pregnant. Use two forms of birth control, including a barrier form (such as a condom and diaphragm with spermicide gel) while you are taking efavirenz, and for at least 12 weeks after your treatment ends. Tell your healthcare provider if you become pregnant during treatment.

Rilpivirine

- This medication may cause depression in some patients. If you notice changes in your mood, such as feeling more sad than you usually do, contact your healthcare provider.

- It is very important to take this medication with a <u>full meal</u> as this helps ensure that your body is absorbing enough of the medication to work against the virus. Ideally, your meal should be at least 500 calories.

- Medications that reduce stomach acid can significantly affect the absorption of this medication and result in failure of HIV treatment. Talk with your healthcare provider or pharmacist before starting any acid suppressant medications.

PI Patient Counseling

- Diarrhea, nausea, vomiting, heartburn, stomach pain, loss of appetite, headache, dizziness, drowsiness, fatigue, weakness, or changes in taste may occur. If any of these effects persist or worsen, tell your healthcare provider or pharmacist promptly.

- A mild rash (redness and itching) may occur within the first few weeks after the medicine is started and usually goes away within 2 weeks with no change in treatment. If a severe rash develops with symptoms of fever, body or muscle aches, mouth sores, shortness of breath, or swelling of the face, contact your healthcare provider immediately.

- Before using this medication, tell your healthcare provider or pharmacist your medical history, especially of: diabetes, heart problems (coronary artery disease, heart attack), hemophilia, high cholesterol/triglycerides, gout/high uric acid in the blood, liver problems (such as hepatitis B or hepatitis C), kidney problems, and/or pancreatitis.

- This medication may increase blood sugar levels. If you have diabetes, check your blood sugar levels regularly as directed by your healthcare provider. Tell your healthcare provider immediately if you have symptoms of high blood sugar, such as increased thirst, increased urination, confusion, drowsiness, flushing, rapid breathing, or fruity breath odor.

- Changes in body fat may occur while taking this medication (such as increased fat in the upper back and neck, breasts, and belly areas). Discuss the risks and benefits of treatment with your healthcare provider, as well as the possible use of exercise to reduce this side effect.

- <u>This medication interacts with many other medications</u>. Tell your healthcare provider about all the medications you are taking, including any over-the-counter medications and herbal supplements. Do not start, stop or change the dosage of any medicine before checking with your doctor or pharmacist first.

- Seek immediate medical attention if any of these rare but serious side effects occur: symptoms of a heart attack (such as chest/jaw/left arm pain, shortness of breath or profuse sweating), change in heart rhythm, dizziness, lightheadedness, severe nausea or vomiting, severe stomach pain, extreme weakness or trouble breathing.

Atazanavir

- Take this medication once daily <u>with food</u>. If you are also prescribed ritonavir, make sure to take both atazanavir and ritonavir at the same time.
- Although rare, some patients have developed kidney stones while on this medication. Take this medication with <u>plenty of water</u> to reduce chances of developing kidney stones. Seek immediate medical attention if you notice signs of a kidney stone (e.g., pain in side/back/abdomen, painful urination or blood in the urine).
- <u>Acid-lowering medications</u> for indigestion, heartburn, or ulcers (e.g., prescription or over-the-counter medications such as antacids, famotidine or omeprazole) can significantly affect the absorption of atazanavir and result in failure of your HIV treatment. Ask your healthcare provider or pharmacist how to use these medications together with atazanavir safely.
- May cause skin or the whites of eyes to turn yellow. This is usually not a dangerous side effect, however, if this becomes bothersome, talk with your healthcare provider. If you develop yellowing of skin/eyes along with severe abdominal pain and/or nausea/vomiting, contact your healthcare provider immediately as these could be signs of liver problems.

Darunavir

- Take darunavir with ritonavir at the same time(s) each day <u>with food</u>.
- This medication may cause rash in some people, which is usually mild and will resolve on its own over time. If you develop a severe, bothersome rash, contact your healthcare provider immediately. If you have a <u>sulfonamide allergy</u>, tell your healthcare provider or pharmacist right away.

INSTI Patient Counseling

- <u>This medication can interact with antacids, multivitamins, iron and other supplements</u>. Talk with your healthcare provider before taking these two medications together. Generally, you should separate this HIV medication at least 2 hours before or 6 hours after the antacids.
- May cause rash in some people. Notify your healthcare provider if it becomes bothersome. If you develop severe rash, accompanied with fever and/or difficulty breathing, seek medical attention immediately.
- May cause muscle pain or tenderness, or weakness. Inform your healthcare provider if you notice these symptoms, especially if you develop these out of proportion to your actual level of activity.
- May cause headache or difficulty sleeping.
- Rarely, may cause kidney or liver problems. Your healthcare provider will be checking your labs from time to time to monitor your kidney and liver functions.

Dolutegravir

- Take this medication with or without food.
- Follow the dosing instructions as prescribed by your healthcare provider (once vs. twice a day).
- Do not take this medication if you are also taking dofetilide. Contact your healthcare provider to discuss alternative HIV therapy options.

Raltegravir

- This medication is generally tolerated by most people who take it.
- Take with or without food. This medication is to be taken twice a day.
- The chewable tablets should not be taken by patients with phenylketonuria (PKU). Talk to your healthcare provider about alternative options if you have been diagnosed with PKU.

Stribild and _Genvoya_ (also see emtricitabine and tenofovir counseling points)

- This medication contains 4 medications in one pill: elvitegravir, cobicistat, emtricitabine, and tenofovir.

- Take this medication <u>once a day with food</u>. Keep the medication in the original container.

- If you have hepatitis B, it's very important that you do not suddenly stop this medication unless instructed to do so by your healthcare provider. Abruptly stopping this medication may result in worsening of your hepatitis symptoms.

- <u>This medication interacts with many medications.</u> Tell your healthcare provider and pharmacist about all the medications you are taking, including any over-the-counter medications and herbal supplements. Do not start, stop, or change the dosage of any medication before checking with your healthcare provider or pharmacist first.

PULMONARY ARTERIAL HYPERTENSION & PULMONARY FIBROSIS

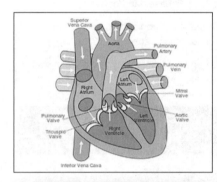

We gratefully acknowledge the assistance of Heather R. Bream-Rouwenhorst, PharmD, BCPS, Clinical Assistant Professor, University of Iowa College of Pharmacy, in preparing this chapter.

BACKGROUND

Pulmonary Arterial Hypertension (PAH) is characterized by continuous high blood pressure in the pulmonary arteries. The average blood pressure in a normal pulmonary artery (called pulmonary artery pressure) is 8 – 20 mmHg when a person is resting. A mean pulmonary artery pressure (mPAP) greater than 25 mmHg in the setting of normal fluid status defines PAH. Other hemodynamic parameters are affected as well.

CLASSIFICATION

Pulmonary hypertension (PH) may occur with various disease states. The World Health Organization (WHO) classifies PH into five groups (see box on the following page).

Group 1 is PAH, which may arise from genetic inheritance, connective tissue disease, advanced liver disease, and HIV among others. Some patients have no identifiable cause of the disease; this is primary, or idiopathic, PAH (versus secondary, which has a known cause). Less commonly, medications can be the causative factor (see box on the following page). PH treatments discussed in this chapter have only been approved for the treatment of PAH with the exception of riociguat *(Adempas)*.

Treatment of the other PH groups is aimed at the underlying causes. Group 2 is pulmonary venous hypertension, which arises from left-sided heart disease (left ventricular systolic or diastolic dysfunction, valvular disease, congenital heart disease, etc.). Group 3 is PH from hypoxia or chronic lung disease, such as chronic obstructive pulmonary disease or interstitial lung disease. Group 4 is chronic thromboembolic PH (CTEPH), which occurs in a minority of PE survivors. Warfarin anticoagulation to an INR goal of 2 – 3 is recommended given the history of a clot, and for patients who are not thrombectomy candidates, riociguat *(Adempas)* is an approved treatment. Group 5 is PH due to causes that do not fit in the above categorization (e.g., sarcoidosis).

GUIDELINES/REFERENCES

ACCF/AHA 2009 Expert Consensus Document on Pulmonary Hypertension. *J Am Coll Cardiol.* 2009;53:1573-1619.

Galie N, Corris PA, Frost A, et al. Updated Treatment Algorithm of Pulmonary Arterial Hypertension. *J Am Coll Cardiol* .2013;62:D60-72.

PATHOPHYSIOLOGY

PAH stems from an imbalance of vasoconstrictor and vaso-dilator substances and an imbalance of proliferation and apoptosis in the pulmonary arteries. The vasoconstrictor substances such as endothelin-1 and thromboxane A_2 (TxA$_2$) are increased in PAH, whereas the vasodilators (e.g., pros-tacyclins, others) are decreased. Vasoconstriction results in reduced blood flow and high pressure within the pulmonary vasculature. The walls of the pulmonary arteries thicken as the amount of muscle increases and scar tissue can form on the artery walls (vasoproliferation). As the walls thicken and scar, the arteries become increasingly narrower. These changes make it hard for the right ventricle to pump blood through the pulmonary arteries and into the lungs due to the increased pressure. As a result of the heart working harder, the right ventricle becomes enlarged and right heart failure can result. Heart failure is the most common cause of death in people who have PAH.

The biochemical changes mentioned above ($\uparrow$ TxA$_2$, $\downarrow$ pros-tacyclin), along with other altered pathways, lead to a pro-thrombotic state, and anticoagulation is suggested to pre-vent blood clots from forming. Warfarin, titrated to an INR of 1.5 – 2.5, is recommended in PAH.

Symptoms of PAH include fatigue, dyspnea, chest pain, syncope, edema, tachycardia and/or Raynaud's phenom-enon. In Raynaud's, the reduced blood supply causes dis-coloration and coldness in the fingers, toes, and occasion-ally other areas.

There is no cure for PAH, but in the last decade, the knowl-edge of PAH has increased significantly and many more treatment options have become available. Without treat-ment, life expectancy is three years. In some cases, a lung or heart-lung transplant may be an option, at least for younger patients.

WORLD HEALTH ORGANIZATION (WHO) CLINICAL CLASSIFICATION OF PULMONARY HYPERTENSION

Group 1 – Pulmonary arterial hyperten-sion (PAH) – includes idiopathic PAH, heritable, drug and toxin induced, PAH associated with connective tissue diseases, HIV infection, portal hyperten-sion, and persistent pulmonary hyper-tension of a newborn

Group 2 – Pulmonary hypertension due to left heart disease

Group 3 – Pulmonary hypertension due to lung diseases and/or hypoxia

Group 4 – Chronic thromboembolic pulmonary hypertension (CTEPH)

Group 5 – Pulmonary hypertension with unclear multifactorial mechanisms

SELECT DRUGS THAT CAN CAUSE PAH

Cocaine

Dasatinib (*Sprycel*)

Diazoxide (*Proglycem*)

Methamphetamine

SSRI use during pregnancy $\uparrow$ risk in newborns

Weight loss agents (diethylpropion, lor-caserin, phendimetrazine, phentermine)

NON-DRUG TREATMENT

Patients with PAH should follow a sodium restricted diet (< 2.4 grams/day) and manage volume status, especially if they have right ventricular failure. Routine immunizations against influenza and pneu-mococcal pneumonia are advised. Exposure to high altitudes may contribute to hypoxic pulmonary vasoconstriction and may not be tolerated by patients. Oxygen is used to maintain oxygen saturation above 90%.

PAH Treatment Algorithm

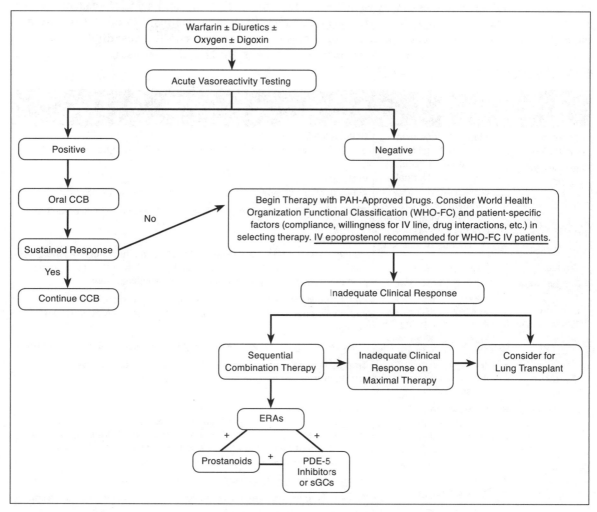

DRUG TREATMENT

After background therapy with warfarin, loop diuretics for volume overload, oxygen therapy, and/or possibly digoxin (if low cardiac output or in atrial fibrillation), patients should be referred to a PAH specialty center. Patients will likely undergo right heart catheterization to determine if they respond to acute vasoreactivity testing. While the pulmonary artery pressures are being measured during right heart catheterization, short-acting vasodilators (such as inhaled nitric oxide, IV epoprostenol, or IV adenosine) are given. If the mPAP falls by at least 10 mmHg to an absolute value less than 40 mmHg, patients are termed responders and should be initiated on calcium channel blockers. Approximately 10 percent of patients respond to and are candidates for calcium channel blocker therapy, although only half have a sustained response. The calcium channel blockers used most frequently are long-acting nifedipine, diltiazem, and amlodipine. The use of verapamil is not recommended due to its more pronounced negative inotropic effects relative to diltiazem.

For most cases, drug therapy will reduce symptoms and improve exercise tolerance. Parenteral prostacyclin therapy appears to prolong life. Medications include prostacyclin analogues which cause vasodilation. These drugs can be given by continuous IV infusion, infusion under the skin, inhalation, or as oral therapy. Endothelin receptor antagonists block endothelin, a vasoconstrictor. Phosphodiesterase-5 inhibitors (the same drugs used for erectile dysfunction but with different brand names and doses) and a soluble guanylate cyclase (sGC) stimulator relax the blood vessels in the lungs. Some patients may benefit from combination therapy.

Prostacyclin Analogues (or Prostanoids)

Prostacyclin analogues act as <u>potent vasodilators</u> (on both pulmonary and systemic vascular beds). They are also <u>inhibitors of platelet aggregation</u>. Prostacyclin synthase is reduced in PAH resulting in inadequate production of prostacyclin I_2, which normally stimulates cAMP, a vasodilator with anti-proliferative effects, in pulmonary artery smooth muscle cells. Drugs which ↓ prostaglandins (<u>NSAIDs</u>) <u>should be avoided</u> in patients with PAH.

DRUG	DOSING	SAFETY/SIDE EFFECTS/MONITORING
Epoprostenol *(Flolan, Veletri)* AKA prostacyclin and PGI$_2$	Start at 2 ng/kg/min and ↑ by 1 ng/kg/min in at least 15 minute increments. Normal dose is 25-40 ng/kg/min (can be up to 200 ng/kg/min titrated over months to years) via continuous IV infusion	**CONTRAINDICATIONS** Severe hepatic impairment (Child-Pugh class C) - oral treprostinil only **WARNINGS** Avoid alcohol with oral treprostinil due to accelerated absorption. Oral treprostinil's shell does not dissolve and can lodge in diverticuli. **SIDE EFFECTS** <u>During Dose Titration</u> – vasodilation (hypotension, headache, flushing; dose-limiting; if this happens, ↓ dose of the drug), N/V/D, anxiety, chest pain/palpitations, tachycardia, edema, and jaw claudication
Treprostinil *(Remodulin* is SC/IV, *Tyvaso* is inhaled, *Orenitram* is oral)	*Remodulin:* start at 1.25 ng/kg/min and ↑ by 1.25 ng/kg/min at weekly intervals for the first month and 2.5 ng/kg/min increments thereafter up to 40-160 ng/kg/min via continuous SC or IV infusion	<u>With Chronic Use</u> – anxiety, flu-like symptoms, jaw pain, thrombocytopenia, neuropathy in addition to those seen during dose titration Treprostinil (inhaled) and iloprost: cough (in addition to above side effects) Treprostinil (oral): side effects as above with more pronounced gastrointestinal adverse effects **NOTES** <u>Avoid interruptions in therapy</u>. Immediate access to back up pump, infusion sets and medication is essential – particularly for epoprostenol – to prevent treatment interruptions (epoprostenol half-life ~ 5 minutes vs. treprostinil half-life ~ 4 hours).
	Inhalation form *(Tyvaso):* Inhale 18 mcg (3 inhalations) 4 times/day to start and ↑ Q1-2 weeks to 9 breaths 4 times/day	<u>Avoid large, sudden reductions or increases in dose.</u> *Flolan:* pump needs to be on ice packs for proper cooling. Requires light protection during administration. *Veletri:* thermostable (no need for ice packs).
	Oral, ER tablets *(Orenitram):* start at 0.25 mg BID with food and ↑ by 0.25-0.5 mg BID every 3-4 days up to ~ 20 mg BID as tolerated	*Remodulin:* SC very painful (85% of patients), may need analgesic to tolerate. Also thermostable – no ice packs needed. <u>Parenteral agents</u> are considered the <u>most potent</u> of all PAH medications.
Iloprost *(Ventavis)*	2.5-5 mcg/inhalation given 6-9 times/day	Patients must be instructed on central catheter maintenance to ↓ infections and to avoid interruption of therapy – both which can be fatal.

Prostacyclin Analogue Drug Interactions

■ Can ↑ the effects of antihypertensive and antiplatelet agents.

■ Treprostinil levels are ↑ by the CYP450 2C8 inhibitor gemfibrozil and ↓ by 2C8 inducers such as rifampin.

Endothelin Receptor Antagonists

Endothelin receptor antagonists (ERAs) block endothelin receptors on pulmonary artery smooth muscle cells. Endothelin is a vasoconstrictor with cellular proliferative effects.

DRUG	DOSING	SAFETY/SIDE EFFECTS/MONITORING
Bosentan *(Tracleer)*	< 40 kg: 62.5 mg BID ≥ 40 kg: 62.5 mg BID (for 4 wks), then 125 mg BID	**BOXED WARNINGS** Hepatotoxicity Use in pregnancy is contraindicated (Pregnancy Category X) Because of the risks of hepatic impairment and possible teratogenic effects, bosentan is only available through the *Tracleer* Access Program (TAP). Prescribers and pharmacists must be certified and enroll patients in the TAP REMS program. **CONTRAINDICATIONS** Pregnancy; concurrent use of cyclosporine or glyburide **WARNINGS** Avoid use in moderate-to-severe hepatic impairment **SIDE EFFECTS** Headache, ↓ Hgb (usually in first 6 weeks of therapy), ↑ LFTs (dose related), upper respiratory tract infections, edema (all > 10%) Spermatogenesis inhibition (25%) leading to male infertility (with bosentan only) **MONITORING** LFTs and bilirubin (baseline and every month thereafter), hemoglobin and hematocrit (baseline and at 1 month and 3 months, then every 3 months thereafter) **NOTES** Women of childbearing potential must have a negative pregnancy test prior to initiation of therapy and monthly thereafter (prior to shipment of the monthly refill). Barrier techniques of contraception are recommended. MedGuide required.
Ambrisentan *(Letairis)*	5-10 mg daily	**BOXED WARNING** Use in pregnancy is contraindicated (Pregnancy Category X) Because of the risk of possible teratogenic effects, ambrisentan is only available through the *Letairis* Education and Access Program (LEAP) restricted distribution program. Prescribers and pharmacists must be certified and enroll patients in the LEAP REMS program. **CONTRAINDICATIONS** Pregnancy, idiopathic pulmonary fibrosis **SIDE EFFECTS** Peripheral edema, headache, ↓ Hgb, flushing, palpitations, and nasal congestion **MONITORING** Hemoglobin and hematocrit (baseline and at 1 month, then periodically thereafter) **NOTES** Women of childbearing potential must have a negative pregnancy test prior to initiation of therapy and monthly thereafter (prior to shipment of the monthly refill). MedGuide required.

Endothelin Receptor Antagonists (ERAs) Continued

DRUG	DOSING	SAFETY/SIDE EFFECTS/MONITORING
Macitentan (Opsumit)	10 mg daily	**BOXED WARNING** Use in pregnancy is contraindicated (Pregnancy Category X) Because of the risk of possible teratogenic effects, macitentan is only available through the *Opsumit* restricted distribution program. Prescribers and pharmacists must be certified and enroll patients in the *Opsumit* REMS program. **CONTRAINDICATIONS** Pregnancy **SIDE EFFECTS** ↓ Hgb, headache, pharyngitis, bronchitis, anemia (all > 10%) **MONITORING** Hemoglobin, hematocrit, and LFTs at baseline and repeat as clinically indicated **NOTES** Women of childbearing potential must have a negative pregnancy test prior to initiation of therapy and monthly thereafter (prior to shipment of the monthly refill). MedGuide required.

Endothelin Receptor Antagonist Drug Interactions

- Avoid use with St. John's wort or grapefruit juice.

- Bosentan is a substrate of 3A4 (major) and 2C9 (minor) and an inducer of 3A4 (weak/moderate) and 2C9 (weak/moderate); monitor for drug interactions. Levels of bosentan can ↑ with 2C8/9 and 3A4 inhibitors. Bosentan can ↓ the effectiveness of hormonal birth control. Avoid concurrent use of cyclosporine or glyburide.

- Ambrisentan is a substrate of 3A4 (major), 2C19 (minor), P-glycoprotein and other pathways. The dose should not exceed 5 mg/d when given concomitantly with cyclosporine.

- Macitentan is a substrate of 3A4 (major) and 2C19 (minor). Strong 3A4 inhibitors and inducers should be avoided with macitentan.

Phosphodiesterase-5 Inhibitors

These agents inhibit phosphodiesterase-5 (PDE-5) in smooth muscle cells of the pulmonary vasculature. PDE-5 is responsible for the degradation of cyclic guanosine monophosphate (cGMP); ↑ cGMP concentrations lead to <u>pulmonary vasculature relaxation and vasodilation</u>.

DRUG	DOSING	SAFETY/SIDE EFFECTS/MONITORING
Sildenafil *(Revatio)* *Viagra* - ED	IV: 2.5-10 mg TID Oral: 5-20 mg TID, taken 4-6 hours apart	**CONTRAINDICATIONS** <u>Concurrent use of nitrates or riociguat</u>. Avoid using sildenafil for PAH in patients taking PI-based (ritonavir, others) ART regimens. **WARNINGS** Color discrimination impairment (dose related) Hearing loss, with or without tinnitus Vision loss, rare but may be due to nonarteritic anterior ischemic optic neuropathy (NAION)
Tadalafil *(Adcirca)* *Cialis* - ED, BPH	40 mg daily (two 20 mg tabs) 20 mg daily if mild to moderate renal/hepatic impairment CrCl < 30 mL/min: avoid	Priapism – seek emergency medical care if erection lasts > 4 hours **SIDE EFFECTS** <u>Dizziness, sudden drop in blood pressure, headache</u>, flushing, dyspepsia, back pain, and epistaxis **NOTES** Avoid use in severe hepatic impairment

PDE-5 Inhibitor Drug Interactions

- Do not give with PDE-5 inhibitors used for erectile dysfunction.

- Concurrent use of nitrate medications [any nitroglycerin-containing drug including *Nitrolingual, Nitrostat*, isosorbide dinitrate/hydralazine *(BiDil)*, among others and the sGC stimulator riociguat], increases the potential for excessively low blood pressure. Taking nitrates is an <u>absolute contraindication</u> to the use of these medicines. These include the illicit drugs such as amyl nitrate and butyl nitrate ("poppers").

- Caution with PDE-5 inhibitors and concurrent alpha blocker therapy (or other antihypertensives): PDE-5 inhibitors can ↑ the hypotensive effect of an alpha blocker. When tadalafil is used, concurrent alpha 1-blockers are not recommended for the treatment of BPH.

- These are 3A4 substrates; avoid use of strong 3A4 inhibitors and inducers.

Soluble Guanylate Cyclase Stimulator

Soluble Guanylate Cyclase (sGC) stimulator increases the conversion of GTP to cGMP, leading to ↑ relaxation and antiproliferative effects in the pulmonary artery smooth muscle cells. Riociguat is approved for use in both PAH and CTEPH.

DRUG	DOSING	SAFETY/SIDE EFFECTS/MONITORING
Riociguat *(Adempas)*	0.5-1 mg TID, increasing by 0.5 mg TID every 2 weeks to target 2.5 mg TID	**BOXED WARNING** Use in pregnancy is contraindicated (Pregnancy Category X) Because of the risk of possible teratogenic effects, riociguat is only available through the *Adempas* restricted distribution program. Prescribers and pharmacists must be certified and enroll patients in the *Adempas* REMS program. **CONTRAINDICATIONS** Pregnancy; concomitant use of PDE-5 inhibitors or nitrates **SIDE EFFECTS** Headache, dyspepsia, dizziness, hypotension, N/V/D (all > 10%). Bleeding appears to be more common with riociguat than placebo. **NOTES** MedGuide required

Riociguat Drug Interactions

- Smoking ↑ riociguat clearance; the dose may need to be ↓ with smoking cessation.

- Separate from antacids by > 1 hour.

- Strong enzyme inhibitors (e.g., ketoconazole, ritonavir) may warrant a lower starting dose.

PULMONARY FIBROSIS

Pulmonary fibrosis (PF), sometimes called usual interstitial pneumonia (UIP), is scarred and damaged lung tissue. The common presentation is exertional dyspnea with a nonproductive cough. As the condition worsens, breathing becomes more labored. There are a variety of causes of PF: toxin

SELECT DRUGS THAT CAN CAUSE PF	
Amiodarone	Nitrofurantoin
Methotrexate	Sulfasalazine

exposure (including asbestos, silica and many others), medical conditions, drugs (see box) or due to a multitude of factors. Often the contributing factor is not identified and the PF is called idiopathic pulmonary fibrosis (IPF).

If the condition is drug-induced, the offending drug should be discontinued. Aside from treatment with chronic oxygen supplementation, two drugs were approved over the past year for IPF. Both pirfenidone and nintedanib slow the rate of decline in lung function. In addition to the two new drugs below, several of the drugs approved for pulmonary arterial hypertension (particularly sildenafil) may be used off-label for PF. The prognosis of IPF is poor; 20-30% of patients survive for 5 years after diagnosis.

DRUG	DOSING	SAFETY/SIDE EFFECTS/MONITORING
Pirfenidone *(Esbriet)* Mechanism not fully known. May ↓ production of fibrosis-associated proteins & cytokines and fibroblast proliferation, may ↓ formation of collagen; anti-inflammatory properties	Days 1-7: 267 mg (1 cap) TID Days 8-14: 534 mg (2 caps) TID Days 15+: 801 mg (3 caps) TID (max 2,403 mg/day) Take with food, at same time of day.	**WARNINGS** Photosensitivity reactions, ↑ LFTs **SIDE EFFECTS** N/V/D, rash, fatigue, dyspepsia, photosensitivity reaction, headache **MONITORING** LFTs at baseline, monthly for 6 months, and then every 3 months thereafter.
Nintedanib *(Ofev)* Tyrosine kinase inhibitor, blocks intracellular signaling and prevents proliferation, migration, and transformation of fibroblasts	150 mg Q12H (max 300 mg/d) Take with food, swallow whole with a full glass of water. Do not crush or chew.	**WARNINGS** May ↑ bleeding, cause thromboembolic events (MI), ↑ LFTs **SIDE EFFECTS** N/V/D, abdominal pain, ↑ LFTs, ↓ appetite **MONITORING** LFTs at baseline, monthly for 3 months, every 3 months thereafter, and as clinically indicated. **NOTES** Pregnancy Category D. Avoid becoming pregnant during therapy and at least 3 months after use. Use appropriate precautions when handling/disposing, drug is hazardous.

Pirfenidone and Nintedanib Drug Interactions

- Moderate-strong 1A2 inhibitors such as ciprofloxacin and fluvoxamine may necessitate a pirfenidone dose ↓.

- P-glycoprotein (P-gp) and 3A4 inhibitors ↑ nintedanib levels; monitor for tolerability. P-gp and 3A4 inducers will ↓ nintedanib levels.

- Nintedanib ↑ bleeding risk. Use caution when combining it with anticoagulants or antiplatelets.

- Smoking ↓ levels of pirfenidone and nintedanib.

ALLERGIC RHINITIS, COUGH & COLD

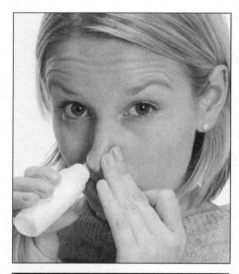

GUIDELINES/REFERENCES

Seidman MD, Gurgel RK, Lin SY et al. Clinical Practice Guideline: Allergic Rhinitis. *Otolaryngology-Head and Neck Surgery.* 2015;152(IS):S1-S43.

Krinsky DL, Berardi RR, Ferreri SP, eds. Handbook of Nonprescription Drugs. 18th ed. Washington DC: APhA; 2015:172-208.

We gratefully acknowledge the assistance of Christina L. Mnatzaganian, PharmD, BCACP, Assistant Clinical Professor, University of California San Diego Skaggs School of Pharmacy and Pharmaceutical Sciences, in preparing this chapter.

ALLERGIC RHINITIS

Background

Allergic rhinitis is inflammation of the nasal airways and is very common, affecting up to 20% – 40% of the population. It is classified as intermittent (infrequent or seasonal) or persistent (chronic or perennial), and symptoms can be mild, moderate or severe. It represents an opportunity for pharmacists to help patients select self care over the counter products, and to use prescription medication correctly. Allergic rhinitis is a major reason for decreased work productivity, or lost work or school days each year. Symptoms include sneezing, itchy nose, eyes or throat, watery eyes, rhinorrhea (runny nose), nasal congestion, and postnasal drip. It can also result in fatigue, irritability, sleep disturbance and reduced cognitive ability. Untreated allergic rhinitis can lead to sinusitis, otitis media (in children) and asthma exacerbation in susceptible people. Unlike the common cold or the flu, onset of symptoms occurs quickly (within minutes) after allergen exposure.

NON-DRUG TREATMENT

Environmental control is required to minimize allergic symptoms and involves avoiding exposure to known or suspected allergens, if possible. An IgE-mediated skin or blood allergy test by an allergy or pulmonary specialist can help determine patient-specific allergens. Common allergens include house-dust mites, outdoor mold spores, pollen from trees and ragweed, cat-derived allergens, cockroaches, and urban pollutants such as a diesel exhaust particles. Ventilation systems with high-efficiency particulate air (HEPA) filters can help with some allergens (pollen, mold), however, these systems are expensive and ineffective for some patients. Vacuuming carpets, drapes, and upholstery with a HEPA vacuum cleaner weekly or more often will reduce household allergens. Removing carpets, upholstered furniture, encasing mattresses, pillows and boxsprings in allergen-impermeable covers, and washing bedding and soft toys in hot water weekly reduces dust mite allergens. Patients with air pollutants as triggers should be aware of the air quality index (AQI) and plan outdoor activities accordingly. Patients with pollen as a trigger should monitor pollen counts and plan accordingly. Staying indoors, closing windows in the house or car and using air-conditioning can help reduce exposure. However, keeping an environment that is "too clean" reduces exposure to microbes and helminths and may not be ideal: children need exposure to various "germs" to build a healthy immune system.

Nasal Irrigation and Wetting Agents

Nasal wetting agents (saline, propylene and polyethylene glycol sprays) or nasal irrigation with warm saline (isotonic or hypertonic) may reduce symptoms. Nasal irrigation rinses out allergens and mucus, increases ciliary function and reduces swelling. Saline solutions are either isotonic (0.9%) or hypertonic (2 – 3.5%). A popular product, the "neti pot", looks like a small genie lamp or teapot. It is used to hold salt water (saline solution) that is poured into one nostril and drained out of the other nostril. Nasal irrigation is safe for children and pregnant women. Instruct to use boiled, bottled or distilled water (not directly from the faucet). The most common side effects are nasal burning, stinging, pain or irritation, which are increased with higher concentrations of saline. Pots and rinse bottles should be washed with hot soapy water after every use and should never be shared with others. Nasal gels with petrolatum *(Allergen Block)* can be applied around the nostrils to physically block pollens and allergens from entering the nose.

DRUG TREATMENT

Selecting appropriate pharmacologic management depends on the person's severity of illness and symptoms. Intranasal corticosteroids are first-line for chronic, moderate-to-severe rhinitis. Milder, intermittent symptoms can be treated with oral antihistamines. Decongestants are used for congestion (if present) and come in nasal and oral formulations. Agents for itchy eyes can be found in the Glaucoma, Ophthalmics & Otics chapter. A variety of other agents can be modestly useful.

Intranasal Corticosteroids

Intranasal corticosteroids work by decreasing inflammation. They are the most effective medication class in controlling symptoms of chronic allergic rhinitis and are considered first-line treatment for moderate-severe rhinitis. They are especially effective in reducing the nasal symptoms of allergic rhinitis (sneezing, itching, rhinorrhea, congestion). Triamcinolone (*Nasacort* Allergy 24HR), fluticasone (*Flonase Allergy Relief*) and budesonide *(Rhinocort Allergy Spray)* are approved for nonprescription use to treat nasal allergy symptoms. Take note that steroids used to treat chronic allergic rhinitis have different brand names and delivery vehicles than those used to treat asthma. For example, fluticasone for nasal allergy relief is *Flonase* ("-nase" for nose) and for asthma is *Flovent*.

DRUG	DOSING	SAFETY/SIDE EFFECTS/MONITORING
Beclomethasone (*Beconase AQ, Qnasl*)	Adult: 1-2 sprays per nostril BID *(Beconase AQ)*; 2 sprays per nostril daily *(Qnasl)*	**WARNINGS** Adrenal suppression: Can occur when used in high doses for prolonged periods
	Age 6-11 yrs.: 1-2 sprays per nostril BID *(Beconase AQ)*	Delayed wound healing: Avoid use if recent nasal septal ulcers, nasal surgery, or nasal trauma until healing has occurred.
Budesonide (*Rhinocort Aqua, Rhinocort Allergy Spray OTC*)	Adult: 1 spray per nostril daily (max 4 sprays per nostril daily)	Pediatrics: can ↓ growth velocity in pediatric patients (~1 centimeter/yr and is dose and duration related). To minimize, use lowest effective dose. Monitor growth.
	Age ≥ 6 yrs.: 1 spray per nostril daily (max 2 sprays per nostril daily)	Infections: Prolonged use can ↑ the risk of secondary infection or limit response to vaccines. Avoid exposure to chickenpox. Caution in patients with untreated fungal, viral, or bacterial infections.
Ciclesonide (*Omnaris, Zetonna*)	Adult: 2 sprays per nostril daily *(Omnaris)*; 1 spray per nostril daily *(Zetonna)*	Ocular disease: Caution in patients with cataracts and/or glaucoma; ↑ intraocular pressure, open-angle glaucoma, and cataracts have occurred with prolonged use. Consider routine eye exams in chronic users.
	Age ≥ 6 yrs.: use adult dose	
Flunisolide	Adult: 2 sprays per nostril BID or TID	**SIDE EFFECTS** Headache, dry nose, epistaxis (nose bleeds), unpleasant taste, localized infection
	Age 6-14 yrs.: 1 spray per nostril TID or 2 sprays per nostril BID	
Fluticasone (*Flonase, Flonase Allergy Relief OTC, Veramyst*) + azelastine (*Dymista*)	Adult: 2 sprays per nostril daily *(Flonase)*; 1-2 sprays per nostril daily *(Veramyst)*	**NOTES** Can take up to one week to get full relief.
	Age ≥ 4 yrs.: 1 spray per nostril daily *(Flonase)*	Budesonide is Pregnancy Category B and is the preferred inhaled steroid in pregnancy.
	Age ≥ 2 yrs.: 1-2 sprays per nostril daily *(Veramyst)*	If using regularly for several months, recommend periodic nasal exams to evaluate for nasal septal perforation or ulcers.
	Dymista: Adult and age ≥ 6 yrs: 1 spray per nostril BID	Advise patients to discontinue if they come into contact with a person who has chickenpox, measles or TB, if they develop symptoms of an infection, have a change in vision, or experience frequent nose bleeds. Instruct patients to shake bottle well before each use and discard product after total number of estimated doses, even if bottle does not feel completely empty.
Mometasone (*Nasonex*)	Adult: 2 sprays per nostril daily	
	Age 2-11 yrs.: 1 spray per nostril daily	
Triamcinolone (*Nasacort AQ*, **Nasacort Allergy 24HR OTC**)	Adult: 1-2 sprays per nostril daily	
	Age ≥ 6 yrs.: use adult dose	
	Age 2-5 yrs.: 1 spray per nostril daily	

Oral Antihistamines

Oral antihistamines are considered <u>first-line agents for patients with mild-moderate disease. They are effective in reducing symptoms of itching, sneezing, rhinorrhea, and other types of immediate hypersensitivity reactions, but have little effect on nasal congestion</u>. Antihistamines work by blocking histamine at the histamine-1 (H1) receptor site. The <u>second-generation agents are generally preferred</u> since they cause less sedation and cognitive impairment. Antihistamines can help if symptoms of allergic conjunctivitis (itchy, red eyes) are present. See Glaucoma, Ophthalmics & Otics chapter.

DRUG	DOSING	SAFETY/SIDE EFFECTS/MONITORING

Select First Generation Oral Antihistamines

DRUG	DOSING	SAFETY/SIDE EFFECTS/MONITORING
Clemastine *(Tavist Allergy, Dayhist Allergy 12 HR Relief)* Tablet, syrup	Adult: 1.34-2.68 mg PO Q8-12H (max 8.04 mg/day) Age 6-11 yrs.: 0.67-1.34 mg PO BID (max 4.02 mg/day)	**CONTRAINDICATIONS** Newborns or premature infants, lactating women, narrow-angle glaucoma, acute asthma exacerbation, stenosing peptic ulcer, symptomatic BPH, and bladder-neck and pyloroduodenal obstruction. Avoid concurrent use of MAO inhibitors.
DiphenhydrAMINE HCl *(Benadryl, many others)* Capsule, tablet, chewable, elixir, strip, syrup, suspension, injection, cream, gel, solution, stick	Adult: <u>25-50 mg PO Q4-6H</u> (max 300 mg/day) Age 6-11 yrs.: 12.5-25 mg PO Q4-6H (max 150 mg/day) Age < 6 yrs.: <u>do not use</u> for self care	**WARNINGS** Due to strong anticholinergic effects, avoid use in elderly (Beers criteria), caution with cardiovascular disease, prostate enlargement, glaucoma, asthma, pyloroduodenal obstruction, thyroid disease. Caution for excessive sedation. In 2008 the FDA advised that OTC cough and cold preparations, including first generation antihistamines (chlorpheniramine, diphenhydramine, brompheniramine and clemastine) should not be used in children < 2 years due to the risk of potentially serious and life threatening side effects.
Carbinoxamine *(Arbinoxa, Karbinal ER)* Capsule, tablet, solution	**IR** Adult: 4-8 mg PO Q6-8H 6-11 yrs.: 2-4 mg PO Q6-8H 2-5 yrs.: 1-2 mg PO Q6-8H **ER** Adult: 6-16 mg PO Q12H 6-11 yrs.: 6-12 mg PO Q12H 4-5 yrs.: 3-8 mg PO Q12H 2-3 yrs.: 3-4 mg PO Q12H	**SIDE EFFECTS** <u>Somnolence</u>, cognitive impairment, strong anticholinergic effects (dry mouth, blurred vision, urinary retention, constipation), and seizures/arrhythmias in higher doses **NOTES** Pregnancy Category B/Pregnancy Category C (carbinoxamine) First generation antihistamines should not be taken by lactating women; second generation agents, such as loratadine or fexofenadine, are preferred. All antihistamines should be discontinued at least 4 days prior to allergy skin testing.
Chlorpheniramine *(Chlor-Trimeton, Chlorphen, Ed ChlorPed, others)* Tablet, liquid, suspension, syrup	**IR** Adult: 4 mg PO Q4-6H (max 24 mg/day) 6-11 yrs.: 2 mg PO Q4-6H (max 12 mg/day) 2-5 yrs.: 1 mg PO Q4-6H (max 6 mg/day) **ER** Adult: 12 mg PO Q12H (max 24 mg/day) no pediatric dosing	1st generation antihistamines are photosensitizing; advise patients to use sunscreens and wear protective clothing while taking them.

Oral Antihistamines Continued

DRUG	DOSING	SAFETY/SIDE EFFECTS/MONITORING

Second Generation Oral Antihistamines

DRUG	DOSING	SAFETY/SIDE EFFECTS/MONITORING
Cetirizine (*ZyrTEC, ZyrTEC-D*, others) Capsule, tablet, solution, syrup, chewable, ODT	Adult: 5-10 mg PO daily (max 5 mg daily in elderly) ≥ 6 yrs.: use adult dose 2-5 yrs.: 2.5-5 mg PO daily	**CONTRAINDICATIONS** Levocertirizine: end-stage renal disease (CrCl < 10 mL/min), hemodialysis, infants and children 6 months to 11 years of age with renal impairment **WARNINGS** CNS depression: can cause sedation when used with other sedating drugs **SIDE EFFECTS** Somnolence can still be seen occasionally with the 2nd generation agents (more with cetirizine and levocetirizine) **NOTES** Fexofenadine: take with water (not juice due to ↓ absorption). Avoid concurrent administration with aluminum or magnesium-containing products. All antihistamines should be discontinued at least 4 days prior to allergy skin testing. If a 2nd generation antihistamine is preferred in pregnancy, loratidine and cetirizine are considered low risk.
Levocetirizine (*Xyzal*) Tablet, solution	Adult: 5 mg PO QHS 6-11 yrs.: 2.5 mg PO QHS 6 mos-5 yrs.: 1.25 mg PO QHS	
Fexofenadine (*Allegra, Allegra D 12H, Allegra D 24H, Children's Allegra ODT, Mucinex Allergy*) Tablet, suspension, ODT	Adult: 60 mg PO BID or 180 mg daily 2-11 yrs.: 30 mg PO BID	
Loratadine (*Claritin, Claritin-D 24 hour, Claritin RediTabs, Alavert*) Tablet, capsule, chewable, solution, syrup, ODT	Adult: 10 mg PO daily or 5 mg PO BID (*RediTabs*) Age ≥ 6 yrs.: use adult dose 2-5 yrs.: 5 mg PO daily	
Desloratadine (*Clarinex, Clarinex D, Clarinex RediTabs*) Tablet, syrup, ODT	Adult: 5 mg PO daily 6-11 yrs.: 2.5 mg PO daily 12 mos-5 yrs.: 1.25 mg PO daily 6-11 mos.: 1 mg PO daily	

Intranasal Antihistamines

DRUG	DOSING	SAFETY/SIDE EFFECTS/MONITORING
Azelastine (*Astelin, Astepro*) + fluticasone (*Dymista*)	Adult: 1-2 sprays per nostril BID 6-11 yrs.: 1 spray per nostril BID	**SIDE EFFECTS** Bitter taste, headache, somnolence, nasal irritation, minor nosebleed, sinus pain **NOTES** Helps with nasal congestion as well.
Olopatadine (*Patanase*)	Adult: 2 sprays per nostril BID 6-11 yrs.: 1 spray per nostril BID	

Decongestants

These agents are effective in reducing sinus and nasal congestion. Decongestants are <u>alpha-adrenergic agonists</u> (sympathomimetics) that work by causing vasoconstriction that decreases sinusoid vessel engorgement and mucosal edema. If <u>a product contains a D after the name</u> (such as *Mucinex D* or *Robitussin D*), it usually contains a decongestant (phenylephrine or pseudoephedrine).

DRUG	DOSING	SAFETY/SIDE EFFECTS/MONITORING

Systemic (Oral)

DRUG	DOSING	SAFETY/SIDE EFFECTS/MONITORING
Phenylephrine HCl *(Sudafed PE, others)* Tablet, liquid, solution, injection	Adult: 10 mg PO Q4H PRN (max 60 mg/day) 6-11 yrs.: 5 mg PO Q4H PRN (max 30 mg/day) 4-5 yrs.: 2.5 mg PO Q4H PRN (max 15 mg/day)	**CONTRAINDICATIONS** Do not use within 14 days of MAO inhibitors. **WARNINGS** Avoid in children < 2 years Use with caution in patients with CV disease and uncontrolled hypertension (can ↑ BP), hyperthyroidism (can worsen), diabetes (can ↑ blood glucose), bowel obstruction, glaucoma (can ↑ IOP), BPH (can cause urinary retention), and in the elderly
Pseudoephedrine *(Sudafed, Nexafed, Zephrex-D*, others)* Tablet, liquid, syrup	Adult: 60 mg PO Q4-6H PRN, or 120 mg PO ER Q12H, or 240 mg PO ER daily (max 240 mg/day) 6-12 yrs.: 30 mg PO Q4-6H PRN (max 120 mg/day) 4-5 yrs.: 15 mg PO Q4-6H PRN (max 60 mg/day)	**SIDE EFFECTS** Cardiovascular stimulation (tachycardia, palpitations, ↑ BP), CNS stimulation (anxiety, tremors, insomnia, nervousness, restlessness, fear, hallucinations), dizziness, headache, anorexia **NOTES** Pregnancy Category C Phenylephrine has low bioavailability (~38%); pseudoephedrine is more effective Onset of 15-60 minutes

Topicals (Intranasal)

DRUG	DOSING	SAFETY/SIDE EFFECTS/MONITORING
Naphazoline 0.05% *(Privine)*	Adult: 1-2 sprays per nostril Q6H PRN	**CONTRAINDICATIONS** Phenylephrine: hypertension, ventricular tachycardia
Oxymetazoline 0.05% *(Afrin, Neo-Synephrine Nighttime 12-Hour, Vicks Sinex, Zicam Extreme Congestion Relief)*	Adult: 2-3 sprays per nostril Q12H PRN ≥ 6 yrs.: use adult dose	**WARNINGS** Do not use with MAO inhibitors, or if have closed angle glaucoma
Phenylephrine 0.125%, 0.25%, 0.5%, 1% *(Neo-Synephrine 4-Hour, Little Noses Decongestant Drops)*	Adult: 2-3 sprays of 0.25% to 1% per nostril Q4H PRN 6-12 yrs.: 2-3 sprays of 0.25% per nostril Q4H PRN 2-5 yrs.: 2-3 sprays of 0.125% per nostril QH PRN	**SIDE EFFECTS** Stinging, burning, sneezing, dryness (vehicle-related), trauma from the tip of the device, rhinitis medicamentosa (rebound congestion if used longer than 3 days)
Tetrahydrozoline 0.05%, 0.1% *(Tyzine)* – Rx	Adult: 3-4 sprays of 0.1% per nostril Q3-4H PRN or 2-4 drops per nostril Q3-4H PRN > 6 yrs.: use adult dose 2-6 yrs.: 2-3 drops of 0.05% per nostril Q4-6H PRN	**NOTES** Effective with a fast onset of 5-10 minutes <u>Limit use to ≤ 3 days to prevent rebound congestion</u>

Additional Allergy Agents

Intranasal cromolyn (Nasalcrom)

Cromolyn is a mast cell stabilizer used for treatment and prophylaxis. It must be started at the onset of allergy season and used regularly (not PRN), 1 spray per nostril every 6 – 8 hours, to be effective. Symptoms start to improve in 3 – 7 days but can take as long as 2 – 4 weeks of continued use to see maximal effect. Although generally not as effective as other agents, it is used in children 2 years and older and pregnancy due to its safety profile.

Intranasal ipratropium bromide

(Atrovent Nasal Spray)

This agent is effective for decreasing rhinorrhea by causing nasal dryness (not effective for other nasal symptoms).

Oral antileukotrienes (Montelukast – Singulair)

Montelukast has similar efficacy to antihistamines or pseudoephedrine and can be recommended for adjunctive relief. The dose of montelukast is 10 mg PO daily (15 years and up), 5 mg chewable tablet PO daily (ages 6 – 14 years), 4 mg chewable tablet PO daily (ages 2 – 5 years), or one packet of 4 mg oral granules PO daily (ages 6 months-5 years). See Asthma chapter for more information.

Sublingual Immunotherapy

In 2014 the FDA approved 3 new sublingual (SL) treatments for allergic rhinitis due to specific types of grass pollen. They are alternatives to allergy shots, which must be given in a physician office. The first dose must be given in the doctor's office with all 3 of these agents, but subsequent doses can be taken at home. The patient must be monitored for at least 30 minutes for signs of allergic reactions (boxed warning) and the patient should be prescribed autoinjectable epinephrine.

- *Oralair* contains 5 different grass pollen extracts. Place 1 SL tablet under the tongue daily; initiate treatment 4 months before and during grass pollen season.

- *Grastek* contains Timothy grass pollen extract. Place 1 SL tablet under the tongue daily; initiate treatment 3 months before and during grass pollen season.

- *Ragwitek* contains ragweed pollen extract. Place 1 SL tablet under the tongue daily; initiate treatment 3 months before and during pollen season.

COMBAT METHAMPHETAMINE EPIDEMIC ACT 2005

Pseudoephedrine (PSE) is located behind pharmacy counters as part of the "Combat Meth Act" (CMEA), under the Patriot Act, to crack down on the methamphetamine epidemic. Meth causes unpredictable and often violent behavior. The waste created in the production is very toxic and is usually dumped illegally. The act applies to any non-prescription product containing pseudoephedrine, phenylpropanolamine and ephedrine, all of which can be converted rather easily into methamphetamine.

To sell these products (primarily PSE, the others are not easily available), they must be kept behind the counter or in a locked cabinet. They often are, but do not need to be, located in the pharmacy. Stores must keep a logbook of sales (exception is the single dose package that contains a maximum of 60 mg – this is 2 of the 30 mg tablets.) For any sale above this amount, customer must show photo ID issued by the state (e.g., license, ID card, expired or unexpired US passport, unexpired foreign passport).

Customers record their name, date and time of sale, and sign the logbook. Store staff must verify the name matches the photo ID and that the date and time are correct. Store staff must also record the address; some stores can swipe the driver's license electronically to do this. The store staff must record what the person received as well as the quantity purchased. The maximum dose allowed for purchase is 3.6 grams or 120 of the 30 mg tablets, and 9 grams (300 tablets) in a 30-day period. The logbook must be kept for a minimum of 2 years and must be kept secured and readily available upon request by board inspectors or law enforcement. The logbook cannot be shared with the public.

Many states now have their own restrictions in addition to the federal restriction, such as age restrictions, prescription required or stricter limits.

COUGH AND COLD

Background

The common cold, a viral infection of the upper respiratory tract, is caused by over 200 viruses including rhinoviruses, coronaviruses, influenza and is transmitted primarily by mucus secretions via patient's hands or by the air from coughing or sneezing. Coughing or sneezing into the elbow or into a tissue is preferable over coughing into a hand, which can then touch surfaces and spread illness. Frequent hand cleansing with soap or soap substitutes (e.g., hand sanitizers) should be encouraged. Refer to the Medication Safety chapter for correct hand washing technique. Refer to the Infectious Diseases II chapter for a table that compares viral and bacteria infections. Although colds are usually self-limiting, they are the leading cause of absenteeism in work and school due to bothersome symptoms.

Natural Products used for Colds

Zinc, in various formulations including lozenges, is used for cold prevention and treatment. There is little efficacy data for cold prevention, but zinc lozenges or syrup may decrease cold duration if used correctly (taken every 2 hours while awake, starting within 24 hours of symptom onset). For this purpose zinc supplements are rated as "possibly effective" by the *Natural Medicines Database*. Zinc lozenges can cause mouth irritation, a metallic taste and nausea. Do not use for more than 5 – 7 days as long term use can cause copper deficiency. Due to loss of smell, zinc nasal formulations were removed from the market. Vitamin C (ascorbic acid) supplements are commonly used, with no efficacy for cold prevention. Some data has shown a decrease in the duration of the cold by 1 – 1.5 days at doses of 1 – 3 grams/day. There may also be a dose-dependent response; doses of at least 2 grams/day appears to work better than 1 gram/day. Vitamin C is rated as "possibly effective" for cold treatment by the *Natural Medicines Database*. However, high doses of vitamin C (4 g/day or greater) may cause diarrhea as well as kidney stones in male patients. Echinacea is also rated as "possibly effective" for cold treatment. With any of these products it is important to use the correct dose from a reputable manufacturer. *Airborne* and *Emergen-C Immune+* are popular products that contains a variety of ingredients, including vitamins C, vitamin E, zinc and echinacea. They are costly and have no proven benefit in the combinations provided.

Expectorants

Cough associated with colds is usually nonproductive. However, expectorants can be used for a productive cough to ↓ phlegm viscosity in the lower respiratory tract and ↑ secretions in the upper respiratory tract to help move phlegm upwards and out.

DRUG	DOSING	SAFETY/SIDE EFFECTS/MONITORING
GuaiFENesin *(Mucinex, Robitussin Mucus + Chest Congestion)* Tablet, caplet, liquid, syrup, granule	200-400 mg Q4H PRN, or 600-1,200 mg ER Q12H (max 2.4 g/day) Age 6-11 yrs:1,200 mg/day (max) Age 4-5 yrs: 600 mg/day (max)	**WARNINGS** Some formulations may contain phenylalanine. **SIDE EFFECTS** Nausea (dose-related), vomiting, dizziness, headache, rash, diarrhea, stomach pain **NOTES** Not for OTC use in children < 2 years of age

Cough Suppressants

Cough suppressants are used for dry, unproductive cough, or to suppress productive cough at night to allow for restful sleep. Dextromethorphan (DM) and codeine have high affinity to several regions of the brain, including the medullary cough center, suppressing the cough reflex. DM also acts as a serotonin reuptake inhibitor. DM is a nonopioid agent without analgesic, sedative, respiratory depressant, or addictive properties when used at usual antitussive doses. However, DM is a drug of abuse as it acts as an NMDA-receptor blocker in high doses leading to euphoric and hallucinogenic properties similar to PCP, termed "robo-tripping". Its safety and efficacy in children has not been established and due to it's abuse potential, California became the first state to ban the sale of DM to minors < 18 years of age. A few other states have followed, some with more stringent requirements. Codeine products scheduled as C-V drugs must contain one or more noncodeine active ingredients and no more than 200 mg of codeine/100 mL. Codeine is commonly abused, particularly in combination with promethazine, known by street names "purple drank" and "lean". Benzonatate suppresses cough by topical anesthetic action on the respiratory stretch receptors.

DRUG	DOSING	SAFETY/SIDE EFFECTS/MONITORING
Dextromethorphan (*Delsym, DayQuil Cough*) Capsule, liquids, lozenge, strips	10-20 mg Q4H PRN, or 30 mg Q6-8H PRN, or 60 mg ER Q12H PRN (max 120 mg/day) Age 6-12 yrs: 60 mg/day max Age 4-6 yrs: 30 mg/day max	**CONTRAINDICATIONS** All dextromethophan-containing products should not be used within 14 days of MAO inhibitor use. **SIDE EFFECTS** N/V, drowsiness, serotonin syndrome if co-administered with other serotonergic drugs **NOTES** If the product name has DM at the end, such as *Robitussin DM*, it contains dextromethorphan. Additive CNS depression may occur with alcohol, antihistamines, and psychotropic medications.
Codeine C-II	Adults: 10-20 mg Q4-6H PRN (max 120 mg/day)	**BOXED WARNING** Respiratory depression and death have occurred in children who received codeine following tonsillectomy and/or adenoidectomy and had evidence of being ultra-rapid metabolizers of codeine due to a CYP2D6 polymorphism, avoid. **CONTRAINDICATIONS** Paralytic ileus, children who have undergone tonsillectomy and/or adenoidectomy, known codeine hypersensitivity, during labor when a premature birth is anticipated **SIDE EFFECTS** N/V, sedation, constipation, hypotension **NOTES:** Use with CNS depressants causes additive CNS depression
Benzonatate (*Tessalon Perles, Zonatuss*)	100-200 mg TID PRN (max 600 mg/day)	**WARNINGS** Accidental ingestion and fatal overdose has been reported in children < 10 years of age, avoid. **SIDE EFFECTS** Somnolence, confusion, hallucinations
Diphenhydramine (*Benadryl*)	25 mg Q4H PRN (max 150 mg/day)	See First Generation Oral Antihistamine table

Decongestants

Systemic and nasal decongestants are used to relieve congestion and rhinorrhea. These agents are discussed in the previous section.

Analgesics/Antipyretics

Analgesics and antipyretics such as acetaminophen and ibuprofen are used to relieve sore throat, body malaise, and/or fever. See Pain chapter for more information.

Select Cough and Cold Combination Products

DRUG	ADULT DOSING
Dextromethorphan/promethazine	15 mg/6.25 mg per 5 mL; 5 mL Q4-6H PRN (max 30 mL/day)
Brompheniramine/pseudoephedrine/ dextromethorphan *(Bromfed DM)*	2 mg/30 mg/10 mg per 5 mL; 10 mL Q4H PRN (max 60 mL/day)
Promethazine/phenylephrine/codeine (Promethazine VC/Codeine) C-V	6.25 mg/5 mg/10 mg per 5 mL; 5 mL Q4-6H PRN (max 30 mL/day)
GuaiFENesin/codeine *(Robafen AC, Virtussin AC)* C-V	100 mg/10 mg per 5 mL; 10 mL PO Q4H PRN (max 60 mL/day)
GuaiFENesin/codeine/pseudoephedrine *(Cheratussin DAC, Mytussin DAC)* C-V	100 mg/10 mg/30 mg per 5 mL; 10 mL Q4H PRN (max 40 mL/day)
Chlorpheniramine/hydrocodone *(TussiCaps, Tussionex, Vituz)* C-II	8 mg/10 mg ER per 5 mL; 5 mL Q12H PRN (max 10 mL/day)
Chlorpheniramine polistirex/codeine polistirex *(Tuzistra XR)*, C-III	10 mL PO Q12H PRN (max 20 mL/day)

Cough and Cold Products in Children

In 2008, the FDA warned that OTC cough and cold products should not be used in children under 2 years old due to safety concerns (under 6 years old per the American Academy of Pediatrics). Later that same year, many manufactures voluntarily re-labeled these cough and cold products to state: "do not use in children under 4 years of age." These cough and cold products include any product containing decongestants and the antihistamines diphenhydramine, brompheniramine or chlorpheniramine. Do not use promethazine in any form in children less than 2 years old. The FDA advises against the use of promethazine with codeine cough syrups in children < 6 years of age, due to the risk of respiratory depression, cardiac arrest and neurological problems.

If a young child has a cold, it is safe and useful to recommend proper hydration, nasal bulbs for gentle suctioning, saline drops/sprays (*Ocean* and generics), vaporizers/humidifiers, and ibuprofen and acetaminophen, if needed for fever or pain. Do not use aspirin in children due to the risk of Reye's syndrome. OTC cough and cold medications have not been shown to work in young children and can be dangerous. Over the past year there have been rare cases of severe skin reactions in patients using acetaminophen and NSAIDs. Symptoms of the common cold usually resolve in a few days (up to 2 weeks). If the child is a small infant, seems seriously ill, or if symptoms worsen or do not go away, the child should be seen by a pediatrician.

Non-pharmacological treatments should be initiated first. A cool mist humidifier helps nasal passages shrink, allowing for easier breathing. Avoid using warm mist humidifiers as they can cause nasal passages to swell (making breathing more difficult) and can cause burns if spilled. Wash humidifiers daily when in use. Saline nose drops or sprays keep nasal passages moist and reduce congestion. Nasal suctioning with a bulb syringe, either with or without saline nose drops, works especially well for infants less than a year old. Older children often resist its use.

Acetaminophen or ibuprofen can be used to reduce fever, aches and pains. If a parent purchases OTC infant drops for fever (let pediatrician recommend if under age 2), remind them to use the calibrated dropper or oral syringe that came with the bottle and do not mix and match dosing devices or overdose can occur. Advise against using kitchen teaspoons to measure out medication since these come in different sizes.

- Acetaminophen infants' or children's liquid suspensions (both 160 mg/5 mL): 10-15 mg/kg/dose Q4-6H PRN, max 5 doses/24H.

- Ibuprofen infants' drops (50 mg/1.25 mL) or children's liquid suspensions (100 mg/5 mL): 5-10 mg/kg/dose Q6-8H PRN. Max daily dose 40 mg/kg/day for both formulations.

Some doctors recommend alternating ibuprofen with acetaminophen at each dosing interval to avoid acetaminophen toxicity or ibuprofen-induced GI discomfort.

Menthol and camphor used topically, such as in *Vick's VapoRub*, do not work well and should not be used in children less than 2 years. Menthol can result in aspiration and cardiac and CNS toxicity if ingested. Camphor is generally considered safe but lacks sufficient data. *Vick's BabyRub* contains petrolatum, eucalyptus oil, lavender oil, rosemary oil and aloe extract and is also considered relatively safe but lacks sufficient efficacy data.

Patient Counseling for *Flonase* (Fluticasone Nasal Inhaler) and *Nasacort 24 HR* (Triamcinolone Nasal Spray)

Before using

- Shake the bottle gently and then remove the dust cover/cap.

- It is necessary to prime the pump into the air the first time it is used, or when you have not used it for awhile (7 days for *Flonase*, 14 days for *Nasacort*). To prime the pump, hold the bottle with the nasal applicator pointing away from you, with your forefinger and middle finger on either side of the nasal applicator and your thumb underneath the bottle. When you prime the pump for the first time, press down and release the pump a few times. The pump is now ready for use. If the pump is not used for awhile (7 days for *Flonase*, 14 days for *Nasacort*) prime until a fine spray appears.

Using the spray

- Blow your nose to clear your nostrils.

- Close one nostril. Tilt your head forward slightly and, keeping the bottle upright, carefully insert the nasal applicator into the other nostril.

- Start to breathe in through your nose, and while breathing in, press firmly and quickly down once on the applicator to release the spray. To get a full actuation, use your forefinger and middle finger to spray while supporting the base of the bottle with your thumb. Avoid spraying in eyes. Breathe gently inwards through the nostril.

- Breathe out through your mouth. If a second spray is needed in that nostril, repeat the above 3 steps. Repeat the above 3 steps in the other nostril.

- Wipe the nasal applicator with a clean tissue and replace with dust cover.

- Do not use the bottle for more than the labeled number of sprays even though the bottle is not completely empty.

- Do not blow your nose right after using the nasal spray. Clean the nasal applicator tip regularly (at least once a week for *Flonase*, after every use for *Nasacort)* by gently pulling it off and rinsing it under warm water. Let it air dry before replacing back onto the bottle.

ASTHMA

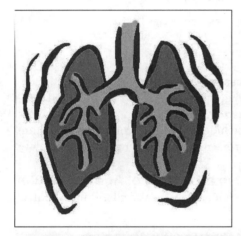

We gratefully acknowledge the assistance of Jean-Venable "Kelly" R. Goode, PharmD, BCPS, FAPhA, FCCP, Professor, Virginia Commonwealth University School of Pharmacy, in preparing this chapter.

BACKGROUND

Asthma is a disease that affects the airways (bronchi) of the lungs. It is one of the most common, chronic diseases among children and the prevalence is increasing each year. Many adults have asthma, affecting 8% of the population in the United States. Asthma is characterized by a predisposition to chronic airway inflammation leading to bronchial smooth muscle constriction (narrowed airways) making breathing more difficult. This inflammation causes recurrent episodes of the classic signs and symptoms of asthma such as <u>wheezing, breathlessness, chest tightness, and coughing</u>, particularly at night or early in the morning. These symptoms vary over time and in intensity, and can be triggered by a variety of factors (see table on the following page). The expiratory airflow limitation (difficulty with exhalation) that results is reversible with medication. An episodic flare-up, called an asthma exacerbation, can occur, particularly when the disease state worsens due to exposure of allergen(s) or non-adherence to the medication regimen.

PATHOPHYSIOLOGY

Atopy, the genetic predisposition for the development of an immunoglobin E (IgE)-mediated response to common allergens, is the strongest identifiable factor for developing asthma. Proinflammatory mediators and cytokines are produced or released by many cells within the airways (e.g., mast cells, eosinophils, neutrophils, T lymphocytes, macrophages, epithelial cells) leading to inflammation. The acute and chronic inflammation affect airflow but also increases bronchial hyperresponsiveness, which enhances susceptibility to bronchospasm (bronchial constriction). Chronic inflammation is associated with permanent changes in the airway structure, referred to as airway remodeling. These structural changes (subepithelial fibrosis, mucous gland hypersecretion, etc.) increase airflow obstruction and may render a person less responsive to treatment.

GUIDELINES/REFERENCES

Expert Panel Report 3. Guidelines for the Diagnosis and Management of Asthma. National Heart, Lung and Blood Institute, August 2007. http://www.nhlbi.nih.gov/guidelines/asthma (accessed 2015 Nov. 6).

The Global Strategy for Asthma Management and Prevention, Global Initiative for Asthma (GINA) 2015. http://www.ginasthma.org/ (accessed 2015 Nov. 6).

ENVIRONMENTAL FACTORS AND COMORBID CONDITIONS (TRIGGERS)

CATEGORIES	EXAMPLES
Airborne Allergens	Airborne pollens (grass, trees, weeds), house-dust mites, animal dander, cockroaches, fungal spores, tobacco smoke
Medication Sensitivities	Aspirin/NSAIDs, non-selective beta blockers
Sulfite Sensitivity	Processed potatoes, shrimp, dried fruit, beer, wine
Environment	Cold air, fog, ozone, sulfur dioxide, nitrogen dioxide, tobacco smoke, wood smoke
Exercise	Particularly cold, dry air
Occupational	Bakers (flour dust), farmers (hay mold), spice and enzyme workers; painters (arabic gum), chemical workers (azo dyes, toluene diisocyanates, polyvinyl chloride); plastics, rubber, and wood workers (formaldehyde, dimethyethanolamine)
Respiratory Infections	Respiratory synctial virus (RSV), rhinovirus, influenza, others
Comorbid Conditions	Allergic bronchopulmonary Aspergillosis, gastroesophageal reflux, obesity, obstructive sleep apnea, rhinitis/sinusitis, chronic stress/depression

DIAGNOSIS

Spirometry is performed to determine airflow obstruction and assess reversibility. Reversibility is defined as either an increase of > 12% in FEV_1 from baseline or by an increase of > 10% of predicted FEV_1 after using a short-acting bronchodilator. A detailed medical history, physical exam, assessment of the patient's signs and symptoms and other tests may be done to exclude other conditions. It is important to classify the severity of asthma to select the appropriate pharmacologic treatment. See table below.

Classifying Asthma Severity and Initiating Treatment in ≥ 12 Years of Age and Adults

Assessing severity and initiating treatment for patients who are not currently taking long-term control medications.

Components of Severity		Classification of Asthma Severity ≥ 12 years of age			
		Intermittent	Persistent		
			Mild	Moderate	Severe
Impairment Normal FEV_1/ FVC 8–19 yr 85% 20 –39 yr 80% 40 –59 yr 75% 60 –80 yr 70%	Symptoms	≤ 2 days/week	> 2 days/week but not daily	Daily	Throughout the day
	Nighttime awakenings	≤ 2x/month	3–4x/month	> 1x/week but not nightly	Often 7x/week
	Short-acting beta-2 agonist use for symptom control (not prevention of EIB)	≤ 2 days/week	> 2 days/week but not daily, and not more than 1x on any day	Daily	Several times per day
	Interference with normal activity	None	Minor limitation	Some limitation	Extremely limited
	Lung function	■ Normal FEV_1 between exacerbations ■ FEV_1 > 80% predicted ■ FEV_1/FVC normal	■ FEV_1 > 80% predicted ■ FEV_1/FVC normal	■ FEV_1 > 60% but < 80% predicted ■ FEV_1/FVC reduced 5%	■ FEV_1 < 60% predicted ■ FEV_1/FVC reduced 5%
Risk	Exacerbations requiring oral systemic corticosteroids	0–1/year	≥ 2/year ————————————————→		
		←———— Consider severity and interval since last exacerbation. ————→ Frequency and severity may fluctuate over time for patients in any severity category..			
Recommended Step for Initiating Treatment		Step 1	Step 2	Step 3 and consider short course of oral systemic corticosteroids	Step 4 or 5
Adapted from NHLBI 2007 EPR.		In 2–6 weeks, evaluate level of asthma control that is achieved and adjust therapy accordingly.			

FEV_1: forced expiratory volume in 1 second, FVC: forced vital capacity, ICU: intensive care unit

DRUG TREATMENT

Drugs used to treat asthma are classified as <u>controllers</u> (maintenance) or <u>relievers</u> (rescue). <u>All patients</u> with asthma (Steps 1 – 6) need a <u>"rescue" inhaler</u> for acute asthma symptoms. <u>Controllers</u> are taken on a chronic, <u>daily basis</u> to keep asthma <u>under control</u>, primarily by <u>reducing inflammation</u>. <u>Relievers</u> are used <u>as-needed</u> to quickly <u>reverse bronchoconstriction</u>, or preventively for <u>exercise-induced broncho-spasm</u> (EIB). Asthma drugs come in oral, inhaled and injectable formulations. <u>Inhaled forms</u> deliver drugs directly into the lungs, have reduced toxicity, and are the <u>preferred</u> delivery vehicle. <u>Inhaled steroids</u> are the <u>most effective</u> and the recommended <u>first-line maintenance medication</u>. Short-acting beta-2 agonists (primarily <u>albuterol</u>) are the drugs of choice for acute bronchospasm, and for prevention of EIB, in both adults, children and during pregnancy. Increased use of a short-acting beta-2 agonist indicates worsening asthma control, and a need to reassess treatment. The primary treatment is to increase the inhaled steroid dose. Steroids can be given by injection in acute cases, and oral steroids are used for severely uncontrolled asthma, but the use of steroids in other formulations than inhaled is limited by the risk of adverse effects. Theophylline can be helpful in some cases, but has significant adverse effects and drug interactions. Patients should attempt to identify what environmental factors cause symptoms and reduce exposure to these factors. Adults aged 19 – 64 years of age with asthma, and children 2 – 18 years of age treated with high-dose oral corticosteroid therapy, should receive the pneumococcal polysaccharide vaccine (PPSV23 or *Pneumovax*). An annual influenza vaccine should be given to those with asthma.

"RESCUERS" – COMMONLY USED IN ASTHMA EXACERBATIONS	"CONTROLLERS" – LONG-TERM, MAINTENANCE THERAPY
Short-acting beta-2 agonists (SABA)	Inhaled steroids
Systemic steroids (injection or oral)	Long-acting beta-2 agonists (taken with inhaled steroids)
Inhaled anticholinergics	Leukotriene modifying agents
	Theophylline
	Inhaled anticholinergics
	Omalizumab (*Xolair*), mepolizumab (*Nucala*)

Stepwise Approach For Managing Asthma In Children 0 – 4 Years of Age

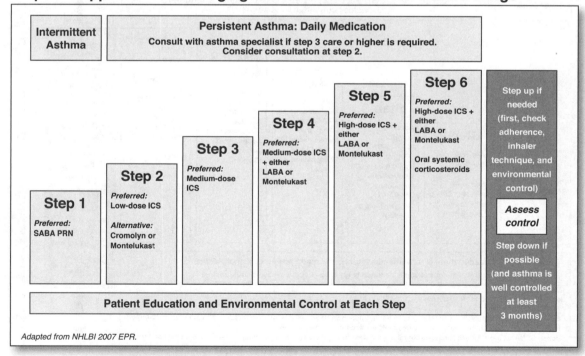

Adapted from NHLBI 2007 EPR.

Stepwise Approach For Managing Asthma In Children 5 – 11 Years of Age

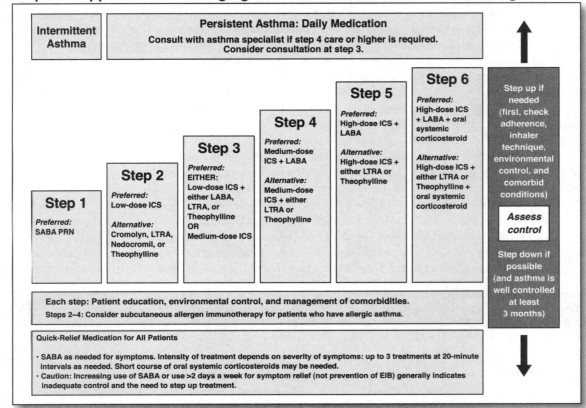

Stepwise Approach For Managing Asthma In Youths ≥ 12 Years Of Age and Adults

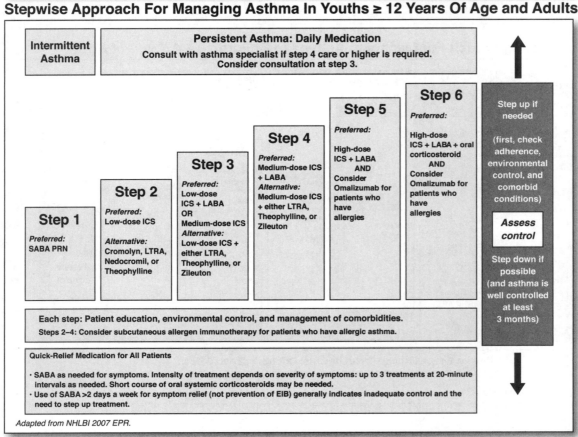

Adapted from NHLBI 2007 EPR.

Beta-2 Agonists

These agents bind to beta-2 receptors, causing <u>relaxation of bronchial smooth muscle</u> and leading to <u>bronchodilation</u>. <u>Inhalation</u> is the <u>preferred</u> route of administration. Inhaled devices come as metered-dose inhalers (MDIs) or dry powder inhalers (DPIs) including a breath-actuated DPI.

DRUG	DOSING	SAFETY/SIDE EFFECTS/MONITORING

Short-Acting Beta-2 Agonists (SABAs)

DRUG	DOSING	SAFETY/SIDE EFFECTS/MONITORING
Racepinephrine *(Asthmanefrin EZ Breathe Atomizer)* OTC	<u>Should not be used</u> since it is <u>non-selective</u>	**WARNINGS** Caution in CVD, glaucoma, hyperthyroidism **SIDE EFFECTS** <u>Nervousness, tremor, tachycardia, palpitations, cough,</u> <u>hyperglycemia</u>, ↓ K **MONITORING** Number of days of SABA use, symptom frequency, peak flow, pulmonary function tests, BP, HR, blood glucose, K **NOTES** Pregnancy Category C
Albuterol *(**ProAir HFA, ProAir RespiClick, Proventil HFA, Ventolin HFA,** VoSpire ER)* 90 mcg/inh, 0.5% and 0.083% nebulizer solution, syrup, tablet	MDI/DPI: 1-2 inhalations Q4-6H PRN Nebulizer: 1.25-5 mg Q4-8H PRN IR: 2-4 mg Q4-6H PO PRN ER: 8 mg Q12H PRN	MDIs: Shake well before use. <u>Beta-2 selective</u> drugs are <u>preferred</u> via <u>inhaled route</u>. These are rescue medications used <u>PRN in all patients with asthma</u>. Regular daily use is not recommended.
Levalbuterol *(**Xopenex, Xopenex Concentrate, Xopenex HFA**)* 45 mcg/inh, nebulizer solution	MDI: 1-2 inhalations Q4-6H PRN Nebulizer: 0.63-1.25 mg Q6-8H PRN	If using <u>SABA > 2 days/week for symptom control</u>, then asthma is not controlled and need to ↑ <u>maintenance therapy</u>. Drugs of choice for exercise-induced bronchospasm (EIB). Levalbuterol contains R-isomer of albuterol. Most albuterol inhalers contain <u>200 inhalations/canister</u>.

Long-Acting Beta-2 Agonists (LABAs)

DRUG	DOSING	SAFETY/SIDE EFFECTS/MONITORING
Salmeterol *(Serevent Diskus)* 50 mcg/inh	DPI: 1 inhalation BID	**BOXED WARNING** ↑ <u>risk of asthma-related deaths</u>, should only be used in asthma patients as <u>adjunctive therapy</u> in patients who are currently receiving but are not adequately controlled on a <u>long-term asthma control medication (an inhaled corticosteroid)</u>. Once <u>asthma control</u> is achieved and maintained, assess the patient at regular intervals and <u>step down therapy if possible</u> without loss of asthma control
+ fluticasone *(**Advair Diskus, Advair HFA**)* ***Advair Diskus*** – 100, 250, 500 mcg fluticasone + 50 mcg salmeterol/inh	DPI: 1 inhalation BID	
Advair HFA – 45, 115, 230 mcg fluticasone + 21 mcg salmeterol/inh	MDI: 2 inhalations BID	**CONTRAINDICATIONS** Monotherapy in the treatment of asthma, treatment of status asthmaticus or other acute episodes of asthma or COPD
Formoterol *(Foradil Aerolizer)* **+ budesonide** *(**Symbicort**)*	DPI: 1 capsule (12 mcg) via *Aerolizer* BID	**SIDE EFFECTS** and **MONITORING** - same as SABAs
Symbicort – 80, 160 mcg budesonide + 4.5 mcg formoterol/inh	MDI: 2 inhalations BID	**NOTES** Pregnancy Category C
+ mometasone *(Dulera)* 100, 200 mcg mometasone + 5 mcg formoterol/inh	DPI: 2 inhalations BID	Refrigerate *Foradil* capsules in the pharmacy, patient can keep at room temp. for 4 months Vilanterol + fluticasone *(Breo Ellipta)* is discussed on the following page MedGuide required

Corticosteroids

Corticosteroids inhibit the inflammatory response, depressing migration of polymorphonuclear (PMN) leukocytes and fibroblasts, and reversing capillary permeability and lysosomal stabilization at the cellular level. They block late-phase reaction to the allergen, reduce airway hyperresponsiveness and are the most potent and effective anti-inflammatory medications available. Inhaled corticosteroids (ICSs) are used in the long-term control of asthma. Short courses of oral systemic steroids are used in asthma exacerbations.

Inhaled Corticosteroids

DRUG	DOSING	SAFETY/SIDE EFFECTS/ MONITORING
Beclomethasone HFA *(QVAR)* 40, 80 mcg/inh	MDI: 1-2 inhalations BID	**CONTRAINDICATIONS** Primary treatment of status asthmaticus or acute episodes of asthma (not for relief of acute bronchospasm)
Budesonide *(Pulmicort Flexhaler, Pulmicort Respules)* *Pulmicort Flexhaler* 90, 180 mcg/in *Pulmicort Respules* nebulizer suspension **+ formoterol *(Symbicort)*** 80, 160 mcg budesonide + 4.5 mcg formoterol/inh	DPI: 1-2 inhalations BID *Pulmicort Respules* (ages 1-8 years): 0.25-0.5 mg via jet nebulizer daily or BID *Symbicort* MDI: 2 inhalations BID	**WARNINGS** Adrenal suppression with high doses for prolonged period of time **SIDE EFFECTS (INHALED)** Dysphonia (difficulty speaking), oral candidiasis (thrush), cough, HA, hoarseness, URTIs, hyperglycemia, ↑ risk of fractures and pneumonia (with high dose, long-term use), growth retardation (in children with high doses)
Ciclesonide *(Alvesco)* 80, 160 mcg/inh	MDI: 1-2 inhalations BID	
Flunisolide HFA *(Aerospan HFA)* – has built-in spacer 80 mcg/inh	MDI: 2 inhalations BID	**MONITORING** Use of SABA, symptom frequency, peak flow, growth (children/adolescents) and signs/symptoms of HPA axis suppression/adrenal insufficiency, signs/symptoms of oral candidiasis, bone mineral density
Fluticasone *(Flovent HFA, Flovent Diskus, Arnuity Ellipta)* *Flovent HFA* 44, 110, 220 mcg/inh *Flovent Diskus* 50, 100, 250 mcg/inh *Arnuity Ellipta* 100, 200 mcg/inh + vilanterol *(Breo Ellipta)* 100, 200 mcg fluticasone + 25 mcg vilanterol/inh **+ salmeterol *(Advair Diskus, Advair HFA)***	MDI: 2 inhalations BID *Flovent Diskus* DPI: 1-2 inhalations BID *Arnuity Ellipta* DPI: 1-2 inhalations daily *Breo Ellipta* DPI: 1 inhalation daily *Advair Diskus*: 1 inhalation BID *Advair HFA*: 2 inhalations BID	**NOTES** To prevent oral candidiasis, rinse mouth and throat with warm water and spit out or use a spacer device if using a MDI Inhaled steroids are first-line for long term control for all ages with persistent asthma *QVAR* and *Alvesco* are MDIs that do not need to be shaken before use Only use *Pulmicort Respules* with a jet nebulizer machine that is connected to an air compressor. Do not use an ultrasonic nebulizer
Mometasone *(Asmanex HFA, Asmanex Twisthaler)* *HFA* 100, 200 mcg/inh *Twisthaler* 110, 220 mcg/inh + formoterol *(Dulera)* 100, 200 mcg mometasone + 5 mcg formoterol/inh	MDI: 1-2 inhalations BID DPI: 1-2 inhalations daily or BID MDI: 2 inhalations BID	Pregnancy Category C/B (budesonide) To ↓ fracture risk, recommend: smoking cessation, exercise, using lowest, effective steroid dose, Ca and vitamin D supplementation with prescription therapies if needed and obtaining regular bone density screening

Daily Dosages for Inhaled Corticosteroids of ≥ 12 Years of Age

DRUG	LOW DAILY DOSE	MEDIUM DAILY DOSE	HIGH DAILY DOSE
Beclomethasone HFA 40 or 80 mcg/inh	80–240 mcg	> 240–480 mcg	> 480 mcg
Budesonide DPI 90, 180, or 200 mcg/inh	180–600 mcg	> 600–1,200 mcg	> 1,200 mcg
Ciclesonide 80, 160 mcg/inh	80–160 mcg	> 160–320 mcg	> 320 mcg
Flunisolide HFA 80 mcg/inh	320 mcg	> 320–640 mcg	> 640 mcg
Fluticasone HFA/MDI: 44, 110, or 220 mcg/inh	88–264 mcg	> 264–440 mcg	> 440 mcg
DPI: 50, 100, or 250 mcg/inh	100–300 mcg	> 300–500 mcg	> 500 mcg
Mometasone DPI 200 mcg/inh	200 mcg	400 mcg	> 400 mcg

DPI: dry powder inhaler, HFA: hydrofluoroalkane, MDI: metered dose inhaler

Leukotriene Modifying Agents

Zafirlukast and montelukast are leukotriene receptor antagonists (LTRAs) of leukotriene D4 (LTD4 – both drugs) and E4 (LTE4 – zafirlukast only). Zileuton is a 5-lipoxygenase inhibitor which inhibits leukotriene formation. All agents help ↓ airway edema, constriction and inflammation.

DRUG	DOSING	SAFETY/SIDE EFFECTS/MONITORING
Zafirlukast (*Accolate*)	20 mg BID Age 5-11 years: 10 mg BID Taken 1 hr before or 2 hrs after meals (empty stomach)	**CONTRAINDICATIONS** Hepatic impairment – zafirlukast Active liver disease or LFTs ≥ 3 x ULN – zileuton **WARNINGS** Neuropsychiatric events; monitor for signs of aggressive behavior, hostility, agitation, depression, suicidal thinking Systemic eosinophilia, sometimes presenting with clinical features of vasculitis consistent with Churg-Strauss syndrome (rare)
Montelukast (***Singulair***)	10 mg daily in the evening Age 6-14 years: 5 mg daily in the evening Age 1-5 years: 4 mg daily in the evening	**SIDE EFFECTS** Headache, dizziness, abdominal pain, ↑ LFTs, URTIs, pharyngitis, sinusitis
Zileuton (*Zyflo, Zyflo CR*)	*Zyflo*: 600 mg QID *Zyflo CR*: 1,200 mg BID within 1 hour of morning and evening meals Age < 12 years: not recommended	**MONITORING** Zileuton – LFTs at baseline, every month for first 3 months, every 2-3 months for the rest of the first year, then periodically; use of SABAs **NOTES** Pregnancy Category B/C (zileuton) Zafirlukast: keep in the original container

Leukotriene Modifying Agents Drug Interactions

- Zafirlukast: substrate of 2C9 (major); inhibitor of 1A2 (weak), 2C9 (moderate), 2C19 (weak), 2D6 (weak), 2C8 (weak) and 3A4 (weak) – may ↑ levels of carvedilol, pimozide, theophylline, warfarin and 2C9 substrates. Levels of zafirlukast may be ↓ by erythromycin, theophylline, and food (↓ bioavailability by 40%) – take 1 hour before or 2 hours after meals

- Montelukast: substrate of 3A4 (minor) and 2C8/9 (minor); inhibitor of 2C8/9 (weak). Gemfibrozil may ↑ levels of montelukast and lumacaftor may ↓ levels of montelukast.

- Zileuton: substrate of 1A2 (minor), 2C9 (minor), 3A4 (minor); inhibitor of 1A2 (weak) – may ↑ levels of pimozide, propranolol, theophylline, and warfarin

Theophylline

Blocks phosphodiesterase causing ↑ cyclic adenosine monophosphate (cAMP) which promotes release of epinephrine from adrenal medulla cells. This results in <u>bronchodilation</u>, mild anti-inflammatory effects, diuresis, CNS and cardiac stimulation and gastric acid secretion. Theophylline may help as add-on therapy, but use is <u>limited by ↓ effectiveness, drug interactions</u> and adverse effects.

DRUG	DOSING	SAFETY/SIDE EFFECTS/MONITORING
Theophylline *(Elixophyllin, Theo-24, Theochron)* Capsule, tablet, elixir, solution, injection Active metabolites are <u>caffeine</u> and <u>3-methylxanthine</u>	300-600 mg daily Therapeutic range: <u>5-15 mcg/mL</u> (measure <u>peak</u> level after 3 days of oral dosing, at steady state)	**WARNINGS** Caution in patients with cardiovascular disease, hyperthyroidism, PUD and seizure disorder since use may exacerbate these conditions **SIDE EFFECTS** <u>Nausea, loose stools</u>, headache, tachycardia, insomnia, tremor, and nervousness Signs of toxicity – persistent and repetitive vomiting, ventricular tachycardias, seizures **MONITORING** Theophylline levels, use of SABA, HR, respiratory rate, CNS effects **NOTES** <u>Dosing is based on IBW</u> If no theophylline given within past 24 hrs, LD = 5 mg/kg If theophylline given within past 24 hrs, LD = (Cp-Co)(Vd) where Vd = 0.5 L/kg; Cp = desired theophylline concentration; Co = initial theophylline concentration If <u>using IV aminophylline</u>, then <u>multiply by 0.8</u> (aminophylline contains 80% theophylline) Pregnancy Category C

Theophylline Drug Interactions

Theophylline is a substrate of 1A2 (major), 3A4 (major), 2E1 (major), 2C9 (minor) and 2D6 (minor) and an inhibitor of 1A2 (weak). It has first order kinetics, followed by zero order kinetics. A <u>small increase in dose</u> can result in a <u>large increase in</u> the theophylline <u>concentration</u>.

- <u>Drugs that may ↑ theophylline levels</u> due to 1A2 inhibition: ciprofloxacin, fluvoxamine, propranolol, zafirlukast, zileuton and possibly others

- <u>Drugs that may ↑ theophylline levels</u> due to 3A4 inhibition: clarithromycin, conivaptan, erythromycin and possibly others

- Drugs that may ↑ theophylline levels due to other mechanisms: alcohol, allopurinol, antithyroid agents, disulfiram, estrogen-containing oral contraceptives, methotrexate, pentoxifylline, propafenone, verapamil and possibly others. Also conditions such as acute pulmonary edema, CHF, cirrhosis or liver disease, cor-pulmonale, fever, hypothyroidism or shock can ↓ clearance.

- Drugs that may ↓ theophylline levels: carbamazepine, fosphenytoin, phenobarbital, phenytoin, primidone, rifampin, ritonavir, tobacco/marijuana smoking, St. John's wort, thyroid hormones (levothyroxine), high-protein diet and charbroiled meats. Conditions such as hyperthyroidism and cystic fibrosis can ↑ clearance.

- Theophylline will ↓ lithium (theophylline ↑ renal excretion of lithium) and will ↓ zafirlukast

Anticholinergics

Anticholinergics inhibit muscarinic cholinergic receptors and reduce intrinsic vagal tone of the airway, leading to bronchodilation. These agents are mainly used with other medications in the emergency department in acute exacerbations. In September 2015, tiotropium (*Spiriva Respimat*) was approved for asthma in patients 12 years of age and older. See COPD chapter for more information on anticholinergics.

Omalizumab *(Xolair)*

IgG monoclonal antibody that inhibits IgE binding to the IgE receptor on mast cells and basophils. Omalizumab is indicated for moderate to severe persistent, allergic asthma in patients 12 years of age and older with a positive skin test to perennial aeroallergen and inadequately controlled symptoms on inhaled steroids (Step 5 or 6 per guidelines).

DRUG	DOSING	SAFETY/SIDE EFFECTS/MONITORING
Omalizumab *(Xolair)*	Dose and frequency based on pretreatment total IgE serum levels and body weight – given SC every 2 or 4 weeks Drug should always be given in a healthcare setting Dosing should be adjusted during therapy for significant changes in body weight	**BOXED WARNING** Anaphylaxis, including delayed-onset, can occur. Anaphylaxis has occurred after the first dose but also has occurred beyond 1 year after beginning treatment. Closely observe patients for an appropriate period of time after administration and be prepared to manage anaphylaxis that can be life-threatening. **WARNING** Slightly ↑ risk of serious cardiovascular and cerebrovascular adverse events Malignancies have been observed in clinical studies **SIDE EFFECTS** Injection site reactions, arthralgias, pain, dizziness, fatigue, leg pain, arm pain, pruritus, dermatitis, bone fracture, earache **MONITORING** Baseline IgE, FEV_1, peak flow, s/sx of anaphylaxis and infection **NOTES** Pregnancy Category B Doses > 150 mg should be divided over more than one injection site

Mepolizumab *(Nucala)*

An interleukin-5 (IL-5) receptor antagonist monoclonal antibody (IgG1 kappa) that inhibits IgE binding to the IgE receptor on mast cells and basophils. Approved in November 2015, mepolizumab is indicated as add-on treatment for severe asthma with an eosinophilic phenotype in ages > 12 years. The dose is 100 mg SC once every 4 weeks.

SPECIAL SITUATIONS

Exercise-Induced Bronchospasm

- If indicated, appropriate long-term control therapy with anti-inflammatory medication is associated with a reduction in the frequency and severity of exercise-induced bronchospasm (EIB). Pretreatment before exercise with SABAs, LABAs or montelukast is recommended. SABAs are the drugs of choice generally.

- SABAs can be taken 5 – 15 minutes before exercise and have a duration of 2 – 3 hours.

- If longer duration of symptom control is needed, LABAs can be used. These agents need to be taken 15 minutes (formoterol) or 30 minutes (salmeterol) prior to exercise. If already using a LABA for asthma maintenance, then do not use additional doses for EIB. Remember LABAs should not be used as monotherapy in patients with persistent asthma.

- Montelukast must be taken 2 hours prior to exercise and it lasts up to 24 hours. However, it only works in 50% of patients. Daily administration to prevent EIB has not been evaluated. Patients receiving montelukast for asthma or another indication should not take an additional dose to prevent EIB.

Pregnancy

Asthma should be monitored in pregnant women as the condition may become worse. To ensure oxygen supply to the fetus, it is safer to be treated with asthma medications than to have poorly controlled asthma. Albuterol is the preferred short-acting beta-2 agonist and budesonide is the preferred inhaled corticosteroid due to more data in pregnancy.

Sample Asthma Action Plan (Adult)

My Asthma Action Plan

Patient Name: _____

Medical Record #: _____

Physician's Name: _____   DOB: _____

Physician's Phone #: _____   Completed by: _____   Date: _____

Long-Term-Control Medicines	How Much To Take	How Often	Other Instructions
		_____ times per day EVERY DAY!	
		_____ times per day EVERY DAY!	
		_____ times per day EVERY DAY!	
		_____ times per day EVERY DAY!	

Quick-Relief Medicines	How Much To Take	How Often	Other Instructions
		Take ONLY as needed	NOTE: If this medicine is needed frequently, call physician to consider increasing long-term-control medications.

Special instructions when I feel ● good, ○ not good, and ● awful.

GREEN ZONE

I feel *good.*

(My peak flow is in the GREEN zone.)

PREVENT asthma symptoms everyday:

☐ Take my long-term-control medicines (above) every day.

☐ Before exercise, take _____ puffs of _____

☐ Avoid things that make my asthma worse like:

YELLOW ZONE

I do *not* feel *good.*

(My peak flow is in the YELLOW zone.)

My symptoms may include one or more of the following:
- Wheeze
- Tight chest
- Cough
- Shortness of breath
- Waking up at night with asthma symptoms
- Decreased ability to do usual activities
- _____

CAUTION. I should continue taking my long-term-control asthma medicines every day AND:

☐ Take _____

If I still do not feel good, or my peak flow is not back in the *Green Zone* within 1 hour, then I should:

☐ Increase _____

☐ Add _____

☐ Call _____

RED ZONE

I feel *awful.*

(My peak flow is in the RED zone.)

Warning signs may include one or more of the following:
- It's getting harder and harder to breathe
- Unable to sleep or do usual activities because of trouble breathing

MEDICAL ALERT! Get help!

☐ Take _____ until I get help immediately.

☐ Take _____

☐ Call _____

My Personal Best Peak Flow

80% Personal Best

50% Personal Best

Liters/Min.

Peak Flow Meter

Danger! Get help immediately!   Call 9–1–1 if you have trouble walking or talking due to shortness of breath or lips or fingernails are gray or blue.

Adapted from NHLBI 2007 EPR.

PEAK FLOW METERS

Background

Peak flow meters are devices that measure a patient's peak expiratory flow rate (PEFR) – the greatest velocity attained during a forced expiration starting from fully inflated lungs. The patient's best PEFR is known as a <u>Personal Best (PB)</u> and is determined by spirometry, taking into account the patient's height, gender, and age. Patients may also find their PB by taking peak flow readings twice a day (morning and evening) for 2 – 3 weeks. The most frequent highest reading is the PB. Typically, a PB can be found after a short burst of steroids to maximize lung function. The PEFR and PB is <u>effort-dependent</u>. Peak flow meters are beneficial in patients with frequent asthma exacerbations, worsening asthma, persistent asthma (Step 3 – 6), poor perception of airflow obstruction and unexplained response to environmental factors. These devices can identify exacerbations early (even before the patient is symptomatic), allowing the patient to initiate treatment sooner. A treatment action plan, is developed by the health care provider so the patient can manage symptoms and avoid hospitalizations due to an exacerbation (see previous page).

Technique

■ Use the peak flow meter every morning upon awakening and <u>before</u> the use of any asthma medications. <u>Proper technique and best effort are essential</u>. Less than <u>best effort</u> can lead to false 'exacerbation' and unnecessary medication treatment.

■ Move the indicator to bottom of numbered scale. Stand up straight. Exhale comfortably.

■ Inhale as deeply as possible. Place lips firmly around mouthpiece, creating a tight seal.

■ Blow out as <u>hard</u> and as <u>fast</u> as possible. Write down the PEFR.

■ Repeat steps two more times, allowing enough rest in between. Record the highest value.

Peak Flow Meter Care

■ Patients should always use the same brand of peak flow meter.

■ Peak flow meters should be cleaned at least <u>once a week</u>; if patient has an infection, they should clean more frequently. Wash peak flow meters in warm water with mild soap. Rinse gently but thoroughly. Do not use brushes to clean inside the peak flow meters. Do not place peak flow meters in boiling water. Allow to air dry before taking next reading.

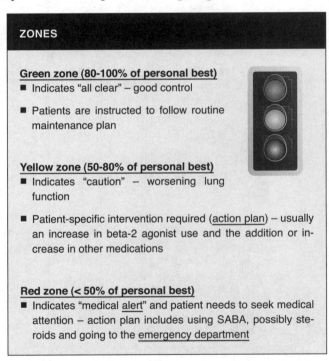

ZONES

<u>Green zone (80-100% of personal best)</u>
■ Indicates "all clear" – good control

■ Patients are instructed to follow routine maintenance plan

<u>Yellow zone (50-80% of personal best)</u>
■ Indicates "caution" – worsening lung function

■ Patient-specific intervention required (<u>action plan</u>) – usually an increase in beta-2 agonist use and the addition or increase in other medications

<u>Red zone (< 50% of personal best)</u>
■ Indicates "medical <u>alert</u>" and patient needs to seek medical attention – action plan includes using SABA, possibly steroids and going to the <u>emergency department</u>

SPACERS

Spacer is a generic term that refers to simple open tubes that are placed on the mouthpiece of an MDI to extend it away from the mouth of the patient. Flunisolide *(Aerospan)* has a built-in spacer. A valve holding chamber (VHC), one type of spacer, has a one-way valve that does not allow the patient to exhale into the device. This benefits patients who have difficulty coordinating actuation (pressing down on the canister) and inhalation as they can press and have a short time delay before the need for inhalation. Therefore, VHC spacers enhance the coordination necessary to administer inhaled medication from an MDI. Patients should use the same combination of an MDI and VHC.

- Spacer devices help prevent thrush from inhaled corticosteroids and can reduce cough associated with some inhalers.
- Clean at least once a week in warm, soapy water.
- Spacer devices are not to be shared.

DEVICES

Nebulizers

A nebulizer is a device that turns liquid medication into a fine mist. This fine mist can be inhaled through a face mask or mouthpiece and into the lungs. Nebulizers use natural breathing, making medication delivery easy for infants, children and the elderly. There are two types of nebulizers, jet nebulizers and ultrasound nebulizers. Check the medication information to see which nebulizer device is indicated. Please see online video course for a demonstration of the nebulizer devices and accessory parts that are required for appropriate use.

Albuterol comes as a nebulized solution and 2 common concentrations are a 0.083% solution containing 2.5 mg/3mL and a 0.5% solution containing 2.5 mg/0.5 mL as a unit-dose and in a 20 mL vial. The 0.083% solution is a ready-to-use preparation that can be placed directly into the nebulizer without further dilution. The 0.5% concentrated solution must be diluted with 2.5 mL of normal saline prior to use. Nebulizers are covered by CMS' Durable Medical Equipment (DME) under the medical insurance component (Part B).

Metered-Dose Inhalers (MDIs)

A metered-dose inhaler is a handheld device that delivers a specific amount of medication in aerosol form. MDIs consist of a pressurized canister inside a plastic case, with a mouthpiece attached. MDIs use a chemical propellant (HFA) to push medication out of the inhaler. MDIs require a slow and deep breathe in from the device. All MDIs need to be shaken since they are suspensions except *QVAR* and *Alvesco*. They can be used with spacer devices.

Dry Powder Inhaler (DPIs)

DPIs are devices that contain the drug in a dry powder. They do not contain propellants; therefore, they require a quick and forceful breathe in during use. Once the medication has been loaded (after "clicking" in place - see directions on the following pages), the device needs to remain flat (or upright) so the medication does not spill inside the device. These devices cannot be used with spacers (since they do not fit the back of the spacer). Some DPIs are breath-actuated which eliminates the need for hand-breath coordination and a spacer. Please see online video course for complete demonstration of all devices.

PATIENT COUNSELING

Metered-Dose Inhalers

Ventolin, ProAir HFA, Proventil, Symbicort, QVAR, Flovent HFA, Alvesco, others

STEP 1	STEP 2	STEP 3

© RxPrep

STEP 1

Make sure the canister is fully inserted into the actuator (if it comes separately). Always use the actuator that came with the canister. Shake the inhaler well for 5 seconds immediately before each spray (except for *QVAR* or *Alvesco* which do not need to be shaken). Remove cap from the mouthpiece and check mouthpiece for foreign objects prior to use.

STEP 2

Breathe out fully through your mouth expelling as much air from your lungs as possible. Holding the inhaler upright (as shown in the picture), place the mouthpiece into your mouth and close your lips around it.

STEP 3

While breathing in slowly and deeply through your mouth, press the top of the canister all the way down with your index finger. Right after the spray comes out, take your finger off the canister. After you have inhaled all the way, take the inhaler out of your mouth and close your mouth. Hold your breath as long as possible, up to 10 seconds, then breathe normally. If another inhalation is needed, wait 1 minute and repeat Steps 1-3. Place cap back on the mouthpiece after use.

TO PRIME

Ventolin
Spray 4 times (shaking between sprays) away from the face. Prime again if >14 days from last use or if you drop it.

Flovent HFA
Spray 4 times (shaking between sprays) away from the face. Prime again if > 7 days from last use with just 1 spray.

Symbicort
Spray 2 times (shaking between sprays) away from the face. Prime again if > 7 days from last use.

TO CLEAN

Ventolin
Rinse mouthpiece under warm running water (but not the metal canister) for 30 seconds to prevent medication buildup and blockage. Shake to remove excess water and let air dry. Clean weekly.

Flovent HFA
Use a clean cotton swab dampened with water to clean the small circular opening where the medicine sprays out. Gently twist the swab in a circular motion to remove the medicine buildup. Do not take the canister out of the plastic actuator. Wipe the inside of the mouthpiece with a damp tissue. Let air dry overnight.

Symbicort
Wipe the inside and outside of the mouthpiece opening with a clean, dry cloth. Do not put into water.

Dry Powder Inhalers

Advair Diskus

STEP 1	STEP 2	STEP 3	STEP 4	STEP 5

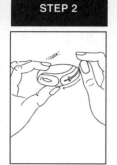 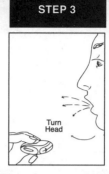 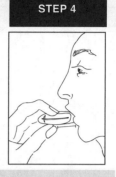 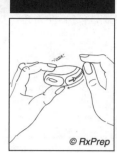

Thumbgrip

Turn Head

© RxPrep

Hold the *Diskus* in your left hand and put the thumb of your right hand in the thumb grip. Push the thumb grip away from you as far as it will go until the mouthpiece appears and the *Diskus* snaps into position.	Hold the *Diskus* in a level, flat position with the mouthpiece towards you. Slide the lever away from the mouthpiece until it clicks.	Before using, breathe out fully while holding the *Diskus* away from your mouth. Do not tilt the *Diskus*.	Put the mouthpiece to your lips. Breathe in quickly and deeply through the inhaler. Do not breathe in through your nose. Remove the *Diskus* from your mouth and hold your breath for 10 seconds, or as long as comfortable. Then, breathe out slowly.	Close the *Diskus* inhaler by putting your thumb in the thumb grip and slide as far back towards you as it will go, until the *Diskus* clicks shut. Rinse your mouth with water and spit out the water to prevent thrush.

TO CLEAN
Do not wash the *Diskus* and store in a dry place.

Pulmicort Flexhaler

STEP 1	STEP 2	STEP 3
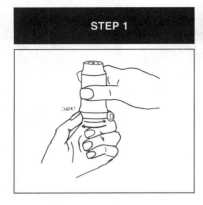	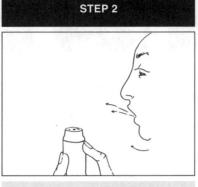	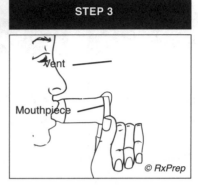

© RxPrep

Twist off the white cover. Holding the middle of the inhaler with one hand, twist the brown base fully in one direction as far as it will go with the other hand. Twist it fully back again in the other direction as far as it will go. You will hear a "click" during one of the twisting movements. The dose is now loaded. Do not shake the inhaler after it is loaded. (Of note, only one dose is loaded at a time, no matter how often you twist the brown base, but the dose counter will continue to advance).

Turn your head away from the inhaler and breathe out fully.

Place the mouthpiece in your mouth and close your lips around the mouthpiece. Breathe in <u>deeply</u> and <u>forcefully</u> through the inhaler. Remove the inhaler from your mouth and breathe out. Replace the white cover on the inhaler and twist shut. Rinse your mouth with water and spit out the water to prevent thrush.

TO PRIME

Twist off the white cover. Holding the inhaler upright, twist the brown base fully in one direction as far as it will go and then fully back. You will hear a click during one of the twisting motions. Repeat twisting motion again (back and forth). The inhaler is now primed and ready to load your first dose. This inhaler does not need to be primed again (even after long periods of no use).

TO CLEAN

Wipe the mouthpiece with a dry tissue weekly. Do not use water or immerse it in water.

ProAir

STEP 1	STEP 2	STEP 3
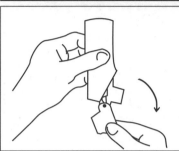	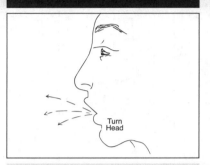	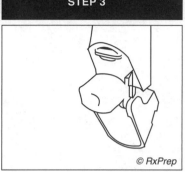

© RxPrep

| Make sure the cap is closed before each dose. Hold the inhaler upright as you open the cap fully. Open the cap all the way back until you hear a "click". Your inhaler is now ready to use. Do not open the cap unless you are taking a dose. Note: <u>Opening and closing the cap without inhaling a dose will waste the medicine and may damage your inhaler.</u> | Breathe out through your mouth and push as much air from your lungs as you can. Be careful not to breathe out into the inhaler mouthpiece. | Put the mouthpiece in your mouth and close your lips around it. Breathe in deeply through your mouth, until your lungs feel completely full of air. Do not let your lips or fingers block the vent above the mouthpiece. Hold your breath for about 10 seconds or as long as you comfortably can. Remove the inhaler from your mouth. Check the dose counter on the back of the inhaler to make sure you received the dose. Close the cap over the mouthpiece after each use of the inhaler. Make sure the cap closes firmly into place. |

TO PRIME
None needed.

TO CLEAN
Keep your inhaler dry and clean at all times. Do not wash or put any part of your inhaler in water. If the mouthpiece needs cleaning, gently wipe it with a dry cloth or tissue after using. Opening and closing the cap without inhaling a dose will waste the medicine and may damage your inhaler.

Foradil Aerolizer

STEP 1	STEP 2	STEP 3	STEP 4	STEP 5

  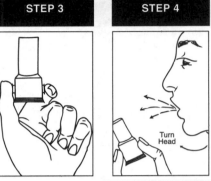 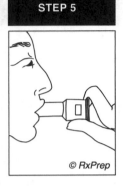

				© RxPrep
Do not remove a *Foradil* capsule from the blister card until time to take the dose. Pull off the *Aerolizer* inhaler cover. Hold the base of the *Aerolizer* firmly and twist the mouthpiece in the direction of the arrow to open.	Place the capsule in the capsule-chamber in the base of the *Aerolizer*. Twist the mouthpiece back to the closed position.	Hold with mouthpiece upright and press both buttons at the same time on the base of the *Aerolizer*. <u>Only press the buttons once</u>. You should hear the capsule being pierced.	Exhale fully away from the device.	Tilt head back slightly. Place mouthpiece in mouth with the buttons on the side (not facing up and down) and close your lips around the mouthpiece. Breathe in <u>quickly</u> and <u>deeply</u> through the inhaler. (You should hear a whirring noise. If not, open the inhaler and loosen the capsule so it can spin freely). Hold your breath as long as you can, then breathe out. Open the *Aerolizer* and make sure capsule is empty, then discard. Close inhaler and replace the cover.

TO CLEAN

Never wash the *Aerolizer*; keep it dry. Always use the new *Aerolizer* that comes with your refill. Always use the *Aerolizer* in a level position.

Patient Counseling for *Singulair*

<u>For adults and children 12 months of age and older with asthma:</u>

- Take this medication once a day in the evening. You may take this medication with food or without food.

- Take every day for as long as your healthcare provider prescribes it, even if you have no asthma symptoms.

- If your asthma symptoms get worse, or if you need to increase the use of your rescue inhaler for asthma attacks, call your healthcare provider right away.

- Do not take this medication for the immediate relief of an asthma attack. If you have an asthma attack, you should follow the instructions your healthcare provider gave you for treating asthma attacks. Always have your rescue inhaler with you.

- The most common side effects with this medication include: stomach pain, upper respiratory infections, headache and sinus infection.

- Rarely, this medication has been associated with behavior and mood changes such as aggressive behavior, hostility, anxiousness, depression and/or suicidal thoughts and actions. Please report any of the symptoms to your healthcare provider immediately.

<u>For patients 6 years of age and older for the prevention of exercise-induced asthma:</u>

- Take this medication at least 2 hours before exercise.

- Always have your rescue inhaler with you for asthma attacks.

- If you are taking *Singulair* daily for chronic asthma or allergies, do not take another dose to prevent exercise-induced asthma. Talk to your healthcare provider about your treatment of exercise-induced asthma.

- Do not take an additional dose of *Singulair* within 24 hours of a previous dose.

- *Singulair* 4 mg oral granules can be given:
  - ❑ directly in the mouth
  - ❑ dissolved in 1 teaspoonful (5 mL) of cold or room temperature baby formula or breast milk
  - ❑ mixed with 1 spoonful of one of the following soft foods at cold or room temperature
  - ❑ applesauce, mashed carrots, rice, or ice cream. Give the child all of the mixture right away (within 15 minutes)

- <u>Important</u> for *Singulair* oral granules: Never store any oral granules mixed with food, baby formula, or breast milk for use at a later time. Throw away any unused portion. Do not mix *Singulair* oral granules with any liquid drink other than baby formula or breast milk.

Patient Counseling for *Pulmicort Respules*

- Take one ampule out of the sealed aluminum envelope, recording the date you opened the envelope.

- Place any unused ampules back into the envelope and store upright, protected from light, at room temperature. Keep in mind, any remaining ampules should be used within two weeks.

- Gently swirl the ampule using a circular motion, making sure to not squeeze the ampule and keeping it in an upright position.

- Twist off the top of the ampule and squeeze all the liquid into the nebulizer and use right away. If using a face mask, make sure it fits snugly.

- Turn the compressor on and continue treatment until the mist stops, generally within 5 to 10 minutes.

- Rinse mouth with water after each dose, and wash face after treatment if a face mask was used.

PRACTICE CASE

Patient Profile

Patient Name Terri Price
Address 108 Morning Road
Age 22
Sex Female
Race White
Height 5'3"
Weight 130 lbs
Allergies NKDA

DIAGNOSES

Asthma - Step 3   GERD
Anemia

MEDICATIONS

Date	No.	Prescriber	Drug and Strength	Quantity	Sig	Refills
7/15	35421	May	*ProAir HFA*	#1	1-2 puffs Q4-6H PRN	6
7/15	35422	May	*Flovent Diskus* 100 mcg/inh	#1	2 inh BID	6
7/15	35423	May	*Singulair* 10 mg	#30	1 PO daily	6
7/15	35424	May	*Aciphex* 20 mg	#30	1 PO daily	6
7/15	35425	May	*Advil* 200 mg		TID PRN headaches	
7/15	35426	May	Ferrous sulfate 325 mg		1 PO daily	
1/18	87242	Horow-itz	Albuterol 0.5% solution	#60	2 nebuliza-tions daily	0

LAB/DIAGNOSTIC TESTS

Test	Reference Value	Results 4/1/13	7/4/15
Glu	65-99 mg/dL		
Na	135-146 mEq/L	135	137
K	3.5-5.3 mEq/L	4.2	4.7
Cl	98-110 mEq/L	102	105
CO_2	21-33 mmHg	26	26
BUN	7-25 mg/dL	10	12
Creatinine	0.6-1.2 mg/dL	0.6	0.7
Calcium	8.6-10.2 mg/dL		9.8
WBC	4-11 cells/mm3		10.2
RBC	3.8-5.1 mL/mm3		4.6

10/29/15 Here for refills on all her asthma medications. Using *ProAir* 4 x/week. Last refilled *ProAir* 18 days ago. Last refilled *Flovent, Singulair* and *Aciphex* 27 days ago. Requests recommendation for sleep agent. Also buying OTC ferrous sulfate, aspirin, *Dexatrim*, Sucrets lozenges and *Maalox*. Per discussion, she is a college student who lives at home with her parents.

Questions

1. TP seems to be exhibiting signs of uncontrolled asthma. Which of the following would be the <u>best</u> recommendation for better control?

   a. Take *ProAir* on a scheduled basis.
   b. Add *Serevent Diskus* 1 inhalation BID.
   c. Take *Singulair* 10 mg BID.
   d. Go to the emergency room as she is having an acute asthma attack.
   e. Elevate the head of the bed by 30 degrees when she sleeps.

2. TP states that she doesn't understand why her asthma is worsening. Which of the following could be contributing to her symptoms?

   a. Living in the same place for many years
   b. NSAID use
   c. Ferrous sulfate use
   d. *Aciphex* use
   e. She could be sleeping on her stomach more

3. TP asks you if the *Sucrets* lozenges will help the sore throat. She was told by her doctor that she has signs of thrush. Which of the following recommendations would you give that would help prevent this from happening in the future? (Select **ALL** that apply.)

   a. Take the *Sucrets* lozenges because they will help with her sore throat and cure thrush.
   b. Recommend that she switch to *Symbicort* instead of *Flovent*.
   c. Recommend that she rinse her mouth after her *Flovent Diskus*, if not already doing so.
   d. Tell her to save her money; *Sucrets* will not work for treating thrush.
   e. Tell her to purchase a spacer device for the *Flovent Diskus*.

4. TP comes back to your pharmacy with a prescription for *Foradil*. Which of the following statements is correct?

   a. The patient can store the medication at room temperature.
   b. This medication needs to be taken with 8 oz of water.
   c. This medication is not recommended in Step 3 asthma.
   d. This medication is taken once daily.
   e. This medication will interact with *Aciphex*.

5. Which of the following side effects is most likely to occur when using *Foradil* therapy?

   a. Neuropsychiatric behavior
   b. Palpitations
   c. Stomach upset
   d. Enuresis
   e. Depression

6. TP is placed on theophylline therapy for treatment of her asthma. Which of the following can decrease theophylline levels? (Select **ALL** that apply.)

   a. Ciprofloxacin
   b. Carbamazepine
   c. Erythromycin
   d. Cirrhosis
   e. High protein diet

Questions 7-11 do not relate to the above case.

7. Emi is a patient weighing 55 lbs. with a prescription for 0.1 mg/kg albuterol in 2.5 mL of normal saline. How many mL of the 0.5% albuterol solution is needed to fill this prescription?

   a. 0.1 mL
   b. 0.4 mL
   c. 0.5 mL
   d. 0.7 mL
   e. 1 mL

8. Omalizumab has a black box warning for:

   a. Increased risk of MI
   b. Stevens-Johnson syndrome
   c. Thrombocytopenia
   d. GI ulcers
   e. Anaphylaxis

9. A patient with asthma has been prescribed *Advair Diskus*. Which of the following statements is correct?

    a. *Advair Diskus* contains fluticasone, a long-acting beta- agonist.
    b. *Advair Diskus* contains flunisolide, an inhaled corticosteroid.
    c. *Advair Diskus* is usually dosed 2 inhalations once daily.
    d. *Advair Diskus* treats both airway constriction and inflammation.
    e. *Advair Diskus* contains formoterol, an anticholinergic agent.

10. Carla is a 10 year old girl with asthma. The physician wants to give her montelukast, but is not sure of the correct dose. Choose the correct dose of montelukast for a 10-year old child:

    a. A 5 mg chewable tablet taken BID
    b. A 5 mg chewable tablet taken once daily
    c. A 10 mg chewable tablet taken once daily
    d. A 10 mg chewable tablet taken BID
    e. A 4 mg packet of granules mixed with milk

11. The therapeutic range for theophylline is:

    a. 10-20 mcg/mL
    b. 5-10 mcg/mL
    c. 5-15 mg/mL
    d. 8-12 mg/mL
    e. 5-15 mcg/mL

Answers

1-b, 2-b, 3-c,d, 4-a, 5-b, 6-b,e, 7-c, 8-e, 9-d, 10-b, 11-e

CHRONIC OBSTRUCTIVE PULMONARY DISEASE

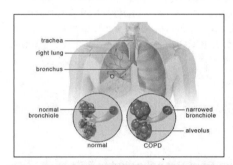

GUIDELINES/REFERENCES

Global Strategy for the Diagnosis, Management and Prevention of COPD, Global Initiative for Chronic Obstructive Lung Disease (GOLD) 2015. Available from http://www. goldcopd.org/uploads/users/files/ GOLD_Report_2015_Sept2.pdf (accessed 2015 Oct. 26).

BACKGROUND

Chronic obstructive pulmonary disease (COPD) is a common, primarily preventable and somewhat treatable disease characterized by persistent airflow limitation that is usually progressive and associated with an enhanced chronic inflammatory response in the airways to noxious particles or gases. In contrast to asthma, the limitation of airflow is not fully reversible and generally worsens over time. COPD is the 3rd leading cause of death in the United States, primarily due to tobacco use and secondhand smoke.

COPD is caused by inhalation of <u>cigarette smoke</u> and other air pollutants (noxious particles, smoke from biomass fuels, etc.) which triggers an abnormal inflammatory response in the lungs. This chronic inflammatory response can lead to lung tissue destruction (resulting in emphysema), and alter normal repair and defense mechanisms (resulting in small airway narrowing and fibrosis). These changes lead to air trapping and worsening airflow limitation, and to the breathlessness and other classic symptoms of COPD.

DIAGNOSIS

A clinical diagnosis of COPD should be considered in any patient who has <u>dyspnea</u> (shortness of breath, which is chronic and progressive), <u>chronic cough or sputum production</u>, and a history of exposure to risk factors for the disease, especially cigarette smoke. <u>Spirometry</u> (testing to measure lung function) is <u>required</u> to make the diagnosis; the presence of a post-bronchodilator $FEV_1/FVC < 0.70$ confirms the presence of persistent airflow limitation and thus of COPD. Spirometry is the most reproducible and objective measurement of airflow limitation available. <u>Smoking cessation</u> is the only management strategy proven to slow progression of disease. Other important management strategies include <u>vaccinations</u>, pulmonary rehabilitation programs, and <u>drug therapy (often using inhalers)</u>. In severe and very severe COPD, fatigue, weight loss and anorexia are common and patients may develop cor pulmonale. Some patients go on to require long-term <u>oxygen</u> therapy, either given in the hospital for acute exacerbations, or used chronically outpatient with the use of portable oxygen systems. In rare cases, lung transplantation is needed.

ASSESSMENT OF COPD

The goals of COPD assessment are to determine the severity of disease, the impact on the patient's health status and the risk of future events (exacerbations, hospital admissions, death) in order to guide therapy. Assess the following aspects of the disease separately:

- Symptoms

- Degree of airflow limitation (using spirometry)

- Risk of exacerbations

- Presence of comorbidities

COPD RISK FACTORS
Cigarette smoking
Smoke exposure (pipe, cigar, marijuana, biomass fuels)
Air pollution
Occupational exposure to dusts and chemicals
Alpha-1 antitrypsin deficiency

Symptoms

The classic symptoms are chronic and progressive dyspnea, cough, and sputum production that varies from day to day. Chronic cough and sputum production may appear years before airflow limitation occurs. Comprehensive symptom assessment is recommended using validated questionnaires such as the COPD Assessment Test (CAT) or the COPD Control Questionnaire (CCQ). The Modified British Medical Research Council (mMRC) is used to assess breathlessness.

Degree of Airflow Limitation

Degree of airflow limitation is assessed using spirometry. Please see table below for classification of severity.

Classification of Severity of Airflow Limitation in COPD (Based on Post-Bronchodilator FEV_1)

CLASSIFICATION	SEVERITY	AIRFLOW
In patients with FEV_1/FVC < 0.70		
GOLD 1	Mild	$FEV_1 \geq 80\%$ predicted
GOLD 2	Moderate	$50\% \leq FEV_1 < 80\%$ predicted
GOLD 3	Severe	$30\% \leq FEV_1 < 50\%$ predicted
GOLD 4	Very Severe	$FEV_1 < 30\%$ predicted

Risk of Exacerbations

An exacerbation of COPD is defined as an acute event characterized by a worsening of the patient's respiratory symptoms that is beyond normal day-to-day variations and leads to a change in medication. The best predictor of having frequent exacerbations (2 or more per year) is a history of previous treated events. The risk of exacerbations will also increase as airflow limitation worsens. Hospitalization for an exacerbation is associated with an increased risk of death.

Comorbidities

Comorbid conditions such as cardiovascular diseases, osteoporosis, depression and anxiety, skeletal muscle dysfunction, metabolic syndrome, GERD and lung cancer may influence mortality and hospitalizations, and should be monitored routinely and treated appropriately.

The combined assessment of COPD takes into account the symptoms, airflow limitation and exacerbation risk of the patient (see table below).

Combined Assessment of COPD

When assessing risk, choose the <u>highest risk</u> according to GOLD grade or exacerbation history.

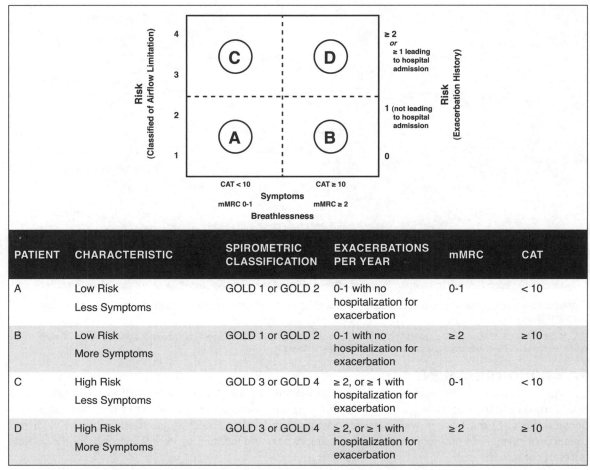

PATIENT	CHARACTERISTIC	SPIROMETRIC CLASSIFICATION	EXACERBATIONS PER YEAR	mMRC	CAT
A	Low Risk Less Symptoms	GOLD 1 or GOLD 2	0-1 with no hospitalization for exacerbation	0-1	< 10
B	Low Risk More Symptoms	GOLD 1 or GOLD 2	0-1 with no hospitalization for exacerbation	≥ 2	≥ 10
C	High Risk Less Symptoms	GOLD 3 or GOLD 4	≥ 2, or ≥ 1 with hospitalization for exacerbation	0-1	< 10
D	High Risk More Symptoms	GOLD 3 or GOLD 4	≥ 2, or ≥ 1 with hospitalization for exacerbation	≥ 2	≥ 10

CAT: COPD Assessment Test, mMRC: Modified British Medical Research Council

Pharmacologic Therapy for Stable COPD*

PATIENT GROUP	RECOMMENDED FIRST CHOICE	ALTERNATIVE CHOICE	OTHER POSSIBLE TREATMENTS**
A	SA anticholinergic PRN or SABA PRN	LA anticholinergic or LABA or SABA and SA anticholinergic	Theophylline
B	LA anticholinergic or LABA	LA anticholinergic and LABA	SABA and/or SA anticholinergic Theophylline
C	ICS + LABA or LA anticholinergic	LA anticholinergic and LABA or LA anticholinergic and PDE-4 inhibitor or LABA and PDE-4 inhibitor	SABA and/or SA anticholinergic Theophylline
D	ICS + LABA and/or LA anticholinergic	ICS + LABA and LA anticholinergic or ICS + LABA and PDE-4 inhibitor or LA anticholinergic and LABA or LA anticholinergic and PDE-4 inhibitor	Carbocysteine N-acetylcysteine SABA and/or SA anticholinergic Theophylline

* Medications in each box are mentioned in alphabetical order and therefore not necessarily in order of preference

** Medications in this column can be used alone or in combination with other options in the First and Alternative Choice columns

SA: short-acting, LA: long-acting, SABA: short-acting beta-2 agonist, LABA: long-acting beta-2 agonist, ICS: inhaled corticosteroid, PDE-4: phosphodiesterase-4, PRN: when necessary

NON-DRUG TREATMENT

Smoking cessation is the most important intervention for all patients who still smoke. Pulmonary rehabilitation helps improve quality of life and symptoms and should be referred to all patients who become short of breath when walking their own pace on level ground. Oxygen therapy has been shown to increase survival in patients with severe resting hypoxemia (defined by $PaO_2 \leq 55$ mmHg or $SaO_2 \leq 88\%$ without complications).

DRUG TREATMENT

The medications used in COPD have <u>not</u> been shown to modify the long-term decline in lung function nor reduce mortality. Therefore, pharmacotherapy is used to <u>decrease symptoms</u> and/or complications such as <u>exacerbations and hospitalizations</u>. Carbocysteine is a mucolytic that has shown a small benefit in patients with viscous sputum. Bronchodilators (beta-2 agonists, anticholinergics) are used as-needed or on a regular basis, depending on symptom severity. If used on a regular basis, <u>long-acting inhaled bronchodilators are more effective and more convenient</u> than treatment with short-acting inhaled bronchodilators. <u>Combining bronchodilators of different pharmacologic classes may improve efficacy and decrease the risk of side effects</u> compared to increasing the dose of a single agent. <u>Long-</u>

term monotherapy with oral or inhaled corticosteroids is not recommended, however, inhaled corticosteroids can be added in severe and very severe COPD. PDE-4 inhibitors reduce inflammation by inhibiting the breakdown of intracellular cyclic AMP and should always be used in combination with at least one long-acting bronchodilator. Treatment with theophylline is not recommended unless other long-term treatment bronchodilators are unavailable or unaffordable.

Vaccines are used to prevent infections and reduce the risk of acute exacerbations. Influenza vaccine (annually) and pneumococcal vaccine (PPSV23, *Pneumovax 23*) x 1 should be given to all smokers from age 19 – 64 years and those with COPD. At age 65 or older repeat PPSV23 x 1 [give ≥ 12 months after PCV13 *(Prevnar 13)* and ≥ 5 years from previous PPSV23].

If patients have severe hereditary alpha-1 antitrypsin deficiency, they may be placed on an alpha-1 proteinase inhibitor *(Prolastin, Aralast* or *Zemaira)* for chronic augmentation therapy. These agents are very expensive, given as weekly IV infusions and are associated with many side effects, including anaphylaxis.

COPD exacerbations may be caused by respiratory tract infections (viral, bacterial) or other factors such as increased air pollution. If there is increased sputum purulence and increased sputum volume or increased dyspnea, or if mechanical ventilation is required, antibiotics should be utilized for 5 – 10 days. Outside of antibiotics, an inhaled short-acting beta-2 agonist with or without a short-acting anticholinergic plus oral steroids (e.g., prednisone 40 mg/day) are effective treatments. For treatment of acute COPD exacerbations, see the Infectious Diseases II chapter.

INHALER DEVICES

There are 2 categories of inhaler devices, metered-dose inhalers (MDIs) and dry powder inhalers (DPIs). See Asthma chapter for a review of these devices. MDIs deliver an aerosolized dose of the medication and generally require a slow and deep breath in from the device. MDIs include products that end in HFA (the propellant in an MDI) and *Respimat*. DPIs deliver the dose of the medication in a powder form and require a quick and forceful breath in from the device. DPIs include devices such as the *Ellipta, Diskus, HandiHaler, Neohaler, Pressair* and *Aerolizer*. Please see the online video course for demonstration of all devices.

ANTICHOLINERGIC AGENTS

Anticholinergics block the action of acetylcholine and ↓ cyclic guanosine monophosphate (cGMP) at parasympathetic sites in bronchial smooth muscle causing bronchodilation.

DRUG	DOSING	SAFETY/SIDE EFFECTS/MONITORING
Short-acting anticholinergics		**WARNINGS** Use with caution in patients with myasthenia gravis, narrow-angle glaucoma, urinary retention, benign prostatic hyperplasia and bladder neck obstruction
Ipratropium bromide (Atrovent HFA) 17 mcg/inh, 0.02% nebulizer solution	*Atrovent* MDI: 2 inhalations QID Nebulizer: 0.5 mg TID-QID	**SIDE EFFECTS** Dry mouth (much more common with tiotropium), upper respiratory tract infections (nasopharyngitis, sinusitis), cough, bitter taste
+ albuterol (Combivent Respimat, DuoNeb) 20 mcg ipratropium + 100 mcg albuterol/inh 0.5 mg ipratropium + 2.5 mg albuterol per 3 mL nebulizer solution	*Combivent Respimat* MDI: 1 inhalation QID Nebulizer (*DuoNeb*): 3 mL QID	**MONITORING** S/sx at each visit, smoking status, COPD questionnaires, annual spirometry **NOTES** Avoid spraying in the eyes
Long-acting anticholinergics		Do not swallow capsules of glycopyrrolate, glycopyrrolate/indacaterol or tiotropium with HandiHaler product
Aclidinium (*Tudorza Pressair*) 400 mcg/inh	DPI: 1 inhalation BID	*Tudorza* – Discard product 45 days after opening pouch, when device locks out or when dose indicator displays "0", whichever comes first.
Glycopyrrolate (Seebri Neohaler) 15.6 mcg/inh	DPI: 1 capsule via *Neohaler* device BID	
+ indacaterol (Utibron Neohaler) 15.6 mcg glycopyrrolate + 27.5 mcg indacaterol/inh	DPI: 1 capsule via *Neohaler* device BID	
Tiotropium (Spiriva HandiHaler, Spiriva Respimat) 18 mcg capsule, 2.5 mcg/inh, (1.25 mcg/inh for asthma)	DPI: 1 capsule inhaled daily via the *HandiHaler* device (requires 2 puffs)	
+ olodaterol (Stiolto Respimat) 2.5 mcg tiotropium + 2.5 mcg olodaterol/inh	**Both** *Respimat* **devices** MDI: 2 inhalations daily	
Umeclidinium (*Incruse Ellipta*) 62.5 mcg/inh + vilanterol (*Anoro Ellipta*) 62.5 mcg umeclidinium + 25 mcg vilanterol/inh	**Both** *Ellipta* **devices** DPI: 1 inhalation daily	

BETA-2 AGONISTS

These agents bind to beta-2 receptors causing relaxation of bronchial smooth muscle, resulting in bronchodilation; the inhaled route is the preferred route of administration. For short-acting beta-2 agonists, see Asthma chapter.

DRUG	DOSING	SAFETY/SIDE EFFECTS/MONITORING
Long-acting Beta-2 agonists		**BOXED WARNING** Long-acting beta-2 agonists (LABAs) increase the risk of asthma-related deaths and should only be used in asthma patients who are currently receiving but are not adequately controlled on a long-term asthma control medication (inhaled corticosteroid)
Salmeterol *(Serevent Diskus)* 50 mcg/inh **+ fluticasone** *(Advair Diskus, Advair HFA)*	DPI: 1 inhalation BID	
Advair Diskus: 100, 250, 500 mcg fluticasone + 50 mcg salmeterol/inh (250/50 is the only one approved for COPD)	DPI: 1 inhalation BID	**CONTRAINDICATIONS** Status asthmaticus, acute episodes of asthma or COPD, monotherapy in treatment of asthma
Advair HFA: 45, 115, 230 mcg fluticasone + 21 mcg salmeterol/inh	MDI: 1 inhalation BID	**SIDE EFFECTS** Tachycardia, tremor, shakiness, lightheadedness, cough, palpitations, hypokalemia and hyperglycemia
Formoterol *(Foradil Aerolizer, Perforomist – nebulizer)* 12 mcg capsule, 20 mcg/2 mL nebulizer solution	DPI: 1 capsule via *Aerolizer* BID Nebulizer: 20 mcg BID	**MONITORING** S/sx at each visit, smoking status, COPD questionnaires, annual spirometry
+ budesonide *(Symbicort)* 80, 160 mcg budesonide + 4.5 mcg formeterol/inh (160/4.5 is the only one approved for COPD)	*Symbicort* MDI: 2 inhalations BID	**NOTES** <u>Bronchodilators</u> are used on a <u>PRN or scheduled</u> basis to reduce symptoms. Long-acting inhaled bronchodilators are more effective and convenient.
Arformoterol *(Brovana)* 15 mcg/2 mL nebulizer solution	Nebulizer: 15 mcg BID	Combination therapy with inhaled steroids can ↑ the risk of pneumonia, however, the combination showed a ↓ in exacerbations and improvement in lung function when compared to the individual components. Indacaterol is more effective than formoterol and salmeterol.
Indacaterol *(Arcapta Neohaler)* 75 mcg capsule **+ glycopyrrolate** *(Utibron Neohaler)* 27.5 mcg indacaterol + 15.6 mcg glycopyrrolate/inh	DPI: 1 capsule via *Neohaler* device daily DPI: 1 capsule via *Neohaler* device BID	Arformoterol contains R-isomer of formoterol. <u>Do not swallow capsules of indacaterol, indacaterol/gylcopyrrolate or formoterol.</u> <u>All steroid-containing inhalers – rinse mouth with water after use and spit.</u>
Fluticasone/vilanterol *(Breo Ellipta)* 100, 200 mcg fluticasone + 25 mcg vilanterol/inh (100/25 is the only one approved for COPD)	DPI: 1 inhalation daily	*Advair* – discard Diskus device 1 month after removal from pouch or when dose counter reads "0" (whichever comes first). *Symbicort* – discard inhaler after the labeled number of inhalations have been used or within 3 months after removal from foil pouch.
Olodaterol *(Striverdi Respimat)* 2.5 mcg/inh + tiotropium *(Stiolto Respimat)* 2.5 olodaterol + 2.5 mcg tiotropium/inh	**Both *Respimat* devices** MDI: 2 inhalations daily	*Serevent Diskus* and all *Ellipta* devices – discard device 6 weeks after removal from the foil tray or when the dose counter reads "0" (whichever comes first). All *Respimat* devices - discard device 3 months after cartridge is inserted into the inhaler or when the inhaler locks (which indicates no doses are left).

PHOSPHODIESTERASE-4 INHIBITOR

PDE-4 inhibitor that ↑ cAMP levels, leading to a reduction in lung inflammation. This medication should always be used in combination with at least one long-acting bronchodilator.

DRUG	DOSING	SAFETY/SIDE EFFECTS/MONITORING
Roflumilast *(Daliresp)* Tablet	500 mcg PO daily	**CONTRAINDICATIONS** Moderate to severe liver impairment **WARNINGS** Psychiatric events (depression, mood changes) including suicidality **SIDE EFFECTS** Diarrhea, weight loss, nausea, ↓ appetite, insomnia, HA **MONITORING** S/sx at each visit, LFTs, smoking status, COPD questionnaires, annual spirometry **NOTES** Use only in severe COPD due to modest benefit

See asthma section for details on theophylline and inhaled corticosteroids

Roflumilast Drug Interactions

Roflumilast is a substrate of 3A4 (major) and 1A2 (minor). Use with strong enzyme inducers (e.g., carbamazepine, phenobarbital, phenytoin, rifampin) is not recommended. Use with 3A4 inhibitors or dual 3A4 and 1A2 inhibitors (erythromycin, ketoconazole, fluvoxamine, cimetidine) will ↑ roflumilast levels.

PATIENT COUNSELING - METERED DOSE INHALERS

Atrovent HFA

STEP 1	STEP 2	STEP 3
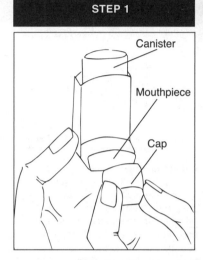		
Insert the metal canister into the actuator. The *Atrovent HFA* plastic actuator should only be used with the *Atrovent HFA* canister. Remove the protective dust cap from the mouthpiece and check mouthpiece for foreign objects prior to use.	Breathe out deeply through your mouth. Holding the inhaler upright (as shown in the picture), place the mouthpiece into your mouth and close your lips around it. Keep your eyes closed so that no medicine will be sprayed into your eyes.	While breathing in slowly and deeply through your mouth, press the top of the canister all the way down with your index finger. Hold your breath as long as possible, up to 10 seconds, then breathe normally. If another inhalation is needed, wait at least 15 seconds and repeat Steps 1-3. Place cap back on the mouthpiece after use.

Tips

PRIMING
Spray 2 times away from the face. Prime again if > 3 days from last use.

CLEANING
Rinse mouthpiece under warm running water (but not the metal canister) for 30 seconds to prevent medication buildup and blockage. Shake to remove excess water and let air dry. Clean at least weekly.

Combivent Respimat, Stiolto Respimat, Striverdi Respimat

STEP 1	STEP 2	STEP 3

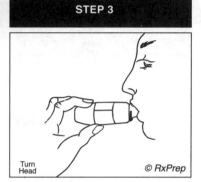

© RxPrep

Hold the inhaler upright with the cap closed to avoid accidentally releasing a dose. Turn the clear base in the direction of the arrows on the label until it clicks (half a turn).	Flip the cap until it snaps fully open. Turn head away from the inhaler and breathe out slowly and fully.	Close lips around the end of the mouthpiece without covering the air vents. While taking a slow, deep breath through your mouth, press the dose release button and continue to breathe in slowly. Hold your breath for 10 seconds or as long as comfortable. Close the cap when finished.

Tips

ASSEMBLE DEVICE FOR FIRST TIME USE

With the cap closed, press the safety catch while pulling off the clear base. Do not touch the piercing element located inside the bottom of the clear base. Write the discard by date on the label of the inhaler (which is 3 months from the date the cartridge is inserted). Push the narrow end of the cartridge into the inhaler. The base of the cartridge will not sit flush with the inhaler; about 1/8 of an inch will stick out when the cartridge is correctly inserted.

PRIMING

Hold the inhaler upright with the cap closed to avoid accidentally releasing a dose. Turn the clear base in the direction of the arrows on the label until it clicks (half a turn). Flip the cap until it snaps fully open. Point the inhaler toward the ground away from your face. Press the dose release button. Close cap. Repeat these steps over again until a spray is visible. Once the spray is visible, repeat the steps 3 more times to make sure inhaler is prepared for use. If inhaler is not used for > 3 days, spray 1 puff toward the ground to prepare the inhaler. If inhaler has not been used for > 21 days, follow priming for initial use instructions.

CLEANING

Clean the mouthpiece, including the metal part inside the mouthpiece, with a damp cloth or tissue weekly.

PATIENT COUNSELING - DRY POWDER INHALERS

Spiriva HandiHaler

STEP 1	STEP 2	STEP 3	STEP 4	STEP 5

© RxPrep

STEP 1	STEP 2	STEP 3	STEP 4	STEP 5
Open the Handi-Haler device by pressing on the green button and lifting the cap upwards. Open the mouthpiece by pulling up and away from the base.	Insert the *SPIRIVA* capsule in the chamber and close the mouthpiece firmly against the gray base until you hear a click.	Press the green piercing button once until it is flat (flush) against the base, then release. Do not shake the device	Turn head away from the inhaler and breathe out fully.	Raise your *Handihaler* to your mouth in a horizontal position and close your lips around the mouthpiece. Breathe in deeply and fully. You should hear or feel the *SPIRIVA* capsule vibrate (rattle). Remove inhaler from your mouth and hold your breath for a few seconds. Breathe normally. Breathe out again and breathe in deeply and fully through the inhaler (you must inhale twice from each capsule). Discard capsule after 2 inhalations. Close the lid of the device.

Tips

CLEANING

Clean inhaler as needed. Rinse inhaler with warm water, pressing the green button a few times so the chamber and piercing needle are under the running water. Make sure any powder build up is removed. Air dry. It takes 24 hours to air dry the *Handihaler* device after it is cleaned.

Tudorza

STEP 1	STEP 2	STEP 3	STEP 4
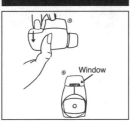	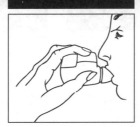		

Window

| Remove the protective cap by lightly squeezing the arrows marked on each side of the cap and pulling outwards. Check the mouthpiece for foreign objects. | A. Before putting into mouth, press the back (green) button all the way down and release.

B. Check the control window to make sure the dose is ready for inhalation; the window will change from <u>red to green</u>. Breathe out completely, <u>away from the inhaler</u>. | Put your lips tightly around the mouthpiece. Breathe in quickly and deeply through your mouth. Breathe in until you hear a <u>"click"</u> sound and <u>keep breathing in</u> to get the full dose.

Note. Do not hold down the back (green) button while breathing in. | Remove the inhaler from your mouth and hold your breath for as long as comfortable. Then breathe out slowly through your nose. Place the protective cap on the inhaler.

Note. Check that the control <u>window has turned to red</u> which indicates the full dose has been inhaled correctly. |

© RxPrep

Tips

CLEANING

You do not need to clean your inhaler. If you wish to clean it, wipe the outside of the mouthpiece with a dry tissue or paper towel. Do not use water.

Anoro Ellipta, Breo Ellipta, Incruse Ellipta

STEP 1	STEP 2	STEP 3
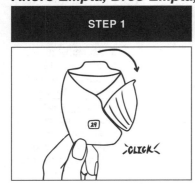		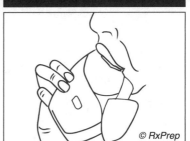

CLICK

© RxPrep

| Open the cover of the inhaler by sliding the cover down to expose the mouthpiece. You should hear a "click." The counter will count down by 1 number, indicating that the inhaler is ready to use. Note: if you open and close the cover without inhaling the medicine, the dose will be lost. <u>It is not possible to accidentally take a double dose or an extra dose in 1 inhalation</u>. | While holding the inhaler away from your mouth, breathe out fully. Do not breathe out into the mouthpiece. | Put the mouthpiece between your lips and close your lips firmly around it. Take one long, steady, deep breath in through your mouth. <u>Do not block the air vent</u> with your fingers. Remove inhaler from mouth and hold your breath for 3-4 seconds or as long as comfortable. Breathe out slowly and gently. Close the inhaler. Rinse your mouth. |

Tips

CLEANING

You can clean the mouthpiece if needed, using a dry tissue, before you close the cover. Routine cleaning is not required.

Arcapta Neohaler, Seebri Neohaler, Utibron Neohaler

STEP 1	STEP 2	STEP 3	STEP 4

  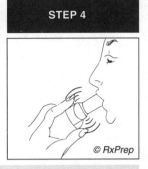

© RxPrep

STEP 1
Pull off cap.

STEP 2
Hold the base of the inhaler firmly and tilt the mouthpiece to open the inhaler. Place the capsule into the capsule chamber. Close the inhaler fully, until you hear a "click" sound.

STEP 3
Hold the inhaler upright. Press both buttons fully one time. You should hear a "click" as the capsule is being pierced. Release the buttons fully. The inhaler is now ready to be used. Before using, breathe out fully, away from the inhaler.

STEP 4
Place the mouthpiece in your mouth and close your lips around the mouthpiece. Hold the inhaler with the buttons to the side (not up and down). Breathe in rapidly and deeply (you should hear a whirring sound when breathing in). Hold your breath as long as comfortable while removing the inhaler from your mouth. Then, breathe out. The capsule should be empty of all powder. If it is not, inhale again. Remove capsule and replace the cap.

Tips

CLEANING
Cleaning the device is not necessary, however, if desired, a clean, dry, lint-free cloth or a clean, dry soft brush may be used to wipe the inhaler between uses.

36

TOBACCO CESSATION

We gratefully acknowledge the assistance of Beth A. Martin, PhD, MS, RPh, Associate Professor, University of Wisconsin-Madison School of Pharmacy, and Megan Heim, PharmD, BCACP, Clinical Pharmacist, William S. Middleton Memorial Veterans Hospital, in preparing this chapter.

BACKGROUND

Smoking is the leading cause of preventable death in the U.S. and a known cause of multiple cancers, heart disease, stroke, complications of pregnancy, COPD, and many other diseases. Tobacco dependence is a chronic disease that often requires repeated intervention and multiple attempts to quit. Effective treatments exist that can significantly increase rates of long-term abstinence. It is essential healthcare providers <u>ask</u> patients <u>about tobacco use</u>, document the response and provide treatment. A national network of tobacco quitlines is available for patients at 1-800-QUIT-NOW (1-800-784-8669).

<u>The combination of counseling and medication</u> is more effective than either counseling or medication alone. Two counseling components that are especially effective are practical counseling (problem-solving/skills training) and social support. There is a strong correlation between <u>counseling intensity</u> (length and number of counseling sessions) and <u>quitting success</u>.

There are several effective, first-line medications (5 nicotine and 2 non-nicotine) available for treating tobacco dependence and use should be encouraged for all patients attempting to quit using tobacco, except when medically contraindicated. <u>Combination therapy</u>, such as using the nicotine patch (long-acting) and a short-acting nicotine formulation (e.g. gum, inhaler, nasal spray) or nicotine patch and bupropion SR, can be considered first-line. Medications reduce withdrawal symptoms associated with decreased nicotine use. Symptoms of nicotine withdrawal include the urge to smoke, depressed mood, trouble sleeping, irritability, frustra-

GUIDELINES/REFERENCES

Treating Tobacco Use and Dependence. April 2013. Agency for Healthcare Research and Quality, Rockville, MD. http://www.ahrq.gov/professionals/clinicians-providers/guidelines-recommendations/tobacco/clinicians/update/index.html (accessed 2015 Sept 25).

Fiore MC, Baker TB. Treating smokers in the health care system. *N Engl J Med* 2011; 365:1222-31.

tion, anger, feeling anxious, difficulty concentrating, restlessness, decreased heart rate, and increased appetite or weight gain.

The risks and benefits of electronic cigarettes (e-cigarettes) is presently unknown. There is some risk that non-smokers who use them risk nicotine addiction, and although preliminary evidence suggests that e-cigarettes are safer than smoking cigarettes and may help reduce nicotine-related illness, some evidence of carcinogens in the nicotine vapors released by e-cigarettes has been found. There is also concern that the flavorings are more tempting to children. At this time these should not be recommended as an alternative to approved cessation aids.

Drug Interactions

Compounds in smoke induce hepatic CYP450 enzymes, primarily CYP450 1A2. Therefore, smokers who quit can experience side effects from supratherapeutic drug levels of caffeine, theophylline, fluvoxamine, olanzapine and clozapine. High levels of clozapine have increased risk for agranulocytosis. For smokers quitting tobacco and using warfarin, increased monitoring for bleeding risk is warranted. The combination of smoking and clopidogrel use increases risk of bleeding. Additionally, the interaction between polyaromatic hydrocarbons in tobacco smoke and estrogen therapy increases the risk of cardiovascular adverse effects, especially in women 35 years of age or older and smoking 15 or more cigarettes daily.

THE "5 A'S" MODEL FOR TREATING TOBACCO USE AND DEPENDENCE

Ask about tobacco use
Identify and document tobacco use status for every patient at every visit.

Advise to quit
In a clear, strong, and personalized manner, urge every tobacco user to quit.

Assess willingness to make a quit attempt
Is the tobacco user willing to make a quit attempt at this time (e.g., in the next month)?

Assist in quit attempt
For the patient willing to make a quit attempt, offer medication and provide or refer for counseling or additional behavioral treatment to help the patient quit.

For patients unwilling to quit at this time, provide motivational interventions designed to increase future quit attempts.

For the recent quitter and any with remaining challenges, provide relapse prevention.

Arrange follow up
For the patient willing to make a quit attempt, arrange for follow up contacts, beginning within the first week after the quit date.

For patients unwilling to make a quit attempt at the time, address tobacco dependence and willingness to quit at next clinic visit.

Special Populations

The 2008 National Guidelines promote the use of behavioral interventions over pharmacologic therapies for the following populations: pregnant patients, adolescents, smokeless tobacco users, and "light" smokers using 10 or fewer cigarettes a day. This is different than the ACOG recommendations.

Vaccinations in Smokers

Smokers 19 - 64 years old should receive the pneumococcal polysaccharide vaccine (PPSV23, *Pneumovax)*. If 65 and older and it has been more than 5 years since the last vaccination, a 2nd dose is needed. Smokers should receive the influenza vaccine annually. The ACIP has no recommendation on vaccine use with e-cigarettes. See Immunizations chapter for further discussion.

DRUG TREATMENT

Nicotine Replacement Therapy (NRT)

DRUG	DOSING	SAFETY/SIDE EFFECTS/MONITORING
Nicotine patch (*NicoDerm CQ,* others*)* OTC	7 mg/day, 14 mg/day, 21 mg/day; apply upon waking on quit date If > 10 cigarettes/day: use 21 mg x 6 wks, then 14 mg x 2 wks, then 7 mg x 2 wks If ≤ 10 cigarettes/day: use 14 mg x 6 wks, then 7 mg x 2 wks	**CONTRAINDICATIONS** Recent MI (within 2 weeks), life-threatening arrhythmia, severe or worsening angina, pregnancy **SIDE EFFECTS** For All: Headache, dizziness, nervousness, insomnia, dyspepsia
Nicotine polacrilex gum (*Nicorette,* others*)* OTC	1st cigarette smoked > 30 min after waking up: use 2 mg gum 1st cigarette smoked ≤ 30 min of waking up: use 4 mg gum Weeks 1-6: 1 piece Q1-2H Weeks 7-9: 1 piece Q2-4H Weeks 10-12: 1 piece Q4-8H Max: 24 pieces/day Use up to 12 weeks	Patch: Skin irritation Inhaler: Local irritation in the mouth and throat, coughing, rhinitis Nasal Spray: Nasal irritation, transient changes in taste and smell **NOTES** Patients must show identification for proof of age prior to purchase of nicotine products since the FDA prohibits sale of nicotine products to individuals younger than 18 years of age (REMS).
Nicotine lozenge (*Nicorette, Nicorette Mini,* others*)* OTC	1st cigarette smoked > 30 min after waking up: use 2 mg lozenge 1st cigarette smoked ≤ 30 min of waking up: use 4 mg lozenge Do not exceed 20 lozenges/day Minimum of 9 lozenges/day for 1st 6 wks 1 lozenge Q1-2H x 6 wks, then 1 lozenge Q2-4H x 3 wks, then 1 lozenge Q4-8H x 3 wks	Nicotine patch has highest adherence rate, may need additional product for acute cravings. The gum and lozenge are sugar free. Gum and lozenge (4 mg strengths) have been shown to reduce or delay weight gain. Inhaler mimics hand to mouth smoking action, providing a coping mechanism. Nasal spray has the fastest delivery system and is useful for rapid relief of withdrawal, has highest dependence potential among NRTs. Avoid in severe reactive airway disease.
Nicotine inhaler (*Nicotrol Inhaler*) Rx	6-16 cartridges daily; taper frequency of use over 6-12 weeks Use up to 6 months	Patch should not be cut and should be removed before an MRI. Patch is typically worn for 24 hours, but can remove at bedtime to avoid insomnia and bothersome vivid dreams.
Nicotine nasal spray (*Nicotrol NS*) Rx	1 dose = 2 sprays (1 spray in each nostril), give 1-2 doses per hour, ↑ PRN for symptom relief; Max: 5 doses/hr or 40 doses/day Use 3-6 months	Pregnancy Category C (OTC products)/D (Rx products)

Bupropion and Varenicline

Bupropion blocks neural re-uptake of dopamine and/or norepinephrine resulting in reduced cravings and other withdrawal symptoms. Varenicline is a partial neuronal alpha–4 beta–2 nicotinic receptor agonist resulting in low-level agonist activity at the receptor site and competitive inhibition of nicotine binding. The partial agonist activity induces modest receptor stimulation that attenuates the symptoms of nicotine withdrawal. In addition, by blocking the ability of nicotine to activate nicotinic acetylcholine receptors, it also inhibits the surges of dopamine release believed to be responsible for the reinforcement and reward associated with smoking. These agents do not need to be tapered when they are discontinued.

DRUG	DOSING	SAFETY/SIDE EFFECTS/MONITORING
BuPROPion SR *(Zyban, Buproban)* *Aplenzin, Wellbutrin, Wellbutrin SR, Wellbutrin XL, Forfivo XL* - for depression *Wellbutrin XL* - for Seasonal Affective Disorder (SAD)	Start 1 week before quit date 150 mg QAM for 3 days, then 150 mg BID Max dose: 300 mg/day Use up to 6 months To ↓ insomnia and risk of seizures, take 2nd dose 8 hours after 1st dose and/or no later than dinner If no significant progress by week 7, consider discontinuation	**BOXED WARNING** Serious neuropsychiatric events, including suicidal thinking and behavior, risk ↑ in children, adolescents, and young adults taking antidepressants **CONTRAINDICATIONS** Seizure disorder; history of anorexia/bulimia; abrupt discontinuation of alcohol, benzodiazepines, barbiturates, antiepileptic drugs, use within 14 days of discontinuing either bupropion or MAO inhibitor; initiation of bupropion in a patient receiving linezolid or IV methylene blue **SIDE EFFECTS** Dry mouth, insomnia, N/V, constipation, sweating, agitation, anxiety, tachycardia, tremors, dizziness **NOTES** Do not use with other forms of bupropion Pregnancy Category C Delays weight gain Can be used with CVD risk MedGuide required See Depression chapter for more information
Varenicline *(Chantix)*	Start 1 week before quit date Days 1-3: 0.5 mg daily Days 4-7: 0.5 mg BID Days 8 (quit date) and beyond: 1 mg BID CrCl < 30 mL/min: 0.5 mg daily Use for 12 weeks, can use another 12 weeks to maintain success To ↓ nausea, use lower dosage and take with food and a full glass of water	**BOXED WARNING** Serious neuropsychiatric events, including suicidal thinking and behavior; stop if patient becomes agitated, hostile, depressed, or other abnormal behavior. **WARNINGS** Seizure risk, ↑ effects of alcohol, accidental injury (e.g., traffic accidents) - use caution operating machinery or driving, CVD risk, angioedema, and serious skin reactions (SJS) **SIDE EFFECTS** Nausea (~30% and dose dependent), insomnia, abnormal dreams, constipation, flatulence, vomiting **NOTES** To ↓ insomnia, take 2nd dose at dinner rather than bedtime Pregnancy Category C MedGuide required

Patient Counseling

Nicotine Gum, Inhaler and Lozenge

- Acidic beverages (e.g., coffee, juices, soft drinks) interfere with the buccal absorption of nicotine; avoid eating or drinking anything except water <u>for 15 minutes before</u> and <u>during use</u>.

Nicotine Gum

- Gum should be <u>chewed slowly</u> until a <u>"peppery" or "flavored" taste</u> emerges, then <u>"parked"</u> between cheek and gum to facilitate nicotine absorption through the oral mucosa. Gum should be slowly and intermittently chewed and parked for about 30 minutes or until the taste or tingle goes away.

- Patients often do not use enough gum to obtain optimal clinical effects. Instruct to use at least <u>1 piece every 1 - 2 hours</u> for the first 6 weeks.

Nicotine Inhaler

- <u>Frequent, continuous puffing (similar to a pipe or cigar) for 20 minutes</u> is advised with each cartridge. Once a cartridge is opened, <u>it is only good for one day</u>. Peak effect is achieved within 15 minutes. After your dose is established, it is generally maintained for 3 months and then gradually tapered during the following 3 months. <u>Clean mouthpiece with soap and water regularly</u>. Delivery of nicotine from the inhaler declines significantly below 40°F. <u>In cold weather, the inhaler and cartridge should be kept in an inside pocket or other warm area</u>.

Nicotine Lozenge

- The lozenge should be allowed to <u>dissolve in the mouth</u> rather than chewing or swallowing it. It could take 20 - 30 minutes to completely dissolve.

- Patients often do not use enough PRN nicotine replacement medications to obtain optimal clinical effects. Generally, patients should use <u>1 lozenge every 1 - 2 hours</u> during the first 6 weeks of treatment, using a minimum of 9 lozenges/day, then decrease over time.

Nicotine Nasal Spray

- Patients should <u>not sniff, swallow, or inhale</u> through the nose while administering doses, as this increases irritating effects. To minimize these common side effects (80% occurrence; takes up to 3 weeks to tolerate), the spray is best delivered with the <u>head tilted slightly forward or level, not back</u>. <u>Patients must wait 5 minutes after use before driving</u> or operating heavy machinery due to the side effects of tearing and sneezing with nasal spray use.

Nicotine Patch

- At the start of each day, place the patch on a relatively hairless location, typically <u>between the neck and waist (upper body)</u>, press onto skin for ~10 seconds, and rotate the site to reduce local skin irritation. Wash hands after applying the patch.

- Patches should be applied <u>as soon as the patient wakes on the quit day</u>. With patients who experience <u>sleep disruption, have the patient remove the 24-hour patch prior to bedtime, or use the 16-hour patch</u>.

- Up to 50% of patients using the nicotine patch will experience a <u>local skin reaction</u>. Skin reactions usually are mild and self-limiting, but occasionally worsen over the course of therapy. Local treatment with hydrocortisone cream (1%) or triamcinolone cream (0.5%) and rotating patch sites may lessen the reaction. Fewer than 5% of patients discontinue patch treatment due to skin reactions.

- Wash hands after removing patch. Discard patches by folding adhesive ends together, replace in pouch and put in the trash with a lid to keep away from pets and children.

Bupropion and Varenicline

- Start taking the medication 1 week before your quit date. This allows for the medication to build up in the body to work. You can continue to use tobacco during this time. Try to stop using tobacco on your quit date.

- If behavior changes are noticed, such as agitation, hostility, depression or other abnormal thoughts or behaviors, stop the medication and call your healthcare provider right away.

Bupropion

- The most common side effects are dry mouth and trouble sleeping. These side effects are generally mild and often disappear after a few weeks. The second dose can be taken 8 hours after the first dose to decrease insomnia.

- Do not take if you have a seizure disorder, are taking other forms of bupropion, or have taken an MAO inhibitor within the last 14 days or had an eating disorder.

- Do not chew, cut, or crush the tablets. If you do, the medicine will be released into your body too quickly. If this happens you may be more likely to get side effects including seizures. Tablets must be swallowed whole. Do not exceed 300 mg daily, or 150 mg at each dose due to seizure risk.

- Take the doses at least 8 hours apart.

- If you are able to quit smoking with this medicine, your healthcare provider may keep you on it for several months so you don't go back to smoking.

Varenicline

- The most common side effects are nausea and trouble sleeping. These side effects are generally mild and often disappear after a few weeks. The second dose can be taken 8 hours after the first dose to decrease insomnia.

- Take the medication after eating and with a full glass (8 ounces) of water.

- Most people will take this medicine for up to 12 weeks. If you do not quit using tobacco by 12 weeks, reaffirm your motivation to quit smoking and consider another 12 weeks of therapy may be helpful to become or stay tobacco-free.

- Before taking this medication, tell your healthcare provider if you have ever had depression or other mental health problems.

- Decrease the amount of alcoholic beverages during treatment until you know if this medication affects your ability to tolerate alcohol. Some people have experienced increased drunkenness (intoxication), unusual or sometimes aggressive behavior, and/or having no memory of things that have happened while drinking alcohol and using this medication.

- Some people can have serious skin reactions while taking this medication. These can include rash, swelling, redness, and peeling of the skin. Some of these reactions can become life-threatening. If a rash with peeling skin or blisters in your mouth occurs, stop taking the medication and get medical attention right away.

CYSTIC FIBROSIS

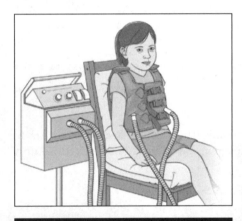

We gratefully acknowledge the assistance of Paul Beringer, PharmD, BCPS, FASHP, Associate Professor of Clinical Pharmacy and Clinical Medicine, University of Southern California, in preparing this chapter.

BACKGROUND

Cystic fibrosis (CF) is an autosomal recessive genetic disorder that leads to abnormal transport of chloride, bicarbonate, and sodium ions across the epithelium, leading to thick, viscous secretions. The thick mucus mostly affects the lungs, pancreas, liver and intestine, primarily causing difficulty breathing and lung infections as well as digestive complications. The name cystic fibrosis refers to the characteristic scarring (fibrosis) and cyst formation that occurs within the pancreas. More than 75% of people with CF are diagnosed by 2 years of age.

CF is caused by a mutation in the gene for the protein cystic fibrosis transmembrane conductance regulator (CFTR). This protein is required to regulate the components of sweat, digestive juices, and mucus. CFTR regulates the movement of chloride, bicarbonate, and sodium ions across epithelial membranes, and mutations can lead to a chronic cycle of lung infection, inflammation, and obstruction which results in a progressive loss of pulmonary function and eventual respiratory failure. CFTR dysfunction also leads to pancreatic dysfunction that can lead to insulin deficiency and diabetes. Infertility, biliary cirrhosis as well as a range of other defects can occur as well.

GUIDELINES/REFERENCES

Cystic Fibrosis Pulmonary Guidelines: Chronic Medications for Maintenance of Lung Health. *Am J Respir Crit Care Med.* 2013; 187:680–689.

Cystic Fibrosis Pulmonary Guidelines: Treatment of Pulmonary Exacerbations. *Am J Respir Crit Care Med.* 2009; 180:802–808.

CLINICAL PRESENTATION

The classic symptoms of CF are salty tasting skin, poor growth and poor weight gain despite adequate food intake, thick and sticky mucus production, frequent lung infections, coughing and shortness of breath. Digital clubbing is often present. Digestive symptoms include steatorrhea (fatty stools) and malnutrition due to poor absorption of nutrients, including fat-soluble vitamins, and a failure to thrive if not treated.

DRUG TREATMENT

Early diagnosis of CF and a comprehensive treatment plan can improve both survival and quality of life. Specialty clinics for cystic fibrosis are helpful and are found in many communities. The prevention and treatment of lung infections are essential; antibiotics (inhaled if possible) are a mainstay of therapy. Patients experience obstruction of pancreatic ducts and cannot digest essential nutrients. Advances in research have led to the development of 2 new targeted gene therapy medications, ivacaftor and ivacaftor/lumacaftor.

Treatments for Lung Problems

Multiple medications are used to help manage the thick mucus and reduce the risk of infection in the lungs. When patients are taking several medications, the order is critical to maximize absorption and effect. The recommended order is as follows: bronchodilator, hypertonic saline, dornase alfa, chest physiotherapy, then inhaled antibiotics.

Controlling Infections in the Lungs

Intermittent Infection

■ Impaired mucociliary clearance predisposes patients with CF to bacterial colonization and lung infections.

TREATMENT OF LUNG PROBLEMS
■ Inhaled bronchodilators: To help open the airways
■ Hypertonic saline *(HyperSal)*: To mobilize mucus and improve airway clearance
■ Dornase alfa *(Pulmozyme)*: To break down extracellular DNA which thins mucus to promote airway clearance
■ Airway clearance technique: Chest physiotherapy, vest, etc.
■ Inhaled antibiotics: For prevention of pulmonary exacerbations
■ Oral azithromycin: To reduce airway inflammation and disrupt *Pseudomonas aeruginosa* biofilm formation
■ Transplantation: For patients with end-stage lung disease

The most common organisms early in the disease are *Staphylococcus aureus* and *Haemophilus influenzae* followed by *Pseudomonas aeruginosa* in adolescents and adults. Acute pulmonary exacerbations characterized by an increase in cough, sputum production with a change in sputum color (greenish), shortness of breath, a rapid decline in FEV_1, loss of appetite and weight are a frequent complication of CF. Treatment often includes an extended course of antibiotics (2 – 4 weeks), modalities to increase airway clearance and nutritional therapies.

■ If the patient has a *Pseudomonas aeruginosa* infection, 2 drugs given IV are recommended to provide potential synergy and prevent resistance. These include aminoglycosides, beta-lactams, quinolones, and others that cover *Pseudomonas aeruginosa*. See Infectious Diseases I chapter for a complete discussion on treatment options of *Pseudomonas aeruginosa*. Doses tend to be larger than normal due to the need to obtain a therapeutic concentration in lung tissue and the reduced susceptibility of the bacteria chronically colonizing the airways of these patients.

Chronic Infection

Lung infections occur intermittently at first, but eventually become chronic. In particular, chronic lung infections with *Pseudomonas aeruginosa* are associated with more rapid decline in pulmonary function. Inhaled antibiotics are recommended for patients with chronic *Pseudomonas aeruginosa* lung infections to reduce the bacterial burden. Treatment is cycled with 28 days on therapy, followed by 28 days off, and is associated with an improvement in lung function and a reduction in the frequency of acute pulmonary exacerbations. The frequency of exacerbations is strongly associated with lung function decline and shortened survival in CF. If a patient is using a bronchodilator and/or mucolytic, these should be given prior to the antibiotic inhalation. See agents in the following chart.

Treatment for Lung Complications

DRUG	DOSING	SAFETY/SIDE EFFECTS/MONITORING

Agents to Promote Mucus Clearance

DRUG	DOSING	SAFETY/SIDE EFFECTS/MONITORING
Albuterol *(AccuNeb, Proventil HFA, others)*	2-4 times daily	Well-tolerated if taken correctly; refer to Asthma chapter for complete information.
Hypertonic saline (HyperSal) 4 mL unit dose vials	4 mL via a nebulizer 2-4 times daily	Hypertonic saline is a high-alert drug, especially with IV administration. For CF therapy, hypertonic saline is supplied as small ampules that are delivered via a nebulizer.
Dornase alfa (Pulmozyme) 2.5 mg single use ampule	2.5 mg daily with recommended nebulizer and compressor system Do not mix with any other drug in the nebulizer	**CONTRAINDICATIONS** Hypersensitivity to Chinese Hamster Ovary (CHO) products **SIDE EFFECTS** Chest pain, fever, rash, rhinitis, laryngitis, voice alteration, throat irritation **NOTES** Store the ampules in the refrigerator (do not expose to room temperature ≥ 24 hours). Protect from light.

Antibiotics, Inhaled

DRUG	DOSING	SAFETY/SIDE EFFECTS/MONITORING
Tobramycin Inhalation Solution *(TOBI, Bethkis, Kitabis Pak)* *TOBI, Kitabis:* 300 mg/5 mL single use ampule *Bethkis:* 300 mg/4 mL single use ampule	300 mg via nebulizer Q12H x 28 days, followed by 28 days off cycle Indicated in patients ≥ 6 years who are colonized with *Pseudomonas aeruginosa* to reduce infection/hospitalization Do not mix with any other drug in the nebulizer	**SIDE EFFECTS** Ototoxicity, tinnitus, voice alteration, dizziness, bronchospasm, mouth and throat pain **NOTES** Little systemic absorption *TOBI:* Use with *PARI LC Plus* reusable nebulizer and *DeVilbiss Pulmo-Aide* air compressor *Bethkis:* Use with *PARI LC Plus* nebulizer and *Vios* air compressor Doses should be taken at least 6 hours apart Recommended to store in refrigerator; can be kept at room temperature up to 28 days (do not use if product has been at room temp > 28 days) In foil to protect from light Not for use if FEV_1 < 40% or > 80% predicted, or if colonized with *Burkholderia cepacia*
Tobramycin Inhalation Powder *(TOBI Podhaler)* 28 mg capsules in blister card	112 mg (4 x 28 mg caps) via podhaler Q12H x 28 days, followed by 28 days off cycle Indicated in patients ≥ 6 years who are colonized with *Pseudomonas aeruginosa* to reduce infection/hospitalization	**SIDE EFFECTS** Similar to above **NOTES** Little systemic absorption Use with *Podhaler* Doses should be taken at least 6 hours apart Store capsules at room temperature in a dry place Not for use if FEV_1 < 25% or > 80% predicted, or if colonized with *Burkholderia cepacia*

Treatment for Lung Complications Continued

DRUG	DOSING	SAFETY/SIDE EFFECTS/MONITORING
Aztreonam Lysine Inhalation Solution *(Cayston)* 75 mg vial	75 mg TID x 28 days, followed by 28 days off cycle Indicated in patients ≥ 7 years who are colonized with *Pseudomonas aeruginosa* to reduce infection/hospitalization Do not mix with any other drug in the nebulizer	**SIDE EFFECTS** Allergic reactions (may be severe), bronchospasm, fever, wheezing, cough, chest discomfort **NOTES** Doses should be taken at least 4 hours apart Use with *Altera* nebulizer system Need to reconstitute with 1 mL of sterile diluent (provided); give immediately Recommend to refrigerate (can be kept at room temperature up to 28 days) Protect from light

Antibiotic, Oral

Azithromycin *(Zithromax)* Off-label	< 40 kg: 250 mg 3 times/ week > 40 kg: 500 mg 3 times/ week Used to decrease inflammation and reduce exacerbations	**SIDE EFFECTS** In CF patients: Tinnitus, nausea, risk of QT prolongation **NOTES** Do not use as monotherapy in individuals with nontuberculous mycobacteria lung infections

Treatment of Malabsorption

Malabsorption, increased energy needs, and reduced appetite are common in CF patients. Correction of maldigestion and malabsorption are essential to meet the increased energy requirements for normal growth, optimal pulmonary function and to prolong life.

- A high-fat and calorically-dense diet: To help with nutrition and normal weight and growth, increased energy needs and to prolong survival

- Pancreatic enzyme replacement: To improve digestion, optimize growth and nutritional status

- Proton pump inhibitors: Required with *Viokace* and used with other pancreatic enzymes to reduce symptoms and for the treatment of GERD

- Vitamin supplements: Especially the fat-soluble vitamins A, D, E, and K for normal cellular function

- Insulin: For treatment of CF-related diabetes mellitus

Pancreatic Enzyme Products

The thick mucus obstructs pancreatic enzyme flow, resulting in a lack of these enzymes reaching the gastrointestinal tract. Frequent, greasy, oily, foul-smelling stools are manifestations of pancreatic insufficiency. Most CF patients need to supplement their diet with appropriate amounts of pancreatic enzyme products (PEPs).

Pancrelipase is a natural product harvested from porcine pancreatic glands which contains a combination of lipase, amylase, and protease. PEPs are formulated to dissolve in the more basic pH of the duodenum so they can act locally to break down fat, starches and protein. The dose is individualized for each patient and is based on the lipase component. Once enzyme therapy is started, the dose is adjusted every 3 – 4 days until stools are normalized. Do not use doses > 6,000 units/kg/meal of lipase due to colonic stricture risk.

Enzymes are given <u>prior to meals and snacks</u>: full doses are given before meals and <u>50% of the mealtime</u> dose is given <u>with snacks</u>. Meals with <u>high fat content</u> require <u>higher doses</u>. Counsel patients <u>not to</u> <u>chew or crush</u> the capsules. If a patient cannot swallow them whole, the microsphere-contents can be <u>sprinkled on soft food with a low pH that does not require chewing</u> (such as applesauce, gelatin, baby food). Do not mix with milk-based foods, such as yogurt or pudding since these have a higher pH. There is also a powder formulation. <u>Take the entire dose at the beginning of each meal or snack along with</u> <u>a generous amount of liquid</u>. Retention in the mouth before swallowing may cause mucosal irritation and stomatitis.

<u>Do not substitute pancreatic enzyme products. This is an FDA recommendation. They do not require</u> <u>refrigeration</u>. If infants spit them out, immediately follow with liquid until swallowed.

DRUG	DOSING	SAFETY/SIDE EFFECTS/MONITORING
Pancrelipase *(Creon, Lip-Prot-Amyl, Pancreaze, Pertzye, Ultresa, Viokace, Zenpep)*	**Initial** Age < 1 year: varies by product Age 1- 3 years: Lipase 1,000 units/kg/meal Age ≥ 4 years: Lipase 500 units/kg/meal **Max (all ages)** Lipase ≤ 2,500 units/<u>kg/</u><u>meal</u> or ≤ 10,000 units/kg/<u>day</u>. Doses > 6,000 units/kg/meal are associated with colonic stricture. Take before or with food, avoid foods with high pH such as dairy. Use ½ meal-time dose with snacks. <u>Keep in original</u><u>container</u>; protect from moisture.	**WARNINGS** Fibrosing colonopathy advancing to colonic strictures (rare): Symptoms include severe abdominal pain, bloating, difficulty passing stools, nausea, vomiting, diarrhea. Risk higher with doses > 10,000 lipase units/kg/day. <u>To avoid oral mucosal irritation</u>, do not chew or retain in the mouth Hyperuricemia **SIDE EFFECTS** <u>Abdominal pain, flatulence, HA, nausea, neck pain</u> **MONITORING** Abdominal symptoms, nutritional intake, weight, height (children), stool, fecal fat **NOTES** <u>Viokace</u> is the only formulation <u>not enteric coated</u> and needs to be given with PPI. All formulations are <u>porcine derived</u> and are <u>not interchangeable</u>. <u>Do not crush or chew</u> contents of capsules. Delayed-release capsules with enteric coated microspheres or microtablets may be opened and sprinkled on soft, acidic foods (pH ≤ 4.5). MedGuide required.

Cystic Fibrosis Transmembrane Conductance Regulator Potentiator

Two therapies are available that work at the cellular level to help where the chloride transport defect occurs. Ivacaftor *(Kalydeco)* works by increasing the time cystic fibrosis transmembrane conductance regulator (CFTR) channels remain open, augmenting chloride transport activity. It is currently indicated in patients ≥ 2 years of age who have one of the following mutations in the CFTR gene: G551D, G1244E, G1349D, G178R, G551S, S1251N, S1255P, S549N, S549R or R117H (which represents 5% of the CF population worldwide). Lumacaftor/ivacaftor *(Orkambi)* is a combination of a CFTR corrector and potentiator therapies. Lumacaftor works by correcting the CFTR folding defect, resulting in an increase in the presence of the protein at the cell surface. Ivacaftor/lumacaftor is approved in patients 12 years and older who are <u>homozygous</u> (two copies) for the CFTR <u>F508del mutation</u> (the most common mutation) in the CFTR gene.

DRUG	DOSING/INDICATIONS	SAFETY/SIDE EFFECTS/MONITORING
Ivacaftor *(Kalydeco)* Tablet, oral packet	150 mg PO Q12H with <u>high fat</u> containing food With CYP3A4 moderate inhibitors or moderate-severe hepatic impairment: 150 mg daily With CYP3A4 strong inhibitors: 150 mg twice weekly	**WARNINGS** ↑ LFTs, cataracts in children Respiratory events: Dyspnea, chest discomfort and abnormal respiration upon initiation (*Orkambi* only) **SIDE EFFECTS** Headache, URTIs, nasopharyngitis, oropharyngeal pain, abdominal pain, nausea, diarrhea, rash
Lumacaftor/ivacaftor *(Orkambi)* Tablet	2 tablets (each containing 200/125 mg) PO Q12H with <u>high fat</u> containing food Moderate hepatic impairment: 2 tablets QAM, 1 tablet QPM Severe hepatic impairment: 1 tablet Q12H With CYP3A4 strong inhibitors: 1 tablet daily	↑ CPK, flatulence (*Orkambi* only) **MONITORING** LFTs (baseline, every 3 months for 1 year, then annually), eye exam (peds), pulmonary tests

Cystic Fibrosis Transmembrane Conductance Regulator Drug Interactions

- Ivacaftor is a substrate of 3A4 (major) and lumacaftor is an inducer of 3A4 (strong); see dosing recommendations above. Inducers of 3A4 will decrease the level of both these medications and should be avoided.

Patient Counseling

TOBI Podhaler

- Use the *Podhaler* <u>device</u> to take the medication. <u>Do not swallow</u> the capsules.

- Use a new *Podhaler* device every 7 days.

- One dose consists of 4 capsules, inhaled 1 at a time, and should be taken as close to 12 hours but <u>no less</u> than 6 hours apart. Remove 1 capsule at a time from the packaging immediately before administration. Inhale one capsule through the *Podhaler* device before removing the next capsule.

- Make sure to finish the whole dose of *TOBI*. Do not leave any medication in the capsules.

- The medication comes in 4 weekly packs containing 7 blister cards of 8 capsules each (4 for each morning and evening). <u>Store capsules at room temperature in a dry place.</u>

TOBI Inhalation for Nebulization

- Open the ampule by twisting off the top. Squeeze all the contents of the ampule into the nebulizer cup.

- Sit or stand in an upright position and breathe through your mouth (may need to use nose clips if easier) and continue until all the medicine is gone and there is no longer any mist being produced.

- Clean the nebulizer as instructed after each use. Wash all parts (except tubing) with warm water and soap, rinse thoroughly, allow to air dry or dry with a lint-free cloth. The nebulizer parts (except tubing) can be washed on the top rack in a dishwasher (in a dishwasher basket).

- Every other treatment day, disinfect the nebulizer parts (except tubing) by boiling them in water for a full 10 minutes.

- Do not share nebulizers.

Pancreatic Enzyme Counseling (Children)

- The most common side effects include stomach pain, bloating, gas, nausea, headache, and neck pain.

- Dispense MedGuide and instruct patient to read it. The MedGuide discusses a rare bowel disorder that can happen with some people.

- This medication is taken at the beginning of a meal or snack. At snacks give half of the meal-time dose.

- Have your child swallow whole. Do not let your child chew or crush or hold the medicine in the mouth or the medicine will cause the mouth to become sore.

- If it is difficult to swallow the capsules, the contents can be sprinkled on a spoonful of soft food such as applesauce, pureed bananas, or pears. Once the contents are sprinkled on the food it needs to be used right away. Do not let your child chew it, just swallow.

- Do not mix with dairy products such as milk or yogurt.

- Have your child drink lots of non-caffeinated liquids every day.

- It is important to follow the diet plan you received for your child to get adequate nutrition and to keep as healthy as possible.

- If you forget to give the medicine with the meal, wait until the next scheduled dose. Do not make up for missed doses.

PRACTICE CASE

PATIENT PROFILE

Patient Name	Gina Alossi								
Address	390 Frost Ave								
Age	13	**Sex**	F	**Race**		**Height**	4'8"	**Weight**	76 lbs
Allergies									

DIAGNOSES

Cystic Fibrosis

MEDICATIONS

Date	No.	Prescriber	Drug & Strength	Quantity	Sig	Refills
3/21		Sanchez	ZenPep	20,000 units	TID	5
3/21		Sanchez	Albuterol 0.5% nebulization solution	2.5 mg/0.5 mL	BID	5
3/21		Sanchez	Multivitamin		QD	

LAB/DIAGNOSTIC TESTS

Test	Normal Value	Results		
		Date 2/9	Date 3/21	Date 4/8
Alk Phos	33-115 u/L	48		
AST	10-35 IU/L	22		
ALT	10-40 IU/L	27		
GLU	65-99 mg/dL	89		
NA	135-146 mEq/L	141		
K	3.5-5.3 mEq/L	4.7		
CL	98-110 mEq/L	104		
HCO3-	22-28 mEq/L	24		
BUN	7-25 mg/dL	19		
Creatinine	0.6-1.2 mg/dL	0.6		
Calcium	8.6-10.2 mg/dL			
WBC	4-11 cells/mm^3	5.5		
CFTR gene testing			F508del/F508del	
Sputum culture (x 2)				*Pseudomonas aeruginosa*

Questions

1. Based on the laboratory testing on 3/21, which of the following medications would be appropriate to add to Gina's regimen?

   a. *TOBI Podhaler*

   b. *Hypersal*

   c. *Pulmozyme*

   d. *Kalydeco*

   e. *Orkambi*

2. Based on the above culture, which of the following represents the best pharmacologic intervention at the present time?

   a. Cephalexin

   b. *Biaxin*

   c. *Kalydeco*

   d. *Cayston*

   e. Chest physiotherapy

3. Which of the following is a correct patient counseling recommendation for pancreatic enzyme replacement therapy?

   a. If the patient has difficulty swallowing the capsules the microspheres can be crushed and sprinkled over food.

   b. The enzymes should be taken with meals.

   c. The enzyme products are equivalent and can be interchanged, depending on formulary requirements.

   d. *Viokace* should be administered with an acidic liquid such as orange juice.

   e. Pancreatic enzymes should not be taken if the meal contains little or no fat content.

Questions 4-7 do not apply to the above case.

4. Which of the following are potential adverse effects associated with *TOBI* therapy? (Select **ALL** that apply.)

   a. Voice alteration

   b. Bronchospasm

   c. Ototoxicity

   d. Tinnitus

   e. Pulmonary infiltrates

5. Which of the following is an appropriate counseling recommendation for *TOBI Podhaler* therapy?

   a. Store capsules in the freezer at all times.

   b. Capsules should be taken orally on an empty stomach.

   c. Take twice daily; doses may be taken 4 hours apart.

   d. Remove only 1 capsule at a time immediately before administration.

   e. Instruct the patient to thoroughly chew (or crush) the tablets.

6. Which of the following therapies are used in promoting mucus clearance in patients with cystic fibrosis?

   a. Pseudoephedrine

   b. Hypertonic saline

   c. Tiotropium

   d. Inhaled aztreonam

   e. Inhaled tobramycin

7. Which of the following are correct statements regarding dosing considerations for ivacaftor? (Select **ALL** that apply).

   a. The brand name is *Kaleidoscope XR*.

   b. Ivacaftor should be administered with a high fat containing meal.

   c. Dosage adjustment is necessary when co-administered with CYP3A4 inhibitors.

   d. Ivacaftor is nephrotoxic and is contraindicated in severe renal insufficiency.

   e. The normal dose is 150 mg by mouth every 12 hours.

Answers

1-e, 2-d, 3-b, 4-a,b,c,d, 5-d, 6-b, 7-b,c,e

DIABETES

We gratefully acknowledge the assistance of Bethany L. Murphy, PharmD, BCACP, Assistant Professor of Pharmacy Practice, Union University School of Pharmacy, in preparing this chapter.

BACKGROUND

Diabetes is a common condition in the United States, affecting ~29 million Americans, or 9.3% of the population. Of the ~29 million, 21 million are diagnosed, and 8 million remain undiagnosed.

Most patients have type 2 diabetes; 1.25 million of the 29 million are children and adults with type 1 diabetes. In some patients, it is difficult to distinguish between type 1 and type 2 diabetes especially early in the disease process. The C-peptide test is used to identify patients who still produce insulin.

Diabetes is characterized by hyperglycemia due to decreased insulin secretion (from the pancreas), decreased insulin sensitivity (primarily in the muscle cells), or both. Continued hyperglycemia leads to many complications, including organ and nerve damage.

GUIDELINES/REFERENCES

American Diabetes Association (ADA) Position Statement. Standards of Medical Care in Diabetes - 2015. *Diabetes Care.* 2015; 38 (suppl 1):S1-93.

American Association of Clinical Endocrinologists (AACE)/American College of Endocrinology. Clinical practice guidelines for developing a diabetes mellitus comprehensive care plan. *Endocr Pract.* 2015; 21 (suppl 1):1-87.

SCREENING/DIAGNOSIS

Screening

Testing for type 2 diabetes and prediabetes should be done in all adults of any age who are overweight or obese (BMI $\geq$ 25 kg/m^2 or $\geq$ 23 kg/m^2 in Asian Americans; this group has a higher risk of diabetes at a lower BMI) and who have one or more additional risk factors for diabetes (see risk factors for type 2 diabetes on the following page). In patients without risk factors, testing should start at 45 years of age.

LONG-TERM COMPLICATIONS OF DIABETES

Microvascular Disease
Retinopathy (most common)

Nephropathy (may progress to ESRD)

Peripheral neuropathy ($\uparrow$ risk for foot infections and amputations)

Autonomic neuropathy (erectile dysfunction, gastroparesis, loss of bladder control/UTIs)

Macrovascular Disease
Coronary artery disease (e.g., MI, HF)

Cerebrovascular disease (e.g., TIA/stroke)

Peripheral artery disease (PAD)

Clinical Signs and Symptoms

Classic symptoms of diabetes that are due to hyperglycemia include polyuria, polyphagia, polydipsia, blurred vision and fatigue. In type 1 diabetes, especially in children, ketoacidosis is commonly the initial presentation and is caused by a total deficiency in insulin. Ketoacidosis seldom occurs in type 2 unless it is associated with the stress of another illness, such as an infection.

Type 2 diabetes frequently goes undiagnosed for years because hyperglycemia develops gradually and the early symptoms may not be severe enough for the patient to notice; however, the hyperglycemia will put the person at increased risk for developing complications. Screening can help to identify these patients.

Prediabetes

Prediabetes indicates an increased risk of developing diabetes. Meeting dietary and exercise recommendations reduces the risk of progression to diabetes. Metformin can be used to help improve blood glucose levels, especially for those with a BMI > 35 kg/m², age < 60 years and in women with a history of gestational diabetes mellitus (GDM). Annual monitoring for development of diabetes and treatment of modifiable CVD risk factors is recommended.

DIAGNOSIS OF PREDIABETES AND DIABETES

Criteria for the Diagnosis of Prediabetes
- Fasting plasma glucose (FPG) 100-125 mg/dL

  or

- 2-hr plasma glucose in the 75-g oral glucose tolerance test (OGTT) 140-199 mg/dL

  or

- A1C 5.7-6.4%

Criteria for the Diagnosis of Diabetes
- Classic symptoms of hyperglycemia (polyuria, polydipsia and unexplained weight loss) or hyperglycemic crisis AND a random plasma glucose ≥ 200 mg/dL

  or

- FPG ≥ 126 mg/dL – fasting is defined as no caloric intake for at least 8 hours*

  or

- 2-hr plasma glucose in the 75-g OGTT ≥ 200 mg/dL*

  or

- A1C ≥ 6.5%*

* In the absence of unequivocal hyperglycemia, result should be confirmed by repeat testing

---

RISK FACTORS FOR TYPE 2 DIABETES

First-degree relative with diabetes

High-risk race/ethnicity (African American, Latino, Native American, Asian American, Pacific Islander)

Overweight (BMI ≥ 25 kg/m² or ≥ 23 kg/m² in Asian Americans)

Physical inactivity

Hypertension (≥ 140/90 mmHg or on medications for hypertension)

HDL < 35 mg/dL and/or TG > 250 mg/dL

History of CVD

A1C ≥ 5.7%, impaired glucose tolerance or impaired fasting glucose on previous testing

Women who delivered a baby weighing > 9 pounds or had gestational diabetes mellitus

Women with polycystic ovary syndrome

Other clinical conditions associated with insulin resistance (e.g. severe obesity, acanthosis nigricans)

Type 1 Diabetes

Type 1 diabetes is caused by the autoimmune destruction of the beta cells in the pancreas. These are the cells that produce insulin; once the beta cells are destroyed, there is no more insulin production. Without insulin, glucose cannot enter muscle cells and fat is used as an alternative energy source. Fat breakdown produces ketones, and the ketones can cause DKA, a life-threatening form of acidosis. Type 1 patients, therefore, must be treated with insulin. Type 1 usually presents in younger, thinner patients, but can appear in older patients. Family history is a risk factor for acquiring type 1, but is much less of a risk factor than with type 2.

Type 2 Diabetes

Type 2 is strongly associated with obesity, physical inactivity and family history. Type 2 diabetes accounts for ~95% of cases and is due to both insulin resistance (at the cellular level) and insulin deficiency. The beta cells produce less insulin over time as they become damaged. This is why the onset of type 2 is often not noticed; the patient is producing some insulin which helps some of the glucose into the cells, but both are inadequate. Type 2 can be managed with lifestyle modifications alone (in a small minority of patients), or lifestyle modifications with some combination of medications, which can be all oral, all injectable (including insulin) or a combination of oral, injectable and/or inhaled formulations.

GESTATIONAL DIABETES MELLITUS

Diabetes in pregnancy consists of two different types: women who develop diabetes during pregnancy (gestational diabetes, or GDM), or women who had diabetes prior to becoming pregnant (pregestational diabetes). In both groups, the blood glucose targets are more stringent than the targets for the non-pregnant population (see box); they are closer to normal levels to help keep the mother and the baby healthy. If the blood glucose is high the baby will be large (macrosomia), will be at risk for hypoglycemia at birth, and will become a child with high risk for obesity and type 2 diabetes. The first step in diabetes management during pregnancy should be lifestyle modifications (diet and exercise). Frequent self-monitoring of blood glucose (SMBG) is used to assess if the lifestyle modifications are adequate; if not, insulin is preferred for add-on treatment. Metformin and glyburide are commonly used during pregnancy, although the guidelines state that the long-term safety data on both oral agents is not available.

GOALS FOR DIABETES IN PREGNANCY

Gestational Diabetes
Preprandial: ≤ 95 mg/dL

1 hour post-meal: ≤ 140 mg/dL

2 hours post-meal: ≤ 120 mg/dL

Pregestational Diabetes
A1C: < 6%

Preprandial, bedtime and overnight: 60-99 mg/dL

Peak postprandial: 100-129 mg/dL

NON-DRUG (LIFESTYLE) TREATMENT

Lifestyle modifications should be used alone or in combination with medications when necessary to meet treatment goals. All patients who smoke should receive cessation counseling. E-

SELECT DRUGS THAT CAN RAISE BLOOD GLUCOSE

Atypical antipsychotics (e.g., olanzapine, clozapine, quetiapine)

Azole antifungals (especially posaconazole)

Beta-agonists

Carvedilol, propranolol (and possibly other beta-blockers)

Cough syrups (sugar content usually modest)

Cyclosporine, tacrolimus, sirolimus

Diazoxide (*Proglycem* - used for low BG due to certain diseases)

Interferon alfas

Niacin

Octreotide (in type 2 diabetes)

Protease Inhibitors

Quinolones

Statins

Systemic steroids

Thiazide and loop diuretics

SELECT DRUGS THAT CAN LOWER BLOOD GLUCOSE

Linezolid

Lorcaserin (*Belviq*)

Octreotide (in type 1 diabetes)

Pentamidine

Propranolol and other non-selective beta-blockers

Quinine

Quinolones

Many anti-diabetic drugs, primarily insulin and insulin secretagogues cigarettes are not recommended as an alternative to smoking or to facilitate smoking cessation. Psychosocial assessment should be routine; emotional well-being is an important part of diabetes care and self-management. Immunizations by age group should be recommended and administered, in accordance with the CDC's Advisory Committee on Immunization Practices (ACIP). Patients with chronic illness, including diabetes, have increased rates of hospitalizations and mortality from influenza and pneumococcal disease, and vaccinations for both are included in the CDC recommendations.

Nutrition

Patients with diabetes should receive individualized medical nutrition therapy (MNT). There is no one-size-fits-all recommendation. Various diets have been shown to provide benefit, including Mediterranean-style, the Dietary Approaches to Stop Hypertension (DASH) plan, plant-based (vegan or vegetarian), and lower-fat or lower-carbohydrate diets. Carbohydrates from vegetables, fruits, whole grains, legumes and dairy products should be selected over other carbohydrate sources, especially those that contain added fat, sugar or sodium. Increased consumption of long-chain omega-3 fatty acids (EPA and DHA) from foods such as fatty fish (2 or more servings per week), and omega-3 linolenic acid (ALA) from foods such as flaxseed and soy, is recommended. The limits recommended for saturated fat, cholesterol and *trans* fat intake are the same as that for the general population.

Overweight or obese patients with diabetes or prediabetes should be encouraged to lose weight by reducing energy intake (decreasing calories), while choosing healthy foods; weight loss improves blood glucose, blood pressure and cholesterol levels. Reducing weekly calorie intake by 3,500 kcal will result in a 1 pound weight loss. The waist circumference should be < 35 inches for females and < 40 inches for males. The recommendation for maximum sodium intake is the same as the general population (< 2,300 mg per day). Reducing sodium intake is important for blood pressure control.

Patients with type 1 diabetes should use the carbohydrate-counting meal planning approach. If the insulin dose is fixed (constant; not adjusted based on the grams of carbohydrates in the meal), then the carbohydrate intake will need to be constant. A carbohydrate serving is measured as 15 grams which is approximately one small piece of fruit, 1 slice of bread, ⅓ cup of cooked rice/pasta, or ½ cup of oatmeal. Many patients with diabetes match the prandial (meal-time) insulin dose to the carbohydrate intake.

High risk individuals should consume 14 grams of fiber for each 1,000 kcal, or about 25 grams per day for women and 38 grams per day for men. Food containing whole grains should be chosen (such as whole wheat flour and brown rice) instead of refined grains (such as white flour and white rice).

PHYSICAL ACTIVITY

Adults should perform at least 150 min/week of moderate-intensity aerobic activity (50 – 70% of maximum heart rate) spread over at least 3 days/week, with no more than 2 consecutive days off.   Changing sedentary habits reduces hyperglycemia and is important for those who watch long hours of television, or who have jobs where they sit all day. Patients should be instructed to "get up and move" every 90 minutes, at the minimum. Resistance training, such as weight lifting is recommended, at least twice weekly.

COMPREHENSIVE CARE

Antiplatelet Therapy

Aspirin (75 – 162 mg/day) should be considered for primary prevention in patients with type 1 and type 2 who have ↑ CVD risk (10-year risk > 10%). This includes men > 50 years of age or women > 60 years of age who have at least one additional major risk factor (family history of CVD, dyslipidemia, albuminuria, smoking or hypertension). Aspirin 75 – 162 mg/day should be used for secondary prevention unless the patient has an allergy or contraindication to use. If the patient has an aspirin allergy, clopidogrel 75 mg/day is recommended.

Blood Pressure Control

Blood pressure (BP) should be measured at every routine visit. Goal BP for patients with diabetes is < 140/90 mmHg. A lower target, < 130/80 mmHg, may be appropriate for certain individuals, such as younger patients or those with a high risk of stroke, if it can be reached without undue treatment burden. An ACE inhibitor or ARB is first-line due to reduction of CVD outcomes and delayed progression of diabetic nephropathy in patients with albuminuria. Most patients with diabetes will require 2 or more medications to achieve BP targets. Choice of additional agents will depend on the patient's comorbidities. Thiazide-like diuretics and dihydropyridine calcium channel blockers are generally used for additional BP control. The ADA and the JNC 8 guidelines recommend one or more antihypertensive medications to be taken at bedtime.

Cholesterol Control

Obtain a lipid profile at diagnosis, at initial medical evaluation, and/or at age 40 and periodically (every 1 – 2 years) thereafter. Lifestyle modification should focus on reducing saturated fat, *trans* fat and cholesterol intake, while increasing intake of omega-3 fatty acids, viscous fiber, plant stanols/sterols and increasing physical activity. Patients with a fasting TG level ≥ 500 mg/dL should be evaluated for secondary causes and consider medical therapy to reduce the risk of pancreatitis and MI. Statin therapy is indicated based on risk status for cardiovascular disease (see below). The most recent ADA guideline for statin therapy closely aligns with the ACC/AHA Blood Cholesterol guideline.

AGE	RISK FACTORS*	RECOMMENDED STATIN INTENSITY DOSE**	MONITORING LIPID PANEL
< 40 years	None	None	Annually or as needed to monitor adherence
	CVD risk factors	Moderate or high	
	Overt CVD	High	
40-75 years	None	Moderate	As needed to monitor adherence
	CVD risk factors	High	
	Overt CVD	High	
> 75 years	None	Moderate	As needed to monitor adherence
	CVD risk factors	Moderate or high	
	Overt CVD	High	

*CVD risk factors include LDL-C ≥ 100 mg/dL, high blood pressure, smoking, overweight/obesity. Overt CVD includes previous CV events or acute coronary syndromes.

**In addition to lifestyle modification

Nephropathy Screening and Treatment

Diabetic nephropathy is the leading cause of end-stage renal disease (ESRD). An <u>annual</u> urine test is used to measure urine albumin excretion. Either an <u>ACE inhibitor</u> or an <u>ARB</u> (but not both in combination) should be started in patients with a <u>urinary albumin excretion ≥ 30 mg/24 hours [or urine albumin-to-creatinine ratio (UACR) ≥ 30 mg/g]</u>. A level < 30 mg/24 hours is considered normal. Optimizing blood glucose (BG) and BP control helps to slow the progression of diabetic nephropathy and delay/prevent renal failure.

Retinopathy Screening and Treatment

Diabetic retinopathy is the leading cause of blindness in adults. An annual dilated, comprehensive eye exam is recommended. If the patient has one or more normal eye exams and their blood glucose is well controlled, screening can be done every 2 years. The comprehensive eye exam should be performed by an ophthalmologist or optometrist. More frequent exams may be required if retinopathy is progressing. Optimizing BG and BP control and cessation of smoking helps to avoid or reduce retinopathy.

Foot Care

All adults with diabetes should have a comprehensive foot exam, at least once per year. This should include visual examination of the skin of the feet for dryness/cracking and for signs of infection, ulcers, bunions, calluses and any deformities such as claw toes. The 10-gram monofilament test (and other tests) can be used to assess the loss of protective sensation (LOPS) and presence of peripheral neuropathy. Screening for peripheral arterial disease (PAD) includes a history for claudication, assessment of pedal pulses and obtaining an ankle-brachial index (ABI).

All patients with diabetes should inspect their feet daily (or have a family member do so if they are unable). Patients with insensate (without feeling) feet, foot deformities and ulcers should have their feet inspected at every physician visit. Patients who smoke or have LOPS, structural abnormalities or a prior lower-extremity complication should be referred to a foot care specialist. Patients should:

- Check feet every day for any changes (red spots, cuts, swelling, blisters and cracks). Be sure to look between the toes. Use a mirror, if needed, to inspect the bottom of the feet. Call or see a healthcare provider if there are cuts or breaks in the skin, ingrown nail(s) or signs of an infection (redness, swelling).

- Wash feet every day and dry them completely, especially between the toes. Rub a thin coat of skin moisturizer over to the tops and bottoms of dry feet, but not between toes due to ↑ risk of tinea pedis.

- Trim toenails straight across and file the edges with an emery board to the contour of the toe.

- Avoid walking barefoot. Wear socks and shoes at all times.

- Wear properly fitting, comfortable, supportive shoes (with orthotics if needed). Use caution when breaking in new shoes. Use extra-wide shoes to accommodate any deformities such as bunions or hammertoes.

- Inspect shoes for foreign objects before inserting feet.

- Keep the blood flowing to feet. Put feet up when sitting. Wiggle toes and move ankles up and down for 5 minutes, 2 – 3 times/day. Do not cross your legs for long periods of time.

- Protect feet from hot or cold. Wear shoes at the beach or on hot pavement. Keep feet away from items that may cause burning such as fireplaces, electric blankets, or heating pads. Use another part of the body to test water (bath or shower) temperature.

Vaccinations for Adults with Diabetes

Patients with diabetes should receive the following vaccines:

- Hepatitis B:
  - Unvaccinated adults 19 – 59 years old
  - Consider in unvaccinated adults ≥ 60 years old
- Influenza injection: annually for all patients ≥ 6 months of age
- Pneumococcal:
  - Age 2 – 64 years: PPSV23 (*Pneumovax 23*) x 1
  - Age ≥ 65 years: PCV13 (*Prevnar 13*) x 1 (must be spaced ≥ 12 months from PPSV23), then ≥ 12 months later give PPSV23 x 1 (must be spaced ≥ 5 years after PPSV23 if previously received)
- Tetanus:
  - Tetanus/diphtheria/pertussis (Tdap) x 1
  - Booster with tetanus/diphtheria (Td) every 10 years, or after 5 years if patient presents with a deep or dirty wound
- Other routine vaccines should be given according to recommendations based on age or risk (see Immunizations chapter)

Durable Medical Equipment

Durable Medical Equipment (DME) covered by CMS under the Part B medical benefit includes glucose monitors, test strips, lancet devices and lancets, and diabetic shoes or inserts. Medicare has an anti-switching rule that prohibits suppliers from encouraging patients to switch glucose meters or test strips. If the supplier does not have the test strip that the meter requires the patient can ask about alternative brands, but the supplier cannot initiate the discussion. CMS does not cover continuous glucose monitoring (CGM) devices. Part B covers some other diabetes services, including self-management training, annual eye exam, foot exam every 6 months, glaucoma tests and nutrition therapy.

Glycemic Targets For Non-Pregnant Adults with Diabetes

Two primary techniques for assessing glycemic control are self-monitoring of blood glucose (SMBG) via a glucometer and glycosylated hemoglobin, or A1C testing. Patients on multiple-dose insulin or insulin pumps should perform SMBG prior to meals and snacks, occasionally postprandially, at bedtime, prior to exercise, when they suspect low blood glucose, after treating low blood glucose until normoglycemic and prior to critical tasks such as driving. In patients on basal insulin or oral medications, there is not enough evidence regarding when to perform SMBG and how often testing is needed.

While SMBG measures the blood glucose at that given moment, the A1C measures the average blood glucose over the past 2 – 3 months. The A1C should be measured:

- Quarterly in patients who are not at goal or when therapy has recently changed

- Twice per year if patients are at goal and have stable glycemic control

Use of point-of-care (POC) testing for A1C allows for more timely treatment changes.

ADULT TREATMENT GOALS	PER ADA GUIDELINES	PER AACE GUIDELINES
A1C	< 7%*	< 6.5%
Preprandial capillary plasma glucose	80-130 mg/dL	< 110 mg/dL
Peak postprandial capillary plasma glucose (1-2 hours after the start of a meal)	< 180 mg/dL	< 140 mg/dL

* Must individualize target goals: per the ADA, a more stringent A1C goal (such as < 6.5%) may be appropriate for patients not experiencing hypoglycemia or other adverse effects of treatment, those with a short duration of diabetes, those with long life expectancy or with no significant CVD. A less stringent A1C goal (such as < 8%) may be appropriate for patients with a history of severe hypoglycemia, limited life expectancy, extensive comorbid conditions, advanced complications or longstanding diabetes where the goal is difficult to attain despite optimal efforts.

Estimated average glucose (eAG) refers to the mean (average) plasma glucose concentrations over 2 – 3 months, and may be easier for patients to understand over A1C. The eAG goal is < 154 mg/dL per the ADA guidelines.

Correlation of A1C with Average Glucose (estimated)

A1C (%)	MEAN PLASMA GLUCOSE (MG/DL)
6	126
7	154
8	183
9	212
10	240
11	269
12	298

ADA TREATMENT GUIDELINES FOR TYPE 2 DIABETES

Mono-therapy

**Lifestyle Modification
(Diabetes Education, Exercise, Weight Loss and Healthy Diet)
+
Start Metformin° (unless contraindicated)**

*° If BG ≥ 300 mg/dL or A1C ≥ 10%, consider mealtime + basal insulin or
if A1C ≥ 9%, consider starting at 2 drug stage*

*If not at target A1C goal after 3 months,
consider adding a 2nd agent**

Dual therapy

Choose 1 of the following agents*:
SU
TZD
DPP-4 inhibitor
SGLT2 inhibitor
GLP-1 agonist
Basal insulin

** Patient and drug factors
to consider include:*
- *Efficacy*
- *Cost*
- *Hypoglycemia risk*
- *Weight gain/loss*
- *Patient preference
  (oral vs. injectable)*
- *Other side effects*

*If not at target A1C goal after 3 months,
consider adding a 3rd agent**

Triple therapy

**Most 3-drug combinations are acceptable.
Combinations that are not recommended include:**

Metformin + DPP-4 inhibitor + GLP-1 agonist
Metformin + SGLT2 inhibitor + GLP-1 agonist

*SU = sulfonylurea, TZD = thiazolidinediones, DPP-4 = dipeptidyl peptidase 4, SGLT2 = sodium glucose
co-transporter 2, GLP-1 = glucagon-like peptide 1*

Factors to Consider When Selecting An Additional Agent to Reach Target A1C Goal

EFFICACY	COST	RISK OF HYPOGLYCEMIA	WEIGHT	FORMULATION
High: Metformin, SUs, TZDs, GLP-1 agonists, insulin, meglitinides	**Low cost:** Metformin, SUs, TZDs, insulin (depends on formulation)	**Low risk:** Metformin, TZDs, DPP-4 inhibitors, GLP-1 agonists, alpha-glucosidase inhibitors, bile acid sequestrant, SGLT2 inhibitors	**Weight loss:** GLP-1 agonists, SGLT2 inhibitors, pramlintide	**Injectable:** Insulin, GLP-1 agonists, pramlintide
Moderate: DPP-4 inhibitors, SGLT2 inhibitors, pramlintide	**Moderate cost:** Meglitinides, alpha-glucosidase inhibitors, insulin	**Moderate risk:** SUs, meglitinides	**Weight neutral:** Metformin, DPP-4 inhibitors, alpha-glucosidase inhibitors, bile acid sequestrant, dopamine agonist	**Oral:** all others
	High cost: all others	**High risk:** Insulin, pramlintide (if insulin dose is not reduced)	**Weight gain:** Insulin, SUs, meglitinides, TZDs	

Primary Mechanism of Action of the Drug Classes

↑/REPLACES INSULIN SECRETION	↓ HEPATIC GLUCOSE OUTPUT	↓ GLUCAGON WHICH ↓ GLUCOSE PRODUCTION (LIVER)	↓ GLUCOSE ABSORPTION	↑ GLUCOSE EXCRETION	↑ INSULIN SENSITIVITY
Insulin SUs Meglitinides	Metformin	GLP-1 agonists DPP-4 inhibitors Pramlintide	Alpha-glucosidase inhibitors	SGLT2 inhibitors	TZDs

BIGUANIDE

Metformin works primarily by ↓ hepatic glucose production, ↓ intestinal absorption of glucose and ↑ insulin sensitivity. Metformin is first-line therapy in type 2 diabetes and used in prediabetes.

DRUG	DOSING	SAFETY/SIDE EFFECTS/MONITORING
MetFORMIN (Glucophage, Glucophage XR, Fortamet, Glumetza, Riomet) IR: 500, 850, 1,000 mg ER: 500, 750, 1,000 mg *Riomet* liquid (500 mg/5 mL) + glipizide *(Metaglip)* + glyburide *(Glucovance)* + pioglitazone *(Actoplus Met, Actoplus Met XR)* + rosiglitazone *(Avandamet)* + **sitagliptin *(Janumet, Janumet XR)*** + saxagliptin *(Kombiglyze XR)* + linagliptin *(Jentadueto)* + repaglinide *(PrandiMet)* + alogliptin *(Kazano)* + canagliflozin *(Invokamet)* + dapagliflozin *(Xigduo XR)* + empagliflozin *(Synjardy)*	IR: 500 mg BID or 850 mg daily initially ER: 500-1,000 mg with dinner initially Titrate in 1-2 week intervals Max dose: 2,000-2,550 mg/day (varies by product) Give with a meal to ↓ GI upset ER: Swallow whole; do not crush, break or chew.	**BOXED WARNING** Lactic acidosis - ↑ risk in acute HF, dehydration, excessive alcohol intake, hepatic/renal impairment or sepsis **CONTRAINDICATIONS** SCr ≥ 1.5 mg/dL (males) or ≥ 1.4 mg/dL (females) or abnormal creatinine clearance, metabolic acidosis. **WARNINGS** Metformin should be stopped in any case of hypoxia, such as decompensated heart failure, respiratory failure, acute MI or sepsis. Avoid in patients with renal/hepatic impairment due to ↑ risk for lactic acidosis. Temporarily discontinue in patients receiving intravascular iodinated contrast media. **SIDE EFFECTS** N/V/D, flatulence, abdominal cramping, long term vitamin B12 deficiency. Weight neutral (few patients may lose weight), little-to-no risk of hypoglycemia when used as monotherapy. **MONITORING** BG, A1C, renal function, B12 **NOTES** ↓ A1C 1-2% Pregnancy Category B The ER formulations may appear in the stool. See counseling section.

Metformin Drug Interactions

- Alcohol can ↑ risk for lactic acidosis especially with renal impairment and advanced heart disease.

- Iodinated contrast dye ↑ risk of lactic acidosis – hold prior to procedure and <u>wait 48 hours</u> after and restart only once renal function has been confirmed as normal.

- Metformin can ↓ vitamin B12 absorption (and possibly folic acid), leading to megaloblastic anemia. Consider vitamin supplementation.

- The combination of metformin and topiramate can ↑ risk of metabolic acidosis.

Metformin Counseling

- Diarrhea, nausea, vomiting, abdominal discomfort and flatulence may occur and often go away with time. If taking the immediate release formulation, it should be given twice daily with meals. Taking with food will help decrease stomach upset. You may find relief with the extended release formulation which is taken with dinner.

- Some people have developed a very rare, life-threatening condition called lactic acidosis while taking metformin. Seek emergency medical help if you have any of these symptoms of lactic acidosis: weakness, somnolence, slow heart rate, shivers, muscle pain, shortness of breath, stomach pain, lightheadedness and/or fainting. Drinking alcohol while taking this medication increases the risk.

- If you need to have any type of X-ray or CT scan using contrast dye that is injected into your vein, you may need to temporarily stop taking metformin.

- Do not crush, chew, or break an extended-release tablet. Swallow the pill whole. It is specially made to release medicine slowly in the body. Breaking the pill would cause too much of the drug to be released at one time.

- If using *Glumetza, Fortamet* or *Glucophage XR*, you may see a shell of the medicine in the stool. This is normal, the medicine is in your body and the tablet is empty.

SULFONYLUREAS

Sulfonylureas (SUs) work by stimulating insulin secretion from the pancreatic beta cells. Do not use with meglitinides due to similar MOA. These are also known as insulin secretagogues.

DRUG	DOSING	SAFETY/SIDE EFFECTS/MONITORING
ChlorproPAMIDE *(Diabinese)* TOLAZamide TOLBUTamide	These older, first-generation agents should not be used as they cause a longer duration of hypoglycemia than the second-generation agents below	**CONTRAINDICATIONS** Type 1 diabetes mellitus, diabetic ketoacidosis, concurrent use with bosentan (glyburide) **WARNINGS** Sulfa allergy (not likely to cross-react – see cautionary statement in Drug Sensitivities, Allergies, Desensitization & Reporting chapter)
GlipiZIDE *(Glucotrol, Glucotrol XL, GlipiZIDE XL)* + metformin *(Metaglip)*	IR: 5-10 mg daily-BID, max 40 mg/day XL: 5-10 mg daily, max 20 mg daily	
Glimepiride *(Amaryl)* + pioglitazone *(Duetact)* + rosiglitazone *(Avandaryl)*	1-2 mg daily, max 8 mg daily	**SIDE EFFECTS** Moderate risk of hypoglycemia, weight gain, nausea **MONITORING** BG, A1C
GlyBURIDE *(DiaBeta)* Micronized glyburide *(Glynase)* + metformin *(Glucovance)*	*DiaBeta*: 2.5-5 mg daily, max 20 mg daily *Glynase*: 1.5-3 mg daily, max 12 mg daily Glyburide regular tablets cannot be used interchangeably with micronized tablet formulations, which have better absorption	**NOTES** ↓ A1C 1-2% Pregnancy Category C ↓ efficacy after long-term use (low durability) Glyburide has a weakly active metabolite that is renally cleared, and is not a preferred agent *Glucotrol XL* is in an OROS formulation (see Routes of Drug Delivery, Self-Administration Techniques and Counseling chapter) and can leave a ghost tablet (empty shell) in the stool

Sulfonylurea Drug Interactions

- Insulin and meglitinides should not be used concurrently with sulfonylureas due to ↑ risk of hypoglycemia.

- Use caution with drugs that can alter blood glucose, see chart at the beginning of the chapter.

- Sulfonylurea dose reduction may be required when a TZD, GLP-1 agonist, DPP-4 inhibitor or SGLT2 inhibitor is initiated.

- These agents are CYP 2C9 substrates, use caution with drugs that are 2C9 inducers or inhibitors.

- Alcohol may place patients with diabetes at ↑ risk for delayed hypoglycemia, especially if taking insulin or insulin secretagogues.

Sulfonylurea Counseling

- Do not crush, chew, or break an extended-release tablet. Swallow the pill whole. It is specially made to release medicine slowly in the body. Breaking the pill would cause too much of the drug to be released at one time.

- Keep away from children, even 1 tablet can be dangerous.

- Take medication with breakfast (except for glipizide IR which is taken 30 minutes before breakfast).

- This medicine can cause low blood sugar and this is more likely if you skip a meal, exercise too long, drink alcohol or are under stress. Symptoms of low blood sugar including shakiness, irritability, hunger, headache, confusion, somnolence, weakness, dizziness, sweating and fast heartbeat. Very low blood sugar can cause seizures (convulsions), fainting or coma. Always keep a source of sugar available in case you have symptoms of low blood sugar.

MEGLITINIDES

Meglitinides work by stimulating insulin secretion from the pancreatic beta cells. Do not use with sulfonylureas due to similar MOA. These are also known as rapid-acting insulin secretagogues as they have a quick onset (15 - 60 minutes) and a shorter duration of action compared to the SUs.

DRUG	DOSING	SAFETY/SIDE EFFECTS/MONITORING
Repaglinide (Prandin) + metformin (PrandiMet)	A1C < 8%: 0.5 mg before each meal (TID) A1C ≥ 8%: 1-2 mg before each meal (TID), max 16 mg daily Take 15-30 minutes before meals	**CONTRAINDICATIONS** Type 1 diabetes, diabetic ketoacidosis, concurrent gemfibrozil therapy (repaglinide) **WARNINGS** Caution in severe liver and/or renal impairment
Nateglinide (Starlix)	60-120 mg before each meal (TID) Take 1-30 minutes before meals	**SIDE EFFECTS** Hypoglycemia, mild weight gain, upper respiratory tract infections (URTIs) **MONITORING** BG, A1C **NOTES** ↓ A1C 0.5-1.5%; ↓ postprandial BG Pregnancy Category C Nateglinide is slightly less effective than repaglinide

Meglitinide Drug Interactions

- Insulin and sulfonylureas should not be used concurrently with meglitinides due to ↑ risk of hypoglycemia.

- Meglitinide dose reduction may be required when a TZD, GLP-1 agonist, DPP-4 inhibitor or SGLT2 inhibitor is initiated.

- Gemfibrozil can ↑ repaglinide concentrations and can ↓ blood glucose.

- Use caution with drugs that can alter blood glucose, see chart at the beginning of the chapter.

- Alcohol may place patients with diabetes at ↑ risk for delayed hypoglycemia, especially if taking insulin or insulin secretagogues.

Meglitinide Counseling

- Take this medication before meals (15 – 30 minutes for repaglinide; 1 – 30 minutes for nateglinide). If you forget to take a dose until after eating, skip that dose and take only your next regularly scheduled dose, before a meal.

- If you plan to skip a meal, skip the dose for that meal.

- This medicine can cause low blood sugar. Be able to recognize the symptoms of low blood sugar including shakiness, irritability, hunger, headache, confusion, somnolence, weakness, dizziness, sweating and fast heartbeat. Very low blood sugar can cause seizures (convulsions), fainting or coma. Always keep a source of sugar available in case you have symptoms of low blood sugar.

- Keep away from children, even ingesting 1 tablet can be dangerous.

THIAZOLIDINEDIONES

Thiazolidinediones (TZDs) are peroxisome proliferator-activated receptor gamma (PPARγ) agonists causing ↑ peripheral insulin sensitivity (↑ uptake and utilization of glucose by the peripheral tissues; insulin sensitizers).

DRUG	DOSING	SAFETY/SIDE EFFECTS/MONITORING
Pioglitazone *(Actos)* + metformin *(Actoplus Met, Actoplus Met XR)* + glimepiride *(Duetact)* + alogliptin *(Oseni)*	15-30 mg daily, max 45 mg daily	**BOXED WARNING** May cause or exacerbate heart failure **CONTRAINDICATIONS** NYHA Class III/IV heart failure **WARNINGS** Avoid pioglitazone in patients with active bladder cancer; bladder risk is increased with duration of use Risk for macular edema; monitor for visual symptoms
Rosiglitazone *(Avandia)* + metformin *(Avandamet)* + glimepiride *(Avandaryl)*	4-8 mg daily, max 8 mg daily	↑ fracture risk Hepatic failure Anovulatory, premenopausal women with insulin resistance may resume ovulation, which could lead to unintended pregnancy; use contraception in these premenopausal women. **SIDE EFFECTS** Peripheral edema, weight gain, URTIs, myalgia, pharyngitis, low risk of hypoglycemia when used as monotherapy ↑ HDL, ↓ TGs and ↓ total cholesterol (pioglitazone only) **MONITORING** LFTs, BG, A1C, and s/sx of heart failure **NOTES** ↓ A1C 0.5-1.4% Pregnancy Category C

Thiazolidinedione Drug Interactions

- These agents can reduce the amount of insulin or insulin secretagogue required. Monitor blood glucose closely after initiation of therapy.

- These agents are CYP 2C8 major substrates; use caution with drugs that are 2C8 inducers (e.g., rifampin) or inhibitors (e.g., gemfibrozil).

Thiazolidinedione Counseling

- May take several weeks for the drug to lower blood sugar, monitor your blood sugar carefully.

- Take once daily, with or without food.

- Contact your healthcare provider right away if you are passing dark-colored urine, have pale stools, feel more tired than usual or if your skin and/or whites of your eyes become yellow. These may be signs of liver damage.

- This drug can cause water retention and can cause your ankles to swell. You may develop trouble breathing. If this happens, inform your healthcare provider right away.

- Women may be more likely than men to have bone fractures in the upper arm, hand or foot while taking this medication. Talk with your healthcare provider if you are concerned about this possibility.

- Tell your healthcare provider if you have heart failure, heart disease or liver problems. For pioglitazone, tell your healthcare provider if you have or have had bladder cancer.

ALPHA-GLUCOSIDASE INHIBITORS

These agents reversibly inhibit membrane-bound intestinal alpha-glucosidases which hydrolyze oligosaccharides and disaccharides to glucose and other monosaccharides in the brush border of the small intestine. In patients with diabetes, this enzyme inhibition results in delayed glucose absorption and lowering of postprandial hyperglycemia. These agents inhibit the metabolism of sucrose to glucose and fructose therefore glucose should be used to treat hypoglycemia (not sucrose).

DRUG	DOSING	SAFETY/SIDE EFFECTS/MONITORING
Acarbose (Precose)	25 mg with the first bite of each main meal; ↑ by 25 mg every 1-2 months, max 300 mg/day in divided doses CrCl < 25 mL/min: use not recommended Start low and titrate slow to ↓ GI effects	**CONTRAINDICATIONS** Inflammatory bowel disease (IBD), colonic ulceration, partial or complete intestinal obstruction, cirrhosis (acarbose) **SIDE EFFECTS** GI effects (flatulence, diarrhea, abdominal pain), weight neutral, no hypoglycemia, ↑ LFTs (acarbose)
Miglitol (Glyset)		**MONITORING** Postprandial BG, A1C, LFTs every 3 months during 1st year (acarbose) **NOTES** ↓ A1C 0.5-0.8%; ↓ postprandial BG Pregnancy Category B Most effective with diets rich in complex carbohydrates

Alpha-Glucosidase Inhibitor Counseling

- Take with a full glass of water with the first bite of food (the medicine needs to be in the stomach with your food). If you plan to skip a meal, skip the dose for that meal.

- This medicine can cause flatulence (gas), diarrhea and abdominal pain, but this usually goes away with time. The dose may be increased as you get over these side effects.

- These agents, by themselves, do not cause low blood sugar. If you get low blood sugar after taking acarbose or miglitol, you <u>cannot treat it with sucrose (present in fruit juice) or table sugar or candy.</u> If you are using this agent with a drug that causes low blood sugar (such as insulin, a sulfonylurea or a meglitinide), you will need to purchase <u>glucose tablets or gel</u> to have on-hand to treat any hypoglycemic episode.

SODIUM GLUCOSE CO-TRANSPORTER-2 INHIBITORS

Sodium glucose co-transporter-2 (SGLT2), expressed in the <u>proximal renal tubules</u>, is responsible for the majority of the reabsorption of filtered glucose from the tubular lumen. By inhibiting SGLT2, these agents reduce reabsorption of filtered glucose and lower the renal threshold for glucose, which ↑ urinary glucose excretion.

DRUG	DOSING	SAFETY/SIDE EFFECTS/MONITORING
Canagliflozin *(Invokana)* + metformin *(Invokamet)*	100 mg daily prior to first meal of the day; can ↑ to 300 mg daily CrCl 45-60 mL/min: 100 mg max dose CrCl 30-44 mL/min: not recommended CrCl < 30 mL/min: contraindicated	**CONTRAINDICATIONS** Severe renal impairment (CrCl < 30 mL/min), ESRD, or on dialysis **WARNINGS** Genital mycotic infections, symptomatic hypotension due to intravascular volume depletion, ↑ LDL, urinary tract infections, <u>ketoacidosis</u>, renal insufficiency, ↑ risk of hyperkalemia (canagliflozin), ↑ risk of bladder cancer (dapagliflozin), ↑ risk of fractures and ↓ bone mineral density (canaglifozin)
Dapagliflozin *(Farxiga)* + metformin *(Xigduo XR)*	5 mg daily in the morning; can ↑ to 10 mg daily CrCl 30-59 mL/min: not recommended CrCl < 30 mL/min: contraindicated	**SIDE EFFECTS** <u>Genital mycotic infections, serious UTIs, hypoglycemia, weight loss,</u> ↑ urination, hypotension, ↑ thirst **MONITORING** Renal function, BG, A1C, LDL, BP
Empagliflozin *(Jardiance)* + linagliptin *(Glyxambi)* + metformin *(Synjardy)*	10 mg daily in the morning; can ↑ to 25 mg daily CrCl 30-44 mL/min: not recommended CrCl < 30 mL/min: contraindicated	**NOTES** ↓ A1C 0.7-1% Pregnancy Category C Monitoring glycemic control with urine glucose tests is not recommended in patients taking SGLT2 inhibitors as SGLT2 inhibitors increase urinary glucose excretion and will lead to positive urine glucose tests. Use alternative methods to monitor glycemic control.

SGLT2 Inhibitor Drug Interactions

- Consider a lower dose of insulin or insulin secretagogue when used in combo with SGLT2 inhibitors to reduce risk of hypoglycemia. Monitor blood glucose closely after initiation of therapy.

- UGT inducers (e.g., rifampin) can ↓ level of canagliflozin, consider ↑ dose to 300 mg.

- Monitor digoxin levels if taking digoxin and canagliflozin concurrently due to ↑ AUC of digoxin.

- Diuretics can worsen volume depletion seen with SGLT2 inhibitors, increasing risk of hypotension.

- Monitor potassium levels closely in patients taking canagliflozin with other medications, such as ACE inhibitors, ARBs and other medications that can cause hyperkalemia.

SGLT2 Inhibitor Patient Counseling

- Take this medication in the morning (canagliflozin is before the first meal).

- This medication can cause dehydration causing dizziness, lightheadedness, increased urination and thirst. Yeast infections of the penis or vagina can occur.

- If you miss a dose, take it as soon as you remember. If it is almost time for the next dose, skip the missed dose and take at the next regularly scheduled time.

DIPEPTIDYL PEPTIDASE 4 INHIBITORS

Dipeptidyl peptidase 4 (DPP-4) inhibitors prevent the enzyme DPP-4 from breaking down incretin hormones, glucagon-like peptide-1 (GLP-1) and glucose-dependent insulinotropic polypeptide (GIP). These hormones help to regulate blood glucose levels by ↑ insulin release from the pancreatic beta cells and ↓ glucagon secretion from pancreatic alpha cells. A reduction in glucagon results in ↓ hepatic glucose production. These medications enhance the effects of the body's own incretins.

DRUG	DOSING	SAFETY/SIDE EFFECTS/MONITORING
SitaGLIPtin *(Januvia)* + metformin *(Janumet, Janumet XR)*	100 mg daily CrCl 30-49 mL/min: 50 mg daily CrCl < 30 mL/min: 25 mg daily	**WARNINGS** Hypoglycemia when used with an insulin secretagogue or insulin, consider dose reduction of the insulin secretagogue or insulin
Saxagliptin *(Onglyza)* + metformin *(Kombiglyze XR)*	2.5-5 mg daily CrCl < 50 mL/min or with strong CYP 3A4 inhibitors: 2.5 mg daily *Kombiglyze XR* is given daily with evening meal	Acute pancreatitis has been reported - discontinue if suspected Severe and disabling arthralgia (joint pain) has been reported in patients taking DPP-4 inhibitors
Linagliptin *(Tradjenta)* + metformin *(Jentadueto)* + empagliflozin *(Glyxambi)*	5 mg daily No renal dose adjustment	Hepatotoxicity (alogliptin only) **SIDE EFFECTS** Nasopharyngitis, upper respiratory <u>tract</u> <u>infections, UTIs, weight neutral</u>, peripheral edema (especially if combined with a TZD), rash
Alogliptin *(Nesina)* + metformin *(Kazano)* + pioglitazone *(Oseni)*	25 mg daily CrCl 30-59 mL/min: 12.5 mg daily CrCl < 30 mL/min: 6.25 mg daily	**MONITORING** BG, A1C, renal function **NOTES** ↓ A1C 0.5-0.8%; ↓ postprandial BG Pregnancy Category B FDA is investigating the risk of heart failure and death with saxagliptin and alogliptin

DPP-4 Inhibitor Drug Interactions

- Consider a lower dose of insulin or insulin secretagogue when used in combo with DPP-4 inhibitors to reduce risk of hypoglycemia. Monitor blood glucose closely after initiation of therapy.

- Saxagliptin is a major 3A4 and P-glycoprotein substrate. Limit the dose to 2.5 mg with strong CYP 3A4 inhibitors including atazanavir, clarithromycin, indinavir, itraconazole, ketoconazole, nefazodone, nelfinavir, ritonavir, saquinavir and telithromycin.

- Linagliptin is a major 3A4 and P-glycoprotein substrate. Linagliptin levels are ↓ by strong inducers (carbamazepine, efavirenz, phenytoin, rifampin, St. John's wort).

DPP-4 Inhibitor Counseling

- Take this medication once daily in the morning, with or without food.

- If you have trouble breathing, or any kind of rash, see your healthcare provider at once.

- Contact your healthcare provider right away if you develop symptoms of pancreatitis, which include severe stomach pain that does not go away, with or without vomiting. The pain can radiate from the abdomen through to the back.

GLUCAGON-LIKE PEPTIDE-1 AGONISTS

Glucagon-like peptide-1 (GLP-1) agonists are analogs of GLP-1 which ↑ glucose-dependent insulin secretion, ↓ glucagon secretion, slow gastric emptying, improve satiety and may result in weight loss. These are incretin mimetics.

DRUG	DOSING	SAFETY/SIDE EFFECTS/MONITORING
Exenatide *(Byetta)* 5 mcg, 10 mcg multidose pen	Start: 5 mcg SC BID for 1 month, then 10 mcg SC BID Give within 60 minutes before the morning and evening meal	**BOXED WARNING** **For All Except *Byetta*** Thyroid C-cell carcinomas seen in rats – unknown if this could happen in humans. Contraindicated in patients with a personal or family history of medullary thyroid carcinoma (MTC) or patients with Multiple Endocrine Neoplasia syndrome type 2 (MEN 2)
Exenatide extended release *(Bydureon)* 2 mg single-dose vial/tray and pen	2 mg SC once weekly Give without regard to meals	**WARNINGS** Pancreatitis (fatal and usually in patients with risk factors: history of pancreatitis, gallstones, alcoholism or ↑ TGs) Renal impairment - use with caution in patients with renal impairment, not recommended in severe impairment (CrCl < 30 mL/min) *(Byetta, Bydureon)*
Liraglutide *(Victoza)* 18 mg/3 mL multidose pen *Saxenda* – for weight loss	Start: 0.6 mg SC daily x 1 week, then 1.2 mg SC daily x 1 week. Can ↑ to 1.8 mg SC daily, if needed. Give without regard to meals	Not recommended in severe GI disease Hypoglycemia can occur when used with insulin secretagogues or insulin. Consider lowering sulfonylurea or insulin dosage when starting.
Dulaglutide *(Trulicity)* 0.75 mg/0.5 mL, 1.5 mg/0.5 mL single-dose pen	Start: 0.75 mg SC once weekly Can ↑ to 1.5 mg SC once weekly Give without regard to meals	**SIDE EFFECTS** Nausea (primary side effect), vomiting, diarrhea, constipation, antibodies, hypoglycemia, weight loss **MONITORING** BG, A1C, renal function
Albiglutide *(Tanzeum)* 30 mg/0.5 mL, 50 mg/0.5 mL single-dose pen	Start: 30 mg SC once weekly Can ↑ to 50 mg SC once weekly Give without regard to meals Use within 8 hours of reconstitution	**NOTES** ↓ A1C 0.5-1.1%; ↓ postprandial BG Pregnancy Category C (*Saxenda* category X) Exenatide is a synthetic version of exendin, a substance found in Gila monster saliva. Can be used as mono- or combination therapy only in type 2 diabetes. Pen injection devices should never be used for more than one person (even when the needle is changed) because of the risk of infection. Abdomen is the preferred SC injection site, but can use thigh or upper arm. MedGuide required.

GLP-1 Agonist Drug Interactions

- Consider a lower dose of insulin or insulin secretagogue when used in combination with GLP-1 inhibitors to reduce risk of hypoglycemia. Monitor blood glucose closely after initiation of therapy.

- These drugs slow gastric emptying and can reduce the extent and rate of absorption of orally administered drugs. Caution is warranted.

Byetta

- Oral contraceptive levels may be ↓ in patients taking *Byetta*. Patients should be advised to take oral contraceptives at least 1 hour before *Byetta* injection.

- Can ↑ the INR in patients on warfarin, monitor INR.

GLP-1 Agonist Counseling

- Pancreatitis, or inflammation of the pancreas, can rarely happen with the use of this drug. Seek immediate medical care if you develop stomach pain that does not go away, with or without vomiting. The pain can radiate from the abdomen through to the back. Alcohol consumption should be limited.

- The most common side effects include nausea, vomiting, diarrhea and headache. These symptoms will decrease over time. Talk to your healthcare provider about any side effect that bothers you or does not go away.

- Administer (using a fresh needle) by SC injection in stomach area (preferred), upper leg (thigh) or the back of the upper arm. Rotate sites with each injection.

- Store in the refrigerator, most GLP-1 agonists are stable at room temperature for 28 to 30 days (*Trulicity* is stable at room temperature for up to 14 days). Never freeze.

- Keep pens and needles out of the reach of children.

- Do not store your pen with the needle attached. If the needle is left on, medication may leak from the pen and air bubbles may form in the cartridge.

For all except Byetta:

- Do not take this medication if you or any family members have had thyroid cancer, especially medullary thyroid cancer. While taking this medication, tell your healthcare provider if you get a lump or swelling in your neck, hoarseness, trouble swallowing, or shortness of breath. These may be symptoms of thyroid cancer.

Byetta

- Inject two times each day, within 60 minutes before the morning and evening meals (or before the 2 main meals of the day, at least 6 hours apart). Count to 5 before withdrawing the needle.

- Never inject after a meal due to the risk of hypoglycemia.

- After the first month, if the nausea is manageable, the dose will be increased from 5 mcg twice daily to a more concentrated pen that provides a 10 mcg dose twice daily.

- After 30 days of use, throw away the *Byetta* pen, even if it is not completely empty. Mark the date when you first used your pen and the date 30 days later.

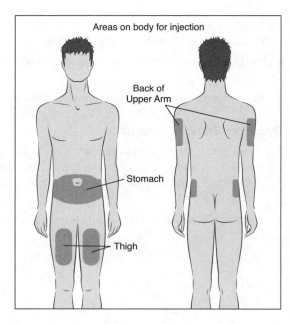

Areas on body for injection

Back of Upper Arm

Stomach

Thigh

Bydureon

- *Bydureon* must be injected immediately after it is mixed; otherwise clumps will form.

- *Bydureon* pen: Remove from refrigerator and let stand at room temperature for 15 minutes. Check the liquid inside the inspection window to make sure the liquid is clear. Do not use if the liquid is colored, has particles, or is not clear.

- Screw needle on pen. With pen upright, slowly turn the knob at the end of the pen. Stop when you hear the click and the green label disappears.
- Hold the end with orange label and tap the pen firmly against the palm of your hand. Tap about 80 times, rotating the pen every 10 taps.
- When mixed, *Bydureon* (both formulations) will be a uniformly cloudy solution.
- After injecting with the *Bydureon* pen, count to 10 before withdrawing the needle.

Victoza

- *Victoza* is taken once daily. After injecting *Victoza*, count to 6 before withdrawing the needle.
- If a dose is missed, skip the dose and resume at the next scheduled dose.

Trulicity

- Remove the base cap and place the clear base flat against the skin at the injection site. Unlock by turning the Lock Ring. Press and hold the green injection button; you will hear a loud click.
- Continue to hold the clear base against the skin until a second click is heard; this happens when the needle starts retracting in about 5 – 10 seconds. You will know the injection is complete when the gray plunger is visible.

Tanzeum

- Check that the pen has a "1" in the number window. Hold the pen upright and twist the clear cartridge in the direction of the arrow until you hear a click and see "2" in the number window.
- Slowly and gently rock the pen side to side (like a windshield wiper) 5 times to mix. Do not shake hard to avoid foaming.
- Place the pen into an empty cup pointing up for 15 minutes (30 mg pen) or 30 minutes (50 mg pen). After this time has elapsed, again slowly and gently rock the pen side to side for 5 times to mix the medicine.
- Look through the view in window to make sure the solution is clear and slightly yellow in color. Push the needle down onto the cartridge until it clicks in place.
- Twist the clear cartridge in the direction of the arrow until it clicks and "3" is present in the number window.
- After injecting, count to 5 before withdrawing the needle.

Bydureon, Trulicity, Tanzeum

- These medications are taken once weekly. If a dose is missed, take as soon as remembered, provided the next regularly scheduled dose is at least 3 days (72 hours) later. If the next dose is < 3 days later, the missed dose should be skipped entirely and resume therapy on the next regularly scheduled dosing day.
- Each prefilled pen comes with 1 dose of medication and the pen should be disposed of after a single use.

PRAMLINTIDE

Pramlintide is a synthetic analog of the human neuroendocrine hormone, amylin. Amylin is produced by pancreatic beta cells to assist in postprandial glucose control. Amylin helps slow gastric emptying, suppresses glucagon secretion following a meal and ↑ satiety. This is an amylinomimetic agent.

DRUG	DOSING	SAFETY/SIDE EFFECTS/MONITORING
Pramlintide *(Symlin Pen 60, SymlinPen 120)* Can use in both types 1 and 2 DM: ↓ mealtime insulins by 50% when starting. MedGuide required REMS drug	Type 1: Start at 15 mcg immediately prior to meals – titrate at 15 mcg increments every 3 days up to 60 mcg if no significant nausea. Type 2: Start at 60 mcg prior to meals – can ↑ to 120 mcg if no significant nausea. Administered SC in abdomen or thigh prior to each meal (≥ 250 kcal or ≥ 30 grams of carbohydrates, if consuming less than the above quantity, skip dose).	**BOXED WARNING** Co-administration with insulin ↑ risk of hypoglycemia (usually within 3 hours following administration) **CONTRAINDICATIONS** Gastroparesis, hypoglycemia unawareness **WARNINGS** Hypoglycemia - reduce mealtime insulin by 50% when starting and monitor BG; do not mix with insulin Never share pens between patients even if needle is changed **SIDE EFFECTS** N/V, anorexia, hypoglycemia, headache, weight loss **MONITORING** BG, A1C **NOTES** ↓ A1C 0.5-1% Pregnancy Category C

Pramlintide Drug Interactions

- Slows gastric emptying; administer concomitant oral medications at least 1 hour before and 2 hours after if rapid onset or threshold concentration is critical.

BILE ACID BINDING RESINS

The mechanism by which colesevelam improves glycemic control is unknown. The other indication is for the treatment of hyperlipidemia. It binds to bile acids and reduces bile acid absorption.

DRUG	DOSING	SAFETY/SIDE EFFECTS/MONITORING
Colesevelam *(Welchol)* Tablets: 625 mg Oral susp. packets: 3.75 gram and 1.875 gram Also approved for hyperlipidemia	3.75 grams/day: 6 tablets daily or 3 tablets BID or 3.75 gram packet daily or 1.875 gram packet BID Tablets need to be taken with a meal and liquid Powder packets need to be dissolved in 4-8 oz of liquid and taken with a meal	**CONTRAINDICATIONS** History of bowel obstruction, TG > 500 mg/dL, history of hypertriglyceridemia-induced pancreatitis **WARNINGS** Can ↑ TGs, particularly when used with insulin or insulin secretagogues Can ↓ absorption of fat-soluable vitamins or other drugs **SIDE EFFECTS** Constipation (> 10%), dyspepsia, nausea, bloating, weight neutral **MONITORING** BG, A1C, LDL, TG **NOTES** ↓ A1C 0.5% Pregnancy Category B

Colesevelam Drug Interactions

- The following medications should be taken 4 hours prior to colesevelam: cyclosporine, glimepiride, glipizide, glyburide, levothyroxine, olmesartan, phenytoin and oral contraceptives containing ethinyl estradiol + norethindrone.

- Colesevelam ↑ levels of metformin when coadministered with metformin extended release; monitor.

- Colesevelam can ↓ INR, monitor INR frequently during initiation and after dose change.

Colesevelam Counseling

- This drug may cause you to feel constipated. Talk to your pharmacist to see if you need a laxative (senna) or stool softener (docusate). Be sure to drink enough water while taking this medication.

- Take this medication at a different time than your multivitamin because *Welchol* ↓ absorption of vitamins A, D, E and K.

BROMOCRIPTINE

Bromocriptine is indicated as an adjunct to diet and exercise to improve glycemic control in adults with type 2 diabetes. It is a <u>dopamine agonist</u> and the mechanism by which it improves glycemic control is unknown; thought to reset hypothalamic circadian activities and ↓ insulin resistance and ↓ glucose production.

DRUG	DOSING	SAFETY/SIDE EFFECTS/MONITORING
Bromocriptine (*Cycloset*) *Parlodel* (higher dose) is indicated for hyperprolactinemia, acromegaly, Parkinson Disease	Start 0.8 mg daily within 2 hours of waking, take with food to ↓ nausea. Titrate in 0.8 mg increments weekly to usual dose of 1.6-4.8 mg daily. If a dose is missed, skip it and take at next scheduled dose.	**CONTRAINDICATIONS** Syncopal migraines, breastfeeding *(Cycloset)* **WARNINGS** Hypotension and orthostasis particularly upon initiation and dose titration Psychosis - use in severe psychosis disorders is not recommended Somnolence **SIDE EFFECTS** Nausea, dizziness due to orthostasis, fatigue, headache, vomiting, psychiatric effects, ↓ prolactin levels, <u>weight neutral</u> **MONITORING** BG, A1C **NOTES** ↓ A1C by 0.5% Pregnancy Category B

Bromocriptine Drug Interactions

- Bromocriptine is a major CYP 3A4 substrate; inducers or inhibitors of 3A4 can lower or raise the bromocriptine concentration.

- Do not use with other ergot medications. May ↑ ergot-related side effects or reduce ergot effectiveness for migraines if co-administered within 6 hours of ergot-related drug.

- Concomitant use with dopamine agonists and antagonists is not recommended.

- Bromocriptine is highly protein bound; may ↑ the unbound fraction of other concomitantly used highly protein-bound drugs.

- May decrease the vasodilatory effects of nitroglycerin.

INSULIN

Insulin is a hormone required by muscle and adipose tissue for glucose uptake. Insulin also has a role in regulating fat storage and inhibits the breakdown of fat for energy. Commercially available insulins differ in their onset and duration of action. Insulins are high-risk medications.

INSULIN TYPE	UNIQUE CONCERNS	SAFETY/SIDE EFFECTS/MONITORING
Rapid-acting insulins		
Aspart (*NovoLOG, NovoLOG FlexPen*) **Glulisine (*Apidra, Apidra SoloStar*)** **Lispro (*HumaLOG, HumaLOG KwikPen*)**	All come as 100 units/mL except *HumaLOG KwikPen* comes as 200 units/mL – use when patient requires > 20 units/day of rapid-acting insulin Give up to 15 minutes before or immediately after meals; lasts 3-5 hours Duration of action is shorter than short-acting insulin	**WARNINGS** Hypoglycemia Hypokalemia - shifts K from extracellular space to intracellular space Renal/hepatic impairment – use caution Pen devices should never be used for more than one person even when the needle is changed due to risk of infection **SIDE EFFECTS** Hypoglycemia, hypokalemia, weight gain, lipodystrophy, injection site reactions **MONITORING** BG, A1C, weight
Rapid-acting insulin (*Afrezza*) – Inhaled Available as 4, 8, and 12 unit cartridges	Cartridges should be at room temperature for 10 minutes before administration Inhale before meals; lasts 3-5 hours Replace the inhaler every 15 days to maintain accurate drug delivery Has a shorter duration of action of 2-3 hours (compared to 5 hours for the injectable rapid-acting insulins) and a shorter t½	Same as above plus: **BOXED WARNING** Contraindicated in patients with chronic lung disease such as asthma or COPD. Before initiating inhaled insulin, perform a detailed medical history, physical examination, and spirometry (FEV1) to identify potential lung disease in all patients. **WARNINGS** Not recommended in smokers or patients who have recently stopped smoking **MONITORING** Pulmonary function tests (FEV1) at baseline, after 6 months, then annually
Short-acting insulins (Regular insulin)		
Regular insulin (*HumuLIN R, NovoLIN R, ReliOn*) Available without a prescription	Give 30 minutes before meals; lasts 6-10 hours Can be used in IV solutions Available alone or combined with intermediate-acting insulins (N, NPH)	Same as above

Insulin Drugs Continued

INSULIN TYPE	UNIQUE CONCERNS	SAFETY/SIDE EFFECTS/MONITORING
Concentrated Regular insulin (*Humulin R U-500*) 20 mL vial	<u>5 times as concentrated;</u> recommended when patient requires <u>> 200 units/day</u> of short-acting insulin Give 30 minutes before meals; lasts up to 24 hours <u>Do not mix with other insulins</u> **Dosing formula for U-100 insulin syringe:** Divide prescribed dose (actual units of Humulin R U-500) by 5 = unit markings in a U-100 insulin syringe **Dosing formula for volumetric (tuberculin or allergy) syringe:** Divide prescribed dose (actual units of *Humulin R U-500*) by 500 = volume (mL) in a volumetric syringe	Same as above plus: The prescribed dose of *Humulin R U-500* should always be expressed in actual units of *Humulin R U-500* along with corresponding markings on the syringe the patient is using (i.e., a U-100 insulin syringe or tuberculin syringe). A conversion chart should always be used when administering *Humulin R U-500* doses with U-100 insulin syringes or tuberculin syringes.

Intermediate-acting (NPH) insulins

Intermediate insulin (*HumuLIN N, NovoLIN N, ReliOn*) <u>Available without a prescription</u>	Typically given once or twice daily. These are <u>cloudy</u> (all mixed preparations containing protamine are cloudy). Onset ~1-2 hours and duration up to 24 hours (varies by patient). Can mix with rapid and short-acting insulins; draw up regular insulin first (the <u>clear</u> before <u>cloudy</u>).	

Long-acting (Basal) insulins

Insulin Detemir (*Levemir, Levemir FlexTouch*) **Insulin Glargine (*Lantus, Lantus SoloStar, Toujeo SoloStar*)** **Insulin Degludec (*Tresiba FlexTouch*)**	Give once (at bedtime) or twice daily Do not mix with other insulins All are 100 units/mL except: *Toujeo* is 300 units/mL and lasts a few hours longer than *Lantus* *Tresiba* comes as a 100 units/mL and a 200 units/mL pen	Glargine has acidic pH and may sting upon injecting

Insulin Drugs Continued

INSULIN TYPE	UNIQUE CONCERNS	SAFETY/SIDE EFFECTS/MONITORING

Pre-Mixed insulins

70% insulin degludec, 30% insulin aspart (*Ryzodeg*) 70% insulin aspart protamine suspension, 30% insulin aspart solution (*NovoLog Mix 70/30*) 75% insulin lispro protamine suspension, 25% insulin lispro solution (*HumaLog Mix 75/25*) 50% insulin lispro protamine suspension, 50% insulin lispro solution (*HumaLog Mix 50/50*) 70% NPH, 30% Regular (*Humulin* 70/30, *Novolin* 70/30, *ReliOn*)	*Humulin* 70/30, *Novolin* 70/30 and *ReliOn* are <u>available without a prescription</u>	

Insulin Drug Interactions

■ Many drugs can ↑ the risk of hypoglycemia when used concurrently with insulin (sulfonylureas, TZDs, DPP-4 inhibitors, SGLT2 inhibitors, others – see chart at the beginning of the chapter). Use caution and/or reduce the dose of insulin.

INSULIN	ONSET	PEAK	DURATION

Rapid-acting Insulin

INSULIN	ONSET	PEAK	DURATION
Insulin aspart (*NovoLOG, NovoLOG FlexPen*) **Insulin glulisine (*Apidra, Apidra SoloStar*)** **Insulin lispro (*HumaLOG, HumaLOG KwikPen*)** **Insulin (*Afrezza*)**	10-30 minutes	0.5-2.5 hours	3-5 hours

Short-acting Insulin

INSULIN	ONSET	PEAK	DURATION
Regular (*HumuLIN R, NovoLIN R, ReliOn*)	30-60 minutes	1-3.5 hours	6-10 hours

Intermediate-acting Insulin

INSULIN	ONSET	PEAK	DURATION
NPH (*HumuLIN N, NovoLIN N, ReliOn*)	1-2 hours	4-8 hours	14-24 hours
Insulin NPH/insulin regular (*HumuLIN 70/30, NovoLIN 70/30, ReliOn*)	30 minutes	2-12 hours	14-24 hours

Long-acting Insulin

INSULIN	ONSET	PEAK	DURATION
Insulin detemir (*Levemir, Levemir FlexTouch*)	1-2 hours	–	14-24 hours
Insulin glargine (*Lantus, Lantus SoloStar, Toujeo SoloStar*)	1-2 hours (6 hours - *Toujeo*)	–	24 hours
Insulin degludec (*Tresiba FlexTouch*)	1-2 hours	–	42 hours

Insulin Vials, Pens and Pumps

Most insulin vials contain 10 mL, except *Humulin R* U-500 insulin which comes in a 20 mL vial. Most insulin pen cartridges contain 3 mL, except *Toujeo SoloStar* pens contain 1.5 mL. In general, pens are easier to use and cause fewer dosing errors if used correctly. They are easier to use for patients with hand tremor, arthritis or vision difficulty. Insulin pumps are devices that consist of a pump, insulin reservoir, tubing and cannula. The devices can be programmed to mimic the insulin secretion of the pancreas. Insulin pumps infuse a basal rate of insulin throughout the day, and boluses of rapid-acting or regular insulin are also administered through the pump. Pumps are most often used by type 1 patients but are increasingly used by type 2 patients. Candidates for insulin pumps must be receiving multiple daily doses of insulin, be experienced in carbohydrate counting, be highly motivated and understand how to operate the pump and willing to test their blood sugar frequently throughout the day. Insulin pumps are not appropriate for newly diagnosed patients.

INSULIN DOSING

Initiating Insulin Therapy for Patients with Type 1 Diabetes

Most people with type 1 diabetes should be treated with pumps or multiple daily injections of insulin (3-4 injections/day of basal and prandial insulin). Patients should be educated on matching the prandial insulin dose to carbohydrate intake, premeal blood glucose and anticipated activity. Insulin analogs are preferred to reduce hypoglycemia risk and mimic the physiologic pattern of the insulin made by our body. Insulin analogs include rapid-acting and basal insulins. Patients with type 1 diabetes should be screened for other autoimmune disorders (thyroid disorders, vitamin B12 deficiency, celiac disease). Insulin should be started at a total daily dose (TDD) of 0.6 units/kg/day based on actual body weight. If using rapid-acting (bolus) and long-acting (basal) insulins, known as a basal-bolus strategy (preferred as these are insulin analogs), 50% of the TDD is used as the long-acting insulin dose and 50% of the TDD is used as the rapid-acting (bolus) insulin. The rapid-acting insulin is divided evenly among the 3 meals (or can give more for a larger meal or less for a smaller meal). If using NPH and regular insulins (NPH/R strategy), take $^2/_3$ of the TDD as the intermediate-acting (NPH) dose and $^1/_3$ as the regular insulin dose. These are generally dosed twice daily, 30 minutes prior to breakfast and dinner (evening meal).

Insulin-to-Carbohydrate Ratio (ICR)

Because every person responds differently to insulin (some are more sensitive than others to insulin's effects), meal time insulin may be adjusted based on the number of carbohydrates an individual is eating with a meal. An insulin-to-carbohydrate ratio (ICR) is patient specific and helps determine the units of insulin required to cover the grams of carbohydrate included in a meal. It can be calculated using the Rule of 500 (for rapid-acting insulins) or Rule of 450 (for regular insulin):

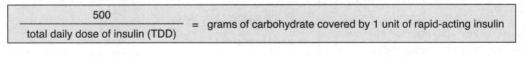

$$\frac{500}{\text{total daily dose of insulin (TDD)}} = \text{grams of carbohydrate covered by 1 unit of rapid-acting insulin}$$

$$\frac{450}{\text{total daily dose of insulin (TDD)}} = \text{grams of carbohydrates covered by 1 unit of regular insulin}$$

Correction Factor and Correction Dose

Patients with diabetes should know how to calculate their correction dose, which is the amount of insulin needed to return their blood glucose to normal range. For example, if a patient's glucose is higher than desired before a meal, a correction dose of insulin will account for this. The correction dose of insulin would be added to the dose they would normally take for that meal, in order to ensure that the patient will reach his or her glycemic target after the meal. The correction dose of insulin is determined based on an individual's correction factor, which provides the number of points that each unit of insulin will decrease the glucose.

Correction Factor – 1,800 Rule (Rapid-acting Insulin)

$$\frac{1,800}{\text{total daily dose of insulin (TDD)}} = \text{correction factor for 1 unit of rapid-acting insulin}$$

Correction Factor – 1,500 Rule (Regular Insulin)

$$\frac{1,500}{\text{total daily dose of insulin (TDD)}} = \text{correction factor for 1 unit of regular insulin}$$

Correction Dose

$$\frac{(\text{Blood glucose now}) - (\text{target blood glucose})}{\text{correction factor}} = \text{correction dose}$$

Initiation and Adjustment of Insulin for Patients with Type 2 Diabetes

In patients with type 2 diabetes, basal insulin is often initiated when a patient fails to reach glycemic goals on multiple oral agents. Basal insulin is started at 0.1 – 0.2 units/kg/day (using actual body weight) or 10 units/day. This dose is titrated by 10 – 15% or 2 – 4 units once or twice weekly to reach the fasting blood glucose goal. If the A1C remains above goal in spite of controlled fasting glucose levels, the addition of one to three injections of rapid-acting mealtime insulin and titrate to achieve post-prandial targets is recommended.

Insulin Conversions*

INSULIN TYPE	CONVERSION
NPH daily to glargine (*Lantus*, *Toujeo*)	1:1
NPH BID to glargine (*Lantus*, *Toujeo*)	Reduce daily dose by 20%
NPH to detemir (or vice versa)	1:1
Glargine (*Lantus*, *Toujeo*) to detemir (or vice versa)	1:1
Glargine (*Lantus*) to glargine (*Toujeo*)	1:1 (patient may require a higher dose of *Toujeo*)
Regular to rapid (or vice versa)	1:1
Premixed to premixed	1:1 if the percent mixture is same/similar (e.g. 70/30 to 75/25 or 50/50 to 50/50)

*adjustment if BG is under good control (otherwise, may increase dose if warranted)

Insulin Stability

For all insulins: Discard insulin if it is frozen, discolored, or contains particulates. If needle is attached for use, discard used needle after use. Do not store under direct sunlight or heat. All insulins should be refrigerated when not in-use. If refrigerated and unopened, the insulin is stable until the expiration date on label. Stability of the different insulins at room temperature, once in-use, is listed in the box.

Hospitalized Patients

Hospitalized patients on insulin should have the BG maintained between 140 – 180 mg/dL. More stringent goals may be appropriate for select patients. The sole use of sliding scale insulin (SSI) in the hospital setting is strongly discouraged. A more physiological insulin regimen including basal, prandial and correctional insulin is preferred over sliding scales, however many hospitals currently use sliding scales as the sole method to control BG. This is against AACE and ADA recommendations.

SLIDING SCALE EXAMPLE

Blood Glucose Reading (mg/dL)	Instruction
BS < 60	Hold insulin; contact MD
150-200	Give 2 units of insulin
201-250	Give 4 units of insulin
251-300	Give 6 units of insulin
301-350	Give 8 units of insulin
351-400	Give 10 units of insulin
401-450	Call MD

Insulin Administration

- Keep unused vials or cartridges in the refrigerator. Vials or pens in current use are good at room temperature for a limited time. Please see stability information to the right.

- Wash hands and lay out all supplies.

- Check insulin for any discoloration, crystals or particles.

- If insulin is a suspension, roll bottle gently between hands (do not shake). If it is a pen, invert 4 – 5 times.

- Clean injection site area of the skin and wipe the top of the insulin vial with an alcohol swab.

- Inject an equal volume of air into the vial that is going to be taken out so not to create negative pressure in the vial. Make sure to limit the bubbles in the syringe.

- The abdomen is the preferred injection site. For alternate sites, see the diagram on the following page. Inject at least two fingers away from the belly button.

- Alternate injection sites around the abdomen regularly to prevent inflammation and atrophy.

STABILITY AT ROOM TEMP WHEN IN-USE

Rapid-Acting Insulin

Apidra, Humalog, Novolog (vials and pens)	28 days

Regular Insulin

Humulin R (U-100, U-500 vial)	31 days
Novolin R (U-100 vial)	42 days
Afrezza	10 days (if unopened); 3 days once opened

NPH Insulin

Humulin N (vial)	31 days
Humulin N (pens)	14 days
Novolin N (vial)	42 days

Mixed Insulin

Humalog 50/50, 75/25, Novolog 70/30 (vials)	28 days
Humulin 70/30 (vial)	31 days
Humalog 50/50, 75/25 and Humulin 70/30 (pens)	10 days
Novolin 70/30 (vial)	42 days
Novolog 70/30 (pen)	14 days

Long-Acting Insulin and Other Injectables

Lantus (vials and pens)	28 days
Toujeo (pen)	28 days
Levemir (vials and pens)	42 days
Tresiba (pen)	56 days (8 weeks)
Byetta (pen)	30 days
Bydureon (vials and pen)	4 weeks
Victoza (pen)	30 days
Symlin (pen)	30 days
Trulicity (pen)	14 days
Tanzeum (pen)	4 weeks

- To inject subcutaneously, gently pinch a 2 inch portion of skin and fat between your thumb and first finger and insert the needle all the way at a 90 degree angle (or 45 degree if patient is thin). If using a syringe, inject insulin and remove needle slowly. If using an insulin pen, inject insulin and count 5 – 10 seconds before removing the needle.

- Properly dispose of needles or entire syringes in a sharps container. These containers can be taken to any proper disposal site (e.g., public health clinic or local needle exchange). Ask the local health department for guidelines or check out the website www.safeneedledisposal.org.

Choosing the correct syringe is important. Choose the smallest syringe that will hold the dose. The smaller the syringe barrel, the easier it is to read the scale markings in order to draw up an accurate dose. This is also helpful for patients with vision problems. If the patient's largest dose is close to the maximum syringe capacity, choose the next syringe size up.

Syringe Size/Volume

- If injecting < 30 units of insulin, use a 0.3 mL syringe (markings in 1 unit increments)

- If injecting 30-49 units of insulin, use a 0.5 mL syringe (markings in 1 unit increments)

- If injecting ≥ 50 units of insulin, use a 1 mL syringe (markings in 2 unit increments; holds up to 100 units)

Needle Length

- ½″ (12.7 mm), $^5/_{16}$″ (8 mm), $^3/_{16}$″ (5 mm), $^5/_{32}$″ (4 mm)

- Many users feel that shorter needles are more comfortable. Use ½″ needles for obese patients and if back leakage of insulin is a problem.

Insulin Injection Sites

Insulin absorption is fastest and most predictable when injected into the abdomen followed by the posterior upper arm, superior buttocks area and lateral thigh area. Because of these variations, the injections should be rotated within a specific region to limit fluctuations in blood glucose.

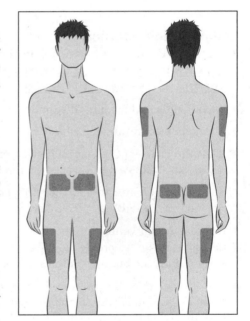

Hypoglycemia

Normal fasting blood glucose in a person without diabetes is 70 – 99 mg/dL. Hypoglycemia occurs when blood glucose falls below this level, or < 70 mg/dL. The lower the level, the more symptomatic the patient. At a blood glucose < 20 mg/dL, seizures, coma and death can occur.

Diabetes Drugs That Cause Hypoglycemia

Insulin is the #1 drug that can cause hypoglycemia. Drugs that make the body secrete more insulin such as sulfonylureas and meglitinides (insulin secretagogues) are also high-risk for causing hypoglycemia. Pramlintide is high risk since it is used concurrently (but injected separately) with insulin at mealtimes. Hypoglycemia is a serious risk, especially if mealtime insulin is not reduced appropriately. Look at the patient case for combination products which may contain a sulfonylurea such as *Glucovance* (metformin + glyburide).

The GLP-1 agonists, DPP-4 inhibitors, thiazolidinediones and SGLT2 inhibitors can ↑ the risk of hypoglycemia, primarily in patients using a hypoglycemic agent (insulin or an insulin secretagogue). Concurrent use may necessitate a dose reduction due to hypoglycemic risk. Other drugs may list hypoglycemia as possible, but it is generally due to the medical condition rather than the agent. These are isolated cases.

Hypoglycemic Symptoms

Hypoglycemic symptoms include dizziness, headache, anxiety, irritability, shakiness, diaphoresis (sweating), hunger, nausea, confusion, lack of coordination, tremors, palpitations or fast heart rate and blurred vision.

Beta-blockers can mask the symptoms of shakiness, palpitations and anxiety. That is why the beta-blocker propranolol is used for stage fright. However, sweating or hunger is not masked. This is most notable with the non-cardioselective agents such as carteolol, carvedilol, propranolol and others. The cardioselective beta-blockers (atenolol, metoprolol) are used more commonly.

Hypoglycemia Treatment

Glucose is the preferred treatment of hypoglycemia, but any form of carbohydrate that contains glucose will raise blood sugar (see box). Added fat will slow absorption and prolong the hypoglycemia.

1. Consume 15 – 20 grams of glucose or simple carbohydrates
2. Recheck blood glucose after 15 minutes.
3. If hypoglycemia continues, repeat treatment (step #1).
4. Once blood glucose returns to normal, the patient should eat a small meal or snack to prevent recurrence.

15 GRAMS OF SIMPLE CARBOHYDRATES USED TO TREAT HYPOGLYCEMIA

3-4 glucose tablets (follow package instructions)

1 serving of gel tube (follow package instructions)

2 tablespoons of raisins

4 ounces (1/2 cup) of juice or regular soda (not diet)

1 tablespoon sugar, honey, or corn syrup

8 ounces (1 cup) of milk

Glucagon

Glucagon should be prescribed for all patients at significant risk of severe hypoglycemia, and caregivers and family members should be instructed on its administration. Glucagon administration is not limited to health care professionals. Glucagon (GlucaGen) is only used if the patient is unconscious or not conscious enough to self-treat the hypoglycemia. If using glucagon, place the patient in a lateral recumbent position (on side) to protect airway and prevent choking when consciousness returns. A fast infusion rate will increase nausea. Glucagon 1 mg is given by SC, IM or IV injection. Of note, glucagon must be reconstituted prior to administration. Once conscious, administer a carbohydrate source. Glucose may be given intravenously (Dextrose 25%, Dextrose 50%). The patient does not need to be unconscious to receive glucose intravenously.

After treating the low blood glucose, check the BG in 15 minutes. If the BG < 70 mg/dL or if the patient is still symptomatic, repeat the treatment and check the BG again in 15 minutes. All episodes of hypoglycemia are dangerous and should be reported to the physician. Hypoglycemia unawareness or one or more episodes of severe hypoglycemia should trigger re-evaluation of the treatment regimen.

Self-Monitoring Blood Glucose (SMBG)

This is important to prevent hypo- and hyperglycemia and complications. Patients on multiple-dose insulin (MDI) or insulin pump therapy should do SMBG at least prior to meals and snacks, occasionally post-prandial, at bedtime, prior to exercise, when they suspect low blood sugar, after treating low blood sugar until they are normoglycemic, and prior to critical tasks such as driving. For patients using less frequent insulin injections, non-insulin therapies or medical nutrition therapy, SMBG may be useful as a guide to the success of therapy.

Preparing to Test

- Some machines require calibration before first use, if a new package of strips is opened, machine is left in extreme conditions, machine is dropped or if the level does not match how the patient is feeling.

- Read the test strip packaging to make sure the strips are compatible with the glucose meter.

- Do not use test strips from a damaged or expired bottle.

- Enter in the correct calibration code, if required.

- Thoroughly wash hands vigorously with warm water and mild soap to clean the site and increase circulation at the fingertip.

- Dry hands thoroughly since water can affect the blood sample and create an error or false reading.

- Allow arm to hang down at the side of the body for 30 seconds so blood can pool into the fingertips.

Testing Blood Glucose

- In order to minimize pain, lance the finger on the side where there are fewer nerves, instead of on the finger pads. Keep hand below the level of the heart.

- Make sure there is a large enough drop of blood as directed by the meter. Allow the blood to flow freely and do not squeeze the finger.

- Use a new test strip for each test.

- Insert test strip completely into the glucose meter prior to applying blood sample.

Maintaining Blood Glucose Meter

- Clean meter regularly.

- Test meter regularly with control solution.

- Store meter and supplies properly, away from heat and humidity.

- Keep extra batteries charged and ready.

- Close the lid of the strips container after every use, as air and moisture can destroy the strips and affect results.

Notes on Alternative Site Testing

- Select meters are approved for testing on other areas, most commonly the forearm, palm or thigh. Always verify with individual meter which sites are appropriate. A different cap on the lancing device is often required for alternate site testing.

- Alternative sites, such as the forearm or thigh, can give a test result that is 20 to 30 minutes old. Alternative testing sites are not recommended in cases where the blood sugar is changing rapidly (after a meal or after exercise) or when hypoglycemia is suspected.

Diabetic Ketoacidosis (DKA) & Hyperglycemia Hyperosmolar State (HHS)

DKA

Diabetic ketoacidosis (DKA) is a hyperglycemic crisis most commonly presenting in <u>type 1</u> and rarely in type 2 diabetes. DKA occurs due to <u>insulin non-compliance</u> (ran out, lost/homeless, refused to take), sub-therapeutic insulin dose (due to a stressor, such as infection, MI or trauma), or as the initial presentation in a type 1 patient. <u>Ketones are present</u> because triglycerides and amino acids are used for energy, which produces free fatty acids (FFAs). Glucagon converts the FFAs into ketones. Normally, insulin prevents this conversion but, in DKA, insulin is absent.

- DKA Symptoms: BG <u>> 250 mg/dL, ketones</u> (urine and serum, or picked up as "fruity" breath), with an <u>anion gap</u> metabolic acidosis (<u>arterial pH < 7.35, anion gap > 12</u>).

- DKA Treatment:

  - <u>Fluids first</u>. <u>Normal saline</u> (NS) infused at a rate of $15 - 20$ mL/kg/hr (1 liter) during the first hour. Continue fluids (type of fluid will be based on hydration, Na and BG status). When blood glucose reaches 250 mg/dL, D5W with 1/2 NS is used (along with insulin).

  - Potassium replacement when needed. Monitor K frequently.

  - Give <u>regular insulin</u> 0.15 units/kg bolus, followed by an IV <u>infusion</u> at a <u>rate of 0.1 units/kg/hr</u>.

  - Sodium bicarbonate may be used when pH < 7.0.

HHS

Hyperglycemia hyperosmolar state (HHS) is a hyperglycemic crisis that most often occurs in type 2 diabetes and is due to some type of severe stress. <u>Serum ketones</u> would be negligible or <u>not present</u> because the type 2 diabetes patient has enough insulin to suppress ketogenesis. The blood glucose is usually much higher at presentation because acidosis is not present and the patient can endure the symptoms longer.

- <u>HHS Symptoms</u>: BG > 600 mg/dL, high serum osmolality > 320 mOsm/L, extreme dehydration, altered consciousness (confusion, dizziness), pH > 7.3, bicarbonate > 15 mEq/L, risk of seizures.

- <u>HHS Treatment</u>: NS and insulin; potassium (as needed).

PRACTICE CASE

PATIENT PROFILE

Patient Name	Emma Hoffman				
Address	577 Ridge Rd				
Age	21	Sex F	Race White	Height 5'9"	Weight 65 kg
Allergies	NKDA				

DIAGNOSES

Type 1 Diabetes
General Anxiety Disorder

Date	Prescriber	Drug & Strength	Sig
4/26	Callihan	Apidra SoloStar	3 units AC meals
4/26	Callihan	Lantus SoloStar	15 units QHS
4/26	Callihan	Ativan	1 mg BID
5/8	Wong	Regular Insulin 100 units/100 mL NS	6.5 units/hr x 6 hrs
5/8	Wong	0.9% NaCl	15 mL/kg/hr x 1 hr, followed by
5/8	Wong	0.45% NaCl D5W1/2NS	500 mL/hr x 2 hrs, followed by 200 mL/hr x 3 hrs

LAB/DIAGNOSTIC TESTS

Test	Normal Value	Results Date 5/8 @ 1300	Results Date 5/8 @ 1400	Results Date 5/8 @ 1500
NA	135-146 mEq/L	139	140	141
K	3.5-5.3 mEq/L	4.5	3.9	3.3
CL	98-110 mEq/L	107	106	107
HCO3-	22-28 mEq/L	17	17	18
BUN	7-25 mg/dL	45	39	32
Creatinine	0.6-1.2 mg/dL	0.8	0.7	0.9
Glucose	65-99 mg/dL	593	361	301
Calcium	8.6-10.2 mg/dL			
WBC	4-11 cells/mm^3			
Urine ketones		Positive		

Questions

1. Which of the following would be the most likely diagnosis for Emma on 5/8?

   a. Sepsis
   b. Diabetic ketoacidosis
   c. Hyperglycemia hyperosmolar state
   d. Serotonin syndrome
   e. Insulin overdose

2. What is Emma's anion gap on 5/8 at 1300?

   a. 16
   b. 15
   c. 13
   d. 9
   e. 8

3. On 5/8, how much total fluid volume from all sources did Emma receive?

   a. 2,614 mL
   b. 2,575 mL
   c. 1,615 mL
   d. 1,600 mL
   e. 1,000 mL

4. According to Emma's labs on 5/8 at 1500, which of the following should be administered?

   a. Magnesium sulfate
   b. Calcium gluconate
   c. 3% hypertonic saline
   d. 5% albumin
   e. Potassium chloride

5. Per the ADA guidelines, what is Emma's goal blood glucose while she remains in the hospital?

   a. < 180 mg/dL
   b. 140 - 180 mg/dL
   c. 110 - 140 mg/dL
   d. 100 - 120 mg/dL
   e. 80 - 130 mg/dL

6. Emma is being transitioned to her outpatient regimen but the hospital does not have *Apidra* or *Lantus* on formulary. Which therapeutic interchange would be most appropriate?

   a. *Tresiba, Toujeo*
   b. *Humulin R U-500, Toujeo*
   c. *Humulin N, Levemir*
   d. *HumaLOG, Levemir*
   e. *HumaLOG 70/30, NovoLOG*

Questions 7-10 do not apply to the case.

7. A patient currently uses 30 units of *Lantus* daily and 10 units of *Humalog* with breakfast, lunch, and dinner. She is going to be started on pramlinitide and needs to be counseled on how to adjust her dose of insulin. Select the correct adjustments.

   a. Reduce *Lantus* to 15 units and *Humalog* to 5 units with meals
   b. Reduce *Lantus* to 10 units and *Humalog* to 5 units with meals
   c. Reduce *Lantus* to 15 units and keep *Humalog* at 10 units with meals
   d. Do not adjust *Lantus* and reduce *Humalog* to 5 units with meals
   e. Do not adjust *Lantus* or *Humalog*

8. A patient is taking *Novolog Mix* 70/30, 10 units twice a day. How many units of insulin aspart does the patient inject in the morning?

   a. 20 units
   b. 10 units
   c. 7 units
   d. 6 units
   e. 3 units

9. Which of the following insulins has the shortest duration?

   a. Glulisine
   b. Detemir
   c. Regular
   d. Glargine
   e. NPH

10. A patient is prescribed *Glucovance*. What are the individual components?

    a. Metformin/glyburide
    b. Metformin/pioglitazone
    c. Metformin/sitagliptin
    d. Metformin/repaglinide
    e. Metformin/glipizide

Answers

1-b, 2-b, 3-a, 4-e, 5-b, 6-d, 7-d, 8-e, 9-a, 10-a.

THYROID DISORDERS

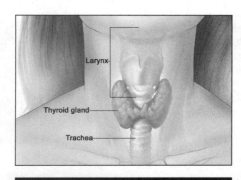

Larynx

Thyroid gland

Trachea

GUIDELINES/REFERENCES

Guidelines for the Treatment of Hypothyroidism: Prepared by the American Thyroid Association Task Force on Thyroid Hormone Replacement. http://online.liebertpub.com/doi/full/10.1089/thy.2014.0028 (accessed 2015 Oct 27).

Garber JR, Cobin RH, Gharib H, et al. Clinical Practice Guidelines for Hypothyroidism in Adults: Cosponsored by the American Association of Clinical Endocrinologists and the American Thyroid Association. *Endocr Pract.* 2012; 18(6):988-1028.

Addtl. guidelines included with the video files (RxPrep Online).

BACKGROUND

The thyroid gland is a butterfly-shaped organ composed of two symmetrical lobes, one on each side of the windpipe, connected by the isthmus. The thyroid gland synthesizes and releases thyroid hormones, and is the only organ containing cells that have the ability to absorb iodine. Thyroid hormones affect metabolism, brain development, respiration, cardiac and nervous system functions, body temperature, muscle strength, skin dryness, menstrual cycles, body weight, and cholesterol levels. Hyperthyroidism (overactive thyroid) and hypothyroidism (underactive thyroid) are the most common problems of the thyroid gland. Hypothyroidism occurs more commonly in women, and its incidence increases with age.

PATHOPHYSIOLOGY

The thyroid gland produces two thyroid hormones, triiodothyronine (T_3) and thyroxine (T_4). Iodine and tyrosine are used to form both T_3 and T_4. Less than 20% of T_3 is produced by the thyroid gland; T_3 is primarily formed from the breakdown of T_4 by peripheral tissues. T_3 is more potent than T_4 but has a shorter half-life. Thyroid hormone production is regulated by thyroid-stimulating hormone (TSH or thyrotropin), which is secreted by the pituitary gland in the brain. Elevations in T_4 levels will inhibit the secretion of TSH, and create a negative feedback loop. Since T_3 and T_4 are transported in the blood and bound by proteins, it is important to measure the free T_4 (FT_4) levels as this is the active form. In hypothyroidism, there is a deficiency in T_4, and consequently, an elevation in TSH. In hyperthyroidism, there is over-secretion of T_4, and consequently, a decrease in TSH.

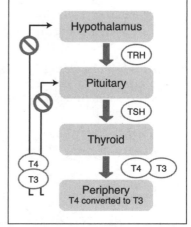

TRH = thyrotropin-releasing hormone

HYPOTHYROIDISM

In hypothyroidism, the decrease in thyroid hormone causes the body to slow down and the classic symptoms of low metabolism appear (fatigue and weight gain). Other signs and symptoms are included in the box to the right. The most common cause of hypothyroidism is Hashimoto's disease, an autoimmune condition in which a patient's antibodies attack their own thyroid gland. Drugs and other conditions that can cause hypothyroidism are included in the box. Complications of hypothyroidism include depression, infertility and cardiovascular disease. When hypothyroidism decompensates or goes untreated for a long period, myxedema coma can result. Myxedema coma is a life-threatening emergency characterized by poor circulation, hypothermia, and hypometabolism. Due to unpredictable absorption of oral thyroid hormone from the gastrointestinal tract, intravenous thyroid hormone products should be administered.

S/SX OF HYPOTHYROIDISM	
Cold intolerance/sensitivity	Coarseness or loss of hair
Dry skin	Menorrhagia (heavier than normal menstrual periods)
Fatigue	
Muscle cramps	Memory and mental impairment
Voice changes	Myalgias
Constipation	Weakness
Weight gain	Depression
Goiter (possible, can be due to low iodine intake)	Bradycardia

Diagnosis

Low free thyroxine (↓ FT$_4$): normal range 0.9 – 2.3 ng/dL

High thyroid stimulating hormone (↑ TSH): normal range 0.3 – 3 mIU/L

Screening for hypothyroidism should be considered in patients > 60 years old.

SELECT DRUGS AND CONDITIONS THAT CAN CAUSE HYPOTHYROIDISM

Hashimoto's disease – most common cause

Pituitary failure

Surgical removal of part or all of the thyroid gland

Congenital hypothyroidism

Thyroid gland ablation with radioactive iodine

External irradiation

Iodine deficiency

Drugs (e.g., amiodarone, carbamazepine, eslicarbazepine, interferons, lithium, oxcarbazepine, phenytoin, tyrosine kinase inhibitors – most notably sunitinib)

Monitoring Parameters

TSH is the primary screening test for thyroid function and it is the most reliable therapeutic endpoint for treatment. Check TSH levels (rarely serum FT$_4$) and clinical symptoms every 4 – 6 weeks until levels are normal, then 4 – 6 months later, then yearly. It is important to monitor as the person ages; they may need a dose reduction. Too high of a dose of thyroid hormone replacement in elderly patients leads to atrial fibrillation and fractures. Serum FT$_4$ is monitored, in addition to TSH, in central hypothyroidism (rare) because the defect is pituitary production of TSH. FT$_4$ is also monitored when treating hypothyroidism in pregnancy.

Pregnancy and Hypothyroidism

Levothyroxine is FDA Pregnancy Category A. Pregnant women with thyroid hormone deficiency or TSH elevation during pregnancy may have children at risk of impairment in their intellectual function and motor skills, unless properly treated. Pregnant women being treated with thyroid hormone replacement will require a 30 – 50% increase in the dose throughout the course of their pregnancy. The mother will need an elevated dose for several months after giving birth. In 2011, the guidelines called for more aggressive control of hypothyroidism in pregnancy. Preferably, treatment should start prior to pregnancy.

Drug Treatment

The goals of therapy are to resolve signs and symptoms of hypothyroidism, normalize serum TSH, and avoid overtreatment (causing hyperthyroidism). Patients should be counseled on clinical symptoms of both hypo and hyperthyroidism as the dose will be titrated to the individual's needs. Levothyroxine (T_4) is the drug of choice and current recommendations encourage the use of a consistent preparation for an individual patient to minimize variability from refill to refill. There are patients who state they just do not "feel right" on T_4 alone, and may supplement with other formulations, such as liothyronine (T_3, *Cytomel* and *Triostat*) or desiccated thyroid (T_3 and T_4, *Armour Thyroid*). Desiccated thyroid is not favored since the preparations can contain variable amounts, although newer formulations have become standardized. This is called "natural thyroid" and it is dosed in grains. Some patients choose to use these alternatives alone.

Levothyroxine should be taken with water consistently 60 minutes before breakfast or at bedtime (at least 3 hours after the last meal) for optimal absorption. It should be stored properly and patients should be counseled regarding drug interactions.

Iodine supplementation, including kelp or other iodine-containing functional foods, is not required in the U.S. because most of the salt has iodine added (iodized salt). This has eliminated almost all cases of iodine deficiency goiter. Individuals who are restricting salt intake can consume foods high in iodine (dairy, seafood, meat, some breads), and can take a multivitamin containing iodine.

Hypothyroidism Treatment

DRUG	DOSING	SAFETY/SIDE EFFECTS/MONITORING
Levothyroxine (T_4) *(Synthroid, Levothroid, Levoxyl, Tirosint, Unithroid)* Capsule, tablet, injection Available strengths: 13, 25, 50, 75, 88, 100, 112, 125, 137, 150, 175, 200, 300 mcg Check AB-rating of a generic to a brand. Not all generic levothyroxine formulations are AB-rated to various brands.	Full replacement dose = 1.6 mcg/kg/day (IBW) Start with full replacement dose in otherwise healthy, young and middle age patients with markedly ↑ TSH. Start with partial replacement dose (25-50 mcg daily) in the elderly, milder hypothyroidism, and those with comorbidities. If known CAD, start with 12.5-25 mcg daily. **Usual Dose** 0.5 mcg/kg/day for elderly; see above 1.6 mcg/kg/day in younger patients (< 50 years of age)	**BOXED WARNING** Thyroid supplements are ineffective and potentially toxic when used for the treatment of obesity or for weight reduction, especially in euthyroid patients. High doses can cause serious or even life-threatening toxic effects particularly when used with some anorectic drugs (e.g., sympathomimetic amines). **CONTRAINDICATIONS** Acute MI, thyrotoxicosis, uncorrected adrenal insufficiency **WARNINGS** ↓ dose in cardiovascular disease (chronic hypothyroidism predisposes to coronary artery disease), ↓ bone mineral density which can lead to osteoporosis **SIDE EFFECTS** If patient is euthyroid, no side effects should exist. If dose is too high, patient will experience hyperthyroid symptoms such as ↑ HR, palpitations, sweating, weight loss, arrhythmias, irritability, others. **MONITORING** Check TSH levels (rarely FT_4) and clinical symptoms every 4-6 weeks until levels are normal, then 4-6 months later, then yearly. Monitor as the patient ages; dose reduction may be necessary. Overdosing levothyroxine in elderly patents leads to atrial fibrillation and fracture. Assessment of serum FT_4, in addition to TSH, can be used selectively in some patients. **SEE NOTES ON NEXT PAGE**

DRUG	DOSING	SAFETY/SIDE EFFECTS/MONITORING
Thyroid, Desiccated USP (T_3 and T_4) *(Armour Thyroid, Nature-Throid, Westhroid, NP Thyroid, WP Thyroid)* Tablet	Start 15-30 mg daily (15 mg in cardiac disease); titrate in 15 mg increments. Usual dose is 60-120 mg daily	**SEE WARNINGS, SIDE EFFECTS AND MONITORING ABOVE** **NOTES** Pregnancy Category A Highly protein bound (> 99%) Levothyroxine is the drug of choice due to chemical stability, once-daily dosing, low cost, lack of antigenicity and more uniform potency
Liothyronine (T_3) *(Cytomel, Triostat)* Tablet, injection	Start 25 mcg daily; titrate in 12.5-25 mcg increments. Usual dose is 25-75 mcg daily	**Levothyroxine IV** Use immediately upon reconstitution. IV to PO ratio is 0.75:1 **Thyroid USP** Natural porcine-derived thyroid that contains both T_3 and T_4; less predictable potency and stability. Not preferred, but some feel better using it
Liotrix (T_3 and T_4 in 1:4 ratio) *(Thyrolar)* Tablet	Start 25 mcg levothyroxine/6.25 mcg liothyronine daily. Usual dose is 50-100 mcg levothyroxine/12.5-25 mcg liothyronine	**Liothyronine** Shorter t½ causes fluctuations in T_3 levels

Levothyroxine Drug Interactions

Drugs that ↓ Thyroid Hormone Levels

- These drugs can ↓ absorption:

  - Aluminum (antacids), calcium, cholestyramine, iron, magnesium, multivitamins (containing ADEK, folate, iron), orlistat *(Xenical, Alli)*, sevelamer, sodium polystyrene *(Kayexalate)*, sucralfate: separate doses by 4 hours from thyroid replacement therapy

  - Lanthanum: separate doses by 2 hours from thyroid replacement therapy

  - Patiromer *(Veltassa)*: separate doses by 6 hours from thyroid replacement therapy

- Estrogen, SSRIs and hepatic inducers ↓ thyroid hormone levels

- Beta-blockers, amiodarone, systemic steroids, and propylthiouracil (PTU) can ↓ the effectiveness of levothyroxine by ↓ the conversion of T_4 to T_3

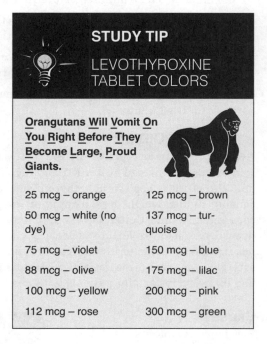

STUDY TIP

LEVOTHYROXINE TABLET COLORS

Orangutans Will Vomit On You Right Before They Become Large, Proud Giants.

25 mcg – orange	125 mcg – brown
50 mcg – white (no dye)	137 mcg – turquoise
75 mcg – violet	150 mcg – blue
88 mcg – olive	175 mcg – lilac
100 mcg – yellow	200 mcg – pink
112 mcg – rose	300 mcg – green

- Thyroid hormone is highly-protein bound (> 99%). Drugs that can cause protein-binding site displacement include salicylates (> 2 g/day), heparin, phenytoin, NSAIDs, others

Thyroid hormone can change concentrations/effects of these drugs:

- ↑ effect of anticoagulants (e.g., ↑ PT/INR with warfarin)

- ↓ digoxin levels

- ↓ theophylline levels

- ↓ effect of antidiabetic agents

Levothyroxine Counseling

- Levothyroxine is a replacement for a hormone that is normally produced by your body to regulate your energy and metabolism. Levothyroxine is given when the thyroid does not produce enough of this hormone on its own.

- There are many medicines that can alter levothyroxine effects; tell the pharmacist about all medications you are taking. This includes over-the-counter vitamins, supplements and heartburn medications.

- Different brands of levothyroxine may not work the same. If you get a prescription refill and your new pills look different, ask the pharmacist.

- This medicine is safe to use while you are pregnant. It is also safe to use while you are breast-feeding a baby. It does pass into breast milk, but it is not harmful to a nursing infant.

- Tell your healthcare provider if you become pregnant during treatment; it is likely that your dose will need to be increased during pregnancy or if you plan to breast-feed.

- Take this medication with water 60 minutes before breakfast or at bedtime at least 3 hours after your last meal.

- If you are taking other medicines on an empty stomach first thing in the morning, discuss the best dosing with your pharmacist. Medications for your bones (osteoporosis) like *Actonel* or *Fosamax* should be taken 30 minutes before your thyroid medicine.

- Some patients will notice a slight reduction in symptoms within 1 to 2 weeks, but the full effect from therapy is often delayed for a month or two before people start to feel normal.

- Even if you feel well, you still need to take this medicine every day for the rest of your life to replace the thyroid hormone your body cannot produce.

- To be sure the dose being used is optimal for you, your blood will need to be tested on a regular basis (at least annually).

HYPERTHYROIDISM

Hyperthyroidism (overactive thyroid or thyrotoxicosis) occurs when there is over-production of thyroid hormones. Instead of low FT_4 and high TSH, FT_4 is high and TSH is low and symptoms are nearly opposite of those seen in hypothyroidism. Hyperthyroidism can significantly accelerate metabolism, causing sudden weight loss, a rapid or irregular heartbeat, sweating, nervousness, irritability, diarrhea and insomnia. Goiter and exophthalmos (protrusion of the eyeballs) can occur. Without treatment, hyperthyroidism can lead to tachycardia, arrhythmias, heart failure and osteoporosis. No one should use thyroid hormone to lose weight; it can lead to irritability and severe cardiac complications. Interestingly, older cats often get hyperthyroidism (more frequently than dogs) and pharmacists occasionally fill prescriptions for patients with names like Kitty.

Causes

The most common cause of hyperthyroidism is Graves' disease, which tends to occur in females in their 30's and 40's. Graves' disease is an autoimmune disorder (like Hashimoto's) but instead of destroying the gland, the antibodies stimulate the thyroid to produce too much T_4. Less commonly, a single nodule is responsible for the excess hormone secretion. Thyroiditis (inflammation of the thyroid) can also cause hyperthyroidism. Drugs that can cause hy-

S/SX OF HYPERTHYROIDISM	
Heat intolerance or increased sweating	Insomnia
Weight loss (or gain)	Light or absent menstrual periods
Agitation, nervousness, irritability, anxiety	Goiter (possible)
Palpitations and tachycardia	Thinning hair
Fatigue and muscle weakness	Tremor
Frequent bowel movements or diarrhea	Exophthalmos (exophthalmia), diplopia

perthyroidism include iodine, amiodarone and interferons. Hyperthyroidism can also occur in patients who take excessive doses of any of the available forms of thyroid hormone.

Drug Treatment

Treatment involves anti-thyroid medications, destroying part of the gland via radioactive iodine (RAI-131) or surgery. RAI-131 is the treatment of choice in Graves' disease. With any option, the patient can be treated with beta blockers first for symptom control (to reduce palpitations, tremors and tachycardia). Propylthiouracil (PTU) or methimazole can be used as a temporary measure until surgery is complete. Initially, when treating with drugs, it takes 1 – 3 months at higher doses to control symptoms, at which point the dose is reduced to prevent hypothyroidism from occurring.

Hyperthyroidism Treatment

DRUG	DOSING	SAFETY/SIDE EFFECTS/MONITORING
Thionamides – inhibit synthesis of thyroid hormones by blocking the oxidation of iodine in the thyroid gland; PTU also inhibits peripheral conversion of T_4 to T_3		
Propylthiouracil (PTU) Tablet	50-150 mg Q8H initially (or higher) until euthyroid, followed by dose reduction	**BOXED WARNING** Severe liver injury and acute liver failure (with PTU) Pregnancy Category D. PTU preferred in 1st trimester – change to methimazole for 2nd and 3rd trimesters (due to increased risk of liver toxicity from PTU and fetal abnormalities from methimazole) **SIDE EFFECTS** GI upset, headache, rash (exfoliative dermatitis, pruritus), fever, constipation, loss of taste/taste perversion, drug-induced lupus erythematosus (DILE), lymphadenopathy, bleeding Hepatitis, agranulocytosis (rare): see MD at once for yellow skin, abdominal pain, high fever, or severe sore throat
Methimazole (*Tapazole*) Tablet	Mild hyperthyroidism: 5 mg Q8H initially until euthyroid (↑ doses for more severe hyperthyroidism), then 5-15 mg daily	**MONITORING** CBC, LFTs, PT and thyroid function tests (TSH, FT_4, total T_3) every 4-6 weeks until euthyroid **NOTES** PTU is preferred in thyroid storm Take with food to reduce GI upset Patient must monitor for liver toxicity (abdominal pain, yellow skin/eyes, dark urine, nausea, weakness) PTU is not a first line treatment for hyperthyroidism except in patients who cannot tolerate other options or conditions where other antithyroid therapies are contraindicated.

DRUG	DOSING	SAFETY/SIDE EFFECTS/MONITORING

Iodides – temporarily inhibit secretion of thyroid hormones; T_4 and T_3 levels will be reduced for several weeks but effect will not be maintained

Potassium iodide and Iodine solution (*Lugol's solution*) Oral solution	Preparation for thyroidectomy: 5-7 drops Q8H for 10 days prior to surgery (off-label)	**CONTRAINDICATIONS** Hypersensitivity to iodide or iodine; dermatitis herpetiformis; hypocomplementemic vasculitis, nodular thyroid condition with heart disease **SIDE EFFECTS** Rash, metallic taste, sore throat/gums, GI upset, urticaria, hypo/hyperthyroidism with prolonged use
Saturated solution of potassium iodide (*SSKI, ThyroShield*) Oral solution	Preparation for thyroidectomy: 1-2 drops Q8H for 10 days prior to surgery (off-label)	**MONITORING** Thyroid function tests, s/sx of hyperthyroidism **NOTES** Pregnancy Category D Dilute in a glassful of water, juice, or milk. Take with food or milk to reduce GI upset *SSKI* is also used as an expectorant

Thionamide Drug Interactions
- Can ↓ the anticoagulant effect of warfarin; monitor.

POTASSIUM IODIDE USE AFTER EXPOSURE TO RADIATION
Potassium iodide (KI) blocks the accumulation of radioactive iodine in the thyroid gland; thus preventing thyroid cancer. Potassium iodide should be taken as soon as possible after radiation exposure on the advice of public health or emergency management personnel only. The correct dose must be used and higher doses do not offer greater protection. The doses below provide protection for 24 hours. If the radiation exposure is longer, refer to the CDC website for repeat-dose instructions. Iodized salt and foods do not contain enough iodine to block radioactive iodine and are not recommended.

- Birth – 1 month: 16.25 mg KI
- Infants and children between 1 month – 3 years: 32.5 mg KI
- Children 3 – 8 years: 65 mg KI
- Adults and children > 68 kg: 130 mg KI

THYROID STORM
Thyroid storm is a <u>life-threatening</u> medical emergency characterized by decompensated hyperthyroidism that can be precipitated by infection, trauma, surgery, radio-active iodine treatment or non-adherence to antithyroid medication. The following treatment measures must be implemented promptly.

S/SX OF THYROID STORM	
Fever (> 103°F)	Agitation
Tachycardia	Delirium
Tachypnea	Psychosis
Dehydration	Coma
Profuse sweating	

Drug Treatment
- Antithyroid drug therapy (<u>PTU is preferred</u>; 500 – 1,000 mg loading dose, then 250 mg PO Q4H) <u>PLUS</u>
    - Can crush tablets and administer through NG-tube if needed
    - Given ≥ 1 hour before iodide to block synthesis of thyroid hormone

- Inorganic iodide therapy such as *SSKI* 3 – 5 drops PO Q8H or *Lugol's solution* 4 – 8 drops PO Q6-8H <u>PLUS</u>

- Beta blocker (e.g., propranolol 40 – 80 mg PO Q6H) <u>PLUS</u>

- Systemic steroid (e.g., dexamethasone 2 – 4 mg PO Q6H) <u>PLUS</u>

- Aggressive cooling with acetaminophen and cooling blankets and other supportive treatments (e.g., antiarrhythmics, insulin, fluids, electrolytes, etc.)

PRACTICE CASE

> MT is a 45 y/o white female who comes to the clinic complaining of more fatigue than normal and constipation. On exam, the patient has some dry skin patches and looks a bit depressed. Her past medical history is significant for GERD.
>
> **Allergies:** NKDA
>
> **Medications:**
> *Dexilant* 30 mg PO daily
> *Maalox* 2 tablespoonfuls PRN heartburn
>
> **Vitals:**
> Height: 5'4" Weight: 122 lbs
> BP: 139/82 mmHg HR: 62 BPM RR: 15 BPM Temp: 38°C Pain: 0/10
>
> **Labs:** Na (mEq/L) = 138 (135 - 145)
> K (mEq/L) = 4.5 (3.5 - 5)
> Cl (mEq/L) = 98 (95 - 103)
> HCO_3 (mEq/L) = 29 (24 - 30)
> BUN (mg/dL) = 11 (7 - 20)
> SCr (mg/dL) = 0.9 (0.6 - 1.3)
> Glucose (mg/dL) = 87 (100 - 125)
> Ca (mg/dL) = 10.1 (8.5 - 10.5)
> Mg (mEq/L) = 1.8 (1.3 - 2.1)
> PO_4 (mg/dL) = 3.0 (2.3 - 4.7)
> TSH (mIU/L) = 44 (0.3 - 3)
> Free T_4 (ng/dL) = 0.5 (0.9 - 2.3)
>
> Initiate therapy for new diagnosis of hypothyroidism and educate patient.

Questions

1. The physician is considering starting thyroid medication for MT. Which of the following options is considered most appropriate for initial therapy?

   a. Levoxyl

   b. Armour Thyroid

   c. Thyrolar

   d. RAI 131

   e. Propranolol

2. What is the full replacement starting dose of *Synthroid* for MT?

   a. 12.5 mcg daily

   b. 25 mg daily

   c. 75 mg daily

   d. 88 mcg daily

   e. 125 mg daily

Questions 3 – 10 do not relate to the case.

3. Which of the following medications can decrease the levels of levothyroxine? (Select **ALL** that apply.)

   a. Magnesium – Aluminum hydroxide *(Maalox)*
   b. Iron
   c. Warfarin
   d. *Kayexalate*
   e. *Dilantin*

4. Propylthiouracil is associated with which of the following serious adverse effects?

   a. Pregnancy
   b. Liver failure
   c. Renal failure
   d. Rhabdomyolysis
   e. Priapism

5. What is the most common cause of hypothyroidism?

   a. Graves' disease
   b. Hashimoto's disease
   c. Surgery
   d. Amiodarone
   e. Lithium

6. A patient is beginning levothyroxine therapy. Patient counseling points should include the following:

   a. You should feel much better by this afternoon or tomorrow morning.
   b. Your healthcare provider will need to recheck your thyroid hormone levels in 4-6 weeks.
   c. If you get pregnant, stop using this medicine.
   d. A and C only
   e. All of the above

7. Which of the following are symptoms of hypothyroidism? (Select **ALL** that apply.)

   a. Fatigue
   b. Weight gain or increased difficulty losing weight
   c. Diarrhea
   d. Tachycardia
   e. Exophthalmos

8. Which of the following is the best way to instruct a patient to take levothyroxine?

   a. First thing in the morning, with food
   b. First thing in the morning, about 60 minutes before food or other medicines
   c. With the largest meal to reduce nausea
   d. With dinner since levothyroxine is sedating
   e. At bedtime

9. A pregnant female is being started on levothyroxine therapy. Levothyroxine has the following pregnancy rating:

   a. Pregnancy Category A
   b. Pregnancy Category B
   c. Pregnancy Category C
   d. Pregnancy Category D
   e. Pregnancy Category X

10. What is the most common cause of hyperthyroidism?

    a. Hashimoto's disease
    b. Pituitary failure
    c. Lithium
    d. Amiodarone
    e. Graves' disease

Answers
1-a, 2-d, 3-a,b,d,e, 4-b, 5-b, 6-b, 7-a,b, 8-b, 9-a, 10-e

SYSTEMIC STEROIDS & AUTOIMMUNE CONDITIONS

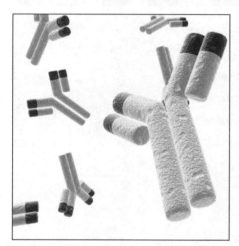

We gratefully acknowledge the assistance of James D. Nash, PharmD, MPH, BCPS, Associate Dean, Regis University School of Pharmacy, in preparing this chapter.

SYSTEMIC STEROIDS

Corticosteroid refers to glucocorticoids and mineralocorticoids.

The primary endogenous <u>glucocorticoid</u> is <u>cortisol</u>. Synthetic steroids used for replacement or to treat inflammation include hydrocortisone, prednisone, triamcinolone, etc. The primary endogenous <u>mineralocorticoid</u> is <u>aldosterone</u>. <u>Fludrocortisone</u> is a synthetic steroid used for mineralocorticoid replacement. These endogenous steroids (cortisol and fludrocortisone) are produced by the adrenal glands.

It is important to distinguish between <u>replacement</u> of endogenous steroids versus <u>treatment</u>. In <u>Addison's disease</u> (also called adrenal insufficiency) the amount of steroids produced is too little and will require <u>replacement</u>. In <u>treatment</u>, steroids are used commonly because they are potent inhibitors of many inflammatory processes. They are given to <u>reduce inflammation</u> due to a <u>chronic condition</u> (such as asthma or an autoimmune disease) or to <u>reduce inflammation</u> due to an <u>acute cause</u> (such as treatment of an allergic reaction). Steroids are used for other indications such as to reduce chemotherapy-induced nausea and vomiting. In this text, the term systemic (or topical) steroids is used instead of glucocorticoids, since most of the use involves glucocorticoids. The mineralocorticoid <u>fludrocortisone</u> is used to replace aldosterone in Addison's, or with another condition that causes adrenal insufficiency. These patients also require glucocorticoids.

GUIDELINES/REFERENCES

Singh JA, Saag KG, Bridges SL Jr, et al. 2015 American College of Rheumatology Guideline for the Treatment of Rheumatoid Arthritis. *Arthritis Care Res.* 2015;doi10.1002/acr.22783.

Hahn BH, McMahon MA, Wilkinson A, et al. American College of Rheumatology Guidelines for Screening, Treatment and Management of Lupus Nephritis. *Arthritis Care Res.* 2012;64(6):797-808.

Additional guidelines included with the video files (RxPrep Online).

Steroid Dosing

Systemic steroids are associated with many risks: adrenal suppression, osteoporosis, hyperglycemia, hypertension, cardiovascular disease, glaucoma and cataracts, immunosuppression, and others (see box on the following page). Dosing designed to reduce risk is required because dosing correlates to adverse effects--even when chosen carefully, adverse effects will remain significant. Minimally, the <u>lowest</u>

possible dose for the <u>shortest</u> possible time should be used. The formulation/route should be selected to reduce risk: inhaled steroids are used for asthma since the medication is delivered directly to the lung, maximizing efficacy while minimizing system absorption and adverse effects. Other steroids are injected directly into inflamed joints, and others are chosen for a gut condition that have low absorption (such as budesonide in the *Entocort EC* formulation). Alternate day dosing can help reduce adrenal suppression. In other cases, a high initial dose is started, then sequentially tapered down to continue to reduce the ongoing inflammation or to prevent a rebound episode. These tapered dosing regimens often come prepackaged such as methylprednisolone *(Medrol Dosepak)* and dexamethasone *(DexPak)*.

Systemic steroids used in high doses for a prolonged time will require a steady reduction in the dose (<u>a taper</u>) in order to provide time to increase the (previously-suppressed) endogenous cortisol production due to the extended use. Tapering is recommended in patients taking systemic steroids for longer than 10 – 14 days.

LONG-TERM SIDE EFFECTS OF SYSTEMIC STEROIDS

Cushing Syndrome
A condition due to excess endogenous <u>cortisol</u> or exogenous <u>steroid</u> therapy.

- Central redistribution of fat (fat deposits in the abdomen)
- Moon facies (fat deposits in the face)
- Buffalo hump (fat deposits between the shoulders)
- Impaired wound healing
- Dermal thinning/bruising

Other Side Effects
Psychiatric disturbances (mood swings, delirium, psychoses)

Sodium and water retention/hypertension

Hypokalemia

Hyperglycemia/diabetes

Increased appetite/weight gain

Immunosuppression

Glaucoma/cataracts

Growth retardation

Amenorrhea

Osteoporosis/fractures

Hirsutism (in women)

Acne

Insomnia/nervousness

GI bleeding/esophagitis/ulcers (do not use with NSAIDs due to ↑ risk)

Oral Steroid Dose Equivalents

STEROID	DOSE	
Cortisone	25 mg	Short-acting
Hydrocortisone	20 mg	Short-acting
Prednisone	5 mg	Intermediate-acting
Prednisolone	5 mg	Intermediate-acting
Methylprednisolone	4 mg	Intermediate-acting
Triamcinolone	4 mg	Intermediate-acting
Dexamethasone	0.75 mg	Long-acting
Betamethasone	0.6 mg	Long-acting

Glucocorticoids (Systemic Steroids)

DRUG	DOSING	SAFETY/SIDE EFFECTS/MONITORING
Cortisone Tablet **Hydrocortisone** *(Solu-CORTEF* – injection, *A-Hydrocort* – injection, *Cortef* – tablet) **MethylPREDNISolone** *(Medrol* – tablet, *Medrol Dosepak* – tablet, *Solu-MEDROL* – injection, *A-Methapred* – injection, *Depo-Medrol* – injection) **PredniSONE** *(PredniSONE Intensol* –soln, *Deltasone* – tablet, *Rayos* – delayed-release tablet) **PrednisoLONE** *(Millipred* – tablet, solution, *Orapred* – tablet, ODT, soln, *AsmalPred* – solution, *Pediapred* – solution, *Veripred* – solution, *Prelone* – syrup, *Flo-Pred* – suspension) **Triamcinolone** *(Aristospan* – injection, *Kenalog* – injection)	Dosing varies by disease severity and patient response The steroid dose (if used once daily) should be given between 7-8 AM to mimic the body's diurnal release of cortisol	**CONTRAINDICATIONS** Live vaccines, serious systemic infections **WARNINGS** Adrenal suppression - HPA axis suppression may lead to adrenal crisis and death. If taking longer than 10-14 days, <u>must taper slowly</u> Immunosuppression, psychiatric disturbances, caution in HF, DM, HTN, osteoporosis, others **SIDE EFFECTS** <u>Short-term side effects (used < 1 month):</u> ↑ appetite/weight gain, fluid retention, emotional instability (euphoria, mood swings, irritability), insomnia, indigestion, bitter taste. Higher doses ↑ in BP and ↑ blood glucose <u>Long-term side effects</u>: listed in chart on previous page **MONITORING** BP, weight, appetite, mood, growth (children/adolescents), bone mineral density, blood glucose, electrolytes, infection, IOP if > 6 weeks therapy **NOTES** Cortisone is a prodrug for cortisol. Prednisone is a prodrug for prednisolone. Prednisolone is used most commonly in children (comes in many formulations).

Relative anti-inflammatory potency: betamethasone/dexamethasone > methylprednisolone/triamcinolone > prednisone/prednisolone > hydrocortisone > cortisone

Fludrocortisone has the highest mineralocorticoid potency causing Na^+ and H_2O retention – indicated for Addison's disease; not for inflammation

AUTOIMMUNE CONDITIONS

Autoimmune diseases are conditions that occur when the body's immune system attacks and destroys healthy body tissue. The immune system is a complex organization of cells and antibodies designed to "seek and destroy" invaders of the body, particularly infections. Symptoms vary based on the type of autoimmune disease and the location of the immune response. Common symptoms to all autoimmune diseases include fatigue, weakness and pain.

Rheumatoid arthritis (RA), systemic lupus erythematosus (SLE), multiple sclerosis (MS), celiac disease, Sjögren's syndrome, Raynaud's and psoriasis are discussed in this chapter. Other autoimmune diseases covered elsewhere in the book include type 1 diabetes (discussed in the Diabetes chapter), Hashimoto's thyroiditis and Graves disease (discussed in the Thyroid Disorders chapter).

TREATMENT

Treatment of autoimmune diseases is typically with immunosuppressive drugs which decrease the immune response. The use of strong immunosuppressants can increase the risk of certain conditions due to the strong depression of the immune system. These conditions include:

- Tuberculosis and hepatitis B (if present) re-activation; testing (and treatment if needed) must be done prior to the start of immunosuppressive agents.

- Viruses; if the virus can be prevented by a live vaccine, the vaccine must be given prior to the start of immunosuppressive treatment.

- Lymphomas and certain skin cancers: these cancer types are normally suppressed by a competent immune system.

- Infections of various types (e.g., bacterial, fungal); this requires CBC monitoring, symptom monitoring (by the patient) and may require infection control mechanisms.

RHEUMATOID ARTHRITIS

Rheumatoid arthritis (RA) is a chronic, symmetrical, systemic and progressive disease that causes inflammation of the joints and other organs in the body, including the kidneys, eyes, heart and lungs. Like many of the autoimmune conditions discussed in this chapter, the disease course is highly variable and some patients have much more aggressive disease than others. RA typically presents first in the hands and feet. Macrophages, cytotoxins, and free oxygen radicals promote cellular damage and inflammation. The inflammation leads to cartilage and bone destruction.

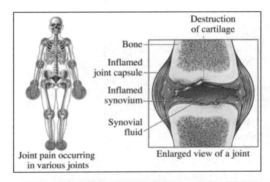

Joint pain occurring in various joints — Bone, Inflamed joint capsule, Inflamed synovium, Synovial fluid — Destruction of cartilage — Enlarged view of a joint

Clinical Presentation

The classic symptoms of RA include joint swelling, stiffness, pain and eventually, bone deformity (see box) as well as the constitutional symptoms of fatigue, fever, weakness and loss of appetite. Patients experience articular (affecting the joints) manifestations that are almost always polyarticular and symmetrical. Any synovial joint can be involved, but the finger joints of the hand are most often affected. The wrists, knees and toe joints are also frequently involved. Morning stiffness, swelling, redness, edema, pain, decreased range

ARTICULAR SYMPTOMS OF RA	
Joint swelling	Edema
Pain	Muscle atrophy
Stiffness	Redness
Bone deformity	Weakness
Decreased range of motion	

of motion, muscle atrophy, weakness, and deformity are typical articular symptoms of RA. Morning stiffness is a clue for RA and may last for up to 2 hours. Osteoarthritis (OA) does not cause prolonged stiffness.

Patients may also experience extra-articular (outside of the joints) manifestations, including firm lumps, called rheumatoid nodules, which are subcutaneous nodules in places such as the elbow or hands. Other extra-articular symptoms may include vasculitis, pulmonary complications (fibrosis, effusions, nodules), lymphadenopathy, splenomegaly, eye inflammation, dry eyes and/or mouth from a related condition (Sjögren's syndrome), pericarditis/myocarditis, and atherosclerosis.

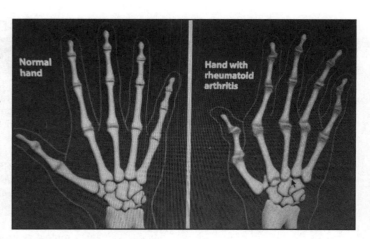

Normal hand

Hand with rheumatoid arthritis

DIAGNOSIS

Criteria 1-4 must be present for ≥ 6 weeks and 4 or more criteria must be present.

Diagnostic Criteria

1. Morning stiffness around joints lasting > 1 hour

2. Soft tissue swelling (arthritis) ≥ 3 joints

3. Swelling (arthritis) of hand, foot, or wrist joints

4. Symmetric involvement

5. Rheumatoid nodules

6. Positive serum rheumatoid factor (present in ~ 70% of patients)

7. Radiographic erosions or periarticular osteopenia in hand or wrist joints

Non-Drug Treatment

Non-drug treatments include rest, physical therapy, occupational therapy, exercise, diet and weight control, and surgical intervention (e.g., a joint replacement).

Drug Treatment

Patients with symptomatic RA should be started on disease-modifying antirheumatic drug (DMARD) monotherapy, regardless of the severity of disease. DMARDs work via various mechanisms to slow the disease process and help prevent further joint damage. The ideal treatment target goal is remission of the disease (or low disease activity). Methotrexate (MTX) is the preferred initial therapy for most patients. For patients with moderate or high disease activity despite MTX (with or without a systemic steroid), a combination of DMARDs or a tumor necrosis factor (TNF) inhibitor biologic or a non-TNF biologic, with or without MTX, is recommended. Never use two biologics in combination due to the risk of serious (fatal) infection. Low dose steroids (defined as ≤ 10 mg/day of prednisone or equivalent) may be added in patients with moderate or high disease activity when starting a DMARD (known as bridging) and in patients with DMARD failure. NSAIDs are an option for bridging; anti-inflammatory doses must be used. Steroids are commonly used in RA flares and should be used at the lowest dose for the shortest duration (< 3 months) possible.

Traditional (Non-Biologic) Disease-Modifying Anti-Rheumatic Drugs (DMARDs)

DRUG	DOSING	SAFETY/SIDE EFFECTS/MONITORING
Methotrexate ***(Otrexup, Rasuvo, Rheumatrex, Trexall)*** *Otrexup* and *Rasuvo* are SC auto-injectors used weekly *Rheumatrex* and *Trexall* are oral tablets Injection (IV/IT) - for oncology use Irreversibly binds and inhibits dihydrofolate reductase, inhibiting folate, thymidylate synthetase and purine; has immune modulator and anti-inflammatory activity	7.5-20 mg once weekly Low weekly doses are used for RA (divided oral dosages of 2.5 mg Q12H x 3 doses as a course once weekly) never dose daily for RA Take weekly; numerous incidences of adverse events (mouth sores, intestinal bleeding, etc.) have occurred due to patients taking daily. May give PO, IM or SC	**BOXED WARNINGS** Hepatotoxicity, acute renal failure, pneumonitis, myelosuppression, mucositis/stomatitis, dermatologic reactions, malignant lymphomas, potentially fatal opportunistic infections, others – renal and lung toxicity more likely when using oncology doses **CONTRAINDICATIONS** Pregnancy, breastfeeding, alcoholism, chronic liver disease, blood dyscrasias, immunodeficiency syndrome **SIDE EFFECTS** (vary by route and dosage) N/V/D, ↑ LFTs, stomatitis, alopecia, photosensitivity, arthralgia, myalgia **MONITORING** CBC, SCr, LFTs at baseline and Q2-4 weeks for first 3 months or following dose increases, then Q8-12 weeks for 3-6 months, then less frequently. Also at baseline: chest X-ray, hepatitis B and C serologies (if at high risk); pulmonary function tests (if lung-related symptoms), TB test **NOTES** Pregnancy Category X Folate can be given to ↓ hematological, gastrointestinal and hepatic side effects associated with MTX. Give 5 mg PO weekly on the day following MTX administration.
Hydroxychloroquine ***(Plaquenil)*** +/- MTX Tablet Immune modulator	400-600 mg/day initially, then 200-400 mg/day for maintenance dose Take with food or milk	**CONTRAINDICATIONS** Retinopathy, hypersensitivity to 4-aminoquinoline compounds, long-term use in children **WARNINGS** Ophthalmic effects such as loss of visual acuity and macular pigment changes; neuromuscular weakness, cardiomyopathy and hematologic reactions with prolonged use; caution in patients with G6PD deficiency **SIDE EFFECTS** N/V/D, abdominal pain, rash, pruritus, HA, vision changes (dose-related), pigmentation changes of the skin and hair (rare) **MONITORING** CBC and LFTs at baseline and periodically. Eye exam and muscle strength at baseline and every 3 months during prolonged therapy **NOTES** Should be avoided in pregnancy

Traditional (Non-Biologic) Disease-Modifying Anti-Rheumatic Drugs (DMARDs) Continued

DRUG	DOSING	SAFETY/SIDE EFFECTS/MONITORING
SulfaSALAzine *(Azulfidine, Azulfidine EN-tabs, Sulfazine, Sulfazine EC)* Tablet +/- MTX Immune modulator	500-1,000 mg/day initially, then 1,000 mg BID for maintenance dose (max 3 grams/day) Take with food and 8 oz. of water to prevent crystalluria	**CONTRAINDICATIONS** Patients with a <u>sulfa or salicylate allergy</u>, GI or GU obstruction, porphyria **WARNINGS** Blood dyscrasias, severe skin reactions (SJS/TEN), hepatic failure, and pulmonary fibrosis; use caution in patients with <u>G6PD deficiency</u> **SIDE EFFECTS** <u>HA, rash, anorexia, dyspepsia, N/V/D, oligospermia (reversible)</u>; <u>folate deficiency</u>, arthralgias, crystalluria **MONITORING** CBC and LFTs (baseline, then every other week for first 3 months, then monthly for 3 months, then once every 3 months), renal function **NOTES** Can cause <u>yellow-orange</u> coloration of skin/urine <u>Impairs folate absorption</u>, may give 1 mg/day folate supplement Pregnancy Category B
Leflunomide *(Arava)* Tablet +/- MTX Inhibits pyrimidine synthesis resulting in antiproliferative and anti-inflammatory effects Prodrug	100 mg PO x 3 days, then 20 mg PO daily, can use 10 mg PO daily if unable to tolerate 20 mg (may omit loading dose if at higher risk of liver or myelosuppression) Must have negative pregnancy test prior and use 2 forms of birth control. If pregnancy is desired, must wait 2 years after discontinuation or use accelerated drug elimination procedure	**BOXED WARNINGS** Embryo-Fetal Toxicity: Exclude pregnancy prior to starting therapy Hepatotoxicity: Avoid in pre-existing liver disease or ALT > 2x upper limit of normal (ULN) **CONTRAINDICATION** Pregnancy, severe hepatic impairment, current teriflunomide therapy **WARNINGS** Severe infections, serious skin reactions (SJS/TEN), peripheral neuropathy, interstitial lung disease, hypertension Upon discontinuation of treatment, use accelerated drug elimination procedure to reduce levels of active metabolite, teriflunomide **SIDE EFFECTS** ↑ LFTs, nausea, diarrhea, respiratory infections, rash, HA **MONITORING** LFTs and CBC at baseline and monthly for first 6 months, BP at baseline and regularly. Screen for TB and pregnancy prior to starting therapy. **NOTES** <u>Pregnancy: Contraindicated</u>. Females/Males of Reproductive Potential: May cause fetal harm; consider discontinuing use (formerly Pregnancy Category X) <u>Accelerated drug elimination options</u>: 1. Cholestyramine 8 grams PO TID x 11 days, 2. Activated charcoal suspension 50 grams PO Q12H x 11 days

Traditional (Non-Biologic) Disease-Modifying Anti-Rheumatic Drugs (DMARDs) Continued

DRUG	DOSING	SAFETY/SIDE EFFECTS/MONITORING
Tofacitinib *(Xeljanz)* Tablet +/- non-biologic DMARDs (MTX), <u>do not use</u> with biologic DMARDs or potent immunosuppressants <u>Inhibits Janus Kinase (JAK) enzymes</u>, which stimulate immune cell function	5 mg PO BID With strong 3A4 inducers: avoid use With strong 3A4 inhibitors or with concomitant moderate 3A4 inhibitors and strong 2C19 inhibitors: 5 mg daily ↓ dose to 5 mg daily in moderate hepatic impairment and mod-severe renal impairment Do not start therapy if: absolute lymphocyte count < 500 cells/mm^3, Hgb < 9 g/dL, or ANC < 1,000 cells/mm^3	**BOXED WARNINGS** Serious infections including tuberculosis, fungal, viral, bacterial, or other opportunistic infections; screen for active and latent TB and treat before starting therapy Malignancy: ↑ risk for lymphomas and other malignancies **WARNINGS** GI perforation, ↑ LFTs, avoid live vaccines **SIDE EFFECTS** Upper respiratory tract infections (URTIs), diarrhea, HA, ↑ lipids **MONITORING** CBC (for lymphopenia, neutropenia and anemia) and lipids at baseline, then 4-8 weeks later, then Q3 months; LFTs (at baseline and periodically thereafter), signs of infection **NOTES** Pregnancy Category C MedGuide required Caution in patients of Asian descent (↑ frequency of side effects)

Methotrexate Drug Interactions

- <u>Methotrexate should not be taken with alcohol</u>; this combination ↑ the risk of liver toxicity.

- Active transport renal elimination is ↓ by aspirin/NSAIDs, beta-lactams, and probenecid, resulting in toxicity. Caution if using concurrently.

- Sulfonamides and topical tacrolimus ↑ adverse effects of methotrexate. Avoid concurrent use.

- Methotrexate can ↓ effectiveness of loop diuretics; loop diuretics can ↑ the methotrexate concentration. Use caution if using these agents concomitantly.

- Methotrexate and cyclosporine concentrations will both ↑ when used concomitantly, leading to toxicity; avoid.

Methotrexate Patient Counseling

- Common side effects of this medication include nausea, vomiting, abdominal pain, diarrhea, mouth sores, and rash.

- If you are receiving this medicine for rheumatoid arthritis or psoriasis, the dosage is usually given once weekly. Some patients are told to divide the once weekly dose in half and take it over two consecutive days per week for better tolerability. Do not use this medicine daily or double-up on doses. Serious side effects could occur if it is used more frequently than directed. Choose a day of the week to take your medicine that you can remember.

- Methotrexate has caused birth defects and death in unborn babies (Pregnancy Category X). If you are pregnant or plan on becoming pregnant, you should not use this medicine. Use an effective form of birth control, whether you are a man or a woman. Tell your healthcare provider if you or your sexual partner become pregnant during treatment.

- Do not use methotrexate if you are breastfeeding.

- If you have kidney problems or excess body water (ascites, pleural effusion), you must be closely monitored and your dose may be adjusted or stopped by your healthcare provider.

- Your healthcare provider will perform periodic blood tests to measure your liver function to ensure it stays healthy. Tell your healthcare provider right away if you develop any new or worsening symptoms, including black, tarry stools or symptoms of liver damage (unusual tiredness or weakness, yellow skin or eyes or darkened urine, stomach upset or pain).

- Methotrexate (usually at high dosages) has rarely caused severe (sometimes fatal) bone marrow suppression (decreasing your body's ability to fight infections) and stomach/intestinal disease (e.g., bleeding) when used at the same time as NSAIDs. Therefore, NSAIDs should not be used with high-doses of methotrexate. Caution is advised if you also take aspirin. If you are using low-dose aspirin (81-325 milligrams per day) for heart attack or stroke prevention, continue to take it unless directed otherwise.

- Methotrexate use has rarely resulted in serious (sometimes fatal) lung problems such as scarring and lung infections (*Pneumocystis* pneumonia).

- For *Rasuvo* and *Otrexup* auto-injectors: Inspect syringe. Liquid should be yellow (*Otrexup*) to yellow-brown (*Rasuvo*). Discard if cloudy or containing particles. Select an injection site on the abdomen (2 inches from navel) or upper thigh only. Do not inject in the arms or any other areas of the body. Swab with alcohol pad and allow to dry – do not fan or blow on the area. For *Otrexup*, twist cap to break seal and remove the safety clip. For *Rasuvo* pull the yellow cap directly off without twisting. Pinch the skin and inject at a 90° angle. Press firmly until you hear a click. Hold 3 seconds for *Otrexup* and 5 seconds for *Rasuvo*. Check the viewing window to be sure the medicine was given. Dispose of the used injector in a sharps container. Store at room temperature.

Biologic Agents

<u>Tumor Necrosis Factor (TNFα) Inhibitors (Anti-TNF biologics)</u>

TNF inhibitor dosing is provided for RA. Recommended dosing for psoriatic arthritis, plaque psoriasis, Crohn's disease, ulcerative colitis, and other indications may vary.

DRUG	DOSING	SAFETY/SIDE EFFECTS/MONITORING
Etanercept *(Enbrel, Enbrel SureClick)* Prefilled syringe and auto-injector +/- MTX	50 mg SC weekly	**BOXED WARNINGS** <u>Serious infections</u>, some fatal, including TB, fungal, viral, bacterial or opportunistic; screen for latent TB and treat prior to therapy Lymphomas and other malignancies **CONTRAINDICATIONS** Active systemic infection, dose > 5 mg/kg in mod-severe heart failure (infliximab), sepsis (etanercept) **WARNINGS** TNF inhibitors can cause demyelinating disease, hepatitis B reactivation, <u>heart failure, hepatotoxicity</u>, lupus-like syndrome, myelosuppression and severe infections. Do not use with other TNF inhibitors or immunosuppressive biologics, or live vaccines. **SIDE EFFECTS** Infections and injection site reactions (redness, rash, swelling, itching, or bruising), positive anti-nuclear antibodies, headache, nausea, ↑ CPK (adalimumab)
Adalimumab *(Humira)* Prefilled syringe and pen +/- MTX	40 mg SC <u>every other week</u> (if not taking MTX, can ↑ dose to 40 mg SC <u>weekly</u>)	
InFLIXimab *(Remicade)* Injection (IV) + MTX	3 mg/kg <u>IV</u> at weeks 0, 2, and 6, then every 8 weeks (can ↑ dose to 10 mg/kg or treat as often as every 4 weeks based on need but ↑ infection risk) IV infliximab requires a <u>filter</u> and is stable in <u>NS only</u> <u>Infusion reactions</u>: hypotension, fever, chills, pruritus (may pre-medicate with acetaminophen, antihistamine, steroids) <u>Delayed hypersensitivity reaction</u> 3-12 days after administration (fever, rash, myalgia, HA, sore throat)	**MONITORING** <u>TB test</u> (prior to initiation and annually if risk factors for TB are present), <u>s/sx of infection</u>, CBC, LFTs, HBV (prior to initiation), HF, malignancies, vitals (during infliximab infusion) **NOTES** Do not shake. <u>Requires refrigeration</u> (biologics will denature if hot). Do not freeze. Etanercept and adalimumab may be stored at room temperature for a maximum of 14 days. Allow to reach room temperature before injecting (15-30 min).
Certolizumab pegol *(Cimzia)* Prefilled syringe and syringe kit +/- MTX	400 mg SC at weeks 0, 2, and 4, then 200 mg SC every other week (may consider 400 mg every 4 weeks)	<u>MTX is used 1st-line</u> and these agents are <u>add-on therapy</u>. <u>However</u>, if the initial presentation is severe, these <u>can be started as initial therapy</u>. <u>Do not use two biologics concurrently</u>.
Golimumab *(Simponi, Simponi Aria)* Prefilled syringe, auto-injector, and injection (IV) + MTX	SC: 50 mg monthly *(Simponi)* IV: 2 mg/kg infused over 30 minutes at weeks 0 and 4, then every 8 weeks *(Simponi Aria)* IV golimumab requires a <u>filter</u>	<u>Do not use live vaccines if using these drugs</u>. Antibody induction can occur and will ↓ usefulness of drug. Pregnancy Category B Rotate injection sites MedGuide required

Other Biologics (Non-TNF Biologics)

Rituximab

<u>Depletes CD20 B cells.</u> B cells are believed to have a role in RA development and progression.

DRUG	DOSING	SAFETY/SIDE EFFECTS/MONITORING
RiTUXimab *(Rituxan)* Injection (IV) + MTX	1,000 mg IV on day 1 and 15 in combination with MTX for 2 doses. Can repeat treatment if needed at 24 weeks (or no sooner than every 16 weeks) Pre-medicate with a steroid, acetaminophen, and an antihistamine Start infusion at 50 mg/hr; can ↑ by 50 mg/hr every 30 min if no reaction (max 400 mg/hr) Gently invert the bag to mix the solution, do not shake	**BOXED WARNINGS** Serious, and fatal, infusion-related reactions usually with the first infusion Progressive multifocal leukoencephalopathy (PML) due to JC virus infection, may be fatal <u>Hepatitis B virus (HBV)</u> reactivation; some cases resulting in fulminant hepatitis, hepatic failure and death Serious skin reactions (SJS/TEN) **WARNINGS** Serious infections, discontinue if a serious infection develops. <u>Screen for latent TB and HBV</u> prior to initiating therapy. Do not give with other biologics or live vaccines. **SIDE EFFECTS** In patients treated for RA: infusion-related reactions, URTIs, UTIs, N/V/D, peripheral edema, weight gain, hypertension, HA, angioedema, fever, insomnia, pain **MONITORING** Cardiac monitoring during and after infusion, vital signs, infusion reactions, CBC, CD20+ cells, renal function **NOTES** Pregnancy Category C MedGuide required

Anakinra

IL-1 receptor antagonist. During inflammation, endogenous IL-1 is induced which mediates immunologic reactions in RA (degrades cartilage, increases bone resorption). Not recommended as a first line option in the guidelines.

DRUG	DOSING	SAFETY/SIDE EFFECTS/MONITORING
Anakinra *(Kineret)* Prefilled syringe	100 mg SC daily (same time each day) Give only after failure of one or more DMARDs CrCl < 30 mL/min: 100 mg SC every other day	**WARNINGS** Malignancies and serious infections, discontinue if a serious infection develops. <u>Screen for TB</u> prior to initiating therapy. Do not give with other biologics or live vaccines. **SIDE EFFECTS** URTIs, HA, nausea, abdominal pain, diarrhea, injection site reactions, arthralgia **MONITORING** CBC (baseline, monthly x 3 months, then Q3 months for first year), SCr, signs of infection **NOTES** Pregnancy Category B

Abatacept

Selective T cell costimulator; inhibits T cell activation by binding to CD80 and CD86 on cells that present these antigens (activated cells are detected in the synovium of RA joints).

DRUG	DOSING	SAFETY/SIDE EFFECTS/MONITORING
Abatacept (Orencia) Prefilled syringe, injection (IV)	IV: 500-1,000 mg (based on body weight) at 0, 2, and 4 weeks, then every 4 weeks, infuse over 30 min SC: 125 mg weekly SC with IV loading dose: give first IV dose as above, followed by 125 mg SC within 24 hours, then 125 mg SC weekly	**WARNINGS** Malignancies and serious infections, discontinue if a serious infection develops. Screen for latent TB and HBV prior to initiating therapy. Do not give with other biologics or live vaccines. Caution in patients with COPD - may worsen symptoms. **SIDE EFFECTS** Headache, nausea, injection site reactions, infections, nasopharyngitis, antibody development **MONITORING** Signs of infection, hypersensitivity **NOTES** Pregnancy Category C Stable in NS only. Requires a filter and light protection during administration; do not shake.

Tocilizumab

IL-6 receptor antagonist. IL-6 mediates immunologic reactions in RA.

DRUG	DOSING	SAFETY/SIDE EFFECTS/MONITORING
Tocilizumab (Actemra) Prefilled syringe, injection (IV) +/- MTX	IV: 4 mg/kg every 4 weeks given over 60 min (may ↑ to 8 mg/kg based on clinical response). Max: 800 mg SC: If < 100 kg, 162 mg every other week (may ↑ to weekly based on response) If ≥ 100 kg, 162 mg SC weekly Do not start if: ALT or AST are > 1.5 times ULN, ANC < 2,000 cells/mm³, or platelets < 100,000 cell/mm³	**BOXED WARNING** Serious infections, discontinue if a serious infection develops. Screen for latent TB prior to initiating therapy. **WARNINGS** GI perforation, hypersensitivity reactions, lipid abnormalities, ↑ LFTs, neutropenia, thrombocytopenia, do not give with other biologics or live vaccines **SIDE EFFECTS** URTIs, HA, hypertension, injection-site reactions, ↑ LDL and total cholesterol, ↑ LFTs **MONITORING** LFTs, CBC (baseline, 4-8 weeks after start of therapy, and every 3 months thereafter), lipid panel, signs of infection **NOTES** MedGuide required

Patient Counseling

Adalimumab, Etanercept and Golimumab

- Read the medication guide that comes with this medicine.

- Common side effects include injection site reactions such as redness, swelling, itching, or pain. These symptoms usually go away within 3 to 5 days. If you have pain, redness or swelling around the injection site that does not go away or gets worse, call your healthcare provider. Other side effects can include upper respiratory infections (sinus infections), headache, dizziness or coughing.

- People taking this medicine should not get live vaccines. Make sure your vaccines are up-to-date before starting this medicine. You can continue to take the annual influenza shot (but not the nasal mist vaccine, since this is a live vaccine).

- Because this medicine works by blocking the immune system, it lowers your ability to fight infections. This may make you more likely to get a serious (rarely fatal) infection or can make any infection you have worse. You should be tested for tuberculosis (TB skin test or chest X-ray) before treatment with this medicine. Tell your healthcare provider immediately if you have any signs of infection such as a fever of 100.5°F (38°C) or higher, chills, very bad sore throat, ear or sinus pain, a cough or more sputum or a change in the color of sputum.

- This medicine has a possibility of causing liver damage. Call your healthcare provider right away if you have any of these symptoms: feel very tired, yellowing of your skin or eyes, poor appetite or vomiting, pain on the right side of your stomach (abdomen).

- This medicine may worsen heart failure (HF). Notify your healthcare provider if you experience sudden weight gain or shortness of breath.

- This medicine is injected subcutaneously (SC) under the skin of the thigh or abdomen (or upper arm for etanercept and golimumab), exactly as prescribed by your healthcare provider (once weekly for etanercept, every 1 – 2 weeks for adalimumab, monthly for golimumab).

- Store the medication (single-use syringes or multiple-use vials) in the refrigerator (etanercept and adalimumab may be stored at room temperature for a maximum of 14 days with protection from light and sources of heat). Allow the medicine to warm to room temperature. Do not warm to room temperature any other way than letting the product sit at room temperature outside the carton for before injecting (takes 15 – 30 minutes). Do not shake the medicine. Before using, check for particles or discoloration. If either is present, do not use the medicine. Injectors require protection from light prior to administration.

- Before injecting each dose, clean the injection site with rubbing alcohol. Do not wave the hand over the wet area to dry. It is important to change the location of the injection site each time you use this drug to prevent problems under the skin. New injections should be given at least 1 inch (2.5 centimeters) from the last injection site. Do not inject into areas of the skin that are sore, bruised, red, broken or hard.

- For adalimumab *(Humira)*: Inject into the abdomen or thigh. A loud click is heard when the plum-colored activator button is pressed. Continue to hold injector against the skin until the yellow marker fully appears in the window view and stops moving (may take 10 seconds).

- For etanercept *(Enbrel)* syringe or auto-injector: Inject into abdomen, thigh, or upper arm. A loud click is heard when injection begins, continue to hold autoinjector against skin for 15 seconds. You may hear a second click as the purple button pops back up, indicating all of the medicine has been injected.

- For etanercept *(Enbrel)* vials for reconstitution: When reconstituting Enbrel powder from the multidose vial, some foaming is normal. The final solution should be clear and colorless, with no particulate matter.

- For golimumab *(Simponi)*: Inject into abdomen, thigh, or upper arm. A loud click is heard when the injection begins, continue to hold autoinjector against skin until second click is heard (3-15 seconds).

SYSTEMIC LUPUS ERYTHEMATOSUS

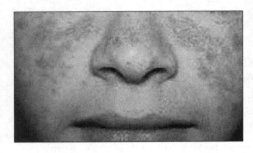

Background

Systemic lupus erythematosus (SLE), or lupus, is a multisystem autoimmune disease that affects primarily young women, with a female-to-male ratio of 10:1. The disease predominantly occurs in persons 15-45 years of age, and it is more common in women of African-American and Asian descent. Patients experience flare-ups to varying degrees as well as periods of disease remission. As the disease progresses, symptoms may be present in almost every organ system, with the heart, lungs, kidneys, and brain being most affected. The hallmark of SLE is the development of auto-antibodies by B cells to cellular components that leads to chronic inflammation and tissue damage.

Clinical Presentation

The most common symptoms include fatigue, depression, anorexia, weight loss, myalgias, arthritis, discoid rash, malar rash (butterfly rash), photosensitivity, and joint pain and stiffness. Over half of the people with SLE develop a characteristic red, flat facial rash over the bridge of their nose and cheeks. Because of its shape, it is frequently referred to as the SLE "butterfly rash." Usually, the rash is not painful or itchy. The facial rash, along with inflammation in other organs, can be precipitated or worsened by exposure to sunlight. Arthritis and cutaneous manifestations are most common, but renal, hematologic and neurologic manifestations contribute largely to morbidity and mortality. Lupus nephritis (kidney disease) develops in over 50% of patients with SLE. Common laboratory findings may include positive antinuclear antibodies (ANA - with titers ≥ 1:160), positive anti-single stranded DNA (anti-ssDNA), positive anti-double stranded DNA (anti-dsDNA), positive anti-Sm, positive antiphospholipid antibodies, low complement (C3, C4, CH50) and elevated acute phase reactants (such as ESR, CRP).

NON-DRUG AND DRUG TREATMENT

Non-drug treatment consists of rest and proper exercise to manage the fatigue. Smoking cessation is encouraged since tobacco smoke can be a trigger for disease flare. Photosensitivity is common with the condition and the treatment; sunscreens and sun protection/avoidance is required. Drug treatment for SLE consists of immunosuppressants, cytotoxic agents, and/or anti-inflammatory

SELECT DRUGS ASSOCIATED WITH DRUG-INDUCED LUPUS ERYTHEMATOSUS (DILE)		
Procainamide	Quinidine	Minocycline
Hydralazine (alone, and in *BiDil*)	Methyldopa	Terbinafine
	Propylthiouracil	Anti-TNF agents
Isoniazid	Methimazole	

agents. Treatment approaches emphasize using a combination of drugs to minimize chronic exposure to corticosteroids.

Patients with mild disease may do well on an NSAID (dosed at anti-inflammatory doses to ↓ swelling and pain) but use caution since the doses are high and these patients are more sensitive to the GI and renal side effects. Concurrent use with a PPI is generally recommended to reduce GI side effects. Other agents are discussed below.

Agents Used in SLE

DRUG	DOSING	SAFETY/SIDE EFFECTS/MONITORING

Antimalarial agents – impair complement-dependent antigen-antibody reactions; have anti-inflammatory, immunomodulatory and antithrombotic properties

DRUG	DOSING	SAFETY/SIDE EFFECTS/MONITORING
Hydroxychloroquine *(Plaquenil)*	400-800 mg/day PO in 1-2 divided doses initially then decrease after weeks to months to 200-400 mg/day PO in 1-2 divided doses Take with food or milk	Hydroxychloroquine has less adverse effects (preferred); takes 6 months to see maximal effect Effective for cutaneous symptoms, arthralgias, fatigue and fever; Use as chronic therapy
Chloroquine *(Aralen)*	250 mg PO daily CrCl < 10 mL/min: 125 mg PO daily	

Corticosteroids

DRUG	DOSING	SAFETY/SIDE EFFECTS/MONITORING
PredniSONE (or **methylPREDNISolone**)	0.5-1 mg/kg/day PO; then taper 500-1,000 mg/day IV for 3 days (acute flare, life threatening-disease), then taper	Used acutely to control flares at higher doses; taper to lower doses for chronic, suppressive therapy

Select cytotoxic agents – used in severe disease (flares)

DRUG	DOSING	SAFETY/SIDE EFFECTS/MONITORING
Cyclophosphamide	500-1,000 mg/m² IV monthly for 6 months, then every 3 months for 2.5 years; or 1-1.5 mg/kg daily if using PO	**SIDE EFFECTS** Myelosuppression, infections, hemorrhagic cystitis, malignancy, sterility, teratogenesis **MONITORING** CBC and urinalysis **NOTES** Pregnancy Category D
AzaTHIOprine *(Azasan, Imuran)*	2 mg/kg PO daily CrCl 10-50 mL/min: 75% of dose CrCl < 10 mL/min: 50% of dose	**BOXED WARNING** Malignancy (especially lymphomas) **WARNINGS** Severe N/V/D, hematologic (leukopenia, thrombocytopenia, anemia) toxicities, hepatotoxicity, infections; patients with genetic deficiency of thiopurine methyltransferase (TPMT) are at ↑ risk for myelosuppression and may require lower dose. **SIDE EFFECTS** N/V/D, rash, ↑ LFTs, myelosuppression **MONITORING** LFTs, CBC, renal function **NOTES** Pregnancy Category D
Mycophenolate mofetil *(CellCept)* Off-label	Initial: 1-3 grams PO daily (can be divided BID) in combination with a glucocorticoid for 6 months Maintenance: 0.5-3 grams daily (can be divided BID)	See Transplant chapter

Agents Used in SLE Continued

DRUG	DOSING	SAFETY/SIDE EFFECTS/MONITORING
CycloSPORINE *(Gengraf, Neoral, SandIMMUNE)* Off-label	Initial: 4 mg/kg PO daily for 1 month; reduce dose by 0.5 mg/kg every 2 weeks until maintenance dose Maintenance: 2.5-3 mg/kg PO daily	See Transplant chapter

IgG1-lambda monoclonal antibody that prevents the survival of B lymphocytes by blocking the binding of soluble human B lymphocyte stimulator protein (BLyS) to receptors on B lymphocytes. This reduces the activity of B-cell mediated immunity and the autoimmune response.

| Belimumab *(Benlysta)* | 10 mg/kg IV Q2 weeks x 3 doses, then Q4 weeks thereafter; infuse over 1 hour

Consider giving pre-medication for infusion reactions and hypersensitivity reactions

Stable in NS only | **WARNINGS**
Serious (sometimes fatal) <u>infections</u>, PML, acute hypersensitivity reactions, malignancy, psychiatric events

SIDE EFFECTS
Infections, nausea, diarrhea, fever, depression, insomnia

NOTES
Live vaccines should not be given 30 days prior or concurrently with therapy.

MedGuide required

Pregnancy Category C |

MULTIPLE SCLEROSIS

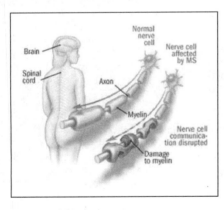

Background

Multiple sclerosis (MS) is a chronic, progressive autoimmune disease in which the patient's immune system attacks the myelin sheath, the fatty substance that surrounds and insulates nerve fibers, of the axons in the brain and spinal cord (CNS). As demyelination progresses, the symptoms worsen because the nerves can no longer properly conduct electrical transmission. Similar to other autoimmune conditions, most patients experience periods of disease activity followed by intervals of remission. The presentation is highly variable with some patients having a much more aggressive course while others have occasional discrete attacks.

Early symptoms include fatigue, weakness, tingling, numbness and blurred vision. As the condition worsens, a variety of physical and psychological issues can make life very challenging, including deterioration of cognitive function, muscle spasms, pain, incontinence, depression, heat sensitivity, sexual dysfunction, difficulty walking and gait instability and visual disturbances. If left untreated, about 30% of patients will develop significant physical disability. Up to 10% of patients have a milder phenotype in which no significant physical disability develops, although these patients may develop mild cognitive dysfunction. Male patients with primary progressive MS generally have the worst prognosis. Symptoms are characterized as primary (due to demyelination, such as muscle weakness), secondary (which result from primary symptoms, such as incontinence due to muscle impairment) and tertiary, which involve psychological and social concerns, such as depression.

MS occurs in both men and women, but (also similar to other autoimmune conditions) is more common in women (ratio 2:1). The typical age of onset is between 20 to 40 years old. Various tests are performed to make a diagnosis including magnetic resonance imaging (MRI), spinal fluid analysis and evoked potentials (tests that measure electrical conduction of the brain). A primary goal of therapy is prevention of disease progression; what is lost in neuronal function cannot be regained. The agents that can modify disease progression are costly. The beta interferons cost about $40,000/year. The newer oral immune modulator fingolimod costs about $48,000/year. The newest agent, dimethyl fumarate, costs about $60,000/year.

Drug Treatment

Medications are used to modify disease, treat relapses, and manage symptoms. Mitoxantrone (*Novantrone*) is a chemotherapeutic agent that may be used for MS and is approved for this condition; a review of mitoxantrone can be found in the Oncology II chapter. Steroids are used to help with relapses. Corticotropin (*HP Acthar*) can be administered SC or IM daily for 2 – 3 weeks. Other drugs used for various related symptoms are summarized at the end of this chapter, and detailed information on these agents can be found in other chapters.

Disease-Modifying Therapies

Interferon beta formulations (*Betaseron, Avonex, Rebif, Extavia, Plegridy*) and glatiramer acetate (*Copaxone, Glatopa*) have been the mainstay of treatment for patients with relapsing forms of MS. Fingolimod (*Gilenya*) and teriflunomide (*Aubagio*) were the first oral disease-modifying agents to be approved for MS. In 2013, a third oral agent, dimethyl fumarate (*Tecfidera*) was approved. Pegylated interferon beta (*Plegridy*) was approved in 2014. It allows for more convenient SC dosing every 14 days. If these are not effective the monoclonal antibodies or chemotherapy drugs can be tried; these have significant toxicities and are used in refractive cases.

If the drug is a powder that is reconstituted, the drug powder may require refrigeration or be kept at room temperature. If a drug is reconstituted, immediate use is necessary (at most within a few hours; a few reconstituted injections permit short storage in the refrigerator). Some of the powders that are reconstituted contain albumin and some patients will not wish to or cannot use albumin-containing products.

DRUG	DOSING	SAFETY/SIDE EFFECTS/MONITORING

Glatiramer acetate is an immune modulator thought to induce and activate T-lymphocyte suppressor cells in relapsing form of MS. Exact mechanism not well-defined.

Glatiramer acetate (Copaxone, Glatopa) Pre-filled syringes (20 and 40 mg/mL), these are not interchangeable	20 mg SC daily or 40 mg SC 3 times per week (at least 48 hours apart)	**WARNINGS** Immediate post-injection reaction, chest pain, lipoatrophy **SIDE EFFECTS** Injection site reactions (inflammation, erythema, pain, pruritus, residual mass), infection, pain, flushing, diaphoresis, dyspnea, weakness, anxiety, rash, nausea, nasopharyngitis, vasodilation, antibody development **NOTES** Pregnancy Category B. Check solution for discoloration; if present, discard. Can be kept at room temp for up to one month, or in the refrigerator (preferred). If cold, let stand to room temp for 20 minutes prior to injecting.

Multiple Sclerosis Drugs Continued

DRUG	DOSING	SAFETY/SIDE EFFECTS/MONITORING

Interferons have antiviral and antiproliferative effects. They reduce antigen presentation and T-cell proliferation, alter cytokine and matrix metalloproteinase (MMP) expression, and restore suppressor function.

DRUG	DOSING	SAFETY/SIDE EFFECTS/MONITORING
Interferon beta-1a *(Avonex, Avonex Pen, Rebif, Rebif Rebidose)* Powder (for reconstitution), pre-filled syringe and pen	**Target Dose** *Avonex* IM: 30 mcg <u>weekly</u> *Rebif* SC: 22 mcg or 44 mcg <u>three times per week</u> (at least 48 hours apart)	**WARNINGS** Psychiatric disorders (depression/suicide), injection site necrosis, myelosuppression, ↑ LFTs, thyroid dysfunction (hyper and hypo), infections, anaphylaxis, worsening cardiovascular disease, seizure risk **SIDE EFFECTS** <u>Flu-like symptoms</u> following administration (lasting min to hrs and ↓ with continued treatment - can use acetaminophen or NSAIDs prior to injection or start with lower doses titrating weekly to target dose)
Interferon beta-1b *(Betaseron, Extavia, Betaconnect)* Powder (for reconstitution), and auto-injector	**Target Dose** SC: 0.25 mg <u>every other day</u>.(use within 3 hrs of reconstitution)	<u>Injection site reactions</u>: mild erythema to severe skin necrosis Visual disturbances, fatigue, depression, pain, urinary tract infections, HA **MONITORING** LFTs, CBC (at 1, 3 and 6 months, then periodically); thyroid function every 6 months (in patients with thyroid dysfunction or as clinical necessary)
Peginterferon beta-1a *(Plegridy, Plegridy Starter Pack)* Pre-filled syringe and pen	**Target Dose** SC: 63 mcg on Day 1, 94 mcg on Day 15, then 125 mcg <u>every 14 days</u> starting on Day 29	**NOTES** Pregnancy Category C. Refrigerate all except *Betaseron* and *Extavia* (which can be stored at room temp). <u>If refrigerated, let stand to room temp prior to injection. Do not expel small air bubble in pre-filled syringes due to loss of dose</u>. Do not shake *Avonex, Betaseron or Extavia*. Some formulations contain albumin – risk of Creutzfeldt-Jakob disease transmission (rare); avoid in albumin-sensitive patients. MedGuide required.

Oral Immune Modulators

DRUG	DOSING	SAFETY/SIDE EFFECTS/MONITORING
Teriflunomide *(Aubagio)* Tablet Active metabolite of leflunomide	7 mg or 14 mg PO daily	**BOXED WARNINGS** Severe hepatotoxicity and teratogenicity **CONTRAINDICATIONS** Severe hepatic impairment, pregnancy, current leflunomide treatment **WARNINGS** Severe infections, peripheral neuropathy, neutropenia, hypertension, serious risk reactions (SJS/TEN), interstitial lung disease Upon discontinuation, can use accelerated drug elimination procedure to remove drug - see leflunomide in this chapter **SIDE EFFECTS** ↑ LFTs, alopecia, diarrhea, nausea, hypophosphatemia, HA, renal impairment **MONITORING** LFTs and bilirubin (within 6 months of starting and monthly for 6 months), SCr, BUN, BP, CBC, s/sx of infection **NOTES** Pregnancy Category X MedGuide required

Multiple Sclerosis Drugs Continued

DRUG	DOSING	SAFETY/SIDE EFFECTS/MONITORING
Fingolimod *(Gilenya)* Capsules	0.5 mg PO daily Blister packs; protect from moisture Patient must be monitored for at least 6 hours after the first dose	**CONTRAINDICATIONS** Recent (within the last 6 months) MI, unstable angina, stroke, TIA, HF requiring hospitalization, or NYHA Class III/IV HF; history of 2nd or 3rd degree heart block or sick sinus syndrome (without a functional pacemaker), QTc interval ≥ 500 msec, concurrent use of Class Ia or III anti-arrhythmics **WARNINGS** Bradycardia (must monitor), BP, macular edema, PML, infections, posterior reversible encephalopathy syndrome (PRES - rare but can cause stroke/hemorrhage), decrease in pulmonary function tests, hepatotoxicity **SIDE EFFECTS** Headache, diarrhea, flu-like syndrome, back pain, ↑ LFTs, cough, hypertension, nausea, abdominal pain **MONITORING** CBC (baseline and periodically thereafter); ECG (baseline; repeat after initial dose observation period); HR, BP and s/sx of bradycardia (hourly at least for first 6 hrs); if pre-existing cardiac condition, perform continuous ECG monitoring overnight after first dose Eye exam at baseline and 3-4 months after initiation of treatment **NOTES** Pregnancy Category C Avoid live vaccines until 2 months after stopping treatment Caution when used with drugs that slow HR, monitor continuous ECG overnight after first dose if concomitant use is necessary MedGuide required
Dimethyl fumarate *(Tecfidera)* Capsules	120 mg PO BID for 7 days, then 240 mg BID Do not crush, chew, or sprinkle capsule contents on food	**WARNINGS** PML, anaphylaxis and angioedema, and lymphopenia/infection risk Flushing: can give aspirin 30 min prior and administer with food to prevent flushing **SIDE EFFECTS** Flushing, N/V/D, abdominal pain **MONITORING** CBC **NOTES** Pregnancy Category C

Multiple Sclerosis Drugs Continued

DRUG	DOSING	SAFETY/SIDE EFFECTS/MONITORING

Dalfampridine: Potassium channel blocker that may increase nerve signal conduction; indicated to improve walking. Takes up to 6 weeks to show efficacy; most patients do not respond.

DRUG	DOSING	SAFETY/SIDE EFFECTS/MONITORING
Dalfampridine (*Ampyra*) Tablet	10 mg BID Take tablets whole; do not crush, chew, divide, or dissolve	**CONTRAINDICATIONS** History of seizures, CrCl ≤ 50 mL/min **WARNINGS** Seizures can occur especially with higher doses, anaphylaxis **SIDE EFFECTS** Urinary tract infections, insomnia, dizziness, HA, nausea, weakness, back pain **MONITORING** ECG, walking ability, SCr (baseline and annually) **NOTES** Pregnancy Category C MedGuide required

Monoclonal Antibodies

DRUG	DOSING	SAFETY/SIDE EFFECTS/MONITORING
Natalizumab (*Tysabri*) Injection (IV) Monoclonal antibody that binds to the alpha-4 subunit of integrins expressed on the surface of leukocytes	300 mg IV given over 1 hour, every 4 weeks Stable in NS only REMS: Only available through the TOUCH prescribing program	**BOXED WARNING** PML - risk factors include anti-JC virus antibodies, duration of therapy and prior use of immunosuppressants. **CONTRAINDICATIONS** History of PML **WARNINGS** Herpes encephalitis and meningitis, hepatotoxicity, immunosuppression/ infections **SIDE EFFECTS** Infusion-related reactions, HA, fatigue, arthralgia, UTIs, vaginitis, nausea, depression, gastroenteritis, abdominal pain, diarrhea **MONITORING** Baseline brain MRI if PML suspected, LFTs, hypersensitivity reactions for 1 hour after infusion **NOTES** MedGuide required Pregnancy Category C

Multiple Sclerosis Drugs Continued

DRUG	DOSING	SAFETY/SIDE EFFECTS/MONITORING

Recombinant humanized monoclonal antibody

Alemtuzumab *(Lemtrada)* Injection (IV) CD52-directed cytolytic monoclonal antibody *Campath* - for leukemia	First course: 12 mg IV (over 4 hours) daily x 5 days Second course: 12 mg IV daily x 3 days <u>12 months after first course</u> <u>Total duration of therapy is 24 months</u> Pre-medicate with 1 gram methylprednisolone (or equivalent) immediately prior to the infusion and for the first 3 days	**BOXED WARNINGS** Serious, sometimes fatal, autoimmune conditions; serious infections; serious and fatal cytopenias; serious, sometimes fatal, infusion reactions; malignancies REMS program: only available through *Lemtrada* REMS **CONTRAINDICATIONS** HIV (causes prolonged ↓ CD4 count) **SIDE EFFECTS** <u>Rash, HA,</u> fever, fatigue, insomnia, urticaria, pruritus, N/V/D, arthralgia, pain, paresthesia, dizziness, flushing **MONITORING** CBC with differential and SCr (initial and monthly until 48 months after last infusion), TSH, ECG, HPV screen, baseline and annual skin exams (for melanoma) **NOTES** Indicated for those with inadequate response to ≥ 2 MS drugs. Complete all vaccinations 6 weeks before therapy. Start <u>antiviral prophylaxis</u> on first day of each course and continue for 2 months or until CD4 count ≥ 200 (whichever is later). Do not shake. MedGuide required. Pregnancy Category C.

Glatiramer Counseling

- This medication is given by injection under the skin as directed by your healthcare provider. This medication is available in 2 different doses. Depending on your dose, this medication is injected daily or 3 times a week at least 48 hours apart. Administer consistently on the same three days each week (e.g., M, W, F schedule).

- Common side effects include redness, warmth and itchy skin where you inject. Other common side effects include sweating, chest pain, weakness and anxiety. These should be mild; if they are not, contact your healthcare provider.

- The syringes can be kept at room temperature for up to one month. If it has been in the refrigerator keep the syringe at room temperature for 20 minutes. Do not inject the medication cold because this will be painful. This liquid in the syringe should be clear and colorless to slightly yellow. If particles or discoloration are present, do not use it.

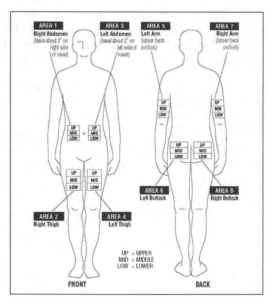

- Change the injection site daily to prevent skin problems (rotate injection sites between your arms, abdomen, hips and thighs). Keep track of your injections and do not inject into the same site for at least 1 week.

- After pulling out the needle, apply gentle pressure on the injection site. Do not rub the area. Discard any unused portion after a single use and put the used syringe into a sharps container.

Fingolimod Counseling

- An electrocardiogram (ECG) is performed before your first dose; once you take the medication, your pulse and blood pressure will be checked frequently and the ECG will be repeated 6 hours later. This is to check your heart rate to make sure it does not go too low.

- It is important not to take other drugs that lower your heart rate with this medication; discuss any questions about other drugs with your pharmacist.

- If you miss a dose, take it as soon as you remember but skip it if it is getting close to the next dose.

- Keep the capsules in the original container. This medication needs to be kept away from moisture. Do not store in the bathroom.

- Contact your healthcare provider right away if you are passing brown or dark-colored urine, have pale stools, feel more tired than usual or if your skin and/or whites of your eyes become yellow. These may be symptoms of liver damage.

- This drug has a risk of causing vision problems, including blurry vision, eye pain, increased sensitivity to light, or having a blind spot or shadows in the center of your vision (vision problems may occur 3 to 4 months after you start taking fingolimod). If you develop any vision problems tell your healthcare provider right away.

Drugs Used for Symptom Control

Patients with MS may use <u>a variety of medications for symptom control</u>. The individual agents used can be found in different chapters in this book. Commonly used symptom-control agents for MS include anticholinergics for incontinence, laxatives for constipation (or loperamide if diarrhea), skeletal muscle relaxants for muscle spasms/spasticity, or various pain agents for muscle spasms and pain. For localized pain and spasms botulinum toxin (*Botox*) injections can provide relief for up to three months. Propranolol can help with tremor. For depression many antidepressants are used; if an SNRI is chosen it may help both neuropathic pain and depression. Fatigue is often treated with modafinil or similar agents, or stimulants used for ADHD, such as methylphenidate. Meclizine and scopolamine are used for dizziness and vertigo. Acetylcholinesterase inhibitors, including donepezil, are used to help cognitive function. Erectile dysfunction can be treated with the phosphodiesterase inhibitors.

<u>Notice that the drugs used for symptom control can worsen other symptoms.</u> For example, anticholinergics can mildly worsen cognitive function (not all of them do, and this is patient-specific), but it happens. The vertigo agents can worsen cognitive function. Propranolol can worsen cognitive function, depression and cause problems with sexual performance. The SSRI and SNRI antidepressants can worsen sexual concerns. Opioids, if used for pain, will worsen constipation, can decrease cognition and have dependence concerns. Managing the various medications used for MS requires competent pharmacists.

RAYNAUD'S PHENOMENON

Raynaud's is a common condition which does not have drug tables discussed separately because the drugs used for treatment are common and are used for several other conditions. It is useful to know the presentation and which drugs are used for symptom relief. Raynaud's is triggered by exposure to cold and/or stress, which causes vasospasm in the extremities (most commonly in the fingers and/or toes). Laboratory findings that can signify other autoimmune conditions are generally absent. The vasospasm causes the skin to turn white and then blue, which is followed by painful swelling when the affected areas warm. The calcium channel blocker (CCB) nifedipine is commonly used for prevention – other CCBs can be used. Additional agents used for vasodilation include iloprost, topical nitroglycerin and the phosphodiesterase-5 inhibitors. Various other classes are used less commonly.

CELIAC DISEASE

Background

Celiac disease (celiac sprue) is an immune response to eating gluten, a protein found in wheat, barley and rye. The primary and effective treatment is to avoid gluten entirely. Gluten is present in many foods, food additives and in many drug excipients. Pharmacists assist patients in avoiding gluten-containing drugs completely, even a small exposure will trigger a reaction. To emphasize this point, the FDA permits food products to be labeled "gluten-free' only if the food contains less gluten than 20 parts per million.

The common symptoms of celiac disease are diarrhea, abdominal pain, bloating and weight loss. Constipation (rather than diarrhea) can be present, and is more common in children. Vitamin deficiencies are common due to decreased absorption in the small intestine. Other complications include nutritional deficiencies, small bowel ulcers, amenorrhea and infertility, and increased risk of cancer (primarily lymphomas). Ninety-five percent of cases will respond well to dietary changes, although avoiding gluten entirely is not a simple task.

Dermatitis herpetiformis is an extremely itchy, blistery skin rash with chronic eruptions that is present in 20-25% of celiac patients, and occurs more often in males. The rash can be present with or without overt intestinal symptoms. The rash is often mistaken for eczema or psoriasis which leads to a delay in diagnosis and treatment.

Treatment

The FDA has strict regulations regarding the active ingredients in drug formulations, but there is little oversight for the excipients in a formulation, making the identification of gluten difficult. The active drug is gluten-free, however the excipients may contain gluten. And, it is not safe to assume that the generic formulations will contain the same excipients as the brand; there is no legal requirement to match the excipients.

Package inserts may contain information on the excipient components. Look for the key work "starch" which will be either corn, potato, tapioca or wheat. If the package insert lists "starch" alone then the manufacturer must be consulted to find out if the starch is wheat. The manufacturer may report that they do not use gluten in the manufacturing process, but they cannot state whether the excipients purchased from outside vendors are gluten-free; there may be cross-contamination. The risk of cross-contamination is low, but not absent, and this information should be provided to the patient who ultimately must decide, hopefully in consult with the prescriber, whether to take the drug or not.

SJÖGREN'S SYNDROME

Sjögren's syndrome is an autoimmune disease, most often characterized by severe dry eyes and dry mouth. Many other symptoms can be associated with Sjögren's, including thyroiditis, Raynaud's phenomenon, neuropathy, and lymphadenopathy. Sjögren's syndrome can be primary or secondary, associated with another autoimmune disease such as RA or SLE. Dry mouth and dry eyes are a source of significant morbidity for these patients and can lead to complications such as dental caries, corneal ulceration and chronic oral infections. There is no known cure for Sjögren's; therefore, treatment focuses on reducing the symptoms of dry eyes and dry mouth.

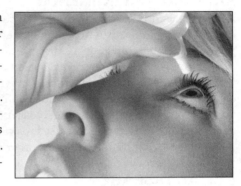

Dry Eyes Treatment

The use of artificial teardrops is the primary treatment for dry eyes. Popular OTC artificial teardrops available are *Systane, Refresh, Clear Eyes* and *Liquifilm*.

It may be necessary to try a couple of different OTC eye drops before finding one that provides the most comfort. If the preservative is irritating (likely benzalkonium chloride) preservative-free artificial tear drops packaged in individual use containers are available. If the eyes dry out while sleeping, an ointment is preferable.

Cyclosporine eye drops (*Restasis*) can be used in patients who do not have satisfactory relief from other measures, including ductal occlusion (lacrimal duct plugs). *Restasis* provides benefit for a small percentage of users and is expensive. Patients should be instructed to monitor a reduction in symptoms and a reduction in the use of OTC eye drops and to use properly to avoid infection, which is more likely due to the dry eye state. Counsel patients that it may take up to 3 – 6 months to notice an increase in tear production.

Eye Drops for Dry Eyes

DRUG	DOSING	SAFETY/SIDE EFFECTS/MONITORING
CycloSPORINE Emulsion Eye Drops (*Restasis*)	1 drop in each eye Q12H	**SIDE EFFECTS** Burning, stinging, redness, pain, blurred vision, foreign body sensation, discharge, itching eye **NOTES** Pregnancy Category C. Prior to use, invert the vial several times to make uniform emulsion. One single-use vial is to be used immediately after opening in one or both eyes, and the remaining contents should be discarded immediately after administration. Do not allow the tip of the vial to touch the eye or any surface, as this can contaminate the emulsion. Remove contact lenses prior to administration, re-insert 15 min afterwards. Separate from artificial tears by 15 min.

Dry Mouth Treatment

Non-drug treatment for dry mouth includes salivary stimulation, using sugar-free chewing gum (with xylitol) and lozenges, and daily rinses with antimicrobial mouthwash. Salivary substitutes are available in lozenges, rinses, sprays, and swabs (*Plax, Oralube, Salivart*). These contain carboxymethylcellulose or glycerin. If OTC treatments do not provide sufficient relief, prescription muscarinic agonists such as pilocarpine or cevimeline (*Evoxac*) can be used. <u>Glycopyrrolate</u> is an anticholinergic agent used to <u>decrease excessive salivation</u>; this may be used in a few conditions, such as myasthenia gravis. Check that the dry mouth is not due to inappropriate use of glycopyrrolate.

Muscarinic Agonists for Dry Mouth

DRUG	DOSING	SAFETY/SIDE EFFECTS/MONITORING
Pilocarpine (*Salagen*) Tablet **Pilocarpine ophthalmic** (*Isopto Carpine, Pilopine HS*) is used for glaucoma	5 mg PO four times daily Fat decreases absorption, avoid taking with a high-fat meal	**CONTRAINDICATIONS** Uncontrolled asthma, narrow-angle glaucoma **MONITORING** Intraocular pressure, fundoscopic exam, visual acuity testing **SIDE EFFECTS** Diaphoresis, flushing, nausea, urinary frequency, chills, weakness, rhinitis, dizziness **NOTES** Pregnancy Category C
Cevimeline (*Evoxac*) Capsule	30 mg PO TID	**CONTRAINDICATIONS** Uncontrolled asthma, narrow-angle glaucoma, acute iritis **SIDE EFFECTS** Diaphoresis, nausea, URTIs (sinusitis, rhinitis) **NOTES** Pregnancy Category C

PSORIASIS

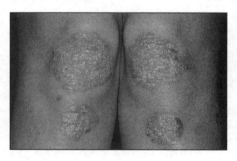

Background

Psoriasis is a chronic, autoimmune disease that appears on the skin. There are several types of psoriasis. The most common is plaque psoriasis, which appears as <u>raised, red patches</u> covered with a <u>silvery white buildup</u> of dead skin cells, on any part of the body. Treatments can be divided into three main types: topical, light therapy, and systemic medications. Most psoriasis is treated with topicals and UV light therapy. Soaking helps loosen and remove the plaques.

Non-Drug Treatment

Ultraviolet (UV) light exposure causes activated T cells in the skin to die. This slows skin turnover and ↓ scaling and inflammation. Brief, daily exposures to small amounts of sunlight can improve psoriasis, but intense sun exposure can worsen symptoms and cause skin damage. UVB phototherapy, in controlled doses from an artificial source, can improve mild to moderate psoriasis symptoms. Other non-drug treatments include photochemotherapy (ultraviolet A light with psoralen, a light sensitizer), and laser light therapy.

Drug Treatment

There are many topical options for treating psoriasis including steroids, vitamin D analogues (calcipotriene), anthralin, topical retinoids (some of the same drugs used for acne), salicylic acid (primarily in medicated shampoo), coal tar and moisturizers. If these fail, calcineurin inhibitor topicals (*Protopic, Elidel*) can be tried. Treatment for more severe symptoms may require immune suppressing agents, including methotrexate, cyclosporine, hydroxyurea and the immunomodulators, such as etanercept and infliximab. Newer systemic agents approved for plaque psoriasis include *Stelara, Otezla, and Cosentyx.*

DRUG	DOSING	SAFETY/SIDE EFFECTS/MONITORING
Topical Steroids	Monotherapy: 1-2 times daily (product dependent)	Use high-potency steroids only short-term due to risk of side effects. Can be used with other therapies See Common Skin Conditions chapter
Retinoids Tazorotene *(Tazorac)*		See Common Skin Conditions chapter
Coal tar, in many products, including *Neutrogena T, Denorex, Psoriasin, Pentrax Gold* Topical (cream, foam, emulsion, ointment, oil, shampoo), bath products (topicals, bar soap) + salicylic acid (*Sebutone, Tarsum, X-Seb T*, others)	Body: Apply 1-4 times per day, usually at bedtime Scalp psoriasis: Apply sparingly to lesions 3-12 hrs before each shampoo	<u>Coal tar products</u> are <u>messy</u>, time consuming and can stain clothing and bedding. Some patients get relief at a reasonable cost. Also used for dandruff and dermatitis Do not use salicylic acid products with other salicylates, systemic absorption can occur **SIDE EFFECTS** Skin irritation, photosensitivity
Anthralin (*Zithranol, Dritho-Crème HP*, others)	Body: once daily or as directed	Keratolytic with irritant potential, ↑ contact time as tolerated up to 30 min
Calcipotriene (*Dovonex, Calcitrene, Sorilux*) Cream, foam, ointment, solution + betamethasone (*Taclonex* ointment, *Taclonex* scalp suspension, *Enstilar* foam)	Plaque psoriasis: Cream, foam, solution: Apply BID Ointment: Apply daily-BID *Taclonex*: Apply once daily for up to 4 weeks for ointment or up to 8 weeks suspension. Do not use > 100 g ointment weekly or use on > 30% of BSA	**CONTRAINDICATIONS** Avoid in hypercalcemia or vitamin D toxicity, do not use on face **NOTES** Vitamin D analog If suspension shake well Do not apply to face, axillae or groin
Acitretin (*Soriatane*) Tablet	25-50 mg daily with main meal of the day (lower doses ↓ side effects)	**BOXED WARNING** Hepatotoxicity, pregnancy, female (must sign informed consent before dispensing) **NOTES** Used <u>only in severe cases</u> when patient is unresponsive to other therapies due to numerous contraindications and side effects Pregnancy Category X MedGuide required

Psoriasis Drugs Continued

DRUG	DOSING	SAFETY/SIDE EFFECTS/MONITORING
Ustekinumab *(Stelara)* Injection Monoclonal antibody	Plaque psoriasis ≤ 100 kg: 45 mg SC at 0 and 4 weeks, then every 12 weeks thereafter > 100 kg: 90 mg SC at 0 and 4 weeks, then every 12 weeks thereafter Avoid injecting into areas where psoriasis is present. Do not shake. Requires protection from light prior to administration.	**WARNINGS** Serious infections (including active TB, fungal, viral, bacterial or opportunistic infections; screen for latent TB and treat before starting therapy, no live vaccines, reversible posterior leukoencephalopathy syndrome (RPLS), lymphomas and other malignancies. **SIDE EFFECTS** Infection, headache, fatigue, diarrhea **NOTES** Pregnancy Category B
Apremilast *(Otezla)* Tablet Phosphodiesterase-4 inhibitor	10 mg daily in the morning, titrate daily to 30 mg BID ↓ dose in severe renal impairment	**WARNINGS** Depression and suicidal ideation, weight loss **SIDE EFFECTS** Diarrhea, N/V, headache **NOTES** Pregnancy Category C
Secukinumab *(Cosentyx)* Prefilled syringe	300 mg SC at weeks 0, 1, 2, 3, and 4, then every 4 weeks thereafter Each dose is given as two SC injections of 150 mg Requires refrigeration. Avoid injecting into areas where psoriasis is present. Do not shake. Bring to room temperature before injecting.	**WARNINGS** Serious infections (including active TB); screen for latent TB and treat before starting; exacerbation of Crohn's disease, latex hypersensitivity, avoid live vaccines **SIDE EFFECTS** Diarrhea, URTIs **NOTES** Pregnancy Category B

Apremilast Drug Interactions

- Apremilast is a major CYP450 3A4 substrate. Strong 3A4 inducers should be avoided concomitantly.

PRACTICE CASE

PATIENT PROFILE

Patient Name	Jennifer Cranford						
Address	4780 Valley Drive						
Age	46	Sex	F	Race	Height	5'3"	Weight 140 lbs
Allergies							

DIAGNOSES

Rheumatoid Arthritis
Hypertension
Depression

MEDICATIONS

Date	No.	Prescriber	Drug & Strength	Quantity	Sig	Refills
5/1/15	48201	Pepper	Lisinopril 20 mg	30	1 PO daily	9
5/1/15	48202	Pepper	Methotrexate 7.5 mg	8	2 tabs weekly	3
5/1/15	48290	Pepper	Prednisone 10 mg	30	1 PO daily	3
5/1/15	51025	Lai	Alendronate 70 mg	4	1 PO weekly	5
			Calcium 500+ D 400 IU	OTC	1 tab daily	

LAB/DIAGNOSTIC TESTS

Test	Normal Value	Results Date 5/22/15	Date	Date
Rheum Fact	<40 IU/mL	88		
ESR	≤30 mm/hr	81		
Alk Phos	33-115 u/L			
AST	10-35 IU/L	48		
ALT	6-40 mEq/L	82		
GLU	65-99 mg/dL			
NA	135-146 mEq/L			
K	3.5-5.3 mEq/L			
CL	98-110 mEq/L			
HCO3-	22-28 mEq/L			
BUN	7-25 mg/dL			
Creatinine	0.6-1.2 mg/dL			
Calcium	8.6-10.2 mg/dL			
WBC	4-11 cells/mm^3	6.5		
TB test, PPD		Negative		

ADDITIONAL INFORMATION

Date	Notes
6/14/15	BP on this visit is 129/85 mmHg. Patient reports morning stiffness for past 2 months which improves as the day progresses. Reports wrists, arms and feet joints are sore and tender and is tired all the time. No chest pain or breathing problems reported.

Questions

1. The prescriber is deciding whether to change the dose of methotrexate to daily therapy or begin etanercept. Choose the correct response:

   a. The methotrexate can be increased safely to 50 mg daily for rheumatoid arthritis.

   b. The methotrexate can be increased safely to 100 mg daily for rheumatoid arthritis.

   c. The methotrexate can be increased safely to 150 mg daily for rheumatoid arthritis.

   d. The methotrexate can be increased safely to 200 mg daily for rheumatoid arthritis.

   e. Methotrexate is not given daily for this.

2. The pharmacist will counsel the patient on her methotrexate therapy. She should include the following counseling points: (Select **ALL** that apply.)

   a. Common side effects include GI upset, nausea and diarrhea.

   b. She should not get pregnant while using this medication.

   c. Her liver will need to be checked periodically with a blood test.

   d. Choose a day of the week that you will remember to take the medicine.

   e. She should be taking leucovorin as well.

3. The patient is using prednisone 10 mg daily and weekly bisphosphonate therapy. Choose the correct statement:

   a. She does not need supplemental calcium and vitamin D with the alendronate.

   b. The prednisone may improve her blood pressure control

   c. If she is able, her healthcare provider should try and help her decrease the prednisone dose.

   d. Prednisone is not bad for bones; in fact, it builds strong bones.

   e. A, B and C.

4. The physician decides to begin etanercept therapy. Choose the correct administration route for this medication:

   a. Oral tablets

   b. Suppository

   c. Subcutaneous injection

   d. Intramuscular injection

   e. Intravenous infusion

Questions 5-7 are NOT based on the above case.

5. The pharmacist will counsel the patient on the etanercept therapy. She should include the following counseling points: (Select **ALL** that apply.)

   a. Store the medication in the freezer.

   b. Inject subcutaneously in the deltoid muscle.

   c. This medication can activate latent tuberculosis; you will need to have a TB test prior to starting therapy.

   d. This medication does not cause increased risk of infections, except for tuberculosis.

   e. You can receive live vaccines, but not the annual influenza vaccine.

6. A physician has written a prescription for *Humira*. Choose the appropriate therapeutic interchange:

   a. Adalimumab

   b. Etanercept

   c. Rituximab

   d. Anakinra

   e. Infliximab

7. A physician has written a prescription for *Remicade*. Choose the appropriate therapeutic interchange:

   a. Adalimumab

   b. Etanercept

   c. Rituximab

   d. Anakinra

   e. Infliximab

Answers

1-e, 2-a,b,c,d, 3-c, 4-c, 5-c, 6-a, 7-e

TRANSPLANT

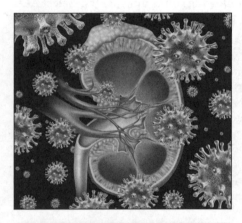

GUIDELINES/REFERENCES

Kidney Disease: Improving Global Outcomes (KDIGO) Transplant Work Group. KDIGO clinical practice guideline for the care of kidney transplant recipients. *Am J Transplant*. 2009; 9 (Suppl 3):S1-155.

Lucey MR, Terrault N, Ojo L et al. Long-Term Management of the Successful Adult Liver Transplant: 2012 Practice Guideline by AASLD and the American Society of Transplantation. http://www.aasld.org/sites/default/files/guideline_documents/managementadultltenhanced.pdf (accessed 2015 Sep 13).

Costanzo MR, Dipchand A, Starling R et al. The International Society of Heart and Lung Transplantation Guidelines for the care of heart transplant recipients. *J Heart Lung Transplant*. 2010; 29:914-56.

We gratefully acknowledge the assistance of Heather R. Bream-Rouwenhorst, PharmD, BCPS, Clinical Assistant Professor, University of Iowa College of Pharmacy, in preparing this chapter.

BACKGROUND

Transplantation is one of the most challenging and complex areas of modern medicine. Some of the key areas for medical management are the problems of transplant rejection, during which the body has an immune response to the transplanted organ, possibly leading to transplant failure and the need to immediately remove the organ from the recipient. The majority of transplant cases are kidneys (1st) and livers (2nd), in addition to others such as pancreases, hearts, lungs, etc. Prior to any transplant, tissue typing or crossmatching is performed to assess donor-recipient compatibility for human leukocyte antigen (HLA) and ABO blood group. A mismatch in either instance would lead to a fast, acute rejection. This is followed by a Panel Reactive Antibody (PRA) test that is taken to gauge the degree to which the recipient is "sensitized" to foreign (or "non-self") proteins. A high score correlates with the likelihood of graft rejection and could necessitate some type of desensitization protocol prior to the transplant. Patients with a higher PRA result are likely to wait longer for a suitable donor.

An allograft is the transplant of an organ or tissue from one individual to another of the same species with a different genotype. This can also be called an allogenic transplant or homograft. A transplanted organ from a genetically identical donor (such as an identical twin) is called an isograft. An autograft is when a tissue is a transplant from one site to another on the same patient, also termed autologous transplant (or autologous stem cell transplant).

AVOIDING AN "ABO MISMATCH" OR INCOMPATIBILITY REACTION

Type A blood will react against type B or type AB blood.

Type B blood will react against type A or type AB blood.

Type O blood will react against type A, type B, or type AB blood.

Type AB blood will not react against type A, type B, or type AB blood.

Type O blood does not cause an immune response when it is received by people with type A, type B, or type AB blood. This is why type O blood cells can be given to patients of any blood type. People with type O blood are called "universal donors."

However, type O can only receive type O blood.

Hyperacute rejection occurs in the operating room within hours of the transplant and is due to some type of mismatch; no treatment exists, and the transplanted organ must be removed to avoid death.

Induction immunosuppressant therapy is given before or at the time of transplant to prevent an acute rejection during the early post-transplant period by providing a high degree of immune suppression. It consists of a short course of very effective intravenous (IV) agents using either a biological drug or monoclonal antibody (these end in -mab) sometimes combined with high-dose IV steroids. The most commonly used induction drug is basiliximab, an interleukin-2 (IL-2) receptor antagonist. The IL-2 receptor is expressed on activated T-lymphocytes and is a critical pathway for activating cell-mediated rejection. As an alternative to basiliximab, patients at higher risk of rejection will receive the lymphocyte-depleting agent antithymocyte globulin. In some cases, induction can be achieved with higher doses of the same drugs used for maintenance. Induction agents may not be required if the transplant is from an identical twin.

Maintenance immunosuppressant therapy is generally provided by the combination of:

- A calcineurin inhibitor (CNI; tacrolimus is the 1st line CNI), plus:
  - An antiproliferative agent (mycophenolate is 1st line in most protocols), or everolimus, sirolimus, belatacept or azathioprine.
  - ± steroids (typically prednisone).

If the patient is low immunological risk, the steroids will be discontinued; otherwise, they are not, and the long-term adverse effects will need to be considered. Suppressing the immune system via multiple mechanisms through different drug classes is designed to both lower toxicity risk of the individual immunosuppressants and to reduce the risk of graft rejection.

Cardiovascular Disease: The Common Cause of Death in Transplant Patients

A concerted effort must be made to reduce risk factors for cardiovascular disease (CVD). This is challenging considering that the patient is using transplant-rejection drugs that cause metabolic syndrome. Nonetheless, these patients are among the highest risk for CVD, and blood pressure, blood glucose, cholesterol and weight must be tightly controlled. For instance, in a renal transplant patient, the blood pressure must be well-controlled with goals provided by the transplant center. Specific goals based on transplant protocols are managed by specialists, including pharmacists, that specialize in transplant medicine. Blood glucose is managed to the ADA guidelines and cholesterol to the NCEP guidelines. Weight is measured at each visit, with reduction programs used as-needed. Refer to the individual chapters for treatment of these conditions.

Cancer: Higher Risk in Transplant Patients

Cancer risk is higher in transplant recipients compared to the general population. Some cancer types are viral-mediated and related to the immune suppression, which causes increased cancer incidence. The cancer risk is similar to that seen with the use of the stronger agents used for autoimmune conditions. For example, the Epstein-Barr virus infects most people without serious consequences. In transplant recipients, there is a marked increase in the risk of malignancies associated with the infection. Age-appropriate cancer screening should be performed prior to getting on the list as a transplant candidate, and post-transplant, according to nationally recognized guidelines. Screening for common cancers should be routine, along with lifestyle measures known to reduce risk. Skin cancer is common with transplant, and sunscreen must be used routinely, along with sun avoidance or sun protection with clothing. In addition, CNIs cause photosensitivity. The skin should be assessed professionally at least annually.

TRANSPLANT DRUGS: WHAT'S USED, WHEN

Immunosuppression protocols will vary by center and type of transplant.

Induction Drugs, to avoid acute early rejection are either:
Basiliximab, an interleukin-2 (IL-2) receptor antagonist (the primary induction agent), or antithymocyte globulin in patients at higher risk of rejection, or the maintenance drugs at higher doses.

Primary Immunosuppressive Drugs
The calcineurin inhibitors (CNIs), which are tacrolimus (primarily) or cyclosporine.

Adjuvant Agents (given with the primary drugs), also called Antiproliferative or Antimetabolite Agents
Given with the CNI (to enable lower doses of the CNI to reduce nephrotoxicity risk). These include steroids, azathioprine or mycophenolate mofetil (*CellCept*). The majority of transplant patients use a CNI + *CellCept* ± steroids. Or, patients may be using one of the drugs that bind to the mTOR protein (such as everolimus) to reduce the CNI nephrotoxicity risk. This class may act synergistically with the CNIs.

With the use of adjuvants, adequate immunosuppression can be achieved while decreasing the dose and toxicity of the individual agents.

Infection Risk Reduction
Protocols for which prophylactic drugs to use will vary by the transplant center and the type of transplant. Vaccines are discussed in a separate sidebar. Opportunistic infections use the same treatments as used for HIV; refer to Infectious Disease IV.

All transplant recipients must self-monitor for symptoms of infection: fever of 100.5°F (38°C) or higher (or lower if elderly), chills, sore throat, ear or sinus pain, cough, more sputum or change in color of sputum, pain with passing urine, mouth sores, or a wound that will not heal.

Monitoring by Patient & Health Care Team

Monitoring Questions
Is it a symptom of drug **toxicity**?

Is it a symptom of **organ rejection**?

Is it a symptom of an **infection**?

In addition to drug toxicity symptoms, patients will need to monitor for symptoms of organ rejection. Common symptoms of an acute rejection include flu-like symptoms, such as chills, body aches, nausea, cough, shortness of breath and organ-specific symptoms that depend on the transplant type. For example, heart failure symptoms or a new arrhythmia could be due to a heart transplant rejection, and a decrease in urine output/fluid retention/blood pressure elevation/graft tenderness could be due to a kidney transplant rejection.

All immunosuppressive agents require careful monitoring (including drug trough levels) to minimize toxicities and decrease the incidence of rejection. Keep in mind which maintenance agents have the highest incidence of nephrotoxicity (tacrolimus, cyclosporine), the most likely to worsen diabetes or cause new-onset diabetes (tacrolimus, steroids, cyclosporine, the most likely to worsen lipid parameters (mTOR inhibitors, steroids, cyclosporine) and which are most likely to cause hypertension (steroids, cyclosporine, tacrolimus).

Reducing Infection Risk

The use of potent drugs has made solid organ transplant widely available and successful. However, the use of strong agents correlates with infection risk. The majority of infections are opportunistic, and these are a major cause of death in transplant recipients. Opportunistic infections are caused by organisms that are ubiquitous (everywhere) in the environment, but rarely cause disease in the immunocompetent host (persons with a functional immune system). Infection prophylaxis is essential; review the basics in the sidebars. Infection control must include reducing risk from transmission, such as proper hand-washing techniques (see Medication Safety chapter), air filtration systems, keeping the mouth clean, and keeping away from dusty, crowded areas and sick people. Often the drugs used for opportunistic infection prophylaxis are used for treatment, but in larger doses and possibly given IV. Treatment may require drugs used in combination. Vaccine-preventable illness is an important consideration pre-transplant since live vaccines cannot be given post-transplant.

VACCINE-PREVENTABLE ILLNESS

Required vaccines should be given pre-transplant if the recipient is not current. The inactivated vaccines can be given post-transplant in 3-6 months (once the immune system has recovered from the induction immunosuppression), if needed; live vaccines cannot be given post-transplant.

Influenza (inactivated, not live) annually (recurring, each October-November) should be given when the vaccine is available.

Pneumococcal vaccine in adults ≥ 19 years who are immunocompromised: receive PCV13 first, followed by PPSV23 at least 8 weeks later. Subsequent doses of PPSV23 should follow current PPSV23 recommendations for adults at high risk (5 years after the first PPSV23 dose). Some transplant centers recommend PPSV23 every 5 years.

Transplant patients are at high risk for serious varicella infections, with a very high risk of disseminated disease with a primary infection. The best protection is to vaccinate the close contacts (in addition to the recipient pre-transplant). Although there is a small risk that transmission could occur (from the vaccine recipient to the transplant recipient), ACIP states that "the benefits of vaccinating susceptible household contacts of immunocompromised persons outweigh the potential risk for transmission of vaccine virus to immunocompromised contacts."

If a vaccinated household contact develops a rash they are considered contagious. They should avoid contact with the transplant recipient and should contact their physician. If the transplant patient develops a rash, they will need to be seen right away.

INDUCTION AGENTS

DRUG	SAFETY/SIDE EFFECTS/MONITORING

Antithymocyte globulins – reverse rejection by binding to antigens on T-lymphocytes (killer cells) and interfering with their function. These drugs are made by injecting human T-lymphocytes into animals, allowing the animals to make antibodies against the T-lymphocytes, and then administering the animals' purified antibodies back to the human transplant recipients. Because they deplete both mature and immature T-lymphocytes, they may be used for both induction and treatment of rejection.

Antithymocyte Globulin *(ATGAM-Equine)* *(Thymoglobulin-Rabbit)*	**BOXED WARNING** Should be administered under the supervision of a physician experienced in immunosuppressive therapy. Adequate laboratory and supportive medical resources must be readily available (e.g., epinephrine). Anaphylaxis (intradermal skin testing recommended prior to 1st dose). **SIDE EFFECTS** Infusion-related reactions (fever, chills, pruritus, rash, hypotension; particularly common with the first dose), leukopenia, thrombocytopenia, chest pain, hypertension, edema and others **MONITORING** Lymphocyte profile (T-cell count), CBC with differential, vital signs during administration **NOTES** Pre-medicate (diphenhydramine, acetaminophen and steroids) to lessen infusion-related reactions. Epinephrine and resuscitative equipment should be nearby. There is a difference in dosing. Normal equine doses are approximately 10-fold greater than the rabbit product (10-15 mg/kg/day vs. 1-1.5 mg/kg/day IV, respectively, for 5-14 days).

Interleukin 2 (IL-2) receptor antagonist – Chimeric (murine/human) monoclonal antibody that inhibits the IL-2 receptor on the surface of activated T-lymphocytes preventing cell-mediated allograft rejection. Basiliximab does not deplete immature T-lymphocytes and therefore cannot be used for treatment of rejection. Because the protein is humanized, infusion-related reactions are unlikely, and pre-medication is generally not necessary.

Basiliximab *(Simulect)* Dosing: 20 mg IV post-op day 1 then repeat dose 4 days after transplant	**BOXED WARNING** Should only be used by physicians experienced in immunosuppressive therapy. **SIDE EFFECTS** Well tolerated; side effects listed are rated as severe and >10%: hypertension, fever, weakness, stomach upset/nausea/vomiting/cramping, peripheral edema, dyspnea/upper respiratory irritation/infection, cough, tremor, painful urination **MONITORING** Signs and symptoms of hypersensitivity and infection.

MAINTENANCE MEDICATIONS

DRUG	DOSING	SAFETY/SIDE EFFECTS/MONITORING

Systemic steroids – naturally occurring hormones that prevent or suppress inflammation and humoral immune responses

PredniSONE, others	2.5-5 mg PO daily, or on alternate days (dose individualized to patient's history of rejection and other factors)	**SHORT-TERM SIDE EFFECTS** Fluid retention, stomach upset, emotional instability (euphoria, mood swings, irritability), insomnia, ↑ appetite, weight gain, acute rise in blood glucose and blood pressure with high dose **LONG-TERM SIDE EFFECTS** Adrenal suppression/Cushing's syndrome, impaired wound healing, hypertension, diabetes, acne, osteoporosis, impaired growth in children. See Autoimmune chapter for further information on chronic steroid use.

Antiproliferative Agents – inhibit T-lymphocyte proliferation by altering purine synthesis

Mycophenolate Mofetil (*CellCept*) **Mycophenolic Acid (*Myfortic*)**	1-1.5 g PO/IV BID *(Cellcept)* or 360-720 mg PO BID *(Myfortic)*, depending on transplant type	**BOXED WARNINGS** ↑ risk of infection; ↑ development of lymphoma and skin malignancies; ↑ risk of congenital malformations and spontaneous abortions when used during pregnancy; should only be prescribed by healthcare providers experienced in immunosuppressive therapy. **SIDE EFFECTS** Diarrhea, GI upset, vomiting, leukopenia, hyper- and hypotension, edema, tachycardia, pain, hyperglycemia, hypo/hyperkalemia, hypomagnesemia, hypocalcemia, hypercholesterolemia, tremor, acne, infections **MONITORING** CBC, intolerable diarrhea, renal function, LFTs, signs of infection **NOTES** *CellCept* and *Myfortic* should not be used interchangeably due to differences in absorption. Myfortic is enteric coated to decrease diarrhea (1% absolute difference in rates of reported diarrhea with *Cellcept* vs. *Myfortic*). Protect tablets from moisture and light. *CellCept IV* is stable in D5W only. Do not use IV if allergy to polysorbate 80. Should be taken on an empty stomach to avoid variability in absorption. Pregnancy Category D, and decreases efficacy of oral contraceptives.

Maintenance Medications Continued

DRUG	DOSING	SAFETY/SIDE EFFECTS/MONITORING
AzaTHIOprine (***Azasan, Imuran***)	1-3 mg/kg PO daily, for maintenance	**BOXED WARNINGS** Chronic immunosuppression can ↑ risk of neoplasia (esp. lymphomas); hematologic toxicities (leukopenia, thrombocytopenia) and mutagenic potential. **WARNINGS** GI (severe N/V/D), hematologic (leukopenia, thrombocytopenia, anemia) and hepatotoxicity; patients with genetic deficiency of thiopurine methyltransferase (TPMT) are at ↑ risk for myelosuppression and may require lower dose. **SIDE EFFECTS** GI upset (N/V), rash, ↑ LFTs, myelosuppression **MONITORING** LFTs, CBC, renal function **NOTES** Pregnancy Category D

Calcineurin inhibitors – suppress cellular immunity by inhibiting T-lymphocyte activation

DRUG	DOSING	SAFETY/SIDE EFFECTS/MONITORING
Tacrolimus (***Prograf**, Astagraf XL, Envarsus XR*) *Protopic* – topical for eczema	Initial: 0.1-0.2 mg/kg/day PO (depending on transplant type) in 2 divided doses for *Prograf*, given every 12 hours Goal trough level varies, dependent on: 1. Transplant type 2. Time since transplant 3. Concurrent medications 4. Center's protocol Goal trough 3-15 ng/mL	**BOXED WARNINGS** ↑ susceptibility to infection; possible development of lymphoma; should be administered under the supervision of a physician experienced in organ transplantation in a facility appropriate for monitoring and managing therapy; extended-release tacrolimus associated with increased mortality in female liver transplant recipients (*Astagraf XL*) **SIDE EFFECTS** Hypertension, nephrotoxicity, hyperglycemia, neurotoxicity, (tremor, headache, dizziness, parasthesias), hyperkalemia, hypomagnesemia, edema, chest pain, insomnia, generalized pain, rash/pruritus, diarrhea, abdominal pain, nausea, dyspepsia, anorexia, constipation, urinary tract infection, anemia, leukopenia, leukocytosis, thrombocytopenia, elevated liver enzymes, arthralgia, hypophosphatemia, hyperlipidemia, QT prolongation **MONITORING** Trough levels, serum electrolytes (K and Mg), renal function, LFTs, BP, blood glucose, lipid profile **NOTES** Consistently take with or without food; food decreases absorption. Higher fat food decreases absorption the most. Do not interchange XL to immediate release. PO IR doses are 3-4 times that of IV. Start oral dosing 8-12 hours after last IV dose. Numerous drug interactions: this is a CYP 3A4 and P-gp substrate. Avoid alcohol.

Maintenance Medications Continued

DRUG	DOSING	SAFETY/SIDE EFFECTS/MONITORING
CycloSPORINE (modified: *Neoral, Gengraf;* **non-modified:** *SandIMMUNE)* *Restasis* – drops for dry eyes	Dose depends on transplant type and formulation Cyclosporine (modified): initial dosing of ~8 ± 4 mg/kg/day, divided BID and then individualized to achieve target trough level Cyclosporine (non-modified): 3-10 mg/kg/day, divided BID, for maintenance, individualized to achieve target trough level IV cyclosporine (*Sandimmune*) is available; the IV dose is 1/3 of the PO dose Conversion to cyclosporine (modified) from cyclosporine (non-modified): Start with daily dose previously used and adjust to obtain pre-conversion cyclosporine trough concentration; monitor every 4-7 days and dose adjust as necessary Goal trough 100-400 ng/mL (nephrotoxicity can occur at any level)	**BOXED WARNINGS** Renal impairment (with high doses); ↑ risk of lymphoma and other malignancies; ↑ risk of skin cancer; ↑ risk of infection; may cause hypertension; dose adjustments should only be made under the direct supervision of an experienced physician, cyclosporine (modified – *Gengraf/Neoral)* has 20-50% greater bioavailability compared to cyclosporine (non-modified – *Sandimmune)* and cannot be used interchangeably. **SIDE EFFECTS** Hypertension, nephropathy, hyperkalemia, hypomagnesemia, hirsutism, gingival hyperplasia, edema, hyperglycemia, neurotoxicity (tremor, headache, paresthesia), abdominal discomfort/nausea/diarrhea, photosensitivity, increased triglycerides, viral infections, QT prolongation **MONITORING** Trough levels, serum electrolytes (K and Mg), renal function, LFTs, BP, blood glucose, lipid profile **NOTES** Numerous drug interactions: this is a CYP 3A4 and P-gp substrate.

Mammalian target of rapamycin (mTOR) kinase inhibitor which inhibits T-lymphocyte activation and proliferation; **may be synergistic with CNIs**

DRUG	DOSING	SAFETY/SIDE EFFECTS/MONITORING
Everolimus *(Zortress, Afinitor)* *Afinitor Disperz* is available for treatment of breast, pancreatic, and renal cancers	Initial: 0.75-1 mg PO BID; adjust maintenance dose if needed to reach serum trough of 3-8 ng/mL	**BOXED WARNINGS** Only experienced prescribers should prescribe everolimus; ↑ risk of infection and cancers; reduced doses of cyclosporine are recommended when used concomitantly; ↑ risk of renal thrombosis may result in graft loss; not recommended in heart transplant. **SIDE EFFECTS** Peripheral edema, constipation, hypertension, hyperglycemia, hyperlipidemia/hypertriglyceridemia, impaired wound healing, pneumonitis (discontinue drug if this develops), proteinuria, fatigue, fever, headache, rash/pruritus, xeroderma, acne, onychoclasis (nail disease), abdominal discomfort, nausea, stomatitis, diarrhea, dysgeusia, weight loss, dry mouth, anemia, lymphocytopenia, thrombocytopenia, risk of renal and hepatic artery thrombosis (do not use within 30 days of transplant), angioedema **MONITORING** Trough levels, renal function, LFTs, lipids, blood glucose, BP, CBC, signs of infection **NOTES** Everolimus is metabolized by CYP 3A4; concomitant use of inducers or inhibitors will necessitate everolimus dose adjustments.

Maintenance Medications Continued

DRUG	DOSING	SAFETY/SIDE EFFECTS/MONITORING
Sirolimus (*Rapamune*)	Usually 1-5 mg/day Serum trough concentrations should be determined 3-4 days after loading doses and 7-14 days after dosage adjustments; approximate range 4-12 ng/mL, level dependent on concurrent drug use, including potent inhibitors or inducers of CYP 3A4 or P-gp.	**BOXED WARNINGS** ↑ risk of infection; ↑ risk of lymphoma; not recommended for use in liver transplantation (hepatic artery thrombosis); not recommended for use in lung transplantation (anastomotic dehiscence) **SIDE EFFECTS** Impaired wound healing, irreversible pneumonitis/bronchitis/cough (discontinue therapy if this develops), hyperglycemia, hyperlipidemia, peripheral edema, hypertension, headache, pain, insomnia, acne, constipation, abdominal pain, diarrhea, nausea, anemia, thrombocytopenia, arthralgia **MONITORING** Trough levels, LFTs, renal function, blood glucose, lipids, BP, CBC, signs of infection **NOTES** Tablets and oral solution are not bioequivalent due to differences in absorption. Sirolimus is metabolized by CYP 3A4; concomitant use of inducers or inhibitors will necessitate sirolimus dose adjustments.

Belatacept binds to CD80 and CD86 to ultimately block T-cell costimulation and production of inflammatory mediators

DRUG	DOSING	SAFETY/SIDE EFFECTS/MONITORING
Belatacept (*Nulojix*) Administer with silicone-free disposable syringe (comes with drug)	Initial: 10 mg/kg on days 1, 5 and then at the end of weeks 2, 4, 8, and 12 after transplantation Maintenance: 5 mg/kg at the end of week 16 after transplantation and then monthly thereafter Dose using TBW and round dose to the nearest 12.5 mg	**BOXED WARNINGS** Increased risk of post-transplant lymphoproliferative disorder (PTLD) with highest risk in recipients without immunity to Epstein-Barr Virus (EBV). Use in EBV seropositive patients only. Increased susceptibility to infection and malignancies; avoid use in liver transplant patients due to risk of graft loss and death; should be administered under the supervision of a prescriber experienced in immunosuppressive therapy. **WARNINGS** Increased risk of opportunistic infections, sepsis, and/or fatal infections. Increased risk of tuberculosis (TB); test patients for latent TB prior to initiation, and treat latent TB infection prior to use **SIDE EFFECTS** Headache, anemia, leukopenia, constipation, diarrhea, nausea, peripheral edema, hypertension, cough, photosensitivity, insomnia, urinary tract infection, pyrexia, hypo/hyperkalemia **MONITORING** New-onset or worsening neurological, cognitive, or behavioral signs/symptoms (consider progressive multifocal leukoencephalopathy (PML), post-transplant lymphoproliferative disorder (PTLD), or CNS infection); signs/symptoms of infection, TB screening prior to therapy initiation, EBV seropositive verification prior to therapy initiation

Drug Interactions

Transplant drugs affect the levels of each other and the following interactions must be considered: Cyclosporine will ↓ mycophenolate and ↑ sirolimus and everolimus (and will increase some of the statins, which transplant patients are usually taking). Both cyclosporine and tacrolimus are CYP 3A4 and P-glycoprotein (P-gp) substrates. Inducers of either enzyme (examples: carbamazepine, nafcillin, rifampin, etc.) will decrease the CNI concentration, and inhibitors (examples: azole antifungals, diltiazem, erythromycin, etc.) will increase the CNI concentration. Both will interact with the majority of drugs. Consistency is essential; the drug dose will be adjusted to the trough level. Tacrolimus absorption is decreased by food; take with or without, but be consistent.

- Azathioprine is metabolized by xanthine oxidase. The dose will need to be reduced by 75% if concomitant allopurinol, a xanthine oxidase inhibitor, is used. ACE inhibitors should not be used with allopurinol due to a risk of severe anemia. Using allopurinol with other drugs that may cause myelosuppression (such as sulfamethoxazole/trimethoprim) should be undertaken cautiously.

- Mycophenolate – can ↓ levels of hormonal contraception; mycophenolate levels can be ↓ by antacids and multivitamins, cyclosporine, metronidazole, PPIs, quinolones, sevelamer, bile acid resins, and rifampin and derivatives. Monitor for additive myelosuppression when using mycophenolate with other marrow suppressing drugs.

- Avoid grapefruit juice and St. John's wort with either CNI.

- Caution with additive drugs that are nephrotoxic with tacrolimus and cyclosporine.

- Caution with additive drugs that raise blood glucose with tacrolimus, steroids, cyclosporine and the mTOR inhibitors (everolimus/sirolimus).

- Caution with additive drugs that worsen lipids with the mTOR inhibitors, steroids and cyclosporine.

- Caution with additive drugs that raise blood pressure with steroids, cyclosporine and tacrolimus.

Patient Counseling for All Immunosuppressants

- Take the medication exactly as prescribed by your healthcare provider. It is important that you take your medication at the same time every day. Also, stay consistent on how you take your medication.

- Never change or skip a dose of medication. Remember, if you stop taking your immunosuppressive medications, your body will reject your transplanted organ.

- Monitor your health at home and keep daily records of your temperature, weight, blood pressure, and glucose (if diabetes is present).

- Do not take any NSAIDs (e.g., *Advil, Naprosyn, Aleve*) as these drugs could cause harm to your kidney.

- Do not take any over-the-counter, herbal, or alternative medications without consulting with your healthcare provider.

- Do not get immunizations/vaccinations without the consent of your healthcare provider. The use of live vaccines should definitely be avoided. Avoid contact with people who have recently received oral polio vaccine, nasal flu vaccine, or zoster vaccine.

- Patients are vulnerable to developing infections (severe infections) due to their suppressed immune system. Avoid contact with people who have the flu or other contagious illness. Practice infection control techniques such as good hand washing and staying away from sick people.

- Chronic immunosuppression has been associated with an increased risk of cancer, particularly lymphoma and skin cancer. Protect and cover your skin from the sun. Be sure to use sunscreen with an SPF of 30 or higher. Avoid using tanning beds or sunlamps. People who take immunosuppressive agents have a higher risk of getting skin cancer.

- If getting a blood test to measure the drug level, take your medication after you had your blood drawn (not before). It is important to measure the lowest (trough) level of drug in your blood.

Patient Counseling for Mycophenolate

- Take <u>exactly</u> as prescribed, every 12 hours (8 AM and 8 PM). It is important that you take your medication at the same time every day.

- If you miss a dose and it is <u>less than 4 hours after the scheduled dose, take the missed dose</u> and continue on your regular schedule. If you miss a dose and it is <u>more than 4 hours after your scheduled dose, skip the missed dose</u>, and return to your regular dosing schedule. Never take 2 doses at the same time. Record any missed doses.

- Take capsules, tablets and oral suspension <u>on an empty stomach</u>, either 1 hour before or 2 hours after a meal.

- Do not open or crush tablets or capsules. If you are not able to swallow tablets or capsules, your healthcare provider may prescribe an oral suspension. Your pharmacist will mix the medicine before giving it to you.

- Do not mix the oral suspension with any other medicine.

- This medication can cause <u>diarrhea</u>. Call your healthcare provider right away if you have diarrhea. Do not stop the medication without first talking with your healthcare provider. Other side effects include nausea, vomiting, abdominal pain/cramping, headache, and decreased white blood cells and platelets.

- Do not get pregnant while taking this medication. Women who take this medication during pregnancy have a higher risk of losing a pregnancy (miscarriage) during the first 3 months (first trimester), and a higher risk that their baby will be born with birth defects. Birth control pills do not work as well with this drug.

- <u>Do not take with antacids or multivitamins concurrently. Separate the doses by 2 hours. Avoid use with bile acid resins.</u>

- <u>Limit the amount of time you spend in sunlight.</u> Avoid using tanning beds or sunlamps. Use sunscreen with a SPF of 30 or higher. People who take this medicine have a higher risk of getting skin cancer.

- <u>Mycophenolic acid *(Myfortic)* and mycophenolate mofetil *(CellCept)* are not interchangeable. Do not switch between products unless directed by your healthcare provider. These medicines are absorbed differently. This may affect the amount of medicine in your blood.</u>

Patient Counseling for Tacrolimus

- Take this medication as directed by your healthcare provider, usually every 12 hours. It is best to take on an empty stomach for best absorption. However it is taken, you must be consistent (with food or without food), and take this medication the same way every day so that your body always absorbs the same amount of drug.

- It is important to take all doses on time to keep the amount of medicine in your body at a constant level. Remember to take it at the same times each day. You will need repeated appropriate laboratory tests while receiving tacrolimus; at a minimum, expect a monthly trough level with renal function and electrolyte monitoring. Follow your prescriber's dosage instructions exactly, and do not change your dose without first discussing it with your prescriber. Tacrolimus increases your risk of cancer; do not become pregnant without discussing pregnancy with your prescriber first.

- If you miss a dose and it is <u>less than 4 hours after the scheduled dose, take the missed dose</u> and continue on your regular schedule. If you miss a dose and it is <u>more than 4 hours after your scheduled dose, skip the missed dose</u>, and return to your regular dosing schedule. Never take 2 doses at the same time. Record any missed doses.

- As with other immunosuppressive agents, owing to the potential risk of malignant skin changes, exposure to sunlight and ultraviolet (UV) light should be limited by wearing protective clothing and using a sunscreen with a SPF of 30 or higher.

- Avoid eating grapefruit or drinking grapefruit juice while being treated with tacrolimus. Grapefruit can increase the amount of tacrolimus in your bloodstream. Tacrolimus has many drug interactions; never start or stop any medication without first discussing the change with the transplant team FIRST.

- Tacrolimus may cause your blood pressure to increase. You may be required to check your blood pressure periodically and/or take another medication to control your blood pressure.

- Side effects of tacrolimus also include tremors/shaking, headache, diarrhea, nausea/vomiting, upset stomach, loss of appetite, tingling of the hands/feet, increased blood pressure, increased cholesterol, increased blood sugar, decreased kidney function, and an increase in potassium levels.

- Tacrolimus may cause diabetes. Tell your healthcare provider if you experience any of the following symptoms of high blood sugar: increased thirst/hunger or frequent urination.

- Tacrolimus may cause a condition that affects the heart rhythm (QT prolongation). QT prolongation can infrequently result in serious fast/irregular heartbeat and other symptoms (such as severe dizziness, fainting) that require immediate medical attention.

- High (or low) levels of potassium or magnesium in the blood may also increase your risk of QT prolongation. This risk may increase if you use certain drugs (such as diuretics/"water pills") or if you have conditions such as severe sweating, diarrhea, or vomiting. This drug may increase your potassium and lower your magnesium levels.

Patient Counseling for Cyclosporine (using *Neoral* as an example)

- Because different brands deliver different amounts of medication, do not switch brands of cyclosporine without your prescriber's permission and directions.

- Take *Neoral* on a consistent schedule with regard to time of day and relation to meals. Avoid eating grapefruit or drinking grapefruit juice while being treated with this medication. Grapefruit can increase the amount of the cyclosporine in your bloodstream. Cyclosporine has many drug interactions; never start or stop any medication without first discussing the change with the transplant team.

- If you miss a dose and it is less than 4 hours after the scheduled dose, take the missed dose and continue on your regular schedule. If you miss a dose and it is more than 4 hours after your scheduled dose, skip the missed dose, and return to your regular dosing schedule. Never take 2 doses at the same time. Record any missed doses.

- Repeated laboratory tests (trough blood levels, renal function, and electrolytes) will be needed while you take cyclosporine. If getting a blood test to measure the drug level, take your medication after you had your blood drawn.

- *Neoral* oral solution (cyclosporine oral solution, USP) Modified should be diluted, preferably with orange or apple juice that is at room temperature. Do not administer oral liquid from plastic or styrofoam cup. The combination of *Neoral* Oral Solution (cyclosporine oral solution, USP) Modified with milk can be unpalatable. (*Sandimmune* may be diluted with milk, chocolate milk, or orange juice). Avoid changing diluents frequently. Mix thoroughly and drink at once. Use the syringe provided to measure the dose, mix in a glass container, and rinse the container with more diluent to ensure the total dose was taken.

- Cyclosporine can also cause high blood pressure and kidney problems. The risk of both problems increases with higher doses and longer treatment with this drug.

- Side effects of cyclosporine also include increased cholesterol, headache, nausea, vomiting, diarrhea, stomach upset, increased hair growth on the face/body, tremor, and acne. If any of these effects persist or worsen, notify your healthcare provider promptly.

- This drug may increase your risk for developing skin cancer. Avoid prolonged sun exposure, tanning booths and sunlamps. Use a sunscreen, SPF 30 or higher, and wear protective clothing when outdoors.

- This medication <u>may cause swelling and growth of the gums (gingival hyperplasia).</u> Brush your teeth and floss daily to minimize this problem. See your dentist regularly.

REJECTION

Rejection of the transplanted organ arises from either <u>T-cell (cellular) or B-cell (humoral or antibody) mediated mechanisms.</u> Both types can occur simultaneously. Distinguishing the type of rejection <u>via biopsy</u> is essential in order to determine treatment.

In general, the initial approach is administration of high-dose corticosteroids. For cellular rejection, the steroids and increased levels of maintenance immunosuppression may be adequate to treat the rejection. For steroid-resistant rejection, administration of antithymocyte globulin is often the next step.

Humoral rejection is more challenging to treat as the preformed antibodies against the graft must be removed and then suppressed from recurring. This process if often done via a course of plasmapheresis and administration of immunomodulatory intravenous immunoglobulin (IVIG), followed by a dose of rituximab. Rituximab, a monoclonal antibody against the CD20 antigen on B-cells, will prevent further antibody development.

CONTRACEPTION & INFERTILITY

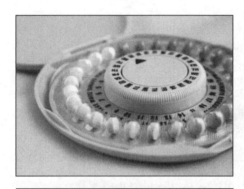

We gratefully acknowledge the assistance of Sally Rafie, PharmD, BCPS, Assistant Clinical Professor, University of California San Diego Skaggs School of Pharmacy and Pharmaceutical Sciences, in preparing this chapter.

BACKGROUND

There are 61 million U.S. women in their childbearing years (ages 15 – 44 years). Seven in 10 women of reproductive age (43 million) are sexually active and do not want to become pregnant, but could become pregnant if they or their partner fails to use a contraceptive method. The typical U.S. woman wants two children. To achieve this goal, she must use contraceptives for roughly three decades of her life.

Among the 43 million women who do not want to become pregnant and are at risk of unintended pregnancy, 68% use some form of contraception correctly and consistently (accounting for 5% of unintended pregnancies), 18% use their contraceptive method incorrectly or inconsistently (accounting for 41% of unintended pregnancies, and 14% do not use any form of contraception or have long gaps in use (accounting for 54% of unintended pregnancies). In the women using contraception, 67% use nonpermanent methods, including hormonal methods (such as the pill, patch, implant, injectable, vaginal ring, and hormonal IUDs) and nonhormonal methods (such as the copper IUD and barrier methods). The remaining women use female or male sterilization. Hormonal methods provide health benefits, including decreased menstrual pain, menstrual irregularity, endometriosis, acne, ectopic pregnancy, noncancerous breast cysts/lumps, and risk of endometrial and ovarian cancer.

Contraceptive choices vary markedly with age. For women in their teens and 20s, the pill is the leading method. Among women 35 years and older, more rely on sterilization, which is often performed post-partum (following a birth). Male contraception options are limited. Presently, male condoms and vasectomy are the only options. A long-acting, nonhormonal contraceptive injection for men is in development.

GUIDELINES/REFERENCES

Emergency Contraception Information
http://ec.princeton.edu/index.html
(accessed 2015 Nov 18).

Association of Reproductive Health Professionals (ARHP)
http://www.arhp.org/topics/contraception
(accessed 2015 Nov 18).

www.plannedparenthood.org
(accessed 2015 Nov 18).
For referrals of low income/lack of insurance to get contraception at reduced or no cost (sliding scale based on inccme).

Centers for Disease Control (CDC)
http://www.cdc.gov/reproductivehealth/
unintendedpregnancy/
contraception.htm and http://
www.cdc.gov/reproductivehealth/
unintendedpregnancy/contraception_
guidance.htm (accessed 2015 Nov 18).

MENSTRUAL CYCLE PHASES AND TEST KITS

A normal menstrual cycle ranges from 23 - 35 days (average 28 days). Menstruation starts on day 1 and typically lasts a few days. Refer to the diagram on female sex hormones and cycle in the Mechanisms chapter.

Ovulation: The mid-cycle luteinizing hormone (LH) surge results in release of the oocyte (egg) from the ovary into the fallopian tube.

The oocyte lives for one day once released. Ovulation kits test for LH and are positive if LH is present. There are also kits to help women track basal body temperature where a spike in temperature predicts ovulation the following day, and can identify a fern-shaped pattern in the saliva that occurs 3 - 5 days prior to ovulation. They predict the best time for intercourse in order to try to conceive (get pregnant).

Pregnancy: A female has the highest chance to become pregnant on days 8 - 16 of her cycle, although pregnancy can occur during any time – no time is considered 100% "safe". Pregnancy test kits are positive if human chorionic gonadotropin (hCG) is present in the urine.

Preconception Health

Teratogens: a drug that is a teratogen can terminate a pregnancy or cause a baby to be born with a birth defect. Medications should be evaluated for teratogens and, if found, these should be discontinued entirely (if possible) or switched to another drug that is safer in pregnancy. Well-known teratogens include alcohol, ACE inhibitors, angiotensin receptor blockers, benzodiazepines, carbamazepine, ergotderivatives, isotretinoin, leflunomide, lithium, methimazole, nafarelin, NSAIDs, paroxetine, phenytoin, phenobarbital, propylthiouracil, quinolones, ribavirin, tazarotene, tetracyclines, topiramate, valproic acid, misoprostol, methotrexate, statins, dutasteride, finasteride, warfarin, lenalidomide and thalidomide. Women considering pregnancy or who are already pregnant should be advised to stop drinking, smoking, and using illicit substances. No amount of alcohol is known to be safe during pregnancy. Refer to the Drug Use in Pregnancy chapter for a further discussion of teratogenic drugs.

Folate Supplementation: Any woman planning to conceive (and all women of child-bearing age) should be taking a folic acid (folate) supplement (400 mcg/

BIRTH CONTROL PILLS: WHAT'S IN A NAME?

0.5/35 (or similar)
Monophasic formulation (progestin/estrogen)

Tri or 7/7/7 or Cycl-
Triphasic formulation

Lo
Low estrogen < 35 mcg

Fe
Contains iron

Progestin only
Often have "nor" in name-for norethindrone (in HRT products "pro" means containing a progestin)

DO NOT USE ANY FORM OF ESTROGEN WITH THESE CONDITIONS

History of blood clot disorders (DVT, PE)

History of stroke or heart attack

Heart valve disease with complications

Severe hypertension

Diabetes for > 20 years or with end organ damage (retinopathy, nephropathy, neuropathy)

Severe headaches (for example, migraines – some forms helpful)

Recent major surgery with prolonged bed rest

Breast cancer

Liver cancer or disease

Uterine cancer or other known or suspected estrogen-dependent cancers

Unexplained abnormal bleeding from the uterus

Jaundice during pregnancy or jaundice with prior hormonal contraceptive use

Known or possible pregnancy

Boxed Warning
Do not use if > 35 years and smoke due to cardiovascular risk (contraindicated)

day) to help prevent birth defects of the brain and spinal cord (neural tube defects). Folate should be taken daily for at least one month before pregnancy and during the entire pregnancy, since it takes time to build up adequate body stores. Folate is in many healthy foods, including fortified cereals, dried beans, leafy green vegetables and orange juice. A couple of the newer combined oral contraceptive pill formulations contain folate – see chart of formulations later in this chapter.

CLOTTING RISK! WATCH FOR HIGH RISK PATIENTS

3 things to keep in mind (in addition to the patient's risk factors):

- Higher estrogen dose, higher clotting risk.

- Drospirenone-containing pills may have higher relative risk for clotting than other progestins; absolute risk is low and is lower than with pregnancy.

- *Ortho Evra* patch: higher systemic estrogen exposure than most COC pills (*NuvaRing* has lower systemic exposure).

FORMULATION CONSIDERATIONS

Breastfeeding
Choose progestin only pill or non-hormonal method 1st 42 days (1st 21 days if no VTE risk factors.

Elevated clotting risk
Avoid drospirenone.

Avoid the *Ortho Evra* patch.

Use lower dose estrogen content.

Choose progestin-only pill or non-hormonal method.

Estrogen contraindication, including clotting risk
Choose progestin-only pill.

Estrogenic side effects
Use low estrogen formulation.

Spotting/"breakthrough bleeding"
(This is more common with *Seasonale*, *Seasonique* and *Amethyst*.) When starting the conventional formulations, wait for three cycles before switching. If early or mid-cycle spotting the estrogen dose may be too low. If later in the cycle the progestin dose may need to be increased.

Avoiding monthly cycle/menses
Use extended (91-day) or continuous formulations. Alternative: monophasic 28-day formulation and skip placebo pills.

Migraine
Choose among various formulations, if with aura choose progestin-only or nonhormonal method.

Fluid retention/bloating
Choose a product containing drospirenone, if low clotting risk. Progestin component helps reduce water retention.

The progestin component is a mild diuretic. It retains potassium, and is contraindicated with renal or liver disease. Check potassium, renal function and use of other potassium-retaining agents.

Premenstrual dysphoric disorder
Choose *Yaz* or sertraline or fluoxetine *(Sarafem)* – see Depression chapter.

Nausea
Take at night, take with food, can consider decreasing estrogen dose or switching to progestin-only or nonhormonal method (ideally after 3 month trial). Change to ring.

Acne
Use COC with lower androgenic activity

Heavy menstrual bleeding
The COC *Natazia* and the levonorgestrel-releasing IUD *Mirena* is indicated for this condition (menorrhagia).

COCs with only 4 placebo pills (rather than 7) or continuous/extended regimens will minimize bleeding. The bleeding loss is slight with the injectables, implants and IUDs.

Before becoming pregnant, a woman should be up-to-date on routine adult vaccines to protect herself and her children. Live vaccines should be given a month or more before pregnancy. Inactivated vaccines can be given before or during pregnancy, if needed. Once pregnant, the inactivated influenza vaccine (the shot) is required, irrespective of the pregnancy trimester. A pregnant woman who contracts influenza is at risk for serious complications and hospitalization. The Tdap vaccine is given between weeks 27 – 36 in each pregnancy, to protect the newborn from pertussis.

EFFECTIVENESS OF CONTRACEPTIVE METHODS

This section focuses on methods that are available as OTC or Rx products in pharmacies. Under the sponge, parous refers to women who have given birth and nulliparous refers to women who have not given birth. Contraceptive methods, except for condoms, do not provide protection from sexually transmitted infections (STIs). Condoms provide some protection. The best protection from STIs (and pregnancy) is abstinence.

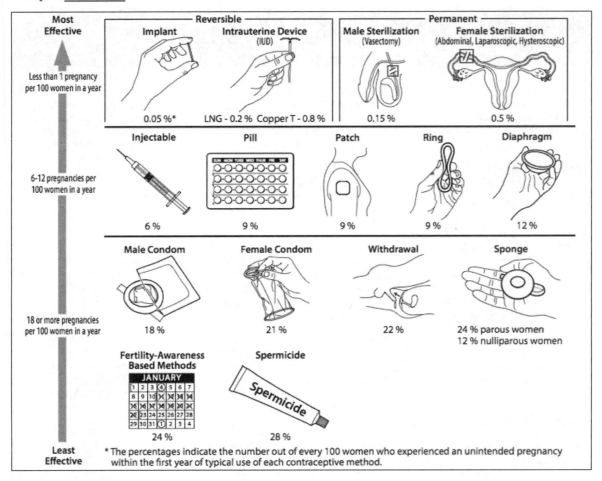

HORMONAL CONTRACEPTIVES

These contain progestin only (pill or injectable) or estrogen/progestin combinations (pills, a patch, and a ring). The patch and the ring have unique considerations (such as how to apply) but contain the same hormones that are present in pill formulations. A contraindication to use of the pill will remain a contraindication for the patch or the ring.

Progestin-only pill (POPs): The use of POPs as a contraceptive method is primarily recommended for lactating (breastfeeding) women, because estrogen reduces the milk production. They are sometimes used for women who cannot tolerate or have a contraindication to estrogen, however they must be taken on a tight schedule and are less "forgiving" if a pill is late or forgotten; it is easier to get pregnant on a POP if the woman is not breastfeeding. They are sometimes used for reduction in premenstrual migraine (a common migraine in women). The POPs are useful for migraine prophylaxis, and are safest for migraines with aura (in this type of migraine, estrogen should not be used due to stroke risk).

Estrogen and progestin combination oral contraceptives (COCs): The primary method of the COCs involves inhibition of follicle stimulating hormone (FSH) and LH production, which in turn prevents ovulation. COCs may also prevent pregnancy by altering the endometrial lining, altering cervical mucus, interfering with fertilization or transport of an egg, or preventing implantation. COCs are used for various indications, including dysmenorrhea, PMS, perimenopausal pregnancy prevention and symptoms (hot flashes, night sweats), anemia due to excessive period-related blood loss, acne (in females), and premenstrual migraine prophylaxis. The use of COCs to regulate menses is first-line treatment for polycystic ovary syndrome (PCOS), a common condition (~15% of women) with a typical presentation of infrequent or prolonged menstrual periods, hirsutism, acne and excessive weight, often with insulin resistance.

Adverse Effects Due to Estrogen

Estrogen can cause nausea, breast tenderness/fullness, bloating, weight gain and elevated blood pressure. The incidence of side effects correlates with the dose; low-dose estrogen formulations are chosen for this purpose, which are generally well-tolerated, but can result in spotting in some women. There can also be insufficient estrogen if the woman is a fast metabolizer, or is using an enzyme inducer. If the spotting

---

ORAL CONTRACEPTIVE TYPES (REPRESENTATIVE LIST)

Monophasic COCs
all active pills with the same level of hormones throughout the 3 active weeks
Alesse, Loestrin, Gildess Fe, Junel Fe 1/20, Sprintec 28 and MonoNessa, Ortho-Cyclen, Yaz

Biphasic or Triphasic ("Multiphasic"); hormone dose changes over the course of 21 days *Kariva, Mircette*

and triphasic forms:
Cyclessa, Ortho-Novum 7/7/7. Ortho Tri-Cyclen Lo, Tri Lo Sprintec, Nortrel 7/7/7, Enpresse

1 formulation is four-phasic *(Natazia)*, with four phases of estradiol valerate and the progestin dienogest

Low-dose pills; less withdrawal symptoms (emotional/physical), less estrogen side effects, including lower clotting risk; these contain 20-35 mcg estrogen (compared to 50 mcg)
Ortho Tri-Cyclen Lo, Lo Loestrin Fe, Gildess Fe, Junel Fe 1/20 Tri Lo Sprintec, Nortrel 7/7/7, Enpresse, Kariva, Mircette, Cyclessa, Ortho-Novum 7/7/7.

Drospirenone formulations (see following page on issues with this progestin)
Yasmin, Yaz, Gianvi, Loryna, Ocella, Zarah, Daylette, Angeliq, Nikki, Safyral, Syeda, Vestura, Beyaz (Safyral & Beyaz contain folate)

Progestin Only Mini-Pills (POPs) with norethindrone
Camila, Micronor, Nor-QD, Nora-BE, Errin, *Heather, Jolivette,* (some names include "nor")

EXTENDED CYCLE COCs
Placebo days are < 1 week (or none at all), either containing norethindrone, drospirenone or levonorgestrel (LNG) with ethinyl estradiol (EE)

24 days active tx + 4 days ferrous fumarate 75 mg (iron takes place of placebo for 4-days hormone-free)
Loestrin 24 Fe, Minastrin 24 Fe (chewable), Lomedia 24 Fe

26 days active tx, 24 days are the same as above followed by 2 days with EE 10 mcg followed by 2 days ferrous fumarate 75 mg
Lo Loestrin Fe, Lo Minastrin Fe

3 months (91 days total) with 84 days of EE 30 mcg/LNG 0.15 mg + 7 days of EE 10 mcg (low dose EE in "placebo" week)
Seasonique, Amethia

Similar to above but lower doses: EE 20 mcg/LNG 0.1 mg in the 84 days, with the same EE 10 mcg in the placebo week
LoSeasonique, Amethia Lo

Continuous EE 20 mcg/LNG 0.09 mg with no placebo. The packets look like regular pill packets; they contain 28 tablets each, all the same – when done, go straight to the next packet, no placebo
Amethyst

(breakthrough bleeding) occurs <u>early</u> or <u>mid-cycle</u>, it may require a higher estrogen dose. The general practice is to wait <u>three monthly cycles</u> prior to changing the dose to see if spotting dissipates.

Serious adverse effects are rare but can include thrombogenic disorders, including heart attack, stroke and DVT/PE. The risk for clotting disorders increases as the woman ages, if she smokes, if she has diabetes or hypertension, if she requires prolonged bed rest, and if she is overweight. Refer to the box on contraindications to estrogen. The progestin drospirenone, as well as the *Ortho Evra* patch (due to a higher systemic estrogen level) are linked to a higher risk of blood clots and are best avoided in at-risk women. Higher dose estrogen formulations have higher risk. When evaluating risks from use of the pill, consider risks with an unintended pregnancy: the risk of blood clots during pregnancy and postpartum is much higher than clotting risk with any birth control pill formulation.

Adverse Effects Due to Progestin

Progestin can cause breast tenderness, headache, fatigue or changes in mood. If <u>late</u> cycle breakthrough bleeding occurs, a <u>higher</u> progestin dose may be required.

The injectable depot medroxyprogesterone acetate can cause a transient loss in bone mineral density. This can be especially important for teens and young women who are still accumulating bone mass. Advise users to supplement their diets as needed to obtain their daily recommended doses of calcium and vitamin D (see recommendations in the Osteoporosis chapter).

Drug Interactions that can Decrease Efficacy of Hormonal Contraceptives

Use back-up while taking the antibiotics listed (with rifampin, use other form of birth control since the induction will last – if switching back, a back-up method needs to be used for 1½ months after rifampin has been discontinued). Rifapentine and rifabutin are also strong inducers. A strong inducer, used long-term, will require an alternate form of birth control, such as condoms/spermicide, an IUD or the birth control injection. The birth control injection does not have drug interactions.

Decreases Hormone Efficacy

- Antibiotics (rifampin, rifapentine, rifabutin); some antibiotics packaging states to use back-up with contraception pills; this list includes agents with evidence of decreased efficacy. If in doubt, it is safest to use back-up.

- Anticonvulsants (barbiturates, carbamazepine, oxcarbazepine, phenytoin, primidone, topiramate and lamotrigine)

- St John's wort

- Ritonavir-boosted protease inhibitors (PIs) Bosentan (*Tracleer*), Mycophenolate (*CellCept, Myfortic*)

- Separate from colesevelam by at least 4 hours. Take at least 1 hour prior to *Byetta* injection.

- Smoking tobacco

The hepatitis C antivirals, *Technivie* and *Viekira Pak*, cannot be used with any formulation containing ethinyl estradiol due to the risk of liver toxicity: With all new drugs being dispensed to a patient using contraception, the package insert should be checked to avoid missing an interaction that could decrease the contraceptive efficacy, or cause toxicity.

POP Start Day Options

- Start at any time. Use another method of birth control for the first 48 hours of progestin-pill use – protection begins after two days. All come in 28-day packs and all pills are active.

- POPs need to take exactly around the same time of day, everyday; if 3 hours have elapsed from the regular scheduled time, back-up is needed for 48 hours after taking the late pill. If a dose is missed, there is a risk of pregnancy and emergency contraception (EC) may be an option.

COC Start Day Options

- Start today. Best practice recommendation. Requires back-up method for 7 days. Maximizes time protected from unintended pregnancy. Known as "quick start."

- Start on the Sunday following the onset of menses (will menstruate during the week – most common start is a Sunday start.) Requires back-up method for 7 days. Avoid Sunday start because requires Sunday refills (problematic if no more refills on prescription).

- Start on 1st day of menses – if COCs are started within five days after the start of the period, no back-up method of birth control is needed; protection is immediate. If not within 5 days, use back-up for first week of use.

Missed COC Pills – Instructions for Typical Formulations

Missed pills (particularly if the seven-day hormone-free interval is extended on either end) are a common cause of contraceptive failure. Unintended pregnancies are often due to picking up the refill late. There may be different instructions in the package insert of the formulation dispensed. These are the standard instructions from the CDC.

PILLS MISSED	NOTES
If **one** pill is **late** (< 24 hours since it should have been taken) or **missed** (24 to < 48 hours since a pill should have been taken)	Take the late or missed dose as soon as possible.
	Continue taking remaining pills at the usual time.
	No back-up contraception needed.
	EC not needed but can be considered if hormonal pills were missed earlier in the cycle or in the last week of the previous cycle and unprotected intercourse occurred in the previous 5 days.
If **two or more** consecutive pills have been **missed** (≥ 48 hours since a pill should have been taken)	Continue taking remaining pills at the usual time (even if it means two pills in one day).
	Use back-up contraception or avoid intercourse for 7 days.
	If hormonal pills were missed in the last week of the cycle:
	Omit the hormone-free interval by finishing the hormonal pills in current pack and start new pack next day.
	If unable to start a new pack, use back-up contraception or avoid intercourse until first 7 days of new pack taken.
	Consider EC if missed pills were during the first week and unprotected intercourse occurred in the previous 5 days.
	Consider EC at other times as appropriate.

Select Different Formulation Overview, Start Day, Gap in Treatment

Seasonale (and generics, several), _Seasonique (Amethia), Lo Seasonique (Amethia Lo)_ contain 91-pills:

- These all contain a 91-day pill regimen with 84 active pills. The difference is the placebo week: _Seasonale_ has 7 days of placebo, and the _Seasonique_-type formulations have 7 days of low dose estrogen. This is not the only formulation where the placebo week has been replaced with low dose estrogen, to decrease symptoms, bleeding and menstrual migraines. These are started on the Sunday after the period starts, even if the patient is still bleeding. If the period began on Sunday, they should start that same day.

- They must use another method of birth control (such as condom or spermicide) as a back-up method if they have sex anytime from the Sunday they start until the next Sunday (the first 7 days). These formulations require that the pill be taken at the same time each day.

COC Counseling

- It is important to take at the same time each day. Have the patient pick the time of day preferred.

Continuous Pills With No Monthly Cycle (*Amethyst*)

- *Amethyst* comes in 28 day packets of all active (yellow) pills, with no placebo pills; the packets are taken continuously. When finished, start the next pack.

- With this formulation, it can be difficult to tell if a woman is pregnant.

- There is a higher discontinuation rate with the continuous formulations than with other COCs, due to spotting; counsel patients that the spotting should decrease over time.

- Beginning: If no previous contraception, begin on the first day of menstrual cycle. If previously taking a 21-day or 28-day combination hormonal contraceptive: Begin on day 1 of the withdrawal bleed (at the latest, 7 days after the last active tablet). If on POP, begin next day after stopping. Back-up is needed for 7-days only after switching from a POP or from an implant or injection.

- Missed doses: If one missed, take as soon as remembered (2 tablets in 1 day), then continue. If more than two missed, see package insert or CDC recommendations. Any missed pills requires back-up for 7 days and may require EC.

Drospirenone Formulations: *Yasmin, Yaz, Gianvi, Loryna, Ocella, Zarah, Daylette, Angeliq, Nikki, Safyral, Syeda, Vestura, Beyaz* (*Safyral* & *Beyaz* contain folate)

These are popular COCs, since they decrease bloating, PMS symptoms and weight gain. This is due to the progestin drospirenone, which is a potassium-sparing diuretic.

- Drospirenone-containing formulations have a risk of increased K^+ and caution must be used with K^+-sparing agents, including aldosterone antagonists, potassium supplements, salt substitutes (KCl), ACE inhibitors, angiotensin receptor blockers, heparin, canaglifozin and calcineurin inhibitors (see hyperkalemia discussion on Renal chapter).

- Avoid use if kidney, liver, or adrenal gland disease. On a case, check the potassium level. It should be in the safe range of 3.5-5 mEq/L.

- This type of progestin has a slightly higher risk of clotting, and should be avoided in women with clotting risk.

Ortho Evra, Xulane Contraceptive Patch

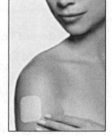

- Thin, beige, plastic patch placed on clean, dry skin of buttocks, stomach, upper arm, or upper torso once a week for 21 out of 28 days. Do not apply to breasts.

- Start on either Day 1 (no back-up needed) or Sunday (back-up 7-days if not day 1).

- If patch becomes loose or falls off > 24 hours during the 3 weeks of use or if > 7 days have passed during the 4th week where no patch is required, there is a risk of pregnancy; thus a back-up method should be used for 1 week while a new patch is put in place.

- Has the same side effects, contraindications and drug interactions as the pills except that the patch causes a higher systemic estrogen exposure; avoid use in anyone with clotting risk factors.

- Less effective in women > 198 pounds. Do not use if smoker and over 35 years old.

NuvaRing Vaginal Contraceptive Ring

- Small flexible ring inserted into the vagina once a month.

- Similar to OCs in that the ring is inserted in place for 3 weeks and taken out for 1 week before replacement with a new ring. The ring can be kept in place for up to 4 weeks for women who want an extended or continuous cycle.

- For starting: insert the ring between day 1 and day 5 of menses.

- Exact position of ring in vagina does not matter.

- If ring is out > 3 hours during week 1, rinse with cool to lukewarm water and reinsert; use back-up method for 1 week while the ring is in place, consider EC if intercourse within last 5 days.

- If ring is out < 3 hours during week 2 or 3, rinse and re-insert ring.

- If ring is out > 3 hours during week 2 or 3, rinse and re-insert ring and use back-up for 7 days.

- If starting 1st cycle of birth control, use back-up method for the 1st week.

- Has the same side effects, contraindications and drug interactions as the pills.

- Patient can store for up to 4 months at room temperature – refrigerated at pharmacy.

Combination Oral Contraceptives Patient Counseling

- The FDA requires that the <u>Patient Package Insert</u> (PPI) be <u>dispensed with oral contraceptives</u> – it will be in the product packaging. The PPI has important safety information and instructions how to use them properly and what to do if pills are missed.

- For the majority of women, birth control pills can be taken safely. But there are some women who are at high risk of developing certain serious conditions that can be life-threatening. The risks increase significantly if you:

  - ❑ Have or have had clotting disorders, heart attack, stroke, angina, cancer of the breast or sex organs, jaundice, or malignant or benign liver tumors.

  - ❑ Smoke; cigarette smoking increases the risk of serious effects on the heart and blood vessels. This risk increases with age and with heavy smoking and is quite marked in women over 35 years of age. Women who use oral contraceptives should not smoke.

- You should not take the pill if you have unexplained vaginal bleeding.

- Most side effects of the pill are mild and not serious. The most common are nausea, bleeding between menstrual periods (spotting), weight gain and breast tenderness. These side effects, especially nausea, often improve after three months of use. Taking the pill with food or at night helps to reduce the nausea.

- For any estrogen-containing product, watch for severe pain in your leg/calf, severe abdominal (stomach) pain, chest pain/shortness of breath/cough, blurred or loss of vision – which can be due to a blood clot. If this occurs you will need to get medical care right away. Make sure to discuss with your pharmacist if you start any new medicines, including over-the-counter products or antibiotics for an infection.

The Shot

- The injection *(Depo-Provera, Depo-subQ Provera)* is depot medroxyprogesterone acetate (DMPA), a progestin. Suppresses ovulation, thickens cervical mucus, and causes thinning of the endometrium.

- Given by IM (150 mg) or SC (104 mg) injection every 3 months.

- Can decrease bone mineral density so all users should be advised to consume recommended daily intake of calcium and vitamin D (see Osteoporosis chapter for recommended daily intake by age). About half of users will be amenorrheic (no menses) after 1 year of use; this is an advantage for some and a disadvantage for others.

ADDITIONAL METHODS OF BIRTH CONTROL AND "SAFE" OR "SAFER SEX"

<u>Abstinence</u> is the only 100% way to prevent pregnancy and STIs. Safer sex recommendations:

- Alcohol and other drugs can make people forget safer sex; avoid use when in high-risk situations.

- Condoms form a barrier between the penis and anus, vagina or mouth. The barrier keeps one partner's fluids from getting into or on the other. Latex or synthetic plastic (not natural sheepskin) condoms must be used for maximum protection. Male or female condoms can be used. Skin-to-skin contact not covered by the condom is not protected from transmission of infection.

- Oral sex is safer than vaginal or anal sex to reduce HIV risk, but will still put the person at risk for herpes, syphilis, hepatitis B, gonorrhea, and HPV. The *Sheer Glyde* dental dam is FDA-approved for safer sex; it blocks passage of infectious organisms during oral contact.

- Lubricant is important for safer sex because it makes condoms and dams slippery and less likely to break by reducing dry friction. Never recommend oil-based lubricant (called "lube") with a latex or non-latex synthetic condom; only recommend water or silicone-based lubricants. These products are discussed in the Osteoporosis chapter.

Condoms

- Male condoms are a thin latex or plastic sheath worn on the penis. Female condoms are inserted into the vagina. Both are OTC and most effective when used with spermicide for contraception. Condoms help protect against many STIs (only if latex or synthetic condoms, not "natural" sheepskin).

- To increase the efficacy for contraception, use with nonoxynol-9 spermicide.

- Do not use spermicide with anal sex. It is irritating and can increase the risk of STIs. Some of the condoms are lubricated with nonoxynol-9.

OTC contraceptive methods (and some condoms) all contain the spermicide nonoxynol-9.

- Available as foams, film, creams, suppositories, and jellies.

- Place deep into the vagina right before intercourse where they melt (except for foam, which bubbles).

Diaphragm, Caps and Shields

These three options are soft latex or silicone barriers that cover the cervix and prevent sperm passage. The new *Caya* diaphragm is a single size and does not require fitting.

Diaphragm Directions for Use

- Wash hands thoroughly.

- Place 1 tablespoon of spermicide in the diaphragm and disperse inside and around the rim.

- Pinch the ends of the cup and insert the pinched end into the vagina.

- Leave in for six hours after intercourse.

- Reapply spermicide if intercourse is repeated, by inserting jelly with applicator.

- Diaphragms should not be in place greater than 24 hours.

- Wash with mild soap and warm water after removal, air dry.

Long-Acting Reversible Contraceptives

- These devices are generally not dispensed from community pharmacies. They must be placed and removed by trained healthcare professionals. They are the most effective forms of contraception that are reversible, and as effective as sterilization.

- Intrauterine devices *(Mirena, Skyla, Liletta)* are both hormonal IUDs. These cause lighter menstrual bleeding and minor or no cramping. *Mirena* is FDA-approved for heavy menstrual bleeding. *Mirena* lasts up to 5 years and *Skyla and Liletta* up to 3 years. About 20% of women using these hormonal IUDs will become amenorrheic.

- The copper-T IUD *(Paragard)* can be used for EC and/or regular birth control, and lasts up to 10 years, but causes heavier menstrual bleeding and cramping, which can be painful. Some women prefer this nonhormonal method.

- Implant *(previously Implanon, now Nexplanon)* is a plastic rod that is placed subdermally *and* releases the progestin etonogestrel for 3 years.

EMERGENCY CONTRACEPTION (EC)

Emergency contraception (EC) is a form of hormonal or nonhormonal contraception that prevents pregnancy after unprotected intercourse. The copper IUD *(Paragard)* is the most effective form of EC if inserted within 5 days. There are two oral EC (also known as the "morning after pill") options, levonorgestrel *(Plan B One-Step)* and ulipristal acetate *(Ella)*, that can be used within 5 days, with effectiveness diminishing over time. This means that the sooner EC is used, the higher the efficacy. The use of higher doses of combination oral contraceptives is no longer a common practice as it is less effective than these options. EC has been available for 30 years and there have been no reports of serious complications or birth defects.

EC can be an important resource after unprotected sex, such as from missed pills, a condom breaking during intercourse, a diaphragm or cap that moved out of place during intercourse, or if a woman may have been sexually assaulted. If sexual assault has occurred the woman may require STI treatment, including HIV prevention and HBV and HPV vaccines. Pharmacists should have referrals for other providers available to provide to patients.

Occasionally, women may be using EC after sex as their regular method of birth control; this may be done when a woman has occasional (not regular) sexual activity and is willing to accept the effectiveness of the method. Depending on insurance coverage, it may also be more expensive. If it is prescribed, it will be covered by insurance plans as required by the Affordable Care Act (ACA), except grandfathered plans, which were included in the ACA without this requirement.

Levonorgestrel

The two common formulations are *Plan B One-Step* and generics, which come as one 1.5 mg tab or two 0.75 mg tabs of levonorgestrel. This formulation of EC reduces the risk of pregnancy by up to 89 percent when started within 72 hours after unprotected intercourse. The sooner it is started, the higher the efficacy.

Plan B One-Step and generics *(Take Action, Next Choice One-Dose, My Way)* are OTC with no age or other restrictions. The pharmacy does not need to be present or open to sell these products. Per the FDA, these should be placed in the OTC aisles with the other family-planning products, such as condoms and spermicides. The generics cost $35 - $45, about $10 less than the brand *Plan B One-Step*. Two-pill generics (levonorgestrel 0.75 mg tablets) are still available only behind the counter without a prescription for ages 17 or older; ages 16 and under still need a prescription. Both sexes require proof of age if getting behind the counter formulations. There is no reason to use a prescription with the formulations available OTC (unless someone wanted the 2 pill formulation), except to use insurance coverage.

If the EC is coming from behind the counter, there is no requirement for purchasers to sign a registry. They can receive multiple packets and the American College of Obstetrics and Gynecologists (ACOG) recommends an additional packet for future use, if needed, since EC is more effective the sooner it is used.

- Mechanism of action: primarily works by preventing or delaying ovulation, but also thickens the cervical mucus.

- This type of EC is indicated for up to 5 days (the sooner, the better) after unprotected intercourse. The package indicates use within 3 days, but is used up to 5 days off-label according to evidence-based guidelines.

- Preferred regimen is 1.5 mg as a single dose (*Plan B One-Step*). Older formulation of two divided doses (0.75 mg) separated by 12 hours is equally effective but can have problems with adherence.

- Primary side effect is nausea, which occurs in 23% of women, and 6% have vomiting. If the women is easily nauseated, an OTC anti-emetic (1 hour prior to use, and caution if driving home due to sedation) should be recommended to avoid losing the dose. If a patient vomits within 2 hours of taking the pill/s, she should consider repeating the dose.

Ulipristal acetate (Ella)

Some patients may not wish to use this EC option because it is a chemical cousin to mifepristone (*Mifeprex*), also known as the "abortion pill" or RU-486. They are not the same drug and are used differently. The mifepristone product available in the US is used for pregnancy terminations only. The dose of ulipristal is much lower potency and is used to delay ovulation. It may also prevent implantation and this is a cause of concern for some.

- Single 30 mg dose. Requires a prescription.

- Works primarily by delaying ovulation. May also prevent implantation in the uterus – this mechanism is more controversial than levonorgestrel.

- Indicated for up to 5 days after unprotected intercourse. More effective than levonorgestrel if 72-120 hours since unprotected intercourse or if woman is overweight.

- Primary side effects are headache, nausea and abdominal pain. Some women have changes in their menstrual cycle, but all should get their period within a week. Can only use once per cycle. Use a barrier method of contraception the rest of the cycle as ovulation may occur later than normal.

Counseling for EC

- If you vomit after taking emergency contraception you may need to take another dose. Before you do, contact a pharmacist or other healthcare provider immediately. If you get easily nauseated, the pharmacist can recommend an OTC medication that helps to lessen nausea that you can use before you take the EC pill.

- If you do not get your period in 3 weeks (or it is more than a week late), a pregnancy test should be taken. If you develop severe abdominal pain or irregular bleeding, you may have an ectopic pregnancy (outside of the uterus) and will need immediate medical attention.

- It is important to visit your healthcare provider for a regular birth control method and information about preventing sexually transmitted infections. If you may have contracted an infection, you should get care right away.

- You may wish to get a package of Emergency Contraception for future use, if needed.

- Regular hormonal contraceptives (OCs, the shot, the ring, the patch), should be started on the same or the following day as taking the EC.

INFERTILITY

Infertility affects 10-15% of persons trying to conceive, or over 2 million American couples annually. One in sixteen babies are now conceived by women using fertility medications. From a business perspective, the sale of infertility medications is profitable. Detailed knowledge of this topic is a "specialty" area; this section provides "basic competency" knowledge.

The chance of pregnancy in couples attempting pregnancy is about 25% per month, and 85% will become pregnant within a year. If pregnancy has not occurred at one year's time, the couple should be referred for medical consultation. Infertility can be due to either the male or female. Males can be contributory due to various problems with sperm production. Females could have one or more contributory factors, including congenital defects, infectious pathogens (including damage from chlamydia or trichomoniasis), abdominal conditions, ectopic pregnancy, scarring from previous surgeries, hypothyroidism or polycystic ovary syndrome (PCOS).

In the beginning part of this chapter there is a brief description of ovulation kits; these are a reasonable place to start, prior to outside referral. Ovulation kits test for luteinizing hormone (LH), which is present in the urine and surges 24-48 hours prior to ovulation. The LH surge triggers the release of an egg from an ovary (ovulation). Ovulation is the most fertile time of the cycle. The three days immediately following the positive result is the highest chance for pregnancy. The kits are simple to use and require either running the test stick under the urine stream, or collecting the urine in a small container and dipping the test strip.

There are other more complex ways to assess ovulation, including testing body temperature, cervical mucus, and using fertility monitors. Any women trying to conceive should have possible teratogens discontinued, if possible. The pharmacist should check the woman's OTC and Rx medication use and consult with the prescriber. It may also be necessary to eliminate medications from the male partner's regimen. Possible teratogens are discussed in more detail in the Drug Use in Pregnancy chapter.

Patient-Specific Infertility Treatment Goals

- Address any underlying medical condition.

- Increase quantity of quality sperm

- Increase number of eggs

- In-vitro fertilization (IVF) and other assisted reproductive technologies (ART) (e.g., cervical or intra-uterine insemination)

The common fertility medications are in the table. They are either oral, or must be given by injection.

DRUG	DOSING	SAFETY/SIDE EFFECTS/MONITORING

Oral

Clomiphene (*Clomid, Serophene*) GnRH ↑ FSH & ↑ LH, to ↑ ovulation Selective Estrogen Receptor Modulator (SERM)	50 mg x 5 days, taken on days 3, 4 or 5 after period starts. Can increase to 100 mg, 5 days/cycle.	**CONTRAINDICATIONS** Liver disease, pregnancy, ovarian cyst, uncontrolled adrenal or thyroid disorders. History of breast cancer as a contraindication is controversial. **SIDE EFFECTS** Hot flashes, ovarian enlargement, abdominal bloating/discomfort, blurred vision, headache, fluid retention. Increases chance of multiple births (but less than injectables), increases thrombosis risk.

Injectable

Human Chorionic Gonadotropin (hCG) (*Ovidrel*), SC (*Pregnyl, Novarel*), IM **Gonadotropins** Follitropin Beta (*Follistim AQ*), IM, SC **Urofollitropin** (*Bravelle, Fertinorm HP*), IM, SC **Follitropin Alpha** (*Gonal-F*), *Gonal-F RFF*, SC **Menotropins** (*Menopur, Repronex*), IM, SC **Gonadotropin Releasing Hormone Agonist (GnRH agonist)** Sometimes used: Leuprolide (*Lupron*), Goserelin (*Zoladex*), Nafarelin (*Synarel*), IM, SC **Gonadotropin Releasing Hormone Antagonist (GnRH antagonist)** Cetrorelix (*Cetrotide*), SC	These come in either prefilled syringes, or as pens that may be preloaded, or pens with prefilled cartridges, or in ampules that are reconstituted, with supplied diluent. If reconstituting: insert syringe needle into vial, invert, slowly draw entire contents into syringe. Make sure tip of needle is not sticking through the solution or it will not be pulled into the syringe. Remove needle and syringe, replace syringe with injection needle. If air bubbles they can be tapped out. Some multiple dose pens require priming – these pens have dose counters on them and the instructions will designate the priming dose. The pen is primed when liquid appears at the tip. All SC injections: keep needle in skin for at least 5 seconds; some are longer, to avoid the drug "popping" out onto the skin. If multiple use, recap. Otherwise, discard entire device without recapping into appropriate container (sharps container, milk container, unbreakable plastic container).	**SIDE EFFECTS** Injection site pain, CNS (depression, fatigue, headache), ovarian hyper-stimulation syndrome (ovaries become enlarged and tender, small risk multiple pregnancies). **NOTES** SC: abdomen is generally preferred due to a more even absorption, or other SC sites. Instructions will indicate either 45 or 90 degrees. See immunization chapter for more details: these are short needles (½" or less). For IM: Upper outer quadrant is often used, as marked in this picture. These are 1" or longer needles; more information on injections in the Immunization chapter. 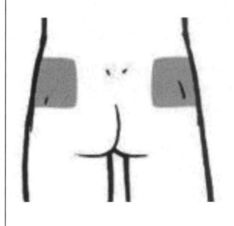

OSTEOPOROSIS, MENOPAUSE & TESTOSTERONE USE

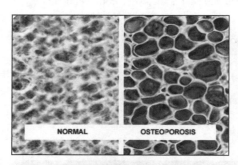

NORMAL   OSTEOPOROSIS

GUIDELINES/REFERENCES

National Osteoporosis Foundation: Clinician's Guide to Prevention and Treatment of Osteoporosis, 2014. http://nof.org/hcp/clinicians-guide (accessed 2015 Jul 20).

American College of Obstetricians and Gynecologist's Practice Bulletin No. 141: Management of Menopausal Symptoms. 2014; 123(1):202-216.

Dandona, P. and Rosenberg, MT. A practical guide to male hypogonadism in the primary care setting. *Int J Clin Pract.* 2010; 64:6:682-696.

WHO Fracture Risk Assessment Tool, accessed at https://www.shef.ac.uk/FRAX/tool.jsp (2015 Oct 11).

We gratefully acknowledge the assistance of Sally Rafie, PharmD, BCPS, Assistant Clinical Professor, University of California San Diego Skaggs School of Pharmacy and Pharmaceutical Sciences, in preparing this chapter.

BACKGROUND

Osteoporosis, which means "porous bones," causes bones to become weak and brittle. It is estimated that more than one-quarter of all adults in the U.S. have osteoporosis, low bone density, or low bone mass. Half of all women and one in five men will have an osteoporosis-related fracture during their life. Falls are a common cause of fracture, but with extremely porous bones, coughing or rolling over in bed can cause fractures. The most common locations for fractures are the vertebrae (spine), proximal femur (hip), and distal forearm (wrist). Vertebral fractures can often occur without a fall and can initially be painless. The only clue to collapsing vertebrae may be a gradual loss of height.

Hip fractures are the most devastating type of fracture, with higher costs, disability, and mortality than all other fractures combined. They are also more common after age 75. A hip fracture in a woman has a 25% risk of mortality at one year, with a higher risk of mortality in men, since men may be in poorer health at baseline. Wrist, or other fractures appear in younger people and serve as an early indicator of poor bone health.

Phases of Bone Loss

Bone accumulates until approximately age 30. After that, bone loss occurs throughout life. Men lose bone at a rate of 0.2 - 0.5% per year, unless they use drugs that accelerate bone loss. Women lose bone slowly after peak bone growth, and then at an increased rate in the 10 years from menopause (1-5% bone loss per year), and then at a slower rate thereafter.

OSTEOPOROSIS IN MEN

Age-related bone loss occurs in men, not just women, and is frequently underdiagnosed. In addition, secondary bone loss can occur from drugs used for prostate cancer (androgen-blocking agents) or with

COPD (receiving series of systemic steroids), with rheumatoid arthritis, or other bone-debilitating conditions. In these patients, fractures have high fatality as the patient is weak. Typically, bisphosphonates are used. It is still necessary to limit treatment duration (3 - 5 years), as is done with women. High-risk agents *(Forteo, Prolia)* are other options, depending on the risk and condition. Men, as with women, will require adequate calcium and vitamin D.

DIAGNOSIS/DEFINITIONS

Osteoporosis is defined by a T-score equal to or < -2.5. This indicates that the bone mineral density (BMD) is at least 2.5 standard deviations below that of an average BMD for normal, young adults. Osteopenia, or low bone mass, is lower bone density than normal, but not as low as osteoporosis. Osteopenia is defined by a T-score between -1 and -2.5. Similarly, this indicates that the BMD is between 1 and 2.5 standard deviations below that of an average BMD for normal, young adults.

Notice that the scores are negative; a T-score of -1 and higher indicates normal bone density. A greater number correlates with stronger (denser) bones, which are less likely to fracture. The T-score is calculated by comparing a person's BMD to the average peak BMD of a normal, young, white adult of the same sex. Z-scores are scored the same way as T-scores but they compare the patient's bone mineral density (BMD) to the mean BMD of an age, sex and ethnicity-matched population.

Osteoblasts are the cells involved in bone formation, and osteoclasts break-down bone; that is, they are involved in resorption. Bone is not "dead tissue"; it is living and constantly remodels, although some types of bone remodels very slowly, and others remodel at a faster rate. Some medications (bisphosphonates, raloxifene, estrogens, denosumab) slow down bone break-down, or resorption. Teriparatide *(Forteo)* does both – it helps prevent bone break-down and helps build bone.

The gold standard to diagnose osteoporosis is a bone scan of the hip and spine performed by a dual energy x-ray absorptiometry (DEXA, or DXA) machine. Ultrasound devices are not optimal, yet they are less expensive, portable, and do not emit radiation. An ultrasound reading provides bone density in one location, such as the heel. An ultrasound reading, if low, should encourage the patient to get a DXA scan. All women at age 65

CONDITIONS WITH OSTEOPOROSIS RISK

Genetic factors are most important, with Caucasian and Asian American women at highest risk

Advanced age

Irritable bowel disease, gastric bypass, and celiac disease

Alcohol abuse (generally, > 3 drinks per day)

Epilepsy, Parkinson's disease, stroke, and multiple sclerosis, HIV/AIDS

Excessive thinness

A decline in adult estrogen levels, from menopause, anorexia nervosa, lactation, hypogonadism

Rheumatoid arthritis and Lupus

Low level of physical activity and adequate nutrition – low over the life span

Calcium and vitamin D – low intake over life span

Smoking

DRUGS WITH OSTEOPOROSIS RISK

Steroid use, long-term, is the major drug-contributing factor to poor bone health (≥ 5 mg/d of prednisone equivalent for ≥ 3 months). Other medications that lower bone density include:

Depot medroxyprogesterone acetate

Anticonvulsants (carbamazepine, fosphenytoin, phenobarbital, phenytoin, primidone, others) (↓ calcium by ↑ breakdown of vitamin D)

Heparin

Lithium

Excess thyroid hormone

Loop diuretics (↓ calcium by ↑ renal excretion)

Aromatase inhibitors used for breast CA

GnRH (gonadotropin-releasing hormone agonists; nafarelin, goserelin) – used for endometriosis

Androgen blockers used for prostate CA and CA Tx

Proton pump inhibitors used chronically (↓ calcium absorption due to ↑ gastric pH)

Selective serotonin reuptake inhibitors

Thiazolidinediones (pioglitazone, rosiglitazone)

and men at age 70 should receive a DXA, and in women younger than 65 years or men between 50 – 69 years, bone density can be determined earlier if there is a history of a fragility fracture (e.g., fall from standing height or less that results in a fracture) after age 50, medical or drug-induced bone loss, parental history of hip fracture, current smoker, alcoholism, rheumatoid arthritis, or other clinical risk factors. Since vertebral fractures are so common in older adults and usually lack symptoms, vertebral imaging may be done if height loss is observed or if BMD indicates osteopenia. In addition to monitoring the BMD over time, biochemical markers of bone turnover are also useful.

Fracture Risk Assessment Tool (FRAX)

The FRAX tool estimates the risk of osteoporotic fracture in the next 10 years (see guidelines box for link). It has been well-validated and its usefulness and limitations are outlined in the National Osteoporosis Foundation (NOF) guidelines. FRAX is a computer-based algorithm developed by the World Health Organization (WHO) and adapted versions are available for Caucasian, Black, Hispanic, and Asian patients in the United States.. The patient's age, sex, BMI, previous fracture, parental hip fracture, femoral neck BMD, current smoking status, steroid use, alcohol intake, disorders strongly associated with osteoporosis (e.g., Type I diabetes, chronic liver disease, premature menopause), and rheumatoid arthritis are entered to calculate the 10-year probabilities of a major osteoporotic fracture and a hip fracture.

Lifestyle Modifications/Fall Prevention Measures

If the bone density is low, care must be taken to avoid falls. Factors that put a patient at increased fall risk include a history of recent falls, the use of drugs that cause CNS changes or cause falls by another mechanism (such as SSRIs or initiation of anti-hypertensives), any condition that causes physical instability or poor coordination, impaired vision, dementia, poor health/frailty, low physical activity and urinary or fecal urgency. A home safety assessment should ensure that lighting is appropriate, floors are safe (throw rugs/clutter/cords have been removed), storage is at reasonable heights, bathrooms have safety bars and nonskid floors, handrails are present on all stairs, and the stairs are well-lit with non-skid treads or carpet.

Exercise and Social Habit Measures

In addition to the changes in the environment listed above, all patients with low bone density should be encouraged to perform weight-bearing exercise (such as walking, jogging, Tai-Chi) and muscle-strengthening exercise (weight training, yoga), take adequate vitamin D and calcium, stop smoking and avoid secondhand smoke, reduce alcohol intake and adopt fall prevention strategies.

Preventing falls requires measures to improve muscle strength, balance and vision. Adequate corrective lenses, safe shoes and appropriate clothing (that will not cause falls) are required. If a disability is present, canes or walkers should be strongly recommended.

CALCIUM AND VITAMIN D

All prescription medications for low bone density require adequate calcium and vitamin D taken concurrently. Dietary intake of calcium is preferred, with supplements to be used if insufficient. Over half of the U.S. population has low calcium and vitamin D intake. Adequate calcium intake is required throughout life, and is critically important in children (who can build bone stores), in pregnancy (when the fetus can deplete the mother's stores if intake is insufficient) and during the years around menopause, when bone loss is rapid. Vitamin D is required for calcium absorption, and low levels contribute to various health conditions, including autoimmune conditions and cancer. Vitamin D deficiency in children causes rickets, and in adults causes osteomalacia (softening of the bone, with low levels of collagen and calcium). Intake in excess of recommended allowances may contribute to kidney stones, cardiovascular disease, and stroke, though the evidence remains controversial. Recommend levels and ensure adequate intake of calcium with vitamin D.

NIH's Recommended Dietary Allowances (RDAs) for Calcium (2013)

AGE	MALE	FEMALE	
0-6 months	200 mg	200 mg	
7-12 months	260 mg	260 mg	
1-3 years	700 mg	700 mg	
4-8 years	1000 mg	1000 mg	
9-13 years	1,300 mg	1,300 mg	
14-18 years	1,300 mg	1,300 mg	same for pregnant/lactating
19-50 years	1,000 mg	1,000 mg	same for pregnant/lactating
51-70 years	1,000 mg	1,200 mg	
71+ years	1,200 mg	1,200 mg	

Notes on Calcium Selection & Absorption

- Calcium absorption is saturable; doses above 500 - 600 mg should be divided.

- Dietary calcium is generally not sufficient; most women need an additional 600 – 900 mg/day (2 to 3 dairy portions) to reach recommended levels.

- Calcium requires vitamin D for absorption.

- Calcium citrate (Citracal, others) has better absorption and can be taken with or without food; usual tab has 315 mg of elemental calcium (21% elemental calcium). It may be preferable with little or no stomach acid – such as what occurs with elderly patients and/or with the use of PPIs, which have been shown to increase fracture risk due to impaired calcium carbonate absorption (including the dietary calcium).

- Calcium carbonate (Oscal, Tums, others) has acid-dependent absorption and should be taken with meals; usual tab is 500 – 600 mg of elemental calcium (40% elemental calcium).

- There is no known benefit of using more expensive formulations – recommend products made by reputable manufacturers, since lead may be present in untested products, especially those containing calcium from dolomite, oyster shell, or bone meal.

- Both forms come as chewables, liquids, and additives in food products.

Notes On Vitamin D Selection

- The NOF recommends an intake of 800 – 1,000 international units of vitamin D for adults age 50 years and older. The Institute of Medicine and NIH's recommended intake for vitamin D for people up to age 70 years is 600 international units daily, and 71+ years is 800 international units daily. However, these levels are currently controversial and many endocrinologists are recommending a higher intake of 800 – 2,000 international units daily. The Institute of Medicine and ACOG guidelines has a recommended safe upper limit of 4,000 international units daily for adolescents and adults. A few years ago vitamin D levels were not routinely tested; this has become commonplace. A serum vitamin D level [25 (OH) D] should be measured and supplements given to reach a level of 30 mg/mL (75 nmol/L).

- The 50,000 unit vitamin D2 supplement (ergocalciferol; the green capsules) are taken weekly for 8 to 12 weeks in adults with deficiency to replenish stores. Cholecalciferol, or vitamin D3, is the preferred source, although vitamin D2 is often the type in supplements and will provide benefit. See Renal Disease & Dosing Considerations chapter for information on vitamin D analogs and calcitriol.

- Sunlight exposure is another source of vitamin D3. Patients should be advised to obtain any required intake from food and supplements rather than sunlight due to the risk of skin cancer.

DRUG TREATMENT

Current FDA-approved options for the prevention and/or treatment of postmenopausal osteoporosis include: bisphosphonates (alendronate, ibandronate, risedronate, and zoledronic acid), calcitonin, estrogens (estrogen and/or hormone therapy), estrogen agonist/antagonist (raloxifene), tissue-selective estrogen complex (conjugated estrogens/bazedoxifene), parathyroid hormone (PTH[1-34], teriparitide), receptor activator of nuclear factor kappa-B ligand (RANKL) inhibitor (denosumab). These medications have been studied in women with postmenopausal osteoporosis and there is limited data in men with glucocorticoid-induced osteoporosis.

Bisphosphonates are used first-line in most patients. They increase bone density and reduce both vertebral and hip fracture risk, except ibandronate which has only been shown to reduce vertebral fractures. Taking bisphosphonates correctly takes time and requires a routine to use properly. If adherence is an issue for this or another reason, it may be useful to use a weekly or monthly oral formulation. Adherence or GI issues (such as stomach upset/heartburn) can be a rationale for the use of parenteral (quarterly or yearly) formulations.

Due to the rare risk of atypical (or low trauma) femur fracture and osteonecrosis of the jaw, bisphosphonates can be stopped after 3-5 years in patients at low risk for fracture. A high risk patient can be continued indefinitely (sometimes after a one year drug holiday) or be switched to a completely different class of drug.

Teriparatide injection (Forteo) is used in patients with osteoporosis who are at high risk for having fractures, have already had an osteoporotic fracture while taking a bisphosphonate, have OP and need to take long-term steroids, or cannot tolerate bisphosphonates. Denosumab (Prolia) is difficult to administer (it must be given in a medical setting) and is expensive; it is also reserved for those with high risk.

Estrogen is no longer used first-line for osteoporosis treatment because of health risks. However, if used for menopausal symptoms, estrogen does increase bone density and reduce vertebral and hip fractures. Estrogen with or without a progestin can be used for osteoporosis prevention in post-menopausal women with vasomotor symptoms of menopause, and should be given at the lowest possible dose for the shortest duration. Conjugated estrogens/bazedoxifene (Duavee) contains estrogen plus an estrogen agonist/antagonist (bazedoxifene) which is also used for prevention of osteoporosis in post-menopausal women with a uterus. Bazedoxifene prevents endometrial hyperplasia in women with a uterus, just like progestin. Raloxifene prevents vertebral fractures only and can be used for treating or preventing osteoporosis and is used most commonly in postmenopausal women who are at risk or have fear of breast cancer.

Calcitonin has fallen out of favor due to reducing only vertebral fractures and has cancer risk; it is reserved for use when alternatives are not suitable.

Osteoporosis Prevention & Treatment Options

DRUG	DOSING	SAFETY/SIDE EFFECTS/MONITORING

Bisphosphonates work by inhibiting osteoclast activity and bone resorption. They are used for prevention and treatment of osteoporosis, as well as Paget's disease, glucocorticoid-induced osteoporosis (and zoledronic acid is also used for hypercalcemia of malignancy.) Bisphosphonates are first-line for most patients.

Oral Bisphosphonates

DRUG	DOSING	SAFETY/SIDE EFFECTS/MONITORING
Alendronate *(Fosamax, Fosamax Plus D, Binosto)*	**Prevention (post-menopausal women)** 5 mg PO daily, or 35 mg PO weekly **Treatment (post-menopausal women and men)** 10 mg PO daily, or 70 mg PO weekly alone, or with vitamin D3 2,800 or 5,600 IU (cholecalciferol), or 70 mg/75 mL solution – drink with at least 2 oz plain water **Glucocorticoid-Induced Osteoporosis** 5 mg PO daily, or 10 mg PO daily if postmenopausal woman not on estrogen	**CONTRAINDICATIONS** Inability to stand or sit upright for at least 30 minutes (60 minutes with once-monthly *Boniva*), difficulty swallowing, esophageal stricture, or at high risk for aspiration Hypocalcemia **WARNINGS** Rare risk of atypical femur fracture (AFF), esophageal cancer and osteonecrosis of the jaw (ONJ). Risk increases with dental surgery, poor dental hygiene, and with high doses used for hypercalcemia of malignancy. AFF and ONJ risk ↑ with duration of exposure. Bone, joint or muscle pain, which may be severe. Esophagitis, dysphagia, esophageal ulcers, esophageal erosions and esophageal stricture (rare). Hypocalcemia must be corrected prior to use. Ensure adequate calcium and vitamin D intake. Do not use or use not recommended: CrCl < 35 mL/min: alendronate, zoledronic acid CrCl < 30 mL/min: ibandronate, risedronate **SIDE EFFECTS** <u>Hypocalcemia</u> (mild, transient), <u>musculoskeletal pain, abdominal pain, dyspepsia, N/V, dysphagia, heartburn, esophagitis</u>, skin rash, eye inflammation, hypertension, headache, UTI
Risedronate *(Actonel, Atelvia)* *Actonel with Calcium:* 35 mg/1250 mg *Atelvia* is delayed-release risedronate that is taken after breakfast, with 4 oz. plain water	**Treatment (post-menopausal women)** 5 mg PO daily, or 35 mg PO weekly, or 75 mg PO on two consecutive days/month, or 150 mg PO monthly **Treatment (males)** 35 mg PO weekly **Glucocorticoid-Induced Osteoporosis** 5 mg PO daily	**NOTES** *Binosto* (effervescent alendronate tablet) contains 650 mg Na⁺. Avoid in sodium restricted patients, such as those with HF or hypertension. Tablets need to be taken with 6-8 oz of plain water. With *Atelvia*, no H₂RAs or PPIs. For all bisphosphonates, separate calcium, antacids, iron and magnesium supplements by at least 2 hours. Caution when using with aspirin or NSAIDs; will worsen gastric irritation. Due to risk of jaw decay/necrosis, dental work should be done prior to starting therapy. Due to transient hypocalcemia when initiating, check calcium and vitamin D levels prior to starting therapy.
Ibandronate *(Boniva)*	**Prevention or Treatment (post-menopausal women)** 2.5 mg PO daily, or 150 mg PO monthly (on same date every month)	Consider injectable bisphosphonate due to the risk of esophageal cancer risk if esophagitis is present, or with other GI issues, or with adherence issues. MedGuide required.

Osteoporosis Treatment & Prevention Options Continued

DRUG	DOSING	SAFETY/SIDE EFFECTS/MONITORING

Injectable Bisphosphonates

DRUG	DOSING	SAFETY/SIDE EFFECTS/MONITORING
Ibandronate (*Boniva*)	**Treatment (post-menopausal women)** 3 mg IV every 3 months **Prevention (post-menopausal women)** 0.5, 1, or 2 mg every 3 months	**CONTRAINDICATIONS** CrCl < 35 mL/minute and if evidence of acute renal impairment (*Reclast* only). **WARNINGS** Renal injury and death can occur due to renal failure. Monitor serum creatinine before every dose. Use with caution in dehydrated patients, elderly, other conditions/drugs that can predispose to renal impairment.
Zoledronic Acid (*Reclast*) *Zometa* – hyperglycemia of malignancy	**Prevention (post-menopausal women)** 5 mg IV every 2 years **Treatment (post-menopausal women and men)** 5 mg IV once yearly **Glucocorticoid-Induced Osteoporosis** 5 mg IV once yearly	**SIDE EFFECTS** No GI problems (bypasses gut), but can cause all others, and an acute phase reaction in patients starting within 3 days post-injection: flu-like symptoms such as fever, achiness, runny nose, headache **NOTES** MedGuide required.

Raloxifene is an estrogen agonist/antagonist, previously called a Selective Estrogen Receptor Modulator (SERM). It acts to ↓ bone resorption. Conjugated estrogens/bazedoxifene (*Duavee*) is an equine (horse) estrogen/SERM combination indicated for osteoporosis prevention (in postmenopausal women with a uterus) and for vasomotor symptoms (raloxifene causes vasomotor symptoms). Used often in women at risk or with fear of breast CA.

DRUG	DOSING	SAFETY/SIDE EFFECTS/MONITORING
Raloxifene (*Evista*)	**Prevention and treatment of postmenopausal osteoporosis** 60 mg PO daily Favorable lipid effects (↓ lipids and LDL; no effect on HDL)	**BOXED WARNINGS** ↑ risk of thromboembolic events (DVT, PE), especially in the first 4 months of use ↑ risk of death due to stroke in women with coronary heart disease or in women at risk for coronary events **SIDE EFFECTS** Hot flashes, peripheral edema, arthralgia, leg cramps/muscle spasms, flu symptoms, infection **NOTES** Separate raloxifene and levothyroxine by several hours. Discontinue at least 72 hours prior to and during prolonged immobilization. MedGuide required.

Osteoporosis Treatment & Prevention Options Continued

DRUG	DOSING	SAFETY/SIDE EFFECTS/MONITORING
Conjugated equine estrogens/bazedoxifene (*Duavee*)	**Osteoporosis prevention (in postmenopausal women <u>with a uterus</u>) & for vasomotor symptoms** 1 tablet (0.45/20 mg) PO daily	**BOXED WARNINGS** Breast CA, Endometrial CA, dementia Do not use with additional estrogens Do not use to prevent cardiovascular disease due to ↑ VTE, and stroke risk in postmenopausal women 50-79 years of age **WARNINGS** Breast cancer risk (from use of estrogen alone), patients with inherited thrombophilias at ↑ VTE risk, changes in lipid values (↑ HDL, ↑ TGs, ↓ LDL), ↑ risk of ovarian cancer, ↑ risk of retinal vascular thrombosis **SIDE EFFECTS** Diarrhea, nausea, dyspepsia, abdominal pain, muscle spasms, oropharyngeal pain (all 7-9%) **NOTES** Not recommended for women over 75 years of age As with other estrogens, use the lowest effective dose for the shortest duration possible (no supplementation with a progestin required; no uterus)

Calcitonin Nasal Spray and Injection – inhibits osteoclastic bone resorption

Calcitonin (*Miacalcin, Fortical*)	**Treatment of osteoporosis in women > 5 years post-menopause** Inhale 1 spray (200 units) in one nostril daily (<u>alternate nostril daily</u>) SC or IM: 100 units daily	**CONTRAINDICATIONS** Allergy to calcitonin salmon **WARNINGS** Risk of malignancy with long-term use Nasal spray: risk nasal ulceration, epistaxis, rhinitis (nasal exams recommended) Hypocalcemia (monitor levels, supplement calcium + vitamin D) Fracture reduction not established; use when alternative treatments are not suitable **SIDE EFFECTS** Back pain, myalgia, headache, nausea, flushing, local inflammation, rhinitis **NOTES** Keep unused bottles refrigerated. Have *EpiPen* available in case of hypersensitivity reaction to first dose. Possible antibody development to salmon. May have a role in elderly patients or short-term in patients with acute pain from vertebral fractures.

Osteoporosis Treatment & Prevention Options Continued

DRUG	DOSING	SAFETY/SIDE EFFECTS/MONITORING

Teriparatide Injection – new bone formation by stimulating osteoblast over osteoclast activity

Teriparatide *(Forteo)*	Treatment of osteoporosis in postmenopausal women and men at risk of fracture 20 mcg <u>SC daily</u> for <u>max of 18-24 months</u>	**BOXED WARNING** Osteosarcoma (bone cancer) **WARNINGS** Orthostatic hypotension with initial doses, use cautiously if history or current urolithiasis (urinary stones) **SIDE EFFECTS** <u>Hypercalcemia (transient, post-dose), arthralgias, pain, nausea, orthostasis/dizziness and ↑ HR</u> **NOTES** 28-day pen, keep refrigerated and protect from light, inject in thigh or abdomen. MedGuide required.

Denosumab – Monoclonal antibody that binds to nuclear factor-kappa ligand (RANKL) and blocks the interaction between RANKL and RANK (a receptor on osteoclasts), preventing osteoclast formation; leads to ↓ bone resorption and ↑ bone mass

Denosumab *(Prolia)* *Xgeva* – hypercalcemia of malignancy, bone cell tumor, prevention of bone metastasis	Treatment of osteoporosis in post menopausal women at high risk of fracture Treatment of androgen deprivation-induced bone loss in men with prostate CA, aromatase inhibitor-induced bone loss in women with breast CA 60 mg SC (in medical setting) every 6 months	**CONTRAINDICATIONS** <u>Hypocalcemia</u> – (must be corrected prior to using), pregnancy **WARNINGS** Osteonecrosis of the jaw (rare); risk ↑ with dental surgery or poor dental hygiene; serious infections, atypical femur fractures (rare), dermatitis/eczema/rash, severe bone/joint/muscle pain, anaphylaxis risk, hypocalcemia (monitor levels), use cautiously if hypoparathyroidism or thyroid surgery or infection **SIDE EFFECTS** <u>Back pain, limb pain, dermatitis, eczema, rash, skin infections, hypocalcemia, increased serum cholesterol.</u> **NOTES** Pregnancy Category X (*Prolia*)/D (*Xgeva*). If/when discontinued, bone loss can be rapid; consider alternative agents to maintain BMD. MedGuide required.

Bisphosphonate Patient Counseling

- Take first thing in the morning <u>before you eat or drink anything, with 6-8 oz</u> (1 cup) of plain water. If you are using formulations that are not once daily (such as weekly), choose the day of the week that is easy to remember (such as Sunday if going to church, or bridge day, etc.)

- Take the medicine while you are <u>sitting up or standing and stay upright for at least 30 minutes (60 minutes with monthly *Boniva)*</u>. During this time, you cannot eat or drink anything else except more plain water. You cannot take any other medicines or vitamins. Nothing but plain water. If you plan to lie down again, you must first eat food.

- This medicine must be <u>swallowed whole</u>, and washed down with water. Do not crush or chew the tablet.

- For effervescent tablets (*Binosto*), dissolve one tablet in 4 oz (1/2 cup) of room temperature water. Wait 5 minutes after effervescence is completed before stirring well and then drinking.

- For oral solution, administer in the morning with at least 2 oz (1/4 cup) of plain water.

- <u>This medicine does not work well if you are not taking enough calcium and vitamin D</u>. Some formulations contain calcium or vitamin D. Discuss with your pharmacist if you need to use calcium or vitamin D supplements.

- If you are using a proton pump inhibitor for heartburn, discuss with your pharmacist. <u>These drugs may increase fracture risk</u>. You may need to use a calcium citrate tablet, with adequate vitamin D.

- Your bone and muscle strength will improve faster if you are doing <u>exercise</u>. Your healthcare provider should discuss with you safe and healthy ways to exercise.

- <u>Common side effects include GI upset, joint or muscle pain, back pain, dyspepsia or heartburn</u>.

- <u>Stop taking the medicine</u> if you develop difficult or painful swallowing, have chest pain, have very bad heartburn that does not go away, or have severe pain in the bones, joints or muscles.

- Tell your healthcare provider right away if you develop thigh or groin pain while on this medication. Some patients have developed serious <u>jaw-bone problems</u> after using this medicine, which may include infection and slower healing after teeth are pulled. Tell your healthcare providers, including your dentist, right away if you have these symptoms. <u>If you have dental work due now, you should have it done before starting the medicine</u>.

- *Atelvia*: This is a long-acting form of risedronate. Take the medicine <u>after breakfast with 4 oz (1/2 cup) of plain water</u>. Sit or stand upright for 30 minutes or longer after taking. <u>Do not use</u> acid suppressing "heartburn" therapy with this medicine. Do not take calcium, iron, magnesium, antacids or multivitamin supplements until later in the day.

Bisphosphonate Missed Doses

- If on a daily schedule and missed one dose, skip that dose. Take the next dose at the regularly scheduled time.

- If on a weekly schedule and missed one dose, take the following morning (but not 2 doses on the same day).

- If on a monthly schedule and miss a dose, take it as soon as you remember (in the morning before eating) except if it is less than one week to the next dose, skip it (do not take 2 doses in the same week).

Raloxifene Patient Counseling

- Take with or without food.

- This drug has a risk of dangerous blood clots. If any of the following occurs it could be due to a blood clot and you should get medical treatment quickly: any sudden leg pain, chest pain, shortness of breath, vision changes, an inability to speak or slurred speech, loss of movement on any side of your body.

- This drug can cause hot flashes during the day and can make you feel hot and sweaty during the night. If these occur and are bothersome discuss treatment options with your healthcare provider.

- Discontinue *Evista* at least 72 hours prior to and during prolonged immobilization, such as after a surgery or with prolonged bed rest.

Teriparatide Patient Counseling

- This medication is similar to a hormone made by the body called parathyroid hormone or PTH. This medication helps to form new bone and increase the bone strength.

- Please read the Medication Guide. During the drug testing process, *Forteo* caused some rats to develop a bone cancer called osteosarcoma. Osteosarcoma has been reported rarely in people who took *Forteo*. The warning states that it is not known if people who use *Forteo* have a higher chance of having osteosarcoma.

- You may feel dizzy or light-headed after the first few doses. This usually happens within 4 hours of taking the medication and goes away within a few hours. For the first few doses, inject this medication where you can sit or lie down right away if these symptoms occur.

- Inform your healthcare provider if you develop bone or joint pain.

- The medicine comes in a prefilled injection pen that lasts 28 days. Each injection provides a 20-mcg dose. You should change the needle each day.

- The pen should be kept in the refrigerator and re-capped after each use. After 28 days, the pen should be discarded even if some medicine remains. There is a place at the end of the user manual to mark the date when the pen is started and the date (28 days later) when the pen should be thrown away.

- Inject one time each day in your thigh or abdomen (lower stomach area). The injection sites must be rotated.

- Do not transfer the medicine from the delivery device to a syringe. The injection pen is set at the right dose and does not require any dose adjustment.

- You can inject at any time of the day. Take it at about the same time each day.

- If you forget or cannot take the medicine at your usual time, take it as soon as you can on that day. Do not take more than one injection in the same day.

- Do not exceed 2 years of use.

- This medicine does not work well if you are not taking enough calcium and vitamin D. Discuss with your pharmacist if you need to use calcium or vitamin D supplements.

- If you are using a proton pump inhibitor for heartburn, discuss with your pharmacist. These drugs may increase fracture risk. You may need to use a calcium citrate tablet, with adequate vitamin D.

Calcitonin Nasal Spray Counseling.

- Keep unused bottles in the refrigerator, but not the one being used. When a new bottle is used it should be allowed to reach room temperature prior to priming. To prime the pump, hold the bottle upright and press the 2 white side arms toward the bottle to release at least 5 sprays until a full spray is produced. Once the pump is primed, it does not have to be re-primed if the bottle is stored in an upright position.

- To use the nasal spray, remove the protective cap, keep head upright and insert the tip into a nostril. Press down firmly on the pump to deliver the medication. Use the other nostril the next day.

- After 30 doses, the pump may not deliver the correct amount of medicine with each spray and should be discarded.

- Call 9-1-1 if you have an allergic reaction (such as swelling of your face or throat or trouble breathing).

- Some nose irritation may occur. Discuss with your healthcare provider if you get nasal crusting, dryness, redness or swelling, nose sores (ulcers) or nose bleeds.

- This medicine does not work well if you are not taking enough calcium and vitamin D. Some formulations contain calcium or vitamin D. Discuss with your pharmacist if you need to use calcium or vitamin D supplements.

- If you are using a proton pump inhibitor for heartburn, discuss with your pharmacist. These drugs may increase fracture risk. You may need to use a calcium citrate tablet, with adequate vitamin D.

MENOPAUSE

Hormone treatment is sometimes used for women who are postmenopausal. Menopause means that the last menstrual period was over 12 months ago. Menopause normally occurs between the ages of 45 and 55. More than half of women experience vasomotor symptoms during the menopause transition (also known as perimenopause) as their ovaries produce less estrogen. A decrease in estrogen and progesterone causes an increase in follicle stimulating hormone (FSH), resulting in hot flashes and night sweats (hot flashes that occur during sleep). Sleep can be disturbed, and mood changes may be present. Due to a decline in estrogen in the vaginal mucosa, vaginal dryness, burning and painful intercourse may be present.

Some women remain largely asymptomatic during menopause, while others suffer from severe symptoms and a reduced quality of life. Women who have both their ovaries removed, or receive chemotherapy or radiation for cancer, will undergo induced menopause and can experience similar symptoms, but more acutely initially due to a sudden, rather than a gradual, estrogen decline.

Estrogen-Progestin Use: Health Risks/Considerations For Use

The most effective therapy for vasomotor symptoms (hot flashes, night sweats) is systemic hormone therapy with estrogen, which causes a decrease in LH, and, consequently, more stable temperature control. Estrogen improves bone density as well.

In women with a uterus, estrogen should never be given alone and should always be accompanied by a progestin. Unopposed estrogen will put the woman at elevated risk for endometrial cancer. Progestins can cause mood disturbances in some women, and may be hard to tolerate. If given intermittently, such as with *Premphase*, spotting can be a nuisance. Progestins (norethindrone, levonorgestrel, norgestimate, drospirenone) are given in combination with the estrogen, or as a separate tablet (generally medroxyprogesterone, or MPA).

In 2002, the data from large trials on hormone therapy became available – these were the Women's Health Initiative (WHI) postmenopausal hormone therapy trials. At first, the news was scary and led to several boxed warnings on the use of HT (hormone therapy), including warnings for increased risk of stroke, heart attacks and probable risk of dementia. As the data was reanalyzed, it became apparent that the majority of risk was highest in older women. Currently, the following considerations for use should be followed according to the North American Menopause Society:

- To maximize safety, the initiation of HT should be considered for healthy symptomatic women who are within 10 years of menopause or aged younger than 60 years and who do not have contraindications to use of HT.

- Provided that the woman has been advised of the increase in risks associated with continuing HT beyond age 60 and has clinical supervision, extending HT use with the lowest effective dose is acceptable under some circumstances.

- Consideration should be given to the woman's quality-of-life priorities as well as her personal risk factors, such as age, time since menopause, and her risk of blood clots, heart disease, stroke, and breast cancer.

Formulation Considerations

Both transdermal and low-dose oral estrogen therapy have been associated with lower risks of VTE and stroke than standard doses of oral estrogen. Topical formulations, given as a patch, gel or emulsion, bypass first pass metabolism, and lower doses can be used. Topical formulations usually cause less nausea, have little or no effect on cholesterol levels and may expose the woman to lower systemic estrogen. Estrogen use is generally well tolerated, but can cause <u>nausea, dizziness, headaches, mood changes, vaginal bleeding, bloating and breast tenderness/fullness</u>.

Local estrogen products are <u>preferred</u> for patients who have <u>vaginal symptoms</u> only (vaginal dryness and/or painful intercourse). Any of the vaginal products included in this chapter (creams, vaginal tablets, vaginal rings) or OTC lubricants can be helpful. Common OTC lubricants include *Replens* and *Luvena*. A lubricant marketed specifically for dyspareunia (dry, painful intercourse) is *Astroglide*. Do not use oil-based lubricants with condoms – the condom can tear. *Astroglide* or silicon-based lubricants are safe to recommend with condoms. Ospemifene *(Osphena)* is a newer drug indicated for dyspareunia; see the warnings concerning this drug – it is not used lightly.

Bioidentical Hormone Therapy (BHT), other "Natural" Formulations

The warnings for hormone therapy are based on the analysis of the WHI data and do not distinguish between hormone type. In the future, if more information is available, these warnings will be refined. It is safest to assume that the known risks for one estrogen formulation will apply to other formulations. Some women will prefer to use bioidentical hormones, that include commercially available products approved by the FDA, and others will prefer compounded preparations.

The term "bioidentical" generally refers to plant-derived hormones that have the same chemical and molecular structure as hormones that are produced in the human body. Many woman, physicians and compounding pharmacists believe that BHT is safer, but keep in mind that there are no well-designed studies to confirm risk or benefit and compounded preparations are not regulated by the FDA. If a woman is using BHT products and feels better, this is important. She should understand the risks that may be present [it is safest to assume risks known from available trial data (above) for any hormone therapy, until proven otherwise].

Natural Products Used for Vasomotor Symptoms

Natural products used for vasomotor symptoms include <u>black cohosh, red clover, soy, flaxseed, dong quai, St. John's wort,</u> and evening primrose oil. The mild "plant estrogens," found in soy and red clover, are called phytoestrogens; phyto means plant. These natural products may help a little bit with mild symptoms, but would not provide the benefit of estrogen.

SSRI to ↓ Vasomotor Symptoms

Paroxetine *(Brisdelle)* is the first non-hormonal FDA-approved treatment of moderate-severe vasomotor symptoms associated with menopause. Women who are taking warfarin or tamoxifen should not use *Brisdelle*. As an SSRI, it will increase the risk of bleeding, and <u>as a CYP450 2D6 inhibitor, it will block the effectiveness of tamoxifen</u>. There is an interaction with warfarin, causing bleeding risk, but the mechanism is unknown.

Contraception

Perimenopausal women who wish to avoid an unintended pregnancy should be counseled about contraceptive options. Women in the perimenopause may have an accidental pregnancy as the menstrual cycle has become irregular; they should be counseled to use effective birth control. SNRIs (desvenlafaxine), clonidine and gabapentin also show effectiveness for treating vasomotor symptoms related to menopause, but these are not FDA approved for this indication.

Ospemifene to ↓ Dyspareunia due to Vulvar/Vaginal Atrophy

Ospemifene (*Osphena*), is an oral estrogen agonist/antagonist indicated for dyspareunia (painful intercourse). Topical vaginal products are safer for this purpose. One of the boxed warnings is for risk versus benefit; this drug has <u>VTE risk</u> and is <u>not indicated for mild symptoms</u>. It is only for a short treatment period for moderate-to-severe symptoms.

DRUG	DOSING	SAFETY/SIDE EFFECTS/MONITORING
PARoxetine (*Brisdelle*) *Paxil, Pexeva, Paxil CR*-for depression	**For the treatment of moderate to severe symptoms associated with menopause** 7.5 mg PO QHS	**BOXED WARNING** Suicide risk; same as with other SSRIs **CONTRAINDICATIONS/WARNINGS** Same as with other SSRIs; see Depression chapter. **SIDE EFFECTS** Same sexual side effects (see Depression chapter), and in the *Brisdelle* trials > 10% incidence for sedation, insomnia, restlessness, tremor, dizziness/weakness, nausea, dry mouth, constipation, diaphoresis **NOTES** Lag time to effect (~4 weeks) <u>Do not use with warfarin (↑ bleeding risk) or tamoxifen (↓ efficacy tamoxifen)</u>
Ospemifene (*Osphena*)	60 mg PO daily Take with food	**BOXED WARNINGS** Endometrial cancer, CVD, Risk vs Benefit **CONTRAINDICATIONS** Undiagnosed abnormal vaginal bleeding, DVT or PE (current or history of), active or history of arterial thromboembolic disease (e.g., stroke, MI), estrogen-dependent tumor (known or suspected), women who are or may become pregnant **SIDE EFFECTS** Hot flashes, vaginal discharge, hyperhidrosis

Common Hormone Products

Estradiol is used primarily for vasomotor symptoms, vaginal atrophy and osteoporosis prevention. The products below have one or more of these indications. Oral contraceptives contain ethinyl estradiol (primarily) and the estrogen dose is higher than with HT.

COMPONENTS	FORMULATION	SAFETY/SIDE EFFECTS/MONITORING
Estradiol	Topical gel (*Divigel, Elestrin, EstroGel*) Topical spray (*Evamist*) Transdermal patch (*Alora, Climara, Minivelle, Vivelle-Dot, Menostar*) Vaginal ring (*Femring*)*	**BOXED WARNINGS, ESTROGEN** Endometrial cancer (if used without a progestin in women with a uterus) Dementia risk in women ≥ 65 years of age taking estrogen alone (without a progestin) Do not use to prevent CVD due to ↑ VTE risk in postmenopausal women 50-79 years
17-b-Estradiol	Vaginal cream (*Estrace*) Vaginal ring (*Estring*) Vaginal tablet (*Vagifem*)	Breast cancer risk in postmenopausal women taking estrogen with medroxyprogesterone acetate (MPA); use lowest effective dose for shortest duration consistent with treatment goals and risks
Estradiol and Levonorgestrel	Transdermal patch (*ClimaraPro*)* *"Pro" in name includes a progestin	For *Evamist* only: breast budding, breast masses (prepubertal females), gynecomastia, prepubertal males who had unintentional exposure developed
Estradiol and Norethindrone	Transdermal patch (*CombiPatch*) Oral tablet (*Activella, Mimvey*)	breast masses; keep children away from spray
Estradiol and Norgestimate	Oral tablet (*Prefest*) – cyclic treatment, estradiol x 3 days, E+P x 3 days, repeat	**CONTRAINDICATIONS** Undiagnosed abnormal vaginal bleeding, any clotting incident or disorder (DVT, PE, MI, CVA, etc.), liver disease, pregnancy, any hormone-dependent cancer
Estradiol and drospirenone	Oral tablet (*Angeliq*)	
Conjugated Equine Estrogens	Oral tablet (*Premarin*) – 0.3, 0.45, 0.625, 0.9, 1.25 mg Vaginal cream (*Premarin*) – 0.625 mg/gram Injection (*Premarin*)	**WARNINGS** Breast cancer risk (from use of estrogen alone), patients with inherited thrombophilias at ↑ VTE risk, changes in CH values (↑ HDL, ↑ TGs, ↓ LDL), ↑ risk of ovarian cancer, ↑ risk of retinal vascular thrombosis
Conjugated estrogens and MedroxyPROGESTERone (MPA)	Oral tablet (*Prempro*) – 0.3-0.625 conjugated E + 1.5-5 MPA Oral tablet (*Premphase*) – 0.625 mg CEE + 5 mg MPA days 15-28 (phasic dosing)	**SIDE EFFECTS** Nausea, dizziness, bloating, breast tenderness/fullness, ↑ triglycerides, ↑ HDL, edema, depression Patch: redness/irritation at the application site
MedroxyPROGESTERone *Depo-Provera* – contraception	2.5, 5, 10 mg oral tablets, suspension available (*Provera*)	**NOTES** Some formulations come in patches – check if the patch must be removed prior to MRI. Patch summary in Drug Formulations chapter.
Conjugated estrogens/bazedoxifene	Oral tablet (*Duavee*)	*Vivelle-Dot, Alora, Minivelle* patches are applied twice weekly. *Climara* and *Menostar* patches are once weekly. *Evamist* spray: Each morning spray on inside of the forearm between the elbow and the wrist. Gels and *Evamist* spray are flammable. Gels: wash hands after application. Applied once daily: *Divigel* (upper thigh, alternate sides), *Elestrin* (upper arm/shoulder), *Estrogel* (arm).

Estrogen Counseling

- This product does not contain a progestin, which should be used by any woman with a uterus taking estrogen therapy. <u>Estrogen taken alone</u> increases the risk of <u>cancer of the uterus</u>.

- Report any unusual vaginal bleeding right away while you are taking estrogen. Vaginal bleeding after menopause may be a warning sign of cancer of the uterus. Your healthcare provider should follow up on any unusual vaginal bleeding to find out the cause.

- Do not use hormone therapy to prevent heart disease, heart attacks, or strokes.

- Using estrogens may increase your chances of heart attacks, strokes, breast cancer, and blood clots. Using estrogens may increase your risk of dementia. You and your healthcare provider should talk regularly about whether you still need treatment with this product.

- Estrogen use is primarily for menopausal symptoms, and should not be continued indefinitely. When you are ready to stop discuss with your healthcare provider the best way to stop the medicine. The goal is to use the lowest dose of hormone therapy for the shortest period of time possible.

- Estrogen can help keep your bones healthy. Ask your pharmacist for help in figuring out if you need to take calcium and vitamin D – these are important for healthy bones.

Patch Application

- <u>Mark the schedule</u> you plan to follow on your medication package's inner flap, or on your calendar.

- If you forget to change your patch on the correct date, apply a new one as soon as you remember.

- <u>Apply patch to lower abdomen, below the waistline</u>. Avoid the waistline, since clothing may cause the patch to rub off.

- The area must be clean, dry, free of powder, oil or lotion. Do not apply the patch to cut or irritated skin.

- <u>Do not apply the patch to breasts</u>. (Never apply any estrogen patch to the breasts.)

- If any adhesive residue remains on your skin after removing the patch, allow the area to dry for 15 minutes. Then, gently rub the area with oil or lotion to remove the adhesive from your skin.

TESTOSTERONE TREATMENT (FOR HYPOGONADISM IN MALES)

Hypogonadism in older males can be due to a normal age-related decline in testosterone, or it can be secondary to a medical condition, surgical procedure, or medication use that lowers testosterone. Treating opioid dependence with <u>methadone</u> lowers testosterone levels significantly. Other opioids may have an effect; the risk should be considered. <u>Chemotherapy</u> drugs used for prostate cancer, <u>cimetidine</u> and <u>spironolactone</u> can lower testosterone. The increased use of testosterone over the past few years is largely due to older males requesting testosterone therapy for Low T" symptoms: <u>improved sexual interest</u> (↑ libido) and performance, increased muscle mass, increased bone density, sharpened memory and concentration, and increased energy. The use of testosterone replacement for conditions other than for accepted medical uses is controversial, and a clear benefit of improved sexual function <u>has not been established</u>. In 2015, the FDA added a warning about the risk of <u>cardiovascular complications</u> and included the recommendation to use only in men with <u>low testosterone</u> levels caused by certain <u>medical conditions</u> and <u>confirmed by laboratory tests</u>.

Recently, there have been reports of <u>increased clotting risk</u> in men using testosterone therapy, but the men with clotting may have had higher risk at baseline; at present, the link is unclear. Testosterone <u>increases hematocrit</u>, which can cause polycythemia and may increase clotting risk. Testosterone can cause non-cancerous <u>prostate growth</u> in men with benign prostatic hypertrophy (BPH). Testosterone replacement is <u>restricted</u> in men with <u>severe BPH</u>. However, even with mild or moderate BPH, if dispensing a 5-alpha-reductase inhibitor for BPH that blocks the conversion of testosterone to the active form, it would not make sense to dispense another drug that provides testosterone directly. Common side effects of testosterone include increased male pattern <u>baldness, acne and gynecomastia</u>.

Testosterone Formulations

Testosterone comes in <u>intramuscular injections</u> which are <u>painful</u> and require medical visits. Patients complain that they feel symptomatic when it is getting close to the time for the next dose. The injections may increase the hematocrit more than topical formulations. The injectable pellets in *Testopel* require medical visits. The pellets are a little smaller than a *Tic-Tac* mint and have the unfortunate tendency of popping out. *Striant* is a buccal form that is held inside the cheek twice daily; it has a high incidence of <u>buccal irritation</u>. The *Androderm* patch has a high incidence of <u>skin irritation</u>. In some cases it is tolerated with prior application of a topical steroid.

The gel formulations (*AndroGel* and other topical gels) are the most popular formulations and are relatively well-tolerated. *AndroGel* is the top-selling "Low-T" product and it is applied to the upper body. The man does not put his shirt on until the gel is dry; the biggest problem with the gel is when others touch the gel. Topical testosterone products require a MedGuide, primarily due to the risk of drug transfer from dad or grandpa to children. This causes "early virilization" and can affect both boys and girls. Depending on the dose received, the child could have enlarged genital organs, aggressive behavior and premature pubic hair growth. The risk of <u>early virilization</u> is a boxed warning. Pharmacists need to counsel men to wash their hands after each application and to be careful that no one touches the areas of application when wet.

There are new topical formulations that reduce accidental exposure risk: *Axiron* is applied to the <u>underarms</u> using an applicator that looks like deodorant, *Fortesta* is applied to the <u>thighs</u> with one finger (the amount is small) and *Natesto* is applied to the <u>nostrils</u>. Testosterone products are usually applied in the morning.

Testosterone Products: C-III

TESTOSTERONE	COUNSELING	SAFETY/SIDE EFFECTS/MONITORING
Topical Gels and Solutions		**BOXED WARNINGS** Secondary exposure to testosterone in children and women can occur with use of testosterone. Cases of secondary exposure resulting in virilization of children have been reported. Women and children should avoid contact with any unwashed or unclothed application sites in men using testosterone gel.
AndroGel 1%, 1.62% Meter-dose pumps (# of pumps depends on dose) or foil packets of 2.5 g or 5 g gel *Vogelxo* meter-dose pump	*AndroGel* 1.62% is applied to the area of the upper arms and shoulders, but not the abdomen; with the 1% the abdomen can be used.	
Testosterone gel *(Vogelxo)*	Applied to upper arms and shoulders once daily	Injection only: Pulmonary oil microembolism (POME) reactions.
Testosterone solution *(Axiron)*	Applied to armpits once daily	**CONTRAINDICATIONS** Breast or prostate cancer.
Testosterone gel *(Fortesta)*	Applied to thighs once daily	**WARNINGS** Patients with benign prostatic hyperplasia (BPH) treated with androgens are at an increased risk for worsening signs and symptoms of BPH.
Testim gel 1%	Applied to arms and shoulders, not abdomen, once daily	$\uparrow$ risk of thromboembolic events (DVT, PE). The FDA is evaluating risk of stroke, MI, and death with testosterone products. Use only for men with low testosterone levels caused by certain medical conditions and confirmed by laboratory tests.
Testosterone nasal gel *(Natesto)*	1 actuation per nostril TID	
Alternative Formulations		Never apply to breast or genitals.
Androderm patch	2 mg, 4 mg patch Apply to back, abdomen, thighs or upper arms each <u>night</u>; causes <u>skin irritation</u>, rotate site and do not use same site for at least 7 days; see notes	**SIDE EFFECTS** $\uparrow$ <u>appetite</u>, $\uparrow$ SCr, sensitive nipples, acne, gynecomastia, dyslipidemia, edema, $\uparrow$ PSA, $\uparrow$ risk of <u>hepatotoxicity</u>, reduced sperm count, sleep apnea
Striant buccal tabs	30 mg to the gum region BID	**Additional Issues By Formulation Type** Patch: skin irritation
Testopel pellets	SC every 3-6 months	Buccal tabs: buccal irritation Nasal gel: nasal irritation
Testosterone undecanoate *(Aveed)* injection	IM every 10+ weeks	
Testosterone cypionate *(Depo-Testosterone)* injection	IM every 2-4 weeks	**MONITORING** Testosterone levels, PSA, liver function, cholesterol, some products recommend checking hematocrit
Testosterone enanthate injection	IM every 2-4 weeks	
First-Testosterone ointment/cream	Apply daily, as directed	**NOTES** *Androderm*: avoid showering, washing the site, or swimming for ≥3 hours after application. After removal, can treat irritation with OTC <u>hydrocortisone</u>. <u>Remove</u> patch before MRI. <u>Gels</u> are flammable until dry. Wash hands after application. Do not dress until skin dry.

AndroGel Patient Counseling

Pump

- Before using the pump for the first time, you will need to prime the pump. To prime *AndroGel*, fully push down on the pump 3 times. Do not use any *AndroGel* that came out while priming. Wash it down the sink or throw it in the trash to avoid accidental exposure to others.

- Your healthcare provider will tell you the number of times to press the pump for each dose.

Packets

- Tear open the packet completely at the dotted line.

- Squeeze all of the *AndroGel* out of the packet into the palm of your hand. Squeeze from the bottom of the packet to the top.

For Both

- This medication should not be used by women or children. Testosterone can cause birth defects in unborn babies. A pregnant woman should avoid coming into contact with testosterone topical gel, or with a man's skin areas where a testosterone topical patch has been worn or the gel has been applied. If contact does occur, wash with soap and water right away.

- Topical testosterone is absorbed through the skin and can cause side effects or symptoms of male features in a child or woman who comes into contact with the medication. Contact with the medication can cause enlarged genitals, premature pubic hair, increased libido, aggressive behavior, male-pattern baldness, excessive body hair growth, increased acne, irregular menstrual periods, or any signs of male characteristics.

- The testosterone transdermal patch may burn your skin if you wear the patch during an MRI (magnetic resonance imaging). Remove the patch before undergoing such a test.

How to apply (1+ push from pump/day or 1 packet/day), or topical gels

- Apply the medication as directed to clean, dry skin of the shoulders/upper arms and/or abdomen (1% only to abdomen) once daily in the morning. Apply only to areas that would be covered if you were to wear a short sleeve t-shirt. Avoid applying this medication to broken, irritated skin. Do not apply to genitals (penis or scrotum). Do not let others apply this medication to your body.

- After applying, wash your hands thoroughly with soap and water to reduce the risk of accidentally spreading it from your hands to other people. Before dressing, wait a few minutes for the application site to dry completely. Be sure to always wear clothing (such as a t-shirt) to cover the application site until you wash the areas well with soap and water.

- If you expect to have skin-to-skin contact with another person, first wash the application area well with soap and water.

- For best effect, wait at least 2 to 6 hours after applying the medication before showering or swimming.

- This medication is <u>flammable</u> until dry. Let the gel dry before smoking or going near an open flame.

- *Axiron* gel (applied to underarms): Apply deodorant first.

- *Fortesta* (applied to the front and inner thighs with one finger), *Natesto* (prime pump 10x first, insert actuator into nostril, depress slowly, remove from nose, wipe tip to transfer gel to lateral side of nostril then press on the nose and lightly massage. Try not to blow nose or sniff for one hour).

44

PAIN

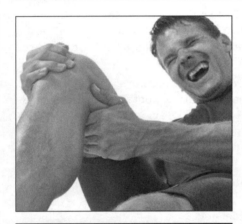

We gratefully acknowledge the assistance of Charles D. Ponte, BS, PharmD, FAADE, FAPhA, FASHP, FCCN, FNAP, Professor of Clinical Pharmacy and Family Medicine, West Virginia University Schools of Pharmacy and Medicine, in preparing this chapter.

GUIDELINES/REFERENCES

Many resources, including guidelines, at the American Pain Society Website: www.ampainsoc.org. Selected resources include:

Common Elements in Guidelines for Prescribing Opioids for Chronic Pain. http://www.cdc.gov/drugoverdose/prescribing/common-elements.html (accessed 2015 Nov 18).

American Pain Society's Principles of Analgesic Use in the Treatment of Acute Pain and Cancer Pain, 6th Edition, 2008.

Additional guidelines included with the video files (RxPrep Online).

BACKGROUND

The word pain is derived from the Latin term "poena" which means "punishment". Despite this literal translation, pain should never be viewed by the patient or provider as a form of retribution for past actions. Pain is the physical suffering or discomfort caused by illness or injury. Pain originating from the same source can be both acute and chronic. Acute pain shares some of the same physical findings associated with anxiety such as sweating and tachycardia.

Chronic pain can be the result of an acute injury or secondary to various diseases such as osteoarthritis or rheumatoid diseases. It can also result from various neuropathies associated with poor glucose control in diabetes or from viruses such as HIV or herpes zoster. Chronic pain can be associated with sleep disorders, anxiety, depression and poor appetite. Pharmacists and prescribers should be concerned about inadequate pain treatment, but must often balance this against the potential abuse and misuse of opioid therapy. Drug interactions and side effects (both short and long-term) are always a concern.

The Joint Commission (TJC) standards require that pain be treated in the same manner as vital signs, making it compulsory for health care professionals in accredited facilities to inquire about, measure, and treat pain as they would blood pressure, pulse or respiratory rate. Pain is considered to be the "fifth vital sign."

TREATMENT PRINCIPLES

Pain is always subjective, and thus, the primary measurement for assessing pain is the patient's own report, along with behavioral observations. Patients should be taught to monitor and document their pain. This will enable the clinician to better evaluate pain and adjust medications more precisely. Pain scales (visual analog example shown here) can be used as guides to assess pain severity. The patient should record the pain level or severity, pain type or quality (using words such as burning, shooting, stab-

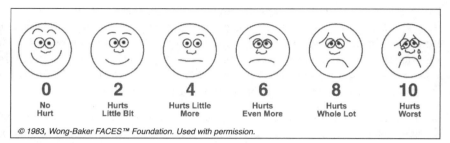

© 1983, Wong-Baker FACES™ Foundation. Used with permission.

bing, aching, etc.) and the time of day that pain is better or worse. Timing is important; the frequency of breakthrough or "end-of-dose" pain can indicate the need for continuous scheduled extended release (ER) pain medication.

It is preferable to prevent severe pain since delaying treatment until the pain worsens may require a higher total analgesic dose. The lowest dose that adequately reduces the pain is considered to be the appropriate dose. Using medicines with multiple mechanisms of action (termed "multimodal" pain control) can produce a better response via additive effects or synergism. Opioid agents in particular can be difficult to manage even for the patient who needs them, and an appropriate goal may be to try and reduce or avoid the use of opioids altogether. The addition of non-opioids (e.g., acetaminophen) to a regimen can often reduce the total opioid dose required while providing superior analgesia. This has been shown to be true in both the ambulatory setting and in acute medical-surgical settings. Additionally, access to non-medication techniques and modalities, such as physical therapy, heat/cold, massage therapy and directed exercise, is essential.

In recent years there has been an increased concern over the incorrect use of chronic opioids. Headache (described in the Migraine chapter) and low back pain are treated commonly. For low back pain, non-drug measures are useful: medium-firm mattress, active lifestyle with exercise, smoking cessation (smokers rate pain higher), weight loss and other modalities. If medications are used, acetaminophen or NSAIDs are helpful. Many patients find benefit with chronic use of amitriptyline or duloxetine (a SNRI). SSRIs have not been found to be beneficial. If severe, tramadol or opioids (lowest effective dose, shortest time required) can be tried next. Steroids have not been found to be helpful. In some cases skeletal muscle relaxants are used although their efficacy is questionable.

OPIOID TERMINOLOGY

Patients taking opioids chronically will often develop physiological adaptation ("physical dependence") and ultimately may live "dose to dose." Such patients will suffer withdrawal symptoms including anxiety, tachycardia, shakiness, shortness of breath or GI symptoms if the dose is missed or taken late.

It is important to distinguish between physiological adaptation and addiction. All patients, including addicts, become physiologically adapted to opioids after repeated exposure. By contrast, addiction involves a strong desire or compulsion to take the drug despite harm, and is manifested by drug-seeking behavior (exaggerated physical problems) or criminal activity (prescription forgery or theft).

Occasionally, patients exhibit "pseudo-addiction." The patient is anxious about running out of drug and may have used up the medication too quickly (signs which can be mistaken for addiction), but these may actually be due to poorly controlled pain. The response to this type of patient is not to scold, but to determine which aspects of their pain are inadequately controlled, and counsel them to return to their pain management provider for reassessment and additional help in developing a tailored pain management regimen. Frequently, the reason for "pseudo-addiction" is the over-reliance on a short-acting opioid combination, such as hydrocodone/acetaminophen. In such cases, if continuation of opioids is appropriate, consideration of conversion to an ER agent is warranted. Over-use of combination agents could put the patient at risk of hepatotoxicity (with combination acetaminophen-containing products) or nephrotoxicity (with NSAID-containing products).

Tolerance to opioids develops over time and necessitates a higher dose to produce the same analgesic response. It occurs in nearly every person taking chronic opioids and is often first recognized as a decrease in the duration of analgesia experienced from a given dose. It is important to distinguish whether the condition causing the pain has worsened (e.g., cancer), or there is a decrease in effectiveness of the medication, or both. Tolerance can usually be overcome by adjusting the dose and/or schedule of the opioid or switching to an equianalgesic dose of another opioid.

Different pain types may be treated better with alternative agents such as NSAIDs for bone and connective tissue pain, and SNRIs and antiepileptic drugs (AEDs) for neuropathic pain. In some patients chronic opioid use can worsen pain sensitivity, a phenomenon known as opioid hyperalgesia. In cases where this is suspected it is prudent to switch patients to a different opioid, or to consider weaning off opioids and using other types of analgesics.

"Break-through" pain (BTP), also called end of dose pain, is acute pain that occurs despite use of an ER or scheduled opioid. It is treated with an immediate release (IR) opioid. If repeat doses of BTP medication are required, then the baseline opioid dose should be increased or substituted with a different opioid. New or adjusted baseline opioids should be dispensed with a BTP medication until the dose of the scheduled opioid is stabilized. In the surgical setting, this can be done with the use of patient-controlled analgesia (PCA): the infusion pump provides a patient-controlled bolus or in some situations a continuous basal rate infusion.

Constipation is the most bothersome complication associated with the use of chronic opioids. Since tolerance does not occur to this adverse effect, careful attention to constipation prophylaxis is essential. Inpatients on intravenous opioids must be carefully monitored for sedation; sedation is the most important predictor of respiratory depression, the usual cause of fatality with an opioid overdose.

DRUG TREATMENT
Choosing the correct analgesic requires that the pain be characterized correctly. Pain is either nociceptive (physical trauma to an organ) or neuropathic (due to damage to a nerve or damage in the CNS).

Nociceptive pain is one of two types: somatic (from the skin, muscles, bones, joints and ligaments which is commonly called musculoskeletal pain) or visceral (from the internal organs, such as the heart or lungs). Neuropathic pain is associated with injury to a nerve or the central nervous system. Common causes of neuropathic pain are uncontrolled diabetes and neurotoxic chemotherapy. Neuropathic pain often responds best to antidepressants that affect norepinephrine reuptake and/or antiepileptic drugs (gabapentin, pregabalin, carbamazepine). In severe cases, other classes of agents are used, including opioids. See discussion at end of chapter.

Pain can be treated using a stepped approach, based on the patient's self-reported pain severity. Adjuvants (e.g., antiepileptic drugs, antidepressants, muscle relaxants) can be added at any step.

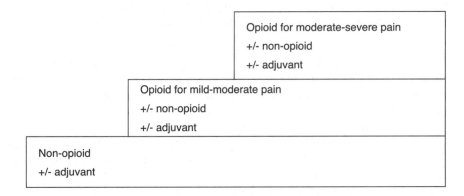

ACETAMINOPHEN

Acetaminophen reduces pain (analgesia) and reduces fever (antipyretic) but does not provide a significant anti-inflammatory effect nor does it inhibit thromboxane and therefore, has no effect on platelets. The mechanism of action is not well defined but is thought to involve inhibition of prostaglandin synthesis in the CNS and reduced pain impulse generation. Other mechanisms may include the endogenous cannabinoid system and inhibition of N-methyl-D-aspartate (NMDA) receptors. The antipyretic action is mediated by inhibition of heat regulating centers in the brain.

Acetaminophen Overdose

Antidote: N-Acetylcysteine (NAC, *Mucomyst*) PO and *Acetadote* IV (more costly)

MOA: Restores intracellular glutathione (acts as a glutathione substitute)

Administer immediately, even before the results of APAP level are obtained; within 8 hours of ingestion

Give 140 mg/kg PO loading dose, followed by 70 mg/kg PO Q4H x 17 doses (unless the initial APAP level is non-toxic)

Has an odor of rotten eggs and often causes N/V

Acetaminophen

DRUG	DOSING	SAFETY/SIDE EFFECTS/MONITORING
Acetaminophen *(Tylenol,* most "Non-Aspirin" pain relievers, *Ofirmev, FeverAll)* Tablet/caplet, chewable tablet, ODT, injection, suspension, infant drops, suppository *FeverAll:* Rectal suppository ***Ofirmev:* Injection** used inpatient to enable ↓ opioid doses, and when other routes are not feasible **+ Hydrocodone** *(Norco, Vicodin, Lortab)* **+ OxyCODONE** *(Percocet, Endocet)* **+ Codeine:** *(Tylenol #2, 3, 4)* **+ TraMADol** *(Ultracet)* + Diphenhydramine *(Tylenol PM)* And in multiple cough & cold products and OTC combos	**Adults** Max < 4,000 mg/day and max of 325 mg per prescription dosing unit in combo products, per the FDA. OTC dosing ranges depend on the formulation or are weight-based. 325 mg, max 2 tabs Q4-6H, NTE 10 tabs per 24 hr (3,250 mg) 500 mg, max 2 tabs Q6H, NTE 6 tabs per 24 hr (3,000 mg) 650 ER, max 2 tabs Q8H, NTE 6 tabs per 24 hr (3,900 mg) Rectal supp: 650 mg supp Q4-6H, NTE 6 supp per 24 hr (3,900 mg) IV (≥ 50 kg): 650 mg Q4H or 1,000 mg Q6H, max dose 4 grams/day *Recommended doses and max doses may differ for combination products.* **Pediatrics (< 12 yrs)** 10-15 mg/kg Q4-6H, max 5 doses/day or use weight and age based dosing table on container Infant drops are now the same concentration as the children's suspension (160 mg/5 mL) to ↓ dosing confusion and thus ↓ toxicity risk Rectal supp: 80, 120, 325, 650 mg	**BOXED WARNING** May cause severe hepatotoxicity (potentially requiring liver transplant or resulting in death), usually associated with excessive acetaminophen intake (> 4 grams/day) or use of more than one acetaminophen-containing product; risk of 10-fold dosing errors with injection. **SIDE EFFECTS** Hepatotoxicity (can be fatal) Cases of severe skin rash (rare) including SJS, TEN, AGEP. Stop drug, seek immediate medical help. Nephrotoxicity (rare, usually with chronic overdose); generally safer than NSAIDs in renal disease **NOTES** Pregnancy Category C (IV formulation); often used for mild pain in pregnancy. Avoid the "APAP" abbreviation on patient labels so they understand that they are getting acetaminophen. **SAFETY CONSIDERATIONS** Use dosing syringe or cup provided with the medicine. Caution with dosing IV acetaminophen: Concentration is 10 mg/mL (in 100 mL vials). Order in mg, not mLs (for example, a 75 mg dose is not 75 mL, it is 7.5 mL). Do not permit nurses to prepare doses in the units. All IV acetaminophen doses should be prepared in the pharmacy.

Acetaminophen Drug Interactions

- May be used with warfarin; however, if used chronically (doses > 2 grams/day), can ↑ INR. Monitor accordingly.

- Avoid or limit alcohol use due to the risk of hepatotoxicity. See counseling section.

Acetaminophen Counseling

- Contact your healthcare provider right away for any condition that is being self-treated if the condition worsens, if it lasts for more than two days, if there is a high fever (> 102.5°F), or with rash, nausea, vomiting or blood in the stool. These are true also for children. Infants should be seen by a pediatrician.

- Many products contain acetaminophen, including prescription pain medicines and over-the-counter pain and cough-and-cold products. The name may be written as acetaminophen, *Tylenol*, APAP, non-aspirin pain reliever, etc. The total daily dose of all products should not exceed the limits above.

- Too much acetaminophen can cause kidney damage, and can permanently harm the liver. This can be worsened by the use of too much alcohol. Women should not exceed more than 1 drink per day, and men should not exceed more than 2 drinks per day.

NON-STEROIDAL ANTI-INFLAMMATORY DRUGS

Non-steroidal anti-inflammatory drugs (NSAIDs) include the traditional (non-selective) NSAIDs such as ibuprofen, the salicylates, which includes aspirin, and the cyclooxygenase 2 (COX-2) inhibitors. The cyclooxygenase (COX) 1 and 2 enzymes catalyze the conversion of prostaglandins (PGs) and thromboxane A2 (TxA$_2$) from arachidonic acid. The non-selective NSAIDs block the synthesis of both COX enzymes. The COX-2 selective agents block the synthesis of COX-2 only, which ↓ GI risk because COX-1 protects the gastric mucosa. Both groups ↓ the formation of the PGs that are involved in ↓ inflammation, ↓ pain and ↓ fever. Blocking COX-1 ↓ the synthesis of PG-H2, which ↓ the formation of TxA$_2$. TxA$_2$ is required for both platelet activation and aggregation and blocking TxA$_2$ ↓ clotting and provides the cardiovascular benefit. Aspirin is a more effective antiplatelet agent than other non-selective NSAIDs because aspirin inhibits COX-1 irreversibly (with a covalent, irreversible bond). The other non-selective NSAIDs bind to COX-1 reversibly.

NSAID Boxed Warnings

A MedGuide is required for all NSAIDs (even OTC written on a prescription) due to these risks below. These boxed warnings are not repeated in the tables that follow.

All NSAIDs, Including Aspirin

- GI Risk: NSAIDs cause an ↑ risk of serious GI adverse events including bleeding, ulceration and perforation of the stomach and intestines, which can be fatal. These events can occur at any time during use and without warning. Elderly patients, those with history of GI bleed, patients taking corticosteroids and those taking SSRIs or SNRIs are at greatest risk for serious GI events.

All Non-Aspirin NSAIDs

- Cardiovascular Risk: NSAIDs may cause ↑ risk of serious cardiovascular thrombotic events, MI and stroke, which can be fatal. Risk may be ↑ with duration of use and in patients with CV disease or risk factors for CV disease.

  - In 2015, the FDA mandated updates to labeling of all non-aspirin NSAIDs (prescription and OTC) to reflect the following: ↑ risk of MI or stroke (as early as the first weeks of NSAID use). Increased risk with higher doses/longer duration of use and is present in patients without history or risk factors. NSAIDs can also ↑ risk of heart failure.

- CABG: Use is contraindicated for the treatment of perioperative pain in the setting of CABG surgery.

NSAIDs, Salicylates

DRUG	DOSING	SAFETY/SIDE EFFECTS/MONITORING
Aspirin/ Acetylsalicylic Acid *(Ascriptin, Bufferin, Ecotrin, Durlaza)* Tablet/caplet, chewable tablet, suppository *Ascriptin, Bufferin, Ecotrin:* EC/buffered *Durlaza* (Rx)*:* **ER capsule** Bayer *"Advanced" Aspirin:* dissolves slightly faster + acetaminophen and caffeine *(Excedrin, Excedrin Migraine)* + caffeine +/- acetaminophen *(Goody's* and *BC Headache Powders)* + antacid *(Alka-Seltzer)* + calcium *(Bayer Women's Low Dose)* And in multiple other OTC combos	Primarily used for cardioprotection: 81-162 mg *Durlaza* (Rx): 162.5 mg once daily Analgesic dosing: 325-650 mg Q4-6H All NSAIDs: known risk factors for GI bleeding: Elderly, previous bleed, chronic or high dose use, hypoxic gut. Check for dark, tarry stool, stomach upset, weakness, coffee-ground emesis (indicates a more serious, fast GI bleed).	**WARNINGS** Avoid with NSAID hypersensitivity (past reaction with trouble breathing), nasal polyps, asthma. Avoid aspirin (not other NSAIDs) in children and teenagers with any viral infection due to potential risk of Reye's syndrome (symptoms include somnolence, N/V, lethargy, confusion). Severe skin rash (rare) including SJS/TEN. Stop drug, seek immediate medical help. Upper GI events (ulcers), avoid if possible 1-2 weeks before surgery due to antiplatelet effects. **SIDE EFFECTS** Dyspepsia, heartburn, bleeding, renal impairment, ↑ blood pressure, CNS effects (fatigue, confusion, dizziness; caution in the elderly), photosensitivity, fluid retention/edema, hyperkalemia (in renal impairment or with potassium-retaining agents), blurred vision **NOTES** Pregnancy Category: most are C/D (avoid, esp in 3rd trimester). To ↓ nausea, use EC/buffered product or take with food. PPIs may be used to protect the gut with chronic NSAID; consider the risks from chronic PPI use (↓ bone density, ↑ infection risk). Do not use *Durlaza* when immediate effect is needed (e.g., MI). **Salicylate-Specific** Salicylate overdose can cause tinnitus. Take with food or water or milk to minimize GI upset. All NSAIDs should be taken with food, but salicylates usually cause more nausea. Methyl salicylate is a popular OTC topical found in *Bengay, Icy Hot, Flexal, Thera-Gesic, Salonpas*. See end of chapter.
Non-Acetylated Salicylates		
Salsalate	Up to 3 grams/day, divided BID-TID	
Magnesium Salicylate *(Doans, Doans ES, Momentum, Keygesic)*	ES: 580 mg/tablet 2 tablets Q6H, max 8 tablets/day	
Choline Magnesium Trisalicylate	1 gram BID-TID or 3 grams at bedtime	
Diflunisal	500 mg BID-TID (max 1.5 grams daily)	
Salicylate salts *(Arthropan, Asproject, Magan, Mobidin, Rexolate, Tusal)*	No longer commonly used	

NSAIDs, Others

DRUG	DOSING	SAFETY/SIDE EFFECTS/MONITORING
Ibuprofen *(Motrin, Advil, Caldolor, Neoprofen)* Tablet/capsule, chewable tablet, suspension, injection *Caldolor:* IV injection For mild-mod pain, can ↓ opioid dose, and can be used when oral routes are not available; must be diluted	**Adult** OTC: 200-400 mg Q4-6H, max 1.2 grams/day, limit self-treatment to ≤ 10 days Rx: 400-800 mg Q6-8H, max 3.2 grams/day ↑ doses required for inflammation **Pediatric** 5-10 mg/kg/dose Q6-8H (as an antipyretic), max daily dose 40 mg/kg/day	**NOTES** Similar to aspirin except for the risk of Reye's in children is not present (ibuprofen is used in pediatrics). Take with food to ↓ nausea. *Neoprofen* injection is indicated for closure of patent ductus arteriosis (PDA) in premature infants.
Naproxen (OTC: *Aleve,* Rx: *Naprelan, Naprosyn, Anaprox*) Tablet/capsule, suspension + sumatriptan *(Treximet)* + esomeprazole *(Vimovo)* And in OTC combos with diphenhydramine and pseudoephedrine	**OTC** Pain, fever: 200 mg (or 220 mg, if naproxen Na) 1 tab Q8-12H (may take 2 tabs for 1st dose); do not exceed 3 tabs in 24 hours **Rx** Inflammation, mild-mod pain: 500 mg Q12H (or occasionally 250 mg Q6-8H); max daily dose is 1,250 mg (Day #1) followed by 1,000 mg thereafter	**NOTES** Prescribers and patients sometimes prefer naproxen since it can be dosed BID. Naproxen base 200 mg = Naproxen Na 220 mg. The PPI in *Vimovo* is used to protect the gut from damage caused by the NSAID.
Diclofenac *(Cataflam, Voltaren-XR, Zorvolex, Zipsor, Cambia, Dyloject, Flector, Pennsaid)* Tablet/capsule, packet, gel, patch, topical solution, injection *Voltaren, Solaraze* gel *Pennsaid* topical solution + misoprostol *(Arthrotec)*	Oral tablets: 50-75 mg BID-TID *Zipsor* capsules: 25 mg four times per day *Zorvolex* capsules: 18 mg or 35 mg TID *Dyloject* IV: 37.5 mg Q6H *Flector* patch: 1 patch (180 mg) to most painful area BID *Cambia* packet: 1 packet (50 mg) mixed in water for acute migraine	**BOXED WARNING** *Arthrotec:* not to be used in women of childbearing potential unless woman is capable of complying with effective contraceptive measures. **NOTES** Possible risk of GI/renal issues; *Zorvolex* is lower dose. Oral diclofenac formulations are not bioequivalent even if mg strength is the same. Misoprostol is used to replace the gut-protective prostaglandin to ↓ the risk of GI damage from the NSAID. This used to be more popular before the advent of PPIs. In addition to ↑ uterine contractions (which can terminate pregnancy), misoprostol component causes cramping and diarrhea.
Indomethacin *(Indocin, Tivorbex)* Capsule, oral suspension, suppository, injection	IR: 25-50 mg BID-TID CR: 75 mg daily-BID *Tivorbex:* 20 mg TID or 40 mg BID-TID	High risk for CNS SEs (avoid in psych conditions) and GI toxicity. The IR formulation is an older NSAID approved for gout; any NSAID can be used. *Tivorbex* is micronized for faster dissolution. Injection indicated for closure of patent ductus arteriosis (PDA) in premature infants.
Piroxicam *(Feldene)*	10-20 mg daily	High risk for GI toxicity and severe skin reactions, including SJS/TEN Used when other NSAIDs have failed; may need agent to protect gut (PPI, misoprostol)

NSAIDs, Others Continued

DRUG	DOSING	SAFETY/SIDE EFFECTS/MONITORING
Ketorolac (Sprix, Toradol) Tablet, injection, nasal spray, ophthalmic *Acular:* ophthalmic	Oral: 10-20 mg x 1, then 10 mg Q4-6H PRN (max 40 mg/day) IV (≥ 50 kg): 30 mg x 1 or 30 mg Q6H (↓ dose if ≥ 65 y/o) IM (≥ 50 kg): 60 mg x 1 or 30 mg Q6H (↓ dose if ≥ 65 y/o) *Sprix:* < 65 y/o and ≥ 50 kg: 1 spray in each nostril Q6-8H ≥ 65 y/o or < 50 kg: 1 spray in one nostril Q6-8H Always start IV, IM or nasal spray and continue with oral, if necessary. Not to be used in any situation with increased bleeding risk. 5 days total max treatment.	**BOXED WARNINGS** For short-term moderate to severe acute pain only as continuation of IV or IM ketorolac (max combined duration IV/IM and PO/nasal is 5 days in adults), not for intrathecal or epidural use, contraindicated in advanced renal impairment or risk due to volume depletion; ↓ dose if ≥ 65 years old, < 50 kg and ↑ SCr. **NOTES** Can cause severe adverse effects including GI bleeding and perforation, post-op bleeding, acute renal failure, liver failure and anaphylactic shock. Usually used in post-op setting (never pre-op). Prime *Sprix* nasal spray 5 times before 1st dose each day.
Sulindac *(Clinoril)*	150-200 mg BID	Sometimes used with reduced renal function, and in patients on lithium who require an NSAID.
Other less-commonly used NSAIDs include: meclofenamate, mefenamic acid *(Ponstel)*, ketoprofen, fenoprofen *(Nalfon)*, flurbiprofen *(Ansaid)*, oxaprozin *(Daypro* – caution similar to piroxicam – higher risk of side effects).		

COX-2 Selective: Lower risk for GI complications (but still present), ↑ risk MI/stroke (avoid with CVD risk, avoid ↑ doses and longer duration in patients at risk for CVD), same risk for renal complications

Celecoxib (CeleBREX) Capsule	OA: 100 mg BID or 200 mg daily RA: 100-200 mg BID Indications: OA, RA, juvenile RA, acute pain, primary dysmenorrhea, ankylosing spondylitis	Highest COX-2 selectivity Contraindicated with sulfonamide allergy Same Boxed Warnings as other NSAIDs Pregnancy Category C prior to 30 weeks gestation; Category D starting at ≥ 30 weeks gestation
Meloxicam (Mobic, Vivlodex) Tablet/capsule, oral suspension	*Mobic:* 7.5-15 mg once daily *Vivlodex:* 5-10 mg once daily	These agents have some COX-2 selectivity. *Vivlodex* capsules and other meloxicam formulations are not interchangeable.
Etodolac *(Lodine)* Tablet/capsule	300-500 mg Q6-8H	
Nabumetone *(Relafen)* Tablet	1,000-2,000 mg daily (can be divided BID)	

NSAID Drug Interactions

- Caution for additive bleeding risk with other agents that can ↑ bleeding risk (e.g., anticoagulants, antiplatelet drugs, some herbals, SSRIs, SNRIs, thrombolytics and possibly others). See Drug Interactions chapter.

- Do not use NSAIDs with steroids due to very high risk GI bleeding.

- There is no reason to use two different NSAIDs concurrently (exception: low dose aspirin for cardio-protection but the cardioprotective effects may be blocked by ibuprofen and other NSAIDs). If using aspirin for cardioprotection and ibuprofen for pain, take aspirin one hour before or eight hours after ibuprofen.

- NSAIDs can ↑ the levels of lithium (avoid concurrent use) and methotrexate.

- Caution with use of aspirin and other ototoxic agents (aminoglycosides, IV loop diuretics, etc.)

NSAID Patient Counseling

- Dispense MedGuide and instruct patient to read it. This medicine can increase the chance of a heart attack or stroke that can lead to death. The risk increases in people who have heart disease. If you have heart disease, please discuss using this medicine with your healthcare provider.

- This medicine can cause ulcers and bleeding in the stomach and intestines at any time during treatment. The risk is highest if you use the drugs at higher doses, and when used long-term. To help reduce the risk, limit alcohol use while taking this medicine, and use the lowest possible dose for the shortest possible time. This medicine should not be used with medicines called steroids (such as prednisone) or anticoagulants (such as warfarin, *Pradaxa* or *Xarelto)*. [There are some exceptions in very high risk (clotting) patients who use both aspirin and warfarin. In general, using them together is not recommended.]

- Do not use after coronary heart surgery, unless you have been instructed to do so by your healthcare provider. Do not use this medicine before any elective surgery.

- Take with food if this medicine upsets your stomach.

- The risk of bleeding with these medicines is higher with many antidepressants, including SSRIs and SNRIs.

- Do not use this medicine if you have experienced breathing problems or allergic-type reactions after taking aspirin or other NSAIDs.

- This medicine can raise your blood pressure. If you have high blood pressure, you will need to check your blood pressure regularly. You may have to stop using this medicine if your blood pressure increases too much.

- This medicine can cause fluid and water to accumulate, particularly in your ankles. If you have heart disease, discuss the use of this medicine with your healthcare provider and monitor your weight.

- Photosensitivity: Limit sun exposure, including tanning booths, wear protective clothing, use sunscreen that blocks both UVA and UVB (this actually applies to some of the NSAIDs, but there is a class risk).

- Do not use this medicine if you are pregnant.

OPIOIDS

Opioid drugs interact in a variety of ways with the three primary types of opioid receptors: μ (mu), κ (kappa) and δ (delta). Opioids are mu receptor agonists in the CNS, and this is the primary mechanism for pain relief.

Opioids are available in many formulations (e.g., IR, ER, solution, patch, SL spray and film, transmucosal lozenge "lollipop", injection, suppository, nasal spray, iontophoretic transdermal system and abuse-deterrent formulations) and in many combination products. Brand names for some discontinued products (e.g., *Avinza*) are included here so they can be recognized. The names may continue to be used in clinical practice.

Opioid Boxed Warnings and Warnings

ER Opioid Formulations Boxed Warnings

On July 9, 2012, the FDA approved a <u>risk evaluation and mitigation strategy (REMS)</u> for <u>all ER opioid</u> medications. Primary components of the REMS: <u>Education for prescribers</u>, and requirement that the prescribers <u>counsel the patients</u>. Common <u>boxed warnings</u> include:

- <u>Addiction, abuse and misuse</u> with ER products, which can lead to overdose and death. Assess risk before prescribing and monitor regularly for these behaviors or conditions.

- <u>Respiratory depression</u> (highest risk at initiation and with dosage increases). Swallow whole. <u>Crushing, dissolving, or chewing</u> of the long acting products can cause the delivery of a <u>potentially fatal dose</u>. <u>Accidental ingestion/exposure</u> of even one dose in children can be fatal. Never give this medication to anyone else (includes patch formulations).

- Life-threatening neonatal opioid withdrawal with prolonged use during pregnancy.

- *Avinza, Kadian, Embeda, Zohydro, Opana ER and Nucynta ER:* Do not consume alcohol or alcohol <u>containing products</u> while taking this medication. Doing so can cause <u>increased plasma levels and a potentially fatal overdose</u>. *MS Contin, MorphaBond, Hysingla and Exalgo* have a similarly worded warning regarding alcohol, but it is not a boxed warning.

Warnings For All Opioids

- Additive sedation: Concomitant use with CNS depressants (including alcohol) may cause profound sedation, respiratory depression and death.

- Monitor closely in elderly, debilitated, cachectic patients and patients with chronic pulmonary disease (conditions associated with hypoxia) or head injury/increased intracranial pressure. All are at increased risk of respiratory depression.

- Risk of hypotension.

OPIOID AUXILLARY LABELS

Controlled substance: Do not share with others.

May cause dizziness or drowsiness.

Do not operate machinery.

Keep away from children and animals.

If ER: Do not crush, chew or dissolve. Swallow whole.

Do not drink alcoholic beverages.

Take with food or milk.

Opioid Allergy

True opioid allergies are rare. Most complaints of itching or rash are not a true allergic response. Symptoms of an opioid allergy (rare, but dangerous if present) include difficulty breathing, severe drop in blood pressure, serious rash, swelling of face, lips, tongue and larynx. In a true opioid allergy, <u>use an agent in a different chemical class</u> (see box).

CLASS	MEDICATIONS
Morphine-like (phenanthrenes)	Morphine, codeine, hydrocodone, hydromorphone, oxycodone, oxymorphone
Meperidine-like (phenylpiperidines)	Meperidine, fentanyl
Methadone (diphenylheptane)	Methadone
Central analgesics	Tapentadol, tramadol

These agents (less commonly used) also cross-react with morphine: pentazocine, nalbuphine, buprenorphine, butorphanol, levorphanol, naloxone, heroin (diacetyl-morphine). Tramadol package labeling warns of increased risk of reactions to tramadol in those with previous anaphylatoid reactions to opioids. Tapentadol does not have this warning in the U.S., though tramadol and tapentadol are structurally similar. If allergic to tramadol, an allergy to tapentadol is likely and vice versa.

DRUG	DOSING	SAFETY/SIDE EFFECTS/MONITORING
Morphine (ER: *MS Contin,* *Kadian, MorphaBond* *AVINza;* IR solution: *Roxanol;* injection: *Astramorph,* *Duramorph,* *Infumorph)* C-II Tablet (IR/ER), capsule (ER), injection, solution, suppository + naltrexone *(Embeda)* ER formulations, including *Embeda*, are REMS drugs.	Common dosing IR (including solution): 10-30 mg <u>Q4H</u> PRN ER: 15, 30, 60, 100, 200 mg <u>Q8-12H</u> *MorphaBond* BID, *Kadian* daily or BID, *Avinza* daily IV (opioid naïve): 2.5-5 mg <u>Q3-4H</u> PRN <u>Do not crush or</u> <u>chew any ER/</u> <u>CR opioids. Can</u> <u>open and sprinkle</u> <u>contents on</u> <u>applesauce, soft</u> <u>food.</u> If <u>renally impaired</u>, start at a lower dose, or avoid morphine, oxycodone, tramadol or tapentadol due to accumulation of parent drug and/or active metabolite(s).	**BOXED WARNINGS** Medication errors with oral solution (note strength), appropriate staff and equipment needed for intrathecal/epidural administration **SIDE EFFECTS** **GI effects** <u>Constipation, N/V</u> (may need anti-emetics) **CNS effects** <u>Somnolence, dizziness</u>, changes in mood, confusion, delirium **Skin reactions** Flushing, <u>pruritus</u>, diaphoresis; may need <u>antihistamine</u> **Respiratory depression** Caused by opioid overdose or combination with other sedatives and CNS depressants, and can be fatal (see opioid antagonist section that follows). **NOTES** Do not use MSO4 or MS abbreviations for morphine or magnesium, due to risk of errors. **Constipation** Tolerance usually develops to opioid side effects <u>except</u> constipation. When opioids are used around the clock (ATC), docusate alone will rarely be enough to treat constipation. It will likely require <u>stimulant</u> laxatives (senna, bisacodyl), osmotic laxatives (e.g., MOM) or commonly <u>docusate + stimulant</u> combinations. Methylnaltrexone (*Relistor*) is a laxative (given SC) for constipation due to opioids (it blocks gut opioid-receptors). The patient <u>must have failed</u> DSS + laxative (senna, bisacodyl). Alternatives to *Relistor* include oral naloxone solution, lubiprostone and naloxegol (see Opioid-Induced Constipation in this chapter).

Opioids Continued

DRUG	DOSING	SAFETY/SIDE EFFECTS/MONITORING
FentaNYL *(Duragesic)* C-II Injection, buccal/ SL tablet, lozenge, SL film, SL spray, nasal spray, patch, iontophoretic transdermal system *Actiq* oral transmucosal lozenge (on a stick "lollipop"): Always start with 200 mcg, can titrate to 4 BTP episodes/day. Only for cancer BTP. *Lazanda:* nasal spray *Fentora:* buccal tabs *Ionsys:* iontophoretic transdermal system *Abstral:* tabs, SL *Onsolis:* film, SL *Subsys:* spray, SL Fentanyl transmucosal forms and *Ionsys* system (not patch or injection) are REMS drugs.	Patch: <u>Apply 1 patch Q72H (occas. Q48H)</u> 12 (delivers 12.5 mcg/hr), 25, 50, 75, 100 mcg/h patch strengths <u>Do not ↑ dose if pain is controlled but doesn't last long enough. In this case shorten the interval</u> (change to Q48H) as you would do with any ER opioid. Otherwise, you risk overdose or higher degree of side effects.	**BOXED WARNINGS** Potential for <u>medication errors</u> when converting between different dosage forms, use with <u>strong or moderate CYP 3A4 inhibitors</u> may result in increased effects and potentially fatal respiratory depression **SIDE EFFECTS** Constipation, bradycardia, confusion, dizziness, somnolence, diaphoresis, dehydration, dry mouth, N/V, muscle rigidity, weakness, miosis, dyspnea **NOTES** <u>Fentanyl, in any form, is for chronic pain management only</u>. Can convert a patient who has been using <u>morphine 60 mg/day</u> or equivalent <u>for at least 7 days</u>. Fentanyl is not used in opioid-naïve patients (especially the potent SL forms, which are for cancer-related BTP). Cut off stick and flush unused/unneeded *Actiq*. Short t½ when given IV. IV boluses are given Q1-2H, but commonly given as continuous infusion or PCA. *Ionsys:* iontophoretic transdermal system for <u>hospital use only</u> (for short-term post-op pain); patient presses button to deliver on-demand doses. Healthcare providers must wear gloves when handling the device. <u>Remove before discharge</u>. Similar drugs (IV only): alfentanil *(Alfenta)*, <u>remifentanil</u> *(Ultiva)*, sufentanil *(Sufenta)*

Fentanyl Patch Information

- Analgesic effect can be seen 8 – 16 hrs after application. Do not stop other analgesic immediately (↓ dose 50% for the first 12 hrs).

- <u>Do not apply > 1 patch each time.</u>

- <u>Do not heat patch or skin area before or after applying. Do not cover with heating pad or any bandage</u>. Caution with <u>fever</u> (tell patient to <u>call healthcare provider</u> if they have a fever).

- Do not switch generic fentanyl patches. Try to use the same one.

- <u>Some patches need to be removed prior to MRI.</u>

- Apply to hairless skin (<u>cut</u> short if necessary) on flat surface (chest, back, flank, upper arm) and change every 72 hrs. <u>Press in place for 30 seconds</u>.

- Do not use soap, alcohol, or other solvents to remove transdermal gel if it accidentally touches skin. Use large amount of water.

- <u>Dispose of patch in toilet or cut it up and put it in coffee grounds.</u>

- <u>Keep away from children and animals, including used patches.</u>

- Keep in child-resistant box.

Opioids Continued

DRUG	DOSING	SAFETY/SIDE EFFECTS/MONITORING
Hydrocodone IR (combination products only) C-II (including combo products) **+ acetaminophen** (***Norco,*** Lorcet, Lortab, Vicodin, Zydone, Anexsia, Co-Gesic) Select combination products: + chlorpheniramine (*TussiCaps*) + chlorpheniramine and pseudoephedrine (*Zutripro*) + pseudoephedrine (*Rezira*) + homatropine (*Tussigon*) + ibuprofen (*Vicoprofen, Reprexain*)	*Norco:* 2.5, 5, 7.5, 10 mg hydrocodone + 325 mg acetaminophen Usual starting dose: 5/325 or 10/325 PO Q6H (or 4 times per day)	**BOXED WARNING** Acetaminophen may cause severe <u>hepatotoxicity</u> (potentially requiring liver transplant or resulting in death), usually associated with <u>excessive acetaminophen intake</u> (> 4 grams/day) or <u>use of more than one acetaminophen-containing product</u>. **WARNINGS** Those that apply to acetaminophen and opioids: respiratory and/or CNS depression, constipation, hypotension, skin reactions (rare), caution in liver disease (avoid or limit alcohol intake) and in 2D6 poor metabolizers **SIDE EFFECTS** N/V, dizziness, lightheadedness, sedation, constipation, risk of respiratory depression and rare side effects related to acetaminophen **NOTES** Products with > 325 mg acetaminophen per dosage unit are no longer considered safe by the FDA.
Hydrocodone ER (*Zohydro, Hysingla ER*) C-II REMS drugs	*Zohydro* (capsule): start at 10 mg <u>Q12H</u> (opioid-naïve) Range 10-50 mg *Hysingla ER* (tablet): start at 20 mg <u>Q24H</u> (opioid-naïve) Range 20-120 mg	**BOXED WARNINGS** Initiation of <u>3A4 inhibitors</u> (or stopping 3A4 inducers) can cause fatal overdose. **NOTES** Both are substrates of 3A4 (major) & 2D6 (minor). Preferably avoid use if breast feeding. Monitor for respiratory depression and sedation. Abuse-deterrent formulations. *Hysingla* QT prolongation has occurred at doses > 160 mg/day.
HYDROmorphone (***Dilaudid, Dilaudid-HP***) C-II Tablet, injection, solution *Exalgo:* ER tablet *Exalgo* is a REMS drug.	Initial (opioid-naïve) Oral: 2-4 mg <u>Q4-6H</u> PRN <u>IV: 0.2-1 mg Q2-3H</u> PRN May cause less nausea, pruritus	**BOXED WARNINGS** Risk of medication error with high potency (HP) injection (use in opioid-tolerant patients only) **NOTES** <u>Potent</u>; start low, convert carefully. <u>High risk for overdose.</u> Caution with 3A4 inhibitors, use lower doses initially. Commonly used in PCAs and epidurals. *Dilaudid HP* (10 mg/mL) is a higher potency injection than *Dilaudid* (1 mg/mL). *Exalgo* is an abuse-deterrent formulation (crush and extraction resistant). *Exalgo* is contraindicated in opioid-naïve patients. Two week washout required between *Exalgo* and MAO inhibitors.

Opioids Continued

DRUG	DOSING	SAFETY/SIDE EFFECTS/MONITORING
OxyCODONE C-II (full opioids and combos) Tablet/capsule (IR), tablet (ER), solution IR: *Oxaydo,* ***Roxicodone*** CR: ***OxyCONTIN*** **+ acetaminophen (*Endocet, Percocet, Roxicet,* *Xartemis XR*)** + naloxone *(Targiniq ER)* + ibuprofen + aspirin *(Percodan)* CR formulations are REMS drugs.	IR: 5-20 mg Q4-6H CR: 10-80 mg Q12H (60, 80 mg only for opioid-tolerant patients) Do not use or ↓ dose with renal impairment. If ER ↓ by ½ - ⅓	**BOXED WARNINGS** Initiation of 3A4 inhibitors (or stopping 3A4 inducers) can cause fatal overdose, caution with oxycodone oral solution and oral concentrate (confusion between mg and mL and different concentrations) **NOTES** *Oxaydo, OxyContin* and *Targiniq ER* are abuse-deterrent formulations. Substrate of 3A4 (major) & 2D6 (minor). Preferably avoid use if breast feeding. Avoid high fat meals with higher doses (except reformulated *OxyContin*).
Oxymorphone (*Opana, Opana ER*) C-II Tablet (IR/ER), injection *Opana ER* is a REMS drug.	IR (opioid-naïve): 5-10 mg Q4-6H PRN ER (opioid-naïve): 5 mg Q12H Take on empty stomach (most other analgesics are with food to help avoid stomach upset)	**NOTES** Do not use with moderate-to-severe liver impairment. Use low doses in elderly, renal or mild liver impairment; there will be higher drug concentrations in these patients. *Opana ER:* abuse-deterrent formulation. *Opana ER* is not suitable for use as an "as needed" analgesic. Tablets should not be broken, chewed, dissolved, or crushed; tablets should be swallowed whole. *Opana ER* is intended for use in long-term, continuous management of moderate-to-severe chronic pain.
Methadone (*Dolophine, Methadone Intensol, Methadose*) C-II Tablet, soluble tablet, solution Methadone is a REMS drug.	Initial: 2.5-10 mg Q8-12H Methadone 40 mg is indicated for detox and maintenance treatment of opioid-addicted patients. Useful for detox because it relieves opioid craving and blocks euphoric effects of abusable opioids.	**BOXED WARNINGS** Life-threatening QT prolongation and serious arrhythmias (e.g., TdP) have occurred during treatment (most involve large, multiple daily doses). Should be prescribed by professionals who know requirements for safe use. **NOTES** Due to variable half-life from 15-60 hrs and in some cases up to 100 hrs due to polymorphism, methadone is hard to dose safely and has a risk of QT prolongation (proarrhythmic) which will be aggravated if dosed incorrectly. Can ↓ testosterone and contribute to sexual dysfunction (others opioids can also, but methadone is notable). In combo with other drugs, it is serotonergic and can raise risk of serotonin syndrome. Methadone also blocks reuptake of norepinephrine. Methadone is a major 3A4 substrate; avoid inhibitors concurrently or lower methadone dose.

Opioids Continued

DRUG	DOSING	SAFETY/SIDE EFFECTS/MONITORING
Meperidine *(Demerol, Meperitab)* C-II Tablet, solution, injection	Oral/IM: 50-150 mg Q3-4H PRN <u>Short duration of action</u> (pain controlled for max 3 hrs)	**WARNING** <u>Renal impairment/elderly at risk for CNS toxicity</u>, avoid with or within 2 weeks of MAO inhibitor **SIDE EFFECTS** Lightheadedness, dizziness, somnolence, N/V, sweating **NOTES** Normeperidine (metabolite) is renally cleared and can accumulate and cause CNS toxicity, including <u>seizures</u>. In combo with other drugs, it is <u>serotonergic</u> and can raise risk of serotonin syndrome. <u>No longer recommended as an analgesic</u> (especially in elderly and renally impaired). <u>Avoid for chronic pain management</u> and even short-term in elderly. Acceptable for short-term acute or single use (e.g., sutures in ER) and used off-label for post-operative rigors (shivering).
Codeine **+ acetaminophen** *(Tylenol #2, 3, 4)* C-II: codeine C-III: combos (w/ acetaminophen) C-V: antitussives (anti-cough), codeine cough syrups	*Tylenol #3:* 1 tab (acetaminophen 300 mg + codeine 30 mg) Q4-6H PRN, range 15-120 mg codeine	**BOXED WARNING** Respiratory depression and death have occurred in children who received codeine following tonsillectomy and/or adenoidectomy and were found to have evidence of being <u>ultra-rapid metabolizers of codeine due to a 2D6 polymorphism</u>. Deaths have also occurred in nursing infants after being exposed to high concentrations of morphine because the mothers were ultra-rapid metabolizers. Use is contraindicated in the postoperative pain management of children who have undergone tonsillectomy and/or adenoidectomy. **SIDE EFFECTS** Codeine has a high degree of GI side effects: constipation, N/V/D

Centrally Acting Analgesics

Both tramadol and tapentadol are <u>mu-opioid receptor agonists</u> and <u>inhibitors</u> of <u>norepinephrine reup-take</u>. Tramadol also inhibits reuptake of <u>serotonin</u>. Tapentadol has the <u>same boxed warnings as other opioids</u> (see previous discussion), while tramadol has no boxed warnings.

DRUG	DOSING	SAFETY/SIDE EFFECTS/MONITORING
TraMADol *(Ultram, Ultram ER, Conzip)* C-IV Tablet (IR/ER), capsule (ER) **+ acetaminophen** *(Ultracet)*	IR: 50-100 mg Q4-6H, max 400 mg/day ER: 100 mg once daily, max 300 mg/day CrCl < 30 mL/min: IR: ↓ dose ER: do not use	**WARNINGS** <u>Seizure risk</u> (avoid in patients with seizure history, head trauma), risk of <u>serotonin syndrome</u> when used alone or with other serotonergic drugs or <u>inhibitors of 2D6 or 3A4</u>, CNS depression (avoid alcohol and do not crush/chew/dissolve ER capsules), respiratory depression (rare), avoid in patients who are suicidal; misuse, abuse and diversion (similar to opioids) **SIDE EFFECTS** Dizziness, nausea, constipation, loss of appetite, flushing, dry mouth, dyspepsia, pruritus, insomnia (some patients find tramadol sedating but for most it is not; this can be an advantage over hydrocodone), possible headache, ataxia. <u>Lower severity of GI side effects versus strong opioids</u>. **NOTES** Tramadol requires conversion to active metabolite by 2D6. Use with 2D6 inhibitors can have variable effects due to mixed MOA of tramadol. <u>Off-label use</u> of tramadol in <u>children < 17 years</u> of age can cause <u>slowed or difficult breathing</u>; ↑ risk following tonsillectomy/adenoidectomy and/or ultra rapid metabolizers.

Centrally Acting Analgesics Continued

DRUG	DOSING	SAFETY/SIDE EFFECTS/MONITORING
Tapentadol *(Nucynta, Nucynta ER)* C-II Tablet (IR/ER) *Nucynta ER* is a REMS drug.	IR: 50-100 mg Q4-6H PRN ER: 50-250 mg BID CrCl < 30 mL/min: Use not recommended (not studied). Use with severe renal insufficiency is a CI in Canada.	**CONTRAINDICATIONS** Use of MAO inhibitors concurrently or within 14 days **WARNINGS** May increase seizure risk (avoid in patients with seizure history or seizure risk), risk of serotonin syndrome when used alone or with other serotonergic drugs **SIDE EFFECTS** Dizziness, somnolence, nausea but lower severity of GI side effects than stronger opioids

Opioid Drug Interactions

- Caution with use of concurrent CNS depressants: Additive somnolence, dizziness, confusion, increased risk of respiratory depression. These include alcohol, hypnotics, benzodiazepines, muscle relaxants, etc. Avoid alcohol with all opioids, especially ER formulations. Boxed warning to avoid alcohol with *Avinza, Kadian, Embeda, Zohydro, Opana ER and Nucynta ER.*

- Increased risk of hypoxemia with underlying respiratory disease (e.g., COPD) and sleep apnea.

- Methadone: Caution with agents that worsen cardiac function or increase arrhythmia risk. Caution with other serotonergic agents.

- Meperidine: Caution with agents that worsen renal function, elderly and those with seizure history. Caution with other serotonergic agents.

- Tramadol and tapentadol: Caution with other agents that lower seizure threshold. Caution with other serotonergic agents. Avoid tramadol with 2D6 inhibitors (requires conversion). Possibility of increased INR with warfarin; monitor. Tapentadol may enhance the adverse/toxic effect of MAO inhibitors; avoid concurrent use.

Opioid Counseling

- Do not crush, chew, break, or open controlled-release forms. Breaking them would cause too much drug to be released into your blood at one time.

- *Avinza* and *Kadian* must be swallowed whole or may be opened and the entire bead contents sprinkled on a small amount of applesauce immediately prior to ingestion. The beads must not be chewed, crushed, or dissolved due to the risk of exposure to a potentially toxic dose of morphine. *Avinza* can be put down a G-tube.

- *Opana* and *Opana ER*: take on empty stomach (1 hr before, 2 hr after eating).

- Avoid alcohol with all opioids, especially ER formulations. Boxed warning to avoid alcohol with *Avinza, Kadian, Embeda, Zohydro, Opana ER and Nucynta ER.*

- To ensure that you get a correct dose, measure liquid forms with a special dose-measuring spoon or cup, not with a regular tablespoon. If you do not have a dose-measuring device, ask your pharmacist.

- This medicine will cause drowsiness and fatigue. Avoid alcohol, sleeping pills, antihistamines, sedatives, and tranquilizers that may also make you drowsy, except under the supervision of your healthcare provider.

- Take with a full glass of water. Take with food or milk if it upsets your stomach.

- Do not stop taking suddenly if you have been taking it continuously for more than 5 to 7 days. If you want to stop, your healthcare provider will help you gradually reduce the dose.

- This medicine is constipating. Increase the amount of fiber and water (at least six to eight full glasses daily) in your diet to prevent constipation (if not fluid restricted due to heart failure). Your pharmacist or healthcare provider will recommend a stronger agent for constipation if this is not adequate. (If asked, recommend stool softener if hard stool, stimulants for most scheduled opioid patients.)

- Do not share this medication with anyone else.

- Never take more pain medicine than prescribed. If your pain is not being adequately treated, talk to your healthcare provider.

Opioid Dose Conversions

The correct dose is the lowest dose that provides effective pain relief. If the dose has been increased and the pain relief is not adequate or if the side effects are intolerable (patients react differently to different opioids) or if the drug is unaffordable or not included on formulary, then switch. Switch safely and monitor for hyperalgesia, which should be suspected when opioids increase pain (rather than decreasing pain) due to a paradoxical situation. This happens occasionally, and if so, increasing the dose will not work. If switching to morphine and the patient has renal insufficiency, a 50% reduction in the total daily dose or similar would be wise; morphine has an active metabolite that is renally cleared, thus a lower dose is required. Always use breakthrough medication, as-needed, when converting.

For opioid conversions (not methadone) you can use ratio conversion. Make sure the units and route in the numerator match, and the units and route in the denominator match. You can technically convert with fentanyl (note no oral dose conversion as fentanyl is not absorbed orally) but it is often done differently using a dosing table (see table and example). Some clinicians use this estimation: morphine 60 mg total daily dose = 25 mcg/hr fentanyl patch. If converting fentanyl using the chart, remember that you are finding the total daily dose in mg, and will then need to convert it to mcg (multiply by 1,000) and then divide by 24 to get the patch dose; fentanyl is dosed in mcg per hour.

When converting one opioid to another, round down (do not round up) and use breakthrough doses for compensation. A patient may respond better to one agent than another (likely due to less tolerance) and estimating lower will reduce the risk of overdose.

DRUG	IV/IM (MG)	ORAL (MG)
Morphine	10	30
Hydromorphone	1.5	7.5
Oxycodone	–	20
Hydrocodone	–	30
Codeine	130	200
Fentanyl	0.1	–
Meperidine	75	300
Oxymorphone	1	10

If the medicine is effective, but runs out too fast, do not increase the dose. This will cause a risk of respiratory depression. Rather, shorten the dosing interval.

To convert

- Calculate total 24 hr dose requirement of the current drug.

- Use ratio-conversion to calculate the dose of the new drug: make sure the numerators and denominators match in both drug and route of administration.

- Calculate 24 hr dose of new drug and <u>reduce dose at least 25%</u>. (If the problem on the exam does not specify to reduce it, but just to find the equivalent dose, then do not reduce it.)

- Divide to attain appropriate interval and dose for new drug.

- Always have breakthrough pain (BTP) medication available while making changes. Guideline recommendation for BTP dosing ranges from 5 – 17% of the total daily baseline opioid dose.

Example of Opioid Conversion:

A hospice patient has been receiving 12 mg/day of IV hydromorphone. The pharmacist will convert the hydromorphone to morphine ER, to be given Q12H. The hospice policy for opioid conversion is to reduce the new dose by 50%, and to use 5 – 17% of the total daily dose for breakthrough pain.

The conversion factors (the left fraction) are taken from the above table. The right fraction has the patient's current total daily IV dose of hydromorphone in the denominator, and the total daily dose of morphine in the numerator:

$$\frac{30 \text{ mg oral morphine}}{1.5 \text{ mg IV hydromorphone}} = \frac{X \text{ mg oral morphine}}{12 \text{ mg IV hydromorphone}} \qquad X = 240 \text{ mg of oral morphine}$$

Multiply the top left numerator (30) by the bottom right denominator (12), and then divide by the left denominator (1.5). This will give a total daily dose of morphine (PO) of 240 mg.

Reduce by 50%, as instructed in the problem:

50% of 240 mg = 120 mg, the correct dose of morphine ER would be 60 mg BID

Whenever possible, use an immediate release version of the long-acting opioid for BTP. Typically 10 – 15% of the total daily dose is administered Q1-2H for BTP (~5% administered Q4H in the elderly). For example, a rescue dose of 15 mg IR morphine Q1-2H could be used with morphine ER 60 mg BID in the example above and this would adhere to the hospice policy stated in the question. Other agents commonly used for BTP include combo agents, such as hydrocodone/acetaminophen. In an inpatient setting, injections can be given. Injections will have a faster onset and since BTP is typically severe, they may be preferable. However, if the patient does not have a port, the injection itself will cause discomfort. In real life, morphine IR may not be available. Hydrocodone/acetaminophen is often used for breakthrough pain. The hydrocodone dose is roughly the same as the morphine dose. If the patient is using acetaminophen alone for more mild pain, or the combination for moderate pain, the total daily acetaminophen intake will need to be monitored. Keep in mind that any drug that requires oral absorption will take time; if the patient has cancer pain (in which case the breakthrough pain is likely to be quite severe) a sublingual form of fentanyl may be used, which has faster onset.

Example of Conversion to Fentanyl Patch using a Fentanyl Patch Conversion Table

MJ is a 52 year old male patient who has been using *OxyContin* 40 mg BID and *Endocet* 5-325 mg as-needed for breakthrough pain. He uses the breakthrough pain medication 2 – 3 times weekly. Using the *OxyContin* dose only select the fentanyl patch strength that should be chosen for this patient, using the following table:

OPIOID CONVERSION TO FENTANYL PATCH USING CHART IN THE DURAGESIC PACKAGE INSERT

Table 1: DOSE CONVERSION TO DURAGESIC				
Current Analgesic	Daily Dosage (mg/day)			
Oral morphine	60–134	135–224	225–314	315–404
Intramuscular or Intravenous morphine	10–22	23–37	38–52	53–67
Oral oxycodone	30–67	67.5–112	112.5–157	157.5–202
Oral codeine	150–447			
Oral hydromorphone	8–17	17.1–28	28.1–39	39.1–51
Intravenous hydromorphone	1.5–3.4	3.5–5.6	5.7–7.9	8–10
Intramuscular meperidine	75–165	166–278	279–390	391–503
Oral methadone	20–44	45–74	75–104	105–134
	↓	↓	↓	↓
Recommended DURAGESIC Dose	25 mcg/hour	50 mcg/hour	75mcg/hour	100 mcg/hour

Table 1 should not be used to convert from DURAGESIC to other therapies because this conversion to DURAGESIC is conservative. Use of Table 1 for conversion to other analgesic therapies can overestimate the dose of the new agent. Overdosage of the new analgesic agent is possible

SOLUTION

Oxycodone 80 mg daily is in the range of 67.5 – 112 mg daily which correlates to the 50 mcg/hr patch.

Methadone Conversion: Not straight-forward; should be done by pain specialists

Methadone conversion from morphine ranges from 1 – 20:1; this is highly variable due to patient tolerance and duration of therapy. The half-life of methadone varies widely. There are separate conversion charts for pain specialists to estimate methadone dosing. This should be done only by specialists with experience in using methadone. In addition to the variable half-life, methadone is proarrhythmic and has other safety issues. Methadone is used both for the treatment of opioid addiction and for chronic pain. When used for chronic pain syndromes, it is administered 2 – 3 times per day after the proper dose is determined by titration. It should be started at very low doses of no more than 2.5 mg PO BID or TID, and escalated slowly.

OPIOID-INDUCED CONSTIPATION

Methylnaltrexone and naloxegol are peripherally-acting mu-opioid receptor antagonists (PAMORAs) indicated for opioid-induced constipation (OIC). These drugs block opioid receptors in the gut to reduce constipation without affecting analgesic effects of opioids. Lubiprostone works by activating chloride channels in the gut, leading to increased fluid in the gut and peristalsis. Refer to the Constipation & Diarrhea chapter for discussion of lubiprostone for IBS.

DRUG	DOSING	SAFETY/SIDE EFFECTS/MONITORING
Methylnaltrexone *(Relistor)* Injection	OIC with chronic non-cancer pain: <u>12 mg SC daily</u> OIC with advanced illness: weight-based dose SC every other day Administer SC in the upper arm, abdomen or thigh CrCl < 30 mL/min: ↓ dose Discontinue all laxatives prior to use	**CONTRAINDICATION** GI obstruction **WARNINGS** Risk of GI perforation (rare reports; monitor for severe abdominal symptoms), risk of opioid withdrawal (evaluate risk vs benefit and monitor), use > 4 months has not been studied, discontinue if opioid is discontinued or if severe/persistent diarrhea **SIDE EFFECTS** Abdominal pain, flatulence, N/D **NOTES** Stay close to toilet after injecting. <u>Only for patients on opioids who have failed DSS + laxative</u> (senna, bisacodyl). <u>Do not use routinely</u>; can often increase laxative to obtain effect. MedGuide required.
Naloxegol *(Movantik)* Tablet	OIC with chronic non-cancer pain: 25 mg once daily in the morning on empty stomach CrCl < 60 mL/min: 12.5 mg once daily Discontinue all laxatives prior to use; can reintroduce laxatives as needed if suboptimal response to naloxegol after 3 days	**CONTRAINDICATIONS** GI obstruction, use with strong 3A4 inhibitors **WARNINGS** Risk of GI perforation (rare reports; monitor for severe abdominal symptoms), risk of opioid withdrawal (evaluate risk vs benefit and monitor) **SIDE EFFECTS** Abdominal pain, diarrhea, headache, flatulence **NOTES** Discontinue if opioid is discontinued. Do not use with strong 3A4 inhibitors. Avoid use or reduce dose to 12.5 mg daily with moderate 3A4 inhibitors. Do not use with grapefruit juice. MedGuide required.
Lubiprostone *(Amitiza)* Tablet	OIC: 24 mcg BID	**CONTRAINDICATION** GI obstruction **NOTES** See Constipation & Diarrhea chapter

BUPRENORPHINE AND NALOXONE FORMULATIONS

Buprenorphine is a <u>partial</u> mu-opioid agonist, meaning is acts as an agonist at low doses and an antagonist at higher doses. It is used in lower doses to treat pain and higher doses to treat addiction. <u>Naloxone is an opioid antagonist</u>; it replaces the opioid on the mu receptor. Given by itself, <u>naloxone</u> (injection or nasal spray) <u>is used for opioid overdose</u>. Buprenorphine/naloxone combination products are used as alternatives to methadone for opioid dependence (buprenorphine suppresses withdrawal symptoms and naloxone helps prevents misuse). Naltrexone is an opioid blocker normally used to help treat alcoholism *(ReVia)*; the IV form *(Vivitrol)* is used for alcohol and opioid dependence.

S/SX OF ACUTE OPIOID OVERDOSE
Somnolence
Respiratory depression with shallow breathing
Constricted (pinpoint) pupils (miosis)
Cold and clammy skin
Overdose can lead to coma and death

DRUG	DOSING	SAFETY/SIDE EFFECTS/MONITORING
Naloxone *(Narcan, Evzio)* Injection, nasal spray *Narcan* nasal spray *Evzio* auto-injector	IV/IM/SC: 0.4-2 mg Q2-3 min or IV infusion at 100 mL/hr (0.4 mg/hr) Nasal spray: 1 spray (4 mg), may repeat <u>Repeat dosing may be required</u> (opioid may last longer than blocking agent) The *Evzio* auto-injector (0.4 mg) has voice directions. Can be given by patients or friends for overdose emergency; give in thigh through clothing, hold for 5 seconds, if any doubt, inject, then call 911.	**NOTES** Naloxone will cause an <u>acute withdrawal</u> syndrome (<u>pain</u>, anxiety, tachypnea) in patients physically dependent on opioids. Due to low bioavailability, can be given orally to prevent opioid-induced constipation (off-label). Highest risk of respiratory depression from opioids: opioid-naïve patients (new users), if dose is ↑ too rapidly, and in illicit substance abuse (e.g., heroin).
Buprenorphine C-III Injection, patch, buccal film **Butrans:** patch (only for mod-severe pain in patients who need ATC opioid) *Buprenex:* injection **Belbuca:** buccal film **+ naloxone** *(Bunavail:* buccal tablets, **Suboxone:** buccal film, **Zubsolv**: sublingual tablets) REMS drugs (all)	*Butrans* (opioid-naïve): 5 mcg/hr patch <u>once weekly</u> *Belbuca* (opioid-naïve): 75 mcg daily or Q12H *Bunavail, Suboxone, Zubsolv:* Used daily for addiction <u>To prescribe for opioid dependence:</u> Prescribers need Drug Addiction Treatment Act (DATA 2000) waiver. If they have it, the DEA number will start with X. **PATCH APPLICATION** Apply to upper outer arm, upper chest, side of chest, upper back. <u>Change weekly</u>. Do not use same site for at least 3 weeks. Disposal: Fold sticky sides together, flush or put in disposal unit that comes with drug.	**BOXED WARNINGS (***BUTRANS* **PATCH)** Risk of addiction, abuse and misuse; risk of serious or fatal <u>respiratory depression</u>; life-threatening neonatal opioid withdrawal with prolonged use during pregnancy, <u>accidental ingestion</u> (especially in children) can be fatal **WARNINGS** CNS depression, QT prolongation (do not exceed one 20 mcg/hr patch) **SIDE EFFECTS** <u>Sedation</u>, dizziness, headache, confusion, mental and physical impairment, diaphoresis, QT prolongation, respiratory depression (dose-dependent) Patch: nausea, headache, application site pruritus/rash, dizziness, constipation, somnolence, vomiting, application site erythema, dry mouth **NOTES** Do not expose patch to heat.

Buprenorphine Drug Interactions

- Caution with use of concurrent CNS depressants: Additive sedation (somnolence), dizziness, confusion. These include alcohol, hypnotics, benzodiazepines, skeletal muscle relaxants, etc.

- Prolongs the QT interval. Do not use with other QT-prolonging agents or in patients at risk of arrhythmia.

MUSCLE RELAXANTS

Muscle relaxants have various, poorly-understood mechanisms of action. Some work predominantly by CNS depression leading to relaxation of skeletal muscles (carisoprodol, chlorzoxazone, metaxalone, methocarbamol), while others work by decreasing transmission of reflexes at the spinal level.

DRUG	DOSING	SAFETY/SIDE EFFECTS/MONITORING

Antispasmodics with analgesic effects

DRUG	DOSING	SAFETY/SIDE EFFECTS/MONITORING
Baclofen *(Lioresal)* Tablet, injection **AUX LABELS** May cause drowsiness. Do not operate machinery....	5-20 mg TID-QID PRN Injection given via intrathecal pump for severe spasticity	**BOXED WARNING** Abrupt withdrawal of intrathecal baclofen has resulted in severe effects (hyperpyrexia, obtundation, rebound/exaggerated spasticity, muscle rigidity, and rhabdomyolysis), leading to organ failure and some fatalities. **SIDE EFFECTS** For all muscle relaxants: excessive sedation, dizziness, confusion **NOTES** Do not overdose in elderly (e.g., start low, titrate carefully), watch for additive side effects.
Cyclobenzaprine *(Fexmid,* Amrix ER, *Flexeril)* Tablet/capsule	IR: 5-10 mg TID PRN ER: 15-30 mg once daily	Dry mouth. May have efficacy with fibromyalgia. Serotonergic: should not be combined with other serotonergic agents. May precipitate or exacerbate cardiac arrhythmias; caution in elderly or those with heart disease (similar to TCAs).
TiZANidine *(Zanaflex)* Tablet/capsule	2-4 mg Q6-8H PRN (max 36 mg/day)	Central alpha-2 agonist: hypotension, dizziness, xerostomia, weakness, QT prolongation

Drugs that exert their effects by sedation

DRUG	DOSING	SAFETY/SIDE EFFECTS/MONITORING
Carisoprodol *(Soma)* C-IV (due to dependence, withdrawal symptoms, and diversion and abuse)	250-350 mg QID PRN	Somnolence Poor 2C19 metabolizers will have higher carisoprodol concentrations (up to 4-fold).
Metaxalone *(Skelaxin)*	800 mg TID-QID PRN	Decreased cognitive/sedative effects; hepatotoxic; monitor
Methocarbamol *(Robaxin, Robaxin-750)*	1,500-2,000 mg QID PRN	Hypotension; monitor BP

Rarely used muscle relaxants include dantrolene *(Dantrium,* sometimes used for malignant hyperthermia), chlorzoxazone *(Parafon Forte DSC)*, orphenadrine *(Norflex)*

Muscle Relaxant Drug Interactions

- Caution with use of concurrent agents that are CNS depressants: Additive somnolence, dizziness, confusion. These include alcohol, hypnotics, benzodiazepines, opioids, etc.

- Carisoprodol: Poor 2C19 metabolizers will have higher carisoprodol concentrations (up to 4-fold).

- Tizanidine: Contraindicated with moderate-strong 1A2 inhibitors (e.g., ciprofloxacin and fluvoxamine) due to elevated tizanidine levels.

Muscle Relaxant Counseling

- This medicine will cause somnolence and fatigue and can impair your ability to perform mental and physical activities. Do not drive when using this medicine.

- Avoid alcohol, sleeping pills, antihistamines, sedatives, pain pills and tranquilizers that may also make you drowsy, except under the supervision of your healthcare provider.

COMMON ADJUVANTS FOR PAIN MANAGEMENT

Adjuvants [e.g., antiepileptic drugs (AEDs), antidepressants, topical anesthetics] are useful in pain management though they are not classified as analgesics. They can be added to opioid or non-opioid analgesics (multimodal treatment). Adjuvants are commonly used in pain associated with neuropathy (from diabetes or spinal cord injury), fibromyalgia, postherpetic neuralgia (PHN), and other disorders. See Epilepsy/Seizure and Depression chapters for more detail on these drugs.

DRUG	DOSING	SAFETY/SIDE EFFECTS/MONITORING
Pregabalin (Lyrica) C-V Capsule, solution	Initial: 75 mg BID or 50 mg TID, max 450 mg/day CrCl < 60 mL/min: ↓ dose and/or extend interval	**WARNINGS** Angioedema, hypersensitivity reactions, risks of suicidal thoughts or behavior (all AEDs), ↑ seizure frequency if rapidly discontinued in those with seizures; can cause peripheral edema, dizziness and somnolence **SIDE EFFECTS** Dizziness, somnolence, peripheral edema, weight gain, ataxia, diplopia, blurred vision, dry mouth, mild euphoria **NOTES** Approved for use in fibromyalgia, PHN and neuropathic pain associated with diabetes and spinal cord injury. MedGuide required.
Gabapentin (Neurontin, Fanatrex) Capsule, tablet, solution, suspension *Gralise* (tablet): for PHN *Horizant* (ER tablet): for PHN and restless legs syndrome	Initial: 300 mg TID, max 3,600 mg/day CrCl < 60 mL/min: ↓ dose and/or extend interval IR, ER and gabapentin enacarbil are are not interchangeable	**WARNINGS** Angioedema/anaphylaxis, mulitorgan hypersensitivity (DRESS) reactions, suicidal thoughts or behavior (all AEDs), ↑ seizure frequency if rapidly discontinued in those with seizures, CNS effects **SIDE EFFECTS** Dizziness, somnolence, ataxia, peripheral edema, weight gain, diplopia, blurred vision, dry mouth **NOTES** Used more often off-label for fibromyalgia, pain (neuropathic), headache, drug abuse, alcohol withdrawal. Take ER formulation with food. MedGuide required.
DULoxetine (Cymbalta, *Irenka)* Capsule	30-60 mg/day	**BOXED WARNING** Antidepressants ↑ risk of suicidal thoughts and behaviors in children, adolescents and young adults. **CONTRAINDICATIONS** Concomitant use or within 2 weeks of MAO inhibitors, avoid with linezolid or IV methylene blue **SIDE EFFECTS** **Common to all SNRIs** ↑ BP, HR; sexual side effects (20-50%) include ↓ libido, ejaculation difficulties, anorgasmia; increased sweating (hyperhidrosis), restless leg (see if began when therapy was started) **Duloxetine-Specific Side Effects** Nausea, dry mouth, somnolence, fatigue, ↓ appetite **NOTES** MedGuide required

Common Adjuvants for Pain Management Continued

DRUG	DOSING	SAFETY/SIDE EFFECTS/MONITORING
Amitriptyline *(Elavil)* Tablet	10-50 mg QHS, sometimes higher	**SIDE EFFECTS** Uncommon with low doses used for pain, but could include: QT prolongation (with overdose), orthostatic hypotension, tachycardia, <u>anticholinergic</u> (dry mouth, blurred vision, urinary retention, constipation, delirium in elderly) **NOTES** TCAs can be used for suicide. Counsel carefully.
Milnacipran *(Savella, Savella Titration Pack)* Tablet	Day 1: 12.5 mg daily Days 2-3: 12.5 mg BID Days 4-7: 25 mg BID Then 50 mg BID (CrCl < 30 mL/min, max dose is 25 mg BID)	**BOXED WARNINGS** Milnacipran is a <u>SNRI</u> similar to SNRIs used to treat depression and other psychiatric disorders. Antidepressants ↑ the risk of suicidal thinking and behavior in children, adolescents, and young adults (18-24 years of age) with major depressive disorder (MDD) and other psychiatric disorders (not approved for depression or in pediatric patients). **CONTRAINDICATIONS** Concomitant use or within 2 weeks of MAO inhibitors, avoid with linezolid or IV methylene blue **SIDE EFFECTS** <u>Nausea, headache, constipation, dizziness, insomnia, hot flashes</u> **DRUG INTERACTIONS** Digoxin: Milnacipran may enhance the adverse/toxic effect of digoxin. The risk of postural hypotension and tachycardia may be increased, particularly with IV digoxin. Do not use IV digoxin in patients receiving milnacipran. Increased bleeding risk with anticoagulants or antiplatelets. **NOTES** Indicated for fibromyalgia only.

Topical Pain Agents, For Localized Pain

DRUG	DOSING/NOTES	SAFETY/SIDE EFFECTS/MONITORING
Lidocaine 5% patches *(Lidoderm)* Lidocaine viscous gel (Rx) *LidoPatch*, OTC, 3.99%	Apply to affected area 1-3 patches/day for up to 12 hrs/day (5% patch) Approved for postherpetic neuralgia (<u>shingles</u>)	**SIDE EFFECTS** Minor topical burning, pruritus, rash **NOTES** <u>Can cut into smaller pieces</u> (before removing backing). <u>Do not apply more than 3 patches at one time.</u> Caution with used patches; can harm children and pets; fold patch in half and discard safely. Do not cover with heating pads/electric blankets.

Topical Pain Agents Continued

DRUG	DOSING/NOTES	SAFETY/SIDE EFFECTS/MONITORING
Capsaicin 0.025% and 0.075% (Zostrix, Zostrix HP) *Qutenza 8%:* Rx capsaicin patch	Apply to affected area TID-QID ↓ TRPV1-expressing nociceptive nerve endings (↓ substance P)	**SIDE EFFECTS** Topical burning, which dissipates with continued use **NOTES** *Qutenza* is given in the healthcare provider's office only – it causes topical burning and requires pre-treatment with lidocaine – applied for 1 hour and lasts for months – works in ~ 40% of patients to reduce pain, indicated for post-herpetic neuralgia (PHN) pain.
Diclofenac topical (Voltaren gel, Flector patch)	Apply to affected area TID-QID NSAIDs, for OA	**NOTES** *Flector* patch: apply to <u>most painful area</u>, twice daily. Remove if bathing/showering. Remove for MRI.
Methyl salicylate topical OTCs (*BenGay, Icy Hot, Precise, SalonPas, Thera-Gesic,* store brands) Methyl salicylate plus other ingredients	Patches, creams	**NOTES** OTC counseling: contact healthcare provider if rash, pruritus, or excessive skin irritation occurs, or symptoms persist for > 7 days. Do not apply over wounds or damaged skin and do not cover with tight bandage or apply heat source. Occasionally the topicals have caused first to third-degree <u>burns</u>, mostly in patients with neuropathic damage: Discontinue use and seek medical attention if signs of skin injury (pain, swelling, or blistering) occur following application.

Lidoderm Patient Counseling

- Patches may be cut into smaller sizes with scissors before removal of the release (plastic) liner.
- Safely discard unused portions of cut patches where children and pets cannot get to them.
- Apply up to three (3) patches at one time to cover the most painful area. Apply patches only once for up to 12 hr in a 24-hr period (12 hr on and 12 hr off).
- Remove patch if skin irritation occurs.
- Fold used patches so that the adhesive side sticks to itself and safely discard used patches or pieces of cut patches where children and pets cannot get to them. Even a used patch contains enough medicine to harm a child or pet.
- Do not use on broken, abraded, severely burned or skin with open lesions (can significantly increase amount absorbed).

Capsaicin Patient Counseling

- Apply a thin film of cream to the affected area and gently rub in until fully absorbed.
- Apply 3 to 4 times daily.
- Best results typically occur after 2 to 4 weeks of continuous use. Do not use as-needed, since frequent, long-term use is required for benefit.
- Unless treating hand pain, wash hands thoroughly with soap and water immediately after use.
- If treating hands, leave on for 30 minutes, then wash hands as above.
- Do not touch genitals, nasal area, mouth or eyes with the medicine; it will burn the sensitive skin.
- The burning pain should dissipate with continual use; starting at the lower strength will help.
- Never cover with bandages or a heating pad; serious burning could result.

PRACTICE CASE

PATIENT PROFILE

Patient Name	Gene Schneider
Address	11188 Country Club Drive

Age:	50	**Sex:**	Male	**Race:**	Caucasian	**Height:**	5'6"	**Weight:**	239 lbs
Allergies	Sulfa								

DIAGNOSES

Hypertension
Osteoarthritis

MEDICATIONS

Date	No.	Prescriber	Drug & Strength	Quantity	Sig	Refills
12/13/15	57643	Suhlbach	Atenolol 100 mg	30	1 PO daily	11
12/13/15	57647	Suhlbach	Amlodipine 5 mg	30	1 PO daily	11
12/13/15	57648	Suhlbach	HCTZ 25 mg	30	1 PO daily	11
OTC			Acetaminophen 500 mg		1-2 PO prn 4-5x daily	
OTC			Capsaicin cream 0.025%		Apply QID	

LAB/DIAGNOSTIC TESTS

Test	Normal Value	Date: 12/11/15	Date:	Date:
		Results		
Na	135-146 mEq/L	130		
K	3.5-5.3 mEq/L	3.7		
Cl	98-110 mE1/L	104		
C02	21-33 mmHg	28		
BUN	7-20 mg/dL	24		
Creatinine	0.6-1.3 mg/dL	1.5		
Glucose	65-99 mg/dL	118		

ADDITIONAL INFORMATION

Date	Notes
12/15/2015	BP today 152/92. Patient reports pain at 5-7 out of 10 throughout day, describes knee as "grating." Capsaicin and APAP used regularly; asking for stronger pain medicine.

Questions

1. Gene's wife asks if OTC ibuprofen would be useful when the pain is not relieved with acetaminophen. The pharmacist counsels Gene and his wife that this may be unsafe due to the following reasons. (Select **ALL** that apply).

   a. It could cause acute kidney problems.

   b. It could cause his blood pressure to increase.

   c. It could cause an interaction with the acetaminophen.

   d. Ibuprofen is contraindicated with a sulfa allergy.

   e. Ibuprofen is not safe to use with concurrent capsaicin.

2. Gene's physician prescribes *Ultracet*. This drug contains the following ingredients:

   a. Tramadol + acetaminophen

   b. Tramadol + ibuprofen

   c. Hydrocodone + acetaminophen

   d. Hydrocodone + ibuprofen

   e. Codeine + acetaminophen

3. Gene's wife uses *Percocet*, and she suggests that this might help Gene. Which of the following statements is correct?

   a. This drug contains an NSAID.

   b. It is no more effective for pain than aspirin and can be dangerous.

   c. There are no significant side effects.

   d. It is more effective for pain than acetaminophen alone.

   e. It may raise blood pressure.

4. Gene fills a prescription for *Ultracet*, and finds that the pain relief is satisfactory for about one year. After this time, the physician tries *MS Contin*, and eventually switches Gene over to the *Duragesic* patch. Choose the correct statement:

   a. *Duragesic* is the brand name for hydromorphone.

   b. This is a poor choice due to his degree of renal insufficiency.

   c. This medication can only be used in patients who have dysphagia.

   d. The starting application frequency is one patch Q48 hours.

   e. The starting application frequency is one patch Q72 hours.

Questions 5-11 are not based on the above case.

5. Tramadol is not a safe choice in patients with this condition:

   a. Muscle spasticity

   b. Aspirin allergy

   c. Seizures

   d. Peptic ulcer disease

   e. Gout

6. A physician has called the pharmacist. He has a patient on morphine sulfate extended-release who is having difficulty with regular bowel movements. The patient is using docusate sodium 100 mg BID. The patient reports that his stools are difficult to expel, although they are not particularly hard or condensed. Which of the following recommendation is most appropriate to prevent the constipation?

   a. Senna

   b. Bismuth subsalicylate

   c. *Relistor*

   d. Mineral oil

   e. Phosphate soda

7. A patient with cancer is using the fentanyl patch along with the *Actiq* transmucosal formulation for breakthrough pain. Which statement is correct?

   a. *Actiq* contains hydromorphone for sublingual absorption.

   b. No more than 4 BTP episodes per day should be treated with *Actiq*; if more are required, the patient should consult with his/her physician.

   c. A patient who is not taking an extended-release version of an opioid may still use *Actiq* for occasional, breakthrough cancer pain.

   d. *Actiq* contains oxymorphone for sublingual absorption.

   e. This drug is contraindicated in patients older than 65 years of age.

8. Which of the following brand-generic combinations is correct?

   a. Celecoxib *(Mobic)*

   b. Naproxen *(Motrin)*

   c. Morphine *(Opana)*

   d. Hydromorphone *(Dilaudid)*

   e. Methadone *(Demerol)*

9. Choose the correct statement regarding the medication *Celebrex*:

   a. This may be a safer option for patients with GI bleeding risk.

   b. This may be a safer option for patients with reduced renal function.

   c. This is a non-selective NSAID, and has a better safety profile.

   d. This drug is safe to use in patients with any type of sulfonamide allergy.

   e. The maximum dose for inflammatory conditions, such as RA, is 200 mg daily.

10. A patient with poor pain control has been taking hydrocodone-acetaminophen 10 mg-325 mg 8 tablets daily. The physician will convert the patient to *Kadian* to provide adequate pain relief. Using the hydrocodone component only, calculate the total daily dose of *Kadian* that is equivalent to the hydrocodone dose, and then reduce the dose by 25% (to lessen the possibility of excessive side effects from the initial conversion). The final daily dose of *Kadian* is:

    a. 10 mg *Kadian*

    b. 40 mg *Kadian*

    c. 60 mg *Kadian*

    d. 80 mg *Kadian*

    e. 110 mg *Kadian*

11. Which is the correct antidote for acetaminophen toxicity?

    a. Flumazenil

    b. N- Acetylcysteine

    c. Pyridoxine

    d. Physostigmine

    e. Atropine

Answers

1-a,b, 2-a, 3-d, 4-e, 5-c, 6-a, 7-b, 8-d, 9-a, 10-c, 11-b

45

MIGRAINE

GUIDELINES/REFERENCES

Evidence-Based Guidelines for Migraine Headache in the Primary Care Setting: Pharmacologic Management for Prevention of Migraine, American Academy of Neurology. http://tools.aan.com/professionals/practice/pdfs/gl0087.pdf (accessed 2015 Nov 2).

ICSI Health Care Guideline: Diagnosis and Treatment of Headache, 2013. https://www.icsi.org/_asset/qwrznq/Headache.pdf (accessed 2015 Nov 2).

BACKGROUND

Headache treatment is a common concern in the community pharmacy, one of the most common complaints in neurologists' offices and the most common pain complaint seen in family practice. Most headaches are migraine and tension-type headaches.

Migraines are chronic headaches that can cause significant pain for hours or days. In addition to severe pain, most migraines cause nausea, vomiting, and sensitivity to light and sound. Some migraines are preceded or accompanied by sensory warning symptoms or signs (auras), such as flashes of light, blind spots or tingling in the arms or legs. Most migraines do not have an aura.

Rarely, a migraine could occur with a serious cardiovascular, cerebrovascular or infectious event. Patients should be seen at once if the headache is accompanied by fever, stiff neck, rash, mental confusion, seizures, double vision, weakness, numbness, chest pain, trouble breathing or trouble speaking.

Children get migraines and parents may ask the pharmacist for advice. OTC agents, usually ibuprofen, are used first. Almotriptan, rizatriptan and zolmitriptan nasal spray are approved for use in children (see table).

MIGRAINE CAUSES

Migraines may be caused by changes in the trigeminal nerve and imbalances in neurotransmitters, including serotonin, which decreases during a migraine causing a chemical release of neuropeptides that trigger vasodilation in cranial blood vessels. Serotonin-receptor agonists (triptans) are selective agonists for the 5-HT$_1$ receptor and cause vasoconstriction of cranial blood vessels, inhibit neuropeptide release and ↓ pain transmission.

The cause of migraines is not well-understood but identifying "triggers" can be useful so the patient can avoid them and reduce migraine incidence. A common type of migraine is a menstrually-associated migraine in women. These may be treated with oral contraceptives or the estradiol patch or creams to decrease migraine frequency. Women who have migraine with aura are at higher risk for stroke and should not use estrogen-containing contraceptives.

DIAGNOSIS

Migraine can be diagnosed when an adult has at least 5 attacks (not attributed to another disorder) fulfilling the following criteria:

1. Headaches last 4 – 72 hrs and recur sporadically.

2. Headaches have ≥ 2 of the following characteristics: unilateral location, pulsating, moderate-severe pain and aggravated by (or causing avoidance of) routine physical activity.

3. One of the following occurs during the headache: nausea and/or vomiting, photophobia and phonophobia.

NATURAL PRODUCTS

Caffeine is effective in combination with acetaminophen or aspirin for migraine headaches and is available in combination products for this purpose. Butterbur, coenzyme Q10, feverfew, magnesium, peppermint (usually applied topically) and riboflavin (alone or in combination) are listed as "possibly effective" by the Natural Medicines Database.

NON-DRUG TREATMENT

A headache diary can assist patients in identifying triggers. Non-pharmacologic interventions involve avoiding triggers, mental relaxation, stress management, or applying cold compresses/ice to the head. The ICSI guidelines mention that acupuncture can be helpful for reducing migraines.

COMMON MIGRAINE TRIGGERS

Hormonal Changes in Women
Fluctuations in estrogen trigger headaches in many women. Some women will use monophasic oral contraceptive formulations to keep estrogen levels more constant and help reduce pre-menstrual migraines, the most common type of female migraine. ACOG recommends progestin-only pills for women with migraine with aura, due to stroke risk with estrogen-containing contraceptives.

Foods
Common offending agents include alcohol, especially beer and red wine, aged cheeses, chocolate, aspartame, overuse of caffeine, monosodium glutamate (MSG), salty foods and processed foods.

Stress
Stress is a major cause of migraines.

Sensory Stimuli
Bright lights, sun glare, loud sounds and scents (which may be pleasant or unpleasant odors).

Changes in Wake-Sleep Pattern
Either missing sleep or getting too much sleep (including jet lag).

Changes in the Environment
A change of weather or barometric pressure.

DRUG TREATMENT

Migraine treatment is divided into <u>acute</u> or abortive (for a headache that is present) and <u>prophylactic</u> (to <u>reduce headache frequency</u>).

There are many drug options for acute treatment, including OTC options: acetaminophen, *Advil Migraine* (which is plain ibuprofen), *Excedrin Migraine* (aspirin, acetaminophen and caffeine), *Aleve* or other agents, including store brands of these options. OTC agents can be tried for migraines that are mild to moderate. Triptans (5-HT$_1$ agonists) are considered <u>first-line</u> for acute treatment. Some patients get more relief from OTC products, some from triptans and others need to use combinations of both. Diclofenac *(Cambia)* in packet formulation is available by prescription and specifically indicated for migraine treatment. In patients with <u>contraindications</u> to triptans or who <u>do not find benefit</u> with a triptan, <u>ergotamine</u> is generally used next. *Fiorinal* and *Fioricet*, although commonly used for migraines, contain butalbital, which can cause physical dependence and has abuse potential. These are not as effective as the first-line migraine treatments and are <u>not recommended</u>. Tramadol, tapentadol and opioids are not recommended for the same reasons. However, if other agents have failed, these are used in select cases. Patients with nausea/vomiting may benefit from combined treatment with an antiemetic.

Some patients will require a <u>prophylactic</u> medication to decrease the frequency of migraines. Agents used for migraine prophylaxis include antihypertensives, antidepressants, antiepileptic drugs and others. This is discussed at the end of the chapter.

DRUG	DOSING	SAFETY/SIDE EFFECTS/MONITORING
Naratriptan *(Amerge)* Tablet	Initial: 1-2.5 mg, can repeat x 1 after 4 hrs Max 5 mg/day	**CONTRAINDICATIONS** Cerebrovascular disease (stroke/TIA), uncontrolled hypertension, ischemic heart disease, peripheral vascular disease, history of hemiplegic or basilar migraine, severe hepatic impairment A few are contraindicated with MAO inhibitors (see below); all must be used with caution with other serotonergic drugs
Almotriptan *(Axert)* Tablet	Initial: 6.25-12.5 mg, can repeat x 1 after 2 hrs Max 25 mg/day	
Frovatriptan *(Frova)* Tablet	Initial: 2.5 mg, can repeat x 1 after 2 hrs Max 7.5 mg/day	**SIDE EFFECTS** Somnolence, nausea, paresthesias (tingling/numbness), throat/neck pressure, dizziness, hot/cold sensations, chest pain/tightness Triptan sensations (pressure in the chest or heaviness or pressure in the neck region) that usually dissipate after administration
SUMAtriptan *(Imitrex, Imitrex STATdose, Alsuma*, Sumavel DosePro, *Zecuity)* *Imitrex:* tablet, SC injection, nasal spray *Alsuma:* SC injection *Sumavel DosePro:* needle-free SC delivery (jet air injector) *Zecuity* transdermal + naproxen 85-500 mg *(Treximet)*	PO: 25, 50 or 100 mg, can repeat x 1 after 2 hrs Max 200 mg/day Intranasal: 5, 10, or 20 mg in one nostril can repeat x 1 after 2 hrs Max 40 mg/day SC: 4, 6 mg, can repeat x 1 after 1 hr Max 12 mg/day Transdermal: apply 1 patch, may apply 2nd patch after 2 hrs *Treximet*: 1 tab, may repeat x 1 after 2 hrs Max 2 tabs/24 hrs	**NOTES** ODTs, nasal sprays and injections are useful if nausea is present. No water is required for ODTs. Nasal sprays and injections work faster. *Imitrex* and *Zomig* nasal sprays contain only 1 dose (do not prime). Almotriptan tablets and zolmitriptan nasal spray are approved for children and adolescents ≥ 12 years of age; rizatriptan is approved for children and adolescents 6-17 years of age. *Treximet:* keep in original container (contains desiccant).
Rizatriptan *(Maxalt, Maxalt-MLT)* Tablet, ODT	Initial: 5-10 mg, can repeat x 1 after 2 hrs *Maxalt MLT:* 5 mg, no water needed Max 30 mg/day	**Duration of Action** The longest-acting triptans (longer acting, but slower onset) are frovatriptan (the longest, with t½ of 26 hrs) and naratriptan. Choose if HA recurs after dosing or lasts a long time. Can use agents with shorter durations of action if fast onset required. The ones with a shorter half-life have a faster onset: almotriptan, eletriptan, rizatriptan, sumatriptan and zolmitriptan.
Eletriptan *(Relpax)* Tablet	Initial: 20-40 mg, can repeat x 1 after 2 hrs Max 80 mg/day	
ZOLMItriptan *(Zomig, Zomig-ZMT)* Tablet, ODT, nasal spray	PO: 1.25-5 mg, can repeat x 1 after 2 hrs Intranasal: 5 mg, can repeat x 1 after 2 hrs Max 10 mg/day (all formulations)	

Triptan Drug Interactions

- FDA warning about combining triptans with serotonergic drugs such as SSRIs and SNRIs. However, many patients take both types together. It may present a problem when another serotonergic agent is added to the combination. Counsel patients on both medications to report restlessness, sweating, poor coordination, confusion, hallucinations.

- Sumatriptan, rizatriptan and zolmitriptan are contraindicated with MAO inhibitors, the others are not.

- Eletriptan *(Relpax)* is contraindicated with strong CYP 3A4 inhibitors.

Patient Counseling

All Triptans

- Side effects that you may experience include sleepiness, nausea, numbness, throat or neck pressure, dizziness, hot or cold sensations, and a heaviness or pressure in the chest or neck region. These usually occur after the drug is taken and go away shortly.

- If nausea prevents you from swallowing or holding down your medicine, your healthcare provider can prescribe a tablet that dissolves in your mouth, an injection or a nasal spray.

- If you have migraines that come on very quickly, a nasal spray or SC injection will provide faster relief.

- Serious, but rare, side effects such as heart attacks and strokes have occurred in people who have used this type of medicine; because of this, triptans cannot be used in patients who have had a stroke, have heart disease or have blood pressure that is not well-controlled. If any of this applies to you, please inform your healthcare provider.

- There is a chance of serotonin syndrome when using this drug with some drugs for low mood (depression) or weight loss. The syndrome is caused by too much serotonin in the body. Signs include agitation, changes in blood pressure, loose stools, a fast heartbeat, hallucinations, upset stomach and throwing up, change in balance, and change in thinking clearly and with logic.

- Take the medicine with or without food, at the first sign of a migraine. The medicine will not work as well if you wait to use it.

- If you use the orally disintegrating tablets *(Maxalt-MLT* and *Zomig-ZMT)*, peel open the blister pack and place the orally disintegrating tablet on your tongue, where it will dissolve and be swallowed with saliva. You do not need to use water with the medicine. These formulations should not be used in patients with phenylketonuria, due to the sweetener.

- If your symptoms are only partly relieved, or if your headache comes back, you may take a second dose in the time period explained to you by the pharmacist.

- If you use migraine treatments more than twice a week or if they are severe, you should be using a daily medicine to help reduce the number of migraines. Please discuss using a "prophylaxis" medicine with your healthcare provider if you are not using one.

Imitrex Injection using the *STATdose* system

Imitrex injections can be administered by prefilled SC syringe, or commonly using the *STATdose* injection device. *Alsuma* is a prefilled auto injector. Protect all from light.

- Inject the medication just below the skin (always SC) as soon as the symptoms of your migraine appear.

- Use the *STATdose* system to administer your injection. This system includes a carrying case and two syringes which will assist you in taking your subcutaneous shot. The shot is relatively mild as it is not a large needle.

- Clean the area of skin, usually in the upper outside arm, with rubbing alcohol prior to administering the injection.

- Open the *Imitrex* injection carrying case and pull off the tamper-proof packaging from one of the cartridge packs. Open the lid of the cartridge. Pull the unused *STATdose* cartridge from the carrying case.

- Load the *STATdose* pen by inserting it into the cartridge and turning it clockwise. The cartridge is loaded when you are no longer able to turn the pen clockwise.

- Gently pull the loaded pen out of the carrying case. The blue button on the side triggers the injection. There is a safety feature that does not allow the injection to be triggered unless it is against your skin

- Hold the loaded pen to the area that you have cleaned to receive the shot. Push the blue button on the side of the pen. To make sure you receive all of the medicine, you must hold the pen still for 5 seconds.

- Follow safety procedures and return the used injection needle to the cartridge. Insert the pen once again into the cartridge. This time turn it counterclockwise to loosen the needle. Remove the empty *STATdose* pen from the cartridge and store it in the carrying case.

- Replace the cartridge pack after both doses of have been used. Discard the pack and insert a new refill.

Sumavel DosePro

- Select a delivery site on the stomach area or thigh. Do not deliver *Sumavel DosePro* in the arm or within 2 inches of navel (belly button). Change delivery sites with each use.

- Snap: When ready to take the dose, hold the device firmly in one hand. Grip the top and bottom of the snap-off tip where the finger grips are located. Break off the tip by snapping it in a downward motion. You do not need to pull or twist it.

- Flip: Firmly press the lever down until it clicks and locks into the handle. Once the lever has been flipped, do not touch the end of the chamber and keep it pointed away from your face and eyes.

- Pinch and Press: Pinch about 2 inches of the skin at the selected delivery site (abdomen or thigh only) and place the end of the device with the clear medication chamber against your skin. Steadily press straight down against skin until you hear a burst of air.

- There is no button to push. Once you hear the burst of air, you can remove the device from the skin.

Zomig Nasal Spray

- Blow your nose gently before use.

- Remove the protective cap.

- Hold the nasal sprayer device gently with your fingers and thumb.

- There is only one dose in the nasal sprayer. <u>Do not prime</u> (test) the nasal sprayer or you will lose the dose.

- Do not press the plunger until you have put the tip into your nostril or you will lose the dose. Insert into nose about a half an inch, close your mouth, press the plunger, keep head level for 10 – 20 seconds, gently breathe in through your mouth.

Zecuity Transdermal Patch

- This is a transdermal patch that runs on lithium batteries. The red light indicates the drug is being released. Use on upper arm or thigh (dry, clean, relatively hair-free). Remove for MRI. Most common side effect is application site irritation.

Ergotamine Drugs

Used primarily in patents with contraindications to or lack of response to triptans. Ergotamine is a nonselective agonist of serotonin receptors, which causes cerebral vasoconstriction.

DRUG	DOSING	SAFETY/SIDE EFFECTS/MONITORING
Dihydroergotamine (DHE 45, Migranal) Injection *(DHE 45)*, nasal spray *(Migranal)*	IM/SC/IV: 1 mg at first sign of headache, repeat hourly to a max dose of 2 mg/day (IV) and 3 mg/day (IM/SC) and max 6 mg/week Intranasal: 1 spray (0.5 mg) into each nostril, can repeat after 15 minutes, up to a total of 4 sprays (2 mg)	**BOXED WARNING** Serious and life-threatening peripheral ischemia associated with the coadministration of DHE with potent CYP 3A4 inhibitors including protease inhibitors and macrolide antibiotics. **CONTRAINDICATIONS** Uncontrolled hypertension, pregnancy; ischemic heart disease, angina, MI; peripheral vascular disease; hemiplegic or basilar migraine; avoid use within 24 hours of sumatriptan, zolmitriptan, ergot or serotonin agonists; avoid during or within 2 weeks of discontinuing MAO inhibitors, avoid pressors/vasonconstrictive drugs. **WARNINGS** Cardiac valvular fibrosis: Ergot alkaloids have been associated with fibrotic valve thickening (aortic, mitral, tricuspid), usually with long-term, chronic use. Cardiovascular effects: Vasospasm or vasoconstriction risk. Do not use in any patient with baseline risk. Cerebrovascular events have occurred after injection. Ergotism (intense vasoconstriction) resulting in peripheral vascular ischemia and possible gangrene can occur with overdose or prolonged chronic use; do not exceed dosing limits. Pleural/retroperitoneal fibrosis: Rare cases of pleural and/or retroperitoneal fibrosis have been reported with prolonged daily use. **SIDE EFFECTS** Nasal spray: rhinitis, dysgeusia, nausea, dizziness. **NOTES** Nasal spray: prime by pumping 4 times. Do not inhale deeply (to let drug absorb into skin in nose). Use at first sign of attack, but can be used at any time during migraine. Pregnancy Category X, do not use in pregnancy or lactation. Many drug interactions; see above.

OTC MIGRAINE AGENTS

If recommending an OTC product, any OTC NSAID such as *Advil Migraine* (ibuprofen only, or generics), *Excedrin Migraine* (acetaminophen/aspirin/caffeine) or *Aleve* are reasonable options. Aspirin may not be a good choice due to nausea. Always ask the patient what they have tried in the past, and if it was useful.

LESS COMMONLY USED ACUTE MIGRAINE MEDICATIONS

Acetaminophen/butalbital/caffeine (*Fioricet*), also comes with codeine, C-III (*Fioricet with Codeine*).

Aspirin/butalbital/caffeine (*Fiorinal*), also comes with codeine, C-III (*Fiorinal with Codeine*).

- Neither are recommended agents for this purpose due to abuse/dependence issues and lower efficacy.

- *Fioricet* generic is a popular drug. It contains a barbiturate; if used regularly, and long-term, it must be tapered off or the patient will get worsening of headache, tremors, and be at risk of delirium and seizures.

- If using codeine-containing formulations, counsel on possible nausea, constipation.

- Do not mix with alcohol.

- Do not exceed safe doses of acetaminophen.

Can also use hydrocodone/APAP combinations *(Vicodin,* etc), or other opioid combo products.

Butorphanol *(Stadol NS)*, C-IV, intranasal spray may provide fast and effective relief of migraine. Onset within 15 mins.

MIGRAINE PROPHYLAXIS

Consider using a prophylactic medication if the patient requests it, if they use acute treatments ≥ 2 days/week or ≥ 3 times per month, if the migraines decrease their quality of life or if acute treatments are ineffective or contraindicated. Typically, the reduction in migraines is ~50% with prophylaxis, but a patient may have to try more than one agent to find one that works well for them. A full trial, at a reasonable dose, should be 2 – 6 months. Choose the prophylactic agent based on the patient and the side effect profile because the efficacy data is similar. Topiramate is used commonly since it has a better side effect profile than most of the other agents, and causes weight loss. If hypertension, using a beta blocker may be the most practical. If weight loss is desirable, topiramate may be chosen. Valproic acid has numerous safety concerns (see Epilepsy/Seizures chapter) and is Pregnancy Category X when used for migraine prophylaxis.

Therapies for migraine prophylaxis in adults include:

- Antihypertensives: Most experience is with beta blockers (best evidence with propranolol, timolol, metoprolol). Other beta blockers, lisinopril and verapamil have been used.

- Antiepileptic drugs: Topiramate *(Topamax)* and valproic acid

- Antidepressants: Amitriptyline is used at a lower dose than for depression. This is why venlafaxine is often used first, but amitriptyline can be added on (low dose at bedtime) for migraine if the patient is using an SSRI.

- Extended-cycle oral contraceptives if premenstrual migraine, or start NSAIDs or triptan (specifically those with longer half life: frovatriptan or naratriptan) 2 days prior to menses, continue for 5 – 7 days.

- Other: Natural products (see beginning of chapter) and botulinum toxin type A *(Botox)* injections. *Botox* is for chronic migraines only (15 or more days/month).

DRUG	TYPICAL DOSING RANGE	COMMENTS/SIDE EFFECTS

Beta Blockers (see Hypertension chapter for complete discussion)

DRUG	TYPICAL DOSING RANGE	COMMENTS/SIDE EFFECTS
Propranolol (*Inderal*)	40-120 mg, divided BID	Fatigue, ↓ HR, possible depression with propranolol (most lipophilic)
Timolol	10-15 mg twice daily	Both propranolol and timolol are non-selective beta blockers; do not use in COPD, emphysema
Metoprolol (*Lopressor, Toprol XL*)	100-200 mg daily	Metoprolol is beta-1 selective. Caution with all beta blockers if low HR (they will ↓ HR), monitor for hypotension, dizziness

Antiepileptic Drugs (see Epilepsy/Seizures chapter for complete discussion)

DRUG	TYPICAL DOSING RANGE	COMMENTS/SIDE EFFECTS
Divalproex (*Depakote, others*), Valproic acid (*Depakene, others*)	250-500 mg twice daily	Liver toxicity, pancreatitis, sedation, weight gain, tremor, teratogenicity, thrombocytopenia, alopecia, nausea (less with divalproex), polycystic ovarian syndrome Pregnancy Category X (migraine prophylaxis)/D (other indications): Avoid in women of childbearing age
Topiramate (*Topamax*)	Start 25 mg QHS, titrate to 50 mg BID	Nephrolithiasis, open angle glaucoma, hypohidrosis (children), depression, metabolic acidosis, 6-13% weight loss, reduced efficacy of oral contraceptives, cognitive impairment Pregnancy Category D: Avoid in women of childbearing age

Medication-Overuse ("Rebound") Headaches

Mediation overuse headaches (MOH) result from overuse of most headache medicines (e.g., NSAIDs, opioids, the butalbital-containing drugs, analgesic combination products, triptans, and ergotamines except DHE) and are characterized by headaches on more than 10 – 15 days per month. Pharmacists are in a position to see many patients who chronically use headache medicines, and have daily headaches. It may be best to discuss this with a healthcare provider if the patient seems at risk or is unlikely to try and cut down on analgesic use independently. To prevent MOH, educate patients to limit acute treatment medications to 2 or 3 times per week, at most. The most important thing is to stop the "over-used" medication. If the drug is an opioid or contains butalbital (*Fioricet, Fiorinal*), a slow taper will be needed to discontinue.

46

GOUT

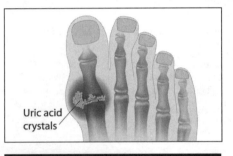

Uric acid crystals

GUIDELINES/REFERENCES

Khanna D, Fitzgerald JD, Khanna PP, et al. 2012 American College of Rheumatology Guidelines for Management of Gout. *Arthritis Care and Research*. 2012;64(10):1431-1461.

BACKGROUND

Gout is a type of arthritis caused by a buildup of uric acid crystals, primarily in the joints. Uric acid is a breakdown product of purines, which are one of the base pairs of DNA and are present in many foods. Gout attacks are sudden with severe pain, burning, and swelling. Gout typically occurs in one joint, which is most often the metatarsophalangeal joint (MTP, the big toe). If left untreated, the attacks can occur over and over, and will eventually damage the joints, tendons and other tissues.

Another type of "gout" is an acute condition called tumor lysis syndrome (TLS). This is a potentially life-threatening complication of aggressive chemotherapy. When cells are "lysed" open, many purines are released into the blood and are quickly converted to uric acid, which can cause acute gout as well as electrolyte abnormalities (hyperkalemia, hyperphosphatemia, and hypocalcemia).

CAUSES

Uric acid is produced as an end-product of purine metabolism (see following figure). Under normal conditions, uric acid is excreted ⅔ renally and ⅓ by the GI tract. When uric acid builds up in the blood, the patient may remain asymptomatic (many people with high uric acid, or hyperuricemia, never get gout) or the uric acid can crystallize in the joints, resulting in a severe, painful gout attack. Gout typically strikes after many years of persistent hyperuricemia.

Risk Factors

Risk factors for gout include male sex, obesity, excessive alcohol consumption (particularly beer), hypertension, chronic kidney disease (CKD), lead intoxication, advanced age and using medications that increase uric acid. To reduce the risk of recurrent gout attacks patients should avoid organ meats, high-fructose corn syrup and alcohol. Servings of fruit juices, table sugar, sweetened drinks and desserts, salt, beef, lamb, pork and seafood with high purine content (sardines, shellfish) should be limited. A healthy diet (including low fat dairy products and vegetables), hydration, weight control, smoking cessation and exercise are recommended in the guidelines to reduce the risk for gout attacks.

MEDICATIONS WITH HIGHEST KNOWN RISK TO INCREASE URIC ACID (THERE ARE OTHERS WITH POSSIBLE RISK OR CASE REPORTS)

Aspirin, higher doses*

Diuretics (thiazides, loops)

Niacin

Pyrazinamide

Ribavirin

Tacrolimus, Cyclosporine

*   No need to discontinue low-dose aspirin used for cardioprotection.

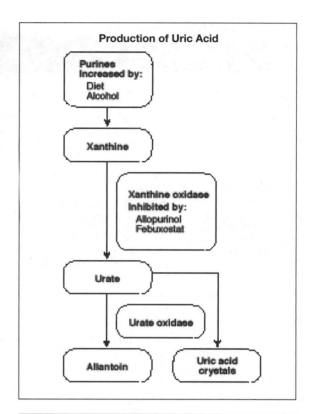

Production of Uric Acid

Laboratory Parameters

A normal serum uric acid (urate) level is ~2.0 – 7.2 mg/dL. Do not start treatment until gout has occurred; asymptomatic hyperuricemia is not treated. The treatment goal is a urate level < 6 mg/dL.

DRUG TREATMENT

The goal of treatment is to treat acute attacks, prevent future flare-ups, and reduce uric acid levels. Note that the drugs used to treat an acute attack (colchicine, NSAIDs, steroids) are different than the drugs used to prevent attacks. Colchicine or NSAIDs, however, are recommended during the initiation of prophylactic treatment to reduce the risk of acute attacks which can occur when uric acid is lowered rapidly. Colchicine is on the Beer's list of potentially harmful drugs in the elderly if the CrCl is < 30 mL/min due to increased risk of adverse effects.

Acute Gout Attack Treatment

Gout attacks are painful and treatment should be started within 24 hours. Single agent treatment with an NSAID, systemic corticosteroid or oral colchicine is recommended for most cases. In more severe disease, combination therapy is suggested with colchicine and NSAIDs, oral corticosteroids and colchicine, or intra-articular steroids (injected into the joint) with one of the other options.

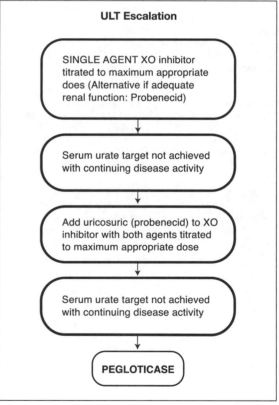

ULT Escalation

Any of these drugs can be supplemented with topical ice therapy as needed. If patients were taking chronic urate-lowering therapy (ULT) (allopurinol, febuxostat), they should continue the ULT without interruption.

Acute Gout Attack Treatment

DRUG	DOSING	SAFETY/SIDE EFFECTS/MONITORING

Colchicine

Colchicine (*Colcrys*, *Mitigare*) + probenecid Patients receiving prophylaxis with colchicine who receive colchicine for acute gout should wait 12 hours before resuming prophylaxis dose	**Treatment** 1.2 mg orally (this is two 0.6 mg tablets) followed by 0.6 mg in 1 hr (do not exceed a total of 1.8 mg in 1 hr, or 2.4 mg/day Dose to be repeated no earlier than 3 days CrCl < 30 mL/min: the treatment dose is the same, but do not give again for 2 weeks **Prophylaxis** 0.6 mg once or twice daily CrCl < 30 mL/min, ↓ to 0.3 mg/day	**CONTRAINDICATIONS** Concomitant use of a P-gp or strong CYP 3A4 inhibitor in the Concomitant use of a P-gp or strong CYP 3A4 inhibitor in the presence of renal or hepatic impairment, or use with both renal and hepatic impairment. **WARNINGS** Blood dyscrasias, gastrointestinal symptoms (↓ dose if anorexia, diarrhea, N/V), neuromuscular toxicity (including rhabdomyolysis), concomitant use of cyclosporine, diltiazem, verapamil, fibrates, and statins ↑ myopathy risk **SIDE EFFECTS** Diarrhea, nausea, vomiting, ↓ vitamin B12 Myelosuppression, myopathy, neuropathy (dose-related) **NOTES** Recommended only when treatment is started within 36 hrs of onset of symptoms. Beer's criteria in elderly with CrCl < 30 mL/min: risk myelosuppression, GI and neuromuscular adverse effects. ↓ dose and monitor, or use steroid as an alternative.

NSAIDs

Indomethacin (*Indocin*)	50 mg TID until attack resolved	See Pain chapter for more complete information. **NOTES** Avoid use in severe renal disease (uric acid is renally cleared and patients with gout may have renal insufficiency); consider risk of bleeding (however risk of GI bleeding is less due to short duration of therapy), CVD risk (most with celecoxib). Indomethacin was the 1st NSAID approved and is the traditional DOC; however, it is more toxic than ibuprofen (↑ risk for GI toxicity) and has psychiatric side effects. Indomethacin, naproxen and sulindac are approved for gout; the ACR guideline does not limit treatment to these NSAIDs.
Naproxen (*Naprosyn, others*)	750 mg x 1, then reduce to 250 mg Q8H until attack resolved	
Sulindac (*Clinoril*)	200 mg BID, until attack resolved	
Celecoxib (*CeleBREX*)	800 mg x 1, then 400 mg x 1 (later in day), then 400 mg BID x 1 week	

Acute Gout Attack Treatment Continued

DRUG	DOSING	SAFETY/SIDE EFFECTS/MONITORING

Steroids: Can be given PO, IM, IV, intra-articular or via ACTH (adrenocorticotropic hormone) which triggers endogenous glucocorticoid secretion.

PredniSONE/ PredniSOLONE	0.5 mg/kg/day PO for 5-10 days (no taper) or 0.5 mg/kg/ day for 2-5 days, then taper (reduce dose by 5 mg each day) over 7-10 days	See Asthma chapter for more complete information. **NOTES** Acute side effects of steroids (e.g., hyperglycemia, hypertension, nervousness, insomnia, increased appetite, edema).
MethylPREDNISolone *(Medrol, Solu-Medrol)*	Intra-articular: If 1-2 large joints involved Oral: Methylprednisolone dose pack	Systemic side effects with intra-articular steroid injections are infrequent. There may be mild pain at the injection site.
Triamcinolone	IM: Triamcinolone 60 mg, then start PO prednisone	Repeated injections can increase the risk of joint damage.

Colchicine Drug Interactions

- Colchicine is a substrate (major) of CYP 3A4 and the efflux transporter P-glycoprotein (P-gp). <u>Fatal toxicity can occur if colchicine is combined with strong 3A4 inhibitors</u>, such as clarithromycin <u>or a strong inhibitor of P-gp</u>, such as cyclosporine. Check for inhibitors prior to dispensing drug. If using a moderate 3A4 inhibitor, the maximum dose for acute treatment is 1.2 mg (2 tablets).

- Myopathy and rhabdomyolysis are higher risk with concomitant colchicine and cyclosporine, diltiazem, verapamil and statins; have patients monitor muscle pain/soreness.

Colchicine Counseling

- At the first sign of an attack, take 2 tablets. You can take 1 more tablet in one hour. Do not use more than this amount in an hour, and do not use more than 4 tablets in 24 hours. Taking too much colchicine can lead to serious side effects.

- You should not take the 2nd dose if you have upset stomach, nausea or diarrhea.

- Report any serious nausea, vomiting, diarrhea, fatigue, unusual bleeding, tingling in your fingers or toes or muscle soreness to your healthcare provider right away.

- <u>Wait at least 3 days</u> before initiating another acute course of therapy.

Chronic Urate Lowering Therapy

Chronic urate lowering therapy (ULT) should be started in all patients with gout who experience intermittent symptoms or tophi (uric acid crystals that can form under the skin in long-term gout). First-line agents for ULT are the xanthine oxidase (XO) inhibitors allopurinol or febuxostat. Blocking XO stops the production of uric acid at an earlier step, and produces a non-toxic end product. These agents are titrated up (<u>slowly for allopurinol</u>) to lower the uric acid to a target level of <u>< 6 mg/ dL</u>. Allopurinol is started at a <u>lower dose with moderate or severe CKD</u>. Patients who are at high risk of a severe allopurinol <u>hypersensitivity reaction</u> (including certain Asian groups) should be screened prior to use for the <u>HLA-B*5801 allele</u>. <u>Probenecid</u> is a 2nd line agent and can be used if XO inhibitors are contraindicated or not tolerated, or can be added when the uric acid level is not at goal despite maximal doses of XO inhibitors. Probenecid <u>inhibits reabsorption</u> of uric acid in the proximal tubule of the nephron, thus promoting uric acid excretion. It requires <u>adequate</u> renal function to be effective. <u>Pegloticase</u> is a recombinant uricase enzyme, which converts uric acid to an inactive, water-soluble metabolite that can be easily excreted. Pegloticase is reserved for <u>severe, refractory disease</u>.

Prophylaxis for tumor lysis syndrome is given in high-risk patients receiving certain types of chemotherapy. If TLS occurs, treatment to lower uric acid is initiated, and the electrolyte levels are corrected. The usual prophylaxis and treatment medication is high-dose allopurinol. Another option is rasburicase (urate oxidase), which has a mechanism of action similar to pegloticase (converts uric acid to water-soluble allantoin).

DRUG	DOSING	SAFETY/SIDE EFFECTS/MONITORING

Xanthine Oxidase Inhibitors

DRUG	DOSING	SAFETY/SIDE EFFECTS/MONITORING
Allopurinol (Zyloprim, Aloprim) Due to the high rate of gout attacks when beginning ULT, colchicine at a dose of 0.6 mg once or twice daily or NSAIDs are used concurrently for the first 3 – 6 months.	Start at 100 mg daily, then slowly titrate up until uric acid is < 6 mg/dL (doses > 300 mg may be necessary and should be divided BID) Take after a meal (with food in stomach) to ↓ nausea	**WARNINGS** Hypersensitivity reactions can occur, including severe rash (SJS/TEN). Can test for HLA-B*5801 prior to starting treatment (consider testing in Koreans with stage 3 or worse CKD, and Han Chinese or Thai irrespective of renal function), and renal impairment alone ↑ risk. Hepatotoxicity, caution in liver impairment, bone marrow suppression. Do not use to treat asymptomatic hyperuricemia (high uric acid, no history gout). **SIDE EFFECTS** Rash, acute gout attacks, nausea, diarrhea, ↑ LFTs **MONITORING** UA level, with goal < 6 mg/dL, CBC (for bone marrow suppression), LFTs, renal function **NOTES** Higher doses used for tumor lysis syndrome (in chemotherapy).
Febuxostat (Uloric)	Start at 40 mg daily,↑ to 80 mg if UA not < 6 mg/dL at 6 weeks	**CONTRAINDICATIONS** Concomitant use with didanosine, mercaptopurine and pegloticase (↑ toxicity). **WARNINGS** Hepatotoxicity, use with caution in patients with liver impairment and discontinue if LFTs > 3x ULN, possible ↑ in thromboembolic events. Administer concurrently with an NSAID or colchicine (up to 6 months) to prevent gout flare, which may occur upon initiation of therapy (this is done with allopurinol as well). Do not use to treat asymptomatic hyperuricemia. **SIDE EFFECTS** Rash, nausea,≠ LFTs, arthralgia **MONITORING** LFTs at 2 months, 4 months, then periodically **NOTES** Tablet contains lactose. Expensive compared to allopurinol, but no dose reduction necessary in renal impairment and ↓ risk hypersensitivity.

Chronic UA – Lowering Therapy Continued

DRUG	DOSING	SAFETY/SIDE EFFECTS/MONITORING

Probenecid (a uricosuric) inhibits reabsorption of uric acid in the kidneys, which ↑ uric acid excretion. Competes with penicillins and cephalosporins in the kidneys, which ↓ the beta lactam excretion and ↑ the plasma levels.

| **Probenecid**
2nd line agent | Start 250 mg BID, can increase to 2 g/day | **CONTRAINDICATIONS**
Concomitant aspirin therapy, blood dyscrasias, uric acid kidney stones (nephrolithiasis), children < 2 years, initiation in acute gout attack

WARNINGS
↓ effectiveness with < 30 mL/min (ACR guidelines: do not use < 50 mL/min)
↑ risk of hemolytic anemia in patients with G6PD deficiency

SIDE EFFECTS
Hypersensitivity reactions, hemolytic anemia

NOTES
Requires adequate renal function; not recommended as monotherapy in patients with CrCl < 50 mL/min; avoid use in patients with CrCl < 30 mL/min.

Used to ↑ penicillin levels; ↓ penicillin's renal excretion. |
| Colchicine-Probenicid | 0.5/500 mg daily for 1 week, then BID (for starting probenecid, to reduce risk acute attack) | |

Pegloticase is a pegylated form of uricase, an enzyme which converts uric acid to allantoin (an inactive and water soluble metabolite of uric acid); it does not block uric acid formation.

| Pegloticase (*Krystexxa*) – injection, costly, refractory cases only | 8 mg IV every 2 weeks | **BOXED WARNING**
Anaphylactic reactions; monitor, and premedicate with antihistamines and corticosteroids. Risk is highest if uric acid is > 6 mg/dL.

CONTRAINDICATIONS
G6PD deficiency

WARNINGS
Acute gout flares may occur upon initiation; an NSAID or colchicine should be given 1 week prior to infusion; continue for at least 6 months

SIDE EFFECTS
Antibody formation, gout flare, infusion reactions, nausea, bruising, urticaria, erythema, pruritus

NOTES
Do not use in combination with allopurinol (increased risk of anaphylaxis) |

Chronic UA – Lowering Therapy Continued

DRUG	DOSING	SAFETY/SIDE EFFECTS/MONITORING
Rasburicase (Elitek)	IV: 0.2 mg/kg daily, max 5 days	**BOXED WARNINGS** Anaphylaxis, hemolysis, methemoglobinemia, interference with uric acid measurements **CONTRAINDICATIONS** History of anaphylaxis or severe hypersensitivity to rasburicase, history of hemolytic reaction or methemoglobinemia associated with rasburicase, G6PD deficiency **WARNINGS** Patients at risk for tumor lysis syndrome should receive appropriate IV hydration as part of uric acid management **SIDE EFFECTS** Peripheral edema, headache, anxiety, rash, N/V abdominal pain, diarrhea or constipation (both 20%), mucositis, hypophosphatemia, hypovolemia, hyperbilirubinemia, ↑ ALT, ↑ antibodies, sepsis, pharyngolaryngeal pain **MONITORING** Uric acid, CBC

Allopurinol Drug Interactions

- Allopurinol ↑ the concentration of mercaptopurine, the active metabolite of azathioprine. Avoid concurrent use of either drug with allopurinol, or ↓ dose, and monitor for toxicity. Antacids ↓ the absorption of allopurinol.

- Avoid concurrent use with didanosine; allopurinol can ↑ didanosine levels.

Probenecid Drug Interactions

- Probenecid may decrease the renal clearance of other medications taken concurrently, including aspirin (do not use salicylates concurrently), methotrexate, penicillins, cephalosporins and carbapenems.

- Probenecid may be used with penicillins to ↑ the penicillin plasma concentrations; this will ↑ adverse reactions. Probenecid can decrease the efficacy of loop diuretics, but increases the loop's toxicity.

Allopurinol Counseling

- Take after a meal to reduce stomach upset (higher doses can be divided). Drink plenty of fluids..

- If you feel ill or get a rash, you should seek medical help quickly. The rash could become serious.

PRACTICE CASE

BK is a 62 y/o white male with hypertension. He presents to the clinic today with pain described as 10/10. He is trying to avoid putting weight on his right foot. Physical exam reveals a swollen, tender, enlarged big toe. His blood pressure has a daily range of 155-178/88-99 mmHg. The patient reports that he consumes low fat yogurt with berries or nuts for breakfast each day. He walks each night around the track at the neighborhood high school. He reports "weekend" alcohol use (3-4 beers on Saturday/Sunday). No past or present history of tobacco use.

Allergies: NKDA

Medications:
Norvasc 10 mg PO daily
Zestril 10 mg PO daily
Chlorthalidone 25 mg PO daily
Aspirin EC 81 mg daily
Fish oil capsule with dinner
Coenzyme Q10 with dinner

Vitals:
Height: 5'11" Weight: 255 pounds
BP: 177/95 mmHg HR: 89 BPM RR: 16 BPM Temp: 98.8ϓF Pain: 10/10

Labs: Na (mEq/L) = 142 (135 - 145)
K (mEq/L) = 4.8 (3.5 - 5)
Cl (mEq/L) = 100 (95 - 103)
HCO_3 (mEq/L) = 28 (24 - 30)
BUN (mg/dL) = 22 (7 - 20)
SCr (mg/dL) = 1.4 (0.6 - 1.3)
Glucose (mg/dL) = 119 (100 - 125)
Ca (mg/dL) = 10.2 (8.5 - 10.5)
Mg (mEq/L) = 1.8 (1.3 - 2.1)
PO_4 (mg/dL) = 4.2 (2.3 - 4.7)

AST (IU/L) = 12 (8 - 48)
ALT (IU/L) = 14 (7 - 55)
Albumin (g/dL) = 4.8 (3.5 - 5)
Uric Acid (mg/dL) = 18.3 (3.5 - 7.2 male, 2 - 6.5 female)

April 1st: 62 y/o male with first episode of acute gout in right great toe. Provide therapy for gout and optimize therapy for uncontrolled HTN. Prescription written for *Dilacor XR* 120 mg Q daily.

Questions

1. What is BK's creatinine clearance (in mL/min), using the Cockcroft-Gault equation and his ideal body weight?

   a. 89
   b. 71
   c. 58
   d. 34
   e. 11

2. The physician is considering allopurinol to treat the acute attack. Choose the correct statement:

   a. This is not appropriate therapy for an acute attack.
   b. He should receive a starting dose of 50 mg daily.
   c. He should receive a starting dose of 75 mg daily.
   d. He should receive a starting dose of 100 mg daily.
   e. He should receive a starting dose of 150 mg daily.

3. BK will receive a short-course of prednisone therapy, with taper, that will last less than 2 weeks. Which of the following side effects are possible and should be explained to BK?

   a. Growth suppression
   b. Insomnia/spaciness
   c. Osteoporosis
   d. Cataracts
   e. Seizures

4. Choose the correct dosing regimen for colchicine for an acute gout attack:

   a. 1.2 mg followed by 0.6 mg every 2 hours, not to exceed 6 tablets/24 hours
   b. 1.2 mg followed by 0.6 mg every 2 hours, not to exceed 8 tablets/24 hours
   c. 1.2 mg followed by 0.6 mg in 2-4 hours (total 1.8 mg)
   d. 1.2 mg followed by 0.6 mg in 1 hours, then as-needed for 3 additional doses (total 3.6 mg)
   e. 1.2 mg followed by 0.6 mg in 1 hours (total 1.8 mg)

Questions 5 – 8 do not apply to the above case.

5. A pharmacist receives a prescription for *Zyloprim*. Which medication is an acceptable alternative?

   a. Probenecid
   b. Colchicine
   c. Allopurinol
   d. Naproxen
   e. Febuxostat

6. Which of the following are true regarding pegloticase? (Select **ALL** that apply.)

   a. The brand name is *Krystexxa*
   b. The recommended dose is 8 mg PO daily
   c. It should not be given in combination with allopurinol
   d. It is a first-line treatment for acute gout
   e. Patients must be monitored for anaphylactic reactions when receiving this agent

7. Which of the following side effects are likely to occur with colchicine therapy?

   a. Nausea, cramping, loose stools
   b. Xerostomia, xerophthalmia
   c. Mental confusion
   d. Skeletal bone loss
   e. Risk of severe rash/hypersensitivity reactions

8. A pharmacist has just attended an education program on the use of febuxostat. He wants to present the main points about this drug to his pharmacy colleagues. He should include the following points: (Select **ALL** that apply.)

   a. Febuxostat works by increasing the renal excretion of uric acid.
   b. Febuxostat appears to have lower risk of hypersensitivity reactions than allopurinol, including less of a risk of serious rash.
   c. Febuxostat costs much more than generic allopurinol and is reserved for refractory cases.
   d. The brand name of febuxostat is *Zyloprim*.
   e. Febuxostat is a xanthine oxidase inhibitor.

Answers

1-c, 2-a, 3-b, 4-e, 5-c, 6-a,c,e, 7-a, 8-b,c,e

DYSLIPIDEMIA

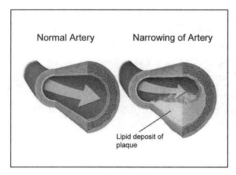

Normal Artery   Narrowing of Artery

Lipid deposit of plaque

We gratefully acknowledge the assistance of Joel C. Marrs, PharmD, FCCP, FASHP, FNLA, BCPS-AQ Cardiology, BCACP, CLS, Associate Professor at the University of Colorado Skaggs School of Pharmacy and Pharmaceutical Sciences, in preparing this chapter.

BACKGROUND

Cholesterol is required for good health. It is a structural component of cells, is a precursor in hormone synthesis, and is used in the production of bile acids. The liver produces cholesterol, and makes bile acids from cholesterol. The bile acids travel from the liver through the bile ducts (along with free cholesterol and waste products) and into the small intestine. Bile acids present in the small intestine are required for fat absorption. The acid in the intestine converts the bile acids into bile salts, which are continually recycled from the intestine and returned to the liver. This process involves the gut (enteric system) and the liver (hepatic), and is referred to as enterohepatic recycling.

The recycling system decreases the liver's requirement for new cholesterol. Cholesterol has two primary methods of exiting the body: either as free cholesterol or as bile acid. If the absorption of free cholesterol is blocked in the intestine (such as with ezetimibe) or the enterohepatic recirculation of bile salts is blocked (by the bile acid sequestrants, such as colesevelam), the end result is a decrease in cholesterol.

GUIDELINES/REFERENCES

Stone NJ, Robinson JG, Lichtenstein AH, et al. 2013 ACC/AHA Guideline on the Treatment of Blood Cholesterol to Reduce Atherosclerotic Cardiovascular Risk in Adults: A Report of the American College of Cardiology/American Heart Association Task Force on Practice Guidelines. *Circulation.* 2014; 129:S1-S45.

Eckel RH, Jakicic JM, Ard JD, et al. 2013 AHA/ACC guideline on lifestyle management to reduce cardiovascular risk: a report of the American College of Cardiology/American Heart Association Task Force on Practice Guidelines. *Circulation.* 2014; 129 (25 Suppl 2):S76-99.

Jacoboson TA, Ito MK, Maki KC, et al. National Lipid Association Recommendations for Patient-Centered Management of Dyslipidemia: Part 1 - Executive Summary. *J Clin Lipidol.* 2014; 8(5):473-488.

Goff DC Jr, Lloyd-Jones DM, Bennett G, et al. 2013 ACC/AHA Guideline on the Assessment of Cardiovascular Risk: A Report of the American College of Cardiology/American Heart Association Task Force on Practice Guidelines. JACC 2014;63:2935-59.

Addtl guidelines included with the video files (RxPrep Online)

Cholesterol is an umbrella term for different types of lipoproteins, and abnormalities in specific lipoprotein levels are called dyslipidemias. Cholesterol cannot dissolve in the blood and is transported in lipoproteins (lipid + a protein carrier). The different types of lipoproteins are important as some contribute to risk. Most importantly, elevations in non-HDL, LDL and triglycerides (TG) will put a patient at elevated risk for atherogenic disease, including coronary, cerebrovascular and peripheral artery disease. With each of these conditions, fatty deposits accumulate in the arteries (atherosclerosis). It is helpful to identify areas of risk, but it is also important to realize that the process itself is generally systemic and occurs throughout the body.

Dyslipidemias can be inherited, which are called primary or familial, but are most often secondary to poor diet, lifestyle, medications or other causes. Refer to the table for a summary of secondary causes. When the dyslipidemia is due to diet and lifestyle, improving eating habits, obtaining regular exercise and, when required, using medications, can correct the dyslipidemia. Elevated TGs can cause acute pancreatitis.

CLASSIFICATION OF DYSLIPIDEMIA

Dyslipidemia refers to any lipoprotein disorder including ↑ total cholesterol (TC), ↑ low-density lipoprotein cholesterol (LDL), ↑ triglycerides (TGs) and/or ↓ high-density lipoprotein cholesterol (HDL). Non-high-density lipoprotein (non-HDL) cholesterol has emerged as a stronger predictor of atherosclerotic cardiovascular disease (ASCVD) than LDL and can be calculated from the values obtained in a traditional lipid panel. Non-HDL is the difference between the TC and the HDL concentration: Non-HDL = TC-HDL. Non-HDL includes atherogenic cholesterol such as LDL, intermediate density lipoproteins (IDL), very low-density lipoproteins (VLDL), chylomicron remnants and lipoprotein (a). Additionally, apolipoprotein B (apoB) is both a high-risk marker and is itself an indicator of the progression of atherosclerosis, which begins when an apoB particle becomes trapped within the vascular wall.

Primary (or Familial)

- Familial dyslipidemias are classified according to the Fredrickson classification. Familial hypercholesterolemias (FH) are genetic defects resulting in severe cholesterol elevations and increased risk of premature ASCVD. FHs include heterozygous familial hypercholesterolemia (HeFH) and homozygous familial hypercholesterolemia (HoFH), which is much more difficult to treat.

Secondary (or Acquired)

- Some common causes of secondary dyslipidemia are listed in the table below. Severe elevations (including LDL ≥ 190 mg/dL and TG ≥ 500 mg/dL) must be evaluated and treated appropriately.

Secondary Causes of Dyslipidemia

SECONDARY CAUSE	↑ LDL	↑ TRIGLYCERIDES
Diet	Weight gain, saturated or *trans* fats, anorexia	Weight gain, very low-fat diets, high intake of refined carbohydrate, excessive alcohol intake
Drugs	Cyclosporine, tacrolimus, protease inhibitors, atypical antipsychotics, glucocorticoids, anabolic steroids, some progestins, diuretics, amiodarone, danazol, isotretinoin, thiazolidinediones, sodium-glucose co-transporter 2 inhibitors, fibric acids (with ↑ TGs)	Cyclosporine, tacrolimus, protease inhibitors, atypical antipsychotics, glucocorticoids, oral estrogen, bile acid sequestrants, retinoids, anabolic steroids, sirolimus, raloxifene, tamoxifen, beta blockers, thiazides, alpha interferons, propofol
Diseases	Nephrotic syndrome, biliary obstruction	Nephrotic syndrome, chronic renal failure, lipodystrophies
Disorders and altered states of metabolism	Obesity, hypothyroidism, pregnancy, polycystic ovary syndrome	Obesity, hypothyroidism, pregnancy, diabetes (poorly controlled)

Cholesterol (Lipoprotein) Types and Normal Values

Many clinicians recommend checking lipoprotein levels after a 9 – 12 hour fast. If the patient is not fasting, the TG level may be <u>falsely elevated resulting in a falsely low calculation of LDL</u>. Non-HDL and apoB do not require fasting for accurate assessment.

LDL may need to be calculated if it is not given using the <u>Friedewald equation: LDL = TC - HDL - (TG/5)</u>. This formula is not used when the TGs are > 400 mg/dL.

Natural Products

Red yeast rice is the product of yeast grown on rice that contains naturally occurring HMG-CoA reductase inhibitors, and is similar to low-dose statins. The *Natural Medicines Database* recommends against the use of red yeast rice products. Some contain too little drug, some contain too much, and some contain contaminants that have caused renal damage. Plant stanols, sterols, fibrous foods (such as in psyllium, barley, oat bran) and a specific type of artichoke extract are each effective in lowering LDL to various extents. OTC fish oils can be used to lower TGs. They can increase LDL in some patients. Garlic used to be recommended for this purpose but the effect is not significant. Fish oils and niacin are discussed later in this chapter. With any of these products, the benefit may have been with a specific formulation and dose, and there are quality concerns with individual products. Refer to the *Natural Medicines Database* for guidance.

NON-DRUG TREATMENT

Lifestyle modifications are an important part of management. These recommendations apply to adults < 80 years old with and without ASCVD and should be emphasized, monitored and reinforced.

- Consuming a diet rich in vegetables and fruits, choosing whole-grain, high-fiber foods, consuming fish, especially oily fish, and limiting intake of saturated fat, *trans* (partially hydrogenated) fat and cholesterol by choosing lean meats, non-meat alternatives and low-fat dairy products. Minimize the consumption of added sugars and salt. The diet should be modified for the individual's calorie requirements, personal preferences and in consideration of other medical conditions. Specific targets:

- Aim for 5 – 6% of calories from saturated fat; ↓ % of calories from *trans* fat.

- Engage in aerobic physical activity 3 – 4 times per week, lasting 40 minutes/session and involving moderate-to-vigorous intensity (↓ LDL 3 – 6 mg/dL).

- Maintain a healthy weight (BMI 18.5 – 24.9 kg/m²).

- Avoid tobacco products, limit alcohol consumption.

CLASSIFICATION OF CHOLESTEROL AND TG LEVELS (MG/DL)

Non-HDL*

< 130	Desirable
130-159	Above desirable
160-189	Borderiine high
190-219	High
≥ 220	Very high

LDL

< 100	Desirable
100-129	Above desirable
130-159	Borderiine high
160-189	High
≥ 190	Very high

HDL

< 40 (men)	Low
< 50 (women)	Low

Triglycerides

< 150	Normal
150-199	Borderiine high
200-499	High
≥ 500	Very high†

HDL = high-density lipoprotein cholesterol, LDL = low-density lipoprotein cholesterol, non-HDL = non-high-density lipoprotein cholesterol

* Non-HDL = total cholesterol minus HDL

† Severe hypertriglyceridemia is another term used for very high triglycerides in pharmaceutical product labeling.

TREATING DYSLIPIDEMIAS

There are two treatment guidelines that address cholesterol management: the American College of Cardiology and the American Heart Association guidelines (ACC/AHA) and the National Lipid Association (NLA) guidelines. The primary difference involves a focus on statin use by risk (ACC/AHA) rather than treating to LDL target levels (NLA).

ACC/AHA GUIDELINES

The ACC/AHA national cholesterol treatment guidelines include significant changes from the previous cholesterol guidelines (NCEP ATP III), which had focused on treating LDL and non-HDL to target values. The current guideline identifies <u>four key patient groups</u> who should consider statin initiation with appropriate <u>intensity</u> to obtain relative reductions in LDL (for example, a target could be a 50% reduction, rather than a specific LDL value). Non-statins are <u>not</u> <u>recommended</u> unless <u>statins are not tolerated</u>. After

> **KEY POINT: ACC/AHA**
>
> The ACC/AHA guidelines state that there is no evidence to support continued use of specific LDL treatment targets. Statins (primarily), dosed at the appropriate intensity, are used in patients with ASCVD and patients at risk for ASCVD.

the release of the guideline, the IMPROVE-IT study showed a further reduction in CV events in stable patients with a recent ACS <u>when ezetimibe was added to a statin</u>, compared to using a statin alone. Previously, ezetimibe was not widely used due to a lack of demonstrated benefit. Now, some patients will be using ezetimibe in addition to a statin.

Identification of 4 Statin Benefit Groups

The following 4 groups of patients should be initiated on statin therapy:

1. Clinical atherosclerotic cardiovascular disease (ASCVD), including coronary heart disease (ACS, S/P MI, stable or unstable angina, coronary or other arterial revascularization), stroke, TIA or peripheral arterial disease thought to be of atherosclerotic origin

2. Primary elevations of LDL ≥ 190 mg/dL

3. Diabetes and 40 – 75 years of age with LDL between 70 – 189 mg/dL

4. Patients 40 – 75 years of age with LDL between 70 – 189 mg/dL and estimated 10-year ASCVD risk of ≥ 7.5% (using the global risk assessment tool)

Global Risk Assessment Tool

The global risk assessment tool is used to provide an estimate of an individual's <u>risk</u> of having a cardiovascular event (e.g., MI, stroke or death) <u>during the next</u> <u>10 years</u>. This is called the 10-year ASCVD risk. When healthcare providers understand the risk level of a patient they are more likely to prescribe risk-reducing treatments, including statins and antihypertensives. The risk level can also motivate the patient to address modifiable risk factors. To calculate a patient's risk, the clinician inputs the patient's gender, age, race, TC, HDL, systolic blood pressure, whether antihypertensive treatment is used, the presence of diabetes and smoking status. A 10-year ASCVD risk of ≥ 7.5% is an indication to start statin therapy in individuals between the age of 40 – 75 years of age. This risk assessment should be repeated every 4 – 6 years in those who

> **ADDITIONAL FACTORS* PER ACC/AHA GUIDELINES**
>
> If after quantitative risk assessment, a risk-based treatment decision is uncertain, additional factors may be considered to assist with decision making. These factors include:
>
> - LDL ≥ 160 mg/dL or other evidence of genetic hyperlipidemia
>
> - Family history of premature ASCVD with onset < 55 years in a first degree male relative or < 65 years in a first degree female relative
>
> - High-sensitivity C-reactive protein ≥ 2 mg/L
>
> - Coronary Artery Calcium score ≥ 300 Agatston units or ≥ 75 percentile for age, sex and ethnicity
>
> - Ankle Brachial Index < 0.9
>
> *   *These factors support revising risk assessment upward*

are found to be at a low 10-year risk (< 7.5%). The link for the tool is provided in the References box on the first page of this chapter. Other factors may be included to measure risk and those are found in the additional factors box.

Determining Appropriate Statin Treatment Intensity Based on Patient Risk

PREVENTION LEVEL	STATIN TREATMENT

Primary Prevention

Primary elevation of LDL ≥ 190 mg/dL	High-intensity*
Diabetes and 40-75 years with LDL between 70-189 mg/dL with estimated 10-year ASCVD risk < 7.5%	Moderate-intensity
Diabetes and 40-75 years with LDL between 70-189 mg/dL with estimated 10-year ASCVD risk ≥ 7.5%	High-intensity*
Ages 40-75 years with LDL between 70-189 mg/dL with estimated 10-year ASCVD risk < 7.5%	Consider risk benefit
Ages 40-75 years with LDL between 70-189 mg/dL with estimated 10-year ASCVD risk ≥ 7.5%	Moderate-to-high intensity

Secondary Prevention

Clinical ASCVD ≤ 75 years	High-intensity*
Clinical ASCVD > 75 years	Moderate-intensity

Use moderate-intensity statin if not candidate for high-intensity

Statin Treatment Intensity Definitions and Selection Options

HIGH-INTENSITY	MODERATE-INTENSITY	LOW-INTENSITY
DAILY DOSE ↓ LDL ≥ 50%	**DAILY DOSE ↓ LDL 30%-49%**	**DAILY DOSE ↓ LDL < 30%**
Atorvastatin 40-80 mg daily	Atorvastatin 10-20 mg daily	Simvastatin 10 mg daily
Rosuvastatin 20-40 mg daily	Rosuvastatin 5-10 mg daily	Pravastatin 10-20 mg daily
	Simvastatin 20-40 mg daily	Lovastatin 20 mg daily
	Pravastatin 40-80 mg daily	Fluvastatin 20-40 mg daily
	Lovastatin 40 mg daily	Pitavastatin 1 mg daily
	Fluvastatin XL 80 mg daily	
	Fluvastatin 40 mg BID	
	Pitavastatin 2-4 mg daily	

NLA Expert Panel Recommendations

In the year following the ACC/AHA guideline, the NLA released part 1 of their cholesterol recommendations, which emphasize treating cholesterol values to specific goal values. The focus was shifted from targeting LDL (such as had been done with ATP III), to primarily targeting non-HDL and LDL, but, like ATP III, include target values rather than percentage reductions. The NLA released part 2 of the recommendations in June 2015, which included an emphasis on active participation of the patient in both lifestyle management and in drug treatment. It includes specific advice for certain groups, such as advice based on race or gender. First, the patient's ASCVD risk is calculated, then lifestyle counseling is initiated, and statins, when indicated, are started. Non-statins are recommended only as add-ons in select patients and only after the statin has been titrated to the maximally tolerated dose.

DRUG TREATMENT

Statins are the drugs of choice in treating ↑ non-HDL and LDL. Although statins ↑ risk of diabetes and myalgias (see box), they are still recommended given their reduction in cardiovascular disease and mortality.

If a patient is completely statin intolerant, it is reasonable to use other cholesterol-lowering drugs. Many of the cholesterol-lowering drugs can cause liver damage (niacin, fibrates, ezetimibe and potentially statins). Liver enzymes should be monitored and the drug stopped if the AST (10 – 40 units/L) or ALT (10 – 40 units/L) is > 3 times the upper limit of normal. Increases in liver enzymes in patients using statins are similar to that of the population not using statins; however, LFTs should be monitored at baseline and periodically thereafter.

In 2015, alirocumab (*Praluent*) and evolocumab (*Repatha*) were FDA-approved for treating familial hypercholesterolemia or for patients with ASCVD who require additional ↓ in LDL. Both drugs are PCSK9 inhibitors which block the protein that binds the liver's LDL receptors. This increases the amount of the receptors, which ↑ LDL degradation, and ↓ LDL ~60%. These are monoclonal antibodies which must be given by SC injections, are costly, and at present lack long-term safety data.

Metreleptin *(Myalept)* is not discussed in the drug tables. This is a recombinant human leptin analog used as an adjunct to diet to treat leptin deficiency with lipodystrophy. The drug may be a breakthrough for some patients with leptin deficiency, but has safety issues, including the development of leptin antibodies and lymphoma risk. It is a REMS drug, with restricted use.

STATINS & MUSCLE DAMAGE

TERMINOLOGY

Myopathy: muscle disease +/- ↑ CPK

Myalgia: muscle soreness

Myositis: muscle inflammation

Rhabdomyolysis: muscle symptoms + very high CPK > 10,000 + muscle protein in the urine (myoglobinuria), which leads to acute renal failure

SYMPTOMS

Most often occur within 6 weeks of starting tx but can occur after years of tx, and include muscle tenderness/soreness (myalgias), weakness, stiffness/cramps.

Often symmetrical (on both sides of the body) and in large adjacent muscle groups in the legs, back or arms.

REDUCE THE RISK

Check for drug interactions.

Do not use simvastatin 80 mg/day.

Do not use gemfibrozil + statin.

MANAGE MYALGIAS

1st: Hold statin if intolerable, check CPK, investigate other possible causes.

2-4 weeks: Re-challenge with same statin at same or ↓ dose.

Most patients who did not tolerate a statin will tolerate it when re-challenged, or will tolerate a different statin.

If original statin and myalgias return, discontinue original statin. Once muscle symptoms resolve, use a low dose of a different statin.

If low dose of a different statin is tolerated, gradually ↑ dose, as tolerated.

STATINS

Statins inhibit the enzyme 3-hydroxy-3-methylglutaryl coenzyme A (HMG-CoA) reductase, which prevents the conversion of HMG-CoA to mevalonate. This is the rate-limiting step in cholesterol synthesis. Evidence supports the use of statin treatment to ↓ ASCVD risk, in those most likely to benefit. It is important to know the statin intensity dosing to provide patients the most benefit from these drugs.

STATIN EQUIVALENT DOSES	
Atorvastatin 10 mg =	Pitavastatin 2 mg
	Rosuvastatin 5 mg
	Simvastatin 20 mg
	Lovastatin 40 mg
	Pravastatin 40 mg
	Fluvastatin 80 mg

DRUG	DOSING	SAFETY/SIDE EFFECTS/MONITORING
AtorvaSTATin **(Lipitor)** + amlodipine (Caduet) + ezetimibe (Liptruzet)	10-80 mg daily	**CONTRAINDICATIONS** Active liver disease (including any unexplained ↑ LFTs), pregnancy, breastfeeding; concurrent use of strong 3A4 inhibitors (simvastatin and lovastatin); concurrent use with cyclosporine (pitavastatin) **WARNINGS** Skeletal muscle effects (e.g., myopathy, rhabdomyolysis) – risk ↑ with higher concentrations, advanced age (≥ 65), uncontrolled hypothyroidism and renal impairment
Fluvastatin **(Lescol, Lescol XL)**	20-80 mg Lescol is taken in the evening Lescol XL is taken daily	Diabetes, ↑ A1C and fasting blood glucose; benefits of statin therapy far outweigh the risk of hyperglycemia Hepatotoxicity, ↑ LFTs (rare) Immune-mediated necrotizing myopathy (IMNM) can occur in rare cases
Lovastatin **(Mevacor, Altoprev)** + niacin (Advicor)	20-80 mg Mevacor (immediate release) is taken with evening meal Altoprev (extended release) is taken at bedtime	**SIDE EFFECTS** Myalgias, arthralgias, myopathy, diarrhea, cognitive impairment **MONITORING** LFTs at baseline and as clinically indicated thereafter; obtain a lipid panel
Pitavastatin **(Livalo)**	1-4 mg daily	4-12 weeks after initiation or up titration of therapy to assess for medication adherence; then every 3-12 months thereafter
Pravastatin **(Pravachol)**	10-80 mg daily	**NOTES** Pregnancy Category X
Rosuvastatin **(Crestor)**	5-40 mg daily	Can take Crestor, Lipitor, Livalo, Lescol XL and Pravachol at any time of day. When CrCl < 30 mL/min, use lower starting doses (lovastatin, simvastatin, rosuvastatin). When CrCl < 60 mL/min, use lower starting dose of pitavastatin.
Simvastatin **(Zocor)** + ezetimibe **(Vytorin)** + niacin (Simcor)	10-40 mg daily in the evening	**Lipid Effects** ↓ LDL ~20-55%, ↑ HDL ~5-15%, ↓ TG ~10-30%

Statin Drug Interactions

All Statins

■ Use with fibrates (avoid statins with gemfibrozil) and niacin products containing ≥ 1 gram ↑ the risk of myopathies.

■ Cases of myopathy, including rhabdomyolysis, have been reported with statins coadministered with colchicine

DRUG	SIGNIFICANT DRUG INTERACTIONS
Simvastatin 3A4 substrate (major)	Avoid Strong 3A4 inhibitors (see box below) Max 10 mg/day – verapamil, diltiazem, dronedarone Max 20 mg/day – amiodarone, amlodipine, lomitapide, ranolazine Max 40 mg/day – ticagrelor
Lovastatin 3A4 substrate (major), P-gp substrate	Avoid Strong 3A4 inhibitors (see box below) Max 20 mg/day – danazol, diltiazem, dronedarone, verapamil Max 40 mg/day – amiodarone, ticagrelor
Atorvastatin 3A4 substrate (major), P-gp substrate	Avoid – cyclosporine, gemfibrozil, tipranavir + ritonavir Max 20 mg/day – clarithromycin, itraconazole, darunavir + ritonavir, fosamprenavir, fosamprenavir + ritonavir, saquinavir + ritonavir Max 40 mg/day – nelfinavir Caution (use lowest dose) with lopinavir + ritonavir Levels of norethindrone and ethinyl estradiol can increase
Rosuvastatin 3A4 (minor) and 2C9 (minor) substrate	Max 5 mg/day – cyclosporine Max 10 mg/day – atazanavir + ritonavir, lopinavir + ritonavir Warfarin – can ↑ INR
Pravastatin 3A4 (minor), P-gp substrate	Max 20 mg/day – cyclosporine Max 40 mg/day – clarithromycin
Fluvastatin 2C9, 2D6, 3A4 substrate (all minor); inhibitor of 1A2 (weak), 2C8 (weak), 2C9 (moderate), 2D6 (weak)	Max 20 mg/day – cyclosporine Max 40 mg/day – fluconazole ↑ levels of glyburide, phenytoin Warfarin - can ↑ INR
Pitavastatin	Cyclosporine contraindicated Max 1 mg/day – erythromycin Max 2 mg/day – rifampin Warfarin – monitor PT/INR after dose change/initiation

STRONG 3A4 INHIBITORS – AVOID WITH SIMVASTATIN AND LOVASTATIN

Itraconazole	Erythromycin	Cobicistat-containing regimens	Gemfibrozil
Ketoconazole	Clarithromycin	Nefazodone	Danazol (with simvastatin)
Posaconazole	Telithromycin	Cyclosporine	Grapefruit juice
Voriconazole	HIV protease inhibitors		

EZETIMIBE

Inhibits absorption of cholesterol at the brush border of the small intestine. Recently (early 2015), the IMPROVE-IT study showed the addition of ezetimibe to moderate intensity statin therapy in stable patients with recent ACS and had LDL cholesterol levels within guideline recommendations further lowered the risk of cardiovascular events.

DRUG	DOSING	SAFETY/SIDE EFFECTS/MONITORING
Ezetimibe *(Zetia)* **+ simvastatin *(Vytorin)*** **+ atorvastatin *(Liptruzet)***	10 mg daily If CrCl < 60 mL/min, do not exceed simvastatin 20 mg/day when using combination product *(Vytorin)*	**CONTRAINDICATIONS** Concomitant use with a statin in patients with active liver disease (including any unexplained ↑ in LFTs), and who are pregnant/breastfeeding is contraindicated. **WARNINGS** Avoid use in moderate-or-severe hepatic impairment Skeletal muscle effects (e.g., myopathy, including risk of rhabdomyolysis), risk ↑ when combined with a statin **SIDE EFFECTS** URTIs, diarrhea, arthralgias, myalgias, pain in extremities, sinusitis **MONITORING** When used with a statin and/or fibrate, obtain LFTs at baseline and as clinically indicated thereafter **NOTES** Pregnancy Category C **Lipid effects with ezetimibe monotherapy** ↓ LDL 18-23%, ↑ HDL 1-3%, ↓ TG 5-10%

Ezetimibe Drug Interactions

- When ezetimibe and cyclosporine are given together, the concentration of both can ↑; monitor levels of cyclosporine.

- Concomitant bile acid sequestrants ↓ ezetimibe; give ezetimibe 2 hours before or 4 hours after bile acid sequestrants.

- Can ↑ risk of cholelithiasis when used with fenofibrate; avoid use with gemfibrozil.

- If using warfarin, monitor INR/bleeding after dose initiation or dose change.

BILE ACID SEQUESTRANTS/BILE ACID BINDING RESINS

Binds bile acids in the intestine forming a complex that is excreted in the feces. This non-systemic action results in a partial removal of the bile acids from the enterohepatic circulation, preventing their reabsorption.

DRUG	DOSING	SAFETY/SIDE EFFECTS/MONITORING
Cholestyramine (*Questran, Questran Light, Prevalite*) Also approved for pruritus due to increased levels of bile acids, regression of arteriosclerosis 4 gram powder packet	4 grams initially (max 24 grams/day), divided BID with meals	**CONTRAINDICATIONS** Cholestyramine – Complete biliary obstruction Colesevelam – Bowel obstruction, TG > 500 mg/dL, history of hypertriglyceridemia-induced pancreatitis **SIDE EFFECTS** <u>Constipation</u> (may need dose reduction or laxative), dyspepsia, nausea, <u>abdominal pain, cramping, gas</u>, bloating, ↑ TGs, esophageal obstruction, ↑ LFTs
Colesevelam (*Welchol*) 625 mg tablet, 1.875 g and 3.75 g granule packet Also approved for Type 2 DM (↓ A1C ~ 0.5%)	Tablets/granules: 3.75 grams daily or in divided doses <u>with a meal and liquid</u>	**NOTES** Pregnancy Category B (*Welchol*)/C (others) ACC/AHA guidelines do not recommend using these agents when TGs are ≥ 300 mg/dL. Cholestyramine packet – Mix powder with 2-6 oz. water or non-carbonated liquid. Sipping or holding the resin suspension in the mouth for prolonged periods may lead to changes in the surface of the teeth resulting in discoloration, erosion of enamel or decay; good oral hygiene should be maintained.
Colestipol (*Colestid*) 1 gram tablet, 5 gram packet and granules	Tablets: 2 grams daily or BID (max 16 grams/day) Packet and Granules: 5 grams daily or BID (max 30 grams/day)	Colesevelam packet – Empty 1 packet into a glass; add 4-8 oz. of water, fruit juice, or a diet soft drink and mix well. Colestipol packet - Empty 1 packet into at least 3 oz. of liquid and stir until completely mixed. **Lipid Effects** ↓ LDL ~10-30% ↑ HDL ~3-5% No change or <u>↑ TG</u> (~5%)

Bile Acid Sequestrants Drug Interactions

- Colesevelam has less drug interactions than the other 2 bile acid sequestrants and is more commonly used. For cholestyramine or colestipol, separate all other drugs by 1 – 4 hours before or 4 – 6 hours after the bile acid sequestrants.

- The following medications should be taken 4 hours prior to colesevelam: cyclosporine, glimepiride, glipizide, glyburide, levothyroxine, olmesartan, phenytoin, and oral contraceptives containing ethinyl estradiol and norethindrone. Consider separation with other drugs as well. Colesevelam ↑ levels of metformin ER.

- With warfarin, monitor INR frequently during initiation and after dose change.

- Bile acid sequestrants may ↓ absorption of fat-soluble vitamins (A, D, E, K), folate and iron. Separate administration times with concurrent multivitamin use as noted above.

FIBRATES

Fibrates are peroxisome proliferator receptor alpha (PPARα) activators, which upregulate the expression of apolipoprotein CII and apolipoprotein A-I. Apo CII ↑ lipoprotein lipase activity leading to ↑ catabolism of VLDL particles. This will ↓ TG significantly, but in the setting of high TG (increased VLDL particles) fibrate therapy may lead to an ↑ LDL particles and subsequently an ↑ LDL cholesterol. The ↓ TG may lead to an ↑ in HDL cholesterol. Also ↑ Apo A-I will lead to ↑ HDL since Apo A-I is the building block of HDL particles. The ACCORD Lipid Study showed no significant difference in experiencing a major cardiac event between patients treated with fenofibrate plus simvastatin compared with simvastatin alone.

DRUG	DOSING	SAFETY/SIDE EFFECTS/MONITORING
Fenofibrate, Fenofibric Acid *(Antara, Fenoglide, Fibricor, Lipofen, Lofibra, TriCor, Triglide, Trilipix, generics)*	*Antara* (micronized capsule): 30-90 mg daily *Fenoglide*: 40-120 mg daily <u>with meals</u> *Fibricor:* 35-105 mg daily *Lofibra* (micronized capsule): 67-200 mg daily <u>with meals</u> *Lofibra* (tablet): 54-160 mg daily *Lipofen:* 50-150 mg daily <u>with meals</u> *TriCor:* 48-145 mg daily *Triglide:* 160 mg daily *Trilipix:* 45-135 mg daily	**CONTRAINDICATIONS** Severe liver disease including primary biliary cirrhosis Severe renal disease (CrCl < 30 mL/min) Gallbladder disease Nursing mothers (fenofibrate derivatives only) Concurrent use with repaglinide (gemfibrozil only) **WARNINGS** Myopathy, ↑ risk when co-administered with a statin particularly in the elderly, diabetes, renal failure, or hypothyroidism Cholelithiasis Reversible ↑ SCr (> 2 mg/dL); clinical significance unknown **SIDE EFFECTS** ↑ LFTs (dose-related), abdominal pain, ↑ CPK, <u>dyspepsia</u>, URTIs **MONITORING** LFTs, renal function
Gemfibrozil *(Lopid)*	600 mg BID, 30 minutes before breakfast and dinner	**NOTES** Pregnancy Category C Reduce dose if CrCl 30-80 mL/min with fenofibrates **Lipid Effects** ↓ TGs ~20-50% ↑ HDL ~15% ↓ LDL ~5-20% (<u>but can ↑ LDL when TG are high</u>)

Fibrate Drug Interactions

- Fibrates (especially gemfibrozil) can ↑ the risk of myopathies and rhabdomyolysis. Gemfibrozil should not be given concurrently with ezetimibe, statins or tizanidine.

- Fibrates may ↑ cholesterol excretion into the bile, leading to cholelithiasis.

- Colchicine can ↑ the risk of myopathy when coadministered with fenofibrate.

- Gemfibrozil is contraindicated with repaglinide as it may ↑ hypoglycemic effects.

- Fibrates may increase the effects of sulfonylureas and warfarin.

NIACIN

Decreases the rate of hepatic synthesis of VLDL (↓ TGs) and LDL; may also ↑ rate of chylomicron TG removal from plasma. Alters the binding of HDL particles to scavenger receptor B-1 in the liver which removes the cholesterol inside but does not take up the HDL particle which leaves it free to return to the circulation for reverse cholesterol transport. Also known as nicotinic acid or vitamin B3, although doses for cholesterol reduction are much higher than doses found in multivitamin products.

DRUG	DOSING	SAFETY/SIDE EFFECTS/MONITORING
Immediate-Release (crystalline) niacin (*Niacor*) – OTC	250 mg with dinner; can ↑ every 4-7 days to max dose 6 grams daily, divided in 2-3 doses	**CONTRAINDICATIONS** Active liver disease, active PUD, arterial bleeding **WARNINGS** Use with caution in patients with unstable angina or in the acute phase of an MI Hepatotoxicity
Extended-Release Niacin (*Niaspan*) 500, 750, 1,000 mg + lovastatin (*Advicor*) + simvastatin (*Simcor*)	500 mg QHS x 4 weeks Can ↑ every 4 weeks to a max dose of 2 grams daily	**SIDE EFFECTS** Flushing, pruritus (itching), N/V/D, hyperglycemia, hyperuricemia (or gout), cough, orthostatic hypotension, hypophosphatemia **MONITORING** Check LFTs at the start (baseline), every 6 to 12 weeks for the first year, and then ~ 6-months; blood glucose (if have diabetes); uric acid (if have gout); INR (if on warfarin), lipid profile **NOTES** Pregnancy Category C
Controlled-(or sustained) Release Niacin (*Slo-Niacin*, OTC) 250, 500, 750 mg	250-750 mg daily	Immediate-release niacin has poor tolerability due to flushing/itching. Extended-release forms (CR and SR) have less (but still significant) flushing but more hepatotoxicity. Therefore, the best clinical choice is *Niaspan* with less flushing and less hepatotoxicity – but it is the most expensive. Take aspirin 325 mg (or ibuprofen 200 mg) 30-60 minutes before the dose to ↓ flushing. Formulations of niacin (IR vs ER) are not interchangeable. Flush-free niacins (inositol hexaniacinate or hexanicotinate), niacinamide or nicotinamide are not effective. Take with food, avoid hot beverages and spicy food which can worsen flushing. **Lipid Effects** ↓ LDL 5-25%, ↑ HDL 15-35%, ↓ TG 20-50%

Niacin Drug Interactions

- Monitor for other concurrent drugs that are potentially hepatotoxic. The combination drug lovastatin/niaspan (*Advicor*) has a max dose of 2,000/40 mg and simvastatin/niaspan (*Simcor*) has a max dose of 2,000/40 mg.

- Take niacin 4 – 6 hours after bile acid sequestrants.

FISH OILS

The mechanism is not completely understood; may be due to reduction of hepatic synthesis of TGs. These are indicated as an adjunct to diet in patients with TGs ≥ 500 mg/dL. Also known as omega-3 fatty acids.

DRUG	DOSING	SAFETY/SIDE EFFECTS/MONITORING
Omega-3 Acid Ethyl Esters (*Lovaza*) 1 gram capsule contains 465 mg EPA (eicosapentaenoic acid) and 375 mg DHA (docosahexaenoic acid)	4 capsules daily or 2 capsules BID	**WARNINGS** Use with caution in patients with known hypersensitivity to fish and/or shellfish. *Lovaza* and *Epanova* can ↑ levels of LDL; monitor. There is a possible association between *Lovaza* and more frequent recurrences of symptomatic atrial fibrillation or flutter in patients with paroxysmal or persistent atrial fibrillation, particularly within the first months of initiating therapy.
Icosapent ethyl (*Vascepa*) contains 1 gram of icosapent ethyl, an ethyl ester of omega-3 fatty acid eicosapentaenoic acid (EPA)	2 capsules BID with or following meals	**SIDE EFFECTS** Eructation (burping), dyspepsia, taste perversions *(Lovaza, Epanova)*, arthralgias *(Vascepa)* **MONITORING** LFTs (in patients with hepatic impairment) and LDL periodically during therapy **NOTES** Pregnancy Category C
Omega-3-carboxylic acids (*Epanova*) 1 gram capsule contains omega-3-carboxylic acids with 850 mg of polyunsaturated fatty acids (mostly EPA+DHA)	2 capsules or 4 capsules daily	There are many OTC omega-3 fatty acid products marketed as dietary supplements. Only prescription medications *Epanova, Lovaza, Omtryg* and *Vascepa* are FDA approved for TG lowering when TG ≥ 500 mg/dL in addition to diet. Stop prior to elective surgeries due to increased risk of bleeding. **Lipid Effects** ↓ TGs up to 45%, ↑ HDL ~9%
Omega-3-acid ethyl esters A *(Omtryg)*	4 capsules daily or 2 capsules BID with meals	Can ↑ LDL (up to 44% with *Lovaza*; 25% with *Omtryg*, and 15% with *Epanova*). No ↑ seen with *Vascepa*.

Fish Oil Drug Interactions

- Omega-3-acids may prolong bleeding time. Monitor INR if patients are taking warfarin at dose initiation or dose change. Caution with other medications that can ↑ bleeding risk.

PROPROTEIN CONVERTASE SUBTILISIN KEXIN TYPE 9 INHIBITORS

Alirocumab and evolocumab are human monoclonal antibodies that bind to proprotein convertase subtilisin kexin type 9 (PCSK9). PCSK9 binds to the low-density lipoprotein receptors (LDLR) on hepatocyte surfaces to promote LDLR degradation within the liver. LDLR is the primary receptor that clears circulating LDL; therefore, the decrease in LDLR levels by PCSK9 results in higher blood levels of LDL. By inhibiting the binding of PCSK9 to LDLR, these agents increase the number of LDLRs available to clear LDL, thereby lowering LDL levels. Both medications are indicated for Heterozygous familial hypercholesterolemia (HeFH) and atherosclerotic cardiovascular disease (ASCVD) as an adjunct to diet and maximally tolerated statin therapy (or other therapies in HeFH) who require additional LDL lowering. Evolocumab is also indicated as an adjunct in homozygous familial hypercholesterolemia (HoFH).

DRUG	DOSING	SAFETY/SIDE EFFECTS/MONITORING
Alirocumab (*Praluent*) 75 mg/mL, 150 mg/mL prefilled syringes or pen-injector	**HeFH or ASCVD** 75-150 mg SC once every 2 weeks	**WARNING** Allergic reactions **SIDE EFFECTS** Nasopharyngitis, injection site reactions, influenza; URTIs, UTI, and back pain (evolocumab), ↑ LFT (alirocumab)
Evolocumab (*Repatha, Repatha Sureclick*) 140 mg/mL prefilled syringe or autoinjector	**HeFH or ASCVD** 140 mg SC once every 2 weeks or 420 mg monthly **HoFH** 420 mg SC once monthly The 420 mg dose is given as 3 injections consecutively within 30 minutes	**MONITORING** LDL-C at baseline and at 4-8 weeks to assess response **NOTES** Special storage and handling required (see Patient Counseling) Long-term outcome data is lacking Expensive (~$14,000/yr) **Lipid Effects** ↓ LDL ~60%, ↓ Non-HDL ~35%, ↓ ApoB ~50%, ↓ TC ~36%

LOMITAPIDE

Lomitapide binds to and inhibits microsomal triglyceride transfer protein (MTP) in the endoplasmic reticulum. MTP inhibition prevents the assembly of apoB containing lipoproteins in enterocytes and hepatocytes resulting in reduced production of chylomicrons and VLDL and subsequently reduced plasma LDL concentrations.

DRUG	DOSING	SAFETY/SIDE EFFECTS/MONITORING
Lomitapide (*Juxtapid*)	5-60 mg daily Initiate at 5 mg daily. If tolerated, increase after 2 weeks to 10 mg daily; double the dose at 4 week intervals to a max of 60 mg Take whole with water and without food, at least two hours after the evening meal	**BOXED WARNING** Hepatotoxicity **CONTRAINDICATIONS** Pregnancy; concomitant use with moderate or strong CYP3A4 inhibitors; moderate or severe hepatic impairment; active liver disease including unexplained persistent ↑ LFTs **WARNINGS** Diarrhea and vomiting occur commonly and can affect absorption of concomitant oral medications **SIDE EFFECTS** N/V/D, dyspepsia, abdominal pain, constipation, flatulence, ↑ LFTs, chest pain, back pain, fatigue, weight loss, influenza, nasopharyngitis **MONITORING** ALT, AST, alkaline phosphatase, total bilirubin and pregnancy test in females of reproductive potential at baseline; measure LFTs prior to any increase in dose or monthly (whichever occurs first) during the first year, and then every 3 months and prior to dosage increases **NOTES** <u>Pregnancy Category X</u> Due to the risk of hepatotoxicity, this agent is only available through a *Juxtapid* Risk Evaluation and Mitigation Strategy (REMS) program. MedGuide required.

Lomitapide Drug Interactions

- Strong and moderate CYP3A4 inhibitors are contraindicated with lomitapide. Refer to the Drug Interactions chapter for a complete list of moderate and strong 3A4 inhibitors.

- If using weak CYP3A4 inhibitors concomitantly, do not exceed 30 mg/day of lomitapide. See Drug Interactions chapter.

- Warfarin: ↑ INR; monitor after dose initiation or dose change.

- Simvastatin, lovastatin; concomitant use may increase risk of myopathy. Do not exceed simvastatin 20 mg/day (may use 40 mg/day if patients have previously tolerated simvastatin 80 mg/day for 12 months or more without evidence of muscle toxicity). Lovastatin dose should also be reduced when starting lomitapide concomitantly.

- Lomitapide is an inhibitor of P-glycoprotein (P-gp), which may increase drugs that are P-gp substrates (See Drug Interactions chapter). Dose reduction of the P-gp substrates should be considered when used concomitantly.

- Monitor for other concurrent drugs that are potentially hepatotoxic. This includes isotretinoin, amiodarone, high dose acetaminophen, methotrexate, tetracyclines and tamoxifen.

- Lomitapide reduces absorption of fat soluble vitamins from the small intestine.

- Separate dosing from bile acid sequestrants by 4 hours.

MIPOMERSEN

Mipomersen is an oligonucleotide inhibitor of apo B-100 synthesis. ApoB is the main component of LDL and very low density lipoprotein (VLDL), which is the precursor to LDL.

DRUG	DOSING	SAFETY/SIDE EFFECTS/MONITORING
Mipomersen (Kynamro)	200 mg SC once weekly Maximal LDL reduction seen after ~ 6 months	**BOXED WARNING** Hepatotoxicity **CONTRAINDICATIONS** Active Liver disease (including unexplained ↑ LFTs), moderate or severe hepatic impairment **WARNINGS** Injection site reactions and flu-like symptoms **SIDE EFFECTS** Injection site reactions, flu-like symptoms, nausea, headache, ↑ ALT, antibody formation, fatigue **MONITORING** ALT, AST, total bilirubin, alkaline phosphatase at baseline; then monthly for the first year of treatment, then every 3 months thereafter, lipids every 3 months for the first year **NOTES** Pregnancy Category B Due to the risk of hepatoxicity, this agent is only available through a *Kynamro* Risk Evaluation and Mitigation Strategy (REMS) program. MedGuide required.

Mipomersen Drug Interactions

- Monitor for other concurrent drugs that are potentially hepatotoxic. This includes isotretinoin, amiodarone, high dose acetaminophen, methotrexate, tetracyclines, and tamoxifen.

Patient Counseling

- For all cholesterol medicines: Your healthcare provider should recommend lifestyle changes including a heart healthy food pattern and exercise.

Statins

- Contact your healthcare provider right away if you have muscle weakness, tenderness, aching, cramps, stiffness or pain that happens without a good reason, especially if you also have a fever or feel more tired than usual. These may be symptoms of muscle damage.

- Contact your healthcare provider right away if you are passing brown or dark-colored urine, have pale stools, feel more tired than usual or if your skin and/or whites of your eyes become yellow. These may be symptoms of liver damage.

- Grapefruit and grapefruit juice may interact with this medicine. This could lead to higher amounts of drugs in your body. Do not consume grapefruit products without discussing with your healthcare provider (for lovastatin, simvastatin, atorvastatin).

- Do not use if pregnant or nursing or if you think you may be pregnant. This drug may harm your unborn baby. If you become pregnant, stop statin therapy and call your healthcare provider right away.

Ezetimibe

- Contact your healthcare provider right away if you are passing brown or dark-colored urine, have pale stools, feel more tired than usual or if your skin and/or whites of your eyes become yellow. These may be symptoms of liver damage.
- Contact your healthcare provider right away if you have muscle weakness, tenderness, aching, cramps, stiffness or pain that happens without a good reason, especially if you also have a fever or feel more tired than usual. These may be symptoms of muscle damage.
- Take this medicine once daily, with or without food.

Fish Oil

- This medication is taken in addition to a healthy diet.
- *Lovaza* and *Omtryg* can be taken once daily, or split BID. *Epanova* is taken once daily.
- Take *Omtryg* and *Vascepa* with food. Take *Epanova* and *Lovaza* with or without food.
- Take whole; do not break, crush, dissolve or chew.
- This medicine does not usually cause side effects, but can cause indigestion (stomach upset), burping or a distorted sense of taste *(Lovaza)* or joint pain *(Vascepa)*.

Niacin

- *Niaspan*: Take at bedtime after a low-fat snack. Other niacins: Take with food.
- Do not crush or chew long-acting formulations.
- Contact your healthcare provider right away if you are passing brown or dark-colored urine, feel more tired than usual or if your skin and/or whites of your eyes become yellow. These may be symptoms of liver damage.
- Flushing (warmth, redness, itching and/or tingling of the skin) is a common side effect that may subside after several weeks of consistent use. Pretreatment with 325 mg aspirin (or 200 mg of ibuprofen) 30 – 60 minutes before the dose (for a few weeks) may help to ↓ flushing. With *Niaspan*, flushing will occur mostly at night; use caution if awakened due to possible dizziness.
- Avoid using alcohol or hot beverages or eating spicy foods around the time of taking this medicine to help reduce flushing.
- If you have diabetes, check your blood sugar when starting this medicine because there may be a mild increase.

Bile Acid Sequestrant

- See notes section in chart for instructions regarding food/fluid intake for specific agents.
- Take this medication at mealtime with plenty of water or other liquid. Never take dry.
- This medication can cause constipation, your pharmacist can recommend a laxative (senna) or stool softener (docusate). Drink plenty of water and eat food with fiber such as fruits, vegetables and grains.
- Separate the dose of this medication from multivitamin dosing due to ↓ absorption of vitamins A, D, E and K (mostly K), folate and iron. You may need to take a multivitamin (especially in women and children) while taking this medication.

Fibrate

- *Antara, Fibricor, TriCor, Triglide* and *Trilipix*: Take once daily, with or without food.
- *Fenoglide, Lofibra* (micronized capsules) *and Lipofen*: Take once daily, with food.
- *Lopid*: Take twice daily, 30 minutes before breakfast and dinner.
- Do not crush or chew. Contact your healthcare provider if you experience muscle aches.
- Contact your healthcare provider right away if you experience abdominal pain, nausea or vomiting. These may be signs of inflammation of the gallbladder or pancreas.
- Contact your healthcare provider right away if you are passing brown or dark-colored urine, feel more tired than usual or if your skin and/or whites of your eyes become yellow. These may be signs of liver damage.

PCSK9 Inhibitor Patient Counseling

- The most common side effects include runny nose, sore throat, symptoms of the common cold or flu, back pain, and redness, pain, or bruising at the injection site.
- This medication may cause an allergic reaction. Seek emergency medical care right away if symptoms of rash, redness, severe itching, a swollen face or trouble breathing develop.
- Do not freeze, expose to extreme heat or shake.
- If removed from the refrigerator, keep at room temperature up to 77°F (25°C) in the original carton and must be used within 30 days.

Alirocumab

- Prior to administration, allow prefilled pen/syringe to warm to room temperature for 30 to 40 minutes and inspect visually for particulate matter and discoloration.
- Administer by subcutaneous injection into the thigh, abdomen or upper arm using a single-dose prefilled pen/syringe. It may take up to 20 seconds to inject all contents of the pen.
- Rotate the injection site with each injection. Do not inject into areas of active skin disease or injury such as sunburns, skin rashes, inflammation or skin infections.
- Store in refrigerator in the outer carton in order to protect from light. Should be used as soon as possible after it has warmed up (time out of refrigeration should not exceed 24 hours).
- Do not freeze, expose to extreme heat or shake.
- If you miss a dose, inject the missed dose as soon as you remember, within 7 days of your missed dose. Then, take the next dose 2 weeks from the missed dose. If the missed dose is not given within 7 days, skip the dose and wait until the next scheduled dose.

Evolocumab

- Given as an injection under the skin (subcutaneously), every 2 weeks or 1 time each month.
- Available as a single-use (1 time) pre-filled autoinjector or as a single-use pre-filled syringe.
- If your healthcare provider prescribes the monthly dose, you will give yourself 3 separate injections in a row, using a different syringe or autoinjector for each injection. Give all of these injections within 30 minutes.
- Do not inject together with other injectable medicines at the same injection site.
- If you miss a dose, inject the missed dose as soon as you remember, as long as there are more than 7 days until the next scheduled dose. If there are 7 days or less until your next scheduled dose, administer the next dose according to the original schedule.

PRACTICE CASE

PATIENT PROFILE

Patient Name DA

Address 1882 Peekaborn

Age 57   **Sex** Male   **Race** White   **Height** 5'11"   **Weight** 246 lbs

Allergies NKDA

DIAGNOSES

Coronary Heart Disease, stent placement 7/15

Dyslipidemia

Hypertension

Type 2 Diabetes

MEDICATIONS

Date	No.	Prescriber	Drug & Strength	Quantity	Sig	Refills
5/15/15	77328	Gallagher	*Actos* 45 mg	#30	1 PO daily	2
5/15/15	73768	Gallagher	Metformin 1000 mg	#60	1 PO BID	2
5/15/15	73554	Gallagher	Lisinopril-HCT 20-25 mg	#30	1 PO daily	2
			Fish oils 1000 mg cap		1 PO BID	
			Aspirin 81 mg EC		1 PO daily	
			Multivitamin		1 PO daily	

LAB/DIAGNOSTIC TESTS

Test	Normal Value	Results Date 5/12/15	Date	Date
Protein, T	6.2-8.3 g/dL			
Albumin	3.6-5.1 g/dL			
Alk Phos	33-115 units/L			
AST	10-35 units/L	32		
ALT	6-40 units/L	20		
TC	125-200 g/dL	224		
TG	<150 g/dL	248		
HDL	> 40 mg/dL	36		
LDL	< 100 mg/dL			
GLU	65-99 mg/dL	114		
Na	135-146 mEq/L	131		
K	3.5-5.3 mEq/L	3.8		
Cl	98-110 mEq/L	105		
HCO3-	22-28 mEq/L	25		
BUN	7-25 mg/dL	18		
Creatinine	0.6-1.2 mg/dL			
Calcium	8.6-10.2 mg/dL			
WBC	4-11 x 10^3 cells/mm³	4.6		
RBC	3.8-5.1 x 10^6 mL/mm³			
Hemoglobin	Male: 13.8- 17.2 g/dL Female: 12.1-15.1 g/dL	14.2		
Hematocrit	Male: 40.7-50.3% Female: 36.1- 44.3%	38		
MCHC	32-36 g/dL			
MCV	80-100 μm			
Platelet count	140-400 x 10^3/mm³	210		
TSH	0.4-4.0 mIU/L	3.2		
FT4	4.5- 11.2 mcg/dL			
Hgb A1c	4-6%	7.2%		

ADDITIONAL INFORMATION

Date	Notes
11/11/15	Patient reports walking more since heart procedure. He has lost 13 lbs in last 5 months by decreasing "donuts and sugar." No EtOH, no tobacco use (past Hx smoking). Patient states he prefers not to take more pills, and is scared about his heart. BP today is 145/88.

Questions

1. What is DA's calculated LDL?

   a. 188
   b. 176
   c. 138
   d. 105
   e. 99

2. DA needs to be placed on statin therapy. According to the ACC/AHA Treatment of Blood Cholesterol Guideline, which would be the most appropriate statin regimen for DA?

   a. Pravastatin 40 mg daily
   b. Rosuvastatin 10 mg daily
   c. Lovastatin 40 mg daily
   d. Atorvastatin 40 mg daily
   e. Pitavastatin 4 mg daily

3. DA returns to the clinic for follow up and complains of pain in his legs with occasional weakness. The statin therapy is stopped and the pain resolves. What is the best course of action to take for treatment of DA's dyslipidemia according to the ACC/AHA Treatment of Blood Cholesterol Guideline?

   a. Restart the same statin at a lower dose
   b. Switch to a different statin
   c. Consider the patient unable to tolerate statin therapy and start a non-statin cholesterol medication
   d. Recommend angiography to evaluate the leg for claudication
   e. Recommend a venous ultrasound to evaluate the leg for a DVT

Questions 4-8 do not relate to the case.

4. Which of the following cholesterol medications are available as injectable agents? (Select **ALL** that apply.)

   a. Praluent
   b. Juxtapid
   c. Kynamro
   d. Livalo
   e. Vascepa

5. A patient is going to be started on *Niaspan* therapy. Which of the following statements is correct?

   a. *Niaspan* is immediate-release niacin.
   b. *Niaspan* has a higher degree of hepatotoxicity than all the other niacin formulations.
   c. *Niaspan* must be taken on an empty stomach.
   d. *Niaspan* is taken with breakfast.
   e. *Niaspan* causes less flushing than immediate-release niacin.

6. A physician has called the pharmacist. He has a patient on phenytoin who cannot tolerate statins. He wishes to begin *Welchol*. Which of the following statements is correct?

   a. The phenytoin should be given 4 hours before *Welchol*.
   b. He cannot use this class of drugs with phenytoin.
   c. *Questran* would be a better option due to a lower risk of drug interactions.
   d. The dose of *Welchol* is 5 g twice daily, with food and water.
   e. There is no drug interaction between phenytoin and *Welchol*.

7. Which of the following medications has been shown to further lower the risk of cardiovascular events when added to statin treated patients with recent ACS? (Select **ALL** that apply.)

   a. *TriCor*
   b. *Lovaza*
   c. *Praluent*
   d. *Zetia*
   e. *Niacor*

8. Which of the following generic/brand combinations is correct?

   a. Alirocumab (*Repatha*)
   b. Fenofibric Acid (*Trilipix*)
   c. Amlodipine/Rosuvastatin (*Caduet*)
   d. Fluvastatin (*Crestor*)
   e. Pitavastatin (*Lescol*)

Answers
1-c, 2-d, 3-a, 4-a,c, 5-e, 6-a, 7-d, 8-b

HYPERTENSION

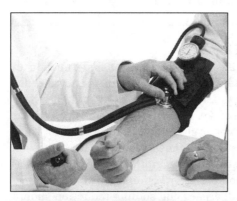

We gratefully acknowledge the assistance of Kim M. Jones, PharmD, BCPS, Assistant Dean of Student Services and Associate Professor of Pharmacy Practice, Union University, in preparing this chapter.

GUIDELINES/REFERENCES

James PA, Oparil S, Carter BL, et al. 2014 Evidence-Based Guideline for the Management of High Blood Pressure in Adults: Report From the Panel Members Appointed to the Eighth Joint National Committee (JNC 8). *JAMA.* 2014; 311:507-520.

Eckel RH, Jakicic JM, Ard JD, et al. 2013 AHA/ACC Guideline on Lifestyle Management to Reduce Cardiovascular Risk: A Report of the American College of Cardiology/American Heart Association Task Force on Practice Guidelines. *Circulation.* 2014; 129:S76-S99.

Hypertension in Pregnancy. Report of the American College of Obstetricians and Gynecologists' Task Force on Hypertension in Pregnancy. American College of Obstetricians and Gynecologists. 2013; 122(5):1122–1131.

BACKGROUND

One in three American adults have hypertension. It is one of the most common conditions seen in primary care. Hypertension is largely asymptomatic and often remains untreated which can leave patients at greater risk of heart disease, stroke and kidney disease. Only when the blood pressure is very high (such as with hypertensive crisis) are symptoms such as throbbing, headache, fatigue and shortness of breath likely to appear. Pharmacists should screen patients for hypertension and advise adherence to medication therapy and lifestyle management. One in four patients discontinue antihypertensive treatment within 6 months. Diuretics can increase urination, angiotensin converting enzyme (ACE) inhibitors can cause cough and calcium channel blockers (CCBs) can cause edema, especially at higher doses. These side effects can each lead to discontinuation, but the major cause of non-adherence is a lack of understanding of the necessity for treatment and cost.

Counseling should include healthy lifestyle measures that can decrease blood pressure, such as a healthy diet, physical activity, maintaining a healthy weight, smoking cessation and sodium restriction. A home blood pressure monitoring device can help the patient get involved and improve motivation and success of therapy.

PATHOPHYSIOLOGY

Most patients have primary or essential hypertension, which is not linked to a specific cause. Poor lifestyle and genetics can be contributory. Secondary hypertension is linked to a specific cause, such as renal disease, adrenal disease and/or drug-induced hypertension.

DRUGS THAT CAN CAUSE OR WORSEN HYPERTENSION

Adrenocorticotropic hormone (ACTH)

Alcohol (excessive)

Amphetamines (e.g., ADHD drugs)

Appetite suppressants (e.g., phentermine)

Caffeine

Calcineurin inhibitors (e.g., cyclosporine, tacrolimus)

Cocaine

Decongestants (e.g., pseudoephedrine)

Erythropoiesis-Stimulating Agents

Estrogen

Herbals [e.g., bitter orange, ephedra (ma-huang), ginseng, guarana, St. John's wort]

Mirabegron (Myrbetriq)

NSAIDs

Select oncology drugs

SNRIs (at higher doses)

Systemic steroids

Thyroid hormone (if overdosed)

THE EIGHTH JOINT NATIONAL COMMITTEE GUIDELINE

The Joint National Committee, 8th edition (JNC 8) has simplified the treatment of hypertension in adults. Treatment is based on age, and the presence of diabetes (DM) and/or chronic kidney disease (CKD). Treatment recommendations are also specified for blacks and nonblacks. Black patients have been separated out for 2 reasons: this group is at high risk for stroke, and BP reduction is not as great with ACE inhibitors or angiotensin receptor blockers (ARBs) compared with other drug classes. Thiazides are more protective against stroke and CCBs also have better outcomes, including BP reduction, in black patients. However, when CKD and proteinuria are present, an ACE inhibitor or ARB is recommended as initial therapy instead because of the higher likelihood of progression to ESRD (these drug classes help slow progression to kidney disease). Medication adherence and sodium reduction should be emphasized with patients.

Key Points with the JNC 8 Guidelines

- Thiazides are no longer the preferred first-line drug class but are now one of four preferred first-line groups. If a thiazide is used, chlorthalidone or indapamide may have better evidence over hydrochlorothiazide (not all experts agree; if a patient is on hydrochlorothiazide and is doing well they do not need to switch).

- In the general nonblack patient population, drug therapy for hypertension should be initiated using one or more agents from 4 medication classes – ACE inhibitors, ARBs, CCBs or thiazide-type diuretics.

- In black hypertensive patients, initial therapy should include a CCB and/or thiazide-type diuretic unless CKD and/or proteinuria is present.

- There are 3 ways to manage BP once a drug is chosen: titrate the first drug up to the maximum dose and then add a 2nd drug or start a 2nd drug before the 1st one is at the maximum dose or begin with 2 drugs at the same time. Two drugs will be needed if the systolic blood pressure (SBP) is > 20 mmHg or the diastolic blood pressure (DBP) is > 10 mmHg above goal.

- Do not use ACE inhibitors and ARBs together.

- If CKD is present (± diabetes) and regardless of race, ACE inhibitors or ARBs are used first-line.

- Beta blockers are no longer among the initial recommended drug classes for uncomplicated hypertension.

- Once daily regimens are preferred for increased patient compliance. Check BP 2-4 weeks after starting therapy and until goal BP is reached.

JNC 8: When to Treat*

TARGET GROUP	TARGET SBP (in mmHg)	TARGET DBP (in mmHg)
18-59 years or those with diabetes or CKD regardless of age	< 140	< 90
≥ 60 years	< 150	< 90

*The American Diabetes Association (ADA) recommends a BP goal < 140/90 mmHg although the SBP/DBP can be targeted to < 130/80 mmHg in younger patients. KDIGO recommends a BP goal of < 130/80 mmHg in CKD patients with moderate to severe albuminuria (see Renal Disease chapter). If an exam question wanted the ADA goal versus JNC 8, it should specify.

JNC 8 Drug Treatment Recommendations

TARGET GROUP	JNC 8 RECOMMENDATION
Nonblack ± diabetes	Thiazide or CCB or ACE inhibitor or ARB
Black patients ± diabetes	Thiazide or CCB
CKD – all races	ACE inhibitor or ARB
All: if BP > 20/10 mmHg above goal	Consider initial therapy with 2 drugs
All: if BP remains elevated with current drugs	Encourage adherence, lifestyle changes, titrate to the maximum dose or add on another drug

Combination Blood Pressure Drugs

The majority of patients require more than one drug to reach goal blood pressure. Many of the common (and a few less common) drugs used together are available in combinations. One of the recommendations in the JNC 8 guideline is to use a combination before titrating one drug to the maximum dose; this may be done as initial therapy, especially in patients with higher blood pressure. Lower doses used in combination may reduce side effects compared to high doses of one agent. Counseling includes each of the components, including any of the side effects or adverse reactions from either drug. Using a diuretic with any other agent requires caution for dizziness and risk of falls. The more commonly used agents are bolded. Notice that for many combinations you can figure out the brand name: <u>diuretic combinations</u> often have part of the brand name at the front and <u>HCT or -ide or -etic at the end</u>.

COMBINATION BLOOD PRESSURE DRUGS

ACE INHIBITOR OR ARB + DIURETIC
Losartan/Hydrochlorothiazide (Hyzaar)

Olmesartan/Hydrochlorothiazide (Benicar HCT)

Lisinopril/Hydrochlorothiazide (Prinzide, Zestoretic)

Benazepril/Hydrochlorothiazide (Lotensin HCT)

Quinapril/Hydrochlorothiazide (Accuretic, Quinaretic)

Valsartan/Hydrochlorothiazide (Diovan HCT)

Telmisartan/Hydrochlorothiazide (Micardis HCT)

Moexipril/Hydrochlorothiazide (Uniretic)

Azilsartan/Chlorthalidone (Edarbyclor)

Candesartan/Hydrochlorothiazide (Atacand HCT)

Captopril/Hydrochlorothiazide (Capozide)

Enalapril/Hydrochlorothiazide (Vaseretic)

Eprosartan/Hydrochlorothiazide (Teveten HCT)

Fosinopril/Hydrochlorothiazide (Monopril HCT)

Irbesartan/Hydrochlorothiazide (Avalide)

ACE INHIBITOR OR ARB + CCB
Benazepril/Amlodipine (Lotrel)

Trandolapril/Verapamil (Tarka)

Perindopril/Amlodipine (Prestalia)

Valsartan/Amlodipine (Exforge)

Olmesartan/Amlodipine (Azor)

Telmisartan/Amlodipine (Twynsta)

ALISKIREN + DIURETIC
Aliskiren/Hydrochlorothiazide (Tekturna HCT)

ALISKIREN + CCB
Aliskiren/Amlodipine (Tekamlo)

ALPHA AGONIST + DIURETIC
Clonidine/Chlorthalidone (Clorpres)

Methyldopa/Hydrochlorothiazide (Aldoril)

BETA BLOCKER + DIURETIC
Atenolol/Chlorthalidone (Tenoretic)

Bisoprolol/Hydrochlorothiazide (Ziac)

Metoprolol tartrate/Hydrochlorothiazide (Lopressor HCT)

Metoprolol succ/Hydrochlorothiazide (Dutoprol)

Nadolol/Bendroflumethiazide (Corzide)

Propranolol/Hydrochlorothiazide (Inderide)

VASODILATOR + DIURETIC
Hydralazine/Hydrochlorothiazide (Hydra-Zide)

K-SPARING DIURETIC + THIAZIDE DIURETIC
Amiloride/Hydrochlorothiazide (Moduretic)

Spironolactone/Hydrochlorothiazide (Aldactazide)

Triamterene/Hydrochlorothiazide (Maxzide, Maxzide 25, Dyazide)

TRIPLE COMBINATIONS
Aliskiren/Amlodipine/Hydrochlorothiazide (Amturnide)

Olmesartan/Amlodipine/Hydrochlorothiazide (Tribenzor)

Valsartan/Amlodipine/Hydrochlorothiazide (Exforge HCT)

PREGNANCY AND HYPERTENSION

Planning for pregnancy includes the discontinuation of teratogenic drugs that could cause fetal harm. If pregnancy is detected, ACE inhibitors, ARBs and the direct renin inhibitor aliskiren should be discontinued immediately. When making antihypertensive treatment recommendations in pregnancy, it must first be determined if the patient is experiencing preeclampsia or chronic hypertension, as these are treated differently. Preeclampsia includes elevated blood pressure and proteinuria in the majority of cases. Preeclampsia occurs after week 20 of pregnancy and is more common in women who are overweight, and/or have hypertension, renal disease or diabetes. Drug therapy is recommended in pregnant patients with <u>chronic hypertension</u> with a SBP ≥ 160 mmHg or DBP ≥ 105 mmHg. First-line recommended agents include labetalol, nifedipine extended-release and methyldopa. BP should be maintained between 120-160 mmHg systolic and 80-105 mmHg diastolic.

LIFESTYLE MANAGEMENT

Weight
Maintain normal BMI and waist circumference.

Moderate Alcohol Consumption
Alcohol should be limited to 1 drink/day (most women) and 2 drinks/day (most men).

Increase Physical Activity
Engage in regular aerobic physical activity: 3-4 sessions per week, lasting 40 minutes on average per session and involving moderate-to-vigorous intensity.

Reduce Sodium Intake
Limit sodium to < 1,500 mg/day.

Smoking Cessation
Pharmacists should be able to recommend how to quit and assist with therapy (see Tobacco Cessation chapter).

Diet
Consume a dietary pattern that emphasizes intake of vegetables, fruits and whole grains; includes low-fat dairy products, poultry, fish, legumes, nontropical vegetable oils and nuts; and limits intake of sweets, sugar-sweetened beverages and red meats. Adapt this dietary pattern to appropriate calorie requirements, personal and cultural food preferences and nutrition therapy for other medical conditions (such as diabetes mellitus). Achieve this pattern by following plans such as the DASH dietary pattern, the USDA Food Pattern or the AHA Diet. Aim for 5-6% of calories from saturated fat and reduce *trans* fat intake.

Control Blood Glucose And Lipids To Reduce Cardiovascular Disease Risk!

AHA - American Heart Association, DASH - Dietary Approaches to Stop Hypertension, USDA - United States Department of Agriculture

THIAZIDE-TYPE DIURETICS

Thiazide-type diuretics are inexpensive, effective and have mild side effects. Thiazides are one of the four recommended treatment groups for treating hypertension per JNC 8. Loop diuretics are used primarily in heart failure (see Chronic Heart Failure chapter).

Thiazides and thiazide-type diuretics inhibit Na reabsorption in <u>the distal convoluted tubules</u> of the nephron causing ↑ excretion of Na and water, as well as K and H ions.

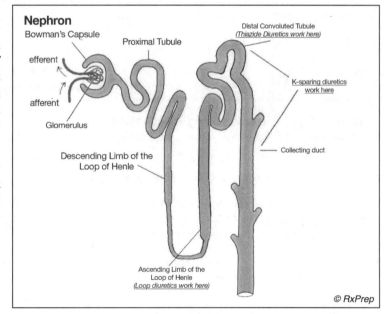

DRUG	DOSING	SAFETY/SIDE EFFECTS/MONITORING
Chlorothiazide *(Diuril)* Tablet, suspension, injection	500-2,000 mg/day	**CONTRAINDICATIONS** Hypersensitivity to sulfonamide-derived drugs, anuria, and renal decompensation
Chlorthalidone *(Thalitone)*	12.5-25 mg daily, max 50 mg daily (little additional clinical benefit seen > 25 mg/day)	**WARNINGS** Sulfa allergy (not likely to cross-react – see cautionary statement in Drug Sensitivities, Allergies, Desensitization & Reporting chapter); electrolyte disturbances; gout can be precipitated in those with a predisposition
Hydrochlorothiazide *(Microzide* – capsule, *Oretic* – tablet)	12.5-50 mg/day, max 100 mg/day (little additional clinical benefit and more electrolyte disturbances seen > 50 mg/day)	**SIDE EFFECTS** Hypokalemia (can usually be avoided with regular intake of potassium rich foods), hyperuricemia ($\uparrow$ UA), elevated lipids ($\uparrow$ LDL, $\uparrow$ TG), hyperglycemia ($\uparrow$ BG), hypercalcemia ($\uparrow$ Ca), $\downarrow$ Na, $\downarrow$ Mg, dizziness, photosensitivity, rash
Indapamide	1.25-5 mg daily	Rarely, can cause hypochloremic alkalosis **MONITORING** Renal function, fluid status (input and output, weight), BP, electrolytes
Methyclothiazide	2.5-5 mg/day	**NOTES** Thiazides may not be effective if CrCl < 30 mL/min, except metolazone, which may work in patients with reduced renal function or in patients with diuretic resistance.
Metolazone *(Zaroxolyn)*	2.5-5 mg, max 20 mg daily	Take early in the day to avoid nocturia. Chlorothiazide is the only medication in this class available IV. Thiazides come in combination with most other classes. Pregnancy Category B.

Thiazide-Type Diuretic Drug Interactions

- All antihypertensives can potentiate the therapeutic effect of other blood pressure lowering drugs; always carefully monitor BP when adding on therapy.

- Diuretics may $\downarrow$ lithium's renal clearance and $\uparrow$ risk of lithium toxicity. Avoid if possible.

- Patients with hypertension should not be routinely using agents that can cause Na and H_2O retention, such as NSAIDs, COX-2 inhibitors or systemic steroids. These agents can lower the effectiveness of antihypertensive medications.

- Thiazide-type diuretics can $\uparrow$ dofetilide concentration leading to $\uparrow$ risk of QT prolongation; concurrent use is contraindicated.

CALCIUM CHANNEL BLOCKERS

There are 2 types of calcium channel blockers (CCBs): dihydropyridines and non-dihydropyridines. With CCBs, be careful to check the Orange Book since there are many long-acting formulations of nifedipine and diltiazem; choose a generic that is AB-rated to the brand.

Dihydropyridine CCBs

The dihydropyridines, which end in (-pine), are used for hypertension (HTN) and Prinzmetal's angina. These agents inhibit Ca ions from entering the "slow" channels or voltage-sensitive areas of <u>vascular smooth muscle</u>, causing peripheral arterial vasodilation and ↓ peripheral vascular resistance and ↓ BP. The <u>peripheral vasodilation</u> leads to <u>reflex tachycardia, headache, flushing, and peripheral edema</u>. Nifedipine extended-release and amlodipine are used often since they are less likely to cause these effects.

Dihydropyridine CCBs

DRUG	DOSING	SAFETY/SIDE EFFECTS/MONITORING
AmLODIPine (Norvasc)	2.5-10 mg daily	**WARNINGS** Increased angina and/or MI has occurred with initiation or dosage titration of dihydropyridine CCBs
Felodipine (Plendil)	2.5-10 mg daily	Use with caution in patients with aortic stenosis; may reduce coronary perfusion resulting in ischemia
Isradipine	2.5-10 mg BID	
NIFEdipine ER (Adalat CC, Afeditab CR, Nifediac CC, Nifedical XL, Procardia XL) NIFEdipine IR (Procardia)	30-90 mg/day	**SIDE EFFECTS** <u>Peripheral edema, fatigue, dizziness, headache, palpitations, flushing, tachycardia/reflex tachycardia, hypotension, gingival hyperplasia</u>
Nisoldipine ER (Sular)	8.5-34 mg/day	**MONITORING** BP, HR, <u>peripheral edema</u>
Nisoldipine ER (original formulation)	10-60 mg/day	
NiCARdipine ER (Cardene SR) NiCARdipine IR (Cardene) is TID **NiCARdipine IV (Cardene IV)** Capsule, Injection	30-60 mg BID 20-40 mg TID	**NOTES** <u>Do not use immediate-release nifedipine for acute BP reduction</u> (not effective and is harmful) Pregnancy Category C Nifedipine: protect from light and moisture Adalat CC and Procardia XL are in an OROS/gel matrix formulation (see Routes of Drug Delivery, Self-Administration Techniques and Counseling chapter) and can leave a ghost tablet (empty shell) in the stool Adalat CC, Afeditab CR and Nifediac CC should be taken on an empty stomach Amlodipine/felodipine are considered the safest CCB in patients with HFrEF Cardene IV <u>requires light protection during administration</u>
Clevidipine (Cleviprex) Injection	1-21 mg/hr	**CONTRAINDICATIONS** Do not use in soy or egg allergy, acute pancreatitis, severe aortic stenosis, lipoid nephrosis **SIDE EFFECTS** Headache, N/V Rare: <u>hypertriglyceridemia, infections</u> **MONITORING** BP, HR **NOTES** Pregnancy Category C In a lipid emulsion (<u>provides 2 kcal/mL</u>); it is <u>milky-white</u> in color Use <u>strict aseptic technique</u> upon administration due to infection risk. Maximum hang time per vial/bottle is <u>12 hours</u>

Non-dihydropyridine CCBs

The non-dihydropyridines consist of verapamil and diltiazem and are used primarily for arrhythmias to control/slow HR, and sometimes for HTN and angina. Diltiazem and verapamil are <u>negative inotropes</u> (↓ contraction force) and <u>negative chronotropes</u> (↓ HR). The dihydropyridines do not have these properties. These agents inhibit Ca ions from entering the "slow" channels or voltage-sensitive areas of vascular smooth muscle and myocardium during depolarization, resulting in coronary vasodilation and decreased HR and BP.

DRUG	DOSING	SAFETY/SIDE EFFECTS/MONITORING
Diltiazem *(Cardizem, Cardizem CD, Cardizem LA, Cartia XT, Dilacor XR, Dilt-CD, Dilt-XR, Diltzac, Taztia XT, Tiazac)* Tablet, Capsule, Injection	60-360 mg/day in 1-2 divided doses; max 480-540 mg daily	**CONTRAINDICATIONS** Hypotension (SBP < 90 mmHg), 2nd or 3rd degree heart block or sick sinus syndrome (unless the patient has a functioning artificial ventricular pacemaker), cardiogenic shock, pulmonary congestion and MI **WARNINGS** First degree AV block or sinus bradycardia, ↑ LFTs
Verapamil *(Calan, Calan SR, Covera HS, Verelan, Verelan PM)* Tablet, Capsule, Injection	240-480 mg/day in 1-3 divided doses	**SIDE EFFECTS** <u>Edema, headache, dizziness, bradycardia, hypotension, arrhythmias, HF, constipation (more with verapamil), gingival hyperplasia</u> **MONITORING** BP, HR, ECG, LFTs **NOTES** Pregnancy Category C *Covera HS* is in an OROS/gel matrix formulation (see Routes of Drug Delivery, Self-Administration Techniques and Counseling chapter) and can leave a ghost tablet (empty shell) in the stool <u>Verapamil requires light protection during administration</u>

Calcium Channel Blocker Drug Interactions

- Diltiazem and verapamil are both major CYP 3A4 substrates <u>and</u> moderate 3A4 inhibitors. They will raise the concentration of many other drugs, and 3A4 inducers and inhibitors will affect their concentration; check for interactions prior to dispensing. Avoid grapefruit juice.

RENIN-ANGIOTENSIN ALDOSTERONE SYSTEM INHIBITORS

- Renin-angiotensin aldosterone system (RAAS) inhibitors reduce vasoconstriction, ↓ aldosterone release, and some agents have shown benefit in renal protection and heart failure. The use of 2 RAAS inhibitors (ACE inhibitor ± ARB ± aliskiren) is not recommended due to poor clinical outcomes per JNC 8.

- <u>Angioedema</u> is more common in <u>black patients</u>. Although angioedema is more likely with ACE inhibitors than ARBs or aliskiren, if a patient has had angioedema with any of these drugs, the others in these classes are contraindicated since angioedema can be fatal. Counsel patients to report any swelling of lips, mouth, tongue, face, or neck immediately.

- RAAS inhibitors ↑ potassium; patients on these medicines should avoid salt substitutes that contain potassium chloride (instead of sodium chloride).

Angiotensin-Converting Enzyme Inhibitors

This class of medications block the conversion of angiotensin I to angiotensin II (Ang II) by inhibiting angiotensin converting enzyme (ACE). They block the degradation of bradykinin, which is thought to contribute to the vasodilatory effect (and side effects of cough and angioedema). Angiotensin II constricts the efferent arterioles to a greater extent than the afferent arterioles within the kidney causing increased perfusion pressure in the glomeruli resulting in kidney damage over time. Therefore, blocking Ang II formation will cause vasodilation reducing BP and glomerular filtration pressure. ACE inhibitors have been shown to slow progression of renal disease in patients with diabetes and/or hypertension who have albuminuria; they also slow progression of heart failure.

DRUG	DOSING	SAFETY/SIDE EFFECTS/MONITORING
Benazepril *(Lotensin)*	10-40 mg/day in 1-2 divided doses	**BOXED WARNING** Fetal toxicity: can cause injury and death to developing fetus; discontinue as soon as pregnancy is detected
Captopril *(Capoten)*	50-100 mg BID-TID Take 1 hour before meals (empty stomach)	**CONTRAINDICATIONS** History of angioedema, bilateral renal artery stenosis, concurrent use with aliskiren in patients with diabetes
Enalapril, Enalaprilat IV injection *(Vasotec, Epaned)* Tablet, Solution, Injection	10-40 mg/day in 1-2 divided doses	**WARNINGS** Angioedema (if occurs, do not use), renal impairment, hypotension (particularly in salt- or volume-depleted patients), hyperkalemia, avoid use with ARB or aliskiren Rare: cholestatic jaundice and hepatic failure
Fosinopril	10-40 mg daily	
Lisinopril *(Prinivil, Zestril)*	5-40 mg daily	**SIDE EFFECTS** Cough, hyperkalemia, hypotension, dizziness, HA, rash
Moexipril *(Univasc)*	3.75-30 mg/day in 1-2 divided doses Take 1 hour before meals (empty stomach)	**MONITORING** BP, K, renal function **NOTES** Pregnancy Category D Patients inadequately treated with once daily dosing may be treated with twice daily dosing
Perindopril *(Aceon)*	4-8 mg daily in 1-2 divided doses	
Quinapril *(Accupril)*	10-40 mg daily	
Ramipril *(Altace)*	2.5-20 mg daily	
Trandolapril *(Mavik)*	2-8 mg daily	

Angiotensin Receptor Blockers

These medications block angiotensin II from binding to the angiotensin II type-1 (AT_1) receptor on vascular smooth muscle, preventing vasoconstriction. ARBs have been shown to slow progression of renal disease in patients with diabetes and/or hypertension who have albuminuria; they also slow progression of heart failure.

DRUG	DOSING	SAFETY/SIDE EFFECTS/MONITORING
Azilsartan *(Edarbi)*	40-80 mg daily	**BOXED WARNING** Fetal toxicity: can cause injury and death to developing fetus; discontinue as soon as pregnancy is detected
Candesartan *(Atacand)*	8-32 mg/day in 1-2 divided doses	**CONTRAINDICATIONS** History of angioedema, bilateral renal artery stenosis, concurrent use with aliskiren in patients with diabetes
Eprosartan *(Teveten)*	400-800 mg/day in 1-2 divided doses	**WARNINGS** Angioedema (if occurs, do not use), renal impairment, hypotension (particularly in salt- or volume-depleted patients), hyperkalemia, avoid use with ACE inhibitor or aliskiren
Irbesartan *(Avapro)*	75-300 mg daily	Olmesartan only: Sprue-like enteropathy – severe, chronic diarrhea with substantial weight loss has been reported in patients taking olmesartan months to years after drug initiation
Losartan *(Cozaar)*	25-100 mg/day in 1-2 divided doses	**SIDE EFFECTS** Hyperkalemia, hypotension, dizziness, HA
Olmesartan *(Benicar)*	20-40 mg daily	
Telmisartan *(Micardis)*	40-80 mg daily	**MONITORING** BP, K, renal function
Valsartan *(Diovan)*	80-320 mg daily	**NOTES** Pregnancy Category D Azilsartan: keep in original container

RAAS Inhibitor Drug Interactions

- All RAAS inhibitors ↑ the risk of hyperkalemia. Monitor K and renal function frequently.

- Dual inhibition of the renin-angiotensin system leads to ↑ risks of renal impairment, hypotension, and hyperkalemia; avoid per JNC 8.

- Patients with hypertension should not routinely use agents that can cause Na and water retention, such as NSAIDs, COX-2 inhibitors or systemic steroids.

- RAAS inhibitors can ↓ lithium's renal clearance and ↑ the risk of toxicity.

ALTERNATIVE AGENTS FOR TREATING HYPERTENSION

Potassium-Sparing Diuretics

Potassium-sparing diuretics are not as effective and are not used as monotherapy for reducing BP, however, they are commonly used in combination with HCTZ *(Maxzide/Dyazide)* to counter thiazide's mild potassium loss and help (a little) with BP. If any potassium-retaining agent is used, there will be a risk of hyperkalemia, especially with reduced renal function. Spironolactone and eplerenone, also known as aldosterone receptor antagonists, are used for HF and ↑ K is a considerable risk with these agents.

Spironolactone is a non-selective aldosterone receptor blocker (also blocks androgen). Eplerenone is a selective aldosterone receptor blocker and does not exhibit the endocrine side effects. These agents compete with aldosterone at the receptor sites in the distal convoluted tubule and collecting ducts of the nephron, increasing Na and water excretion while conserving K and H ions.

DRUG	DOSING	SAFETY/SIDE EFFECTS/MONITORING
AMILoride *(Midamor)*	5-20 mg daily	**BOXED WARNINGS** Tumor risk with spironolactone; tumorigenic in chronic rat toxicity studies. Avoid unnecessary use. **CONTRAINDICATIONS** Anuria, significant renal impairment, hyperkalemia (Addison's disease or other conditions that ↑ K)
Eplerenone *(Inspra)*	HF: 25-50 mg daily HTN: 50-100 mg daily	For eplerenone: do not use with strong 3A4 inhibitors, type 2 diabetes with microalbuminuria, SCr > 2 mg/dL in males, SCr > 1.8 mg/dL in females, CrCl < 50 mL/min **SIDE EFFECTS** Hyperkalemia, ↑ SCr, dizziness. For eplerenone, ↑ TGs.
Spironolactone *(Aldactone)*	HF: 12.5-25 mg daily, max 50 mg daily HTN: 25-100 mg/day in 1-2 divided doses	For spironolactone: gynecomastia, breast tenderness, impotence, irregular menses, amenorrhea. Rare for all: hyperchloremic metabolic acidosis.
Triamterene *(Dyrenium)* **+ HCTZ** *(Maxzide, Maxzide-25, Dyazide)*	37.5 mg/25 mg daily – BID	**MONITORING** Check K before starting and frequently thereafter; BP, electrolytes, renal function, fluid status (input and output, weight) **NOTES** Pregnancy Category B (amiloride, eplerenone)/C (spironolactone, triamterene)

K-Sparing Diuretic Drug Interactions

- Eplerenone is a CYP 3A4 substrate; use with strong 3A4 inhibitors is contraindicated.

- Potassium-sparing diuretics have a risk of hyperkalemia. Monitor K and renal function frequently and be careful of other medications that can increase potassium (see Drug Interactions chapter).

Beta Blockers

Beta blockers are no longer recommended as first-line agents for uncomplicated hypertension unless the patient has a condition where these agents are recommended first-line (e.g., S/P MI, HF, others). These agents competitively block the beta-1 and beta-2 adrenergic receptors, resulting in decreases in BP, HR, myocardial contractility and myocardial oxygen demand. Beta blockers with intrinsic sympathomimetic activity (ISA) partially stimulate beta receptors while blocking against additional stimulation and are contraindicated in S/P MI patients. These agents are carteolol, acebutolol, penbutolol, and pindolol (CAPP).

DRUG	DOSING	SAFETY/SIDE EFFECTS/MONITORING

Beta-1 Selective Blockers

DRUG	DOSING	SAFETY/SIDE EFFECTS/MONITORING
Acebutolol (Sectral)	200-1,200 mg/day in 1-2 divided doses	**BOXED WARNING** Beta blockers should not be withdrawn abruptly (particularly in patients with CVD), gradually taper over 1-2 weeks to avoid acute tachycardia, HTN, and/or ischemia.
Atenolol (Tenormin)	25-100 mg daily	**CONTRAINDICATIONS** Sinus bradycardia, 2nd or 3rd degree heart block or sick sinus syndrome (unless patient has a functioning artificial pacemaker) or cardiogenic shock, do not initiate in patients with active asthma exacerbation.
Betaxolol	5-20 mg daily	**WARNINGS** Caution in patients with diabetes particularly with recurrent hypoglycemia, asthma, severe COPD, or peripheral vascular disease and Raynaud's disease. May mask signs of hyperthyroidism; may potentiate hypoglycemia and/or mask s/sxs; may aggravate psychiatric conditions.
Bisoprolol (Zebeta)	2.5-20 mg daily	**SIDE EFFECTS** ↓ HR, hypotension, fatigue, dizziness, depression, ↓ libido, impotence, hyperglycemia (non-selective agents can ↓ insulin secretion in type 2 diabetes), hypoglycemia (more common with non-selective agents), hypertriglyceridemia, ↓ HDL
Esmolol (Brevibloc) Injection	0.5-1 mg/kg bolus followed by 50-150 mcg/kg/min infusion, titrate as needed	**MONITORING** HR (↓ dose if HR < 55 BPM), BP, titrate every 2 weeks (as tolerated)
Metoprolol tartrate (Lopressor) Tablet, Injection **Metoprolol succinate extended release (Toprol XL)** Tablet	IR: 100-450 mg/day in 2-3 divided doses XL: 25-100 mg daily; max dose 400 mg daily HF: Start 12.5-25 mg extended release daily (target 200 mg XL daily)	**NOTES** Take metoprolol immediate-release tablets with food. Metoprolol extended-release tablets are taken preferably with or following a meal. Pregnancy Category B (acebutolol)/C/D (atenolol) Caution: Metoprolol IV is not equivalent to oral doses (IV:PO ratio 1:2.5) Beta-1 selective agents – AMEBBA – Atenolol, Metoprolol, Esmolol, Bisoprolol, Betaxolol, Acebutolol

Beta-1 Blocker and Produces Nitric Oxide-Dependent Vasodilation

DRUG	DOSING	SAFETY/SIDE EFFECTS/MONITORING
Nebivolol (Bystolic)	5-10 mg daily; max 40 mg daily With a CrCl < 30 mL/min or moderate liver impairment, start at 2.5 mg daily	**CONTRAINDICATIONS** Same as above plus severe liver impairment **WARNINGS** Same as above **SIDE EFFECTS** Headache, fatigue, dizziness, nausea, diarrhea, bradycardia, ↑TGs, ↓ HDL **NOTES** Nitric oxide causes peripheral vasodilation; clinical benefit unclear Pregnancy Category C

Beta Blockers Continued

DRUG	DOSING	SAFETY/SIDE EFFECTS/MONITORING

Beta-1 and Beta-2 Blockers (non-selective)

Nadolol *(Corgard)*	40-320 mg daily	**NOTES** Propranolol has high lipid solubility (lipophilic); therefore, it is associated with more CNS side effects since it crosses the blood brain barrier. CNS side effects include sedation, depression, cognitive effects and others. Pregnancy Category B (pindolol)/C
Penbutolol *(Levatol)*	10-80 mg daily	
Pindolol	5-30 mg BID	
Propranolol *(Inderal LA, InnoPran XL, Hemangeol)* Capsule, Tablet, Solution, Injection	40-640 mg/day in 1-2 divided doses	
Timolol	10-30 mg BID	

Non-selective Beta Blocker and Alpha-1 Blockers

Carvedilol *(Coreg, Coreg CR)* Tablet, Capsule (CR)	HTN: Start IR 6.25 mg BID (max 25 mg BID) or CR 20 mg daily (max 80 mg daily) HF: Start IR 3.125 mg BID (max 50 mg BID if > 85 kg; 25 mg BID if ≤ 85 kg) or CR 10 mg/day (max 80 mg)	Same as above **WARNINGS** Intraoperative floppy iris syndrome has occurred in cataract surgery patients who were on or were previously treated with an alpha-1 blocker **SIDE EFFECTS** Same plus weight gain and edema **NOTES** Take all forms of carvedilol <u>with food</u> to ↓ rate of absorption and ↓ risk of orthostatic hypotension Pregnancy Category C Carvedilol CR has less bioavailability than carvedilol IR, therefore, dose conversions are not 1:1. Dosing conversion from *Coreg* to *Coreg CR:* *Coreg* 3.125 mg BID = *Coreg CR* 10 mg daily *Coreg* 6.25 mg BID = *Coreg CR* 20 mg daily *Coreg* 12.5 mg BID = *Coreg CR* 40 mg daily *Coreg* 25 mg BID = *Coreg CR* 80 mg daily The IR and CR dose doubles with each increment from the starting dose
Labetalol *(Trandate)* Tablet, Injection	100-1,200 mg BID	Same as above Injection is commonly used in the hospital setting Can be used in cocaine overdose Pregnancy Category C

Beta Blocker Drug Interactions

- Beta blockers can enhance the hypoglycemic effects of insulin and sulfonylureas. Non-selective beta blockers can ↓ insulin secretion in type 2 diabetes causing hyperglycemia. Monitor blood glucose in patients with diabetes.

- Beta blockers, particularly the non-selective agents, can mask the symptoms of hypoglycemia (e.g., shakiness, palpitations, anxiety). Sweating and hunger are symptoms that are not masked.

- Use caution when administering other drugs that ↓ HR; see Drug Interactions chapter.

- 2D6 inhibitors can ↑ carvedilol levels and rifampin can ↓ carvedilol levels.

- Carvedilol can ↑ digoxin and cyclosporine levels; can require dose adjustments.

- Nebivolol should be used with caution in patients taking 2D6 inhibitors.

Direct Renin Inhibitor

Aliskiren directly inhibits renin which is responsible for the conversion of angiotensinogen to angiotensin I (Ang I). A decrease in the formation of Ang I results in a decrease in the formation of Ang II, a potent vasoconstrictor.

DRUG	DOSING	SAFETY/SIDE EFFECTS/MONITORING
Aliskiren *(Tekturna)*	150-300 mg daily Avoid high fat foods (reduces absorption) Take with or without food and take the same way each day. Protect from moisture.	**BOXED WARNING** Fetal toxicity: can cause injury and death to developing fetus; discontinue as soon as pregnancy is detected **CONTRAINDICATIONS** History of angioedema, bilateral renal artery stenosis, concurrent use with ACE inhibitors or ARBs in patients with diabetes **WARNINGS** Angioedema (if occurs, do not use); renal impairment, hypotension (particularly in salt- or volume-depleted patients), hyperkalemia, avoid use with ACE inhibitors or ARBs (particularly in patients with CrCl < 60 mL/min) **SIDE EFFECTS** ↑ SCr and BUN, hyperkalemia, diarrhea, hypotension **MONITORING** BP, K, renal function **NOTES** Pregnancy Category D

Direct Renin Inhibitor Drug Interactions

- Aliskiren is metabolized by CYP 3A4; concentration is affected by 3A4 inducers and inhibitors. Do not use with cyclosporine or itraconazole due to increased aliskiren levels.

- Aliskiren ↓ the level of furosemide; monitor effectiveness.

Centrally-Acting Alpha-2 Adrenergic Agonists

These agents stimulate alpha-2 adrenergic receptors in the brain which results in reduced sympathetic outflow from the CNS. Clonidine is used commonly for resistant hypertension and in patients who can not swallow (due to dysphagia, dementia) since it is available as a patch formulation. Since the patch is changed weekly, it can help with adherence.

DRUG	DOSING	SAFETY/SIDE EFFECTS/MONITORING
CloNIDine *(Catapres, Catapres-TTS patch*, *Duraclon* inj*)* *Kapvay* – for ADHD Tablet, Patch, Injection	0.1-0.3 mg PO BID **Patch - weekly** *Catapres-TTS*-1 = 0.1 mg/24 hr *Catapres-TTS*-2 = 0.2 mg/24 hr *Catapres-TTS*-3 = 0.3 mg/24 hr	**CONTRAINDICATIONS** Active liver disease and concurrent use with MAO inhibitor (methyldopa only) **SIDE EFFECTS** Dry mouth, somnolence, headache, fatigue, dizziness, constipation, bradycardia, hypotension, depression, behavioral changes, sexual dysfunction; skin rash, pruritus, erythema, contact dermatitis – with clonidine patch For methyldopa: same side effects as above plus hypersensitivity reactions, hepatitis, myocarditis, positive Coombs test (risk for hemolytic anemia), drug-induced fever, drug-induced lupus erythematosus (DILE) and can ↑ prolactin levels
GuanFACINE *(Tenex)* *Intuniv* – for ADHD	0.5-2 mg daily	**MONITORING** BP, HR, mental status **NOTES** Clonidine patch is applied weekly. Apply patch to a hairless area on upper, outer arm or on upper chest. Place white round adhesive cover over patch to hold it in place. Rotate application site. Remove patch before MRI. Dispose of safely, away from children and pets.
Methyldopa Tablet, Injection	250 mg BID-TID; max 3 grams/day	Rebound hypertension (with sweating/anxiety/tremors), if stopped abruptly (less likely with the patches). Do not stop abruptly, must taper. Pregnancy Category B (methyldopa oral, guanfacine)/C (methyldopa injectable, clonidine)

Direct Vasodilators

These agents cause direct vasodilation of arterioles with little effect on veins causing a decrease in systemic vascular resistance and a reduction in BP.

DRUG	DOSING	SAFETY/SIDE EFFECTS/MONITORING
HydrALAZINE Tablet, Injection	10-50 mg PO QID (max 300 mg/ day) 10-20 mg IV Q4-6H PRN	**CONTRAINDICATIONS** Mitral valvular rheumatic disease, CAD **WARNING** Drug-induced lupus erythematosus (DILE – dose and duration related) **SIDE EFFECTS** Headache, reflex tachycardia, palpitations **MONITORING** HR, BP **NOTES** Pregnancy Category C

Direct Vasodilators Continued

DRUG	DOSING	SAFETY/SIDE EFFECTS/MONITORING
Minoxidil *Rogaine –* OTC topical for hair growth	5-40 mg/day, in 1-2 divided doses (max 100 mg/ day)	**BOXED WARNING** May cause pericardial effusion or exacerbate angina. Must administer with a beta blocker and loop diuretic. **CONTRAINDICATION** Pheochromocytoma **SIDE EFFECTS** Fluid retention, tachycardia, aggravation of angina, pericardial effusion, <u>hair growth</u> **NOTES** Pregnancy Category C

Alpha Blockers

Alpha blockers bind to alpha-1 adrenergic receptors which results in vasodilation of arterioles and veins; not first-line therapy for HTN.

DRUG	DOSING	SAFETY/SIDE EFFECTS/MONITORING
Doxazosin *(Cardura, Cardura XL)*	1-4 mg daily	**WARNINGS** Orthostatic hypotension and syncope, especially with the 1st dose, restarting the dose, rapidly ↑ the dose, or initiation with another anti-hypertensive agent or PDE-5 inhibitor
Prazosin *(Minipress)*	1-5 mg BID-TID	Intraoperative floppy iris syndrome has occurred in cataract surgery patients who were on or were previously treated with an alpha-1 blocker Angina can occur or worsen Priapism
Terazosin *(Hytrin)*	1-2 mg QHS	**SIDE EFFECTS** Dizziness, fatigue, headache, fluid retention/edema **NOTES** *Cardura XL* is in an OROS formulation (see Routes of Drug Delivery, Self-Administration Techniques and Counseling chapter) and can leave a ghost tablet (empty shell) in the stool

Hypertensive Urgencies and Emergencies

There are many options for treating hypertensive urgency and emergency and drug selection often depends on the patient's other medical conditions. IV medications from the various drug classes and vasodilators (discussed in the Critical Care & Fluid/Electrolytes chapter) are used in hypertensive emergencies, while oral therapy is preferred in hypertensive urgencies. Below is a summary of the conditions and treatment goals.

	URGENCY: NOT LIFE-THREATENING	EMERGENCY: POTENTIALLY LIFE-THREATENING
Definition	BP (generally ≥ 180/110-120) <u>without</u> acute target organ damage	BP (generally ≥ 180/110-120) <u>with</u> acute target organ damage (e.g., encephalopathy, MI, unstable angina, pulmonary edema, stroke, aortic dissection, renal impairment, etc).
Treatment	Any oral medication with an onset of action within 15-30 minutes; reduce BP gradually over 24-48 hrs.	Reduce MAP or BP by no more than 10-25% (within the first hour), then if stable, to 160/100-110 mmHg within the next 2-6 hrs. Use IV medications such as hydralazine, labetalol, sodium nitroprusside, nicardipine, or others.

Patient Counseling

All Hypertension Medications

- Hypertension often has no symptoms, so you may not even feel that you have high blood pressure. Continue using this medicine as directed, even if you feel well. You may need to use blood pressure medication for the rest of your life to prevent complications such as kidney damage, stroke and heart attack.

- To be sure this medication is helping your condition, your blood pressure will need to be checked on a regular basis. It is important that you do not miss any scheduled visits to your healthcare provider.

- This medicine is only part of a complete program of treatment for hypertension that also includes diet, exercise, and weight control. Follow your diet, medication, and exercise routines very closely.

- You may have been instructed to check your blood pressure at home. Record the measurements in a notebook for your provider to see.

Diuretics

- This medication will cause you to urinate more throughout the day. This is expected from your medication. If you require 2 doses per day, be sure to take your 2nd dose no later than 4 P.M. to avoid getting up at night to urinate.

- This medicine may make you feel dizzy and lightheaded when getting up from a sitting or lying position. Get up slowly. Let your feet hang over the bed for a few minutes before getting up. Hang on to the bed or nearby dresser when standing from a sitting position.

- Be sure that all objects are off the floor as you make your way to the bathroom. It is best to have a clear path to prevent falls.

- Potassium supplements may be needed while you are on this medication to ensure you have enough potassium for your heart. (Do not include if counseling on potassium-sparing diuretics.)

- If you have diabetes, your blood sugar may have to be monitored more frequently in the beginning as this medication can affect your blood sugar.

ACE Inhibitors, ARBs, and Aliskiren

- Do not use this medicine without telling your healthcare provider if you are pregnant or planning a pregnancy. This medicine could cause birth defects if you take the medication during pregnancy. Use an effective form of birth control. Stop using this medication and tell your healthcare provider right away if you become pregnant during treatment.

- Take the missed dose as soon as you remember. If it is almost time for your next dose, skip the missed dose and take the medicine at the next regularly scheduled time. Do not take extra medicine to make up the missed dose.

- Do not use salt substitutes or potassium supplements while taking this medication, unless your healthcare provider has told you to do so. Be careful of your potassium intake.

- Get emergency medical help if you have any of these signs of an allergic reaction: hives; difficulty breathing; swelling of your face, lips, tongue, or throat.

- Tell your healthcare provider if you develop a bothersome, dry occasional cough while taking this medicine (with ACE inhibitors only).

Beta Blockers

- Remember to take this medicine at the same time every day.

- This medication can cause a few side effects, including dizziness and fatigue, and can rarely cause sexual problems. If the side effects bother you, let your healthcare provider know. Do not stop this medication suddenly.

- Do not skip doses. If you miss a dose, take the missed dose as soon as you remember. If it is almost time for your next dose, skip the missed dose and take the medicine at the next regularly scheduled time. Do not take extra medicine to make up the missed dose.

- Do not discontinue your medication without consulting your physician. Stopping this medicine suddenly may make your condition worse.

- Contact your healthcare provider if you experience any difficulty in breathing (for non-selective beta-blockers).

- If taking carvedilol *(Coreg/Coreg CR)*, take with food.

- If taking immediate-release metoprolol *(Lopressor)*, take with food. *Toprol XL* is preferably taken with or after a meal.

Calcium Channel Blockers

- This medication helps lower your blood pressure. This will decrease your risk of having a stroke or heart attack.

- This medication can cause a few side effects, including swelling of the ankles, tiredness, dizziness, headache, hot or warm feeling in your face, and irregular or fast heart beat.

- Do not start any new prescription or non-prescription medicines or supplements unless you check with your healthcare provider first.

- *Adalat CC, Afeditab CR* and *Nifediac CC* should be taken on an empty stomach.

- *Adalat CC, Procardia XL* and *Covera HS* can leave an empty shell in your stool. If you see the tablet in your stool, it is nothing to worry about.

- Avoid eating grapefruit or drinking grapefruit juice while using this medication.

Clonidine

- Do not stop clonidine suddenly; this can cause your blood pressure to become dangerously high. Make sure you do not run out of medicine.

- Clonidine can cause a variety of side effects, including drowsiness, dizziness, fatigue, dry mouth, and can aggravate depression and contribute to sexual dysfunction. If the side effects bother you, let your healthcare provider know. Do not stop this medication suddenly.

- The clonidine patch *(Catapres-TTS)* is changed weekly. Apply the patch to a hairless area of the skin on the upper outer arm or chest every 7 days. An adhesive cover can be applied over the patch to keep it in place. Do not place the patch on broken or irritated skin. After 7 days, remove the used patch and apply a new patch to a different area than the previous site to avoid skin irritation.

- This patch will need to be removed before an MRI to prevent a potential burn.

- When removing the patch, be sure to discard of safely, away from the reach of any children or pets.

PRACTICE CASE

FP is a 58 y/o black male at the clinic today for a routine follow-up visit. His past medical history includes hypertension and chronic lower back pain. He states that he feels fine except for his back pain and does not understand why he has to take any other medications. His diet consists of mostly processed and pre-packaged foods. He is a non-smoker and does not drink alcohol.

Allergies: NKDA

Medications:
Norco 1-2 tabs PRN pain NTE 8 tabs/day
Prinzide 20/25 mg 1 tab daily

Vitals:
BP: 162/95 mmHg HR: 88 BPM RR: 18 BPM Temp: 38°C Pain: 3/10

Labs: Na (mEq/L) = 141 (135 - 145)
K (mEq/L) = 3.8 (3.5 - 5)
Cl (mEq/L) = 100 (95 - 103)
HCO_3 (mEq/L) = 27 (24 - 30)
BUN (mg/dL) = 35 (7 - 20)
SCr (mg/dL) = 1.2 (0.6 - 1.3)
Glucose (mg/dL) = 160 (100 - 125)
Ca (mg/dL) = 9.1 (8.5 - 10.5)
Mg (mEq/L) = 1.7 (1.3 - 2.1)
PO_4 (mg/dL) = 4.1 (2.3 - 4.7)

Reinforce disease state education and adjust medication.

Questions

1. Which of the following medication combinations is *Prinzide*?

   a. Benazepril and hydrochlorothiazide
   b. Enalapril and hydrochlorothiazide
   c. Irbesartan and hydrochlorothiazide
   d. Lisinopril and hydrochlorothiazide
   e. Triamterene and hydrochlorothiazide

2. FP has a risk factor for developing angioedema. Which of the following increases his risk of angioedema?

   a. Age
   b. Gender
   c. Ethnicity
   d. Concurrent medications
   e. Electrolyte profile

3. FP needs better BP control. Which of the following medications would be the best recommendation to add to his profile?

   a. *Lasix*

   b. *Zaroxolyn*

   c. *Hytrin*

   d. *Avalide*

   e. *Norvasc*

Questions 4-9 do not apply to the above case.

4. What is the mechanism of action for *Bystolic*? (Select **ALL** that apply.)

   a. Beta-2 selective blocker

   b. Beta-1 selective blocker

   c. Increases nitric oxide production

   d. Alpha-1 selective blocker

   e. Alpha-2 agonist

5. Choose the correct statement(s) concerning *Coreg CR*: (Select **ALL** that apply.)

   a. The generic name is nebivolol.

   b. The starting dose for hypertension is 12.5 mg BID.

   c. The drug is a non-selective beta and alpha-1 blocker.

   d. The drug decreases heart rate.

   e. The drug should be taken without food.

6. Shantal is a 62 year old black female who comes to the clinic for a regular check up. She has chronic kidney disease with proteinuria and is taking *Accupril* 20 mg daily. Her 3 BP readings on this visit are 143/93, 149/91 and 146/95. What would be the best recommendation to make at this time?

   a. Discontinue her *Accupril* and start *Norvasc*.

   b. Add on *Diovan*.

   c. Add on hydrochlorothiazide.

   d. Discontinue her *Accupril* and start *Trandate*.

   e. No additional medication is needed at this time.

7. A patient comes in with a new prescription for *Exforge*. Which of the following medications are the correct match for this prescription?

   a. Aliskiren and hydrochlorothiazide

   b. Aliskiren and valsartan

   c. Amlodipine and benazepril

   d. Valsartan, amlodipine, and hydrochlorothiazide

   e. Amlodipine and valsartan

8. A patient develops angioedema while taking *Altace*. Which of the following medications would be a safe, alternative agent to use for BP control?

   a. *Maxzide*

   b. *Atacand*

   c. *Lotrel*

   d. *Lotensin*

   e. *Tekturna*

9. Which one of the following beta blockers has intrinsic sympathomimetic activity (ISA)?

   a. Atenolol

   b. Acebutolol

   c. Carvedilol

   d. Timolol

   e. Nadolol

Answers

1-d, 2-c, 3-e, 4-b,c, 5-c,d, 6-c, 7-e, 8-a, 9-b

CHRONIC STABLE ANGINA

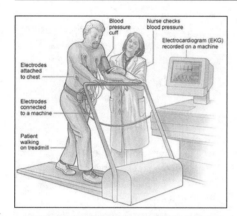

We gratefully acknowledge the assistance of Kim M. Jones, PharmD, BCPS, Assistant Dean of Student Services and Associate Professor of Pharmacy Practice, Union University, in preparing this chapter.

GUIDELINES/REFERENCES

2014 ACC/AHA/AATS/PCNA/SCAI/STS Focused Update of the Guideline for the Diagnosis and Management of Patients With Stable Ischemic Heart Disease. *Circulation.* 2014;130:1749-1767.

2012 ACCF/AHA/ACP/AATS/PCNA/SCAI/STS Guideline for the Diagnosis and Management of Patients with Stable Ischemic Heart Disease. *Circulation.* 2012;126(25):e354-471.

BACKGROUND

Angina is chest pain, pressure, tightness or discomfort due to ischemia of the heart muscle or spasm of the coronary arteries. The chest pain is described as "squeezing," "grip-like," "heavy," or "suffocating," and typically does not vary with position or respiration. Angina is categorized as stable angina or unstable angina (UA). UA is a medical emergency where the chest pain is increasing (in frequency, intensity or duration) and is not relieved with nitroglycerin or rest. Stable angina, also known as stable ischemic heart disease (SIHD), is associated with predictable chest pain often brought on by exertion or emotional stress and relieved within minutes by rest or with nitroglycerin. Stable angina is due to plaque build up within the inner walls of the coronary arteries (atherosclerosis), causing narrowing of the arteries and reduced blood flow to the heart. The reduced blood flow causes ischemia (lack of oxygen) to the heart which causes the chest pain.

Angina can also be present in patients with normal coronary arteries, where symptoms are caused by vasospasm in the arteries. This type of angina is called Prinzmetal's (variant or vasospastic) angina, which is often caused by illicit drug use, particularly cocaine.

Some patients (women, elderly and those with diabetes) may not experience the classic symptoms of angina and recognize the need for medical attention. This is known as silent ischemia as it is unnoticed by the patient.

DIAGNOSIS

A cardiac stress test is performed to assess the presence of myocardial ischemia and diagnose ischemic heart disease (also known as coronary artery disease, or CAD). The cardiac stress test is done with heart stimulation, either by exercise on a treadmill, pedaling a stationary exercise bicycle, or with intravenous pharmacological stimulation. During exercise, the patient's ECG, heart rate, and blood pressure are monitored and recorded as the intensity of exercise increases incrementally. The patient is monitored for the development of symptoms (e.g., chest pain, dyspnea, lightheadedness, etc.), transient rhythm disturbances or ST segment abnormalities on the ECG, and other manifestations of cardiac ischemia. In patients for whom the diagnosis of CAD is certain, stress testing is often used for risk stratification or prognostic assessment to determine the need for possible coronary angiography or revascularization.

For patients with disabilities or other medical conditions that limit their exercise capacity, pharmacologic stress testing with dipyridamole, adenosine (*Adenoscan*), regadenoson (*Lexiscan*) or dobutamine can be performed.

NON-DRUG TREATMENT

Multiple risk factors for heart disease, vascular disease and stroke are typically present in patients with SIHD, including hypertension, smoking, dyslipidemia, diabetes, obesity and physical inactivity. Patients should be encouraged to follow a heart healthy dietary pattern (saturated fats < 7% of total calories and *trans* fat < 1% of total calories, intake of fresh fruits and vegetables, low-fat dairy products, etc.) Encourage patients to stop smoking and avoid secondhand smoke, maintain a BMI of 18.5 – 24.9 kg/m², and maintain a waist circumference < 35 inches in females and < 40 inches in males. Encourage physical activity, 30 – 60 minutes of moderate-intensity aerobic activity, at least 5 days and preferably 7 days per week, supplemented by an increase in daily lifestyle activities (e.g., walking breaks at work, gardening) to improve cardiopulmonary fitness. Medically supervised programs such as cardiac rehabilitation, and physician-directed, home-based programs are recommended for at-risk patients at first diagnosis. Please note these recommendations are different from the obesity guideline recommendations (see Weight Loss chapter for more information). Alcohol intake should be limited to 1 drink/day (4 oz wine, 12 oz beer, or 1 oz of spirits) for women and 1 – 2 drinks/day for men, unless alcohol is contraindicated.

DRUG TREATMENT

The treatment goals for chronic angina are to reduce the mortality risk of an acute coronary syndrome (unstable angina/myocardial infarction) and provide relief from the anginal pain. An antiplatelet agent and an antianginal regimen are used together for this purpose. Aspirin is the recommended antiplatelet agent; clopidogrel *(Plavix)* is used in patients with an allergy or other contraindication to aspirin or in combination in high-risk patients with SIHD. Beta blockers are first-line therapy for stable angina. Calcium channel blockers (both DHPs and non-DHPs) or long-acting nitrates should

---

DIAGNOSTIC PROCEDURES

History and physical

CBC, CK-MB, troponins (I or T), aPTT, PT/INR, lipid panel, glucose

ECG (at rest and during chest pain)

Cardiac stress test/stress imaging

Cardiac catheterization/angiography

TYPES OF ANGINA

Stable Angina
Decreased myocardial O_2 supply due to reduced blood flow from arteries narrowed by atherosclerotic plaque

Symptoms have been occurring for weeks but without worsening

Unstable Angina
Cause is the same as stable angina but is severe, acute chest pain not relieved by rest or nitroglycerin; acute medical care is needed

Prinzmetal's Angina
Decreased myocardial O_2 supply due to vasospasm of the artery

Silent Ischemia
Transient myocardial ischemia without symptoms of angina

be utilized when beta blockers are contraindicated or when additional symptomatic relief is needed. Ranolazine can also be utilized as a substitute for or in addition to beta blocker therapy. Nitroglycerin as a sublingual tablet or translingual spray, is recommended for immediate relief of angina in all patients. Chronic stable angina is one of the atherosclerotic cardiovascular diseases (ASCVD), as defined by the ACC/AHA lipid guideline. Patients ≤ 75 years should be placed on high-intensity statin therapy. For patients > 75 years, moderate-intensity statin therapy is recommended. Patients should be aggressively managed if they have hypertension, heart failure and diabetes with the guideline-driven therapies for each of these conditions. The pneumococcal vaccine (PCV13 followed by PPSV23 12 months later) and an annual influenza vaccine is recommended.

TREATMENT APPROACH FOR STABLE ANGINA
A – Antiplatelet and antianginal drugs
B – Blood pressure and beta blockers
C – Cholesterol (statins) and cigarettes (cessation)
D – Diet and diabetes
E – Exercise and education

ANTIPLATELET AGENTS

Aspirin binds irreversibly to cyclooxygenase-1 and 2 (COX-1 and 2) enzymes which results in ↓ prostaglandin (PG) and ↓ thromboxane A_2 (TxA_2) production; TxA_2 is a potent vasoconstrictor and ↑ platelet aggregation. Aspirin has antiplatelet, antipyretic, analgesic and anti-inflammatory properties. Clopidogrel is a prodrug that irreversibly inhibits $P2Y_{12}$ ADP-mediated platelet activation and aggregation.

DRUG	DOSING	SAFETY/SIDE EFFECTS/MONITORING
Aspirin (Bayer, Ascriptin, Bufferin, Durlaza, Ecotrin, Halfprin, others) See Pain chapter for more information on aspirin	75-162 mg daily	**CONTRAINDICATIONS** NSAID or salicylate allergy; patients with the syndrome of asthma, rhinitis, and nasal polyps; children and teenagers with viral infection (due to Reye's syndrome risk) **WARNINGS** Risk of bleeding (GI bleed/ulceration, others) Renal impairment **SIDE EFFECTS** Dyspepsia, heartburn, nausea, bleeding, tinnitus (in toxicity) **MONITORING** Bleeding, bruising **NOTES** Shown to ↓ incidence of MI, CV events, and death; used in all acute and chronic ischemic heart disease patients indefinitely (unless contraindicated) Enteric coated aspirin must be chewed if patient is having an ACS *Durlaza* is a new, extended-release capsule; not to be used when rapid onset is needed (e.g., ACS, pre-PCI)

Antiplatelet Agents Continued

DRUG	DOSING	SAFETY/SIDE EFFECTS/MONITORING
Clopidogrel *(Plavix)*	75 mg daily	**BOXED WARNING** Clopidogrel is a prodrug. Effectiveness depends on the activation to an active metabolite mainly by CYP 2C19. Poor metabolizers exhibit higher cardiovascular events than patients with normal CYP 2C19 function. Tests to check CYP 2C19 genotype can be used as an aid in determining a therapeutic strategy. Consider alternative treatment strategies in patients identified as 2C19 poor metabolizers. The CYP 2C19*1 allele corresponds to fully functional metabolism while the CYP 2C19*2 and *3 alleles have reduced function. Patients with 2C19*2 and *3 alleles are poor metabolizers. **CONTRAINDICATIONS** Active pathological bleed (e.g., PUD, ICH) **WARNINGS** CYP 2C19 inhibitors: Avoid concomitant use of omeprazole or esomeprazole ↑ bleeding risk, discontinue 5 days prior to elective surgery Thrombotic thrombocytopenic purpura (TTP) has been reported **SIDE EFFECTS** Bleeding, bruising, pruritus **MONITORING** Symptoms of bleeding; Hgb/Hct as necessary **NOTES** Do not start in patients likely to undergo CABG surgery. Used in patients with a contraindication to aspirin or in addition to aspirin in certain high-risk patients with SIHD for mortality reduction.

Aspirin Drug Interactions

- Most drug interactions are due to additive effects with other agents that can ↑ bleeding risk (e.g., anticoagulants, other antiplatelet drugs, ginkgo and other natural products, NSAIDs, SSRIs, SNRIs, thrombolytics and others). See Drug Interactions chapter for more information on drugs that can ↑ bleeding risk.

- Salicylates may ↑ the serum concentration of methotrexate.

- Caution with the use of aspirin and other ototoxic agents (see Drug Interactions chapter).

Clopidogrel Drug Interactions

- Most drug interactions are due to additive effects with other agents that can ↑ bleeding risk (e.g., anticoagulants, other antiplatelet drugs, ginkgo and other natural products, NSAIDs, SSRIs, SNRIs, thrombolytics and others). See Drug Interactions chapter for more information on drugs that can ↑ bleeding risk.

- Clopidogrel is a prodrug metabolized mainly by CYP 2C19. Avoid concomitant use with omeprazole and esomeprazole as these agents can reduce the effectiveness of clopidogrel due to 2C19 inhibition.

ANTI-ANGINAL TREATMENT

DRUG	MECHANISM OF CLINICAL BENEFIT	CLINICAL NOTES
Beta Blockers Used 1st line in stable angina See Hypertension chapter for a complete review of these agents	Reduce myocardial oxygen demand by ↓ HR (negative chronotropic effect), ↓ contractility (negative inotropic effect) and ↓ left ventricular wall tension with long-term use	Start low, go slow; titrate to resting HR of 55-60 BPM; avoid abrupt withdrawal. Do not use a beta blocker with intrinsic sympathomimetic activity (ISA). More effective than nitrates and CCBs in silent ischemia; avoid use in Prinzmetal's angina; effective as monotherapy or in combination with CCBs, nitrates, and/or ranolazine. Provide mortality reduction and symptom improvement.
Calcium Channel Blockers Preferred agent for Prinzmetal's (variant) angina See Hypertension chapter for a complete review of these agents	Decrease oxygen demand by ↓ HR and contractility (non-DHPs); produce vasodilation, ↓ SVR and BP to improve myocardial oxygen supply (DHPs)	Can be used when beta blockers are contraindicated or as add-on therapy for treatment of symptoms in stable angina. Slow-release or long-acting dihydropyridine and nondihydropyridine CCBs are effective; avoid short-acting CCBs (e.g., nifedipine IR).
Nitrates	Forms free radical nitric oxide which ↑ cGMP, producing vasodilation of veins more than arteries; ↓ myocardial oxygen demand by ↓ preload; improves collateral blood flow	**SL tablets or spray** Recommended for all patients for fast relief of angina. Call 911 if chest pain does not go away after the first SL tab or first spray. Nitrate tolerance does not develop with SL tablets. **Long-acting nitrates** Long-acting nitrates are used when beta blockers are contraindicated or as add-on therapy for treatment of symptoms. Long-acting nitrates require a nitrate-free interval to prevent tolerance. See nitroglycerin formulations table on next page.
Ranolazine (Ranexa)	Selectively inhibits the late phase Na current; ↓ intracellular Ca; may ↓ myocardial oxygen demand	**CONTRAINDICATIONS** Hepatic impairment, concurrent use of strong 3A4 inhibitors and inducers **WARNING** Can cause QT prolongation Acute renal failure has been observed in some patients with CrCl < 30 mL/min **SIDE EFFECTS** Dizziness, constipation, headache, nausea **MONITORING** ECG, K, renal function **NOTES** Can use in place of beta blockers or as add-on therapy for treatment of symptoms. Has little to no clinical effects on HR or BP. Do not crush, break, or chew.

NITROGLYCERIN FORMULATIONS

NITROGLYCERIN (NTG) FORMULATIONS	SAFETY/SIDE EFFECTS/MONITORING
Nitroglycerin SL tablet *(Nitrostat)* **0.3, 0.4, 0.6 mg**	**CONTRAINDICATIONS** Hypersensitivity to organic nitrates, concurrent use with PDE-5 inhibitors or riociguat; ↑ intracranial pressure; severe anemia **SIDE EFFECTS** Headache, dizziness, lightheadedness, flushing, hypotension, tachyphylaxis (↓ effectiveness/tolerance), syncope
Nitroglycerin translingual spray 0.4 mg/spray *(NitroMist, Nitrolingual Pump Spray)*	**MONITORING** BP (continuously if receiving IV), HR, chest pain
Nitroglycerin IV	**NOTES** Counsel patients to dose the medication so they have a 10-12 hour nitrate-free period to ↓ tolerance (some products require more than 12 hours of a nitrate-free interval). **Nitroglycerin SL tablets** Keep in the original amber glass bottle.
Nitroglycerin ointment 2% *(Nitro-BID)*	**Nitroglycerin IV** Prepare in glass bottles or polyolefin bags (non-PVC) due to sorption of the drug in PVC. Use administration sets (tubing) intended for nitroglycerin (non-PVC as well). Use with infusion pump.
Nitroglycerin transdermal patch *(Nitro-Dur, Minitran)* **0.1, 0.2, 0.3, 0.4, 0.6, 0.8 mg/hr**	**Nitroglycerin ointment 2%** Dosed BID, 6 hours apart with 10-12 hour nitrate-free interval.
Isosorbide mononitrate IR/ER tablet *(Monoket, Imdur)* IR: 10 mg, 20 mg ER: 30 mg, 60 mg, 120 mg	**Nitroglycerin patch** On for 12-14 hours, off for 10-12 hours; rotate sites. Dispose of safely, away from children and pets. **Isosorbide mononitrate** IR: BID at least 7 hours apart (e.g., 8 AM and 3 PM) ER: QAM
Isosorbide dinitrate IR/ER *(Isordil Titradose, Dilatrate-SR)* – preferred for systolic HF IR: 5 mg, 10 mg, 20 mg, 30 mg, 40 mg ER: 40 mg	**Isosorbide dinitrate** IR is dosed BID-TID. If TID, give at 8 AM, 12 PM and 4 PM for a 14 hour nitrate-free interval (or similar). SR/ER is daily in the morning or divided BID for an 18 hour nitrate-free interval.

Nitrate Drug Interactions

- Avoid concurrent use with PDE-5 inhibitors; use caution with other antihypertensive medications and alcohol as these can potentiate the hypotensive effect and cause a significant ↓ in BP.

Ranolazine Drug Interactions

- Ranolazine is a substrate of 3A4 (major), 2D6 (minor) and P-gp and an inhibitor of 3A4 (weak), 2D6 (weak) and P-gp. Do not use with strong 3A4 inhibitors or CYP 3A4 inducers. Limit the dose to 500 mg BID in patients taking moderate CYP 3A4 inhibitors. Limit simvastatin to 20 mg/day if used concurrently.

Patient Counseling

All Nitroglycerin Products

- This drug should not be used with the following medications: sildenafil (*Viagra, Revatio*), tadalafil (*Cialis, Adcirca*), vardenafil (*Levitra, Staxyn*) or avanafil (*Stendra*). A dangerous drop in blood pressure could occur.

Nitroglycerin Sublingual Tablet and Translingual Spray

- Nitroglycerin sublingual tablets should not be chewed, crushed or swallowed. Take one tablet at the first sign of chest pain. This medication may also be taken prophylactically 5 - 10 minutes before activities that bring on chest pain. The tablet should be placed under the tongue or in the area between the inside of the cheek and the gums/teeth.

- Take the medicine while sitting or lying down to avoid dizziness, lightheadedness or fainting which may be associated with use. Do not eat, drink, or smoke for at least 5 – 10 minutes after use of the product or while experiencing chest pain.

- Call 911 immediately if chest pain/angina persists after one dose of sublingual NTG (tablet or spray). Continue to take 2 additional doses (up to 3 doses total) at 5 minute intervals while waiting for the ambulance to arrive.

- If NTG products are stored and handled properly, tablets should be stable until the manufacturer provided expiration date. If the tablets start to get powdery, get a new bottle.

- You may feel a slight burning or tingling sensation when taken sublingually. This sensation is not a sign of how well the medication is working. Do not use more medication just because you do not feel a burning or tingling sensation.

- Nitroglycerin SL tablets should be kept in the original amber glass bottle, at room temperature, and must be tightly capped after each use to prevent loss of potency. Shake out 1 tablet only; do not let the other tablets get wet.

- For the *Nitrolingual Pump Spray*: The pump must be sprayed 5 times into the air to prime the pump before use. If not used within 6 weeks, prime the pump with 1 spray before use. Do not shake. Press the button firmly with the forefinger to release the spray onto or under the tongue. Close your mouth after the spray. Do not inhale the spray and try not to swallow too quickly afterwards. Do not eat or drink or rinse the mouth for 5 – 10 minutes after the dose. You can use 1 spray every 5 minutes as needed for chest pain but no more than 3 sprays in 15 minutes.

Nitroglycerin Patches

- Remove the patch from its pouch and remove the protective clear liner. Select any area of skin on the body except the extremities below the knee or elbow. The chest is the preferred site.

- Apply the patch to a clean, dry, and hairless area. Hair in the area may be clipped, but not shaved. Avoid areas with cuts or irritation. Do not apply the patch immediately after bathing or showering. Wait until your skin is completely dry. However, you may bathe, shower, and swim while wearing the patch.

- Press the patch firmly in place with the palm of your hand. Wash your hands after applying the patch.

- Wear 1 patch a day for 12 to 14 hours.

- For the medicine to work well, there must be a 10 – 12 hour "patch free" interval between patches (where the patch is left off).

- To reduce skin irritation, apply each new patch to a different area of skin. After removing the old patch, fold it in half with the sticky sides together, and discard out of the reach of children and pets.

Nitroglycerin Ointment

- Measure desired dosage of ointment with the dose measuring applicator supplied with the tube. Place the applicator on a flat surface, printed side down. Squeeze the necessary amount of ointment from the tube onto the applicator, and place the applicator (ointment side down) on the desired area of the skin.

- Spread the ointment using the dose measuring applicator lightly onto the chest (or other area of skin if preferred). Do not rub into the skin.

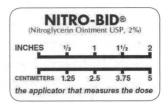

- Tape the applicator into place.

- This <u>medication can stain clothing</u>. Care should be taken to completely cover the dose measuring applicator.

Isosorbide Mononitrate

- Take this medication by mouth, once or twice daily or as directed by your healthcare provider. <u>Take the first dose of the day when you wake up, then take the second dose 7 hours later</u> (if on a twice daily regimen). It is important to take the drug at the same times each day. <u>Do not change the dosing times</u> unless directed by your healthcare provider.

- Side effects can include headache (can be severe), dizziness, lightheadedness, redness, mild warmth, or nausea. The redness and mild warmth is called flushing which will go away when your body adjusts to the medicine. Headache is often a sign that this medication is working. Your healthcare provider may recommend treating headaches with the over-the-counter pain reliever acetaminophen. <u>The headache should become less bothersome as your body gets used to the medicine.</u> If the headaches continue or become severe, tell your healthcare provider promptly.

- This drug may make you dizzy. Do not drive, use machinery, or do any activity that requires alertness until you are sure you can perform such activities safely. Limit alcoholic beverages.

- To reduce the risk of dizziness and lightheadedness, get up slowly when rising from a sitting or lying position. Hold onto the side of the bed or chair to avoid falling.

Ranolazine

- Ranolazine is used to decrease the number of times you may get chest pain.

- Ranolazine works differently than other drugs for angina, so it can be used with your other angina medications (beta blockers, nitrates and calcium channel blockers).

- Take this medication by mouth twice daily with or without food or as directed by your healthcare provider. Swallow the tablet whole. Do not crush or chew the tablets.

- Use this medication regularly in order to get the most benefit from it. Take it at the same times each day. It should not be used to treat chest pain when it occurs. Use other medications (sublingual nitroglycerin) to relieve an angina attack as directed by your healthcare provider.

- Inform your healthcare provider if your condition does not improve or if it worsens (if the chest pain happens more often).

- Dizziness, headache, lightheadedness, nausea, and constipation may occur. If any of these effects persist or worsen, notify your healthcare provider or pharmacist promptly.

- Ranolazine may cause a condition that affects the heart rhythm (<u>QT prolongation</u>). This heart rhythm can infrequently result in serious fast/irregular heartbeat and other symptoms (such as severe dizziness, fainting) that require immediate medical attention. The risk may be increased if you are taking other drugs that may affect the heart rhythm. Check with your healthcare provider or pharmacist before using any herbal or OTC medications.

ACUTE CORONARY SYNDROMES

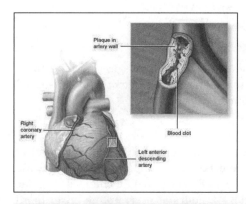

GUIDELINES/REFERENCES

2014 AHA/ACC Guideline for the Management of Patients with Non-ST-Elevation Acute Coronary Syndromes: A Report of the American College of Cardiology/American Heart Association Task Force on Practice Guidelines. *Circulation*. 2014.130:e344-e426.

2013 ACCF/AHA Guideline for Management of ST-Elevation Myocardial Infarction: A Report of the American College of Cardiology Foundation/American Heart Association Task Force on Practice Guidelines. *Circulation*. 2013; 127:e362-e425.

2011 AHA/ACCF Secondary Prevention and Risk Reduction Therapy for Patients with Coronary and Other Atherosclerotic Vascular Disease: 2011 Update. *Circulation*. 2011;124:2458-2473.

We gratefully acknowledge the assistance of Kim M. Jones, PharmD, BCPS, Assistant Dean of Student Services and Associate Professor of Pharmacy Practice, Union University, in preparing this chapter.

BACKGROUND

Acute coronary syndrome (ACS) is a set of clinical conditions brought on by sudden, reduced blood flow causing an imbalance between myocardial oxygen supply and demand. This results from plaque buildup in the coronary arteries (coronary atherosclerosis). These plaques are made up of fatty deposits and cause the arteries to narrow, making blood flow more difficult. The surface of the plaque can rupture, leading to clot formation and an acute reduction in blood flow, causing ischemia. This ischemia may lead to myocyte necrosis and subsequent release of biochemical markers into the bloodstream, mainly cardiac troponins I and T. The measurement of these enzymes is routine when establishing the diagnosis of acute myocardial infarction (MI). The cardiac troponins I and T (TnI and TnT) are the most sensitive and specific biomarkers for ACS. The troponins are detectable in the blood within 2 - 12 hours (depending on the assay) after myocardial necrosis and can remain detectable for up to 5 – 14 days. Creatine kinase myocardial isoenzyme (CK-MB) and myoglobin are less sensitive markers than troponins, but may still be monitored in clinical practice.

Acute coronary syndrome encompasses the clinical conditions of non-ST segment elevation acute coronary syndromes (NSTE-ACS) and ST segment elevation myocardial infarction (STEMI). NSTE-ACS describes both unstable angina (UA) and non-ST-segment elevation myocardial infarction (NSTEMI) since patients are indistinguishable upon presentation and the term emphasizes the continuum between UA and NSTEMI.

ACS is a medical emergency. When patients experience ACS symptoms, 911 should be called immediately. Emergency medical personnel should immediately perform a 12-lead ECG at the site of first medical contact. Patients who are having an acute MI (STEMI or NSTEMI) should be urgently transported to a hospital with percutaneous coronary intervention (PCI) capability, if possible. Coronary heart disease is the leading cause of death in the United States.

Signs and Symptoms of ACS

The classic symptoms of ACS include chest pain ("pain" encompasses not only pain, but also symptoms of discomfort, pressure and squeezing) lasting ≥ 10 minutes, severe dyspnea, diaphoresis, syncope/presyncope, and/or palpitations. The pain may radiate to the arms, back,

RISK FACTORS
Age (men > 45 years of age, women > 55 years of age or had early hysterectomy)
Family history (1st degree relative) of coronary event before 55 years of age (men) or 65 years of age (women)
Smoking
Hypertension
Dyslipidemia
Diabetes
Chronic angina
Known coronary artery disease
Sedentary lifestyle; lack of exercise

neck, jaw or epigastric area. Female, elderly, and diabetic patients are less likely to present with these classic symptoms. Precipitating factors include exercise, cold weather, extreme emotions, stress and sexual intercourse, but symptoms can occur at rest or with minimal exertion.

Diagnosis

A 12-lead ECG should be performed and evaluated within 10 minutes upon the patient's arrival to the emergency department (ED). If not diagnostic, but the patient remains symptomatic, serial ECGs should be performed every 15 – 30 minutes during the first hour to detect ischemic changes. Cardiac troponin I or T levels should be obtained at presentation and 3 – 6 hours after symptom onset in all patients with ACS symptoms. B-type natriuretic peptide (BNP) or N-terminal pro-B-type natriuretic peptide (NT-proBNP) level may be obtained to assess risk.

- UA: chest pain with negative cardiac enzymes; and no or transient ischemic ECG changes (ST-segment depression or prominent T-wave inversion).

- NSTEMI: chest pain with positive cardiac enzymes (↑ troponin I or T levels) and no or transient ischemic ECG changes (ST-segment depression or prominent T-wave inversion).

- STEMI: chest pain with positive cardiac enzymes and positive ST segment elevation in at least 2 contiguous leads of ≥ 0.2 mV (2 mm) in men or ≥ 0.15 mV (1.5 mm) in women in leads V2 – V3 and/or ≥ 0.1 mV (1 mm) in other contiguous leads. New or presumably new left bundle branch block (LBBB) is considered a STEMI equivalent.

DRUG TREATMENT

Acute treatment is aimed at providing immediate relief of ischemia and preventing MI expansion and death. Treatment includes the use of antianginal, antiplatelet and anticoagulant therapy. A combination of morphine, oxygen, nitroglycerin and aspirin are given upon presentation (acronym MONA). Other mainstay therapies for an evolving MI may include P2Y$_{12}$ inhibitors and an anticoagulant such as heparin, low-molecular weight heparin (LMWH), bivalirudin or fondaparinux. Additionally, a GP IIb/IIIa antagonist (eptifibatide, tirofiban or abciximab) may be given in select patients. All patients without contraindications should receive a beta blocker within 24 hours of presentation; ACE inhibitors and aldosterone antagonists should be used in select NSTEMI and STEMI patients (see below). High-intensity statin therapy should be initiated or continued in all patients, pending no contraindications to use, per the NSTE-ACS and STEMI guidelines.

When patients arrive at the hospital, the medical team decides on a treatment strategy for the patient depending on the diagnosis and symptom severity. Patients may be treated with medications alone (referred to as medical management) or with PCI (referred to as early invasive strategy). For patients presenting with STEMI, a fibrinolytic should be administered if the patient is not able to receive PCI within 2 hours (120 minutes) of first medical contact. Patients may also go directly for urgent coronary artery bypass surgery graft (CABG) if there is significant multi-vessel disease within the coronary arteries.

Treatment of Non-ST-Segment Elevation Acute Coronary Syndrome (NSTE-ACS)

Treatment acronym is MONA + GAP-BA (see chart below).

Summary of Drugs Used Acutely for ACS

DRUG	MOA OF CLINICAL BENEFIT	CLINICAL COMMENTS
MONA (acronym)		
Morphine	Produces arterial and venous dilation; leading to a ↓ in myocardial O$_2$ demand; provides pain relief	Morphine sulfate (2-5 mg IV repeated at 5- to 30-minute intervals PRN) may be used in patients with ongoing chest discomfort despite nitroglycerin (NTG) therapy. Side effects: hypotension, bradycardia, N/V, sedation, and respiratory depression. Avoid use in bradycardia, right ventricular infarct, confusion, and hypotension. Antidote: naloxone *(Narcan, Evzio)*. See Pain chapter.
Oxygen		Supplemental oxygen should be administered to patients with arterial oxygen saturation < 90% (SaO$_2$ < 90%), or who are in respiratory distress.
Nitrates	Dilates coronary arteries and improves collateral blood flow; ↓ cardiac O$_2$ demand by ↓ preload	Sublingual NTG (0.3-0.4 mg) every 5 minutes for up to 3 doses should be taken for immediate relief of ischemic pain. If chest pain/discomfort is not improved or worsening 5 minutes after the first dose, call 911. Administer IV NTG (start at 10 mcg/min, titrate to desired BP effect) for persistent ischemic pain, hypertension or heart failure. Do not use NTG if patient's SBP < 90 mmHg, HR < 50 BPM or experiencing a right ventricular infarction. NTG or other nitrates should not be administered to patients receiving PDE-5 inhibitors for erectile dysfunction within 12 hrs of avanafil, 24 hrs of sildenafil/vardenafil, or 48 hrs of tadalafil use. See Chronic Stable Angina chapter for more information on nitrates.
Aspirin	Inhibits platelet aggregation/clot formation by inhibiting production of thromboxane A$_2$ (TxA$_2$) via irreversible COX-1 and COX-2 inhibition	Non-enteric-coated, chewable aspirin (162-325 mg) should be given to all patients immediately if no contraindications are present (do not use *Durlaza*). Maintenance dose of aspirin 81-162 mg daily should be continued indefinitely. If intolerant to aspirin, use clopidogrel or ticagrelor. Give loading dose, followed by the maintenance dose (discussed later in this chapter).

Summary of Drugs Used Acutely for ACS Continued

DRUG	MOA OF CLINICAL BENEFIT	CLINICAL COMMENTS
GAP-BA (acronym)		
Glycoprotein (GP) IIb/ IIIa receptor antagonists	Blocks fibrinogen binding to the GPIIb/IIIa receptors on platelets, preventing platelet aggregation	May be used in medical management or for patients going for a percutaneous coronary intervention (PCI +/- stent). Agents include abciximab, eptifibatide, or tirofiban. Abciximab should only be given to patients in whom PCI is planned. Of note: these agents are not used for all patients undergoing PCI; if used, they are given concurrently with heparin.
Anticoagulants	Inhibits clotting factors and can reduce infarct size	Used to prevent further clotting. Agents include heparin, LMWHs (enoxaparin, dalteparin), fondaparinux and bivalirudin. See Anticoagulation chapter.
P2Y$_{12}$ inhibitors	Inhibits P2Y$_{12}$ receptor on platelets, preventing platelet aggregation	Ticagrelor (slightly preferred) or clopidogrel can be given to all patients (medical management as well as PCI). Prasugrel should only be given if the patient is going for PCI. Administer the loading dose followed by a maintenance dose. Do not give these agents if patient is going for urgent CABG surgery.
Beta Blockers	↓ O$_2$ demand by ↓ BP, HR, and contractility; ↓ ischemia, reinfarction, and arrhythmias; prevents cardiac remodeling; ↑ long-term survival	An oral, low dose beta blocker (beta-1 selective blocker without intrinsic sympathomimetic activity preferred) should be started within the first 24 hours in patients who do not have any of the following: 1) signs of HF, 2) evidence of a low-output state, 3) ↑ risk for cardiogenic shock, 4) other contraindications to beta blockade (PR interval > 0.24 sec., 2nd or 3rd degree heart block without a pacemaker, active asthma or reactive airway disease). If patient has concomitant HFrEF and is stable, choose 1 of the 3 beta blockers used in HFrEF (bisoprolol, metoprolol succinate or carvedilol – see HF chapter). IV beta blocker therapy may be reasonable especially if ongoing ischemia or hypertension is present, in STEMI patients. Oral long-acting nondihydropyridine calcium channel blockers (verapamil or diltiazem) are reasonable to use in patients with recurrent ischemia without contraindications after beta blockers and nitrates have been fully used. See Hypertension chapter for more information.
ACE Inhibitors	Inhibits Angiotensin Converting Enzyme and blocks the production of Angiotensin II; prevents cardiac remodeling; ↓ preload and afterload	An oral ACE inhibitor should be started within the first 24 hours and continued indefinitely in all patients with left ventricular ejection fraction (LVEF) < 40%, those with HTN, DM, or stable CKD unless contraindicated (use ARB if patient is ACE inhibitor intolerant). ACE inhibitors may be reasonable in all patients with other cardiac or vascular disease. Do not use an IV ACE inhibitor within the first 24 hours due to the risk of hypotension. See Hypertension chapter for more information.

Medications to Avoid in the Acute Setting

- NSAIDs (except for aspirin), whether nonselective or COX-2-selective agents, should <u>not</u> be administered during hospitalization due to ↑ risk of mortality, reinfarction, hypertension, cardiac rupture, renal insufficiency and heart failure associated with their use.

- Immediate-release nifedipine should <u>not</u> be used due to ↑ risk of mortality.

- IV fibrinolytic therapy should not be administered unless patient has ST-segment elevation MI or a new left bundle branch block (which is a STEMI equivalent).

Glycoprotein IIb/IIIa Receptor Antagonists

Glycoprotein IIb/IIIa receptor antagonists block the platelet glycoprotein IIb/IIIa receptor, which is the binding site for fibrinogen, von Willebrand factor, and other ligands. Inhibition of binding at this <u>final common</u> receptor blocks platelet aggregation and prevents further thrombosis. Eptifibatide and tirofiban have reversible blockade and abciximab has irreversible blockade.

DRUG	DOSING	SAFETY/SIDE EFFECTS/MONITORING
Abciximab *(ReoPro)*	LD: 0.25 mg/kg IV bolus MD: 0.125 mcg/kg/min (max 10 mcg/min) IV infusion for 12 hrs (PCI, STEMI with PCI) or 18-24 hrs (UA/NSTEMI unresponsive to conventional medical therapy with planned PCI within 24 hrs) Abciximab is not recommended for NSTE-ACS without PCI	**CONTRAINDICATIONS** Thrombocytopenia (platelets < 100,000/mm^3) History of bleeding diathesis (predisposition) Active internal bleeding Severe uncontrolled HTN Recent major surgery or trauma (within past 4 weeks for tirofiban, past 6 weeks for abciximab//eptifibatide) History of stroke within 2 years (abciximab); history of stroke within 30 days or any history of hemorrhagic stroke (eptifibatide)
Eptifibatide *(Integrilin)*	LD: 180 mcg/kg IV bolus (max 22.6 mg), repeat bolus in 10 mins if undergoing PCI MD: 2 mcg/kg/min (max 15 mg/hour) IV infusion started after the first bolus. Continue for 18-24 hours after PCI or for 12-72 hours if PCI was not performed CrCl < 50 mL/min: Reduce infusion dose to 1 mcg/kg/min (max 7.5 mg/hour)	**For abciximab** Recent (within 6 weeks) GI or GU bleeding of clinical significance ↑ prothrombin time Hypersensitivity to murine proteins Intracranial neoplasm, arteriovenous malformation or aneurysm **For eptifibatide** Dependency on renal dialysis **SIDE EFFECTS** <u>Bleeding, thrombocytopenia</u> (esp. abciximab), <u>hypotension</u>
Tirofiban *(Aggrastat)*	LD: 25 mcg/kg IV bolus over 3 min MD: 0.15 mcg/kg/min IV infusion for up to 18 hours CrCl ≤ 60 mL/min: same LD, reduce MD to 0.075 mcg/kg/min	**MONITORING** Hgb, Hct, platelets, s/sx of bleeding, renal function **NOTES** Do not shake vials upon reconstitution <u>Must filter abciximab with administration</u> Platelet function returns in ~24-48 hours after discontinuing abciximab and ~4-8 hours after stopping eptifibatide/tirofiban

P2Y$_{12}$ Inhibitors

P2Y$_{12}$ inhibitors bind the adenosine diphosphate (ADP) P2Y$_{12}$ receptor on the platelet surface which prevents ADP-mediated activation of the GPIIb/IIIa receptor complex, thereby reducing platelet aggregation. Clopidogrel and prasugrel are prodrugs and have irreversible binding to the receptor. Ticagrelor is not a prodrug and has reversible binding to the receptor. Cangrelor (*Kengreal*) is an intravenous P2Y$_{12}$ inhibitor approved in 2015 and has not been incorporated into the guidelines. Please see indication below.

DRUG	DOSING	SAFETY/SIDE EFFECTS/MONITORING
Clopidogrel *(Plavix)* Indicated for ACS, recent MI, stroke, and PAD	LD: 300-600 mg PO (600 mg for PCI) MD: 75 mg PO daily If patient received fibrinolytic therapy for STEMI and is > 75 years of age, omit the loading dose and start 75 mg daily	**BOXED WARNING** Clopidogrel is a prodrug. Effectiveness depends on the activation to an active metabolite mainly by CYP 2C19. Poor metabolizers exhibit higher cardiovascular events than patients with normal CYP 2C19 function. Tests to check CYP 2C19 genotype can be used to guide therapeutic strategy. Consider alternative treatment strategies in patients identified as 2C19 poor metabolizers. The CYP 2C19*1 allele corresponds to fully functional metabolism while the CYP 2C19*2 and *3 alleles have reduced function. Patients with 2C19*2 and *3 alleles are poor metabolizers. **CONTRAINDICATIONS** Active pathological bleed (e.g., PUD, ICH) **WARNINGS** CYP 2C19 inhibitors: Avoid concomitant use of omeprazole or esomeprazole. ↑ bleeding risk, discontinue 5 days prior to elective surgery Thrombotic thrombocytopenic purpura (TTP) has been reported **SIDE EFFECTS** Bleeding, bruising, pruritus **MONITORING** Symptoms of bleeding; Hgb/Hct as necessary **NOTES** Do not start in patients likely to undergo CABG surgery MedGuide required
Prasugrel *(Effient)* Indicated for patients with ACS who are to be managed with PCI	LD: 60 mg PO (no later than 1 hour after PCI) MD: 10 mg PO daily (5 mg daily if patient weighs < 60 kg) Once PCI is planned, give the dose promptly and no later than 1 hour after the PCI. Keep in original container.	**BOXED WARNING** Significant, sometimes fatal, bleeding **CONTRAINDICATIONS** Active pathological bleed; history of TIA or stroke **WARNINGS** ↑ bleeding risk, discontinue 7 days prior to elective surgery Thrombotic thrombocytopenic purpura (TTP) has been reported **SIDE EFFECTS** Bleeding (more than clopidogrel) **NOTES** Do not start in patients likely to undergo urgent CABG surgery Not recommended in patients > 75 years due to high bleeding risk, except in high risk patients (DM or prior MI) MedGuide required

P2Y₁₂ Inhibitors Continued

DRUG	DOSING	SAFETY/SIDE EFFECTS/MONITORING
Ticagrelor *(Brilinta)* Indicated for patients with ACS	LD: 180 mg MD: 90 mg PO BID for 1 year. After 1 year, give 60 mg BID Tablets can be crushed and mixed with water to be swallowed or given via NG tube	**BOXED WARNINGS** Significant, sometimes fatal, bleeding <u>Maintenance doses of aspirin above 100 mg</u> reduce the effectiveness of ticagrelor and <u>should be avoided</u>. After any initial aspirin dose, maintenance aspirin dose should not exceed 100 mg daily **CONTRAINDICATIONS** Active pathological bleed, history of ICH **WARNING** ↑ bleeding risk, discontinue 5 days prior to elective surgery Hepatic impairment **SIDE EFFECTS** <u>Bleeding, dyspnea (> 10%)</u>; ↑ SCr, bradyarrhythmias **NOTES** Do not start in patients likely to undergo CABG surgery MedGuide required
Cangrelor *(Kengreal)* Indicated as adjunct to PCI to ↓ risk of periprocedural MI, repeat revascularization and stent thrombosis in patients who are P2Y₁₂ inhibitor naïve and are not receiving a GP IIb/IIIa inhibitor	30 mcg/kg IV bolus prior to PCI, then 4 mcg/kg/min IV infusion for 2 hours or duration of procedure (whichever is longer)	**CONTRAINDICATIONS** Significant active bleeding **SIDE EFFECTS** Bleeding **NOTES** Pregnancy Category C No reversal agent, effects are gone 1 hour after drug discontinuation Transition to oral P2Y₁₂ inhibitor as follows: ticagrelor 180 mg given during or immediately after stopping cangrelor, <u>prasugrel 60 mg and clopidogrel 600 mg immediately after stopping cangrelor</u> (do not give prior to stopping cangrelor)

P2Y₁₂ Inhibitor Drug Interactions

- All P2Y₁₂ inhibitors: Avoid use, if possible, with other agents that ↑ bleeding risk, including other antiplatelets (Note: P2Y₁₂ inhibitors are used with aspirin), NSAIDs, anticoagulants, SSRIs, SNRIs, thrombolytics and others. See Drug Interactions chapter for drugs that can ↑ bleeding risk. If a patient experiences bleeding while on a P2Y₁₂ inhibitor, manage bleeding without discontinuing the P2Y₁₂ inhibitor, if possible. Stopping the P2Y₁₂ inhibitor (particularly within the first few months after ACS) ↑ the risk of subsequent cardiovascular events.

- Clopidogrel is a prodrug metabolized mainly by CYP 2C19. Avoid concomitant use with omeprazole and esomeprazole as these agents can reduce the effectiveness of clopidogrel due to 2C19 inhibition.

- Ticagrelor is a 3A4 (major) substrate; avoid use with strong 3A4 inhibitors and inducers. See Drug Interactions chapter for more information. Avoid simvastatin and lovastatin doses greater than 40 mg/day. Monitor digoxin levels with initiation of or any change in ticagrelor dose.

Treatment of ST Segment Elevation Myocardial Infarction (STEMI)

MONA + GAP-BA + PCI or fibrinolytic therapy (PCI is preferred).

Fibrinolytics

These agents cause fibrinolysis by binding to fibrin in a thrombus (clot) and converting entrapped plasminogen to plasmin. Once a STEMI is confirmed on 12-lead ECG performed by emergency medical services (EMS), a treatment course of PCI or fibrinolytic therapy must be determined. PCI is preferred if it can be performed within 90 minutes (optimal door-to-balloon time) or within 120 minutes of first medical contact. If PCI is not possible within 120 minutes of first medical contact, fibrinolytic therapy is recommended and should be given within 30 minutes of hospital arrival (door-to-needle time). In the absence of contraindications and when PCI is not available, fibrinolytic therapy is reasonable in STEMI patients who are still symptomatic within 12-24 hours of symptom onset.

DRUG	DOSING	SAFETY/SIDE EFFECTS/MONITORING
Alteplase (t-PA, rt-PA, Activase)	**Accelerated Infusion** > 67 kg: 100 mg IV over 1.5 hrs; given as 15 mg bolus, 50 mg over 30 min, 35 mg over 1 hr ≤ 67 kg: 15 mg bolus, 0.75 mg/kg (max 50 mg) over 30 min, 0.5 mg/kg (max 35 mg) over 1 hr (max 100 mg total)	**CONTRAINDICATIONS** **Absolute** Active internal bleeding or bleeding diathesis Any prior intracranial hemorrhage Recent intracranial or intraspinal surgery or trauma (last 2-3 months) Intracranial neoplasm, arteriovenous malformation, or aneurysm
Tenecteplase (TNKase)	Single IV bolus dose: < 60 kg: 30 mg 60-69 kg: 35 mg 70-79 kg: 40 mg 80-89 kg: 45 mg ≥ 90 kg: 50 mg	Severe uncontrolled hypertension (unresponsive to emergency therapy) **SIDE EFFECTS** Bleeding, hypotension, intracranial hemorrhage **MONITORING** Hgb, Hct, s/sx of bleeding
Reteplase (r-PA) (Retevase)	2 dose regimen: 10 units IV, followed by 10 units IV given 30 minutes later	**NOTES** Door-to-needle time should be < 30 minutes (for fibrinolytics)

Long-Term Medical Management in Patients S/P MI (Secondary Prevention)

TREATMENT	CONSIDERATIONS
Aspirin	Aspirin 81-325 mg daily indefinitely unless there is a contraindication; 81 mg is the preferred maintenance dose, per the guidelines. The recommended maintenance dose of aspirin to be used with ticagrelor is 81 mg daily.
P2Y$_{12}$ inhibitor	Clopidogrel 75 mg daily, prasugrel 10 mg daily (or 5 mg daily if weight < 60 kg), or ticagrelor 90 mg BID for 1 year in all patients. Continuation beyond 12 months may be considered in patients following drug eluting stent placement. Ticagrelor has been approved for use beyond 1 year at a new dose of 60 mg BID.
Nitroglycerin	SL tabs or spray PRN chest pain for all patients. Verbal or written instructions for use should be reviewed with the patient.
Beta blocker	Given for 3 years in the absence of HF or HTN, per ACC/AHA secondary prevention guidelines. Dose titrated to a resting HR of 50-60 BPM. Patient should take indefinitely if HF is present or needed as additional therapy for HTN.

Long-Term Medical Management in Patients S/P MI (Secondary Prevention) Continued

TREATMENT	CONSIDERATIONS
ACE inhibitor	Indefinitely if patient has LVEF < 40%, HTN, CKD, or diabetes. Reasonable for all MI patients with no contraindications to therapy.
Aldosterone Antagonist	Indefinitely for patients with LVEF ≤ 40% and either symptomatic HF or DM who are receiving target doses of an ACE inhibitor and beta blocker without significant renal impairment (SCr > 2.5 mg/dL in men, SCr > 2 mg/dL in women) or hyperkalemia (K > 5 mEq/L).
Statin	Patients ≤ 75 years of age, use high-intensity statin therapy.
	Patients > 75 years of age, use moderate-intensity statin therapy (see Dyslipidemia chapter).

Other Considerations for Patients S/P MI

- Pain relief – patients with chronic musculoskeletal pain should use acetaminophen, nonacetylated salicylates, tramadol or small doses of narcotics before considering the use of NSAIDs. If these options are insufficient, it is reasonable to use nonselective NSAIDs such as naproxen (lowest CV risk). COX-2 selective agents have high CV risk and should be avoided.

- Warfarin use – if patients need to take warfarin (AFib patients, etc.) along with aspirin and P2Y$_{12}$ inhibitor, it may be reasonable to lower the INR goal to 2 - 2.5. Use this triple combination for the shortest time possible to limit the risk of bleeding. Proton pump inhibitors should be prescribed in any patient with a history of GI bleeding while taking triple antithrombotic therapy.

- Lifestyle counseling – should include smoking cessation, managing chronic conditions (such as HTN, DM), encouraging physical exercise and a healthy diet. All patients should be referred to a comprehensive cardiovascular rehabilitation program.

WHAT MEDICATIONS TO STOP/CONTINUE WHEN PATIENT GOES FOR CABG SURGERY

Continue:

Aspirin

UFH

Discontinue:

Clopidogrel and ticagrelor 5 days before elective CABG; prasugrel 7 days before elective CABG

Eptifibatide/tirofiban 2-4 hours before CABG; 12 hours before CABG for abciximab

Enoxaparin 12-24 hours before CABG and dose with UFH

Fondaparinux 24 hours before CABG and dose with UFH

Bivalirudin 3 hours before CABG and dose with UFH

PROTEASE-ACTIVATED RECEPTOR-1 ANTAGONIST

Vorapaxar is a reversible antagonist of the protease-activated receptor-1 (PAR-1) expressed on platelets, but its long half-life makes it effectively irreversible. As an anti-platelet agent, it decreases platelet aggregation and clot formation, thereby decreasing the risk of heart attacks and strokes. Vorapaxar is indicated in patients with a history of MI or with peripheral arterial disease (PAD) to reduce thrombotic cardiovascular events (CV death, MI, stroke and urgent coronary revascularization). This agent was used in addition to aspirin and/or clopidogrel in clinical trials. Vorapaxar has not yet been incorporated into clinical guidelines.

DRUG	DOSING	SAFETY/SIDE EFFECTS/MONITORING
Vorapaxar *(Zontivity)*	One tablet (2.08 mg) PO daily	**BOXED WARNING** Bleeding risk; contraindicated in patients with history of stroke, TIA, or ICH, or active pathological bleeding. Vorapaxar ↑ the risk of bleeding, including ICH and fatal bleeding. **WARNING** Do not use in severe liver impairment **SIDE EFFECTS** Bleeding, anemia **NOTES** Pregnancy Category B No antidote MedGuide required

Vorapaxar Drug Interactions

- Vorapaxar is a substrate of 3A4 and inhibitor of P-gp. Avoid concomitant use with strong 3A4 inhibitors and strong 3A4 inducers.

Patient Counseling for Clopidogrel

- Take this medication once daily. Clopidogrel can be taken with or without food.

- Clopidogrel helps prevent platelets from sticking together and forming a clot that can block an artery.

- It is important to take this medication every day. Do not stop taking clopidogrel without talking to the healthcare provider who prescribed it. Stopping this medication can put you at risk of developing a clot which can be life-threatening.

- If you miss a dose, take it as soon as you remember. If it is almost time for your next dose, skip the missed dose. Take the next dose at your regular scheduled time. Do not take 2 doses at the same time unless instructed by your healthcare provider.

- You may bleed and bruise more easily, even from a minor scrape. It may take longer to stop bleeding.

- Call your healthcare provider at once if you have black or bloody stools, or if you cough up blood or vomit that looks like coffee grounds. These could be signs of bleeding in the digestive tract.

- One rare but serious side effect is thrombotic thrombocytopenic purpura (TTP). Seek prompt medical attention if you experience any of these symptoms that cannot otherwise be explained: fever, weakness, extreme skin paleness, purplish spots or skin patches (called purpura), yellowing of the skin or eyes (jaundice), or mental status changes.

- Avoid drinking alcohol while taking clopidogrel. Alcohol increases the risk of bleeding in the stomach or intestines.

- If you need to have any type of surgery or dental work, tell the surgeon or dentist ahead of time that you are using clopidogrel. You may need to stop using the medicine for at least 5 days before having major surgery, to prevent excessive bleeding.

- While taking this medication, do not take NSAIDs (non-steroidal anti-inflammatory drugs) or acid-reducing medications without consulting your healthcare provider.

CHRONIC HEART FAILURE

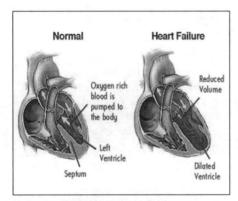

Normal **Heart Failure**

Oxygen rich blood is pumped to the body

Reduced Volume

Left Ventricle

Septum

Dilated Ventricle

GUIDELINES/REFERENCES

Yancy CW, Jessup M, Bozkurt B, et al. 2013 ACCF/AHA Guideline for the Management of Heart Failure: A Report of the American College of Cardiology Foundation/American Heart Association Task Force on Practice Guidelines. *Circulation* 2013;128:e240-e327.

Executive Summary: HFSA 2010 Comprehensive Heart Failure Practice Guideline. *Journal of Cardiac Failure.* June 2010;16(6):475-539.

We gratefully acknowledge the assistance of Tien M. H. Ng, PharmD, FCCP, BCPS (AQ-C), Associate Professor, University of Southern California School of Pharmacy, in preparing this chapter.

BACKGROUND

Heart failure (HF) is a common condition in the U.S., especially in older adults. Heart disease, which is largely composed of heart failure, affects ~11% of the adult population. Heart "failure" occurs when the heart is not able to supply sufficient oxygen-rich blood to the body. The blood that is pumped from the heart to the rest of the body is called cardiac output (CO). Perfusion is the process of delivering blood to the tissues. HF is caused by a reduced ability of the heart to eject blood, known as low-output HF. Low CO commonly occurs because the left ventricle is not ejecting enough blood or there is impaired ability of the left ventricle to fill with blood due to high filling pressure. When the heart is not able to meet the body's needs, symptoms, such as shortness of breath (dyspnea) and fatigue appear as heart failure begins to worsen.

Ejection fraction (EF) measures the fraction of blood pumped from a ventricle with each heartbeat. A normal EF has a range from 55 – 70%. Left ventricular ejection fraction (LVEF) is the measure of blood pumped out of the left ventricle (into the systemic circulation). An LVEF, or simply EF, less than 40% indicates systolic dysfunction, or heart failure with a reduced ejection fraction (HFrEF). HF can also occur with an LVEF greater than 40% with an impaired ability of the left ventricle to fill with blood. This is called diastolic dysfunction, or heart failure with a preserved ejection fraction (HFpEF). In diastolic dysfunction, the LVEF is normal or mildly reduced (> 40 – 50%).

Many patients have components of both systolic and diastolic dysfunction. Less commonly, the reason for the mismatch in blood flow and metabolic need is caused by very high requirements due to an acute medical condition, such as sepsis or severe viral infections. This is called "high output" heart failure. For the purposes of this chapter, the term "heart failure" will refer to systolic heart failure, or HFrEF.

HF is the most common condition causing hospitalization in patients greater than 65 years old. HF admissions are caused by either new-onset HF (known as acute HF) or worsening HF (known as acute decompensated HF, or ADHF). The majority of HF hospitalizations are due to nonadherence with medications and/or lifestyle recommendations. Avoidable HF admissions are a major cause of increased healthcare costs. Pharmacist involvement in optimizing medications (such as making sure the right medications are being used and harmful medications are not being used) and in medication adherence strategies, reduces readmissions and healthcare costs. Up to 25% of HF patients do not fill one or more discharge medications, and ~34% stop taking one or more medications within a month of discharge. Lifestyle adherence is essential, including healthy eating and sodium restriction. Medicare has started penalizing hospitals for excessive readmissions due to HF exacerbations. In order to decrease hospital readmissions, patients need to know what steps to take if symptoms worsen. The steps are outlined in the patient's HF action plan, which is discussed at the end of this chapter.

TERMINOLOGY

Cardiac output (CO) is the volume of blood that is pumped by the heart in one minute. CO is a function of the heart rate (HR) and the stroke volume (SV), or the volume of blood ejected from the left ventricle during one complete heartbeat (cardiac cycle). The cardiac index (CI) relates the CO to the size of the patient, and is calculated by dividing the CO by the body surface area (BSA). Refer to the CO and CI formulas in the box later in this chapter.

PATHOPHYSIOLOGY OF SYSTOLIC HF

HF is commonly classified as either ischemic (due to a decrease in blood supply, such as from an MI) or non-ischemic, such as from long-standing uncontrolled hypertension. Other less common causes include valvular disease, excessive alcohol intake or illicit drug use, congenital heart defects, viral infections, diabetes, and cardiotoxic drugs/chest radiation. In the U.S. most HF cases are due to damage from an MI or from long-standing hypertension.

During low cardiac output states, the body compensates by activating pathways that will temporarily increase CO. Neurohormones are released that increase the blood volume or increase the force or speed of contractions. These changes provide temporary relief, but over time will further compromise the heart. Chronic neurohormonal activation increases the workload of the heart which causes damage to the myocytes and produces changes in the size and shape of the heart. This is called cardiac remodeling. Altering the heart's compensatory neurohormonal pathways is essential to prevent the damage and improve heart function. Medications used to treat heart failure target the different compensatory mechanisms and/or symptoms of HF and are described in the drug treatment section.

The three main neurohormonal pathways activated in heart failure are: the renin angiotensin aldosterone system (RAAS), sympathetic nervous system (SNS) and vasopressin. The RAAS begins with renin which splits angiotensinogen to produce angiotensin I. Angiotensin I is further converted into angiotensin II (Ang II) by the angiotensin-converting enzyme (ACE). There are also non-ACE pathways for the formation of Ang II. Ang II causes blood vessel constriction (vasoconstriction), and stimulates

SELECT DRUGS THAT CAUSE OR WORSEN HEART FAILURE

Some chemotherapeutic drugs, particularly anthracyclines [doxorubicin (*Adriamycin, Doxil*), daunorubicin] and some tyrosine kinases inhibitors such as lapatinib (*Tykerb*) and sunitinib (*Sutent*). These cause fluid retention: trastuzumab (H*erceptin*), ado-trastuzumab (*Kadcyla*), imatinib (*Gleevec*) and docetaxol (*Taxotere*)

Amphetamines and other sympathomimetics (stimulants) and illicit drugs such as cocaine

Nondihydropyridines calcium channel blockers (diltiazem, verapamil) in systolic HF

Antiarrhythmic drugs (lower risk with amiodarone and dofetilide). Do not use class I antiarrhythmics with HF (mexiletine, tocainide, procainamide, quinidine, disopyramide, flecainide and propafenone)

Itraconazole

Strong immunosuppressants, including interferons, TNF inhibitors such as etanercept (*Enbrel*) and rituximab

NSAIDs, all, including celecoxib (*Celebrex*)

Steroids, systemic

Triptan migraine drugs (contraindicated with history of cardiovascular disease or uncontrolled hypertension)

Thiazolidinediones, due to increased risk of edema

Excessive alcohol use

the release of aldosterone (from the adrenal gland) and vasopressin (from the pituitary gland). Aldosterone causes sodium and water retention, and increases potassium excretion. Vasopressin causes vasoconstriction and water retention. Activation of the SNS results in the release of norepinephrine (NE) and epinephrine (EPI). These catecholamines cause an increase in heart rate, contractility (positive inotropy) and vasoconstriction. All three neurohormonal systems also promote cardiac remodeling. Importantly, each neurohormonal system potentiates the others, contributing to the vicious cycle of chronic neurohormonal activation.

Clinical Presentation and Assessment

The classic symptoms of heart failure include dyspnea (shortness of breath), cough, peripheral edema and fatigue. Hypoperfusion or congestion of essential organs can lead to end-organ damage, especially in the kidneys, resulting in renal failure.

Heart failure patients are categorized by the presence of signs and symptoms, which are used to classify the stage (degree) of the disease, or by the severity of the HF symptoms (how severely the patient is affected by the physical limitations, such as shortness of breath and fatigue). The American College of Cardiology and the American Heart Association (ACC/AHA) recommend categorizing patients by the HF stage (see table). The staging system is used to guide treatment in order to slow progression in asymptomatic patients (stages A and B) or in symptomatic patients (stages C and D). HF patients can also be classified by the level of limitation in physical functioning using the New York Heart Association (NYHA) classification system.

ACC/AHA STAGING SYSTEM		NYHA FUNCTIONAL CLASS	
A	At high risk for development of HF, but without structural heart disease or symptoms of HF (e.g., patients with HTN, CAD, DM, obesity, metabolic syndrome)		No corresponding category
B	Structural heart disease present, but without signs or symptoms of HF (e.g., LVH, low EF, valvular disease, previous MI)	I	No limitations of physical activity. Ordinary physical activity does not cause symptoms of HF (e.g., fatigue, palpitations, dyspnea)

Clinical Diagnosis of HF

C	Structural heart disease with prior or current symptoms of HF (e.g., patients with known structural heart disease, SOB and fatigue, reduced exercise tolerance)	I	No limitations of physical activity. Ordinary physical activity does not cause symptoms of HF (e.g., fatigue, palpitations, dyspnea)
		II	Slight limitation of physical activity. Comfortable at rest, but ordinary physical activity results in symptoms of HF
		III	Marked limitation of physical activity. Comfortable at rest but minimal exertion (bathing, dressing) causes symptoms of HF
		IV	Unable to carry on any physical activity without symptoms of HF, or symptoms of HF at rest
D	Advanced structural heart disease with symptoms of HF at rest despite maximal medical treatment (Refractory HF requiring specialized interventions)		

NON-DRUG (LIFESTYLE) TREATMENT

Patients with heart failure should be instructed to:

- Monitor and document body weight daily. This should be done in the morning after voiding and before eating.

- Notify the provider when weight ↑ by 2 – 4 pounds in 1 day or 3 – 5 pounds in 1 week, or when the symptoms have worsened: ↑ shortness of breath with activity, ↑ in cough or wheezing, ↑ swelling in the feet/ankles/legs, ↑ number of pillows needed to sleep, needing to sleep in a chair (upright), or feeling more fatigued than usual. A HF action plan should be provided and explained to the patient.

- Maintain sodium restriction of less than 1,500 mg/day.

- Maintain fluid restriction (1.5 – 2 L/day) in stage D, especially in patients with hyponatremia, to reduce congestive symptoms.

- Stop smoking. Limit alcohol intake. Avoid illicit drug use.

- Obtain recommended vaccines: Influenza (annually), pneumococcal vaccines if 65 years of age or older, and any patient-specific requirements.

- Consider weight reduction to BMI < 30 kg/m². Weight reduction is important to reduce the heart's workload and preserve function.

- Exercise training (or regular physical activity) is recommended as safe and effective in patients with HF who are able to participate to improve functional status. Cardiac rehabilitation can be useful in stable HF patients.

OTC and Alternative Medications

- Omega-3 polyunsaturated fatty acid (PUFA) supplementation is reasonable to use as adjunctive therapy in patients with NYHA Class II – IV symptoms to ↓ mortality and cardiovascular hospitalizations. The dose of 1 gram daily is commonly used although the optimal dose has not been established.

- Avoid the use of products containing ephedra (ma huang) or ephedrine. Patients should consult with their healthcare provider prior to the use of sympathomimetics (stimulants), such as decongestants.

- Avoid NSAIDs (including COX-2 inhibitors) due to the risk of renal impairment and fluid retention.

- Hawthorn and coenzyme Q10 may improve HF symptoms based on small studies; patients should consult with their healthcare provider prior to use.

HF S/SX AND FORMULAS

GENERAL HF S/SX

Dyspnea/shortness of breath (SOB, at rest or on exertion)

Weakness/fatigue

Reduction in exercise capacity

Left ventricular hypertrophy (LVH)

↑ BNP (B-type Natriuretic Peptide): normal < 100 pg/mL

↑ NT-proBNP (N-terminal pro B-type Natriuretic Peptide): normal < 300 pg/mL

BNP and proBNP are used to distinguish between cardiac and non-cardiac causes of dyspnea

LEFT-SIDED HF S/SX

Orthopnea (SOB when lying flat)

Paroxysmal nocturnal dyspnea (PND) or nocturnal cough

Bibasilar rales (crackling lung sounds due to fluid back-up)

S3 gallop (abnormal heart sound)
EF < 40%*

RIGHT-SIDED HF S/SX

Edema

Ascites (abdominal fluid accumulation)

Jugular venous distention (JVD)

Hepatojugular reflux (HJR)

Hepatomegaly

HF FORMULAS

$CO = HR \times SV$

$$CI = \frac{CO}{BSA}$$

*EF is measured with a heart ultrasound (echo, echocardiography) or with other tests.

DRUG TREATMENT

The cornerstones of HF treatment are <u>ACE inhibitors</u> or <u>ARBs</u>, <u>beta blockers</u> and <u>loop diuretics</u>. The following diagram and summary of standard treatment, treatment of select patients, and the role of the new drugs is brief. Additional specifics on each drug class are provided with the drug tables on the following pages. Review the summaries here and study the specifics when reviewing the drugs in the class.

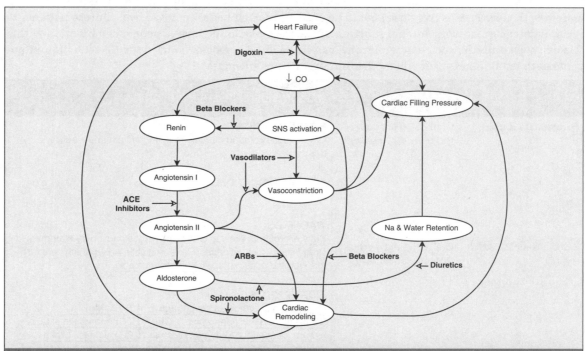

STANDARD CHRONIC HF TREATMENT

Loop diuretics reduce blood volume, which reduces edema and congestion and provides symptom relief.

ACE inhibitors or angiotensin receptor blockers (ARBs) block neurohormonal activation of the RAAS, which results in vasodilation and improvement in EF. ACE inhibitors and ARBs reduce morbidity and mortality.

Beta blockers block the neurohormonal activation of the sympathetic nervous system (SNS) by blocking epinephrine and norepinephrine. Beta blockers also provide benefit in controlling heart rate and reducing arrhythmia risk. Beta blockers reduce morbidity and mortality.

TREATMENT FOR SELECT PATIENTS

Hydralazine and nitrates improve ventricular function in patients who cannot tolerate an ACE inhibitor/ARB or are used as an add-on to standard treatment in the black population. The combination of hydralazine and isosorbide dinitrate (*BiDil*) reduces morbidity and mortality in black patients with NYHA Class III-IV and in nonblack patients who cannot tolerate an ACE inhibitor or ARB.

Aldosterone receptor antagonists (ARAs) provide added diuresis, improve symptoms and improve EF. ARAs reduce morbidity and mortality in NYHA Class II-IV.

Digoxin provides a small increase in cardiac output, improves symptoms and decreases cardiac hospitalizations.

NEW DRUGS FOR SELECT PATIENTS

Ivabradine (*Corlanor*) is used to reduce the risk of hospitalization in stable, symptomatic HF with a normal sinus rhythm, a resting heart beat of 70 BPM or higher and with an LVEF of < 35%, who are either on maximally tolerated doses of beta blockers or have a contraindication to beta blocker use.

Sacubitril/valsartan (*Entresto*) is used to reduce the risk of cardiovascular death and hospitalization for heart failure (NYHA Class II-IV) patients who have a decreased EF.

Loop Diuretics

Loop diuretics are used to ↓ fluid volume to make it easier for the heart to pump. Loop diuretics block sodium and chloride reabsorption in the thick <u>ascending limb of the loop of Henle</u>, interfering with the chloride-binding co-transport system. <u>They ↑ excretion of sodium, chloride, magnesium, calcium, and water</u>. They are used to reduce congestive symptoms (reduction in preload) and restore euvolemia (or "dry" weight). Loop diuretics have <u>not been shown</u> to <u>alter the survival</u> of stable heart failure patients; therefore, the lowest effective dose should be used. Care must be taken not to over-diurese patients to avoid hypotension or worsen renal function. If the response to the loop is poor, a combination with a thiazide-type diuretic, such as metolazone, can be useful. Loops can be used for BP reduction in patients with renal impairment when other options are not adequate.

DRUG	DOSING	SAFETY/SIDE EFFECTS/MONITORING
Furosemide *(Lasix)*	Oral: 20-40 mg daily or BID, max 600 mg/day	**BOXED WARNING** Can lead to profound diuresis resulting in fluid and electrolyte depletion **CONTRAINDICATIONS** Anuria **WARNINGS** <u>Sulfa allergy</u> (not likely to cross-react – see cautionary statement in Drug Sensitivities, Allergies, Desensitization & Reporting chapter) – <u>this warning does not apply to ethacrynic acid</u>
Bumetanide *(Bumex)*	Oral: 0.5-1 mg daily or BID, max 10 mg/day	**SIDE EFFECTS** <u>Hypokalemia</u>, orthostatic hypotension, ↓ Na, ↓ Mg, ↓ Cl, ↓ Ca (different than thiazides which ↑ Ca), ↑ HCO$_3$/metabolic alkalosis, hyperuricemia (↑ UA), hyperglycemia (↑ BG), ↑ TGs, ↑ total cholesterol, photosensitivity, ototoxicity (more with <u>ethacrynic acid</u>) including hearing loss, tinnitus and vertigo
Torsemide *(Demadex)*	Oral: 10-20 mg daily, max 200 mg/day	**MONITORING** <u>Renal function, fluid status</u> (input and output, weight), BP, electrolytes, audiology testing with high doses or rapid IV administration, s/sx of HF **NOTES** IV formulations of furosemide and bumetanide are light-sensitive (in amber bottles); IV admixtures do not require light protection.
Ethacrynic Acid *(Edecrin)*	Oral: 50-200 mg daily or divided, max 400 mg/day	All, except torsemide, are available in IV and PO formulations. <u>Furosemide IV:PO ratio 1:2</u> (furosemide 20 mg IV = furosemide 40 mg PO). Store at room temp (refrigeration causes precipitation – warming may dissolve crystals). Do not use furosemide solutions if they are yellow in color; must be clear. <u>Bumetanide, torsemide and ethacrynic acid IV:PO ratio 1:1.</u> Take early in the day to avoid nocturia. Pregnancy Category B (torsemide, ethacrynic acid)/C (furosemide, bumetanide). <u>Oral equivalent dosing: Furosemide 40 mg = bumetanide 1 mg = torsemide 20 mg = ethacrynic acid 50 mg</u>

Loop Diuretic Drug Interactions

- Can acutely ↓ blood pressure. Always carefully monitor BP when adding on therapy.

- Loop diuretics can ↑ the ototoxic potential of other ototoxic drugs (see Drug Interactions chapter), especially with impaired renal function. This combination should be avoided if possible.

- Diuretics can ↓ lithium's renal clearance and ↑ risk of lithium toxicity.

- Do not use NSAIDs in patients with HF. NSAIDs ↑ sodium and water retention and ↓ the effect of the loop diuretics and can lead to renal impairment.

- The combination of a loop and a thiazide-type diuretic may ↑ diuretic response. Electrolyte abnormalities are more likely and must be monitored closely.

ACE Inhibitors and Angiotensin Receptor Blockers

ACE inhibitors block the conversion of angiotensin I to angiotensin II (Ang II) by inhibiting the angiotensin converting enzyme (ACE). They block the degradation of bradykinin, which is thought to contribute to the vasodilatory effect (and the side effects of cough and angioedema). ARBs compete with Ang II for binding to the type-1 angiotensin II receptor (AT1) subtype, which is responsible for the vasoconstrictive, aldosterone-stimulating, and remodeling effects of Ang II. Overall, these agents ↓ RAAS activation, specifically ↓ the effects of Ang II and aldosterone. This results in a ↓ in preload and afterload. They ↓ pathologic cardiac remodeling, improve left ventricular function, and ↓ morbidity and mortality. The clinical benefits appear to be a drug class effect. The use of an ACE inhibitor (or ARB if intolerant to ACE inhibitors) is indicated for all HF patients regardless of symptoms (NYHA Class I – IV). Other important points include:

- The target doses for these medications are the doses used in clinical trials demonstrating their benefit or the maximum tolerated dose for a given patient. Titrate the drug to target doses, if possible. Titrate the dose to reduce symptoms, not BP.

- The combination of an ACE inhibitor and ARB has been shown to ↓ hospitalizations for HF, however, this is not frequently done as it is more common to combine with an aldosterone receptor antagonist (ARA). Triple combination of ACE inhibitor/ARB/ARA is not recommended due to a higher risk of hyperkalemia and renal insufficiency.

- There is an increased incidence of angioedema in black patients. Angioedema is more likely with ACE inhibitors than ARBs, but if a person had angioedema with either class of agents (or aliskiren), these agents should not be used since angioedema can be fatal. Counsel to report any swelling of lips, mouth, tongue, face or neck immediately.

- ACE inhibitors and ARBs ↑ potassium; patients on these medicines should avoid using salt substitutes (which contain KCl rather than NaCl) or OTC potassium supplements.

DRUG	DOSING	SAFETY/SIDE EFFECTS/MONITORING

ACE Inhibitors – only those mentioned in the guidelines (see complete list in Hypertension chapter)

Captopril (Capoten)	Start 6.25 mg TID, 1 hr before meals Target dose: 50 mg TID	**BOXED WARNING** Fetal toxicity: can cause injury and death to developing fetus; discontinue as soon as pregnancy is detected
Enalapril (Vasotec), Enalaprilat (Vasotec IV)	Start 2.5 mg PO BID Target dose: 10-20 mg PO BID	**CONTRAINDICATIONS** History of angioedema, bilateral renal artery stenosis, concurrent use with aliskiren in patients with diabetes
Fosinopril	Start 5-10 mg daily Target dose: 40 mg daily	**WARNINGS** Angioedema (if occurs, do not use), renal impairment, hypotension (particularly in salt- or volume-depleted patients), hyperkalemia, avoid use with ARB or aliskiren
Lisinopril (Prinivil, Zestril)	Start 2.5-5 mg daily Target dose: 20-40 mg daily	Rare: cholestatic jaundice and hepatic failure
Perindopril (Aceon)	Start 2 mg daily Target dose: 8-16 mg daily	**SIDE EFFECTS** Cough, hyperkalemia, hypotension, dizziness, HA, rash
Quinapril (Accupril)	Start 5 mg BID Target dose: 20 mg BID	**MONITORING** BP, K, renal function, s/sx of HF
Ramipril (Altace)	Start 1.25-2.5 mg daily Target dose: 10 mg daily	**NOTES** Pregnancy Category D
Trandolapril (Mavik)	Start 1 mg daily Target dose: 4 mg daily	

Angiotensin Receptor Blockers (ARBs) – only those mentioned in the guidelines (see complete list in Hypertension chapter)

Candesartan (Atacand)	Start 4-8 mg daily Target dose: 32 mg daily	Same as above except lack of cough and less angioedema with ARBs
Losartan (Cozaar) – benefit in clinical trials but no FDA indication	Start 25-50 mg daily Target dose: 50-150 mg daily	
Valsartan (Diovan)	Start 20-40 mg BID Target dose: 160 mg BID	

ACE Inhibitor/ARB Drug Interactions

- All RAAS inhibitors ↑ the risk of hyperkalemia (most significant side effect). Monitor K and renal function frequently.
- Dual inhibition of the RAAS with ACE inhibitors and ARBs leads to ↑ risks of renal impairment, hypotension, and hyperkalemia; avoid the combination.
- The triple combination of ACE inhibitor, ARB and ARA is not recommended due to a higher risk of hyperkalemia and ↑ renal insufficiency.
- ACE inhibitors or ARBs should not be used in combination with the renin inhibitor aliskiren in patients with diabetes.
- All RAAS inhibitors can have additive antihypertensive effects; monitor BP.
- RAAS inhibitors can ↓ lithium's renal clearance and ↑ risk of lithium toxicity.

Angiotensin Receptor and Neprilysin Inhibitor

Entresto is a combination of a neprilysin inhibitor (sacubitril) and valsartan. Neprilysin is the enzyme responsible for the degradation of several vasodilatory peptides, including natriuretic peptides, adrenomedullin, substance P, and bradykinin. These peptides counteract the effects of RAAS activation, and produce vasodilation. It is indicated in NYHA Class II-IV patients to <u>reduce HF hospitalizations</u> and <u>cardiovascular death</u>, and is being considered as a first-line option (in place of an ACE inhibitor or ARB monotherapy).

DRUG	DOSING	SAFETY/SIDE EFFECTS/MONITORING
Sacubitril/valsartan (***Entresto***)	Start: 50-100 mg BID Target dose: 200 mg BID CrCl < 30 mL/min = 50 mg BID The dose is the sum of the two compounds: 50 mg = 24/26 mg sacubitril/valsartan 100 mg = 49/51 mg sacubitril/valsartan 200 mg = 97/103 mg sacubitril/valsartan	**BOXED WARNING** Fetal toxicity: can cause injury and death to developing fetus; <u>discontinue as soon as pregnancy is detected</u> **CONTRAINDICATIONS** History of angioedema, bilateral renal artery stenosis, concurrent use with aliskiren in patients with diabetes, concurrent use with ACE inhibitors **WARNINGS** Angioedema, hypotension, hyperkalemia and renal dysfunction **SIDE EFFECTS** <u>Hypotension, hyperkalemia, cough</u>, dizziness and renal failure **MONITORING** BP, K, renal function, s/sx of HF **NOTES** Do <u>not use concomitantly</u> with an <u>ACE inhibitor</u> or <u>another ARB</u>. Must have <u>36 hour wash-out period</u> between discontinuation of <u>ACE inhibitor</u> and initiation of sacubitril/valsartan.

Sacubitril/Valsartan Drug Interactions

- Do not use in combination with an ACE inhibitor or ARB. Avoid use with aliskiren in patients with diabetes or patients with CrCl < 60 mL/min.

- Can ↑ serum potassium if used with potassium-sparing diuretics.

- Concomitant use of NSAIDs can ↑ the risk of renal impairment.

- Sacubitril/valsartan can ↓ lithium's renal clearance and ↑ risk of lithium toxicity.

Beta Blockers

Beta-adrenergic receptor antagonists, or simply beta blockers, antagonize the effects of catecholamines (especially NE) at the beta-1 and beta-2 adrenergic receptors. Beta blockers ↓ vasoconstriction. Beta blockers improve cardiac function and ↓ morbidity and mortality. Beta blockers are recommended for all HF patients. Unlike ACE inhibitors (or ARBs), the clinical benefits of beta blockers are not considered a class effect. Only bisoprolol, carvedilol (IR and ER), and metoprolol succinate ER are recommended in the guidelines. The target doses for these agents are the doses used in clinical trials demonstrating their benefit, or the maximum tolerated dose for a given patient. Beta blockers with intrinsic sympathomimetic activity (ISA) should be avoided. Beta blockers should only be stopped in ADHF if hypotension or hypoperfusion is present.

DRUG	DOSING	SAFETY/SIDE EFFECTS/MONITORING

Beta blockers – only those mentioned in the guidelines (see complete list in Hypertension chapter)

DRUG	DOSING	SAFETY/SIDE EFFECTS/MONITORING
Bisoprolol (*Zebeta*) – benefit in clinical trials but no FDA indication	Start 1.25 mg daily Target dose: 10 mg daily Titrate every 2 weeks as tolerated	**BOXED WARNING** Beta blockers should not be withdrawn abruptly (particularly in patients with CVD), gradually taper over 1-2 weeks to avoid acute tachycardia, HTN, and/or ischemia **CONTRAINDICATIONS** Sinus bradycardia, 2nd or 3rd degree heart block, or sick sinus syndrome (unless patient has a functioning artificial pacemaker) or cardiogenic shock; do not initiate in patients with active asthma exacerbation **WARNING** Caution in patients with diabetes particularly with recurrent hypoglycemia, asthma, severe COPD or peripheral vascular disease and Raynaud's disease; may mask signs of hyperthyroidism; may aggravate psychiatric conditions
Metoprolol succinate extended-release (*Toprol XL*) Metoprolol tartrate (*Lopressor*) is not recommended in the guidelines	Start 12.5-25 mg/day Target dose: 200 mg daily Titrate every 2 weeks as tolerated	**SIDE EFFECTS** ↓ HR, hypotension, fatigue, dizziness, depression, ↓ libido, impotence, hyperglycemia (non-selective agents can ↓ insulin secretion in type 2 diabetes), hypoglycemia (more common with non-selective agents), ↑ TGs, ↓ HDL; weight gain and edema especially with carvedilol **MONITORING** HR (↓ dose if HR < 55 BPM), BP, s/sx of HF, renal function, LFTs **NOTES** Caution: Metoprolol tartrate IV dose is not equivalent to oral dose (IV:PO ratio 1:2.5) Toprol XL can be cut at the score line; preferably taken with or following a meal

Beta Blockers Continued

DRUG	DOSING	SAFETY/SIDE EFFECTS/MONITORING

Non-selective Beta Blocker and Alpha-1 Blocking Agent

| **Carvedilol** *(Coreg, Coreg CR)* | **IR**:
Start 3.125 mg BID
Target dose:
≤ 85 kg: 25 mg BID
> 85 kg: 50 mg BID

CR:
Start 10 mg daily
Target dose: 80 mg daily

Titrate every 2 weeks as tolerated | Same as above

WARNINGS
Intraoperative floppy iris syndrome has occurred in cataract surgery patients who were on or were previously treated with an alpha-1 blocker

NOTES
Take all forms of carvedilol with food to decrease rate of absorption, thus ↓ risk of orthostatic hypotension

Dosing conversion from *Coreg* to *Coreg CR*:
Coreg 3.125 mg BID = *Coreg CR* 10 mg daily
Coreg 6.25 mg BID = *Coreg CR* 20 mg daily
Coreg 12.5 mg BID = *Coreg CR* 40 mg daily
Coreg 25 mg BID = *Coreg CR* 80 mg daily
The IR and CR dose doubles with each increment from the starting dose |

Beta Blocker Drug Interactions

- Beta blockers, particularly the non-selective drugs, can mask many symptoms of hypoglycemia (shakiness, palpitations, anxiety). Sweating and hunger are not masked.

- Beta blockers can ↑ the effects of insulin and oral hypoglycemic drugs such as sulfonylureas. Non-selective beta blockers can ↓ insulin secretion in type 2 diabetes. Monitor blood glucose in patients with diabetes.

- Use caution with other drugs that ↓ HR.

- 2D6 inhibitors can ↑ carvedilol levels and rifampin can ↓ carvedilol levels.

- Carvedilol can ↑ digoxin and cyclosporine levels; may require dose adjustments.

Aldosterone Receptor Antagonists

Aldosterone is a mineralocorticoid, with receptors in the kidneys, as well as on the heart, brain, vasculature, adipose tissue and immune cells. As part of the compensatory RAAS system, aldosterone causes retention of Na and water in the distal convoluted tubule and collecting ducts. Aldosterone receptor antagonists (ARAs) reduce sodium and water retention, cardiac remodeling (especially myocardial fibrosis), and the risk of sudden cardiac death. Overall, ARAs reduce morbidity and mortality. An ARA should be added to standard treatment in patients with NYHA Class II – IV.

DRUG	DOSING	SAFETY/SIDE EFFECTS/MONITORING

Aldosterone Receptor Antagonists

DRUG	DOSING	SAFETY/SIDE EFFECTS/MONITORING
Spironolactone (*Aldactone*)	Start 12.5-25 mg daily Target dose: 25 mg daily or BID	**BOXED WARNING** Tumor risk with spironolactone; tumorigenic in chronic rat toxicity studies **CONTRAINDICATIONS** Anuria, significant renal impairment (CrCl ≤ 30 mL/min), hyperkalemia (Addison's disease or other conditions that ↑ K); concomitant use of strong 3A4 inhibitors with eplerenone **WARNINGS** Do not initiate treatment in heart failure patients with K > 5 mEq/L; SCr > 2.0 mg/dL (females) or SCr > 2.5 mg/dL (males) **SIDE EFFECTS** Hyperkalemia, ↑ SCr, dizziness. Rare: hyperchloremic metabolic acidosis For spironolactone: gynecomastia, breast tenderness, impotence, irregular menses
Eplerenone (*Inspra*)	Start 25 mg daily Target dose: 50 mg daily, titrate based on K level	For eplerenone: ↑ TGs **MONITORING** Check K (before starting and frequently thereafter), BP, renal function; fluid status (input and output, weight), s/sx of HF **NOTES** To minimize risk of hyperkalemia: Avoid in severe renal impairment (CrCl ≤ 30 mL/min) Do not start if K > 5 mEq/L Start at a low dose; ↑ risk when concurrent ACE inhibitors or ARBs are used at higher doses Do not use NSAIDs concurrently (which should be avoided in HF) Monitor frequently There is an ↑ risk if dehydration occurs

ARA Drug Interactions

- Eplerenone is a CYP 3A4 substrate; use with strong 3A4 inhibitors is contraindicated.

- All RAAS inhibitors ↑ the risk of hyperkalemia (most significant side effect). Monitor K and renal function frequently.

- The triple combination of ACE inhibitor, ARB, and ARA is not recommended due to high risk of hyperkalemia and renal insufficiency.

- All RAAS inhibitors can have additive antihypertensive effects, monitor BP.

- RAAS inhibitors can ↓ lithium's renal clearance and ↑ risk of lithium toxicity.

Hydralazine/Nitrate

Hydralazine is a direct arterial vasodilator which ↓ afterload. Nitrates ↑ the availability of nitric oxide which causes venous vasodilation and ↓ preload. Hydralazine also decreases the development of nitrate tachyphylaxis (tolerance). The combination improves the survival of heart failure patients, although not as much as ACE inhibitors. Therefore, this combination is used as alternative treatment for patients who cannot tolerate ACE inhibitors or ARBs due to poor renal function, angioedema, or hyperkalemia. And, it can be added to standard treatment in black patients based on a study demonstrating improved survival. The combination product, *BiDil*, is indicated in self-identified black patients with NYHA Class III or IV who are symptomatic despite optimal treatment with ACE inhibitors and beta blockers. Hydralazine or oral nitrates may be used as monotherapy for other indications, however, they have not individually been shown to affect HF outcomes. Isosorbide dinitrate was the oral nitrate used in clinical trials – there are no data with isosorbide mononitrate although it is used in practice. As with ACE inhibitors or ARBs, the target doses are those shown to be beneficial in clinical trials.

DRUG	DOSING	SAFETY/SIDE EFFECTS/MONITORING
HydrALAZINE	Start 25-50 mg TID-QID Target dose: 300 mg/day in divided doses	**CONTRAINDICATION** Mitral valve rheumatic heart disease **WARNING** Drug-induced lupus erythematosus (DILE) – dose and duration related, fluid/sodium retention, peripheral neuritis **SIDE EFFECTS** Headache, reflex tachycardia, palpitations **MONITORING** HR, BP, s/sx of HF, ANA titer
Isosorbide dinitrate *(Isordil Titradose, Dilatrate SR)* - preferred formulation for systolic HF **Isosorbide mononitrate (Monoket, Imdur)**	Dinitrate: Start 20-30 mg TID-QID Target dose: 120 mg daily in divided doses Mononitrate: not listed in the guidelines	**CONTRAINDICATIONS** Concurrent use with PDE-5 Inhibitors and riociguat **SIDE EFFECTS** Headache, dizziness, lightheadedness, flushing, hypotension, tachyphylaxis (need 10-12 hour nitrate-free interval), syncope **MONITORING** HR, BP, s/sx of HF
Isosorbide dinitrate + hydralazine (*BiDil*)	Start 20/37.5 mg TID (1 tab TID) Target dose: 40/75 mg TID (2 tabs TID) No nitrate tolerance	**CONTRAINDICATIONS** Concurrent use with PDE-5 Inhibitors and riociguat **WARNING** Drug-induced lupus erythematosus (DILE) – dose and duration related, peripheral neuritis **SIDE EFFECTS** Headache, dizziness, lightheadedness, hypotension **MONITORING** HR, BP, s/sx of HF, CBC and ANA titer (if s/sx of DILE)

Hydralazine/Nitrate Drug Interactions

- Must avoid nitrate administration within 12 hours of avanafil, within 24 hours of sildenafil or vardenafil and within 48 hours of tadalafil. Do not dispense nitrates to patients using PDE-5 inhibitors. Avoid use with riociguat.

Digoxin

Digoxin <u>inhibits the Na/K ATPase pump</u> which results in a <u>positive inotropic effect (↑ in CO)</u>. It also exerts a parasympathetic effect which provides a <u>negative chronotropic effect (↓ HR)</u>. Digoxin is added in patients who remain symptomatic despite receiving standard treatment of an ACE inhibitor (or ARB) with a beta blocker. Digoxin <u>improves symptoms, exercise tolerance, and quality of life</u>. Overall, digoxin <u>does not improve survival</u> of heart failure patients, but it does <u>reduce hospitalizations for heart failure</u>. Dosing should take into account the patient's renal function, body size, age and gender (<u>lower dose for renal insufficiency, smaller, older, female</u>), with the majority of patients being on no more than 0.125 mg daily. Serum digoxin concentrations for HF should be kept < 1.0 ng/mL (range 0.5 – 0.9 ng/mL). Patients on digoxin should maintain the serum potassium between 4 – 5 mEq/L.

DRUG	DOSING	SAFETY/SIDE EFFECTS/MONITORING
Digoxin *(Digitek, Digox, Lanoxin)* Tablet, solution, injection	Available as 0.0625, 0.125, 0.1875, 0.25 mg Typical dose: 0.125-0.25 mg daily Loading doses not used in HF <u>Therapeutic range for HF = 0.5-0.9 ng/mL (higher range for AFib)</u> CrCl < 50 mL/min; ↓ dose or frequency ↓ dose by 20-25% when going from PO to IV <u>Antidote: *DigiFab*</u>	**CONTRAINDICATIONS** Ventricular fibrillation **WARNINGS** 2nd/3rd degree heart block without a pacemaker, Wolff-Parkinson-White syndrome (WPW) with AFib, vesicant - avoid extravasation **SIDE EFFECTS** Dizziness, mental disturbances, headache, N/V/D **MONITORING** ECG, HR, BP, electrolytes, renal function and digoxin level (drawn optimally 12-24 hrs after dose) **TOXICITY** <u>Initial s/sx of toxicity are N/V, loss of appetite and bradycardia.</u> Severe s/sx of toxicity include blurred/double vision, altered color perception, greenish-yellow halos around lights or objects, abdominal pain, confusion, delirium, prolonged PR interval, arrhythmias

Digoxin Drug Interactions

- Use caution when administering other drugs that ↓ HR.

- Digoxin is mostly renally cleared and partially cleared hepatically. Decreased renal function requires a ↓ digoxin dose. In acute renal failure, digoxin is held.

- Digoxin is a P-gp and 3A4 substrate (minor). Digoxin levels ↑ with amiodarone, dronedarone, quinidine, verapamil, erythromycin, clarithromycin, itraconazole, cyclosporine, propafenone, and many other drugs. Reduce digoxin dose by 50% if patient is on amiodarone or dronedarone.

- <u>Hypokalemia, hypomagnesemia, and hypercalcemia ↑ risk of digoxin toxicity.</u>

- Hypothyroidism can ↑ digoxin levels.

Ivabradine

High resting heart rate is associated with increased morbidity and mortality in heart failure. Ivabradine is an inhibitor of the "funny" current (If) in the sinus node and belongs to a class of drugs known as hyperpolarization-activated cyclic nucleotide-gated channel blockers (HCN blockers). Inhibition of this current results in a reduction in sinus rate and hence heart rate. Ivabradine reduces the risk of hospitalizations for worsening heart failure, but does not affect mortality. Although its exact place in therapy remains to be addressed in treatment guidelines, ivabradine provides another option to improve morbidity in select HFrEF patients.

DRUG	DOSING	SAFETY/SIDE EFFECTS/MONITORING
Ivabradine (Corlanor) Indicated in patients with: - stable, symptomatic chronic HF - LVEF ≤ 35% - sinus rhythm with resting heart rate ≥ 70 BPM - either are on maximally tolerated doses of beta blockers or have a contraindication to beta blocker use	Starting dose: 5 mg PO twice daily; after two weeks, adjust dose based on heart rate Maintenance dose: 2.5-7.5 mg PO twice daily Target: resting heart rate between 50-60 BPM	**CONTRAINDICATIONS** Acute decompensated HF; BP < 90/50 mmHg; sick sinus syndrome, sinoatrial block or 3rd degree AV block unless patient has a functioning pacemaker; resting heart rate < 60 BPM prior to treatment; severe hepatic impairment; pacemaker dependence (heart rate maintained exclusively by the pacemaker); use in combination with strong 3A4 inhibitors **WARNINGS** Fetal toxicity: Females should use effective contraception as drug can cause fetal harm Atrial fibrillation, HR, and bradycardia Not recommended in patients with 2nd degree AV block unless patient has a functioning pacemaker **SIDE EFFECTS** Bradycardia, hypertension, atrial fibrillation, luminous phenomena (phosphenes - seeing flashes of light) **MONITORING** HR, ECG, BP **NOTES** MedGuide required

Ivabradine Drug Interactions

- Ivabradine is a substrate of CYP3A4 and is contraindicated with strong 3A4 inhibitors. Ivabradine should be avoided in patients taking strong 3A4 inducers and moderate 3A4 inhibitors.

Potassium Oral Supplementation

Potassium supplementation is an important aspect of managing HF since loop diuretics cause ↓ K while other HF drugs (RAAS inhibitors, ARAs) ↑ K. Maintenance of potassium levels is essential to reduce the proarrhythmic risk of digoxin, especially as HF ↑ arrhythmia risk. There are different formulations (tablets, capsules and liquids) which also vary by salt form (acetate, bicarbonate, citrate, chloride, gluconate and phosphate). The salt used depends on patient factors including acid-base status and deficiency of other electrolytes such as phosphate. Potassium chloride is used most commonly.

Potassium levels should be monitored with the frequency dependent on the stability of the renal function, medication regimen, and the clinical status. Check potassium levels if the renal function changes, and after any change in diuretic, ACE inhibitor, ARB or ARA dose. Magnesium deficiency aggravates hypokalemia. The magnesium level may need to be checked and should be corrected prior to correcting the potassium level.

The usual range of K is 3.5 – 5 mEq/L. Supplementation may not be needed in patients who are able to supplement their intake of potassium through dietary sources (e.g., bananas, potatoes, orange juice, beans, dark leafy greens, apricots, peaches, avocados, white mushrooms, tomatoes, and some varieties of fish).

DRUG	DOSING	SAFETY/SIDE EFFECTS/MONITORING
Potassium chloride *(K-Tab, K-Vescent, Kaon-Cl, Klor-Con, Klor-Con 10, Klor-Con M10, Klor-Con M15, Klor-Con M20, Micro-K,* others)	Prevention of hypokalemia: 20-40 mEq/day in 1-2 divided doses Treatment of mild hypokalemia: Generally 40-100 mEq/day in 2-5 divided doses; adjust dose according to laboratory values No more than 20-25 mEq should be given as a single dose to avoid GI discomfort	**CONTRAINDICATIONS** Severe renal impairment, hyperkalemia Oral solid dosage forms are contraindicated in patients with delayed or obstructed passage through the GI tract **WARNINGS** Caution in patients with mild-moderate renal impairment, patients with disorders that alter K (untreated Addison's disease, heat cramps, severe tissue trauma/burns) and in patients taking other medications that ↑ K **SIDE EFFECTS** N/V/D, abdominal pain, flatulence, hyperkalemia **MONITORING** K, Mg, Cl, pH, urine output **NOTES** Take with meals and a full glass of water or other liquid to minimize the risk of GI irritation *Micro-K*: Capsules can be opened and contents sprinkled on a spoonful of applesauce or pudding and immediately swallowed without chewing *K-Tab, Klor-Con*: Swallow whole; do not crush, cut, chew, or suck on tablet *Klor-Con M:* Swallow whole; do not crush, chew, or suck on tablet; tablet can also be cut in half and swallowed separately, or can dissolve the whole tablet in 4 oz. of water – stir for 2 mins. and drink immediately

ACUTE DECOMPENSATED HEART FAILURE

Stable heart failure patients may experience episodes of worsening symptoms such as sudden weight gain, inability to lie flat without becoming short of breath, decreasing functionality (e.g., unable to perform their daily routine), increasing shortness of breath and fatigue, known as acute decompensated heart failure (ADHF). ADHF presents with either worsening congestion and/or hypoperfusion. Treatment consists of IV loop diuretics, vasodilators such as nesiritide and/or inotropes. Nesiritide (*Natrecor*) is a recombinant B-type natriuretic peptide that binds to vascular smooth muscle, ↑ cGMP resulting in smooth muscle cell relaxation which causes vasodilation. Nesiritide is not commonly used due to side effects, cost and lack of clinical outcome data. Vasodilators and inotropes are discussed in the Critical Care & Fluids/Electrolytes chapter.

Congestive Heart Failure Management/Action Plan

1. **Green means Go.**   Follow medication, weight and diet advice.
2. **Yellow means Caution.**   You may need to change your medicines.
3. **Red means Danger.**   Get help from a doctor today. Call 911.

1. Green – Go

- No shortness of breath
- Usual amount of swelling in legs
- No weight gain
- No chest pain
- No change in usual activity

Weigh yourself every day

Take all your medicines

Eat a low salt diet

Go to your doctor appointments

Bring all your medicines to every appointment

2. Yellow – Caution

Weight gain of:
- 2-3 pounds in 1 day
- 5 pounds in a week

Increased number of pillows to sleep

You may need to change your medicines

Call your doctor for instructions

Increased swelling or coughing

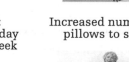

Shortness of breath with activity

3. Red – Danger

Weight gain of more than 5 pounds in 1 week

Dizziness or falling

Call your doctor <u>today</u> to report symptoms and request an appointment.

Waking at night due to shortness of breath

Shortness of breath at rest, chest tightness or wheezing

<u>Call 911 if having severe chest pain</u>

www.ccwjc.com

Patient Counseling

All Heart Failure Patients

- Monitor body weight daily, in the morning before eating and after using the restroom. Weight should be recorded in a notebook.

- Follow the steps in your HF action plan or contact your healthcare provider if your symptoms worsen or if you gain weight (2-4 pounds in one day or 3-5 pounds in one week).

- Follow a sodium restricted diet. Foods high in sodium include:

  ❑ Prepared sauces and condiments (such as soy sauce, BBQ sauce, Worcestershire sauce or salsa)

  ❑ Canned vegetables and soups

  ❑ Frozen dinners

  ❑ Deli meats (sandwich meats, bacon, ham, hot dogs, sausage or salami)

  ❑ Salty foods (pickles, olives, cheese, nuts, chips or crackers)

- Take nutrition classes and learn to read nutrition labels. Choose "no sodium added" or "low sodium" options. Healthy ways of cooking include broiling, baking, poaching, and steaming without added salt.

- <u>Stop smoking</u>. Do not use any illegal drugs; they can badly damage the heart. Alcohol, including beer and wine, should be <u>avoided</u> or limited to 1 drink per day for females and 2 drinks per day for males.

- Avoid pain medicines like ibuprofen (NSAIDs) without checking with the pharmacist or cardiologist. Also, do not use nutritional supplements, vitamins or herbals for HF without discussing with the pharmacist if they are safe to use.

- Take your medications as directed. Discuss with your healthcare provider if the medications are too expensive. Not taking the medications and not following the food and salt recommendations will usually cause worsening of the HF symptoms and possible hospitalization.

Beta Blockers in HF

- Do not stop taking the medication unless your healthcare provider tells you to do so.

- If you miss a dose, take your dose as soon as you remember, unless it is time to take your next dose. Do not double the dose.

- This medication can cause you to feel dizzy, tired or faint. Do not drive a car, use machinery or do anything that requires you to be alert until you adjust to the medication and the symptoms subside. These effects will go away in a few days. However, call your healthcare provider if the symptoms feel severe or you have weight gain or increased shortness of breath.

- This medication can cover up some of the signs and symptoms of low blood sugar (hypoglycemia); make sure to test your blood sugar often and take a fast-acting sugar source if needed.

- Medications used to treat severe allergic reactions may not work as well while taking this medication.

Toprol XL

- If you have been told to cut the *Toprol XL* or its generic equivalent tablet in half, you must use a pill cutter and cut only at the score line. Otherwise, the medicine will enter your body too quickly. Swallow the ½ tablet whole. The tablets cannot be crushed or chewed and should be taken preferably with or following a meal.

Coreg CR

- Take with food, to help reduce dizziness.

- Swallow *Coreg CR* capsules whole. Do not chew or crush the capsules.

- If you have trouble swallowing *Coreg CR* whole: The capsule can be carefully opened and the beads sprinkled over a spoonful of applesauce which should be taken right away. The applesauce should not be warm. Only use applesauce.

Digoxin

- This medicine helps make the heart beat stronger. Keep taking as directed, even if you feel well.

- Do not stop taking this medicine without talking to your healthcare provider. Stopping this medication suddenly may make your condition worse.

- Avoid becoming overheated or dehydrated as an overdose can easily occur if you are dehydrated.

- Symptoms of overdose include poor or no appetite, nausea, vomiting, diarrhea, vision changes (such as blurred or yellow/green vision), uneven heartbeats and feeling like you might pass out. If any of these occur, see a healthcare provider right away.

- There are many medications that can interact with digoxin. Check with your physician or pharmacist before starting any new medicines, including over the counter, vitamin and/or herbal products.

- To be sure that this medication is not causing harmful effects, your blood may need to be tested on a regular basis. Your kidney function will also need to be monitored.

Sacubitril/valsartan

- This medication is used with other heart failure therapies, in place of an ACE inhibitor or other ARB therapy.

- Do not take this medication if you have had an allergic reaction including swelling of your face, lips, tongue, throat or trouble breathing while taking a type of medicine called an angiotensin-converting enzyme (ACE) inhibitor or angiotensin II receptor blocker (ARB).

- This medication cannot be used for at least 36 hours after stopping an ACE inhibitor.

- Do not take this medication if you have diabetes and take a medicine that contains aliskiren.

- Tell you healthcare provider if you are pregnant, plan to become pregnant or are breastfeeding or plan to breastfeed.

- Tell you healthcare provider about all the medications that you take, especially if you take potassium supplements or salt substitutes, non-steroidal anti-inflammatory drugs (NSAIDs), lithium or other medications for high blood pressure or heart problems.

Ivabradine

- This medication can cause an abnormal heart rhythm. Tell your healthcare provider if you have symptoms of an irregular heartbeat, such as feeling that your heart is pounding or racing (palpitations), chest pressure or pain, or worsened shortness of breath.

- This medication can cause a low heart rate. Contact your healthcare provider if you have symptoms such as dizziness, fatigue, lack of energy, or have low blood pressure.

- Tell your healthcare provider if you are pregnant, plan to become pregnant or are breastfeeding or plan to breastfeed.

- Avoid drinking grapefruit juice and taking St. John's wort during treatment with ivabradine. Tell your pharmacist all the medications, herbals and OTC medications you are taking.

PRACTICE CASE

PATIENT	FACILITY	ENCOUNTER
JF	**San Diego Medical Group Tower**	**NOTE TYPE** SOAP Note
DOB 08/29/1940	T (444) 444-4444	**SEEN BY** Alison James
AGE 75 yrs	F (444) 444-5555	**DATE** 10/06/2015
SEX Female	35 La Jolla Drive	Not signed
PRN JF120303	San Diego, CA 92130	

Chief complaint

"Shortness of breath and puffy legs"

Vitals	Height: 61 in	Weight: 148 lb	BMI: 27.96	BP: 117/75 mmHg
	Temperature: 98.7 °F	Pulse: 104 BPM	Respiratory rate: 23 BPM	

Subjective

JF is a pleasant 74 y/o female accompanied by her husband.

HPI: Per her husband, JF was doing well with her heart failure regimen over the past several months. Over the weekend, they visited family and ate ham, canned vegetables, and casseroles. JF's shortness of breath started to get worse at that time and continued to worsen over the next 2 days. JF reports a 5 pound weight gain over the last 2 days. She gets short of breath with activity. Her legs and feet are puffy by noon. Her urine output is good, but the fluid is not going away. If she sits in a chair and does nothing, she does not have shortness of breath. She states that she is compliant with her medications. Review of the prescription bottles and refill history support this statement.

JF consulted her heart failure action plan, which instructed her to visit the clinic if her weight increased by > 5 pounds in one week.

Allergies: NKDA

Objective

Past Medical History:
HF (LVEF 35% documented by ECHO in 2014) / HTN / Type 2 DM (diet controlled) / Depression

Medications:
Lasix 40 mg PO daily / Prinivil 40 mg PO daily / Digox 0.25 mg PO daily / Toprol XL 100 mg PO daily / Celexa 20 mg PO daily

Social History: No alcohol, drugs, or tobacco
Family History: Mother with HTN, dyslipidemia, and MI. Father with HTN. Both deceased. Sister with Type 2 DM.

Labs (reference range)

Na 142 (135 - 145 mEq/L)	SCr 1.5 (0.6 - 1.3 mg/dL)
K 4.7 (3.5 - 5.0 mEq/L)	Glu 218 (70 - 110 mg/dL)
Cl 101 (95 - 103 mEq/L)	Digoxin 1.8 ng/mL (indication specific)
HCO3 25 (24 - 30 mEq/L)	BNP 372 pg/mL (< 100 pg/mL)
BUN 30 (7 - 20 mg/dL)	

Tests
ECG: sinus tachycardia, no ST or T wave changes
Chest xray: cardiomegaly and bilateral pleural effusions

Assessment

1) Symptomatic heart failure likely secondary to recent dietary indiscretion
2) Hypertension
3) Type 2 Diabetes
4) Depression

Plan

JF has taken all of her home medications for today. An additional 40 mg of *Lasix* was given in clinic today.

Questions

1. Looking at JF's chart note, how much total *Lasix* will JF receive on October 6, 2015?

   a. 10 mg
   b. 20 mg
   c. 40 mg
   d. 80 mg
   e. 100 mg

2. JF is taking *Digox* for her heart failure. Which of the following statements is the best interpretation for the use of *Digox* for JF?

   a. She is receiving the correct amount of *Digox* for her condition.
   b. She is receiving too much *Digox* for her condition.
   c. She is not receiving enough *Digox* given her current HR.
   d. She has a contraindication to *Digox* at this time.
   e. She is receiving too much *Digox* given her current HR.

3. The equivalent dose of *Lasix* JF is receiving on a daily basis when converted to the IV route:

   a. 5 mg
   b. 10 mg
   c. 20 mg
   d. 40 mg
   e. None of the above.

4. Which of the following objective findings support the diagnosis of HF in JF? (Select **ALL** that apply.)

   a. Echo results
   b. BNP level
   c. ECG results
   d. Chest X-ray
   e. Pulse

5. Which of the following medications should JF generally avoid as they may worsen her heart failure? (Select **ALL** that apply.)

   a. Celecoxib
   b. Verapamil
   c. Amiodarone
   d. Pioglitazone
   e. Naproxen

6. The healthcare provider decides to increase the *Toprol XL* dose to 200 mg daily. Which of the following patient counseling points should be discussed with JF regarding this change? (Select **ALL** that apply.)

   a. The increase in medication may make you feel more tired and dizzy at first and should disappear over time.
   b. This increase in medication can cause a loss of appetite, blurred vision, lightheadedness, and/or visual changes.
   c. This medication may be cut in half (if directed to do so) with a pill cutter, but do not crush or chew the tablets.
   d. This medication can cause metabolic acidosis.
   e. The increase in medication will cause an increase in your heart rate. Call your healthcare provider if you feel your heart racing.

Questions 7-8 do not pertain to the above case.

7. A 70 kg patient is beginning carvedilol therapy for heart failure. The starting dose is 3.125 mg BID. What should the target dose for carvedilol be in this patient?

   a. 6.25 mg BID
   b. 12.5 mg BID
   c. 25 mg BID
   d. 50 mg BID
   e. 100 mg BID

8. What is the trade name for eplerenone?

   a. *Invega*
   b. *Invanz*
   c. *Invirase*
   d. *Isuprel*
   e. *Inspra*

Answers

1-d, 2-b, 3-c, 4-a,b,d, 5-a,b,d,e, 6-a,c, 7-c, 8-e

ARRHYTHMIAS

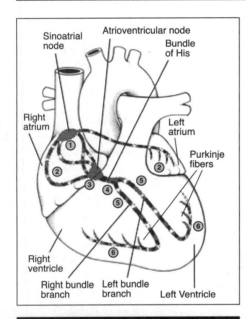

Sinoatrial node — Atrioventricular node — Bundle of His — Right atrium — Left atrium — Purkinje fibers — Right ventricle — Right bundle branch — Left bundle branch — Left Ventricle

GUIDELINES/REFERENCES

January CT, Wann LS, Alpert JS, et al. 2014 AHA/ACC/HRS Guideline for the Management of Patients With Atrial Fibrillation: A Report of the American College of Cardiology/American Heart Association Task Force on Practice Guidelines and the Heart Rhythm Society. *Journal of the American College of Cardiology*. 2014; doi:10.1016/j.jacc.2014.03.022.

We gratefully acknowledge the assistance of Tien M. H. Ng, PharmD, FCCP, BCPS (AQ-C), Associate Professor at the University of Southern California School of Pharmacy, in preparing this chapter.

BACKGROUND

A normal heart beats in a regular, coordinated way because electrical impulses traveling down the cardiac conduction system trigger a sequence of organized contractions. Arrhythmias are caused by abnormalities in the formation and/or conduction of these electrical impulses. Heart rate describes the frequency of depolarization of the ventricles. Arrhythmias can occur with the heart rate being slow (bradyarrhythmias) or fast (tachyarrhythmias). Normally the resting heart rate (HR) in adults is 60 to 100 beats per minute (BPM). An arrhythmia can be silent (asymptomatic) which may only be detected during a routine physical exam. However, most patients experience symptoms. Common complaints of patients experiencing arrhythmias include palpitations (feeling like there is fluttering or racing), dizziness, light-headedness, shortness of breath, chest pain and fatigue. In severe cases, arrhythmias can lead to syncope, heart failure and death.

NORMAL SINUS RHYTHM

Activation of the heart in the normal sequence through the cardiac conduction system, and at the usual rate of 60 to 100 BPM, is called normal sinus rhythm (NSR). The diagram above traces the normal sequence of formation and conduction of an electrical impulse in the heart. The sinoatrial (SA) node (1) initiates an electrical impulse that spreads throughout the right and left atria (2), resulting in atrial contraction. The electrical impulse reaches the atrioventricular (AV) node (3), where its conduction is slowed. Once through the AV node, the impulse travels down the bundle of His (4), which divides into the right bundle branch for the right ventricle (5) and the left bundle branch for the left ventricle (5). The impulse then spreads through the ventricles via Purkinje fibers (6), resulting in a coordinated and rapid contraction of both ventricles. Any disruption in the normal sequence of impulse formation or conduction can result in an arrhythmia.

CARDIAC ACTION POTENTIAL

The cardiac action potential of ventricle myocytes is generated by the movement of ions through the transmembrane ion channels in the cardiac cells. The cardiac action potential is depicted below and consists of 5 phases (numbered 0-4).

- Phase 0: The upstroke or rapid depolarization, which initiates the heartbeat in response to an influx of Na

- Phase 1: Early rapid repolarization

- Phase 2: Plateau in response to an influx of Ca and efflux of K

- Phase 3: Final rapid repolarization in response to an efflux of K

- Phase 4: Resting membrane potential and diastolic depolarization

Abnormalities of the heart or its conduction system that alter the cardiac action potential lead to the development of cardiac arrhythmias.

Many factors can contribute to the development of arrhythmias. The most common cause of arrhythmias is myocardial ischemia or infarction. Other conditions resulting in damage to cardiac tissue, including heart valve disorders, hypertension and heart failure, can cause arrhythmias. Non-cardiac conditions can trigger or predispose a patient to arrhythmias. Electrolyte imbalances, especially those involving potassium, magnesium, sodium and calcium (since these are important to cardiac electrophysiology), can result in arrhythmias. Elevated sympathetic states, including hyperthyroidism and infection, can contribute. Drugs can cause or worsen arrhythmias; this includes the drugs used to treat arrhythmias. Many drugs can affect conduction and/or prolong repolarization through effects on ion currents in the heart. Drug-induced slowing of repolarization, as indicated by prolongation of the QT interval on an electrocardiogram, can result in a particularly dangerous ventricular tachyarrhythmia called Torsade de Pointes (TdP).

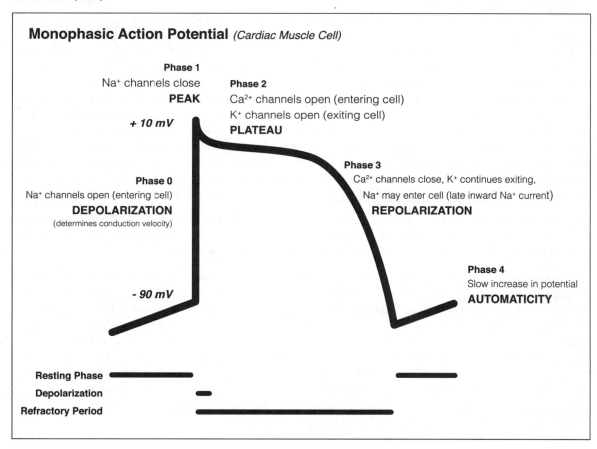

CLASSIFICATION OF ARRHYTHMIAS

Arrhythmias are generally classified based on their location of origin into two broad categories: supraventricular (originating above the atrioventricular node) or ventricular (originating below the atrioventricular node). Arrhythmias originating in or just below the atrioventricular node are called junctional rhythms, but these are less common. Supraventricular tachyarrhythmias include sinus tachycardia, atrial fibrillation, atrial flutter, focal atrial tachycardias and supraventricular re-entrant tachycardias (formerly known as paroxysmal supraventricular tachycardias or PSVTs). Common ventricular arrhythmias include premature ventricular contractions (PVCs), ventricular tachycardia and ventricular fibrillation.

Atrial fibrillation (AFib) is the most common type of arrhythmia. AFib results from multiple waves of electrical impulses in the atria, resulting in an irregular and usually rapid ventricular response. The rapid ventricular rate can result in hypotension and worsen underlying ischemia and heart failure. Due to the disorganized depolarization of the atria, coordinated atrial contraction is impaired, which increases the risk of thromboembolism and stroke. Therefore, the management of atrial fibrillation usually involves anticoagulation (see Anticoagulation chapter), and antiarrhythmics to either slow the ventricular rate (rate-control) and/or terminate the atrial fibrillation to restore normal sinus rhythm (rhythm-control). Beta blockers (preferred) or nondihydropyridine calcium channel blockers are recommended for controlling ventricular rate in patients with AFib. Of note, patients with underlying heart failure should not receive a nondihydropyridine calcium channel blocker. Amiodarone and digoxin are not first-line agents for ventricular rate control, but may be added for refractory patients or in those who cannot tolerate beta blockers or calcium channel blockers. Digoxin does not control the ventricular rate during exertion. The goal resting HR is < 80 BPM in patients with symptomatic AFib; however, a more lenient rate-control strategy of < 110 BPM may be reasonable in patients who are asymptomatic and have preserved left ventricular function. Rhythm-control consists of 1) methods for conversion to NSR and 2) maintenance of NSR. Conversion to NSR is most effective with direct current cardioversion. Medications can be used as well and include amiodarone (oral and IV), dofetilide, flecainide, ibutilide and propafenone. For maintenance of NSR, dofetilide, dronedarone, flecainide, propafenone or sotalol is recommended. Due to toxicities, amiodarone should only be used when other agents have failed or are contraindicated. Rhythm control antiarrhythmics should not be used when AFib becomes permanent.

TYPE OF AFIB	DEFINITION
Paroxysmal	AFib that terminates spontaneously or with intervention within 7 days of onset; episodes may recur with variable frequency
Persistent	Continuous AFib that is sustained > 7 days
Longstanding Persistent	Continuous AFib of > 12 months duration
Permanent	Term used when a joint decision has been made by clinician and patient to cease further attempts to restore and/or maintain NSR; this represents a therapeutic attitude rather than an inherent attribute of the AFib

Atrial flutter is caused by one or more rapid re-entry circuits in the atrium. Atrial flutter is usually more organized and regular than atrial fibrillation. This arrhythmia occurs most often with heart disease, and in the first week after heart surgery. Atrial flutter often converts to AFib.

Premature ventricular contractions (PVCs) are among the most common arrhythmias and occur in people with and without heart disease. This is a "skipped heartbeat" that anyone can experience. These electrical impulses are generated from within the ventricular tissue. In some people, it can be related to stress, too much caffeine or nicotine, or too much exercise. A series of PVCs in a row resulting in a heart rate of greater than 100 BPM is known as ventricular tachycardia. Ventricular tachycardia is further classified based on the presence or absence of a detectable peripheral pulse. Ventricular tachycardia with a pulse is treated with certain antiarrhythmics, whereas, ventricular tachycardia without a pulse is a medical emergency and advanced cardiac life support should be initiated. Untreated ventricular tachycardia can degenerate into ventricular fibrillation (complete disorganized electrical activation of the ventricles) which is always a medical emergency.

QT Prolongation & Torsade de Pointes

Prolongation of the QT interval is a risk factor for Torsade de Pointes (TdP), a particularly lethal ventricular tachyarrhythmia which is most commonly associated with drugs capable of prolonging repolarization of ventricular myocytes and can result in sudden cardiac death. The QT interval is measured from the beginning of the QRS complex to the end of the T wave. It reflects ventricular depolarization and repolarization. A QT interval is considered prolonged when it is > 440 milliseconds (msec). Drug-induced QT prolongation is dose-dependent (concentration-dependent). Combining different drugs that can cause QT prolongation can have additive effects, and the benefit-risk of using multiple QT prolonging medications must be evaluated carefully. Reduced drug clearance or drug interactions which result in increased concentrations of QT prolonging drugs will also accentuate the effect on the QT interval and increased risk for TdP. Therefore, if a patient is using a low dose of amitriptyline for neuropathic pain, this may not be considered particularly risky due to the low dose, although the risk may be additive with other drugs or if the elimination of amitriptyline is impaired.

Additive QT Prolongation

The following QT interval prolonging drugs must be used with caution in patients with any arrhythmia risk (including those with any pre-existing cardiac condition or history of arrhythmia, electrolyte abnormalities or those taking other proarrhythmic drugs).

DRUG TREATMENT

Antiarrhythmic drugs are used for two main purposes in the treatment of cardiac arrhythmias. Some antiarrhythmic drugs are used to terminate the arrhythmia and restore and maintain normal sinus rhythm (class I and III antiarrhythmics). Other agents are used to slow the ventricular rate during a supraventricular arrhythmia (class II and IV antiarrhythmics, digoxin).

Antiarrhythmics work by affecting the electrical currents in the cells of the heart. By blocking the movement of ions in different phases of the cardiac action potential (see figure), select drugs can reduce conduction velocity and/or automaticity, or prolong the refractory period which can slow or terminate abnormal electrical activity which results in arrhythmias. They can also occasionally worsen the existing arrhythmia or cause other arrhythmias. All patients should be instructed to be seen if they suspect they have "worse heartbeat problems" or have an increase in their symptoms. Prior to starting any medication for a non-life-threatening arrhythmia, be sure to check the patient's electrolytes and obtain a toxicology screen.

SELECT DRUGS THAT CAN INCREASE/PROLONG THE QT INTERVAL

Antiarrhythmics - Class I (Class Ia in particular) and Class III agents

Antibiotics including quinolones, macrolides, foscarnet, telavancin, telithromycin and others

Azole antifungals

Antidepressants including tricyclics (amitriptyline, clomipramine, desipramine, doxepin, imipramine), SSRIs (citalopram, escitalopram, others), SNRIs, mirtazapine and trazodone. Sertraline is preferred in cardiac patients.

Antiemetic agents including the 5-HT3 receptor antagonists, droperidol and phenothiazines

Antipsychotics (aripiprazole, asenapine, chlorpromazine, clozapine, haloperidol, iloperidone, olanzapine, paliperidone, pimozide, quetiapine, risperidone, thioridazine, ziprasidone)

Oncology agents (arsenic, bortezomib, bosutinib, ceritinib, crizotinib, dasatinib, lapatinib, nilotinib, pazopanib, sorafenib, sunitinib, vandetanib, others)

Protease inhibitors (atazanavir, saquinavir) and rilpivirine

Other agents: alfuzosin, apomorphine, atomoxetine, buprenorphine, chloroquine, diphenhydramine, donepezil, ezogabine, fingolimod, galantamine, methadone, mirabegron, pentamidine, propofol, quinine, ranolazine, sevoflurane, solifenacin, tacrolimus, tizanidine, others

Vaughan Williams Classification of Antiarrhythmics

The Vaughan Williams classification system is the most commonly used classification system for anti-arrhythmic drugs. Here the drugs are split into categories based on their dominant electrophysiological effect. It has the virtue of simplicity, although many drugs overlap into more than one category.

CLASS	DRUGS
Ia	Procainamide, Disopyramide, Quinidine
Ib	Lidocaine, Mexiletine, (Phenytoin)
Ic	Flecainide, Propafenone
II	Beta blockers (e.g., esmolol, propranolol)
III	Amiodarone, Dronedarone, Sotalol, Ibutilide, Dofetilide
IV	Diltiazem, Verapamil

STUDY TIP

VAUGHAN WILLIAMS CLASSIFICATION

Class I
Ia – Police Department Questions
(Procainamide, Disopyramide, Quinidine)

Ib – Liquored Man
(Lidocaine, Mexiletine)

Ic – For Peeing
(Flecainide, Propafenone)

Class II
(Beta Blockers)

Class III
After Drinking Scotch In Dark
(Amiodarone, Dronedarone, Sotalol, Ibutilide, Dofetilide)

Class IV
Dirty Vehicle
(Diltiazem, Verapamil)

CLASS I ANTIARRHYTHMICS

Class I antiarrhythmics are sodium channel blockers. All sodium channel blockers have the potential for negative inotropic effects. They are further sub-classified based on the duration of time they bind to the sodium channel. Class Ia are intermediate on-off sodium channel blockers and they also block the potassium channels. Class Ib are fast on-off sodium channel blockers. Class Ic are slow on-off sodium channel blockers. All Class I agents are proarrhythmic.

The Cardiac Arrhythmia Suppression Trial (CAST) was a negative study in which patients with premature ventricular contractions (PVCs) after an MI were randomized to flecainide, encainide (discontinued) or placebo. Those taking flecainide or encainide had an increase in mortality compared to patients taking placebo. This led to the following boxed warning for all the Class I antiarrhythmics, particularly the Class Ic agents:

"In the Cardiac Arrhythmia Suppression Trial (CAST), recent (> 6 days but < 2 years ago) myocardial infarction patients with asymptomatic, non-life-threatening ventricular arrhythmias did not benefit and may have been harmed by attempts to suppress the arrhythmia with flecainide or encainide." This boxed warning is not repeated in the following charts.

Class Ia Antiarrhythmics

Class Ia antiarrhythmics block both <u>sodium channels</u> and potassium channels. Quinidine and disopyramide also have <u>strong anticholinergic effects</u>. Procainamide is metabolized by acetylation to N-acetyl-procainamide (<u>active metabolite</u>). Class Ia antiarrhythmic drugs ↓ conduction velocity, ↑ refractory period and ↓ automaticity.

DRUG	DOSING	SAFETY/SIDE EFFECTS/MONITORING
QuiNIDine Tablet, Injection	IR: 400 mg PO Q6H ER: 300-648 mg PO Q8-12H Take with food or milk to ↓ GI upset Different salt forms are not interchangeable (267 mg of gluconate = 200 mg of sulfate form)	**BOXED WARNING** Quinidine may ↑ mortality in treatment of AFib or flutter; control AV conduction before initiating **CONTRAINDICATIONS** Concurrent use of quinolones that prolong the QT interval or ritonavir; 2nd/3rd degree heart block or idioventricular conduction delays (unless patient has a functional artificial pacemaker), thrombocytopenia, thrombocytopenic purpura, myasthenia gravis **WARNINGS** Proarrhythmic Hepatotoxicity Drug-Induced Lupus Erythematosus (DILE) - discontinue drug Hemolysis risk in G6PD deficiency - discontinue drug Can cause positive Coombs test - discontinue drug (hemolysis risk) **SIDE EFFECTS** <u>Diarrhea (35%), stomach cramping (22%)</u>, lightheadedness, N/V, <u>cinchonism</u> (tinnitus, hearing loss, blurred vision, headache, delirium), rash **MONITORING** ECG, electrolytes, BP, CBC, LFTs, renal function **NOTES** Avoid changes in Na intake; ↓ Na intake can ↑ quinidine levels Alkaline foods/alkaline urine ↑ quinidine levels and can lead to toxicity
Procainamide Injection	<u>Active metabolite, N-acetyl procainamide (NAPA), is renally cleared</u>; ↓ dose when CrCl < 50 mL/min **Therapeutic levels:** Procainamide: 4-10 mcg/mL NAPA: 15-25 mcg/mL Combined: 10-30 mcg/mL Draw levels 6-12 hours after IV infusion has started	**BOXED WARNINGS** Potentially <u>fatal blood dyscrasias (e.g., agranulocytosis)</u>, monitor patient closely in the first 3 months of therapy and periodically thereafter. Long-term use leads to positive antibody (ANA) test in 50% of patients which may result in <u>drug-induced lupus erythematosus (DILE) in 20-30% of patients</u>. **CONTRAINDICATIONS** 2nd/3rd degree heart block (unless patient has a functional artificial pacemaker), SLE, TdP, procaine or other ester-type local anesthetics **WARNINGS** Proarrhythmic **SIDE EFFECTS** <u>Hypotension, rash</u> **MONITORING** ECG, electrolytes, BP, renal function, procainamide and NAPA levels, CBC, ANA titers

Class Ia Antiarrhythmic Agents Continued

DRUG	DOSING	SAFETY/SIDE EFFECTS/MONITORING
Disopyramide (*Norpace, Norpace CR*) Capsule	IR: 100-200 mg PO Q6H CR: 200-400 mg PO Q12H CrCl ≤ 40 mL/min: Decrease frequency of IR and do not use CR formulation Take on an empty stomach	**CONTRAINDICATIONS** $2^{nd}/3^{rd}$ degree heart block (unless patient has a functional artificial pacemaker), cardiogenic shock, congenital QT syndrome, sick sinus syndrome **WARNINGS** Proarrhythmic; HF; BPH/urinary retention/narrow-angle glaucoma; myasthenia gravis (due to anticholinergic effects) **SIDE EFFECTS** Anticholinergic effects > 10% (dry mouth, constipation, urinary retention), hypotension **MONITORING** ECG, electrolytes, BP, s/sx of HF

Class Ia Antiarrhythmic Drug Interactions

- Quinidine is a substrate of CYP450 3A4 (major), 2C9 (minor) and P-gp; inhibits 2D6 (strong), 2C9 (weak), 3A4 (weak) and P-gp. Some major drug interactions with quinidine include digoxin (↓ digoxin dose by 50%), warfarin (↑ INR), potent 3A4 inhibitors will ↑ quinidine levels (e.g., avoid grapefruit juice). Drugs that alkalinize the urine (carbonic-anhydrase inhibitors, sodium bicarbonate, thiazide diuretics) ↓ renal elimination of quinidine.

- Procainamide is a substrate of 2D6 (major). Moderate and strong 2D6 inhibitors ↑ levels of procainamide.

- Disopyramide is a substrate of 3A4 (major). Inhibitors of 3A4 and drugs with anticholinergic side effects can ↑ risk of side effects; 3A4 inducers can ↓ the effects of disopyramide.

- All Class Ia antiarrhythmic agents can have additive QT prolongation with other agents that also prolong the QT interval.

Class Ib Antiarrhythmics

Class Ib antiarrhythmics are pure sodium channel blockers. They are <u>only useful for ventricular arrhythmias</u> (no efficacy for supraventricular arrhythmias such as atrial fibrillation). They <u>cross the blood-brain-barrier</u> and, therefore, can cause <u>CNS</u> adverse effects. Class Ib antiarrhythmic drugs have little effect on conduction velocity at normal heart rates but will have greater effects on ↓ conduction and automaticity at higher heart rates with little effect on ↓ refractory period.

DRUG	DOSING	SAFETY/SIDE EFFECTS/MONITORING
Lidocaine *(Xylocaine)* Injection Available in many formulations for local anesthetic effects	1-1.5 mg/kg IV bolus; can repeat bolus 0.5-0.75 mg/kg every 5-10 mins up to 3 mg/kg (cumulative dose); followed by 1-4 mg/min IV infusion Can be given via endotracheal tube (need higher dose – 2-2.5x the IV dose)	**BOXED WARNINGS** Hepatotoxicity (mexiletine only) **CONTRAINDICATIONS** 2nd/3rd degree heart block (unless patient has a functional artificial pacemaker). Lidocaine: Wolff-Parkinson-White syndrome, Adam-Stokes syndrome, allergy to corn or corn-related products or amide type anesthetic
Mexiletine Capsule	200 mg PO Q8H; max 1.2 g/day Take with food	**WARNINGS** Caution in the elderly, hepatic impairment and in patients with HF **SIDE EFFECTS** Lightheadedness, dizziness, incoordination, N/V, tremor, CNS (hallucinations, disorientation, confusion, ataxia) **MONITORING** ECG, BP, LFTs, mental status, electrolytes

Class Ib Antiarrhythmic Drug Interactions

- Lidocaine is a substrate of 3A4 (major), 1A2 (major), and 2C9 (minor); inhibits 1A2 (weak). Amiodarone, beta blockers, and 3A4 inhibitors (e.g., diltiazem, verapamil, grapefruit juice, erythromycin, clarithromycin, itraconazole, ketoconazole, protease inhibitors) ↑ lidocaine levels.

- Mexiletine is a substrate of 1A2 (major) and 2D6 (major); inhibits 1A2 (strong).

Class Ic Antiarrhythmics

Class Ic antiarrhythmic agents are <u>sodium channel blockers</u> and exhibit negative inotropic properties. Propafenone also has significant beta-adrenergic receptor blocking effects. These drugs are <u>absolutely contraindicated in patients with heart failure, significant left ventricular hypertrophy</u> or with a <u>recent myocardial infarction</u> (due to negative inotropic properties). Class Ic antiarrhythmic drugs significantly ↓ conduction velocity and automaticity, but have little-to-no effect on refractory period.

DRUG	DOSING	SAFETY/SIDE EFFECTS/MONITORING
Flecainide Tablet	50-100 mg PO Q12H; max 400 mg/day Store in tight, light-resistant container	**BOXED WARNINGS** When treating atrial flutter, 1:1 atrioventricular conduction may occur; pre-emptive negative chronotropic therapy (e.g., digoxin, beta blockers) may ↓ the risk Proarrhythmic **CONTRAINDICATIONS** 2nd/3rd degree heart block (unless patient has a functional artificial pacemaker), cardiogenic shock, coronary artery disease (heart failure, myocardial infarction), concurrent use of ritonavir **SIDE EFFECTS** <u>Dizziness, visual disturbances</u>, dyspnea **MONITORING** ECG, BP, HR, electrolytes
Propafenone *(Rythmol, Rythmol SR)* Capsule, tablet	IR: 150-300 mg PO Q8H SR: 225-425 mg PO Q12H	**CONTRAINDICATIONS** Sinoatrial and atrioventricular disorders (unless patient has a functional artificial pacemaker), sinus bradycardia, cardiogenic shock, hypotension, bronchospastic disorders **SIDE EFFECTS** <u>Taste disturbance (metallic), dizziness, visual disturbances</u>, N/V **MONITORING** ECG, BP, HR, electrolytes

Class Ic Antiarrhythmic Drug Interactions

- Flecainide is a substrate of 2D6 (major) and 1A2 (minor); inhibits 2D6 (weak).

- Propafenone is a substrate of 2D6 (minor), 3A4 (minor) and 1A2 (minor); inhibits 1A2 and 2D6 (weak).

Class II Antiarrhythmics

Class II antiarrhythmic drugs are <u>beta blockers</u> which block beta-adrenergic receptors and indirectly block <u>calcium channels</u> in the SA and AV nodes, resulting in ↓ automaticity and conduction velocity in the nodes. These drugs are used to <u>slow the ventricular rate</u> in supraventricular tachyarrhythmias. Do not use beta blockers with intrinsic sympathomimetic activity since they do not slow ventricular rate. Please refer to the Hypertension chapter for review of the beta blockers.

Class III Antiarrhythmics

Class III antiarrhythmic drugs all significantly prolong the refractory period. Most drugs in this class act through blockade of potassium channels. Ibutilide is the exception, and works by activating the late inward sodium current which also results in a significant ↑ in refractory period. Amiodarone and drone-darone also block alpha- and beta-adrenergic receptors, and calcium and sodium channels. Sotalol also has significant beta-adrenergic receptor blocking activity.

DRUG	DOSING	SAFETY/SIDE EFFECTS/MONITORING
Amiodarone (Cordarone, Pacerone, Nexterone) Tablet, Injection	**Pulseless VT/VF** 300 mg IV push x 1, may repeat 150 mg x 1 if needed **VT with pulse** 150 mg IV bolus, 1 mg/min x 6 hours, then 0.5 mg/min x 18 hours or longer **AFib** 600-800 mg/day for a 10 gram loading dose, followed by 200 mg daily **Maintenance of NSR in AFib** 400-600 mg/day for 2-4 weeks; then 100-200 mg daily **Ventricular arrhythmias** 800-1,600 mg/day x 1-3 weeks, then 600-800 mg/day x 4 weeks, then 400 mg/day t½ = 40-60 days	**BOXED WARNINGS** For life-threatening arrhythmias only due to toxicity: Patients should be hospitalized when therapy is initiated Pulmonary toxicity Liver toxicity Proarrhythmic: exacerbation of arrhythmias making them more difficult to tolerate or reverse **CONTRAINDICATIONS** Severe sinus-node dysfunction causing marked bradycardia, 2nd/3rd degree heart block (unless patient has a functional artificial pacemaker), bradycardia causing syncope, cardiogenic shock, hypersensitivity to iodine **WARNINGS** Hyper- and hypo-thyroidism (hypo is more common) - amiodarone partially inhibits peripheral conversion of T4 to T3, neurotoxicity (peripheral neuropathy), optic neuropathy (visual impairment), severe skin reactions (SJS/TEN), photosensitivity (slate blue skin discoloration) **SIDE EFFECTS** Hypotension, bradycardia, corneal microdeposits, dizziness, ataxia, N/V constipaton, tremor **MONITORING** ECG, BP, HR, electrolytes, pulmonary function (including chest X-ray) at baseline and annually, LFTs at baseline and every 6 months, thyroid function at baseline and every 3-6 months, ophthalmic exams **NOTES** Pregnancy Category D Infusions longer than 2 hours must be administered in a non-polyvinyl chloride (PVC) container such as polyolefin or glass. Premixed *Nexterone* comes in GALAXY containers which are non-PVC and non-DEHP and can be stored up to 24 months at room temperature. PVC tubing is fine to use. Use a 0.22 micron filter, incompatible with heparin (flush with saline). Premixed IV bag advantages: Longer stability, PVC bag not an issue, available in most commonly used concentrations. If hypotension or bradycardia occurs, slow infusion rate or discontinue. Recommended as a drug of choice in patients with concomitant heart failure. MedGuide required.

Class III Antiarrhythmic Agents Continued

DRUG	DOSING	SAFETY/SIDE EFFECTS/MONITORING
Dronedarone *(Multaq)* Tablet	400 mg PO BID <u>with meals</u> t½ = 13-19 hrs (less lipophilic than amiodarone)	**BOXED WARNINGS** Increased risk of death, stroke, HF in patients with decompensated HF (NYHA Class IV or any class with a recent hospitalization due to HF) or permanent AFib **CONTRAINDICATIONS** 2nd/3rd degree heart block (unless patient has a functional artificial pacemaker), symptomatic HF, HR < 50, concomitant use of strong 3A4 inhibitors, concomitant use of drugs that prolong the QT interval, QT ≥ 500 msec, PR interval > 280 msec, lung or liver toxicity related to previous amiodarone use, severe hepatic impairment, pregnancy, nursing mothers **WARNINGS** Hepatic failure (esp. in the first 6 months), lung disease (including pulmonary fibrosis and pneumonitis), marked ↑ SCr, prerenal azotemia and acute renal failure have been reported usually in the setting of heart failure or hypovolemia, hypokalemia or hypomagnesemia with concomitant administration of potassium-depleting diuretics **SIDE EFFECTS** QT prolongation, ↑ SCr, N/V/D, abdominal pain, diarrhea, bradycardia, asthenia **MONITORING** ECG, BP, HR, electrolytes, renal function, LFTs (especially in the first 6 months) **NOTES** <u>Pregnancy Category X</u> Noniodinated derivative of amiodarone MedGuide required
Sotalol *(Betapace, Betapace AF, Sotylize, Sorine)* Tablet, Solution, Injection Non-selective beta blocker	80 mg PO BID; can ↑ to 160 mg PO BID (monitor QT interval and renal function closely) <u>CrCl 40-60 mL/min:</u> ↓ frequency <u>CrCl < 40 mL/min:</u> varies by formulation	**BOXED WARNINGS** Sotalol can cause life-threatening ventricular tachycardia and QT prolongation; to minimize risk of arrhythmias, initiation (or reinitiation) and dosage increase should be done in a hospital with continuous monitoring and staff familiar with recognizing and treating life-threatening arrhythmias <u>Adjust dosing interval</u> based on <u>creatinine clearance</u> to ↓ risk of proarrhythmia, QT prolongation is directly related to sotalol <u>concentration</u> *Betapace* should not be substituted with *Betapace AF* since *Betapace AF* is distributed with educational information specifically for patients with AFib/Atrial flutter **CONTRAINDICATIONS** 2nd/3rd degree heart block (unless patient has a functional artificial pacemaker), congenital or acquired long QT syndrome, sinus bradycardia, uncontrolled HF, cardiogenic shock, asthma For *Betapace AF, Sotylize, sotalol inj.*: QT > 450 msec, bronchospastic conditions, CrCl < 40 mL/min, K < 4 mEq/L, sick sinus syndrome **SIDE EFFECTS** Bradycardia, palpitations, chest pain, dizziness, fatigue, dyspnea, N/V, hypotension, TdP, HF, bronchoconstriction **MONITORING** ECG, BP, HR, electrolytes, renal function

Class III Antiarrhythmic Agents Continued

DRUG	DOSING	SAFETY/SIDE EFFECTS/MONITORING
Ibutilide *(Corvert)* Injection	≥ 60 kg: 1 mg IV over 10 min < 60 kg: 0.01 mg/kg over 10 min, may repeat x 1 after 10 minutes	**BOXED WARNING** Potentially fatal arrhythmias can occur **SIDE EFFECTS** Ventricular tachycardias (e.g., TdP), headache, hypotension, QT prolongation
Dofetilide *(Tikosyn)* Capsule	500 mcg PO BID CrCl 40-60 mL/min: 250 mcg BID CrCl 20-39 mL/min: 125 mcg BID CrCl < 20 mL/min: avoid T.I.P.S. *(Tikosyn* In Pharmacy System) REMS program – designated to allow retail pharmacies to stock and dispense *Tikosyn*; must be enrolled and staff must be educated. Pharmacists must verify that the hospital/prescriber is a confirmed participant before drug is dispensed.	**BOXED WARNING** Must be initiated (or reinitiated) in a setting with continuous ECG monitoring for a minimum of 3 days **CONTRAINDICATIONS** Patients with congenital or acquired long QT syndromes; concurrent use of cimetidine, dolutegravir, hydrochlorothiazide, itraconazole, ketoconazole, megestrol, prochlorperazine, trimethoprim, verapamil; HR < 50, CrCl < 20 mL/min, QT > 440 msec **SIDE EFFECTS** Headache, dizziness, ventricular tachycardias (e.g., TdP), ↑ QT interval **MONITORING** ECG, BP, HR, electrolytes, renal function; QT interval and CrCl every 3 months (discontinue if corrected QT > 500 msec) **NOTES** A recommended option in patients with heart failure MedGuide required REMS program – available to prescribers and hospitals through *Tikosyn* Education Program. This program provides comprehensive education about the importance of in-hospital treatment initiation and individualized dosing.

Class III Antiarrhythmic Drug Interactions

- All Class III antiarrhythmic agents can have additive QT prolongation with other agents that also prolong the QT interval.

- Use extreme caution with other negative chronotropes (e.g., beta blockers, verapamil, diltiazem, ivabradine) which can ↑ risk of bradycardia with sotalol, amiodarone and dronederone.

- Electrolyte abnormalities (K, Na, Ca, Mg, etc.) should be corrected before any antiarrhythmic treatment is initiated or the risk of arrhythmia is ↑ (true for all antiarrhythmics).

- Do not use grapefruit juice/products. Avoid ephedra and St. John's wort (P-gp inducer).

Amiodarone Drug Interactions

- Amiodarone is an inhibitor of 2C9 (moderate), 2D6 (moderate), 3A4 (weak) and P-gp; major substrate of 3A4 and 2C8 and P-gp. Strong/moderate inhibitors of 3A4, 2C8 and P-gp will ↑ levels of amiodarone and strong/moderate inducers of 3A4, 2C8 and P-gp will ↓ levels of amiodarone.

- When starting amiodarone, ↓ dose of digoxin by 50% and ↓ dose of warfarin by 30 - 50%. Do not exceed 20 mg/day of simvastatin or 40 mg/day of lovastatin in patients taking amiodarone.

- Sofosbuvir may enhance the bradycardic effect of amiodarone.

Dronedarone Drug Interactions

- Dronedarone is a moderate inhibitor of 2D6, 3A4, and P-gp; major substrate of 3A4. Avoid use with strong inhibitors and inducers of 3A4 and other drugs that can prolong the QT interval. If using digoxin, reduce dose of digoxin by 50%. Caution with the use of statins at higher doses (see above under amiodarone).

- Monitor INR after initiating dronedarone in patients taking warfarin.

Dofetilide Drug Interactions

- Dofetilide is a minor 3A4 substrate. Avoid concurrent use with cimetidine, dolutegravir, HCTZ, itraconazole, ketoconazole, megesterol, prochlorperazine, trimethoprim, verapamil and with other QT prolonging agents.

Class IV Antiarrhythmics

Class IV antiarrhythmic drugs block L-type calcium channels, slowing SA and AV nodal conduction velocity. These drugs are used to slow the ventricular rate in supraventricular tachyarrhythmias. Non-dihydropyridine calcium channel blockers should not be used in patients with LV systolic dysfunction (HFrEF) and decompensated HF due to their negative inotropic effects, but they may be used in patients with HF with preserved LV systolic function (HFpEF).

DRUG	DOSING	SAFETY/SIDE EFFECTS/MONITORING
Diltiazem *(Cardizem, Cardizem CD, Cardizem LA, Cartia XT, Dilacor XR, Dilt-CD, Dilt-XR, Diltzac, Tiazac, Taztia XT)* Tablet, Capsule, Injection	120-360 mg PO daily	**CONTRAINDICATIONS** Severe hypotension (systolic < 90 mmHg), 2nd/3rd degree heart block or sick sinus syndrome (unless the patient has a functioning artificial pacemaker), cardiogenic shock, systolic HF, Wolff-Parkinson-White syndrome (WPW) with AFib **WARNINGS** First degree AV block with sinus bradycardia, ↑ LFTs **SIDE EFFECTS** Edema, headache, dizziness, hypotension, arrhythmias, HF, constipation (more with verapamil), gingival hyperplasia
Verapamil *(Calan, Calan SR, Covera HS, Verelan, Verelan PM)* Tablet, Capsule, Injection	180-480 mg PO daily	**MONITORING** ECG, BP, HR, electrolytes, LFTs, renal function **NOTES** Only non-dihydropyridine CCBs are used as antiarrhythmics

For drug interactions/counseling of calcium channel blockers, see Hypertension chapter.

Drugs Not Included In Vaughan Williams Classification

- Adenosine slows conduction through the AV node via activation of adenosine-1 receptors. Adenosine is used to restore normal sinus rhythm (NSR) in paroxysmal supraventricular tachyarrhythmias (PSVTs).

- Digoxin causes direct AV node suppression, ↑ refractory period and ↓ conduction velocity. Digoxin enhances vagal tone, resulting in ↓ ventricular rate in supraventricular tachyarrhythmias. Digoxin reduces the resting heart rate but it is ineffective at controlling the ventricular response during exercise; therefore, it is not used first line for rate control.

DRUG	DOSING	SAFETY/SIDE EFFECTS/MONITORING
Adenosine *(Adenocard)* Injection	Used in paroxysmal supraventricular tachycardia (PSVTs) and not for converting AFib/Atrial flutter or ventricular tachycardia 6 mg IV push (may increase to 12 mg if not responding) t½: less than 10 sec	**CONTRAINDICATIONS** 2nd/3rd degree heart block, sick sinus syndrome or symptomatic bradycardia (except in patients with a functional pacemaker), bronchospastic lung disease **SIDE EFFECTS** Transient new arrhythmia, facial flushing, chest pain/pressure, neck discomfort, dizziness, headache, GI distress, transient ↓ in blood pressure, dyspnea
Digoxin *(Digitek, Digox, Lanoxin)* Tablet, solution, Injection	Available as 0.0625, 0.125, 0.1875, 0.25 mg Typical dose: 0.125-0.25 mg PO daily Loading dose [called total digitalizing dose (TDD)] is: 8-12 mcg/kg. Give ½ of the TDD as the initial dose, followed by ¼ of the TDD in 2 subsequent doses at 4-8 hour intervals. Alternatively, give 0.25 mg IV and repeat dosing to a max of 1.5 mg over 24 hours Therapeutic range for AFib = 0.8-2 ng/mL (lower range for heart failure) When CrCl < 50 mL/min, ↓ dose or ↓ frequency ↓ dose by 20-25% when going from oral to IV Antidote: *DigiFab*	**CONTRAINDICATIONS** Ventricular fibrillation **WARNINGS** 2nd/3rd degree heart block without a pacemaker, Wolff-Parkinson-White syndrome (WPW) with AFib, vesicant - avoid extravasation **SIDE EFFECTS** Dizziness, mental disturbances, headache, N/V/D **MONITORING** ECG, HR, BP, electrolytes, renal function and digoxin level (drawn optimally 12-24 hrs after dose) **Toxicity** Initial s/sx of toxicity are N/V, loss of appetite and bradycardia; severe s/sx of toxicity include blurred/double vision, altered color perception, greenish-yellow halos around lights or objects, abdominal pain, confusion, delirium, prolonged PR interval, arrhythmias **NOTES** Pregnancy Category C Digoxin is not usually given alone; used in combination with a beta blocker or CCB

Digoxin Drug Interactions

- Use caution when administering other drugs that slow HR.

- Digoxin is 50 – 70% cleared by the kidney (unchanged) and partially cleared hepatically. Decreased renal function requires a ↓ digoxin dose. In acute renal failure, digoxin is held.

- Digoxin is a substrate of 3A4 (major) and P-gp. Digoxin levels ↑ with amiodarone, dronedarone, quinidine, verapamil, erythromycin, clarithromycin, itraconazole, propafenone and many other drugs. Reduce digoxin dose by 50% if patient is on amiodarone or dronedarone.

- Hypokalemia, hypomagnesemia and hypercalcemia ↑ the risk of digoxin toxicity.

- Hypothyroidism can ↑ digoxin levels.

Amiodarone Patient Counseling

- Dispense Medication Guide.

- This medication is used to treat certain types of serious (possibly fatal) irregular heartbeat problems called arrhythmias. It is used to restore and maintain the normal heart rhythm and keep a regular, steady heartbeat. Amiodarone works by blocking certain electrical signals in the heart that can cause an irregular heartbeat. This medication has not been shown to help people with these arrhythmias live longer. Treatment should be started in a hospital to monitor your condition.

- Take this medication by mouth, usually once or twice daily or as directed by your healthcare provider. If stomach upset occurs, take the medication with food.

- Severe (sometimes fatal) lung or liver problems have occurred in some rare instances with amiodarone use. Tell your healthcare provider immediately if you experience any of these serious side effects: cough, fever, chills, chest pain, difficult or painful breathing, coughing up blood, severe stomach pain, nausea, vomiting, fatigue, yellowing eyes or skin, or dark-colored urine and new shortness of breath. Your blood will need to be checked, and possibly a chest X-ray during treatment.

- Like other medications used to treat irregular heartbeats, amiodarone can infrequently cause them to become worse. Seek immediate medical attention if your heart continues to pound or skips a beat.

- This drug may infrequently cause serious vision changes. Tell your healthcare provider immediately if you develop any vision changes (such as seeing halos or blurred vision). You will need to have your eyes checked before and during the time you are taking amiodarone.

- You may develop "pins and needles" or numbness in your legs, hands and feet, or muscle weakness or trouble walking. Discuss with your healthcare provider if this happens.

- This drug can change how your thyroid gland works and may cause your metabolism to speed up or slow down. Tell your healthcare provider if you develop any symptoms of low or overactive thyroid including cold or heat intolerance, unexplained weight loss/gain, thinning hair, unusual sweating, nervousness, irritability or restlessness. Discuss this with your healthcare provider; tests can be ordered to check your thyroid function.

- This drug may cause your skin to be more sensitive to the sun. Stay out of the sun during the mid-day and use protective clothing and broad spectrum sunscreen. Infrequently, this medication has caused the skin to become a blue-gray color. This effect is not harmful and usually goes away months after the drug is stopped.

- Do not consume grapefruit or drink grapefruit juice while using this medication. Grapefruit juice can increase the amount of medication in your blood.

- This drug can interact with other medicines. Before starting a new medicine including any over-the-counter medications, discuss with your pharmacist if it is safe to use with amiodarone.

- If you miss a dose, do not take a double dose to make up for the dose you missed. Continue with your next regularly scheduled dose.

Digoxin Patient Counseling

- This medicine helps the heart beat with a more regular rate. Keep taking as directed, even if you feel well.

- Do not stop taking this medicine without talking to your healthcare provider. Stopping suddenly may make your condition worse.

- Avoid becoming overheated or dehydrated as an overdose can occur more easily if you are dehydrated.

- Symptoms of overdose may include nausea, vomiting, diarrhea, loss of appetite, vision changes (such as blurred or yellow/green vision), confusion and hallucinations and feeling like you might pass out. If any of these occur, see your healthcare provider right away.

- There are many medications that can interact with digoxin. Check with your healthcare provider before starting any new medicines, including over the counter, vitamin and/or herbal products.

- To be sure that this medication is not causing harmful effects, your blood may need to be tested on a regular basis. Your kidney function will also need to be monitored.

PRACTICE CASE

AH is a 57 y/o Hispanic male who had an appointment in the clinic this morning. He has asked to speak to the pharmacist at the clinic pharmacy. He tells you that he went to the clinic because he felt like his heart was racing and he felt dizzy. The doctor told him that he has atrial fibrillation. He is concerned that this will affect his life span. You are able to access his clinic records and learn that his past medical history includes heart failure (NYHA Class 3) and hypertension. He is a smoker.

Allergies: Sulfa

Medications:
Digox 0.25 mg PO daily
Lasix 40 mg PO daily
Spironolactone 12.5 mg PO daily
Coreg CR 20 mg PO daily
Lisinopril 40 mg PO daily

Vitals:
BP: 152/83 mmHg   HR: 84 BPM   RR: 15 BPM   Temp: 98.5°F

Labs: Na (mEq/L) = 137 (135 - 145)
K (mEq/L) = 5.2 (3.5 - 5)
Cl (mEq/L) = 99 (95 - 103)
HCO_3 (mEq/L) = 28 (24 - 30)
BUN (mg/dL) = 43 (7 - 20)
SCr (mg/dL) = 1.4 (0.6 - 1.3)
Glucose (mg/dL) = 112 (100 - 125)
Ca (mg/dL) = 9.5 (8.5 - 10.5)
Mg (mEq/L) = 1.8 (1.3 - 2.1)
PO_4 (mg/dL) = 3.8 (2.3 - 4.7)

The cardiologist has written a new prescription for amiodarone 200 mg PO daily that AH would like to have filled.

Questions

1. Before the prescription for amiodarone is filled, the pharmacist should call the doctor to decrease the dose of which of AH's medications?

   a. *Digox*
   b. *Lasix*
   c. Spironolactone
   d. *Coreg CR*
   e. Lisinopril

2. When counseling AH on the use of amiodarone, he should be told to expect periodic monitoring of these organ systems:

   a. Liver, kidney, and eyes
   b. Liver, colon, and kidney
   c. Kidney, gall bladder, and CNS
   d. Thyroid, kidney, and liver
   e. Thyroid, liver, and lungs

3. Which of the following are side effects of amiodarone? (Select **ALL** that apply.)

    a. Skin discoloration

    b. Corneal deposits

    c. Pulmonary fibrosis

    d. Taste perversions

    e. Hypothyroidism

4. AH develops thyroid dysfunction. His doctor switches him to *Multaq* to try and alleviate the problem. Choose the correct therapeutic equivalent for *Multaq*:

    a. Mexiletine

    b. Flecainide

    c. Lidocaine

    d. Dronedarone

    e. Dofetilide

Questions 5-10 do not apply to the above case.

5. What class of antiarrhythmic is disopyramide in the Vaughan Williams classification system?

    a. Ia

    b. Ib

    c. Ic

    d. III

    e. IV

6. A patient has a long QT interval. She is at risk for fatal arrhythmias. Which of the following medications will increase her risk of further QT prolongation? (Select **ALL** that apply.)

    a. *Biaxin*

    b. Ketorolac

    c. Docusate

    d. Escitalopram

    e. Ondansetron

7. A patient is takng *Betapace AF*. Which of the following creatinine clearance values would represent when *Betapace AF* should be taken once daily?

    a. 70 mL/min

    b. 55 mL/min

    c. 29 mL/min

    d. 5 mL/min

    e. *Betapace AF* does not need to be adjusted in renal impairment.

8. A patient is beginning digoxin 0.125 mg daily in addition to her *Lopressor* therapy. After a few weeks, the patient develops an infection with nausea and vomiting. She is weak and dehydrated and is admitted to the hospital. Her work up is significant for new onset acute renal failure, mental confusion, pneumonia and atrial fibrillation. She is started on levofloxacin for her pneumonia. Which of the following statements regarding this patient and her digoxin therapy is true? (Select **ALL** that apply.)

    a. The digoxin may have become toxic due to her decreased renal function.

    b. An elevated digoxin level can worsen nausea and vomiting.

    c. The digoxin level will increase due to the initiation of levofloxacin.

    d. Mental confusion may be due to an elevated digoxin level.

    e. The patient will need to stay on digoxin therapy regardless of the level.

9. Which of the following statement(s) are true regarding *Tikosyn*? (Select **ALL** that apply.)

    a. *Tikosyn* does not need to be dose-adjusted in renal impairment.

    b. *Tikosyn* comes orally and can be started at home.

    c. The generic name is dronedarone.

    d. *Tikosyn* is considered first-line therapy for rate control in patients with atrial fibrillation.

    e. Monitoring of the QT interval and renal function is essential in patients receiving *Tikosyn*.

10. A patient is slightly bradycardic. The physician does not wish to further lower the heart rate. Choose the agent that will least likely cause the patient's heart rate to drop any lower:

    a. Verapamil

    b. Sotalol

    c. Digoxin

    d. Amlodipine

    e. Diltiazem

Answers

1-a, 2-e, 3-a,b,c,e, 4-d, 5-a, 6-a,d,e, 7-b, 8-a,b,d, 9-e, 10-d

ANTICOAGULATION

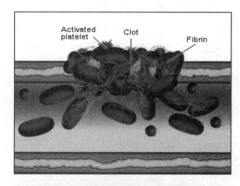

Activated platelet · Clot · Fibrin

GUIDELINES/REFERENCES

January CT, Wann LS, Alpert JS, et al. 2014 AHA/ACC/HRS Guideline for the Management of Patients With Atrial Fibrillation: A Report of the American College of Cardiology/American Heart Association Task Force on Practice Guidelines and the Heart Rhythm Society. *Journal of the American College of Cardiology*. 2014; doi:10.1016/j. jacc.2014.03.022.

Executive Summary of Antithrombotic Therapy and Prevention of Thrombosis, 9th ed: American College of Chest Physicians Evidence-Based Clinical Practice Guidelines. *CHEST* 2012;141(2):7S-47S.

ISMP has many resources on safe use of anticoagulants available at www. ismp.org

BACKGROUND

Anticoagulants are used to prevent blood clots from forming and to keep existing clots from becoming larger or expanding. They do not break down existing clots (like thrombolytics such as tPA). Anticoagulants must be carefully monitored due to the risks involved with either clotting or bleeding. A deep vein thrombosis (DVT) is a blood clot (thrombus) in a vein. DVTs can occur anywhere in the body but are most frequently found in the deep veins of the legs, thighs, and pelvis. A blood clot which has traveled from its point of origin is called an embolus (plural emboli). When a clot forms in a deep vein, the clot or a piece of the clot can break off, travel to the heart and be pumped into the arteries of the lung. This can cause a pulmonary embolism (PE). Venous thromboembolism (VTE) refers to a DVT and/or a PE. Patients with atrial fibrillation or patent foramen ovale (PFO) can form clots in the heart which can travel to the brain causing a transient ischemic attack (TIA) or ischemic stroke. Anticoagulants are used for the prevention and treatment of venous thromboembolism (DVT/PE), for the prevention of stroke, and in the treatment of acute coronary syndrome (ACS).

CLOT FORMATION

Coagulation is the process by which blood clots form. A number of factors can lead to activation of the coagulation process such as blood vessel injury, blood stasis, and prothrombotic conditions. The coagulation process involves activation of platelets and the clotting cascade which leads to fibrin formation and a stable clot. All of the clotting factors have an inactive and an active form. Once activated, the clotting factor will serve to activate the next clotting factor in the sequence until fibrin is formed. The coagulation cascade has two pathways which lead to fibrin formation: the contact activation pathway (or the intrinsic pathway) and the tissue factor pathway (or the extrinsic pathway). Anticoagulants are used to inhibit the clotting cascade, thereby preventing or reducing clot formation.

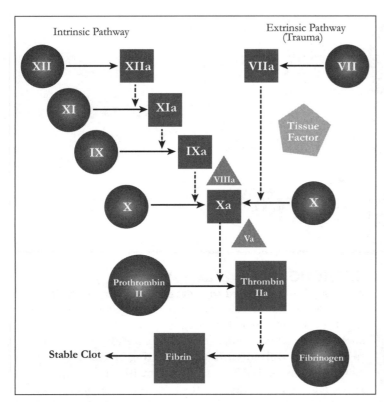

DRUG TREATMENT

Anticoagulants work by various mechanisms. Unfractionated heparin, low molecular weight heparins (LMWHs), and fondaparinux work by binding to antithrombin (AT) causing a conformational change which increases ATs activity 1,000-fold. AT inactivates thrombin and other proteases involved in blood clotting, including factor Xa. LWMHs inhibit factor Xa more specifically than unfractionated heparin. Fondaparinux (Arixtra) is a synthetic pentasaccharide that requires AT binding to selectively inhibit Factor Xa.

Direct thrombin inhibitors (which block thrombin directly, as the name suggests) decrease the amount of fibrin available for clot formation. The intravenous direct thrombin inhibitors have been very important clinically since they do not cross-react with heparin-induced thrombocytopenia (HIT) antibodies. Once HIT develops in the hospital setting, the injectable direct thrombin inhibitor argatroban is the drug of choice. The oral direct thrombin inhibitor, dabigatran (Pradaxa), does not require blood tests to monitor for effectiveness, is not subject to food interactions and has few drug interactions; these are advantages over warfarin. It does, however, cause significant dyspepsia/gastritis and has an increased risk of GI bleeding compared to other oral anticoagulants.

Rivaroxaban (Xarelto), apixaban (Eliquis) and edoxaban (Savaysa) work by inhibiting Factor Xa. These oral agents are taken once or twice daily and require no laboratory monitoring for efficacy. Dabigatran, rivaroxaban, apixaban and edoxaban should not be used in patients with prosthetic heart valves. Warfarin is the drug of choice for these patients.

Warfarin is a vitamin K antagonist. Vitamin K is required for the carboxylation of clotting factors II, VII, IX, and X. Without adequate vitamin K, the liver produces the clotting factors, but they have reduced coagulant activity. Warfarin requires careful patient monitoring with frequent blood tests to measure the INR (international normalized ratio), the test used to measure warfarin's safety and efficacy. Warfarin has a narrow therapeutic range and the INR is highly variable and is affected greatly by many drugs and changes in dietary vitamin K intake.

High Alert Medications

All of the anticoagulants can cause significant bleeding and are classified as "High Alert" medications by the Institute for Safe Medication Practices (ISMP). Bleeding events associated with anticoagulants put patients at risk for increased mortality. The Joint Commission's National Patient Safety Goals require the implementation of policies and protocols to properly initiate and manage anticoagulant therapy. Patients receiving anticoagulants should receive individualized care through a defined process that includes standardized ordering, dispensing, administration, monitoring and patient/caregiver education (for treatment doses). When pharmacists are involved in managing anticoagulants, patient care and outcomes are improved and costs are decreased. Pharmacists are also involved with ensuring that patients who need anticoagulants for VTE prophylaxis – such as orthopedic and cardiac surgical patients – receive them.

VTE PROPHYLAXIS

The CHEST guidelines provide specific recommendations for the prevention of VTE depending on the patient's level of risk. Risk factors for the development of VTE are found in the box. If patients have a contraindication to anticoagulants (such as an active bleed) or have a high risk for bleeding, they will need non-drug alternatives to prevent clotting. These options include intermittent pneumatic compression (IPC) devices or graduated compression stockings (GCS). For acutely ill hospitalized medical patients at increased risk for thrombosis, the recommended drugs and their respective regimens are listed below.

Anticoagulant Recommendations for Acutely Ill Hospitalized Patients at Increased Risk of VTE

DRUG	DOSE
Unfractionated heparin (UFH)	5,000 units SC Q8-12H
Low Molecular Weight Heparin (LMWH)	Enoxaparin 30 mg SC BID or 40 mg SC daily (if CrCl < 30 mL/min, give 30 mg SC daily)
	Dalteparin 2,500-5,000 units SC daily
Factor Xa inhibitor	Fondaparinux 2.5 mg SC daily (do not use if CrCl < 30 mL/min or if patient weighs < 50 kg)
	After Knee/Hip Surgery: Rivaroxaban 10 mg PO daily (do not use if CrCl < 30 mL/min)
	After Knee/Hip Surgery: Apixaban 2.5 mg PO BID
Direct Thrombin Inhibitor	Reduce risk of recurrent DVT: Dabigatran 150 mg BID
	After Hip Replacement Surgery: 110 mg on day 1, then 220 mg daily (do not use if CrCl ≤ 30 mL/min)

RISK FACTORS FOR THE DEVELOPMENT OF VENOUS THROMBOEMBOLISM

Surgery

Major trauma or lower extremity injury

Immobility

Cancer or chemotherapy

Venous compression (tumor, hematoma, arterial abnormality)

Previous venous thromboembolism

Increasing age

Pregnancy and postpartum period

Estrogen-containing medications or selective estrogen receptor modulators

Erythropoiesis-stimulating agents

Acute medical illness

Inflammatory bowel disease

Nephrotic syndrome

Myeloproliferative disorders

Paroxysmal nocturnal hemoglobinuria

Obesity

Central venous catheterization

Inherited or acquired thrombophilia

For long distance travelers at risk for VTE (previous VTE, recent surgery or trauma, active malignancy, pregnancy, estrogen use, advanced age, limited mobility, severe obesity, or known thrombophilic disorder), the following recommendations will ↓ VTE risk: frequent ambulation, calf muscle exercise, sitting in an aisle seat and using graduated compression stockings with 15 – 30 mmHg of pressure at the ankle during travel. Aspirin or anticoagulants should not be used.

VTE TREATMENT

Any VTE that is provoked (caused) either by surgery or a transient (reversible) risk factor should be treated for 3 months. If the VTE is unprovoked, extending therapy longer than 3 months is recommended, as long as the bleeding risk is low-to-moderate. If the risk of bleeding is high, limit the treatment to 3 months. When patients have 2 episodes of unprovoked VTE, long-term treatment may be warranted.

Heparin-Induced Thrombocytopenia (HIT) Overview

Heparin-induced thrombocytopenia is an immune-mediated IgG drug reaction that is associated with a high risk of venous and arterial thrombosis. The immune system forms antibodies against heparin when it binds to platelet factor 4 (PF 4). These IgG antibodies form a complex with heparin and PF 4. In HIT, this complex binds to the Fc receptors on platelets, which leads to further platelet activation, and causes a release of PF 4 and other pro-coagulant microparticles from platelet granules. If left untreated, HIT can lead to a pro-thrombotic state causing many complications including heparin-induced thrombocytopenia and thrombosis (HITT). HITT causes amputations, post-thrombotic syndrome, and/or death. The estimated incidence of HIT is ~3% of those patients exposed to heparin for more than four days. It is lower with a shorter duration of treatment. The typical onset of HIT occurs 5 – 14 days after the start of heparin or within hours if a patient has been exposed to heparin within the past 3 months. A diagnosis is made by a compatible clinical picture, a profound, unexplained drop in platelet count (defined as > 50% drop from baseline) and laboratory confirmation of antibodies or platelet activation by heparin. Although thrombocytopenia is the most common presenting feature of HIT, in up to 25% of patients with HIT, the development of thrombosis precedes the development of thrombocytopenia. Platelets should be checked at baseline and monitored frequently.

Management of HIT Complicated by Thrombosis (HITT) per the CHEST 2012 Guidelines

- If HIT is suspected/confirmed, stop all forms of heparin and LMWH including heparin flushes (can use regional citrate) and heparin-coated catheters. If the patient is on warfarin and diagnosed with HIT, the warfarin should be discontinued and vitamin K should be administered. Although the patient is at a high risk of thrombosis, warfarin use with a low platelet count has a high correlation with warfarin-induced limb gangrene and necrosis.

- In patients with HIT, nonheparin anticoagulants are recommended, in particular, argatroban, over the further use of heparin or LMWH or initiation/continuation of vitamin K antagonists. Argatroban is also favored in patients with renal impairment.

- Do not start warfarin therapy until the platelets have recovered to at least 150,000/mm³. Warfarin should be initiated at lower doses (5 mg maximum). Overlap warfarin with a nonheparin anticoagulant for a minimum of 5 days and until the INR is within target range for 24 hours.

- If urgent cardiac surgery or PCI is required, bivalirudin is the preferred anticoagulant.

UNFRACTIONATED HEPARIN

Unfractionated heparin (UFH) binds to antithrombin (AT) and inactivates thrombin (Factor IIa) and Factor Xa (as well as factors IXa, XIa, XIIa, and plasmin) and prevents the conversion of fibrinogen to fibrin.

DRUG	DOSING	SAFETY/SIDE EFFECTS/MONITORING
Unfractionated Heparin Anticoagulation Treatment/ Prophylaxis Many strengths and volumes (ranging from 1 unit/mL to 20,000 units/mL), including total units of 5,000, 10,000, 12,500, 20,000, 25,000 & others. Usual infusion for treatment is 25,000 units in 250 mL (concentration: 100 units/ mL) in D5W, ½ NS or NS. Line Flush 10 units/mL, 100 units/mL syringes (in 1, 2, 2.5, 3, 5, 10, 30 mL), others **SAFETY NOTE** Heparin lock-flushes *(HepFlush)* are used to keep IV lines open (patent), not used for anticoagulation. There have been fatal errors, especially in neonates, made by choosing the incorrect heparin strength. Heparin injection 10,000 units/ mL and heparin flushes 10 or 100 units/mL look and sound alike. Using a higher dose to flush a line could cause fatal hemorrhage. Refer to the Medication Safety & Quality Improvement chapter for safe use of antithrombotics.	**Prophylaxis of VTE** 5,000 units SC Q8-12H **Treatment of VTE** 80 units/kg IV bolus followed by 18 units/kg/hr infusion or a fixed dose of 5,000 units IV bolus followed by 1,000 units/hr infusion. If treating as an outpatient, give 333 units/kg x 1 dose SC, then 250 units/kg SC Q12H **Treatment of ACS/STEMI** 60 units/kg IV bolus (max 4,000 units); 12 units/kg/hr (max 1,000 units/hr) infusion Use actual body weight for dosing Onset IV: immediate; SC: 20-30 min t½ = 1.5 hrs. Monitor for a ↓ in platelet count of > 50% from baseline. HIT has cross-sensitivity with LMWHs Antidote: Protamine – 1 mg protamine will reverse ~100 units of heparin; max dose 50 mg	**CONTRAINDICATIONS** Uncontrolled active bleed (ICH), severe thrombocytopenia, history of HIT, hypersensitivity to pork products. Some products contain benzyl alcohol as a preservative, use of these products is contraindicated in neonates, infants, pregnancy and breastfeeding **WARNING** Do not give IM due to hematoma risk Fatal medication errors: must examine product that the correct concentration is chosen **SIDE EFFECTS** Bleeding (epistaxis, ecchymosis, gingival, GI), thrombocytopenia, heparin induced thrombocytopenia (HIT), hyperkalemia and osteoporosis (with long-term use) **MONITORING** aPTT (or anti-Xa level: 0.3-0.7 units/mL) aPTT is taken 6 hours after initiation, every 6 hours until therapeutic range of 1.5-2.5 x control (patient's baseline) is reached, then every 24 hours. Also check aPTT after every dosage change. Platelets, Hgb, Hct at baseline and daily to monitor for thrombocytopenia and bleeding **NOTES** Pregnancy Category C Unpredictable anticoagulant response – has variable and extensive binding to plasma proteins and cells

Heparin Drug Interactions

- Most drug interactions are due to additive effects with other drugs that can ↑ bleeding risk (other anticoagulants, antiplatelet drugs, some herbals, NSAIDs, SSRIs, SNRIs, thrombolytics, others). See the Drug Interactions chapter.

LOW MOLECULAR WEIGHT HEPARINS

Low molecular weight heparins (LMWHs) bind to AT and have a greater affinity of inhibiting Factor Xa than Factor IIa.

DRUG	DOSING	SAFETY/SIDE EFFECTS/MONITORING
Enoxaparin *(Lovenox)* Multidose vial (300 mg/3 mL) and prefilled syringes: 30 mg/0.3 mL, 40 mg/0.4 mL, 60 mg/0.6 mL, 80 mg/0.8 mL, 100 mg/mL, 120 mg/0.8 mL, 150 mg/mL 1 mg = 100 units Anti-Xa activity	**Prophylaxis of VTE** 30 mg SC Q12H or 40 mg SC daily CrCl < 30 mL/min: 30 mg SC daily **Treatment of VTE and UA/NSTEMI** 1 mg/kg SC Q12H (or 1.5 mg/kg SC daily for VTE inpatient treatment only) CrCl < 30 mL/min: 1 mg/kg SC daily **Treatment for STEMI** Patients < 75 years: 30 mg IV bolus plus a 1 mg/kg SC dose followed by 1 mg/kg SC Q12H (max 100 mg for the first two doses only) CrCl < 30 mL/min: 30 mg IV bolus plus a 1 mg/kg SC dose, followed by 1 mg/kg SC daily Patients ≥ 75 years: 0.75 mg/kg SC Q12H (no bolus – max 75 mg for the first two doses only) CrCl < 30 mL/min: 1 mg/kg SC daily (no bolus) Patients managed with percutaneous coronary intervention (PCI): if the last SC dose was given 8-12 hours before balloon inflation, give 0.3 mg/kg IV bolus	**BOXED WARNING** Patients receiving neuraxial anesthesia (epidural, spinal) or undergoing spinal puncture are at risk of hematomas and subsequent paralysis. **CONTRAINDICATIONS** History of HIT, active major bleed, hypersensitivity to pork **SIDE EFFECTS** Bleeding, anemia, ↑ LFTs, thrombocytopenia, hyperkalemia, injection site reactions (bruising) **MONITORING** Anti-Xa level monitoring is recommended in pregnancy and in patients with mechanical heart valves. Monitoring may be done in obesity, low body weight, pediatrics, elderly or renal insufficiency. aPTT is not used. Obtain peak anti-Xa levels 4 hours post dose. VTE treatment (enoxaparin daily): 1-2 anti-Xa units/mL VTE treatment (enoxaparin Q12H): 0.6-1 anti-Xa units/mL Recurrent VTE prophylaxis in pregnancy: 0.2-0.6 anti-Xa units/mL Monitor platelets, Hgb, Hct, SCr **NOTES** Pregnancy Category B More predictable anticoagulant response compared to heparin and does not require anti-Xa level monitoring in most cases. This makes LMWH more cost effective even though the actual drug costs more than UFH. Do not expel air bubble from syringe prior to injection. Do not administer IM. Store at room temperature. Largely neutralized by protamine.
Dalteparin *(Fragmin)*	**Prophylaxis of VTE** 2,500-5,000 units SC daily **Treatment of UA/NSTEMI** 120 units/kg (max 10,000 units) Q12H	

LMWH Drug Interactions

- Most drug interactions are due to additive effects with other drugs that can ↑ bleeding risk (other anticoagulants, antiplatelet drugs, some herbals, NSAIDs, SSRIs, SNRIs, thrombolytics, others). See the Drug Interactions chapter.

FACTOR Xa INHIBITORS

Fondaparinux *(Arixtra)* is a synthetic pentasaccharide that selectively inhibits Factor Xa via antithrombin (AT). Therefore, it is an indirect inhibitor of Factor Xa. Rivaroxaban *(Xarelto)*, apixaban *(Eliquis)* and edoxaban *(Savaysa)* are direct Factor Xa inhibitors and are available orally. Fondaparinux is often used off label in clinical practice for HIT.

DRUG	DOSING	SAFETY/SIDE EFFECTS/MONITORING

Injectable Indirect Factor Xa Inhibitor (SC)

Fondaparinux *(Arixtra)* Prefilled syringes: 2.5 mg/0.5 mL, 5 mg/0.4 mL, 7.5 mg/0.6 mL, 10 mg/0.8 mL	**Prophylaxis of VTE** ≥ 50 kg: 2.5 mg SC daily < 50 kg: contraindicated **Treatment of VTE** < 50 kg: 5 mg SC daily 50-100 kg: 7.5 mg SC daily > 100 kg: 10 mg SC daily	**BOXED WARNING** Patients receiving neuraxial anesthesia (epidural, spinal) or undergoing spinal puncture are at risk of hematomas and subsequent paralysis. **CONTRAINDICATIONS** Severe renal impairment (CrCl < 30 mL/min), active major bleed, bacterial endocarditis, thrombocytopenia with positive test for anti-platelet antibodies in presence of fondaparinux, body weight < 50 kg (prophylaxis only) **SIDE EFFECTS** Bleeding (epistaxis, ecchymosis, gingival, GI, etc.), anemia, local injection site reactions (rash, pruritus, bruising), thrombocytopenia, hypokalemia, hypotension **MONITORING** Anti-Xa levels, CBC, platelets, Hgb, Hct, SCr Anti-Xa levels should be obtained 3 hours post dose. **NOTES** Pregnancy Category B Do not expel air bubble from syringe prior to injection. No antidote. Do not administer IM. Store at room temperature.

Factor Xa Inhibitors Continued

DRUG	DOSING	SAFETY/SIDE EFFECTS/MONITORING

Oral Direct Factor Xa Inhibitors

DRUG	DOSING	SAFETY/SIDE EFFECTS/MONITORING
Rivaroxaban *(Xarelto)* Tablet **Missed Dose** Administer the dose as soon as possible on the same day as follows: If taking 15 mg twice daily: take immediately to ensure intake of 30 mg/day. In this particular instance, two 15 mg tablets may be taken at once. Then resume regular schedule on the following day. If taking 10, 15 or 20 mg once daily: take immediately on the same day; otherwise skip.	**Nonvalvular AFib** CrCl > 50 mL/min: 20 mg PO daily with evening meal CrCl 15-50 mL/min: 15 mg PO daily with evening meal CrCl < 15 mL/min: avoid use **Treatment of DVT/PE** 15 mg PO BID with food x 21 days, then 20 mg PO daily with food. CrCl < 30 mL/min: avoid use **Prophylaxis for DVT (after knee/hip replacement)** 10 mg PO daily – without regards to meals (for 12 days after knee or 35 days after hip replacement surgery). Give first dose 6-10 hours after surgery CrCl < 30 mL/min: avoid use **Reduction in the Risk of Recurrence of DVT and PE** 20 mg PO daily with food CrCl < 30 mL/min: avoid use	**BOXED WARNINGS** Patients receiving neuraxial anesthesia (epidural, spinal) or undergoing spinal puncture are at risk of hematomas and subsequent paralysis Premature discontinuation ↑ risk of thrombotic events **CONTRAINDICATIONS** Active pathological bleed **WARNINGS** Avoid in patients with moderate to severe hepatic impairment Not recommended with prosthetic heart valves **SIDE EFFECTS** Bleeding, anemia **MONITORING** CBC with differential; renal function, LFTs **NOTES** Pregnancy Category C/B (apixaban) No antidote. No monitoring of efficacy required. Discontinue 24 hours prior to elective surgery (rivaroxaban). Discontinue 48 hours prior to elective surgery with moderate-high bleeding risk or 24 hours prior with a low bleeding risk (apixaban). Can be crushed and put on applesauce (rivaroxaban) or down NG tube (rivaroxaban, apixaban).
Apixaban *(Eliquis)* Tablet **Missed Dose** Take immediately on the same day and twice daily administration should be resumed. The dose should not be doubled to make up for a missed dose.	**Nonvalvular AFib** 5 mg BID Unless patient has at least 2 of the following: age ≥ 80 years, body weight ≤ 60 kg, or SCr ≥ 1.5 mg/dL, give 2.5 mg BID **Treatment of DVT/PE** 10 mg PO BID x 7 days, then 5 mg PO BID **Prophylaxis for DVT (after knee/hip replacement)** 2.5 mg PO BID (for 12 days after knee or 35 days after hip replacement surgery). Give first dose 12-24 hours after surgery **Reduction in the Risk of Recurrence of DVT and PE** 2.5 mg PO BID after at least 6 months of treatment for DVT or PE	

Factor Xa Inhibitors Continued

DRUG	DOSING	SAFETY/SIDE EFFECTS/MONITORING
Edoxaban *(Savaysa)* Tablet **Missed Dose** Take immediately on the same day. The dose should not be doubled to make up for a missed dose.	**Nonvalvular AFib** CrCl > 95 mL/min: do not use CrCl 51-95 mL/min: 60 mg daily CrCl 15-50 mL/min: 30 mg daily **Treatment of DVT/PE** 60 mg daily CrCl 15-50 mL/min or body weight ≤ 60 kg or on certain P-gp inhibitors: 30 mg daily CrCl < 15 mL/min: use not recommended	**BOXED WARNINGS** Reduced efficacy in nonvalvular AFib patients with CrCl > 95 mL/min Patients receiving neuraxial anesthesia (epidural, spinal) or undergoing spinal puncture are at risk of hematomas and subsequent paralysis Premature discontinuation ↑ risk of ischemic events **CONTRAINDICATIONS** Active pathological bleed **WARNINGS** Not recommended with prosthetic heart valves, moderate to severe hepatic impairment **SIDE EFFECTS** Bleeding, anemia, rash, ↑ LFTs **MONITORING** Renal function, LFTs, CBC **NOTES** Pregnancy Category C No antidote. No monitoring of efficacy required. Discontinue 24 hours prior to elective surgery.

Factor Xa Inhibitor Drug Interactions

- Rivaroxaban is a substrate of 3A4 (major) and P-gp. Avoid concomitant use with drugs that are combined P-gp and strong 3A4 inducers (e.g., carbamazepine, phenytoin, rifampin, St. John's wort) or combined P-gp and strong 3A4 inhibitors (e.g., ketoconazole, itraconazole, lopinavir/ritonavir, ritonavir, indinavir, and conivaptan). The benefit must outweigh the potential risks in these situations: CrCl 15-80 mL/min who are receiving combined P-gp and moderate 3A4 inhibitors (e.g., diltiazem, verapamil, dronedarone, erythromycin).

- Apixaban is a substrate of 3A4 (major) and P-gp. Avoid concomitant use with strong dual inducers of 3A4 and P-gp (e.g., carbamazepine, phenytoin, rifampin, St. John's wort). For patients receiving doses > 2.5 mg BID, the dose of apixaban should be decreased by 50% when coadministered with drugs that are strong dual inhibitors of 3A4 and P-gp (e.g., clarithromycin, itraconazole, ketoconazole, or ritonavir). For patients taking 2.5 mg BID, avoid these strong dual inhibitors.

- Edoxaban is a substrate of P-gp; avoid concomitant use with rifampin.

- See Drug Interactions chapter for drugs that can ↑ bleeding risk.

- Drugs that ↑ clotting risk (including estrogen and SERMs) should be discontinued.

Conversion Between Anticoagulants

ORAL FACTOR XA INHIBITORS	
Oral Factor Xa inhibitors to warfarin	Stop Factor Xa inhibitor and start parenteral anticoagulant and warfarin at next scheduled dose of the Factor Xa inhibitor
Warfarin to apixaban	Stop warfarin and start apixaban when INR < 2
Warfarin to edoxaban	Stop warfarin and start edoxaban when INR ≤ 2.5
Warfarin to rivaroxaban	Stop warfarin and start rivaroxaban when INR < 3
ORAL DIRECT THROMBIN INHIBITOR	
Dabigatran to warfarin	CrCl > 50 mL/min: Start warfarin 3 days before stopping dabigatran CrCl 30-50 mL/min: Start warfarin 2 days before stopping dabigatran CrCl 15-30 mL/min: Start warfarin 1 day before stopping dabigatran CrCl < 15 mL/min: No recommendations can be made
Warfarin to dabigatran	Stop warfarin and start dabigatran when INR < 2

DIRECT THROMBIN INHIBITORS

These agents directly inhibit thrombin (Factor IIa); they bind to the active thrombin site of free and clot-associated thrombin.

DRUG	DOSING	SAFETY/SIDE EFFECTS/MONITORING

Direct Thrombin Inhibitors (injectable; IV or SC)

DRUG	DOSING	SAFETY/SIDE EFFECTS/MONITORING
Argatroban Indicated for HIT and in patients undergoing PCI who are at risk for HIT **Bivalirudin _(Angiomax)_** Indicated for patients with ACS undergoing PCI and are at risk for HIT	**HIT** Initial: 2 mcg/kg/min – titrate to target aPTT. Max: 10 mcg/kg/min **PCI** IV drugs given as a bolus followed by an infusion; all are weight-based Used in patients with a history of HIT Argatroban – ↓ dose in hepatic impairment Bivalirudin – ↓ dose when CrCl < 30 mL/min	**CONTRAINDICATIONS** Active major bleeding **SIDE EFFECTS** Bleeding, anemia, hematoma **MONITORING** aPTT and/or ACT (for bivalirudin), platelets, Hgb, Hct, renal function **NOTES** Pregnancy Category B No cross-reaction with HIT. No antidote. Argatroban can ↑ INR; if starting on warfarin concurrently do not use a loading dose of warfarin; dose cautiously.
Desirudin _(Iprivask)_ Indicated for VTE prevention after hip arthroplasty	15 mg SC Q12H CrCl < 60 mL/min: ↓ dose	**BOXED WARNING** Patients receiving neuraxial anesthesia (epidural, spinal) or undergoing spinal puncture are at risk of hematomas and subsequent paralysis. **MONITORING** aPTT, renal function, CBC **NOTES** Pregnancy Category C No antidote

Direct Thrombin Inhibitors Continued

DRUG	DOSING	SAFETY/SIDE EFFECTS/MONITORING

Direct Thrombin Inhibitor (oral)

Dabigatran *(Pradaxa)* Capsules **Missed Dose** Take immediately <u>unless it is within 6 hours</u> of next scheduled dose; do not double up.	**Nonvalvular AFib** 150 mg BID CrCl 15-30 mL/min: 75 mg BID CrCl < 15 mL/min: no recommendations **Treatment of DVT/PE and Reduction in the Risk of Recurrence of DVT and PE** 150 mg BID, start after 5-10 days of parenteral anticoagulation CrCl ≤ 30 mL/min: no recommedations **Prophylaxis of DVT/PE following hip replacement surgery** 110 mg on day 1, then 220 mg daily CrCl ≤ 30 mL/min: no recommendations <u>Take with a full glass of water (with or without food). Swallow capsules whole. Do not break, chew, crush or open.</u> <u>Keep in original container. Discard 4 months after opening the original container.</u> Keep bottle tightly closed to protect from moisture. Blister packs are good until the date on the pack	**BOXED WARNINGS** Patients receiving neuraxial anesthesia (epidural, spinal) or undergoing spinal puncture are at risk of hematomas and subsequent paralysis. Premature discontinuation ↑ risk of thrombotic events. **CONTRAINDICATIONS** Active pathological bleed and patients with mechanical prosthetic heart valve(s) **SIDE EFFECTS** <u>Dyspepsia, gastritis-like symptoms, bleeding (including more GI bleeding)</u> **MONITORING** Renal function, CBC with differential **NOTES** Pregnancy Category C Can ↑ aPTT, PT/INR Dabigatran prevents 5 more strokes per 1,000 patients/year than warfarin (therefore preferred by CHEST guidelines for stroke prevention in nonvalvular AFib). These guidelines came out before rivaroxaban and apixaban were approved. Discontinue if undergoing invasive surgery (1-2 days before if CrCl ≥ 50 mL/min, 3-5 days before if CrCl < 50 mL/min). <u>No antidote. No monitoring of efficacy required.</u> <u>Store in a cool, dry place; not in bathrooms.</u> <u>Do not put down an NG tube.</u>

Dabigatran Drug Interactions

- Dabigatran is a substrate of P-gp; avoid concomitant use with rifampin.

- Nonvalvular AFib: If patients have a CrCl 30-50 mL/min and taking P-gp inhibitors (dronedaone or systemic ketoconazole), reduce dose to 75 mg BID. In severe renal impairment (CrCl 15-30 mL/min), avoid concomitant use of P-gp inhibitors.

- Other indications: Avoid concomitant P-gp inhibitors in patients with CrCl < 50 mL/min.

- See Drug Interactions chapter for drugs that can ↑ bleeding risk.

- Drugs that ↑ clotting risk (including estrogen and SERMs) should be discontinued.

WARFARIN (COUMADIN, JANTOVEN)

Warfarin <u>competitively inhibits</u> the C1 subunit of the multi-unit <u>vitamin K epoxide reductase (VKORC1) enzyme complex</u>, thereby reducing the regeneration of vitamin K epoxide and causing <u>depletion of active clotting factors II, VII, IX and X and proteins C and S.</u>

DRUG	DOSING	SAFETY/SIDE EFFECTS/MONITORING
Warfarin *(Coumadin, Jantoven)* Tablet <u>Racemic mixture of R- and S- enantiomers with the S- enantiomer being 2.7-3.8 times more potent</u> **Missed Dose** Take immediately on the same day. Do not double the dose the next day to make up for a missed dose	Healthy outpatients: 10 mg daily for first 2 days, then adjust dose per <u>INR</u> values <u>Lower doses (≤ 5 mg)</u> for elderly, malnourished, taking drugs which can ↑ warfarin levels, liver disease, heart failure, or have a high risk of bleeding Take at the same time each day Tablet colors: 1 mg (pink) 2 mg (lavender) 2.5 mg (green) 3 mg (tan) 4 mg (blue) 5 mg (peach) 6 mg (teal) 7.5 mg (yellow) 10 mg (white) See Study Tip on the next page Highly protein bound (99%)	**BOXED WARNING** Major or fatal bleeding **CONTRAINDICATIONS** Hemorrhagic tendencies, blood dyscrasias, uncontrolled hypertension, non-compliance, recent or potential surgery of the eye or CNS, major regional lumbar block anesthesia or traumatic surgery resulting in large open surfaces, pericarditis or pericardial effusion, bacterial endocarditis, (pre-)eclampsia, threatened abortion, pregnancy (except with mechanical heart valves at high risk for thromboembolism) **WARNINGS** <u>Tissue necrosis/gangrene</u>, systemic atheroemboli and cholesterol microemboli, <u>HIT</u> (contraindicated as monptherapy in the initial treatment of active HIT), <u>presence of 2C9*2 or *3 alleles and/or polymorphism of VKORC1</u> gene may increase bleeding risk (routine genetic testing is not currently recommended - see Pharmacogenomics chapter) **SIDE EFFECTS** <u>Bleeding, skin necrosis, purple toe syndrome</u> **MONITORING** INR target is 2.5, range 2-3, for most indications (DVT, AFib, bioprosthetic mitral valve, mechanical aortic valve, antiphospholipid syndrome) and should be <u>2.5-3.5</u> for some high-risk indications such as a <u>mechanical mitral</u> valve or <u>2 mechanical heart valves</u>. INR monitoring to begin after the initial 2 or 3 doses, or if on a chronic, stable dose of warfarin, monitor at intervals up to 12 weeks. Hct, Hgb, signs of bleeding **NOTES** <u>Pregnancy Category X/D</u> (women with mechanical heart valves) <u>Antidote: vitamin K</u> Dental cleanings and single tooth extraction do not generally require a change in warfarin dosing if INR is in therapeutic range.

Warfarin – Pharmacokinetic Drug Interactions

- Warfarin is a substrate of CYP 2C9 (major), 1A2 (minor), 2C19 (minor) and 3A4 (minor) and an inhibitor of 2C9 (weak) and 2C19 (weak). Avoid use with tamoxifen.

- 2C9 inducers – including aprepitant, bosentan, carbamazepine, phenobarbital, phenytoin, primidone, <u>rifampin</u> (large ↓ INR), licorice, St. John's Wort – can ↓ INR.

- 2C9 inhibitors – including amiodarone, azole antifungals (e.g., <u>fluconazole</u>, ketoconazole, voriconazole), capecitabine, etravirine, fluvastatin, fluvoxamine, macrolide antibiotics, <u>metronidazole</u>, tigecycline, <u>TMP/SMX</u>, zafirlukast – can ↑ INR. See Drug Interactions chapter.

- Antibiotics: Penicillins, including amoxicillin, some cephalosporins, fluoroquinolones, macrolides, TMP/SMX and tetracyclines can enhance the anticoagulant effect of warfarin – monitor INR.

- Check for 1A2, 2C19 and 3A4 interactions; these occur, but usually have less of an effect on INR.

- When starting <u>amiodarone</u>, ↓ the dose of warfarin by 30-50%.

Warfarin – Pharmacodynamic Drug Interactions

- The most common pharmacodynamic interactions are with NSAIDs, antiplatelet agents, other anticoagulants, SSRIs and SNRIs. <u>These interactions ↑ bleeding risk, but the INR may be in the usual range or slightly elevated.</u>

- Drugs that ↑ clotting risk (including estrogen and SERMs) should be discontinued.

Herbal/Natural Product Drug Interactions

- Several natural medicines may ↑ bleeding risk including bromelain, danshen (can ↑ INR), dong quai (can ↑ INR), vitamin E, evening primrose oil, high doses of fish oils, garlic, ginger, ginkgo biloba, ginseng, glucosamine (can ↑ INR), goldenseal, grapefruit (can ↑ INR), policosanol, willow bark and wintergreen oil (can ↑ INR). There are other herbal products that can ↑ the bleeding risk with warfarin.

- Some products may ↓ the effectiveness of warfarin including alfalfa, American ginseng, green tea and coenzyme Q-10. Per the package insert, American ginseng may decrease the effects of warfarin. There is evidence that both American and Panax ginseng inhibit platelet aggregation, which potentially has the opposite effect. Monitor INR closely if patients are taking ginseng.

- Any additions of vitamin K will ↓ the INR. Check any nutritional products for vitamin K content. Stay consistent with the amount of vitamin K consumed through the diet (see foods high in vitamin K box).

FOODS HIGH IN VITAMIN K

Broccoli	Lettuce (red leaf or butterhead)
Brussels sprouts	
Cabbage	Mustard greens
Canola oil	Parsley
Cauliflower	Soybean Oil
Chickpeas	Spinach
Cole Slaw	Swiss chard
Collard Greens	Tea (green or black)
Coriander	
Endive	Turnip greens
Green kale	Watercress

Warfarin Use – Key Points from CHEST 2012 Guidelines

- In healthy outpatients, the initial starting dose of warfarin should be 10 mg daily for the first 2 days, then adjust per INR values.

- For patients with stable therapeutic INRs presenting with a single subtherapeutic INR value, routinely bridging with heparin is not recommended.

- Routine pharmacogenomic testing is not recommended at this time.

- For patients with consistently <u>stable</u> INRs on warfarin therapy, INR testing can be done up to every 12 weeks rather than every 4 weeks.

- For patients with previously stable therapeutic INRs who present with a single out-of-range INR of ≤ 0.5 below or above the therapeutic range, continue current dose and obtain another INR within 1-2 weeks.

- Routine use of vitamin K supplementation is not recommended in patients taking warfarin.

- Start warfarin therapy on the same day as the parenteral anticoagulant (e.g., enoxaparin) and continue <u>both anticoagulants for a minimum of 5 days and until the INR is 2 or above for at least 24 hours</u>. Once the INR is therapeutic for 24 hours, the parenteral anticoagulant can be discontinued.

- Warfarin is highly protein bound, therefore caution is advised with other highly protein bound drugs that may displace warfarin such as phenytoin, valproic acid and others.

Use of Vitamin K for High (Supratherapeutic) INRs

Variable INRs are a norm of clinical practice. Elevated INRs can scare the clinician due to increased risk of bleeding. It is important to know how to treat patients with high INR values. Vitamin K is used for reversal (to ↓ INR quickly) by itself or with other agents for life-threatening bleeds described later in this section. Bleeding, at any INR, will warrant more serious intervention.

<u>Oral formulations of vitamin K (generally at doses of 2.5-5 mg) are preferred in patients without significant or major bleeding</u>. Vitamin K given subcutaneous (SC) has a slow onset and a variable response; therefore, <u>SC injections should be avoided</u>. The <u>intramuscular (IM) route should also be avoided</u> due to the risk of hematoma formation. Intravenous administration should be given <u>only</u> when the patient is experiencing serious bleeding. <u>IV injection</u> is reported to cause anaphylaxis in 3 of out 100,000 patients: <u>infuse slowly</u>.

Use of Vitamin K for Overanticoagulation

SYMPTOMS/INR VALUE	WHAT TO DO
INR above therapeutic range but < 4.5	Reduce or skip warfarin dose. Monitor INR. Resume warfarin when INR therapeutic. Dose reduction may not be needed if only slightly above therapeutic range.
For patients with a supratherapeutic INR of 4.5-10 without bleeding	Routine use of vitamin K is <u>not</u> recommended if no evidence of bleeding. Hold 1-2 doses of warfarin. Monitor INR. Resume warfarin at lower dose when INR therapeutic. Vitamin K can be used if urgent surgery needed (≤ 5 mg, with additional 1-2 mg in 24 hours if needed) or bleeding risk is high (1-2.5 mg).
For patients with INR > 10 without bleeding	Hold warfarin. Give <u>oral</u> vitamin K 2.5-5 mg even if not bleeding. Monitor INR. Resume warfarin at a lower dose when INR is therapeutic.
For patients with major bleeding from warfarin	Hold warfarin therapy. Give vitamin K 5-10 mg by slow <u>IV</u> injection and four-factor prothrombin complex concentrate (PCC). PCC suggested over fresh frozen plasma (FFP) due to risks of allergic reactions, infection transmission, longer preparation time, slower onset and higher volume.

Anticoagulant Antidotes

Protamine combines with strongly acidic heparin to form a stable salt complex neutralizing the anticoagulant activity of both drugs. Phytonadione provides an essential vitamin for liver synthesis of clotting factors (II, VII, IX, X). *Kcentra* is a newer product available as a single-use vial containing coagulation Factors II, VII, IX and X, and antithrombotic proteins C and S as a lyophilized concentrate. It is <u>indicated for the urgent reversal of warfarin</u> along with vitamin K.

ANTIDOTE	DOSING	SAFETY/SIDE EFFECTS/MONITORING

For heparin/LMWH reversal

| **Protamine**

Injection
10 mg/mL
(5 mL, 25 mL) | 1 mg protamine will reverse ~100 units of heparin – reverse the amount of heparin given in the last 2-2.5 hours; max dose: 50 mg

Enoxaparin given within last 8 hours:
1 mg protamine per
1 mg of enoxaparin

Enoxaparin given
> 8 hours ago: 0.5 mg protamine per
1 mg of enoxaparin

Dalteparin: 1 mg protamine for each 100 anti-Xa units of dalteparin | **BOXED WARNING**
Hypotension, cardiovascular collapse, non-cardiogenic pulmonary edema, pulmonary vasoconstriction, and pulmonary hypertension may occur.

SIDE EFFECTS
Hypotension, bradycardia, flushing, anaphylaxis

MONITORING
aPTT, anti-Xa levels, cardiac monitoring required (ECG, BP, HR)

NOTES
Rapid IV infusion causes hypotension. Administer slow IV push (50 mg over 10 minutes). Inject without further dilution over 1-3 minutes. |

For warfarin reversal

| **Vitamin K or Phytonadione** *(Mephyton)*

5 mg tablets

1 mg/0.5 mL, 10 mg/mL injection | 1-10 mg PO/IV

If given IV, infuse slowly; rate of infusion should not exceed 1 mg/min

To ↓ risk of anaphylaxis, dilute dose in a minimum of 50 mL of compatible solution and administer using an infusion pump over at least 20 minutes | **BOXED WARNINGS**
Severe reactions resembling hypersensitivity reactions (e.g., anaphylaxis) have occurred rarely during or immediately after IV administration (even with proper dilution and rate of administration); some patients had no previous exposure to phytonadione

SIDE EFFECTS
Anaphylaxis, flushing, rash, dizziness

NOTES
Requires light protection during administration

SC route not recommended due to variable absorption

IM route not recommended due to risk of hematoma

Orlistat and mineral oil ↓ vitamin K oral absorption |
| **Four Factor Prothrombin Complex Concentrate** (Human) *(Kcentra)*

Injection

Factors II, VII, IX, X, Protein C, Protein S | IV dose is based on patient's INR and body weight

Do not let drug back-up into line; will clot.

Refrigerate; allow to reach room temp prior to administration.

Do not repeat dose | **BOXED WARNING**
Arterial and venous thromboembolic complications have been reported

CONTRAINDICATIONS
Disseminated intravascular coagulation (DIC) and known heparin-induced thrombocytopenia (contains heparin)

WARNINGS
Made from human blood and may carry risk of transmitting infectious agents

SIDE EFFECTS
HA, N/V/D, arthralgia, hypotension, ↓ K, thrombotic events

NOTES
Administer vitamin K concurrently |

Anticoagulant Antidotes Continued

ANTIDOTE	DOSING	SAFETY/SIDE EFFECTS/MONITORING
Three Factor Prothrombin Complex Concentrates (Human) (*Bebulin, Profilnine*) Off label	Weight-based dosing given IV slowly Given with Fresh Frozen Plasma (FFP) or Factor VIIa	**BOXED WARNINGS** HIT *(Bebulin)* **WARNINGS** *Bebulin* and *Profilnine* contain Factors II, IX and X but low or nontherapeutic levels of factor VII and should not be confused with Prothrombin Complex Concentrate (Human) [(Factors II, VII, IX, X), Protein C, Protein S] (*Kcentra*) which contains therapeutic levels of factor VII. Made from human blood and may carry risk of transmitting infectious agents (e.g., viruses) **SIDE EFFECTS** Chills, fever, flushing, nausea, headache, risk of thrombosis **NOTES** Due to ADRs may need to slow infusion and give antihistamine Administer vitamin K concurrently
Factor VIIa Recombinant (*NovoSeven RT*) Off label	10-20 mcg/kg IV bolus over 5 minutes	**BOXED WARNING** Serious thrombotic events are associated with the use of factor VIIa outside labeled indications.

For dabigatran reversal - binds only to dabigatran molecules without interfering with the coagulation cascade

IdaruCIZUMAB (Praxbind) Injection 2.5 g/50 mL single-use vial	5 grams IV (given as 2 separate 2.5 gram doses no more than 15 minutes apart) Do not confuse with IDArubicin	**WARNINGS** Thromboembolic risk, risk of serious adverse events with hereditary fructose intolerance due to sorbitol excipient **SIDE EFFECTS** HA, ↓ K, delirium, constipation, fever

Perioperative Management of Patients on Warfarin

- Stop warfarin therapy approximately 5 days before major surgery. In patients with a mechanical heart valve, AFib, or VTE at high risk for thromboembolism, <u>bridging therapy</u> with LMWH or UFH is recommended (bridging means stopping the warfarin and using anticoagulant doses of the LMWH or UFH for a short period to prevent clotting). Discontinue therapeutic-dose SC LMWH 24 hours before surgery (stop the UFH IV therapy 4 – 6 hours before surgery). <u>Patients at low risk for thromboembolism do not require bridging</u>; stop the warfarin and restart after surgery when hemostasis is achieved (see below).

- If INR is still elevated 1 – 2 days before surgery, give low-dose vitamin K (1 – 2 mg).

- If reversal of warfarin is needed in a patient requiring an urgent surgical procedure, give low-dose (2.5 – 5 mg) IV or oral vitamin K.

- Resume warfarin therapy 12 – 24 hours after the surgery, when there is adequate hemostasis.

- In patients receiving bridge therapy with SC LMWH undergoing high-bleeding risk surgery, resume therapeutic dose of LMWH therapy 48 – 72 hours after surgery, when there is adequate hemostasis. If low bleeding risk, may resume therapeutic dose LMWH therapy 24 hours after surgery.

- Continue warfarin or aspirin in patients undergoing minor dental, dermatologic, or cataract surgery.

- Antiplatelet therapies (such as $P2Y_{12}$ inhibitors) may need to be stopped 5 – 10 days prior to major surgery. The risks/benefit of stopping therapy must be evaluated on a case-by-case basis.

ANTICOAGULATION FOR PATIENTS WITH NONVALVULAR ATRIAL FIBRILLATION/ATRIAL FLUTTER (PER CHEST GUIDELINES)

This section refers only to nonvalvular AFib and AFlutter anticoagulation for primary and seconardary prevention of cardioembolic stroke. Valvular patients can have mechanical heart valves; these patients have the highest risk for clotting/strokes. Valvular patients with <u>mechanical</u> heart valves are treated with <u>warfarin</u> and the treatment is non-controversial.

The majority of patients with AFib/AFlutter do not have heart valve involvement and these patients may require anticoagulation depending on their risk of having a cardioembolic stroke. With AFib/AFlutter, there is blood stasis in the left ventricle, which may clot in high risk patients with these arrhythmias. If the clot forms and is then ejected out during a heart's contraction, the clot will travel up to the brain causing a stroke or TIA. This is known as a cardioembolic stroke. Therefore, prevention with anticoagulation is key.

The latest 2012 CHEST guideline uses the $CHADS_2$ scoring system to estimate risk of stroke in AFib/AFlutter and to guide anticoagulation therapy. They do not include the newer oral Factor Xa inhibitors. After the 2012 CHEST guideline was released, a newer guideline by the ACC/AHA/HRS group was released that does include the two newer drugs and uses the CHA_2DS_2-VASc scoring system. This means there are two current guidelines for the same condition. First, focus on the simpler CHEST guideline recommedations (1st set of boxes), and then focus on the differences in the newer guideline (the 2nd set of boxes).

$CHADS_2$ scoring system: First <u>count the number of risk factors</u> the patient has in the case that are listed in the box on the <u>left</u>. Second, use the box on the <u>right</u> to <u>select</u> the <u>correct/recommended anticoagulant</u>.

The higher the value, the higher the risk and the more intensive anticoagulation that is required to reduce the chance that the patient will have a stroke.

ANTICOAGULATION FOR PATIENTS WITH AFIB WHO ARE GOING TO UNDERGO CARDIOVERSION

- AFib > 48 hours or unknown duration: anticoagulation (if warfarin, target INR 2–3) for at least 3 weeks prior to and 4 weeks after cardioversion (regardless of method – electrical or pharmacologic) when normal sinus rhythm is restored.

- AFib ≤ 48 hours duration undergoing elective cardioversion: start full therapeutic anticoagulation at presentation, do cardioversion, and continue full anticoagulation for at least 4 weeks while patient is in normal sinus rhythm.

- For patients staying in AFib, chronic anticoagulation therapy may be needed for stroke prevention. Treatment depends on the number of risk factors present. See text.

$CHADS_2$ SCORING SYSTEM
Add up the total number of risk factors for a given patient.
C – CHF.....................................1
H – HTN.....................................1
A – Age ≥ 75 years 1
D – Diabetes..............................1
S_2 – prior Stroke/TIA*..................2
*Does not include thromboembolism (TE) per CHEST guideline

RISK CATEGORY	RECOMMENDED THERAPY
$CHADS_2$ score = 0	No therapy. For patients wanting anticoagulant therapy, ASA 75-325 mg daily should be used over oral anticoagulation or combination therapy with ASA and clopidrogrel.
$CHADS_2$ score = 1	Oral anticoagulation* rather than ASA 75 mg-325 mg daily or combination therapy with ASA and clopidogrel. For patients unable to take oral anticoagulants, ASA and clopidogrel should be used.
$CHADS_2$ score ≥ 2	Oral anticoagulation*. For patients unable to take oral anticoagulants, ASA and clopidogrel should be used.

Oral anticoagulation favors dabigatran 150 mg BID rather than adjusted-dose warfarin therapy (target INR 2-3).

ANTICOAGULATION FOR PATIENTS WITH NONVALVULAR ATRIAL FIBRILLATION/ ATRIAL FLUTTER (PER THE ACC/AHA/HRS AFIB GUIDELINE)

The boxes below are the CHA_2DS_2-VASc scoring boxes. Notice that there are more risk factors than in the first table – the additions are the three on the bottom called "VASc" (Vascular disease, Age and Sex category). Notice that the newer agents rivaroxaban and apixiban are included as treatment options if the score is 2 or higher. Anticoagulation for patients with AFib who are undergoing cardioversion is the same as the CHEST guidelines.

CHA_2DS_2-VASc SCORING SYSTEM
Add up the total number of risk factors for a given patient.
C – CHF... 1
H – HTN... 1
A – Age ≥ 75 years 2
D – Diabetes.. 1
S_2 – prior Stroke/TIA 2
V – Vascular Disease .... 1 (prior MI, PAD, aortic plaque)
A – Age 65-74 years 1
S – Sex category, female..................... 1

RISK CATEGORY	RECOMMENDED THERAPY
CHA_2DS_2-VASc Score = 0	No anticoagulation recommended.
CHA_2DS_2-VASc Scoring = 1	No anticoagulation or oral anticoagulation or ASA may be considered.
CHA_2DS_2-VASc Scoring ≥ 2	Oral anticoagulation is recommended. Options include warfarin, dabigatran, rivaroxaban and apixaban.

For patients who are unable to maintain a therapeutic INR on warfarin, a direct thrombin inhibitor or factor Xa inhibitor is recommended.

Important – Patients with valvular AFib (those with mechanical heart valves) should only be treated with warfarin (with the INR goals given in the warfarin section of this chapter).

Patient Counseling: For All Anticoagulants

- This medication can interact with many other drugs. Check with your healthcare provider before taking any other medication, including over the counter medications, vitamins, or herbal products.
- This medication can cause you to bruise and/or bleed more easily. Report any unusual bleeding, bruising, or rashes to your healthcare provider.
- Tell physicians and dentists that you are using this medication before any surgery is performed.
- Call your healthcare provider right away if you fall or injure yourself, especially if you hit your head. Alcoholic drinks should be avoided.
- Do not start, stop, or change any medicine without talking with your healthcare provider.
- This medication is very important for your health, but it can cause serious and life-threatening bleeding problems.

- Call your healthcare provider right away if you develop any of these symptoms:
  - Unexpected pain, swelling, or discomfort
  - Headaches, dizziness, or weakness
  - Unusual bruising that develops without known cause
  - Frequent nose bleeds
  - Unusual bleeding gums
  - Bleeding from cuts that take longer than normal to stop
  - Menstrual bleeding or vaginal bleeding that is much heavier than normal
  - Pink or brown urine
  - Red or black stools that look like tar
  - Coughing up blood or blood clots
  - Vomiting blood or material that looks like coffee grounds

Enoxaparin

- Wash and dry hands.
- Sit or lie in a comfortable position so you can see your abdomen. Choose an area on the right or left side of your abdomen, at least 2 inches from the belly button.
- Clean the injection site with an alcohol swab and allow the site to dry.
- Remove the needle cap by pulling it straight off the syringe and discard it in a sharps collector. Do not twist the cap off as this can bend the needle.
- Hold the syringe like a pencil in your writing hand.
- Do not expel the air bubble in the syringe prior to injection unless your healthcare provider has advised you to do so.
- With your other hand, pinch an inch of the cleansed area to make a fold in the skin. Insert the full length of the needle straight down – at a 90 degree angle – into fold of skin.
- Press the plunger with your thumb until the syringe is empty.
- Pull the needle straight out at the same angle that it was inserted, and release the skin fold.
- Point the needle down and away from yourself and others, and push down on the plunger to activate the safety shield.
- Do not rub the site of injection as this can lead to bruising. Place the used syringe in the sharps collector.

Dabigatran

- Do not stop taking dabigatran without talking to your prescriber. Stopping dabigatran increases your risk of having a stroke.
- Take with a full glass of water and swallow the capsules whole. Do not break, chew, or empty the pellets from the capsule. It is fine to take with or without food.
- Common side effects of dabigatran include indigestion, upset stomach or stomach burning and/or pain.
- Only open 1 bottle of dabigatran at a time. Finish your opened bottle of dabigatran before opening a new bottle. After opening a bottle of dabigatran, use within 4 months.
- Keep dabigatran in the original bottle or blister package to keep it dry and protect the capsules from moisture. Do not put dabigatran in pill boxes or pill organizers.

- Tightly close your bottle of dabigatran right after you take your dose.

- If you miss a dose of dabigatran, take it as soon as you remember. <u>If your next dose is less than 6 hours away, skip the missed dose.</u> Do not take two doses of dabigatran at the same time.

- Dabigatran is not for patients with artificial heart valves.

Rivaroxaban

- Rivaroxaban is not for patients with artificial heart valves.

- If you take rivaroxaban for atrial fibrillation: Take rivaroxaban once daily <u>with your evening meal</u>.
  - ❑ If you miss a dose of rivaroxaban, take it as soon as you remember on the same day. Take your next dose at your regularly scheduled time.

- If you take rivaroxaban for blood clots in the veins of your legs or lungs: Take rivaroxaban once or twice daily as prescribed <u>with food</u> at the same time each day.
  - ❑ If you miss a dose of rivaroxaban and take rivaroxaban <u>twice daily</u>: Take rivaroxaban as soon as you remember on the same day. You may take 2 doses at the same time to make up for the missed dose. Take your next dose at your regularly scheduled time.
  - ❑ If you miss a dose of rivaroxaban and take rivaroxaban <u>once daily</u>: Take rivaroxaban as soon as you remember on the same day. Take your next dose at your regularly scheduled time.

- If you take rivaroxaban for hip or knee replacement surgery: Take rivaroxaban once daily with or without food.
  - ❑ Take rivaroxaban once daily with or without food.
  - ❑ If you miss a dose of rivaroxaban, take it as soon as you remember on the same day. Take your next dose at your regularly scheduled time.

Warfarin

- Take warfarin at the same time every day as prescribed by your doctor. You can take warfarin either with food or on an empty stomach.

- Warfarin lowers the chance of blood clots forming in your body.

- If you miss a dose, take the dose as soon as possible on the same day. Do not take a double dose the next day to make up for a missed dose.

- You will need to have your blood tested frequently to monitor your response to this medication. This test is called an INR. Your dose may be adjusted to keep you INR in a target range.

- Do not make changes in your diet, such as eating large amounts of green, leafy vegetables. Be consistent with the amount of leafy green vegetables and other foods rich in vitamin K.

- Avoid drinking alcohol.

- Other side effects besides bleeding include purple toe syndrome that can cause your toes to become painful and purple in color. Also, death of skin tissue can occur. Report any unusual changes or pain immediately to your healthcare provider.

PRACTICE CASE

AM is a 57 y/o female who has been admitted to the hospital with shortness of breath, difficulty breathing, chest pain, coughing and sweating. She states she saw blood in a tissue that she coughed into while coming to the hospital. Her past medical history includes hypertension, neuropathic pain in her feet and atrial fibrillation. She is recovering from a bad fall two days ago but reports "no broken bones, just bruises." She states that she is having difficulty taking care of her grandson who she watches during the day because she is "too tired."

Medications:
Aspirin 325 mg one EC tablet daily
Cordarone 200 mg one daily
Lyrica 75 mg one capsule BID
Chlorthalidone 25 mg one daily
Effexor XR 150 mg one daily

Labs: Ca (mg/dL) = 8.3 (8.5 - 10.5)
Cl (mEq/L) = 98 (95 - 103)
Mg (mEq/L) = 1.3 (1.3 - 2.1)
K (mEq/L) = 4.2 (3.5-5)
PO_4 (mg/dL) = 3.9 (2.3 - 4.7)
Na (mEq/L) = 142 (135 - 145)
HCO_3 (mEq/L) = 22 (24 - 30)
BUN (mg/dL) = 41 (7 - 20)
SCr (mg/dL) = 1.5 (0.6 - 1.3)

AST (U/L) = 27 (0-33)
ALT (U/L) = 23 (0-45)

INR = 1.1 (0.00-1.2)
PTT (seconds) = 27.4 (24.8-35.6)

BP: 152/96 Temp: 98.4°F, Wt 176 lbs. Ht 5'4". Computerized tomography and ultrasound are ordered. Acute PE and DVT are confirmed. The patient will be started on a heparin drip.

Adult Heparin Drip Protocol

PTT	Rebolus or Hold	Rate Adjustment	Recheck PTT
≤ 60	Bolus: 80units/kg	↑ 4 units/kg/hr	6hrs
61-78	Bolus: 40units/kg	↑ 2 units/kg/hr	6hrs
GOAL 79-118	**NONE**	**NONE**	**In AM**
119-135	NONE	↓ 2 units/kg/hr	6hrs
≥ 136	HOLD 60 minutes	↓ 3 units/kg/hr	6hrs

QUESTIONS

1. The medical team asks the clinical pharmacist to dose the heparin for AM. Using the protocol provided, what should the correct bolus and infusion rate of heparin be for AM?

    a. 10,000 units bolus, followed by 2,300 units/hr infusion
    b. 14,000 units bolus, followed by 3,500 units/hr infusion
    c. 7,000 units bolus, followed by 1,400 units/hr infusion
    d. 6,400 units bolus, followed by 1,440 units/hr infusion
    e. None of the above

2. The bolus and infusion are given. After 6 hours, the aPTT comes back at 66 sec. Per the protocol, what is the correct dose adjustment for heparin?

    a. Give a 6,400 unit bolus now and increase the infusion rate to 1,900 units/hr
    b. Give a 3,200 unit bolus now and increase the infusion rate to 1,600 units/hr
    c. Make no change to the dose
    d. Do not give a bolus and reduce the infusion rate to 1,500 units/hr
    e. None of the above

3. The pulmonary embolism was confirmed. It is AM's third day in the hospital, and the medical team would like to discharge her. She starts bridge therapy and receives 5 mg of warfarin at bedside. Which of the statements is true regarding warfarin? (Select **ALL** that apply.)

    a. Warfarin is a direct thrombin inhibitor that helps to prevent clot formation.
    b. Warfarin has a high risk of bleeding. Careful monitoring is advised.
    c. Warfarin should be taken with a low fat meal and never double up on the dose.
    d. Warfarin is a racemic mixture and the R-isomer is more potent than the S-isomer.
    e. Warfarin should overlap the heparin therapy until she is at a therapeutic INR for 24 at least hours.

4. In addition to warfarin, what other medication will AM need for bridge therapy until her INR is therapeutic? Select the appropriate agent, route of administration, and dose for AM's treatment of PE.

    a. Lovenox 30 mg SC daily
    b. Lovenox 30 mg SC Q12H
    c. Lovenox 80 mg SC Q12H
    d. Lovenox 80 mg SC daily
    e. Lovenox 180 mg SC daily

5. AM will need to be counseled on subcutaneous administration of enoxaparin. List the steps in order that the patient should take to administer the drug.

    a. Place injection in the abdomen at least 2" from the navel.
    b. Insert full length of the needle at a 90 degree angle.
    c. Place the used syringe in a sharps container.
    d. Wash hands thoroughly.
    e. The patient should clean the injection site with alcohol.

6. AM should be careful not to take other products that can increase the bleeding risk while on warfarin. Which of the following would *not* increase her risk of bleeding? (Select **ALL** that apply.)

    a. Calcium with Vitamin D
    b. Large amounts of garlic
    c. Dong quai
    d. Fidaxomicin
    e. Ginkgo biloba

Questions 7-10 do not relate to the case.

7. Which of the following medications can significantly interact with warfarin? (Select **ALL** that apply.)

    a. Amiodarone
    b. Morphine
    c. Rifampin
    d. Levetiracetam
    e. Fluconazole

8. A patient comes to the hospital with a DVT. He has developed HIT with thrombosis in the past. Which of the following agents is considered first-line treatment in this patient?

   a. *Arixtra*
   b. Argatroban
   c. *Xarelto*
   d. *Fragmin*
   e. Desirudin

9. Which of the following is a possible side effect of heparin? (Select **ALL** that apply.)

   a. Xerostomia
   b. Thrombocytopenia
   c. Osteoporosis
   d. Hyperkalemia
   e. Bleeding

10. Which of the following parameters need to be monitored during heparin therapy?

    a. Hematocrit, hemoglobin, platelets, AST, and ALT
    b. Hematocrit, hemoglobin, platelets, and aPTT
    c. Hematocrit, hemogloblin, platelets, and PT
    d. CBC and Chem 7 panel
    e. Chem 7 panel and aPTT

Answers

1-d, 2-b, 3-b,e, 4-c, 5-d,e,a,b,c, 6-a,d, 7-a,c,e, 8-b, 9-b,c,d,e, 10-b

ONCOLOGY I: OVERVIEW & SIDE EFFECT MANAGEMENT

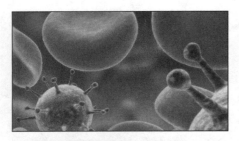

We gratefully acknowledge the assistance of Doreen Pon, PharmD, BCOP, BCPS, Assistant Professor at Western University of Health Sciences and Muoi Gi, PharmD, BCPS, BCOP, Oncology Pharmacy Residency Director, VA San Diego Healthcare System and D. Raymond Weber, PharmD, BSPharm, BCOP, BCPS, RPh, Associate Professor, Notre Dame of Maryland University School of Pharmacy, in preparing this chapter.

GUIDELINES/REFERENCES

National Comprehensive Cancer Network (NCCN). www.nccn.org (accessed 2015 October 15)

American Society of Clinical Oncology (ASCO). www.asco.org (accessed 2015 October 15)

WARNING SIGNS

The American Cancer Society lists seven warning signs of cancer in an adult. Any of these warning signs should warrant referral to a physician:

Change in bowel or bladder habits

A sore that does not heal

Unusual bleeding or discharge

Thickening or lump in breast or else where

Indigestion or difficulty swallowing

Obvious change in wart or mole

Nagging cough or hoarseness

BACKGROUND

Cancer is a group of diseases characterized by uncontrolled growth and spread of abnormal cells and is also referred to as malignancy. The process by which abnormal cells spread to other parts of the body is called metastasis, and this process can result in death. Cancer is caused by both external factors (such as chemicals, radiation, bacteria and viruses) and internal factors (heredity, hormones, immune disorders, and genetic mutations). Sunlight exposure, tobacco use, excessive alcohol intake, obesity, older age, poor diet and low physical activity level increases the risk for certain cancers.

CLASSIFICATION

There are more than 100 types of cancer. Types of cancer are usually named for the orgrans or tissues where the cancer forms. Malignancies are classified based on the tissue type as epithelial, connective, lymphoid or nerve. Most malignant cells retain enough traits to identify their basic tissue type, and therefore a sample of tissue (biopsy) should be taken for diagnosis along with X-rays, CT scans, MRIs and other diagnostic tools to evaluate the stage of cancer. Lab work is required for blood chemistries, urine analysis and tumor markers.

CANCER SCREENING RECOMMENDATIONS

Cancer Screening Guidelines for Average Risk Patients (American Cancer Society)

CANCER	SEX	AGE	SCREENING
Breast	F	40-44 years	Talk with healthcare provider; women may choose to start annual screening with mammograms
		45-54 years	Begin yearly mammograms
		≥ 55 years	Mammograms every 2 years or continue yearly
Cervical	F	21-29 years	Pap smear every 3 years
		30-65 years	Pap smear + HPV test every 5 years
			or
			Pap smear every 3 years
Colon	M/F	≥ 50 years	Preferred tests (find polyps and cancer - choose one of the following):
			Colonoscopy every 10 years
			Flexible sigmoidoscopy every 5 years
			Double-contrast barium enema every 5 years
			CT colonography every 5 years
			Alternative tests (find only cancer - choose one of the following):
			Stool DNA test every 3 years
			Fecal occult blood test every year
			Fecal immunochemical test every year
Lung	M/F	55-74 years	Low dose CT scan of the chest every year can be considered if (all of the following):
			In fairly good health
			Have at least a 30 pack-year smoking history
			Still smoking or quit smoking within the past 15 years

HPV: Human papillomavirus

ABCDE's Warning Signs of Melanoma Skin Cancer

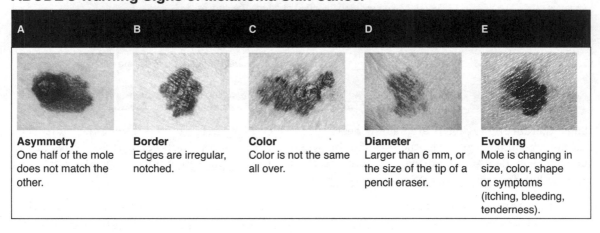

A	B	C	D	E
Asymmetry One half of the mole does not match the other.	**Border** Edges are irregular, notched.	**Color** Color is not the same all over.	**Diameter** Larger than 6 mm, or the size of the tip of a pencil eraser.	**Evolving** Mole is changing in size, color, shape or symptoms (itching, bleeding, tenderness).

TREATMENT OVERVIEW

Cancer can be treated with surgery, radiation, chemotherapy, hormone therapy, biological therapy, targeted therapy, immunotherapy and/or vaccines. Treatment decisions are based on the cancer type and stage and patient characteristics such as tumor markers. For most cancers (including breast, lung, prostate and colon cancer), the stage is classified by the size of the tumor and whether it has spread. As a cancer grows, it can invade nearby tissues and enter the lymphatic system. Cancer cells can travel through the blood or lymphatic system to distant organs, such as the lungs, liver and brain. This process of metastasis usually represents the most advanced stage of cancer, or stage IV. Stage IV cancers are rarely curable. Goals of treatment depend on prognosis. The plan may attempt to achieve remission (with curative intent) or be palliative (to reduce tumor size and symptoms). If a patient remains cancer-free for 5 years, it is unlikely that their cancer will recur. Although these patients may be "cured," they are typically considered cancer-free survivors. Response to treatment is classified as complete (no evidence of disease for at least 1 month) or partial (≥ 30% ↓ in tumor size). Stable disease means < 30% decrease or < 20% increase in tumor size, and progression is ≥ 20% increase in tumor size or tumor growth in a new site.

TO REDUCE RISK OF DEVELOPING CANCER

Everyone should be encouraged to maintain a healthy lifestyle:

- Avoid tobacco (enroll in smoking cessation program if needed).
- Maintain a healthy weight.
- Exercise regularly.
- Eat healthy with plenty of fruits and vegetables.
- Limit alcohol intake.
- Protect skin from harmful UV rays.
- Assess cancer risk, family history, and individual history.
- Have regular check-ups and cancer screening tests.

Often, the primary treatment modality is surgery if the cancer is resectable. Neoadjuvant therapy (e.g., radiation or chemotherapy) may be used prior to surgery to shrink the tumor initially. Adjuvant therapy (may include radiation and/or chemotherapy) is given after surgery in an attempt to eradicate residual disease and ↓ recurrence.

Sometimes, surgery is not an option for initial treatment and the treatment regimen begins with chemotherapy.

Terminology Used in Cancer Therapy

TYPE OF THERAPY	DEFINITION
Curative	Therapy given with the intention of curing the cancer.
Palliative	Therapy given with the intention of reducing symptoms and/or slowing the growth of the cancer.
Adjuvant	Therapy given after the primary therapy (usually surgery) to eradicate residual disease and ↓ recurrence.
Neoadjuvant	Therapy given before the primary therapy (usually surgery) to shrink the size of the tumor.

Chemotherapeutic regimens are usually designed for synergism. Drugs with different mechanisms of action that complement each other are chosen. Synergy will not work unless each drug is active on the tumor independently. Most drugs are more effective at killing rapidly dividing cancer cells since they work by interfering with the DNA replication cycle.

Due to their various mechanisms of action, chemotherapeutic regimens can be highly toxic. The majority of adverse effects are due to damaging effects on non-cancerous, rapidly dividing cells in the GI tract, hair follicles and bone marrow (where the production of blood cells takes place). Thus, diarrhea, alopecia, and myelosuppression are common side effects of most chemotherapeutic regimens. Pharmacists can play an important role in helping patients manage the side effects of chemotherapeutic regimens.

Due to these severe side effects, the patient's <u>physical functioning must be assessed</u> with rating systems such as the Karnofsky and the ECOG (Eastern Cooperative Oncology Group) performance status scales. Many patient factors can affect treatment choice such as: age, co-morbidities and/or previous treatments. A patient's quality of life may lead the clinician and family to choose palliative measures (to reduce the symptoms) over a more aggressive treatment plan with side effects that could be intolerable to the patient.

Pregnancy & Breastfeeding

Chemotherapy should be avoided during pregnancy and breastfeeding, although some patients treated while pregnant have delivered healthy babies. Counsel both male and female patients to avoid conceiving during treatment and to consider using barrier methods to avoid contact with body fluids. Some of the medications can cause long-term sterility.

SUMMARY OF TOXICITIES

For studying purposes, it is helpful to know the common toxicities of chemotherapy drugs and the specific agents most commonly associated with those toxicities. It is important to know the chemoprotectant drugs (or antidotes) and the situations in which they should be used, along with maximum doses of select chemotherapy drugs. These common toxicities are discussed here and the drugs are discussed in more detail in the next chapter.

Common Toxicities of Select Chemotherapeutic Agents

TOXICITY	COMMON DRUGS	MONITORING	MANAGEMENT
Myelosuppression	Almost all, <u>except</u>: Asparaginase, bleomycin, vincristine, most monoclonal antibodies and many tyrosine kinase inhibitors (TKIs)	Complete blood count (CBC) with differential, temperature, bleeding, fatigue, shortness of breath	Neutropenia: Colony-stimulating factors (CSFs) Anemia: RBC transfusions and erythropoiesis-stimulating agents (ESAs) Thrombocytopenia: Platelet transfusions
Nausea & Vomiting	<u>Cisplatin, doxorubicin, epirubicin, cyclophosphamide and ifosfamide</u> are highly emetogenic	Patient symptoms of nausea and vomiting and hydration status	Highly emetogenic chemotherapy: Neurokinin-1 receptor antagonist (NK_1-RA) + corticosteroid + serotonin-3 receptor antagonist $(5HT_3-RA)$ Moderately emetogenic chemotherapy: Corticosteroid + $5HT_3-RA$ IV/PO fluid hydration
Mucositis	<u>Fluorouracil, capecitabine, irinotecan, methotrexate</u> and many TKIs including afatinib, pazopanib, ponatinib, regorafenib, sorafenib, sunitinib, everolimus	S/sx of superinfection of oral ulcers with herpes simplex virus or thrush (*Candida* spp.)	Symptomatic Treatment: Mucosal coating agents, topical local anesthetics

Common Toxicities of Chemotherapeutic Agents Continued

TOXICITY	COMMON DRUGS	MONITORING	MANAGEMENT
Diarrhea	Fluorouracil, capecitabine, irinotecan and many TKIs	Frequency of bowel movements, hydration status, potassium	IV/PO fluid hydration, antimotility agents (e.g., loperamide) Irinotecan: atropine for early onset diarrhea
Constipation	Vincristine, pomalidomide, thalidomide	Frequency of bowel movements	Stimulant laxatives, polyethylene glycol
Xerostomia	Caused by radiation therapy to the head or neck regions.	Dry mouth	Artificial saliva substitutes, pilocarpine
Cardiotoxicity	**Cardiomyopathy:** Anthracyclines, HER2 inhibitors (ado-trastuzumab, trastuzumab, pertuzumab), fluorouracil **QT prolongation:** Arsenic trioxide, most tyrosine kinase inhibitors (dasatinib, nilotinib, vemurafenib, dabrafenib, trametinib, crizotinib, ceritinib, erlotinib, gefitinib, lapatinib, pazopanib, regorafenib, sorafenib, sunitinib) and leuprolide	**Cardiomyopathy:** Left ventricular ejection fraction (LVEF), lifetime cumulative dose of anthracycline **QT prolongation:** ECG, K, Mg, Ca	**Cardiomyopathy:** Do not exceed recommended lifetime cumulative dose of 450-550 mg/m^2 for doxorubicin, dexrazoxane can be administered prophylactically in selected patients receiving doxorubicin. **QT prolongation:** Ensure K, Mg, Ca within normal limits, consider holding therapy if QTc > 500 msec.
Hepatotoxicity	Antiandrogens (bicalutamide, flutamide, nilutamide), folate antimetabolites (methotrexate, pemetrexed, pralatrexate), pyrimidine analog antimetabolites (cytarabine, gemcitabine), many tyrosine kinase inhibitors, ipilimumab	LFTs, jaundice, ascites	Symptomatic management. Consider stopping therapy.
Nephrotoxicity	Cisplatin, methotrexate (especially high doses), pemetrexed, pralatrexate, carfilzomib, bevacizumab, nivolumab, pembrolizumab, ipilimumab	BUN, SCr, urinalysis, urine output, creatinine clearance	Amifostine *(Ethyol)* may be given prophylactically with cisplatin to reduce the risk of nephrotoxicity. Ensure adequate hydration. Do not exceed maximum dose of 100 mg/m^2/cycle for cisplatin.
Hemorrhagic Cystitis	Ifosfamide, cyclophosphamide	Urinalysis for blood, symptoms of dysuria	Mesna (*Mesnex*) is always given prophylactically with ifosfamide (and sometimes with cyclophosphamide) to reduce the risk of hemorrhagic cystitis. Ensure adequate hydration.

Common Toxicities of Chemotherapeutic Agents Continued

TOXICITY	COMMON DRUGS	MONITORING	MANAGEMENT
Neuropathy	**Peripheral Sensory Neuropathy:** Vinca alkaloids (vincristine, vinblastine, vinorelbine), platinums (cisplatin, oxaliplatin), taxanes (paclitaxel, docetaxel, cabazitaxel), proteosome inhibitors (bortezomib, carfilzomib), thalidomide, ado-trastuzumab, cytarabine (high doses), brentuximab **Autonomic Neuropathy:** Vinca alkaloids		Symptomatic treatment with drugs for neuropathic pain. **Vincristine:** Many recommend limiting the dose of vincristine to 2 mg per week (regardless of BSA calculated dose). **Oxaliplatin:** Causes an acute cold-mediated sensory neuropathy. Instruct patients to avoid cold temperatures and drinking cold beverages. **Bortezomib:** SC administration is associated with less peripheral neuropathy than IV administration.
Clotting Risk	Aromatase inhibitors (e.g., anastrazole, letrozole), SERMs (e.g., tamoxifen), immunomodulators (thalidomide, lenalidomide, pomalidomide)	S/sx of DVT/PE, stroke, MI	Consider thromboprophylaxis based on patient's risk factors

Chemotherapy Adjunctive Medications

CHEMOTHERAPEUTIC AGENT	ADJUNCTIVE MEDICATION	INDICATION FOR ADJUNCTIVE MEDICATION
Cisplatin	Amifostine *(Ethyol)*	Prophylaxis to prevent nephrotoxicity
Doxorubicin	Dexrazoxane *(Zinecard)*	Prophylaxis to prevent cardiomyopathy
	Dexrazoxane *(Totect)*	Treatment for extravasation
Fluorouracil	Leucovorin or levoleucovorin *(Fusilev)*	Given with fluorouracil to enhance efficacy
Ifosfamide	Mesna *(Mesnex)*	Prophylaxis to prevent hemorrhagic cystitis
Irinotecan	Atropine	Prophylaxis to prevent acute diarrhea
Methotrexate	Leucovorin or levoleucovorin *(Fusilev)*	Given after methotrexate (MTX) to reduce myelosuppresion and mucositis
	Glucarpidase *(Voraxaze)*	Given in acute renal failure/high concentration of MTX

MANAGEMENT OF SIDE EFFECTS

Myelosuppression Overview

Myelosuppression ($\downarrow$ in bone marrow activity resulting in fewer RBCs, WBCs and platelets) is a complication of most chemotherapeutic agents. Neutrophils and platelets are often affected since these cells have shorter life spans and thus, the turnover is rapid. If WBCs decrease, the immune system will become depressed and the patient will have trouble fighting an infection. If RBCs decrease, the patient becomes anemic, experiencing weakness and fatigue. If platelets decrease, there is an increased risk of severe bleeding.

The lowest point that WBCs and platelets reach (the nadir) occurs about 7 – 14 days after chemotherapy, although some agents have a delayed effect. RBC nadir is much later, generally after several months of therapy, due to the long life span of RBCs (~120 days). WBCs and platelets generally recover 3 – 4 weeks post treatment. The next dose of chemotherapy is given after the WBCs and platelets have returned to a safe level. If the WBCs and/or platelets have not recovered to a safe level, the next cycle of chemotherapy may need to be delayed to allow for recovery. Medications may be necessary to help restore blood cell counts. Severe cases may require a transfusion (providing the deficient cell line directly, such as giving packed RBCs for severe anemia). All agents used for myelosuppression discussed here are usually given by subcutaneous injection, either by the patient, caregiver or healthcare provider.

Anemia

Hemoglobin (Hgb) levels are used to assess anemia. Normal Hgb levels are 12 – 16 g/dL for females and 13.5 – 18 g/dL for males (hematocrit is 36 – 46% females; 38 – 50% males). Anemia may recover on its own, be treated with a RBC transfusion, or rarely, with an erythropoiesis-stimulating agent (ESA). ESAs can shorten survival and ↑ tumor progression or recurrence as shown in clinical studies of patients with breast, non-small cell lung, head and neck, lymphoid, and cervical cancers. Therefore, ESAs are not recommended to be used in patients receiving chemotherapy with curative intent. To make sure that patients are aware of the risks, MedGuides are dispensed at the initiation of therapy. For cancer, the use of ESAs must fulfill the requirements of the ESA APPRISE Oncology Program. This is a REMS (Risk Evaluation and Mitigation Strategies) program to make sure healthcare providers are trained and patients receive proper counseling on the risks and benefits of therapy. To minimize the risks of ESAs in patients with chemotherapy-induced anemia, the following guidelines are adopted from the ESA APPRISE Oncology Program:

- Use ESA therapy only in patients with non-myeloid malignancies where anemia is due to the effect of concomitant myelosuppressive chemotherapy

- Upon initiation of ESA therapy, there is a minimum of 2 additional months of planned chemotherapy

- Initiate ESA therapy when the Hgb is < 10 g/dL

- Use the lowest dose needed to avoid RBC transfusions

Serum ferritin, transferrin saturation (TSAT) and total iron-binding capacity (TIBC) may be ordered to assess iron storage and transport since the ESAs will not work well to correct the anemia if iron levels are inadequate. Levels of folate and vitamin B12 may need to be evaluated, especially if there is a poor response to the ESA. For further information regarding ESAs and ESA dosing in cancer, refer to the Anemia chapter.

Neutropenia

A low neutrophil count ↑ infection risk and makes it difficult for the human body to fight an infection. The more neutropenic the patient is, the higher the risk of infection.

Neutropenia Definition (American Society of Clinical Oncology)

CATEGORY	ABSOLUTE NEUTROPHIL COUNT (ANC)
Neutropenia	< 1,000 cells/mm^3
Severe Neutropenia	< 500 cells/mm^3
Profound Neutropenia	< 100 cells/mm^3

Know how to calculate the ANC; this is reviewed in the Calculations chapter.

Colony stimulating factors (CSFs), also called "myeloid growth factors," are a class of biologic agents that regulate the proliferation, differentiation, survival, and activation of cells in the myeloid lineage. Myeloid refers to the granulocyte precursor cell, which differentiates into neutrophils, eosinophils, and basophils. These agents are expensive and have not been shown to improve overall survival outcomes. They do shorten the time that a patient is at risk for infection due to neutropenia and <u>reduce mortality from infections</u> when <u>given prophylactically in patients at high risk for febrile neutropenia</u>. The National Comprehensive Cancer Network (NCCN) recommends that all patients with > 20% chance of developing chemotherapy-induced febrile neutropenia receive myeloid growth factors. There are three types: GM-CSF (sargramostim), G-CSF (filgrastim) and pegylated G-CSF (pegfilgrastim). GM-CSF is limited to use in stem cell transplantation. Both forms of G-CSF are indicated for prevention of febrile neutropenia.

Effect of CSF Prophylaxis on the Duration of Chemotherapy-Induced Neutropenia

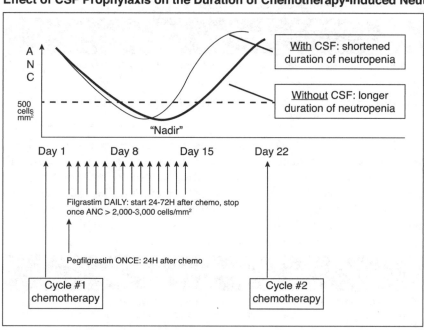

DRUG	DOSING	SAFETY/SIDE EFFECTS/MONITORING
Filgrastim (Neupogen, Zarxio) Tbo-filgrastim (*Granix*) G-CSF	5 mcg/kg/day given IV/SC daily (round to the nearest 300 mcg or 480 mcg vial size); treat through post-nadir recovery (until ANC > 2,000-3,000 cells/mm³) 10 mcg/kg/day used for bone marrow transplant	**SIDE EFFECTS** Filgrastim/pegfilgrastim/tbo-filgrastim: <u>bone pain</u>, fever, generalized rash, injection site reaction Sargramostim: <u>fever, bone pain, arthralgias, myalgias, rash</u>, dyspnea, peripheral edema, pericardial effusion, cardiovascular edema, HTN, chest pain
Pegfilgrastim (Neulasta) Pegylated G-CSF Long acting: relatively equivalent to 14 daily doses of filgrastim	1 prefilled syringe (6 mg) SC once per chemo cycle	**MONITORING** CBC with differential, pulmonary function, weight, vital signs **NOTES** Store in refrigerator. Protect vials from light. Administer first dose 24-72 hours after chemo.
Sargramostim (Leukine) GM-CSF Limited to use in stem cell transplantation	250 mcg/m²/day given IV/SC daily; treat through post-nadir recovery	Patients should report any signs of enlarged spleen (pain in left upper abdomen or respiratory distress syndrome). Must document when pegfilgrastim was given. Pegfilgrastim should <u>not</u> be given until 24 hours after the end of chemo infusion or within 14 days prior to the next cycle of chemo. Filgrastim and sargramostim should <u>not</u> be given within 24 hours before or after chemo.

Febrile Neutropenia

Patients receiving cytotoxic chemotherapy are at risk for infections with enteric bacteria and fungi due to alterations in gastrointestinal mucosa caused by chemotherapy. These patients also commonly have central venous access devices, which places them at risk for infections due to skin flora. When these patients become neutropenic following cytotoxic chemotherapy, they may be unable to fight off these infections, placing them at risk for death due to sepsis syndrome. Because a fever may be the only sign of infection in a neutropenic patient, appropriate empiric antibiotics must be started immediately in neutropenic patients who develop fevers.

The Infectious Diseases Society of America defines febrile neutropenia as:

FEVER	NEUTROPENIA
Single oral temperature > 38.3 C (101 F) or Oral temperature > 38.0 C (100.4 F) sustained for greater than 1 hour	Absolute neutrophil count (ANC) < 500 cells/mm³ or ANC that is expected to decrease to < 500 cells/mm³ during the next 48 hours

Although both Gram-positive and Gram-negative bacteria may be isolated from patients with febrile neutropenia, infection with Gram-negative bacteria pose the greatest risk for causing sepsis syndrome in these patients. Therefore, initial empiric antibiotics in febrile neutropenia should provide adequate coverage against Gram-negative bacteria, including *Pseudomonas aeruginosa*. The individual patient's risk of developing serious complications should also be considered when determining the initial empiric antibiotics regimen. Modification of the initial empiric antibiotic regimen may be necessary based on culture results, if a patient continues to have fevers or clinical deterioration.

PATIENT RISK	RISK DEFINITION	INITIAL EMPIRIC ANTIBIOTICS
Low-risk	Expected ANC < 500 cells/mm³ for ≤ 7 days No comorbidities	**Oral anti-pseudomonal antibiotics:** Ciprofloxacin + amoxicillin-clavulanate or Ciprofloxacin +/– clindamycin or Levofloxacin
High-risk	Expected ANC ≤ 100 cells/mm³ for > 7 days Presence of comorbidities Evidence of renal or hepatic impairment (CrCl < 30 mL/min or LFTs > 5x ULN)	**Intravenous anti-pseudomonal ß-lactams:** Cefepime or Ceftazidime or Meropenem or Imipenem-cilastatin or Piperacillin-tazobactam

Thrombocytopenia

Low platelets (thrombocytes) can result in spontaneous, uncontrolled bleeding. The normal range for platelets is 150,000 – 450,000/mm³. The risk for spontaneous bleeding is increased when the platelet count is <10,000 cells/mm³. Platelet transfusions are generally indicated when the count falls below 10,000 cells/mm³ (or 20,000 cells/mm³ if active bleed is present). Chemotherapy dose may be reduced or placed on hold until the platelet count recovers. Intramuscular injections and medications that affect platelet functioning, such as NSAIDs, should be avoided in patients who are thrombocytopenic.

Chemotherapy-Induced Nausea and Vomiting (CINV)

Nausea and vomiting are common with chemotherapy. Patient factors which ↑ risk of nausea and vomiting include: female gender, < 50 years of age, dehydration, history of motion sickness, and history of nausea and vomiting with prior regimens. For chemotherapy-induced nausea and vomiting (CINV), <u>administer anti-emetics at least 30 minutes prior</u> to chemotherapy and provide take-home anti-emetic medication (such as ondansetron, prochlorperazine, or metoclopramide) for breakthrough nausea and vomiting. There are 3 subtypes of CINV: acute, delayed and anticipatory.

SUBTYPE	RISK FACTORS	ONSET	MAJOR NEURO-TRANSMITTERS	DRUG THERAPY
Acute	See text above for patient risk factors and the table below for high risk drugs	Within 24 hours after chemo	Serotonin	$5HT_3$ receptor antagonists
Delayed	Anthracyclines, platinum analogs, cyclophosphamide, ifosfamide, any chemo regimens with a high risk for causing acute CINV	1 to 7 days after chemo	Substance P	NK_1 receptor antagonists, corticosteroids, palonosetron (the only $5HT_3$-RA with a labeled indication for delayed emesis)
Anticipatory	History of CINV with previous chemo regimen	Before chemo		Benzodiazepines

Emetic Risk Potential of Select IV Antineoplastic Agents (per NCCN guidelines)

HIGH EMETIC RISK	MODERATE EMETIC RISK	LOW EMETIC RISK	MINIMAL EMETIC RISK
> 90% frequency of emesis	30%-90% frequency of emesis	10%-30% frequency of emesis	< 10% frequency of emesis
AC combination (doxorubicin or epirubicin with cyclophosphamide)	Aldesleukin > 12-15 million units/m^2	Aldesleukin ≤ 12 million units/m^2	Majority of the monoclonal antibodies (bevacizumab, cetuximab, ipilimumab, panitumumab, pertuzumab, rituximab, trastuzumab)
<u>Cisplatin</u>	Arsenic trioxide	Cabazitaxel	
Cyclophosphamide > 1,500 mg/m^2	Bendamustine	Carfilzomib	
	Carboplatin	Docetaxel	Bleomycin
Dacarbazine	Cyclophosphamide ≤ 1,500 mg/m^2	Etoposide	Bortezomib
Doxorubicin ≥ 60 mg/m^2	Daunorubicin	Fluorouracil	Vinca alkaloids
Epirubicin > 90 mg/m^2	Doxorubicin < 60 mg/m^2	Gemcitabine	
Ifosfamide ≥ 2 g/m^2 per dose	Epirubicin ≤ 90 mg/m^2	Ixabepilone	
	Idarubicin	Mitoxantrone	
	Ifosfamide < 2 g/m^2 per dose	Paclitaxel	
	Interferon alfa ≥ 10 million units/m^2	Pemetrexed	
	Irinotecan	Topotecan	
	Oxaliplatin		

Emetic Risk Potential of Select Oral Antineoplastic Agents (per NCCN guidelines)

MODERATE TO HIGH RISK	MINIMAL TO LOW RISK
Cyclophosphamide ≥ 100 mg/m²/day	Capecitabine
Crizotinib	Mercaptopurine
Etoposide	Methotrexate
Lomustine (single day)	Temozolomide ≤ 75 mg/m²/day
Procarbazine	Majority of the TKIs (dasatinib, erlotinib, imatinib, nilotinib, sunitinib, sorafenib)
Temozolomide > 75 mg/m²/day	
Vismodegib	Immunomodulators (lenalidomide, pomalidomide, thalidomide)

Anti-Emetic Regimens for Acute/Delayed Nausea & Vomiting

High Emetic Risk Chemotherapy

High emetic risk is managed by a 3-drug combination of either 1) a neurokinin-1 receptor antagonist (NK$_1$-RA) + corticosteroid + 5HT$_3$ receptor antagonist (5HT$_3$-RA) or 2) olanzapine + corticosteroid + 5HT$_3$-RA.

Regimen/Dosing Recommendations for Highly-Emetogenic Chemotherapy (per NCCN guidelines)

Acute:
Either NK$_1$-RA + corticosteroid + 5HT$_3$ antagonist **or** olanzapine + corticosteroid + 5HT$_3$ antagonist
Delayed:
NK$_1$-RA + corticosteroid

NEUKOKININ 1 RECEPTOR ANTAGONIST-CONTAINING REGIMEN

AGENT	DAY 1	DAY 2	DAY 3	DAY 4

NK$_1$-RA

AGENT	DAY 1	DAY 2	DAY 3	DAY 4
Aprepitant	125 mg PO	80 mg PO	80 mg PO	–
Fosaprepitant	150 mg IV	–	–	–
Rolapitant	180 mg PO	–	–	–
Netupitant (only in combination with palonosetron)	300 mg PO	–	–	–

Corticosteroid

AGENT	DAY 1	DAY 2	DAY 3	DAY 4
Dexamethasone (with aprepitant and netupitant)	12 mg PO/IV	8 mg PO	8 mg PO	8 mg PO
Dexamethasone (with fosaprepitant)	12 mg PO/IV	8 mg PO	8 mg PO BID	8 mg PO BID
Dexamethasone (with rolapitant)	20 mg PO/IV	8 mg PO BID	8 mg PO BID	8 mg PO BID

Neurokinin 1 Receptor Antagonist Containing Regimen Continued

DRUG	DAY 1	DAY 2	DAY 3	DAY 4

5HT$_3$ Receptor Antagonist

DRUG	DAY 1	DAY 2	DAY 3	DAY 4
Dolasetron	100 mg PO	–	–	–
Granisetron	2 mg PO or 10 mcg/kg or 1 mg IV or 3.1 mg patch (apply 24-48 hrs before chemo)	–	–	–
Ondansetron	16-24 mg PO or 8-16 mg IV	–	–	–
Palonosetron	0.25 mg IV or 0.5 mg PO (in combination with netupitant, *Akynzeo*)	–	–	–

+/- Lorazepam 0.5-2 mg PO/IV/SL Q6H on days 1-4

+/- H$_2$RA or proton pump inhibitor

OLANZAPINE-CONTAINING REGIMEN

DRUG	DAY 1	DAY 2	DAY 3	DAY 4
Olanzapine and	10 mg PO	10 mg PO	10 mg PO	10 mg PO
Dexamethasone and	20 mg IV	–	–	–
Palonosetron	0.25 mg IV	–	–	–

± Lorazepam 0.5-2 mg PO/IV/SL Q4-6H on days 1-4

± H$_2$RA or proton pump inhibitor

Moderate Emetic Risk Chemotherapy

Moderate emetic risk is managed by a 2-drug combination of a corticosteroid and 5-HT$_3$ antagonist, with or without a neurokinin 1 antagonist (for select patients, where appropriate). As an alternative, an olanzapine-containing regimen could be used as well.

Low Emetic Risk Chemotherapy

Low emetic risk is managed by a 1-drug regimen of either a 5-HT$_3$ antagonist, dexamethasone, prochlorperazine or metoclopramide.

Antiemetics for Breakthrough CINV

Despite receiving antiemetic prophylaxis for acute and/or delayed CINV, some patients may experience breakthrough nausea and vomiting. Various antiemetics may be used, including 5HT$_3$-RAs, dopamine receptor antagonists, and cannabinoids. 5HT$_3$-RAs are usually well-tolerated by most patients, with migraine-like headaches and constipation being common side effects. They also cause minimal sedation, compared to dopamine receptor antagonists and cannabinoids. Dopamine receptor antagonists, such as prochlorperazine, promethazine, and metoclopramide, are commonly prescribed, although some patients may experience unpleasant side effects. These agents commonly cause sedation and some anticholinergic side effects. Extrapyramidal symptoms (EPS), such as acute dystonic reactions, can occur, especially in younger patients. Acute dystonic reactions should be treated with anticholinergics (benztropine, diphenhydramine).

Cannabinoids, such as Dronabinol *(Marinol)* and nabilone *(Cesamet)* can be used as second line agents. These are synthetic analogs of delta-9-tetrahydrocannabinol, a naturally occurring component of *Cannabis sativa* (marijuana). Although these agents may be legally prescribed, they may cause side effects similar to *Cannabis*, such as sedation, dysphoria, or euphoria. The DEA classifies *Cannabis*, (marijuana, used in the plant form) as a schedule I drug, however it can be purchased for medical and nonmedical use in some states, and in some jurisdictions can be purchased for medical use only.

Antiemetic Agents

DRUG	DOSING	SAFETY/SIDE EFFECTS/MONITORING

5HT-3 Receptor Antagonists: work by blocking serotonin, both peripherally on vagal nerve terminals and centrally in the chemoreceptor trigger zone. All may be given once prior to chemotherapy on day 1, with the exception of the granisetron transdermal patch.

DRUG	DOSING	SAFETY/SIDE EFFECTS/MONITORING
Ondansetron *(Zofran, Zuplenz film)*	PO: 16-24 mg IV: 8-16 mg	**CONTRAINDICATIONS** Concomitant use of apomorphine *(Apokyn)* with ondansetron (enhances hypotensive effects of apomorphine) **WARNINGS** Dose-dependent ↑ in QT interval (torsade de pointes) - more common with IV Serotonin syndrome when used in combination with other serotonergic agents **SIDE EFFECTS** Headache, fatigue, dizziness, constipation **NOTES** Pregnancy Category B
Granisetron *(Kytril, Sancuso patch)*	PO: 2 mg IV: 10 mcg/kg or 1 mg Patch: 3.1 mg/24hr patch, apply 24-48hrs before chemo; may leave in place up to 7 days	
Dolasetron *(Anzemet)*	PO: 100 mg IV: Not indicated for CINV due to ↑ risk for QT prolongation	
Palonosetron *(Aloxi)* + netupitant *(Akynzeo)*	PO: 0.5 mg IV: 0.25 mg	

Antiemetic Agents Continued

DRUG	DOSING	SAFETY/SIDE EFFECTS/MONITORING

Dopamine Receptor Antagonists: work by blocking dopamine receptors in the CNS, including the chemoreceptor trigger zone (among other mechanisms).

DRUG	DOSING	SAFETY/SIDE EFFECTS/MONITORING
Prochlorperazine *(Compazine, Compro)*	10 mg IV/PO Q6H PRN May give 25 mg suppository PR Q12H PRN	**BOXED WARNING** Prochlorperazine: ↑ mortality in elderly patients with dementia-related psychosis. Promethazine: Do not use in children < 2 years old due to risk of respiratory depression. Do not give via intra-arterial or SC administration. IV route can cause serious tissue injury if extravasation occurs.
Promethazine *(Phenergan, Phenadoz, Promethegan)*	12.5-25 mg PO/IV/PR Q4-6H PRN	Metoclopramide: Tardive dyskinesia (TD) that can be irreversible. Discontinue metoclopramide in patients who develop signs or symptoms of TD. The risk of developing TD increases with duration of treatment and total cumulative dose. Avoid treatment with metoclopramide for longer than 12 weeks. **WARNINGS** Symptoms of Parkinson's disease may be exacerbated. Avoid use in patients with Parkinson's disease. **SIDE EFFECTS** Sedation, lethargy, hypotension, neuroleptic malignant syndrome (NMS), QT prolongation, acute EPS (common in children – antidote is diphenhydramine or benztropine), can lower seizure threshold, strong anticholinergic side effects (not metoclopramide)
Metoclopramide *(Reglan, Metozolv ODT)*	10-40 mg PO/IV Q6H PRN For highly emetic regimens: 0.5-2 mg/kg/dose PO/IV Q6H PRN CrCl < 40 mL/min: Give 50% of the dose	**NOTES** MedGuide required (metoclopramide) Pregnancy Category B (metoclopramide) Pregnancy Category C (promethazine)

Corticosteroids: unknown

DRUG	DOSING	SAFETY/SIDE EFFECTS/MONITORING
Dexamethasone *(Decadron)*	All off label dosing High risk: 12 mg PO/IV on day 1 of chemo, then 8 mg PO daily days 2-4 (with aprepitant or netupitant) or 8 mg PO day 2, then 8 mg PO BID days 3 and 4 (with fosaprepitant) or 20 mg PO/IV on day 1, then 8 mg PO BID on days 2-4 (with rolapitant) Moderate risk: 12 mg PO/IV on day 1 of chemo, then 8 mg PO/IV days 2-3 Low risk: 12 mg PO/IV on day(s) of chemo	**CONTRAINDICATIONS** Systemic fungal infections, cerebral malaria **SIDE EFFECTS** Short-term side effects include ↑ appetite/weight gain, fluid retention, emotional instability (euphoria, mood swings, irritability, acute psychosis), insomnia, GI upset. Higher doses can cause ↑ in BP and blood glucose (especially in patients with diabetes).

Antiemetic Agents Continued

DRUG	DOSING	SAFETY/SIDE EFFECTS/MONITORING

Cannabinoids: may work by activating cannabinoid receptors within the central nervous system and/or by inhibiting the vomiting control mechanism in the medulla oblongata.

| Dronabinol *(Marinol)*
 <u>Refrigerate</u> capsules
 C-III | Labeled dosing: 5 mg/m² PO prior to chemo and Q2-4H after chemo for up to 6 doses/day. Most patients respond to 5 mg 3-4 times/day. | **SIDE EFFECTS**
 Somnolence, euphoria, ↑ appetite, orthostatic hypotension, dysphoria, lowering of the seizure threshold, use with caution in patients with histories of substance abuse or psychiatric disorders |
| Nabilone *(Cesamet)*
 No refrigeration needed
 C-II | 1-2 mg PO BID, continue for up to 48H after last chemo dose | |

<u>Substance P/Neurokinin-1 Receptor Antagonists</u>: inhibit the substance P/neurokinin 1 receptor, therefore augmenting the antiemetic activity of 5HT₃ receptor antagonists and corticosteroids to inhibit acute and delayed phases of chemotherapy-induced emesis.

Aprepitant *(Emend)* Capsule	PO: 125 mg 1 hour before chemo on day 1, then 80 mg daily x 2 days	**CONTRAINDICATIONS** Aprepitant/Fosaprepitant: do not use with pimozide or cisapride (CYP3A4 substrates)
Fosaprepitant *(Emend IV)* Injection	IV: 150 mg 30 minutes before chemo	Rolapitant: do not use with thioridazine (CYP2D6 substrate)
Netupitant + palonosetron *(Akynzeo)* Capsule	PO: 300/0.5 mg 1 hour before chemo	**SIDE EFFECTS** Dizziness, fatigue, constipation, weakness, hiccups **NOTES** Aprepitant/Fosaprepitant/Netupitant are CYP3A4 inhibitors. Dose of dexamethasone should be decreased when used concurrently as an antiemetic.
Rolapitant *(Varubi)* Tablet	PO: 180 mg 1-2 hours before chemo	Rolapitant is a CYP2D6 inhibitor. Dose of dexamethasone should not be decreased when used concurrently as an antiemetic.

Gastrointestinal Complications

Cells of the GI tract are rapidly dividing and are therefore susceptible to being killed by chemotherapy agents that interfere with DNA replication or cell division. Damage to the epithelium of the GI tract results in diarrhea. Damage to oral mucosal epithelial cells leads to painful oral ulcerations, also called oral <u>mucositis</u>. Damage to the salivary glands usually caused by radiation therapy to the head or neck regions may cause dry mouth, also called <u>xerostomia</u>.

Chemotherapy-Induced Diarrhea (CID)

Chemotherapy-induced diarrhea can lead to life-threatening dehydration and electrolyte imbalances. <u>Antimotility agents</u>, such as loperamide and diphenoxylate + atropine may be prescribed to treat CID. Although the usual maximum dose of loperamide is 16 mg/day, this dose may be increased to 24 mg/day when treating CID under medical supervision. <u>Fluorouracil, capecitabine, and irinotecan</u> commonly cause CID that occurs several days after chemotherapy. The risk of diarrhea is increased when fluorouracil (or the prodrug capecitabine) is used in combination with leucovorin or when used in patients with dihydropyrimidine dehydrogenase (DPD) deficiencies (not common). Irinotecan also causes an early onset diarrhea that occurs during the infusion of the drug and is often accompanied by symptoms of cholinergic excess such as abdominal cramping, rhinitis, lacrimation and salivation. The treatment is the anticholinergic drug atropine. Many <u>TKIs</u>, especially those targeting VEGFR or EGFR, such as sorafenib and sunitinib, commonly cause diarrhea.

Oral Mucositis

Oral mucositis usually occurs several days after chemotherapy, with the severity of symptoms usually peaking around 7 days after chemotherapy and slowly resolving approximately 4 - 8 days later. Many chemotherapy agents that cause diarrhea also cause oral mucositis. No therapy is approved for the prevention of oral mucositis caused by standard doses of chemotherapy. Patients should be instructed to practice good oral hygiene to help reduce the risk of oral complications. Agents that coat or anesthetize the oral mucosa may be prescribed for control of oral pain and discomfort. Patients who develop oral mucositis may also develop oral infections with herpes simplex virus or *Candida spp.* Antiviral or antifungal medications may be prescribed.

Medications for Oral Complications of Chemotherapy

DRUG	DOSING	SAFETY/SIDE EFFECTS/MONITORING

Oral Mucositis

DRUG	DOSING	SAFETY/SIDE EFFECTS/MONITORING
Mucosal Barrier Gel Spray, solution, wafer *(Episil, Gelclair, Mucotrol, MuGard, Orafate, ProThelial)*	Varies depending on product. Most are applied to the oral mucosa several times per day.	**SIDE EFFECTS** Burning, stinging sensation in the mouth
Lidocaine 2% topical solution for mouth/throat	15 mL swish and spit/swallowed Q3H PRN	**BOXED WARNING** Avoid use in patients < 3 years of age due to reports of seizures, cardiopulmonary arrest and death. **WARNINGS** Exceeding the recommended dose can result in high plasma levels and serious adverse effects (seizures, cardiopulmonary arrest) **SIDE EFFECTS** Dizziness, drowsiness, confusion, hypotension **NOTES** Avoid ingestion of food for 60 minutes following dose due to risk of impaired swallowing and aspiration.

Xerostomia

DRUG	DOSING	SAFETY/SIDE EFFECTS/MONITORING
Artificial Saliva Substitutes Spray, solution, lozenge *(Aquoral, Biotene, Caphosol, Entertainer's Secret, Moi-Stir, Mouth Kote, NeutraSal, Numoisyn, Oasis, SalivaSure)*	Varies depending on product. Most can be applied to oral mucosa PRN.	

Medications for Oral Complications of Chemotherapy Continued

DRUG	DOSING	SAFETY/SIDE EFFECTS/MONITORING
Pilocarpine *(Salagen)*	5-10 mg PO TID Hepatic impairment Moderate: 5 mg PO BID Severe: avoid use	**WARNINGS** Use with caution in patients with cholelithiasis, nephrolithiasis, cardiovascular disease, asthma, bronchitis, COPD **SIDE EFFECTS** Cholinergic side effects: flushing, sweating, nausea, urinary frequency **NOTES** Avoid administering with high-fat meal

Hand-Foot Syndrome

Hand-foot syndrome (also known as palmar-plantar erythrodysesthesia) frequently occurs following treatment with fluorouracil, capecitabine, cytarabine, and liposomal doxorubicin. It can also occur following treatment with multitargeted TKIs, such as sorafenib and sunitinib. The mechanism for this toxicity is unclear. Patients may present with redness, swelling, tenderness, pain, blisters and possibly peeling of the palms and soles. Dose reductions or delays in treatment are recommended if symptoms do not improve.

Cooling procedures with cold compresses provide temporary relief of pain and tenderness. Emollients provide excellent moisturizing for hands and feet. Corticosteroids and pain medications may be used to help alleviate inflammation and pain.

HYPERCALCEMIA OF MALIGNANCY

Hypercalcemia occurs commonly in patients with breast cancer, lung cancer and multiple myeloma and causes significant symptoms for the patient, including nausea, vomiting, fatigue, dehydration, renal failure and mental status changes. Because of the risk of intravascular volume depletion due to hypercalcemia, all patients should be treated with hydration. Patients with mild hypercalcemia (corrected calcium < 12 mg/dL and no symptoms) may receive oral or IV hydration, all others should receive IV hydration. Loop diuretics, such as furosemide, should only be given after dehydration is corrected. Patients with moderate to severe hypercalcemia (corrected calcium > 12 mg/dL or symptomatic) should be treated with an IV bisphosphonate. Denosumab is an alternative in patients who cannot receive or have not responded to bisphosphonates. Calcium lowering effects of bisphosphonates and denosumab are expected to be observed in 1-3 days. Calcitonin lowers serum calcium in 4-6 hours and can be used concurrently with bisphosphonates or denosumab in patients with symptomatic hypercalcemia. Tachyphylaxis to calcitonin develops with repeated dosing, so therapy should be limited to 48 hours.

HAND-FOOT SYNDROME PREVENTION

Limit daily activities to reduce friction and heat exposure to hands and feet for 1 week after IV medication (e.g., 5-Fluorouracil) or during the duration of oral exposure (e.g., capecitabine).

Avoid long exposure to hot water (washing dishes, showers). Take short showers in luke warm water.

Avoid use of dishwashing gloves as the rubber will hold in the heat.

Avoid increased pressure on soles of feet (no jogging, aerobics, power walking, jumping).

Avoid increased pressure on palms of hands (do not use garden tools, screwdrivers, knives for chopping or performing other tasks that require squeezing hand(s) on a hard surface).

Hypercalcemia of Malignancy Treatment

TREATMENT	MOA	ONSET	DURATION	DEGREE OF HYPERCALCEMIA*
Hydration with normal saline and loop diuretics	↑ renal calcium excretion	Minutes to hours	Only during length of infusion	Mild (oral or IV hydration) Moderate Severe
Calcitonin (Miacalcin) 4-8 units/kg IM/SC Q12H	Inhibits bone resorption, ↑ renal calcium excretion	4-6 hours	48 hours max (risk of tachyphylaxis)	Moderate Severe
IV Bisphosphonates **Zoledronic acid (Zometa)** 4 mg IV once, may repeat in 7 days if needed. Do not infuse over < 15 minutes due to increased risk of renal toxicity. Dose does not need to be adjusted for mild-moderate renal insufficiency when used for hypercalcemia. (Do not confuse with _Reclast_, which is dosed at 5 mg IV yearly for osteoporosis) Pamidronate (Aredia) 60-90 mg IV over 2-24 hrs once, may repeat in 7 days if needed.	Inhibits bone resorption by stopping osteoclast function	24-72 hours	2-4 weeks	Mild Moderate Severe
Denosumab (Xgeva) 120 mg SC on days 1, 8 and 15 of the first month, then monthly (Do not confuse with _Prolia_, which is dosed at 60 mg SC every 6 months for osteoporosis - see Osteoporosis chapter)	Monoclonal antibody that blocks the interaction between RANKL and RANK (a receptor on osteoclasts), preventing osteoclast formation	24-72 hours	~1 month	Moderate Severe

• Degree of Hypercalemia: Mild: corrected calcium < 12 mg/dL, Moderate: corrected calcium 12-14 mg/dL, Severe: corrected calcium >14 mg/dL

Safe Handling of Hazardous Agents

Chemotherapy agents are hazardous drugs that are considered carcinogenic, mutagenic, and teratogenic. To limit exposure to these agents, pharmacies should have written procedures for handling these drugs safely. The United States Pharmacopeia (USP) chapters 797 and 800 regulate the preparation and handling of hazardous drugs and should be used by centers that prepare chemotherapy. Refer to the Sterile Compounding chapter for further information.

Routes of exposure include inhalation, ingestion, dermal contact, and accidental injections. The most common type of accidental exposure is inhalation of the aerosolized drug. A vertical flow class II biological safety or biosafety cabinet should be used at all times in addition to chemo-gowns and chemo-block gloves (preferably double gloving). The gowns should be made of lint-free, low-permeability fabric with a solid front, long sleeves, and tight-fitting elastic cuffs. Negative-pressure techniques should be employed during drug preparation. Chemotherapy spill kits should be readily available and located in areas of the institution in which chemotherapy is handled. Cytotoxic waste should be disposed of properly, IV bags should be labeled "Chemotherapeutic: Dispose of Properly" or similar, and patients should be informed of proper methods of disposing of potentially contaminated body waste (such as flushing the toilet twice).

Many chemotherapy agents are vesicants, which means they may cause tissue necrosis if the IV drug accidentally leaks from the vein into which it is being administered into the surrounding tissue (also called extravasation). Vesicant drugs include anthracyclines, vinca alkaloids, ixabepilone, mitomycin, mechlorethamine and teniposide. Care should be taken to avoid extravasation of these drugs by administering them through freshly started peripheral IVs or central venous catheters. If extravasation occurs, apply cold compresses (except with the vinca alkaloids and etoposide, use warm compresses) and the antidotes below depending on the drug extravasated:

- Anthracyclines: dexrazoxane (*Totect*) or dimethyl sulfoxide (off label use)
- Vinca alkaloids: hyaluronidase (off label use)

Based on clinical experience, a limited number of chemotherapy agents may be administered intrathecally. This is usually accomplished by performing a lumbar puncture and injecting the drug into the cerebrospinal fluid. Drugs that may be administered intrathecally include cytarabine, methotrexate, hydrocortisone, and thiotepa and they must be preservative-free.

Unfortunately, accidental intrathecal administration of vincristine has been reported. Intrathecal administration of vincristine is <u>fatal</u>. Care must be taken to properly label syringes of vincristine to avoid accidental intrathecal administration. Preparation of vincristine in small volume IVPB solutions (50 – 100 mL) is preferred to avoid the risk of accidental intrathecal administration.

Timing of Vaccinations

Vaccination during chemotherapy should be avoided because the antibody response is suboptimal. When chemotherapy is being planned, vaccination should precede the initiation of chemotherapy by ≥ 2 weeks. Patients on chemotherapy may receive the inactivated seasonal influenza vaccine in between cycles of chemotherapy. The administration of live vaccines to immunocompromised patients must be avoided.

Patient Counseling for Ondansetron

- Common side effects of this medication include headache, constipation, fatigue and dizziness.
- Take this medicine by mouth with a glass of water. It may be taken as needed or at scheduled times. Follow the directions on your prescription label. Do not take your medicine more often than directed.
- Do not take this medicine if you are taking apomorphine.
- If you are prescribed the oral disintegrating tablets: Do not attempt to push the tablets through foil backing. With <u>dry hands</u>, peel back the foil of 1 blister and remove the tablet. Place tablet on the tongue; it will dissolve in seconds. Once dissolved, you may swallow with saliva. Administration with liquid is not necessary. Wash hands after administration.
- If you are prescribed the oral soluble film *(Zuplenz)*: with dry hands, fold the pouch along the dotted line to expose the tear notch. While still folded, tear the pouch carefully along the edge and remove the oral soluble film just prior to dosing. Place the film on the tongue, it will dissolve in a few seconds. Allow each film to dissolve completely before taking the next film if more than one is needed to reach the desired dose (i.e., 16 mg given as two 8 mg films).

ONCOLOGY II: COMMON CANCER TYPES & TREATMENT

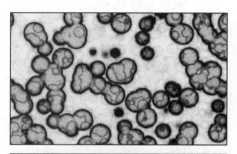

We gratefully acknowledge the assistance of Doreen Pon, PharmD, BCOP, BCPS, Assistant Professor at Western University of Health Sciences and Muoi Gi, PharmD, BCPS, BCOP, Oncology Pharmacy Residency Director at the VA San Diego Healthcare System and D. Raymond Weber, PharmD, BSPharm, BCOP, BCPS, RPh, Associate Professor, Notre Dame University of Maryland School of Pharmacy, in preparing this chapter.

GUIDELINES/REFERENCES

National Comprehensive Cancer Network (NCCN). www.nccn.org (accessed 2015 October 15)

American Society of Clinical Oncology (ASCO). www.asco.org (accessed 2015 October 15)

CHEMOTHERAPY REGIMENS AND DOSING

Cancer treatment depends on multiple factors, including cancer type, extent of disease and patient factors. When chemotherapy is used, the regimens are usually in combinations chosen for efficacy, synergy and ability to target cells with different resistance mechanisms and different stages of replication. Regimens are usually administered in cycles involving one or more drugs, given once, or multiple times, such as over several consecutive days, followed by days or weeks without treatment. The break in treatment will allow the patient time to recover from side effects.

CANCER THERAPEUTIC AGENTS

Traditional cytotoxic cancer therapeutic agents kill cancer cells by interfering with cellular replication. Cell cycle specific agents, such as antimetabolites and microtubule inhibitors, kill cancer cells during specific phases of the cell cycle, while cell cycle non-specific agents, such as alkylating agents and anthracyclines, can kill cancer cells in any phase of the cell cycle. Regardless of cell cycle specificity, traditional cytotoxic cancer therapeutic agents are more effective at killing cells undergoing cell division. Therefore, cancers that are characterized by more rapid cell growth, such as acute leukemias, are very susceptible to the cytotoxic effects of traditional cytotoxic cancer therapeutic agents. However, because other cells in the body are also rapidly dividing, such as those in the gastrointestinal tract and bone marrow, they are also susceptible to being killed by cytotoxic chemotherapy. This is why many cytotoxic cancer therapeutic agents cause common toxicities such as diarrhea, mucositis, and myelosuppression.

Some of the other cancer therapeutic agents are considered to be more targeted. Rather than non-specifically affecting any cell undergoing replication, these agents are designed to recognize specific biomarkers that are present on cancer cells or other cells that are essential for cancer cell growth. Drugs that are considered "targeted" include monoclonal antibodies and tyrosine kinase inhibitors (TKIs). In general, these targeted agents have side effect profiles that are very different from traditional cytotoxic agents.

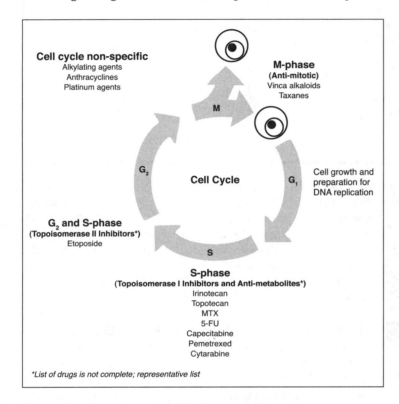

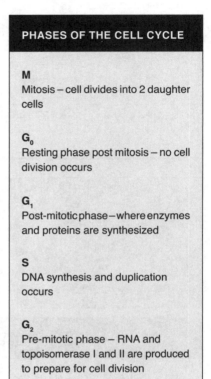

Body Surface Area (BSA) Calculations

Chemotherapy may be dosed using flat or fixed dosing, patient's weight (mg/kg), or patient's body surface area (BSA). There are several BSA formulas, but the most commonly used are: DuBois and DuBois, and Mosteller. The weight that is commonly used for calculating the dose in oncology is the actual body weight. Use the patient's actual body weight for BSA and oncology dosage calculations unless instructed otherwise.

Dubois and Dubois Equation

$$\text{BSA (m}^2) = 0.007184 \times \text{Height(cm)}^{0.725} \times \text{Weight(kg)}^{0.425}$$

Example

A patient has a weight of 175 pounds and height of 6′1″. Calculate the patient's BSA using the DuBois and DuBois formula. Round to the nearest hundredth.

Convert weight in pounds to kilograms by dividing by 2.2: 175/2.2 = 79.5 kg
Convert height in inches to centimeters by multiplying by 2.54: 73″ x 2.54 = 185.4 cm

$$\text{BSA (m}^2) = 0.007184 \times \text{Height(cm)}^{0.725} \times \text{Weight(kg)}^{0.425}$$

$$\text{BSA (m}^2) = 0.007184 \times (185.4)^{0.725} \times (79.5)^{0.425}$$

$$\text{BSA (m}^2) = 2.03 \text{ m}^2$$

Mosteller Equation

$$BSA\ (m^2) = \sqrt{\frac{Ht\ (cm)\ x\ Wt\ (kg)}{3,600}}$$

Example

A patient has a weight of 175 pounds and height of 6'1". Calculate the patient's BSA using the Mosteller formula. Round to the nearest hundredth.

Convert weight in pounds to kilograms by dividing by 2.2: 175/2.2 = 79.5 kg
Convert height in inches to centimeters by multiplying by 2.54: 73" x 2.54 = 185.4 cm

$$BSA\ (m^2) = \sqrt{\frac{185.4\ cm\ x\ 79.5\ kg}{3,600}} = 2.02\ m^2$$

A patient with a BSA of 2.02 m² is going to receive paclitaxel for lung cancer at a dose of 175 mg/m². Calculate the dose of paclitaxel that this patient will receive.

$$175\ mg/m^2\ \ x\ \ 2.02\ m^2\ =\ 354\ mg$$

A patient with a BSA of 2.02 m² is going to receive paclitaxel for lung cancer at a dose of 175 mg/m². Paclitaxel is available as a 6 mg/mL solution. If the patient's dose is 354 mg, how many milliliters will be needed for the dose?

$$354\ mg\ \ x\ \ \frac{1\ mL}{6\ mg}\ =\ 59\ mL$$

TRADITIONAL CYTOTOXIC CANCER THERAPEUTIC AGENTS

The discussion that follows highlights the more commonly encountered "prototype drugs" in each class, but is not intended to be comprehensive in scope. Throughout this section, the traditional cytotoxic cancer therapeutic agents will be categorized into either cell cycle non-specific agents or cell cycle specific agents.

CELL CYCLE NON-SPECIFIC AGENTS

Alkylating Agents

Alkylating agents work by cross-linking DNA strands and inhibiting protein synthesis and DNA synthesis.

- Many of the agents are available in oral or oral and intravenous formulations.

- Can cause DNA mutations that lead to "secondary malignancies" (usually acute leukemia).

- Cyclophosphamide and ifosfamide produce a metabolite, acrolein, that concentrates in the bladder and can cause hemorrhagic cystitis. Mesna is a chemoprotectant that inactivates this toxic metabolite.

DRUG	UNIQUE CONCERNS	SAFETY/SIDE EFFECTS/ MONITORING
Cyclophosphamide *(Cytoxan)* Ifosfamide *(Ifex)*	Hemorrhagic Cystitis: Ensure adequate hydration and give mesna Mesna (*Mesnex*) is a chemoprotectant that must be given prophylactically with ifosfamide and with high doses of cyclophosphamide	**BOXED WARNINGS** Myelosuppression Hemorrhagic cystitis (ifosfamide, cyclophosphamide) Pulmonary toxicity (carmustine) Neurotoxicity (ifosfamide)
Carmustine *(BiCNU, Gliadel wafer)*	Use non-PVC bag and tubing due to absorption to PVC	
Dacarbazine *(DTIC-Dome)*	Protect from light (decomposed drug turns pink)	**SIDE EFFECTS** Pulmonary toxicity (busulfan, carmustine, lomustine)
Procarbazine *(Matulane)*	MAO inhibitor, avoid interacting drugs/foods	SIADH (cyclophosphamide)
Altretamine *(Hexalen)* Bendamustine *(Treanda)* Busulfan *(Myleran)* Lomustine *(CeeNU)* Mechlorethamine *(Mustargen)* Melphalan *(Alkeran)* Temozolomide *(Temodar)*		Mucositis, moderate-high emetic potential, alopecia, secondary malignancies, neurotoxicity

Platinum-Based Compounds

Similar to alkylating agents in that they cross-link DNA and interfere with DNA synthesis and cell replication.

- Due to the platinum content, they can cause a few toxicities that are similar to symptoms of heavy metal poisoning, such as peripheral sensory neuropathy, ototoxicity, and nephrotoxicity.

- Cisplatin is associated with the highest incidence of nephrotoxicity and chemotherapy-induced nausea and vomiting (CINV).

DRUG	UNIQUE CONCERNS	SAFETY/SIDE EFFECTS/MONITORING
CISplatin *(Platinol)*	Nephrotoxicity, ototoxicity (both cumulative) Doses are usually limited to ≤ 100 mg/m²/cycle Nephrotoxicity: Monitor renal function, intake/output, Mg and K as levels may decrease, ensure adequate IV hydration (1-2 L) before each dose. Amifostine (*Ethyol*) is a chemoprotectant that may be given prophylactically to prevent nephrotoxicity. Ototoxicity: Perform audiograms at baseline and before each dose. Highly emetogenic: 3 drug antiemetic regimen required for prevention.	**BOXED WARNINGS** Anaphylactic-like reactions (risk ↑ with number of exposures; caution when administering > 6 cycles of platinum-based compounds) Myelosuppression, N/V, renal toxicity, ototoxicity, doses > 100 mg/m²/cycle must be confirmed with prescriber (cisplatin) MyelosuOncology_I_V10_MS SB edits. pdfion, N/V (carboplatin) **CONTRAINDICATIONS** Pre-existing renal impairment, hearing impairment, myelosuppression (cisplatin)
CARBOplatin *(Paraplatin)*	Myelosuppression is dose-related. Doses for adults are commonly calculated by target AUC using the Calvert Formula: Total carboplatin dose (mg) = (Target AUC) x (GFR + 25) where: - AUC can range from 2-8 mg/mL x min - GFR is commonly "capped" at 125 mL/min	**SIDE EFFECTS** Peripheral neuropathy (cumulative dose-related), myelosuppression, ↑ LFTs
Oxaliplatin *(Eloxatin)*	Acute sensory neuropathy: Occurs 1-7 days after administration and can be exacerbated by exposure to cold, including drinking cold beverages	

Anthracyclines

Work by several mechanisms, including intercalation into DNA, inhibiting topoisomerase II, and creating oxygen-free radicals that damage cells.

- Cardiotoxicity is associated with all anthracyclines and is manifested as cardiomyopathy and heart failure. The risk for cardiotoxicity is related to the total cumulative anthracycline dose the patient has received over their lifetime. The recommended lifetime maximum cumulative anthracycline dose differs for each anthracycline, but is most well-defined for doxorubicin. Dexrazoxane (Zinecard) is a chemoprotectant indicated for prevention of doxorubicin-induced cardiotoxicity (see box).

TO REDUCE DOXORUBICIN CARDIOTOXICITY:

1. Keep track of the lifetime cumulative doxorubicin dose for each patient

   [Doxorubicin Dose in mg/m²/cycle] x [total number of cycles received] = Cumulative Doxorubicin Dose in mg/m²

   Example: [Doxorubicin 50 mg/m²/cycle] x [6 cycles] = 300 mg/m²

2. Lifetime maximum cumulative doxorubicin dose = 450-550 mg/m²

3. Monitor left ventricular ejection fraction (LVEF) before and after treatment (with MUGA or ECHO)

4. Dexrazoxane (Zinecard) is a chemoprotectant that may be considered when the doxorubicin cumulative dose exceeds 300 mg/m²

- Anthracyclines are potent vesicants, however, liposomal anthracyclines are not. Dexrazoxane (Totect) is an antidote that can be used for accidental doxorubicin extravasation. Note dexrazoxane has two brand names, each used for a different indication.

DRUG	UNIQUE CONCERNS	SAFETY/SIDE EFFECTS/MONITORING
DOXOrubicin (Adriamycin) DAUNOrubicin (Cerubidine) EPIrubicin (Ellence) IDArubicin (Idamycin) VALrubicin (Valstar)	Potent vesicants (tissue necrosis if extravasated) Red urine discoloration Doxorubicin: do not exceed 450-550 mg/m² (total lifetime cumulative dose) Dexrazoxane (Totect) for extravasation; (Zinecard) for cardio-protection at higher doses N/V - give antiemetics	**BOXED WARNINGS** Myocardial toxicity, vesicant, myelosuppression, hepatotoxicity, secondary malignancy Renal impairment (daunorubicin, idarubicin) **CONTRAINDICATIONS** Pre-existing myocardial insufficiency Severe hepatic impairment
DOXOrubicin liposomal (Doxil) DAUNOrubicin liposomal (DaunoXome)	Not vesicants Red urine discoloration Not interchangeable with non-liposomal formulations	**BOXED WARNINGS** Myocardial toxicity, infusion-related reactions, myelosuppression Hepatotoxicity (daunorubicin) **SIDE EFFECTS** Hand-foot syndrome
MitoXANtrone (Novantrone) an anthracenedione, related to the anthracyclines	Irritant with vesicant-like properties Blue urine discoloration	**BOXED WARNINGS** Myocardial toxicity, myelosuppression, secondary malignancy

CELL CYCLE SPECIFIC AGENTS

Vinca Alkaloids

Vinca alkaloids inhibit the function of microtubules during <u>M phase</u>.

- <u>Peripheral</u> sensory and <u>autonomic neuropathies</u> (<u>constipation</u>) are common. Neuropathies are common side effects because microtubules play an important role in axonal transport in neurons. Vin<u>C</u>ristine is associated with more <u>C</u>NS toxicity (neuropathy) than the other vinca alkaloids. Accidental <u>intrathecal administration</u> will cause a progressive <u>paralysis and death</u>. Label products to prevent accidental intrathecal administration.

> ## FOR INTRAVENOUS USE ONLY.
> ## FATAL IF GIVEN BY OTHER ROUTES.

- Vin<u>B</u>lastine and vinorel<u>B</u>ine are associated with more <u>B</u>one marrow suppression (myelosuppression) than vincristine.

- Vinca alkaloids are potent <u>vesicants</u>. Use warm compresses and hyaluronidase (off-label use) if extravasation occurs.

DRUG	UNIQUE CONCERNS	SAFETY/SIDE EFFECTS/MONITORING
VinCRIStine *(Vincasar)*	Not myelosuppressive Often "capped" at <u>2 mg/dose</u>, regardless of the calculated mg/m² dose. Higher doses may be associated with ↑ risk of neuropathy	**BOXED WARNINGS** Vesicants <u>For IV administration only</u> (intrathecal administration is <u>fatal</u>)
VinBLASTine *(Velban)* VinORELbine *(Navelbine)*	Myelosuppressive	**SIDE EFFECTS** Peripheral sensory neuropathy (paresthesias), autonomic neuropathy (gastroparesis, constipation), SIADH
VinCRIStine liposomal *(Marqibo)*	<u>Not</u> interchangeable with vincristine	

Taxanes

Taxanes inhibit the function of microtubules during <u>M phase</u>.

- <u>Peripheral sensory neuropathies</u> are common side effects since the microtubules play an important role in axonal transport in neurons.

- Severe <u>infusion-related hypersensitivity reactions</u> (HSR) and <u>fatal anaphylaxis</u> can occur with all taxanes. Premedication regimens vary depending on the specific taxane.

- For all taxanes, use <u>non-PVC IV bag</u> and tubing due to leaching of DEHP (except *Abraxane*).

- Drug interaction: elimination of taxanes is reduced when given after cisplatin/carboplatin. Give taxanes <u>before</u> platinum-based compounds.

DRUG	UNIQUE CONCERNS	SAFETY/SIDE EFFECTS/MONITORING
PACLitaxel *(Taxol)*	HSR: Premedicate with diphenhydramine, corticosteroid, H₂RA	**BOXED WARNINGS** Severe hypersensitivity reactions, myelosuppression Fluid retention (docetaxel)
DOCEtaxel *(Taxotere)*	HSR: Premedicate with corticosteroids for 3 days, starting 1 day prior to docetaxel Causes <u>severe fluid retention</u> (characterized by pleural effusion, cardiac tamponade and/or edema); premedicate with dexamethasone 1 day prior to administration	**SIDE EFFECTS** Peripheral sensory neuropathy, myalgias, arthralgias, hepatotoxicity
Cabazitaxel *(Jevtana)*	HSR: Premedicate with diphenhydramine, corticosteroid, H₂RA	
Paclitaxel albumin-bound *(Abraxane)*	No premedication required	

Topoisomerase I Inhibitors

These agents block the coiling and uncoiling of the double-stranded DNA helix during <u>S phase</u>; causes single and double strand breaks in the DNA and prevents religation (sealing the DNA strands back together again) of single strand breaks.

DRUG	UNIQUE CONCERNS	SAFETY/SIDE EFFECTS/MONITORING
Irinotecan *(Camptosar)*	<u>Acute cholinergic symptoms:</u> Flushing, sweating, abdominal cramps, diarrhea (treat with atropine) <u>Delayed diarrhea:</u> Treat with loperamide (up to 24 mg/day) <u>Pharmacogenomics:</u> Patients homozygous for the UGT1A1*28 allele are at ↑ risk for neutropenia	**BOXED WARNINGS** Myelosuppression Diarrhea (early and late) (irinotecan) **SIDE EFFECTS** N/V/D, alopecia, diarrhea, abdominal pain
Topotecan *(Hycamtin)*		

Topoisomerase II Inhibitors

Block the coiling and uncoiling of double-stranded DNA during the G2 phase; causes single and double strand breaks in the DNA and prevents religation (sealing the DNA strands back together again) of single strand breaks.

DRUG	UNIQUE CONCERNS	SAFETY/SIDE EFFECTS/MONITORING
Etoposide IV *(Toposar)*	Infusion rate-related hypotension: Infuse over at least 30-60 minutes IV preparation: Prepare infusion solution to a concentration ≤ 0.4 mg/mL to avoid precipitation Use non-PVC IV bag and tubing due to leaching of DEHP	**BOXED WARNING** Myelosuppression **SIDE EFFECTS** Hypersensitivity reactions, anaphylaxis, secondary malignancies
Etoposide phosphate *(Etopophos)*	Does not have infusion solution concentration limits like etoposide (primarily used if the concentration needs to be ≥ 0.4 mg/mL)	
Etoposide capsules *(VePesid)*	Refrigerate capsules Etoposide IV:PO ratio 1:2 (50% bioavailability) Doses > 200 mg need to be given in divided doses due to reduced bioavailability	

Pyrimidine Analog Antimetabolites

These agents inhibit pyrimidine synthesis during S phase; an active metabolite (F-UMP) is incorporated into RNA to replace uracil and inhibits cell growth, while another active metabolite (5-dUMP) inhibits thymidylate synthetase.

DRUG	UNIQUE CONCERNS	SAFETY/SIDE EFFECTS/MONITORING
Fluorouracil, "5-FU" *(Adrucil)* *Efudex, Carac, Tolak* and *Fluoroplex* are topical formulations used for actinic keratosis. *Efudex* is also used for basal cell carcinoma.	Leucovorin: Given with fluorouracil to ↑ the efficacy of fluorouracil; helps fluorouracil bind more tightly to its target enzyme, thymidylate synthetase Pharmacogenomics: Dihydropyrimidine dehydrogenase (DPD) deficiency ↑ risk of severe toxicity	**BOXED WARNINGS** Significant ↑ in INR during and up to 1 month after treatment, monitor INR frequently (capecitabine) **CONTRAINDICATIONS** Severe renal impairment (CrCl < 30 mL/min) (capecitabine) **SIDE EFFECTS** Hand-foot syndrome, cardiotoxicity, diarrhea, photosensitivity, dermatitis, mucositis
Capecitabine *(Xeloda)* Given as 2 divided doses 12 hrs apart, with water within 30 min after a meal	Oral prodrug of fluorouracil Pharmacogenomics: Dihydropyrimidine dehydrogenase (DPD) deficiency ↑ risk of severe toxicity	
Cytarabine conventional (called "ara-C") Cytarabine liposomal *(DepoCyt)* for intrathecal administration	Cytarabine Syndrome: Fever, flu-like symptoms, myalgia, bone pain, rash	**BOXED WARNINGS** Myelosuppression and GI toxicities (conventional); Chemical arachnoiditis (N/V, HA, fever) is common and can be fatal if untreated - give dexamethasone (liposomal formulation) **SIDE EFFECTS** Pulmonary toxicity, encephalopathy, hepatotoxicity, hand-foot syndrome
Gemcitabine *(Gemzar)*	Infusion rate affects efficacy and toxicity; infuse per institutional protocol	**SIDE EFFECTS** Myelosuppression, flu-like symptoms, hepatotoxicity, pulmonary toxicity

Folate Antimetabolites

Interfere with the enzymes involved in the folic acid cycle, blocking purine and pyrimidine biosynthesis during S phase.

- Folic acid or folic acid analogs +/- vitamin B12 may be required to reduce toxicity caused by interference with the folic acid cycle (myelosuppression, mucositis, diarrhea). With high doses of methotrexate, leucovorin (or levoleucovorin) "rescue" must be given. Leucovorin is the active form of folic acid that is able to bypass the enzyme block of dihydrofolate reductase caused by methotrexate. Note that folic acid is ineffective for high dose methotrexate "rescue".

- Nephrotoxicity is associated with all the folate antimetabolites, but most frequently with high doses of methotrexate ($\geq$ 1 gram/m^2).

DRUG	UNIQUE CONCERNS	SAFETY/SIDE EFFECTS/ MONITORING
Methotrexate *(Trexall, Rheumatrex)* Doses used for cancer are much higher than doses used for RA or psoriasis. RA/psoriasis doses are given weekly, not daily. If given intrathecally, use only the preservative-free formulation of methotrexate	High doses of methotrexate (MTX) require leucovorin (folinic acid) "rescue" to reduce toxicities. Levoleucovorin *(Fusilev)* is also available as the levo (L) isomer (the active biological moiety) of leucovorin and is dosed at 1/2 the dose of leucovorin. Monitor MTX levels and renal function daily and continue leucovorin until MTX level is $\leq$ 0.05-0.1 micromolar. Hydration and IV sodium bicarbonate must be given to alkalinize the urine and $\downarrow$ risk of nephrotoxicity caused by high dose MTX. Ensure patient does not have 3rd spacing (ascites, pleural effusions, severe edema) prior as this can cause delayed clearance of drug. Glucarpidase *(Voraxaze)* can rapidly lower methotrexate levels that remain high despite adequate hydration and urinary alkalinization; turns extracellular MTX into inactive metabolites (DAMPA and glutamate); very expensive Drug Interactions NSAIDs, salicylates, beta-lactams, proton pump inhibitors, sulfonamide antibiotics, probenecid – all can $\downarrow$ clearance of methotrexate	**BOXED WARNINGS** Myelosuppression and aplastic anemia, renal damage, hepatotoxicity (fibrosis and cirrhosis with long-term use), interstitial pneumonitis, dermatologic reactions (SJS/TEN), diarrhea, stomatitis, immunosuppression, tumor lysis syndrome **SIDE EFFECTS** Nephrotoxicity (dose related), hepatotoxicity (more common with chronic use), hand-foot syndrome
PEMEtrexed *(Alimta)*	To $\downarrow$ risk of side effects, give folic acid, vitamin B12 and dexamethasone	**SIDE EFFECTS** Nephrotoxicity, hepatotoxicity, dermatologic toxicity (premedicate with dexamethasone)
PRALAtrexate *(Folotyn)*	To $\downarrow$ risk of side effects, give folic acid and vitamin B12	**SIDE EFFECTS** Nephrotoxicity, hepatotoxicity

DOSING CONSIDERATIONS FOR CANCER THERAPEUTIC AGENTS

DRUG	MAXIMUM DOSES	REASON
Bleomycin	Lifetime cumulative dose 400 units	Pulmonary toxicity
Doxorubicin	Lifetime cumulative dose 450-550 mg/m^2	Cardiotoxicity
Cisplatin	Dose per cycle not to exceed 100 mg/m^2	Nephrotoxicity
Vincristine	Single dose "capped" at 2 mg	Neuropathy

Miscellaneous Agents

DRUG	UNIQUE CONCERNS	SAFETY/SIDE EFFECTS/MONITORING
Tretinoin, AKA **All-trans Retinoic Acid,** *ATRA* ↓ proliferation and ↑ differentiation of acute promyelocytic leukemia (APL) cells First line therapy for APL	Retinoids (vitamin A analogues) <u>Pregnancy Category D</u> Retinoic Acid-Acute Promyelocytic Leukemia (RA-APL) differentiation syndrome: fever, dyspnea, weight gain, edema, pulmonary infiltrates, pericardial or pleural effusions – treat with dexamethasone.	**BOXED WARNINGS** <u>RA-APL differentiation syndrome</u>, leukocytosis, pregnancy **SIDE EFFECTS** Leukocytosis, RA-APL differentiation syndrome, QT prolongation, N/V/D, skin/mucous membrane dryness, hyperlipidemia, GI bleeding
Arsenic trioxide *(Trisenox)* ↑ apoptosis of APL cells and damages fusion protein PML-RAR alpha Second line therapy for acute promyelocytic leukemia (APL)	<u>QT prolongation</u>: monitor ECG, avoid concurrent QT prolonging agents, keep Mg, Ca, and K within normal range. If acute vasomotor reactions (lightheadedness, dizziness, or hypotension) occur, prolong infusion.	**BOXED WARNINGS** <u>RA-APL differentiation syndrome</u>, ECG abnormalities (AV block, <u>QT prolongation</u>), ECG and electrolyte monitoring **SIDE EFFECTS** Leukocytosis, APL differentiation syndrome, <u>QT prolongation</u>, N/V/D, GI bleeding, stomatitis, electrolyte imbalance, acute vasomotor reactions (lightheadedness, dizziness, or hypotension), fatigue, edema, headache, insomnia, anxiety, infection
Asparaginase *(Erwinaze)* – derived from Erwinia chrysanthemi Pegaspargase *(Oncaspar)* – modified form of L-asparaginase (derived from *E. coli*) and conjugated with polyethylene glycol	Deprives leukemia cells of asparagine which is an essential amino acid in leukemia. The pegylated form (pegaspargase) allows for every 2 week dosing and ↓ incidence of allergic reactions. Monitor fibrinogen, PT, aPTT, LFTs	**CONTRAINDICATIONS** Bleeding, thrombosis or pancreatitis with prior asparaginase treatment **SIDE EFFECTS** <u>Hypersensitivity reactions, pancreatitis</u>, hyperglycemia, hepatotoxicity, CNS toxicity (lethargy, somnolence), encephalopathy, N/V, <u>prolonged prothrombin time (PT/INR)</u>
Bleomycin Intercalating agent blocking topoisomerase II	Due to risk of anaphylactoid reaction, a test dose may be given. May premedicate with acetaminophen to ↓ incidence of fever or chills. ↑ risk of pulmonary fibrosis when given with G-CSF (filgrastim). Recommend to not use G-CSF on days of bleomycin administration. <u>Not myelosuppressive.</u> <u>Maximum lifetime dose of 400 units due to pulmonary toxicity risk.</u>	**BOXED WARNINGS** <u>Pulmonary fibrosis</u>, anaphylaxis **SIDE EFFECTS** <u>Hypersensitivity reaction</u>, pulmonary reactions (such as pneumonitis which may progress to pulmonary fibrosis), mucositis, hyperpigmentation, fever, chills, N/V (mild)

Miscellaneous Agents Continued

DRUG	UNIQUE CONCERNS	SAFETY/SIDE EFFECTS/MONITORING
Mitomycin *(Mutamycin)* Free radical formation and alkylator	Vesicant, do not extravasate. Antidote is dimethyl sulfoxide (DMSO) and cool compresses. Mitomycin IV solutions are a hazy blue in color and can make the urine blue-green.	**BOXED WARNINGS** Bone marrow suppression, hemolytic-uremic syndrome **CONTRAINDICATIONS** Thrombocytopenia, coagulopathy, bleeding **SIDE EFFECTS** Leukopenia, thrombocytopenia, N/V, fatigue, alopecia, mucous membrane toxicity, cystitis or dysuria (from intravesical administration into bladder)

Mammalian Target of Rapamycin (mTOR) Inhibitors - Inhibit downstream regulation of vascular endothelial growth factor (VEGF) reducing cell growth, metabolism, proliferation and angiogenesis.

DRUG	UNIQUE CONCERNS	SAFETY/SIDE EFFECTS/MONITORING
Everolimus *(Afinitor)* Tablet *Zortress* is indicated for <u>transplantation</u> and used in various doses	CYP 3A4 major substrate	**BOXED WARNINGS** See Transplant chapter for *Zortress* **CONTRAINDICATIONS** Hypersensitivity to rapamycin derivatives **SIDE EFFECTS** <u>Dyslipidemia</u>, hyperglycemia, myelosuppression, <u>rash</u>, pruritus, hand-foot syndrome, <u>stomatitis</u>, fatigue, N/V/D, peripheral edema, <u>interstitial lung disease</u>, renal impairment, ↑ LFTs MedGuide required
Temsirolimus *(Torisel)* Injection	CYP 3A4 major substrate Premedicate with diphenhydramine <u>Use non-PVC bag & tubing</u> due to leaching of DEHP	**CONTRAINDICATION** Moderate to severe hepatic impairment **SIDE EFFECTS** <u>Dyslipidemia, hyperglycemia, myelosuppression, interstitial lung disease</u>, acute hypersensitivity reactions (polysorbate 80 solvent system), N/V/D, peripheral edema, renal impairment

Immunomodulators - oral agents that block angiogenesis and kill abnormal cells in the bone marrow while stimulating the bone marrow to produce normal healthy cells. Usually indicated for multiple myeloma. These agents are <u>Pregnancy Category X</u> and patients must not become pregnant while using these drugs. All three have strict REMS programs.

DRUG	UNIQUE CONCERNS	SAFETY/SIDE EFFECTS/MONITORING
Lenalidomide *(Revlimid)* **Pomalidomide (Pomalyst)** **Thalidomide *(Thalomid)***	<u>Pregnancy Category X</u>: Severe birth defects. Only available under restricted distribution program: patient, prescriber and pharmacist must be registered with *Revlimid* REMS program, *Pomalyst* REMS program and/or *Thalomid* REMS program if using drug. MedGuide required Consider prophylactic anticoagulation due to ↑ VTE risk, <u>seek medical care</u> if signs and symptoms of DVT/PE develop: <u>shortness of breath, chest pain, or arm or leg swelling</u>.	**BOXED WARNINGS** Fetal risk/pregnancy, thrombosis (DVT/PE), hematologic toxicity (lenalidomide) **CONTRAINDICATIONS** Pregnancy **SIDE EFFECTS** <u>Neutropenia, thrombocytopenia</u>, constipation, N/V/D, fatigue, fever, cough, pruritus, rash, arthralgias, back pain, peripheral edema, DVT/PE. Neuropathy, confusion, somnolence (thalidomide) Hypercalcemia (pomalidomide)

Miscellaneous Agents Continued

DRUG	UNIQUE CONCERNS	SAFETY/SIDE EFFECTS/MONITORING

Proteasome Inhibitors - Inhibit proteosomes, which help to regulate intracellular protein homeostasis by inhibiting cell cycle progression and inducing apoptosis.

Bortezomib *(Velcade)* SC administration has less neuropathy than IV administration	<u>Give antiviral (acyclovir, valacyclovir) to prevent herpes (zoster and simplex) reactivation</u>	**CONTRAINDICATIONS** Hypersensitivity to boron or mannitol, intrathecal administration (fatal) **SIDE EFFECTS** <u>Peripheral neuropathy</u>, psychiatric disturbances, insomnia, weakness, paresthesias, arthralgias/myalgias, cardiotoxicity, pulmonary toxicity, hypotension, <u>thrombocytopenia, neutropenia,</u> N/V/D, tumor lysis syndrome
Carfilzomib *(Kyprolis)*	Premedicate with dexamethasone and fluids ↑ alkaline phosphatase correlates with ↑ efficacy	**SIDE EFFECTS** <u>Peripheral neuropathy (but less than bortezomib)</u>, fatigue, pulmonary toxicity, acute renal failure, tumor lysis syndrome, hepatotoxicity, anemia, thrombocytopenia, N/V/D, pyrexia, cardiotoxicity

TARGETED THERAPIES

Monoclonal Antibodies

Monoclonal antibodies work in various ways to inhibit cancer cell growth. Some bind to specific antigens or receptors on the surface of cancer cells and cause cell death. Some of these agents are conjugated to cytotoxic drugs or radioactive compounds. Some help to activate the immune system to recognize and destroy tumor cells. Representative monoclonal antibody targets and the associated drugs are listed below.

- All are given as intravenous infusions.

- Most are associated with infusion-related reactions, including hypersensitivity reactions, anaphylaxis, hypotension, and bronchospasm. Some infusion-related reactions may be fatal. Premedication is usually required.

- Agents that are conjugated to cytotoxic drugs are associated with additional side effects due to the cytotoxic conjugate.

- Agents that activate the immune system can be associated with autoimmune-mediated side effects.

Monoclonal Antibodies Nomenclature

PREFIX	TARGET			SOURCE				STEM
	Substem	Meaning	Example	Substem	Meaning	% Human	Example	
variable	*ci*	circulatory system	beva*ci*zumab	*o*	m*o*use	0	Blinatum*o*mab	-mab
	li	immune system	ipi*li*mumab	*xi*	*Chi*meric*	~34	Cetu*xi*mab	
	os	bone	den*os*umab	*zu*	Humani*z*ed*	~90-95	Bevaci*zu*mab	
	tu	tumor	per*tu*zumab	*u*	h*u*man	100	Panitum*u*mab	

Chimeric/humanized are designated as human and animal source

"AMA (USAN) Monoclonal antibodies". United States Adopted Names. 2007-2008.

"The use of stems in the selection of International Nonproprietary Names (INN) for biological and biotechnical substances". World Health Organization. 2011. pp. 51-52.

COMMON MABs	TARGET
Bevacizumab *(Avastin)*	Binds to VEGF
Cetuximab *(Erbitux)*	Binds to EGFR
Trastuzumab *(Herceptin)*	Binds to HER2
Rituximab *(Rituxan)*	Binds to CD20
Ipilimumab *(Yervoy)*	Binds to cytotoxic T-lymphocyte antigen-4 (CTLA4) receptor

DRUG	UNIQUE CONCERNS	SAFETY/SIDE EFFECTS/MONITORING

Vascular Endothelial Growth Factor (VEGF) Inhibitors

DRUG	UNIQUE CONCERNS	SAFETY/SIDE EFFECTS/MONITORING
Bevacizumab *(Avastin)* Ramucirumab *(Cyramza)*	Use 0.22 micron filter for ramucirumab Impairs wound healing: Do <u>not</u> administer for <u>28 days before or after surgery</u> Monitor blood pressure and proteinuria prior to each dose	**BOXED WARNINGS** <u>Severe/fatal bleeding</u>, <u>GI perforation</u>, surgical wound dehiscence (splitting) **SIDE EFFECTS** <u>Hypertension</u>, proteinuria, nephrotic syndrome, heart failure, thrombosis

Human Epidermal Growth Factor Receptor 2 (HER2) Inhibitors

DRUG	UNIQUE CONCERNS	SAFETY/SIDE EFFECTS/MONITORING
Trastuzumab (Herceptin) Pertuzumab *(Perjeta)* **Ado-Trastuzumab emtansine (Kadcyla)** Trastuzumab conjugated to a microtubule inhibitor	Use 0.22 micron filter for Ado-Trastuzumab Pharmacogenomics: Test for HER2 gene expression; must have HER2 over-expression to use. Monitor LVEF (ECHO or MUGA) at baseline and during treatment.	**BOXED WARNINGS** Heart failure, embryo-fetal death and birth defects Severe infusion-related reactions and pulmonary toxicity (trastuzumab) Hepatotoxicity (ado-trastuzumab) Ado-trastuzumab emtansine and conventional trastuzumab are <u>not</u> interchangeable **SIDE EFFECTS** Infusion-related reactions, N/V/D, alopecia

Monoclonal Antibodies Continued

DRUG	UNIQUE CONCERNS	SAFETY/SIDE EFFECTS/MONITORING

Epidermal Growth Factor Receptor (EGFR) Inhibitors

DRUG	UNIQUE CONCERNS	SAFETY/SIDE EFFECTS/MONITORING
Cetuximab *(Erbitux)* Panitumumab *(Vectibix)*	Premedicate 1st dose with diphenhydramine Use 0.22 micron filter Pharmacogenomics: Test for EGFR gene expression and KRAS mutation. EGFR positive expression correlates with better response rates in NSCLC. Must be KRAS wild type to use. KRAS mutation predicts poor response to treatment in colorectal cancer.	**BOXED WARNINGS** Severe/fatal infusion-related reactions Cardiac arrest (cetuximab) Dermatologic toxicities (panitumumab) **SIDE EFFECTS** Acneiform rash, serious skin toxicities (SJS/TEN), ocular toxicities, infusion-related reactions, N/V/D, Mg and Ca wasting **NOTES** Acneiform rash usually occurs within the 1st 2 weeks of treatment and may correlate with response. Advise patients to avoid direct sunlight, use sunscreen and topical emollients. Contact MD if skin blistering, bullae, or exfoliation occur.

Leukocyte Cluster of Differentiation (CD) Antigens (CD20, CD30, CD19, CD3) Inhibitors

DRUG	UNIQUE CONCERNS	SAFETY/SIDE EFFECTS/MONITORING
Rituximab *(Rituxan)* Ofatumumab *(Arzera)* Obinutuzumab *(Gazyva)*	Premedicate with diphenhydramine, acetaminophen, corticosteroid; slowly titrate rate of first infusion to lower risk of infusion reactions Pharmacogenomics: Test for B-cell antigen CD20; must be CD20 positive to use MedGuide required	**BOXED WARNINGS** Hepatitis B reactivation, progressive multifocal leukoencephalopathy (all) Serious skin reactions (SJS/TEN), severe/fatal infusion-related reactions (rituximab) **SIDE EFFECTS** Rash, peripheral edema, hypertension, renal impairment, tumor lysis syndrome **NOTES** Check hepatitis B panel prior to administration Can cause severe infusion-related reactions (urticaria, hypotension, angioedema, bronchospasm, hypoxia, anaphylaxis)
Brentuximab vedotin *(Adcetris)* Conjugated to MMAE, a microtubule inhibitor		**BOXED WARNINGS** Progressive multifocal leukoencephalopathy **CONTRAINDICATIONS** Concurrent use with bleomycin **SIDE EFFECTS** Myelosuppression, neuropathy, pulmonary toxicity, hepatotoxicity, infusion-related reactions, SJS/TEN
Blinatumomab *(Blincyto)* Bispecific antibody targeting CD19 on B-cells and engaging CD3 on T-cells, causing lysis of B-cells	MedGuide required	**BOXED WARNINGS** Cytokine release syndrome, neurotoxicity **SIDE EFFECTS** Myelosuppression, hepatotoxicity, leukoencephalopathy, tumor lysis syndrome

Monoclonal Antibodies Continued

DRUG	UNIQUE CONCERNS	SAFETY/SIDE EFFECTS/MONITORING

Programmed Death Receptor-1 (PD-1) Inhibitors - monoclonal antibodies that selectively inhibit programmed cell death-1 (PD-1) activity by binding to the PD-1 receptor to block ligands from binding and inducing antitumor responses

Pembrolizumab (Keytruda)	MedGuide required	**SIDE EFFECTS** Immune-mediated toxicities: colitis, hepatotoxicity, pulmonary toxicity, nephrotoxicity, thyroid disorders **NOTES** Immune-mediated toxicities may require interruption or permanent discontinuation of treatment and treatment with corticosteroids
Nivolumab (Opdivo)	MedGuide required	

Cytotoxic T-Lymphocyte Antigen-4 (CTLA-4) Inhibitor - monoclonal antibody that binds to the cytotoxic T-lymphocyte associated antigen 4 (CTLA-4) receptors, which effectively removes the "brake" from T-cell activation. Induces antitumor responses through increased T-cell recognition of cancer cells

Ipilimumab (Yervoy)	MedGuide required REMS program	**BOXED WARNINGS** Fatal immune-mediated reactions (enterocolitis, hepatitis, dermatitis, endocrinopathy, neuropathy) **NOTES** Immune-mediated toxicities may require interruption or permanent discontinuation of treatment and administration of corticosteroids.

Tyrosine Kinase Inhibitors

There are a large number of different tyrosine kinase proteins that play roles in intracellular signaling pathways that control the growth and differentiation of cells. Tyrosine kinase inhibitors (TKIs) are orally administered small molecules that are active against different types of cancers. Some TKIs are "targeted" to inhibit specific abnormal tyrosine kinases that are associated with certain types of cancers. Pharmacogenomic testing must be done to identify patients likely to respond to these targeted TKIs. Other TKIs are considered to be "multitargeted". They inhibit multiple different tyrosine kinases involved in the cell signaling pathway and/or cell growth. Representative TKI targets and the associated drugs are listed below. Some characteristics common to many of the TKIs include:

- For many of the TKIs, oral bioavailability may be altered if taken with food. It is very important for patients to follow the dosing instructions with regards to taking the specific TKI with or without food.

- Many TKIs have limited distribution through specialty pharmacies.

- Most TKIs are substrates of CYP3A4 and should be used cautiously with CYP3A4 inhibitors or inducers, including grapefruit and grapefruit juice.

- Many TKIs are associated with causing QT prolongation, hepatic toxicity, thyroid dysfunction, and diarrhea.

- Many TKIs cause skin toxicity. Stevens-Johnson Syndrome (SJS) or toxic epidermal necrolysis (TEN) have been associated infrequently with most of the TKIs. An acneiform rash that occurs within the first 2 weeks of initiation of treatment is common with TKIs that target the epidermal growth factor receptor (EGFR).

- TKIs that target vascular endothelial growth factor, such as multitargeted TKIs and VEGF targeted TKIs, are commonly associated with causing hypertension and hand-foot syndrome, both of which are probably due to these agents effects on interfering with the growth of blood vessels.

DRUG	UNIQUE CONCERNS	SAFETY/SIDE EFFECTS/MONITORING

BCR-ABL Inhibitors

| Imatinib *(Gleevec)*
 Dasatinib *(Sprycel)*
 Nilotinib *(Tasigna)*
 PONATinib *(Iclusig)*
 Bosutinib *(Bosulif)* | Pharmacogenomics: Test for Philadelphia chromosome (BCR-ABL gene translocation). Must be Philadelphia chromosome (BCR-ABL) positive to use.

 MedGuide required (nilotinib, ponatinib) | **BOXED WARNINGS**
 QT prolongation (nilotinib)

 Vascular occlusions (strokes, MIs), heart failure, hepatotoxicity (ponatinib)

 SIDE EFFECTS
 Myelosuppression, N/V/D, fluid retention, edema, skin rash, ↑ LFTs, HF, QT prolongation (dasatinib, nilotinib, bosutinib) |

BRAF Inhibitors

| Vemurafenib *(Zelboraf)*

 Dabrafenib *(Tafinlar)* | Pharmacogenomics: Test for BRAF mutations. Must be BRAF V600E or V600K mutation positive to use. | **WARNINGS**
 New malignancies such as squamous cell carcinoma and basal cell carcinoma, QT prolongation, serious skin reactions, hepatotoxicity

 SIDE EFFECTS
 Skin rash, photosensitivity, N/V/D, peripheral edema, fatigue, arthralgia |

Mitogen-Activated Extracellular Kinase (MEK) 1 and 2 Inhibitors

| Trametinib *(Mekinist)* | Pharmacogenomics: Test for BRAF mutations. Must be BRAF V600E or V600K mutation positive to use. | **SIDE EFFECTS**
 Hypertension, HF, hepatotoxicity, skin rash, hand-foot syndrome, N/V/D |

Epidermal Growth Factor Receptor (EGFR) Inhibitors

| Afatinib *(Gilotrif)*

 Erlotinib *(Tarceva)*

 Gefitinib *(Iressa)* | Pharmacogenomics: Must be EGFR mutation positive (exon 19 or 21) to use. | **WARNINGS**
 Interstitial lung disease, hepatotoxicity, GI perforation, skin reactions (SJS/TEN), ocular toxicity (keratitis), fetal harm; diarrhea (afatinib/gefitinib)

 SIDE EFFECTS
 Acneiform rash, dry skin, pruritus, N/V/D, mucositis

 NOTES
 Acneiform rash usually occurs within the 1st 2 weeks of treatment and may correlate with response. Advise patients to avoid direct sunlight, use sunscreen and topical emollients. Report if skin blistering, bullae or exfoliation occur. |

Anaplastic Lymphoma Kinase (ALK) Inhibitors

| Crizotinib *(Xalkori)*

 Ceritinib *(Zykadia)* | Pharmacogenomics: Must be ALK mutation positive to use | **WARNINGS**
 Hepatotoxicity, bradycardia, interstitial lung disease, QT prolongation; ocular toxicities (crizotinib), pancreatitis (ceritinib)

 SIDE EFFECTS
 Skin rash, N/V/D, edema, hyperglycemia (ceritinib) |

Tyrosine Kinase Inhibitors Continued

DRUG	UNIQUE CONCERNS	SAFETY/SIDE EFFECTS/MONITORING

Human Epidermal Growth Factor Receptor 2 (HER-2) Inhib tor (also inhibits EGFR)

Lapatinib *(Tykerb)*	Pharmacogenomics: Must have <u>HER2</u> over-expression to use	**BOXED WARNINGS** Hepatotoxicity **WARNINGS** <u>Decreased LVEF</u>, serious skin reactions (SJS/TEN), interstitial lung disease, <u>QT prolongation</u> **SIDE EFFECTS** Diarrhea, N/V, skin rash

Vascular Endothelial Growth Factor (VEGF) Inhibitor

Axitinib *(Inlyta)*		**WARNINGS** Hypertension (hypertensive crisis), cardiac failure, thrombotic events, proteinuria, GI perforation **SIDE EFFECTS** Hand-foot syndrome, N/V/D, hypothyroidism, mucositis, impaired wound healing

Multitargeted

PAZOPanib *(Votrient)* Regorafenib *(Stivarga)* SORAfenib *(NexAVAR)* SUNItinib *(Sutent)*		**BOXED WARNINGS** Hepatotoxicity (except sorafenib) **WARNINGS** Hepatotoxicity, cardiac toxicity, hypertension, proteinuria, hemorrhagic events, SJS/TEN, impaired wound healing **SIDE EFFECTS** Skin changes, hand-foot syndrome, N/V/D, QT prolongation, thyroid dysfunction, mucositis

PROSTATE CANCER

Prostate cancer is the most commonly diagnosed cancer and the second most common cause of cancer deaths among males in the US. Most patients are diagnosed at earlier stages of the disease, before the prostate cancer has metastasized to other organs. At 5 years after diagnosis, almost all patients with nonmetastatic prostate cancer will still be alive, whereas only approximately one-third of patients with metastatic prostate cancer will still be alive. Nonmetastatic prostate cancer can be treated with surgery, radiation with or without pharmacologic androgen deprivation therapy (ADT), or watchful waiting. First-line treatment for metastatic prostate cancer is usually pharmacologic ADT ("chemical castration") with a gonadotropin releasing hormone (GnRH) agonist or antagonist. Metastatic prostate cancer that has failed to respond to ADT is called "castration-resistant" and may be treated with additional hormonal agents listed below or cytotoxic cancer therapeutic agents.

Hormonal Therapies for Prostate Cancer

Hormonal therapy for prostate cancer is referred to as ADT. The goal is to reduce the concentration of testosterone in the body. GnRH agonists and antagonists cause symptoms of hypogonadism, such as hot flashes, loss of libido/impotence, gynecomastia, hair thinning and peripheral edema. Long-term therapy can be associated with osteoporosis and metabolic complications, such as weight gain, hyperlipidemia, and diabetes. They are also associated with QT prolongation.

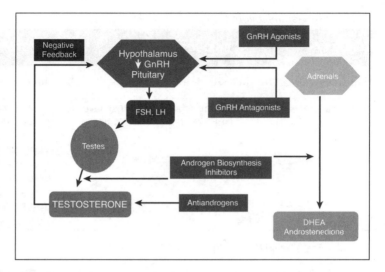

DRUG	UNIQUE CONCERNS	SAFETY/SIDE EFFECTS/MONITORING

Gonadotropin-Releasing Hormone (GnRH) Agonists - also referred to as luteinizing hormone releasing hormone (LHRH) agonists - these drugs reduce testosterone synthesis through a negative feedback mechanism. They cause an initial surge in testosterone concentrations, followed by a gradual reduction in testosterone. This initial surge in testosterone may cause symptoms of "tumor flare" in patients with metastatic prostate cancer. Symptoms of tumor flare may include bone pain or problems with urination. To prevent symptoms of tumor flare, antiandrogens are given for several weeks in conjunction with the initiation of GnRH agonists.

DRUG	UNIQUE CONCERNS	SAFETY/SIDE EFFECTS/MONITORING
Leuprolide (Lupron, Eligard, Viadur) **Goserelin (Zoladex)** Histrelin (Supprelin LA, Vantas) Triptorelin (Trelstar) Given SC or IM monthly or less frequently (up to once yearly) depending on formulation	Osteoporosis Risk: Consider calcium, vitamin D supplementation, weight bearing exercise, DEXA screening Tumor Flare: Consider antiandrogen therapy when initiating GnRH agonists in patients with metastatic prostate cancer Leuprolide and goserelin can be used to treat breast cancer in women	**CONTRAINDICATIONS** Pregnancy (all) Breastfeeding, vaginal bleeding (leuprolide) **SIDE EFFECTS** Hot flashes, impotence, gynecomastia, peripheral edema, bone pain, injection site pain, QT prolongation, dyslipidemia, hyperglycemia

Gonadotropin Releasing Hormone Antagonist - this agent does not cause an initial surge in testosterone concentrations.

DRUG	UNIQUE CONCERNS	SAFETY/SIDE EFFECTS/MONITORING
Degarelix (Firmagon) Given SC monthly	Osteoporosis Risk: Consider calcium, vitamin D supplementation, weight bearing exercise, DEXA screening Does not cause tumor flare	**CONTRAINDICATIONS** Pregnancy **SIDE EFFECTS** Similar to GnRH agonists plus hypersensitivity reactions

Hormonal Therapies for Prostate Cancer Drugs Continued

DRUG	UNIQUE CONCERNS	SAFETY/SIDE EFFECTS/MONITORING

First Generation Antiandrogens - competitively inhibit the binding of testosterone to prostate cancer cells. They are only used in combination with GnRH agonists. Monotherapy is ineffective due to an up-regulation in the expression of androgen receptors.

Bicalutamide *(Casodex)* 50 mg PO daily		**BOXED WARNINGS** Hepatotoxicity (flutamide), interstitial pneumonitis (nilutamide)
Flutamide *(Eulexin)* 250 mg PO Q8H	Causes more diarrhea than others in class	**CONTRAINDICATIONS** Use in women, especially in pregnancy (bicalutamide); severe hepatic impairment (flutamide, nilutamide)
Nilutamide *(Nilandron)*	Can cause night blindness and disulfiram reactions (avoid alcohol)	**SIDE EFFECTS** Hot flashes, gynecomastia, edema, asthenia, hepatotoxicity, ↑ risk of CVD, N/V/D

Second Generation Antiandrogen - unlike first generation antiandrogens, it does not cause an up-regulation in the expression of androgen receptors and can be used as monotherapy.

Enzalutamide *(Xtandi)* 160 mg (4 x 40 mg capsules) daily	**CONTRAINDICATIONS** Pregnancy **SIDE EFFECTS** Hypertension, peripheral edema, hot flashes, fatigue, seizures

Androgen Biosynthesis Inhibitor - interferes with specific enzymes involved in the biosynthesis of steroid hormones in the testes and adrenal gland and decreases production of testosterone. It must be given with prednisone to cause a negative feedback on the production of aldosterone and prevent symptoms of hyperaldosteronism (hypertension, fluid retention and hypokalemia).

Abiraterone *(Zytiga)* 1,000 mg (4 x 250 mg tablets) daily on an empty stomach (1 hr before or 2 hrs after food) Given with prednisone 5 mg BID	**CONTRAINDICATIONS** Pregnancy **SIDE EFFECTS** Mineralocorticoid excess: fluid retention, HTN, hypokalemia Hyperglycemia, ↑ TGs, hypophosphatemia, hot flashes

BREAST CANCER

Breast cancer is the most commonly diagnosed cancer and the second most common cause of cancer deaths among females in the US.

Treatment of Early Stage Breast Cancer (Stage I-II)

Most patients with early stage breast cancer are treated with multi-modality therapy, including surgery, radiation therapy, chemotherapy, and hormonal therapy. Adjuvant treatment with chemotherapy and hormonal therapy will help to decrease the risk of disease recurrence and improve long-term survival. Patients whose breast cancer cells overexpress HER2 should receive a HER2-targeted monoclonal antibody, such as trastuzumab, in addition to cytotoxic chemotherapy. HER2 is a human epidermal growth factor receptor that is overexpressed in ~20% of breast cancers.

- Patients who are estrogen and/or progesterone receptor positive (ER+/PR+) are candidates for adjuvant hormonal therapy. The choice of therapy depends on the menopausal status of the patient.

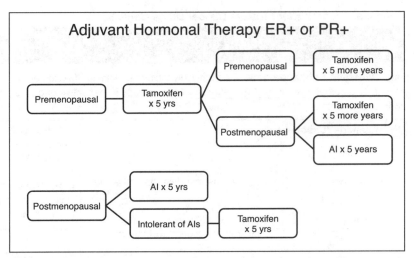

- Patients who are premenopausal should be treated with tamoxifen for 5 years. Their menopausal status should then be reassessed. If they are still premenopausal, they should receive tamoxifen for an additional 5 years. If they are now postmenopausal, they may receive either tamoxifen or an aromatase inhibitor for an additional 5 years.

- Patients who are postmenopausal should be treated with an aromatase inhibitor or tamoxifen for 5 years. However, treatment with an aromatase inhibitor is preferred.

- Patients who are both ER- and PR- do not benefit from adjuvant hormonal therapy.

Treatment of Metastatic Breast Cancer (Stage IV)

Treatment of patients with metastatic breast cancer is influenced by the site of metastases and HER2 status. Patients with metastatic breast cancer may have visceral metastases (involvement of vital organs, such as the lungs, liver, brain) and/or nonvisceral metastases (involvement of the skin or bone).

- Visceral metastases are more immediately life-threatening and are usually treated with cytotoxic chemotherapy, which acts rapidly. HER2-targeted monoclonal antibodies should be given in addition to cytotoxic chemotherapy for patients who are HER2-positive.

- Nonvisceral metastases are less life-threatening and can be treated with hormonal therapy, which acts more slowly but is better tolerated than cytotoxic chemotherapy.

Hormonal Therapies for Breast Cancer

Hormonal therapies for breast cancer work by interfering with estrogen-stimulated growth of breast cancer cells. In premenopausal women, the ovaries are the primary producers of endogenous estrogen. In postmenopausal women and women who have had their ovaries removed, the adrenal glands are the primary producers of endogenous estrogen.

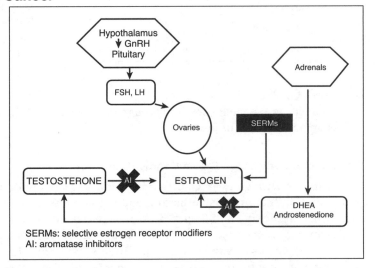

- Selective estrogen receptor modifiers (SERMs) have estrogen antagonist activity in breast tissue, but act as estrogen agonists in some other tissues, including bone. There are used for breast cancer in hormone receptor positive tumors. Most SERMs are used in post-menopausal women, however, tamoxifen is used in both pre- and postmenopausal women and in men.

- Aromatase inhibitors (AIs) block the enzyme required for the peripheral conversion of adrenally produced estrogen precursors to estrogen. Since the majority of estrogen in premenopausal women is produced in the ovaries, not the adrenal glands, AIs are ineffective in adequately suppressing estrogen-stimulated cancer cell growth in premenopausal women. Therefore, AIs are approved for post-menopausal women only (and not in men with breast CA).

DRUG	UNIQUE CONCERNS	SAFETY/SIDE EFFECTS/MONITORING

Selective Estrogen Receptor Modulators

Tamoxifen (Nolvadex, Soltamox) 20 mg PO daily **Fulvestrant (Faslodex)** 500 mg IM days 1, 15, 29, then monthly Raloxifene (Evista) 60 mg PO daily Toremifene (Farestron)	Tamoxifen ↑ risk of uterine or endometrial cancers, others decrease risk Tamoxifen is a major substrate of CYP 3A4, 2C9 and 2D6. Watch for drug interactions, particularly with 2D6 inhibitors. Recommend venlafaxine for hot flashes (over fluoxetine and paroxetine which are strong 2D6 inhibitors) for patients on tamoxifen.	**BOXED WARNINGS** ↑ risk of uterine or endometrial cancers (tamoxifen), ↑ risk of thromboembolic events such as VTE, PE, stroke (tamoxifen, raloxifene), QT prolongation (toremifene) **CONTRAINDICATIONS** Concomitant warfarin therapy (tamoxifen), history of DVT/PE (tamoxifen, raloxifene), pregnancy and breastfeeding (raloxifene), QT prolongation, hypokalemia, hypomagnesemia (toremifene) **SIDE EFFECTS** DVT/PE, menopausal symptoms, hot flashes, flushing, edema, weight gain, hypertension, mood changes, amenorrhea, vaginal bleeding/discharge, arthralgia/myalgia, skin changes, cataracts (tamoxifen) **NOTES** Pregnancy Category D/X (raloxifene) MedGuide required (tamoxifen, raloxifene)

Aromatase Inhibitors

Anastrozole (Arimidex) 1 mg PO daily **Letrozole (Femara)** 2.5 mg PO daily **Exemestane (Aromasin)** 25 mg PO daily	Higher risk of osteoporosis due to decreased bone mineral density; consider Ca and vitamin D supplementation, weight bearing exercise, DEXA screening Higher risk of CVD compared to SERMs	**CONTRAINDICATIONS** Pregnancy **SIDE EFFECTS** Arthralgia/myalgia, bone pain, lethargy/fatigue, menopausal symptoms, hot flashes, N/V, rash, hepatotoxicity, hypertension, dyslipidemia

Administration and Safe Handling of Oral Chemotherapeutic Agents

GENERIC (BRAND)	PREGNANCY CATEGORY	ADMINISTRATION	SPECIAL HANDLING
Imatinib (Gleevec)	D	Take with food or within 1 hour after a meal	Thalidomide, pomalidomide, and lenalidomide: female patients of reproductive potential must have 2 negative pregnancy tests prior to starting treatment and use 2 forms of birth control. REMS drugs and only available through a specialty pharmacy.
Thalidomide (Thalomid)	X		
Capecitabine (Xeloda)	D		
Nilotinib (Tasigna)	D	Take on an empty stomach (1 hour before or 2 hours after food, pomalidomide is taken 2 hours before or 2 hours after food)	
Erlotinib (Tarceva)	D		
Sorafenib (Nexavar)	D		
Pazopanib (Votrient)	D		
Temozolomide (Temodar)	D		
Abiraterone (Zytiga)	X		
Pomalidomide (Pomalyst)	X		
Dasatinib (Sprycel)	D	Take without regards to food	
Sunitinib (Sutent)	D		
Tamoxifen (Nolvadex, Soltamox)	D		
Anastrozole (Arimidex)	X		
Bicalutamide (Casodex)	X		
Lenalidomide (Revlimid)	X		

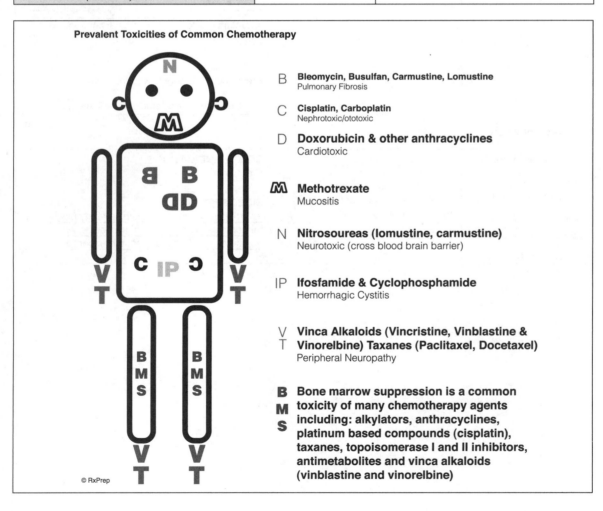

Prevalent Toxicities of Common Chemotherapy

B **Bleomycin, Busulfan, Carmustine, Lomustine**
Pulmonary Fibrosis

C **Cisplatin, Carboplatin**
Nephrotoxic/ototoxic

D **Doxorubicin & other anthracyclines**
Cardiotoxic

M **Methotrexate**
Mucositis

N **Nitrosoureas (lomustine, carmustine)**
Neurotoxic (cross blood brain barrier)

IP **Ifosfamide & Cyclophosphamide**
Hemorrhagic Cystitis

VT **Vinca Alkaloids (Vincristine, Vinblastine & Vinorelbine) Taxanes (Paclitaxel, Docetaxel)**
Peripheral Neuropathy

BMS **Bone marrow suppression is a common toxicity of many chemotherapy agents including: alkylators, anthracyclines, platinum based compounds (cisplatin), taxanes, topoisomerase I and II inhibitors, antimetabolites and vinca alkaloids (vinblastine and vinorelbine)**

© RxPrep

Patient Counseling

Tamoxifen

- This medication can be used to reduce your chance of getting breast cancer, reduce the spread of breast cancer or be used to cure breast cancer.
- Swallow the tablet whole daily, with water or another non-alcoholic liquid. You can take it with or without food.
- If you forget a dose, take it when you remember, then take the next dose as usual. If it is almost time for your next dose or you remember at your next dose, do not take extra tablets to make up the missed dose.
- Do not become pregnant while taking this medication or for 2 months after you stop. This medication can stop hormonal birth control methods from working correctly (birth control pills, patches, injections, rings and implants). Therefore, while taking this medication, another method of contraception should be used, such as condoms, diaphragms with spermicide, or IUDs.
- If you become pregnant, stop taking this medication right away and call your healthcare provider.
- Be sure to have regular gynecology check-ups, breast exams and mammograms. Your healthcare provider will tell you how often. These will check for signs of breast cancer and cancer of the endometrium (lining of the uterus).
- This medication can cause some serious, but rare, side effects such as endometrial cancer, stroke, or a blood clot. This medication can also increase the risk of getting cataracts.
- The most common side effects include hot flashes, hypertension, peripheral edema, mood changes, depression, skin changes, and vaginal discharge.
- You should call your healthcare provider right away if you develop:
  - ❑ vaginal bleeding or bloody discharge that could be a rusty or brown color, change in your monthly bleeding, such as in the amount or timing of bleeding or increased clotting, or pain or pressure in your pelvis (below your belly button).
  - ❑ sudden chest pain, shortness of breath, coughing up blood, pain, tenderness, or swelling in one or both of your legs.
  - ❑ sudden weakness, tingling, or numbness (in your face, arm or leg, especially on one side of your body), sudden confusion, trouble speaking or sudden trouble seeing in one or both eyes, sudden trouble walking, dizziness, loss of balance or coordination, or sudden severe headache with no known cause.
  - ❑ signs of liver problems like lack of appetite and yellowing of your skin or whites of your eyes.
- For *Evista* – discontinue at least 72 hours prior to and during prolonged immobilization (e.g., post-surgical recovery, prolonged bed rest), and avoid prolonged restrictions of movement during travel because of the increased risk of thromboembolic event (blood clots).

Aromatase Inhibitors

- This medication is used to treat breast cancer in women who have finished menopause. This medication does not work in women who have not finished menopause. It can be taken with or without food.
- If you miss a dose, take it as soon as you remember. If it is almost time for your next dose, skip the missed dose. Take your next regularly scheduled dose. Do not take two doses at the same time.
- Common side effects include hot flashes, weakness, joint pain, bone pain, osteoporosis, mood changes, high blood pressure, depression, and rash.

- This medication can cause rare, but serious, adverse effects such as heart disease, increased cholesterol, skin reactions, allergic reactions, and liver problems.
- Call your healthcare provider right away if you develop:
  - ❑ chest pain, shortness of breath.
  - ❑ any skin lesions, ulcers, or blisters.
  - ❑ swelling of the face, lips, tongue, or throat, trouble swallowing, or trouble breathing.
  - ❑ a general feeling of not being well with yellowing of the skin or whites of the eyes or pain on the right side of your abdomen.
- Tell your healthcare provider about all the medicines you take, including prescription and non-prescription medicines, vitamins, and herbal supplements. This medication should not be taken with tamoxifen or any medicines containing estrogen regardless of formulation (pills, patches, creams, rings, or suppositories).

Leuprolide for Prostate Cancer

- This medication is used to treat your prostrate cancer and will lower sex hormones (testosterone and estrogen) produced by the body.
- If you are taking this medication for metastatic prostate cancer, then some patients experience worsening of their prostate cancer symptoms upon starting the this medication due to "tumor flare". To minimize this side effect, an anti-androgen (such as bicalutamide) may be started at least 1 week prior to your injection.
- Common side effects include hot flashes and impotence.
- During the first few weeks of treatment you may experience increased bone pain and increased difficulty in urinating.
- If you have a change in strength on one side of your body that is greater than the other side, trouble speaking or thinking, change in balance, or blurred eyesight you will need to see a healthcare provider right away.

PRACTICE CASE

> TO is a 53 y/o Indian male diagnosed with non-Hodgkin's lymphoma. His past medical history is significant for mild heart failure (NYHA Class I). He is to receive 6 cycles of "CHOP" chemotherapy.
>
> **Allergies**: NKDA
>
> **Chemotherapy Regimen:**
> Cyclophosphamide 750 mg/m^2 IV on Day 1
> Doxorubicin 50 mg/m^2 IV on Day 1
> Vincristine 1.4 mg/m^2 IV on Day 1
> Prednisone 100 mg PO on Days 1-5 given first
>
> **Vitals**:
> Height: 5'10" Weight: 200 pounds
> BP: 145/97 mmHg   HR: 79 BPM   RR: 15 BPM   Temp: 98.5°F   Pain: 0/10
>
> **Labs**: Na (mEq/L) = 136 (135 - 145)
> K (mEq/L) = 3.7 (3.5 - 5)
> Cl (mEq/L) = 98 (95 - 103)
> HCO_3 (mEq/L) = 26 (24 - 30)
> BUN (mg/dL) = 15 (7 - 20)
> SCr (mg/dL) = 1.1 (0.6 - 1.3)
> Glucose (mg/dL) = 106 (100 - 125)
> Ca (mg/dL) = 9.1 (8.5 - 10.5)
> Mg (mEq/L) = 1.5 (1.3 - 2.1)
> PO_4 (mg/dL) = 2.9 (2.3 - 4.7)
> AST (IU/L) = 20 (8 - 48)
> ALT (IU/L) = 12 (7 - 55)
> Albumin (g/dL) = 3.4 (3.5 - 5)
> T Bili (mg/dL) = 0.8 (0.1 - 1.2)
>
> Start chemotherapy today. Monitor for acute toxicities from chemotherapy regimen and begin any supportive care as needed.

Questions

Questions 1-4 refer to the above case.

1. The pharmacist must first calculate the patient's BSA and will use the Dubois and Dubois equation: BSA (m^2) = 0.007184 x [weight (kg)$^{0.425}$] x [height (cm)$^{0.725}$]. The patient's BSA is:

   a. 1.15 m^2

   b. 1.03 m^2

   c. 2.09 m^2

   d. 2.18 m^2

   e. 3.15 m^2

2. What is the correct milligram dose of doxorubicin that the patient should receive on Day 1?

   a. 104.5 mg

   b. 510 mg

   c. 949.5 mg

   d. 948.5 mg

   e. 300 mg

3. The physician wants to know if there are any medications that can reduce the likelihood of cardiotoxicity with doxorubicin therapy. Which of the following would you suggest?

    a. Totect
    b. Zinecard
    c. Lasix
    d. Epogen
    e. Mesna

4. What is the dose limiting toxicity of vincristine?

    a. Neuropathy
    b. Nephrotoxicity
    c. Hypersensitivity reaction
    d. Ototoxicity
    e. Pulmonary toxicity

Questions 5-13 do not relate to the above case.

5. A patient is using apomorphine *(Apokyn)* injections for advanced Parkinson disease. The patient has been suffering from nausea. Which of the following antiemetics should be avoided with apomorphine?

    a. Lorazepam
    b. Metoclopramide
    c. Prochlorperazine
    d. Granisetron
    e. All of the above

6. A patient will begin raloxifene therapy. Choose the correct counseling points: (Select **ALL** that apply.)

    a. This drug can increase your risk of breast cancer.
    b. Avoid long periods of immobility, such as during long airplane flights – get up and move when you can.
    c. This medication can cause weakened bones and fractures.
    d. This medication should only be used by men.
    e. This drug should be taken once daily.

7. Which of the following medications should be taken with food? (Select **ALL** that apply.)

    a. Gleevec
    b. Xeloda
    c. Nexavar
    d. Votrient
    e. Zytiga

8. An antidote for toxicity from high-dose methotrexate is:

    a. Folic acid
    b. Leucovorin
    c. Vitamin B12
    d. Cholestyramine
    e. Vitamin D

9. A pharmacist received a prescription for *Gleevec*. An appropriate generic interchange is:

    a. Aprepitant
    b. Imatinib
    c. Temozolomide
    d. Anastrozole
    e. Capecitabine

10. A pharmacist received a prescription for *Arimidex*. An appropriate generic interchange is:

    a. Aprepitant
    b. Anastrozole
    c. Exemestane
    d. Letrozole
    e. Tamoxifen

11. A patient is receiving dronabinol for nausea. Appropriate counseling points should include:

    a. The capsules should be kept in the refrigerator.
    b. Your appetite may increase.
    c. This medication cannot be shared with others.
    d. A and B only.
    e. A, B and C.

12. A patient has chemotherapy-induced anemia. She states she is weak. The pharmacist has access to her labs and finds that the current hemoglobin level is 11 g/dL. Ferritin, serum iron, TIBC, folate and vitamin B12 are all at acceptable levels. Her oncologist has prescribed *Procrit*. The patient has brought the *Procrit* prescription to the pharmacy. Choose the correct statement:

    a. The prescription can be filled after the pharmacist confirms that the patient is registered with the ESA APPRISE program.
    b. The generic name of *Procrit* is darbepoetin.
    c. The patient should be aware that they may experience euphoria and increased appetite.
    d. The prescription should not be filled; the pharmacist should contact the prescriber.
    e. A and B only.

13. A patient with end stage breast cancer has been experiencing fatigue and dehydration. She has a corrected calcium of 11.5 mg/dL. What is most appropriate for treating her hypercalcemia?

    a. Instruct patient to drink 8 glasses of water
    b. IV hydration, loop diuretic, and zoledronic acid
    c. Calcitonin
    d. Vitamin D
    e. No treatment is necessary since her calcium is within the normal range

Answers

1-c, 2-a, 3-b, 4-a, 5-d, 6-b,e, 7-a,b, 8-b, 9-b, 10-b, 11-e, 12-d, 13-b

56

ANEMIA

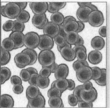
Normal amount of red blood cells

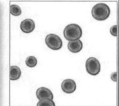
Anemic amount of red blood cells

We gratefully acknowledge the assistance of Charlotte Ricchetti, PharmD, BCPS, CDE, Associate Professor, Regis University School of Pharmacy, in preparing this chapter.

BACKGROUND

Anemia is the most common blood disorder and affects approximately 3.5 million Americans. It is characterized by a decrease in hemoglobin (Hgb) and/or hematocrit (Hct) concentration below the normal range for age and gender. Red blood cells (RBCs), known as erythrocytes, are the most common type of blood cell whereas Hgb is an iron-rich protein in RBCs that carries oxygen from the lungs to the tissues. Reticulocytes are immature RBCs which circulate in the blood for 1 – 2 days before maturing into an erythrocyte. Normally, RBCs have a lifespan of about 120 days after which they are removed from circulation by macrophages, mainly in the spleen. A decrease in Hgb or RBC volume results in decreased oxygen carrying capacity of the blood. The main cause of anemia can be classified as impaired RBC production, increased RBC destruction (hemolysis), and blood loss. Anemia can be a sign of many medical disorders, including chronic renal disease and malignancy. Therefore, rapid diagnosis of the cause is essential.

SYMPTOMS OF ANEMIA

Most patients with mild or early stage anemia are asymptomatic. If anemia becomes severe and prolonged, the lack of oxygen in the blood can lead to classic symptoms including <u>fatigue, malaise, weakness, shortness of breath, exercise intolerance, headache, dizziness, anorexia, and/or pallor</u>. More severe symptoms, usually due to acute blood loss, may include chest pain, angina, fainting, palpitations, and tachycardia. <u>Glossitis</u> (an inflamed, sore tongue), <u>koilonychias</u> (thin, concave, spoon-shaped nails), or <u>pica</u> (craving and eating non-foods such as chalk or clay) may develop in iron deficiency anemia. In addition, patients with vitamin B12 (cobalamin) deficiency can present with neurologic symptoms including peripheral neuropathies and visual disturbances. Psychiatric symptoms can also result from vitamin B12 deficiency.

GUIDELINES/REFERENCES

Kidney Disease: Improving Global Outcomes (KDIGO) Anemia Work Group. KDIGO Clinical Practice Guideline for Anemia in Chronic Kidney Disease. Kidney International. Suppl 2012; 2:279-335.

National Kidney Foundation. KDOQI Clinical Practice Guideline and Clinical Practice Recommendations for Anemia in Chronic Kidney Disease: 2007 Update of Hemoglobin Target http://www2.kidney.org/professionals/DOQI/guidelines_anemiaUP/ (access 2015 November 3)

Note: Iron requirements for infants, per the American Pediatric Association, are in the Dietary Supplements & Natural and Complementary Medicine chapter.

Additional guidelines included with the video files (RxPrep Online).

A decreased oxygen supply can cause ischemic damage to many organs. Chronic anemia is most notable in causing heart damage, the heart tries to compensate for low oxygen levels by pumping faster (tachycardia), thereby increasing the mass of the ventricular wall, which can eventually lead to heart failure.

TYPES OF ANEMIA

Once the diagnosis of anemia is made using Hgb, the most common way to classify the anemia is by the mean corpuscular volume (MCV) or the average volume of RBCs. While the symptoms may be similar for both macrocytic and microcytic anemia, the MCV differs. In microcytic anemia, the MCV is low, < 80 mm³, and iron deficiency is the most common cause. Macrocytic (megaloblastic) anemia presents with an elevated MCV, > 100 mm³, and can be due to folate or vitamin B12 deficiency. An anemia presenting with a normal MCV, 80 – 100 mm³, is called normocytic anemia. This type of anemia can result from acute blood loss (surgery or trauma), hemolysis, bone marrow failure (aplastic anemia), or anemia of chronic disease. Certain genetic conditions cause dysfunctional RBCs resulting in anemia, such as sickle cell anemia. Please refer to the Sickle Cell Disease chapter for more information.

Additional laboratory tests are utilized to determine the type and cause of the anemia. RBC indices help determine the size of the RBCs, the amount of Hgb within the RBCs and the variations in RBC size. Iron studies are used to evaluate the iron status in patients with anemia.

TEST	NORMAL ADULT RANGE
Hemoglobin (Hgb)	Males: 13.5–18 g/dL Females: 12–16 g/dL
Hematocrit (Hct)	Males: 38–50% Females: 36–46%
Red Blood Cell Count (RBCs)	Males: 4.5–5.5 x 10⁶ cells/µL Females: 4.1–4.9 x 10⁶ cells/µL
Reticulocyte Count	0.5–2.5% of RBCs

RBC Indices

Mean Corpuscular Volume (MCV)	80–100 mm³
Mean Corpuscular Hemoglobin (MCH)	26–34 pg/cell
Mean Corpuscular Hemoglobin Concentration (MCHC)	31–37 g/dL
Red Blood Cell Distribution Width (RDW)	11.5–14.5%

Iron Studies

Serum Iron	65–150 mcg/dL
Serum Ferritin	11–300 ng/mL
Total Iron-Binding Capacity (TIBC)	250–400 mcg/dL
Transferrin Saturation (TSAT)	Males: 15–50% Females: 12–45%

Additional Tests

Serum Folate	5–25 mcg/L
Vitamin B12	200–900 pg/mL

IRON DEFICIENCY ANEMIA

Iron deficiency is the most common nutritional deficiency in the United States. It can result from inadequate dietary intake (e.g., vegetarian diet, malnutrition, dementia, psychiatric illnesses), ↑ iron loss (e.g., acute/chronic hemorrhage, blood donation), ↓ iron absorption (e.g., high gastric pH, celiac disease, partial gastrectomy, achlorhydria), or ↑ iron requirements (e.g., pregnancy and lactation). Dietary iron is available in two forms: heme iron (found in meat) and non-heme iron (found in plant and dairy foods). Absorption of heme iron is minimally affected by dietary factors and is much more absorbable than non-heme iron. The bioavailability of non-heme iron <u>requires gastric acid</u> and varies greatly depending on the concentration of enhancers (e.g., meat, ascorbate) and inhibitors (tannins found in tea, calcium, phytates found in legumes and whole grain) in the diet. Vegetarians may or may not require iron supplementation; even if the intake is adequate, the absorption can be decreased by concurrent foods. Patients with iron deficiency anemia (IDA) present with a <u>low Hgb</u> and <u>low MCV</u>. Other abnormal laboratory findings include <u>↓ ferritin level</u> (most sensitive marker), ↓ serum iron, ↓ TSAT, and ↑ TIBC.

QUANTITATIVE LABORATORY FINDINGS	TEST
Low	RBC, Hgb, Hct, MCV (< 80 mm^3), ferritin, serum iron, TSAT, MCHC, reticulocyte count
High	RDW, TIBC

At-Risk Patients

Pregnant women, pre-term and low birth weight infants, children under the age of 2 years, teenage girls, women with heavy menstrual periods, and patients with renal failure are at an increased risk for iron deficiency. Gastrointestinal diseases, including Crohn's, celiac disease and weight loss surgery, can reduce absorption and require replacement therapy. Total dietary iron intake in vegetarian diets may meet recommended levels; however, non-heme iron is less available for absorption than heme-containing iron found in meat. In addition, IDA can be caused by medications that can result in bleeding (e.g., aspirin, non-steroidal anti-inflammatory drugs, anticoagulants).

Women taking hormonal contraception experience less bleeding during menstrual periods and therefore have a lower risk of developing iron deficiency. A pharmacist may occasionally dispense hormonal contraception to a female to reduce anemia, this is usually in younger females since young women tend to have heavier blood loss.

The CDC recommends routine low-dose iron supplementation (30 mg/day) for all pregnant women, beginning at the first prenatal visit. Usually the low iron dose is provided in the prenatal vitamin. When a low Hgb or Hct is confirmed by testing, larger doses of iron are required.

TREATMENT OF IRON DEFICIENCY ANEMIA

Oral Iron Therapy

- <u>Oral iron therapy can adequately treat patients with IDA, except for patients on hemodialysis (discussed in the parenteral iron therapy section)</u>.

- Compared to parenteral iron, oral preparations have a lower risk of serious side effects and have low cost and low administration burden.

- There are several types of oral iron. It is important to note the amount of elemental iron per dose. The normal dose for treatment of IDA is 100 – 200 mg elemental iron per day in divided doses.

- There is no evidence that one oral formulation is more effective than another. Even if the % of elemental iron is higher in one formulation, it would not be expected to be more effective as long as each product is dosed appropriately. <u>Please know the % of elemental iron in each iron salt form</u>.

- Ferrous iron (Fe^{2+}) is absorbed more readily than the ferric (Fe^{3+}) form. Polysaccharide iron complex is the only oral formulation in the ferric form, and may have less GI irritation.

- Although sustained-release or enteric coated formulations may have lower risk of GI irritation, they are not recommended as initial therapy because they reduce the amount of iron that is present for absorption in the duodenum, the site of maximal absorption.

- Absorption of iron is enhanced in an acidic gastric environment. Administering iron with ascorbic acid (vitamin C 200 mg) may enhance absorption to a minimal extent.

- Food decreases the absorption of iron. It is best to take iron at least 1 hour before or 2 hours after meals. However, many patients must take iron with food because they experience GI upset (nausea) when iron is administered on an empty stomach.

- An increase in Hgb level by 1 g/dL should occur every 2 – 3 weeks on iron therapy. Treatment should continue for 3 – 6 months after the anemia is resolved to allow for iron stores to return to normal and to prevent relapse.

Oral Iron Therapy

DRUG	DOSING	SAFETY/SIDE EFFECTS/MONITORING
Ferrous sulfate (*Ferro-Bob, FerrouSul, Fer-In-Sol, Poly-Vi-Sol With Iron, Flinstones MVI With Iron*)	325 mg (65 mg elemental iron) PO daily to TID Most commonly prescribed and is the least expensive	**Iron Salt** / **Elemental Iron** table below
Ferrous sulfate, dried (exsiccated) Controlled Release (*Slow Fe, Feosol*)	160 mg (50 mg elemental iron) PO daily to TID (other doses available)	
Ferrous fumarate (*Ferretts, Hemocyte*)	324 mg (106 mg elemental iron) PO daily to TID (other doses available)	
Ferrous gluconate (*Fergon*)	324 mg (38 mg elemental iron) PO daily to TID (other doses available)	
Carbonyl iron (*Feosol with Carbonyl Iron, Ferralet 90*)	45 mg (45 mg elemental iron) PO daily to 4x/day (*Ferralet* is a combination of ferrous gluconate and carbonyl iron)	
Polysaccharide Iron Complex (*Iferex 150, Ferrex 150, Niferex 150*)	150 mg PO daily	

Safety/Side Effects/Monitoring column contents:

Iron Salt	Elemental Iron
Ferrous gluconate	12%
Ferrous sulfate	20%
Ferrous sulfate, exsiccated	30%
Ferrous fumarate	33%
Carbonyl iron	100%
Polysaccharide iron complex	100%

CONTRAINDICATIONS
Hemochromatosis, hemolytic anemia

WARNING
Accidental overdose of iron-containing products is a leading cause of fatal poisoning in children under 6. Keep iron out of reach of children. In case of accidental overdose, go to ED or call poison control center immediately.

SIDE EFFECTS
Nausea, stomach upset, constipation (dose-related), dark and tarry stools

MONITORING
Hgb, iron studies, RBC indices, reticulocyte count

NOTES
Although fiber is first line treatment for constipation, a stool softener such as docusate is often recommended for iron-induced constipation.

Oral Iron Drug Interactions

- Antacids and agents that raise pH (H$_2$RAs, PPIs) ↓ iron absorption by ↑ pH. Patients should take iron 2 hours prior to or 4 hours after antacids. H$_2$RAs and PPIs raise gastric pH for up to 24 hours, therefore separating the dose of these agents and iron supplements does not improve absorption.

- Antibiotics, primarily tetracycline (less of a concern with doxycycline and minocycline) and quinolones, can decrease iron absorption through chelation. Take iron 1 – 2 hours before or 4 hours after tetracycline; 2 hours before or 6 hours after ciprofloxacin; 2 hours before or 2 hours after levofloxacin; 4 hours before or 8 hours after moxifloxacin.

- Iron should be taken 60 minutes after oral ibandronate or 30 minutes after alendronate/risedronate.

- Iron can interact and ↓ the levels of the following medications: bisphosphonates, cefdinir, dolutegravir, levothyroxine, levodopa, methyldopa and mycophenolate. Separate the doses by 1 – 4 hours (see prescribing information).

- High dose vitamin C (~200 mg) ↑ acidity, and thus ↑ the absorption of iron; little benefit with low doses.

- Food ↓ absorption as much as 50%; advise patients to take on an empty stomach. If unable to tolerate, take with a small amount of food. If taken with food, it will take longer to correct the anemia.

Iron Toxicity

Accidental iron poisoning is the leading cause of poisoning deaths among young children. As little as 5 tablets in a small child can lead to overdose. The child can initially appear asymptomatic or have already developed severe nausea, vomiting, gastrointestinal bleeding (most often vomiting blood) and diarrhea. If a parent suspects their child ingested iron pills or liquid, they should be directed to the nearest emergency room immediately – whether symptomatic or not. Left untreated, iron overdose damages most organs and can be fatal. The antidote for iron overdose is deferoxamine *(Desferal)*. This is different from deferiprone *(Ferriprox)*, which is for transfusional iron overload unresponsive to chelation therapy.

Parenteral Iron Therapy

Parenteral iron therapy is as effective but has a risk of severe adverse reactions and is much more expensive than oral therapy. The following clinical situations can warrant IV administration:

- Hemodialysis (most common use of IV iron) – the KDIGO guidelines state, to reduce symptoms of anemia and avoid transfusions, most hemodialysis patients will require IV iron on a regular basis.

- Unable to tolerate oral iron or losing iron too fast for oral replacement.

- Intestinal malabsorption, such as Crohn's disease, celiac disease, certain gastric bypass procedures, achlorhydria and bacterial overgrowth syndromes.

Intravenous (Parenteral) Iron Therapy

DRUG	SAFETY/SIDE EFFECTS/MONITORING
Iron dextran (INFeD, Dexferrum)	**BOXED WARNING (IRON DEXTRAN AND FERUMOXYTOL)** Serious and sometimes fatal anaphylactic reactions have occured with the use of iron dextran or ferumoxytol. All patients receiving iron dextran should be given a test dose prior to first therapeutic dose. Fatal reactions have occurred even in patients who tolerated the test dose. History of drug allergy and/or concomitant use of ACE inhibitor may ↑ risk.
Sodium ferric gluconate (Ferrlecit)	
Iron sucrose (Venofer)	**SIDE EFFECTS** Muscle aches, hypotension, hypertension, tachycardia, chest pain and peripheral edema All parenteral iron products carry a risk for hypersensitivity reactions including anaphylaxis
Ferumoxytol (Feraheme)	**MONITORING** Hgb, Hct, serum ferritin, serum iron, TSAT, TIBC, reticulocyte count, vital signs, adverse reactions especially anaphylaxis
Ferric carboxymaltose (Injectafer)	**NOTES** Give by slow IV injection to ↓ risk of hypotension. All agents are stable in NS; maximum of 100 mL of NS for *Ferrlecit* and *Venofer*. *Feraheme* is stable in NS or D5W.
Ferric pyrophosphate citrate (Triferic)	*Triferic* should only be added to the bicarbonate concentrate of the hemodialysate for patients receiving hemodialysis.

MACROCYTIC ANEMIA

Macrocytic anemia is caused by either a vitamin B12 or folate deficiency or both. Pernicious anemia is a type of macrocytic anemia that results in low vitamin B12 levels due to lack of intrinsic factor, which is required for adequate vitamin B12 absorption in the small intestine. Since gut absorption of vitamin B12 is impaired in those who lack intrinsic factor, pernicious anemia requires lifelong vitamin B12 replacement therapy. The Schilling test can diagnose vitamin B12 deficiency due to lack of intrinsic factor. Vitamin B12 deficiency can result in serious neurologic consequences including cognitive dysfunction and peripheral neuropathies. Neurologic symptoms can precede development of anemia. If vitamin B12 deficiency is not identified for more than 6 – 12 months, the neurologic symptoms may become irreversible. Folic acid deficiency does not result in neurologic symptoms.

Alcoholism, poor nutrition, Crohn's disease, and celiac disease are other causes of macrocytic anemia. Macrocytic anemia is diagnosed by a low Hgb and a high MCV (> 100 mm³). Vitamin B12 and/or serum folate levels will be low.

QUANTITATIVE LABORATORY FINDINGS	TEST
Low	Hgb, Hct, RBC, reticulocyte count, serum folate and/or serum vitamin B12
Normal	MCHC
High	MCV (> 100 mm³), RDW, serum homocysteine Serum methylmalonate in vitamin B12 deficiency

Treatment of Macrocytic Anemia

Vitamin B12 deficiency is treated initially with vitamin B12 injections (since injections bypass absorption barriers) and followed with oral supplements. <u>Vitamin B12 injections</u> are <u>recommended as first line</u> for anyone with a severe deficiency or neurological symptoms.

DRUG	DOSING	SAFETY/SIDE EFFECTS/MONITORING
Cyanocobalamin, vitamin B12 *(Physicians EZ Use B-12* inj, *Nascobal* nasal spray, oral generics)	IM or deep SC: 100-1,000 mcg daily/weekly/monthly (various dosing regimens depending on severity of deficiency) Oral/Sublingual: 1,000-2,000 mcg/day for mild-moderate deficiencies Intranasal *(Nascobal)*: 500 mcg in one nostril once weekly	**CONTRAINDICATIONS** Cobalt allergy **SIDE EFFECTS** Pain with injection, rash **MONITORING** Hgb, Hct, vitamin B12, reticulocyte count **NOTES** Do not use sustained-release B12 supplements as the absorption is not adequate.
Folic Acid, folate *(FA-8)* Tablet, capsule, injection	0.4-0.8 mg daily	**SIDE EFFECTS** Bronchospasm, flushing, rash, pruritus, malaise (rare) **MONITORING** Hgb, Hct, folate, reticulocyte count

Drug Interactions

Vitamin B12

- Chloramphenicol, colchicine, ethanol, long-term use of <u>metformin or a PPI (≥ 2 years)</u> may ↓ B12 absorption.

Folic Acid

- Folic acid ↓ the efficacy of raltitrexed (a chemotherapeutic agent); avoid concurrent use.

- Folic acid may ↓ the serum concentration of fosphenytoin, phenytoin, primidone and phenobarbital. Monitor therapy.

- Green tea and sulfasalazine may ↓ the serum concentration of folic acid. Monitor therapy.

NORMOCYTIC ANEMIA

Anemia Of Chronic Kidney Disease

<u>Chronic kidney disease (CKD)</u> causes anemia primarily due to a <u>deficiency in erythropoietin (EPO)</u>, a hormone produced by the kidneys. EPO stimulates the bone marrow to produce RBCs in response to decreasing levels of oxygen in the tissues. To a lesser degree, this type of anemia is also attributed to a shortened red cell survival and reduced responsiveness to the hormone. Iron therapy and <u>erythropoiesis-stimulating agents</u> (ESAs) are the mainstay of anemia treatment in patients with CKD. Before treating this type of anemia, iron levels are important to assess. <u>If the iron stores are low, ESAs are ineffective.</u> <u>The majority of patients receiving hemodialysis require iron therapy</u> as hemodialysis results in a 6 – 7 mg of iron loss per day of dialysis which is further compounded by physiologic and venipuncture losses. <u>Parenteral (IV) iron is first line therapy in patients receiving hemodialysis.</u> In practice, most healthcare institutions primarily follow the KDIGO (Kidney Disease Improving Global Outcomes) and/or the KDOQI (Kidney Disease Outcomes Quality Initiative) guidelines when initiating ESAs in patients with anemia of CKD. Prior to initiating ESA treatment, the KDIGO guidelines recommend that TSAT should be > 30% and ferritin levels should be > 500 ng/mL in both non-dialysis and dialysis patients. On the other hand, KDOQI guidelines recommend that TSAT should be > 20% in both non-dialysis and

dialysis patients and ferritin levels should be >100 ng/mL in non-dialysis patients and > 200 ng/mL in dialysis patients. Per the ESAs package insert, TSAT should be at least 20% and ferritin levels should be at least 100 ng/mL in non-dialysis or 200 ng/mL in dialysis patients prior to starting ESA therapy.

ESA therapy reduces the need for blood transfusions but has no beneficial effect on mortality in patients with CKD. Levels of folate and vitamin B12 may also be assessed, especially if there is a poor response to ESA.

Erythropoiesis-Stimulating Agents (ESAs)

DRUG	DOSING	SAFETY/SIDE EFFECTS/MONITORING
Epoetin alfa *(Epogen, Procrit)* IV, SC	**Chronic Kidney Disease** 50-100 units/kg 3x/week, then individualize maintenance dose Initiate when Hgb < 10 g/dL Reduce or interrupt dose when Hgb approaches or exceeds 11 g/dL for CKD on HD, or > 10 g/dL for CKD not on HD If Hgb increases > 1 g/dL in any 2-week period, interrupt or ↓ dose by 25% If Hgb does not ↑ by 1 g/dL after 4 weeks, ↑ dose by 25% **Cancer** 150 units/kg 3x/week or 40,000 units weekly Initiate when Hgb < 10 g/dL and when at least 2 additional months of chemotherapy planned If Hgb increases > 1 g/dL in any 2-week period, interrupt or ↓ dose by 25%	**BOXED WARNINGS** ESAs ↑ risk of death, MI, stroke, VTE, thrombosis of vascular access, and tumor progression or recurrence. **Chronic Kidney Disease** ESAs ↑ risk of death, serious cardiovascular events, and stroke when administered to target a Hgb level > 11 g/dL. No trial has identified a Hgb target level, ESA dose, or dosing strategy to minimize these risks. Use the lowest effective dose to reduce the need for RBC transfusions. **Cancer** ESAs ↓ overall survival and/or ↑ risk of tumor progression or recurrence in clinical studies of patients with breast, head and neck, non-small cell lung, lymphoid, and cervical cancers. Prescribers and hospitals must enroll in and comply with the ESA APPRISE Oncology Program to prescribe and/or dispense these agents to cancer patients. ESAs are not indicated when the anticipated outcome is cure. Use the lowest effective dose to avoid RBC transfusions. Discontinue following completion of a chemotherapy course. **Perisurgery** Due to ↑ risk of DVT, DVT prophylaxis is recommended.
Darbepoetin *(Aranesp)* IV, SC	**Chronic Kidney Disease on HD** 0.45 mcg/kg weekly or 0.75 mcg/kg every 2 weeks **Chronic Kidney Disease Not on HD** 0.45 mcg/kg every 4 weeks Initiate when Hgb < 10 g/dL Reduce or interrupt dose when Hgb approaches or exceeds 11 g/dL for CKD on HD, or > 10 g/dL for CKD not on HD If Hgb increases > 1 g/dL in any 2-week period, interrupt or ↓ dose by 25% **Cancer** 2.25 mcg/kg weekly or 500 mcg every 3 weeks Initiate when Hgb < 10 g/dL and when at least 2 additional months of chemotherapy planned If Hgb increases > 1 g/dL in any 2-week period, ↓ dose by 40%	**CONTRAINDICATIONS** Uncontrolled hypertension; pure red cell aplasia (PRCA) that begins after treatment; multidose vials containing benzyl alcohol are contraindicated in neonates, infants, pregnancy and lactation. **SIDE EFFECTS** Hypertension, fever, headache, arthralgia/bone pain, pruritus/rash, nausea, cough, injection site pain, thrombosis, edema, chills, dizziness **MONITORING** Hgb, Hct, TSAT, serum ferritin, BP **NOTES** IV route is recommended for patients on hemodialysis. Do not ↑ the dose more frequently than once every 4 weeks. Store in refrigerator. Protect vials from light. The t½ of darbepoetin is 3-fold longer than epoetin alfa (hence given less frequently) MedGuide required

Aplastic Anemia

Aplastic anemia occurs when the bone marrow fails to make enough RBCs, WBCs and platelets. It can be caused by drugs, infectious diseases, autoimmune disorders or hereditary conditions, but in many cases, the cause is unknown. Patients become at risk for life-threatening infections or bleeding. Treatment may include immunosuppressants, blood transfusions or a stem cell transplant. Eltrombopag (Promacta), a thrombopoietin nonpeptide agonist which increases platelet counts, was recently approved for treatment of severe aplastic anemia. The initial dose is 50 mg PO daily.

Hemolytic Anemia

Hemolytic anemia is a type of anemia where RBCs are destroyed and removed from the bloodstream before their normal lifespan of 120 days. This type of anemia can be acquired (e.g., drug-induced) or inherited (e.g., sickle cell anemia, G6PD deficiency). Acquired hemolytic anemia, such as drug-induced, occurs when the medication binds to the RBC surface and causes antibodies to develop against the RBC proteins. This autoimmune reaction can persist for several weeks despite the medication being discontinued. The direct Coombs test is used to detect antibodies that are stuck to the surface of RBCs. Medications that can cause a positive Coombs test, hence hemolytic anemia, are listed to the right.

Glucose-6-phosphate dehydrogenase (G6PD) deficiency is an X-linked inherited disorder that most commonly affects persons of African, Asian, Mediterranean, or Middle Eastern descent. G6PD deficiency is the result of a deficient enzyme produced from RBCs or a nonfunctional enzyme. Without sufficient levels of the enzyme to protect the RBCs, the RBCs become damaged or destroyed via hemolysis 24 to 72 hours after exposure to oxidative stress such as infections, certain foods (e.g., fava beans), severe stress, and certain drugs (see box). When hemolysis is severe, patients present with weakness, tachycardia, jaundice and hematuria, but these symptoms are self-limiting with resolution after 8 to 14 days. Most individuals do not need treatment but should be instructed on what foods and medications to avoid that cause oxidative stress.

Oral Iron Patient Counseling

- This medication is used to treat low levels of iron in your body.

- This medication should be taken on an empty stomach. If taking it on an empty stomach is too nauseating, it can be taken with food.

- Limit consumption of tannins, calcium, polyphenols, and phytates (found in legumes and whole grains), as these can decrease iron absorption.

- This medication needs to be taken for at least a few months for your anemia symptoms to improve; do not stop until directed by your healthcare provider.

- Iron can cause your stool to become dark. This is expected.

- If you develop constipation, ask your pharmacist for a recommendation for a stool softener (such as docusate sodium) and a fiber product (such as psyllium).

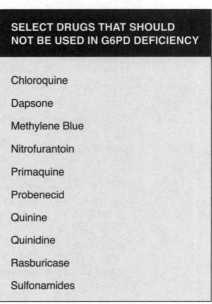

SELECT DRUGS THAT CAN CAUSE HEMOLYTIC ANEMIA

Cephalosporins

Isoniazid

Levodopa

Methyldopa

Nitrofurantoin

Penicillins

Quinidine

Quinine

Rifampin

Sulfonamides

SELECT DRUGS THAT SHOULD NOT BE USED IN G6PD DEFICIENCY

Chloroquine

Dapsone

Methylene Blue

Nitrofurantoin

Primaquine

Probenecid

Quinine

Quinidine

Rasburicase

Sulfonamides

ESA Patient Counseling

- This medication is used to treat anemia. It can help reduce your need for a blood transfusion.

- This drug can increase your risk of life-threatening heart or circulation problems, including heart attack or stroke. This risk will increase the longer you use this drug. Seek emergency medical help if you have symptoms of blood clots such as: crushing chest pain, sudden numbing pain spreading to the arm or shoulder, sudden trouble thinking/seeing/walking, or feeling short of breath, even with mild exertion.

- This drug may increase risk of disease progression or recurrence for breast cancer, non-small cell lung cancer, head and neck cancer, cervical cancer, or lymphoid cancer. Talk with your healthcare provider about your individual risk.

- This drug may cause other serious side effects such as high blood pressure, or serious allergic reactions (causing rash, shortness of breath, wheezing, fainting, sweating, facial swelling). If you experience any of these, stop using the drug and contact your healthcare provider right away.

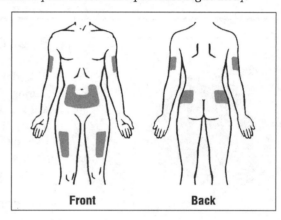

Front   **Back**

- Less serious side effects may include body aches, headache, fever, or pain or tenderness where you injected the medication.

- Do not draw up the drug dose into a syringe until you are ready to give yourself an injection.

- Do not shake the medication bottle. Vigorous shaking will ruin the medicine.

- Do not use the medication if it has changed colors or has any particles in it.

- Recommended sites for injection are the outer area of the upper arms, the abdomen (except for 2 inches around the navel), the front of the middle thighs, and the upper outer area of the buttocks. See shaded areas for injection above.

- Do not inject into an area that is tender, red, bruised, hard or has scars or stretch marks.

- Use each disposable needle only once.

- Throw away used needles in a puncture-proof container (ask your pharmacist where you can get one and how to dispose of it). Keep this container out of the reach of children and pets. Store this drug in the refrigerator and do not allow it to freeze.

- Your healthcare provider may occasionally change your dose to make sure you get the best results from this medication.

- To be sure this medication is working safely and helping your body produce red blood cells, your blood will need to be tested on a regular basis. You may also need to check your blood pressure during treatment. Do not miss any scheduled appointments.

57

SICKLE CELL DISEASE

GUIDELINES/REFERENCES

National Heart, Lung, and Blood
Institute. Evidence-based management
of sickle cell disease. Expert panel
report, 2014. http://www.nhlbi.nih.gov/
sites/www.nhlbi.nih.gov/files/sickle-
cell-disease-report.pdf (accessed 2015
Sep 25).

BACKGROUND

Sickle cell disease (SCD) is a group of inherited red blood cell disorders resulting from a genetic abnormality that causes hemoglobin to be misshapen. Normal red blood cells (RBCs) are shaped like a donut (without the hole), which allows flexibility to move through large and small blood vessels to deliver oxygen to the tissues. Patients with SCD make RBCs that are rigid with a concave "sickle" shape. The irregularly shaped RBCs are unable to transport oxygen effectively and stick together, blocking smaller blood vessels and causing patients with SCD to experience a wide array of complications.

The normal lifespan of RBCs is 90 – 120 days; sickled cells burst (hemolyze) after 10 – 20 days, causing anemia and fatigue.

The hallmark of SCD is a sickle cell crisis or vaso-occlusive crisis (VOC). When tissues become ischemic and oxygen-deprived, severe painful episodes occur. These often begin at night, most commonly in the lower back, legs, hips, abdomen and chest, and last from 3 to 14 days. If the pain is in the chest, it is called acute chest syndrome (ACS), which is extremely painful and can be life-threatening. ACS is the leading cause of illness in SCD and is the most common condition at the time of death.

The spleen has several physiologic functions, including removal of old or damaged RBCs. It also aids in immune function, as it makes and stores white blood cells and serves a unique role in clearing some types of bacterial pathogens, particularly encapsulated organisms, including *Streptococcus pneumoniae, Haemophilus influenzae,* and *Neisseria meningitidis*. Decreased or absent spleen function (functional asplenia) typically manifests within the first year of life in patients with SCD. Due to repetitive sickling and infarctions, the spleen becomes fibrotic and eventually shrinks in size. This places patients at increased risk for serious infections. Patients with SCD should seek medical attention whenever temperature > 101.3°F occurs.

In light of increased stroke risk in patients with SCD, if contraception is needed, progestin-only contraceptives, levonorgestrel intrauterine devices (IUDs) and barrier methods are preferred.

NON-DRUG TREATMENT

Blood transfusions are often essential for treating SCD. Transfusions protect against many of the life-threatening complications by providing healthy red blood cells. These are given either chronically or for acute episodes of ACS, stroke and anemia. The goal hemoglobin level is no higher than 10 g/dL post-infusion. Transfusions carry risk, including iron overload, which can lead to hemosiderosis (excess iron that affects organ function). There is no physiologic means to remove excess iron, necessitating chelation therapy to remove iron, which is discussed later in this chapter.

Children with severe sickle cell disease have been cured with bone marrow transplant after undergoing a regimen in which their own marrow was completely destroyed with chemotherapy first, followed by the healthy donor marrow replacement. This regimen is considered too toxic for adults who have accumulated organ damage. Some adults have been successfully treated in recent years with a partial bone marrow transplant in combination with immunosuppressants.

DRUG TREATMENT

The primary drug classes used in SCD are immunizations and antibiotics (primarily penicillin) to reduce infection risk, analgesics to control pain, hydroxyurea to reduce the frequency of pain episodes and acute chest syndrome, and iron chelation therapy.

Immunizations and Antibiotics

Infections are common in children and young adults.

SICKLE CELL DISEASE COMPLICATIONS
Acute chest syndrome
Anemia
Bones – abnormal growth (long legs and arms) pain, osteomyelitis, osteonecrosis
Gallstones
Hand-foot syndrome (painful swelling)
Infection
Large urine volume (can result in nocturnal enuresis)
Leg ulcers
Liver enlargement
Pain
Pregnancy complications and loss
Priapism
Pulmonary hypertension
Renal impairment
Renal medullary carcinoma
Retinopathy
Spleen – acute sequestration, decreased function
Stroke
Vision loss

Infections are the major cause of death for children with SCD under 5 years of age; 35% of infants with SCD die from infections, most commonly due to *Streptococcus pneumoniae* and *Haemophilus influenzae.* This results in part from a lack of spleen function. Bacteria proliferate and cause increased risk of infection, including septicemia with encapsulated bacteria (*S. pneumoniae, H. influenzae, Salmonella* spp.). Infections with atypical organisms (*Chlamydophila* and *Mycoplasma pneumoniae*) are also increased.

Children under the age of 2 years are at highest risk for invasive pneumococcal disease. In addition to the routine childhood vaccines [pneumococcal conjugate vaccine, (PCV13, *Prevnar*) and *H. influenzae*, type B vaccine], infants with SCD should receive the meningococcal vaccine series. Those older than 2 years with SCD should receive the pneumococcal polysaccharide vaccine (PPSV23, *Pneumovax*) and meningococcal vaccines as recommended. (See Immunizations chapter).

Because vaccine efficacy is not 100%, prophylactic penicillin, usually given orally, has been shown to dramatically reduce the mortality associated with invasive pneumococcal infection in young children and should be initiated in early infancy and continued minimally until age 5 years. If a patient undergoes surgical splenectomy or if invasive pneumococcal infection develops despite antibiotic prophylaxis, indefinite antibiotic prophylaxis should be used.

Analgesics

Mild to moderate pain can often be managed at home with rest, fluids, application of warm compresses applied to affected areas, and the use of NSAIDs or acetaminophen. For severe pain and VOC, opioids are recommended. There is no test or lab assay to definitively diagnose VOC. Pain management must be guided by the patient's self-reported pain severity. Outpatient analgesic use should be reviewed and treatment initiated within 30 minutes of triage. Many patients will require patient-controlled analgesia (PCA) for severe pain. Blood transfusion is not recommended in uncomplicated VOC.

SICKLE CELL PAIN MANAGEMENT PRINCIPLES
Believe the patient's pain
Appoint <u>one healthcare provider</u> to write prescriptions for long-term opioids
Use a <u>partnership agreement and individualized treatment plan</u> (patient rights and responsibilities, including random drug testing)
Patient should be seen every 2-3 months
Encourage fluids, fiber, stool softeners, and stimulant laxatives PRN

Hydroxyurea

Fetal hemoglobin, or HbF, is the form of hemoglobin present in the fetus and young infants. Fetal hemoglobin blocks the sickling action of red blood cells, which is why infants with SCD do not develop symptoms until HbF levels have decreased and been replaced with the defective sickle hemoglobin, HbS. Hydroxyurea is a disease-modifying agent that blocks the enzyme ribonucleotide reductase, which <u>stimulates production of HbF</u>. This reduces the frequency of acute pain crises and episodes of ACS as well as the need for transfusions. Hydroxyurea is indicated for adults with ≥ 3 moderate–severe <u>pain crises in 1 year</u> or patients with severe ACS, anemia, or disability. Use should be considered in all children > 9 months regardless of disease severity.

DRUG	DOSE	SAFETY/SIDE EFFECTS/MONITORING
Hydroxyurea (*Droxia, Hydrea*)	Start: 15 mg/kg daily (round up to nearest capsule), max 35 mg/kg daily (divide higher doses) CrCl < 60 ml/min: start at 5-10 mg/kg daily (round up to nearest capsule) Infants and children: start at 20 mg/kg daily Titrate by 5 mg/kg/day every 8 weeks to a goal Absolute Neutrophil Count (ANC) 2,000-4,000.	**BOXED WARNING** Myelosuppression Malignancy **SIDE EFFECTS** <u>Myelosuppression</u>, macrocytosis, alopecia, hyperpigmentation or atrophy of skin and nails, leukemia, skin cancer, skin ulcers **MONITORING** CBC with differential every 4 weeks during initiation dose escalation, then every 2-3 months when stable. If toxicity, withhold hydroxyurea until bone marrow recovers, then restart at dose reduced by 5 mg/kg. Hemoglobin F, uric acid, renal function, LFTs **NOTES** Pregnancy Category D <u>Hazardous agent</u>-wear gloves when dispensing and wash hands before and after contact MedGuide required Clinical response can take 3-6 months

Hydroxyurea Drug Interactions

- Hydroxyurea can increase the effects of clozapine, didanosine, natalizumab, pimecrolimus, stavudine, tacrolimus (topical), tofacitinib, and live vaccines. Concomitant use should be avoided. Concurrent treatment with antiretrovirals (including didanosine and stavudine), has higher risk for potentially fatal pancreatitis, hepatotoxicity, hepatic failure, and severe peripheral neuropathy.

Hydroxyurea Patient Counseling

- Anyone handling the capsules (patient or caregiver) should <u>wear disposable gloves when handling</u> to reduce risk of exposure. Wash hands before and after handling. The capsules should not be opened.

- If you accidentally spill any of the contents, immediately wipe up with a damp cloth and throw cloth away in a sealed plastic bag, then clean the area three times with detergent solution followed by clean water.

- For males and females of reproductive age:

  - This medicine can harm an unborn baby and is not recommended during pregnancy. Discuss effective birth control and family planning with your healthcare provider.

  - Effective <u>contraception should be used during and even after stopping this medication</u> (for males at least one year, females at least 30 days).

- Hydroxyurea can lower your body's ability to fight infection and make you more prone to illness or bleeding.

- Wear sun protection, as this medicine can increase risk of skin cancer.

- Call your healthcare provider immediately if you experience fever, chills, sores in the mouth, easy bruising/bleeding, purple or red pinpoint spots under the skin, pale skin, rash, shortness of breath, rapid heart rate, painful or difficult urination, and/or confusion.

Iron Chelation Treatment

Chronic RBC <u>transfusions cause iron overload</u>, which damages the liver, heart and other organs. Chelation therapy is used to remove excess iron stores in the body. Historically, deferoxamine (the antidote for iron toxicity) has been used, but it requires an infusion pump for intravenous (IV) or subcutaneous (SC) administration over 8-12 hours daily, and has significant toxicities. Deferasirox is taken orally once daily with less toxicity. Deferasirox is indicated for the treatment of chronically elevated levels of iron in the blood caused by repeated blood transfusions (transfusional hemosiderosis) in patients 2 years of age and older. It is also used for iron overload from chronic transfusions in patients with beta-thalassemia, a blood disorder causing decreased hemoglobin production.

DRUG	DOSING	SAFETY/SIDE EFFECTS/MONITORING
Deferoxamine (*Desferal*) Injection	SC, IV, or IM, dosed by weight. CrCl 10-50 mL/min: decrease by 25-50% CrCl < 10 mL/min, hemodialysis, peritoneal dialysis: Avoid use Pediatric IV or IM dosed by weight	**CONTRAINDICATIONS** Severe renal disease **SIDE EFFECTS** Ototoxicity, visual impairment, arthralgia, headache, acute respiratory distress syndrome (dyspnea, cyanosis, and/or interstitial infiltrates), agranulocytosis, growth failure, hypersensitivity reactions (e.g., urticaria, angioedema), injection-site reactions (erythema, pruritus), hypotension **MONITORING** Serum iron, ferritin, total iron-binding capacity, CBC with differential, renal function, LFTs, growth and body weight, audiometry and ophthalmologic exams (if used long-term) **NOTES** Pregnancy Category C. Can cause reddish brown discoloration of the urine. Avoid ascorbic acid-containing supplements during first month of treatment to avoid cardiac impairment. After first month, can be started at doses ≤ 200 mg/day in adults, 100 mg/day for children ≥ 10 years of age, or 50 mg/day in children < 10 years of age.

DRUG	DOSING	SAFETY/SIDE EFFECTS/MONITORING
Deferasirox (*Exjade*, *Jadenu*)	*Exjade,* tablet for oral suspension: Initial: 20 mg/kg Take 30+ min before eating, mixed into orange or apple juice or water *Jadenu*, oral tablet: Improved bioavailability; dose is 30% less than *Exjade* Initial: 14 mg/kg Take on an empty stomach or with a light meal	**BOXED WARNINGS** Renal failure, hepatic failure, gastrointestinal hemorrhage/ulceration **CONTRAINDICATIONS** Renal impairment, platelets < 50,000/mm³, advanced malignancies, high-risk myelodysplastic syndromes **SIDE EFFECTS** Headache, rash (including SJS), N/V/D, abdominal pain, increased SCr, proteinuria, cough, viral infection **MONITORING** LFTs, bilirubin, renal function, ferritin, iron, CBC **NOTES** Pregnancy Category C Can cause reddish brown discoloration of the urine
Deferiprone (*Ferriprox*)	Initial: 25 mg/kg TID Max: 33 mg/kg Dose to the nearest ½ tab	**BOXED WARNING** Agranulocytosis **SIDE EFFECTS** N/V, reddish brown discoloration of the urine, neutropenia, agranulocytosis, abdominal pain **MONITORING** Absolute neutrophil count (ANC) weekly during treatment **NOTES** Pregnancy Category D. Hazardous agent-wear gloves when dispensing and wash hands before and after contact. If breaking tablets, double glove, gown, and use respiratory protection. Can cause reddish brown discoloration of the urine. MedGuide required.

Deferasirox Drug Interactions

- Deferasirox is a substrate of UGT1A1 as well as an inhibitor of CYP450 1A2, 2C8, and an inducer of 3A4 and can be affected by many drugs; check prior to dispensing.

- Avoid concomitant use of aluminum hydroxide, bile acid sequestrants (e.g., cholestyramine), and potent UGT inducers (e.g., rifampin, phenobarbital, phenytoin) as they can reduce the efficacy of chelation therapy.

Deferasirox Patient Counseling

- Administer tablets for oral suspension in water, orange juice or apple juice. Avoid carbonated drinks due to foaming. Do not chew or swallow tablet whole. Take on an empty stomach at least 30 minutes before eating, using this method:

  - SET the timer to 3 minutes.

  - MIX the *Exjade* tablet(s) into water, orange juice, or apple juice until the timer beeps. You can use the *Exjade* mixer or a glass of water.

  - DRINK all of the *Exjade* mixture. If any *Exjade* remains, add a small amount of liquid, stir, and drink until completely finished.

- Oral tablets should be swallowed whole on an empty stomach or with a light meal.

- Avoid aluminum-containing products as they can bind the chelation therapy and reduce its effectiveness. Ask your healthcare provider if you have questions about a specific product.

- Seek immediate medical attention if you experience any of these signs of an allergic reaction, including difficulty breathing, hives, and/or swelling of your face, lips, tongue, or throat.

Deferiprone Drug Interactions

- Deferiprone is a substrate of UGT1A6. Use caution with UGT1A6 inhibitors or inducers.

- Administration of products containing polyvalent cations (e.g., aluminum, calcium, magnesium hydroxide, and zinc) should be separated by at least 4 hours from deferiprone to prevent decreased deferiprone serum concentrations.

Deferiprone Patient Counseling

- Disposable gloves should be worn by anyone handling the tablets (patient or caregiver) to reduce risk of exposure. Wash hands before and after handling.

- Anyone (patient or caregiver) handling broken tablets should wear 2 pairs of gloves, a gown, and use respiratory protection.

- This medicine can harm an unborn baby and is not recommended during pregnancy. Discuss effective birth control and family planning with your healthcare provider.

- Take deferiprone at least 4 hours away from aluminum- or calcium-containing antacids or multivitamins with minerals as they can bind the chelation therapy and reduce its effectiveness. Ask your healthcare provider if you have questions about a specific product.

58

DEPRESSION

BACKGROUND

Major Depressive Disorder (MDD, or referred to here as "depression") is one of the most common health conditions in the world. The statistics are sobering. In any given year, approximately 15 million U.S. citizens will experience an episode of MDD. Although approximately half of these people seek help for this condition, only 20 percent – 10 percent of the total population with MDD – receive adequate treatment, and just 30 percent of those who receive adequate treatment reach the treatment goal of remission. People with depression suffer greatly with persistent feelings of hopelessness, dejection, constant worry, poor concentration, a lack of energy, an inability to sleep and, sometimes, suicidal tendencies.

Healthcare providers should remember that depression is usually a chronic illness that requires long-term treatment, much like diabetes or high blood pressure. Although some people experience only one episode, the majority have recurrent episodes. A significant treatment problem is patients who discontinue their medication, or, continue medication despite an inadequate response. This is discussed under "Treatment-Resistant Depression." Due to high rates of inadequate response, pharmacists should attempt to ensure adequate treatment trials: 6-8 weeks, at a therapeutic dose (the VA/DoD guideline recommends an 8-12 week trial).

CAUSES OF DEPRESSION

Depression's causes are poorly understood, but involve some combination of genetic, biologic and environmental factors. Pharmacists are most concerned with biological factors, since these are treated with medications. Serotonin (5HT) may be the most important neurotransmitter (NT) involved with feelings of well being. Other NTs include acetylcholine (ACh) and catecholamines [including dopamine (DA), norepinephrine (NE), and epinephrine (EPI)]. Recent research has focused on complex or completely novel pathways that may be involved in depression. Since it is not possible at this time to measure brain chemical imbalances, treatment for mood disorders, including depression, depends on a competent assessment and trial. If a drug does not work, after a suitable trial of at least 6 – 8 weeks, a combination or different set of NTs can be targeted (see treatment resistance section). Patient history is critical in treating any mental illness; what worked in the past, or did not work, should help guide current and future therapy. Pharmacists should always counsel patients, family and caregivers that mood may worsen;

this is essential, since the majority of antidepressants are prescribed by primary care providers, and patient follow-up (after the prescription has been written) rarely occurs. The patient needs instructions on how to respond to worsened mood. This is critical for adolescents and young adults in particular.

CONCURRENT BIPOLAR OR ANXIETY DISORDERS

It is necessary to rule-out bipolar disorder prior to initiating antidepressant therapy in order to treat the patient properly and avoid rapid-cycling (cycling rapidly from one phase to the other). This is why screening forms for MDD now include questions designed to identify mania symptoms such as "There are times when I get into moods where I feel very speeded up or irritable." Benzodiazepines (BZDs) are often used adjunctively in depression with concurrent anxiety, although in many cases the BZD is the only "treatment" and the depression itself is left untreated. BZDs can cause and/or mask depression and put the patient at risk for physiological dependence and withdrawal symptoms when the dose is wearing off (tachycardia, anxiety, amongst others). Prescribers should also select BZDs carefully and monitor closely if patients have co-occurring substance use disorders.

DEPRESSION DIAGNOSIS

DSM-5 criteria includes presence of at least 5 of the following symptoms (even if they are in response to a significant loss like bereavement or financial ruin) during the same two week period (must include symptom 1 or 2):

1. Depressed mood
2. Marked diminished interest/pleasure
3. Significant weight loss or weight gain
4. Insomnia or hypersomnia
5. Psychomotor agitation or retardation
6. Fatigue or loss of energy
7. Feelings of worthlessness
8. Diminished ability to concentrate
9. Recurrent suicidal ideation

LAG EFFECT AND SUICIDE PREVENTION

Patients should be told that the medicine must be used daily, and will take time to work. It is important to inform the patient that physical symptoms such as low energy improve within a few weeks but psychological symptoms, such as low mood, may take a month or longer. If a patient reports suicidal ideation, refer to the ED or elsewhere for help. If someone has a plan to commit suicide, it is more likely that the threat is real.

DRUG TREATMENT

The guidelines state that because the effectiveness of the different antidepressant classes is generally comparable, the initial choice of an agent should be based on the side effect profile, safety concerns and the patient-specific symptoms. For most patients an SSRI, SNRI or (with specific concurrent conditions or considerations) mirtazapine or bupropion is preferred.

Due to safety concerns (the risk of drug-drug and drug-food interactions) the use of the oral nonselective monoamine oxidase inhibitors (MAO inhibitors) such as phenelzine, tranylcypromine and isocarboxazid is restricted to patients unresponsive to other treatments. Serotonin syndrome can occur with administration of one or more serotonergic medications (and higher doses increase risk) but is most severe when an MAO inhibitor is administered with another serotonergic medication.

All drug therapy trials should preferably be given with competent, concurrent psychotherapy, although this is not typically done. If a drug is being discontinued it should be tapered off over several weeks. In some instances a drug with a longer half-life (e.g., fluoxetine) can be used to minimize withdrawal symptoms. Withdrawal symptoms (anxiety, agitation, insomnia, dizziness, flu-like symptoms) can be quite distressing to the patient. Paroxetine and some other agents carry a high risk of withdrawal symptoms and must be tapered upon discontinuation.

Treatment-Resistant Depression

Prescribers should supervise a trial of 6-8 weeks at an adequate (therapeutic) dose before concluding that it is not working well. Only about half of patients respond to the prescribed antidepressant and just about one-third will reach remission (the elimination of depressive symptoms). The goal of therapy is remission. An incomplete response can necessitate any of the following:

- A dosage increase.

- A combination of antidepressants (which may or may not be appropriate).

- Augmentation with buspirone *(BuSpar)* or a low dose of an atypical antipsychotic. Agents approved as augmentation therapy with antidepressants are aripiprazole *(Abilify)*, olanzapine + fluoxetine *(Symbyax)* and quetiapine ext-rel *(Seroquel XR)*.

- Other guideline recommendations (as there are several, with various recommendations) include augmentation with lithium, thyroid hormone, and in some cases, electroconvulsive therapy (ECT).

- In 2012, good trial results were reported with the use of ketamine, which suggests alternative mechanisms may be targeted for improved treatment response.

Antidepressant Use in Pregnancy, Postpartum Depression

Untreated maternal depression, especially in the late second or early third trimesters, is associated with increased rates of adverse outcomes (e.g., premature birth, low birth weight, fetal growth restriction, postnatal complications). Depression in pregnant women often goes unrecognized and untreated in part because of safety concerns. All drugs carry risk, and the risk/benefit must be considered individually.

If a woman is on antidepressants and wishes to become pregnant, it may be possible to taper the drug if the depression is mild and she has been symptom-free for the previous six months. In more severe cases, medications may need to be continued, or started. The ACOG guidelines for mild depression in pregnancy recommend psychotherapy first, followed by drug treatment if-needed. SSRIs are often used initially and are pregnancy category C, except for paroxetine, which is D, due to potential cardiac effects. Paroxetine is the most difficult SSRI to discontinue, and requires a slow titration if stopped. The new formulation of paroxetine, *Brisdelle*, is pregnancy category X. Although SSRIs have historically been preferred, in December of 2011 the FDA issued a warning regarding SSRI use during pregnancy and the potential risk of persistent pulmonary hypertension of the newborn (PPHN). Tricyclics, also pregnancy category C, are the second group most commonly used.

Postpartum depression is common but often unrecognized and under-treated, with adverse outcomes for the mother, baby, and family. Breast-feeding is helpful for most women for physical and emotional symptoms, and is considered beneficial for the baby. Drug safety in breastfeeding, therefore, is essential. SSRIs or tricyclics are generally preferred (with the exception of doxepin, per the ACOG recommendations).

MEDICATIONS THAT CAN CAUSE OR WORSEN DEPRESSION

Beta-blockers (particularly propranolol)

Clonidine

Corticosteroids

Cyclosporine

Ethanol

Isotretinoin

Indomethacin

Interferons

Methadone, and possibly other chronic opioid use that can lower testosterone or estrogen levels

Oral contraceptives, anabolic steroids (medication-specific, patient specific)

Methyldopa

Methylphenidate/Other ADHD Stimulants/Atomoxetine: Monitor mood

Procainamide

Reserpine

Statins (patient specific, some cases)

Varenicline

Antidepressants require monitoring for worsening mood, especially among younger people

---

In addition to the medications listed, medical conditions such as stroke, Parkinson disease, dementia, multiple sclerosis, thyroid disorders (particularly hypothyroidism), low vitamin D levels (possible link), metabolic conditions (e.g., hypercalcemia), malignancy, OAB and infectious diseases can be contributory.

NATURAL PRODUCTS

St. John's wort or SAMe (S-adenosyl-L- methionine) may be helpful. Both are classified as "likely effective" for treating depression in the *Natural Medicines Database*, but there is less evidence of efficacy than with standard treatments. Both agents cannot be used with other serotonergic agents. St. John's wort is a broad-spectrum CYP 450 enzyme inducer and has many significant drug interactions. It is a photosensitizer and is serotonergic; use caution with other 5HT drugs.

SSRIs: Selective Serotonin Reuptake Inhibitors

DRUG	DOSING	SAFETY/SIDE EFFECTS/MONITORING
FLUoxetine (PROzac, *Sarafem, PROzac Weekly)* + OLANZapine *(Symbyax)* – taken QHS, for resistant depression	10-60 mg/day (titrate to 60 mg/d for bulimia) 90 mg weekly 20 mg/5 mL liquid Premenstrual dysphoric disorder (PMDD): *Sarafem* 20 mg every day of menstrual cycle or 20 mg daily starting 14 days prior to menstruation through 1st full day of bleeding	**BOXED WARNING** Antidepressants increase the risk of suicidal thinking and behavior in children, adolescents, and young adults (18-24 years of age) with major depressive disorder (MDD) and other psychiatric disorders; consider risk prior to prescribing. **CONTRAINDICATIONS** Concurrent use with MAO inhibitors, linezolid, IV methylene blue, or pimozide; concurrent use with thioridazine (fluoxetine, paroxetine); concurrent use with alosetron, ramelteon, or tizanidine (fluvoxamine); concurrent use with disulfiram (sertraline); pregnancy *(Brisdelle)*
PARoxetine (Paxil, *Pexeva, Paxil CR, Brisdelle)* Preg Cat D *Brisdelle:* Preg Cat X	IR: 10–60 mg/day CR: 12.5–75 mg/day 10 mg/5 mL Each 10 mg IR = 12.5 mg CR	**SIDE EFFECTS** Sexual side effects: include ↓ libido, ejaculation difficulties, anorgasmia Somnolence, insomnia, nausea, xerostomia, diaphoresis (dose-related), weakness, tremor, dizziness, headache (but may help for migraines if taken continuously)
FluvoxaMINE *(Luvox, Luvox CR)*	100-300 mg/day Fluvoxamine has more drug interactions	Fluoxetine can cause activation; take dose in AM, others AM (usually) or PM, if sedating SIADH, hyponatremia (elderly at higher risk)
Sertraline (Zoloft)	50-200 mg/day 20 mg/mL liquid Premenstrual dysphoric disorder (PMDD): 50-150 mg every day of menstrual cycle or 50-150 mg daily starting 14 days prior to menstruation through 1st full day of bleeding	Restless leg syndrome (see if this began when treatment was started) ↑ bleeding risk with concurrent use of anticoagulants, antiplatelets, NSAIDs, gingko, thrombolytics ↑ fall risk; use extreme caution in frail patients, osteopenia/ osteoporosis, use of CNS depressants **NOTES** All approved for depression and a variety of anxiety disorders except fluvoxamine which is only approved for OCD.
Citalopram (CeleXA)	20-40 mg/day 2011 FDA warning not to use > 40 mg/day due to QT risk; Max 20 mg/day in poor CYP 2C19 metabolizers or concurrent use of 2C19 inhibitors	Note FDA warning regarding QT risk and citalopram at > 40 mg/day or > 20 mg/day if 60+ years, if liver disease, with CYP 2C19 poor metabolizers or on 2C19 inhibitors. Similar, but lower risk for escitalopram at > 20 mg/day; do not exceed 10 mg/day in elderly. Bottom line: if cardiac risk is present, best to avoid citalopram. Sertraline is often the top choice for an SSRI in cardiac patients.
Escitalopram (Lexapro – **S-enantiomer of citalopram)**	10 mg/day (can ↑ 20 mg/d) 1 mg/mL liquid Do not exceed > 20 mg/day due to QT risk; Max 10 mg/day in CYP 2C19 poor metabolizers.	In 2011, the FDA issued a warning regarding SSRI use during pregnancy and the potential risk of persistent pulmonary hypertension of the newborn (PPHN). SSRIs are pregnancy category C, except paroxetine, which is considered more dangerous, and is D/X *(Brisdelle)*. Citalopram/escitalopram not approved for use in children. To switch to fluoxetine 90 mg/weekly from fluoxetine daily, start 7 days after last daily dose.

SSRI and Combined Mechanism

DRUG	DOSING	SAFETY/SIDE EFFECTS/MONITORING

SSRI and 5-HT$_{1A}$ Partial Agonist

DRUG	DOSING	SAFETY/SIDE EFFECTS/MONITORING
Vilazodone (*Viibryd*) Dosing to the right is in the patient starter kit.	Start at 10 mg x 7 days, then 20 mg x 7 days, then 40 mg all with food	**BOXED WARNING** Antidepressants increase the risk of suicidal thinking and behavior in children, adolescents, and young adults (18-24 years of age) with major depressive disorder (MDD) and other psychiatric disorders; consider risk prior to prescribing. **CONTRAINDICATIONS** Potentially lethal drug interaction with MAO inhibitors; see wash-out information. Do not initiate in patients being treated with linezolid or methylene blue IV. **SIDE EFFECTS** Diarrhea, nausea/vomiting, insomnia, ↓ libido (less sexual SEs compared to SSRIs and SNRIs) **NOTES** ↑ bleeding risk with concurrent use of anticoagulants, anti-platelets, NSAIDs, gingko, thrombolytics. Pregnancy Category C

SSRI, 5-HT Receptor Antagonist, 5-HT$_{1A}$ Agonist

DRUG	DOSING	SAFETY/SIDE EFFECTS/MONITORING
Vortioxetine (*Brintellix*)	10 mg/d, can ↑ 20 mg/day, with or without food (5 mg/d if higher doses not tolerated)	**BOXED WARNING** Antidepressants increase the risk of suicidal thinking and behavior in children, adolescents, and young adults (18-24 years of age) with major depressive disorder (MDD) and other psychiatric disorders; consider risk prior to prescribing. **CONTRAINDICATIONS** Potentially lethal drug interaction with MAO inhibitors; see washout information. Do not initiate in patients being treated with linezolid or methylene blue IV. **SIDE EFFECTS** Nausea, constipation, vomiting ↑ bleeding risk with concurrent use of anticoagulants, antiplatelets, NSAIDs, gingko, thrombolytics **NOTES** Pregnancy Category C

SSRI Drug Interactions

- MAO Is and hypertensive crisis: allow 2 weeks either going to an MAO inhibitor or from an MAO inhibitor to an SSRI except fluoxetine which requires a 5 week wash-out period if going from fluoxetine to an MAO inhibitor (due to the long half-life of fluoxetine of at least 7 days).

- Fluoxetine: 2D6, 2C19 inhibitor. Fluvoxamine: 1A2, 2D6, 2C9, 2C19, 3A4 inhibitor. Paroxetine: 2D6 inhibitor. Note all three are 2D6 inhibitors and some other psych drugs are 2D6 substrates. Psych drugs are sometimes used in combination.

- Tamoxifen's effectiveness decreases with fluoxetine, paroxetine and sertraline (and duloxetine and bupropion).

- ↑ bleeding risk with concurrent use of anticoagulants, antiplatelets, NSAIDs, gingko, thrombolytics.

- Do not use with thioridazine or pimozide.

- Do not use with cimetidine.

- Do not initiate in patients receiving linezolid or methylene blue IV.

- Caution with drugs that cause orthostasis or CNS depressants due to risk of falls.

- FDA warning regarding QT risk and citalopram at > 40 mg/day or > 20 mg if 60+ years, if liver disease, with 2C19 poor metabolizers and on 2C19 inhibitors. Similar, but lower risk for escitalopram at > 20 mg/day; do not exceed 10 mg/day in elderly. Bottom line: if cardiac risk is present, avoid citalopram. Sertraline is often the top choice for an SSRI in cardiac patients.

SSRI Counseling

- Dispense MedGuide and instruct patient to read it. Especially in adolescents and young adults: counsel on risk of suicide – particularly during therapy initiation.

- Fluoxetine is taken in the morning; the others morning or at bedtime.

- To reduce your risk of side effects, your healthcare provider may direct you to start taking this drug at a low dose and gradually increase your dose.

- Take this medication exactly as prescribed. To help you remember, use it at the same time each day. Antidepressants do not work if they are taken as-needed.

- It is important to continue taking this medication even if you feel well. Do not stop taking this medication without consulting your healthcare provider. Some conditions may become worse when the drug is suddenly stopped. Your dose may need to be gradually decreased.

- It may take 1 to 2 weeks to feel a benefit from this drug and 6-8 weeks to feel the full effect on your mood. Tell the healthcare provider if your condition persists or worsens. You can try a medication in a different class. One will work or it may take different tries to find the right medicine that will help you feel better.

- Some patients, but not all, have sexual difficulties when using this medicine. If this happens, talk with the healthcare provider. They can change you to a medicine that does not cause these problems.

- Sertraline oral concentrate must be diluted before use. Immediately before administration, use the dropper provided to measure the required amount of concentrate; mix with 4 ounces (1/2 cup) of water, ginger ale, lemon/lime soda, lemonade, or orange juice only. Do not use with disulfiram.

SNRIs – Serotonin and Norepinephrine Reuptake Inhibitors

DRUG	DOSING	SAFETY/SIDE EFFECTS/MONITORING
Venlafaxine (Effexor, Effexor XR) Depression, GAD, Panic Disorder, Social Anxiety Disorder	150-375 mg/day Can start low with 37.5 or 75 mg Different generics; check orange book	**BOXED WARNING** Antidepressants increase the risk of suicidal thinking and behavior in children, adolescents, and young adults (18-24 years of age) with major depressive disorder (MDD) and other psychiatric disorders; consider risk prior to prescribing.
DULoxetine (Cymbalta) Depression, Peripheral Neuropathy (Pain), Fibromyalgia, GAD, Chronic Musculoskeletal Pain	40-60 mg/day (daily, or 20-30 BID); max dose 120 mg/day; doses > 60 mg/day not more effective Duloxetine is a good choice if the patient has both pain and depression	**CONTRAINDICATIONS** Potentially lethal DI: SNRIs and MAO inhibitors – see wash out information. Do not initiate in a patient receiving linezolid or intravenous methylene blue. **SIDE EFFECTS** Similar to SSRIs (due to serotonin reuptake) and side effects due to ↑ NE uptake: ↑ pulse, dilated pupils (possibly leading to an episode of narrow angle glaucoma), dry mouth, excessive sweating and constipation
Desvenlafaxine (Pristiq) Depression	50 mg/day, can ↑ 100 mg/day	SNRIs can affect urethral resistance. Caution is advised when using SNRIs in patients prone to obstructive urinary disorders. All have warning for ↑ BP, but risk is greatest with venlafaxine when dosed > 150 mg/day; yet all have risk especially at higher doses. ↑ BP may respond to dose reduction, use of antihypertensive or change in therapy.
Levomilnacipran (Fetzima) Depression	40-120 mg/day Start at 20 mg/day x 2 days Do not open, chew or crush capsules; take whole. Do not take with alcohol.	↑ bleeding risk with concurrent use of anticoagulants, antiplatelets, NSAIDs, gingko, thrombolytics. **NOTES** The SNRI dose is ↓ in renal impairment. Do not use levomilnacipran or duloxetine with CrCl < 30 mL/min.

SNRI Drug Interactions

- MAO inhibitors and hypertensive crisis: 5-14 day (duloxetine) or 7 day (venlafaxine, desvenlafaxine, levomilnacipran) wash out if going from SNRI to a MAO inhibitor, 14 day wash out if going from MAO inhibitor to SNRI.

- Duloxetine is a moderate 2D6 inhibitor.

- Tamoxifen's effectiveness decreases with duloxetine.

- Do not initiate in patients receiving linezolid or methylene blue IV.

- ↑ bleeding risk with concurrent use of anticoagulants, antiplatelets, NSAIDs, gingko, thrombolytics.

- If on antihypertensive medications, use caution and monitor (can ↑ BP), especially at higher doses.

SNRI Counseling

- Dispense MedGuide and instruct patient to read it. Especially in adolescents and young adults: counsel on risk of suicide – particularly during therapy initiation.

- This medication may cause nausea and stomach upset (if venlafaxine IR can try change to XR).

- You may experience increased sweating; if so, discuss with your healthcare provider. You should check your blood pressure regularly to make sure it stays in a safe range.

- Desvenlafaxine: When you take this medicine, you may see something in your stool that looks like a tablet. This is the empty shell from the tablet after the medicine has been absorbed by your body.

- Levomilnacipran: Take capsules whole. Do not open, chew or crush the capsules. Do not take with alcohol; this could cause the medicine to be released too quickly.

- To reduce your risk of side effects, your healthcare provider may direct you to start taking this drug at a low dose and gradually increase your dose.

- Do not crush or chew extended-release formulations.

- Take this medication exactly as directed. To help you remember, use it at the same time each day. Antidepressants do not work if they are taken as-needed.

- It is important to continue taking this medication even if you feel well. Do not stop taking this medication without consulting your healthcare provider. Some conditions may become worse when the drug is suddenly stopped. Your dose may need to be gradually decreased.

- It may take 1 to 2 weeks to feel a benefit from this drug and 6-8 weeks to feel the full effect on your mood. Tell the healthcare provider if your condition persists or worsens. You can try a medication in a different class. One will work it may take different tries to find the right medicine that will help you feel better.

- Some patients, but not all, have sexual difficulties when using this medicine. If this happens, talk with the healthcare provider. They can change you to a medicine that does not cause these problems.

TRICYCLICS

NE and 5HT reuptake inhibitors (primarily, and block ACh and histamine receptors which contributes to the SE profile).

DRUG	DOSING	SAFETY/SIDE EFFECTS/MONITORING
TERTIARY AMINES **Amitriptyline** *(Elavil* – brand N/A) **Doxepin** – *Zonalon* and *Prudoxin* are cream for pruritus, *Silenor* is for insomnia ClomiPRAMINE *(Anafranil)* Imipramine *(Tofranil, Tofranil PM* – this is different salt, not interchangeable) Trimipramine *(Surmontil)* **SECONDARY AMINES** Amoxapine Desipramine *(Norpramin)* Maprotiline Nortriptyline *(Pamelor)* Protriptyline *(Vivactil)* (Secondary amines are relatively selective for NE – tertiary amines may be slightly more effective but have worse SE profile)	**AMITRIPTYLINE** Depression: 100-150 mg BID Neuropathic pain/ migraine prophylaxis: 10-50 mg QHS **NORTRIPTYLINE** Depression: 25 mg TID-QID **DOXEPIN** Depression: 100-300 mg daily	**BOXED WARNING** Antidepressants ↑ the risk of suicidal thinking and behavior in children, adolescents, and young adults (18-24 years of age) with major depressive disorder (MDD) and other psychiatric disorders; consider risk prior to prescribing. **CONTRAINDICATIONS** Concurrent use with MAO inhibitors, linezolid, IV methylene blue; myocardial infarction, glaucoma (doxepin), urinary retention (doxepin) **SIDE EFFECTS** **Cardiotoxicity** QT-prolongation with overdose – can be used for suicide-counsel carefully; obtain baseline ECG if cardiac risk factors or age > 50 years old Orthostasis, tachycardia **Anticholinergic** Dry mouth, blurred vision, urinary retention, constipation (taper off to avoid cholinergic rebound) Vivid dreams Weight gain (varies by agent and patient), sedation, sweating Myoclonus (muscle twitching-may be symptoms of drug toxicity) **NOTES** ↑ fall risk – especially in elderly due to combination of orthostasis and sedation Tertiary amines more likely to cause sedation and weight gain

Tricyclic Drug Interactions

■ MAO inhibitors and hypertensive crisis: 2 week wash-out if going to or from an MAO inhibitor.

■ Additive QT prolongation risk; see Drug Interaction chapter for other high-risk QT drugs to attempt to avoid additive risk.

■ Metabolized by CYP 2D6 (up to 10% of Caucasians are slow metabolizers); check for drug interactions.

Tricyclic Counseling

■ Dispense MedGuide and instruct patient to read it. Especially in adolescents and young adults: counsel on risk of suicide – particularly during therapy initiation. TCAs are dangerous if the patient wishes to kill themselves; a month's supply can be deadly. Counseling is critical.

■ This drug can cause constipation. You may need to use a stool softener or laxative if this becomes a problem.

■ This drug may cause dry/blurry vision. You may need to use an eye drop lubricant.

■ This drug may make it more difficult to urinate.

■ This drug may cause dry mouth. This can contribute to dental decay (cavities) and difficulty chewing food. It is important to use proper dental hygiene when taking any medication that causes dry mouth, including brushing and flossing. Sugar free lozenges may be helpful.

■ This drug may cause changes in your blood pressure. Use caution when changing from lying down or sitting to a standing position. Hold onto the bed or rail until you are steady.

■ If you experience anxiety, or insomnia (sometimes with vivid dreams), these usually go away. If they do not, contact your healthcare provider.

■ Take this medication exactly as prescribed. To help you remember, use it at the same time each day. Antidepressants do not work if they are taken as-needed.

■ It is important to continue taking this medication even if you feel well. Do not stop taking this medication without consulting your healthcare provider. Some conditions may become worse when the drug is suddenly stopped. Your dose may need to be gradually decreased.

■ It may take 1 to 2 weeks to feel a benefit from this drug and 6-8 weeks to feel the full effect on your mood. Tell the healthcare provider if your condition persists or worsens. You can try a medication in a different class. It may take several tries to find the right medicine that will help you feel better.

Monoamine Oxidase (MAO) Inhibitors

Inhibit the enzyme monoamine oxidase, which breaks down catecholamines, including 5-HT, NE, EPI, DA. If these NTs ↑ dramatically, hypertensive crisis, and death can result.

DRUG	DOSING	SAFETY/SIDE EFFECTS/MONITORING/
Isocarboxazid *(Marplan)*	20 mg/day, divided, max 60 mg/day	**BOXED WARNING** Antidepressants increase the risk of suicidal thinking and behavior in children, adolescents, and young adults (18-24 years of age) with major depressive disorder (MDD) and other psychiatric disorders; consider risk prior to prescribing.
Phenelzine *(Nardil)*	15 mg TID, max 60-90 mg/day	**CONTRAINDICATIONS** Cardiovascular disease, cerebrovascular defect, history of headache, history of hepatic disease, pheochromocytoma. Concurrent use of sympathomimetics and related compounds, CNS depressants, dextromethorphan, ethanol, meperidine, bupropion, or buspirone.
Tranylcypromine *(Parnate)*	30 mg/day in divided doses, max 60 mg/day	**WARNINGS** Not commonly used but watch for drug-drug and drug-food interactions – if missed could be fatal. Hypertensive crisis (VERY high blood pressure) can occur when taken with TCAs, SSRIs, SNRIs, many other drugs and tyramine-rich foods (see interactions below). **SIDE EFFECTS** Anticholinergic effects (taper upon discontinuation to avoid cholinergic rebound) Orthostasis Sedation (except tranylcypromine causes stimulation) Sexual dysfunction, weight gain, headache, insomnia
Selegiline transdermal patch *(EMSAM)* MAO-B Selective Inhibitor Selegiline as *Eldepryl* and *Zelapar* (ODT) are oral drugs for Parkinson disease.	Start at 6 mg patch/day, can ↑ to 9 or 12 mg/day	**CONTRAINDICATIONS** Discontinue at least 10 days prior to elective surgery requiring general anesthesia, do not use with local anesthesia containing sympathomimetic vasoconstrictors, foods high in tyramine, supplements containing tyrosine, phenylalanine, tryptophan, or caffeine. No dietary issues with 6 mg patch. **SIDE EFFECTS** Constipation, gas, dry mouth, loss of appetite, sexual problems

MAO Inhibitor Drug Interactions

- MAO inhibitors and hypertensive crisis: allow 2 week wash-out if going to or from an MAO inhibitor and an SSRI, SNRI or TCA antidepressant (exception: if going from fluoxetine back to an MAO inhibitor, need to wait 5 weeks).

- MAO inhibitors <u>cannot</u> be used with many other drugs or the drugs will not be broken down and hypertensive crisis, serotonin syndrome or psychosis may result. The interaction could be fatal. These include any drugs with effects on the concentrations of epinephrine, norepinephrine, serotonin or dopamine. This includes bupropion, carbamazepine, oxcarbazepine, ephedrine and analogs (pseudoephedrine, etc), buspirone, levodopa, linezolid. lithium, meperidine, SSRIs, SNRIs, TCAs, tramadol, methadone, mirtazapine, dextromethorphan, cyclobenzaprine (and other skeletal muscle relaxants), OTC diet pills/herbal weight loss products and St. John's wort.

- Patients taking MAO inhibitors must avoid tyramine-rich foods, including aged cheese, pickled herring, yeast extract, air-dried meats, sauerkraut, soy sauce, fava beans and some red wines and beers (tap beer and any beer that has not been pasteurized – canned and bottled beers contain little or no tyramine). Foods can become high in tyramine when they have been aged, fermented, pickled or smoked.

MAO Inhibitor Counseling

- Dispense MedGuide and instruct patient to read it. Especially in adolescents and young adults: counsel on risk of suicide – particularly during therapy initiation.

- Warn patients regarding the need to avoid interacting foods and drugs. See list in above drug interaction section. Stay away from tyramine-rich containing foods.

- Seek immediate medical care if you experience any of these symptoms: sudden severe headache, nausea, stiff neck, vomiting, a fast or slow heartbeat or a change in the way your heart beats (palpitations), tight chest pain, a lot of sweating, confusion, dilated pupils, and sensitivity to light.

- Use this medication regularly in order to get the most benefit from it. Take this medication exactly as prescribed. To help you remember, use it at the same time each day. Antidepressants do not work if they are taken as-needed.

- It is important to continue taking this medication even if you feel well. Do not stop taking this medication without consulting your healthcare provider. Some conditions may become worse when the drug is suddenly stopped. Your dose may need to be gradually decreased.

- It may take 1 to 2 weeks to feel a benefit from this drug and 6-8 weeks to feel the full effect on your mood. Tell the healthcare provider if your condition persists or worsens. You can try a medication in a different class. One will work – it may take different tries to find the right medicine that will help you feel better.

- *EMSAM* Patch Application: Change once daily. Pick a time of day you can remember. Apply to either upper chest or back (below the neck and above the waist), upper thigh, or to the outer surface of the upper arm. Rotate site and do not use same site 2 days in a row. Wash hands with soap after applying patch. Do not expose to heat. The wash-out period counseling above includes the patch.

Dopamine (DA) and Norepinephrine (NE) Reuptake Inhibitor

DRUG	DOSING	SAFETY/SIDE EFFECTS/MONITORING
BuPROPion *(Aplenzin, Wellbutrin SR, Wellbutrin XL, Wellbutrin, Forfivo XL)* + naltrexone *(Contrave)* – for weight management *Buproban, Zyban* – for smoking cessation *Wellbutrin XL* is approved for Seasonal Affective Disorder (SAD) – start in early fall, titrate to 300 mg/day, if desired can discontinue in late spring by cutting to 150 mg daily x 2 weeks	300-450 mg daily *Wellbutrin IR* is TID *Wellbutrin SR* is BID (to 200 mg BID) *Wellbutrin XL* is daily Hydrobromide salt *(Aplenzin):* Initial: 174 mg once daily in the morning; may increase as early as day 4 of dosing to 348 mg once daily (target dose); maximum dose: 522 mg daily. In patients receiving 348 mg once daily, taper dose down to 174 mg once daily prior to discontinuing. Do not exceed 450 mg/day due to seizure risk	**BOXED WARNING** Antidepressants increase the risk of suicidal thinking and behavior in children, adolescents, and young adults (18-24 years of age) with major depressive disorder (MDD) and other psychiatric disorders; consider risk prior to prescribing. **CONTRAINDICATIONS** Seizure disorder; history of anorexia/bulimia, abrupt discontinuation of ethanol or sedatives; concurrent use with MAO inhibitors, linezolid, IV methylene blue, or other forms of bupropion **SIDE EFFECTS** Dry mouth, insomnia, headache/migraine, nausea/vomiting, constipation, and tremors/seizures (dose-related), possible blood pressure changes (more hypertension than hypotension – monitor), weight loss No effects on 5HT and therefore no sexual dysfunction; may be used if issues with other antidepressants

Dopamine (DA) and Norepinephrine (NE) Reuptake Inhibitor Continued

DRUG	DOSING	SAFETY/SIDE EFFECTS/MONITORING
Mirtazapine (*Remeron*, *Remeron SolTab*) Used commonly in oncology and skilled nursing since it helps with sleep at night (dosed QHS) & increases appetite (good for weight gain in frail elderly)	Tetracyclic antidepressant that works by its central presynaptic alpha2-adrenergic antagonist effects, which results in increased release of norepinephrine and serotonin 15-45 mg QHS	**BOXED WARNING** Antidepressants increase the risk of suicidal thinking and behavior in children, adolescents, and young adults (18-24 years of age) with major depressive disorder (MDD) and other psychiatric disorders; consider risk prior to prescribing. **WARNINGS** Anticholinergic effects, QT prolongation, blood dyscrasias, CNS depression **SIDE EFFECTS** <u>Sedation and ↑ appetite, weight gain</u>, dry mouth, dizziness Agranulocytosis (rare)
TraZODone (*Oleptro*) Rarely used as an antidepressant due to <u>sedation</u>. Used primarily off-label for sleep (dosed 50-100 mg QHS) TraZODone ER (*Oleptro*) may be less sedating	Inhibits 5-HT reuptake, blocks H1 and alpha1-adrenergic receptors IR: 100-300 mg BID ER: 150-375 mg QHS	**BOXED WARNING** Antidepressants increase the risk of suicidal thinking and behavior in children, adolescents, and young adults (18-24 years of age) with major depressive disorder (MDD) and other psychiatric disorders; consider risk prior to prescribing. **CONTRAINDICATIONS** Concurrent use with MAO inhibitors, linezolid, or IV methylene blue **SIDE EFFECTS** <u>Sedation</u> Orthostasis (risk in elderly for falls) Sexual dysfunction and risk of <u>priapism</u> (medical emergency – requires immediate medical attention if painful erection longer than 4 hrs)
Nefazodone	150-600 mg BID	**BOXED WARNINGS** Antidepressants increase the risk of suicidal thinking and behavior in children, adolescents, and young adults (18-24 years of age) with major depressive disorder (MDD) and other psychiatric disorders; consider risk prior to prescribing, <u>hepatotoxicity</u>. **CONTRAINDICATIONS** Hepatic disease, concurrent use with MAO inhibitors, carbamazepine, cisapride, pimozide, or triazolam **SIDE EFFECTS** Similar to trazodone, but less sedating **NOTES** Rarely used due to <u>hepatotoxicity</u>: monitor LFTs, counsel on symptoms of liver damage

Bupropion Drug Interactions

- Do not use with *Buproban* or *Zyban* for smoking cessation; same drug.

- Do not use in patients with seizure history; drug ↓ seizure threshold. Do not exceed 450 mg daily in anyone.

Key Counseling Points For Above Agents

- Dispense MedGuide and instruct patient to read it. Especially in adolescents and young adults: counsel on risk of suicide – particularly during therapy initiation.

- Counsel on lag time, need to take daily as with other agents.

- Bupropion: Include not to exceed 450 mg daily, or 150 mg at each dose if using immediate-release formulations due to seizure risk.

- Mirtazapine: Counsel to take at night, drug is sedating, and should increase appetite.

TREATMENT RESISTANCE DEPRESSION

Rule-out bipolar disorder, check if antidepressant is at optimal dose, sometimes use combination standard antidepressants, or augment with various options. The antipsychotics below are approved for treatment-resistant depression as adjunctive agents (i.e., in addition to another agent).

All antipsychotics require MedGuides with this Warning:

Medicines like this one can raise the risk of death in elderly people who have lost touch with reality (psychosis) due to confusion and memory loss (dementia). This medicine is not approved for the treatment of patients with dementia-related psychosis.

And because it is being used to augment AD therapy:

Antidepressants have increased the risk of suicidal thoughts and actions in some children, teenagers, and young adults. See Schizophrenia/Psychosis chapter for more detail on the antipsychotics.

DRUG	DOSING	SAFETY/SIDE EFFECTS/MONITORING
ARIPiprazole *(Abilify, Abilify Discmelt)*	Start 2-5 mg/day (QAM), can ↑ to 15 mg	**BOXED WARNINGS** Antidepressants increase the risk of suicidal thinking and behavior in children, adolescents, and young adults (18-24 years of age) with major depressive disorder (MDD) and other psychiatric disorders; consider risk prior to prescribing. Elderly patients with dementia-related psychosis treated with antipsychotic drugs are at ↑ risk of death.
OLANZapine/fluoxetine *(Symbyax)*	Usually started at 6 mg/25 mg capsule QHS (fluoxetine is activating, but olanzapine is more sedating), can ↑ cautiously.	**WARNINGS** Risk of Neuroleptic Malignant Syndrome Risk of Tardive Dyskinesia (TD) Risk of leukopenia, neutropenia, agranulocytosis **CONTRAINDICATIONS** *Symbyax:* Do not use with pimozide, thioridazine & caution with other QT prolonging drugs/conditions
QUEtiapine extended release *(SEROquel, SEROquel XR)*	Start 50 mg QHS, ↑ nightly to 150-300 mg QHS	**SIDE EFFECTS** Each of these drugs can cause metabolic issues, including dyslipidemia, weight gain, diabetes (less with aripiprazole) All can cause orthostasis/dizziness **Abilify** Anxiety, insomnia, constipation
Brexpiprazole *(Rezulti)*	Start 0.5-1 mg/day, can ↑ 3 mg/day (titrate weekly)	**Olanzapine** Sedation Weight gain, ↑ lipids, ↑ glucose, EPS, QT prolongation (lower risk) **Quetiapine** Sedation, orthostasis Weight gain, ↑ lipids, ↑ glucose Little risk EPS **Brexpiprazole** Weight gain, dyspepsia, diarrhea, akathisia

PRACTICE CASE

SA is a 57 y/o male who appears thin and anxious. He is married with two children. His wife brought him to the clinic today due to constant worry, anxiety, and feelings of worthlessness. When he was in college, he had several bouts of depression and was successfully treated with doxepin at that time. He stopped taking the medication when he graduated and moved to California, because he felt the sunshine made him feel better. His wife reports that this is the third or fourth time in the past few years that her husband has felt so low that she became concerned he might harm himself. She reports that he stays up all night with constant worry and probably has not had a good night's sleep in months.

Per clinic records, SA was seen 2 months ago and started on *Celexa* 40 mg daily and lorazepam 1 mg 1-3 times daily as needed. SA has been using these medications, and states that they "help a little, but not much". He is taking the lorazepam 1 mg TID each day. He does not smoke, drink alcohol, or use illicit drugs.

Allergies: shellfish, contrast dye, latex

Medications:
Inderal LA 120 mg daily
Celexa 40 mg daily
Lorazepam 1 mg 1-3 times daily PRN
Fosinopril 20 mg daily

Vitals:
Height: 5'10" Weight: 155 lbs
BP: 158/102 mmHg HR: 80 BPM RR: 16 BPM Temp: 98.2°F Pain: 1/10

Labs: Na (mEq/L) = 140 (135 - 145)
K (mEq/L) = 4.1 (3.5 - 5)
Cl (mEq/L) = 99 (95 - 103)
HCO3 (mEq/L) = 26 (24 - 30)
BUN (mg/dL) = 12 (7 - 20)
SCr (mg/dL) = 0.7 (0.6 - 1.3)
Glucose (mg/dL) = 100 (100 - 125)
Ca (mg/dL) = 10.1 (8.5 - 10.5)
Mg (mEq/L) = 2.0 (1.3 - 2.1)
PO4 (mg/dL) = 4.1 (2.3 - 4.7)

AST (IU/L) = 27 (8 - 48)
ALT (IU/L) = 39 (7 - 55)
Albumin (g/dL) = 3.7 (3.5 - 5)

Patient reports minimal improvement of depression with current prescriptions.

Questions

1. SA has depression that has not responded to an adequate trial of fluoxetine or citalopram. Which of the following options represents the best alternative?

   a. Sertraline
   b. Venlafaxine
   c. Fluvoxamine
   d. Escitalopram
   e. Mirtazapine

2. If SA was started on *Effexor XR* (he won't be), which of the following parameters should be carefully monitored in this patient? (Select **ALL** that apply.)

   a. Blood pressure
   b. Thyroid parameters
   c. White blood cell count
   d. Metabolic acidosis
   e. Symptoms of depression

3. A pharmacist counseling a patient on the use of any antidepressant should include the following counseling points:

   a. Your energy level may pick up before your mood starts to feels better.
   b. Your mood should improve; this usually takes about a month.
   c. If this medicine does not work, the doctor will try a different agent, which may work better.
   d. This medication needs to be taken every day; it does not work if it is taken occasionally.
   e. All of the above.

4. What is the mechanism of action of venlafaxine?

   a. Selective serotonin reuptake inhibitor
   b. Serotonin and dopamine reuptake inhibitor
   c. Serotonin and norepinephrine reuptake inhibitor
   d. Norepinephrine and dopamine reuptake inhibitor
   e. Norepinephrine and acetylcholine reuptake inhibitor

5. The doctor takes a thorough medication history and decides that it would be worthwhile to try doxepin, since the patient had a good history of use with this agent. Which of the following statements is correct? (Select **ALL** that apply.)

   a. Doxepin is a monoamine oxidase inhibitor.
   b. Doxepin can cause excess salivation and has significant food interactions.
   c. He should be carefully evaluated for suicide risk.
   d. The brand name is *Sular*.
   e. The brand name is *Silenor*.

Questions 6-7 do not apply to the case.

6. A patient has been started on bupropion for depression. His other medications include *Lopid*, *Pravachol* and *Zyban*. Which of the following statement is correct?

   a. Bupropion will raise his triglycerides.
   b. Bupropion will raise his HDL cholesterol.
   c. Bupropion will lower his HDL cholesterol.
   d. Bupropion should not be used in this patient.
   e. *Lopid* is an inducer and will decrease the level of bupropion.

7. A patient has been started on bupropion 200 mg TID for depression. His medical conditions include partial seizures and obsessive compulsive disorder. His medications include fluvoxamine and phenytoin. Which of the following statements is correct? (Select **ALL** that apply.)

   a. Bupropion will induce the metabolism of phenytoin.
   b. The bupropion dose is too high.
   c. Bupropion should not be used in this patient.
   d. One of the brand formulation used for depression is called *Contrave*.
   e. Patients with sexual dysfunction should avoid the use of this drug.

Answers

1-e, 2-a,e, 3-e, 4-c, 5-c,e, 6-d, 7-b,c

SCHIZOPHRENIA/ PSYCHOSIS

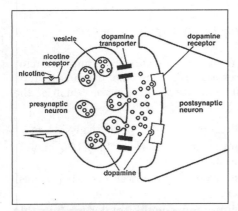

We gratefully acknowledge the assistance of Robin Wackernah, PharmD, BCPP, Regis University School of Pharmacy, Rueckert-Hartman College for Health Professions, in preparing this chapter.

BACKGROUND

Schizophrenia is a chronic, severe and disabling thought disorder that occurs in ~1% of all societies regardless of class, color, religion, or culture. The cause is multifactorial and includes altered brain structure and chemistry, primarily involving dopamine and glutamine. Genetics (inherited susceptibility) and environmental factors are important in disease development. Patients suffer from <u>hallucinations</u>, <u>delusions</u> (false beliefs), <u>disorganized thinking and behavior</u>. They can withdraw from the world around them and enter a world of psychosis, where they struggle to differentiate reality from altered perceptions. Schizophrenia ranges from relatively mild to severe. Some people may be able to function adequately in daily life, while others need specialized, intensive care. <u>Treatment adherence</u> is important and <u>often difficult to obtain</u>, primarily due to the patient's inability to recognize their illness. This is regrettable to the patient's family and to themselves as patients with schizophrenia typically live a life of torment where they may not be able to care for themselves. This condition has one of the highest suicide rates.

The onset of symptoms usually begins in young adulthood. A diagnosis is not based on lab tests, but on the patient's behavior, which should include both <u>negative and positive signs and symptoms</u> (described on the following page). The Diagnostic and Statistical Manual of Mental Disorders, 5th Edition (DSM-5) is the current tool used to diagnose schizophrenia and other psychiatric disorders.

GUIDELINES/REFERENCES

American Psychiatric Association. (2013). Diagnostic and Statistical Manual of Mental Disorders: DSM-5. Washington, D.C: American Psychiatric Association

American Psychiatric Association Guideline Watch (September 2009): Practice Guideline for the Treatment of Patients with Schizophrenia http://meridianhealthplan.com/content/pdf/shared/providers/cpgs/bh/schizophrenia-GuidelineWatch.pdf. (accessed 2015 Oct 12).

PATHOPHYSIOLOGY

Schizophrenia is a thought disorder in which neurotransmitter abnormalities are central. Genetics, environment, stressors and some illicit drugs can be contributing factors. There is increased dopamine in the mesolimbic pathway. The older "dopaminergic model" is being supplemented with a more recent understanding of the role of the glutamatergic N-methyl-D-aspartate (NMDA) receptor and its role in the pathogenesis of schizophrenia. Antipsychotics primarily block dopamine receptors, although newer agents that block serotonin and additional receptors have benefit.

Antipsychotics target the positive symptoms, but the lack of motivation, cognitive and functional impairment remain challenges for many patients and often take longer to respond to antipsychotics, if at all. Researchers hope that a better understanding of glutamate receptors will improve functional levels. One problem with current treatment is that the drugs that target dopamine hyperactivity also target dopamine involved in focus and the ability to pay attention; dopamine and glutamine modulate each other. Glutamine synaptic dysfunction is a large area of current research. It is hoped that as the pathways are better understood, along with drug development, a "fine tuning" of treatment will improve results.

DSM-5 DIAGNOSTIC CRITERIA FOR SCHIZOPHRENIA
Note: Delusions, hallucinations or disorganized speech must be present

Negative signs and symptoms	Positive signs and symptoms
Loss of interest in everyday activities	Hallucinations; can be auditory (hearing voices), visual, or somatic
Lack of emotion (apathy)	
Inability to plan or carry out activities	Delusions: beliefs held by the patient that are without a basis in reality
Poor hygiene	Disorganized thinking/behavior, incoherent speech, often on unrelated topics, purposeless behavior, or difficulty speaking and organizing thoughts, such as stopping in mid-sentence or jumbling together meaningless words
Social withdrawal	
Loss of motivation (avolition)	
Poverty (lack) of speech (alogia)	Difficulty paying attention

NATURAL PRODUCTS

Fish oils are being used for psychosis, as well as other psychiatric disorders including ADHD and depression. The evidence is preliminary, but promising. Considering the debilitating nature of schizophrenia, natural products are not used in lieu of antipsychotics in patients that require them. Do not recommend cod liver oil due to risk of vitamin A toxicity. Keep in mind that natural products have dose-response relationships; check the *Natural Medicines Database* for dosing recommendations that appear to have benefit from clinical trials.

DRUG TREATMENT

Side-effect profiles play an important role in selecting initial treatment for schizophrenia. Second-generation antipsychotics (SGAs) may be used first-line due to a lower risk of extrapyramidal side effects (EPS); however, some patients respond better to a first-generation antipsychotic (FGA).

First Generation Antipsychotics

High-potency FGAs such as haloperidol are associated with a high risk of EPS effects, a moderate risk of sedation and a lower risk of orthostatic hypotension, tachycardia, and anticholinergic effects compared to low-potency FGAs. In contrast, low-potency FGAs are associated with a lower risk of EPS, a high degree of sedation, and a high risk of cardiovascular effects (orthostatic hypotension, tachycardia), and anticholinergic effects. Although other side effects also vary with the specific medication, in general, the first-generation antipsychotic medications are associated with a moderate risk of weight gain, a low risk of metabolic effects, higher risk of EPS with the FGAs when compared with the SGAs, and a risk of sexual side effects. With certain agents (thioridazine particularly), QT risk is significant. Other possible side effects of FGAs include seizures, temperature dysregulation, allergic reactions, and dermatological, hepatic, ophthalmological, and hematological effects.

Second Generation Antipsychotics

SGAs have a variety of side effects. Metabolic side effects are a well known phenomenon with SGAs. These include weight gain, lipid abnormalities and hyperglycemia, which can sometimes lead to diabetes. Although at a lower incidence than FGAs, many SGAs exhibit dose-related EPS. Hormonal issues can be problematic with agents that increase prolactin levels, causing gynecomastia (painful, swollen breast tissue), galactorrhea (breastmilk production without pregnancy), sexual dysfunction and irregular or missed periods. Cardiovascular effects, including QT prolongation can be present with SGAs and ziprasidone has the highest risk. Adverse effects may limit the use of an agent; for example clozapine has superior efficacy, but has multiple boxed warnings and is particularly known for agranulocytosis, seizures and myocarditis – in addition to having high metabolic risk. Clozapine is not recommended for first-line use, but a trial should be considered for very ill patients who have had no or poor response to two trials of antipsychotic medication (at least one should be an SGA).

Due to the potential for significant metabolic side effects when initiating antipsychotics, the American Diabetes Association (ADA) recommends screening and monitoring for overweight and obesity, dyslipidemia, hyperglycemia, hypertension and personal or family history of risk. During treatment, the patient should be monitored for changes in weight, waist circumference, plasma lipid and glucose levels, and acute symptoms of diabetes.

MEDICATIONS/ILLICIT DRUGS THAT CAN CAUSE PSYCHOTIC SYMPTOMS

Anticholinergics (centrally-acting, high doses)

Cannabis

Dextromethorphan

Dopamine or dopamine agonists used for Parkinson disease (*Requip, Mirapex, Sinemet*, etc.)

Illicit substances:

  Bath salts (synthetic cathinones)

  Cocaine, esp. "crack" cocaine

  Lysergic acid diethylamide (LSD) and other hallucinogenics

  Methamphetamine, ice, crack

  MDPV (bath salts)

  Phencyclidine (PCP)

Interferons

Stimulants (especially if already at risk), including amphetamines used for ADHD

Systemic steroids (typically with lack of sleep – ICU psychosis)

Choosing an SGA

The SGAs are chosen based on several considerations, which should be identified when examining a patient case:

- Patient's past history: what drugs have helped control the symptoms (e.g., quieted the voices down), and drugs that did not help (if they were taken, and at a reasonable dose). Likely adherence to treatment should also be considered.

- Side effects: These can be acceptable in some patients but not in others, for example, if the patient is overweight, do not pick an agent which worsens metabolic issues. In patients with a history of tardive dyskinesia (TD), or any type of movement disorder, avoid risperidone, paliperidone and lurasidone, which can be associated with extrapyramidal symptoms. The table at the right lists the drugs most likely to cause major adverse effects – avoid using them in an at-risk patient.

- When assessing treatment resistance or evaluating the best option for a partial response, it is important to evaluate whether the patient has had an adequate trial (at least 4 – 6 weeks) of an antipsychotic, including whether the dose is adequate and whether the patient has been taking the medication as prescribed.

- Prescriber's familiarity with a drug, or formulary considerations, including costs will also factor in to treatment selection.

IMPORTANT ADVERSE EFFECTS OF SECOND GENERATION ANTIPSYCHOTICS
Metabolic side effects
Highest risk – Clozapine, olanzapine, quetiapine
Moderate risk – Risperidone, paliperidone
Lower risk – Aripiprazole, ziprasidone, lurasidone and asenapine
EPS
Lowest risk – Quetiapine (recommended in patients with Parkinson's who require antipsychotics)
Hematological effects
Highest risk – Clozapine (agranulocytosis)
QT prolongation
Highest risk – Ziprasidone
↑ Prolactin
Highest risk – Risperidone, paliperidone
Seizure
Highest risk – Clozapine (dose-dependent)

Formulations

Long-Acting Injections: Haloperidol is an older agent and comes in various formulations, including an IM injection for acute use, a long-acting decanoate, tablets and a solution. Long-acting injectables, including *Haldol* decanoate (every 4 weeks), *Risperdal Consta* (every 2 weeks), *Invega Sustenna* (every 4 weeks), *Invega Trinza* (every 3 months), *Abilify Maintena* (every 4 weeks), and a few others provide the benefit of increased adherence, or compliance, with the medication. They are also used in acute care settings prior to the release of patients without adequate resources (e.g., homelessness).

Orally Disintegrating Tablets (ODTs): Used to help solve the problem of "cheeking" where the patient avoids taking the medication by holding the dose in their cheek and then spitting it out. With ODTs the tablet dissolves rapidly in the mouth, without the need for water. Several of the SGAs are available as ODTs (clozapine, olanzapine, risperidone, aripiprazole and asenapine).

Acute IM Injections: Intramuscular (IM) injections provide "stat" relief to help calm down an acutely agitated, psychotic patient for their own safety and the safety of others. They are often mixed with other drugs, such as benzodiazepines for anxiolytic and sedative effects, and anticholinergics to reduce dystonic risk (for example the "*Haldol* cocktail", which contains haloperidol, lorazepam and diphenhydramine). In contrast, oral absorption could take up to an hour to calm the patient down. The patient will be sedated and hopefully sleep through the acute symptoms. Olanzapine and benzodiazepines should not be given together (IM) due to orthostasis risk.

Boxed Warning

Antipsychotics (APs) <u>increase the risk of mortality in elderly patients with dementia-related psychosis</u>, primarily due to an <u>increased risk of stroke and infection</u>. Note that APs are not particularly helpful to treat dementia-related anger/outbursts, but they are used and pharmacists are required to counsel on this risk. See the counseling section for wording suggestion. Additional drug-specific warnings are listed separately with the drugs.

NEUROLEPTIC MALIGNANT SYNDROME

<u>Antipsychotics used to be called neuroleptics</u>. Neuroleptic malignant syndrome (NMS) is <u>rare but is highly lethal</u>. It occurs most commonly with the FGAs and is due to D_2 blockade. NMS can occur, but is less common with SGAs and with other dopamine blocking agents, including metoclopramide (*Reglan*). The majority of cases occur within two weeks of starting treatment or immediately following high doses of injectables given alongside multiple oral doses. Occasionally, patients develop NMS even after years of antipsychotic use. NMS is a medical emergency as the intense muscle contractions can lead to acute renal injury (due to rhabdomyolysis from the destruction of muscle tissue), suffocation and death.

Signs Include

- <u>Hyperthermia</u> (high fever, with profuse sweating)
- Extreme <u>muscle rigidity</u> (called "lead pipe" rigidity), which can lead to respiratory failure
- Mental status changes
- Other signs can include tachycardia, tachypnea and blood pressure changes

Laboratory Results

- ↑ creatine phosphokinase and ↑ white blood cells

Treatment

- <u>Taper off the antipsychotic quickly</u> and consider another choice (quetiapine or clozapine).
- Provide supportive care: Cardiorespiratory and hemodynamic support and control of electrolyte balance.
- Cool the patient down: Cooling bed, antipyretics, cooled IV fluids.
- Muscle relaxation with benzodiazepines or <u>dantrolene</u> (*Ryanodex, Dantrium, Revonto*) is sometimes used, and some cases may require a dopamine agonist such as bromocriptine.

First-Generation Antipsychotics (FGAs) block D_2 receptors. Minimal $5HT_{2A}$ receptor blockade.

DRUG	DOSING	SAFETY/SIDE EFFECTS/MONITORING
Low Potency		**BOXED WARNING (ALL APs)** Elderly patients with dementia-related psychosis treated with antipsychotics are at an increased risk of death compared to placebo. Most deaths appeared to be either cardiovascular (e.g., heart failure, sudden death) or infectious in nature. This drug is not approved for the treatment of dementia-related psychosis.
ChlorproMAZINE	300-1,000 mg/day, divided	
Thioridazine BOXED WARNING: QT prolongation	300-800 mg/day, divided	**SIDE EFFECTS** All are sedating and all cause EPS, however the lower potency agents have ↑ sedation and ↓ incidence EPS (e.g., chlorpromazine), and the higher-potency agents (e.g., haloperidol) have ↓ sedation (but still sedating) with ↑ EPS.
Mid potency		Dystonias, which are prolonged contraction of muscles (including painful muscle spasms) can occur during initiation. May be life-threatening if airway is compromised. Higher risk with younger males. Centrally-acting anticholinergics (diphenhydramine, benztropine) may be used for prophylaxis during treatment initiation or for treatment if need arises.
Loxapine *(Loxitane, Adasuve* inhalation powder for acute agitation)	30-100 mg/day, divided	
Perphenazine	8-64 mg/day, divided	Akathisia, which is restlessness with anxiety and an inability to remain still. May be treated with anticholinergics, benzodiazepines or propranolol.
High Potency		Parkinsonism, which looks similar to Parkinson disease, with tremors, abnormal gait, bradykinesia, etc. Treat with anticholinergics or propranolol if tremor is the main symptom.
FluPHENAZine Available in **2-wk decanoate** for IM use	6-12 mg/day, divided	Tardive dyskinesias (TD), which are abnormal facial movements, primarily in the tongue or mouth. Risk is higher in elderly females. If TD occurs the drug should be stopped as soon as possible and replaced with an SGA with low EPS risk (quetiapine, clozapine). TD can be irreversible.
Haloperidol *(Haldol)*, see formulations to right Class: butyrophenone (and DA-blocker) Haloperidol is also used for tics and vocal outbursts due to Tourette syndrome	Oral (tablet, solution): start 0.5-2 mg BID-TID, up to 30 mg/day IV: usually 5-10 mg Decanoate (monthly): IM only, for conversion from PO, use 10-20x the oral dose	Dyskinesias, abnormal movements, are possible, however, this is more common with Parkinson drugs. Seizures (phenothiazines, butyrophenones). Cardiovascular Effects: orthostasis, tachycardia, QT prolongation; IV haloperidol has high risk.
Thiothixene *(Navane)*	15-60 mg/day, divided	Sexual dysfunction.
Trifluoperazine	15-50 mg/day, divided	*Adasuve*: dysgeusia (bad, bitter, or metallic taste in mouth), sedation, bronchospasm risk, REMS drug.

Second-Generation Antipsychotics (SGAs) block D$_2$ and 5HT$_{2A}$ receptors.

Aripiprazole and cariprazine are unique; act as a D$_2$ and 5HT$_{1A}$ partial agonist.

DRUG	DOSING	SAFETY/SIDE EFFECTS/MONITORING
ARIPiprazole (Abilify, Abilify Discmelt ODT, Abilify Maintena injection, Aristada injection) Tablet, ODT, IM solution, IM suspension	10-30 mg PO QAM Acute agitation: 9.75 mg IM soln x 1 (Q2H up to 30 mg/day) Abilify Maintena-IM suspension, give monthly Aristada-IM suspension, give every 4-6 weeks, dose-dependent (see notes at right)	**SIDE EFFECTS** Akathisia, anxiety, insomnia Constipation Less weight gain, some QT prolongation **NOTES** Also approved for irritability associated with autism Aristada 882 mg dose can be given Q6 weeks, all other strengths are given Q4 weeks
Asenapine (Saphris) Sublingual tablet	10-20 mg/day, divided BID No food/drink for 10 min after dose	**CONTRAINDICATIONS** Severe hepatic impairment **SIDE EFFECTS** Somnolence, tongue numbness; EPS (5% more than placebo), QT prolongation; aoid use with QT risk
Brexpiprazole (Rexulti) Also indicated for major depressive disorder (MDD)	2-4 mg daily	**SIDE EFFECTS** Weight gain, dyspepsia, diarrhea, akathisia
Cariprazine (Vraylar) Also indicated for bipolar disorder	1.5-6 mg daily	**SIDE EFFECTS** EPS, dystonias, headache, insomnia
CloZAPine (Clozaril, FazaClo ODT, Versacloz suspension) Only if failed to respond to treatment with 2 standard AP treatments, or had significant ADRs	300-900 mg/day, divided (start at 12.5 mg and titrate, also titrate off since abrupt discontinuation can cause seizures) Clozapine is very effective and has ↓ risk of EPS/TD, but used no sooner than 3rd line due to severe side effect potential (metabolic effects, agranulocytosis)	**BOXED WARNINGS, CLOZAPINE-SPECIFIC** Significant risk of potentially life-threatening agranulocytosis. Tachycardia, orthostatic hypotension, syncope, and cardiac arrest; risk is highest during the initial titration period especially with rapid dose increases. Titrate slowly. Myocarditis and cardiomyopathy; discontinue if suspect. Seizures, dose-correlated; start at no higher than 12.5 mg once or twice daily, titrate slowly, using divided doses. Use with caution in patients at seizure risk: seizure history, head trauma, alcoholism, or concurrent treatment with medications which lower seizure threshold. **SIDE EFFECTS** Orthostasis, syncope, weight gain, ↑ lipids, ↑ glucose, somnolence, dizziness, insomnia, GI upset, sialorrhea (hypersalivation), QT prolongation Risk of agranulocytosis, seizures, myocarditis **MONITORING** REMS: Prescribers and pharmacies must be certified and patients enrolled with the Clozapine REMS To start treatment, baseline ANC must be ≥ 1,500/mm³ Check ANC weekly x 6 months, then every 2 weeks x 6 months, then monthly Monitor for metabolic effects; see counseling section **NOTES** Smoking reduces drug levels

Second-Generation (SGA) Antipsychotics Continued

DRUG	DOSING	SAFETY/SIDE EFFECTS/MONITORING
Iloperidone *(Fanapt)*	12-24 mg/day, divided Titrate slowly due to orthostasis/dizziness	**SIDE EFFECTS** Dizziness, somnolence, orthostasis, tachycardia QT prolongation; avoid use with QT risk
Lurasidone *(Latuda)*	40-160 mg/day, divided	**CONTRAINDICATIONS** Use with strong CYP3A4 inducers and inhibitors **SIDE EFFECTS** Somnolence, EPS, dystonias, nausea, agitation, akathisia Nearly weight, lipid and blood glucose neutral **NOTES** Take with food ≥ 350 kcal
OLANZapine *(**ZyPREXA**, Zydis ODT, Relprevv* injection)	10-20 mg QHS IM Injection (acute agitation) *Relprevv* inj suspension lasts 2-4 weeks, restricted use, REMS drug	**BOXED WARNING, OLANZAPINE-SPECIFIC** *Zyprexa Relprevv* – patients should be monitored for 3 hr post-injection. Sedation (including coma) and delirium (including agitation, anxiety, confusion, disorientation) have been observed following use. **SIDE EFFECTS** Somnolence, weight gain, ↑ lipids, ↑ glucose EPS, QT prolongation (lower risk) **MONITORING** For metabolic effects; see counseling section **NOTES** Smoking reduces drug levels
Paliperidone *(**Invega**, Invega Sustenna* and *****Invega Trinza*** are* long-acting injections) Active metabolite of risperidone; SEs similar	PO: 3-12 mg daily CrCl < 50 mL/min: 3 mg daily CrCl < 10 mL/min: Not recommended OROS delivery enables once daily dosing-do not break or crush *Invega Sustenna*, IM injection, give monthly *Invega Trinza*, IM injection, give every 3 months (start only after receiving *Invega Sustenna* x 4 months)	**SIDE EFFECTS** ↑ prolactin – sexual dysfunction, galactorrhea, irregular/missed periods EPS, especially at higher doses Tachycardia, headache, sedation, anxiety QT prolongation; avoid use with QT risk Weight gain, ↑ lipids, ↑ glucose **MONITORING** For metabolic effects; see counseling section
QUEtiapine *(**SEROquel**, **SEROquel XR**)*	400-800 mg/day, divided BID or XR QHS	**SIDE EFFECTS** Somnolence, orthostasis Weight gain, ↑ lipids, ↑ glucose Low EPS risk – often used for psychosis in Parkinson disease, QT prolongation (lower risk) **MONITORING** For metabolic effects; see counseling section **NOTES** Take XR at night, without food or with a light meal (≤ 300 kcal)

Second-Generation (SGA) Antipsychotics Continued

DRUG	DOSING	SAFETY/SIDE EFFECTS/MONITORING
RisperiDONE (RisperDAL, RisperDAL M-TAB ODT), see injection at right Also approved for irritability associated with autism	4-16 mg/day, divided *Risperdal Consta*, Q 2 week injection, 25-50 mg	**SIDE EFFECTS** Somnolence EPS, especially at higher doses ↑ prolactin – sexual dysfunction, galactorrhea, irregular/missed periods Orthostasis Weight gain, ↑ lipids, ↑ glucose QT prolongation **MONITORING** For metabolic effects; see counseling section **NOTES** > 6 mg ↑ prolactin and ↑ EPS
Ziprasidone (Geodon), *Geodon* injection	40-160 mg/day, divided BID Acute injection: *Geodon IM* 10 mg Q2H or 20 mg Q4H Max: 40 mg/day IM	**CONTRAINDICATIONS** QT prolongation; contraindicated with QT risk **SIDE EFFECTS** Somnolence (some have insomnia), respiratory tract infection, headache, dizziness, nausea **NOTES** Take with food

Antipsychotic Drug Interactions

- All antipsychotics can prolong the QT interval – note that some are considered higher risk than others. The higher risk QT SGAs are noted. Thioridazine, an FGA, is high-risk for QT prolongation (boxed warning).

- Smoking can reduce plasma levels of olanzapine and clozapine, patients who smoke may require higher doses.

- High plasma levels of risperidone and paliperidone can ↑ prolactin and cause EPS. Caution when using risperidone concomitantly with CYP 2D6 inhibitors, including paroxetine and fluoxetine.

- With clozapine: avoid concurrent drugs that lower the seizure threshold.

- Some of the APs have CYP450 drug interactions which could require dosing adjustments.

- Monitoring is also required for an increased risk of respiratory depression and hypotension when administered with benzodiazepines.

- Caution with other dopamine blocking agents such as metoclopramide (*Reglan*) as EPS and TD risk may be increased.

ALL ANTIPSYCHOTIC COUNSELING

- Dispense MedGuide and instruct patient to read it. In addition to individual warnings, several of the agents have anti-depressive properties and these include a warning for suicidality, particularly among adolescents.

- This medication can decrease hallucinations (such as voices) and can quiet the noise. It can help you to think more clearly and feel positive about yourself, feel less nervous, and take a more active part in everyday life.

- There may be a slightly increased risk of serious, possibly fatal, side effects when this medication is used in older adults with dementia. This medication is not approved for the treatment of dementia-related behavior problems.

- Contact your healthcare provider right away if you experience uncontrollable movements of the mouth, tongue, cheeks, jaw, arms or legs.

- Contact your healthcare provider immediately and seek immediate medical attention if you experience fever, sweating, severe muscle stiffness (rigidity) and confusion.

- Use caution when driving, operating machinery, or performing other hazardous activities. This drug can cause dizziness, confusion and drowsiness.

- Dizziness may be more likely to occur when you rise from a sitting or lying position. Rise slowly to prevent dizziness and a possible fall.

- Avoid consuming alcohol during treatment with this drug. Alcohol will increase sleepiness and dizziness and can interfere with the drug's ability to work properly.

- Tell your healthcare provider if your condition persists or worsens.

Clozapine

- This medication can cause a serious immune system problem called agranulocytosis (low white blood cells). To make sure you have enough white blood cells, you will need to have a blood test before you begin taking clozapine and then have your blood tested regularly during your treatment.

- Clozapine can also cause seizures, especially with higher doses, or if it is increased too quickly when starting treatment. Let your healthcare provider know if you have ever had seizures. While taking this medication, avoid activities during which a sudden loss of consciousness could be dangerous (e.g., driving, operating machinery, swimming).

- This medication may rarely cause an inflammation of the heart muscle (myocarditis). Seek immediate medical attention if you have weakness, difficult/rapid breathing, chest pain, or swelling of the ankles/legs. The risk is highest during the first month of treatment.

Olanzapine, Clozapine, Risperidone, Paliperidone and Quetiapine

- This drug has a risk of weight gain, elevated cholesterol, elevated blood pressure and high blood glucose. These must be monitored, and treated if they occur. Talk to your healthcare provider if you experience any symptoms of high blood glucose, including excessive thirst, frequent urination, excessive hunger, or fatigue.

- Your healthcare provider will order blood tests during treatment to monitor for side effects.

Different Types of Oral Formulations

- *Saphris*: Place the sublingual tablet under the tongue and allow it to dissolve completely. The tablet will dissolve in saliva within seconds. Do not eat or drink for 10 minutes after taking this medication. Your tongue will feel numb afterwards.

- *FazaClo, Abilify Discmelt, Risperdal M-Tab, Zyprexa Zydis*: Immediately upon opening the foil blister, using dry hands, remove the tablet and place in your mouth. Do not push the tablet through the foil because it may crumble. The tablet dissolves quickly so it can be easily swallowed with or without liquid.

- Most ODTs contain phenylalanine. Do not dispense ODTs to patients with phenylketonuria (PKU).

- *Risperdal* oral solution can be administered directly from the calibrated pipette, or mixed with water, coffee, orange juice, and low-fat milk; it is not compatible with cola or tea.

- *Latuda* is taken with food, which must contain at least 350 kcal. *Geodon* is taken with food.

- Quetiapine immediate-release tablet may be taken without regard to meals. The extended-release tablet *(Seroquel XR)* should be taken without food or with a light meal (up to 300 kcal).

- Olanzapine is usually taken once daily at night (QHS), since it is long-acting and sedating.

- *Invega:* Part of the tablet may pass into your stool after your body has absorbed the medicine. If you see the tablet in your stool, it is nothing to worry about.

PRACTICE CASE

Ruby is a 24 year-old college student. Her parents have attempted to help Ruby over the past year. Her academic performance deteriorated and she began to look unkempt. About a month ago, her mom was sure she saw Ruby mumbling to herself. Ruby began to call her mother "evil" and told her mother that she was destroying her life. Later, Ruby accused her mother of trying to feed her poisoned food. Ruby has dropped her old high-school friendships, except for one girl who her mother feels is more troubled than Ruby. When the mother went to talk to one of Ruby's instructors, she found out that Ruby had accused the teacher of changing what Ruby had written on an exam, and that the teacher had seen Ruby mumbling to herself in class. The teacher also complained that Ruby lacks attention in class, and reported that her work is sloppy and disorganized. The teacher had assumed there was difficulty at home, since Ruby told her that her mother is dying from cancer. This report from Ruby was not truthful.

The crisis in the family came to a head recently when Ruby stole a bottle of vodka from the local convenience store and was caught. Fortunately, the store manager knew the family and declined to press charges. However, later that night Ruby took some unknown medication and attempted to drown herself in the bathtub. She was taken by ambulance to the hospital.

The psychiatric team, after a brief visit with Ruby and a history taken from her family, gave Ruby a tentative diagnosis of schizophrenia. She received an injection of haloperidol and lorazepam, and is sleeping soundly. The psychiatric resident has come to the family to discuss treatment options.

No current medications; no known medical history. Height 5'5", weight 125 lbs.

Questions

1. The physician gave the patient an injection of haloperidol. This medication comes in the following formulations. (Select **ALL** that apply.)

   a. Oral tablets

   b. IM injection

   c. Long-lasting (monthly) decanoate

   d. Oral solution

   e. Orally disintegrating tablet (ODT)

2. If Ruby were to experience neuroleptic malignant syndrome while receiving haloperidol, what therapies could be administered in this emergency situation? (Select **ALL** that apply.)

   a. Fluphenazine injection

   b. Cooled IV fluids, ice beds

   c. Heating blankets

   d. Muscle relaxants

   e. Airway support

Questions 3-7 do not apply to the case.

3. Choose the potential adverse reaction from haloperidol which can be <u>irreversible</u> (and, if it occurs, the medicine should be quickly tapered off):

   a. Dystonic reaction

   b. Tardive dyskinesia

   c. Akathisia

   d. Dizziness

   e. Orthostatic hypotension

4. A patient is started on olanzapine for psychotic symptoms. This agent puts the patient at high risk for the following adverse effects: (Select **ALL** that apply.)

   a. Weight loss

   b. Elevated blood glucose

   c. Increased risk lymphoma or other malignancies

   d. Elevated cholesterol

   e. Elevated creatine phosphokinase

5. A patient has been prescribed *Risperdal Consta*. Choose the correct statement:

   a. The medication lasts four weeks.

   b. The medication is given transdermally.

   c. *Risperdal Consta* is an orally-dissolving formulation for use with dysphagia.

   d. There remains a risk of EPS with this formulation.

   e. The benefit with the *Consta* formulation is little or no risk of elevated prolactin levels.

6. A patient has schizophrenia, with constant auditory hallucinations which have instructed the patient to harm himself and others. He has failed olanzapine and chlorpromazine. His other medications include sertraline for anxiety. His WBC is 3.4 cells/mm^3 with and ANC of 1400 and platelet count of 120,000. Which of the following statements is correct?

   a. He should begin clozapine treatment.

   b. Clozapine treatment is contraindicated due to his ANC.

   c. Clozapine treatment is contraindicated due to his platelet count.

   d. Clozapine treatment is not indicated since he has not tried haloperidol.

   e. He should begin treatment with *Zyprexa*.

7. A patient with psychotic symptoms takes the following medications for chronic conditions: metoprolol, warfarin, amiodarone, lisinopril and insulin. His physician wishes to begin an antipsychotic. Which of the following agents represents the best option for this patient?

   a. Thioridazine

   b. Haloperidol

   c. Ziprasidone

   d. Risperidone

   e. Aripiprazole

Answers

1-a,b,c,d, 2-b,d,e, 3-b, 4-b,d, 5-d, 6-b, 7-e

60

BIPOLAR DISORDER

We gratefully acknowledge the assistance of Robin Wackernah, PharmD, BCPP, Regis University School of Pharmacy, Rueckert-Hartman College for Health Professions, in preparing this chapter.

BACKGROUND

Bipolar disorder is a mood disorder in which moods can fluctuate from an extremely sad or hopeless state of depression to elevated, overexcited moods called mania or hypomania. Each mood episode represents a drastic change from a person's usual mood and behavior. Sometimes, a mood episode includes symptoms of both mania and depression. This is called a mixed state.

The Diagnostic and Statistical Manual of Mental Disorders, Fifth Edition (DSM-5) is the current tool used to diagnose bipolar disorder and other psychiatric disorders. Bipolar disorder is classified as bipolar I and bipolar II, which is differentiated primarily by the severity of the manic episode. Another milder form not specifically addressed in this chapter is called "cyclothymic disorder" where the criteria for depression or mania are not fully met.

Bipolar I is the most severe form of the disorder. The key diagnostic symptom is mania, but patients may also experience bouts of depression. Mania is characterized as an elevated mood where patients have a lot of energy, may feel euphoric, ("on top of the world"), and can be irritable. The symptoms of mania in bipolar I can be so severe that they impair social or occupational functioning, and may require psychiatric hospitalization. Patients can also present with features of psychosis such as hearing voices or delusions (false beliefs).

Bipolar II has the same symptoms as bipolar I disorder, but with less severe episodes called hypomania rather than mania. Hypomania, by definition, does not affect social or occupational functioning, patients do not require hospitalization for mania, and there is no psychosis.

The estimated prevalence of bipolar I ranges from 0.4 – 1.6%. Bipolar II disorder is less common in the general population, but is more common in females. Bipolar disorder can lead to problems with relationships, employment, disrupt lives and can lead to drug abuse and suicide.

GUIDELINES/REFERENCES

Diagnostic and Statistical Manual of Mental Disorders, Fifth Edition (DSM-5).

WFSBP: Update 2012 on the long-term treatment of bipolar disorder. *The World Journal of Biological Psychiatry.* 2013;14:154–219.

APA, Treatment of Patients with Bipolar Disorder. http://psychiatryonline.org/pb/assets/raw/sitewide/practice_guidelines/guidelines/bipolar.pdf (accessed 2015 Oct 13).

VA/DOD, Management of Bipolar Disorder in Adults, 2010. http://www.guideline.gov/content.aspx?id=16314&search=bipolar (accessed 2015 Oct 13).

Diagnostic Criteria

In addition to the elevated or irritable mood, the DSM-5 diagnostic criteria for mania include 3 or more of the following symptoms. Note that 4 symptoms are required if the mood is only irritable:

- Inflated self-esteem or grandiosity (having an exaggerated belief in one's importance or talents)

- Decreased need for sleep

- More talkative than usual

- Flight of ideas (jumping from one topic to the next) or racing thoughts (the mind switches between thoughts very quickly)

- Distractibility

- Increase in goal-directed activity (either social, at work or at school)

- Excessive involvement in pleasurable activities that have a high potential for painful consequences (e.g., buying sprees, sexual indiscretions, gambling)

Bipolar Mania or Illicit Drug Use?

A toxicology screen should be taken first (prior to start of treatment, and as-needed) to rule-out mania due to illicit drug use.

DRUG TREATMENT

Patients with bipolar disorder usually cycle between both mania and depression. The goal of treatment is to stabilize the mood without inducing a depressive or manic state. Mood stabilizers, which include lithium, valproate, lamotrigine and carbamazepine, are important medications in treatment of bipolar disorder, and are used to treat both mania and depression without inducing either state. Antipsychotics are used when a patient presents with mania and exhibits signs of psychosis, and are also indicated as monotherapy for mood stabilization. Patients with bipolar disorder are more susceptible to extrapyramidal symptoms (EPS); antipsychotics should be used with caution in this population, particularly the first generation antipsychotics (FGAs), such as haloperidol, which are associated with a high incidence of EPS. When antipsychotics are needed, the second-generation antipsychotics (SGAs) are preferred.

Antidepressants can induce a manic episode and are not generally recommended unless a mood stabilizer is also part of the patient's medication regimen. While some of the FGAs have been associated with inducing depression, the SGAs do not induce depressive episodes, and some of them have antidepressant effects. For example, lurasidone is indicated for bipolar depression and aripiprazole and quetiapine have FDA approvals for adjunctive therapy in major depressive disorder.

In selecting treatment, the side effect profile must be considered; it is also important to review the patient's medication history to know what has failed or has been beneficial in the past, including family history. If a patient's relative with bipolar disorder responded well to a medication, it is reasonable to consider using the same medication. According to the American Psychiatric Association (APA) guidelines, first-line treatment for a patient who presents in a manic state is to initiate valproate or lithium plus an antipsychotic. For bipolar depression, first-line treatment includes lithium or lamotrigine. Lurasidone can also be used as monotherapy for bipolar depression. After an acute episode, maintenance treatment is used to prevent a relapse.

Lamotrigine is used in bipolar depression and for maintenance treatment, however, it is not beneficial in acute mania due to the slow titration that is required to reach a target dose. Lithium is used in mania, depression and maintenance. Lithium is still commonly used and is often paired with an SGA in severe cases. Carbamazepine (as *Equetro*) and valproate are both approved for bipolar mania. See the Epilepsy/Seizures chapter for detailed information on these agents and the summary table later in this chapter.

MedGuides are required with all antidepressants (primarily due to suicide risk) and with all antipsychotics (primarily due to increased risk of death in elderly patients with dementia-related psychosis).

MOOD STABILIZERS & PREGNANCY

Lithium, valproate and carbamazepine are <u>Pregnancy Category D</u> for treatment of bipolar disorder. They have known fetal risk and the benefit must outweigh the risk. Lamotrigine (pregnancy category C) is often considered the safer option, relative to the other agents. During pregnancy, if the fetal risk is not well defined, an attempt should be made to avoid unnecessary drugs during the first trimester when organogenesis takes place. The SGAs that are approved for bipolar disorder are pregnancy category C. Lurasidone, approved for adjunctive use in depressive episodes of bipolar I, is pregnancy category B.

- Lithium exposure in pregnancy is associated with an increase in congenital cardiac malformations.

- Valproate exposure in pregnancy is associated with increased risk of fetal anomalies, including neural tube defects, fetal valproate syndrome and long term adverse cognitive effects. It should be avoided in pregnancy, if possible, especially during the first trimester.

- Carbamazepine exposure in pregnancy is associated with fetal carbamazepine syndrome. It should be avoided in pregnancy, if possible, especially during the first trimester. Carbamazepine is a third-line agent for treating bipolar disorder but is occasionally used, and a formulation was approved recently with an indication for bipolar I *(Equetro)*.

ANTIEPILEPTIC DRUGS USED IN BIPOLAR DISORDER

See Epilepsy/Seizure chapter for a full discussion including drug interactions and patient counseling.

DRUG	DOSING	SAFETY/SIDE EFFECTS/MONITORING
LamoTRIgine *(LaMICtal, LaMICtal ODT, LaMICtal XR)* Various formulations, including chewables, ODT Supplementation with calcium and vitamin D recommended	Dosing requires slow titration (↑ every other week) due to risk of rash Dose depends on inhibitors (lower doses) and inducers (higher doses): <u>Usual dose</u>: start at 25 mg daily, max 200 mg once daily If using <u>valproic acid</u>, start at 25 mg every other day, max 100 mg once daily If using <u>carbamazepine, phenytoin, phenobarbital, or primidone</u> (and not on valproic acid), start at 50 mg once daily, max 400 mg/day divided BID	**BOXED WARNING** Serious skin reactions, including SJS/TEN **WARNINGS** Risk of aseptic meningitis, blood dyscrasias (aplastic anemia, agranulocytosis), multiorgan hypersensitivity (DRESS) reactions **SIDE EFFECTS CAN ↓ ADHERENCE** <u>Somnolence or insomnia, nausea, dizziness, rash</u> (non-serious, 7%), nystagmus, visual disturbances **NOTES** Pregnancy Category C XR formulation is taken once daily
Valproate/Valproic acid derivatives *(Depakene, Depakote, Stavzor, Depacon)* Various formulations including tablet, capsule, sprinkle capsule Supplementation with calcium and vitamin D recommended	Start at 25 mg/kg/day, max 60 mg/kg/day <u>Therapeutic Range</u> 50-125 mcg/mL	**BOXED WARNINGS** <u>Hepatic failure</u>-most common during the first 6 months Teratogenicity Pancreatitis Mitochondrial disease ↑ risk acute liver failure **CONTRAINDICATIONS** Liver disease, urea cycle disorders, migraine prophylaxis in pregnancy, mitochondrial disorders **WARNINGS** Hyperammonemia, hypothermia, brain atrophy, multiorgan hypersensitivity (DRESS) reactions **SIDE EFFECTS CAN ↓ ADHERENCE** N/V/D, alopecia [recommend a multivitamin w/minerals (selenium & zinc)], <u>weight gain, tremor</u>, diplopia, blurred vision, ↓ platelets (<u>dose-related</u>), flu-like symptoms, infection **NOTES** Pregnancy Category D/X (for migraine prophylaxis)

Antiepileptic Drugs Used In Bipolar Disorder Continued

DRUG	DOSING	SAFETY/SIDE EFFECTS/MONITORING
CarBAMazepine (*Equetro*) – for bipolar Extended-release (ER) capsule (*Carbatrol, Epitol, Tegretol Tegretol XR*) – for seizures Tablet, capsule, suspension Potent CYP450 inducer and autoinducer – ↓ level of many other drugs and of itself	Start at 200 mg BID, max 1600 mg/day Therapeutic range: 4-12 mcg/mL ER capsule contents can be sprinkled on food (do not crush or chew) Supplementation with calcium and vitamin D recommended	**BOXED WARNINGS** Serious skin reactions, including SJS/TEN; if Asian descent, test for HLA-B*1502 allele prior to use Blood cell abnormalities, including agranulocytosis **CONTRAINDICATIONS** Bone marrow depression, use within 14 days of MAO inhibitor, concurrent use of nefazodone, use with non-nucleoside reverse transcriptase inhibitors **WARNINGS** SIADH, multiorgan hypersensitivity (DRESS) reactions, others **SIDE EFFECTS CAN ↓ ADHERENCE** Dizziness, somnolence, headache, N/V, ataxia, rash **NOTES** Pregnancy Category D

Lithium

Lithium has various proposed mechanisms, including influencing the reuptake of serotonin and/or norepinephrine and inhibiting postsynaptic D2 receptor supersensitivity.

DRUG	DOSING	SAFETY/SIDE EFFECTS/MONITORING
Lithium (*Lithobid, Eskalith*) Tablet, capsule, solution	Start at 150-900 mg/day, divided TID, max 900-2,400 mg/day divided TID-QID Extended-release is taken BID **Therapeutic Range** 0.6-1.2 mEq/L (trough level) Acute mania may need up to 1.5 mEq initially Titrate slowly to help patient tolerate SEs Take with food (post-meal) if nausea, try split dosing, or use ER If tremor, thirst, confusion, or nocturia, try QHS dosing Liquid conversion: 5 ml (8 mEq) lithium citrate soln = 300 mg IR lithium carbonate cap/tab	**BOXED WARNING** Serum lithium levels should be monitored to avoid toxicity **SIDE EFFECTS** GI upset, cognitive effects, cogwheel rigidity, fine hand tremor, weight gain, polyuria/polydipsia, hypothyroidism (see monitoring), hypercalcemia, cardiac abnormalities (inverted T waves), edema, worsening of psoriasis, blue-gray skin pigmentation **TOXICITY** > 1.5 mEq/L (coarse hand tremor, vomiting, persistent diarrhea, confusion, ataxia) > 2.5 mEq/L (CNS depression, arrhythmia, seizures, irreversible brain damage, coma) **MONITORING** Serum lithium levels, renal function, thyroid function (TSH, FT4), calcium, ECG (patients > 40 years old) **NOTES** Pregnancy Category D Use cautiously in mild-moderate renal impairment, increased risk of toxicity as lithium is 100% renally cleared Avoid use with other serotonergic agents

Lithium Drug Interactions

- These ↑ lithium: ↓ salt intake, <u>NSAIDs, ACE inhibitors, ARBs</u>, thiazide diuretics. Aspirin and sulindac are safer NSAID options.

- These ↓ lithium: ↑ salt intake, caffeine, and theophylline.

- These ↑ risk of serotonin syndrome if taken with lithium: SSRIs, SNRIs, triptans, linezolid and other serotonergic drugso

- These ↑ risk of neurotoxicity (ataxia, tremors, nausea) if taken with lithium: verapamil, diltiazem, phenytoin and carbamazepine.

Lithium Counseling

- Call your healthcare provider if you experience severe nausea, vomiting, worsened diarrhea, slurred speech, extreme drowsiness, weakness, and noticeable (worsened) tremor. These symptoms can occur when the lithium level is too high in your blood.

- You will need to have your blood checked occasionally during treatment.

- Do not crush, chew, or break any extended-release forms of lithium (*Lithobid*). The drug is specially formulated to release slowly in the body.

- Lithium can cause you to feel confused or "dizzy," especially when the dose is started or increased. Use caution when driving or performing other hazardous activities until you know how you feel taking this medication.

- Lithium is known to be harmful to an unborn baby. Do not take lithium without first talking to your healthcare provider if you are pregnant or are planning a pregnancy. Lithium can pass into breast milk. Discuss with your healthcare provider if you are breastfeeding.

- Maintain adequate fluid intake by drinking 8 to 12 glasses of water or other fluids (not counting any caffeinated sodas, coffee or tea) every day while taking lithium. Vigorous exercise, prolonged exposure to heat or sun, excessive sweating, diarrhea, or vomiting can cause dehydration and increased side effects from lithium.

- Do not change the amount of salt you consume. There is a lot of salt in many fast foods, luncheon meats, "TV dinners" and canned goods.

- Do not stop taking this medication, even if you are feeling better.

SECOND-GENERATION ANTIPSYCHOTICS USED IN BIPOLAR DISORDER

SGAs are often used with or without lithium or valproate in patients with bipolar disorder. The agents listed are those with FDA approval for bipolar mania or bipolar depression; SGAs without FDA approval for these indications are also used clinically. For a more complete review of the SGAs, including drug interactions and counseling, refer to the Schizophrenia/Psychosis chapter.

Second-Generation Antipsychotics Used in Bipolar Disorder

DRUG	DOSING	SAFETY/SIDE EFFECTS/MONITORING
ARIPiprazole (Abilify, Abilify Discmelt) Approved for the acute treatment of manic & mixed episodes	PO: 15-30 mg QAM Acute mania: 9.75 mg IM immediate-release x1	**COMMON SIDE EFFECTS** These drugs can cause metabolic issues, including dyslipidemia, weight gain, diabetes Risk of neuroleptic malignant syndrome (NMS) Risk of tardive dyskinesia (TD)
Asenapine (Saphris) Approved for acute manic or mixed episodes, +/- lithium or valproate	Start at 10 mg SL BID, 5 mg BID if in combination. Max 20 mg/day Must dissolve under tongue, and no food/drink for 10 min	Risk of leukopenia, neutropenia, agranulocytosis All can cause orthostasis/dizziness
Cariprazine (*Vraylar*) Approved for manic or mixed episodes	Day 1: 1.5 mg, can increase to 3 mg daily on day 2 Target dose: 3-6 mg daily	**SPECIFIC SIDE EFFECTS** **Aripiprazole** Akathisia (esp in younger patients), agitation, insomnia, constipation, fatigue, blurred vision
Lurasidone (Latuda) Approved for bipolar depression, +/- lithium or valproate	20-120 mg daily Dose titration NOT required Take with food	**Asenapine** Tongue numbness, sedation, dizziness, weight gain (less than risperidone and olanzapine), some QT risk
OLANZapine/FLUoxetine (*Symbyax*) Approved for bipolar depression, 2nd line option due to metabolic effects from olanzapine	Usually started at 6 mg/25 mg capsule QHS (fluoxetine is activating, but olanzapine is more sedating), can ↑ cautiously CI with MAO inhibitors, pimozide, thioridazine, & caution with other QT prolongating drugs/conditions	**Cariprazine** EPS, dystonia, insomnia, headache, N/V **Olanzapine** Cognitive dysfunction, dry mouth, fatigue, sedation, ↑ appetite/weight, peripheral edema, tremor, blurred vision, ↓ CVD risk than other listed APs, some QT risk with the IM injection
OLANZapine (ZyPREXA, Zydis ODT, Relprevv Inj.) Approved for acute manic or mixed episodes with lithium or valproate, and for maintenance as monotherapy	5-20 mg/day, generally QHS Acute agitation: 10 mg IM short-acting x 1	**Quetiapine** QT risk, sedation, dry mouth, constipation, dizziness, ↑ appetite/weight
QUEtiapine extended release (SEROquel, SEROquel XR) Approved for acute manic or mixed episodes as adjunct with lithium or divalproex, and for maintenance as monotherapy	Bipolar mania/maintenance: 400-800 mg QHS Bipolar depression: 300 mg QHS	**Risperidone** Sedation, ↑ appetite, fatigue, insomnia, Parkinsonism, akathisia, nausea, some QT risk, EPS **Ziprasidone** QT risk (greatest), sedation or insomnia, EPS, dizziness, akathisia, abnormal vision, weakness, nausea, rash/skin reactions (drug reaction with eosinophilia and systemic symptoms, DRESS)
RisperiDONE (RisperDAL, RisperDAL Consta, RisperDAL M-TAB) Approved alone or with lithium or valproate for acute mania or mixed episodes	Start at 2-3 mg daily, can ↑ to 6 mg daily Maintenance: 25-50 mg IM Q2 weeks Tablets, oral solution, M-tabs (ODT), IM suspension	**ADA Screening/Monitoring Recommendations** Patients being started on APs should first be screened for overweight and obesity, dyslipidemia and hyperglycemia, hypertension, and personal or family history of risk. While being treated, the patient should be monitored for treatment-emergent changes in weight, waist circumference, plasma lipid and glucose levels, and acute symptoms of diabetes.
Ziprasidone (Geodon) Approved as monotherapy for manic/mixed episodes, and as adjunct with lithium or valproate for maintenance	Start at 40 mg BID, can ↑ to 80 mg BID Take with food	

PRACTICE CASE

MH is a 65 y/o white female brought to the clinic today (11/1) by her sister. She has a long history of bipolar I that has been reasonably controlled on lithium therapy for many years. MH lives with her sister, who takes good care of her medical and social needs. Occasionally, her sister reports, MH gets "back to her old thing" and becomes convinced that she is on a mission to "change the world." MH can never explain what is involved with this mission. Her sister states that MH has always had a fine hand tremor, but today her hands are visibly shaking. She is nauseous and vomited the little she ate this morning. Her speech is slurred and confused. She appears to have difficulty walking into the examination room. She also has a cold with nasal congestion. Additional past medical history includes hypertension.

Allergies: NKDA

Medications:
Lithobid 450 mg BID
Oscal 500 mg BID with meals
B-complex tablet daily

9/9: Prescription provided for Diovan 80 mg daily for elevated blood pressure.

Vitals:
BP: 129/80 mmHg HR: 75 BPM RR: 15 BPM Temp: 38.1°C Pain: 2/10

Labs:

10/1/2013	11/1/2014
Na (mEq/L) = 136 (135 - 145)	Na (mEq/L) = 140 (135 - 145)
K (mEq/L) = 3.9 (3.5 - 5)	K (mEq/L) = 4.6 (3.5 - 5)
Cl (mEq/L) = 104 (95 - 103)	Cl (mEq/L) = 101 (95 - 103)
HCO3 (mEq/L) = 24 (24 - 30)	HCO3 (mEq/L) = 25 (24 - 30)
BUN (mg/dL) = 14 (7 - 20)	BUN (mg/dL) = 28 (7 - 20)
SCr (mg/dL) = 0.7 (0.6 - 1.3)	SCr (mg/dL) = 1.7 (0.6 - 1.3)
Glucose (mg/dL) = 120 (100 - 125)	Glucose (mg/dL) = 108 (100 - 125)
WBC (cells/mm3) = 8.2 (4 - 11 x 103)	WBC (cells/mm3) = 5.6 (4 - 11 x 103)
Hgb (g/dL) = 12.4	Hgb (g/dL) = 14.3
(13.5 - 18 male, 12 - 16 female)	(13.5 - 18 male, 12 - 16 female)
Hct (%) = 39.2 (38 - 50 male, 36 - 46 female)	Hct (%) = 42.1 (38 - 50 male, 36 - 46 female)
Plt (cells/mm3) = 201 (150 - 450 x 103)	Plt (cells/mm3) = 250 (150 - 450 x 103)
Lithium (mEq/L) = 0.9 (0.6 - 1.2)	Lithium (mEq/L) = 1.8 (0.6 - 1.2)

Questions

1. The following factors are likely contributing to the current symptoms of GI distress, coarse hand tremor, ataxia and confusion: (Select **ALL** that apply.)

   a. The use of a calcium supplement

   b. The patient's decline in renal function

   c. Lithium level of 1.8 mEq/L

   d. The use of a vitamin supplement (B-complex)

   e. The patient's ethnicity

2. MH is using *Lithobid*. Describe *Lithobid* clearance:

   a. 100% renal clearance; no hepatic metabolism.

   b. 50% metabolized by 3A4, 50% excreted unchanged in the urine.

   c. 75% metabolized by 2D6, 25% excreted unchanged in the urine.

   d. 100% metabolized by 2C9, 100% metabolites cleared renally.

   e. Metabolized by 2C19, metabolites cleared renally.

3. Select the correct statement regarding the medication added to the patient's regimen on September 9th:

   a. It will increase the risk of bradycardia.

   b. It will increase her blood pressure.

   c. It will contribute to rapid-cycling.

   d. It will increase appetite and could contribute to weight gain.

   e. It will increase lithium levels.

Questions 4-7 are NOT based on the above case.

4. A patient has a history of two myocardial infarctions. He has bipolar II which is moderately controlled with lithium monotherapy. He has been using lithium for many years. His physician wishes to use an antipsychotic as augmentation therapy. Which of the following antipsychotics can cause QT prolongation? (Select **ALL** that apply.)

   a. *Seroquel*

   b. *Risperdal*

   c. *Geodon*

   d. *Mellaril*

   e. *Haldol*

5. Patient counseling for lithium should include the following points: (Select **ALL** that apply.)

   a. Lithium could become unsafe if taken with over-the-counter ibuprofen or naproxen.

   b. You may notice that your hands develop a fine (light) tremor.

   c. If the tremor becomes worse and you feel nauseated, contact your healthcare provider at once.

   d. A safe level for this drug is 0.6-1.2 mg/L.

   e. You must keep the salt level in your diet around the same amount each day.

6. A patient is being treated with valproate therapy. Boxed warnings for this medication include: (Select **ALL** that apply.)

   a. Neuroleptic Malignant Syndrome

   b. Mitochondrial disease

   c. Hepatotoxicity

   d. Pancreatitis

   e. Teratogenicity

7. Which of the following statements regarding drug treatment of bipolar disorder are true: (Select **ALL** that apply.)

   a. Lithium, valproate/divalproex, lamotrigine, carbamezipine and asenapine are mood stabilizers.

   b. Antidepressants can induce a manic episode.

   c. Antidepressants should only be started if a mood stabilizer is also part of the regimen.

   d. FGAs are preferred in bipolar disease due to lower incidence of metabolic side effects.

   e. Lamotrigine is not useful in acute mania due to the slow titration that is required.

Answers

1-b,c, 2-a, 3-e, 4-a,b,c,d,e, 5-a,b,c,e, 6-b,c,d,e, 7-b, c, e

61

PARKINSON DISEASE

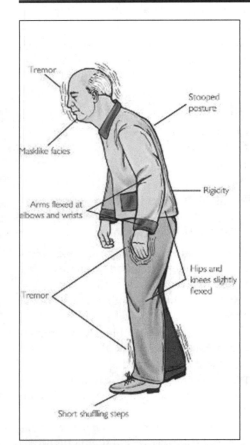

Tremor

Stooped posture

Masklike facies

Rigidity

Arms flexed at elbows and wrists

Tremor

Hips and knees slightly flexed

Short shuffling steps

GUIDELINES/REFERENCES

Diagnosis and prognosis of new onset Parkinson disease (an evidence-based review): Report of the Quality Standards Subcommittee of the American Academy of Neurology. *Neurology.* 2006 Apr 11;66(7):968-75.

We gratefully acknowledge the assistance of George DeMaagd, PharmD, BCPS, Associate Dean of Academic Administration, Professor of Pharmacy, Union University School of Pharmacy, in preparing this chapter.

BACKGROUND

Parkinson disease (PD) is a brain disorder. It occurs when neurons in a part of the brain called the substantia nigra die or become impaired. The cause of neuronal death is not well understood, but is multi-factorial. Normally, these cells produce dopamine. Dopamine allows smooth, coordinated function of the body's muscles and movement. When ~80% of the dopamine-producing cells are damaged, the motor symptoms of the disease appear. Motor symptoms include bradykinesia (slow movement), involuntary shaking and tremor, arm/leg/trunk stiffness, postural instability (trouble with balance, and falls). Non-motor symptoms can precede motor symptoms and may appear much earlier. These include loss of sense of smell (anosmia), constipation, sleep difficulties, low mood/depression and orthostasis. While this disease usually develops after the age of 65, 15% of those diagnosed are under 50. Initially (in what is called Stage I) the disease appears as tremor on one-side (unilateral) and eventually spreads bilaterally. Bradykinesia (slow movement) refers to a reduction in spontaneous movement, which can give the appearance of abnormal stiffness and a decrease in facial expression. This causes difficulty with everyday functions, such as buttoning clothes and cutting food. Walking appears as shuffling steps. Speech is also affected. Rigidity causes stiffness and difficulty with movement. "Cogwheel rigidity" is a ratchet-like movement usually seen in the arms or wrists. Postural instability, another cardinal feature of this condition, is a tendency to be unstable when standing upright, and is due to a decline in reflexes. Some patients will sway backwards, which causes falls. Even with high doses of Parkinson drug treatment, including various combinations, the disease continues to progress, including extended periods of "off time" – this is when symptoms of the disease worsen before the next dose of medication is due. These are among the most frustrating and challenging aspects of disease management. An off episode, with muscle stiffness, slow movements, and difficulty starting movement is one of the most frustrating aspects of living with the disease. Eventually, the patient will be unable to walk and have difficulty feeding themselves and swallowing foods. Amantadine can be useful to help with dyskinesias in later stage disease due to antagonism of the NMDA receptor. Apomorphine treats later stage severe freezing episodes, but it requires subcutaneous (SC) administration, has difficult side effects, and provides increased movement for just about an hour. Patients with Parkinson disease have a high incidence of depression. The agents with the highest efficacy for treatment in these patients are the tricyclic antidepressants, and preferably the secondary amines (such as desipramine and nortriptyline) due to less side effects than with the tertiary amines. The majority of PD patients, however, use SSRIs since many clinicians are familiar with this class and think that they are better tolerated. Although the SSRIs are commonly used, they may contribute to tremor or increase the risk of serotonin syndrome in Parkinson disease patients who are taking MAO-B inhibitors, including the antidepressants and linezolid (Zyvox). Psychosis can present with advanced disease. Quetiapine is the preferred antipsychotic, due to a low risk of movement disorders, but will require monitoring due to metabolic complications, including increased blood glucose and cholesterol. Clozapine is an alternative option with a low risk of aggravating movement disorders, although it

PRIMARY SIGNS/SYMPTOMS

TRAP:

Tremor – seen during resting, usually worsened by anxiety

Rigidity – arms, legs, trunk and face (mask-like face)

Akinesia/bradykinesia – lack of movement or slow initiation of movement

Postural instability – poor balance, which may lead to frequent falls

Other S/Sx of Parkinson Disease
Small, cramped handwriting (micrographia)

Shuffling walk, bent (over) posture

Muffled speech, drooling, dysphagia

Depression, anxiety (psychosis in advanced disease)

Constipation, incontinence

has the added risk of agranulocytosis and other complications, and requires careful monitoring.

Drug-Induced Parkinson Disease

Certain drugs can cause Parkinsonism due to their antagonism of dopamine receptors. These include phenothiazines (prochlorperazine, others), first generation antipsychotics (including haloperidol) the second-generation antipsychotics risperidone (Risperdal), at higher doses, and the newer agent paliperidone (Invega), and the dopamine-blocking agent metoclopramide (Reglan). Metoclopramide is most likely to produce Parkinsonism when it is overdosed, especially in elderly patients who require a dose reduction with renal dysfunction. CNS effects (sedation, dizziness) from metoclopramide are another reason to avoid use in the elderly, if possible. Disorders with these drugs are always dose-dependent; higher doses (especially in elderly patients) are highest risk. Keep in mind that with PD patients drugs that can cause tremor (lithium, tacrolimus, etc.) can worsen the PD symptoms.

DRUG TREATMENT

Medications are used to help improve movement, and for the related issues, such as psychosis and constipation. Levodopa, which is in the commonly used agent carbidopa-levodopa (Sinemet), is the most effective agent and is sometimes better tolerated for initial treatment in the elderly than the dopamine agonists. Initial treatment of tremor in younger patients can be treated with a centrally-acting anticholinergic. The considerable side effects of these agents makes the drug difficult to use in elderly patients; the Beers criteria for potentially inappropriate medication use in older adults lists this group of drugs in the "Avoid" use category. Amantadine is sometimes used

Parkinson Drugs MOA

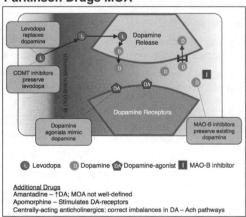

Additional Drugs
Amantadine – ↑DA; MOA not well-defined
Apomorphine – Stimulates DA-receptors
Centrally-acting anticholinergics: correct imbalances in DA – Ach pathways

for <u>initial treatment of tremor</u>, usually in younger patients. A monoamine oxidase inhibitor may also be used as the <u>initial treatment</u> and can provide a mild benefit. The <u>dopamine agonists</u> are often given as the initial option in younger patients (< 65 years). As the disease progresses, treatment will be directed at both <u>reducing off periods</u> and <u>limiting dyskinesias</u>, and will require <u>multiple</u> combinations and adjunctive therapies to manage the progressive nature of the disease. In 2014 a new drug was approved for orthostatic hypotension, which (primarily) affects patients with Parkinson's, although other conditions can present with this complication and in some cases it is idiopathic. The drug is called droxidopa *(Northera)*. It is reviewed at the end of the PD drugs in this chapter.

Dopamine Replacement Agents & Agonists

DRUG	DOSING	SAFETY/SIDE EFFECTS/MONITORING

Carbidopa/Levodopa: Levodopa is a precursor of dopamine. Carbidopa inhibits dopa decarboxylase, preventing peripheral metabolism of levodopa. Tolcapone blocks central and peripheral conversion. Entacapone blocks peripheral conversion only.

Carbidopa/Levodopa (Sinemet, Sinemet CR, Rytary ER, Duopa intestingal gel-suspension given via tube; see notes.)** Levodopa and carbidopa are available separately. If switching from levodopa IR to levodopa-carbidopa CR, dosage should be substituted at an amount that provides ~10-30% more of levodopa/day.	Usual starting dose 25/100 TID IR: 10/100, 25/100, 25/250 mg tab CR: 25/100, 50/200 <u>CR tab can be cut into half</u> – do not crush or chew ER (*Rytary*): start at 23.75/95 mg TID if levodopa-naive; to convert from levodopa use chart in package insert <u>70-100 mg/day of carbidopa is required to inhibit the</u> peripheral conversion (dopa decarboxylase) and to decrease nausea Titrate cautiously due to orthostasis/dizziness risk	**CONTRAINDICATIONS** Non-selective MAO inhibitors within last 14 days, narrow angle glaucoma **SIDE EFFECTS** <u>Nausea, dizziness, orthostasis</u>, vomiting, dry mouth <u>Dyskinesias</u> (abnormal movements), dystonias (occasional, painful) ~1/3 of patients develop confusion, hallucinations, or psychosis (with disease progression; not initially) <u>Can cause brown, black or dark urine</u>, saliva or sweat, and discolor clothing, positive Coombs test, unusual sexual urges, priapism, uric acid elevation (slight) **NOTES** Response <u>fluctuations</u> and <u>dyskinesias</u> after long-term use. <u>Separate from iron</u>, possibly separate from protein (see counseling). *Rytary*: swallow whole or sprinkle on small amount of applesauce; high-fat, high-kcal meal delays absorption. *Duopa* is administered with a feeding tube (J-tube).

COMT-INHIBITORS: <u>Used only with levodopa to ↑ levodopa duration of action.</u> Inhibits the enzyme Catechol-O-methyltransferase (COMT) to prevent peripheral and central conversion of levodopa

Entacapone (Comtan) Levodopa/carbidopa + entacapone (*Stalevo*) Tolcapone (*Tasmar*) – not used much due to hepatotoxicity	200 mg with each dose of carbidopa/levodopa (max 1,600 mg/day) ***Stalevo*** 12.5/50/200 mg 18.75/75/200 mg 25/100/200 mg 31.25/125/200 mg 37.5/150/200 mg 50/200/200 mg	**SIDE EFFECTS** Similar to levodopa, due to extending levodopa duration of action: Nausea, dyskinesias Dizziness, orthostasis, hypotension Can cause orange/brown urine, diarrhea **NOTES** ↓ in levodopa dose of 10-30% is usually necessary when adding on COMT inhibitor.

Dopamine Replacement Agents & Agonists Continued

DRUG	DOSING	SAFETY/SIDE EFFECTS/MONITORING

DA-AGONISTS – Acts similar to dopamine at the dopamine receptor

DRUG	DOSING	SAFETY/SIDE EFFECTS/MONITORING
Pramipexole (Mirapex, Mirapex ER) Both dopamine agonists approved in IR formulations (not long-acting) for restless legs syndrome (RLS), dosed QHS	Start 0.125 mg TID, titrate in 5-7 d to 0.5–1.5 mg TID ER: Start 0.375 mg daily, can ↑ ~5-7 d to max dose of 4.5 mg daily A slow dose titration (no more than weekly) is required due to orthostasis, dizziness, sleepiness	**SIDE EFFECTS** <u>Drowsiness, including sudden daytime sleep attacks</u> <u>Nausea, dizziness, orthostasis</u>, vomiting, dry mouth, peripheral edema, constipation <u>Hallucinations, dyskinesias</u>, impulse control disorders **NOTES** ↓ pramipexole dose if CrCl < 50 mL/min.
Ropinirole (Requip, Requip XL) RLS: see above	Start 0.25 mg TID, titrate weekly to 4-8 mg TID, max 24 mg daily XL: Start 2 mg daily, can ~1-2 weeks to max dose of 24 mg daily	Ropinirole: CYP 450 1A2 substrate; caution with 1A2 inhibitors due to increased drug levels. Bromocriptine *(Parlodel)* – no longer used for PD due to serious pulmonary complications; used as *Cycloset* for type 2 diabetes.
Rotigotine *(Neupro)* Patch formulation only Like the other dopamine agonists, approved for both PD and restless leg syndrome RLS: 1 mg/24 hours, can increase by 1 mg weekly	Patch: 1, 2, 3, 4, 6 or 8 mg/24 hours	**SIDE EFFECTS** <u>Orthostasis, peripheral edema, drowsiness, application site (skin) reactions, hyperhidrosis, dyskinesias, nausea</u>, headache, fatigue, hallucinations, arthralgias **NOTES** Apply once daily, <u>same time each day</u>. Do not apply to same site for at least 14 days. <u>Do not apply heat source over patch</u>. <u>Remove patch in MRI</u>, avoid if sensitivity/allergy to <u>sulfites</u>.

DA-AGONIST injection for advanced disease; a "rescue" movement agent for off periods

DRUG	DOSING	SAFETY/SIDE EFFECTS/MONITORING
Apomorphine *(Apokyn)* Lasts 45-90 minutes For hypomobility in advanced disease – SC injection restores temporary movement Used by patients for "off" periods; can be injected up to 5x/day. Taken in addition to other PD medications.	SC injection Start at 0.2 mL (this is 2 mg, but do not write in mg) and can increase to a maximum recommended dose of 0.6 mL (6 mg). Caution: dosed in mL, not mh Must be started in a medical office.	**CONTRAINDICATIONS** Do not use with 5HT$_3$ antagonists (ondansetron, others) due to severe hypotension and loss of consciousness **SIDE EFFECTS** <u>Severe nausea and vomiting, hypotension</u>, yawning, dyskinesias, somnolence, dizziness, QT-prolongation **NOTES** Supine and standing blood pressure should be checked pre-dose and at 20, 40, and 60 minutes post dose Trimethobenzamide *(Tigan)* 300 mg PO TID or a similar antiemetic should be started 3 days prior to the initial dose of apomorphine and continued at least during the first two months of therapy. This is used to manage the severe nausea and vomiting due to apomorphine use.

Carbidopa/Levodopa *(Sinemet)* Drug Interactions

- Contraindicated with non-selective MAO inhibitors (2 week separation).

- Do not use with dopamine blockers – which will worsen Parkinson disease symptoms (see front section) – this includes phenothiazines, metoclopramide, etc.

- Iron can ↓ absorption.

- Protein-rich foods can ↓ absorption.

Carbidopa/Levodopa *(Sinemet)* Counseling

- Do not stop taking this medicine suddenly. Stopping suddenly could make your condition much worse.

- Do not crush or chew any controlled-release forms of carbidopa and levodopa *(Sinemet CR)*. They are specially formulated to release slowly into your system. If necessary, the tablets can be split in half where they are scored, then swallowed without crushing or chewing.

- Use caution when driving, operating machinery, or performing other hazardous activities. Carbidopa and levodopa may cause dizziness or drowsiness. If you experience dizziness or drowsiness, avoid these activities.

- Call your healthcare provider right away if you have uncontrollable movements of the mouth, tongue, cheeks, jaw, arms, or legs, or if you have a fever and your body feels very hot.

- Do not take carbidopa and levodopa if you are taking or have taken a monoamine oxidase inhibitor (MAOI) such as isocarboxazid *(Marplan)*, phenelzine *(Nardil)*, or tranylcypromine *(Parnate)* in the past 14 days.

- You may have unusual sexual urges. If this happens, you may wish to inform your healthcare provider.

- This drug may cause the urine to become darker, even dark brown, and can stain clothing.

- Iron can decrease the amount of medicine that gets into your body; if you take iron pills they should be taken at a different time.

- Foods high in protein may reduce the amount of drug that gets into your body (however, protein intake is important and usually not reduced).

- For males, in the very unlikely event you have a painful or prolonged erection (lasting more than 4 hours), stop using this drug and seek immediate medical attention or permanent problems could result.

Ropinirole & Pramipexole *(Requip & Mirapex)* Counseling

- This medicine can be taken with or without food. Taking it with food is helpful if the medicine causes nausea.

- Nausea and drowsiness are the most common side effects. This medicine may cause you to fall asleep while you are doing daily activities such as driving, talking with other people, watching TV, or eating. If you experience increased drowsiness or dizziness, or episodes of falling asleep while performing daily activities, do not drive or participate in potentially dangerous activities.

- This drug can cause dizziness, which may be more likely to occur when you rise from a sitting or lying position. Rise slowly and use caution to prevent a fall.

- Alcohol, sleeping pills, antihistamines, antidepressants, pain medicine and other medicines that cause drowsiness can make the drowsiness worse, which could be dangerous. Do not use alcohol.

- Hallucinations may occur, and may be more common in elderly patients. Tell your healthcare provider if you experience thoughts which seem like they are paranoid, or excessive worry, or hearing voices. There is medicine that may help, or the dose may need to be changed.

- It is likely that the dose will be increased slowly, over time. This is normal since the dose has to start low due to dizziness and sleepiness.

Rotigotine *(Neupro)* Patch Counseling

- Side effects from the patch can include ankle swelling, headache, fatigue, nausea, changes in blood pressure, difficulty getting a good night's sleep, and unusual thoughts. If any of these occur and are troublesome, discuss with your healthcare provider.

- This medicine can cause you to become very sleepy. Do not drive a car or operate dangerous machinery until you are sure this can be done safely.

- If you have any unusual body movements, inform your healthcare provider right away.

- You may find that you sweat more than usual. It is important to drink enough fluids and avoid direct sunlight.

- The patch contains aluminum, which can burn your skin if you have certain medical procedures. The patch must be removed prior to magnetic resonance imaging (MRI) or "cardioversion." Do not expose the patch to heat, such as heating pads.

- To apply the patch:
  - ❑ Choose the time of day that works best for you so it is easiest to remember.
  - ❑ Wear the patch for 24 hours. Remove before applying the next patch.
  - ❑ Do not apply to hairy skin, or skin that has cuts. Do not use moisturizer before applying the patch or it will not stick well.
  - ❑ After peeling off one side of the backing, apply to dry skin on the stomach, thigh, hip, side of the body, shoulder or upper arm. Press in place for 30 seconds.
  - ❑ Do not cut the patch. If the patch falls off, you can reapply with bandage tape.
  - ❑ The patch can irritate the skin. Report to your healthcare provider if you get a rash, swelling or itching that persists. Rotate the place where you place the patch. Wait at least 14 days before applying in the same location.
  - ❑ When the patch is removed, fold it in half (sticky sides together) and throw away the folded patch so that children and pets cannot reach it.

Apomorphine *(Apokyn)* Counseling

- Do not take with any of these drugs: ondansetron, dolasetron, granisetron, palonosetron, and alosetron or any drug of the $5HT_3$ antagonist class or group if using apomorphine.

- This drug causes severe nausea, and vomiting. A drug called trimethobenzamide *(Tigan)*, started before using this medicine and during treatment, will help reduce nausea.

- Other possible side effects include yawning, a runny nose, and swelling of your hands, arms, legs, and feet.

- Do not drink alcohol or take any medicines that make you sleepy while you are using this medicine.

- Do not drive a car, operate machinery, or do anything that might put you or others at risk of getting hurt until you know how the medicine affects you.

- This medicine can cause dizziness or fainting. Do not change your body position too fast. Get up slowly from sitting or lying.

- Choose an injection site on your stomach area, upper arm, or upper leg. Change your injection site each time the medicine is used. This will lower your chances of having a skin reaction at the site where you inject.

- This medicine is given by subcutaneous (SC) injection. Never inject into a vein.

Additional Parkinson Disease Medications

DRUG	DOSING	SAFETY/SIDE EFFECTS/MONITORING

Amantadine: blocks dopamine reuptake into presynaptic neurons, increases dopamine release from presynaptic fibers; Used for mild disease, or for dyskinesias in advanced disease

| Amantadine (Symmetrel) | 100 mg BID-TID

↓ dose in renal impairment | **SIDE EFFECTS**
Dizziness (lightheadedness) and insomnia, abnormal dreams, hallucinations
Toxic delirium (with renal impairment, ↓ dose)
Cutaneous reaction called *livedo reticularis* (reddish skin mottling – requires drug discontinuation) |

Selective MAO-B Inhibitors: used as adjunctive therapy with levodopa or as monotherapy (rasagiline has this indication)

Selegiline *(Eldepryl)* *Emsam* – patch for depression May need to reduce levodopa dose when beginning therapy w/selective MAO-B Inhibitor	5 mg BID, with breakfast & lunch Selegiline can be activating; do not dose at bedtime. If dosed twice, take 2nd dose at mid-day.	**CONTRAINDICATIONS** Concomitant use of cyclobenzaprine, dextromethorphan, methadone, propoxyphene, St John's wort, or tramadol; concomitant use of meperidine or an MAO inhibitor. **SIDE EFFECTS** Due to DA-excess, similar to levodopa Rasagiline, when taken as monotherapy, can cause headache, joint pain and indigestion. If taken with levodopa, any of the side effects from dopamine excess are possible.
Selegiline *(Zelapar ODT)*	1.25-2.5 mg daily	
Rasagiline *(Azilect)*	0.5-1 mg daily	**NOTES** Selegiline is metabolized by several CYP450 enzymes to amphetamine metabolites. *Zelapar* ODT has greater liver bypass, with ↓ formation of amphetamine metabolites. Rasagiline is metabolized by CYP1A2 and has no amphetamine metabolites.

Centrally-Acting Anticholinergics: used primarily for tremor in younger patients

| Benztropine *(Cogentin)* | 0.5-2 mg TID (start QHS) | **SIDE EFFECTS**
Dry mouth, constipation, urinary retention, blurred vision
Drowsiness, confusion, tachycardia, high incidence peripheral and central anticholinergic side effects |
| Trihexyphenidyl *(Artane)* | 1-5 mg TID (start 1 mg QHS) | **NOTES**
Used primarily for tremor; avoid use in elderly. |

Additional Parkinson Disease Medications Continued

DRUG	DOSING	SAFETY/SIDE EFFECTS/MONITORING

Alpha/Beta Agonist: used for neurogenic orthostatic hypotension

Droxidopa *(Northera)*	Start at 100 mg TID, can titrate Q 24-48 hour to max 1800 mg/day Take with or without food, with last dose at least 3 hours prior to bedtime (to avoid supine hypertension during sleep)	**BOXED WARNING** Supine hypertension: monitor supine BP prior to and during treatment and more frequently when titrating. To reduce risk, elevate the head of the bed and measure BP in this position. If supine hypertension cannot be managed by elevation of the head of the bed, reduce dose or discontinue. **SIDE EFFECTS** Syncope, falls, headache, UTI **NOTES** Take capsule whole; do not open. Sound-alike drug name (levodopa, carbidopa, *Droxia*).

MAO-B Inhibitor Drug Interactions

- Selegiline and rasagiline should not be used with foods high in tyramine content: (aged or matured cheese, air-dried or cured meats including sausages and salamis; fava or broad bean pods, tap/draft beers, Marmite concentrate, sauerkraut, soy sauce, and other soybean condiments). Food's freshness is also an important concern; improperly stored or spoiled food can create an environment in which tyramine concentrations may increase. Avoid these foods during and for 2 weeks after discontinuation of medication. Avoid products containing dopamine, tyrosine, phenylalanine, tryptophan, or caffeine.

- Selegiline and rasagiline are MAO B inhibitors and at high doses become non-selective; use caution or avoid use with other serotonergic drugs.

- Rasagiline is a CYP 1A2 substrate and should not be dosed above 0.5 mg daily with ciprofloxacin or other CYP 1A2 inhibitors.

PRACTICE CASE

Patient Profile

Patient Name Benjamin Chen
Address 6401 Wisteria Drive
Age 70
Sex Male
Race Asian
Height 5'11"
Weight 185 lbs
Allergies none

DIAGNOSES

Sleepiness

Diziness

MEDICATIONS

Date	No.	Prescriber	Drug and Strength	Quantity	Sig
8/30	76525	Hayes	Carbidopa/Levodopa 25/250 mg	#90	TID
8/30	76526	Hayes	Ropinirole 1 mg	#90	TID (not using, per patient)
8/30	67527	Hayes	Ramipril 10 mg daily	#60	one capsule BID
8/30	76528	Hayes	Amlodipine 10 mg	#30	daily
8/30	76549	Hayes	Multivitamin	#100	daily

LAB/DIAGNOSTIC TESTS

Test	Reference Value	Results 9/15
Ca (mg/dL)	8.5 - 10.5	8.8
Cl (mEq/L)	95 - 103	99
Mg (mEq/L)	1.3 - 2.1	1.4
K (mEq/L)	3.5-5	4.1
P04 (mg/dL)	2.3 - 4.7	4.2
Na (mEq/L)	135 - 145	140
HC03 (mEq/L)	24 - 30	27
BUN (mg/dL)	7 - 20	16
SCr (mg/dL)	0.6 - 1.3	0.9
WBC (mm3)	4,000 - 11,000	5.3
RBC (106/-L)	4.5 - 5.5 male, 4 - 4.9 female	4.8
Hgb (g/dL)	13.5 - 18 male, 12 - 16 female	12.2
Hct (%)	38 - 50 male, 36 - 46 female	36
MCV (mm3)	80 - 96	82
MCHC (g/dL)	31 - 37	33
RDW (%)	11.5 - 14.5	12.1
BP		108/64
Temp		98.6°F
HR		84 BPM

01/11/2016 (today): Patient here for a follow-up due to worsening clinical state. Sinemet use x 3 years, he states it "worked fine" but is now "nearly useless." States he is choking swallowing his food and cannot move well.

Questions

1. Choose the correct statement concerning the patient's carbidopa/levodopa therapy:

   a. The dose of carbidopa is too low.

   b. The dose of carbidopa is too high.

   c. The medication may make his urine turn brown.

   d. The medication will worsen his hypertension.

   e. The medication can cause severe rash.

2. When Benjamin started ropinirole, he found he could not tolerate the medicine due to excessive sleepiness. Choose the correct statement:

   a. The starting dose of ropinirole was too high.

   b. Pramipexole would be less sedating.

   c. The brand name of ropinirole is *Mirapex*.

   d. He should have been started on benztropine instead.

   e. He should have been counseled to increase his caffeine intake during therapy initiation.

3. Choose the correct titration schedule for ropinirole or pramipexole:

   a. Wait at least 2 days before increasing the dose.

   b. Wait at least one week before increasing the dose.

   c. Wait at least two weeks before increasing the dose.

   d. Wait at least three weeks before increasing the dose.

   e. Wait at least four weeks before increasing the dose.

4. Benjamin is using levodopa therapy. He is taking carbidopa concurrently, in the combination medicine *Sinemet*. Choose the correct statements concerning *Sinemet*. (Select **ALL** that apply.)

   a. Carbidopa inhibits decarboxylase and prevents the breakdown of levodopa outside the CNS.

   b. The dose of carbidopa should stay between 30-50 mg.

   c. Using carbidopa with levodopa will decrease nausea.

   d. A typical starting dose of *Sinemet* is 25/250 mg TID.

   e. *Sinemet* is preferred for initial treatment in younger patients with tremor as the only presenting symptom.

5. Which of the following is a common side effect from ropinirole therapy?

   a. Brown urine

   b. Extreme hunger

   c. Somnolence

   d. Loss of consciousness

   e. Hyperglycemia

Questions 6-8 do not apply to the case.

6. A patient has been started on selegiline therapy. What is the mechanism of action of selegiline?

   a. Selective inhibitor of monoamine oxidase A

   b. Selective inhibitor of monoamine oxidase B

   c. Dopamine reuptake inhibitor

   d. Dopamine agonist

   e. Anticholinergic

7. Which of the following medications will require a dose reduction with renal impairment?

   a. Rasagiline

   b. Pramipexole

   c. Benztropine

   d. Levodopa

   e. *Stalevo*

8. Choose the drug which can be safely administered to a patient receiving *Azilect* therapy:

   a. Tramadol

   b. Meperidine

   c. Dextromethorphan

   d. Methadone

   e. Polyethylene glycol

Answers

1-c, 2-a, 3-b, 4-a,c, 5-c, 6-b, 7-b, 8-e

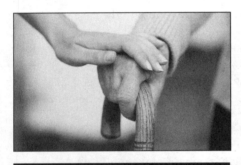

ALZHEIMER'S DISEASE

We gratefully acknowledge the assistance of George DeMaagd, PharmD, BCPS, Associate Dean of Academic Administration, Professor of Pharmacy, Union University School of Pharmacy, in preparing this chapter.

BACKGROUND

Dementia is a group of symptoms affecting intellectual and social abilities severely enough to interfere with daily functioning. There are several types of dementia and Alzheimer's disease is the most common type and the type with well-defined treatment. Unfortunately, the treatments provide modest benefit.

Conditions with mild memory loss without other features of dementia may be referred to as mild cognitive impairment (MCI). Tests to determine whether a patient has dementia are described below. Studies continue to evaluate markers and tests that may help identify the disease at earlier stages. A definitive diagnosis of the actual cause and type of the dementia cannot be made unless an autopsy is conducted post-mortem. If the diagnosis is a dementia that will progressively worsen over time, such as Alzheimer's disease, early diagnosis gives a person time to plan for the future while he or she can still participate in making decisions

Diagnosis

Initial screening should attempt to rule out causes of memory impairment which could be reversible, such as vitamin B12 deficiency, depression and infection. In some patients, analgesics, benzodiazepines or other centrally-acting medications can cause or exacerbate memory loss. Mild memory loss could be age-related. Exams used to identify or screen for dementia include the Folstein <u>Mini-Mental State Exam (MMSE, score < 24 indicates a memory disorder)</u>, DSM-5 criteria, National Institute of Neurological and Communicative Disorders and Stroke and the Alzheimer's Disease and Related Diseases Association (NINCDS-ARDA) criteria.

GUIDELINES

American Geriatrics Society. Guide to the management of psychotic disorders and neuropsychiatric symptoms of dementia in older adults. April 2011. https://www.nhqualitycampaign.org/files/AGS_Guidelines_for_Telligen.pdf (accessed 2015 Sep 29).

Qaseem, A, Snow, V, Cross JT Jr et al. Current pharmacologic treatment of dementia: a clinical practice guideline from the American College of Physicians and the American Academy of Family Physicians. *Ann Intern Med.* 2008;148(5):370-8.

SYMPTOMS

Memory loss

Difficulty communicating

Inability to learn or remember new information

Difficulty with planning and organizing

Poor coordination & motor functions

Personality changes

Inappropriate behavior

Paranoia, agitation, hallucinations

Pathophysiology
Neuritic plaques & tangles in brain tissue; neuron signaling is interrupted

Alteration of neurotransmitters (e.g., decreased acetylcholine)

DRUGS THAT CAN WORSEN DEMENTIA

Peripheral anticholinergics (including incontinence & IBS drugs)

Central anticholinergics (benztropine, etc.)

Antihistamines & antiemetics

Antipsychotics

Barbiturates

Benzodiazepines

Skeletal muscle relaxants

Other CNS depressants

ANTICHOLINERGICS & MEMORY IMPAIRMENT RISK

Anticholinergics are used to treat incontinence (e.g., oxybutinin), allergies or insomnia (e.g., diphenhydramine), dystonic reactions (e.g., benztropine, diphenhydramine), and a few other conditions. A drug with strong central anticholinergic effects (e.g., benztropine) can cause acute cognitive impairment and, occasionally, confusion and hallucinations. The effect depends on the patient's baseline cognitive function, the sensitivity to the medication, the clearance, and the number of drugs and dosing used. In elderly patients, centrally-acting anticholinergics are commonly avoided due to these risks except for the use of anticholinergics used for overactive bladder (OAB). Incontinence is distressing to the patient, to the family, and can lead to nursing home placement; it is not a minor concern. It is difficult to treat adequately – and the cost of disposable diapers is beyond the reach of many families. If used, the effectiveness should be evaluated and if no improvement in OAB symptoms at 6 weeks the drug should be discontinued.

NATURAL PRODUCTS USED FOR DEMENTIA

Vitamin E is sometimes tried for dementia, but doses (> 400 IU) carry health risk. *Ginkgo biloba* is commonly used for memory; at this time, the benefit is not well-defined. *Ginkgo* increases bleeding risk. Huperzine A (derived from Chinese club moss) is an acetylcholinesterase inhibitor and is being used for dementia, with inconsistent results. Mild adverse effects include nausea. Other natural products including A-phosphatidylserine and acetyl-L-carnitine act as acetylcholine precursors, and may be helpful. Recent data suggests older adults with low serum vitamin D levels have an increased risk of developing Alzheimer's disease. If vitamin D is low, it should be supplemented for this and other reasons.

NON-DRUG TREATMENT

In all age groups, physical activity enhances the growth and survival of brain cells. Studies have shown increased brain volume in regions important for memory, learning, concentration and planning in individuals with higher levels of physical activity. The vascular health of the blood vessels in the brain is vital for cognitive function. Healthy blood glucose, blood pressure and cholesterol values will reduce the risk of systemic atherosclerosis and preserve brain function. "Thinking" activities, and healthy diets, including fruits, vegetables, nuts and fish and low in red meat and alcohol can provide benefit in slowing decline.

DRUG TREATMENT

Acetylcholinesterase inhibitors, such as donepezil, are the mainstay of therapy. These are used alone, or with memantine for more advanced disease. At best, one in twelve patients has improvement with these medications. However, for a family, this may mean that the patient who responds can feed themselves for a little while longer, or use the bathroom independently for several more months. Many others do not have noticeable improvement and likely experience side effects (nausea, diarrhea, dizziness). A key clinical pearl with the acetylcholinesterase inhibitors is that although patients may not improve clinically, they may have a slower clinical progression versus if they were not on therapy.

A higher dose of donepezil *(Aricept)* was released in 2010 for advanced disease, however the benefit is very mild (2-point improvement on a 100-point cognition scale). The motivation for the release of this product was the availability of generic donepezil. If a prescriber writes for the higher dose the patient will need to purchase the brand medication. Patients receiving acetylcholinesterase inhibitors should be monitored for both improvement and side effects; if no improvement or intolerable side effects the drug can be discontinued – this may also be advisable if the dementia has advanced to the point where it lacks clinical benefit. However, it may not be acceptable to the family, and in some patients there will be noticeable deterioration when the medicine is discontinued. The timing of the dose should be considered. If nausea is present, evening administration can be helpful. Donepezil is administered QHS for this reason. If insomnia is a concern, the dose can be moved to the morning.

It has become more common to add memantine *(Namenda)* to an acetylcholinesterase inhibitor, especially in the more advanced stages of Alzheimer's disease. Memantine is approved for use alone or with donepezil. *Namzaric* is a combination formulation of donepezil with memantine.

Antidepressants (such as sertraline, citalopram and escitalopram) can be used to treat related depression and anxiety. Antipsychotics are used off-label to treat delusion/anger, but they increase the risk of death in elderly patients (see Boxed Warning in the Schizophrenia chapter) and provide little benefit.

DRUGS TO TREAT ALZHEIMER'S DISEASE

DRUG	DOSING	SAFETY/SIDE EFFECTS/MONITORING

Acetylcholinesterase inhibitors inhibit centrally-active acetylcholinesterase, the enzyme responsible for hydrolysis (breakdown) of acetylcholine, which results in ↑ ACh. Used in mild-moderate disease, and in moderate-advanced disease in combination with memantime.

DRUG	DOSING	SAFETY/SIDE EFFECTS/MONITORING
Donepezil *(Aricept, Aricept ODT, Aricept 23 mg)* ODT, Tablet Used alone or with memantine in more severe disease + memantine *(Namzaric)*	5-10 mg QHS for mild to moderate disease 23 mg QHS, for advanced disease, if stable on lower dose 1st x 3 mos donepezil/memantine 10/14 mg, 10/28 mg	**SIDE EFFECTS** GI side effects: nausea, vomiting, loose stools Bradycardia, fainting, insomnia, tremors, weight loss QT prolongation (donepezil, galantamine) **NOTES** Donepezil is dosed QHS to help ↓ nausea. *Aricept 23 mg* is used for advanced disease – minimal additional benefit with higher dose.
Rivastigmine *(Exelon, Exelon Patch)* Capsule, Patch	1.5-6 mg BID 4.6, 9.5, 13.3 mg/24 hr patch < 6 mg PO daily = 4.6 mg patch 6 - 12 mg PO daily = 9.5 mg Can ↑ to 13.3 mg patch if 9.5 mg tolerated x 4 weeks	Rivastigmine and galantamine IR is with food (breakfast and dinner), galantamine ER is with breakfast. Galantamine solution can be mixed with liquid and taken within 4 hours. Recommend *Exelon* patch or *Aricept ODT* to decrease GI side effects – if the cost difference is acceptable.
Galantamine *(Razadyne, Razadyne ER)* Tablet, Solution	IR: 4-12 mg BID 4mg/mL solution ER: start at 8 mg daily x 4 weeks, then ↑ to 16 - 24 mg	*Exelon* patch: titrate Q 4 weeks, apply first patch the day after last oral dose. Apply daily at same time of day. Rotate; do not use same spot for 14 days. *Namzaric* capsule: can be opened and sprinkled on food.

Drugs to Treat Alzheimer's Disease Continued

DRUG	DOSING	SAFETY/SIDE EFFECTS/MONITORING

Memantine blocks NMDA (N-methyl-D-aspartate), which inhibits glutamate from binding to NMDA receptors & ↓ abnormal activation. Used alone or in combination with donepezil for moderate-advanced disease.

Memantine (Namenda, Namenda XR) Approved for use alone or in combination with donepezil *(Aricept)* for moderate to severe AD + donepezil (*Namzaric*)	IR: 5-10 mg BID (start at 5 mg Q daily, titrate by 5 mg weekly to 10 mg BID) XR: 7, 14 or 28 mg daily (start at 7 mg daily and titrate not faster than weekly) Can switch IR 10 mg BID to 28 mg daily; begin XR the next XR day (not same day) Oral solution 2 mg/mL	**SIDE EFFECTS** Dizziness, constipation, headache **NOTES** Mostly excreted unchanged in urine; do not exceed 5 mg BID or 14 mg XR daily if CrCl < 30 mL/min. XR caps: do not crush or chew, can be opened and sprinkled on applesauce. Oral solution: use provided dosing device, squirt slowly into corner of mouth.

Acetylcholinesterase Drug Interactions

- Use caution with concurrent use of drugs that can lower heart rate (beta blockers, diltiazem, verapamil, digoxin, etc.) and with drugs that cause dizziness (antipsychotics, antihypertensives, alpha blockers, skeletal muscle relaxants, hypnotics, opioids, etc.) due to the risk of dizziness and falls. Drugs that have anticholinergic effects can reduce efficacy (see previous table for drugs that can worsen symptoms). Discontinue incontinence drugs if there is no benefit.

Acetylcholinesterase Counseling

- These medicines can cause nausea and stomach upset. If this remains a problem, talk to your doctor about changing to the longer-acting formulations, or the *Exelon* patch, which has the least nausea. Taking the medicine with food should help.

- The dose of this medication may be increased, but is started low due to the risk of dizziness, falls, and nausea. Use caution when moving from a sitting to a standing position. Try not to use with other drugs that can lower your heart rate and make you feel dizzy. It is best to avoid alcohol when using this medicine.

- Discuss with the pharmacist about all prescription and over-the-counter medicine you use since some of these can worsen memory problems.

- Donepezil is started at 5 mg, at bedtime. It is taken at night to help with nausea. If you experience sleep problems (insomnia), you can take it in the morning. If you have trouble swallowing the medicine, there is a formulation that dissolves in your mouth that can be used instead.

- Rivastigmine is started at 1.5 mg twice daily, with food. Galantamine is started at 4 mg twice daily, with or without food.

Exelon patch application instructions

- Apply a new patch at the same time each day to the upper or lower back, upper arm, or chest; rotate applications site. Do not use the same site within 14 days. Do not apply to an area of the skin that is hairy, oily, irritated, broken, scarred, or calloused.

- Do not apply to an area where cream, lotion, or powder has recently been applied. Do not place the patch under tight clothing.

- Remove the protective liner from one side of the patch. Place the sticky side of the patch on the application site, then remove the second side of the protective liner. Press the patch down firmly until the edges stick well.

- After 24 hours, remove the used patch. Do not touch the sticky side. Fold the patch in half with the sticky sides together and dispose of safely.

Memantine Counseling

- Take this medication by mouth, with or without food. When you first start taking this medication, you will usually take it once daily. Once your dose increases to more than 5 mg daily, take this medication twice daily (5 mg twice daily, and then it usually increases to 10 mg twice daily). *Namenda XR*: S tart at 7 mg once daily.

- For the oral liquid: read the instruction sheet that comes with the bottle. Follow the directions exactly. Use the oral syringe that comes with the product to measure out your dose. Swallow the medication directly from the syringe. Do not mix it with water or other liquids. For the capsule: If you have trouble swallowing, open the capsule and sprinkle on applesauce. Do not crush or chew the capsule.

- You may experience dizziness; use caution when moving from a sitting to a standing position. Try not to use with other drugs that can make you feel dizzy. It is best to avoid alcohol when using this medicine.

- If you become constipated from this medicine, please ask your pharmacist, who can recommend an over-the-counter medicine that will help relieve the constipation.

ATTENTION DEFICIT HYPERACTIVITY DISORDER (ADHD)

GUIDELINES/REFERENCES

Diagnostic and Statistical Manual of Mental Disorders, Fifth Edition (DSM-5).

Dobie C, Donald WB, Hanson M, et al. Institute for Clinical Systems Improvement's Diagnosis and Management of Attention Deficit Hyperactivity Disorder in Primary Care for School-Age Children and Adolescents. https://www.icsi.org/_asset/60nzr5/ADHD-Interactive0312.pdf (accessed 01 Oct 2015).

ADHD: Clinical Practice Guideline for the Diagnosis, Evaluation, and Treatment of Attention-Deficit/Hyperactivity Disorder in Children and Adolescents. *Pediatric Peds*. 2011; 2011-2654.

BACKGROUND

The core symptoms of ADHD are <u>inattention, hyperactivity, and impulsivity</u>. People with ADHD often have difficulty focusing, are easily distracted, have trouble staying still, and frequently are unable to control impulsive behavior. Primary symptoms vary; some patients are more inattentive, and others are more impulsive.

The primary treatments for ADHD are <u>stimulant</u> medications, primarily methylphenidate formulations *(Concerta, Ritalin,* others) and lisdexamfetamine *(Vyvanse)*. Stimulants raise <u>dopamine</u> and <u>norepinephrine</u> levels. In ADHD, it is thought there may be defects in the dopamine pathways that regulate reward anticipation and emotional self-regulation. Providing medications is challenging; similar to other psychiatric conditions, ADHD is marked by a wide variation in treatment response and dosing range. The range in treatment response and dosing has led research into the hypothesis that genetic factors may underlie such differences. Due to the positive response from using methylphenidate, the primary focus of research is on the catecholamine system (dopamine is catalyzed to epinephrine and norepinephrine; refer to Mechanisms chapter).

Keep in mind that a focus on genetics alone is a mechanistic view; it is likely that <u>stressors</u> alter the brain patterns of catecholamine use in some patients, which leads to ADHD symptoms. In the popular book *Scattered* (Gabor Maté, MD), the author focuses on altering the environment to help control symptoms. Environment, as well as genetics, is a determinant in brain chemistry and alterations in the environment can change the chemistry. However, some require medications even with strong social support.

ADHD can cause an emotional response from those who feel stimulant medications are over-used. Parents who rely on the medications to help their children do better in school, and adults who use ADHD medications may be negatively viewed. Pharmacists can make sure that when medications are prescribed, they are used safely. <u>Stimulants are C-II</u>, which means the prescriptions can only be prescribed for one month at a time, which makes it convenient to check blood pressure and heart rate (and weight and height, periodically, in children). Many prescribers issue three months of prescriptions at a time, which are post-dated. Stimulants are a common drug of abuse and have a high street value; these should be dispensed with caution, and counseling must include instructions <u>not to share with others and to store in a safe place</u>. Occasionally the "ADHD" stimulants are used for other conditions, including narcolepsy and shift work sleep disorder; this condition is discussed in the Sleep Disorders chapter.

About 10% of school-aged children are using ADHD medications, with boys outnumbering girls. The guidelines have age-specific treatment recommendations for children ages 4 - 18 years, although a couple of the medications are approved for treating children as young as 3 years old. ADHD should be considered a chronic illness; up to 80% of children will continue to exhibit symptoms into adolescence and up to 65% of children will still exhibit symptoms into adulthood. Inattention and impulsivity often remain as the patient ages, and hyperactivity can be decreased.

DSM-5 DIAGNOSTIC CRITERIA

People with ADHD show a persistent pattern of inattention and/or hyperactivity-impulsivity that interferes with functioning or development. The DSM-5 requirements for an ADHD diagnosis:

<u>Inattention</u>: Six or more symptoms of inattention for children up to age 16, or five or more for ages 17 to adults; symptoms of inattention have been present for at least 6 months, and they are inappropriate for the developmental level:

- Fails to pay attention, has trouble holding attention, does not pay attention when someone is talking, does not follow through on instructions, fails to finish schoolwork, has difficulty organizing tasks, avoids or dislikes tasks which require mental effort, loses things, is easily distracted, and is forgetful.

<u>Hyperactivity and Impulsivity</u>: Six or more symptoms of hyperactivity-impulsivity for children up to age 16, or five or more for ages 17 to adults; symptoms of hyperactivity-impulsivity have been present for at least 6 months to an extent that is disruptive and inappropriate for the person's developmental level:

- Often fidgets or squirms, leaves seat unexpectedly, runs about when not appropriate, unable to play quietly, is "on the go" as if "driven by a motor", talks excessively, blurts out answers, has trouble waiting his/her turn, and interrupts or intrudes on others.

<u>In addition</u>, the following conditions must be met:

- Several inattentive or hyperactive-impulsive symptoms were present <u>before age 12 years</u>, symptoms must have been present in <u>2 or more settings</u> (at home, school, at work, with friends or relatives), symptoms interfere with functioning, and symptoms are not caused by another psychiatric disorder.

NATURAL PRODUCTS

Fish oils are a natural product increasingly used for a variety of psychiatric conditions, including ADHD. Fish oil supplements (which provide omega-3 fatty acids) with or without evening primrose oil (which provides omega-6 fatty acids) may be helpful in some patients. Fish oils are rated as "possibly effective" to improve cognitive function and behavior in children with ADHD by the *Natural Medicines Database*. Check the dose prior to making a recommendation. The combo product used in the study that showed benefit used 6 capsules daily. Other products are occasionally used for ADHD, including SAMe, St. John's wort and ginkgo. If St. John's wort is used, check for drug interactions since this herbal induces CYP 450 enzymes and will lower the concentration of the majority of other drugs. It is serotonergic, and has phototoxicity risk.

DRUG TREATMENT

First-line drug therapy for ADHD are stimulants. When stimulants do not work well enough (after trials of 2 - 3 agents), atomoxetine *(Strattera)*, a non-stimulant medication, can be tried next, or will be used first-line by prescribers who are concerned about the possibility of abuse by the patient or family.

The stimulant agent methylphenidate, which is available in various formulations, is tried first, or lisdexamfetamine (*Vyvanse*), the pro-drug of dextroamphetamine. Longer-acting formulations are preferred for children who would otherwise need dosing at school (which would require a nurse's office visit) and to help maintain more steady symptom control. Other stimulant classes can be tried.

Guanfacine (approved in the extended-release (ER) formulation *Intuniv*), and clonidine (in the ER formulation *Kapvay*) are used most often as adjunctive treatments. For example, it is common to see *Concerta* with *Intuniv*, or *Vyvanse* with *Kapvay*, or vice versa. The guanfacine or clonidine formulation is being added-on to the stimulant after the stimulant was tried and additional benefit was needed. *Intuniv* or *Kapvay* can also be used to help with sleep in the evening as they are sedating. They are also used alone. Diphenhydramine is used to help with sleep at night, however it is important to monitor for a paradoxical reaction in some children (e.g., causing hyperactivity). Another option to help with sleep is immediate-release clonidine, taken at bedtime.

Family therapy/psychotherapy may be required for an improved prognosis. Prior to the start of treatment, the patient should be evaluated for bipolar due to the risk of stimulants aggravating the condition. The medications described in this section are used off-label to help with some of the symptoms of autism.

STIMULANTS FOR ADHD
CNS stimulants that block the reuptake of norepinephrine and dopamine.

DRUG	DOSING	SAFETY/SIDE EFFECTS/MONITORING

Methylphenidate

DRUG	DOSING	SAFETY/SIDE EFFECTS/MONITORING
Methylphenidate IR (Ritalin, Methylin chewable, oral susp) All of the stimulants (including modafinil and armodafinil) and atomoxetine require a MedGuide. *Kapvay* and *Intuniv* do not. All stimulants are C-II.	Start 5 mg BID 60 mg/day max, take 30 min before meals Chewable tabs: 2.5 -10 mg Methylphenidate approved for 6+ yrs	**BOXED WARNINGS** Potential for drug dependency; use caution if a history of ethanol or drug abuse. Avoid abrupt discontinuation. *Adderall:* Misuse may cause sudden death and serious cardiovascular adverse events. **CONTRAINDICATIONS** MAO inhibitor use within the past 14 days. Marked anxiety, tension, and agitation, glaucoma, family history or diagnosis of Tourette's syndrome or tics (excluding *Aptensio XR, Quillivant XR*). *Metadate CD* and *Metadate ER* only: Severe hypertension, heart failure, arrhythmia, hyperthyroidism, recent MI or angina; concomitant use of halogenated anesthetics. *Ritalin* and *Ritalin SR* only: Pheochromocytoma.
Methylphenidate long-acting *(Ritalin LA)* ½ IR, ½ SR in one capsule	Start 20 mg QAM 10-40 mg LA caps	
Methylphenidate IR – ER *(Concerta)* OROS system Somewhat harder to abuse (harder to crush)	Start 18-36 mg QAM 18, 27, 36, 54 mg ER tabs Swallow whole	**WARNINGS** Severe CV events, ↑ risk suicidal thoughts/behaviors, peripheral vasculopathy (Raynaud's Syndrome), priapism, blurry vision, seizures *Daytrana*: loss of skin pigmentation at application site **SIDE EFFECTS** Nausea, loss of appetite, insomnia, dizziness, headache, lightheadedness, irritability, blurry vision, difficulty with visual accomodation, dry mouth
Methylphenidate ER *(Methylin ER, Metadate ER, Quillivant XR* – oral suspension; reconstitute at pharmacy	Start 20 mg QAM 10-60 mg ER tabs Suspension: 25 mg/5 mL	↑ BP ~2-4 mmHg, ↑ HR ~3-8 BPM, monitor; avoid use with CVD Exacerbation of mixed/mania episodes if bipolar disorder, use caution with any pre-existing psychiatric condition, including depression, aggressive behavior, hostility
Methylphenidate *(Aptensio XR)* IR/XR release, lasts for 12 hrs	Start 10 mg QAM 10-60 mg caps	**MONITORING** Consider ECG prior to treatment, monitor BP and HR during treatment (all). Monitor height and weight (children). Cardiac evaluation if symptoms such as chest pain, syncope. Monitor CNS effects, signs of peripheral vasculopathy (e.g., digital changes), signs of misuse, abuse or addiction.
Methylphenidate IR – ER *(Metadate CD)* Beads that dissolve at different rates	Start 20 mg QAM 10-60 mg ER caps	
Methylphenidate transdermal patch *(Daytrana)*	1.1 mg/hr (10 mg/9 hr)-3.3 mg/ hr (30 mg/9 hr)	**NOTES** *Focalin XR, Ritalin LA, Metadate CD, Aptensio XR* and *Adderall XR* can be taken whole or the capsules sprinkled on applesauce (if not warm and used right away, do not chew). *Concerta* OROS delivery: The capsule's outer coat dissolves fast to give immediate action, and the rest is released slowly. May see ghost tablet in stool. *Concerta, Metadate CD* and *Ritalin LA* are all QAM (IRs and some others are divided), and *Daytrana* patch is QAM, applied to alternate hip 2 hours before desired effect (or as soon as the child awakens so it starts to deliver prior to school). Remove after 9 hours (at night, for sleep). If overdosed, symptoms (anxiety, tachycardia) can be ↓ with a benzodiazepine. For all: titrate up (increase dose) weekly, as-needed. Some products contain phenylalanine.

Stimulants for ADHD Continued

DRUG	DOSING	SAFETY/SIDE EFFECTS/MONITORING

Dexmethylphenidate

Dexmethylphenidate IR *(Focalin)*	2.5-10 mg tabs, given QAM 20 mg max/day BID, 4+ hrs apart, with or without food	see Methylphenidate **NOTES** Active isomer of methylphenidate. Conversion from methylphenidate to dexmethylphenidate: One-half the total daily dose of racemic methylphenidate.
Dexmethylphenidate ER *(Focalin XR)*	5-20 mg caps, given QAM 40 mg max/day	

Dextroamphetamine and amphetamine

Dextroamphetamine/ Amphetamine IR *(Adderall)*	5-30 mg scored tabs QAM or BID, without regard to meals 2nd dose 4-6 h after 1st	see Methylphenidate **NOTES** The American Academy of Pediatrics (2011) does not recommend use of dextroamphetamine in children ≤ 5 years due to insufficient evidence (although FDA-approved).
Dextroamphetamine/ Amphetamine ER *(Adderall XR)*	5-30 mg ER caps QAM, with or without food	Avoid use of acidic foods, juice or vitamin C; can decrease amphetamine level.
Dextroamphetamine IR *(Dexedrine, Zenzedi, ProCentra* – solution)	5-10 mg tabs QAM or BID, with or without food Solution: 5 mg/5 mL	
Dextroamphetamine SR and IR *(Dexedrine Spansules)*	5, 10, 15 mg SR caps QAM, with or without food	

Lisdexamfetamine (prodrug of dextroamphetamine)

Lisdexamfetamine *(Vyvanse)*	Start 20-30 mg 20, 30, 40, 50, 60, 70 mg caps QAM, with or without food <u>Can mix contents with water, yogurt or orange juice; take right away</u>	see Methylphenidate **NOTES** Lisdexamfetamine is a prodrug composed of l-lysine (amino acid) bonded to dextroamphetamine (d-amphetamine). It is hydrolyzed in the blood to active d-amphetamine. If injected or snorted, the fast effect (rush) would be muted. The design is to ↓ the abuse potential.

Stimulant Drug Interactions
- 14-Day wash out period after MAO inhibitor use.

Patient Counseling for Stimulants
- Dispense MedGuide and instruct parents/patient to read it. Stimulants should not be used in patients with heart problems or serious psychiatric conditions. Report at once if the child has <u>chest pain, shortness of breath</u>, or fainting. Report at once if the child is <u>seeing or hearing things that are not real</u> or believing things that are not real.
- The healthcare provider should check the child's <u>blood pressure, heart rate, height and weight</u>.
- Some children get nausea or headache when the dose is increased or can act "wired." This is why the dose is increased slowly at the beginning.
- This is a controlled medication and has potential to be abused. Do not share this medicine with anyone else and store in a safe place.

- Your child may not have much of an appetite. Children seem to be less hungry during the middle of the day, but they are often hungry by dinnertime as the medication wears off. Your child should eat a healthy breakfast. Pack healthy snacks for school, such as nuts, cheese and fruit.

- Certain food colorings and preservatives that are common in "junk" foods and candies can worsen hyperactive behavior in some children. If these foods affect your child, you can limit them.

- If the child has trouble sleeping, the formulation may be changed. Or, the prescriber may recommend OTC diphenhydramine or prescription clonidine to take before bedtime.

- Less commonly, a few children develop sudden, repetitive movements or sounds called tics. Changing the medication dosage may make tics go away. Some children also may appear to have a personality change, such as appearing "flat" or without emotion. Talk with your child's healthcare provider if you see any of these side effects.

- If your child develops an erection lasting longer than 4 hours he will need to get immediate medical help to prevent long-term problems with the penis.

- If using a capsule formulation that can be mixed with applesauce *(Focalin XR, Ritalin LA, Metadate CD, Adderall XR* and *Aptensio XR)* and your child has difficulty swallowing the capsules, they can be sprinkled on a small amount of applesauce (if not warm and used right away). Do not chew the applesauce; just swallow. A small amount only so it is not chewed. *Concerta*: may see a ghost tablet in stool; the medication has been absorbed.

- If the child is using the medicine *Vyvanse*, the capsule contents can be mixed in water, yogurt or orange juice. Take right away. It must be taken right after putting into the water.

Daytrana Patch Instruction

- Each morning put a new patch on the hip and alternate the side each day (left hip odd days, right hip even days). Do not apply where the waist of the pants could rub it off. Apply 2 hours before effect is needed.

- Hold patch on skin for 30 seconds and smooth down edges. It should stay on during swimming or bathing. Remove the patch after 9 hours so your child can sleep well at night.

- Wash your hands immediately after applying the patch. Patches should not be reapplied with bandages, tape, or other household adhesives. Do not use hair dryers, heating pads, electric blankets, or other heat sources directly on the patch. If you have to replace a patch that has fallen off, the total wear-time for the first and second patch should not be more than a total of 9 hours in 1 day. Do not reapply the same patch that fell off.

- When peeling off to discard, fold in half, put down the toilet or lidded trash can.

Quillivant XR Suspension Instructions

- The bottle must contain liquid. Return to the pharmacist if it is powder.

- First, shake the bottle for at least 10 seconds. Use the dosing dispenser to measure the milliliters (mL) dose.

- Insert the tip of the dispenser into the upright bottle and push the plunger all the way down. Turn the bottle upside down and remove the correct amount; measure to the white end of the plunger.

- Use the dosing dispenser to slowly squirt the medication into the child's mouth. Cap tightly and rinse the dispenser with tap water or in a dishwasher.

- The medicine can be stored at room temperature for up to 4 months.

NON-STIMULANTS FOR ADHD – 2ND LINE AGENTS – NOT CONTROLLED

DRUG	DOSING	SAFETY/SIDE EFFECTS/MONITORING

Selective Norepinephrine Reuptake Inhibitor

AtoMOXetine *(Strattera)*	Start at 40 mg/day, can Increase after 3+ days to 80 mg, max 100 mg/day, take daily or divide BID 80 mg max with CYP 2D6 inhibitors or if poor 2D6 metabolizer	**BOXED WARNING** Risk of suicidal ideation; monitor for suicidal thinking or behavior, worsening mood, or unusual behavior **CONTRAINDICATIONS** Glaucoma, pheochromocytoma, adrenal gland tumor, severe cardiovascular disorders, MAO inhibitor use within past 14 days **WARNINGS** Aggressive behavior, treatment-emergent psychotic or manic symptoms, orthostasis and syncope, allergic reactions, priapism Rare, but severe hepatotoxicity (most within 120 days of start of treatment) Risk of serious cardiovascular events; avoid use if known problems; conduct cardiac evaluation if needed. Use with caution if BP elevated **SIDE EFFECTS** Headache, insomnia (~10%), somnolence (~10%), dry mouth, nausea, abdominal pain, ↓ appetite, erectile dysfunction, ↓ libido, hyperhidrosis, fatigue, dizziness, hot flashes, dysmenorrhea, menstrual changes, paresthesia, urinary retention Orthostasis; use caution in patients at risk Psychiatric effects, including hallucinations and mania Priapism (more common than with methylphenidate) **MONITORING** HR, BP, ECG, height, weight, agitation **NOTES** Do not open capsule – irritant. Primarily a CYP450 2D6 substrate; 2D6 inducers or inhibitors may necessitate a change in atomoxetine dose.

Central Alpha₂ₐ Adrenergic Receptor Agonist

These agents stimulate alpha-2 adrenergic receptors in the brain. Both are (old) hypertension drugs which are now longer-acting formulations for ADHD (and clonidine is used off-label in the IR form for sleep/benefit, taken QHS).

GuanFACINE ER *(Intuniv)* For patients using stimulants for additional benefit, or alone *Tenex* – for hypertension	1-4 mg, max 4 mg/day Start at 1 mg daily Do not take with high-fat meal (↑ absorption) With CYP 3A4 inducers, max dose 8 mg/day With CYP 3A4 inhibitors, max dose 2 mg/day	**SIDE EFFECTS** Somnolence, dizziness, orthostasis, headache, fatigue, hypotension, nausea, constipation, abdominal pain, skin rash (rare, discontinue if occurs), bradycardia **NOTES** All cardiovascular effects (bradycardia, hypotension, orthostasis, syncope) are dose-dependent; titrate carefully. Sedation can cause risk with physical and mental activities. Cases of skin rash with exfoliation; discontinue if rash develops. Do not interchange with other guanfacine formulations. Do not crush.

Non-Stimulants for ADHD – 2ⁿᵈ Line Agents – Not Controlled Continued

DRUG	DOSING	SAFETY/SIDE EFFECTS/MONITORING
CloNIDine ER (Kapvay) For patients using stimulants for additional benefit, or alone *Catapres* – for hypertension	0.1-0.4 mg/day Start at 0.1 mg at bedtime, ↑ 0.1 mg/day Q 7 days until desired response Dose BID, if uneven give higher dose QHS	**SIDE EFFECTS** Headache, somnolence, abdominal pain, upper resp tract infections **NOTES** Rebound hypertension (with sweating/anxiety/tremors), if stopped abruptly – taper off by ↓ 0.1 mg Q 3-7 days. ER formulation has ↓ SEs. Do not crush.

Atomoxetine Drug Interactions

- Decrease dose if on strong CYP 2D6 inhibitors (e.g., paroxetine, fluoxetine, bupropion, quinidine) or if 2D6 poor metabolizer, up to max 80 mg/day.

- 14-day wash out period after MAO inhibitor use.

Patient Counseling for Atomoxetine

- Dispense MedGuide and instruct parents/patient to read it. The MedGuide includes a warning for risk of suicidal ideation in children and risk of liver injury.

- Common side effects can include headache, insomnia, somnolence, dry mouth, nausea, stomach pain, lessened appetite, nausea, sweating, dizziness and fatigue. Girls and women can get hot flashes, dysmenorrhea, ↓ sexual interest or menstrual changes.

- You may have suicidal thoughts or behavior while taking atomoxetine. Watch for symptoms of depression, unusual behavior, or thoughts of hurting yourself. Your healthcare provider may need to check you at regular visits while you are taking this medication.

- The capsule cannot be opened. Do not use an open or broken capsule. If the medicine from inside the capsule gets into your eyes, rinse thoroughly with water and call your healthcare provider.

- Atomoxetine can cause side effects that may impair your thinking or reactions. Be careful if you drive or do anything that requires you to be awake and alert.

- Monitor for symptoms of liver damage: weakness, abdominal pain, yellowed skin, light colored stool or darkened urine.

Clonidine and Guanfacine Drug Interactions

- Both clonidine and guanfacine are sedating; use caution with other CNS depressants.

- Both clonidine and guanfacine lower blood pressure; use caution with other anti-hypertensives.

- Both clonidine and guanfacine come as other formulations; do not use concurrently.

- Guanfacine is a CYP 3A4 substrate; see dosing in table for use with inducers or inhibitors.

ANXIETY DISORDERS

We gratefully acknowledge the assistance of Christine Fitzgerald, BS, PharmD, BCPS, Temple University School of Pharmacy, in preparing this chapter.

BACKGROUND

Anxiety exists to protect us from harm. For example, if an aggressive dog or bear comes along, fear (a symptom of anxiety) is important to avoid getting attacked and can help us escape from the situation. Occasional anxiety, which is normal, can occur in the general population when faced with challenging issues at work, home or school. The symptoms of <u>occasional</u> anxiety (fear, worry) should dissipate once the issue is gone. Any physical symptoms (tachycardia, palpitations, shortness of breath, stomach upset, chest pain or other pain, insomnia and fatigue) should also resolve. Medical conditions, including hyperthyroidism, can cause anxiety, and if present, will need to be treated.

When a person has an anxiety <u>disorder</u>, the symptoms are <u>continuous and severe</u> and cause great distress. The disorder can interfere with the ability to do well at school or work, and can harm relationships. The major types of anxiety disorders are generalized anxiety disorder (GAD), panic disorder (PD) and social anxiety disorder (SAD). Disorders that have symptoms of anxiety include obsessive compulsive disorder (OCD) and post-traumatic stress disorder (PTSD). Although OCD and PTSD have symptoms of anxiety, the Diagnostic and Statistical Manual of Mental Disorders, Fifth Edition (DSM-5) classifies these disorders differently. OCD has its own category called "obsessive-compulsive and related disorders" and PTSD is categorized under "trauma and stressor- related disorders."

Lifestyle changes can improve symptoms. Increasing physical activity, helping others, community involvement, yoga, meditation, and other methods can broaden the patient's outlook and reduce stress.

<u>Cognitive Behavioral Therapy</u> (CBT) is a type of mental health treatment in which a trained counselor helps the patient explore patterns of thinking that lead to self-destructive actions and behavior. CBT can be beneficial and, in some cases, provides adequate relief without the need for chronic medications.

GUIDELINES/REFERENCES

Diagnostic and Statistical Manual of Mental Disorders, Fifth Edition (DSM-5). American Psychiatric Association. Arlington VA; 2013.

Baldwin DS, Waldman S, Allgulander C. Evidence-based pharmacological treatment of generalized anxiety disorder (DSM-IV-TR). *Int J Neuropsychopharmacol.* 2011 Jun;14(5):697-710.

NATURAL PRODUCTS

Kava is used as a relaxant but can damage the liver and should not be recommended. 5-HTP and L-tryptophan are used for both anxiety and depression, and may provide benefit, but the use has been associated with eosinophilia myalgia syndrome (EMS). St. John's wort is used for depression and anxiety; the primary concern is that St. John's wort is a strong inducer and the concentration of concurrent medications will be lowered. It is serotonergic, has risk with other serotonergic drugs, and causes photosensitivity. Valerian is used for anxiety and sleep, but some valerian products may have been contaminated with liver toxins; if this is being used the liver should be monitored. Passionflower appears to be safe and is rated as "possibly effective" by the Natural Medicines Database.

DRUG TREATMENT

The primary first-line agents used to treat anxiety disorders are selective serotonin reuptake inhibitors (SSRIs), serotonin norepinephrine reuptake inhibitors (SNRIs) and a few of the tricyclic antidepressants. Clomipramine is indicated for OCD and is often used for this purpose. Although only some of the antidepressants (ADs) have specific anxiety indications, these agents are often chosen based on the healthcare

SELECT DRUGS AND CONDITIONS THAT CAN CAUSE ANXIETY
Theophylline
Levothyroxine
Acetazolamide
Albuterol (if used incorrectly-swallowed)
Aripiprazole, haloperidol
Caffeine, in high doses
Stimulants
Decongestants (pseudoephedrine and nasally inhaled agents)
Steroids
Bupropion
Fluoxetine, paroxetine
Illicit drugs, including cocaine, LSD, methamphetamine, others

provider's familiarity and/or the side effect profile. For example, although fluvoxamine was the first SSRI indicated for OCD, it is rarely used due to its drug interaction potential. SSRI and SNRI agents are often initiated at half the initial dose used for depression and are slowly titrated to minimize anxiousness and jitteriness that is common during the first couple of weeks of treatment; dose carefully to avoid worsening the anxiety. Clinicians may overlap SSRIs or SNRIs with a benzodiazepine for 2-4 weeks to help alleviate the initial stimulatory effects and regulate sleep. Patients should be advised that immediate relief is not to be expected when initiating AD treatment for anxiety (or depression); it commonly takes 4 or more weeks for a noticeable benefit. For specifics on the antidepressants see the Depression chapter.

Buspirone (*BuSpar*) is approved for GAD, and is an option with any of the following: a poor response to an antidepressant (including as adjunctive treatment), if at risk for benzodiazepine abuse, or if elderly. Buspirone is less sedating and has less cognitive effects than benzodiazepines, but it does cause some, and is known for causing dizziness. Buspirone does not work right away; it take 2 - 4 weeks to have a beneficial effect.

Hydroxyzine (*Vistaril*) is FDA approved for anxiety and is considered second-line. It is occasionally used for short-term anxiety as an alternative to benzodiazepines. This is a sedating antihistamine and works by sedating the patient, rather than treating any underlying condition. It should not be used long-term. It is used more commonly for pruritus. Review hydroxyzine in the Common Skin Conditions chapter.

Pregabalin (*Lyrica*) is not FDA approved for anxiety but is useful if a patient has anxiety with neuropathic pain. Pregabalin has immediate anxiolytic effects similar to benzodiazepines. It is a controlled substance (C-V) due to mild euphoric properties, which can have a calming effect. Propranolol (*Inderal*, others) is used to reduce symptoms of stage fright or performance anxiety (e.g., tremor, tachycardia). It is dosed at 10-40 mg 1 hour prior to an event such as a public speech. Use caution with this approach due to CNS effects (e.g., confusion, dizziness). This is a non-selective beta blocker and is not used with asthma or COPD.

Benzodiazepines

Benzodiazepines are often used for anxiety. They provide fast relief for acute symptoms. Situations in which benzodiazepines are appropriate include short-term situations where anxiety is acute and can cause extreme stress, prevent proper sleep, and disrupt life. These symptoms can be the result of a recent death of a loved one, a natural disaster, or other stressful situations. In such cases, they should be used less than 1 - 2 weeks, and then discontinued. Benzodiazepines can cover-up anxiety symptoms, but do not treat the causes, and, in most cases, should not be used long-term.

When benzodiazepines are used in the elderly, they pose significant risks for confusion, dizziness and falls – the risk increases with concurrent use of other CNS depressants. The BEERS Criteria for benzodiazepine use in the elderly states: *May be potentially inappropriate for use in geriatric patients (Quality of evidence – high; Strength of recommendation – strong)*. Additionally, elderly patients may have a "paradoxical" reaction to and respond to the drug with insomnia, agitation and excitement. The benzodiazepines are differentiated by their pharmacokinetic parameters, including the onset of action and the duration of action.

Potentiates GABA, an inhibitory neurotransmitter, causing CNS depression and providing anxiolytic, anticonvulsant, sedative and/or muscle relaxant properties.

DRUG	DOSING	SAFETY/SIDE EFFECTS/MONITORING
LORazepam (Ativan) Tablet, injection, *LORazepam Intensol* is solution (sol for solution) LORazepam injection--used commonly for agitation, sedation	1-3 mg PO BID-TID All C-IV All given PRN or scheduled, depending on condition	**CONTRAINDICATIONS** Varies among agents: acute narrow-angle glaucoma, sleep apnea, severe respiratory insufficiency, significant liver disease, use with ketoconazole or itraconazole (alprazolam), not for use in infants < 6 months of age (diazepam oral), myasthenia gravis (diazepam).
ALPRAZolam (Xanax, Xanax XR, *Niravam ODT), Alprazolam Intensol* (solution) Tablet, ODT, solution	0.25-0.5 mg PO TID	**WARNINGS** Anterograde amnesia (after drug is taken some events may not be stored as memories), CNS depression, extravasation with IV use, paradoxical reactions (discontinue if hyperactive/aggressive behavior), potential for abuse, safety risks in elderly (risk of impaired cognition, delirium falls/ fractures, development of tolerance, withdrawal symptoms; taper off slowly Physiological dependence and tolerance develop with chronic use
ChlordiazePOXIDE *(Librium)* Capsule	5-25 mg TID-QID	**SIDE EFFECTS** Somnolence, dizziness, weakness, ataxia, lightheadedness
ClonazePAM (KlonoPIN) Tablet, ODT	0.25-0.5 mg PO BID	**NOTES** Pregnancy Category D; risk of cleft lip and/or palate or floppy baby syndrome. Use in lactation is not recommended; if used, select a short-acting agent such as alprazolam or lorazepam (less risk to infant).
Clorazepate *(Tranxene-T)* Tablet	7.5-15 mg BID-QID	L-O-T (lorazepam, oxazepam, and temazepam) are considered less potentially harmful for elderly or with liver impairment since they are metabolized to inactive compounds (glucuronides).
Diazepam (Valium) Tablet, injection, *Diazepam Intensol* (solution) *Diastat* – rectal, for acute seizure control	2-10 mg PO BID-QID	Diazepam: Lipophilic, fast onset, long half-life, high abuse potential. Alprazolam: Fast onset, often abused due to quick action. To avoid withdrawal symptoms (anxiety, shakiness, insomnia, tachycardia, muscle pain) taper off slowly. These are likely if used > 10 days.
Oxazepam *(Serax)* Capsule	10-30 mg PO TID-QID	Alcohol withdrawal: chlordiazepoxide, diazepam (fastest onset, comes as injection), lorazepam (has injection) or oxazepam (preferred if liver disease). Overdose causes respiratory depression. Antidote is flumazenil.

Benzodiazepine Drug Interactions

- Additive effects with CNS depressants, including most pain medications, skeletal muscle relaxants, antihistamines, antipsychotics, anticonvulsants, mirtazapine, trazodone, alcohol, and others.

- Alprazolam is contraindicated with ketoconazole and itraconazole.

- Diazepam, clonazepam, chlordiazepoxide, alprazolam, clorazepate: ↑ levels with CYP 3A4 inhibitors; caution/lower doses if used in combination.

- Caution if used with clozapine due to ↑ risk of delirium and sedation. Avoid use with methadone, olanzapine and sodium oxybate due to additive CNS depression. Valproate increases lorazepam concentration.

Benzodiazepine Counseling

- Common side effects include drowsiness, dizziness, unsteadiness on your feet, slow reactions, lightheadedness and difficulty remembering what happened after taking the medicine. If any of these persist or worsen, contact your healthcare provider promptly.

- If you have been using the medication regularly on a daily basis (usually for more than 10 days), it cannot be stopped suddenly. To stop using it the dose will have to be decreased slowly or you will experience withdrawal, which is uncomfortable and can be dangerous.

- This medication can cause drug-seeking behavior (addiction/habit forming). Do not increase your dose, take it more frequently or use it for a longer time than prescribed. Keep the bottle in a safe place to prevent others from taking it.

- When used for an extended time, this medication may not work as well and may require a higher dose. Talk with your healthcare provider if this medication stops working well. Do not increase the amount or take it more frequently than prescribed.

- Do not take with other medications that can make you sleepy, unless directed by your healthcare provider. Other sedating medications could cause a great deal of sedation and confusion if taken together with this medication. Do not use alcohol with this medication.

- Avoid driving and doing other tasks or actions that call for you to be alert until you see how this medication affects you.

- Taking this drug during pregnancy can cause harm to the baby. This medication is not recommended during breastfeeding.

Buspirone

The mechanism is unknown, but may be due to buspirone's affinity for 5-HT_{1A} and 5-HT_2 receptors.

DRUG	DOSING	SAFETY/SIDE EFFECTS/MONITORING
BusPIRone Tablet	Start 7.5 mg PO BID Can increase by 5 mg/day Q 2-3 days, max dose is 30 mg PO BID Take with or without food; be consistent. Avoid use if severe kidney or liver impairment.	**WARNINGS** Do not use with MAO inhibitors **SIDE EFFECTS** Nausea, dizziness, drowsiness, headache, lightheadedness, excitement **NOTES** Pregnancy category B. No potential for abuse, tolerance or physiological dependence. When switching from a benzodiazepine to buspirone, the benzodiazepine should be tapered off slowly.

Buspirone Drug Interactions

- Do not use with MAO inhibitors.

- ↓ dose with erythromycin, diltiazem, itraconazole, verapamil; consider dose reduction with any 3A4 inhibitor.

- 3A4 inducers, including rifampin, may require an increase in the buspirone dose.

- Grapefruit increases the buspirone level; avoid concurrent use, or decrease buspirone dose.

Buspirone Counseling

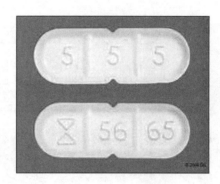

- Common side effects can include dizziness, drowsiness, nausea, or headache.

- Buspirone comes in a *Dividose* tablet designed to make dose adjustments easy. Each tablet is scored and can be broken accurately on the score lines into thirds. It snaps into pieces with finger pressure.

- Take this medication by mouth, usually 2 or 3 times a day, as directed by your healthcare provider. Take this medication with or without food, but it is important to choose one way and always take it the same way so that the amount of drug absorbed will stay the same. This medication does not have immediate effects, but takes 2 to 4 weeks to help reduce anxiety.

- Do not take with other medicines that can make you sleepy, unless directed by your healthcare provider. Do not use alcohol with this medicine.

- Grapefruit will increase the amount of buspirone in your bloodstream.

- Dosage is based on your medical condition and response to therapy. Use this medication regularly in order to get the most benefit from it. To help you remember, use it at the same times each day. When this medication is started, symptoms of anxiety (e.g., restlessness) may sometimes get worse before they improve. It may take up to a month or more to get the full effect of this medication.

- This medication is not recommended during breastfeeding.

65

SLEEP DISORDERS: INSOMNIA, RESTLESS LEGS SYNDROME (RLS) & NARCOLEPSY

GUIDELINES/REFERENCES

American Academy of Sleep Medicine: Practice Parameters for the Treatment of Narcolepsy and other Hypersomnias of Central Origin. *Sleep*. 2006; 29:11:1705-1711.

American Academy of Sleep Medicine: Practice Parameters for the Treatment of Insomnia. *Sleep*. 2007; 30:2:1415-1419.

Cappuccio FP, D'Elia L, Strazzullo P, Miller MA. Sleep duration and all-cause mortality: a systematic review and meta-analysis of prospective studies. *Sleep*. 2010; 33:585-92.

BACKGROUND

There are several types of common sleep disorders. This chapter discusses the primary types for which common prescription drug treatments are available: insomnia, restless leg syndrome and narcolepsy. A lack of restful sleep contributes to poor health and is linked to development of a number of chronic conditions, including cardiovascular disease and depression. Patients who are using chronic OTC sleep agents should be referred to a healthcare provider. The other sleep condition in the "top 4" is sleep apnea, which is treated by non-drug measures.

Insomnia

Insomnia is when a person wants to sleep but cannot. This is the most common sleep condition and occurs either when trying to get sleep (sleep initiation), with reduced duration (sleep is normally 7-9 hours) or is due to a poor sleep quality. A problem with either sleep initiation, duration or quality will contribute to daytime impairment with fatigue, somnolence, poor memory and concentration and, if long-term, chronic health conditions.

Primary treatments for insomnia include cognitive therapy and drug treatment. Cognitive therapy is preferred and includes changes to sleep hygiene (these are called "lifestyle" changes and are in the following box) that can reduce the need for drugs entirely. If a retired elderly person has a daily routine that includes watching television and napping for much of the day they may be able to eliminate night-time sleep problems by reducing the naps and taking a brisk walk earlier in the day. In some cases avoidance of caffeine later in the day is the answer. There is concern about increased mortality with the use of hypnotics--even with occasional use. The hypnotics are over-prescribed. Other cognitive therapy that can be helpful includes biofeedback where the patient is educated to monitor heart rate and muscle tension and record the daily patterns. They receive instruction on how to modify patterns to improve sleep.

DRUGS LIKELY TO CONTRIBUTE TO INSOMNIA

Bupropion

Stimulants (methylphenidate, etc.)

OTC appetite suppressants

Decongestants (pseudoephedrine, etc.)

MAO-B Inhibitors, if taken late in the day

Fluoxetine, if taken late in the day

Caffeine

Steroids

Alcohol (initially induces sleep, but prevents deeper stages of sleep and causes nocturia)

Any drug that causes urinary retention or nocturia, including antihistamines and diuretics taken later in the day.

SLEEP (INCLUDE WITH COUNSELING) HYGIENE METHODS TO IMPROVE SLEEP

Keep the bedroom dark, comfortable, and quiet

Keep a regular sleep schedule

Avoid daytime naps even after a poor night of sleep – or limit to 30 minutes

Reserve bedroom for only sleep and sex

Turn the face of clock aside to minimize anxiety about falling asleep

If unable to sleep, get up and do something to take your mind off sleeping

Establish a pre-bedtime ritual to condition your body for sleep

Relax before bedtime with soft music, mild stretching, yoga, or pleasurable reading

Avoid exercising right before bedtime

Do not eat heavy meals before bedtime

Do not take any caffeine in the afternoon

Heart failure or any condition that causes shortness of breath can worsen sleep. Anxiety and depression cause insomnia; if the condition can be corrected with psychotherapy, a prescription agent, or both, a hypnotic may not be required. When sleep hygiene issues or medical conditions cannot be corrected, or when a problem causing the insomnia has not been identified, hypnotics may be used to help provide a good night's rest.

Natural Products used for Insomnia

If insomnia is due to depression, taking St. John's wort may be helpful but this will interact with many prescription drugs. St. John's wort induces CYP 450, is a photosensitizer and is serotonergic. Chamomile tea taken in the evening helps many people feel calmer. Melatonin is useful for some patients. Valerian can be useful. There have been isolated reports of valerian causing liver toxicity; this risk is unclear at present. Check the Natural Medicines Database for doses and the current safety profile.

DRUG TREATMENT

The OTC first-generation antihistamines diphenhydramine and doxylamine are used for insomnia. Neither should be used chronically but can be helpful short-term for problems with sleep initiation and duration. Diphenhydramine has better evidence of efficacy and is available in many formulations and in less-expensive store brands. In patients using prescription agents long-term the non-benzodiazepines are preferred over benzodiazepines due to a decreased risk of physical dependence and less daytime cognitive effects. The non-controlled prescription agents are not as effective in most patients but are useful in select cases. Most commonly non-benzodiazepines, such as zolpidem, are used chronically and are preferred over the benzodiazepines that are used as hypnotics. Although this is accurate keep in mind that, if possible, drugs used chronically for sleep are now discouraged. Suvorexant *(Belsomra)* is a new agent with a unique mechanism: it blocks the orexin neuropeptide signaling system, which is involved with promoting wakefulness. Non-24-Hour Sleep-Wake Disorder, or "Non-24" is a condition where patients have difficulty with obtaining restful sleep because their circadian rhythm is not synchronized with the 24-hour day-night cycle. This can be present in persons who are totally visually blind and non-blind. Tasimelteon *(Hetlioz)* is the first drug approved for this condition. It is a melatonin receptor agonist (similar to ramelteon).

DRUG	DOSING	SAFETY/SIDE EFFECTS/MONITORING

Non-benzodiazepines: Acts selectively at the benzodiazepine receptors to increase GABA

DRUG	DOSING	SAFETY/SIDE EFFECTS/MONITORING
Zolpidem *(Ambien, Ambien CR,* generic) C-IV *Zolpimist*-spray *Edluar SL* tabs *Intermezzo SL* – for night-time awakening	5-10 mg PO QHS *Ambien CR*: 6.25-12.5 mg PO QHS *Zolpimist* 5 mg/spray (1-2 sprays) QHS *Edluar* 5-10 mg PO QHS *Intermezzo SL* 3.5 mg males, 1.75 mg females, and if using CNS depressants (decrease dose of these as well, if possible)	**WARNINGS** ↑ risk mortality (interferes with breathing at night, causes accidents/falls, confusion, and may ↑ risk infection and cancer) <u>Potential for abuse and dependence</u> **SIDE EFFECTS** <u>Somnolence</u> <u>Dizziness, ataxia</u> Lightheadedness "pins and needles" feeling on skin May cause <u>parasomnias</u> (unusual actions while sleeping – of which the patient may not be aware) Withdrawal symptoms if used longer than 2 weeks **NOTES** ***Intermezzo SL*** Do not take unless planning to sleep 4+ more hours.
Zaleplon *(Sonata)* C-IV	5-10 mg PO QHS	
Eszopiclone *(Lunesta)* C-IV Not limited to short-term use (officially, although all 3 used long-term commonly)	1-3 mg PO QHS 1 mg if difficulty falling asleep, 2 mg if difficulty staying asleep, 3 mg if helpful for longer duration	Lifestyle changes should be the primary method to improve sleep, not drugs. Preferred over benzodiazepines for 1st line treatment of insomnia due to ↓ abuse, dependence and tolerance. Do not take with fatty food, a heavy meal or alcohol.

Orexin-receptor antagonist: The orexin neuropeptide signaling system promotes wakefulness.

DRUG	DOSING	SAFETY/SIDE EFFECTS/MONITORING
Suvorexant *(Belsomra)* C-IV	10 mg QHS if at least 7 hours sleep remaining, max 20 mg	**CONTRAINDICATIONS** Narcolepsy **WARNINGS** Abnormal thinking and behavioral changes, worsening of depression/suicidal ideation, sleep paralysis, hypnagogic/ hypnopompic hallucinations, cataplexy-like symptoms **SIDE EFFECTS** Somnolence, headache, dizziness, abnormal dreams, cough, upper respiratory tract infection **NOTES** *Belsomra* may cause sleep-driving and other complex behaviors while not being fully awake. Use lower dose (5 mg) with moderate CYP 3A4 inhibitors; avoid use with strong CYP3A4 inhibitors.

Insomnia Drugs Continued

DRUG	DOSING	SAFETY/SIDE EFFECTS/MONITORING

Melatonin Receptor Agonists

DRUG	DOSING	SAFETY/SIDE EFFECTS/MONITORING
Ramelteon *(Rozerem)* For insomnia, not controlled Not limited to short-term use	8 mg PO QHS	**SIDE EFFECTS** Somnolence, dizziness **NOTES** Do not take with fatty food.
Tasimelteon *(Hetlioz)* For Non-24-Hour Sleep-Wake Disorder	20 mg PO QHS	**WARNINGS** Use is not recommended in patients with severe hepatic impairment, may have significant drug interactions; check prior to dispensing ↑ ALT, URI **SIDE EFFECTS** Headache, abnormal dreams, ALT, URI **NOTES** Can take weeks to take effect. Take without food.

Tricyclic Antidepressant

DRUG	DOSING	SAFETY/SIDE EFFECTS/MONITORING
Doxepin extended-release *(Silenor)* Not controlled Generic doxepin, traZODone, mirtazapine used off-label for sleep Used for difficulty staying asleep (sleep maintenance)	6 mg PO QHS 3 mg if ≥ 65 years	**CONTRAINDICATIONS** Requires 2 week washout for MAO Is This is an antidepressant and requires MedGuide for unusual thoughts/suicide risk **SIDE EFFECTS** Somnolence, low incidence nausea and upper respiratory infections, possibility of anticholinergic SEs

Ambien, Sonata and *Lunesta* Drug Interactions

- Caution with the use of non-benzodiazepines with potent 3A4 inhibitors (e.g., ritonavir, indinavir, saquinavir, atazanavir, ketoconazole, itraconazole, erythromycin and clarithromycin).

- Additive effects with sedating drugs, including most pain medicines, muscle relaxants, antihistamines, the antidepressant mirtazapine *(Remeron)*, trazodone, alcohol and others.

Ambien, Sonata and *Lunesta* Counseling

- If using *Zolpimist*, spray directly into your mouth over your tongue (once for a 5 mg dose, twice for a 10 mg dose). Prime the bottle if 1st-time use. If using *Edluar* SL tablets, allow tablet to dissolve under tongue; do not swallow. For *Intermezzo*: this drug is not swallowed, it dissolves under the tongue. Do not take unless you are planning to sleep 4 or more hours.

- You should not eat a heavy/high-fat meal within 2 hours of taking this medication; this may prevent the medicine from working properly.

- Call your healthcare provider if the insomnia worsens or is not better within 7 to 10 days. This may mean that there is another condition causing your sleep problem.

- Common side effects include sleepiness, lightheadedness, dizziness, "pins and needles" feeling on your skin and difficulty with coordination.

- You may still feel drowsy the next day after taking this medicine.

- This drug may (rarely) cause abnormal thoughts and behavior. Symptoms include more outgoing or aggressive behavior than normal, confusion, agitation, hallucinations, worsening of depression, and suicidal thoughts or actions. Some people have found that they get out of bed while not being fully awake and do an activity that they do not know they are doing.

- You may have withdrawal symptoms when you stop taking this medicine, if you have been taking it for more than a couple of weeks. Withdrawal symptoms include unpleasant feelings, stomach and muscle cramps, vomiting, sweating and shakiness. You may also have more trouble sleeping the first few nights after the medicine is stopped. The problem usually goes away on its own after 1 or 2 nights.

- Do not take with other medicines that can make you sleepy, unless directed by your healthcare provider. Do not use alcohol with any sleep medicine.

- After taking this medicine, you should not be driving a car or using any dangerous machinery.

- This medicine is a federally controlled substance (C-IV) because it can be abused or lead to dependence. Keep the bottle in a safe place to prevent misuse and abuse.

BENZODIAZEPINES

Potentiate GABA, an inhibitory neurotransmitter, causing CNS depression. BEERS Criteria for use in elderly: May be potentially inappropriate for use in geriatric patients.

DRUG	DOSING	SAFETY/SIDE EFFECTS/MONITORING
LORazepam (Ativan) LORazepam Intensol is solution (sol for solution) Further information on the BZDs is in the Anxiety chapter. C-IV	0.5-2 mg PO QHS	See Anxiety chapter for a full discussion; these are important agents and cause risk of physical (physiological) dependence, abuse (addiction) and tolerance. L-O-T (lorazepam, oxazepam, and temazepam): these are considered less potentially harmful for elderly or those with liver impairment since they are metabolized to inactive compounds (glucuronides); choose L-O-T if need BZD in elderly patient and for sleep. Lorazepam and Oxazepam are approved for sleep (not Temazepam).
Temazepam (Restoril) C-IV	7.5-30 mg PO QHS	
Estazolam (Prosom) C-IV		Cannot use with potent 3A4 inhibitors
Quazepam (Doral) C-IV		Caution when use in elderly due to its long half-life: risk of falls, fractures
Flurazepam C-IV		Caution when use in elderly due to its long half-life: risk of falls, fractures
Triazolam (Halcion) C-IV		Associated with higher rebound insomnia and daytime anxiety; Tapering upon discontinuation. Contraindicated with efavirenz (Sustiva), delavirdine (Rescriptor), azole antifungals, and protease inhibitors & all 3A4 Inhibitors

Benzodiazepine Drug Interactions: refer to Anxiety chapter for complete counseling.

Additional Counseling when Used for Sleep

- This medication should be taken before bedtime. Take the medicine immediately prior to sleep. Do not do anything dangerous, such as driving a car, after taking the medicine. Do not mix with alcohol.

ANTIHISTAMINES

Compete with (block) histamine H1 receptors.

DRUG	DOSING	SAFETY/SIDE EFFECTS/MONITORING
Diphenhydramine *(Benadryl, Sominex, Unisom, others, store brands)*	25-50 mg PO QHS	**SIDE EFFECTS** Possible anticholinergic side effects: Sedation; tolerance to sedative effects can develop after 10 days use. Confusion (can exaccerbate memory/cognition difficulty)
Doxylamine *(Aldex, Unisom Nighttime, store brands)*	25 mg PO QHS	Peripheral anticholinergic side effects: Dry mouth Urinary retention (will make it very difficult for males with BPH to urinate, can slow down/delay urination in females) Dry/blurry vision, risk increased IOP Constipation Best to avoid use in BPH (may worsen symptoms) and glaucoma (may elevate IOP). Beer's drug; avoid use in elderly due to risk of confusion, dry mouth, constipation.

Diphenhydramine *(Benadryl)* Counseling (for all indications – applies to other sedating antihistamines)

- Diphenhydramine is an antihistamine used to relieve symptoms of allergy, hay fever and the common cold. These symptoms include rash, itching, watery eyes, itchy eyes/nose/throat, cough, runny nose and sneezing. It is also used to prevent and treat nausea, vomiting and dizziness caused by motion sickness. Diphenhydramine can also be used to help you relax and fall asleep. It is occasionally used for involuntary movements and muscle stiffness from Parkinson's disease.

- When using this medicine, you will become sleepy. It can also make you feel confused and make it difficult to concentrate.

- Do not take with other medicines that can make you sleepy, unless directed by your doctor. Do not use alcohol with any sleep medicine.

- This medicine should not be used by patients with an enlarged prostate, or BPH, without getting approval. It will temporarily make urination more difficult.

- If you have glaucoma, discuss use with your eye doctor. It may raise your the pressure in your eyes.

- If you have problems with constipation, this medicine will worsen the constipation.

- This medicine can cause your eyes to become dry and your vision to become blurry. It can also cause dry mouth.

- This medicine can make it difficult to urinate (it will take longer for the urine to come out).

- Although this drug is meant to be sedating, some children will experience excitability instead.

- After taking this medicine, you should not drive a car or use any dangerous machinery.

- Take the tablet, capsule, or liquid form by mouth, with or without food. Diphenhydramine may be taken with food or milk if stomach upset occurs. If you are taking the suspension, shake the bottle well before each dose. Measure liquid forms of this medication with a dose-measuring spoon or device, not a regular teaspoon, to make sure you have the correct dose.

- The rapidly-dissolving tablet or strip should be allowed to dissolve on the tongue and then swallowed, with or without water. A second strip may be taken after the first strip has dissolved. The chewable tablets should be chewed thoroughly before being swallowed.

- To prevent motion sickness, take your dose 30 minutes before starting activity such as travel. To help you sleep, take your dose about 30 minutes before bedtime. If you continue to have difficulty sleeping for longer than 2 weeks, contact your doctor.

RESTLESS LEGS SYNDROME

Restless legs syndrome (RLS) is an urge to move the lower legs which is sometimes described as a "creeping" sensation. RLS is worse at night and is relieved with movement. RLS is thought to be due to a dysfunction with dopamine in the brain's basal ganglia circuits. The primary treatment is dopamine agonists (most commonly) and the anticonvulsant gabapentin.

Drug Treatment

Pramipexole *(Mirapex)* and ropinirole *(Requip)* are dopamine agonists primarily used in longer-acting formulations for Parkinson disease, or are taken TID. For RLS these are taken in the immediate-release (IR) formulations 1-3 hours before bedtime. Rotigotine *(Neupro)* is a dopamine agonist that comes in a patch formulation that is also used for Parkinson disease and RLS. For both conditions the patch is applied once daily. Parkinson patients usually start with the 2 mg patch and RLS treatment begins with the 1 mg patch. Patients must be told not to apply a heat source over the patch and to remove the patch if receiving an MRI procedure. This patch causes skin irritation; the same site cannot be used again for 14 days. The patch contains a sulfite (metabisulfite) and in sulfite-sensitive patients will cause an allergic reaction.

Dopamine agonists cause orthostasis, somnolence, and nausea that is dose-related. Even when used for RLS the dose is titrated upwards carefully (slowly). Patients should be monitored for psychiatric concerns (hallucinations, abnormal dreams) and movement disorders.

Gabapentin enacarbil *(Horizant)* is approved for postherpetic neuralgia (PHN) and RLS. With any indication gabapentin requires a reduced dose with renal impairment (CrCl < 60 mL/min) to avoid increased side effects (dizziness, somnolence, ataxia, peripheral edema, weight gain, diplopia, blurred vision, dry mouth). The tablet is taken with food and must be swallowed whole (it cannot be crushed or chewed). For RLS it is taken at ~5:00 PM daily. The IR formulation of gabapentin is used off-label as a less-expensive alternative. Refer to the Parkinson Disease chapter for additional information on the dopamine agonists, and the Epilepsy/Seizures chapter for additional information on gabapentin.

NARCOLEPSY

Narcolepsy is excessive daytime sleepiness with cataplexy (sudden loss of muscle tone) and sleep paralysis. Narcolepsy causes sudden daytime "sleep attacks" especially when the person is in a relaxed setting due to poor control of normal sleep-wake cycles. The sleep attacks last a few seconds to several minutes. Patients have difficulty managing with narcolepsy; they can fall asleep while at work, school, or in the middle of a conversation. And, the sleep quality at night is poor.

Drug Treatment

Narcolepsy is treated with stimulants, such as modafinil or armodafinil or with sodium oxybate, which is derived from the inhibitory neurotransmitter gamma aminobutyric acid (GABA). Several of the stimulants used primarily for ADHD have narcolepsy indications, including dextroamphetamine, dextroamphetamine/amphetamine *(Adderall)* and various methylphenidate formulations *(Metadate ER, Methylin, Ritalin* and *Ritalin SR)*. Patients may be using drugs approved for other indications: selegiline can be useful for daytime sleepiness, and tricyclic antidepressants or fluoxetine can be useful for cataplexy. These are drugs used to improve wakefulness in adult patients with excessive sleepiness associated with narcolepsy, obstructive sleep apnea/hypopnea syndrome, and shift work sleep disorder.

Stimulants for Wakefulness

DRUG	DOSING	SAFETY/SIDE EFFECTS/MONITORING
Modafinil *(Provigil)* C-IV	200 mg daily	**SIDE EFFECTS** Headache, dizziness, anxiety, agitation, nausea, diarrhea, insomnia, dry mouth, risk of severe rash. **WARNINGS** Avoid use with pre-existing cardiac conditions. Use with caution with hepatic impairment, renal impairment, psychiatric disorders and Tourette's. **NOTES** Both of these agents require a MedGuide due to risk of severe rash, which can be life-threatening.
Armodafinil *(Nuvigil)* R-isomer of modafinil; similar drug C-IV	150-250 mg daily	Similar side effects, similar drug to modafinil, including risk of severe rash – give MedGuide.

Note: Additional stimulants indicated for weight loss in weight loss/gain chapter, and the ADHD stimulants are sometimes used for these conditions.

Sodium oxybate is derived from GABA. Indicated for narcolepsy with cataplexy (sudden loss of muscle strength). Helps with sleep at night, generally used with daytime stimulants.

DRUG	DOSING	SAFETY/SIDE EFFECTS/MONITORING
Sodium oxybate *(Xyrem)* C-III (narcolepsy) C-I (abuse) REMS program: this is a "date rape" drug (sedative, called GHB) that requires strict measures to ensure it is going to narcolepsy with cataplexy patients only.	Start 2.25 g QHS and again 2.5-4 hours later after 1st dose; titrate to effect, dosing range ~6-9 g/night	**BOXED WARNINGS** Respiratory depression (strong CNS depressant). Sodium oxybate is a salt form of hydroxybutyrate (GHB), a drug of abuse. Danger is increased when taken with other CNS depressants; coma and death can result. Restricted access through the REMS *Xyrem* Success Program. **SIDE EFFECTS** Dizziness, nausea, somnolence, enuresis (dose-related), daytime hangover effect **NOTES** Taken in ¼ cup water, usually in an empty pharmacy pill container. Patient should lie down immediately after taking and stay in bed. The second dose is taken 2.5-4 hours after the first. Will typically fall asleep within 5-15 minutes after taking 1st dose. Contains a high sodium content.

66

EPILEPSY/SEIZURES

We gratefully acknowledge the assistance of Kimberly B. Tallian, PharmD, BCPP, FASHP, FCCP, FCSHP, Psychiatry/Neurology Pharmacy Specialist, Scripps Mercy Hospital, San Diego, in preparing this chapter.

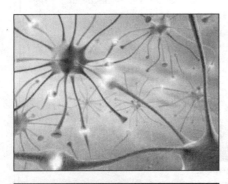

GUIDELINES/REFERENCES

Drugs for Epilepsy Treatment Guidelines, Medical Letter 2013;11(126): 9-18.

Practice Parameter Update: Management Issues for Women with Epilepsy – Focus on Pregnancy (an Evidence-Based Review): Obstetrical Complications and Change in Seizure Frequency: Report of the Quality Standards Subcommittee and Therapeutics and Technology Assessment Subcommittee of the American Academy of Neurology and American Epilepsy Society. *Neurology.* 2009;73:133-141.

Efficacy and tolerability of the new antiepileptic drugs I: Treatment of new onset epilepsy: Report of the Therapeutics and Technology Assessment Subcommittee and Quality Standards Subcommittee of the American Academy of Neurology and the American Epilepsy Society. *Neurology.* 2004;62:1252-1260.

BACKGROUND

Epilepsy is a disorder of the brain that causes seizures and affects 2.9 million adults and children in the United States. Seizures are the outward occurrence that result from abnormal, excessive and synchronous activity from a group of neurons. Seizures can vary widely from uncontrolled jerking movements (tonic-clonic seizure) to a subtle momentary loss of awareness (absence seizure). Unfortunately, many patients do not have complete seizure control, even with medications. Seizures can damage and destroy neurons, which can cause cognitive deficits and be life-threatening.

PATHOPHYSIOLOGY

Seizures can result from an imbalance between excitatory and inhibitory neurotransmitters. Excess excitatory neurotransmitters (norepinephrine, acetylcholine, histamine, corticotropin releasing factor, glutamate), altered receptor sensitivity to the neurotransmitters, or reduced function or deficiency of inhibitory neurotransmitters (gamma-aminobutyric acid, or GABA) can provoke seizures.

DIAGNOSIS

Many factors are evaluated for a diagnosis of epilepsy including age of onset, seizure type and frequency, description of witnessed seizure, identifiable causes or triggers and a thorough neurological exam. An electroencephalogram (EEG), the most common test used to diagnose epilepsy, records electrical activity of the brain, or brain waves. The EEG may show abnormal spike and wave patterns even when the patient is not having a seizure. Imaging of the brain (e.g., CT of the head, MRI) may also be done to detect causes of the seizures such as tumors, bleeding and cysts.

INTERNATIONAL CLASSIFICATION OF SEIZURE TYPES

SEIZURE TYPE	SYMPTOMS

Partial (Focal) Seizures - Partial seizures start in one hemisphere of the brain, but can spread to the other hemisphere resulting in secondarily generalized seizures (see next category below). If there is <u>no loss of consciousness</u>, the seizure is called <u>simple partial</u>. If there is <u>loss of consciousness</u>, the seizure is termed <u>complex partial</u>.

Simple Partial Seizures (<u>consciousness not impaired</u>)	Motor (muscles contract/relax, eye movements, head turning)
	Autonomic (incontinence, nausea, sweating, tachycardia)
	Sensory (flashes of light, noises, dizziness, unpleasant odors/tastes)
	Psychic (detachment, time/memory distortions, unprovoked emotions)
Complex Partial Seizures (<u>impaired consciousness</u>)	Features of simple partial (see above)
	Automatisms (repetitive behaviors that serve no purpose, such as lip smacking, fumbling, picking at something)

Generalized Seizures - begin in both hemispheres of the brain and result in a <u>loss of consciousness</u>.

Absence Seizures (formerly called petit mal)	Brief and abrupt <u>staring</u> spells lasting 10–30 seconds
Myoclonic Seizures	Brief, lightning-like jerk movements of entire body
Tonic-Clonic Seizures (formerly called grand mal)	Characterized by five phases: Flexion, extension, tremor, clonic and loss of consciousness
Tonic Seizures	Flexion and/or extension only (flexion ↓ angle, extension ↑ angle - the hand/arms/feet/legs open and close, or thrash)
Clonic Seizures	Rhythmic, repetitive, jerking muscle movements
Atonic Seizures	Loss of muscle tone and falls to the ground; known as "drop attacks"

STATUS EPILEPTICUS

Seizures lasting <u>longer than 5 minutes</u> or <u>2 or more</u> seizures between which the patient <u>does not regain consciousness</u> are called <u>status epilepticus (SE), which is a medical emergency</u>. Treatment consists of using a rapid-acting benzodiazepine first (e.g., lorazepam), followed by antiepileptic drug (AED) therapy (loading dose followed by maintenance dose). <u>Lorazepam (Ativan) is the benzodiazepine of choice</u> for treating status epilepticus due to the longer duration of action in the CNS which provides longer protection. Diazepam is highly lipophilic (quick onset) but rapidly redistributes into fat causing the CNS half-life to be shorter, with a shorter duration of effect. Drug therapy is often selected depending on the patient's access site (e.g., if no IV access, need to give IM or rectal).

- Lorazepam: 4 mg given slow IV (adults); max rate 2 mg/min, may repeat in 5 – 10 minutes if no response. May be given IM, but IV is preferred. If IV access is not established, midazolam can be given IM.

- Diazepam: 5 – 10 mg given slow IV (≤ 5 mg/minute), may repeat every 5 – 15 min; max dose is 30 mg.

- Diazepam rectal gel *(Diastat AcuDial)*: 2.5 – 20 mg PR (age and weight-based). May repeat once if necessary. It is important to check that the dose has been dialed correctly and locked for both syringes prior to dispensing.

- Follow initial benzodiazepine treatment with phenytoin (max rate 50 mg/minute) or fosphenytoin (max rate 150 mg PE/min).

- If the initial bolus did not control the seizure activity, the patient will be switched to an alternative AED (e.g., IV valproate sodium or levetiracetam) or given a continuous infusion (e.g., IV midazolam, phenobarbital, propofol, thiopental).

NON-DRUG TREATMENT

A ketogenic diet is often used in patients with refractory seizures (not responding to medications), primarily in children. The diet contains high fats, normal protein and low carbohydrates (usually a 4:1 ratio of fats to combined protein and carbohydrates), which forces the body to breakdown fatty acids into ketone bodies as an energy source. Ketone bodies pass into the brain and replace glucose. This elevated ketone state, ketosis, can lead to a reduction in seizure frequency.

MEDICAL MARIJUANA AND EPILEPSY

Presently, it is unknown if marijuana is a safe and effective treatment for epilepsy, including the impact on cognitive function. Safety concerns coupled with a lack of evidence of efficacy in clinical trials does not support the use of marijuana for the treatment of seizures at this time. Two phase III clinical trials are currently underway to evaluate the safety and efficacy of cannabidiol as adjunctive treatment in children and adults with inadequately controlled Dravet or Lennox-Gastaut syndromes. Pharmacists should keep in mind that there are parents who have seen improved seizure control in their child; these are select cases. In such situations, consider the impact of increased drug metabolism, which may require dose adjustments of other medications.

DRUGS/CONDITIONS THAT CAN LOWER THE SEIZURE THRESHOLD
Antipsychotics (e.g., clozapine, phenothiazines, butyrophenones)
Antivirals (e.g., amantadine, rimantadine, foscarnet, ganciclovir, valganciclovir, acyclovir IV)
Bupropion
Carbapenems (with higher doses/renal impairment – especially imipenem)
Cephalosporins
Lindane
Lithium and theophylline (in toxicity)
Mefloquine
Meperidine (chronic dosing with poor renal function)
Metoclopramide
Natural products such as dendrobium, evening primrose oil, gingko, melatonin
Penicillins
Quinolones
Sleep deprivation, alcohol intoxication, menstruation, infection and fever (especially in children) can worsen seizure.
Tramadol

DRUG TREATMENT

An accurate diagnosis of seizure type, classification and frequency is critical to selecting an appropriate AED. Other factors are assessed such age, long-term side effect profile, comorbidities, insurance coverage and willingness to adhere to treatment. Monotherapy is preferred and 50 – 70% of patients are maintained on one drug. Many patients do not become seizure-free on monotherapy, and a second medication may be added. Treatment goals include seizure freedom or a reduction in seizure frequency while minimizing adverse effects of the medication. Roughly 30% of patients will have refractory seizures despite medication. Refer to the table of the most commonly used treatments per seizure type.

The most common side effects with AEDs are CNS-related, including somnolence, fatigue, cognitive impairment and coordination abnormalities such as ataxia and dizziness since these drugs have to penetrate the CNS to be effective. Side effects such as confusion and sedation can make it difficult for children to do well in school and for adults to perform well at work.

When AEDs are used in women of reproductive age, it is important to consider teratogenicity risk and provide proper counseling. Carbamazepine, clonazepam, phenobarbital/primidone, phenytoin/fosphenytoin, topiramate and valproic acid are pregnancy category D – this means that there is known fetal risk, and the benefit must outweigh the risk. Healthcare providers should always consider that untreated or inadequately treated epilepsy during pregnancy ↑ the risk of complications in both the pregnant mother and her developing baby. Valproic acid is thought to have the highest risk of fetal harm. Valproic acid is pregnancy category X for migraine prophylaxis; otherwise, it is category D. Recently, the FDA issued a warning that valproic acid is associated with ↓ IQ scores in children following in utero exposure. All other AEDs are pregnancy category C. The metabolism of some of the AEDs increases during pregnancy (lamotrigine and others), resulting in breakthrough seizures. This can require a higher dose, which can ↑ risk to the fetus. Managing epilepsy during pregnancy is complex.

FIRST AID FOR SEIZURES

First aid for seizures involves responding in ways that can keep the person safe until the seizure stops by itself:

- Keep calm and reassure other people who may be nearby.
- Prevent injury by clearing the area around the person of anything hard or sharp.
- Ease the person to the floor and put something soft and flat, like a folded jacket, under the head. Turn the person gently onto one side. This will help keep the airway clear.
- Remove eyeglasses and loosen ties or anything around the neck that may make breathing difficult.
- Time the seizure with a watch. If the seizure continues for longer than five minutes without signs of slowing down or if the person has trouble breathing afterwards, appears to be injured, in pain, or has an unusual recovery, call 911.
- Do not hold people down or try to stop their movements.
- Contrary to popular belief, it is not true that people having a seizure can swallow their tongue. Do not put anything in the person's mouth. Efforts to hold the tongue down can injure the teeth or jaw.
- Do not attempt artificial respiration except in the unlikely event that a person does not start breathing again after the seizure has stopped.
- Stay with the person until the seizure ends naturally and the person is fully awake.
- Do not offer the person water or food until fully alert.
- Be friendly and reassuring as consciousness returns.
- Offer to call a taxi, friend or relative to help the person get home safely, particularly if the person seems confused or unable to get home without help.

There are many drug interactions with most of the AEDs. Several of the AEDs are strong inducers and can ↓ the concentration of other drugs, including other AEDs the patient may be taking. AEDs that are inducers include carbamazepine, eslicarbazepine, oxcarbazepine, fosphenytoin, perampanel, phenytoin, phenobarbital, primidone and topiramate (≥ 200 mg/day).

Individuals with epilepsy may have ↑ fracture risk. Bone loss can occur as soon as two years after the start of AED therapy. Modifiable factors that affect bone density should be addressed (see Osteoporosis, Menopause & Testosterone Replacement chapter). The mechanism of AED-induced bone loss is not completely understood. Hepatic enzyme inducers ↓ vitamin D levels by ↑ metabolism, which ↓ calcium absorption. All patients on enzyme-inducing AEDs should supplement with vitamin D and calcium.

All AEDs require a MedGuide due to the risk of suicidality. The MedGuide warning states: "Like other antiepileptic drugs, this medication may cause suicidal thoughts or actions in a very small number of people, about 1 in 500." This warning is not repeated in the drug tables.

Seizure drugs are <u>titrated upwards</u> when initiated to ↓ side effects and ↓ toxicity risk. <u>Never discontinue abruptly</u>. This will cause or worsen seizures. <u>Taper</u> the medication off slowly. Often, the new drug is being titrated up while the old drug is being titrated off (to continue providing seizure control), unless the patient is discontinuing treatment entirely.

Treatment of Choice

SEIZURE TYPE	1ST LINE TREATMENT
Partial, including secondarily generalized	Carbamazepine
	Lamotrigine
	Levetiracetam
	Oxcarbazepine
Primary Generalized Tonic-Clonic	Lamotrigine
	Levetiracetam
	Valproic acid
Absence	Ethosuximide
	Valproic acid
Atypical Absence, Myoclonic, Atonic	Ethosuximide
	Lamotrigine
	Levetiracetam
	Valproic acid

COMMONLY USED/IMPORTANT ANTICONVULSANTS

Levetiracetam

Mechanism of action is unknown; may inhibit voltage-dependent N-type calcium channels, facilitate GABA-ergic inhibitory transmission through displacement of negative modulators, reduce delayed rectifier potassium current and/or bind to synaptic proteins which modulate neurotransmitter release.

DRUG	DOSING	SAFETY/SIDE EFFECTS/MONITORING
LevETIRAcetam (Keppra, Keppra XR, Spritam) Tablet, solution, injection Adjunctive therapy for several seizure types (myoclonic, partial and tonic-clonic seizures)	Initial: 500 mg BID or 1,000 mg daily (XR) Maximum: 3,000 mg/d CrCl ≤ 80 mL/min: ↓ dose IV:PO ratio 1:1	**WARNINGS** <u>Behavioral abnormalities and psychotic symptoms</u>, severe skin reactions (SJS/TEN), hematologic abnormalities (mainly anemias) **SIDE EFFECTS** <u>Somnolence, fatigue, irritability, dizziness, weakness</u>, asthenia **MONITORING** Mental status and seizure frequency **NOTES** Pregnancy Category C <u>No significant drug interactions</u> *Spritam* uses ZipDose technology with 3D printing to produce a porous tablet fomulation that <u>rapidly dissolves with a sip of liquid</u>.

Lamotrigine

Lamotrigine inhibits voltage-sensitive sodium channels, thereby stabilizing neuronal membranes and decreasing presynaptic transmitter release of glutamate (an excitatory amino acid).

DRUG	DOSING	SAFETY/SIDE EFFECTS/MONITORING
LamoTRIgine *LaMICtal, LaMICtal Starter, LaMICtal ODT, LaMICtal XR* Tablet, chewable, ODT Adjunctive therapy for partial seizures, or conversion to primary therapy from older drugs, bipolar	Starting Dose Week 1 and 2: 25 mg daily Week 3 and 4: 50 mg daily Week 5 and on: can ↑ by 50 mg daily every 1-2 weeks. Maintenance Dose: 300-400 mg daily Divide BID, unless using XR (daily) Higher doses (50 mg daily week 1 and 2) if taking hepatic inducers of glucuronidation (carbamazepine, phenytoin, phenobarbital, primidone, rifampin, and lopinavir/ritonavir); Lower doses if taking valproic acid (25 mg every other day week 1 and 2)	**BOXED WARNING** Serious skin reactions, including SJS/TEN (rate of rash is greater in pediatrics than adults); ↑ risk with higher than recommended starting doses, dose escalation, or co-administration of valproic acid. To ↓ risk of rash, use correct starting dose and follow the titration schedule– *Lamictal Starter Kit* and *Lamictal ODT Patient Titration Kits* provide the recommended dose/titration schedule for the first 5 weeks. Titration schedule is based on concomitant medications (see dosing). Discontinue at the first sign of rash and do not reinitiate. **WARNINGS** Risk of aseptic meningitis, blood dyscrasias, multiorgan hypersensitivity (DRESS) reactions **SIDE EFFECTS** N/V, somnolence, rash, tremor, ataxia, impaired coordination, dizziness, diplopia, blurred vision, alopecia (treat with a multivitamin with minerals as it needs to contain selenium and zinc) **MONITORING** LFTs, s/sx of rash, seizure frequency **NOTES** Pregnancy Category C Discontinue if any sign of hypersensitivity reaction or unspecified rash Comes in C-R (child-resistant) packaging. Starter kit packaging for those not taking interacting medications is orange; for those taking valproic acid is blue; for those taking an inducer is green.

Lamotrigine Drug Interactions

- Valproic acid ↑ lamotrigine concentrations more than 2-fold. Use the lower dose starter kit (blue box) upon initiation if currently taking valproic acid.

- Carbamazepine, phenytoin, phenobarbital, primidone and rifampin ↓ lamotrigine levels by 40%. Use the higher dose starter kit (green box) when using these drugs concurrently.

- Oral estrogen-containing contraceptives ↓ lamotrigine levels by 50%; monitor as a higher dose of lamotrigine may be needed.

- Lopinavir/ritonavir ↓ lamotrigine levels by 50%; atazanavir/ritonavir ↓ lamotrigine levels by 32%.

- Caution for additive CNS effects, including dizziness, somnolence, fatigue.

Carbamazepine

Fast sodium channel blocker; structurally similar to tricyclic antidepressants (TCAs); stimulates release of antidiuretic hormone (ADH), promoting reabsorption of water. In addition to anticonvulsant effects, carbamazepine has anticholinergic, antineuralgic, antidiuretic, muscle relaxant, antimanic, antidepressive and antiarrhythmic properties.

DRUG	DOSING	SAFETY/SIDE EFFECTS/MONITORING
CarBAMazepine *(TEGretol, TEGretol XR, Carbatrol, Epitol)* Capsule, tablet, chewable, suspension Indicated for many seizure types (except absence seizures) and indicated for trigeminal neuralgia *Equetro* – for bipolar	Initial: 200 mg BID or divided QID (suspension) Maximum: 1,600 mg/day (some patients may require more) **Therapeutic Range** <u>4-12 mcg/mL</u> Carbamazepine levels should be monitored within 3-5 days of initiation <u>and again after 4 weeks</u> due to autoinduction.	**BOXED WARNINGS** <u>Serious skin reactions</u>, including SJS/TEN: Patients of Asian descent should be tested for <u>HLA-B*1502</u> allele prior to initiation; if positive for this allele, carbamazepine cannot be used (unless benefit clearly outweighs risk) <u>Aplastic anemia</u> and <u>agranulocytosis; monitor CBC, platelets, and differential</u> prior to and during therapy; discontinue if significant myelosuppression occurs **CONTRAINDICATIONS** Myelosuppression, hypersensitivity to TCAs, use of MAO inhibitors within past 14 days, concurrent use of nefazodone, concomitant use of delavirdine or other non-nucleoside reverse transcriptase inhibitors **WARNINGS** Risk of developing a hypersensitivity reaction may be ↑ in patients with the variant HLA-A*3101 allele Multiorgan hypersensitivity (DRESS) reactions <u>Hyponatremia (SIADH)</u>, hypothyroidism Mild anticholinergic effects, cardiac conduction abnormalities Renal impairment/hepatic impairment: use with caution **SIDE EFFECTS** <u>Dizziness, somnolence, N/V, ataxia, dry mouth, pruritus, photosensitivity, blurred vision, rash, vitamin D and calcium deficiency (bone loss), ↑ LFTs</u>, alopecia (treat with a multivitamin with minerals as it needs to contain selenium and zinc) **MONITORING** CBC with differential, platelets, LFTs, s/sx of rash, ophthalmic exam, thyroid function tests, electrolytes (especially Na), renal function, mental status, seizure frequency, carbamazepine levels **NOTES** Pregnancy Category D Potent CYP450 <u>inducer</u> and <u>autoinducer</u> – ↓ level of many other drugs and of itself <u>Supplementation with calcium and vitamin D recommended</u>

Carbamazepine Drug Interactions

- Carbamazepine is a strong inducer of many enzymes (1A2, 2C19, 2C8/9, 3A4), P-glycoprotein (P-gp) and is an <u>autoinducer</u>. It will ↓ the levels of many drugs, including hormonal contraceptives, other seizure medications, levothyroxine, warfarin and others. <u>Use of an alternative, nonhormonal contraceptive is recommended</u>.

- Carbamazepine is a major 3A4 substrate. 3A4 inhibitors will ↑ carbamazepine levels and 3A4 inducers will ↓ carbamazepine levels. Avoid use with nefazodone and non-nucleoside reverse transcriptase inhibitors.

- Caution for additive CNS effects, including dizziness, somnolence, fatigue.

Oxcarbazepine

Oxcarbazepine (OXC) is a prodrug that converts to active 10-monohydroxy derivative (MHD). Both OXC and MHD are voltage-sensitive sodium channel blockers, inhibiting repetitive firing and decreasing the propagation of synaptic impulses. Modulates activity at calcium channels.

DRUG	DOSING	SAFETY/SIDE EFFECTS/MONITORING
OXcarbazepine (Trileptal, Oxtellar XR) Tablet, suspension *(Trileptal)*, extended-release tablet *(Oxtellar XR)* Partial seizures	Initial: 300 mg BID *(Trileptal)*; 600 mg daily *(Oxtellar XR)* Maximum: 2,400 mg/day CrCl < 30 mL/min: start 300 mg daily Carbamazepine to oxcarbazepine dose conversion: 1.2 – 1.5x carbamazepine dose Extended release – take on empty stomach 1 hour before or 2 hours after meals	**WARNINGS** Hypersensitivity reactions to carbamazepine have 25-30% cross-sensitivity to oxcarbazepine ↑ risk for SJS/TEN, consider screening patients of Asian descent for HLA-B*1502 prior to initiating therapy Multiorgan hypersensitivity (DRESS) reactions Hyponatremia Hypothyroidism **SIDE EFFECTS** Somnolence, dizziness, N/V, abdominal pain, diplopia, visual disturbances, ataxia, tremor, vitamin D and calcium deficiency (bone loss) **MONITORING** Serum Na levels especially during first 3 months of therapy (hyponatremia more common than with carbamazepine), thyroid function, CBC, mental status, seizure frequency **NOTES** Pregnancy Category C Supplementation with calcium and vitamin D recommended *Trileptal* oral suspension – once bottle is open use within 7 weeks

Oxcarbazepine Drug Interactions

- Oxcarbazepine is a weak 3A4 inducer and 2C19 inhibitor, but is not an auto-inducer. Strong 344 inducers can ↓ oxcarbazepine levels. Oxcarbazepine/MHD can ↑ levels of fosphenytoin, phenytoin and phenobarbital.

- Oxcarbazepine may ↓ hormonal contraceptive levels significantly. Use of an alternative, nonhormonal contraceptive is recommended.

- Caution for additive CNS effects, including dizziness, somnolence, fatigue.

Valproic Acid/Valproate

Valproic acid causes ↑ availability of gamma (γ)-aminobutyric acid (GABA), an inhibitory neurotransmitter. Divalproex sodium is a compound of sodium valproate and valproic acid. Divalproex dissociates to valproate in the GI tract.

DRUG	DOSING	SAFETY/SIDE EFFECTS/MONITORING
Valproate/Valproic acid (Depakene, Stavzor, Depacon) *Depakene* – capsule, syrup *Stavzor* – delayed-release capsule *Depacon* – IV **Divalproex (Depakote, Depakote ER, Depakote Sprinkle)** *Depakote* – delayed-release tablet *Depakote ER* – extended-release tablet *Depakote Sprinkle* – capsules can be opened and sprinkled on food Delayed-release divalproex ↓ GI upset Also used for bipolar and migraine prophylaxis	Initial: 10-15 mg/kg/day Maximum: 60 mg/kg/day **Therapeutic Range** 50-100 mcg/mL (some patients may need higher levels) ER tablets *(Depakote ER)* are not bioequivalent to delayed release tablets *(Depakote)*. For bioequivalence, increase total daily dose by 8-20% when converting to extended-release tablets. If the albumin is low (< 3.5 g/dL) the true valproic acid level will be higher than it appears – adjust with the same formula used for phenytoin.	**BOXED WARNINGS** Hepatic Failure: Occurs rarely in adults (1:50,000) usually during first 6 months of therapy. Children (1:600) under the age of two years and patients with mitochondrial disorders (mutations in mitochondrial DNA polymerase gamma (POLG) gene) are at ↑ risk. Monitor LFTs frequently during the first 6 months Teratogenicity: Including neural tube defects (e.g., spina bifida) and ↓ IQ scores following *in utero* exposure Pancreatitis: Can be fatal in children and adults **CONTRAINDICATIONS** Hepatic disease, urea cycle disorders, prophylaxis of migraine in pregnancy, known mitochondrial disorders caused by mutations in mitochondrial DNA POLG and suspected POLG-related disorder in children < 2 years of age **WARNINGS** Hyperammonemia (treat with carnitine in symptomatic adults only), hypothermia, dose-related thrombocytopenia (↑ bleeding risk), multiorgan hypersensitivity (DRESS) reactions **SIDE EFFECTS** N/V, anorexia, abdominal pain, dizziness, somnolence, tremor, alopecia (treat with a multivitamin with minerals as it needs to contain selenium and zinc), weight gain, edema, polycystic ovary syndrome (PCOS), vitamin D and calcium deficiency (bone loss), diplopia, blurred vision **MONITORING** LFTs (at baseline and frequently during first 6 months), CBC with differential, platelets, serum drug concentrations, mental status changes, seizures **NOTES** Pregnancy Category D/X (for migraine prophylaxis) Supplementation with calcium and vitamin D recommended

Valproic Acid/Valproate Drug Interactions

- Valproic acid is an inhibitor of 2C9 (weak) and is a substrate of 2C19 (minor) and 2E1 (minor).

- Valproic acid can ↑ levels of lamotrigine, phenobarbital, phenytoin, warfarin and zidovudine.

- Use special caution with combination of valproic acid and lamotrigine due to risk of serious rash; use lower starting dose of lamotrigine and titrate slowly.

- Combination with topiramate can lead to hyperammonemia ± encephalopathy.

- Salicylates displace valproic acid from albumin and ↑ levels.

- Carbapenems (imipenem, meropenem etc.) can ↓ the levels of valproic acid.

- Caution for additive CNS effects, including dizziness, somnolence, fatigue.

Phenytoin/Fosphenytoin

<u>Fast sodium channel blockers</u> that stabilize neuronal membranes and reduce seizures by increasing efflux or decreasing influx of Na ions.

DRUG	DOSING	SAFETY/SIDE EFFECTS/MONITORING
Phenytoin *(Dilantin, Dilantin Infatabs, Phenytek)* Capsule, chewable, suspension, injection (IV only) Generalized tonic-clonic, complex partial; prevention of seizures following neurosurgery **Fosphenytoin** *(Cerebyx)* Injection <u>Prodrug of phenytoin (IV/IM)</u>	Phenytoin: 15-20 mg/kg loading dose; up to 300-600 mg/day Fosphenytoin should always be dosed in phenytoin equivalents (PE): 1 mg PE = 1 mg phenytoin (fosphenytoin 1.5 mg = phenytoin 1 mg = 1 mg PE) **Therapeutic Range** <u>Total PHT: 10-20 mcg/mL</u> Free PHT: 1-2.5 mcg/mL (roughly $^1/_{10}$th of the total PHT level) <u>Exhibits saturable, or Michaelis-Menten, kinetics</u>; a <u>small change in dose</u> can cause a <u>large change in serum level</u> <u>If the albumin (alb) is low (< 3.5 g/dL), the true phenytoin level will be higher</u> than it appears – adjust with formula below (if CrCl ≥ 10 mL/min) or measure a free phenytoin level. $$PHT\ correction = \frac{PHT\ measured}{(0.2 \times alb) + 0.1}$$ With CrCl < 10 mL/min and low albumin, use correction formula: $$PHT\ correction = \frac{PHT\ measured}{(0.1 \times alb) + 0.1}$$ IV:PO ratio <u>1:1</u> <u>Enteral feedings ↓ phenytoin absorption; hold feedings 1-2 hours prior and 1-2 hours after phenytoin administration</u> <u>Phenytoin IV is compatible with NS only, requires a filter and is stable for 4 hours</u>; do not refrigerate as may cause precipitation (which may dissolve upon warming). Fosphenytoin can be mixed with NS or D5W and is refrigerated (stable for 48 hrs at room temperature; 30 days if refrigerated).	**BOXED WARNINGS** Phenytoin IV administration should <u>not exceed 50 mg/minute</u> and fosphenytoin IV administration should <u>not exceed 150 mg PE/minute</u> in adults; if faster hypotension and cardiac arrhythmias can occur. **WARNINGS** Extravasation: IV phenytoin is a vesicant; can cause venous irritation and "purple glove syndrome" (discoloration with edema and pain of distal limb); inject into a large vein slowly and follow with a saline flush. Serious skin reactions: ↑ risk of SJS/TEN, Asian patients should be screened for HLA-B*1502 Multiorgan hypersensitivity (DRESS) reactions <u>Blood dyscrasias</u>, caution in cardiac disease patients, hepatic and renal impairment, hypothyroidism **SIDE EFFECTS** With IV route (may need to lower rate): Hypotension, bradycardia, arrhythmias, cardiovascular collapse <u>Dose-related (toxicity): Nystagmus, ataxia, slurred speech, dizziness, somnolence, lethargy, confusion, blurred vision and diplopia</u> Chronic: <u>Skin thickening (children), gingival hyperplasia, hair growth, vitamin D and calcium deficiency (bone loss), morbilliform rash (measles-like), rash, hepatotoxicity, peripheral neuropathy, hyperglycemia</u>, metallic taste, connective tissue changes, enlargement of facial features (lips) **MONITORING** <u>LFTs</u>, CBC with differential, <u>serum trough</u> concentration, mental status, seizure frequency. For IV, continuous cardiac monitoring (ECG, BP, HR) **NOTES** Pregnancy Category D <u>Supplementation with calcium and vitamin D, and possibly folic acid, is recommended</u> <u>Strong CYP450 enzyme inducer</u>

Phenytoin/Fosphenytoin Drug Interactions

- Phenytoin and fosphenytoin are strong inducers of several CYP450 enzymes, including 2B6, 2C19, 2C8/9, 3A4, P-gp and UGT1A1; they are substrates of 2C19 (major), 2C9 (major) and 3A4 (minor). These 2 drugs can lower the concentration of many drugs including other anticonvulsants, contraceptives, warfarin, etc.

- Use of an alternative, non-hormonal contraceptive is recommended.

- Caution for additive CNS effects, including dizziness, somnolence, fatigue.

- These agents have <u>high protein binding</u> [fosphenytoin (95-99%)/phenytoin (90-95%)]; they can displace other highly-protein bound drugs. Other drugs can displace fosphenytoin/phenytoin, causing an ↑ in levels and potential toxicity.

Topiramate

Fast sodium channel blocker that enhances γ-aminobutyric activity (GABA), antagonizes the alpha-amino-3-hydroxy-5-methyl-4-isoxazolepropionic acid (AMPA)/kainate subtype of the glutamate receptors, and weakly inhibits carbonic anhydrase.

DRUG	DOSING	SAFETY/SIDE EFFECTS/MONITORING
Topiramate *(Topamax, Topiragen, Topamax* Sprinkle) Topiramate extended-release *(Qudexy XR, Trokendi XR)* Capsule, extended-release capsule, tablet Adjunctive therapy for partial seizure, primary generalized tonic-clonic seizure, or Lennox-Gastaut syndrome, or conversion to primary therapy from older drugs Also used for migraine prophylaxis	Week 1: 25 mg BID (IR) or 50 mg daily (XR) Week 2: 50 mg BID (IR) or 100 mg daily (XR) Week 3: 75 mg BID (IR) or 150 mg daily (XR) Week 4: 100 mg BID (IR) or 200 mg daily (XR) ↑ by 100 mg weekly until max dose or therapeutic effect Maximum: 400 mg/day CrCl < 70 mL/min: ↓ dose by 50% *Topamax* Sprinkle Capsules: May be swallowed whole or opened to sprinkle the contents on a small amount (~1 teaspoon) of soft food (drug/food mixture should not be chewed; swallow immediately)	**CONTRAINDICATIONS** *Trokendi XR* only – recent alcohol use (within 6 hours prior to and 6 hours after dose), patients with metabolic acidosis and taking metformin **WARNINGS** Hyperchloremic nonanion gap <u>metabolic acidosis</u> due to inhibition of carbonic anhydrase and ↑ renal bicarbonate loss. Dose reduction or discontinuation (by tapering dose) should be considered in patients with persistent or severe metabolic acidosis. <u>Oligohydrosis (reduced perspiration)/hyperthermia</u> (mostly in children) – try to limit sun exposure and hydrate <u>Nephrolithiasis</u> (kidney stones) – keep hydrated; caution in those on a ketogenic diet Acute myopia and secondary angle closure glaucoma <u>Hyperammonemia</u> – alone and with co-administration of valproic acid Visual problems (reversible) – consider discontinuation Cognitive impairment **SIDE EFFECTS** <u>Somnolence, dizziness, psychomotor slowing, cognitive problems (difficulty with memory/concentration/attention), weight loss, anorexia, paresthesias, ↓ sodium bicarbonate concentrations, vitamin D and calcium deficiency (bone loss)</u> **MONITORING** Electrolytes (especially <u>bicarbonate</u>), renal function, hydration status, mental status, intraocular pressure, seizure frequency **NOTES** <u>Pregnancy Category D</u> – use during pregnancy can cause <u>cleft lip and/or palate</u> in newborn <u>Supplementation with calcium and vitamin D recommended</u>

Topiramate Drug Interactions

- Topiramate is an inhibitor of 2C19 (weak) and inducer of 3A4 (weak).

- Phenytoin, carbamazepine, valproic acid and lamotrigine can ↓ topiramate levels.

- Topiramate may ↓ oral contraceptive effectiveness, especially with higher doses (≥ 200 mg/day). Use of an alternative, non-hormonal contraceptive is recommended.

- Caution for additive CNS effects, including dizziness, somnolence, fatigue.

Pregabalin/Gabapentin

These agents bind to the alpha-2-delta subunit of voltage-dependent calcium channels within the CNS, inhibiting excitatory neurotransmitter release including glutamate, norepinephrine, serotonin, dopamine, substance P, and calcitonin gene-related peptide. Although structurally related to GABA, they do not bind GABA or benzodiazepine receptors.

DRUG	DOSING	SAFETY/SIDE EFFECTS/MONITORING
Pregabalin *(Lyrica)* C-V Capsule, solution Adjunctive therapy for adult patients with partial onset seizures Diabetic or spinal cord injury neuropathic pain, postherpetic neuralgia, fibromyalgia	Initial: 75 mg BID Maximum: 600 mg/day CrCl < 60 mL/min: ↓ dose and/or extend the interval	**WARNINGS** Angioedema, peripheral edema **SIDE EFFECTS** Dizziness, somnolence, peripheral edema, weight gain, ataxia, diplopia, blurred vision, dry mouth, mild euphoria **MONITORING** Edema/weight gain, somnolence, mental status, seizure frequency **NOTES** Pregnancy Category C Often used for neuropathic pain treatment
Gabapentin *(Neurontin, Fanatrex)* Capsule, tablet, solution, suspension *Gralise* – postherpetic neuralgia *Horizant* (gabapentin enacarbil)– postherpetic neuralgia and restless legs syndrome	Initial: 300 mg TID Maximum: 3,600 mg/day CrCl < 60 mL/min: ↓ dose and/or extend the interval Immediate-release, extended-release and gabapentin enacarbil are not interchangeable	**WARNINGS** Multiorgan hypersensitivity (DRESS) reactions **SIDE EFFECTS** Dizziness, somnolence, ataxia, peripheral edema, weight gain, diplopia, blurred vision, dry mouth **MONITORING** Edema/weight gain, somnolence, mental status, seizure frequency **NOTES** Pregnancy Category C More often used off-labeled for fibromyalgia, neuropathic pain, drug abuse, alcohol withdrawal

Pregabalin/Gabapentin Drug Interactions

- No significant drug-drug interactions; renally eliminated. Use caution with pregabalin and glitazones concurrently due to risk of additive edema.

- Caution for additive CNS effects, including dizziness, somnolence, fatigue.

Phenobarbital/Primidone

Barbiturate agents that enhance gamma (γ)-aminobutyric acid (GABA) to bind to GABA-A receptors and potentiate GABA-mediated chloride influx; shift in Cl ions results in hyperpolarization (a less excitable state) and membrane stabilization.

DRUG	DOSING	SAFETY/SIDE EFFECTS/MONITORING
PHENobarbital C-IV Tablet, solution, elixir, injection Generalized tonic-clonic, status epilepticus, and partial seizures	Initial: 50-100 mg 2 or 3 times daily t½: ~100 hrs **Therapeutic Range** 20-40 mcg/mL in adults 15-40 mcg/mL in children	**CONTRAINDICATIONS** Severe hepatic impairment, dyspnea or airway obstruction, SC administration **WARNINGS** Do not discontinue abruptly as seizures can result (applies to all anticonvulsants); withdrawal symptoms will ↑ seizure risk Paradoxical reactions including hyperactive or aggressive behavior, particularly in acute pain and pediatric patients Hypotension especially when given IV Serious skin reactions (SJS/TEN) Respiratory depression
Primidone *(Mysoline)* Tablet Prodrug of phenobarbital and phenylethylmalonamide (PEMA) – both are active metabolites Generalized tonic-clonic, psychomotor and focal seizures	Initial: 100-125 mg QHS Maximum: 2 grams/day	**SIDE EFFECTS** Somnolence, cognitive impairment, dizziness/ataxia, physiological dependence, tolerance, hangover effect, depression, vitamin D and calcium deficiency (bone loss), folate deficiency **MONITORING** LFTs, CBC with differential, mental status, serum drug concentration, seizure frequency **NOTES** Pregnancy Category D Supplementation with calcium and vitamin D recommended Strong CYP450 enzyme inducers

Phenobarbital/Primidone Drug Interactions

- Phenobarbital (primidone is the prodrug) is a strong inducer of most CYP enzymes, including 1A2, 2C8/9, 3A4 and P-gp. These two drugs can ↓ the levels of many drugs metabolized by these enzymes.

- Use of an alternative, non-hormonal contraceptive is recommended.

- Caution for additive CNS effects, including dizziness, somnolence, fatigue.

Ethosuximide

T-type calcium channel blocker that ↑ seizure threshold and suppresses paroxysmal spike-and-wave pattern in absence seizures.

DRUG	DOSING	SAFETY/SIDE EFFECTS/MONITORING
Ethosuximide *(Zarontin)* Capsule, solution One of the drugs of choice for absence	Initial: 500 mg daily Maximum: 1,500 mg/day Therapeutic range: 40-100 mcg/mL	**WARNINGS** Serious skin rash (SJS/TEN) and blood dyscrasias **SIDE EFFECTS** N/V, abdominal pain, weight loss, hiccups, dizziness, somnolence **MONITORING** LFTs, CBC with differential, platelets, signs of rash, serum drug concentrations, seizure frequency.

Ethosuximide Drug Interactions

- Ethosuximide is a major 3A4 substrate; look for 3A4 inducers and inhibitors.

- Valproic acid can ↑ ethosuximide levels.

- Caution for additive CNS effects, including dizziness, somnolence, fatigue.

Lacosamide

Slow sodium channel blocker, thereby stabilizing hyperexcitable neuronal membranes.

DRUG	DOSING	SAFETY/SIDE EFFECTS/MONITORING
Lacosamide *(Vimpat)* <u>C-V</u> Tablet, solution, injection Monotherapy or adjunctive therapy for partial-onset seizures	Initial: 50-100 mg BID Maximum: 400 mg/day CrCl ≤ 30 mL/min: maximum dose is 300 mg/day	**WARNINGS** Lacosamide prolongs PR interval and ↑ risk of arrhythmias. Obtain an ECG prior to use and after titrated to steady state in patients with or at risk of cardiac conduction problems. Multiorgan hypersensitivity (DRESS) reactions Syncope, dizziness, ataxia **SIDE EFFECTS** Nausea, dizziness, headache, diplopia, blurred vision, ataxia, tremor, euphoria **MONITORING** ECG (baseline and at steady state) in at-risk patients, mental status, seizure frequency **NOTES** Pregnancy Category C

Lacosamide Drug Interactions

- Lacosamide is a substrate of 2C19 (minor), 2C9 (minor), 3A4 (minor) and an inhibitor of 2C19 (weak). Caution with inhibitors of 2C19, 2C9 and 3A4 as they can ↑ lacosamide levels.

- Use caution with concomitant medications that prolong the PR interval (e.g., beta blockers, CCBs, digoxin) due to the risk of AV block or bradycardia.

OTHER ANTICONVULSANTS

DRUG	MOA	SAFETY/SIDE EFFECTS/MONITORING
Benzodiazepines, including: CloBAZam (*Onfi*) C-IV Tablet, suspension Adjunctive with Lennox-Gastaut syndrome	Enhances GABA resulting in shift in Cl ions and hyperpolarization (a less excitable state)	**WARNINGS** Serious skin reactions (SJS/TEN) Paradoxical reactions including hyperactive or aggressive behavior Anterograde amnesia **NOTES** Causes physiological dependence, tolerance, drooling, pyrexia Supplementation with calcium and vitamin D recommended
Eslicarbazepine (*Aptiom*) Tablet Major <u>active metabolite of oxcarbazepine</u>	Fast Na channel blocker	**NOTES** Same warnings and side effects as oxcarbazepine including ↓ Na; monitor. Inducer of 3A4 (moderate); inhibitor of 2C19 (moderate) Supplementation with calcium and vitamin D recommended
Ezogabine (*Potiga*) C-V Tablet Refractory partial seizures	Binds the KCNQ voltage-gated K channels, enhancing the M-current and suppressing seizure activity	**BOXED WARNING** <u>Retinal abnormalities</u> that can progress to vision loss in ~33% of patients after 4 years of treatment **WARNINGS** Dose-related neuropsychiatric disorders, including confusion, psychosis, and hallucinations, generally within the first 8 weeks of treatment <u>Skin discoloration</u> (mostly blue) in ~ 10% of patients, generally after ≥ 2 years of treatment and at higher dosages (≥ 900 mg/day) Urinary retention, <u>QT prolongation</u> **MONITORING** Eye exam at baseline and every 6 months, monitor QT interval in at-risk patients, electrolytes, LFTs, renal function **NOTES** <u>Urine discoloration</u> (orange, red, brown)
Felbamate (*Felbatol*) Tablet, suspension Refractory seizures	Enhances GABA, NMDA receptor blocker	**BOXED WARNINGS** <u>Hepatic failure</u> and <u>aplastic anemia</u> **MONITORING** LFT and CBC monitoring **NOTES** Informed consent needs to be signed by patient and prescriber prior to dispensing
Perampanel (*Fycompa*) C-III Tablet	Alpha-amino-3-hydroxy-5-methyl-4-isoxazolepropionic acid (AMPA) glutamate receptor blocker	**BOXED WARNING** Neuropsychiatric events (dose-related) including irritability, aggression, anger, paranoia and others mostly in the first 6 weeks **NOTES** Inducer of 3A4 (weak) Supplementation with calcium and vitamin D recommended

Other Anticonvulsants Continued

DRUG	MOA	SAFETY/SIDE EFFECTS/MONITORING
Rufinamide (*Banzel*) Tablet, suspension Lennox-Gastaut syndrome only	Fast Na channel blocker	**CONTRAINDICATIONS** Patients with familial short QT syndrome due to QT shortening (dose-related) **NOTES** Take with food
TiaGABine (*Gabitril*) Tablet	Blocks GABA reuptake in the presynaptic neurons	**WARNINGS** Worsening of seizures/new onset seizures when used off-label for other indications, SJS/TEN **NOTES** Take with food
Vigabatrin (*Sabril*) Tablet, packet for solution Refractory complex partial seizures and infantile spasms	Irreversibly inhibits GABA transaminase, ↑ levels of GABA	**BOXED WARNING** Causes permanent vision loss (≥ 30% of patients) **MONITORING** Eye exam at baseline, every 3 months during therapy and 3-6 months after discontinuation of therapy **NOTES** Only available through SHARE distribution program (Support, Help And Resources for Epilepsy)
Zonisamide (*Zonegran*) Capsule	Fast Na channel blocker, T-type Ca channel blocker and weak carbonic anhydrase inhibitor	**CONTRAINDICATIONS** Hypersensitivity to sulfonamides **WARNINGS** Same as topiramate except: no hyperammonemia warning and there is a serious skin reaction risk (SJS/TEN) **SIDE EFFECTS** Side effects similar to topiramate, including oligohydrosis (primarily in children) and risk of nephrolithiasis **NOTES** Pregnancy Category C

Significant Toxicities

ADVERSE EFFECT	ASSOCIATED DRUGS	
Teratogenicity*	Carbamazepine	Phenytoin/Fosphenytoin
	Clonazepam	Topiramate
	Phenobarbital/Primidone	Valproic Acid
Hepatotoxicity	Carbamazepine	Phenytoin
	Felbamate	Valproic Acid
	Phenobarbital/Primidone	
Decreases efficacy of oral contraceptives	Carbamazepine	Perampanel
	Clobazam	Phenobarbital/Primidone
	Eslicarbazepine	Phenytoin
	Oxcarbazepine	Topiramate (≥ 200 mg/day)

Significant Toxicities Continued

ADVERSE EFFECT	ASSOCIATED DRUGS	
Fatal pancreatitis	Valproic Acid	
Aplastic anemia	Carbamazepine (and agranulocytosis)	Felbamate
Serious skin rash (SJS/TEN)	Carbamazepine	Oxcarbazepine
	Clobazam	Phenobarbital/Primidone
	Ethosuximide	Phenytoin/Fosphenytoin
	Lamotrigine	Tiagabine
	Levetiracetam	Zonisamide
Oligohydrosis – inability to sweat, risk of heat stroke – highest risk in children	Topiramate	Zonisamide
Nephrolithiasis (kidney stones)	Topiramate	Zonisamide
Weight gain	Valproic Acid	Pregabalin
	Gabapentin	
Weight loss	Ethosuximide	Topiramate
	Felbamate	Zonisamide
Hyponatremia	Carbamazepine	Oxcarbazepine (more common)
	Eslicarbazepine	

* *Patients should be encouraged to enroll in the North American Antiepileptic Drug (NAAED) Pregnancy Registry if they become pregnant. This registry is collecting information about the safety of antiepileptic drugs during pregnancy (aed-pregnancyregistry.org).*

Patient Counseling for All Anticonvulsants

- Like other seizure medications, this drug can cause suicidal thoughts or actions in a very small number of people (about 1 in 500). Call your healthcare provider right away if you experience thoughts about suicide or dying, new or worsening depression or anxiety, panic attacks, irritability or other unusual behavior. Dispense MedGuide and instruct patient/family to read it.

- Do not stop taking this medication without consulting your healthcare provider. Seizures may become worse when the drug is suddenly stopped. When stopping therapy, the dose needs to be gradually decreased.

- Seizure medications can impair judgment, thinking and coordination. You may experience dizziness and drowsiness, especially when starting therapy. Do not drive, operate heavy machinery or do other dangerous activities until you know how this medication affects you.

- This medication can have additional drowsiness and dizziness with other drugs such as alcohol, barbiturates, benzodiazepines, hypnotics, opioids and skeletal muscle relaxants (any CNS depressant). Avoid use of other sedating drugs, if possible.

- Avoid drugs that can lower the seizure threshold (see chart at the beginning of the chapter). Avoid St. John's wort with all anticonvulsants.

- Use caution with different generic substitutions; try to stick to the same manufacturer. Small dosage variations can result in loss of seizure control.

Carbamazepine

- The most common side effects include sleepiness, dizziness, nausea, vomiting and problems with coordination. Take with food to decrease stomach upset.

- Carbamazepine can cause rare but very serious (possibly fatal) skin reactions. If you are of Asian descent, you should have a blood test prior to using this medicine to determine if you are at greater risk of developing a serious skin reaction. The serious skin reactions usually develop within the first few months of treatment. Seek immediate medical attention if you feel weak and feverish, develop a skin rash, hives, sores in your mouth or blistering or peeling of the skin.

- Carbamazepine can cause rare but serious blood problems (aplastic anemia or agranulocytosis). You will need to have your blood checked to make sure this is not occurring. Contact your healthcare provider right away if you develop fever, sore throat, other infections, easy bruising or bleeding, red or purple spots on your body or severe weakness and tiredness.

- Carbamazepine is FDA pregnancy category D. This means that the drug is known to be harmful to an unborn baby. Do not take this drug without first talking to your doctor if you are pregnant or are planning a pregnancy.

- This medication can lower the amount of vitamin D and calcium in your body; it is recommended to supplement with calcium and vitamin D while taking this medication.

Lamotrigine

- The most common side effects of this medication include sleepiness, dizziness, rash, nausea, vomiting, insomnia, lack of coordination or blurred or double vision.

- This medication can cause a serious skin rash. These serious skin reactions are more likely to happen in the first 2 to 8 weeks of treatment (but it can happen in people who have taken the medication for any period of time). Call your healthcare provider right away if you develop a fever, skin rash, hives, swollen lymph glands, sores in the mouth or around your eyes or unusual bleeding or bruising.

- This medication can rarely cause aseptic meningitis, which is a serious inflammation of the protective membrane of the brain. Call your healthcare provider right away if you develop a stiff neck, headache, fever, abnormal sensitivity to light, muscle pains, chills and/or confusion.

- Swallow tablets whole.

- The ODT formulation should be placed on the tongue and moved around the mouth to rapidly disintegrate.

- Chewable tablets can be swallowed whole, chewed, or mixed in water or diluted fruit juice. If mixed, take the whole amount right away.

Levetiracetam

- Take levetiracetam with or without food.

- Swallow the tablets whole. Do not chew, break or crush tablets. Ask your healthcare provider for levetiracetam oral solution or dissolvable tablet if you cannot swallow tablets.

- If taking levetiracetam oral solution, be sure to use a medicine dropper or medicine cup to help you measure the correct amount of levetiracetam oral solution. Do not use a household teaspoon or tablespoon.

- This medication can cause serious skin reactions, although this is rare. Seek immediate medical attention if you feel weak and feverish, develop a skin rash, hives, sores in your mouth or blistering or peeling of the skin.

Oxcarbazepine

- This medication can cause low sodium concentrations in the blood. Symptoms of low blood sodium include nausea, tiredness or lack of energy, headache, more frequent or more severe seizures and confusion.

- Take oxcarbazepine with or without food. Take oxcarbazepine extended release *(Oxtellar XR)* on an empty stomach at least 1 hour before or 2 hours after food. Swallow whole.

- Before taking oxcarbazepine oral suspension, shake the bottle for at least 10 seconds and use the oral dosing syringe to withdraw the amount of medicine needed. The dose may be taken directly from the oral syringe or may be mixed in a small glass of water immediately prior to swallowing. Rinse syringe with warm water after use and allow to dry thoroughly. Discard any unused portion after 7 weeks of first opening the bottle.

- This medication can lower the amount of vitamin D and calcium in your body; it is recommended to supplement with calcium and vitamin D while taking this medication.

- This medication can cause serious skin reactions, although this is rare. Seek immediate medical attention if you feel weak and feverish, develop a skin rash, hives, sores in your mouth or blistering or peeling of the skin.

Phenobarbital

- This medication can cause abuse and dependence and can slow your thinking and reflexes. Do not drive, operate heavy machinery, or do other dangerous activities until you know how this medication affects you.

- This medication can lower the amount of vitamin D and calcium in your body; it is recommended to supplement with calcium and vitamin D while taking this medication.

Phenytoin

- The most common side effects of this medication include sleepiness, dizziness, unsteady walking, confusion and slurred speech.

- This medication can lower the amount of folic acid, vitamin D and calcium in your body; it is recommended to supplement with calcium and vitamin D, and possibly folic acid, while taking this medication.

- This medication can cause a serious skin rash. Call your healthcare provider right away if you develop a skin rash, hives, fever, swollen lymph glands, sores in the mouth or unusual bleeding or bruising.

- This medicine can cause inflammation of your gums. Brush and floss regularly; do not miss dental cleanings or appointments.

- This medicine can cause birth defects if taken during pregnancy. Do not take phenytoin without first talking to your healthcare provider if you are pregnant or are planning a pregnancy.

- If using the suspension, shake the bottle well before each dose.

- Use this medication regularly in order to get the most benefit from it. It is important to take all doses on time to keep the amount of medicine in your body at a constant level.

Topiramate

- The most common side effects of this medication include sleepiness, dizziness, tingling of the arms and legs, weight loss and loss of appetite. This medication can cause confusion, problems with concentration, attention, memory, or speech.

- This medication may cause eye problems. Please contact your healthcare provider right away if you experience a sudden decrease in vision with or without eye pain and redness. Rarely, this medicine can increase the pressure in the eye. This can lead to permanent loss of vision if not treated.

- Topiramate may cause decreased sweating and increased body temperature. Children in particular should be watched for signs of decreased sweating and fever especially in hot weather. Keep your child out of direct sunlight and heat and have the child drink plenty of water when going outside when it is hot.

- Topiramate can increase the level of acid in your blood (metabolic acidosis). Contact your healthcare provider right away if you feel tired, have a loss of appetite, feel changes in heartbeat, or have trouble thinking clearly.

- Topiramate Sprinkle Capsules may be swallowed whole or may be opened and sprinkled on a teaspoon of soft food. Drink fluids right after eating the food and medicine mixture to make sure it is all swallowed. Do not chew the food and medicine mixture. Do not store any medicine and food mixture for later use.

- Drink plenty of fluids during the day. This helps prevent kidney stones while taking this medication.

- This medicine can cause birth defects if taken during pregnancy. Do not take without first talking to your healthcare provider if you are pregnant or are planning a pregnancy. An increased risk of oral clefts (cleft lip and/or palate) has been observed, particularly following first trimester exposure.

- This medication can lower the amount of vitamin D and calcium in your body; it is recommended to supplement with vitamin D and calcium while taking this medication.

Valproic Acid

- Common side effects with this medication include nausea, vomiting, sleepiness, weakness, increased appetite, weight gain, double or blurry vision and hair loss.

- This medication can rarely damage the liver. This is more likely to occur in the first 6 months of therapy. Call your healthcare provider right away if you develop severe fatigue, vomiting, loss of appetite, pain on the right side of your stomach, dark urine, light stools or yellowing of your skin or whites of your eyes.

- In rare cases, valproic acid has caused severe, sometimes fatal, cases of pancreatitis (inflammation of the pancreas). Call your healthcare provider right away if you have severe stomach pain that you may also feel in your back or have nausea or vomiting that does not go away. These symptoms may be early signs of pancreatitis.

- Do not crush, chew or break the capsules. Swallow them whole.

- Measure the liquid form of valproic acid with a special dose-measuring spoon or cup, not a regular teaspoon or tablespoon. If you do not have a dose-measuring device, ask your pharmacist for one.

- This medicine can cause birth defects if taken during pregnancy. Do not take without first talking to your healthcare provider if you are pregnant or are planning a pregnancy. Malformations of the face, head, brain and spinal cord have been reported (neural tube defects such as spina bifida). In addition, children born to mothers taking valproic acid products while pregnant may have impaired mental development.

- Take with food to help avoid stomach upset.

- You will need to have blood tests during treatment. It is important for your healthcare provider to know how much medication is in the blood and how well your liver is working.

- This medication can lower the amount of vitamin D and calcium in your body; it is recommended to supplement with vitamin D and calcium while taking this medication.

PRACTICE CASE

LK is a 35 y/o white female s/p MVA. She suffered a closed head injury, two broken ribs and a concussion. She had one seizure in the emergency room. During her hospital stay, she was initially treated with fosphenytoin then continued on phenytoin. She has no past medical history and does not smoke or drink alcohol. Her medications, vitals, and labs on the day of discharge are as follows:

Allergies: PCN, sulfa, "quinolones" and latex

Discharge Medications:
Phenytoin 100 mg PO TID
Norco 5/325 mg 1-2 tabs Q6 hours PRN pain #10
Patient states that she will continue her home medications, which include:
Loestrin 1 tab PO daily
Fish oil softgels 2 with dinner for "cholesterol"
Valerian root 3 capsules at bedtime for "calm sleep"
B complex tablet daily with lunch

Vitals:
BP: 138/76 mmHg   HR: 85 BPM   RR: 14 BPM   Temp: 38°C   Pain: 4/10

Labs: Na (mEq/L) = 133 (135 - 145)
K (mEq/L) = 3.8 (3.5 - 5)
Cl (mEq/L) = 101 (95 - 103)
HCO_3 (mEq/L) = 26 (24 - 30)
BUN (mg/dL) = 10 (7 - 20)
SCr (mg/dL) = 0.7 (0.6 - 1.3)
Glucose (mg/dL) = 98 (100 - 125)
Ca (mg/dL) = 9.9 (8.5 - 10.5)
Mg (mEq/L) = 1.9 (1.3 - 2.1)
PO_4 (mg/dL) = 3.1 (2.3 - 4.7)
AST (IU/L) = 34 (8 - 48)
ALT (IU/L) = 42 (7 - 55)
Albumin (g/dL) = 2.2 (3.5 - 5)
Phenytoin (mcg/mL) = 7.7 (10 - 20)

Discharge patient with follow up in 1 week in the Internal Medicine clinic.

Questions

1. LK is receiving phenytoin for her seizure control. What is LK's true phenytoin level at this time?

   a. 4.8 mcg/mL

   b. 7.7 ng/mL

   c. 7.7 mcg/mL

   d. 10.8 mcg/mL

   e. 14.3 mcg/mL

2. The medical resident asks the pharmacist to explain why a total phenytoin level needs to be adjusted for the albumin level. The pharmacist should give this response:

   a. The total phenytoin level will appear artificially low if the albumin is low – and should be adjusted.

   b. The total phenytoin level will appear artificially high if the albumin is low – and should be adjusted.

   c. The total phenytoin level will appear artificially low if the albumin is high – and should be adjusted.

   d. The total phenytoin level will appear artificially high if the albumin is high – and should be adjusted.

   e. Albumin levels have no effect on total phenytoin levels.

3. LK will be counseled to recognize symptoms of acute phenytoin toxicity. Which of the following should be included? (Select **ALL** that apply.)

   a. Shakiness/walking unsteady

   b. Severe rash

   c. Double vision

   d. Nystagmus

   e. Osteomalacia

4. There is a serious drug interaction between LK's birth control pills and phenytoin. Choose the correct counseling statement(s):

   a. Phenytoin will lower the amount of contraceptive medicine in her body.

   b. She will need to use a different type of contraceptive method.

   c. Phenytoin will increase the amount of contraceptive medicine in her body.

   d. A and B

   e. B and C

5. If LK continues phenytoin long-term, which of the following medical condition(s) could result if she does not use proper supplementation? (Select **ALL** that apply.)

   a. Osteoporosis

   b. Vision loss

   c. Alopecia

   d. Arrhythmias

   e. Progressive multifocal leukoencephalopathy

Questions 6-13 do not apply to the case.

6. A patient is going to receive phenytoin via infusion. Which of the following statements are correct? (Select **ALL** that apply.)

   a. Phenytoin has saturable kinetics.

   b. The maximum infusion rate is 100 mg/minute.

   c. The therapeutic level of total phenytoin is 10-20 mcg/mL.

   d. Phenytoin should be mixed in dextrose only.

   e. The brand name of phenytoin is *Felbatol*.

7. A child has been receiving divalproex for seizure control. Unfortunately, the seizures are not well-controlled. The physician has ordered lamotrigine as adjunctive therapy, with a careful dose-titration. What is the reason that a slow titration is required when initiating lamotrigine?

   a. Risk of multiorgan hypersensitivity reaction

   b. Risk of cardiac myopathy

   c. Risk of fluid retention and heart failure

   d. Risk of severe, and potentially fatal, rash

   e. Risk of fulminant hepatic failure

8. What is the mechanism of action of phenobarbital?

   a. Enhances dopamine

   b. Enhances GABA

   c. Suppresses dopamine

   d. Suppresses GABA

   e. Fast sodium channel blocker

9. Which of the following drugs decrease sweating and can cause heat stroke in children, and requires counseling to parents to help children avoid the sun and keep hydrated? (Select **ALL** that apply.)

    a. Rufinamide
    b. Zonisamide
    c. Felbamate
    d. Topiramate
    e. Oxcarbazepine

10. Which of the following drugs can cause kidney stones and require counseling for adequate fluid intake?

    a. Topiramate
    b. Tiagabine
    c. Pregabalin
    d. Valproic Acid
    e. Carbamazepine

11. Which of the following drugs is a preferred agent for treating typical absence seizures?

    a. Ethosuximide
    b. Lamotrigine
    c. Felbamate
    d. Topiramate
    e. Ezogabine

12. You find a patient actively seizing and call 911. What steps should you take to ensure the patient is safe? (Select **ALL** that apply.)

    a. Turn the patient on their side
    b. Remove sharp or hard objects away from the patient seizing and support their head
    c. Insert a stick into the seizing patient's mouth to prevent them from swallowing their tongue
    d. Loosen the patient's clothes
    e. Time the seizure

13. Which of the following statements are true regarding status epilepticus? (Select **ALL** that apply.)

    a. It is a medical emergency.
    b. Lorazepam is preferred over other benzodiazepines since it has a longer duration of action in the CNS.
    c. Clobazam is preferred for patients still having seizure activity after the first-line agent is given.
    d. It is defined as sub-clinical seizure activity on an EEG.
    e. Phenytoin is the drug that should be used first-line to break status epilepticus.

Answers

1-e, 2-a, 3-a,c,d, 4-d, 5-a, 6-a,c, 7-d, 8-b, 9-b,d, 10-a, 11-a, 12-a,b,d,e, 13-a,b

STROKE

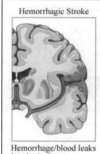
Hemorrhagic Stroke

Hemorrhage/blood leaks into brain tissue

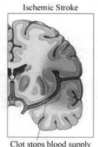
Ischemic Stroke

Clot stops blood supply to an area of the brain

GUIDELINES/REFERENCES

Guidelines for the Prevention of Stroke in Patients with Stroke and Transient Ischemic Attack. AHA/ASA. *Stroke* 2014; 45:2160-2236.

Guidelines for the Early Management of Patients with Acute Ischemic Stroke. AHA/ASA. *Stroke* 2013; 44:870-947.

Guidelines for the Management of Aneurysmal Subarachnoid Hemorrhage. AHA/ASA. *Stroke* 2012; 43:1711-1737.

Guidelines for the Management of Spontaneous Intracerebral Hemorrhage. AHA/ASA. *Stroke* 2010; 41:2108-2129.

BACKGROUND

A stroke, or cerebrovascular accident (CVA), occurs when blood flow to an area of the brain is interrupted by ischemia due to a clot (thrombus or emboli) or a ruptured blood vessel (hemorrhage). When a stroke occurs, brain cells in the immediate area are killed. When brain cells die, they release chemicals that set off a chain reaction that endanger brain cells in the larger, surrounding area of brain tissue called the penumbra. Without prompt medical treatment, this larger area of brain cells can also die. Acute ischemic stroke refers to a stroke caused by a thrombus or embolus and is more common than a hemorrhagic stroke. Intracerebral hemorrhage (ICH), subarachnoid hemorrhage (SAH) and subdural hematoma are all hemorrhagic strokes which indicate bleeding in the brain. <u>Using agents that increase the risk of bleeding can be harmful (and fatal) in these cases</u>.

When brain cells die, the abilities controlled by that area of the brain can be lost or impaired. Some people recover completely from less serious strokes, while others face chronic disability or loss of life. Stroke is the leading cause of disability and the 4th leading cause of death in the United States.

CLINICAL PRESENTATION & DIAGNOSIS

Signs and symptoms of a stroke can include the 5 "suddens":

■ Sudden numbness or weakness of the face, arm or leg, especially on one side of the body (hemiplegia-paralysis on one side of the body, hemiparesis-weakness on one side of the body).

■ Sudden confusion, trouble speaking or understanding

■ Sudden trouble seeing in one or both eyes

■ Sudden trouble walking, dizziness, loss of balance or coordination

■ Sudden, severe headache with no known cause

Instruct the patient to call 9-1-1 immediately if any of these symptoms are present.

The evaluation of a stroke patient should be done expeditiously as time is brain. The clinical assessment (history, general exam, labs, and neurological exam) and stroke scales such as the National Institutes of Health Stroke Scale (NIHSS) assess severity of the stroke and provide prognostic information. Initial treatment includes supportive cardiac and respiratory care and quickly determining the nature of the lesion as ischemic or hemorrhagic via brain imaging. Brain imaging, either by computed tomography (CT) or, less commonly with magnetic resonance imaging (MRI), is essential to the diagnostic process and in selecting the appropriate treatment. Imaging should be interpreted within 45 minutes of the patient's arrival in the emergency department by a physician with expertise in reading these studies.

ACT F.A.S.T. (TEST TO LOOK FOR SIGNS/SYMPTOMS OF STROKE)	
Face	Ask the person to smile. Does one side of the face droop or is it numb?
Arms	Ask the person to raise both arms. Does one arm drift downward?
Speech	Ask the person to repeat a simple sentence. Are the words slurred? Is the sentence repeated correctly?
Time	If the person shows any of these symptoms, even if the symptoms go away, call 9-1-1 immediately. Check the time so you know when the symptoms appeared. Brain cells are dying.

HEMORRHAGIC STROKE

Hemorrhagic strokes include intracerebral hemorrhage (ICH), subarachnoid hemorrhage (SAH) and subdural hematoma. Patients with hemorrhagic stroke should use intermittent pneumatic compression for the prevention of venous thromboembolism in addition to elastic stockings since anticoagulants should not be used while the patient is bleeding. Overall, treatment of a hemorrhagic stroke is largely supportive.

Drug Treatment of Intracerebral Hemorrhage

ICH has the highest mortality rate of all stroke subtypes. The progression of neurological deficits in many patients is frequently due to ongoing bleeding and enlargement of the hematoma during the first few hours of the bleed. This can lead to an increase in intracranial pressure (ICP). Measures should be taken to lower the ICP such as elevating the head of the bed by 30 degrees and using mannitol. Patients with a severe coagulation factor deficiency or severe thrombocytopenia should receive appropriate factor replacement therapy or platelets, respectively. Prophylactic anticonvulsant medication should not be used.

RISK FACTORS FOR STROKE
Hypertension – most common risk factor
Atrial Fibrillation
Gender (males > females)
Ethnicity (highest risk in African Americans)
Age ≥ 55 years
Atherosclerosis
Diabetes
Transient Ischemic Attack (TIA)
Prior history of stroke
Smoking
Dyslipidemia
Patent Foramen Ovale (PFO)
Sickle Cell Disease

Mannitol

Produces osmotic diuresis by increasing the osmotic pressure of glomerular filtrate, which inhibits tubular reabsorption of water and electrolytes and increases urinary output. Mannitol reduces ICP by withdrawing water from the brain parenchyma and excreting water in the urine.

DRUG	DOSING	SAFETY/SIDE EFFECTS/MONITORING
Mannitol *(Osmitrol)*	5%, 10%, 15%, 20%, 25% Mannitol 20% – 0.25-1 g/kg/dose IV Q6-8H PRN: give over 20-30 minutes	**CONTRAINDICATIONS** Severe renal disease (anuria), severe dehydration, progressive heart failure, pulmonary congestion **WARNINGS** May accumulate in the brain (causing rebound increases in ICP) if circulating for long periods of time as with continuous infusion; intermittent boluses preferred. **SIDE EFFECTS** Fluid and electrolyte loss, dehydration, hyperosmolar-induced hyperkalemia, acidosis, ↑ osmolar gap **MONITORING** Renal function, daily fluid in's and out's, serum electrolytes, serum and urine osmolality, cerebral perfusion pressure (CPP), ICP, and BP **NOTES** Vesicant Maintain serum osmolality < 300-320 mOsm/kg

Drug Treatment of Acute Subarachnoid Hemorrhage

Subarachnoid hemorrhage (SAH) is bleeding occurring in the space between the brain and the surrounding membrane (subarachnoid space). SAH usually results from rupture of a cerebral aneurysm or an arteriovenous malformation (AVM) or from traumatic brain injury. Surgical clipping, endovascular coiling or complete obliteration, when feasible, may be performed in patients with an aneurysm or AVM. SAH is associated with a high incidence of delayed cerebral ischemia 2 weeks following the stroke. Vasospasm is thought to be the cause of the delayed ischemia and can occur 4 – 21 days after the bleed. Oral nimodipine is used to prevent the vasospasm associated with delayed ischemia. The use of prophylactic anticonvulsants may be considered in the acute post hemorrhagic period to prevent seizures. The routine use of long-term anticonvulsants is not recommended, but may be considered for patients with known risk factors for delayed seizure disorder (e.g., prior seizure, intracerebral hematoma).

Nimodipine

Dihydropyridine calcium channel blocker shown to be more selective for cerebral arteries due to increased lipophilicity.

DRUG	DOSING	SAFETY/SIDE EFFECTS/MONITORING
NiMODipine *(Nymalize)* Capsule, solution	60 mg PO Q4H for 21 days Start therapy within 96 hours of the onset of SAH Administer on an empty stomach, at least 1 hour before or 2 hours after meals	**BOXED WARNING** Inadvertent IV administration: Nimodipine has inadvertently been administered IV when withdrawn from capsules into a syringe for subsequent nasogastric administration. Severe cardiovascular adverse events including death have occurred. **SIDE EFFECTS** Hypotension, bradycardia, headache, nausea **MONITORING** CPP, ICP, BP, HR, neurological checks **NOTES** Label oral syringes "For oral use only". Pharmacy should draw up the medication to reduce medication errors.

Nimodipine Drug Interactions

- Nimodipine is a major 3A4 substrate; strong 3A4 inhibitors can increase the levels of nimodipine and strong 3A4 inducers can decrease the levels of nimodipine. Avoid concurrent use of grapefruit juice.

ISCHEMIC STROKE

Drug Treatment of Acute Ischemic Stroke

The goal of therapy is to maintain CPP to the ischemic area, maintain normal ICP, control BP and possibly remove the clot (e.g., *Merci Retrieval System* device, others) or dissolve the clot with alteplase *(Activase)* if within the safe time frame.

Alteplase

Recombinant tissue plasminogen activator (rt-PA) causes fibrinolysis by binding to fibrin in a thrombus (clot) and converts entrapped plasminogen to plasmin.

DRUG	DOSING	SAFETY/SIDE EFFECTS/MONITORING
Alteplase *(Activase)* Must confirm clot on brain imaging (head CT scan) before use	Infuse 0.9 mg/kg (maximum dose 90 mg) IV over 60 minutes with 10% of the dose given as a bolus over 1 minute Dosing is different for MI and pulmonary embolism indications Once reconstituted, use within 8 hours.	**CONTRAINDICATIONS** Active bleed, PLT count < 100,000/mm³, INR > 1.7, ↑ aPTT due to recent heparin use (within previous 48 hours), current use of direct thrombin inhibitors or direct factor Xa inhibitors with elevated sensitive laboratory tests (e.g., aPTT, PT/INR or appropriate factor Xa activity assays), previous ICH, severe uncontrolled hypertension (> 185/110 mmHg), recent intracranial or intraspinal surgery, stroke or serious head injury within past 3 months, intracranial neoplasm, and many others. **SIDE EFFECTS** Major bleeding (e.g., ICH), hypotension, angioedema **MONITORING** Neurological assessments every 15 minutes during infusion, then every 30 minutes for next 6 hours, then hourly until 24 hours after treatment. Check BP every 15 minutes for the first 2 hours, then every 30 minutes for 6 hours, then hourly until 24 hours after treatment. Obtain follow-up brain imaging (head CT) at 24 hrs before starting anticoagulants and antiplatelets. **NOTES** Treatment must be initiated within 3 hours of symptom onset (guidelines state benefit in select patients up to 4.5 hours but this is not FDA approved). If severe headache, acute hypertension, nausea, or vomiting occurs, discontinue the infusion and obtain emergency CT scan.

Alteplase Drug Interactions

- Most drug interactions are due to additive effects with other agents that can ↑ bleeding risk. See Drug Interactions chapter for drugs that can increase bleeding risk.

Additional Therapies in the Treatment of Acute Ischemic Stroke

Aspirin Therapy

Aspirin 325 mg PO within 24 – 48 hours after stroke onset is recommended in most patients to prevent early recurrent stroke. Aspirin should not be given within 24 hours of fibrinolytic therapy.

Hypertension Management

Antihypertensives should be used to lower BP < 185/110 mmHg prior giving alteplase. In patients with malignant hypertension (> 220/120 mmHg), the BP should be ↓ by 15% during the first 24 hours after stroke onset.

Hyperglycemia Management

Maintain BG levels in the range of 140 – 180 mg/dL and closely monitor to prevent hypoglycemia.

DVT Prevention

SC anticoagulants should be given for DVT prophylaxis in immobilized patients. However, these agents should not be used within 24 hours of receiving alteplase therapy.

Ischemic Stroke Prevention

Modifiable risk factors should be corrected.

- Hypertension – the use of ACE inhibitors and thiazide-type diuretics have shown a reduction in the risk of stroke in addition to lifestyle modifications. This recommendation also holds for patients without a history of hypertension as long as they can tolerate the BP reduction. It is reasonable to target SBP level < 140 mmHg and DBP < 90 mmHg. It may be reasonable to target a SBP of < 130 mmHg for patients with a lacunar stroke.

- Dyslipidemia – treat according to the ACC/AHA 2013 lipid guidelines (see Dyslipidemia chapter).

- Diabetes – screening for diabetes should be done in the post stroke period; A1C is the preferred test during this time. Use of existing guidelines for glycemic control and BP targets in patients with diabetes is recommended for patients who have had a stroke or TIA.

- Metabolic syndrome – counsel on lifestyle modification (diet, exercise, and weight loss) for vascular risk reduction.

- Lifestyle changes including smoking cessation, increased physical exercise (at least 30 minutes most days of the week), weight reduction if necessary (maintain a BMI 18.5 – 24.9 kg/m² and a waist circumference < 35 inches for women and < 40 inches for men) and limit alcohol intake (≤ 2 drinks/day for males, ≤ 1 drink/day for females).

- Nutrition – it is reasonable to recommend sodium restriction to < 2.4 grams/day and further reduction to < 1.5 grams/day for greater BP reduction. Follow a Mediterranean-type diet emphasizing vegetables, fruits, whole grains, low-fat dairy products, poultry, legumes and olive oil.

Primary Prevention

Primary prevention for ischemic stroke is only recommended for patients with atrial fibrillation. See Anticoagulation chapter for more detail.

Secondary Prevention

Patients with previous cardioembolic stroke should be placed on anticoagulant therapy for secondary stroke prevention. For patients with noncardioembolic ischemic stroke or TIA, the use of antiplatelet agents rather than oral anticoagulation is recommended to reduce the risk of recurrent stroke and other cardiovascular events. Aspirin, aspirin plus extended-release dipyridamole, or clopidogrel are all acceptable options for initial therapy. For patients allergic to aspirin, clopidogrel should be used. The combination of aspirin and clopidogrel can be considered for initiation within 24 hours of a minor ischemic stroke or TIA and continued for 90 days. When this combination is started days to years after a minor stroke or TIA, it ↑ the risk of hemorrhage and should not be used for routine secondary prevention after ischemic stroke or TIA.

For patients who have an ischemic stroke or TIA while taking aspirin, there is no evidence that ↑ the dose of aspirin provides additional benefit. Although alternative antiplatelet agents are often considered, no single agent or combination has been adequately studied in patients who have had an event while receiving aspirin.

Antiplatelet Therapy

Aspirin binds irreversibly to the cyclooxygenase-1 and 2 (COX-1 and 2) enzymes, resulting in ↓ prostaglandin (PG) and ↓ thromboxane A_2 (TxA_2) production; TxA_2 is a potent vasoconstrictor and facilitates platelet aggregation. Aspirin has antiplatelet, antipyretic, analgesic, and anti-inflammatory properties.

Clopidogrel inhibits $P2Y_{12}$ ADP-mediated platelet activation and aggregation. Dipyridamole inhibits the uptake of adenosine into platelets and increases cAMP levels, which indirectly inhibits platelet aggregation.

DRUG	DOSING	SAFETY/SIDE EFFECTS/MONITORING
Aspirin (Ascriptin, Bayer Aspirin, Bufferin, Durlaza, Ecotrin, Halfprin, others) See Pain chapter for more information	50-325 mg daily Do not crush enteric coated tablet. Administer with food or a full glass of water to minimize GI upset	**CONTRAINDICATIONS** NSAID or salicylate allergy; patients with the syndrome of asthma, rhinitis, and nasal polyps; children and teenagers with viral infection (due to Reye's syndrome risk) **WARNINGS** Risk of bleeding (GI bleed/ulceration, others) Renal impairment **RENAL IMPAIRMENT SIDE EFFECTS** Dyspepsia, heartburn, nausea, bleeding, tinnitus (in toxicity) **MONITORING** Bleeding, bruising **NOTES** *Durlaza* is a new, extended-release capsule; not to be used when rapid onset is needed (e.g., ACS, pre-PCI)
Dipyridamole ER/Aspirin *(Aggrenox)*	200 mg/25 mg BID Protect from moisture; keep in original container	**CONTRAINDICATIONS** NSAID allergy; patients with the syndrome of asthma, rhinitis, and nasal polyps; children and teenagers with viral infections **SIDE EFFECTS** Headache (> 10%), dyspepsia, abdominal pain, nausea, diarrhea, and bleeding **MONITORING** Signs of bleeding; Hgb/Hct as necessary **NOTES** Amount of aspirin provided is not adequate for cardiac indications (e.g., MI prophylaxis)

Antiplatelet Therapy Continued

DRUG	DOSING	SAFETY/SIDE EFFECTS/MONITORING
Clopidogrel **(Plavix)**	75 mg daily	**BOXED WARNING** Clopidogrel is a prodrug. Effectiveness depends on the activation to an active metabolite mainly by CYP 2C19. Poor metabolizers exhibit higher cardiovascular events than patients with normal 2C19 function. Tests to check CYP 2C19 genotype can be used as an aid in determining a therapeutic strategy. Consider alternative treatment strategies in patients identified as 2C19 poor metabolizers. The CYP2C19*1 allele corresponds to fully functional metabolism while the CYP2C19*2 and *3 alleles have reduced function. Patients with 2C19*2 and *3 alleles are poor metabolizers. **CONTRAINDICATIONS** Active pathological bleed (e.g., PUD, ICH) **WARNINGS** CYP 2C19 inhibitors: Avoid concurrent use omeprazole or esomeprazole ↑ bleeding risk, discontinue 5 days prior to elective surgery Thrombotic thrombocytopenic purpura (TTP) has been reported **SIDE EFFECTS** Bleeding, bruising, pruritus **MONITORING** S/sx of bleeding; Hgb/Hct as necessary **NOTES** Do not start in patients likely to undergo CABG surgery MedGuide required
Ticlopidine	250 mg BID with food	**BOXED WARNINGS** Life-threatening hematologic reactions, including neutropenia, agranulocytosis, thrombotic thrombocytopenia purpura (TTP), and aplastic anemia. **SIDE EFFECTS** ↑ cholesterol (↑ TGs), N/V/D, rash, neutropenia, bleeding, pruritus **MONITORING** CBC every 2 weeks for first 3 months

Drug Interactions

- Most drug interactions are due to additive effects with other agents that can ↑ bleeding risk. See Drug Interactions chapter for drugs that can increase bleeding risk.

- Clopidogrel is a prodrug metabolized mainly by CYP 2C19. Avoid concomitant use with omeprazole and esomeprazole as these agents may reduce the effectiveness of clopidogrel due to 2C19 inhibition.

GASTROESOPHAGEAL REFLUX DISEASE & PEPTIC ULCER DISEASE

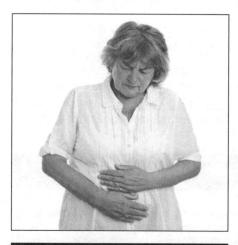

GASTROESOPHAGEAL REFLUX DISEASE

Background

Gastroesophageal reflux disease (GERD) is a condition in which the stomach contents leak backward into the esophagus. Normally, gastric contents are prevented from backflow into the esophagus by a ring of muscle fibers called the lower esophageal sphincter (LES). In GERD, the LES pressure (muscle tone) is reduced (or transiently relaxes) and allows for backflow of the stomach contents. Typical symptoms of GERD include heartburn, hypersalivation, regurgitation and/or an acidic taste in the mouth. Less commonly, symptoms can include recurrent cough, sore throat, hoarseness, and chest pain, which can be difficult to distinguish from cardiac pain. GERD can lead to esophageal erosion, strictures, bleeding and Barrett's esophagus (abnormal cell growth of the esophageal lining due to years of acid reflux which can lead to esophageal cancer).

The stomach epithelial lining contains parietal cells which secrete hydrochloric (HCl) acid and intrinsic factor, G cells which secrete gastrin, mucus-secreting cells, and chief cells which secrete pepsinogen. The parietal cells have receptors for histamine and acetylcholine. These substances stimulate HCl acid secretion by acting on the H^+/K^+ ATPase pumps located on the parietal cell wall.

Treatment Principles

The vast majority of patients self-treat with OTC products and do not seek medical attention unless this fails. Patients with alarm symptoms (chest pain, dysphagia, choking, hematemesis, black bloody stools) and those who do not respond to lifestyle modification and/or self-treatment with OTC products after 2 weeks should be referred for further evaluation. Patient-reported symptoms, history and risk factors are used for the initial diagnosis of GERD; invasive testing is not required when typical symptoms are present. An 8-week course of a proton pump inhibitor (PPI) is the treatment of choice for moderate to severe GERD, and is used to heal any erosive esophagitis. There are no major efficacy differences between the various PPIs. If symptoms persist after an 8-week treatment, maintenance therapy can be used. Histamine-2 receptor antagonists (H_2RAs) can be used for maintenance of mild disease, but a PPI may be required for maintenance in more severe cases. Metoclopramide and sucralfate are not recommended. Caution should be used with chronic acid suppression from H_2RAs and PPIs because of recent concerns of ↑ risk of GI infections (most commonly caused by *C. difficile)* and ↑ risk of nosocomial pneumonia in hospitalized patients. In addition, PPIs ↑ risk of osteoporosis and fractures with long-term use. Both H$_2$RAs and PPIs have risks in the elderly. According to the updated Beers Criteria, PPIs should not be used beyond 8 weeks in elderly patients unless the patient is high-risk or demonstrates need for chronic PPI treatment. All H$_2$RAs should be avoided in elderly patients with delirium (or high risk of), dementia or cognitive impairment because of adverse CNS effects that could make these worse. Be cautious of H$_2$RA doses; renal impairment requires lower doses.

RECOMMENDED NON-DRUG (LIFESTYLE) TREATMENT
■ Weight loss has the best evidence for improvement in symptoms, per guidelines.
■ Avoid foods that ↓ LES pressure, these are patient specific and can include: chocolate, caffeine, acidic/spicy food, and carbonated drinks.
■ Avoid eating meals with high fat content 2-3 hours before bedtime.
■ Elevate the head of the bed 6"-8" (not with pillows, but with a wedge, or by elevating the head-side of the bed under the mattress).

DRUG TREATMENT

Antacids

Antacids work by neutralizing gastric acid (producing salt and water) thus increasing gastric pH. This provides relief within minutes since antacids do not require systemic absorption. Antacids work quickly, but the duration of relief is only 30 – 60 minutes. This makes antacids most suitable for mild, infrequent symptoms.

DRUG	DOSING	SAFETY/SIDE EFFECTS/MONITORING
Calcium carbonate *(Tums, others)* **Magnesium *[Phillips Milk of Magnesia (MOM), others]*** **Magnesium + (Aluminum or Calcium) combo *(Maalox, Mylanta, Rolaids*, others)*** **Mag-Al-Simethicone (anti-gas)** ***(Maalox Max, Mylanta Max Strength*, others)** Sodium bicarbonate + aspirin + citric acid *(Alka-Seltzer Original)* Sodium bicarbonate *(Neut)* Antacid + alginic acid *(Gaviscon)* Calcium carbonate, magnesium hydroxide, famotidine *(Pepcid Complete)*	Many formulations including suspensions, chewable tablets, capsules 10-30 mL or 2-4 tablets 4-6x/day	**WARNINGS** Aluminum and magnesium can accumulate with severe renal dysfunction. Use is not recommended in patients with CrCl < 30 mL/min. **SIDE EFFECTS** Calcium: Constipation or loose stools Aluminum: Constipation Magnesium: Loose stools (may use with aluminum to counter-balance, but still can get loose stools) Unpleasant taste **NOTES** Onset of relief within minutes; lasts 30-60 minutes. Antacids are the drugs of choice in pregnancy. *Alka-Seltzer Original* contains > 500 mg Na and 325 mg aspirin per tab. Sodium bicarbonate also used for metabolic acidosis with renal disease. Alginic acid in *Gaviscon* theoretically forms barrier to combat reflux (questionable efficacy).

Antacid Drug Interactions

Antacids ↓ absorption of numerous medications. Interactions may be specific to the antacid formulation. This list highlights the most important interactions and is not all-inclusive.

- If taken with antacids, drugs that require an acidic gut for absorption will have ↓ absorption and enteric coated products could dissolve and release prematurely. Antacids have a short duration of action and can usually be separated from drugs that could interact. Use caution when antacids are administered with allopurinol, bisacodyl, bisphosphonates, some oral cephalosporins (e.g., cefditoren, cefpodoxime, cefuroxime), oral steroids (esp. budesonide), fosinopril, gabapentin, iron, isoniazid, itraconazole, ketoconazole, ledipasvir, mesalamine, mycophenolate, quinolones, sotalol, tetracycline antibiotics (less clinical concern with doxycycline and minocycline), thyroid products, most tyrosine kinase inhibitors (dasatinib, erlotinib, others), numerous HIV medications (NNRTIs: delavirdine, rilpivirine; PI: atazanavir; INSTIs: dolutegravir, elvitegravir, raltegravir)

- Select medications and recommended separation from antacids: 2 hours before or 6 hours after ciprofloxacin, 2 hours before or 2 hours after levofloxacin and cefuroxime, 4 hours before or 8 hours after moxifloxacin, 1 – 2 hours before or 4 hours after tetracycline. Thyroid products and ledipasvir should be separated from antacids by at least 4 hours. Gabapentin should be administered 2 hours after antacids. Ibandronate should be taken 60 minutes before antacids and alendronate/risedronate at least 30 minutes before antacids. Refer to HIV chapter for specifics involving HIV medications and antacids.

Antacid Patient Counseling

- Recommend lifestyle counseling.
- This medicine provides immediate relief, but lasts only about 30 - 60 minutes. If you need a medication that lasts longer, please ask your healthcare provider.
- If you use this product more than 2 times per week, you may have a condition that requires stronger therapy. Discuss the symptoms with your healthcare provider.
- Do not use aluminum or magnesium products if you have advanced kidney disease.
- If you experience constipation, discontinue use of aluminum-containing products.
- If you experience loose stools, discontinue use of magnesium-containing products.
- Do not use antacids that contain sodium if you are on a sodium restricted diet, have heart disease, high blood pressure, heart failure or kidney disease. Do not use sugar-containing antacids if you have diabetes.
- Seek urgent care if you have bloody stools or vomit blood or material that looks like coffee grounds.

Histamine-2 Receptor Antagonists

Histamine-2 receptor antagonists (H_2RAs) reversibly inhibit the H_2 receptors on the gastric parietal cells, which ↓ gastric acid secretion. H_2RAs are used PRN for heartburn and scheduled for GERD. Higher doses are used for ulcer healing and hypersecretory conditions (Zollinger-Ellison syndrome). H_2RAs can be used as maintenance therapy for GERD in patients who experience relief while taking them (patients without erosions) or for patients who complete 8 weeks of PPI therapy (to heal erosions) and are able to remain symptom free on an H_2RA. This could ↓ side effects associated with long-term use of PPIs.

DRUG	DOSING	SAFETY/SIDE EFFECTS/MONITORING
Famotidine *(Pepcid, Pepcid AC, Pepcid AC Max Strength)* Tablet, suspension, injection **+ calcium carbonate and magnesium hydroxide** *(Pepcid Complete)* + ibuprofen 800 mg *(Duexis)*	**OTC** 10-20 mg 1-2 times daily PRN **Rx** 20 mg BID	**WARNINGS** Confusion, usually reversible [risk factors: age > 50, renal or hepatic impairment (see notes)], ECG changes with renal dysfunction (famotidine), potential for vitamin B12 deficiency with prolonged use (≥ 2 years) **SIDE EFFECTS** Headache, agitation/vomiting in children < 1 year Cimetidine: gynecomastia, impotence
Ranitidine *(Zantac, Zantac Acid Reducer*, Deprizine FusePaq Compounding Kit) Tablet (OTC), capsule (Rx), suspension, syrup, injection	**OTC** 75-150 mg 1-2 times daily PRN **Rx** 150 mg BID	**NOTES** Onset of relief: 30-45 minutes, duration: 4-10 hours. Pregnancy Category B. Generally no benefit to combining with a PPI, except if used at HS for a patient taking a PPI for daytime symptoms.
Nizatidine *(Axid, Axid AR)* Tablet (OTC), capsule (Rx), oral solution	**OTC** 75 mg 1-2 times daily PRN **Rx** 150 mg BID	Decrease dose when CrCl < 50 mL/min (famotidine, ranitidine, nizatidine); CrCl < 30 mL/min (cimetidine). Cimetidine (and to a lesser extent famotidine and ranitidine) can ↑ SCr, without causing renal impairment. Acid suppressive therapy (including H$_2$RAs and PPIs) ↑ risk of GI infections (including *C. difficile* associated diarrhea) and may ↑ risk of pneumonia in hospitalized patients.
Cimetidine *(Tagamet, Tagamet HB)* Tablet, injection	**OTC** 200 mg 1-2 times daily PRN **Rx** 400 mg Q6H	Avoid all H$_2$RAs in elderly with delirium, dementia, cognitive impairment due to risk of adverse CNS effects per Beers Criteria. Avoid cimetidine entirely due to drug interactions and side effects. Take with meals or OTC PRN 30-60 minutes before food causing heartburn.

H$_2$RA Drug Interactions

- Caution with CNS depressants: risk of additive delirium, dementia, cognitive impairment especially in the elderly. Use lower doses in elderly and renal impairment. Avoid cimetidine entirely in elderly.

- If taken with H$_2$RAs, drugs that require an acidic gut for absorption will have ↓ absorption and enteric coated products could dissolve and release prematurely. Use caution when H$_2$RAs are administered with atazanavir and rilpivirine (refer to HIV chapter for specific recommendations), bisphosphonates (exception for *Atelvia* formulation below), itraconazole, ketoconazole, ledipasvir (see Hepatitis & Liver Disease chapter for specific recommendations), mesalamine and many tyrosine kinase inhibitors (exceptions below).

- The following drugs should be avoided with H$_2$RAs: some oral cephalosporins (e.g., cefditoren, cefpodoxime, cefuroxime), delavirdine, dasatinib, pazopanib, posaconazole (oral suspension) and the *Atelvia* formulation of risedronate.

CIMETIDINE

- Cimetidine is a 3A4 inhibitor and weak to moderate inhibitor of other enzymes. Avoid use with clopidogrel, dofetilide and warfarin. Use caution with many drugs including amiodarone, phenytoin, carbamazepine, quinidine, theophylline, SSRIs, and others.

H₂RA Counseling

- Recommend lifestyle counseling.

- This medicine provides fast relief in about 30 – 45 minutes and it lasts 4 – 10 hours. If your symptoms remain bothersome, discuss with your healthcare provider.

- If you are self-treating for more than 14 days or more than 2 times per week and heartburn persists, discuss your symptoms with a healthcare provider.

- If elderly: This medication could cause you to be confused, dizzy, or have memory problems. If you notice this, discuss the symptoms with your healthcare provider.

Proton Pump Inhibitors

Proton pump inhibitors (PPIs) block gastric acid secretion by irreversibly binding to the gastric H^+/K^+-adenosine triphosphatase (ATPase) pump in parietal cells. This shuts down the proton pump. An 8-week course of PPI therapy is recommended for relief of GERD symptoms and to heal erosions that may be present. Any PPI can be selected, see table for recommended dosing. After 8 weeks of PPI therapy, symptoms should be reassessed. If symptoms continue, the lowest effective dose of PPI or H₂RA should be used. Intermittent and on-demand PPI therapy are additional options.

WHAT IS ESOMEPRAZOLE STRONTIUM?

Esomeprazole strontium is not generic *Nexium*, but it has the same indications.

- Not approved for infants/children (concerns about bone growth with strontium)

- Pregnancy Category C vs. *Nexium* Category B

- 24.65 mg capsule = 20 mg esomeprazole base

- 49.3 mg = 40 mg esomeprazole base

Recommended PPI Dosing for GERD

DRUG	TIMING
Dexlansoprazole (*Dexilant*)	Without regard to meals (pre-meal if needed for symptoms)
Esomeprazole magnesium (*Nexium*)	60 minutes before breakfast
Esomeprazole strontium	60 minutes before breakfast
Lansoprazole (*Prevacid*)	Before breakfast (time not specified)
Omeprazole (*Prilosec*)	Before breakfast (time not specified)
Omeprazole + sodium bicarbonate (*Zegerid*)	60 minutes before breakfast (can also control nighttime symptoms if given at HS)
Pantoprazole (*Protonix*)	30 minutes before breakfast
Rabeprazole (*AcipHex*)	30 minutes before meal (capsules) May take with or without food (tablets)

DRUG	DOSING	SAFETY/SIDE EFFECTS/MONITORING
Omeprazole *(PriLOSEC, PriLOSEC OTC; First-Omeprazole, Omeprazole+Syrspend SF Alka suspension compounding kits)* Tablet (OTC), capsule, packet, suspension **+ sodium bicarbonate** *(Zegerid, Zegerid OTC)* Capsule, packet	*Prilosec:* 20 mg daily *Zegerid* dosing based on omeprazole component: 20 mg daily	**WARNINGS** *C. difficile*-associated diarrhea (CDAD), osteoporosis-related fractures (especially with long-term use), pneumonia in hospitalized patients, hypomagnesemia (with long-term use), potential for vitamin B12 deficiency with prolonged use (≥ 2 years), acute interstitial nephritis (hypersensitivity reaction) **SIDE EFFECTS** HA, N/D (all mild and infrequent)
Pantoprazole *(Protonix)* Tablet, injection, packet	40 mg daily	**NOTES** PPIs are the most effective agents for severe disease/symptoms
Lansoprazole *(Prevacid, Prevacid SoluTab, Prevacid 24H-OTC,* First-Lansoprazole suspension compounding kit) Soluble tablet, capsule (OTC), suspension	15-30 mg daily	All PPIs have similar efficacy, although an individual patient may respond better to one agent than another Pregnancy Category B (dexlansoprazole, lansoprazole, pantoprazole)/C (esomeprazole, omeprazole, rabeprazole)
Dexlansoprazole *(Dexilant)* Capsule	30-60 mg daily	Pantoprazole and esomeprazole are the only PPIs available IV
Esomeprazole magnesium *(NexIUM, NeXIUM IV)* Capsule, injection, packet **+ naproxen 375 or 500 mg** *(Vimovo)* Esomeprazole strontium Capsule	20-40 mg daily (esomeprazole base) Esomeprazole strontium 24.65 mg = 20 mg esomeprazole base and 49.3 mg = 40 mg base	Do not crush, cut, or chew tablets or capsules Dexlansoprazole, esomeprazole, lansoprazole, omeprazole, and rabeprazole capsules can be opened (not crushed) and mixed in apple sauce or acidic juice if patient cannot swallow pill or for NG tube delivery *Zegerid* 20 mg and 40 mg have same Na bicarb content; two 20 mg caps ≠ 40 mg cap; caution in patients on Na restricted diet, each cap has 300 mg Na
RABEprazole *(AcipHex)* Tablet, capsule sprinkle	20 mg daily	Suspension kits contain pre-measured powdered drug, suspension liquid (with flavoring) and mixing tools; available in different sizes/strengths

PPI Drug Interactions

- If taken with PPIs, drugs that require an acidic gut for absorption will have ↓ absorption and enteric coated products could dissolve and release prematurely. Use caution when PPIs are administered with atazanavir (refer to HIV chapter for specific recommendations), bisphosphonates (exception for *Atelvia* formulation below), itraconazole, ketoconazole, ledipasvir, (refer to Hepatitis & Liver Disease chapter for specific recommendations), mesalamine and many tyrosine kinase inhibitors (exceptions below).

- The following drugs should be avoided with PPIs due to ↓ absorption: some oral cephalosporins (e.g., cefditoren, cefpodoxime, cefuroxime), delavirdine, rilpivirine, dasatinib, erlotinib, pazopanib, posaconazole oral suspension, the *Atelvia* formulation of risedronate and St. John's wort.

- PPIs inhibit 2C19: Do not use PPIs with nelfinavir. PPIs may ↑ levels of methotrexate, phenytoin, raltegravir, saquinavir, tacrolimus, voriconazole and warfarin.

- PPIs may ↓ the effectiveness of clopidogrel via 2C19 inhibition. If using these agents together, avoid omeprazole and esomeprazole.

PPI Counseling

- Recommend lifestyle counseling.

- Refer to chart and counsel accordingly: It is important to take your medicine 30 minutes before breakfast. It will work best to stop acid if taken this way.

- This medicine is not for immediate relief of heartburn and acid symptoms, you need to take it everyday as prescribed to get relief.

- If taking long-term, ensure that calcium and vitamin D intake is optimal. Recommend calcium citrate formulations (improved absorption in basic pH).

- If you are planning to stop this medicine, you should taper the dose to avoid acid rebound. Please discuss with your healthcare provider (recommend decreased dose, then every other day over at least a couple of weeks.)

- Effervescent and orally dissolving formulations *(Prevacid SoluTab)* contain phenylalanine. Do not use in patients with phenylketonuria (PKU).

- If you are self-treating for more than 14 days and heartburn persists, consult your healthcare provider.

- Do not crush or chew any capsules.

- *Prevacid SoluTab*: Do not swallow whole. Place on tongue and allow to dissolve (with or without water), then swallow.

Cytoprotective Drugs

Misoprostol is a prostaglandin E_1 analog that replaces the gastro-protective prostaglandins removed by NSAIDs.

Sucralfate is in a sucrose-sulfate-aluminum complex and can interact with albumin and fibrinogen to form a physical barrier over an open ulcer. This protects the ulcer from further insult by HCl acid, pepsin, and bile and allows it to heal.

DRUG	DOSING	SAFETY/SIDE EFFECTS/MONITORING
Misoprostol *(Cytotec)* Tablet	Start at 100 mcg right after dinner, increase (if tolerated) to 100 mcg QID or 200 mcg QID. Take right after meals and at bedtime.	**BOXED WARNINGS** Abortifacient – warn patients not to give this drug to others; do not use to ↓ NSAID-induced ulcers in women of childbearing potential unless capable of complying with effective contraceptive measures. **SIDE EFFECTS** Diarrhea, abdominal pain **NOTES** Pregnancy Category X
Sucralfate *(Carafate)* Tablet, suspension	1 g tablets QID <u>before</u> meals and at bedtime (usual), may be given 1 g Q4H (for treatment of active ulcer)	**WARNINGS** Caution in renal impairment; sucralfate is in an aluminum complex and can accumulate. **SIDE EFFECTS** Constipation **NOTES** Pregnancy Category B. No longer recommended for GERD per guidelines. Used only as an adjunct for GERD or peptic ulcer disease.

Sucralfate Drug Interactions

- Avoid taking antacids 30 minutes before or 30 minutes after taking sucralfate.

- Avoid other drugs 2 hours before or 4 hours after administering sucralfate (difficult to use).

Patient Counseling

Misoprostol Counseling

- Do not use in women of childbearing age unless strict compliance with contraceptive measures.

- Can start with 100 mcg right after dinner (with food in stomach), attempt to increase as-directed. Use of psyllium *(Metamucil)* may help decrease diarrhea.

Sucralfate Counseling

- Major side effect is constipation; drink adequate fluids and use laxatives if directed.

- Discuss other drugs, including OTC products you are using, with your healthcare provider. This drug can decrease the absorption of other medicines.

Metoclopramide

Metoclopramide is a dopamine antagonist. At higher doses, it blocks serotonin receptors in the chemo-receptor zone of the CNS. It also enhances the response to acetylcholine in the upper GI tract causing enhanced motility and accelerated gastric emptying (peristaltic speed) and ↑ LES tone.

DRUG	DOSING	SAFETY/SIDE EFFECTS/MONITORING
Metoclopramide (Reglan, *Metozolv ODT)* Tablet, ODT, oral solution, injection	5-15 mg QID 30 min before meals and at bedtime	**BOXED WARNING** Can cause tardive dyskinesia (increased risk in elderly and with high doses and long-term therapy) **CONTRAINDICATIONS** GI obstruction, perforation, hemorrhage; history of seizures; pheochromocytoma; combination with other agents likely to increase extrapyramidal symptoms (EPS) **SIDE EFFECTS** Somnolence, dystonic reactions, restlessness, fatigue, drug-induced Parkinson disease, neuroleptic malignant syndrome (rare) **NOTES** ↓ dose in patients with CrCl < 40 mL/min (use 50% of normal dose) CNS side effects are dose-related and more common in the elderly – use with caution and dose-adjust in renal impairment Avoid use in patients with Parkinson disease Metoclopramide has a short duration of action (must be present in gut when food is present) MedGuide required

Metoclopramide Drug Interactions

- Avoid in patients receiving medications for Parkinson disease (antagonistic effect). Avoid use of antipsychotic agents, promethazine, tetrabenazine, and trimetazidine with metoclopramide due to increase in adverse effects. When used in combination with SSRIs, monitor for possible EPS, NMS, and serotonin syndrome.

- Caution for additive CNS effects, including dizziness, somnolence and fatigue.

Metoclopramide Counseling

- Use caution when driving, operating machinery, or performing other hazardous activities. This drug may cause dizziness or drowsiness.

- Avoid consuming alcohol during treatment with this drug. Alcohol may increase drowsiness and dizziness.

- Contact your healthcare provider right away if you experience any unusual body movements, such as shakiness, stiffness, or uncontrollable movements of the mouth, tongue, cheeks, jaw, arms, or legs.

PEPTIC ULCER DISEASE

GUIDELINES/REFERENCES

Chey WD, Wong BC. American College of Gastroenterology guideline on the management of *Helicobacter pylori* infection. *Am J Gastroenterol*. 2007; 102:1808-25.

Gatta L, Vakil N, Vaira D, Scarpignato C. Global eradication rates for *Helicobacter pylori* infection: systematic review and meta-analysis of sequential therapy. *BMJ*. 2012; 347:4587-99.

Background

Peptic ulcer disease (PUD) occurs from mucosal erosion within the gastrointestinal tract. Unlike gastritis, the ulcers in PUD extend deeper into the mucosa. Most ulcers occur in the duodenum but a small percent also occur in the stomach. The three most common causes of PUD are *Helicobacter pylori (H. pylori)*-positive ulcers, nonsteroidal anti-inflammatory drug (NSAID)-induced ulcers and stress ulcers in the presence of critical illness and in mechanically-ventilated patients. *H. pylori*, a spiral-shaped, pH sensitive, gram-negative bacterium that lives in the acidic environment of the stomach, is responsible for the majority of peptic ulcers (~70 – 80%). Other, less common causes of PUD are hypersecretory states, such as Zollinger-Ellison syndrome (causes ↑ gastric acid), G-cell hyperplasia, mastocytosis, and basophilic leukemias.

Under normal conditions, a physiologic balance exists between gastric acid secretion and the gut's repair mechanism. Mucosal defense and repair mechanisms include mucus and bicarbonate secretion, mucosal blood flow, prostaglandin synthesis, cellular regeneration, and epithelial cell renewal. These mechanisms protect the GI mucosa from damage from NSAIDs (including aspirin), *H. pylori*, acid, pepsin, and other GI irritants.

Symptoms

The primary symptom of PUD is gastric pain which can feel like a gnawing or burning pain in the middle or upper stomach. The pain is usually most bothersome between meals or during the night. Other symptoms are bloating, reflux and nausea. If the ulcer is duodenal (usually caused by *H. pylori)*, eating generally lessens the pain. With gastric ulcers (primarily from NSAIDs), eating generally worsens the pain. Other symptoms include heartburn, belching, bloating, nausea and anorexia.

H. pylori Diagnostic Tests

H. pylori infection, if left untreated, can lead to cancer. If testing is positive for *H. pylori*, the infection should be treated. Common diagnostic tests for the presence of *H. pylori* include:

- Urea breath test (UBT): Breath test that identifies gas (CO_2) produced by the bacteria. False negatives can be secondary to the recent use of H_2RAs, PPIs, bismuth or antibiotics; discontinue H_2RAs and PPIs 1 – 2 weeks and bismuth and antibiotics 4 weeks prior to the test.

- Fecal antigen test: Detects *H. pylori* in the stool. False negatives can be secondary to the recent use of H_2RAs, PPIs, bismuth, or antibiotics (to a lesser extent than the UBT); discontinue these drugs at least 2 – 4 weeks prior to test.

H. pylori Treatment

The American College of Gastroenterology guidelines recommend <u>triple therapy with a PPI + 2 antibiotics (clarithromycin and amoxicillin) for 14 days</u>. Metronidazole can be used in place of amoxicillin if the patient has an allergy. Several of the regimens (with various PPIs) are approved for a 10 day regimen. Due to recent <u>failures with triple therapy</u> (often due to clarithromycin resistance), many patients now receive <u>quadruple</u> therapy. The guidelines do not yet state this recommendation, however many experts discourage the use of triple therapy as first-line due to clarithromycin resistance rates unless local eradication rates are ≥ 90%. Quadruple therapy consists of one of the following regimens: a PPI, clarithromycin, metronidazole/tinidazole and amoxicillin <u>or</u> a PPI, bismuth, tetracycline and metronidazole or the use of <u>sequential therapy</u>, which is now first-line in some countries outside of the U.S. and is used increasingly here. Sequential therapy is a 10-day treatment that switches after 5 days: a PPI plus amoxicillin 1 gram BID is taken for 5 days, followed by triple therapy with a PPI, clarithromycin 500 mg BID and tinidazole/metronidazole BID for the remaining 5 days. If the PPI is continued beyond 14 days, this is to help ulcer healing for a short period of time; it should not be continued indefinitely.

<u>Do not make drug substitutions in *H. pylori* eradication regimens</u>. H_2RAs should not be substituted for a PPI, unless the patient cannot tolerate a PPI. Likewise, other antibiotics in the same class should not be substituted in *H. pylori* eradication regimens (for example, do not use ampicillin instead of amoxicillin).

First-Line *H. pylori* Treatment Regimens

DRUG REGIMEN	NOTES

Triple Drug Therapy: Take for 14 days

PPI BID (or esomeprazole 40 mg daily) + **Amoxicillin 1,000 mg BID +** **Clarithromycin 500 mg BID** *(Prevpac, with lansoprazole as the PPI)*	<u>Penicillin or macrolide allergy:</u> replace amoxicillin or clarithromycin with metronidazole 500 mg BID in this regimen or use alternative therapy below See GERD section for PPI side effects and Infectious Diseases I chapter for more on the antibiotics *Prevpac* contains all medications on one blister card. Take entire contents of one card each day for 14 days.

Quadruple Therapy: Take for 10-14 days
(Use if failed above therapy, cannot tolerate above agents, have taken a macrolide or metronidazole in the past, or if high local resistance rates to clarithromycin)

PPI BID (or esomeprazole daily) + **Bismuth subsalicylate 525 mg QID +** **Metronidazole 250-500 mg QID +** **Tetracycline 500 mg QID** Or Regimen with Combination Product: Bismuth subcitrate potassium 420 mg QID + metronidazole 375 QID + tetracycline 375 mg QID *(Pylera)* + PPI for 10 days	**Alcohol use** Do not use metronidazole **Pregnancy** Do not use tetracycline **Salicylate allergy/children** Do not use bismuth subsalicylate (or tetracycline in children 8 years or less). If patient cannot tolerate a PPI, substitute H_2RA (e.g., ranitidine 150 mg BID, famotidine 40 mg daily, nizatidine 300 mg/d). Swallow all capsules in the *Pylera* regimen.

Drug Interactions

- Refer to previous sections for drug interactions with antacids, H_2RAs, and PPIs and Infectious Diseases I chapter for drug interactions with antibiotics.

H. pylori Counseling

- For all *H. pylori* regimens: These medicines are used for stomach ulcers caused by an infection. It is very important that you take the medicine as prescribed and complete the course of therapy.

- It is common to have some diarrhea while taking these medicines. If it becomes severe or watery, contact your healthcare provider.

- *Prevpac:* Each card has your dose (4 pills) for the morning and the evening. Take your dose before breakfast and before dinner.

- Other side effects to watch for are bad taste in the mouth, headache, or any sign of allergy like a skin rash.

- This medicine may cause a darkening of your tongue and dark stool. It goes away when you stop the medicine.

- *Pylera:* To treat your stomach ulcers correctly, you will need two prescriptions: *Pylera* and a prescription for an acid reducing medication. You will take the acid reducing medicine for 10 days to help the ulcer heal, but you should not continue taking it after that unless your healthcare provider has said to continue. You will take 3 *Pylera* capsules 4 times per day (with breakfast, lunch, dinner and at bedtime), with a full glass of water. Swallow the capsules whole. Take the acid reducing medication as prescribed.

Non-Steroidal Anti-Inflammatory Drug-Induced Ulcers

Background

The use of high dose non-steroidal anti-inflammatory drugs (NSAIDs) or chronic NSAID use greatly increases the risk for <u>gastric</u> (GI) ulcers. NSAIDs (including aspirin) can cause gastric mucosal damage by 2 mechanisms: direct irritation of the gastric epithelium and systemic inhibition of prostaglandin synthesis (by inhibiting COX-1).

RISK FACTORS FOR NSAID-INDUCED ULCERS
Elderly
Previous bleed
Chronic NSAID use or high dose
Concomitant anticoagulant, steroids, SSRIs/SNRIs
Smoking
Poor health

Prevention and Treatment

Concomitant PPI therapy decreases ulcer risk. High-risk patients using a non-selective NSAID chronically can reduce bleeding risk by using concurrent PPI therapy. The clinician will need to consider long-term risks of acid-suppression therapy. Alternatively, a COX-2 selective agent (e.g., celecoxib) with or without a PPI can be used in high-risk patients if they do not have cardiovascular risk factors. Generic NSAID agents that approach the selectivity of celecoxib are meloxicam, nabumetone and etodolac. Some evidence suggests that naproxen may be preferable to other NSAIDs in patients with low-moderate GI risk and high CV risk.

If an ulcer develops, it would be best to discontinue the NSAID, if possible, and treat the ulcer with a PPI for about 8 weeks. Misoprostol is also an option, but diarrhea and cramping along with its four times per day dosing regimen contribute to poor patient compliance. If the NSAID therapy cannot be stopped, then reducing the NSAID dose, switching to acetaminophen or a nonacetylated salicylate or using a more selective COX-2 inhibitor should be considered.

<u>Use caution with NSAIDs in any person with cardiovascular or renal disease</u> since they can elevate blood pressure and decrease renal blood flow. If possible, avoid non-selective NSAIDs and celecoxib in patients with both <u>high GI and CV risk</u> and those at high risk of chronic kidney disease.

Patients who require antiplatelet therapy with a previous history of ulcers should be tested for *H. pylori* and treated, if positive.

PRACTICE CASE

PATIENT PROFILE

Patient Name	Benjamin Spector						
Address	10 Pine Place						
Age:	72	**Sex:** Male	**Race:** Caucasian		**Height:** 5'6"	**Weight:** 160 lbs	
Allergies	Aspirin (hives)						

DIAGNOSES

Prostate enlargement	Seasonal allergies, occasional bronchodilator
Parkinson disease	MI x 2 (last MI ~8 years ago)
Dyslipidemia	GERD

MEDICATIONS

Date	No.	Prescriber	Drug & Strength	Quantity	Sig	Refills
6/23/15	35421	Cooper	Clopidogrel 75 mg	#30	1 PO daily	6
6/23/15	35422	Cooper	Protonix 40 mg	#30	1 PO daily	6
6/23/15	35423	Cooper	Pravastatin 20 mg	#30	1 PO BID	6
6/23/15	35424	Cooper	Sinemet 25/250	#90	1 PO TID	6
			Albuterol inhaler	#1	Occasional use	4
			Loratadine 10 mg		1 tablet PRN	
11/1/15	42877	Kreinfeldt	Metoclopramide 10 mg	#120	1 PO QID	

LAB/DIAGNOSTIC TESTS

Test	Normal Value	Results Date: 11/1/15	Date: 11/1/14	Date:
Protein, T	6.2-8.3 g/dL			
Albumin	3.6-5.1 g/dL			
Alk Phos	33-115 units/L			
AST	10-35 units/L	28		
ALT	10-35 units/L	22		
TC	125-200 g/dL			
TG	<150 g/dL			
Na	135-146 mEq/L		137	
K	3.5-5.3 mEq/L		4.8	
Cl	98-110 mEq/L		105	
CO2	21-33 mmHg		24	
BUN	7-20 mg/dL	26	22	
Creatinine	0.6-1.2 mg/dL	1.9	1.2	
Glucose	65-99 mg/dL			
Calcium	8.6-10.2 mg/dL			
WBC	4-11 cells/mm^3			
RBC	3.8-5.1 mL/mm^3			
Hemoglobin	Male: 13.8-17.2 g/dL Female: 12.1-15.1 g/dL			
Hematocrit	Male: 40.4-50.3% Female: 36.1-44.3%			
MCHC	32-36 g/dL			
MCV	80-100 μm			
Platelet count	140-400 x 10^3/mm^3			
TSH	0.4-4.0 mIU/L			
FT4	4.5-11.2 mcg/dL			
Hgb A1c	4-6%			

ADDITIONAL INFORMATION

Date	Notes
11/1/15 (today)	PCP (Copper) on vacation. Reports bothersome heartburn and reflux after eating dinner and during sleep. Eats dinner at 8:30 pm, falls asleep 9:30-10 pm. Enjoys black tea with honey & smokes a pipe each night after dinner.

Questions

1. The patient is using *Protonix* once daily. Which of the following is an appropriate substitution?

   a. Omeprazole
   b. Esomeprazole
   c. Pantoprazole
   d. Rabeprazole
   e. Lansoprazole

2. The patient is still experiencing symptoms despite his current therapy. The physician decided to add-on metoclopramide to control the reflux symptoms. Choose the correct statement:

   a. Inappropriate therapy; the physician should increase *Protonix* to 60 mg daily.
   b. Inappropriate therapy; the physician should add ranitidine 75 mg at bedtime.
   c. Inappropriate therapy; the physician should add on magnesium citrate PRN.
   d. Inappropriate therapy; the physician should start misoprostol 200 mcg QID.
   e. Metoclopramide is appropriate therapy; no change is required.

3. Benjamin can make several lifestyle changes that may help with his evening symptoms. Which of the following are correct counseling points the pharmacist can provide to the patient?

   a. Consider cessation of evening smoke
   b. Eat dinner at an earlier time
   c. Change his evening drink to a non-caffeinated, non-alcoholic option
   d. Elevate the head of his bead 6-8 inches
   e. All of the above

4. The substituting physician prescribed metoclopramide. Which of the following side effects may be present?

   a. Worsening of his Parkinson disease symptoms
   b. Worsening of his prostate disease symptoms
   c. Dizziness, sleepiness
   d. A and B only
   e. A and C only

5. The prescriber decides to discontinue metoclopramide, but asks the pharmacist about metoclopramide dosing. If metoclopramide was to be used with Mr. Spector's current degree of renal function, what is the correct dose?

   a. 10 mg four times daily
   b. 10 mg twice daily
   c. 10 mg daily
   d. 2.5-5 mg four times daily
   e. 5 mg once daily

Questions 6-14 are not based on the above case.

6. An elderly female presents at the pharmacy. She does not have health insurance coverage. Which of the following PPIs is available over-the-counter?

   a. *Zegerid*
   b. *Prevacid*
   c. *Prilosec*
   d. A and C
   e. All of the above

7. A patient has entered the pharmacy and asked the pharmacy technician to help her locate the store-brand version of *Pepcid*. Which of the following medications should the technician select?

   a. Famotidine
   b. Cimetidine
   c. Ranitidine
   d. Omeprazole
   e. Lansoprazole

8. A physician has written a prescription for *Prevacid*. Which of the following represents an acceptable therapeutic substitution?

   a. Omeprazole
   b. Esomeprazole
   c. Rabeprazole
   d. Pantoprazole
   e. Lansoprazole

9. Which of the following proton pump inhibitors is available in an IV formulation? (Select **ALL** that apply.)

   a. Dexilant
   b. Nexium
   c. Protonix
   d. AcipHex
   e. Prilosec

10. An elderly female patient has hypertension and heartburn. Her family states she has trouble swallowing large pills. She failed H_2RA therapy and has been well-controlled on a PPI. She is currently using *Nexium* 40 mg daily. Which of the following would be a better option?

    a. Gaviscon
    b. Alka-Seltzer Original
    c. Zegerid
    d. Prevacid SoluTab
    e. Maalox

11. A 46 year-old man has received a prescription for lansoprazole 15 mg daily, amoxicillin 500 mg BID and clarithromycin 500 mg BID for *H. pylori* treatment. Choose the correct statement:

    a. Contact prescriber to correct dose of lansoprazole.
    b. Contact prescriber to correct doses of lansoprazole and amoxicillin.
    c. Contact prescriber to correct doses of clarithromycin and amoxicillin.
    d. Contact prescriber to correct doses of lansoprazole and clarithromycin.
    e. Fill as written.

12. A 16 year-old patient has the following allergies noted on her patient profile: ciprofloxacin, aspirin and erythromycin. The allergic reaction is not listed, and the patient is not available by phone. You wish to fill the prescription for *H. pylori* therapy, which includes rabeprazole, amoxicillin and clarithromycin. Choose the correct statement:

    a. It is safe to fill; most allergies to erythromycin are gastrointestinal.
    b. It is safe to fill; there is no cross-reaction with these agents.
    c. It is not safe to fill due to the use of amoxicillin in a patient with ciprofloxacin allergy.
    d. It is not safe to fill due to the patient's age.
    e. It is not safe to fill until the erythromycin allergy is clarified.

13. Proton pump inhibitors can increase the risk of: (Select **ALL** that apply.)

    a. Bone fracture
    b. *C. difficile* infection
    c. Stroke
    d. Hypermagnesemia
    e. Pneumonia in hospitalized patients

14. A pharmacist is dispensing tetracycline. Which of the following are correct counseling points? (Select **ALL** that apply.)

    a. Take this medication 1-2 hours before or 4 hours after taking any products containing magnesium, aluminum, or calcium, iron, zinc including vitamins, supplements and dairy products.
    b. Do not use sunlamps while using this therapy.
    c. You should avoid getting pregnant while using this medicine.
    d. You may experience stomach upset, including loose stools and nausea.
    e. Do not take if you are allergic to penicillin.

Answers

1-c, 2-b, 3-e, 4-e, 5-d, 6-e, 7-a, 8-e, 9-b,c, 10-d, 11-b, 12-e, 13-a,b,e, 14-a,b,c,d

CONSTIPATION & DIARRHEA

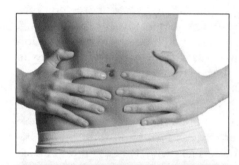

GUIDELINES

American Gastroenterological Association, Bharucha AE, Dorn SD et al. American Gastroenterological Association Medical Position Statement on Constipation. *Gastroenterology*. 2013; 144:211–217.

CONSTIPATION

Background

Constipation is defined as infrequent or hard stools, or difficulty passing stools. More specifically, constipation may involve pain during the passage of a bowel movement, the inability to pass a bowel movement after straining or pushing for more than 10 minutes, requiring digital evacuation, or no bowel movements after more than 3 days. The lifestyle measures in the box may help. In some cases, the patient is using a drug that is constipating (see box that follows). If lifestyle measures are not adequate, and/or if a constipating agent cannot be stopped, laxatives are used. Constipation due to irritable bowel syndrome (IBS)

Drug Treatment

The AGA guidelines recommend <u>increasing fiber intake</u> (dietary and as supplements) with the possibility of adding on a relatively inexpensive <u>osmotic agent</u> (milk of magnesia or polyethylene glycol). These are available OTC. Milk of magnesia contains magnesium and is <u>not</u> used with severe renal impairment. Polyethylene glycol is available OTC as *MiraLax* and in a larger prescription container.

If the patient needs to defecate, a suppository (<u>bisacodyl or glycerol</u>) will provide fast relief. Preferably, these should be administered 30 minutes after a meal when GI peristalsis has increased, but they can be used at any time of day. Oral <u>stimulants (senna, bisacodyl)</u> can be added on at <u>bedtime</u> as chronic agents. Senna is the usual first-line oral stimulant agent and is given as 2 tablets QHS. These agents take ~10 hours to work and will make it will make it possible to have a bowel movement the following morning, which is when most people defecate. Men most often have a bowel movement most mornings. Women have bowel movements less frequently.

Fiber products (such as psyllium) are the first line treatment in most cases, and the

LIFESTYLE MEASURES TO REDUCE CONSTIPATION

Correct fluid intake (64 oz – caution with CVD)

Limit caffeine and alcohol (to avoid dehydration)

Replace refined foods with whole grain products, bran, fruits & vegetables, beans

Increase physical activity

Do not delay going to the bathroom when the urge to defecate is present; may need to schedule time (important for young children)

CONDITIONS/DRUGS THAT ARE CONSTIPATING

Medical conditions where constipation is common

Cerebrovascular events	Multiple sclerosis
Parkinson disease	Irritable Bowel Syndrome (constipation-predominant)
Spinal cord tumors	
Diabetes	Anal disorders (anal fissures, fistulae, rectal prolapse)
Hypothyroidism	

Medications that are constipating

Opioids	Aluminum antacids (magnesium often in combination with aluminum to counteract effect)
Anticholinergic drugs	
Antihistamines, phenothiazines, tricyclic antidepressants, antispasmodics, urge incontinence drugs, especially darifenacin (*Enablex*)	
	Aluminum complex in other drugs (sucralfate [*Carafate*])
	Tramadol, tapentadol
Non-DHP calcium channel blockers, especially verapamil	Colesevelam
	Milnacipran
	Ranolazine
Clonidine	
	Varenicline
Bismuth	
	5-HT$_3$ receptor antagonists (e.g., ondansetron)
Iron (use docusate to avoid hard, compact stools)	
	Phentermine/topiramate
	Aripiprazole

treatment of choice in pregnancy. In addition to providing benefit for constipation, psyllium modestly improves cholesterol and blood glucose levels. Psyllium requires adequate fluids. An elderly female with incontinence would not likely be willing to increase fluid intake. Docusate, a commonly used stool softener, would be reasonable. Patients of any age using iron supplements will generally require docusate. Iron makes the stool hard and compact; it is difficult for fiber to mix in to soften the stool.

Patients using chronic opioids will often require a stimulant laxative because the opioids reduce the ability to push out the stool. Certain opioids are more constipating than others (e.g., morphine causes more constipation than fentanyl) but all are constipating, and some patients have more constipation than others. The stool softener docusate is given with the stimulant laxative if the stool is hard. If the stool is not hard but the patient cannot push it out ("moosh with no push"), a stimulant alone is the usual treatment. There are newer options for opioid-induced constipation for patients who do not find relief with a stimulant + stool softener.

Laxative Agents Used for Bowel Prep

A successful colonoscopy requires a complete and thorough bowel prep. Several of the agents below (the PEGs, and occasionally sodium phosphate) are used for both bowel prep and as laxatives. Sodium phosphate can cause fluid and electrolyte abnormalities, and is particularly risky in patients with renal or cardiac disease. Some of the PEG formulations are only used for bowel prep, such as *Golytely*. General counseling for bowel prep agents must include when to take the agent, what the patient can consume during the bowel cleansing process (i.e., after they have started using the bowel prep agent) and what must be avoided. Although usually safe and well-tolerated, in certain patients fluid and electrolyte loss could be critical. For this reason, some of the bowel prep agents require MedGuides. Use extra caution in patients with cardiovascular disease, renal insufficiency, and if taking diuretics (loops, due to additional fluid loss) and NSAIDs. Refer to the Notes section on the Bowel Prep laxatives for instructions on what is acceptable to consume with these agents.

Laxatives for Chronic Constipation

Bulk-producing laxatives create a gel-like matrix in the stool, soaking up fluid in loose stool and adding bulk to hard stool. Emollients and lubricants (stool softeners) lubricate and soften fecal mass, making defecation easier. Lubiprostone works by activating chloride channels in the gut, leading to increased fluid in the gut and peristalsis. Linaclotide is an agonist of guanylate cyclase C, which increases chloride and bicarbonate secretion into the intestinal lumen, decreasing GI transit time.

Treatment for Constipation associated with Irritable Bowel Syndrome

Lubiprostone and linaclotide are approved for both chronic constipation (called chronic idiopathic constipation, or CIC) and for IBS with constipation. Due to cost considerations, polyethylene glycol is often used first and will provide adequate relief in many cases.

Bulk-Forming Agents

Bulk-producing laxatives create a gel-like matrix in the stool, soaking up fluid in loose stool and adding bulk to the stool. First-line treatment (+/- an osmotic agent), and drug of choice in pregnancy.

DRUG	DOSING	SAFETY/SIDE EFFECTS/MONITORING
Psyllium *(Metamucil)* Capsule, powder Sugar-free options available	2.5-30 g/day in divided doses	**CONTRAINDICATIONS** Fecal impaction, GI obstruction (psyllium) **SIDE EFFECTS** Increased gas, bloating, bowel obstruction if strictures present, choking if powder forms are not taken with enough liquid
Calcium polycarbophil *(FiberCon)* Caplet	1,250 mg 1-4 times/day	**NOTES** Onset of action – 12 to 72 hours. Take <u>2 hours</u> before/after other drugs (caution with other drugs that stick to fiber).
Methylcellulose *(Citrucel)* Caplet, powder	Caplet: 1-3 g/day Powder: 2-6 g/day	Adequate fluids required. Inappropriate for patients on fluid restriction (e.g., heart failure), have difficulty swallowing, or at risk for fecal impactment (e.g., intestinal ulcerations, stenosis).

Osmotics

Osmotic laxatives cause fluid to be retained in the bowel lumen, with a net increase of fluid secretions in the small intestines. This distends the colon and increases peristalsis.

DRUG	DOSING	SAFETY/SIDE EFFECTS/MONITORING
Magnesium hydroxide (*Milk of Magnesia*), magnesium citrate, magnesium sulfate	MgOH: 2.4-4.8 g QHS or in divided doses	**CONTRAINDICATIONS** Anuria (sorbitol), low galactose diet (lactulose)
Polyethylene glycol 3350 (*MiraLax,* GaviLAX, GlycoLax, HealthyLax, PEGyLAX)	17 g in 4-8 oz water daily	**SIDE EFFECTS** Electrolyte imbalance, gas, dehydration, suppositories: rectal irritation
Glycerin (*Pedia-Lax, Sani-Supp Fleet*) Suppository: adult & pediatric sizes	Insert 1 suppository PR	**NOTES** Onset of action – 30 minutes to 96 hours (oral), 15-30 minutes (rectal)
Sorbitol Solution, enema	30-150 mL (70% solution) PO 120 mL (25-30% solution) PR	Magnesium: caution with renal impairment
Lactulose (*Constulose, Enulose, Generlac, Kristalose*)	10-20 g daily	Suppository used commonly in children who need to defecate (soon).

Stimulants

Stimulants/irritants work by reducing water and electrolyte absorption by stimulating colonic neurons and irritating the mucosal lining of the colon.

DRUG	DOSING	SAFETY/SIDE EFFECTS/MONITORING
Senna (*Ex-Lax, Senokot,* others*)*	15 mg PO daily	**CONTRAINDICATIONS** Abdominal pain or obstruction (senna and bisacodyl); acute intestinal inflammation, colitis ulcerosa, appendicitis (senna); N/V (bisacodyl) **Warnings** Avoid use if stomach pain, N/V, or a sudden change in bowel movements which lasts > 2 weeks.
Bisacodyl (*Dulcolax,* others*)*	5-15 mg PO daily 10 mg PR daily; if too soft to insert, can cool in fridge or cold water first Do not crush or chew the enteric coated tablets, do not take within 1 hr of milk, dairy products or antacids.	**SIDE EFFECTS** Cramping, electrolyte imbalance, rectal irritation (supp) **NOTES** Onset of action – 6-10 hours (oral), 15-60 minutes (rectal. Ideally, give 30 minutes after a meal (for ↑ peristalsis). Chronic opioids use often requires a stimulant laxative.

Emollients/Lubricants

Emollients (also referred to as stool softeners) reduce the surface tension of the oil-water interface of the stool, allowing more water and fat to mix with the stool.

DRUG	DOSING	SAFETY/SIDE EFFECTS/MONITORING
Docusate sodium (*Colace*) ,docusate calcium, docusate potassium	Docusate sodium: 50-360 mg PO daily or in divided doses 283 g/5 mL PR daily-TID	**CONTRAINDICATIONS** Abdominal pain, N/V, concomitant use mineral oil **NOTES** Onset of action – 12 to 72 hours (oral), 2-15 mins (rectal). Preferred when straining should be avoided (e.g., postpartum, post-MI, anal fissures, hemorrhoids). Use when stool is hard and/or dry.

Lubricants

Lubricants coat the bowel and the stool mass with a waterproof film. This keeps moisture in the stool and makes defecation easier.

DRUG	DOSING	SAFETY/SIDE EFFECTS/MONITORING
Mineral oil	Dose varies with product, take a multivitamin at a different time due to malabsorption of fat-soluble vitamins Do not take docusate and mineral oil together (absorption of mineral oil)	**CONTRAINDICATIONS** < 6 years, pregnancy, bedridden/aspiration risk, elderly, use > 1 week, difficulty swallowing **NOTES** Onset of action – 6-8 hours (oral), 2-15 mins (rectal). Not preferred due to risk of aspiration (lipid pneumonitis).

Osmotics used for Whole Bowel Irrigation

DRUG	DOSING	SAFETY/SIDE EFFECTS/MONITORING
Polyethylene glycol solution *(Colyte, GaviLyte-C, GaviLyte-G, Gavilyte-N, GoLYTELY, MoviPrep NuLYTELY, TriLyte)* *NuLytely, TriLyte* are sulfate-free; may taste better	Drink 240 mL every 10 minutes until 4 liters are consumed *MoviPrep:* Drink 240 mL every 15 minutes until 2 liters are consumed. Preferable to split the dose, such as half the night before, and half the morning of the procedure	**BOXED WARNING** Nephropathy (*OsmoPrep*) **CONTRAINDICATIONS** Ileus, gastrointestinal obstruction, gastric retention, bowel perforation, toxic colitis, toxic megacolon; Acute phosphate nephropathy, gastric bypass or stapling surgery (*Prepopik*); severe renal impairment (*OsmoPrep*) **SIDE EFFECTS** N/V, abdominal discomfort, bloating, arrhythmias, electrolyte abnormalities, seizures
Sodium picosulfate, magnesium oxide, and citric acid (*Prepopik*)	150 mL x 2 doses Combination stimulant laxative and osmotic, enables lower fluid intake	**NOTES** Onset of action – within 1-6 hours. The following food items are acceptable to consume the day prior to colonoscopy: "Clear liquid diet," which can include water, clear broth (beef or chicken), juices without pulp (apple, white cranberry, white grape, lemonade), soda, coffee or tea (without milk or cream), clear gelatin (without fruit pieces), popsicles (without fruit pieces or cream).
Sodium phosphates (*OsmoPrep*)	32 tablets and 2 quarts of clear liquid	The following food items cannot be consumed prior to colonoscopy: Anything with red or blue/purple food coloring (including gelatin and popsicles), milk, cream, tomato, orange or grapefruit juice, alcoholic beverages, cream soups, and solid or semi-solid foods. MedGuide required for: *GoLYTELY, MoviPrep, NuLYTELY, Prepopik, OsmoPrep.*

Lubiprostone

Lubiprostone works by activating chloride channels in the gut, leading to increased fluid in the gut and peristalsis.

DRUG	DOSING	SAFETY/SIDE EFFECTS/MONITORING
Lubiprostone *(Amitiza)* Chronic idiopathic constipation (CIC) Opioid-induced constipation (OIC) with chronic non-cancer pain Irritable bowel syndrome with constipation (IBS-C) in adult women.	CIC & OIC: 24 mcg BID IBS-C: 8 mcg BID ↓ dose with mod-severe liver impairment	**CONTRAINDICATIONS** Mechanical bowel obstruction **SIDE EFFECTS** Nausea, diarrhea, headache, hypokalemia **NOTES** Take with food and water to decrease nausea. Swallow whole. Do not break, chew or crush.

Linaclotide

Linaclotide is an agonist of guanylate cyclase C, which increases chloride and bicarbonate secretion into the intestinal lumen, decreasing GI transit time. It is used for both chronic constipation, and for IBS with constipation.

DRUG	DOSING	SAFETY/SIDE EFFECTS/MONITORING
Linaclotide *(Linzess)* Chronic idiopathic constipation in adults Irritable bowel syndrome with constipation in adults	CIC: 145 mcg PO daily IBS-C: 290 mcg PO daily Take at least 30 minutes before breakfast on an empty stomach.	**Boxed Warning** Death due to dehydration in animal studies, avoid use in pediatric patients **CONTRAINDICATIONS** < 6 years, mechanical GI obstruction **SIDE EFFECTS** Diarrhea, abdominal distension, flatulence, headache **NOTES** MedGuide required. Swallow whole; do not break, chew or crush. Keep in original container (contains desiccant).

Peripherally-Acting Mu-Opioid Receptor Antagonist

Peripherally-acting mu-opioid receptor antagonists (PAMORAs) act on mu-opioid receptors found in the GI tract, decreasing constipation. Alvimopan is only for hospitalized patients and is given prior to surgery to reduce the risk of ileus that can occur post-op. Methylnaltrexone and naloxegol are used only in patients on opioids only for opioid-induced constipation (OIC).

DRUG	DOSING	SAFETY/SIDE EFFECTS/MONITORING
Alvimopan *(Entereg)* Post-surgical patients to ↓ risk of post-operative ileus REMS drug	12 mg PO, 30 min-5 hrs prior to surgery, and 12 mg BID for up to 7 days total (15 doses) Used inpatient only	***ENTEREG* ONLY:** **BOXED WARNING** Potential risk of MI with long-term use **CONTRAINDICATIONS** <u>Patients who have taken therapeutic doses of opioids for more than 7 consecutive days prior to use</u> **SIDE EFFECTS** ↓ K, dyspepsia, anemia, urinary retention, back pain
Methylnaltrexone (*Relistor*) OIC (chronic opioids being used for non-cancer pain, including palliative care) REMS drug	See Pain chapter.	
Naloxegol (*Movantik*) OIC (chronic opioids being used for non-cancer pain) REMS drug	See Pain chapter.	

Peripherally-Acting Mu-Opioid Receptor Agonist

Eluxadoline is a mu-opioid receptor agonist (in contrast to the PAMORAs, which are mu-receptor antagonists). While the PAMORAs compete and displace the binding of opioids to receptors in the periphery to reduce constipation, eluxadoline binds to the opioid receptors as an agonist to treat diarrhea. Patients who would use this drug would have IBS with diarrhea where the diarrhea is difficult to treat with usual measures. Having a gallbladder increases the risk of the complication of sphincter of Oddi spasm; this is a muscular valve that controls the flow of digestive fluids/enzymes to the first part of the small intestine.

DRUG	DOSING	SAFETY/SIDE EFFECTS/MONITORING
Eluxadoline *(Viberzi)* Controlled substance: Category C-IV REMS drug	100 mg PO BID (with gallbladder) 75 mg BID (without gallbladder) Take with food.	**WARNINGS** Potential risk of MI with long-term use Sphincter of Oddi spasm, which can increase LFTs and cause pancreatitis. Increased risk of pancreatitis with > 3 alcoholic drinks/day. **CONTRAINDICATIONS** Biliary duct obstruction, sphincter of Oddi dysfunction, pancreatic disease, alcoholism, patients who drink > 3 alcoholic drinks/day, severe hepatic impairment (Child-Pugh class C), history severe constipation, known GI obstruction **SIDE EFFECTS** Constipation, nausea, abdominal pain, rash, dizziness LFTs, upper resp infections, nasopharyngitis

DIARRHEA

Background

Diarrhea occurs when there is an increase in the number of bowel movements or bowel movements are more watery and loose than normal. When the intestines push stools through the bowel before the water in the stool can be reabsorbed, diarrhea occurs. Abdominal cramps, nausea, vomiting, or a fever may occur along with the diarrhea. Fluid and electrolyte replacement is essential; review counseling points at end of this section.

MEDICATIONS THAT CAN CAUSE DIARRHEA

Antacids containing magnesium	Laxatives
Antibiotics, especially broad-spectrum antibiotics and clindamycin, erythromycin (due to prokinetic activity) – rule out *C. difficile* infection	Metoclopramide
	Misoprostol
	Quinidine
	Many drugs include diarrhea as a possible side effect
Colchicine	

Treatment

Most cases are viral. Diarrhea can be idiopathic, caused by diseases, or can be caused by stomach flu or food poisoning. Drinking untreated water, not washing fruits/vegetables properly, using untreated ice for drinks, or unpasteurized dairy products can cause viral, bacterial, or parasitic infections. *E. coli* is the most common bacterial cause. The treatment of diarrhea caused by a bacterial infection is discussed in the Infectious Disease chapter.

Treatment for Diarrhea associated with Irritable Bowel Syndrome

In most cases, loperamide offers acceptable relief. Rifaximin (Xifaxan) is an antibiotic with approval for this condition. It is costly, and relapse often occurs within several months of treatment. Alosetron (Lotronex) is useful for women only, but has restricted use due to the risk of ischemic colitis.

Antisecretory Agents

Bismuth subsalicylate exhibits both antisecretory and antimicrobial effects when used as an antidiarrheal.

DRUG	DOSING	SAFETY/SIDE EFFECTS/MONITORING
Bismuth subsalicylate (***Pepto-Bismol***, others)	525 mg Q 30-60 mins PRN or 1,050 mg Q 60 mins PRN Max 4,200 mg/day for 2 days	**CONTRAINDICATIONS** Salicylate allergy, concomitant use of salicylates, ulcer, coagulopathy, bloody/black stool **SIDE EFFECTS** Black tongue/stool, salicylate toxicity if used excessively (N/V, tinnitus, etc) **NOTES** Children and teenagers who are recovering from the flu, chickenpox, or other viral infections should not use this drug due to risk of Reye's syndrome.

Antimotility Agents

Loperamide and diphenoxylate slow intestinal motility, prolonging water absorption.

DRUG	DOSING	SAFETY/SIDE EFFECTS/MONITORING
Loperamide *(Imodium A-D, Loperamide A-D, Anti-Diarrheal, Diamode,* others*)*	4 mg PO after first loose stool, then 2 mg after each subsequent stool Max 16 mg/day	**CONTRAINDICATIONS** Abdominal pain without diarrhea, children < 2 years, acute dysentery (bloody diarrhea and high fever), acute ulcerative colitis, pseudomembranous colitis (*C. difficile*), bacterial enterocolitis caused by invasive organisms (toxigenic *E. coli, Salmonella, Shigella*) **SIDE EFFECTS** Abdominal cramping, constipation, nausea **NOTES** Self-treatment should not be > 48 hours.
Diphenoxylate/atropine *(Lomotil)* Diphenoxylate 2.5 mg with atropine 0.025 mg C-V	Diphenoxylate 5 mg up to QID Max 20 mg/day	**CONTRAINDICATIONS** Children < 2 years, diarrhea caused by enterotoxin-producing bacteria or pseudomembranous colitis, obstructive jaundice **SIDE EFFECTS** Sedation, constipation, urinary retention, tachycardia, blurred vision, dry mouth, depression **NOTES** A subtherapeutic amount of atropine is include in the formulation to discourage abuse.

Counseling for All Diarrhea Cases

- Do not self-treat if high fever (> 101°F) or blood in stool; see healthcare provider if no improvement in 2 days, if severe abdominal pain, infants (< 6 months), or if patient is pregnant.

- Diarrhea treatment should include fluid and electrolytes – this is important for all but especially so in children or adults with chronic medical illness.

- For moderate-severe fluid loss, replacement is best accomplished with oral rehydration solutions (ORS), which are available at stores and pharmacies *(Pedialyte, Infalyte,* etc) in developed countries. *Gatorade* or similar products are used as alternatives.

- Caution with *Imodium* and *Lomotil* if a decrease in intestinal motility may be due to infection from *Shigella, Salmonella*, and toxigenic strains of *E. coli* – toxic megacolon (usually due to *E. coli* or severe IBS) may occur. These products are also not recommended in C. difficile infections – the patient's body must be able to rid itself of the toxin.

- If fever/cold symptoms are present, aspirin rarely causes Reye's Syndrome in children and is avoided except under a healthcare provider's care (it may rarely be used in a child with a heart condition, where benefit may outweigh risk). For fever or mild pain, the parent can treat the child with acetaminophen or ibuprofen but should not exceed recommended daily amounts of acetaminophen or ibuprofen.

- Combination cough and cold products should not be used in children under 2 years old per the FDA (under 6 years old per the American Academy of Pediatrics). Any combination product may contain additional amounts of acetaminophen or ibuprofen – the patient must be counseled to count all sources.
- <u>Rule out lactose intolerance</u> as a cause of the diarrhea by stopping use of dairy products. Physicians can confirm lactose intolerance by tests.
- Bismuth Subsalicylate Counseling
- Do not use if you have an allergy to bismuth, salicylates (including aspirin and NSAIDs, like ibuprofen), or any other part of this drug.
- Tell your healthcare provider prior to starting this medicine if you are also taking a salicylate like aspirin.
- Do not give to children and teenagers who have flu signs, chickenpox, or other viral infections due to the chance of Reye's syndrome.
- Some chewable products have phenylalanine. If you have PKU, do not use this product.
- This medicine may make your tongue and stool dark, this is normal. Contact your healthcare provider right away if you notice tarry or bloody stools or if you are throwing up blood or a substance that looks like coffee grounds.
- If you notice a ringing in the ears or a loss of hearing while taking this medicine, stop taking it and contact your healthcare provider.
- Do not take for longer than 7 days without the approval of your healthcare provider.

INFLAMMATORY BOWEL DISEASE

BACKGROUND

Inflammatory bowel disease (IBD) is a group of <u>inflammatory</u> conditions of the colon and small intestine. The major types of IBD are <u>ulcerative colitis</u> (UC) and <u>Crohn's disease</u> (CD). The classic symptom is <u>persistent bloody diarrhea</u>. Exacerbations can be followed by periods of remission. Other symptoms include rectal urgency and tenesmus (a feeling of having to pass stools, even if the colon is empty). Symptoms can occur at any time with likely <u>flares</u> when the patient develops an infection, uses NSAIDs, or eats foods that trigger the disease. Food triggers include fatty foods, gas-producing foods (lentils, beans, legumes, cabbage, broccoli, onions) and some others. These are patient-specific. When <u>food triggers</u> are identified they can be <u>avoided</u> or prepared in a way that improves tolerability. <u>Irritable bowel syndrome</u> (IBS) is a <u>different condition</u>. <u>Similar to IBD, triggers</u> can cause symptom exacerbation. Unlike IBD, <u>IBS does not cause inflammation</u> and is not as serious a condition; IBS causes abdominal pain, bloating, gas, and either constipation or diarrhea. Drugs used to treat IBS primarily <u>treat the constipation or diarrhea</u>; refer to that chapter for drug specifics.

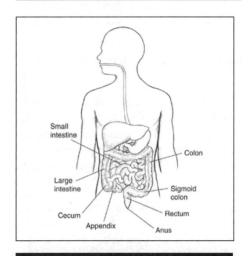

Small intestine

Colon

Large intestine

Sigmoid colon

Cecum

Rectum

Appendix

Anus

GUIDELINES/REFERENCES

Lichtenstein GR, Hanauer SB, Sandborn WJ. Management of Crohn's Disease in Adults. *Am J Gastroenterol.* 2009; 104:465-483.

Kornbluth A, Sachar DB. Ulcerative Colitis Practice Guidelines in Adults. *Am J Gastroenterol.* 2010; 105:501-523.

Ulcerative Colitis

Ulcerative colitis (UC) is characterized by mucosal inflammation confined to the <u>rectum and colon</u> with <u>superficial</u> ulcerations (in contrast to Crohn's, where the ulcers can be deep). When UC is limited to the descending colon and rectum, it is called <u>distal</u> disease and will be accessible with topical (rectal) treatment. Inflammation limited to the rectum is called <u>proctitis</u>. The larger the affected area, the worse the symptoms. When the disease flares, patients can have numerous stools per day, often with pain, which can significantly decrease quality of life. UC is classified as mild, moderate, severe or fulminant. Moderate disease is characterized by > 4 stools per day with minimal signs of toxicity and patients with severe disease have ≥ 6 bloody stools daily with evidence of toxicity [fever, tachycardia, anemia, or an elevated erythrocyte sedimentation rate (ESR)].

Crohn's Disease

Crohn's disease (CD) is characterized by <u>deep</u>, transmural (through the tissue) inflammation that can affect any part of the GI tract. The <u>ileum and colon</u> are most commonly affected. Damage to the bowel wall can cause <u>strictures and fistulas</u> (abnormal connections or openings). Symptoms of CD include chronic diarrhea (often nocturnal), abdominal pain, and weight loss. Perianal symptoms (e.g., bleeding, fissures) can be present before bowel symptoms.

CD and UC Comparison

	CD	UC
Diarrhea	Bloody or non-bloody	Bloody
Smoking	Risk factor	Protective
Location	Entire GI tract (esp. ileum & colon)	Colon (esp. rectum)
Depth	Transmural	Superficial
Pattern	Non-continuous	Continuous
Fistulas/Strictures	Common	Uncommon

Natural Products

For diarrhea in IBD, psyllium (in *Metamucil* and other formulations) or other "bulk-forming" fiber products can be useful.

Peppermint (oil, sometimes teas) can be useful as an antispasmodic. Some use chamomile tea. The probiotic *Lactobacillus* or *Bifidobacterium infantis* can reduce abdominal pain, bloating, urgency, constipation or diarrhea in some patients. Antibiotics and probiotics are <u>not</u> taken at the same time; separate the dosing by at least two hours. Fish oils (for the EPA and DHA, the omega fatty acid components) are used, although the evidence for benefit is contradictory. Indian frankincense gum resin taken TID may be beneficial for UC, based on preliminary studies.

<u>Watch for avoidable problems</u>: Sorbitol is used as a sweetener in some diet foods and is present in various drugs. Sorbitol has laxative properties and can cause considerable GI distress in some patients. Lactose will worsen GI symptoms if lactose-intolerant. Lactose is used in some oral drugs as an excipient. <u>Both sorbitol and lactose are classified as excipients (or binders)</u>; they help hold tablets together.

DRUG TREATMENT

Mild cases of UC and CD may only need antidiarrheal medicines, primarily loperamide *(Imodium)*. Antispasmodics for UC may be useful. The most common antispasmodic is dicyclomine *(Bentyl)* which is an anticholinergic with a high incidence of side effects (e.g., dizziness, dry mouth, somnolence, urinary retention).

Treatments for IBD are used for <u>induction</u> (they induce remission and treat exacerbations), <u>maintenance</u> of remission or both. <u>Short courses of oral or IV steroids</u> are used to treat <u>acute exacerbations</u> in both UC and CD. In UC <u>aminosalicylates</u> are used for <u>maintenance therapy</u> to control inflammation and reduce flare-ups. Mesalamine is the primary aminosalicylate used; it is well tolerated and can be taken once daily. The other aminosalicylates (sulfasalazine, balsalazide, olsalazine) are <u>converted to mesalamine</u>. Sulfasalazine is used less commonly due to the <u>many side effects</u> associated with the sulfapyridine component. The efficacy of <u>aminosalicylates</u> has been <u>proven in UC</u>; however, guidelines <u>no longer recommend</u> their use <u>in CD</u> (they do not maintain remission). <u>Topical steroids or oral budesonide are first line for mild-moderate CD</u>. In moderate-severe cases, an immunosuppressive agent such as azathioprine, mercaptopurine, or methotrexate is used. Steroids may also be used in moderate-severe cases. <u>Anti-TNF agents (e.g., infliximab) are used in patients with IBD that is refractory to steroids and immunosuppressants</u>. These agents are discussed in the Systemic Steroids & Autoimmune Conditions chapter.

Nicotine has been shown to worsen CD but can be protective in UC. In fact, nicotine patches have been used as an adjunct therapy for UC; however, adverse effects (nausea, dizziness) limits the benefit.

Agents Used For Mild Symptom Control: Diarrhea, Cramping/GI Spasms

DRUG	DOSING	SAFETY/SIDE EFFECTS/MONITORING

Antidiarrheals

DRUG	DOSING	SAFETY/SIDE EFFECTS/MONITORING
Loperamide *(Imodium)* Tablet/capsule, chewable tablet, suspension	4 mg PO after first loose stool initially; then 2 mg after each subsequent stool; not to exceed 16 mg/day 2 mg tab/cap; 1 mg/7.5 mL *(Imodium AD)*	**CONTRAINDICATIONS** Abdominal pain without diarrhea, children < 2 years of age, acute dysentery (bloody diarrhea and high fever), acute ulcerative colitis, pseudomembranous colitis *(C. difficile),* bacterial enterocolitis (caused by *Salmonella, Shigella,* and *Campylobacter)* **SIDE EFFECTS** Abdominal cramping, constipation, nausea **NOTES** Do not self-treat for > 2 days
Bismuth subsalicylate *(Pepto-Bismol,* others) Chewable tablet, suspension	524 mg (2 tbsp or 2 tablets) every 30-60 min as needed, up to 8 doses/day; max 2 days	**CONTRAINDICATIONS** Children with viral infections (varicella, influenza) due to risk of Reye's syndrome, patients with a salicylate allergy, history of severe GI bleed/ulcer or coagulopathy **SIDE EFFECTS** Black tongue/stool, hearing loss/tinnitus (toxicity) **NOTES** Caution in patients on aspirin therapy, anticoagulants, or those with renal insufficiency. Salicylate toxicity can occur if used excessively.
Diphenoxylate + atropine *(Lomotil)* Tablet, solution C-V	5 mg daily-QID (max 20 mg/day) Diphenoxylate 2.5 mg + atropine 0.025 mg/tablet or 5 mL solution	**CONTRAINDICATIONS** Children < 2 years of age, pseudomembranous colitis *(C. difficile),* diarrhea caused by enterotoxin-producing bacteria (toxigenic *E. coli, Salmonella, Shigella),* obstructive jaundice **WARNING** Toxic megacolon reported in acute ulcerative colitis patients on agents that inhibit intestinal motility. Observe for abdominal distention and discontinue promptly if noted. **SIDE EFFECTS** Somnolence, urinary retention, tachycardia, dry mouth, dizziness, depression

Antispasmodic

DRUG	DOSING	SAFETY/SIDE EFFECTS/MONITORING
Dicyclomine *(Bentyl)* Tablet/capsule, solution	20 mg QID; max 80 mg/day for > 2 weeks (can use 40 mg QID for < 2 weeks if symptoms respond) Take 30-60 minutes before meals	**CONTRAINDICATIONS** GI obstruction, severe ulcerative colitis, reflux esophagitis, unstable cardiovascular status in acute hemorrhage, obstructive uropathy, breast feeding, narrow-angle glaucoma, myasthenia gravis, infants < 6 months of age **WARNINGS** Anticholinergic (use caution in elderly, per Beer's Criteria), caution in mild-moderate ulcerative colitis (potential for toxic megacolon or paralytic ileus) **SIDE EFFECTS** Dizziness, dry mouth, nausea, blurred vision

Corticosteroids

DRUG	DOSING	SAFETY/SIDE EFFECTS/MONITORING

Oral Steroids

DRUG	DOSING	SAFETY/SIDE EFFECTS/MONITORING
PredniSONE Tablet, solution	5-60 mg/day	**SIDE EFFECTS** Short-term: ↑ appetite/weight gain, fluid retention, emotional instability (euphoria, mood swings, irritability), insomnia, GI upset; higher doses can cause ↑ in BP and blood glucose Long-term: Adrenal suppression/Cushing's syndrome, immuno-suppression/impaired wound healing, hypertension, hyperglycemia, cataracts, osteoporosis, others. Refer to Systemic Steroids & Autoimmune Conditions chapter. **NOTES (FOR ALL STEROIDS)** For management of acute flare, avoid long-term use if possible. May use alternate day therapy (ADT) to ↓ adrenal suppression and adverse effects. If used longer than 2 weeks, must taper (over 3-4 weeks) to avoid withdrawal symptoms. If long-term use is required, assess bone density (consider use of bisphosphonates, optimize calcium and vitamin D intake).
Budesonide **(Entocort EC,** Uceris) Entocort EC: 3 mg extended release capsule Uceris: 9 mg extended release tablet	Active disease: 9 mg once daily in the morning for up to 8 weeks Maintenance of remission: 6 mg once daily for 3 months If changing from prednisone, taper prednisone while starting budesonide	**For Budesonide** Undergoes extensive first-pass metabolism; ↓ systemic exposure than other oral steroids. Entocort EC indicated for mild-moderate Crohn's involving the ileum or ascending colon; Uceris indicated in UC only. Swallow whole – do not crush, chew or break.

Topical Steroids

DRUG	DOSING	SAFETY/SIDE EFFECTS/MONITORING
Hydrocortisone (Cortifoam, Cortenema)	Cortenema: 1 enema (100 mg) QHS for 21 days, then taper Cortifoam: 1 applicatorful (90 mg) 1-2 times daily for 2-3 weeks, then taper	**CONTRAINDICATIONS** Enema and foam: obstruction, abscess, perforation, peritonitis, intestinal anastomoses, extensive fistulas Enema only: systemic fungal infections and ileocolostomy in immediate/early post-op period **NOTES** Topical steroids have not been proven effective for maintenance of remission. Advantages of topical therapy include less systemic absorption and less frequent dosing schedule.
Budesonide rectal foam (Uceris)	1 metered dose BID x 2 weeks, then 1 metered dose daily x 4 weeks (1 metered dose = 2 mg budesonide)	**NOTES** For mild-moderate distal UC. Propellant is flammable; avoid fire and smoking during and after use.

Budesonide Drug Interactions

- Budesonide is a major CYP 3A4 substrate. <u>Potent 3A4 inhibitors may require a budesonide dose reduction</u>; 3A4 inducers may ↓ concentration of oral budesonide

- <u>Avoid grapefruit juice and grapefruit products</u> when using this medication.

- Antacids may effect dissolution and ↓ concentration of oral budesonide. Separate by 2 hours.

Maintenance Therapy

DRUG	DOSING	SAFETY/SIDE EFFECTS/MONITORING

Aminosalicylates

DRUG	DOSING	SAFETY/SIDE EFFECTS/MONITORING
Mesalamine (*Apriso:* ER cap *Asacol HD:* ER tab *Delzicol:* ER cap *Pentasa:* ER cap *Lialda:* ER tab *Canasa:* suppository *Rowasa:* enema) 5-ASA (5-aminosalicyclic acid)	Oral: *Delzicol*: 800 mg TID or 400 mg QID *Pentasa*: 1 g QID *Lialda*: 2.4-4.8 g once daily *Asacol HD*: 1.6 g TID *Apriso* 1.5 g once daily Suppository: 1 g rectally QHS Enema: 4 g QHS	**CONTRAINDICATIONS** Hypersensitivity to salicylates or aminosalicylates or any component of the formulation (see notes) **WARNINGS** Caution in patients with renal or hepatic impairment and active peptic ulcer, ↑ blood dyscrasias in elderly, pericarditis/myocarditis, oligospermia (rare) Patients with hypersensitivity to sulfasalazine may have a similar reaction to mesalamine (most patients do not). *Apriso* contains phenylalanine; avoid in phenylketonuria (PKU). *Rowasa* enema contains metabisulfite salts; caution in sulfite sensitivity. **SIDE EFFECTS** Abdominal pain, nausea, headache, flatulence, eructation (belching), pharyngitis, acute intolerance syndrome (similar to symptoms of IBD exacerbation) **MONITORING** Renal function, CBC, symptoms of IBD **NOTES** Mesalamine is better tolerated than other aminosalicylates. <u>Topical mesalamine</u> is more effective than oral mesalamine and steroids for <u>distal disease/proctitis in UC</u>; can use oral and topical together. Topical agents should not be used in proximal disease. Swallow caps/tabs whole; do not crush, chew, or break due to delayed-release coating. *Apriso:* do not use with antacids (dissolution is pH-dependent)
SulfaSALAzine (*Azulfidine, Azulfidine EN-tabs, Sulfazine, Sulfazine EC*) 5-aminosalicylic acid derivative	2-6 g daily divided TID or QID	Refer to Systemic Steroids & Autoimmune Conditions chapter.

Maintenance Therapy Continued

DRUG	DOSING	SAFETY/SIDE EFFECTS/MONITORING
Balsalazide *(Colazal, Giazo)*	*Colazal*: 2.25 g PO TID *Giazo*: 3.3 g PO BID	**CONTRAINDICATIONS** Salicylate allergy **SIDE EFFECTS** Headache, abdominal pain, diarrhea, vomiting (GI effects more common in children) **MONITORING** Renal function, LFTs, hypersensitivity, symptoms of IBD **NOTES** *Giazo* is only approved in males (failed to show a benefit in females). *Colazal* capsule contents may be sprinkled on applesauce. Beads are not coated, so mixture can be chewed if needed. This may cause staining of teeth/tongue.
Olsalazine *(Dipentum)*	500 mg PO BID	**CONTRAINDICATIONS** Salicylate allergy **SIDE EFFECTS** Diarrhea, abdominal pain **MONITORING** CBC, LFTs, renal function, symptoms of IBD

Immunosuppressive Agents – these agents can be used if patient fails above therapy or they can be used in combination with above therapies; often called "immunomodulators" or "steroid sparing" therapies

AzaTHIOprine *(Azasan, Imuran)*	2-3 mg/kg/day given IV/PO	**BOXED WARNINGS** Chronic immunosuppression can ↑ risk of neoplasia (esp. lymphomas), hematologic toxicities (leukopenia, thrombocytopenia) and mutagenic potential **WARNINGS** GI (severe N/V/D), hematologic (leukopenia, thrombocytopenia, anemia), and hepatotoxicity; patients with genetic deficiency of thiopurine methyltransferase (TPMT) are at ↑ risk for myelosuppression and may require lower dose. **SIDE EFFECTS** Severe N/V/D, rash, ↑ LFTs, hematologic toxicities (leukopenia, thrombocytopenia) **MONITORING** LFTs, CBC (weekly for 1st month), renal function **NOTES** Pregnancy Category D. Azathioprine is metabolized to mercaptopurine (avoid concurrent use due to myelosuppression). Olsalazine and allopurinol inhibit TPMT – may require ↓ dose of azathioprine.
Mercaptopurine *(Purinethol, Purixan)*	1-1.5 mg/kg/day PO	Similar to azathioprine, including TPMT **NOTES** Take on an empty stomach. Avoid old terms "6-Mercaptopurine" and "6-MP" – they caused 6x overdoses.

Maintenance Therapy Continued

DRUG	DOSING	SAFETY/SIDE EFFECTS/MONITORING
Methotrexate (*Rheumatrex, Trexall*) *Rasuvo* and *Otrexup* auto-injectors are used for RA	15-25 mg weekly PO	Refer to Systemic Steroids & Autoimmune Conditions chapter.

Monoclonal Antibodies to TNF

In patients with <u>moderate-severe</u> disease that has <u>not responded</u> to steroids and/or immunosuppressants or in any patient in which a steroid is contraindicated or not desired, treatment with monoclonal antibodies to TNF is likely to be used next. The drugs used in UC and CD are listed below. These are in the Systemic Steroids & Autoimmune Conditions chapter, where they are primarily used. The integrin receptor antagonists are used for both (autoimmune and IBD) and are discussed below.

DRUG	UC	CD
Adalimumab *(Humira)*	FDA approved	FDA approved
InFLIXimab *(Remicade)*	FDA approved	FDA approved
Golimumab *(Simponi)*	FDA approved	
Certolizumab *(Cimzia)*		FDA approved

Monoclonal Antibodies – Integrin Receptor Antagonists

DRUG	DOSING	SAFETY/SIDE EFFECTS/MONITORING
Natalizumab *(Tysabri)* Injection Approved for Crohn's and Multiple Sclerosis	300 mg IV over 1 hour <u>every 4 weeks</u> If taking steroids when initiating *Tysabri*, taper when onset of benefit observed. Stop *Tysabri* if patient cannot taper steroids within 6 months.	**BOXED WARNING** Progressive multifocal leukoencephalopathy (PML): monitor mental status changes; risk factors include: anti-JC virus antibodies, ↑ treatment duration and prior immunosuppressant use. **WARNINGS** Herpes encephalitis and meningitis, hepatotoxicity, immunosuppression/infections **SIDE EFFECTS** <u>Infusion reactions, headache, fatigue</u>, nausea, rash, depression, gastroenteritis, abdominal/back pain **NOTES** Only approved for moderate-severe Crohn's patients who have <u>failed anti-TNF therapy</u>. <u>Discontinue if no response by week 12.</u> Cannot be used with other immunosuppressants. <u>REMS: Must be enrolled in manufacturer TOUCH Prescribing Program.</u> MedGuide required. Do not shake. Stable in NS only.

Monoclonal Antibodies – Integrin Receptor Antagonists Continued

DRUG	DOSING	SAFETY/SIDE EFFECTS/MONITORING
Vedolizumab *(Entyvio)* Injection Approved for Crohn's and UC	300 mg IV at 0, 2, and 6 weeks, then every 8 weeks. Discontinue if no benefit by week 14	**WARNINGS** Infusion reactions (rare), infections, liver injury, and PML (see monitoring). Patients receiving vedolizumab <u>should not receive live vaccines</u>. **SIDE EFFECTS** <u>Headache, nasopharyngitis, arthralgia</u>, antibody development **MONITORING** LFTs, signs and symptoms of infection, hypersensitivity, neurological symptoms and/or progressive weakness (to monitor for PML – not observed with vedolizumab, but Boxed Warning with natalizumab); routine TB screening **NOTES** Refrigerate and store in original packaging. Swirl during reconstitution, do not shake. After reconstitution, use immediately or refrigerate up to 4 hours. Do not freeze. Infuse over 30 min. All immunizations must be up to date before starting therapy. Cannot be used with other immunosuppressants. MedGuide required.

Patient Counseling

Mesalamine

- <u>Do not crush or chew long-acting formulations.</u> You may see a <u>ghost tablet</u> in the feces *(Asacol HD, Delzicol)*; the drug has been absorbed into your body; the tablet is empty.

- *Rowasa* enema: *Rowasa* is an off-white suspension. It can darken over time when removed from the foil pouch. If it has dark brown contents, throw it away. Remove bottle from pouch and shake well. Remove the protective sheath from the applicator tip. Hold the bottle at the neck so as not to cause any of the medicine to be discharged. Best results are obtained by lying on the left side with the left leg extended and the right leg flexed forward for balance. Gently insert the lubricated applicator tip into the rectum to prevent damage to the rectal wall, pointed slightly toward the navel. Grasp the bottle firmly, and then tilt slightly so that the nozzle is aimed toward the back, and squeeze slowly to instill the medication. Steady hand pressure will discharge most of the medicine. After administering, withdraw and discard the bottle. Remain in position for at least 30 minutes, or preferably all night for maximum benefit. *Rowasa* can cause staining of surfaces including clothing and other fabrics, flooring, painted surfaces, marble, granite, vinyl and enamel. Take care in choosing a suitable location for administration of this product.

- *Canasa* suppository: For best results, empty your rectum (have a bowel movement) just before using. This medication should be used at bedtime. Detach one suppository from the strip. Remove foil wrapper; avoid excessive handling. Insert the suppository with the pointed end first completely into your rectum, using gentle pressure. For best results, keep the suppository in your rectum for at least 1 – 3 hours. You may put a little bit of lubricating gel on the suppository. *Canasa* can cause staining of surfaces including, clothing, and other fabrics, flooring, painted surfaces, marble, granite, vinyl and enamel. Keep *Canasa* away from these surfaces to prevent staining.

Hydrocortisone *(Cortifoam)*

- Preparation: Shake the foam container well for 5 – 10 seconds before using. Hold container upright on a level surface. Place the tip of the applicator onto the nose of the container cap. Pull plunger past the fill line on the applicator barrel. To fill the applicator, press down firmly on the cap flanges, hold for 1 – 2 seconds and release. Wait 5 – 10 seconds for the foam to expand and fill the applicator barrel. Repeat until full and then remove applicator from container.

- Use: hold applicator firmly by the barrel (thumb and middle finger on the barrel "wings") and place index finger on the plunger. Insert tip into anus and push plunger to expel foam. Withdraw applicator. The foam container should never be inserted into the anus – only the applicator.

- After use, take apart and clean all parts with warm water for next use.

- Each aerosol container should deliver 14 doses.

- Store at room temperature.

Budesonide *(Uceris)* Rectal Foam

- This medicine is for rectal use only.

- The *Uceris* rectal foam kit has 2 aerosol canisters and 28 lubricated applicators. Each canister contains 14 doses of foam. Store at room temperature. Do not puncture or burn the canisters.

- Empty your rectum completely. Warm the canister in your hands and shake well for 10 – 15 seconds before using. Choose a position to administer – standing, lying or sitting on the toilet. Use the evening dose before bedtime and try not to have a bowel movement until morning.

- The aerosol is flammable. Keep it away from fire, flames or smoking during and after use. Do not spray toward a flame.

- Do not use grapefruit or grapefruit juice with this medication. If you have been using grapefruit do not change the amount without discussing this with your healthcare provider.

Budesonide *(Entocort EC* and *Uceris)*

- Take this medication with a full glass of water before a meal. <u>Do not crush, chew or break open the capsule.</u>

- Tell your healthcare provider if you have changes in the shape or location of body fat (especially in your arms, legs, face, neck, breasts, and waist), high blood pressure, severe headache, fast or uneven heart rate, blurred vision, or a general ill feeling with headache, tiredness, nausea, and vomiting.

- You should have your blood pressure monitored on a regular basis.

- You should have your blood sugar monitored on a regular basis.

- Do not use grapefruit or grapefruit juice products with this medication. If you have been using grapefruit do not change the amount without discussing this with your healthcare provider.

- Avoid being near people who are sick or have infections.

For counseling on the biologic agents, refer to the Systemic Steroids & Autoimmune Conditions chapter.

PRACTICE CASE

Frank Clough: SOAP Note for 09/24/2014 Age on DOS: 75 yrs, DOB: 01/14/1939	**San Diego Medical Group** 35 La Jolla Drive Suite 100 San Diego, CA 92130 (444) 444-4444

seen by: Alison James

seen on: Wednesday 24 September 2014

VS

Height:	Weight:	BMI:	Blood Pressure:	Temp:	Pulse:	Resp Rate:
65.0 in	148.0 lb	24.6	165 / 92 mmHg	98.9 F	97 bpm	16 rpm

CC | Lots of diarrhea for the past few days and now there's blood in it

S | Mr. Clough presents with a 3 day history of 5-6 diarrhea episodes per day. He describes this as similar to his initial diagnosis of ulcerative colitis in Nevada about 5 months ago. He describes some cramping and bloating in the lower abdomen, but no other associated pain. He doesn't think the pain is worse or better with food, but he hasn't eaten much over the past few days. He has no nausea or vomiting. Today he noticed some streaks of blood in the diarrhea and his wife became concerned and made the appointment at the clinic. He states he is compliant with his mesalamine suppositories and they have worked well in controlling his UC over the past months until now. His usual diarrhea frequency is 1-2 episodes her day. Patient reports an allergy to penicillin. He experiences a severe rash.

O | Past Medical History:
Ulcerative colitis (distal disease) and hypertension

Medications:
Canasa 1 gm suppository daily at HS x 5 months / Tenormin 100 mg daily x "many years"
Both prescribed by MD in Nevada and active. Patient states he is compliant.

Labs (reference range):
Na 139 mEq/L (135 - 145)
K 3.8 mEq/L (3.5 - 5)
Cl 100 mEq/L (95 - 103)
HCO3 26 mEq/L (24 - 30)
BUN 27 mg/dL (7 - 20)
SCr 1.4 mg/dL (0.6 - 1.3)
Glu 109 mg/dL (100 - 125)
WBC 8.6 cells/mm3 (4 - 11 x 10^3)
Hgb 16.8 g/dL (13.5 - 18 male, 12 - 16 female)
Hct 48 % (38 - 50 male, 36 - 46 female)
Plt 250 mm3 (150,000 - 450,000)

A | 75 yo otherwise fairly healthy white gentleman here for an ulcerative colitis exacerbation.
(1) Ulcerative colitis (distal) exacerbation:
Patient has been well-controlled on mesalamine suppositories for his disease and finds this therapy acceptable. He has never required steroids of any kind. He is currently dehydrated as evidenced by objective data (BP, HR and BUN/SCr ratio) and requires therapy to control the acute flare.
(2) Hypertension:
BP is not currently at goal. Since this is a new patient to our clinic, we may need to re-assess once he is more stable and rehydrated. Regardless, need to align therapy with JNC 8 guidelines.

P | Prednisone 10 mg daily for ulcerative colitis flare. Follow-up in clinic in 1 week.

Questions

1. The patient was originally prescribed mesalamine suppositories for distal disease classified as mild-moderate. Which of the following statements are correct? (Select **ALL** that apply.)

   a. Oral therapy is preferred for initial treatment.

   b. Mesalamine is available in oral and rectal (suppositories, enema) formulations.

   c. Sulfasalazine is preferred over mesalamine for distal disease.

   d. Mesalamine cannot be used in a sulfa allergy.

   e. Mesalamine is considered first-line therapy for distal disease.

2. Mesalamine rectal suppository counseling should include the following points: (Select **ALL** that apply.)

   a. Peel open the plastic and remove suppository prior to use.

   b. Handle unwrapped suppository as little as possible.

   c. Should be kept in the rectum for at least 1-3 hours.

   d. Lubricating gel may be used to ease application.

   e. Insert suppository just prior to a bowel movement.

3. The physician prescribed prednisone for the acute flare-up. Which of the following are short-term side effects that may occur and should be conveyed to the patient? (Select **ALL** that apply.)

   a. Elevated blood glucose

   b. Elevated blood pressure

   c. Osteoporosis

   d. Changes in mood

   e. Cataracts

4. Guidelines recommend against steroid treatment for long-term control of IBD symptoms; however, many patients use budesonide (or prednisone) daily. Which of the following are long-term side effects that may occur and should be conveyed to the patient? (Select **ALL** that apply.)

   a. Hepatotoxicity

   b. Poor wound healing

   c. Fat redistribution

   d. Adrenal suppression

   e. Peptic ulcers

Questions 5-6 are not based on the above case.

5. A female patient has failed her initial treatment for Crohn's disease, which included cyclosporine and methotrexate. Her symptoms are described as severe. She is prescribed infliximab. Which of the following statements is correct?

   a. She can use *Enbrel* instead.

   b. She should have been prescribed *Tysabri* prior to use of infliximab.

   c. Infliximab suppositories are the preferred formulation.

   d. This medication comes in an IV formulation only.

   e. This medication can suppress TB activation.

6. A patient has been prescribed infliximab. Which of the following tests should be ordered prior to the start of therapy? (Select **ALL** that apply.)

   a. Pulmonary function

   b. TSH and FT4

   c. CBC

   d. TB

   e. HBV

Answers

1-b,e, 2-a,b,c,d, 3-a,b,d, 4-b,c,d, e, 5-d, 6-c,d,e

71

SEXUAL DYSFUNCTION

We gratefully acknowledge the assistance of James D. Nash, PharmD, MPH, BCPS, Associate Dean and Associate Professor, Regis University School of Pharmacy, in preparing this chapter.

BACKGROUND

This chapter will focus on erectile dysfunction in males and hypoactive sexual desire disorder in females. Erectile dysfunction (impotence), refers to difficulty getting or sustaining an erection that is firm enough for sex. This is a common type of sexual dysfunction in men and can generally be treated with phosphodiesterase (PDE)-5 inhibitors. Males can experience other types of sexual dysfunction, including problems with ejaculation and low libido, which is sometimes treated with testosterone and is discussed in the chapter that covers hormone treatment.

In women, sexual dysfunction can be due to either an inability to reach orgasm (anorgasmia), painful intercourse, or low sexual desire (hypoactive sexual desire disorder). Flibanserin (*Addyi*) is the sole drug for females with sexual dysfunction, and claims to treat HSDD. In clinical trials, 1 of every 11 females using flibanserin had an increase of one-half of a satisfying sexual event per month, compared to placebo. It is approved for premenopausal women only, and causes fainting.

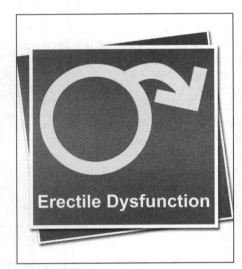

Erectile Dysfunction

GUIDELINES/REFERENCES

Montague DK, Jarow JP, Broderick GA, et al. For The Erectile Dysfunction Guideline Update Panel. Chapter 1: The Management Of Erectile Dysfunction: An AUA Update. *J Urol.* 2005 July; 174(1): 230-239.

ERECTILE DYSFUNCTION

The most common cause of erectile dysfunction (ED) is reduced blood flow to the penis, which is commonly caused by diseases such as <u>peripheral neuropathy, atherosclerosis, and hypertension</u>. Since the arteries supplying blood to the penis are smaller than those supplying blood to the heart, they can become restricted sooner than the larger vessels. ED can be considered an early warning indicator of cardiovascular disease, and men with ED with risk factors should be referred for cardiac evaluation. Psychological issues (including <u>depression</u> and <u>stress</u>) and neurological illness (<u>spinal cord injury, stroke</u>) can be contributory. Low testosterone can be a factor, although the majority of men with low testosterone complain of low desire. Drugs that can contribute to erectile dysfunction are listed in the table.

NON-DRUG TREATMENT

Lifestyle changes, including losing weight, quitting tobacco use or reducing alcohol intake may be able to improve the condition. Underlying diseases that can contribute to ED should be properly managed and any offending agents should be discontinued, if possible.

Non-drug options that are beneficial in some men are vacuum erection devices, implants and surgery.

Natural products used to treat ED include <u>yohimbe, L-arginine, and panax ginseng</u>. *The Natural Medicines Database* rates L-arginine (taken in high doses) and panax ginseng as "possibly effective" for this purpose. Yohimbe is rated as "insufficient evidence to date" with

DRUGS THAT CAN CAUSE ERECTILE DYSFUNCTION
Alcohol
Anticancer drugs - leuprolide, flutamide, busulfan, cyclosphamide
Anticholinergics
Antidepressants – particularly <u>SSRIs and SNRIs</u>
Antihypertensives – <u>beta blockers</u>, clonidine, methyldopa
Antipsychotics – haloperidol, chlorpromazine, fluphenazine, thioridazine
Atomoxetine
BPH medications - <u>finasteride</u>, <u>dutasteride</u>, and <u>silodosin</u> (primarily causes retrograde ejaculation)
Digoxin
H_2RAs – <u>cimetidine</u>, nizatidine, ranitidine
Nicotine
Opioids (chronic use) - methadone

some studies showing benefit and others which did not. There is disagreement over which part of the plant provides benefit; some studies use the yohimbe bark and others use an isolated compound (yohimbine). Yohimbe causes stomach upset, anxiety, and can cause more severe health concerns, including tachycardia and arrhythmias.

DRUG TREATMENT

PDE-5 inhibitors (sildenafil, vardenafil, tadalafil, avanafil) are the first-line treatment for ED. If a patient cannot tolerate or has a contraindication to PDE-5 inhibitors, alprostadil can be used instead. Alprostadil is either injected into the penis, or inserted into the penis with a urethral suppository. The treatment is invasive, painful, and short-acting.

Two of the PDE-5 inhibitors used for ED are indicated for other conditions. Sildenafil (*Viagra*) is indicated for ED and sildenafil (*Revatio*) is indicated for pulmonary arterial hypertension (PAH). Tadalafil (*Cialis*) is indicated for benign prostatic hypertrophy (BPH) and ED, and Tadalafil (*Adcirca*) is indicated for PAH. A PDE-5 inhibitor should not be used concurrently with a PDE-5 inhibitor used for a different condition.

PDE-5 Inhibitors

Following sexual stimulation, PDE-5 inhibitors cause a local release of nitric oxide, which increases <u>cGMP and smooth muscle relaxation. This causes the blood flow to the penis to increase</u>, which results in an erection. PDE-5 inhibitors do not increase libido (sexual interest).

DRUG	DOSING	SAFETY/SIDE EFFECTS/MONITORING
Sildenafil *(Viagra)* *Revatio* – PAH	25-100 mg daily (see diagram for dosing considerations for class) Start at 50 mg, taken ~1 hr (0.5-4 hrs) before sexual activity	**CONTRAINDICATIONS** Concurrent use with <u>nitrates</u> or riociguat. **WARNINGS** Impaired <u>color discrimination</u>, dose-related; patients with retinitis pigmentosa may have higher risk.
Vardenafil *(Levitra, Staxyn ODT)*	*Levitra*: 5-20 mg *Staxyn ODT*: 10 mg Start at 10 mg, taken ~1 hr before sexual activity	<u>Hearing loss</u>, with or without tinnitus/dizziness. <u>Vision loss</u>, rare, can be due to nonarteritic anterior ischemic optic neuropathy. Risk factors include low cup-to-disc ratio, coronary artery disease, diabetes, hypertension, hyperlipidemia, smoking, and > 50 years of age. Avoid use with known degenerative retinal disorders.
Tadalafil *(Cialis)* *Cialis* – ED and BPH *Adcirca* – PAH Known as the "weekend pill"	5-20 mg Start at 10 mg, with or without food, taken ~ 30 mins before sexual activity, or start at 2.5-5 mg daily	<u>Hypotension</u>, due to vasodilation, higher risk if resting BP < 90/50 mmHg, fluid depletion, or autonomic dysfunction. <u>Priapism</u>, instruct to seek emergency medical care if erection lasts > 4 hrs. If chest pain occurs, taking seek immediate medical help. **SIDE EFFECTS** <u>Headache, flushing, dyspepsia, color vision changes</u>, blurred vision, increased sensitivity to light) erythema, epistaxis, diarrhea, myalgia, muscle/back pain (tadalafil)
Avanafil *(Stendra)*	50-200 mg Start at 100 mg, taken ~15 mins prior to sexual activity	**NOTES** If muscle/back pain w/tadalafil it usually lasts < 2 days. Best when taken on an empty stomach, avoid with fatty food (tadalafil can be taken with or without food). For ED, no more than one dose/day is recommended. *Stendra* can be taken closest to sexual activity.

PDE-5 Inhibitor Dosing Guide -  Viagra, Cialis, Levitra, Stendra

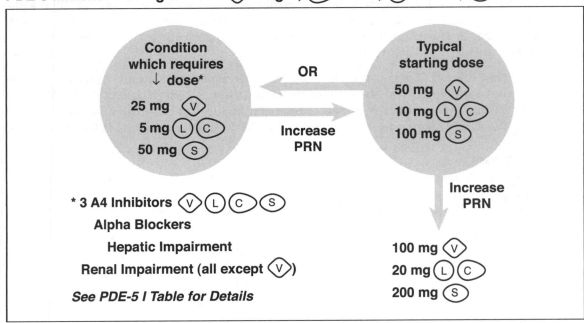

PDE-5 Inhibitor Drug Interactions

- Nitrates are an <u>absolute contraindication</u> for the use of PDE-5 inhibitors. Concurrent use of any prescription nitrates (including *Nitrostat, Nitrolingual,* and *BiDil*) or illicit alkyl nitrates ("poppers" such as amyl nitrate and butyl nitrate) increases the potential for severe hypotension.

- Caution with other agents that cause hypotension (i.e., <u>alpha blockers</u> and <u>antihypertensive drugs</u>).

- If a patient with ED has taken a PDE-5 inhibitor and then develops angina, nitroglycerin should not be used until after 12 hours for avanafil, after 24 hours for sildenafil or vardenafil and after 48 hours for tadalafil. Occasionally, if needed, nitrates are used in an acute emergency, with careful monitoring.

- <u>Caution with PDE-5 inhibitor and concurrent alpha-1 blocker therapy</u>: PDE-5 inhibitors can enhance the hypotensive effect of an alpha-1 blocker. The patient should be stable on the alpha-1 blocker (and be without excessive dizziness/hypotension) prior to starting the PDE-5 inhibitor. If *Cialis* is being used to treat BPH, do not use alpha-1 blockers concurrently.

- <u>Strong CYP450 3A4 inducers ↓ drug serum levels; monitor effectiveness.</u> Moderate and strong 3A4 inhibitors increase the drug serum levels (which can require lower doses and/or extended dosing intervals).

- Grapefruit juice, a 3A4 inhibitor, can increase the PDE-5 inhibitor levels.

PDE-5 Inhibitor Patient Counseling

- Sildenafil, vardenafil, and avanafil work faster when taken on an empty stomach; fatty food will slow down how fast the drug works. Tadalafil can be taken with or without food.

- Take the PDE-5 inhibitor approximately 15 minutes (avanafil), 30 minutes (tadalafil), or 1 hour (sildenafil and vardenafil) before sexual activity.

- Sildenafil, vardenafil, and avanafil last for 4-6 hours; tadalafil lasts for up to 36 hours.

- Sexual activity can put an extra strain on your heart, especially if your heart is already weak from a heart attack or heart disease. Stop sexual activity and get medical help right away if you have chest pain, dizziness, or nausea during sex.

- PDE-5 inhibitors can cause your blood pressure to drop suddenly to an unsafe level if it is taken with certain other medicines. Do not take PDE-5 inhibitors if you take medicines called "nitrates" (such as nitroglycerin) or street drugs called "poppers" (such as amyl nitrate and butyl nitrate). A sudden drop in blood pressure can cause you to feel dizzy, faint, or have a heart attack or stroke.

- PDE-5 inhibitors do not protect you or your partner from getting sexually transmitted diseases, including HIV.

- If you have an erection that lasts more than 4 hours or is painful, get medical help right away or the penis could be severely damaged.

- Sudden vision loss in one or both eyes can be a sign of a serious eye problem that can occur from the use of this medicine. This is a rare occurrence, but if this happens stop taking the medicine and get medical help right away.

- Some people can have ringing in their ears (tinnitus) or dizziness. If you have these symptoms, stop taking the PDE-5 inhibitor and contact a doctor right away. If you cannot hear out of one or both ears, contact your healthcare provider right away.

Alprostadil (Prostaglandin E$_1$)

Alprostadil is prostaglandin E$_1$, which causes vasodilation and allows blood flow into the cavernosal arteries, which enlarges the penis. The drug is either injected into the penis, or inserted into the penis through the urethra. The treatment is invasive, painful and does not last as long as the PDE-5 inhibitors. Alprostadil is used in some men who cannot tolerate or have contraindications to PDE-5 inhibitors.

DRUG	DOSING	SAFETY/SIDE EFFECTS/MONITORING
Alprostadil *(Caverject, Caverject Impulse, Edex)* Intercavernous injection Reconstitute prior to use	Inject 1.25-2.5 mg into the base of the penis, titrate until desired response is achieved. Appropriate dose should cause erection 5-10 min after injection, lasts ~1 hr. Max 1x/day, 3x/week <u>Refrigerate</u>	**CONTRAINDICATIONS** Sickle cell anemia, multiple myeloma, leukemia, anatomical deformation of fibrotic conditions of the penis, penile implants **SIDE EFFECTS** <u>Penile pain</u>, HA, dizziness, hematoma, <u>priapism</u>, scarring at injection site
Alprostadil *(Muse)* Urethral pellets	Insert 125-250 mcg pellet into urethra Urinate before administration Max 2x/day <u>Refrigerate</u>	**CONTRAINDICATIONS** Urethral stricture, balanitis, severe hypospadias and curvature, urethritis, venous thrombosis, sickle cell anemia, multiple myeloma, leukemia **SIDE EFFECTS** <u>Penile pain</u>, HA, dizziness, <u>priapism</u>, syncope

HYPOACTIVE SEXUAL DESIRE DISORDER

Hypoactive sexual desire disorder (HSDD) is characterized by a low sexual desire that causes marked distress or interpersonal difficulty. The low sexual desire is not due a health condition or drug.

5-HT$_{1A}$ Agonist and 5-HT$_{2A}$ Antagonist

Flibanserin exhibits agonist activity at 5-HT$_{1A}$ and antagonist activity at 5-HT$_{2A}$, the exact mechanism of how this treats HSDD is unknown. Flibanserin does <u>not enhance</u> sexual performance. <u>Premenopausal</u> females only; not indicated for post-menopausal females or males.

DRUG	DOSING	SAFETY/SIDE EFFECTS/MONITORING
Flibanserin *(Addyi)* REMS: Providers and pharmacies need to be certified. MedGuide required. Avoid use in pregnancy or breastfeeding.	<u>100 mg QHS</u> Discontinue if no benefit after 8 weeks	**BOXED WARNINGS** ↑ risk severe hypotension and syncope if taken with <u>alcohol</u>, moderate-to-strong <u>3A4 Inhibitors</u>, or <u>hepatic impairment</u> **CONTRAINDICATIONS** <u>Alcohol, concurrent use of moderate-to-strong 3A4 inhibitors</u>, hepatic impairment **WARNINGS** <u>Hypotension, syncope</u>, CNS depression **SIDE EFFECTS** Dizziness, somnolence, nausea, fatigue, insomnia, and dry mouth

Drug Interactions

- CNS depressants: ↑ risk of hypotension and syncope.

- CYP3A4 inhibitors ↑ flibanserin; moderate-strong 3A4 inhibitors are contraindicated. CYP2C19 poor metabolizers: can increase the risk of hypotension and syncope.

PRACTICE CASE

JF is a 60 y/o black male who made an appointment at the Family Medicine clinic to be evaluated for impotence. He cannot sustain an erection. This has caused performance anxiety, which has worsened the situation. His medical conditions include hypertension, anxiety/low mood, obesity and prostate enlargement.

Allergies: NKDA

Medications:
Flomax 0.4 mg daily
Inderal LA 160 mg daily
Fosinopril 10 mg daily
Zoloft 100 mg daily
Vitamin D 200 IU daily
Aspirin 325 mg daily
Acetaminophen 325 mg 1-2 tablets PRN headache

Vitals:
Height: 5'9" Weight: 210 pounds
BP: 118/82 mmHg HR: 90 BPM RR: 16 BPM Temp: 98.6ºF

Labs: Na (mEq/L) = 140 (135 - 145)
K (mEq/L) = 5.1 (3.5 - 5)
Cl (mEq/L) = 100 (95 - 103)
HCO3 (mEq/L) = 25 (24 - 30)
BUN (mg/dL) = 16 (7 - 20)
SCr (mg/dL) = 1.0 (0.6 - 1.3)
Glucose (mg/dL) = 130 (100 - 125)
Ca (mg/dL) = 10.1 (8.5 - 10.5)
Mg (mEq/L) = 1.9 (1.3 - 2.1)
PO4 (mg/dL) = 4.5 (2.3 - 4.7)

Start sildenafil 50 mg - take 1 hour prior to sexual activity. Schedule follow-up appointment in 2 months. The cardiologist has written a new prescription for amiodarone 200 mg PO daily that AH would like to have filled.

Questions

1. Is sildenafil contraindicated in this patient? (Select **ALL** that apply.)

   a. Yes, the combination of *Flomax* and sildenafil is contraindicated.

   b. No, but he must be cautioned about dizziness, lightheadedness and fainting.

   c. No, but he has to begin sildenafil at 12.5 mg once daily.

   d. No, but the *Flomax* should be changed to doxazosin; this is a safer combination.

   e. No, but the dose of the alpha blocker should be stable (well-tolerated) prior to beginning the PDE-5 inhibitor.

2. Which of the following medications could be contributing to JF's problem with erectile dysfunction? (Select **ALL** that apply.)

   a. *Inderal LA*

   b. *Zoloft*

   c. Vitamin D

   d. Aspirin

   e. Acetaminophen

3. If JF begins sildenafil therapy, he should be counseled concerning the risk of priapism. Select the correct counseling statement:

   a. If you sustain an erection that lasts more than 4 hours, you should stop using the medicine. The erection will go away in about 24 hours.

   b. If you sustain an erection that lasts more than 4 hours, you should stop using the medicine and take 25 mg of over-the-counter diphenhydramine. The erection will go away in about 24 hours.

   c. If you sustain an erection that lasts more than 4 hours, you should stop using the medicine and rest in bed until the erection goes away, which takes about 4-6 hours.

   d. If you sustain an erection that lasts more than 2 hours, you will need to get medical help right away. Priapism must be treated as soon as possible or it can cause lasting damage to the penis.

   e. If you sustain an erection that lasts more than 4 hours, you will need to get medical help right away. Priapism must be treated as soon as possible or it can cause lasting damage to the penis.

4. The pharmacist should call the physician and recommend possible medication changes that could reduce or eliminate the ED problem. Reasonable suggestions could include: (Select **ALL** that apply.)

   a. Change the *Zoloft* to a medication that is not in the SSRI or SNRI class.

   b. Change the fosinopril to losartan.

   c. Change *Inderal LA* to a different class of medication, or try a trial with metoprolol.

   d. Change the fosinopril to amlodipine.

   e. Change the *Inderal LA* to furosemide.

Questions 5-7 do not apply to the above case.

5. A patient is using tadalafil three times weekly. He uses 10 mg, taken 1 hour before sexual intercourse. He has asked the physician to change him to the daily form of the medicine, since he uses it more than twice weekly. Choose the correct dosing range for daily tadalafil when used for ED:

   a. 0.125-2.5 mg daily

   b. 2.5-5 mg daily

   c. 5-10 mg daily

   d. 10-15 mg daily

   e. This medicine cannot be used daily

6. The PDE-5 inhibitors require lower doses, and in some cases avoidance, when a patient is using certain drugs, including saquinavir and clarithromycin. This is due to the following reason:

   a. These are strong CYP 3A4 inducers; they could cause the PDE-5 inhibitor level to decrease to a dangerous level.

   b. These are strong CYP 3A4 inhibitors; they could cause the PDE-5 inhibitor level to increase to a dangerous level.

   c. These are strong CYP 3A4 inducers; they could cause the PDE-5 inhibitor level to increase to a dangerous level.

   d. These are strong CYP 3A4 inhibitors; they could cause the PDE-5 inhibitor level to decrease to a dangerous level.

   e. There is no interaction between PDE-5 inhibitors and these medications.

7. A 50 year old female is inquiring about *Addyi*. She has seen some advertisements on television and feels she is a prime candidate. Which of the following should be discussed during counseling:

   a. It is indicated for all female adult patients.
   b. The recommended starting dose is 50 mg daily increasing to 100 mg daily as tolerated.
   c. It may take time to see an effect so it is recommended to continue the medication for at least 90 days.
   d. Avoid drinking alcohol while using *Addyi*.
   e. You cannot use this drug if you have renal impairment.

Answers

1-b,e, 2-a,b, 3-e, 4-a,c, 5-b, 6-b, 7-d

72

BENIGN PROSTATIC HYPERPLASIA (BPH)

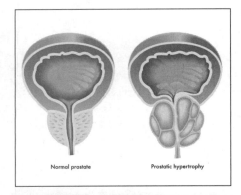

Normal prostate   Prostatic hypertrophy

GUIDELINES/REFERENCES

Update on AUA Guideline on the Management of Benign Prostatic Hyperplasia. *The Journal of Urology.* 2011; 185:1793-1803.

American Urological Association Practice Guidelines Committee. AUA guidelines on management of benign prostatic hyperplasia 2003. Chapter 1: Diagnosis and treatment recommendations. *The Journal of Urology.* 2003; 170:530-547.

BACKGROUND

The prostate is a walnut-sized gland that surrounds the urethra at the base of the bladder. As part of the male reproductive system, the main function of the prostate is to secrete slightly alkaline fluid that becomes part of the seminal fluid carrying sperm.

The prostate is dependent on androgens (mainly testosterone) for development and maintenance of size and function. Testosterone is metabolized to dihydrotestosterone (DHT) by 5 alpha-reductase. DHT is responsible for normal and hyperplastic growth (increase in the number of cells). Benign prostatic hyperplasia (BPH) results from overgrowth of the stromal and epithelial cells of the prostate gland. The enlarged gland contributes to lower urinary tract symptoms (LUTS) via direct bladder outlet obstruction (BOO) and increased smooth muscle tone and resistance. As the prostate enlarges, the layer of tissue surrounding it stops it from expanding, causing the gland to press against the urethra like a clamp on a garden hose. The bladder wall becomes thicker and irritated. The bladder begins to contract even when it contains small amounts of urine, causing more frequent urination. Eventually, the bladder weakens and loses the ability to empty itself. Interestingly, there is not a direct linear correlation between prostate size and symptoms; some men are more bothered even with a smaller prostate size, while others with a larger prostate are not as symptomatic. The enlargement does not usually cause problems until later in life with a peak incidence around 65 years of age. When the prostate becomes larger, prostate specific antigen (PSA) levels can increase; yet, BPH does not increase the risk of prostate cancer.

SYMPTOMS/COMPLICATIONS

The signs and symptoms of BPH are mainly LUTS which include difficulty holding urine (storage) and emptying the bladder (voiding). These disturbances significantly impact the quality of life for the patient. LUTS can include:

- Hesitancy, intermittency, straining or weak stream of urine
- Urinary urgency and leaking or dribbling
- Incomplete emptying of the bladder (bladder always feels full)
- Urinary frequency, especially nocturia (urination at night)
- Bladder outlet obstruction (BOO)

BPH rarely causes more severe symptoms – but, if the blockage is severe, the urine could back up into the kidneys and result in acute renal failure. Urinary tract infections can also be present, but are uncommon in men.

DRUGS THAT CAN WORSEN BPH
Anticholinergics (e.g., benztropine)
Antihistamines (e.g., diphenhydramine, chlorpheniramine)
Caffeine (can worsen symptoms)
Decongestants (e.g., pseudoephrine)
Diuretics (increase urination–be sure to take early in the day to limit nocturia)
SNRIs (affect urethral resistance)
TCAs, phenothiazines and other drugs with anticholinergic properties
Testosterone products

DIAGNOSIS

Prostate cancer symptoms can be similar to the symptoms of BPH. Diagnosis requires a careful patient medical history including surgeries and trauma, current medications including herbal and OTC drugs, focused physical exam including a Digital Rectal Exam (DRE), and urinalysis and serum Prostate Specific Antigen (PSA) to rule out conditions other than BPH (e.g., prostate or bladder cancer, neurogenic bladder, others). Patient may be asked to complete a voiding diary as well to better tailor therapy. PSA, a protein produced by prostate cells, is frequently ↑ in prostate cancer, however, it can also be increased in other conditions including BPH. Note that the recommendations for routine prostate cancer screening have changed (they will be done less frequently than in the past); see Oncology chapter.

DRUG TREATMENT

The patient's perception of the severity of BPH symptoms guides selection of the treatment modality in a patient. Validated questionnaires, such as the AUA Symptom Score, are commonly used to quantify symptoms. The scoring system rates how bothersome the symptoms are to the patient, with higher scores indicating more severe or bothersome symptoms. Treatment options can include watchful waiting, pharmacologic therapy and surgical intervention. Choice of treatment is a shared decision-making process between the patient and the clinician. Mild disease is generally treated with watchful waiting, which entails having the patient return for reassessment yearly. Moderate/severe disease is generally treated with medications, a minimally invasive procedure, or surgery such as transurethral resection of the prostate (TURP). Medications include alpha blockers (selective and non-selective), alone or in combination with a 5 alpha-reductase inhibitor. The 5 alpha-reductase inhibitors should not be used in men with LUTS secondary to BPH without prostatic enlargement (as these medications work by decreasing prostate size). Peripheral-acting anticholinergic agents used for overactive bladder (such as tolterodine) are sometimes a reasonable option for men without an elevated post void residual (PRV) urine and when LUTS are predominately irritative. If anticholinergics are used, PVR should be < 250-300 mL (anticholinergics are discussed in the Overactive Bladder chapter). Another treatment option is using the phosphodiesterase-5 (PDE-5) inhibitor tadalafil. This can be used in men with BPH alone, and can be an attractive option for men with both BPH and erectile dysfunction (ED); the dose is sufficient for both indications. Tadalafil, in combination with an alpha blocker (especially a non-selective agent) would pose risk for additive hypotension and orthostasis in an elderly male.

Historically, alpha blockers have been considered the standard BPH drug treatment. They are used alone in mild symptoms, and often with a 5 alpha-reductase inhibitor with moderate symptoms. Recently, tamsulosin (the most popular alpha-blocker) has been associated with floppy iris syndrome, a condition that makes cataract surgery difficult to complete safely. Cataracts are common in elderly patients, and the use of alpha blockers increases the risk itself. The important thing is to let the ophthalmologist know if a patient has ever taken an alpha-blocker.

Natural Products

Saw palmetto is used for BPH, but it is rated as "possibly ineffective" by *The Natural Medicines Database* due to contradictory and inconsistent data. Pygeum is another natural product and it is rated as "likely effective". Do not recommend a pygeum product unless it has been harvested ethically; ripping the bark off the trees to extract pygeum is not sustainable. Beta-sitosterol (which is available as supplements, in margarine substitutes, in African wild potato extract products, in pumpkin seed and in soy and red clover) is rated as "likely effective" and rye grass pollen is rated as possibly effecitve. Lycopene is used for prostate cancer prevention, however, there is no good evidence for taking the supplement for this purpose. Pharmacists should not recommend natural products until the patient has seen a health care provider; it is not prudent to recommend a product that could be masking cancer symptoms. Although the symptoms will primarily be benign, the small risk of prostate cancer must be considered.

ALPHA BLOCKERS

These agents inhibit alpha-1 adrenergic receptors and relax the smooth muscle of the bladder neck reducing bladder outlet obstruction and improving urinary flow. There are 3 types of alpha receptors: 1A (prostate primarily has these receptors), 1B, and 1D; terazosin and doxazosin are non-selective and this results in more side effects (orthostasis, dizziness, fatigue, headache) than the selective agents (tamsulosin, alfuzosin, silodosin).

DRUG	DOSING	SAFETY/SIDE EFFECTS/MONITORING
Non-Selective Alpha-1 Blockers		**CONTRAINDICATIONS** Concurrent use silodosin or alfuzosin with strong 3A4 inhibitors, hepatic impairment (Child-Pugh class C for silodosin, class B/C for alfuzosin); severe renal impairment (silodosin)
Terazosin	Start at 1 mg at bedtime; <u>titrate slowly</u> to effect – generally 10 mg QHS (may ↑ to 20 mg QHS)	**WARNINGS** <u>Orthostatic hypotension/syncope</u>: typically with first dose, if therapy is interrupted for several days, dosage is increased too rapidly or another antihypertensive agent or PDE-5 inhibitor is started
Doxazosin (*Cardura, Cardura XL*)	IR: Start at 1 mg; <u>titrate slowly</u> up to 4-8 mg daily, usually given at bedtime XL: Start at 4 mg daily with breakfast; titrate to a max of 8 mg daily	<u>Intraoperative floppy iris syndrome</u> has occurred in cataract surgery patients who were on or were previously treated with an alpha-1 blocker Priapism – seek medical attention if erection lasting > 4 hours Angina – D/C if symptoms of angina begin or worsen
Selective Alpha₁ₐ Blockers		**SIDE EFFECTS** <u>Dizziness, fatigue, orthostatic hypotension, headache</u>, fluid retention <u>Rhinitis</u> (tamsulosin)
Tamsulosin (*Flomax*) + dutasteride (*Jalyn*)	<u>0.4 mg</u> daily, 30 min after the same meal each day; max 0.8 mg daily	<u>Abnormal ejaculation</u> (esp. with tamsulosin and silodosin) **MONITORING** BP, PSA, urinary symptoms
Alfuzosin (*Uroxatral*)	10 mg daily, immediately after same meal each day CrCl < 30 mL/min: use with caution	**NOTES** The non-selective agents are often given QHS to help minimize the initial "first dose" effect of orthostasis/dizziness. This requires careful counseling (see below) as the man likely has nocturia, where getting up at night to use the bathroom with dizziness and orthostasis can be dangerous. Alpha blockers work right away, but 4-6 weeks may be required to assess whether beneficial effects have been achieved; they do <u>not</u> shrink the prostate and do <u>not</u> change PSA levels.
Silodosin (*Rapaflo*)	8 mg daily with a meal CrCl 30-50 mL/min: 4 mg daily CrCl < 30 mL/min: do not use	Take *Cardura XL* with breakfast. Cardura XL is an OROS formulation (see Routes of Drug Delivery, Self-Administration Techniques and Counseling chapter) and can leave a ghost tablet (empty shell) in the stool <u>Do not use alfuzosin in patients at risk for QT prolongation – prolongs QT interval</u> <u>Silodosin can cause retrograde ejaculation</u> (28%), reversible upon drug discontinuation Alpha blockers – used for bladder outlet obstruction in women (off label)

Alpha Blocker Drug Interactions

- Use caution when co-administered with PDE-5 inhibitors *(Viagra/Revatio, Cialis/Adcirca, Levitra/Staxyn, Stendra)* due to additive hypotensive effects. Patients should be stable on alpha-blocker therapy before PDE-5 inhibitor therapy is initiated, using the lowest dose. Conversely, if a patient is already taking a PDE-5 inhibitor, the alpha blocker should be started at the lowest dose, and the selective agents will be preferred (over the non-selective agents).

- Use caution with other drugs that lower BP.

- Tamsulosin, alfuzosin and silodosin are major CYP 3A4 substrates; avoid use with strong 3A4 inhibitors.

- Silodosin cannot be used with strong P-gp inhibitors, such as cyclosporine.

- Alfuzosin: can cause QT prolongation; do not use with other QT prolongating agents. Use with caution in patients with known QT prolongation (congenital or acquired).

5 Alpha-Reductase Inhibitors

These agents inhibit the 5 alpha-reductase enzyme which blocks the conversion of testosterone to dihydrotestosterone (DHT). This class of medications is indicated for the treatment of symptomatic BPH in men <u>with an enlarged prostate</u> to improve symptoms, decrease the risk of acute urinary retention, and decrease the risk of need for surgery, including TURP or prostatectomy.

DRUG	DOSING	SAFETY/SIDE EFFECTS/MONITORING
Finasteride *(Proscar)* Affects 5α-receptors type 2 For hair loss (*Propecia* 1 mg daily)	5 mg daily	**CONTRAINDICATIONS** <u>Women of child-bearing potential, pregnancy, children</u> **WARNINGS** May ↑ risk of high-grade prostate cancer. **SIDE EFFECTS** <u>Impotence, ↓ libido, ejaculation disturbances, breast enlargement and tenderness, rash</u> – sexual SEs ↓ with time and approach placebo levels at one year of use in some men; in some men sexual issues persist **MONITORING** PSA, urinary symptoms
Dutasteride *(Avodart)* + tamsulosin (*Jalyn*) Affects both types of 5α-receptors (types 1 and 2)	0.5 mg daily	**NOTES** <u>Pregnancy Category X</u> <u>Pregnant women should not handle or take</u>; can be absorbed through skin, can be detrimental to fetus, semen of male taking this drug may present a danger 6 months (or longer) of treatment may be required for maximal efficacy Usually used in men with larger prostate size (40+ grams) or more severe symptoms; due to the slow-onset, often given with α-blocker <u>5 alpha-reductase inhibitors shrink the prostate and ↓ PSA levels</u> Swallow dutasteride whole. Do not chew or open as contents may cause oropharyngeal irritation. Take *Jalyn* 30 min after same meal each day.

5 Alpha-Reductase Inhibitor Drug Interactions

- Finasteride and dutasteride are minor CYP 3A4 substrates; strong CYP 3A4 inhibitors may ↑ levels.

- Do not use finasteride in a patient using *Propecia* for hair loss; refer to prescriber.

Phosphodiesterase-5 Inhibitor

Phosphodiesterase-5 mediated ↓ in smooth muscle and endothelial cell proliferation, ↓ nerve activity, and ↑ smooth muscle relaxation and tissue perfusion of the prostate and bladder.

DRUG	DOSING	SAFETY/SIDE EFFECTS/MONITORING
Tadalafil *Cialis* – for ED and Benign Prostatic Hypertrophy (BPH) *Adcirca* – for pulmonary arterial hypertension (PAH)	5 mg daily, same time each day CrCl 30-50 mL/min: 2.5 mg initially, max 5 mg daily CrCl < 30 mL/min: do not use Use 2.5 mg if using strong CYP 3A4 inhibitor	**CONTRAINDICATIONS** Concurrent use of nitrates or riociguat **WARNINGS** Impaired color discrimination, dose-related, caution in patients with retinitis pigmentosa Hearing loss, with our without tinnitus/dizziness Vision loss, rare, can be due to non-arteritic anterior ischemic optic neuropathy (NAION), Hypotension due to vasodilation Priapism – seek medical attention if erection lasting > 4 hours Concomitant use with alpha blockers is not recommended–discontinue alpha-blocker at least 1 day before initiating tadalafil. See Erectile Dysfunction chapter for complete review **SIDE EFFECTS** Headache, flushing, nausea, dyspepsia, myalgia, back pain, respiratory tract infection, nasopharyngitis **MONITORING** BP, PSA, urinary symptoms

For drug interactions/counseling for tadalafil, see Erectile Dysfunction chapter.

Patient Counseling

Alpha Blockers

- Especially for non-selective agents, such as doxazosin: This medicine can cause a sudden drop in blood pressure. You may feel dizzy, faint or "light-headed," especially after you stand up from a lying or sitting position. This is more likely to occur after you have taken the first few doses or if you increase your dose, but can occur at any time while you are taking the drug. It can also occur if you stop taking the drug and then restart treatment. When you get up from a sitting or lying position, go slowly and hold onto the bed rail or chair until you are steady on your feet.

- If you take the medicine at bedtime, but need to get up from bed to go to the bathroom, get up slowly and cautiously and hold onto the bed rail or chair until you are steady on your feet.

- You should not drive or do any hazardous tasks until you are used to the effects of the medicine. If you begin to feel dizzy, sit or lie down until you feel better.

- This medicine can cause side effects that may impair your thinking or reactions. Be careful if you drive or do anything that requires you to be awake and alert.

- Drinking alcohol can make the dizziness worse, and increase night-time urination if taken close to bedtime.

- Taking cold and allergy medications such as decongestants and antihistamines can make your symptoms worsen. Discuss what to use with your pharmacist if you need assistance.

- Tell your doctor (or ophthalmologist) about the use of this medication before cataract surgery. The doctor will want to know if you have ever taken this medication.

- Rarely, this medication can cause a painful erection which cannot be relieved by having sex. If this happens, get medical help right away. If it is not treated, you may not be able to get an erection in the future.

Tamsulosin

- The dose should be administered approximately half an hour following the same meal each day.

Alfuzosin

- Do not crush, chew, or break the alfuzosin tablets. Swallow them whole.

- Take after same meal each day (food increases absorption).

Silodosin

- The most common side effect seen with this medication is an orgasm with reduced or no semen (dry orgasm). This side effect does not pose a safety concern and is reversible with discontinuation of the drug (lower risk with tamsulosin).

- Take the same time each day with food.

5 Alpha-Reductase Inhibitor Counseling

- This medicine can take several months or longer to help reduce the BPH symptoms. It is effective, it just takes awhile to work because it shrinks the prostate slowly. If your doctor has given you another medicine called an alpha-blocker, that medicine works faster.

- Women who are or may become pregnant should not handle the tablets. (These drugs can cause birth defects to a developing male fetus – Pregnancy Category X). The semen of males using the medicine may also be harmful.

- Your doctor may perform blood tests or other forms of monitoring during treatment with finasteride. One of the tests that may be performed is called PSA (prostate-specific antigen). This drug can reduce the amount of PSA in the blood.

- Tell your doctor if you experience any of these side effects: decreased sex drive, decreased volume of ejaculate, impotence, breast tenderness or enlargement.

- Taking cold and allergy medications such as decongestants and antihistamines can make your symptoms worsen. Discuss what to use with your pharmacist if you need assistance.

OVERACTIVE BLADDER

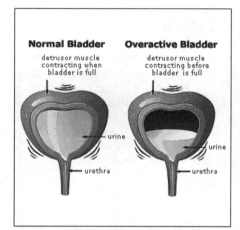

Normal Bladder
detrusor muscle
contracting when
bladder is full

urine

urethra

Overactive Bladder
detrusor muscle
contracting before
bladder is full

urine

urethra

GUIDELINES/REFERENCES

Diagnosis and Treatment of Overactive Bladder (Non-Neurogenic) In Adults: AUA/SUFU Guideline. *J Urol.* 2012 Dec; 188(6):2455-63.

BACKGROUND

Overactive bladder (OAB) is a common, disabling urinary disorder that affects many people (1 in 6 people or over 33 million Americans). It is not a normal sign of aging. In overactive bladder, the detrusor muscle contracts frequently and before the bladder is full, leading to the classic symptoms of:

- Urinary urgency (a sudden, compelling desire to pass urine which is difficult to defer), and

- Urinary frequency (voiding ≥ 8 times in a 24 hour period), and

- Nocturia (≥ 2 awakenings to void per night)

Overactive bladder can lead to urinary urge incontinence. About 1/3 of patients have incontinent episodes (OAB wet) and the other 2/3 of patients do not have incontinence (OAB dry).

IMPLICATIONS OF OVERACTIVE BLADDER

Many co-morbidities exist in patients with OAB including falls and fractures, skin breakdown and infections, UTIs, depression, and sexual dysfunction. Due to embarrassment of their condition, there are many social implications of OAB including low self-esteem, lack of sexual intimacy, social and physical isolation, sleep disturbances, limits on travel and dependence on caregivers; all leading to a reduced quality of life. Many patients become dehydrated because they limit their fluid intake. The cost of pads and adult diapers can be a huge financial burden.

PATHOPHYSIOLOGY

The bladder is commonly referred to as a "balloon" with an outer muscular layer known as the <u>detrusor muscle</u>. The detrusor muscle and the bladder outlet functions are neurologically coordinated to store and expel urine. The detrusor muscle is innervated mainly by the parasympathetic nervous system while the bladder neck is innervated by the sympathetic nervous system. The internal sphincter is also innervated by the sympathetic nervous system and the external sphincter is innervated by the somatic nervous system. Both voluntary and involuntary contractions of the detrusor muscle are mediated by <u>activation of muscarinic receptors via acetylcholine</u>. Of the five known muscarinic receptor subtypes, the human bladder is comprised of M2 and M3 receptors in a 3:1 ratio. It is the <u>M3 receptor</u> that is responsible for both emptying contractions as well as involuntary bladder contractions of incontinence. In overactive bladder, the <u>detrusor muscle</u> is <u>hyperactive</u> (overactive), causing the symptoms of frequent micturitions, urgency, nocturia, and/or incontinence.

Risk Factors for Overactive Bladder

- Age > 40 years
- Diabetes
- Restricted mobility
- Obesity
- Prior vaginal delivery
- Neurologic conditions (e.g., stroke, Parkinson disease, dementia)
- Hysterectomy
- Drugs that can increase incontinence [e.g., ACE inhibitors (due to cough), alcohol, cholinesterase inhibitors, diuretics, sedatives, others]
- Pelvic injury

Diagnosis

Diagnosis requires a careful patient history intake including comorbid conditions, duration of symptoms, baseline symptoms, fluid intake and type of fluids (with and without caffeine), a physical exam and urinalysis. Validated questionnaires such as the Urinary Distress Inventory (UDI) or the Overactive Bladder Questionnaire (OAB-q) are used to quantify symptoms. Patients may be required to

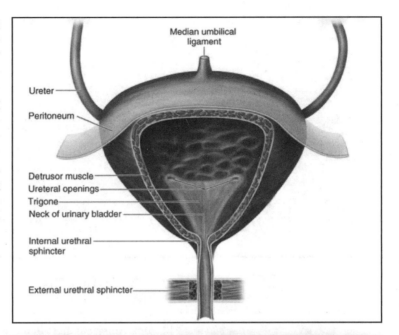

Median umbilical ligament

Ureter

Peritoneum

Detrusor muscle

Ureteral openings

Trigone

Neck of urinary bladder

Internal urethral sphincter

External urethral sphincter

FORMS OF URINARY INCONTINENCE

Functional
There is no abnormality in the bladder, but the patient may be cognitively, socially, or physically impaired thus hindering him or her from access to a toilet (e.g., patients in wheelchairs).

Overflow
Leakage that occurs when the quantity of urine stored in the bladder exceeds its capacity, often occurring without the urge to urinate (BPH is the most common cause).

Stress
Urine leaks out during any form of exertion (e.g., exercise, coughing, sneezing, laughing, etc.) as a result of pressure on the bladder.

Urge
Patient cannot hold in urine long enough to reach the toilet and is associated with neuropathy; often found in those who have diabetes, strokes, dementia, Parkinson disease, or multiple sclerosis (although people without co-morbidities are affected also).

Mixed
Combination of urge and stress incontinence

Approximately 1/3 of incontinence is stress, 1/3 is urge and 1/3 is mixed.

complete a bladder diary to accurately measure intake and voiding information. A urine culture and post-void residual assessment may be performed to rule out other causes.

NON-DRUG TREATMENT

Behavioral therapies are considered first-line to improve OAB symptoms by changing patient behavior and/or their environment. Behavioral treatments include bladder training, delayed or scheduled voiding, pelvic floor muscle exercises (Kegel exercises), urge control techniques (distraction, self-assertions), fluid management, dietary changes (avoiding bladder irritants), weight loss and other lifestyle changes. Behavior therapies can be combined with other treatment modalities such as medications. Surgical intervention should be reserved for the rare non-neurogenic patient who has failed all other therapeutic options and whose symptoms are intolerable.

DRUG TREATMENT

Behavioral and drug therapies are often used in combination in clinical practice to optimize patient symptom control and quality of life. Anticholinergic drugs are second-line therapy. These agents are antagonists of the muscarinic receptor and block acetylcholine, thus limiting contractions of the detrusor muscle. Patients with a post void residual (PVR) > 250 – 300 mL should not be started on an anticholinergic agent. Extended-release formulations are preferred over immediate-release formulations due to a lower rate of dry mouth. More selective (for the M3 receptor) anticholinergic agents (solifenacin, darifenacin, fesoterodine) have less CNS side effects over the nonselective, older agents such as oxybutynin. If a patient fails an antimuscarinic agent or develops an adverse effect, it is recommended to try at least one other anticholinergic agent or a dose adjustment before moving on to third-line recommendations, including onabotulinumtoxin A, nerve stimulation or surgical correction. In-dwelling catheters are used only as a last resort in select patients. Additive antimuscarinic drugs should be avoided, if possible.

PELVIC FLOOR MUSCLE EXERCISES

Pelvic Floor Muscle ("Kegel") Exercises
These exercises are done to strengthen the pelvic floor muscles and can diminish OAB symptoms.

Proper technique is key and this means finding the correct muscles. Instruct the patient to imagine that they are trying to stop urination midstream. Squeeze the muscles they would use. If they sense a "pulling" feeling, those are the correct muscles for pelvic exercise.

Pull in the pelvic muscles and hold for a count of 3. Then relax for a count of 3. Work up to 3 sets of 10 kegel exercises per day. Do these exercises 3 times a day to strengthen pelvic floor muscles and reduce wetting episodes.

CHOLINERGIC & ANTICHOLINERGIC PHARMACOLOGY

Cholinergic drugs act like acetylcholine at the acetylcholine receptors and cause the "SLUD" symptoms: Salivation, Lacrimation (tearing), Urination and Diarrhea. The classic cholinergic drug bethanechol is used occasionally to treat urinary retention by increasing urination, which occurs with neurogenic bladder. Another cholinergic agent is pilocarpine, which is sometimes used for dry mouth (to increase salivation).*

Anticholinergics have the opposite effect: they block acetylcholine, which is present in the periphery (outside of the CNS) and centrally (inside the CNS) and will cause the anti-SLUD peripheral symptoms of dry mouth, dry/blurry vision, urinary retention and constipation along with the central anticholinergic effects such as sedation, dizziness and cognitive impairment.

This is how diphenhydramine, which blocks acetylcholine in the CNS, works as a sedative. Diphenhydramine has to travel through the periphery (to get to the CNS) and will cause the peripheral side effects as well, including urinary retention. However, it is not an appropriate choice for an elderly patient due to the central effects which can increase fall risk and the peripheral effects that are not desired.

When incontinence drugs were first developed, the primary goal was to use agents with lower CNS penetration; therefore, exhibiting fewer central side effects. Oxybutynin is an older drug in this class and the prototype peripheral agent. Later on, drugs were designed to be specific for the M3 muscarinic receptor, the subtype present in high density on the bladder wall (the detrusor muscle). When this muscle contracts, there is a sudden urge to urinate; therefore blocking the M3 receptor can reduce the sudden urge to urinate. Darifenacin is an example of an M3-specific drug. Unfortunately, the M3 receptor is also found in high density on the salivary glands, causing dry mouth when this receptor is blocked. The pharmacist must help the patient to manage dry mouth, which is quite uncomfortable and increases the degree of dental decay. It is possible to reduce this side effect with the use of longer-acting agents (instead of IR formulations) and with drugs that bypass first-pass metabolism (patch and gel) since the drug metabolites contribute to the dry mouth. With the long-acting formulations, there are lower "peaks" and, thus, lower side effects. Although there is more drug to hit the "right" receptors (producing the desired effect) during peak concentrations, there will also be more drug to hit the "wrong" receptors (causing side effects).

Another mechanism to increase acetylcholine is to block the enzyme that breaks it down. These are the acetylcholinesterase inhibitors, which are used for dementia and to reverse neuromuscular blockade.

Anticholinergic Drugs

These agents are competitive antagonists of the muscarinic receptors which inhibit binding of acetylcholine, thus limiting contractions of the detrusor muscle.

DRUG	DOSING	SAFETY/SIDE EFFECTS/MONITORING
Oxybutynin	5 mg PO BID-TID	**CONTRAINDICATIONS**
Oxybutynin XL **(Ditropan XL)**	5-30 mg PO daily	Urinary retention, gastric retention, decreased gastric motility and uncontrolled narrow angle glaucoma
Oxybutynin patch **(Oxytrol, Oxytrol for** **Women – OTC)**	3.9 mg daily (Rx patch is changed every 3-4 days; OTC patch is changed every 4 days)	*Oxytrol for Women* OTC: Pain or burning when urinating, blood in urine, unexplained lower back or side pain, cloudy or foul-smelling urine, males, age < 18 years, urinary or gastric retention, glaucoma, accidental urine loss only due to coughing, sneezing, or laughing
Oxybutynin 10% topical gel *(Gelnique)*	Apply contents of 1 sachet to intact, dry skin daily	**WARNINGS**
Oxybutynin 3% topical gel *(Gelnique 3%)*	3 pumps daily	Anticholinergics may cause agitation, confusion, drowsiness, dizziness, hallucinations, headache, and/or blurred vision, which may impair physical or mental abilities; patients must be cautioned about performing tasks which require mental alertness (e.g., operating machinery or driving).
Tolterodine *(Detrol)*	1-2 mg PO BID	
Tolterodine ER *(Detrol LA)*	2-4 mg PO daily	**SIDE EFFECTS**
Trospium *(Sanctura, Sanctura XR)*	20 mg BID or 60 mg XR daily. Take <u>on an empty stomach</u>	<u>Dizziness and drowsiness</u> (greatest with oxybutynin and less with the newer, selective agents), <u>xerostomia</u> (dry mouth), <u>constipation</u>, dry eyes/blurred vision, urinary retention, application site reactions (with topicals and patch)
Solifenacin (VESIcare)	5-10 mg PO daily	**NOTES** ↓ dose in renal impairment (CrCl < 30 mL/min) with fesoterodine, solifenacin, tolterodine, and trospium (do not use trospium XR formulation in these patients).
Darifenacin *(Enablex)*	7.5-15 mg PO daily	Extended-release formulations have less incidence of dry mouth than their IR counterparts. *Ditropan XL* is in an OROS formulation (see Routes of Drug Delivery, Self-Administration Techniques and Counseling chapter) and can leave a ghost shell (empty shell) in the stool.
Fesoterodine *(Toviaz)*	4-8 mg PO daily	Oxybutynin patch and gel cause less dry mouth and constipation than oral forms.
		Darifenacin causes more constipation.
		Oxytrol patch should be placed on dry, intact skin on the abdomen, hips or buttocks. Avoid reapplication to the same site within 7 days. <u>Available OTC for women ≥ 18 years</u>. Men who are experiencing OAB symptoms should see their doctors to rule out other conditions.
		Antimuscarinic agents should be used with caution in patients using other medications with anticholinergic properties.

Anticholinergic Drug Interactions

- All of the anticholinergics can have additive effects with other medications that have anticholinergic side effects.

- Acetylcholinesterase inhibitors used for dementia (e.g., donepezil) increase acetylcholine in the CNS, whereas the OAB agents primarily stay in the periphery (outside the CNS). However, some patients may experience some CNS side effects (e.g., memory impairment). The risk vs. benefit must be considered. If little to no improvement in OAB symptoms at 6 weeks, the anticholinergic drug should be discontinued.

- Tolterodine ER – do not exceed 2 mg/day when administered with strong 3A4 inhibitors.

- Solifenacin – do not exceed 5 mg/day when administered with strong 3A4 inhibitors.

- Darifenacin – do not exceed 7.5 mg/day when administered with strong 3A4 inhibitors.

- Fesoterodine – do not exceed 4 mg/day when administered with strong 3A4 inhibitors.

Beta-3 Agonist

Mirabegron relaxes the detrusor muscle during the storage phase of the fill-void cycle by activation of beta-3 receptors which increases bladder capacity.

DRUG	DOSING	SAFETY/SIDE EFFECTS/MONITORING
Mirabegron (Myrbetriq)	25-50 mg daily CrCl 15-29 mL/min: 25 mg CrCl < 15 mL/min: not recommended	**SIDE EFFECTS** Hypertension, nasopharyngitis, UTI, headache **MONITORING** BP, HR, urinary symptoms **NOTES** Efficacy seen within 8 weeks

Mirabegron Drug Interactions

- Mirabegron is a moderate CYP2D6 inhibitor. Use caution with co-administration of narrow therapeutic window drugs metabolized by 2D6. Levels of metoprolol and desipramine are increased when co-administered with mirabegron. Use caution when administered concurrently with digoxin (use lowest digoxin dose and monitor levels).

Onabotulinumtoxin A *(Botox)*

Botox is a third-line treatment option for patients who are refractory to first- and second-line treatment options. It affects the efferent pathways of detrusor activity by inhibiting the release of acetylcholine.

DRUG	DOSING	SAFETY/SIDE EFFECTS/MONITORING
Onabotulinumtoxin A *(Botox)*	100 units total dose, as 0.5 mL (5 units) injections, across 20 sites (given intradetrusor) – repeat therapy no sooner than 12 weeks from previous administration In adults treated with *Botox* for more than one indication, do not exceed a total dose of 360 units in a 3 month interval.	**BOXED WARNING** All botulinum toxin products may spread from the area of injection to produce symptoms consistent with botulinum toxin effects. Swallowing and breathing difficulties can be life-threatening. **CONTRAINDICATIONS** Infection at the proposed injection site, urinary tract infection and urinary retention **SIDE EFFECTS** Urinary tract infection, urinary retention, dysuria **MONITORING** Post-void residual volume, symptoms of OAB **NOTES** Potency units of *Botox* are not interchangeable with other preparations of botulinum toxin products. Prophylactic antimicrobial therapy (excluding aminoglycosides) should be administered 1-3 days prior to, on the day of, and for 1-3 days following *Botox* administration. MedGuide required.

Botox Drug Interactions

- Aminoglycosides and other agents affecting neuromuscular transmission can potentiate the effects of *Botox.*

Anticholinergic Patient Counseling

Ditropan XL

- Certain medications can interact with this medication. Tell your healthcare provider or pharmacist of the medications you are currently taking including any over the counter products, vitamins and herbal supplements.

- The tablet must be swallowed whole with liquid; do not crush, divide, or chew; take at approximately the same time each day.

- This medication can be taken without regards to meals (unlike trospium which needs to be taken on an empty stomach).

- If you miss a dose, skip it. Take at your next scheduled dose. Do not take 2 doses within the same day.

- Part of the tablet may pass into your stool after your body has absorbed the medicine. If you see the tablet in your stool, it is nothing to worry about.

- This medicine can cause dry mouth. Some formulations cause more dry mouth than others (the longer-lasting forms tend to cause less dry mouth). If dry mouth is bothersome, please discuss with your healthcare provider. Avoiding mouthwashes with alcohol, taking small sips of water, sucking on ice chips or sugar-free candy or chewing sugar-free gum can help with dry mouth symptoms. Take good care of your teeth since dry mouth contributes to tooth decay.

- Another possible side effect of this medicine is constipation. Some formulations cause more constipation than others with darifenacin *(Enablex)* causing the most. Maintain adequate water and dietary fiber, including vegetables and whole-grains. A stool softener, such as docusate, may be helpful. If not, a laxative such as senna may be helpful. You may need to discuss this with your healthcare provider. If you have any type of serious constipation or constipation for ≥ 3 days, or current stomach problems, you should let your healthcare provider know.
- This medication can make you feel dizzy or drowsy. Using alcohol can make this worse. Heat can make this worse. Do not operate any dangerous machinery (such as driving a car) until you know how this medicine affects your concentration and coordination.
- Doing pelvic floor muscle (Kegel) exercises in combination with this medicine will work better than taking the medicine alone. You should get instructions on how to do this correctly, and do them for a few minutes three times daily, so you can slowly build up these muscles.

Oxytrol Patch

- The patch causes less dry mouth than oral formulations.
- Open one pouch and apply immediately. Do not use if pouch is torn or opened.
- Apply one patch to clean, dry, intact skin on the abdomen, hips, or buttocks.
- Apply to an area of skin that is under clothing and protected from sunlight. Avoid applying the patch on your waistline, since tight clothing may rub the patch off.
- The Rx patch is changed every 3 to 4 days; the OTC patch is changed every 4 days.
- Select a new site for each new patch (avoid reapplication to same site within 7 days).
- Do not apply the patch to areas of skin that are irritated, oily, or to where lotions or powders have been applied.
- The patch must be removed prior to having an MRI procedure.
- Contact with water (e.g., swimming, bathing) will not change the way the drug works. Avoid rubbing the patch area during these activities.
- <u>If the area around the patch becomes red, itchy, or irritated, try a new site. If irritation continues or becomes worse, notify your healthcare provider promptly.</u>

Oxybutynin topical *(Gelnique)*

- For topical use only.
- This formulation causes less dry mouth and less constipation than other formulations.
- For *Gelnique* 10%, each packet is for one use only. For *Gelnique* 3%, use 3 pumps (must prime the pump prior to first use with 4 pumps).
- Apply to clean, dry, intact skin on abdomen, upper arm/shoulders, or thighs. Rub into skin until dry. Use a different site each day (cannot use the same site two days in a row).
- Do not apply to recently shaved skin.
- Do not bathe, swim or shower for 1 hour after application.
- Wash hands after use.
- Cover treated area with clothing after gel has dried to prevent transfer of medication to others.
- Oxybutynin gel is flammable. Avoid an open flame and do not smoke until the gel has completely dried on the skin.

74

GLAUCOMA, OPHTHALMICS & OTICS

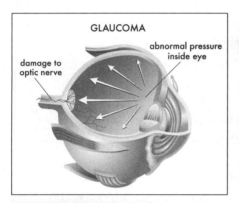

GLAUCOMA

damage to optic nerve

abnormal pressure inside eye

Eye & Ear Rx Interpretation

ABBREVIATION	MEANING	CAUTION
AD, AS, AU	Right Ear, Left Ear, Each Ear	These directions can be mistaken (interchanged) for each other & may mean other things: know how to interpret them but it is safer to write them out: use right eye, left eye, each eye, right ear, left ear, each ear.
OD, OS, OU	Right Eye, Left Eye, Each Eye	
Memory tip: <u>A</u> is from the Latin for ear (auris), <u>O</u> is from eye (oculus), <u>D</u> is from right (dextra) and <u>S</u> is from left (sinistra).		

GUIDELINE

American Academy of Ophthalmology Glaucoma Panel. Preferred Practice Pattern Guidelines. Primary Open-Angle Glaucoma Suspect. 2010. http://one.aao.org/preferred-practice-pattern/primary-openangle-glaucoma-ppp--october-2010 (accessed 2014 Oct 7).

EYE MEDICATION FORMULATIONS

- Solutions

- Suspensions – <u>shake well</u> or disperse prior to use.

- Ointments – apply to the conjunctival sac or over lid margins (for blepharitis). Ointments will make vision blurry and are not used with contact lenses.

- Gels – with cap on, <u>invert and shake once</u> to get medicine into the tip before instilling into the eye.

GLAUCOMA

Glaucoma is an eye disease caused by an increase in intraocular pressure (IOP). If left untreated, glaucoma can result in damage to the optic nerve and gradual loss of vision. There may be no symptoms felt by the patient, although some may experience eye pain, headache, or decreased vision.

There are two main forms of glaucoma. Angle-closure, or closed-angle glaucoma is treated in the hospital and is a medical emergency. The <u>more common type, open-angle glaucoma</u>, is most commonly treated with eye drops and in some cases, surgery. The decision to treat depends on whether damage to the optic nerve is present, the results from a "visual field" test and the IOP value.

RISK FACTORS

Risk factors for glaucoma include family history, increased age, African American ethnicity, and nearsightedness (myopia). A history of eye surgeries and diabetes can be contributory.

DRUG TREATMENT

Prostaglandin (PG) analogs and beta-blockers are used most commonly as initial agents. PG analogs are the most effective drugs at ↓ IOP, are safe and are used once daily. If the pressure is high in one eye and not the other a beta blocker would be more likely used as the initial agent because the iris-darkening/eyelash thickening would not be desirable in one eye only. The other classes of glaucoma medications are used as add-ons.

Adherence & Technique: Improvement Is Needed

There are two likely causes of persistently high IOP: 1) poor eyedrop administration technique and 2) poor adherence. The correct way to administer eye drops is described later in this chapter. The asymptomatic presentation contributes to poor adherence. Counseling is critical for both administration technique and the need for therapy. The patient should understand the consequences of untreated glaucoma (i.e., loss of vision). Yet, even with counseling, the adherence remains poor. For example, in one of the studies referenced in the glaucoma guidelines, less than 45% of the participants took < 75% of the daily doses. The patients had received counseling, and the medication was provided at no charge, and taken once-daily.

DRUGS THAT CAN INCREASE IOP
Cough/cold/motion sickness medications (antihistamines, including scopolamine)
Anticholinergics (e.g., oxybutynin, tolterodine, benztropine, trihexyphenidyl, tricyclics)
Chronic corticosteroids, especially eye drops such as prednisolone
Topiramate (Topamax)

DRUG	DOSING	SIDE EFFECTS/CLINICAL CONCERNS

Beta Blockers, Nonselective: reduce aqueous humor production

DRUG	DOSING	SIDE EFFECTS/CLINICAL CONCERNS
Timolol 0.25% and 0.5% (Timolol GFS, Timoptic, Timoptic-XE, Istalol, Betimol, Timoptic Ocudose) + brimonidine (Combigan) + dorzolamide (Cosopt, Cosopt PF) Levobunolol (Betagan) Carteolol (Ocupress) Metipranolol (OptiPranolol) Betaxolol (Betoptic, Betoptic S)	Timolol 1 drop Q daily-BID Timoptic-XE, Timolol GFS: gels, Q daily Gels: Shake once before use. Wait 10 minutes after other eye drops before inserting gel.	**CONTRAINDICATIONS** Sinus bradycardia; sinus node dysfunction; heart block > than first degree (except in patients with a pacemaker); cardiogenic shock, uncompensated cardiac failure, bronchospastic disease **SIDE EFFECTS** Slight burning, stinging, itching of the eyes or eyelids, changes in vision, increased sensitivity of the eyes to light, bradycardia, bronchospasm with non-selective agents, fatigue **NOTES** All non-selective beta blockers except for betaxolol. Some contain the preservative benzalkonium chloride (BAK) which is absorbed by soft contact lenses. Use eyedrops first, wait 15 minutes before inserting lenses (or remove prior to using eye drops). Occasionally patients have sensitivity to this preservative. The PF in Cosopt PF stands for "preservative free." Some contain sulfites, which can cause allergic reactions.

Glaucoma Medications Continued

DRUG	DOSING	SIDE EFFECTS/CLINICAL CONCERNS

Prostaglandin Analogs: increase aqueous outflow

Travoprost *(Travatan Z)* **Bimatoprost *(Lumigan)*** **Latanoprost *(Xalatan)*** Unoprostone *(Rescula)* Tafluprost *(Zioptan)*	1 drop QHS, except *Rescula* is BID Cannot be administered with contact lenses (preservative BAK will absorb into lenses) – remove and wait 15 min prior to re-insertion (most given QHS-instruct to remove lenses 1st)	**WARNINGS** Ocular effects: <u>darkening of the iris</u>, eyelid skin and <u>eyelashes</u>. Eyelash <u>length and number can increase</u>. Long-term consequences to the eye are not known. Contamination of multiple-dose ophthalmic solutions can cause bacterial keratitis. **SIDE EFFECTS** <u>Blurred vision, stinging</u>, foreign body sensation, <u>increased pigmentation of the iris/eyelashes</u>, eyelash <u>growth</u>/thickening **NOTES** Store unopened bottles of latanoprost in refrigerator. *Zioptan* comes as 10 single-use containers in a foil pouch; store unopened pouches in refrigerator. Once opened the contents are good for 28 days at room temperature. Bimatoprost *(Latisse)* is indicated for eyelash hypotrichosis (to ↑ eyelash growth) – do not use concurrently with same class for glaucoma without MDs approval (using PAs more frequently ↓ effectiveness). *Travatan Z* does not contain BAK, instead has different preservative. This may be helpful to some with reaction to BAK or dry eye, but most are fine with a less expensive generic. *Zioptan:* The single-use containers are sterile, but no preservative. Discard container after use, even if medicine is remaining.

Cholinergics (Miotics): increase aqueous outflow

Carbachol *(Isopto Carbachol, Miostat)*	1-2 drops up to TID	**SIDE EFFECTS** Corneal clouding, poor vision at night (due to pupil constriction), burning (transient), irritation, hypotension, bronchospasm, abdominal cramps/GI distress **NOTES** Use with caution with history of retinal detachment or corneal abrasion.
Pilocarpine *(Isopto Carpine, Pilopine HS)*	Solution: 1-2 drops up to 6x/daily Gel: Instill 0.5" ribbon into lower conjunctival sac once daily, at bedtime	

Glaucoma Medications Continued

DRUG	DOSING	SIDE EFFECTS/CLINICAL CONCERNS

Carbonic Anhydrase Inhibitors: reduce aqueous humor production

Dorzolamide (Trusopt) **+ timolol (Cosopt, Cosopt PF).** AcetaZOLAMIDE (*Diamox Sequels*) Brinzolamide (*Azopt*) + brimonidine (*Simbrinza*) Methazolamide (*Neptazane*)	Trusopt: 1 drop TID Azopt: 1 drop TID Cosopt: 1 drop BID Acetazolamide 250 mg PO 1-4 x daily, or 500 mg ER PO BID	**WARNINGS** Sulfonamide allergy with the eye drops and the oral acetazolamide: caution with allergy due to risk of systemic exposure **SIDE EFFECTS** Ocular agents: blurred vision, blepharitis, dry eye, discharge Oral agent (acetazolamide): CNS effects (ataxia, confusion), photosensitivity/skin rash (including risk of SJS and TEN), anorexia, nausea, risk of hematological toxicities **NOTES** Acetazolamide oral capsules are infrequently used for glaucoma. They are used for prevention and treatment of acute mountain (altitude) sickness. *Cosopt PF* comes in preservative-free (PF), single-use containers.

Adrenergic Alpha-2 Agonists: increase aqueous outflow, reduce aqueous humor production

Brimonidine (Alphagan P) + timolol **(Combigan)** + brinzolamide (*Simbrinza*) Dipivefrin (*Propine, Akpro*) Apraclonidine (*Iopidine*)	*Iopidine, Alphagan* are dosed TID	**WARNINGS** CNS depression: caution with heavy machinery, driving **SIDE EFFECTS** Sedation, burning/stinging/itchy eyes, dry mouth, dry nose

Patient Counseling (Eye Drops)

- Wash your hands.
- Before you open the bottle, shake it a few times. Gels need one shake prior to use (helps the medication reach the tip).
- Bend your neck back a little so that you're looking up. Use one finger to pull down your lower eyelid. It is helpful, at least initially, to use a mirror.
- Without letting the tip of the bottle touch your eye or eyelid, squeeze one drop of the medicine into the space between your eye and your lower eyelid. If you squeeze in more than one drop, you are wasting medicine.
- After you squeeze the drop of medicine into your eye, close your eye. Then press a finger between your eye and the top of your nose. Press for at least one full minute. This way, more of the medicine stays in your eye. You will be less likely to have side effects. Blot extra solution from the eyelid with a tissue.
- If eyedrop contains the preservative benzalkonium chloride and the patient wears soft contact lenses, they should remove the lenses prior to administration (wait 15 minutes to reinsert).
- If you need to take more than one glaucoma medicine:
- Put a drop of the first medicine in your eye. Wait at least 5 - 10 minutes to put the second medicine in your eye. If administering a gel, wait 10 minutes after other eye medicine before use.

- If someone else puts your medicines in your eye for you, remind that person to wait 5 - 10 minutes between each medicine.

Prostaglandin Analog Counseling Specifics

- Remove contact lenses before using this medication because it contains a preservative that can be absorbed by the lenses, and cause them to become discolored. Wait at least 15 minutes after using this medication before putting your lenses back in.

- You may experience an increase in brown pigment in the iris and gradual changes in eye color (for this reason, they are not usually administered to patients with light eyes who have glaucoma in one eye only). Eyelash growth and pigmentation may increase (which is often pleasing to the patient). The skin on the eyelids and around the eyes may darken.

- This medicine is well-tolerated, but occasionally a patient can experience excessive tearing, eye pain, or lid crusting. If this occurs, please discuss with the optometrist or ophthalmologist..

- Latanoprost *(Xalatan)* unopened bottles should be stored in the refrigerator.

- Tafluprost *(Zioptan)* is kept refrigerated. Once opened the pouch of 10 is good at room temperature for 28 days.

- Do not use this medicine if you are also using Bimatoprost *(Latisse)*, to increase eyelash growth, without the the optometrist's or ophthalmologist's approval. *Latisse* may reduce the effectiveness of the glaucoma medicine.

Timolol *(Timoptic)* Counseling Specifics

- Common side effects from beta blockers include burning/stinging or itching of the eyes, and possible light sensitivity.

- Timolol is a non-selective beta blocker, and although proper application should keep most of the medicine in the eye, it is best to avoid in patients with asthma, COPD, chronic bronchitis, emphysema, or advanced cardiac disease. The medicine might exacerbate the disease symptoms. If you have any of these conditions, please discuss if this medicine is safe to use.

- If dispensing the drops in the *Ocudose* dispenser: To open the bottle, unscrew the cap by turning as indicated by the arrows on the top of the cap. Do not pull the cap directly up and away from the bottle. Pulling the cap directly up will prevent your dispenser from operating properly.

- Invert the bottle, and press lightly with the thumb or index finger over the "Finger Push Area" until a single drop is dispensed into the eye.

- If dispensing the gel *(Timoptic XE, Timolol GFS)*: Turn the container upside down once and shake the contents prior to use. The gel is used once daily. If using other eye drop before, wait at least 10 minutes before using gel.

OTHER OCULAR CONDITIONS

Medications can cause ocular adverse effects that disappear once the drug is discontinued (such as blurry vision from an anticholinergic). In other cases the damage can be permanent (such as vision loss with a PDE5-inhibitor). Patients should be instructed to report visual changes immediately; in most cases the damage is reversible if the medication is stopped quickly.

Common Agents Known to Cause Vision Changes/Damage

- Alpha blockers (floppy iris syndrome-causes difficulty in cataract surgery)

- Amiodarone (corneal deposits, optic neuropathy)

- Bisphosphonates (ocular inflammation)

- Digoxin (yellow/green vision, blurriness, halos)

- Chloroquine *(Aralen)* (retinopathy, may cause permanent visual damage)

- Ethambutol *(Myambutol)*, linezolid *(Zyvox)* (optic neuropathy, especially with chronic use)

- Ezogabine *(Potiga)* (retinal changes, vision loss)

- Hydroxychloroquine *(Plaquenil)* (retinopathy)

- Isoniazid (optic neuritis)

- Isotretinoin ($\downarrow$ night vision which may be permanent, dry eyes/irritation)

- Quinolones (retinal detachment)

- Sildenafil *(Viagra)* and other PDE5-Inhibitors used for ED, PAH, BPH (greenish tinge around objects, possible permanent vision loss in one or both eyes)

- Tamoxifen *(Soltamox)* (corneal changes, decreased color perception)

- Telithromycin *(Ketek)* (blurry vision, diplopia)

- Voriconazole *(VFEND)* (abnormal vision, color vision change, photophobia)

Conjunctivitis: Allergic, Bacterial & Viral

Conjunctivitis or "pink eye" occurs in one or both eyes. Symptoms include swelling, itching, burning, and redness of the conjunctiva, the protective membrane that lines the eyelids and covers the white part of the eye (the sclera). Conjunctivitis can be due to a virus, a bacteria, an allergan or from some type of ocular irritant, such as chemicals or contact lenses. In most cases, conjunctivitis causes only mild discomfort, does not harm vision and will clear without medical treatment. Many times, treatment is given even if not clearly indicated. In some cases, treatment is required.

Viral and bacterial conjunctivitis occurs mostly in young children and is highly contagious. Until treatment is initiated, infected children should stay at home and should be allowed to return to school once treatment has begun, unless there are systemic symptoms. Any patient with viral or bacterial conjunctivitis should be instructed to use proper hand hygiene:

- Don't touch your eyes with your hands.

- Wash your hands thoroughly and frequently.

- Change your towel and washcloth daily, and do not share towels with others.

- Discard eye cosmetics, particularly mascara.

- Do not use anyone else's eye cosmetics or personal eye-care items.

For any type of conjunctivitis compresses can help alleviate swelling and mild discomfort. To make a compress, soak a clean cloth in warm water (cool water for viral or allergic conjunctivitis), wring it out and apply gently to the closed eyelids. Artificial tears can be used to provide lubrication and help reduce a "gritty" feeling.

Chemical conjunctivitis has no specific drug treatment and is not described in the following table. The irritant should be flushed out of the eyes with saline and inflammation can be reduced with an NSAID or a steroid eye drop. If contact lenses have caused the irritation they should not be used until the condition has cleared. It may be helpful to change the type of contact lens or the brand of disinfectant solution. If the condition is severe, such as a burn, or the chemical is dangerous or unknown, the patient should be referred for emergency care.

Treatment Common to All Conjunctivitis Types

Most cases are mild and will resolve without treatment directed at the cause, such as an antibiotic for suspected bacterial conjunctivitis. However, these are often used and in some cases are helpful in alleviating symptoms more quickly. Inflammation for any type of conjunctivitis can be reduced with NSAID (if mild) or steroid eye drops (if more severe). Artificial tears can help with a "gritty" feeling and will alleviate dryness. Instruct patients to return for follow-up if they do not recover within a few days (or longer with some types). If antibiotics are used the course should be completed.

Conjunctivitis Types

VIRAL	BACTERIAL	ALLERGIC
Causes: adenovirus (most common), other viruses, most mild but some due to a more severe viral infection (e.g., zoster, HIV)	Causes: *Staph aureus, Strep pneumoniae, H. influenzae, Moraxella catarrhalis* More severe cases can be due to infection with *N. gonorrhoeae* or *Chlamydia*, which will require systemic treatment.	Common allergens include pollen, dust mites, animal dander, molds
No topical treatment for common viral conjunctivitis. The infection will run its course, from several days to 2-3 weeks.	Topical antibiotic eye drops or ointments, selected: Azithromycin (*Azasite*) – stored in refrigerator, 14 days at room temp. Moxifloxacin (*Vigamox*) Besifloxacin (*Besivance*) Tobramycin/Dexamethasone *(TobraDex, TobraDex ST)* Ciprofloxacin (*Ciloxan*) Ofloxacin (*Ocuflox*) Gentamicin *(Garamycin)* Tobramycin *(Tobrex)* Erythromycin Sulfacetamide *(Bleph-10)* Trimethoprim/Polymyxin B (*Polytrim*) Neomycin/Bacitracin/Polymyxin B (*Neosporin*)	**MAST CELL STABILIZER EYE DROPS** Cromolyn Lodoxamide (*Alomide*) Nedocromil (*Alocril*) Pemirolast (*Alamast*) **ANTIHISTAMINE EYE DROPS** Azelastine (*Optivar*) Epinastine (*Elestat*) Olopatadine (*Patanol*)

Eye Drops to Reduce Inflammation and Add Lubrication (Moisture)

DRUG	USAGE NOTES	EXAMPLES
Eye Drops to ↓ Inflammation	Steroid eye drops should be used short-term due to risk of ↑ IOP.	**STEROIDS** Dexamethasone (*Maxidex, Ozurdex*) Loteprednol (*Alrex, Lotemax* suspension, ointment, gel) Fluorometholone (*Flarex, FML Forte, FML Liquifilm* suspension, ointment) Prednisolone acetate (*Pred Forte*) **NSAIDs** Ketorolac (*Acular, Acular LS, Acuvail*) Flurbiprofen (*Ocufen*) Diclofenac Bromfenac
Artificial Tears to Moisturize Eyes	Common lubricants – mineral oil, glycerin, propylene glycol, dextran, hypromellose Administered multiple times daily, as-needed.	*Systane* *Refresh* *Clear Eyes* *Liquifilm* and others

Blepharitis (Eyelid Inflammation)

Blepharitis most commonly involves the part of the eyelid where the eyelashes come out of the skin. In many patients the condition is chronic and is difficult to treat and in others it is an acute, short-term condition. The primary symptoms are <u>inflamed, irritated and itchy eyelids</u>. The <u>preferred treatment</u> is gentle washing and application of <u>compresses</u>: apply a warm compress over the eye for a few minutes to loosen the crusty deposits, then use a <u>warm moist washcloth (water plus a few drops of baby shampoo)</u> to wipe away the debris. In some cases, antibiotic ointments, steroid eye drops and artificial tears are helpful.

OTICS

Background

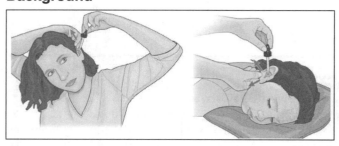

Common conditions treated in the ear include pain (such as from an otitis infection-which may be treated with topical antibiotics, although oral are much more common), inflammation from swimmer's ear (otitis externa) and ear wax (cerumen) impaction. Otitis externa pain can be treated (preferentially) with systemic analgesics (ibuprofen, acetaminophen). During treatment patients should stay out of the water, avoid flying due to the pressure changes, and avoid the use of headphones and ear plugs. Tinnitus (ringing or roaring or buzzing sounds) is caused by drug toxicity (primarily salicylates), noise exposure, or is idiopathic. There is no effective drug treatment for tinnitus. For any condition, eye drops may be used in the ear, but never use ear drops in the eyes; the ear drops may not have an appropriate pH, may not be isotonic and may not be sterile.

Ear drops with antibiotics may also be used for outer ear infections. A few common products:

- Ciprofloxacin and hydrocortisone *(Cipro HC)*

- Ciprofloxacin and dexamethasone *(Ciprodex)*

- Neomycin, colistin, hydrocortisone, and thonzonium *(Cortisporin-TC)*

Ear Wax (Cerumen) Removal

Earwax blockage occurs when earwax (cerumen) accumulates in the ear or becomes too hard to wash away naturally. It is removed in a medical office. If the condition is chronic, ear-wax removal medication [carbamide peroxide *(Debrox)*, triethanolamine *(Cerumenex)]* is sometimes used every 4 - 8 weeks as a preventive measure. Instruct the patient to tilt the head sideways (see below) and instill 5 - 10 drops twice daily for up to four days.

Otic Medication Application

- If cold, hold the bottle for 1 or 2 minutes to warm the solution. Ear drops that are too cold will be uncomfortable and can cause dizziness.

- Lie down or tilt the head so that the affected ear faces up.

- Gently pull the earlobe up and back for adults (down and back for children) to straighten the ear canal.

- Administer the prescribed number of drops into the ear canal. Keep the ear facing up for about 5 minutes to allow the medicine to coat the ear canal.

- Do not touch the dropper tip to any surface. To clean wipe with a clean tissue.

75

MOTION SICKNESS

BACKGROUND

Motion sickness (kinetosis) is also called seasickness or air-sickness. Symptoms are nausea, dizziness and fatigue. People can get motion sickness on a moving boat, train, airplane, car, or amusement park rides. This is a common condition.

NON-PHARMACOLOGIC TREATMENT

Some patients find benefit with a wrist band that presses on an acupuncture point located on the inside of the wrist, about the length of 2 fingernails up the arm from the center of the wrist crease. One popular brand is *Sea-Band* benefit. The best way to stop motion sickness, if possible, is to stop the motion.

Natural Products

Ginger, in teas or supplements, is used most commonly. Peppermint may be helpful.

DRUG TREATMENT

Medications for motion sickness are anticholinergics and may cause drowsiness and may impair judgment. Pilots, ship crew members, or anyone operating heavy equipment or driving a car should not take them. The military uses combinations of products (such as oral scopolamine to reduce nausea, taken with a stimulant, such as dextroamphetamine, to counteract the drowsiness from the scopolamine) but these combinations have significant risk and should not be routinely recommended.

Scopolamine *(Transderm-Scop)* is the most commonly prescribed medication for motion sickness. It is not more effective than generically-available OTC agents but is applied topically (behind the ear) and is taken less frequently (apply 4-6 hours prior to need, lasts three days, do not cut patch, alternate ears, do not get into eyes, wash hands afterwards).All of the antihistamines have anticholinergic effects similar to scopolamine. Make sure the oral agents are taken prior to travel (30-60 minutes prior) and ensure that the patient knows they will get tired. Instruct them not to consume alcohol or other CNS depressants.

Antihistamines used for motion sickness include cyclizine (*Marezine*), diphenhydramine *(Benadryl)*, dimenhydrinate *(Dramamine)* or Meclizine *(Bonine)*. Dimenhydrinate, meclizine and cyclizine are long-acting piperazine antihistamines and are a little less sedating than other antihistamines, but they are still sedating. All of the antihistamines have anticholinergic effects similar to scopolamine. Make sure the oral agents are taken prior to travel (30-60 minutes prior) and ensure that the patient knows they will get tired. Instruct them not to consume alcohol or other CNS depressants.

Promethazine is used and is prescription only. Do not use promethazine in children. All promethazine products carry a black box warning contraindicating use in children less than 2 years and strongly cautioning use in children age 2 and older. The FDA advises against the use of promethazine with codeine cough syrups in children less than 6 years of age, due to the risk of respiratory depression, cardiac arrest and neurological problems.

Anticholinergics

DRUG	DOSING	SAFETY/SIDE EFFECTS/MONITORING
Scopolamine 3-day patch *(Transderm-Scop)* Applied behind ear Q 72 hrs, rotate ears	1.5 mg, patch placed behind ear (hairless), 4-6 hours before needed, or 1 hour prior to cesarean section or evening before AM surgery – remove 24 hours after surgery) Primarily for motion sickness, occasionally used inpatient. Do not use in children.	**WARNINGS** Hypersensitivity to belladonna alkaloids, narrow-angle glaucoma, paradoxical bradycardia, CNS depression, blurry vision/eye pain, withdrawal (high doses with abrupt d/c) **SIDE EFFECTS** Dry mouth, dizziness, stinging eyes (if touch eyes after handling patch), pupil dilation, ↑ risk IOP, confusion (can be significant in elderly, frail), hallucinations (rare), tachycardia (rare) **NOTES** Pregnancy Category C. Remove prior to MRI. Do not cut patch, wash hands before and after application.
Meclizine *(Dramamine Less Drowsy, Motion-Time, Medi-Meclizine, Travel Sickness, Antivert-discontinued)*	25-50 mg PO 1 hour before travel, can repeat Q 24	**WARNINGS** Worsening of BPH symptoms, can ↑ IOP (glaucoma), and worsen cognition (elderly) **SIDE EFFECTS** Sedation, dry mouth, dry/blurry vision, tachycardia **NOTES** Pregnancy Category B.
OTHER ANTIHISTAMINES USED Cyclizine, DiphenhydrAMINE, DimenhyDRINATE, **Promethazine:** Do not use in children due (primarily) to risk of respiratory depression. Do not give IV due to risk of severe tissue necrosis (vesicant). IM route is preferred for injection. Available in oral tablets, rectal suppository and injection.		

Transderm Scop Counseling

- Peel off the clear backing from the patch and apply it to a clean, dry, hairless area of the skin behind the ear. Press firmly for at least 30 seconds to make sure the patch sticks well, especially around the edges. The patch will slowly release the medication into your body over 3 days. Apply at least 4 hours before activity that will cause motion sickness. If getting an MRI procedure, remove patch before the MRI or it will burn your skin.

- Be sure to wash your hands thoroughly with soap and water before and immediately after handling the patch, so that any drug that might get on your hands will not come into contact with your eyes. Wash the area behind the ear where the patch was removed.

- No alcohol. Try to avoid other drugs that make you tired – this drug causes significant drowsiness.

- The most common side effect is dryness of the mouth. Other common side effects are drowsiness, blurry vision and widening of the pupils (especially if the drug is on your hands and you touch your eyes). Rarely, some people get disoriented, and others can get confusion, hallucinations or heart palpitations. If any of these occur remove the patch and contact your healthcare provider.

76

COMMON SKIN CONDITIONS

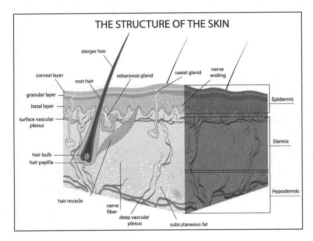

THE STRUCTURE OF THE SKIN

GUIDELINES

There are various conditions presented in this section and treatments for each are presented below. It can be difficult to determine the type of skin condition, which are often presented by the patient to the community pharmacist. *The Handbook of OTC Drugs* has pictures of common conditions, and many more are available at www.dermnet.com. If recommending OTC treatment it is important to tell the patient to be seen by a physician if the condition does not improve or worsens. A pharmacist should be able to recognize a blemish that could be skin cancer; see the pictures and description in the Oncology I chapter.

Natural Products

Aloe is a natural product produced from the aloe vera plant that is used for many skin conditions, including sunburn and psoriasis. It has little proven efficacy but if used as a gel or lotion it may provide a soothing effect. Tea tree oil is used for a variety of skin conditions. It can be useful for treating acne. It may be helpful for onychomycosis symptoms (depending on the dose and application schedule), but is not useful in eradicating the infection in most patients. Lysine is used for cold sore prevention.

DRUGS THAT CAN DISCOLOR SKIN, SECRETIONS

Brown Levodopa, Entacapone Methyldopa	**Brown/Black/Green** Methocarbamol	**Yellow-Green** Propofol Flutamide	**Red** Anthracyclines Deferasirox (urine)
Brown/Yellow Metronidazole, Tinidazole Nitrofurantoin Riboflavin (B2)	**Purple/Ora/Red** Chlorzoxazone **Orange/Yellow** Sulfasalazine **Orange/Red/Brown** Ezogabine	**Red-Orange** Phenazopyridine Rifapentine Rifampin	**Blue** Mitoxantrone Methylene blue **Blue-Gray** Chloroquine Amiodarone

Acne, Background & Treatment

- Most people develop acne, including infants, adults (and women, commonly, around the menstrual cycle) and, primarily, adolescents in puberty.

- Androgens (male sex hormones) are the primary determinant of acne (and is why boys often will have worse acne than girls) and the presence of the bacteria *P. acnes* and fatty acids present in oil glands. Where the oil glands are located is where acne occurs: the face, chest, shoulders and back.

- Lesions are classified as whiteheads, blackheads, small bumps, cysts and nodules.

- Treatment is determined by severity: mild (few, occasional pimples), moderate (inflammatory papules), or severe (nodules and cysts).

- Acne is treated with four primary groups of agents: OTC (benzoyl peroxide and salicylic acid), retinoids, systemic isotretinoin and antibiotics.

- Benzoyl peroxide (BPO) is the most effective OTC agent. It comes as Rx, including in combination with hydrocortisone, the retinoid adapalene or with the antibiotics erythromycin or clindamycin. Start with 2.5-5% BPO, which is generally adequate and less irritating than the higher strengths.

- Salicylic acid is a mildly useful OTC agent, and is primarily used in "medicated pads" for facial cleansing.

- Retinoids, primarily topical tretinoin and derivatives are the usual Rx drug of choice. [They are also used to reduce fine wrinkles.]

  - Retinoids are vitamin A derivatives. The mechanism is primarily to reduce adherence of the keratinocytes (outer skin cells) in the oil gland.

  - They are well-tolerated when used topically, with mild skin irritation (redness, drying) and photosensitivity possible. Start at night (or every other night) with the correct (pea sized) amount. Use moisturizer each morning, followed by sunscreen.

  - Retinoids take 4-12 weeks to work and acne may worsen initially. An antibiotic (often minocycline) taken concurrently can help.

  - They are not used in pregnancy or breastfeeding; some are pregnancy category C, others are X. Tazarotene often works better than tretinoin; it is used with difficult cases and is pregnancy category X.

  - Often a topical antibiotic is used concurrently – the retinoid allows the antibiotic to get into the pores to eradicate the bacteria.

  - The oral retinoic isotretinoin has many safety considerations, including severe teratogenicity, and is reserved for severe nodular acne only. Cholesterol and pregnancy tests are required, among other monitoring.

- Some women find benefit with birth control pills, especially if the acne is in combination with irregular periods or symptoms of androgenic excess.

- Azelaic acid *(Azelex, Finacea)* is a topical dicarboxylic acid cream or gel available OTC and Rx for acne and rosacea. It is well tolerated and can cause mild topical burning or "tingling."

DRUGS	NOTES	SAFETY/COUNSELING

Retinoid topicals are 1st line agents

Tretinoin cream *(Atralin, Renova, Retin-A, Retin-A Micro, Avita, Refissa, Tretin-X)*

Slower-release, less skin irritation with:

- Microsphere gel *(Retin-A Micro)*

- Polymerized cream or gel *(Avita)*

Adapalene *(Differin)* cream, solution

Adapalene + BPO *(Epiduo)*

Tazarotene (*Tazorac*, Avage-creams, Fabior-foam) stronger, more irritating

Dapsone gel *(Aczone)*

Retinoids are popular and there are many other products, such as clindamycin + tretinoin gel *(Ziana)*, others

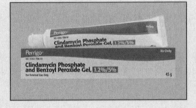

TYPES OF ACNE PIMPLES

Healthy skin   Whiteheads   Blackheads   Papules   Pustules

Apply daily, usually at bedtime, about 20 minutes after washing face.

If irritation use lower strength, or every other night. May need to reduce contact initially (wash off if skin is irritated).

A pea-sized amount is sufficient (for facial application); it should be divided into 4 equal parts and smoothed over the entire surface of the face – not just on acne.

Avoid salicylic acid scrubs or astringents while starting a retinoid; this will worsen irritation.

Wash only with mild soap twice daily.

Takes 4-12 weeks to see response; may worsen acne initially.

Limit sun exposure.

Do not use dapsone gel if G6PD deficiency.

Benzoyl peroxide (most effective OTC agent), salicylic acid is weaker OTC agent

OTC (many products) including *Benoxyl, Benzac, Clearasil*, if needed with a retinoid.

Erythromycin + BPO *(Benzamycin)*

Clindamycin + BPO *(Acanya, BenzaClin, Duac,* Neuac)

BPO+hydrocortisone *(Vanoxide-HC)*

Azelaic acid *(Azelex, Finacea)*, OTC, Rx

Duac
Dispense with 60 day expiration. Apply QHS to affected areas. Can store at room temp, do not freeze.

Limit sun exposure.

Clindamycin Topicals, usual instructions
Clean face, shake (if lotion), apply a thin layer once or twice daily. Avoid contact with eyes; if contact, rinse with cold water.

Takes 2-6 weeks for effect and up to 12 weeks for full benefit.

BPO can bleach clothing, hair

Limit sun exposure; skin will burn more easily.

Benzamycin and BenzaClin
Add indicated amount of purified water to the vial (70% ethyl alcohol for *Benzamycin*) and immediately shake to completely dissolve medication. If needed, add additional purified water to bring level up to the mark. Add the solution in the vial to the gel and stir until homogenous in appearance (1 to 1½ minutes). *Benzamycin* is kept refrigerated. *BenzaClin* is kept at room temp. Place a 3 month expiration date on the label following mixing.

Acne Background & Treatment Continued

DRUGS	NOTES	SAFETY/COUNSELING
Oral isotretinoin *(Amnesteem, Claravis, Myorisan, Absorica)* Only for the treatment of severe recalcitrant nodular acne 0.5–1.0 mg/kg/day, divided BID with food for 15-20 weeks. Comes as 10, 20, and 40 mg capsules. Counseling about contraception and behaviors associated with risk of pregnancy must be repeated on a monthly basis. Two forms of birth control are required while taking this medication (cannot use a progestin-only pill). Dryness: Carry bottled water, eye drops and lip balm.	Female patients must sign patient information/informed consent form about birth defects that contains warnings about the risk of potential birth defects if the fetus is exposed to isotretinoin. Must have had 2 negative pregnancy tests prior to starting treatment. Cannot get pregnant for one month before, while taking the drug, or for one month after the drug is stopped. Do not breastfeed or donate blood until at least one month has passed after the drug is stopped. Do not use with vitamin A supplements, tetracyclines, steroids, progestin-only contraceptives or St. John's wort. Must swallow capsule whole, or puncture and sprinkle on applesauce or ice cream – this may irritate esophagus.	Pregnancy Category X: severe birth defects or miscarriage. Can only be dispensed by a pharmacy registered and activated with the pregnancy risk management iPLEDGE program. 1-month Rx at a time, fill within 7 days with yellow sticker attached. Teratogenicity, arthralgias, skeletal hyperostosis, osteoporosis, psychiatric issues (depression, psychosis, risk of suicide), decreased night vision (may be permanent), difficulty wearing contact lens (dry eyes/irritation), dry skin, chapped lips, elevated cholesterol and BG, transient chest pain and hearing loss, and photosensitivity.
ORAL ANTIBIOTICS USED COMMONLY FOR ACNE **Minocycline ext-rel** *(Solodyn)* 12 years and older, dosed by weight Doxycycline and minocycline are more effective than tetracycline in eradicating *P. acnes* Trimethoprim/Sulfamethoxazole is also used. Erythromycin used to be commonly used but is not currently due to resistance.	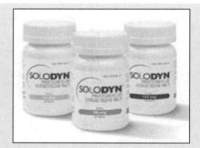	Photosensitivity, rash in susceptible patients, dizziness, diarrhea, somnolence Like other tetracyclines can cause fetal harm if administered during pregnancy. May cause permanent discoloration in teeth if used when teeth are forming (up to 8 years of age).

Alopecia (Hair Loss), Background & Treatment

- As people age, hair tends to gradually thin. Other causes of hair loss include hormonal factors, medical conditions and medications.

- The most common cause of hair loss is a hereditary condition called male-pattern baldness, and less commonly, female-pattern baldness.

- Hormonal changes in women that can result in hair loss are usually associated with pregnancy, childbirth or menopause.

- Medical conditions that cause hair loss include hypothyroidism, alopecia areata (an autoimmune condition), scalp infections and some other conditions, including lupus.

- Drugs that can contribute to alopecia include various chemotherapeutics (primarily because hair cells are rapidly dividing and therefore are targeted by the treatment) and infrequently with the following medications: clomiphene, heparin, hydroxychloroquine, interferons, lithium, some types of oral contraceptives, levonorgestrel, procainamide, valproate, spironolactone and warfarin.

- Zinc and vitamin D deficiency is thought to contribute to hair loss.
- Many people will seek surgical intervention for hair loss. The medications work modestly and are presented here. Bimatoprost in the *Latisse* formulation is for thinning eyelashes (hypotrichosis) and should not be used concurrently in patients using a prostaglandin analog for glaucoma (minimally, contact the optometrist or ophthalmologist to confirm because the IOP may increase if there is excessive use of prostaglandin analogs.)

DRUGS	NOTES	SAFETY/COUNSELING
Finasteride *(Propecia)* 5-alpha reductase type 2 inhibitor Do not dispense with someone on finasteride (*Proscar*) for BPH 1 mg daily, at least 3 months duration to begin to see effect	 Romic Eskandarian, PharmD *(God made a few good heads, and put hair on the rest of them.)*	Preg Categ X: females should not handle – can damage male fetus. Must be used indefinitely or condition reappears. **Side effects** Lower dose than *Proscar*; lower risk of sexual side effects; see overactive bladder chapter for further details
Minoxidil topical OTC 2% and 5% – 5% solution more effective, but more facial hair growth.	Rx tablets indicated for hypertension (very rarely used)	For men and women Must be used indefinitely or condition reappears.
Bimatoprost solution *(Latisse)* For thinning eyelashes (hypotrichosis)	Apply nightly to the skin at the base of the upper eyelashes only (do not apply to the lower lid). Use the applicator brush. Blot any excess. Repeat for other eye. Dispose of the applicator after one use.	May cause itchy eyes and/or eye redness. If discontinued, lashes eventually return to previous appearance. Eyelid skin darkening may occur, which may be reversible. Hair growth may occur in other skin areas that the solution frequently touches. Do not use concurrently with PG analogs used for glaucoma.

Cold Sores, Background & Treatment

- Cold sores (Herpes simplex labialis) are ubiquitous and are highly contagious. Children often pick up the infection from family members. Infection is usually due to herpes simplex virus type 1 (HSV-1) in children, but can be caused by HSV-2 when older due to oral/genital sex. Virus can be shed when asymptomatic but is most commonly spread with active lesions; the infectious exudate should not be transmitted (kissing, sharing drinks).

- Sore eruption is preceded by prodromal symptoms (tingling, itching, soreness). In most patients the sore appears in the same location repeatedly. The most common site is the junction between the upper and lower lip. Triggers that instigate sore outbreaks include fatigue/stress, stress to the skin (sun exposure, acid peels) and dental work. Patients should identify their own trigger/s and attempt to avoid them.

- The prodromal period is the optimal time to apply topical or take oral medication to reduce blister duration. If recurrences are frequent (> 4 times/year), chronic suppression, taken daily, can be used. OTC and Rx topicals shorten the duration by up to one day; oral (systemic) antivirals shorten the duration by up to two days.

■ The natural product lysine is used commonly for cold sore prevention.

DRUGS	NOTES	SAFETY/COUNSELING
Docosanol *(Abreva)* – OTC **Rx** Acyclovir topical cream *(Zovirax)* Acyclovir buccal tablets *(Sitavig)* Penciclovir topical cream *(Denavir)*	Oral antivirals can be used, are more effective, and are discussed in the ID chapter. 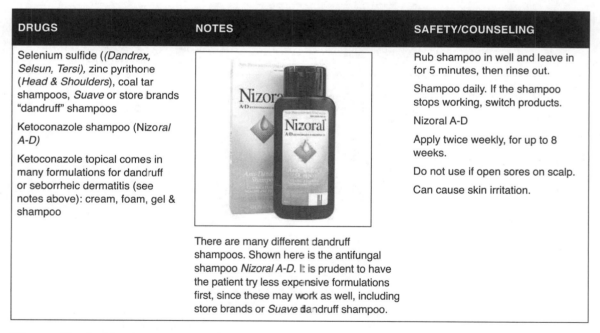	*Abreva* cream: Apply 5x daily at first sign of outbreak, continue until healed. *Zovirax* cream: Apply 5 times daily for 4 days (can be used on genital sores). *Sitavig* tablet: Apply one 50 mg tablet as a single dose to the upper gum region. *Denavir* cream: Apply every 2 hours during waking hours for 4 days.

Dandruff, Background & Treatment

■ Dandruff occurs when the scalp is itchy and/or scaling with white oily flakes (dead skin) in the hair and on the shoulders, back or clothing.

■ Dandruff can be due to either eczema or fungal (yeast) overgrowth, and worsened by hormones, the weather or shampoo. Seborrheic dermatitis is a common form of eczema that causes flaking, itchy skin on the face, back, chest or head. If it is on the scalp it is commonly referred to as dandruff.

■ Patients are not likely to know the cause of the dandruff. A store-brand, inexpensive dandruff shampoo can be tried first, and if this is ineffective, the pricier ketoconazole antifungal shampoo can be used.

DRUGS	NOTES	SAFETY/COUNSELING
Selenium sulfide (*(Dandrex, Selsun, Tersi)*, zinc pyrithone (*Head & Shoulders*), coal tar shampoos, *Suave* or store brands "dandruff" shampoos Ketoconazole shampoo (*Nizoral A-D*) Ketoconazole topical comes in many formulations for dandruff or seborrheic dermatitis (see notes above): cream, foam, gel & shampoo	There are many different dandruff shampoos. Shown here is the antifungal shampoo *Nizoral A-D*. It is prudent to have the patient try less expensive formulations first, since these may work as well, including store brands or *Suave* dandruff shampoo.	Rub shampoo in well and leave in for 5 minutes, then rinse out. Shampoo daily. If the shampoo stops working, switch products. Nizoral A-D Apply twice weekly, for up to 8 weeks. Do not use if open sores on scalp. Can cause skin irritation.

Diaper Rash, Background & Treatment

Diaper rash commonly occurs with nearly all babies. The skin is sensitive, and when exposed to the urine and stools, and a diaper moving back and forth, rash appears. Once the skin is damaged it is susceptible to bacteria and yeast overgrowth.

Prevention

- Change diapers frequently, do not cover diapers with plastic, use absorbent diapers.

- Wipe well with unscented wipes or plain water.

- Leave off the diaper, when possible, to let the skin air-dry. The baby can lie on a towel.

- Use a skin protectant:

  ❏ Petrolatum ointment (*A & D Ointment*, store brands) – this is a good preventative every-day ointment, includes vitamins A and D.

  ❏ Petrolatum with zinc oxide, such as in *Desitin* – is thicker and contains a dessicant (zinc oxide) to dry out the skin; may be preferable for babies more prone to rash.

- *"Butt Paste"* or *"Triple Paste"* – are other alternatives.

- Clotrimazole, miconazole, others – for stubborn rashes, if yeast thought to be involved.

- Hydrocortisone 0.5-1% cream – can be used BID, but not for more than several days at a time.

- Combinations of the above are used.

DRUGS	NOTES	SAFETY/COUNSELING
Desitin (petrolatum + zinc oxide, a dessicant to decrease moisture) *A&D Ointment*, or plain petrolatum, or store-brands. Miconazole+zinc oxide+petrolatum *(Vusion)* Or other products mentioned above.		Review counseling tips above. Infants should be referred to the physician (especially if under 6 months) and older babies if condition appears serious or worsens. Topical antibiotics may be needed if bacterial involvement is suspected. Topical antifungals may be needed if fungal involvement is suspected. Topical steroids, low potency, may be used short-term. Diaper rashes can have more than one contributing organism.

Eczema (Atopic Dermatitis), Background & Treatment

- Eczema is a general term for many types of skin inflammation, and is used interchangeably with the term atopic dermatitis (which is sometimes used to refer to other conditions – this makes the term "atopic dermatitis" confusing).

- Eczema is most common in young children and infants, but can occur at any age.

- Eczema presents as skin rashes, which become crusty and scaly; blisters can develop. The rash is very itchy, red, dry and sore.

- Common locations are the insides of elbows, back of knees, face (often on the cheeks), behind the ears, buttocks, hands and feet.

- Outbreak "triggers" can be environmental irritants or allergens, including soaps, perfumes, pollution, stress or weather changes; patients should attempt to avoid triggers.

- Hydration is <u>essential</u> to reduce disease severity. Use <u>moisturizers</u>. Maintain humidity in the home.

- Treatment can include <u>topical corticosteroids</u> (and occasional oral courses, if-needed), antihistamines (for itching), or the immunosuppressant <u>calcineurin inhibitors</u>, if topical steroids with hydration <u>are not adequate</u>.

- In severe, refractive cases, oral immune-suppressants (cyclosporine, methotrexate, monoclonal antibody-type drugs such as etanercept and others) can be used. These are described in other chapters.

DRUGS	NOTES	SAFETY/COUNSELING
Tx: topical or oral steroids, antibiotics, antihistamines, keep skin well hydrated (moisturized with petrolatum, lanolin, products such as *Aquaphor, Eucerin, Keri* or store brands) Treat first with topical steroids, only use these agents if failed steroids: Tacrolimus (*Protopic*) **Pimecrolimus (*Elidel*)** Do not use in children younger than 2 years of age.	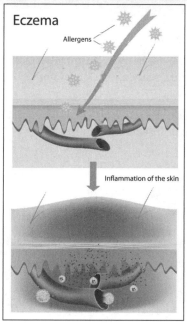 Eczema Allergens Inflammation of the skin	Dispense MedGuide for *Elidel* and *Protopic*: Associated with cases of lymphoma and skin cancer; use only as second-line agents for short-term and intermittent treatment of atopic dermatitis (eczema) in patients unresponsive to, or intolerant of other treatments. Apply a thin layer only to the affected skin areas, twice a day. Use the smallest amount needed to control symptoms. Takes weeks to work; continue to apply. <u>Wash your hands after application.</u> Limit sun exposure; photosensitizer. Side effects can include headache, skin burning, itching, cough, flu-like symptoms

Fungal Infections: Skin, Background & Treatment

Tinea pedis, cruris, corporis, and topical *Candida* infections (vaginal, onychomycosis, diaper rash see separate sections)

Athlete's foot (tinea pedis)

- A fungal infection of the foot caused by various fungi (commonly trichophyton rubrum).

- Symptoms are itching, peeling, redness, mild burning, and sometimes sores. This is a common infection, particularly among those using public pools, showers, and locker rooms. Diagnosis is usually by symptoms, but if unclear (psoriasis and other conditions can cause itchy skin), the skin can be scraped off and viewed under a microscope.

- It is treated topically with antifungals, except in severe cases.

Jock itch (tinea cruris)

- Affects the genitals, inner thighs and buttocks.

- The rash is red, itchy and can be ring-shaped.

- Jock itch is not very contagious, but can be spread person-to-person with close contact.

- Keep the skin dry (use a clean towel after showering) and treat with an antifungal topical. Creams work best.

- Change underwear at least daily.

Ringworm (tinea corporis)

- Not a worm, but a skin fungal infection.

- Ringworm can appear anywhere on the body and typically looks like circular, red, flat sores (one or more, may overlap), usually with dry, scaly skin. Occasionally the ring-like presentation is not present – just itchy red skin.

- The outer part of the sore can be raised while the skin in the middle appears normal. It can spread person-to-person or by contact with infected animals.

- Most cases are treated topically.

- Tinea capitis is "ringworm" on the scalp – this affects primarily young children, mostly in crowded, lower-income situations and requires systemic therapy, with the same drugs used for onychomycosis.

Cutaneous (skin) *Candida* infections

- Topical *Candida* infections cause red, itchy rashes, most commonly in the groin, armpits or anywhere the skin folds.

- These are more likely in obese persons because they will have more skin with folds; the infection can be in unusual places, such as under the breasts, if the skin is moist. Diabetes is another risk factor.

- Occasionally fungal infections appear in the corner of nails (on the skin, not in the nailbed). If this is a suspected bacterial infection, OTC antibiotic topicals or mupirocin (*Bactroban* – excellent gram positive coverage) can be used.

- *Candida* can cause diaper rash in infants (discussed under diaper rash).

DRUGS	NOTES	SAFETY/COUNSELING
Terbinafine and butenafine highly effective: Terbinafine (*Lamisil* AT cream and solution) Butenafine (*Lotrimin Ultra* cream) Clotrimazole (*Lotrimin* cream, lotion, solution, *Desenex*) Miconazole (*Monistat-Derm, Lotrimin* powder and spray) Miconazole+petrolatum (for moisture barrier, used in geriatrics) *(Baza)* *Monistat Derm* cream Tolnaftate (*Tinactin* powder, cream, spray) Undecylenic acid (*Cruex, Desenex*), others **Betamethasone/Clotrimazole (*Lotrisone*)** – popular for tinea with inflammation/itching **Rx** Ketoconazole (cream), ketoconazole foam *(Extina)* Note the same name in OTC products can refer to different active ingredients – do not instruct patient by brand name alone or there could be a product mix-up. The FDA will be attempting to eliminate this confusion by restricting name allocations.	 Tinea corporis (ringworm) – the name "ringworm" is a misnomer; this is a fungal infection. The rings can be single or overlap.	Topical antifungals come in creams, ointments, gels, solutions Creams work best and are used in most cases. Solutions can be easier to apply in hairy areas. Powders do not work well for treatment but may be used for prevention, such as in shoes after a gym workout. Use cotton socks. Apply medicine 1-2 inches beyond the rash. Use for at least 2-4 weeks, even if it appears healed. Reduce moisture to the infected area. If foot infection, do not walk barefoot (to avoid spreading it). Wear sandals in public showers (to avoid catching it).

Fungal Infections: Toenail & Fingernail, Background & Treatment

- Onychomycosis (tinea unguium) can cause pain, discomfort, and disfigurement and can lead to physical limitations, such as difficulty standing and walking. The discoloration and disfigurement can cause loss of self-esteem and psychological issues.

- Topical agents are limited to mild cases, patients who cannot tolerate systemic therapies, or are used concurrently with systemic treatment or as prophylaxis. They are <u>not</u> potent enough to cure most infections.

- Itraconazole and terbinafine are used most commonly and have FDA indications; fluconazole and posaconazole are used off-label. Griseofulvin is rarely used currently.

- It takes a long time for the nail bed to look better – sometimes up to a year in toenails. Toenails take longer to treat than fingernails, and are more commonly infected.

- Pulse therapy (intermittent) can be used to reduce costs and possibly toxicity, but may not be as effective.

- A 20% <u>potassium hydroxide (KOH) smear</u> is essential for diagnosis as other conditions can produce a similar presentation.

DRUGS	NOTES	SAFETY/COUNSELING
Itraconazole *(Sporanox)* Dose 200 mg Q daily x 12 weeks for 12 weeks, or "pulse-dosing" (fingernails only): 200 mg BID x 1 week, repeat 1-week course after 3 weeks off-time Terbinafine *(LamISIL, Terbinex)* – oral (topical is *LamISIL AT,* and is used for fungal skin infections) 250 mg PO daily for 6 weeks (fingernail) or 12 weeks (toenail) Ciclopirox *(Penlac, Loprox)* Apply evenly over entire nail plate QHS (or 8 hours before washing) to all affected nails with applicator brush Tavabarole *(Kerydin)* Efinaconazole *(Jublia)* *Kerydin* & *Jublia*: apply once daily for 48 weeks, both for toenails	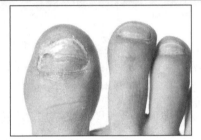 Ciclopirox *(Penlac, Loprox)* – used in combination with orals; poor efficacy when used alone. Occasionally used in patients who cannot tolerate systemic therapy, but generally cannot cure an infection when used alone. Occasionally used as prophylaxis. Tavaborole *(Kerydin)* – oxaborole antifungal, applied topically to toenails Q daily x 48 weeks to entire nail surface and under the nail tip. Efinaconazole *(Jublia)* – azole antifungal, applied topically to toenails Q daily x 48 weeks	For systemic azoles, refer to Infectious Disease chapter III. Systemic drugs used for nail fungal infections are hepatotoxic (monitor LFTs), QT prolongers (avoid in QT risk) and CYP 3A4 substrates & inhibitors (there are many drug interactions). Nausea and diarrhea are common. Itraconazole *(Sporanox)* Boxed warning to avoid use in heart failure. Requires gastric acid for absorption; cannot use strong acid suppressing agents concurrently. Terbinafine *(Lamisil, Terbinex)* – oral Primarily headache, rash, nausea, risk of hepatotoxicity. Recurrence is common. Practice proper foot care and keep the nails dry. Keep blood glucose controlled. Do not smoke.

Fungal Infections: Vaginal

This is a common infection; about 75% women will have at least one episode, and half of these women will have recurrence. In a small percentage of women the recurrence is chronic.

- The infection is uncommon before a girl begins menstruating, and occurs most commonly during the week prior to menstruation – this makes treatment decisions around the period important. The woman can begin treatment during menses, or wait until the bleeding stops. Tampons should not be used when medication is applied.

- Vaginal fungal infections are also common during pregnancy. Pregnant patients are hopefully seeing a physician, and require longer (7 - 10 day) treatment.

- Symptoms are primarily itching, with possible soreness and pain (burning) during urination or sex. Some women have a cottage-cheese like discharge (white, thick, clumpy).

- Diagnosis can be confirmed with either a vaginal culture to check for fungal growth or, via a pH test: a pH greater than 4.5 indicates the presence of either a *Candida* or trichomoniasis infection. OTC test kits such as the *Vagisil Screening Kit* test for vaginal pH. Generally, testing is not necessary if the woman has been seen by the physician for the initial infection and is able to recognize the symptoms.

- If the woman has had the infection before and is able to recognize the symptoms, she can self-treat with OTC products. If there are more than four infections in a year, or if symptoms recur within 2 months, refer to the physician to rule-out an underlying condition that could be causative (most likely diabetes, HIV, receiving steroids or other immune-suppressing agents, pregnancy, or irritation from repeated douching or use of lubricants). Women taking high-dose estrogen in birth control pills or in hormone replacement therapy are at elevated risk. Antibiotic use can be a risk factor; the antibiotic can wipe out the normal flora and lead to fungal overgrowth.

- Lactobacillus or yogurt with active cultures is thought to reduce infection occurrence; however, this is rated as "possibly ineffective" by the *Natural Medicines Database*.

- If self-treating, counsel that condoms and diaphragms may not provide adequate pregnancy protection; the oil in OTC antifungals weakens the latex.

- To avoid future infections, keep the vaginal area clean, wipe from the front to the back, use cotton underwear, avoid tight-fitting clothing, including pantyhose, change pads/tampons often, change out of wet swimsuits or clothing quickly, and recommend against use of vaginal douches, sprays and deodorant tampons; these can alter the vaginal pH and contribute to infection.

DRUGS	NOTES	SAFETY/COUNSELING
Mild-moderate, infrequent infection 1 or 3 day treatment, with vaginal cream, ointment or vaginal suppository/tab **OTC, topical** Butoconazole (*Gynazole-1*, others) Clotrimazole (*Gyne-Lotrimin*, others) Miconazole (*Monistat 3*, others) Terconazole (*Terazol 3*, others) Tioconazole (*Vagistat-1*) **Rx, oral** Fluconazole (*Diflucan*) 150 mg PO x 1 Complicated infections, pregnancy: 7-10 days treatment, or send for referral	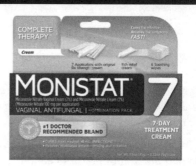 .Always counsel on ways to avoid recurrence: avoid douching, wear cotton underwear, avoid tight-fitting pantyhose and pants, change out of wet swimsuits quickly. Some recommend avoiding hot tubs or very hot baths. The male sexual partner may be tested if the female's infections are recurrent; this is not commonly done	Counseling for OTC antifungals: Prior to using the product, wash the vagina with mild soap and water, and pat dry with a towel. Insert applicator, suppository, or vaginal tab at night before bed. Lying down immediately after insertion helps retain the medicine inside the vagina. It may be helpful to use a protective pad. The creams and suppositories are oil-based medications that can weaken latex condoms and diaphragms; avoid sexual intercourse. If you get your menstrual cycle during treatment, continue the treatment, otherwise a woman can wait until her menstrual cycle is over before starting treatment if she desires (this is not necessary). Do not use tampons during treatment. Complete entire course of treatment. Medical care is warranted if symptoms persist/recur within 2 months after using an OTC product, or if > 4/year.

Genital Warts, Background & Treatment

- Genital warts are caused by the human papillomavirus (HPV), a common sexually transmitted disease (STD), spread easily skin-to-skin. Consider recommending HPV vaccine, if series incomplete. *Gardasil* protects against the strains of HPV that cause most genital warts and reduces risk of cervical cancer. *Cervarix* protects against cervical cancer but not genital warts. Condoms reduce risk of STD transmission.

- Treatment may not be required if no symptoms, but if discomfort or emotional distress, treatment can reduce or remove the warts.

- Imiquimod (*Aldara, Zyclara*) will reduce warts. Avoid sexual contact while the cream is on your skin; weakens condoms, diaphragms and can irritate the partner's skin.

In addition to the treatments below, the warts may be removed by lasers, cryotherapy (with liquid nitrogen to freeze the warts, after which they come off), freezing, electrocautery (electrical current burns off warts) or surgical excision.

DRUGS	NOTES	SAFETY/COUNSELING
Imiquimod cream (*Aldara, Zyclara*) *Aldara* also approved for superficial basal cell carcinoma and actinic keratosis. Podophyllum Resin (*Podocon-25*)	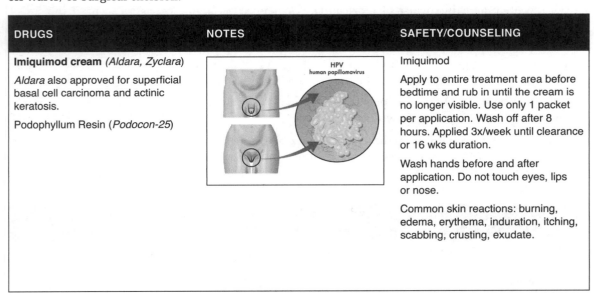	Imiquimod Apply to entire treatment area before bedtime and rub in until the cream is no longer visible. Use only 1 packet per application. Wash off after 8 hours. Applied 3x/week until clearance or 16 wks duration. Wash hands before and after application. Do not touch eyes, lips or nose. Common skin reactions: burning, edema, erythema, induration, itching, scabbing, crusting, exudate.

Hemorrhoids

- Hemorrhoids are swollen blood vessels in the lower rectum. They are in a sensitive location and have a rich blood vessel supply that can result in engorgement. Common symptoms are pruritus, burning and rectal bleeding. The blood is usually bright red.

- If dietary fiber is not optimum, increasing fiber intake can help reduce straining. Products such as psyllium will mix with the stool to make it spongier and easier to push out. A stool softener (such as docusate) will reduce straining.

- Phenylephrine (*Preparation H,* others) is a vasoconstrictor that shrinks the hemorrhoid and reduces burning and itching.

- Hydrocortisone (*Anusol-HC, Preparation H Hydrocortisone,* others) comes in anal suppositories and various topicals including creams and wipes. These reduce itching and inflammation.

- Witch hazel (*Tucks* pads) is a mild astringent that can relieve mild itching. Barriers (skin protectants) to reduce irritation from stool/urine are helpful in some cases (petrolatum, others – see Diaper Rash section).

- There are many combination products. Example: *Tucks* ointment contains mineral oil (skin protectant), zinc oxide (desiccant) and pramoxine (anesthetic).

DRUGS	NOTES	SAFETY/COUNSELING
Preparation H *Anusol-HC* Many others	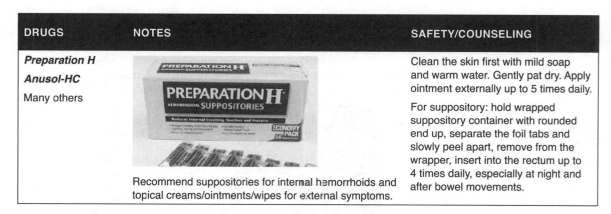 Recommend suppositories for internal hemorrhoids and topical creams/ointments/wipes for external symptoms.	Clean the skin first with mild soap and warm water. Gently pat dry. Apply ointment externally up to 5 times daily. For suppository: hold wrapped suppository container with rounded end up, separate the foil tabs and slowly peel apart, remove from the wrapper, insert into the rectum up to 4 times daily, especially at night and after bowel movements.

Lice & Scabies, Background & Treatment

Note; this section largely discusses lice; scabies (mites) are treated with some of the same medications. Scabies are primarily spread through sexual contact. The primary treatment for scabies is permethrin in a cream formulation (*Elimite*) and the prescription drug ivermectin (*Stromectol*), two doses, taken one week apart. Ivermectin, when taken orally, can be difficult to tolerate due to lymph node enlargement, arthralgias, skin tenderness, pruritus and fever. Ivermectin was approved in 2012 in a topical formulation for lice called *Sklice*. Lindane (*Kwell*, others) used to be commonly used for scabies (and lice) but is not used commonly now due to neurotoxicity. Ivermectin in both topical and oral forms is not first-line for lice; these are options in difficult-to-treat cases. Oral ivermectin requires a body weight of at least 15 kg.

- Lice occurs most commonly in elementary school age children.

- Pyrethrins (permethrin) are the OTC drug of choice; can be used in infants as young as 2 months. Avoid with chrysanthemums or ragweed allergy

- Malathion lotion 0.5% (*Ovide*) is an organophosphate. Only for use on persons 6 years of age and older. Can irritate the skin and is flammable; do not smoke or use electrical heat sources, including hair dryers, curlers, and curling or flat irons, when applying and while the hair is wet.

- Benzyl alcohol lotion (*Ulesfia* 5% lotion) kills live lice but not nits. Can irritate the skin and eyes; avoid eye contact.

- *Lindane* shampoo 1% is no longer recommended due to neurotoxicity and is reserved for refractive cases, and never in pregnancy, on irritated skin, or in infants, children, persons with small frames and the elderly.

- If the same medication has been used several times it may not be working.

- Repeating the procedure, and removing the nits from hair, bedding, and elsewhere is essential:

  - Wash clothes and bedding in hot water, followed by a hot dryer.

  - If something cannot be washed, seal it in an air-proof bag for 2 weeks or dry clean. Vacuum the carpet well. Soak combs and brushes in hot water for 10 minutes. Make sure to check other children in the household.

  - Do not use a combination shampoo/conditioner, or conditioner before using lice medicine. Do not re-wash the hair for 1 - 2 days after treatment.

  - After each treatment, check the hair and use a nit comb to remove nits and lice every 2 - 3 days. Continue to check for 2 - 3 weeks to be sure all lice and nits are gone.

  - Re-treatment is needed for OTC and prescription products (except *Sklice*) on days 7 - 10 (they vary; check the product) in order to kill any surviving hatched lice before they produce new eggs.

DRUGS	NOTES	SAFETY/COUNSELING
Permethrin, pyrethrins, OTC DOC for lice *(Nix, RID, Triple X)* 2 months+ (guideline says to retreat on day 9) Spinosad *(Natroba)* –works well, expensive. 4+ yrs Malathion *(Ovide)* – flammable, do not use near heat source, organophosphate Benzyl Alcohol Lotion *(Ulesfia)* 6+ months Ivermectin *(Sklice)* 6+ months Lindane *(Kwell,* others) is no longer routinely recommended; high risk neurotoxicity/seizures, requires MedGuide – more commonly used for scabies (mites)	 For Camping Use Only. (c)	In addition to OTC treatment, remove the live lice and nits by inspecting the hair in 1-inch segments and using a lice comb. Without removing live lice and nits, the OTC product will not work. Nits are "cemented" to the hair shaft and do not fall off after treatment. Nit removal requires multiple efforts, which should be continued for two weeks after treatment. See bulleted points above for additional counseling. Only in resistant/difficult cases use *Sklice* (topical ivermectin), or can use oral ivermectin *(Stromectol)* in those weighing at least 15 kg.

Minor Cuts, Abrasions & Burns, Background & Treatment

- The basic types of minor wounds are lacerations, abrasions, cuts, bites and burns.

- Some can be effectively treated through simple first aid and others, depending on the severity, may need more medical attention than first aid can provide.

- Anything that involves puncture wounds should be referred out.

- Make sure tetanus vaccine is current (Q 10 years, after series has been completed). If the wound is dirty a repeat tetanus vaccine may be required if it is >5 years since vaccination. The patient should be referred for medical care.

- If wound looks like abuse, contact authorities if able.

- Abrasions are minor injuries to the top layer of skin and are primarily treated with simple first aid.

- Abrasions such as a skinned knee can be cleaned thoroughly, antibiotic ointment applied and allowed to air heal.

- Lacerations are defined as irregular wounds with ragged edges, with the potential for deeper skin damage and bruising under the skin.

- If deep seek medical attention.

- A cut is different than a laceration because the edges will be more uniform or regular.

- After cleaning, if the bleeding does not stop, or it extends far below the surface layers of the skin, seek medical attention because it may require stitching to get the wound to close. If not, regular bandaging should get the edges of the wound to close over time.

- Antibiotic ointment can be applied prior to placing the bandage.

- Tissue adhesives *(Band-Aid Liquid Bandage, Nexcare Skin Crack Care,* others) create a polymer layer, which binds to the skin, keeping the wound clean and keeping moisture out. Some contain topical analgesics. *Seal-On* is a topical sponge (dressing) that can absorb blood and is used for nose-bleeds and other minor bleeds. There are other similar products.

- Bites (except minor insect bites) should never be treated with just simple first aid, because of the high risk of infection, especially with animal or human bites. Certain spider bites in the U.S. can be deadly: the brown recluse, the black widow and the hobo spiders. Spiders tend to stay hidden and are not aggressive. Bites can usually be avoided by inspecting and shaking out clothing or equipment prior to use, and wearing protective clothing. If bitten, stay calm, identify the type of spider if possible, wash with soap and cold water, apply cold compress with ice, elevate extremity, and get emergency medical care.

- Minor, harmless insect bites can be treated with a topical steroid or systemic antihistamine (such as diphenhydramine) to reduce itching.

- Burns are characterized as first degree (red/painful, minor swelling), second degree (thicker, very painful, produce blisters) and third degree (damage to all layers of skin, skin appears white or charred). Burns produced by chemical exposure, or in a person with underlying disease that reduces immunity should be referred for emergency medical care.

- If the burn is first or second degree OTC treatment is acceptable if the area is less than 2 inches in diameter and if the burn is not on the face, over a major joint or on the feet or genitals. In diabetes a burn on a foot, even mild, could lead to an amputation. Vigilance is required.

- Minor burns should be treated first by running the burn under cool running water or soaking in cool water for 5-20 minutes.

- Do not apply ice, which can further damage the injured skin. Bandages should be applied if the skin is broken, or if blisters pop. Burns heal best when kept moist (but not wet). Certain bandages designed for burns keep the environment moist, or ointments, such as antibiotic ointment, can be applied.

- Burned skin itches as it heals; the fingernails of children may need to be cut short and filed, or covered. The skin that has been burned will be more sensitive to the sun for up to a year.

- Ointments (80% oil/20% water, such as *Aquaphor*) should be used for skin protection over a minor burn to hold in moisture and reduce scarring risk.

- Silver sulfadiazene *(Silvadene; SSD; Thermazene)* may be used topically to reduce infection risk and promote healing, although it has not been shown to be very effective. If the skin is broken systemic toxicity could occur. Do not use if sulfa allergy or G6PD deficiency (due to hemolysis risk).

DRUGS	NOTES	SAFETY/COUNSELING
Triple antibiotic ointment (*Neosporin*, store brands) contains polymyxin, bacitracin & neomycin. If reaction to the neomycin component can use *Polysporin* (bacitracin and polymixin) or *Bacitracin* alone. Either of these is often sufficient. **Mupirocin (*Bactroban*)** is an Rx antibiotic cream or ointment; very good staph and strep coverage, including MRSA; can be used for nasal MRSA colonization. (*Bactroban nasal* is used for MRSA-nasal colonization) **Bacitracin, Neomycin, Polymyxin B, and Hydrocortisone (*Cortisporin*** ointment) is a popular Rx topical used for superficial skin infections. Tissue adhesives *(Band-Aid Liquid Bandage, Nexcare Skin Crack Care*, others) – "paint on" bandages to protect/keep moisture in skin via polymer layer. *Seal-On* is a sponge that is used to stop nosebleeds.	If the wound is not in an area that will get dirty or be rubbed by clothing, it does not need to be covered. Leaving a wound uncovered helps it stay dry and helps it heal.	To apply topical antibiotics: Clean the affected area and apply a small amount of medication (an amount equal to the surface area of the tip of a finger) to the affected area 1 to 3 times daily. If area can get dirty (such as a hand) or be irritated by clothing, cover with an adhesive strip (e.g., *Band-Aid*) or with sterile gauze and adhesive tape +/- antibiotic ointment. Change daily. Certain wounds, like large scrapes, should be kept moist and clean to help reduce scarring and speed healing. Bandages used for this purpose are called occlusive or semi-occlusive bandages. Burns require a moist (but not wet) environment by applying either ointment, or a bandage designed for burns.

Pinworm *(Vermicularis)* Infection

- Anthelmintics, such as mebendazole, pyrantel pamoate, and albendazole, are active against *Enterobius vermicularis.*

- Pinworm infection most commonly occurs in children and presents as anal itching. Pyrantel comes in several OTC products including the popular *Pin-X.* The pinworms can be resistant to treatment. Albendazole and mebendazole are prescription only.

- The "tape" test is used to identify eggs: stick a piece of tape around the anus in the morning prior to voiding/defecating. It can take up to 3 morning tape tests to identify the eggs. Reinfection after treatment is common.

DRUGS	NOTES	SAFETY/COUNSELING
Pyrantel pamoate (*Pamix, Pin-X, Reeses*) – OTC Albendazole (*Albenza*), Mebendazole – Rx Wash hands frequently. Treat the entire household.	**HELMINTHS** Small intestine Ascaris male Ascaris female Pinworms	Pyrantel causes headache and dizziness. OTC requires 3 treatments separated by 3 weeks. Mebendazole can be crushed, chewed, and mixed with food. Mebendazole and albendazole causes <u>headache, nausea</u> and are <u>hepatotoxic.</u> Albendazole: give concurrently with <u>anticonvulsants and high-dose glucocorticoids</u> to decrease CNS inflammation. Take with a <u>high-fat</u> meal. Tablets can be crushed or chewed, then follow with water.

Poison Ivy, Oak, Sumac, Background & Treatment

- Poison ivy, oak or sumac poisoning is an allergic reaction that results from touching the sap of these plants, which contain the toxin uroshiol.

- The sap may be on the plant, in the ashes of burned plants, on an animal, or on other objects that came in contact with the plant, such as clothing, garden tools, and sports equipment.

- Small amounts of uroshiol can remain under a person's fingernails for several days unless it is deliberately removed with good cleaning.

- Poison ivy grows around lakes and streams in the midwest and east. Leaves are green in the summer and red in the fall.

- Poison oak grows in the west (along the Pacific coast) and in the east from New Jersey to Texas. The leaves look like oak, usually in clusters of three leaves. The plant has clusters of yellow berries.

- Poison sumac grows in boggy areas, especially in the southeast and west. The leaves have 7-13 smooth-edged leaflets, with pale yellow or cream-colored berries.

DRUGS	NOTES	SAFETY/COUNSELING
Aluminum acetate solution *(Burrow's)* Colloidal oatmeal *(Aveeno)* Calamine lotion – *Caladryl, IvaRest* are calamine + topical analgesics *Zanfel* is supposed to bind urushiol (this is the toxin) – low evidence for efficacy	 *"Leaves of three, Let it be."*	Wash the uroshiol off with soap and water carefully, including under fingernails and on clothing. Topical or oral steroids will help (oral needed in severe rash). Cold compresses can help.

Inflammation (Topical)(From Various Conditions, Rashes), Background & Treatment

- Primary treatment for skin irritation are topical steroids. Two strengths of hydrocortisone (HC) available OTC, 0.5% and 1%; all other topical steroids are prescription. A chart of Rx topical steroids is at the end of this chapter.

- The steroid vehicle influences the strength of the medication. Usual potency, from highest to weakest: ointment > creams > lotions > solutions > gels > sprays. Ointments have low water content; refer to the Compounding chapter for details.

- Parts of the body with thin skin, such as the face, eyelids and genitals, are highly susceptible to the side effects of topical steroids and low potency products should be used on these areas. Use low potency products on areas of the skin with folds, such as the armpits, groin, and under the breasts, where the absorption is higher.

- Local (skin) steroid side effects, if used long-term include skin thinning, pigment changes (lighter or darker), telangectasia (blood vessel) formation, rosacea, perioral dermatitis and acne, increased risk skin infections, delayed wound healing, irritation/burning/peeling, and possibly contact dermatitis from the steroid itself.

- For urticaria (hives) the second-generation antihistamines can be recommended (OTC) as the initial options due to better tolerability than first-generation antihistamines. Cetirizine is a common choice; see the Allergic Rhinitis, Cough & Cold chapter for a discussion of antihistamines. For hives, higher doses are used. The "non-sedating" antihistamines are more sedating with higher doses. First-generation antihistamines (diphenhydramine, others) can be given at bedtime if the sedative effects are desirable.

- H2-blockers (famotidine, others) are helpful in some patients for hives and urticaria. Hydroxyzine is often prescribed and is in the table below.

DRUGS	NOTES	SAFETY/COUNSELING
OTC steroids are low potency: Hydrocortisone 0.5% (infants) and 1% for mild conditions, thin skin (groin area, elderly) and for children. HC 1% lotion *(Aquanil)* See other steroids in chart at end of this section. Apply high potency Rx steroids once daily – Apply OTC/lower potency 1-2x daily. It is common to see a higher potency product, followed by a lower potency product, to treat acute inflammation. Severe rash likely to require oral steroids for 1-2 weeks.	Ointments often more potent than creams; use ointments for thick or dry skin. Ointments have low water content (reduced absorption) and form a skin barrier. Use lotions, gels and foams for hairy skin. No evidence for use of topical diphenhydramine – can use systemic but caution due to side effects. Skin should be lubricated (hydrated) with moisturizers for most conditions. The steroid vehicle can lubricate. Camphor, menthol, local anesthetics (often in combo creams with HC) can help relieve itching. Common <u>topical steroids</u>, ranked by <u>potency</u>, are included at the end of this chapter.	 The "finger-tip" unit is used to estimate amount required: the amount that can be squeezed from the fingertip to the 1st joint covers one adult hand (about ½ g). Topical steroid over-use has risks; see top bullet points. Do not apply for longer than 2 weeks. Encourage patient not to use more than directed.
HydrOXYzine *(Vistaril)* 25 mg TID-QID	Used for general urticaria (hives) with severe itching	Anticholinergic; primarily sedation and dry mouth.

Sunscreens/Sun Protection, Background & Treatment

- Applying sunscreen is important due to the risk of sun damage and skin cancer. Keep in mind that sunscreen blocks vitamin D production in the skin and many Americans are vitamin-D deficient. This is a difficulty in current practice.

- It is advisable to stay out of the sun when it is strongest (between 10AM-4PM). The sun damaging ultraviolet (UV) rays penetrate clouds; this applies to overcast days as well.

- Another method to avoid the sun is to wear protective clothing.

- Where skin is exposed sunscreen can be applied that provides both UVA (A for aging – causes damage below the skin surface) and UVB (B for burning) protection. Both UVA and UVB contribute to skin cancer. A "broad spectrum" sunscreen should be chosen; it protects against both UVA and UVB. SPF stands for sun protection factor, which is a measure of how well the sunscreen deflects UVB rays.

- Some dermatologists recommend <u>SPF 15</u> and others recommend <u>SPF 30</u>. The key is to apply <u>liberally and at least every two hours</u>. The American Academy of Pediatrics says to keep all babies less than 6 months old out of the sun.

- HOW SPF WORKS: If someone would normally burn in 10 minutes, an SPF of 5 would extend the time they would burn to 50 minutes (5 x 10 = 50.) However, it is not accurate to calculate that if one normally would burn in one hour, then a sunscreen with an SPF of 10 would permit the person to stay in the sun for 10 hours (10 times longer) without burning, since the intensity of the sun varies during the day, and the sunscreen would not last more than a couple of hours.

- Sunscreen labeling is no longer permitted to use "waterproof" or "sweatproof" since they all wash off, at least partially, in the water. They can claim to be "water-resistant" but only for 40-80 minutes. Always reapply after swimming, or sweating.

- The American Academy of Dermatology (AAD) recommends sunscreens with any of the following ingredients: avobenzone, cinoxate, ecamsule, menthyl anthranilate, octyl methoxycinnamate, octyl salicylate, oxybenzone or sulisobenzone.

- Oxybenzone irritates some people's skin; this is not common.

DRUGS	NOTES	SAFETY/COUNSELING
Many products, choose one with UVA and UVB coverage, SPF 15+. UVA: Blocks aging (A for aging – wrinkles). Ingredients that block UVA: ecamsule, avobenzone, oxybenzone, sulisobenzone, titanium dioxide, zinc oxide (zinc and titanium are common barrier agents). UVB: Blocks burning (B for burning). SPF (sun exposure factor) – measures how long it takes to burn versus not using sunscreen (measures UVB only). An SPF of 15 takes 15 times longer for skin to redden than without the sunscreen.	 Apply liberally, at least every two hours, prior to sun exposure, and after getting the skin wet from swimming or sweating.	All sunscreens wash off; reapply after going in the water and at least every 2 hours. Avoid peak sun (10AM-4PM), even if overcast. Wear protective clothing. Consider vitamin D deficiency-if avoiding sun or little sun exposure may need supplementation. UVA and UVB exposure increases risk of skin cancer, including most common type (squamous cell). "Broad spectrum" covers both UVA and UVB. Water resistant – means resistant for 40-80 minutes.

Potencies of Topical Steroid Products

TREATMENT	ACTIVE INGREDIENT

Very High Potency

TREATMENT	ACTIVE INGREDIENT
Clobex **Lotion/Spray/Shampoo, 0.05%**	**Clobetasol propionate**
Cormax Cream/Solution, 0.05%	Clobetasol propionate
Diprolene **Ointment, 0.05%**	**Betamethasone dipropionate**
Olux **Foam, 0.05%**	**Clobetasol propionate**
Temovate **Cream/Ointment/Solution, 0.05%**	**Clobetasol propionate**
Ultravate **Cream/Ointment, 0.05%**	**Halobetasol propionate**
Vanos Cream, 0.1%	**Fluocinonide**
Psorcon Ointment, 0.05%	Diflorasone diacetate
Psorcon E Ointment, 0.05%	Diflorasone diacetate

High Potency

TREATMENT	ACTIVE INGREDIENT
Diprolene **Cream AF, 0.05%**	**Betamethasone dipropionate**
Elocon **Ointment, 0.1%**	**Mometasone furoate**
Florone Ointment, 0.05%	Diflorasone diacetate
Halog Ointment/Cream, 0.1%	Halcinonide
Lidex **Cream/Gel/Ointment, 0.05%**	**Fluocinonide**
Psorcon Cream, 0.05%	Diflorasone diacetate
Topicort Cream/Ointment, 0.25%	Desoximetasone
Topicort Gel, 0.05%	Desoximetasone

High-Medium Potency

TREATMENT	ACTIVE INGREDIENT
Cutivate Ointment, 0.005%	Fluticasone propionate
Lidex-E **Cream, 0.05%**	**Fluocinonide**
Luxiq Foam, 0.12%	Betamethasone valerate
Topicort LP Cream, 0.05%	Desoximetasone

Medium Potency

TREATMENT	ACTIVE INGREDIENT
Cordran Ointment, 0.05%	Flurandrenolide
Elocon **Cream, 0.1%**	**Mometasone furoate**
Kenalog **Cream/Spray, 0.1%**	**Triamcinolone acetonide**
Synalar Ointment, 0.03%	Fluocinolone acetonide
Westcort **Ointment, 0.2%**	**Hydrocortisone valerate**

Potencies of Topical Steroid Products Continued

TREATMENT	ACTIVE INGREDIENT

Lower Potency

TREATMENT	ACTIVE INGREDIENT
Capex Shampoo, 0.01%	Fluocinolone acetonide
Cordran Cream/Lotion/Tape, 0.05%	Flurandrenolide
Cutivate Cream/Lotion, 0.05%	Fluticasone propionate
DermAtop Cream, 0.1%	Prednicarbate
***DesOwen* Lotion, 0.05%**	**Desonide**
Locoid Cream/Lotion/Ointment/Solution, 0.1%	Hydrocortisone
Pandel Cream, 0.1%	Hydrocortisone
Synalar Cream, 0.03%/0.01%	Fluocinolone acetonide
***Westcort* Cream, 0.2%**	**Hydrocortisone valerate**

Mild Potency

TREATMENT	ACTIVE INGREDIENT
Aclovate Cream/Ointment, 0.05%	Alclometasone dipropionate
***Derma*-Smoothe/FS Oil, 0.01%**	**Fluocinolone acetonide**
Desonate Gel, 0.05%	Desonide
Synalar Cream/Solution, 0.01%	Fluocinolone acetonide
Verdeso Foam, 0.05%	Desonide

Lowest Potency

TREATMENT	ACTIVE INGREDIENT
Cetacort Lotion, 0.5%/1%	Hydrocortisone
Cortaid Cream/Spray/Ointment	**Hydrocortisone**
Hytone Cream/Lotion, 1%/2.5%	Hydrocortisone
Micort-HC Cream, 2%/2.5%	Hydrocortisone
Nutracort Lotion, 1%/2.5%	Hydrocortisone
Synacort Cream, 1%/2.5%	Hydrocortisone

77

WEIGHT LOSS

We gratefully acknowledge the assistance of Elizabeth Pogge, PharmD, MPH, BCPS, FASCP, Associate Professor of Pharmacy Practice, Midwestern University College of Pharmacy-Glendale, in preparing this chapter.

BACKGROUND

Overweight and obesity is a national health threat and a major public health challenge. Data from the CDC (2011-2012) estimates the percentage of U.S. adults who are overweight (BMI 25-29.9) or obese (BMI ≥ 30) at 69%, and in children and adolescents at 32%. A person who is overweight will have increased risk for coronary heart disease, hypertension, stroke, type 2 diabetes, certain types of cancer, and premature death. In addition to the health risks, being overweight reduces the quality of life and causes social stigmatization and discrimination.

GUIDELINES

2013 AHA/ACC/TOS Guideline for the Management of Overweight and Obesity in Adults: A Report of the American College of Cardiology/AHA Task Force on Practice Guidelines and The Obesity Society. *J Am Coll Cardiol.* 2014; 63:2985-3023.

Pharmacological Management of Obesity: An Endocrine Society Clinical Practice Guideline. *J Clin Endocrinol Metab.* 2015; 100(2):342-62.

Weight loss must involve an "energy deficit" – calories must be decreased in order to force the body to use fat as an energy source. If someone is hungry it is difficult not to eat. The weight loss drugs work primarily by increasing satiety, which decreases appetite. Recent research has focused on how diets high in saturated fat and simple carbohydrates (the typical American diet) are thought to impair the regulation of the hormones leptin (which suppresses appetite) and ghrelin (which increases appetite). Consuming many calories from simple sugars and fats may damage the hypothalamus, which can damage the function of leptin and ghrelin. This impairs the ability to control hunger and lose weight. This research is providing a better understanding of why the types of food a person eats is important and has contributed to the success of best-selling books, including *The Grain Brain* and *Wheat Belly*. These books were written by a neurologist and a cardiologist, respectively, who believe that the simple carbohydrate-based diet causes cellular damage and inflammation, which in turn increases disease risk, including dementia and cardiovascular disease.

Weight loss is successful only when the patient is able to make permanent changes in diet and exercise habits. This will usually require changes in the family's habits. Fad diets may cause an acute weight loss, but are generally not recommended as they are difficult to maintain and can have harmful health consequences. Many people think they are heavier than they would like to be due to a low metabolism.

If low metabolism is an issue it will show up on lab tests (i.e., as hypothyroidism) and can be treated.

GUIDELINE RECOMMENDATIONS

In 2013, updated obesity guidelines were released as a joint project between the American College of Cardiology, the American Heart Association and The Obesity Society. The guidelines support these actions:

Obesity needs to be confronted and addressed – which means it needs to be identified. BMI and waist circumference should be assessed at least annually. Overweight and obese patients should be warned of the health risks.

Counseling should emphasize that lifestyle changes that produce even modest, sustained weight loss of 3% - 5% produce clinically meaningful health benefits (such as decreased triglycerides, A1C, and the risk of developing type 2 diabetes), and greater weight loss produces greater benefits.

Rather than emphasizing one particular type of diet, the guidelines state that "A variety of dietary approaches can produce weight loss in overweight and obese adults." Dietary strategies could consist of any of the following methods:

- Reducing food and calorie intake: 1,200–1,500 kcal/day for women and 1,500–1,800 kcal/day for men or using a 500-750 kcal/day energy deficit; (a 500 kcal decrease per day equals 1 pound weight loss per week (3,500 kcal/pound).

- Using one of the evidence-based diets that restricts certain food types (such as restricting high-carbohydrate foods, low-fiber foods, or high-fat foods), in order to create an energy deficit by reduced food intake.

- In select patients and only under medical monitoring the use of a very low calorie diet (defined as < 800 kcal/day), can be recommended.

All patients who would benefit from weight loss should participate for > 6 months in a comprehensive lifestyle program that includes weight loss support with a trained person, weight and diet monitoring and regular physical activity of 200 - 300 minutes/week.

The guidelines recommend bariatric surgery for adults with a BMI ≥ 40, or with a BMI ≥ 35 with an obesity-related comorbid condition. Using a surgical approach requires adjusting medications and providing nutrient support. Post-bariatric requirements are discussed in more detail later in this chapter. In 2015, additional guidelines issued from the Endocrine Society took a more favorable view on the use of medications to aid weight loss. The new recommendations are primarily due to the availability of new prescription agents that assist with weight loss

Drug Treatment: OTC and Rx

OTC weight loss drugs commonly contain stimulants, such as bitter orange (which is either synephrine alone or with related compounds), and/or excessive amounts of caffeine. Caffeine is packaged under different names, including yerba mate, guarana and concentrated green tea powder. In general, OTC supplements for weight loss are ineffective and can potentially be harmful, especially in patients with cardiovascular disease; therefore, they should not be recommended.

SELECT DRUGS/CONDITIONS THAT CAN CAUSE WEIGHT GAIN
Insulin, sulfonylureas, meglitinides
Thiazolidinediones (pioglitazone—*Actos*, rosiglitazone—*Avandia*)
Prednisone and other corticosteroids, estrogen, testosterone
Pregabalin (*Lyrica*), Gabapentin (*Neurontin*)
Divalproex (*Depakote*), Valproic acid (*Depakene*)
Tricyclic antidepressants (more likely with tertiary amines)
Mirtazapine (*Remeron*)
MAO inhibitors
SSRIs (including paroxetine—*Paxil*)
Antipsychotics (including clozapine—*Clozaril*, olanzapine—*Zyprexa*, quetiapine—*Seroquel*, risperidone—*Risperdal* and paliperidone—*Invega*)
Lithium (*Lithobid*)
Dronabinol (*Marinol*), megestrol (*Megace*)
Conditions: Hypothyroidism

Prescription agents are <u>not appropriate for patients with small amounts of weight to lose</u>. Prescription drugs are indicated in individuals with a BMI > 30, or with a BMI > 27 with at least one weight-related co-morbidity (such as dyslipidemia, hypertension or diabetes). They are only used in <u>addition to a dietary plan and increased physical activity</u>, per the FDA. Diabetes is common in overweight adults. Weight loss can lower the requirement for medications; patients with diabetes who are using prescription weight loss drugs must monitor blood glucose carefully.

In the past, several drugs used to treat obesity have been pulled from the market due to safety concerns. For this reason, pharmacists should consider the "7 year rule" – which roughly translates to: do not recommend new agents until they have been out for awhile and used in millions – in order to get a more complete understanding of the adverse effect profile than might have been evident in clinical trials. This rule never applies to life-saving drugs.

Four new prescription drugs indicated for weight loss have become available since 2012: phentermine/topiramate ER (*Qsymia*), lorcaserin (*Belviq*), naltrexone/bupropion *(Contrave)* and liraglutide (*Saxenda*). The benefit with these agents (weight loss at one year, versus diet and lifestyle alone) is variable; *Qsymia* (~19 pounds), *Belviq* (~8 pounds), *Contrave* (~11 pounds) and *Saxenda* (~13 pounds).

SELECT DRUGS/CONDITIONS THAT CAN CAUSE WEIGHT LOSS
Antiepileptic Drugs (<u>topiramate</u>—*Topamax*, zonisamide—*Zonegran*, ethosuximide—*Zarontin*)
<u>Stimulants used for ADHD</u> (such as methylphenidate IR-ER—*Concerta*, dextroamphetamine-amphetamine—*Adderall*, methylphenidate—*Ritalin*, lisdexamfetamine—*Vyvanse*)
<u>GLP-1 agonists</u> (such as exenatide—*Byetta, Bydureon*, liraglutide—*Victoza*)
Pramlintide (*Symlin*)
<u>Bupropion</u> (*Wellbutrin, Zyban, Buproban*)
Interferons
Acetylcholinesterase inhibitors (donepezil—*Aricept*, rivastigmine—*Exelon*, galantamine—*Razadyne*)
Conditions: <u>Hyperthyroidism</u>, Lupus, Celiac Disease, Crohn's Disease, Cystic Fibrosis, Ulcerative Colitis, Tuberculosis (active disease)

The older stimulant agents are only used short-term to "jump start" a diet. The non-stimulant orlistat is available as an OTC *(Alli)* and as a prescription drug (*Xenical*); orlistat is a useful agent to reduce dietary fat absorption, but has GI tolerability issues (flatulence) and must be taken with a reduced fat diet. The <u>fat</u> contributes to the <u>flat</u>. Orlistat efficacy is modest with ~7 pound weight loss at one year, versus placebo.

Any medication must be taken concurrently with a reasonable dietary plan, and preferably, physical activity that contributes to good health and weight management. *Qsymia, Belviq, Contrave* and *Saxenda,* unlike the stimulants used as single agents for weight loss, can be continued long-term for maintenance. Weight loss drugs should be <u>discontinued</u> if the patient did not obtain <u>at least a 5% weight loss at 12 weeks</u>.

DRUG	DOSING	SAFETY/SIDE EFFECTS/MONITORING

Phentermine: Sympathomimetic (stimulant), with effects similar to amphetamines, causing an increase in norepinephrine.

Topiramate: Effects due to increased satiety and decreased appetite, possibly by enhancing GABA, blocking glutamate receptors and/or weak inhibition of carbonic anhydrase.

Phentermine/Topiramate ER *(Qsymia)* C-IV REMS drug: only through certified pharmacy network; not all stores will carry. Teratogenic risk; obtain pregnancy test before treatment and monthly thereafter; use effective contraception.	Start at 3.75/23 mg PO QAM x 14 days, then titrate up based on weight loss Max 15/92 mg PO QAM CrCl < 50 mL/min the max dose is 7.5/46 mg/day	**CONTRAINDICATIONS** Hyperthyroidism, glaucoma, MAO inhibitor use within past 14 days, pregnancy, lactation **SIDE EFFECTS** <u>Dizziness, tachycardia, headache, cognitive impairment, constipation, dry mouth, insomnia, paresthesias,</u>↓ serum HCO_3, upper respiratory tract infection, pharyngitis **NOTES** <u>Pregnancy Category X.</u> Taper off due to seizure risk.

The naltrexone component ↓ food cravings and the bupropion component ↓ appetite.

Naltrexone/Bupropion *(Contrave)*	ER tab 8 mg/90 mg Week 1: 1 tab QAM Week 2: 1 tab QAM, 1 tab QPM Week 3: 2 tabs QAM, 1 tab QPM Week 4+: 2 tabs QAM, 2 tabs QPM Swallow whole Do not cut, chew, or crush Do not take with high fat meal	**BOXED WARNING** Not approved for treatment of major depressive disorder (MDD) or psychiatric disorders. Antidepressants can increase the risk of suicidal thinking and behavior in children, adolescents, and young adults (18-24 years of age) with MDD and psychiatric disorders; consider risk prior to prescribing **CONTRAINDICATIONS** <u>Chronic opioid or opiate agonist or partial agonist use</u>, or acute opiate withdrawal, abrupt discontinuation of alcohol, benzodiazepines, barbiturates, and antiepileptic drugs, uncontrolled hypertension, <u>seizure disorder, use of other bupropion-containing products, bulimia/anorexia</u>, concomitant use of MAO inhibitors, linezolid, methylene blue, pregnancy **WARNINGS** Use with caution if psychiatric disorder, seizure risk, discontinue if S/Sx hepatotoxicity **SIDE EFFECTS** <u>N/V, constipation, headache, dizziness, dry mouth, sleep disorder</u> (including abnormal dreams), can ↑ HR, ↑ BP; risk is highest during the initial 3 months **NOTES** Pregnancy Category X. Naltrexone will <u>block opioids/buprenorphine</u>, which will <u>block analgesia</u>; do not use concurrently. Discontinue these agents 7-10 days prior to use of *Contrave*.

Weight Loss Drugs Continued

DRUG	DOSING	SAFETY/SIDE EFFECTS/MONITORING

Serotonin 5-HT$_{2c}$ receptor agonist, ↑ satiety, resulting in weight loss.

Lorcaserin *(Belviq)* C-IV Per FDA, company required to monitor cardiovascular outcomes after release	10 mg PO BID	**CONTRAINDICATIONS** Pregnancy **WARNINGS** Valvular heart disease, serotonin syndrome, CNS effects, ↓ WBC, ↓ RBC, ↑ prolactin, ↑ risk PAH, ↑ risk psychiatric disorders (including suicide risk), priapism **SIDE EFFECTS** <u>Headache, dizziness, fatigue, nausea, dry mouth, constipation, hypoglycemia</u> **NOTES** Pregnancy Category X.

GLP-1 receptor agonist, ↑ satiety, resulting in weight loss.

Liraglutide *(Saxenda)* *Victoza*– for diabetes	Start at 0.6 mg SC daily x 1 week, titrate up by 0.6 mg SC daily at weekly intervals Target dose: 3 mg SC daily	**CONTRAINDICATIONS** Patients with a personal or family history of medullary thyroid carcinoma (MTC) or patients with Multiple Endocrine Neoplasia syndrome type 2 (MEN 2), Pregnancy **SIDE EFFECTS** <u>Nausea</u> (even with lower dose), tachycardia, hypogylcemia **NOTES** Pregnancy Category X. May need to ↓ insulin or sulfonylurea/meglitinide dose to ↓ risk of hypoglycemia; see Diabetes chapter for detailed drug information. Medguide required.

Short term appetite suppressants – sympathomimetics (stimulants), with effects similar to amphetamines, causing increase in norepinephrine.

Phentermine *(Adipex-P, Suprenza-ODT)* C-IV	15-37.5 mg PO, before or after breakfast, or in divided doses	**CONTRAINDICATIONS** MAO inhibitors within the past 14 days <u>Avoid use with hypertension, PAH, hyperthyroidism, glaucoma, abuse potential</u>
Diethylpropion *(Tenuate)* C-IV	IR: 25 mg PO TID 1 hour before meals and mid-evening SR: 75 mg PO once in midmorning	**SIDE EFFECTS** <u>Tachycardia, agitation, ↑ BP, cardiovascular complications,</u> insomnia, dizziness, tremor, risk of dependence, risk of psychotic symptoms
Phendimetrazine *(Bontril PDM)* C-IV	IR: 35 mg PO BID-TID, 1 hr before meals ER: 105 mg PO Q daily, 30 - 60 minutes before morning meal	**NOTES** Phentermine is Pregnancy Category X. Stimulants as single agents used <u>up to 12 weeks</u> to "jump-start" a diet. <u>Monitor HR, BP.</u> Taper off due to seizure risk.

Weight Loss Drugs Continued

DRUG	DOSING	SAFETY/SIDE EFFECTS/MONITORING

Long-term lipase inhibitor that decreases the absorption of dietary fats by ~30%.

| Orlistat Rx *(Xenical)* | 120 mg PO w/each meal containing fat, take with meal or up to 1 hr after eating

Indicated in ages > 12 years

Both orlistat formulations must be used with a low-fat diet plan | **CONTRAINDICATIONS**
Pregnancy, chronic malabsorption syndrome, cholestasis

WARNINGS
(Rare) liver damage, cholelithiasis, increased urinary oxalate (and risk kidney stones), hypoglycemia (with diabetes)

SIDE EFFECTS
GI (flatus with discharge, fecal urgency, fatty stool)

NOTES
Take multivitamin with A, D, E, K and beta carotene at bedtime or separated by 2+ hr. Do not use with cyclosporine or separate by 3+ hr. Separate levothyroxine by 4+ hr.

Must stick to dietary plan for both weight improvement and to help lessen GI side effects (max 30% of kcals from fat). |
| **Orlistat OTC** *(Alli)* | 60 mg PO w/each meal containing fat | Same as *Xenical* (above) for counseling, vitamin and diet/fat intake, and drug interactions. |

Patient Counseling for all Weight Loss Agents
- This drug is used in adults who are obese, or who are overweight with at least one weight-related medical problem such as high blood pressure, high cholesterol, or type 2 diabetes.

- If you do not lose an expected amount of weight within the first three months the drug is not effective for you and should be stopped; if you are not losing weight, let your healthcare provider know.

- You must be using a sensible eating plan and getting regular physical activity while taking this medicine.

- If you have diabetes and you lose weight, you could get low blood glucose (hypoglycemia); you will need to monitor your blood glucose carefully, and your diabetes medicine/s may need to be adjusted as you lose weight. If you use insulin or a sulfonylurea or *Prandin* or *Starlix* these are high risk for hypoglycemia. (*Belviq*; warning for hypoglycemia.)

- Do not use this drug if you are pregnant or planning to become pregnant. Attempting to lose weight during pregnancy is not safe. (*Qsymia* has highest risk of causing harm to a baby and will make birth control pills not work as well.)

Orlistat (*Xenical and Alli*)
- Take one capsule with liquid at each main meal or up to one hour after a meal that contains fat, up to three times daily. You should be using a healthy eating plan that contains no more than 30% of calories that come from fat.

- You will need to take a daily multivitamin supplement that contains vitamins A, D, E, and K and beta carotene. Take the multivitamin once a day at least 2 hours before or after taking orlistat, such as at bedtime.

- If you take levothyroxine (for low thyroid), it should be separated from orlistat by at least 4 hours.

- If you take cyclosporine (a transplant medication) it must be separated from orlistat by at least 3 hours. Discuss using orlistat with your transplant team; it is important not to change the amount of transplant medicine that your body is receiving.

Post-Bariatric Surgery; Pharmacists Role

The 2013 obesity guideline recommends advising adults with a BMI ≥ 40 or BMI ≥ 35 with an obesity-related condition who cannot successfully lose weight that bariatric surgery may be an appropriate option. These patients can be offered referral to a bariatric surgeon for evaluation. Bariatric surgery restricts food intake, which leads to weight loss. Patients who have bariatric surgery must commit to a lifetime of healthy eating and regular exercise to sustain the weight loss.

Weight loss surgery requires changes to the drug regimen, and adjustments in nutrients with decreased absorption, depending on the surgery type. This summary will not distinguish between the needs with various surgeries, but rather provides a short review of the common problems.

Micronutrients

- One of the most common problems following bariatric surgery is calcium deficiency. Calcium is mostly absorbed in the duodenum, which may be bypassed. Calcium citrate is preferred as it has non-acid-dependent absorption.

- Anemia may result from vitamin B12 and iron deficiency; both may require supplementation.

- Iron and calcium supplements should be taken 2 hours prior, or 4 hours after antacids.

- Patients may require life-long supplementation of the fat-soluble vitamins A, D, E and K, due to fat malabsorption.

Medications

- Medications may require dose-reduction, and may need to be crushed or put in liquid or transdermal form for up to two-months post-surgery. Pharmacists will need to assess which drugs can be safely crushed and provide alternatives to drugs that cannot be crushed (i.e., extended-release).

- Due to the risk of gallstones with rapid weight loss, patients may need ursodiol (Actigall, Urso 250, Urso Forte), which dissolves gallstones, unless the gallbladder has been removed. This drug is also used for primary biliary cirrhosis. It cannot be administered with aluminum-based antacids (if used, give 2 hours after ursodiol). Urso Forte can be split into halves, but not crushed or chewed. Urso and Urso Forte should be taken with food. Ursodiol can be made into a sweetened suspension. The most common side effects are headache, dizziness, constipation or diarrhea (both about 26%) and nausea.

- Avoid drugs that are GI irritants – such as NSAIDs and bisphosphonates.

APPENDIX

PRESCRIPTION TOP-SELLERS

Brand names are provided as a study aid (generic may be top-seller).

RANK	DRUG	BRAND NAME
1	Hydrocodone/Acetaminophen	*Lortab, Vicodin, Xodol*
2	Lisinopril	*Prinivil, Zestril*
3	Levothyroxine	*Levoxyl, Synthroid*
4	Amlodipine	*Norvasc*
5	Atorvastatin	*Lipitor*
6	Omeprazole	*Prilosec*
7	Simvastatin	*Zocor*
8	Metformin	*Fortamet, Glucophage, Glumetza*
9	Amoxicillin	*Moxatag*
10	Azithromycin	*Zithromax, Z-Pak, Zmax*
11	Alprazolam	*Xanax*
12	Hydrochlorothiazide	*Microzide, Oretic*
13	Gabapentin	*Gralise, Neurontin*
14	Fluticasone Propionate, Nasal Inhaler	*Flonase*
15	Tramadol	*Ultram*
16	Ibuprofen	*Motrin, Advil*
17	Sertraline	*Zoloft*
18	Prednisone	*Deltasone*
19	Metoprolol Tartrate	*Lopressor*
20	Metoprolol Succinate	*Toprol XL*

RANK	DRUG	BRAND NAME
21	Losartan	*Cozaar*
22	Furosemide	*Lasix*
23	Zolpidem	*Ambien*
24	Citalopram	*Celexa*
25	Oxycodone/Acetaminophen	*Endocet, Percocet, Roxicet, others*
26	Pravastatin	*Pravachol*
27	Montelukast	*Singulair*
28	Albuterol	*ProAir HFA, Proventil HFA, Ventolin HFA*
29	Cyclobenzaprine	*Fexmid*
30	Clonazepam	*Klonopin*
30	Potassium Chloride	*Klor-Con, Micro-K, others*
31	Fluoxetine	*Prozac*
32	Lisinopril/HCTZ	*Prinzide, Zestoretic*
33	Atenolol	*Tenormin*
34	Pantoprazole	*Protonix*
35	Meloxicam	*Mobic*
36	Escitalopram	*Lexapro*
37	Trazodone	*Oleptro*
38	Amoxicillin/Clavulanate	*Augmentin*
39	Lorazepam	*Ativan*

Prescription Top-Sellers Continued

RANK	DRUG	BRAND NAME
40	Ciprofloxacin, Oral	*Cipro*
40	Levothyroxine	*Synthroid*
41	Carvedilol	*Coreg*
42	Cephalexin	*Keflex*
43	Clopidogrel	*Plavix*
44	Sulfamethoxazole/ Trimethoprim	*Bactrim, Bactrim DS, Septra DS, Sulfatrim*
45	Warfarin	*Coumadin*
46	Rosuvastatin	*Crestor*
47	Tamsulosin	*Flomax*
48	Ranitidine	*Zantac*
50	Naproxen	*Anaprox, Naprosyn, others*
51	Fluconazole	*Diflucan*
52	Duloxetine	*Cymbalta*
53	Oxycodone	*Roxicodone*
54	Bupropion XL	*Wellbutrin XL*
56	Venlafaxine ER	*Effexor XR*
57	Allopurinol	*Aloprim, Zyloprim*
58	Methylprednisolone	*Medrol, Medrol Dosepak*
59	Amphetamine salts IR	*Adderall*
60	Ondansetron	*Zofran, Zofran ODT*
60	Triamcinolone	*Kenalog, others (topicals)*
61	Esomeprazole	*Nexium*
62	Losartan/HCTZ	*Hyzaar*
63	Diazepam	*Valium*
64	Vitamin D2, Ergocalciferol	*Hyzaar*
65	Amitriptyline	*Catapres, Catapres-TTS*
66	Paroxetine	*Paxil*
67	Clonidine	*Catapres, Catapres-TTS*
68	Fenofibrate	*Antara, Lofibra, Tricor, Trilipix, others*
69	Metformin ER	*Glucophage XR*

RANK	DRUG	BRAND NAME
70	Fluticasone/Salmeterol	*Advair Diskus*
70	Influenza Vaccine	*Fluvirin, Afluria, Fluzone*
71	Doxycycline	*Oracea, Doryx, others*
72	Glimepiride	*Amaryl*
73	Spironolactone	*Aldactone*
74	Triamterene/HCTZ	*Dyazide, Maxzide, Maxzide-25*
75	Levofloxacin	*Levaquin*
76	Valacyclovir	*Valtrex*
77	Acetaminophen/Codeine	*Tylenol #2, #3, #4*
78	Lamotrigine	*Lamictal, Lamictal ODT, Lamictal Starter*
79	Topiramate	*Topamax*
80	Lovastatin	*Altoprev, Mevacor*
81	Quetiapine	*Seroquel*
83	Metronidazole	*Flagyl*
84	Lisdexamfetamine	*Vyvanse*
85	Promethazine	*Phenergan*
86	Folic acid	*Vitamin B6*
87	Alendronate	*Fosamax*
88	Glipizide	*Glucotrol*
90	Insulin Glargine	*Lantus Solostar*
92	Clindamycin Oral	*Cleocin*
93	Latanoprost	*Xalatan*
94	Methylphenidate ER	*Concerta*
95	Enalapril	*Vasotec*
96	Pregabalin	*Lyrica*
97	Benzonatate	*Tessalon Perles, Zonatuss*
98	Propranolol	*Inderal*
99	Cefdinir	
100	Morphine	*MS Contin, Avinza, Kadian, others*
101	Amphetamine Salts ER	*Adderall XR*

Prescription Top-Sellers Continued

RANK	DRUG	BRAND NAME
102	Sumatriptan	Imitrex
103	Tizanidine	Zanaflex
104	Risperidone	Risperdal
105	Tiotropium	Spiriva HandiHaler
106	Bupropion SR	Wellbutrin SR
107	Bactroban	Mupirocin
108	Diclofenac Gel	Voltaren Gel
109	Polyethylene Glycol	Golytely, MoviPrep, Nulytely, TriLyte
110	Buspirone	Buspar
111	Hydroxyzine	Vistaril
112	Isosorbide Mononitrate	Monoket
113	Benazepril	Lotensin
114	Temazepam	Restoril
115	Acyclovir	Zovirax
116	Phentermine	Adipex-P, Suprenza
117	Finasteride	Proscar
118	Estradiol	Alora, Climara, Vivelle-Dot
119	Valsartan/HCTZ	Diovan HCT
120	Sitagliptan	Januvia
121	Mirtazapine	Remeron
122	Aripiprazole	Abilify
123	Ergocalciferol	Vitamin D Analog
124	Tadalafil	Cialis
125	Celecoxib	Celebrex
126	Carisoprodol	Soma
127	Formoterol/Budesonide	Symbicort
128	Insulin Glargine	Lantus
129	Buprenorphine/Naloxone	Suboxone
130	Prednisolone	Orapred, Pediapred, Prelone
130	Sildenafil	Viagra

RANK	DRUG	BRAND NAME
131	Nitrofurantoin	Macrobid, Macrodantin, Furadantin
132	Amlodipine/Benazepril	Lotrel
133	Nystatin	Bio-Statin
134	Donepezil	Aricept
135	Levetiracetam	Keppra
136	Famotidine	Pepcid
137	Clobetasol	Clobex, Olux, Temovate
138	Penicillin VK	
139	Mometasone	Nasonex
140	Baclofen	Lioresal
141	Glipizide ER	Glucotrol XL
142	Valsartan	Diovan
143	Ketoconazole	Prevacid
144	Butalbital/Acetaminophen/ Caffeine	Fioricet
145	Methocarbamol	Robaxin
146	Oseltamivir	Tamiflu
147	Ramipril	Altace
148	Nebivolol	Bystolic
149	Chlorhexidine	Peridex, others
150	Ezetimibe	Zetia
151	Ethinyl Estradiol and Norgestimate	Sprintec 28, Ortho-Tri-Cyclen
152	Methotrexate	Rheumatrex, Trexall
153	Lansoprazole	Prevacid
154	Fluticasone, Oral Inhaler	Flovent HFA, Flovent Diskus
155	Hydralazine	
156	Methylphenidate	Ritalin
157	Diltiazem	Cardizem, Tiazac
158	Rivaroxaban	Xarelto
159	Meclizine	UniVert
160	Prednisolone Opthalmic	Pred Forte

Prescription Top-Sellers Continued

RANK	DRUG	BRAND NAME
161	Influenza Vaccine HD	Fluzone High Dose
162	Fentanyl Patch	Duragesic
163	Ethinyl Estradiol/Etonogestrel	NuvaRing
164	Thyroid, Dessicated	Armour
165	Oxycodone ER	OxyContin
166	Glyburide	Diabeta, Glynase
167	Dicyclomine	Bentyl
168	Minocycline	Minocin, Solodyn
169	Hydroxycholoroquine	Plaquenil
171	Verapamil SR	Calan SR, Isoptin SR
172	Medroxyprogesterone	Depo-Provera
175	Pioglitazone	Actos
176	Nifedipine ER	Adalat CC, Nifediac CC, Procardia
177	Codeine/Promethazine	Armour Thyroid
178	Ropinirole	Requip
179	Ethinyl Estradiol/Norgestimate	Tri-Sprintec, TriNessa, Ortho Tri-Cyclen
180	Hydrocortisone	A-Hydrocort, Cortef, Solu-CORTEF
181	Gemfibrozil	Lopid
182	Doxazosin	Cardura
183	Clindamycin Topical	Cleocin-T, Clindagel, others
184	Dexlansoprazole	Dexilant
186	Beclomethasone	QVAR
187	Clotrimazole/Betamethasone	Lotrisone
189	Phenazopyridine	Pyridium, Uristat, others
190	Olmesartan	Benicar
191	Cyanocobalamin	Vitamin B12
192	Levocetirizine	Xyzal
193	Nortriptyline	Pamelor
194	Dextromethorphan/Promethazine	Depakote ER
196	Divalproex ER	Depakote ER
197	Lithium	Lithobid
198	Diltiazem 24 hr	Taztia XT, Tiazac
199	Olanzapine	Zyprexa, Zyprexa Zydis
200	Nitroglycerin	Nitrostat
201	Chlorthalidone	Thalitone
202	Timolol maleate	Timoptic, Istalol, Betimol
203	Divalproex	Depakote
204	Cetirizine	Zyrtec
205	Methadone	Dolophine, Methadose
206	Oxybutynin	Gelnique, Oxytrol, Ditropan XL
207	Ofloxacin	Ocuflox, Floxin Otic
208	Insulin Aspart	Novolog FlexPen
209	Metoclopramide	Reglan, Metozolv ODT
210	Cefuroxime	Ceftin
211	Digoxin	Digitek, Digox, Lanoxin;
213	Erythromycin	E.E.S., Ery-Tab, EryPed, Erythrocin
216	Colchicine	Colcrys
217	Carbidopa/Levodopa	Sinemet, Sinemet CR
218	Estrogens (conjugated)	Premarin
219	Oxcarbazepine	Trileptal
220	Terazosin	Hytrin
221	Azelastine	Astelin, Astepro

Prescription Top-Sellers Continued

RANK	DRUG	BRAND NAME
222	Zolpidem ER	Ambien CR
223	Hydromorphone	Dilaudid
224	Memantine	Namenda
225	Olmesartan/HCTZ	Benicar HCT
226	Ketorolac	Acular, Toradol
227	Labetalol	Trandate
228	Solifenacin	VESIcare
229	Insulin Lispro	Humalog
230	Benztropine	Cogentin
231	Fluocinonide	Vanos
232	Pramipexole	Mirapex
233	Brompheniramine/ Pseudoephedrine/DM	Bromfed DM
234	Bimatoprost	Lumigan
235	Tretinoin	Atralin, Avita, Refissa, Renova, Retin-A
237	Indomethacin	Indocin
238	Amiodarone	Cordarone, Pacerone
239	Bisoprolol/HCTZ	Ziac
240	Irbesartan	Avapro
241	Ethinyl Estradiol/ Norethindrone	Loestrin, Microgestin Fe, June Fe Gildess Fe
242	Quinapril	Accupril
243	Progesterone	Prometrium
244	Terbinafine	Lamisil, Terbinex
246	Olopatadine	Pataday
247	Cyclosporine, eye drops	Restasis

RANK	DRUG	BRAND NAME
248	Neomycin/Polymyxin B/ Hydrocortisone	Cortisporin, Cortomycin
249	Insulin Detemir	Levemir FlexPen
250	Sitagliptan/Metformin	Janumet
251	Venlafaxine	Effexor
252	Insulin Aspart	Novolog
253	Combivent Respimat	Humalog
254	Desvenlafaxine	Pristiq
256	Insulin Lispro	Humalog Kwikpen
257	Phenytoin	Dilantin, Phenytek
258	Epinephrine SC	Epipen 2-Pak
260	Albuterol/Ipratropium	Combivent
261	Dexmethylphenidate ER	Focalin XR
262	Phenobarbital	Luminal
263	Guanfacine XR	Intuniv
264	Nabumetone	Relafen
265	Polymixin/Trimethoprim	Polytrim
266	Anastrozole	Arimidex
267	Travoprost	Travatan Z
268	Norgestrel/Ethinyl Estradiol	Provera
269	Dexamethasone	DexPak, DoubleDex
270	Valsartan	Diovan
271	Sucralfate	Carafate
272	Clarithomycin	Biaxin
274	Ipratropium Bromide	

Prescription Top-Sellers Continued

RANK	DRUG	BRAND NAME
275	Diphenoxylate/Atropine	*Lomotil*
276	Shingles Vaccine	*Zostavax*
277	Doxepin	*Silenor*
279	Atomoxetine	*Strattera*
280	Atenolol/Chlorthalidone	*Tenoretic*
281	Budesonide	*Pulmicort, Pulmicort Flexhaler*
282	Testosterone Cypionate	
283	Timolol/Dorzolamide	*Cosopt*

RANK	DRUG	BRAND NAME
284	Ciprofloxacin/Dexamethasone Otic	*Ciprodex*
285	Varenicline	*Chantix*
286	Testosterone gel	*AndroGel*
289	Guanfacine IR	*Tenex*
291	Moxifloxacin	*Vigamox*
292	Desonide	*Desonate, DesOwen*
293	Niacin ER	*Niaspan*
294	Hydrocodone/Chlorpheniramine	*TussiCaps, Tussionex*

RxPrep thanks IMS Health and Mr. Robert Hunkler for providing this list to aid the students.

COMMON MEDICAL ABBREVIATIONS

ABBREVIATION	MEANING
AAA	Abdominal Aortic Aneurysm
A&O	Alert & Oriented
ABG	Arterial Blood Gas
ac	Before Meals
ACOG	American Congress of Obstetricians and Gynecologists
ACTH	Adrenocorticotropic Hormone
ad	Right Ear
ADH	Anti-Diuretic Hormone
ADR	Adverse Drug Reaction
ADT	Alternate Day Therapy
AF	Atrial Fibrillation, or A.Fib
AGEF	Acute Generalized Exanthematous Pustulosis
AIN	Acute Interstitial Nephritis
ALT	Alanine Aminotransferase
ANA	Antinuclear Antibody
ANS	Autonomic Nervous System
APTT	Activated Partial Thromboplastin Time
ARDS	Acute Respiratory Distress Syndrome
ARF	Acute Renal Failure
as	Left Ear

ABBREVIATION	MEANING
AST	Aspartate Aminotransferase
ATC	Around the Clock
ATN	Acute Tubular Necrosis
au	Each Ear
AVP	Arginine Vasopressin
BEE	Basal Energy Expenditure
BID	Twice a Day
BIW	Two Times Per Week
BM	Bowel Movement
BMP	Basic Metabolic Panel
BP	Blood Pressure
BPH	Benign Prostatic Hypertrophy
BPM	*Beats Per Minute, Breaths Per Minute*
BUN	Blood Urea Nitrogen
C or w/	With
C-I, C-II, C-III, C-IV,	Calcium Channel Blocker
C-V	Refers to Controlled Drug Categories
C&S	Culture and Sensitivity
C/O	Complaining Of
CA	Cancer

Common Medical Abbreviations Continued

ABBREVIATION	MEANING
CABG	Coronary Artery Bypass Graft
CAD	*Coronary Artery Disease*
cAMP	Cyclic Adenosine Monophosphate
CA-MRSA	Community-Acquired MRSA
CAPES	*Citrobacter, Acinetobacter, Providencia, Enterobacter, Serratia*
CBC	Complete Blood Count
CC	Chief Complaint
CCB	Calcium Channel Blocker
CD	Crohn's Disease
CDI	*C. difficile* infection
CF	Cystic Fibrosis
CH	Cholesterol
CHF	Congestive Heart Failure
CI	Cardiac Index Contraindicated
CMV	*Cytomegalovirus*
CNS	Central Nervous System
CO	Cardiac Output
COPD	Chronic Obstructive Pulmonary Disease
CP	Chest Pain or Cerebral Palsy
CPAP	Continuous Positive Airway Pressure
CPK	Creatine Phosphokinase
CPR	Cardiopulmonary Resuscitation
CrCl	Creatinine Clearance
CRE	Carbapenem-Resistant *Enterobacteriaceae*
CRF	Chronic Renal Failure
CRP	C-reactive Protein
CSF	Cerebrospinal Fluid
CT	Computerized Tomography
CV	Cardiovascular
CVA	Cerebrovascular Accident
CVP	Central Venous Pressure
CXR	Chest X-Ray
D1	Dopamine 1 Receptor
D2	Dopamine 2 Receptor
D/C	Discontinue or Discharge
D5W	5% Dextrose in Water
DDIs	Drug-Drug Interactions
DJD	Degenerative Joint Disease (Osteoarthritis)

ABBREVIATION	MEANING
DKA	Diabetic Ketoacidosis
DM	Diabetes Mellitus
DOC	Drug of Choice
DOE	Dyspnea on Exertion
DRESS Syndrome	Drug Reaction with Eosinophilia and Systemic Symptoms
DVT	Deep Venous Thrombosis
Dx	Diagnosis
EC	Enteric Coated
ECG	Electrocardiogram
EIAD	Extended-Interval Aminoglycoside Dosing (PK chapter)
ESBL	*Extended Spectrum Beta Lactamases*
ESR	Erythrocyte Sedimentation Rate
ETOH	Ethanol
F/U	Follow-Up
FBS	Fasting Blood Sugar
FEV1	Forced Expiratory Volume in 1 second
FT4	Free Thyroxine (T4)
fxn	Function
GFR	Glomerular Filtration Rate
GI	Gastrointestinal
GNR	Gram Negative Rod
gtt, gtts	Drop, Drops
GTT	Glucose Tolerance Test
H/O	History Of
HA	Headache
HACEK	*Haemophilus, Actinobacillus, Cardiobacterium, Eikenella, Kingella*
HBV	Hepatitis B Virus
HCG	Human Chorionic Gonadotropin
HCT	Hematocrit
HCTZ, HCT	Hydrochlorothiazide
HCV	Hepatitis C Virus
HDL, HDL-C	High Density Lipoprotein
HF	Heart Failure
HFrEF	Heart Failure with Reduced Ejection Fraction
HFpEF	Heart Failure with Preserved Ejection Fraction
Hgb	Hemoglobin
HIV	Human Immunodeficiency Virus
HJR	Hepatojugular Reflex

Common Medical Abbreviations Continued

ABBREVIATION	MEANING
HNPEK	Haemophilus influenzae, Neisseria spp, Proteus mirabilis, E. coli, Klebsiella pneumonia
HPI	History of Present Illness
HR	Heart Rate
HS	At Bedtime
HSV	Herpes Simplex Virus
HTN	Hypertension
HUS/TTP	Hemolytic-Uremic Syndrome and Thrombotic Thrombocytopenic Purpura
Hx	History
I&O	Intake and Output
IBD	Inflammatory Bowel Disease
IBS	Irritable Bowel Syndrome
ICU	Intensive Care Unit
ID	Intradermal
IE	Infective Endocarditis
IM	Intramuscular
Inj	Injection
INR	International Normalized Ratio
IV	Intravenous
IVP	Intravenous Push
IVPB	Intravenous Piggyback
LD	Loading Dose
LDH	Lactate Dehydrogenase
LDL, LDL-C	Low-Density Lipoprotein
LFTs	Liver Function Tests
LLSB	Left Lower Sternal Border
LVH	Left Ventricular Hypertrophy
MAO	Monoamine Oxidase
MAO I	Monoamine Oxidase Inhibitor
MAP	Mean Arterial Pressure
MCH	Mean Cell Hemoglobin
MCHC	Mean Cell Hemoglobin Concentration
MCV	Mean Corpuscular Volume
MD	Maintenance Dose
MDI	Metered-Dose Inhaler
MDR	Multidrug-Resistant
MI	Myocardial Infarction

ABBREVIATION	MEANING
MIC	Minimum Inhibitory Concentration
mL	Milliliter
mPAP	*Mean Pulmonary Artery Pressure*
MRI	Magnetic Resonance Imaging
MRSA	Methicillin-Resistant Staph Aureus
MS	Multiple Sclerosis or Morphine Sulfate (Don't use for Morphine – Dangerous)
MSSA	Methicillin-Sensitive Staph Aureus
MVA	Motor Vehicle Accident
MVI	Multivitamin Injection
NTE	Not To Exceed
N/V, N&V	Nausea and Vomiting
N/V/D	Nausea, Vomiting, Diarrhea
NG	Nasogastric
NKA	No Known Allergies
NKDA	No Known Drug Allergies
NOAC	New Oral Anticoagulant
NPO	Nothing By Mouth
NR	No Refills
NRT	Nicotine Replacement Therapy
NSAIDs	Nonsteroidal Anti-Inflammatory Drugs
NSR	Normal Sinus Rhythm
OD	Right Eye
ODT	Orally Disintegrating Tablet
OS	Left Eye
OU	Each Eye
P-gp	P-glycoprotein
PAP	Pulmonary Artery Pressure
pc	After Meals
PCC	Prothrombin Complex Concentrate
PCI	Percutaneous Coronary Intervention
PCN	Penicillin
PCOS	Polycystic Ovary Syndrome
PCV13	Pneumococcal conjugate vaccine (13-valent)
PCWP	Pulmonary Capillary Wedge Pressure

Common Medical Abbreviations Continued

ABBREVIATION	MEANING
PE	Pulmonary Embolus, or Physical Exam
PEK	*Proteus mirabilis, E. coli, Klebsiella pneumonia*
PKU	Phenylketonuria
PMH	Past Medical History
PO	Oral
PPD	Purified Protein Derivative
PPSV23	Pneumococcal polysaccharide valent (23-valent)
PRBC	Packed Red Blood Cells
PR	Per Rectum
PRN	As Needed
PT	Prothrombin Time, or Physical Therapy
Pt	Patient
PTCA	Percutaneous Transluminal Coronary Angioplasty
PTH	Parathyroid Hormone
PUD	Peptic Ulcer Disease
PVC	Polyvinyl Chloride
Q	Every
QD	Every Day
QID	Four Times a Day
QOD	Every Other Day
QS	Sufficient Quantity
QS AD	A Sufficient Quantity to Make
R/O	Rule Out
RA	Rheumatoid Arthritis
RASS	Richmond Agitation and Sedation Scale
RBC	Red Blood Cell
RML	Right Middle Lobe
ROS	Review of Systems
RSI	Rapid Sequence Intubation
RSV	Respiratory Syncytial Virus
Rx	Treatment, Prescription
rxn	Reaction

ABBREVIATION	MEANING
S or w/o	Without
S/P	Status Post
SCr	Serum Creatinine
SIADH	Syndrome of Inappropriate Antidiuretic Hormone
SIG	Write on Label
SJS	Stevens Johnson Syndrome
SL	Sublingual
SLE	Systemic Lupus Erythematous
SOAP	Subjective, Objective, Assessment, Plan
SOB	Shortness of Breath
SC, SQ, subc, subq	Subcutaneous
ss	One-half
S/Sx	Signs and Symptoms
SSTI	Skin and Soft-Tissue Infection or Skin and Skin-Structure Infection
STAT	Immediately
STI	Sexually Transmitted Infection
Supp, sup	Suppository
SVR	Systemic Vascular Resistance
Sx	Symptoms
TB	Tuberculosis
TC	Total Cholesterol
TdP	Torsade de Pointes
TEG	Thromboelastography
TEN	Toxic Epidermal Necrolysis
TG	Triglycerides
TIA	Transient Ischemic Attack
TIBC	Total Iron Binding Capacity
TID	Three Times a Day
TIW	Three Times Per Week
TOP	Topically
TPN	Total Parenteral Nutrition
TSH	Thyroid Stimulating Hormone

Common Medical Abbreviations Continued

ABBREVIATION	MEANING
TTP	Thrombotic Thrombocytopenic Purpura
Tx	Treatment
UA	Urinalysis
UC	Ulcerative Colitis
UFH	Unfractionated Heparin
ULN	Upper Limit of Normal
UNG	Ointment
URTI	Upper Respiratory Tract Infection
UTI	Urinary Tract Infection
V1	Vasopressin 1 Receptor
V2	Vasopressin 2 Receptor

ABBREVIATION	MEANING
VF	Ventricular Fibrillation
VRE	Vancomycin-Resistant Enterococcus
VT	Ventricular Tachycardia
WA	While Awake
WBC	White Blood Cells
WNL	Within Normal Limits
WPW	Wolff-Parkinson-White Syndrome
X	Times
y/o	Years Old
yr	Year

Meanings of abbreviations may vary. Not all of these abbreviations are considered safe, but all are used outpatient. In hospital settings, avoid unapproved abbreviations (See Medication Safety & Quality Improvement chapter)

INDEX

Maxalt-MLT 198, 685
Maxipime 358
Maxzide 722, 728-729
Maxzide/Dyazide 728
meclizine 1048-1049
meclofenamate 661
Medrol 580-581
Medrol Dosepak 580-581
medroxyprogesterone 636, 646, 649
mefloquine 147, 954
Mekinist 152
melatonin 208, 945, 947, 954
meloxicam 661-662, 993-994
Menactra 302
MenB-4c 302
MenB-FHbp 302
Menomune 302
Menveo 302
meperidine 125, 144, 417, 668, 670, 889
Mephyton 256, 809
mepolizumab 489, 496
mercaptopurine 152, 227, 368-596, 828, 1008, 1012
meropenem 397, 359, 405, 407
Merrem 359
mesalamine 124, 202, 1008, 1011, 1014
Metadate CD 201, 934, 936
Metadate ER 934, 950
Metaglip 545-546
Metamucil 990, 1008
metformin 222, 227, 368, 545-546, 550-551, 555-556
Metformin 281
metformin/glipizide 545
metformin/glyburide 545
metformin/pioglitazone 545
metformin/repaglinide 545
metformin/rosiglitazone 545
metformin/saxagliptin 545
metformin/sitagliptin 545
methadone 125,140-142, 145, 419, 446, 449, 454-455, 650, 667, 672-673, 889
methimazole 279, 281, 575
methocarbamol 675, 1050
methotrexate 17, 154, 222, 254-255, 279, 355, 368, 410, 495, 584-588, 713-714, 828, 988, 1008, 1057
methyldopa 222, 226-227, 281, 340, 722, 733, 1050
methylene blue 154, 222, 254-255, 525, 883-887, 890-891, 1050
Methylin 200, 934, 950
Methylin ER 934
methylnaltrexone 664, 672-673
methylphenidate 201, 205, 882, 931, 933-935, 937, 945, 950
methylprednisolone 36, 580-581, 592-593
metoclopramide 198, 320, 825, 827, 829, 900, 917, 954, 983-984, 990, 991, 1004
metolazone 724, 762
metoprolol/HCTZ 722
metoprolol succinate 750, 766
metoprolol tartrate 722, 730, 766
Metozolv ODT 198, 990
MetroCream 376
MetroGel 376
MetroLotion 376
metronidazole 19, 142-143, 343, 375-376, 379, 385, 390, 403, 408-409, 411, 617, 992, 1050
Mevacor 705
mexiletine 758, 782, 785
Miacalcin 199, 642
micafungin 249, 422
Micardis 728
Micardis HCT 722
miconazole 1056, 1059, 1061
Micronor 625

Microzide 724
Midamor 729
midazolam 264, 265, 419, 447, 448, 456, 953
miglitol 549-550
Migranal 687
milk thistle 209, 255, 340
Millipred 581
milnacipran 677, 886-887
milrinone 263
Mimvey 649
Minipress 734
Minitran 205, 744
Minivelle 649
Minocin 366, 385
minocycline 145, 226, 366, 372, 379, 385, 404
minoxidil 734, 1054
mipomersen 714
mirabegron 720, 1037
MiraLAX 287 990
Mirapex 898, 919, 920
Mirapex ER 919
Mircette 625
mirtazapine 142-144, 147, 198, 881, 889, 891-892, 942, 947, 948
misoprostol 279, 660, 989, 993, 1004
mitomycin 847
mitoxantrone 1050
Mobic 661
modafinil 142-143, 934, 950, 951
moexipril 722, 727
moexipril/HCTZ 722
mometasone 478, 492, 1070
mometasone/formoterol 492
mometasone furoate 1070
Monistat 1059
Monistat 3 1061
Monodox 366
MonoNessa 625
montelukast 200-201, 482, 493-494, 496
Monurol 201, 377
morphine 103-104, 111-112, 121, 125, 140, 142, 145, 150-151, 153, 204, 249, 261, 263-264, 266, 288-289, 656, 664-665, 668-669, 670-672, 836, 919, 921
morphine/naltrexone 664
morphine sulfate 749
Motrin 287, 660
Movantik 673
Moxatag 354, 384
Moxeza 363
moxifloxacin 248, 362-364, 379, 399, 403, 405, 437
MS Contin 664
Mutaq 788
mupirocin 199, 386, 404, 1059, 1065
Muse 1022
Mutamycin 847
Myalept 704
Myambutol 400, 1045
Mycamine 249, 422
Mycelex 198
mycophenolate 220, 246, 325-326, 340, 355, 616-618
mycophenolic acid 613, 618
Myfortic 613, 618
Mylanta 13
Mylanta Max Strength 984
Mylicon 287
Myrbetriq 720, 1037
Mysoline 964

N

nabilone 147, 830, 832
nabumetone 661, 993
N-acetylcysteine 252
nadolol 342, 722, 731
nadolol/bendroflumethiazide 722
nafarelin 279

nafcillin 124, 355
naloxegol 673
naloxone 125, 184, 199, 243, 254-255, 275, 663-664, 667, 673-674
naltrexone 341, 664, 672-674, 1074
naltrexone/bupropion 1074-1075
Namenda 928-929
Namenda XR 201
naphazoline 251, 481
Naprosyn 617, 692
naproxen 660, 684, 692-693, 993
naproxen/esomeprazole 988
naratriptan 684
Narcan 255, 749
narcan ns 255
Nardil 889, 920
Naropin 268
Nasacort AQ 478
Nasalcrom 482
natalizumab 246, 598, 876, 1013, 1014
Natazia 623-624
nateglinide 142, 547
Natesto 651-653
Natrecor 772
nebivolol 730, 732
nefazodone 142, 551, 706, 891, 958, 959
nelfinavir 142, 452, 454, 459, 551
Neo-Fradin 343
neomycin 304, 343, 1046-1047, 1065
Neoral 594, 615, 619
Neosporin 1046, 1065
Nesina 551
nesiritide 772
Neulasta 825
Neupogen 825
Neurontin 676
nevirapine 142, 340, 448-449
Nexavar 858
Nexium 201, 987-988
Nexterone 787
niacin 62, 209, 225, 400, 407, 705-706, 710, 715
niacin/lovastatin 705, 710
niacin/simvastatin 705, 710
Niacor 710
Niaspan 710, 715
nicardipine 725, 734
NicoDerm CQ 204-205, 524
Nicorette 524
nicotine 204-205, 255, 522, 524, 526, 780, 1008
Nicotrol 524
Nicotrol NS 524
nifedipine 142, 281, 469, 722, 725, 743, 750
nilotinib 828, 858
Nimbex 269
nimodipine 977-978
nintedanib 475
Niravam 198, 941
nisoldipine 419, 725
Nitro-Dur 205, 744
nitrofurantoin 154, 222, 378-379, 386, 406, 1050
nitroglycerin 24,128, 199, 205, 247, 250-251, 262, 342, 473, 739-740, 741 743-746
Nitrolingual 199, 473-745
NitroMist 199, 744
nitroprusside 249, 253-254, 262
Nitrostat 199, 473, 744
nivolumab 822, 851
nizatidine 986, 992
Nizoral 419, 424
Nora-BE 625
Norco 657
norepinephrine 144, 249, 259-260, 525, 656-657, 667, 880-881, 886-887, 889-892, 1075

Norflex 675
norfloxacin 344, 363, 409
Noritate 376
normal saline 16, 30, 32, 835
Noroxin 363
Norpace 784
Norpace CR 784
Norpramin 887
Nor-QD 625
Northera 918, 923
nortriptyline 143, 887
Norvasc 725
Norvir 453
Novolin 70/30 560
Novolin N 560
Novolin R 560
NovoLog 537, 560, 1072
NovoSeven 270, 810
Noxafil 420
NSAIDs 279-280
Nucala 489, 496
Nucynta 669
Nuvigil 951
nystatin 423, 425

O

Ocella 625
Octagam 271
octreotide 254, 341-342
Ocuflox 1046
Ocupress 1041
ofatumumab 152
Ofev 475
ofloxacin 43, 45, 63, 128, 142, 248, 344, 362-364, 379, 384-385, 397, 402-403, 406-407, 409, 411, 437, 494
olanzapine 142, 197-198, 202, 523, 828-829, 883, 893-894, 899, 903, 905-906, 913
Oleptro 891
olmesartan 556, 708, 722, 728
olmesartan/HCTZ 722
olodaterol 515
olopatadine 480, 1046
Olux 1070
Olysio 152, 335
omalizumab 489, 495-496
ombitasvir 334, 337-339, 345
ombitasvir/paritaprevir/ritonavir 334, 337-339, 345
ombitasvir/paritaprevir/ritonavir co-packaged with dasabuvir 334, 337-339, 345
omega-3-carboxylic acids 711
omeprazole 142-143, 201, 451, 465, 742-743, 753, 982, 987, 988, 992
Omnaris 478
Onbrez 419
Oncaspar 846
ondansetron 142, 197-198, 827, 830, 838, 919, 921, 998
Onglyza 551
Onmel 419
Onsolis 199, 665
Ontak 153
Opana ER 667, 669
Opdivo 851
Opsumit 472
Oracea 366
Oracit 327
Oralair 482
Orapred 197-198, 581
Orbactiv 369
Orencia 246, 248, 590
Orenitram 470
oritavancin 369
Orkambi 533, 536
orlistat 573, 1074, 1076, 1077
orphenadrine 124, 675
Ortho Evra 205, 623
Ortho-Novum 625
Ortho Tri-Cyclen 625

Oscal 76, 638
oseltamivir 120, 393, 426
Oseni 550-551
Osmitrol 248
ospemifene 647-648
Osphena 647-648
Otezla 605
Otrexup 584, 1013
oxacillin 124, 354-355
oxaliplatin 827
oxazepam 941, 948
oxcarbazepine 122, 142-143, 220, 337, 449-450, 889, 891, 955-956, 959, 966, 968, 970
oxybutynin 205, 1035-1037, 1039, 1041
oxycodone 125, 142, 145, 657, 658, 667, 670, 671
oxycodone/acetaminophen 657, 667
oxycodone/naloxone 667
OxyContin 667, 672
oxymetazoline 199, 251, 280, 481
oxymorphone 670, 125, 340, 667
Oxytrol 205, 1036, 1039

P

Pacerone 787
paclitaxel 827, 839
paliperidone 202, 227, 899, 903-905
palonosetron 829, 921
Pamelor 887
pamidronate 835
pancuronium 269
panitumumab 151, 827, 849
pantoprazole 987-988
Parcopa 198
paricalcitol 323-324
Parnate 889, 920
paroxetine 140-141, 145, 279, 647-648, 881-883, 885, 904, 938, 940
passionflower 208
Patanase 480
Patanol 1046
patiromer 326, 573
Paxil 648, 883
Paxil CR 648, 883
pazopanib 858
Pediapred 581
Pediarix 299, 300, 303
PedvaxHIB 300
pegaspargase 846
Pegasys 330, 331
pegfilgrastim 825
peginterferon beta-1a 596
Peg-Intron 199, 331
pegloticase 693-695
pegylated 330-331, 695, 825
pembrolizumab 851
pemetrexed 827
penbutolol 729, 731
penicillin 10, 68, 123-124, 222, 320, 354-356, 358, 360, 367, 386, 392-393, 410, 806, 875, 992
penicillin G aqueous 354
penicillin G benzathine 410, 354
penicillin G procaine 410
Penicillins 354
Pentacel 299, 300, 303
pentamidine 146, 220, 246, 249, 325, 436, 437
Pentasa 1011
Pepcid 986
Pepcid AC 986
Pepcid Complete 984-985
peppermint 208-209, 683, 1008, 1048
Pepto-Bismol 200, 1009
peramivir 122, 425
perampanel 966
Percocet 657, 667
Percodan 667